Teacher's Edition

by
Siegfried Haenisch

AGS Publishing
Circle Pines, Minnesota 55014-1796
800-328-2560
www.agsnet.com

About the Author

Siegfried Haenisch, Ed.D., holds a master's degree in mathematics and has taught mathematics at every level, from elementary to graduate school, most recently as Professor in the Department of Mathematics and Statistics at the College of New Jersey. The Mathematical Association of America granted him the 1995 Award for Distinguished Teaching of Mathematics. Dr. Haenisch was the site director for the training of teachers in the New Jersey Algebra Project. He was a member of the National Science Foundation Institutes in Mathematics at Rutgers University, Oberlin College, and Princeton University. At Yale University, he was a member of the Seminar in the History of Mathematics, sponsored by the National Endowment in the Humanities. Dr. Haenisch currently serves as a mathematics curriculum consultant to school districts.

Photo credits for this textbook can be found on page 526.

The publisher wishes to thank the following educators for their helpful comments during the review process for *Algebra.* Their assistance has been invaluable.

Maria Antonopoulou, Algebra Teacher, Hastings Education Centre, Vancouver, B.C., Canada; **David Arnold,** SLD Teacher, Winter Park Ninth Grade Center, Winter Park, Florida; **Tamara Bell,** Special Education Teacher, Muncie Community Schools, Southside High School, Muncie, Indiana; **Jacqueline DeWitt,** Cooperative Consultant, Umatilla High School, Sorrento, Florida; **Tina Dobson,** Special Education Math Resource Specialist, Sandridge Junior High School; Roy, Utah; **Connie Eichhorn,** Career Center and Adult Education Program, Omaha Public Schools, Omaha, Nebraska; **Dr. Rita Giles,** Program Director, Fairfax County Public Schools, Alexandria, Virginia; **Anne Hobbs,** Special Education Secondary Coordinator, Hobbs Municipal Schools, Hobbs, New Mexico; **Deborah Horn,** Wayne City High School, Wayne City, Illinois; **Rosanne Hudok,** Learning Support Teacher, Keystone Oaks High School, Pittsburgh, Pennsylvania; **Robert Jones,** Mathematics Supervisor, Cleveland Public Schools, Cleveland, Ohio; **Lee Kucera,** Math Teacher, Capistrano Valley High School, Mission Viejo, California; **Anne Lally,** Algebra Teacher, Eli Whitney School, Chicago, Illinois; **Christine Lansford,** Coordinator of Special Education, Melville Comprehensive School, Melville, Saskatchewan, Canada; **Robert Maydak,** Math Specialist, Pittsburgh Mt. Oliver Intermediate Unit, Pittsburgh, Pennsylvania; **Kathe Neighbor,** Math Chair, Crawford High School, San Diego, California; **Rachelle Powell,** Department Chair, Dr. Ralph H. Poteet High School, Mesquite, Texas; **Jacqueline Smith,** Resource Department Chair, Sterling High School, Baytown, Texas; **Carol Warren,** Math Teacher, Crockett County High School, Alamo, Tennessee; **William Wible,** Math Resource Teacher, San Diego Unified, San Diego, California

Publisher's Project Staff

Vice President of Product Development, Kathleen T. Williams, Ph.D., NCSP; Associate Director, Product Development, Teri Mathews; Managing Editor: Patrick Keithahn; Editor: Judy Monroe; Development Assistant: Bev Johnson; Graphic Designer: Katie Sonmor; Creative Services Manager: Nancy Condon; Desktop Publishing Specialist: Linda Peterson; Purchasing Agent: Mary Kaye Kuzma; Senior Marketing Manager/Secondary Curriculum: Brian Holl

4201 Woodland Road
Circle Pines, MN 55014-1796
800-328-2560 • www.agsnet.com

AGS Publishing is a trademark and trade name of American Guidance Service, Inc.

Printed in the United States of America
ISBN 0-7854-3568-9
Product Number 93822

A 0 9 8 7 6 5 4 3 2

Contents

Overview

Lesson Plans

Teacher's Resources

Algebra teaches the basic concepts of algebra in a step-by-step approach and meets the standards set by most states and the National Council of Teachers of Mathematics (NCTM). This text is written for students and young adults who need extra help grasping new concepts. Because students learn in many different ways, emphasis is placed on including instruction using a variety of modalities. When appropriate, manipulatives are suggested to provide a tactile/kinesthetic activity promoting concept mastery.

The text is organized into thirteen discrete chapters. Chapters open with a photograph and description of an application of the chapter content. These examples will give students a better understanding of the diversity of mathematics. Chapter openers also include Goals for Learning that introduce students to key objectives.

Short lessons with lots of examples are included to illustrate and teach each new skill. Rules are highlighted for quick reference. Math terms are defined in the side column and in the glossary. Frequent sets of activities allow students to practice their newly acquired skills. To further facilitate learning, sample solutions are given in the back of the text for the first activity in each exercise set. In addition, the answers to all odd-numbered problems are also provided. These pages are referred to on the appropriate lesson page for easy reference. Combined with the many opportunities for practice within a lesson, supplemental problems in the back of the student text offer extra reinforcement.

As recommended by NCTM, students are encouraged to write about mathematics. Students may record these writings in a notebook or portfolio. To encourage understanding and motivation, problem-solving exercises are integrated throughout the lessons. These exercises present real-life situations that require algebraic thinking and analysis. To extend this concept, application activities are included within each chapter. These activities help students relate concepts to everyday situations, helping them to connect math instruction with the real world.

Skill Track Software

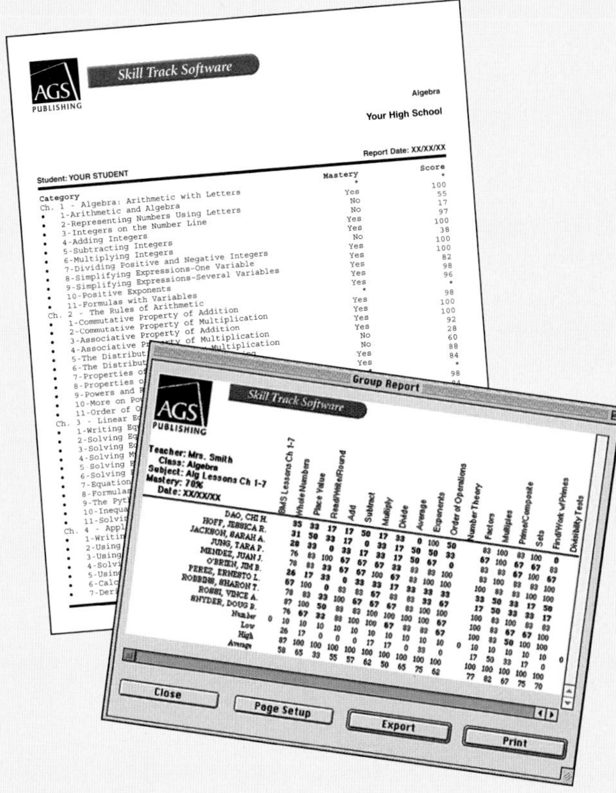

Skill Track Software The Skill Track software program allows students using AGS Publishing textbooks to be assessed for mastery of each chapter and lesson of the textbook. Students access the software on an individual basis and are assessed with multiple choice items.

Students can enter the program through two paths:

Lesson
Six items assess mastery of each lesson.

Chapter
Two parallel forms of chapter assessments are provided to determine chapter mastery. The two forms are equal in length and cover the same concepts with different items. The number of items in each chapter assessment varies by chapter, as the items are drawn from content of each lesson in the textbook.

The program includes high-interest graphics to accompany the items. Students are allowed to retake the chapter or lesson assessments over again at the instructor's discretion. The instructor has the ability to run and print out a variety of reports to track students' progress.

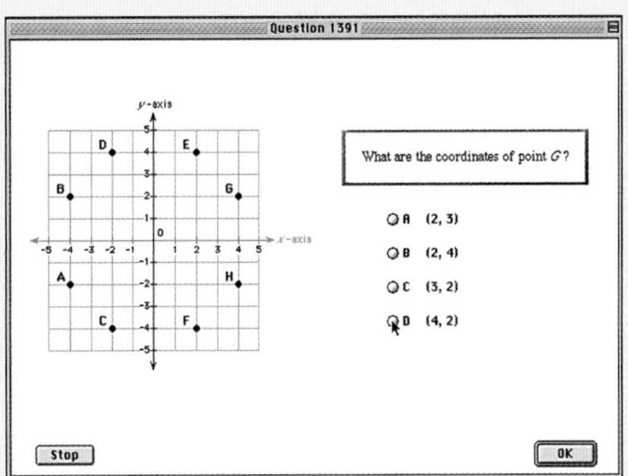

Teaching Strategies in Math Transparencies and The Great Review Game

Interest Level: Grades 6-12

Focus your math lessons with Teaching Strategies in Math Transparencies.

This transparency set contains graphic organizers that present concepts in a meaningful, visual way. They stimulate learning and discussion, while teaching students how to manage information.

Types of graphic organizers include:

- Number Line
- Venn Diagram
- Concept Web
- Spider Map
- Circle Organizer
- Network Tree
- Three-Column Chart
- Problem-Solving Strategy

This transparency set provides teachers with clear objectives and teaching strategies. You're shown how to introduce each transparency to your students, followed by ways to practice, apply, check-up, and extend the use of each graphic organizer.

Make learning a game with The Great Review Game

Extend the use of *Algebra* with this attractive, highly interactive computer game. *The Great Review Game* on CD-ROM contains material based on the *Algebra* text and offers an exciting companion to textbook learning. Vibrant graphics, dynamic animation, sound effects, game controls, and the team/individual play format motivate students to play the game and try their skills at their own level and at their own pace.

The Great Review Game CD-ROM is available in both Windows® and Macintosh® formats for *Algebra* and other AGS Publishing mathematics textbooks.

For more information on AGS Publishing worktexts and textbooks:
call 800-328-2560, visit our Web site at www.agsnet.com, or e-mail AGS Publishing at agsmail@agsnet.com.

AGS Publishing Mathematics Textbooks

Enhance your math program with AGS Publishing textbooks—an easy, effective way to teach students the practical skills they need. Each AGS Publishing textbook meets your math curriculum needs. These exciting, full-color books use student-friendly text and real-world examples to show students the relevance of math in their daily lives. Each presents a comprehensive coverage of skills and concepts. The short, concise lessons will motivate even your most reluctant students. With readabilities of all the texts below fourth grade reading level, your students can concentrate on learning the content. AGS Publishing is committed to making learning accessible to all students.

Guidelines for Using Manipulatives

The manipulative activities in the *Algebra* Teacher's Edition are intended to develop students' mathematical understanding at a concrete level. Manipulatives are used to build visual representations, or models, of algebraic concepts and relationships and their symbols. Students who are introduced to algebraic concepts through the use of manipulatives will develop an understanding of symbolic representations and algorithms more quickly and in a deeper, more internalized manner. For this reason, the manipulative activities are presented along with *Teaching the Lesson* in the three-step lesson plan.

To successfully include manipulatives into your algebra program, here are some general guidelines:

- When an activity or concept is first introduced, spend as much time as necessary on guided practice in order for students to understand the use of the manipulatives before they begin using them independently.
- Students should have manipulatives available at their desks during group instruction so they can practice the activity along with your explanation.
- Present the activities in order. Students will develop their understanding of the use of the manipulatives in small, incremental steps.
- Repetition is important. The suggested exercises represent the minimum amount of practice necessary for most students. For students who require more practice, additional exercises are available in the Student Workbook.
- The term *symbolic equivalent* is used to refer to the mathematical symbols and terms that represent algebraic concepts and relationships. Students need to recognize the connection between the manipulative models and the symbols used to represent them. For this reason, students should sketch each model they build and write the corresponding symbolic equivalent.
- Help students develop the habit of using the manipulatives to check their work. Reviewing and evaluating one's own work is a metacognitive skill that improves problem-solving ability.

Manipulatives Used with Algebra

All of the ETA/Cuisenaire® manipulatives used with *Algebra* are available for purchase from AGS Publishing. Call 800-328-2560 and request product number 93835. For your information and planning, the chart below shows the manipulatives used throughout program. In addition, the Teacher's Resource Library (TRL) includes Manipulatives Masters 1-5 (shown below).

Basics for Using Algebra Tiles™

Algebra Tiles are a set of colorful plastic pieces used to represent positive and negative variables. Instructions for their use follow.

Identifying the Algebra Tiles Pieces The edge of the Algebra Tiles shape represents a variable or a number. A long edge represents x and a short edge represents 1. The large square represents x^2, the rectangle represents $1x$, and the small square represents 1. Shapes that are the same are congruent and represent like terms. Congruency is not affected by color.

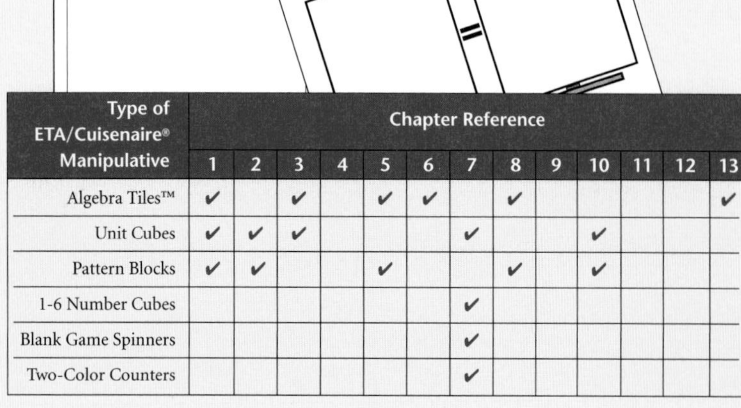

Type of ETA/Cuisenaire® Manipulative	Chapter Reference												
	1	2	3	4	5	6	7	8	9	10	11	12	13
Algebra Tiles™	✔		✔		✔	✔		✔					✔
Unit Cubes	✔	✔	✔				✔			✔			
Pattern Blocks	✔	✔			✔			✔		✔			
1-6 Number Cubes							✔						
Blank Game Spinners							✔						
Two-Color Counters							✔						

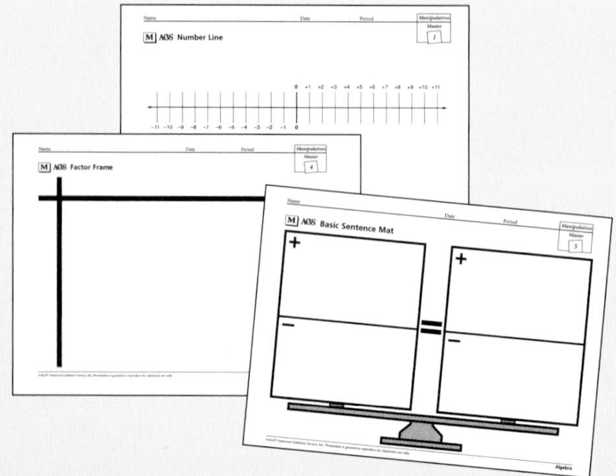

The Zero Rule When a value and its additive inverse are combined, the result is zero. The additive inverse of each Algebra Tiles shape is represented by the congruent piece of a different color. When you combine two pieces of the same shape but different color (and sign), the result is zero. When you combine terms or simplify expressions, you can add or remove pairs of additive inverses without changing the value of the expression. This is referred to as *applying the Zero Rule.*

Modeling Expressions

A variety of first and second degree monomials and polynomials can be modeled with the Algebra Tiles shapes.

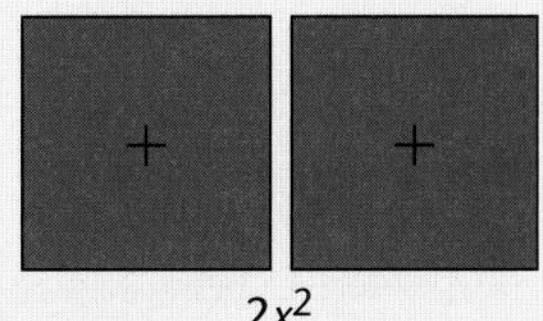

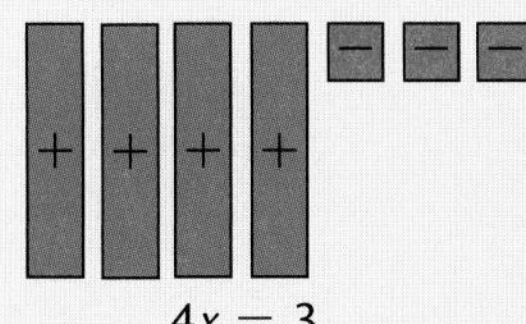

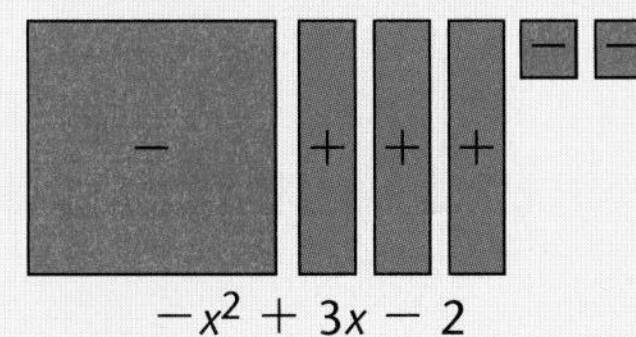

Using the Factor Frame The Factor Frame (Manipulatives Master 4) is used with the Algebra Tiles to model multiplication, division, and factoring.

Multiplication: Area illustrates multiplication of monomials or polynomials. Use the Algebra Tiles to create a frame that represents the multiplicand and the multiplier.

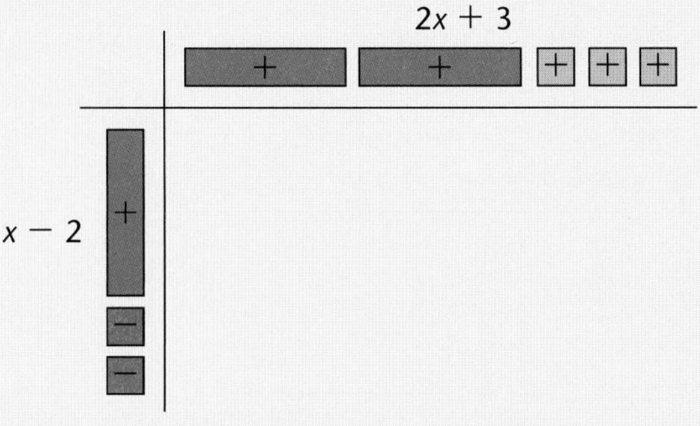

Because of the commutative property of multiplication, the placement of the multiplicand and the multiplier on the top and left parts of the frame is interchangeable. The distributive property is used to multiply the factors on the outside of the frame. The rectangle formed inside the frame is filled with Algebra Tiles to represent the product of the factors.

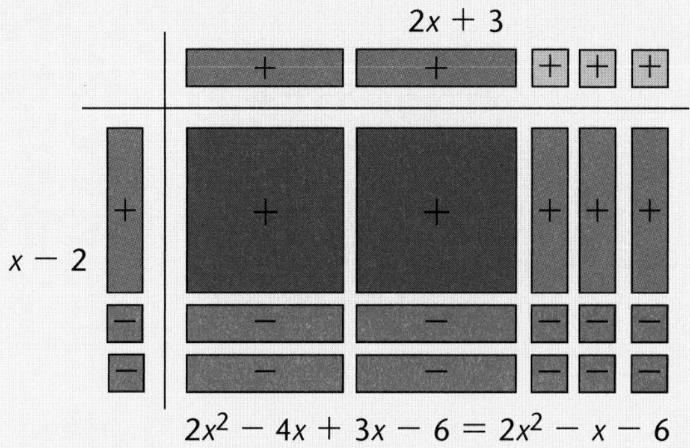

Division: The Algebra Tiles that model the divisor are placed on the outside of the frame along the left side. The pieces that represent the dividend are arranged inside the frame, with the x^2 pieces generally placed in the upper left corner of the rectangle and the small squares in the lower right corner. The pieces are placed to form a rectangle that must meet two conditions: 1) The adjoining edges of adjacent pieces must be the same length; and 2) The rectangle cannot have any open areas.

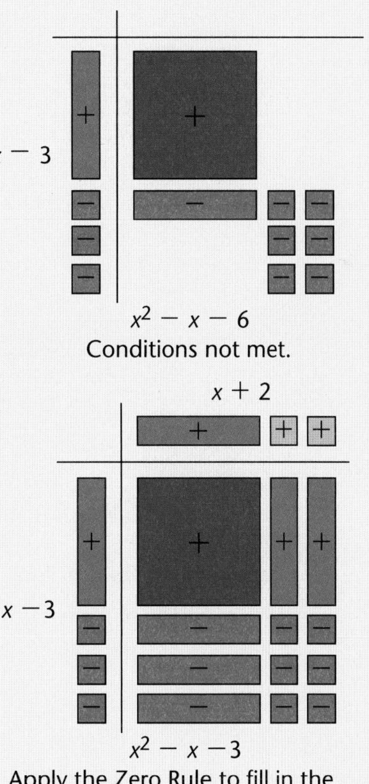

Conditions not met.

Apply the Zero Rule to fill in the rectangle. The quotient is $x + 2$.

If there are not enough Algebra Tiles in the dividend to satisfy these two conditions, the Zero Rule can be applied by using pairs of additive inverses to fill in the open areas of the rectangle. To find the quotient, fill in the top portion of the frame with the appropriate Algebra Tiles pieces.

Factoring: When modeling factoring with the Algebra Tiles, only the rectangular area inside the frame is filled in initially, using the pieces which represent the polynomial to be factored. The pieces inside the frame must meet the same two conditions as in division (adjoining edges must be the same length; no open areas). As with division, it may be necessary to apply the Zero Rule and add extra pieces. To find the factors of the polynomial, fill in the left and top portions of the frame with the appropriate Algebra Tiles pieces.

Student Text Highlights

- Each lesson is clearly labeled to help students focus on the skill or concept to be learned.
- Vocabulary terms are boldfaced and then defined in the margin at the top of the page and in the glossary.
- Reminder notes and tips help students recall and apply what they already know.

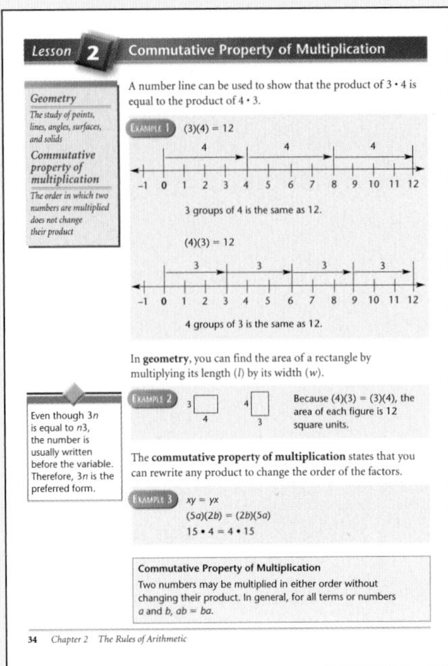

Lesson 2 Commutative Property of Multiplication

Geometry The study of points, lines, angles, surfaces, and solids

Commutative property of multiplication The order in which two numbers are multiplied does not change their product

A number line can be used to show that the product of 3 • 4 is equal to the product of 4 • 3.

EXAMPLE 1 (3)(4) = 12

3 groups of 4 is the same as 12.

(4)(3) = 12

4 groups of 3 is the same as 12.

In **geometry**, you can find the area of a rectangle by multiplying its length (*l*) by its width (*w*).

EXAMPLE 2 Because (4)(3) = (3)(4), the area of each figure is 12 square units.

Even though 3*n* is equal to *n*3, the number is usually written before the variable. Therefore, 3*n* is the preferred form.

The **commutative property of multiplication** states that you can rewrite any product to change the order of the factors.

EXAMPLE 3 $xy = yx$
$(5a)(2b) = (2b)(5a)$
$15 \cdot 4 = 4 \cdot 15$

Commutative Property of Multiplication
Two numbers may be multiplied in either order without changing their product. In general, for all terms or numbers *a* and *b*, *ab* = *ba*.

34 Chapter 2 The Rules of Arithmetic

Geometry
The study of points, lines, angles, surfaces, and solids

Commutative property of multiplication
The order in which two numbers are multiplied does not change their product

Even though 3*n* is equal to *n*3, the number is usually written before the variable.

- Goals for Learning at the beginning of each chapter identify learner outcomes.

Goals for Learning

- To write and solve equations
- To use formulas for perimeter and area to solve problems
- To use the Pythagorean theorem to solve problems
- To graph inequalities on the number line
- To solve inequalities

- Problem-solving exercises give students opportunities to use skills they have learned to solve practical problems.
- Simple, step-by-step examples provide problem-solving strategies students need to complete problems within the lesson.
- Exercise sets parallel the instruction and examples in each lesson.

PROBLEM SOLVING

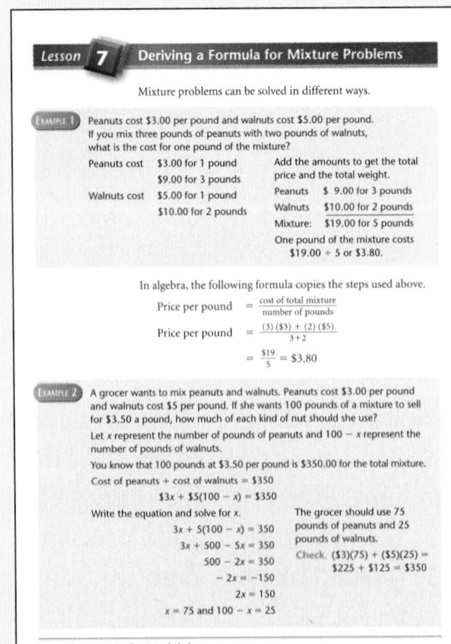

Lesson 7 Deriving a Formula for Mixture Problems

Mixture problems can be solved in different ways.

EXAMPLE 1 Peanuts cost \$3.00 per pound and walnuts cost \$5.00 per pound. If you mix three pounds of peanuts with two pounds of walnuts, what is the cost for one pound of the mixture?

Peanuts cost \$3.00 for 1 pound; \$9.00 for 3 pounds
Walnuts cost \$5.00 for 1 pound; \$10.00 for 2 pounds

Add the amounts to get the total price and the total weight.
Peanuts \$ 9.00 for 3 pounds
Walnuts \$10.00 for 2 pounds
Mixture: \$19.00 for 5 pounds
One pound of the mixture costs \$19.00 ÷ 5 or \$3.80.

In algebra, the following formula copies the steps used above.

$$\text{Price per pound} = \frac{\text{cost of total mixture}}{\text{number of pounds}}$$

$$\text{Price per pound} = \frac{(3)(\$3) + (2)(\$5)}{3+2} = \frac{\$19}{5} = \$3.80$$

EXAMPLE 2 A grocer wants to mix peanuts and walnuts. Peanuts cost \$3.00 per pound and walnuts cost \$5 per pound. If she wants 100 pounds of a mixture to sell for \$3.50 a pound, how much of each kind of nut should she use?

Let x represent the number of pounds of peanuts and $100 - x$ represent the number of pounds of walnuts.

You know that 100 pounds at \$3.50 per pound is \$350.00 for the total mixture.

Cost of peanuts + cost of walnuts = \$350

$\$3x + \$5(100 - x) = \$350$

Write the equation and solve for x.

$3x + 5(100 - x) = 350$
$3x + 500 - 5x = 350$
$500 - 2x = 350$
$-2x = -150$
$2x = 150$
$x = 75$ and $100 - x = 25$

The grocer should use 75 pounds of peanuts and 25 pounds of walnuts.

Check. (\$3)(75) + (\$5)(25) = \$225 + \$125 = \$350

114 Chapter 4 Applications of Algebra

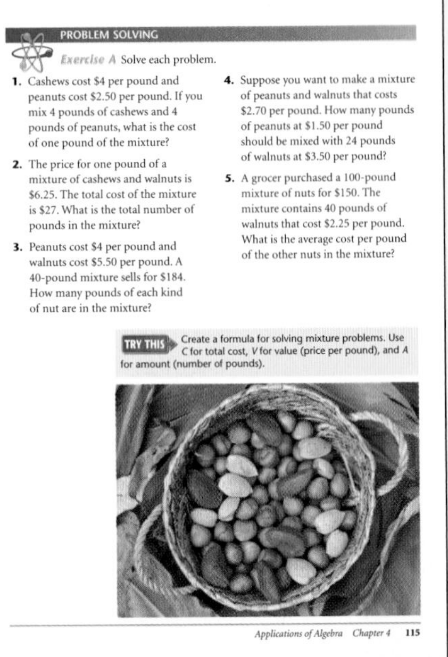

PROBLEM SOLVING

Exercise A Solve each problem.

1. Cashews cost \$4 per pound and peanuts cost \$2.50 per pound. If you mix 4 pounds of cashews and 4 pounds of peanuts, what is the cost of one pound of the mixture?
2. The price for one pound of a mixture of cashews and walnuts is \$6.25. The total cost of the mixture is \$27. What is the total number of pounds in the mixture?
3. Peanuts cost \$4 per pound and walnuts cost \$5.50 per pound. A 40-pound mixture sells for \$184. How many pounds of each kind of nut are in the mixture?
4. Suppose you want to make a mixture of peanuts and walnuts that costs \$2.70 per pound. How many pounds of peanuts at \$1.50 per pound should be mixed with 24 pounds of walnuts at \$3.50 per pound?
5. A grocer purchased a 100-pound mixture of nuts for \$150. The mixture contains 40 pounds of walnuts that cost \$2.25 per pound. What is the average cost per pound of the other nuts in the mixture?

TRY THIS Create a formula for solving mixture problems. Use *C* for total cost, *V* for value (price per pound), and *A* for amount (number of pounds).

Applications of Algebra Chapter 4 115

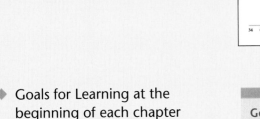

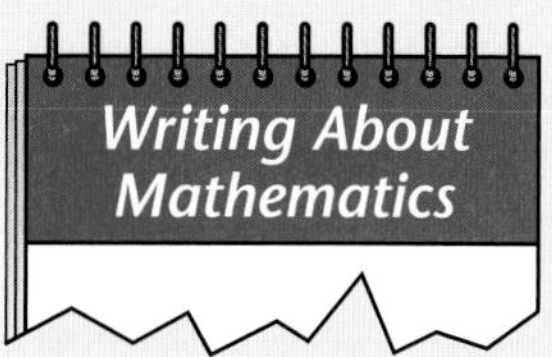

Calculator Practice

Technology Connection

Search Engines

Many Internet search engines use *and statements* to help limit and focus a search. Try this: type a word into a search engine. Notice the number of Web sites that show up. Add a second word to your search phrase (separated from the first by a comma), and you get fewer sites. Type a third word, and you get even fewer sites. That's because you get only the Web sites with all three words—word 1 AND word 2 AND word 3.

- Many features reinforce and extend student learning beyond the lesson content.

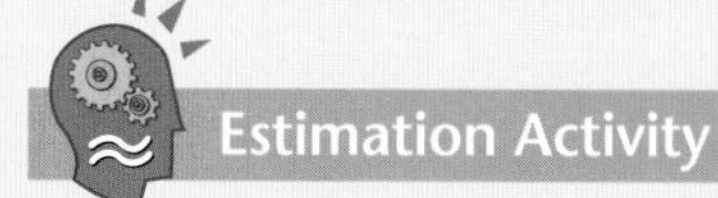

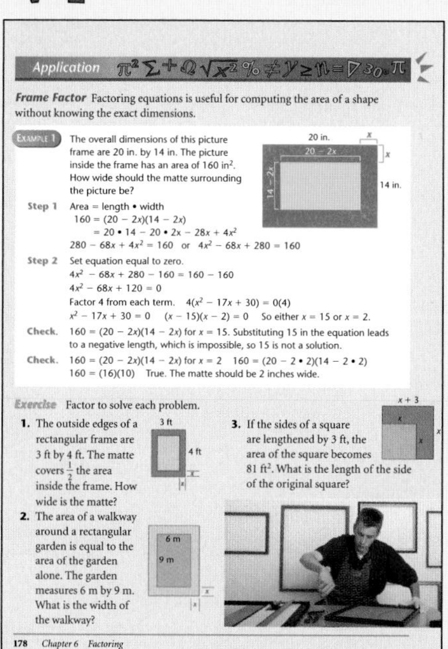

Application

Frame Factor Factoring equations is useful for computing the area of a shape without knowing the exact dimensions.

EXAMPLE 1 The overall dimensions of this picture frame are 20 in. by 14 in. The picture inside the frame has an area of 160 in^2. How wide should the matte surrounding the picture be?

Step 1 Area = length • width
$160 = (20 - 2x)(14 - 2x)$
$= 20 \cdot 14 - 20 \cdot 2x - 28x + 4x^2$
$280 - 68x + 4x^2 = 160$ or $4x^2 - 68x + 280 = 160$

Step 2 Set equation equal to zero.
$4x^2 - 68x + 280 - 160 = 160 - 160$
$4x^2 - 68x + 120 = 0$
Factor 4 from each term. $4(x^2 - 17x + 30) = 0(4)$
$x^2 - 17x + 30 = 0$ $(x - 15)(x - 2) = 0$ So either $x = 15$ or $x = 2$.

Check. $160 = (20 - 2x)(14 - 2x)$ for $x = 15$. Substituting 15 in the equation leads to a negative length, which is impossible, so 15 is not a solution.

Check. $160 = (20 - 2x)(14 - 2x)$ for $x = 2$ $160 = (20 - 2 \cdot 2)(14 - 2 \cdot 2)$
$160 = (16)(10)$ True. The matte should be 2 inches wide.

Exercise Factor to solve each problem.

1. The outside edges of a rectangular frame are 3 ft by 4 ft. The matte covers $\frac{1}{2}$ the area inside the frame. How wide is the matte?
2. The area of a walkway around a rectangular garden is equal to the area of the garden alone. The garden measures 6 m by 9 m. What is the width of the walkway?
3. If the sides of a square are lengthened by 3 ft, the area of the square becomes 81 ft^2. What is the length of the side of the original square?

178 Chapter 6 Factoring

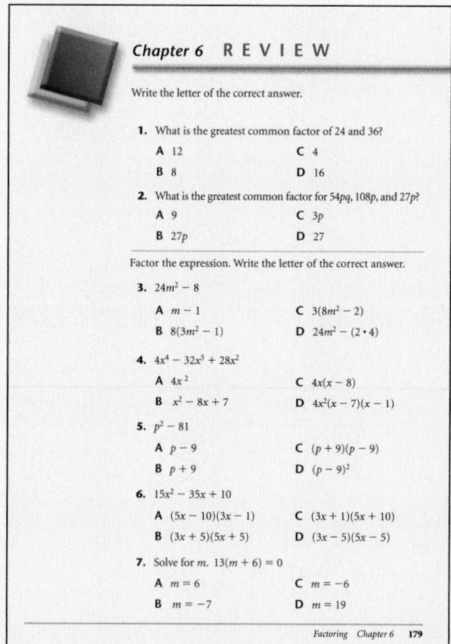

Chapter 6 REVIEW

Write the letter of the correct answer.

1. What is the greatest common factor of 24 and 36?
   A 12 C 4
   B 8 D 16
2. What is the greatest common factor for $54pq$, $108p$, and $27p$?
   A 9 C $3p$
   B $27p$ D 27

Factor the expression. Write the letter of the correct answer.

3. $24m^2 - 8$
   A $m - 1$ C $3(8m^2 - 2)$
   B $8(3m^2 - 1)$ D $24m^2 - (2 \cdot 4)$
4. $4x^4 - 32x^3 + 28x^2$
   A $4x^2$ C $4x(x - 8)$
   B $x^2 - 8x + 7$ D $4x^2(x - 7)(x - 1)$
5. $p^2 - 81$
   A $p - 9$ C $(p + 9)(p - 9)$
   B $p + 9$ D $(p - 9)^2$
6. $15x^2 - 35x + 10$
   A $(5x - 10)(3x - 1)$ C $(3x + 1)(5x + 10)$
   B $(3x + 5)(5x + 5)$ D $(3x - 5)(5x - 5)$
7. Solve for m. $13(m + 6) = 0$
   A $m = 6$ C $m = -6$
   B $m = -7$ D $m = 19$

Factoring Chapter 6 179

- Application activities help students relate the chapter content to real-life situations.
- Chapter Reviews allow students and teachers to check for skill mastery. Multiple choice items are provided for practice in taking standardized tests. Supplementary Problems at the back of the book provide additional practice.

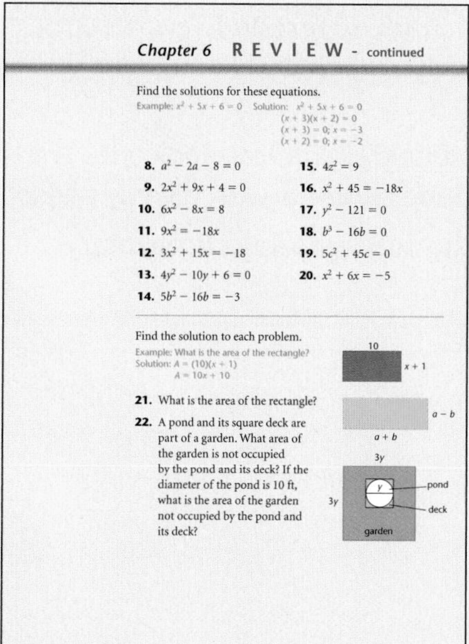

Chapter 6 REVIEW - continued

Find the solutions for these equations.

Example: $x^2 + 5x + 6 = 0$ Solution: $x^2 + 5x + 6 = 0$
$(x + 3)(x + 2) = 0$
$(x + 3) = 0; x = -3$
$(x + 2) = 0; x = -2$

8. $a^2 - 2a - 8 = 0$
9. $2x^2 + 9x + 4 = 0$
10. $6x^2 - 8x = 8$
11. $9x^2 = -18x$
12. $3x^2 + 15x = -18$
13. $4y^2 - 10y + 6 = 0$
14. $5b^2 - 16b = -3$
15. $4z^2 = 9$
16. $x^2 + 45 = -18x$
17. $y^2 - 121 = 0$
18. $b^3 - 16b = 0$
19. $5c^2 + 45c = 0$
20. $x^2 + 6x = -5$

Find the solution to each problem.

Example: What is the area of the rectangle?
Solution: $A = (10)(x + 1)$
$A = 10x + 10$

21. What is the area of the rectangle?
22. A pond and its square deck are part of a garden. What area of the garden is not occupied by the pond and its deck? If the diameter of the pond is 10 ft, what is the area of the garden not occupied by the pond and its deck?

180 Chapter 5 Factoring

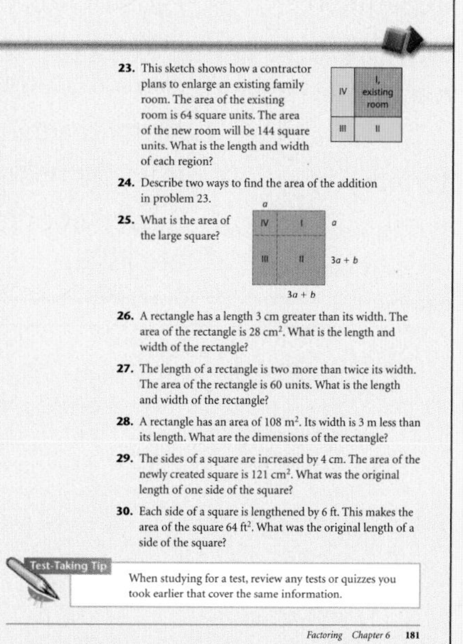

23. This sketch shows how a contractor plans to enlarge an existing family room. The area of the existing room is 64 square units. The area of the new room will be 144 square units. What is the length and width of each region?
24. Describe two ways to find the area of the addition in problem 23.
25. What is the area of the large square?
26. A rectangle has a length 3 cm greater than its width. The area of the rectangle is 28 cm^2. What is the length and width of the rectangle?
27. The length of a rectangle is two more than twice its width. The area of the rectangle is 60 units. What is the length and width of the rectangle?
28. A rectangle has an area of 108 m^2. Its width is 3 m less than its length. What are the dimensions of the rectangle?
29. The sides of a square are increased by 4 cm. The area of the newly created square is 121 cm^2. What was the original length of one side of the square?
30. Each side of a square is lengthened by 6 ft. This makes the area of the square 64 ft^2. What was the original length of a side of the square?

Test-Taking Tip
When studying for a test, review any tests or quizzes you took earlier that cover the same information.

Factoring Chapter 6 181

- Test-Taking Tips at the end of each Chapter Review help reduce test anxiety and improve test scores.

Teacher's Edition Highlights

The comprehensive, wraparound Teacher's Edition provides instructional strategies at point of use. Everything from preparation guidelines to teaching tips and strategies are included in an easy-to-use format. Activities are featured at point of use for teacher convenience.

Chapter 2

Planning Guide

The Rules of Arithmetic

		Student Text Lesson				Student Text Features							Teaching Strategies							Learning Styles						Teacher's Resource Library			
		Student Pages	Vocabulary	Practice Exercises	Solutions Key	Estimation Activity	Algebra in Your Life	Technology Connection	Writing About Mathematics	Try This	Problem Solving	Calculator Practice	Online Connection	Common Error	Applications (Home, Career, Community)	Mental Math	Manipulatives	Calculator	Group Problem Solving	Auditory/Verbal	Visual/Spatial	Logical/Mathematical	Body/Kinesthetic	Interpersonal/Group Learning	LEP/ESL	Activities	Alternative Activities	Workbook Activities	Self-Study Guide
Lesson 1	Commutative Property of Addition	32–33	✓	✓	✓				33						33								33			13	13	13	✓
Lesson 2	Commutative Property of Multiplication	34–35	✓	✓	✓						35		40						35		35	35				14	14	14	✓
Lesson 3	Associative Property of Addition	36–37	✓	✓	✓					37						37									37	15	15	15	✓
Lesson 4	Associative Property of Multiplication	38–41	✓	✓	✓		41	39							39									39		16	16	16	✓
Lesson 5	The Distributive Property—Multiplication	42–43	✓	✓	✓									43										43		17	17	17	✓
Lesson 6	The Distributive Property—Factoring	44–45	✓	✓	✓						45			45					45							18	18	18	✓
Lesson 7	Properties of Zero	46–47	✓	✓	✓				47					47		47									47	19	19	19	✓
Lesson 8	Properties of 1	48–49	✓	✓	✓						49								49	49						20	20	20	✓
Lesson 9	Powers and Roots	50–53	✓	✓	✓	52						53		50			51	52		51						21	21	21	✓
Lesson 10	More on Powers and Roots	54–55		✓	✓							55		54			55	55						49		22	22	22	✓
Lesson 11	Order of Operations	56–57		✓	✓						57								57	57				57		23	23	23–24	✓
Application	Using Square Root	58		✓	✓										58														✓

Chapter Activities

Teacher's Resource Library
Estimation Exercise 2: Estimating Square Roots
Application Activity 2: Using Square Root
Everyday Algebra 2: Finding Volume
Community Connection 2: Transportation and Shipping

Teacher's Edition
Chapter 2 Project

Assessment Options

Student Text
Chapter 2 Review

Teacher's Resource Library
Chapter 2 Mastery Tests A and B

Software Options

Skill Track Software
Use the Skill Track Software for *Algebra* for additional reinforcement of this chapter. The software provides multiple-choice assessment items for students to access by computer.

Solutions Key
Use the Solutions Key with this chapter to help students who may need additional assistance. The Solutions Key CD provides solutions for every exercise in the student edition.

Other Resources

Alternative Activities
The Teacher's Resource Library (TRL) contains a set of worksheets written at a second-grade reading level called Alternative Activities. They cover the same content as the regular Activities.

Manipulatives
See the Manipulative activities in this chapter for hands-on modeling of the content.
Unit Cubes
Pattern Blocks

30A

30B

Chapter Planning Guides

- The Planning Guide saves valuable preparation time by organizing all materials for each chapter.
- A complete listing of lessons allows you to preview each chapter quickly.
- Assessment options are highlighted for easy reference. Options include:
  Chapter Reviews
  Chapter Mastery Tests, Forms A and B
  Midterm and Final Tests
- Page numbers of Student Text and Teacher's Edition features help customize lesson plans to your students.
- Many teaching strategies and learning styles are listed to help include students with diverse needs.
- All activities for the Teacher's Resource Library are listed.

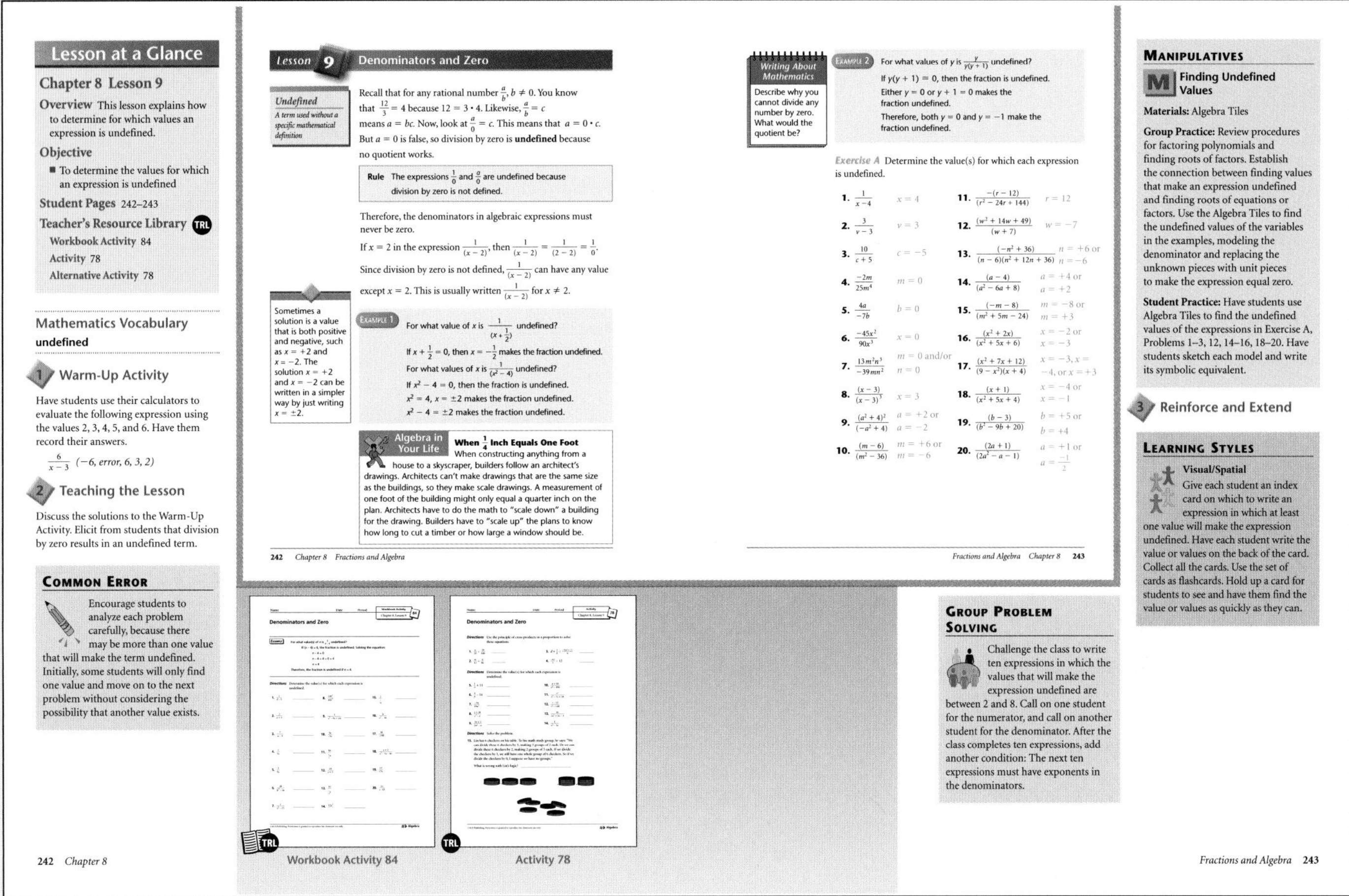

Lesson at a Glance

Chapter 8 Lesson 9

Overview This lesson explains how to determine for which values an expression is undefined.

Objective

- To determine the values for which an expression is undefined

Student Pages 242–243

Teacher's Resource Library TRL

Workbook Activity 84

Activity 78

Alternative Activity 78

Mathematics Vocabulary

undefined

1 Warm-Up Activity

Have students use their calculators to evaluate the following expression using the values 2, 3, 4, 5, and 6. Have them record their answers.

$\frac{6}{x-3}$ (−6, error, 6, 3, 2)

2 Teaching the Lesson

Discuss the solutions to the Warm-Up Activity. Elicit from students that division by zero results in an undefined term.

Common Error

Encourage students to analyze each problem carefully, because there may be more than one value that will make the term undefined. Initially, some students will only find one value and move on to the next problem without considering the possibility that another value exists.

Lesson 9 Denominators and Zero

Undefined — A term used without a specific mathematical definition

Recall that for any rational number $\frac{a}{b}$, $b \neq 0$. You know that $\frac{12}{3} = 4$ because $12 = 3 \cdot 4$. Likewise, $\frac{a}{b} = c$ means $a = bc$. Now, look at $\frac{a}{0} = c$. This means that $a = 0 \cdot c$. But $a = 0$ is false, so division by zero is **undefined** because no quotient works.

Rule The expressions $\frac{1}{0}$ and $\frac{a}{0}$ are undefined because division by zero is not defined.

Therefore, the denominators in algebraic expressions must never be zero.

If $x = 2$ in the expression $\frac{1}{(x-2)}$, then $\frac{1}{(x-2)} = \frac{1}{(2-2)} = \frac{1}{0}$.

Since division by zero is not defined, $\frac{1}{(x-2)}$ can have any value except $x = 2$. This is usually written $\frac{1}{(x-2)}$ for $x \neq 2$.

Sometimes a solution is a value that is both positive and negative, such as $x = +2$ and $x = -2$. The solution $x = \pm 2$ and $x = -2$ can be written in a simpler way by just writing $x = \pm 2$.

Example 1 For what value of x is $\frac{1}{(x+\frac{1}{2})}$ undefined?

If $x + \frac{1}{2} = 0$, then $x = -\frac{1}{2}$ makes the fraction undefined.

For what values of x is $\frac{1}{(x^2-4)}$ undefined?

If $x^2 - 4 = 0$, then the fraction is undefined.

$x^2 = 4$, $x = \pm 2$ makes the fraction undefined.

$x^2 - 4 = \pm 2$ makes the fraction undefined.

Algebra in Your Life — When $\frac{1}{4}$ Inch Equals One Foot

When constructing anything from a house to a skyscraper, builders follow an architect's drawings. Architects can't make drawings that are the same size as the buildings, so they make scale drawings. A measurement of one foot of the building might only equal a quarter inch on the plan. Architects have to do the math to "scale down" a building for the drawing. Builders have to "scale up" the plans to know how long to cut a timber or how large a window should be.

242 Chapter 8 Fractions and Algebra

Writing About Mathematics

Describe why you cannot divide any number by zero. What would the quotient be?

Example 2 For what values of y is $\frac{y}{y(y+1)}$ undefined?

If $y(y+1) = 0$, then the fraction is undefined.

Either $y = 0$ or $y + 1 = 0$ makes the fraction undefined.

Therefore, both $y = 0$ and $y = -1$ make the fraction undefined.

Exercise A Determine the value(s) for which each expression is undefined.

1.	$\frac{1}{x-4}$	$x = 4$	11.	$\frac{-(r-12)}{(r^2-24r+144)}$	$r = 12$
2.	$\frac{3}{v-3}$	$v = 3$	12.	$\frac{(w^2+14w+49)}{(w+7)}$	$w = -7$
3.	$\frac{10}{c+5}$	$c = -5$	13.	$\frac{(-n^2+36)}{(n-6)(n^2+12n+36)}$	$n = +6$ or $n = -6$
4.	$\frac{-2m}{25m^4}$	$m = 0$	14.	$\frac{(a-4)}{(a^2-6a+8)}$	$a = +4$ or $a = +2$
5.	$\frac{4a}{-7b}$	$b = 0$	15.	$\frac{(-m-8)}{(m^2+5m-24)}$	$m = -8$ or $m = +3$
6.	$\frac{-45x^2}{90x^3}$	$x = 0$	16.	$\frac{(x^2+2x)}{(x^2+5x+6)}$	$x = -2$ or $x = -3$
7.	$\frac{13m^2n^3}{-39mn^2}$	$m = 0$ and/or $n = 0$	17.	$\frac{(x^2+7x+12)}{(9-x^2)(x+4)}$	$x = -3, x = -4$, or $x = +3$
8.	$\frac{(x-3)}{(x-3)^3}$	$x = 3$	18.	$\frac{(x+1)}{(x^2+5x+4)}$	$x = -4$ or $x = -1$
9.	$\frac{(a^2+4)^2}{(-a^2+4)}$	$a = +2$ or $a = -2$	19.	$\frac{(b-3)}{(b^2-9b+20)}$	$b = +5$ or $b = +4$
10.	$\frac{(m-6)}{(m^2-36)}$	$m = +6$ or $m = -6$	20.	$\frac{(2a+1)}{(2a^2-a-1)}$	$a = +1$ or $a = \frac{-1}{2}$

Fractions and Algebra Chapter 8 243

Manipulatives

M Finding Undefined Values

Materials: Algebra Tiles

Group Practice: Review procedures for factoring polynomials and finding roots of factors. Establish the connection between finding values that make an expression undefined and finding roots of equations or factors. Use the Algebra Tiles to find the undefined values of the variables in the examples, modeling the denominator and replacing the unknown pieces with unit pieces to make the expression equal zero.

Student Practice: Have students use Algebra Tiles to find the undefined values of the expressions in Exercise A, Problems 1–3, 12, 14–16, 18–20. Have students sketch each model and write its symbolic equivalent.

3 Reinforce and Extend

Learning Styles

Visual/Spatial

Give each student an index card on which to write an expression in which at least one value will make the expression undefined. Have each student write the value or values on the back of the card. Collect all the cards. Use the set of cards as flashcards. Hold up a card for students to see and have them find the value or values as quickly as they can.

Group Problem Solving

Challenge the class to write ten expressions in which the values that will make the expression undefined are between 2 and 8. Call on one student for the numerator, and call on another student for the denominator. After the class completes ten expressions, add another condition: The next ten expressions must have exponents in the denominators.

TRL Workbook Activity 84

TRL Activity 78

242 Chapter 8

Fractions and Algebra 243

Lessons

- Quick overviews of chapters and lessons save planning time.
- Lesson objectives are listed for easy reference.
- Page references are provided for convenience.
- Easy-to-follow lesson plans in three steps saves time: Warm-Up Activity, Teaching the Lesson, and Reinforce and Extend.
- Common Error alerts teachers to possible student errors before they are made.
- Mental Math activities encourage students to think independently.
- Calculator activities provide students with practice using a calculator.
- Applications: Three areas of application—Career Connection, In the Community, and At Home—help students relate math to the world outside the classroom. Applications motivate students and make learning relevant.
- Group Problem Solving provides group work for students.
- Relevant Web sites are listed in Online Connections.
- Learning Styles provide teaching strategies to help meet the needs of students with diverse ways of learning. Modalities include Auditory/Verbal, Visual/Spatial, Body/Kinesthetic, Logical/Mathematical, and Interpersonal/Group Learning. Additional teaching activities are provided for LEP/ESL students.
- Answers are provided in the Teacher's Edition for all exercises in the Student Text. Answers to the Teacher's Resource Library and Student Workbook are provided at the back of this Teacher's Edition and on the TRL CD-ROM.
- Worksheet and Activity pages from the Teacher's Resource Library are shown at point of use in reduced form.

Teacher's Resource Library Highlights

TRL All of the activities you'll need to reinforce and extend the text are conveniently located on the AGS Publishing Teacher's Resource Library (TRL) CD-ROM. All of the reproducible activities pictured in the Teacher's Edition are ready to select, view, and print. Additionally, you can preview other materials by directly linking to the AGS Publishing Web site.

Workbook

Workbook Activities are available to reinforce and extend skills from each lesson of the textbook. Also available in a bound workbook format.

Activities

Lesson activities for each lesson of the textbook give students additional skill practice.

Alternative Activities

These activities cover the same content as the regular Activities but are written at a second-grade reading level.

Application Activities
Everyday Algebra
Community Connections
Estimation Exercises

Relevant activities help students extend their knowledge to the real world and reinforce concepts covered in class.

Self-Study Guide

An assignment guide provides the student with an outline for working through the text independently. The guide provides teachers with the flexibility for individualized instruction or independent study.

Mastery Tests

Chapter, Midterm, and Final Mastery Tests are convenient assessment options.

Answer Key

All answers to reproducible activities are included in the TRL and in the Teacher's Edition.

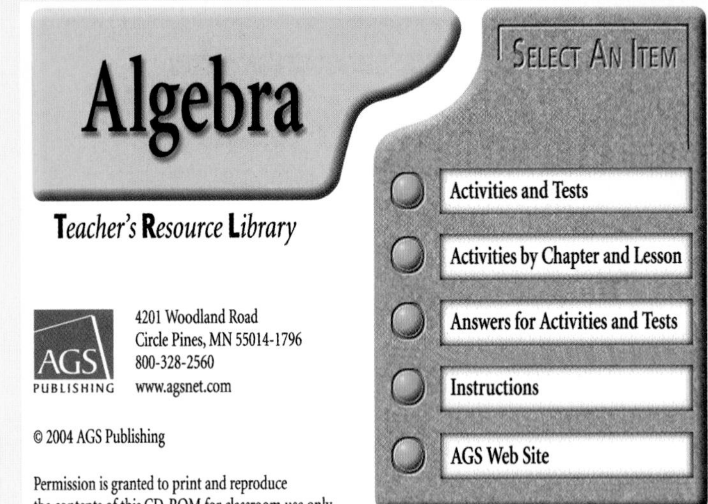

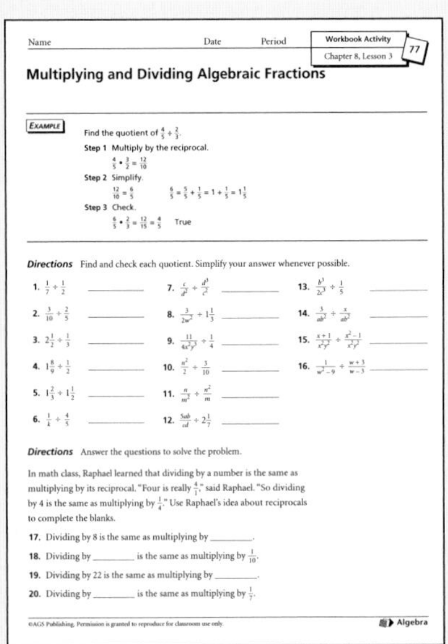

Name Date Period — Workbook Activity 77, Chapter 8, Lesson 3

Multiplying and Dividing Algebraic Fractions

EXAMPLE Find the quotient of $\frac{4}{5} \div \frac{2}{3}$.

Step 1 Multiply by the reciprocal. $\frac{4}{5} \cdot \frac{3}{2} = \frac{12}{10}$

Step 2 Simplify. $\frac{12}{10} = \frac{6}{5}$ $\frac{6}{5} = \frac{5}{5} + \frac{1}{5} = 1 + \frac{1}{5} = 1\frac{1}{5}$

Step 3 Check. $\frac{6}{5} \cdot \frac{2}{3} = \frac{12}{15} = \frac{4}{5}$ True

Directions Find and check each quotient. Simplify your answer whenever possible.

1. $\frac{1}{7} \div \frac{1}{2}$ _____
2. $\frac{3}{10} \div \frac{2}{5}$ _____
3. $2\frac{1}{2} \div \frac{1}{3}$ _____
4. $1\frac{8}{9} \div \frac{1}{2}$ _____
5. $1\frac{2}{3} \div 1\frac{1}{2}$ _____
6. $\frac{1}{k} \div \frac{4}{5}$ _____
7. $\frac{c}{d^2} \div \frac{d^3}{c^2}$ _____
8. $\frac{3}{2w^2} \div 1\frac{1}{3}$ _____
9. $\frac{11}{4x^2y^3} \div \frac{1}{4}$ _____
10. $\frac{n^2}{2} \div \frac{3}{10}$ _____
11. $\frac{n}{m^2} \div \frac{n^2}{m}$ _____
12. $\frac{5ab}{cd} \div 2\frac{1}{7}$ _____
13. $\frac{b^3}{2c^3} \div \frac{1}{5}$ _____
14. $\frac{3}{ab^2} \div \frac{x}{ab^2}$ _____
15. $\frac{x+1}{x^2y^2} \div \frac{x^2-1}{x^2y^2}$ _____
16. $\frac{1}{w^2-9} \div \frac{w+3}{w-3}$ _____

Directions Answer the questions to solve the problem.

In math class, Raphael learned that dividing by a number is the same as multiplying by its reciprocal. "Four is really $\frac{4}{1}$," said Raphael. "So dividing by 4 is the same as multiplying by $\frac{1}{4}$." Use Raphael's idea about reciprocals to complete the blanks.

17. Dividing by 8 is the same as multiplying by _____.
18. Dividing by _____ is the same as multiplying by $\frac{1}{10}$.
19. Dividing by 22 is the same as multiplying by _____.
20. Dividing by _____ is the same as multiplying by $\frac{1}{7}$.

©AGS Publishing. Permission is granted to reproduce for classroom use only. Algebra

Workbook Activities

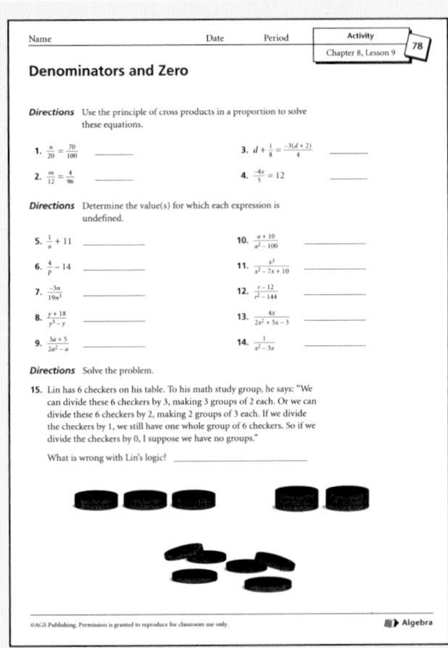

Name Date Period — Activity 78, Chapter 8, Lesson 9

Denominators and Zero

Directions Use the principle of cross products in a proportion to solve these equations.

1. $\frac{n}{20} = \frac{70}{100}$ _____
2. $\frac{m}{12} = \frac{4}{96}$ _____
3. $d + \frac{1}{8} = \frac{-3(d+2)}{4}$ _____
4. $\frac{-4x}{5} = 12$ _____

Directions Determine the value(s) for which each expression is undefined.

5. $\frac{1}{a} + 11$ _____
6. $\frac{4}{p} - 14$ _____
7. $\frac{-3n}{19n^3}$ _____
8. $\frac{y+18}{y^3-y}$ _____
9. $\frac{3a+5}{2a^2-a}$ _____
10. $\frac{a+10}{a^2-100}$ _____
11. $\frac{x^3}{x^2-7x+10}$ _____
12. $\frac{r-12}{r^2-144}$ _____
13. $\frac{4x}{2x^2+5x-3}$ _____
14. $\frac{1}{x^2-3x}$ _____

Directions Solve the problem.

15. Lin has 6 checkers on his table. To his math study group, he says: "We can divide these 6 checkers by 3, making 3 groups of 2 each. Or we can divide these 6 checkers by 2, making 2 groups of 3 each. If we divide the checkers by 1, we still have one whole group of 6 checkers. So if we divide the checkers by 0, I suppose we have no groups."

What is wrong with Lin's logic? _____

©AGS Publishing. Permission is granted to reproduce for classroom use only. Algebra

Activities

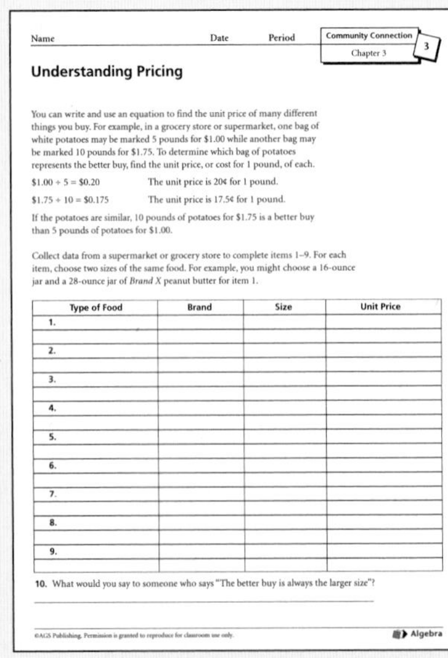

Name Date Period — Community Connection 3, Chapter 3

Understanding Pricing

You can write and use an equation to find the unit price of many different things you buy. For example, in a grocery store or supermarket, one bag of white potatoes may be marked 5 pounds for \$1.00 while another bag may be marked 10 pounds for \$1.75. To determine which bag of potatoes represents the better buy, find the unit price, or cost for 1 pound, of each.

\$1.00 ÷ 5 = \$0.20 The unit price is 20¢ for 1 pound.

\$1.75 ÷ 10 = \$0.175 The unit price is 17.5¢ for 1 pound.

If the potatoes are similar, 10 pounds of potatoes for \$1.75 is a better buy than 5 pounds of potatoes for \$1.00.

Collect data from a supermarket or grocery store to complete items 1–9. For each item, choose two sizes of the same food. For example, you might choose a 16-ounce jar and a 28-ounce jar of *Brand X* peanut butter for item 1.

Type of Food	Brand	Size	Unit Price
1.			
2.			
3.			
4.			
5.			
6.			
7.			
8.			
9.			

10. What would you say to someone who says "The better buy is always the larger size"?

©AGS Publishing. Permission is granted to reproduce for classroom use only. Algebra

Community Connections

Name Date Period — Mastery Test A, Page 1, Chapter 8

Chapter 8 Mastery Test A

Directions Circle the letter of the correct answer.

1. Write the fraction $\frac{-12}{20}$ in simplest form.
   A $\frac{-3}{20}$ C $\frac{-3}{5}$
   B $\frac{6}{10}$ D $\frac{12}{20}$
2. Find the product of $\frac{3}{4} \cdot \frac{5}{12}$. Simplify if possible.
   A $\frac{5}{48}$ C $\frac{1}{2}$
   B $\frac{5}{16}$ D $\frac{3}{12}$
3. Find the difference of $1\frac{1}{2} - \frac{2}{3}$.
   A -1 C $\frac{5}{6}$
   B $\frac{4}{6}$ D $\frac{1}{3}$
4. Find the sum of $\frac{3}{cd} + \frac{5}{de}$.
   A $\frac{(3de + 5cd)}{(cd)(de)}$ C $\frac{15}{ce(d^2)}$
   B $\frac{8}{cde}$ D $\frac{8cde}{(cd)(de)}$
5. Solve for u. $\frac{4u}{7} = \frac{1}{20}$.
   A $u = \frac{1}{35}$ C $u = \frac{5}{27}$
   B $u = \frac{7}{80}$ D $u = \frac{1}{4}$

Directions Write each fraction in simplest form.

6. $\frac{16}{-36}$ _____
7. $\frac{c^4}{c^2}$ _____
8. $\frac{24a^4b^3}{8a^2b^2}$ _____
9. $\frac{(n-5)}{(n^2-25)}$ _____
10. $\frac{(p^2-64)}{(p+8)}$ _____
11. $\frac{(-w-6)}{(w^2+4w-12)}$ _____

©AGS Publishing. Permission is granted to reproduce for classroom use only. Algebra

Mastery Tests

Correlation of Algebra to the NCTM Standards

STANDARD 1 Number and Operations

Instructional programs from pre-kindergarten through grade 12 should enable all students to:

- understand numbers, ways of representing numbers, relationships among numbers, and number systems;
- understand meanings of operations and how they relate to one another;
- compute fluently and make reasonable estimates.

Algebra

Understand numbers: pages 6–15, 20–22, 32–57, 98–113, 124–133, 220–233, 314–321, 328–335, 392–397.

Understand meanings: pages 12–15, 20–21, 50–55, 58, 129–133, 210–213, 314–321.

Compute fluently: pages 8–15, 32–57, 96–117, 131–133, 230–243, 314–321.

Estimation Activities: pages 17, 52, 83, 106, 147, 176, 194, 233, 275, 301, 345, 367, 387.

STANDARD 2 Algebra

Instructional programs from pre-kindergarten through grade 12 should enable all students to:

- understand patterns, relations, and functions;
- represent and analyze mathematical situations and structures using algebraic symbols;
- use mathematical models to represent and understand quantitative relationships;
- analyze change in various contexts.

Algebra

Understand patterns: pages 256–282, 288–313, 322, 348–350, 386–400, 402.

Represent and analyze: pages 16–19, 42–45, 64–89, 96–117, 136–149, 160–177, 224–243, 254–279, 288–305, 310–313, 390–400.

Use mathematical models: Application exercises at the end of each chapter help students to model mathematical situations. See pages 26, 58, 90, 118, 150, 178, 214, 244, 282, 322, 350, 380, 402.

Analyze change: pages 150, 258–260, 348–350, 402.

STANDARD 3 Geometry

Instructional programs from pre-kindergarten through grade 12 should enable all students to:

- analyze characteristics and properties of two- and three-dimensional geometric shapes and develop mathematical arguments about geometric relationships;
- specify locations and describe spatial relationships using coordinate geometry and other representational systems;
- apply transformations and use symmetry to analyze mathematical situations;
- use visualization, spatial reasoning, and geometric modeling to solve problems.

Algebra

Analyze characteristics: pages 80–81, 234–237, 356–377, 380.

Specify locations: pages 282, 294–297.

Apply transformations: pages 372–375, 380.

Use visualization: pages 38–41, 50–52, 80–81, 100–103, 116–117, 140–141, 166–171, 178, 368–377.

STANDARD 4 Measurement

Instructional programs from pre-kindergarten through grade 12 should enable all students to:

- understand measurable attributes of objects and the units, systems, and processes of measurement;
- apply appropriate techniques, tools, and formulas to determine measurements.

Algebra

Understand measurable attributes: not applicable

Apply appropriate techniques, tools, and formulas: pages 34–35, 38–41, 50–52, 138–141, 166–171, 356–359, 364–369.

STANDARD 5 Data Analysis and Probability

Instructional programs from pre-kindergarten through grade 12 should enable all students to:

- formulate questions that can be addressed with data and collect, organize, and display relevant data to answer them;
- select and use appropriate statistical methods to analyze data;
- develop and evaluate inferences and predictions that are based on data;
- understand and apply basic concepts of probability.

Algebra

Formulate questions: pages 100–103, 184–214.

Select and use: pages 184–195.

Develop and evaluate: pages 204–205.

Understand and apply: pages 196–209.

STANDARD 6 Problem Solving

Instructional programs from pre-kindergarten through grade 12 should enable all students to:

- build new mathematical knowledge through problem solving;
- solve problems that arise in mathematics and in other contexts;
- apply and adapt a variety of appropriate strategies to solve problems;
- monitor and reflect on the process of mathematical problem solving.

Algebra

Problem Solving exercises: pages 5, 7, 11, 13, 35, 45, 49, 57, 67, 69, 73, 75, 83, 89, 99, 103, 105, 107, 109, 113, 115, 117, 137, 139, 141, 163, 167, 171, 177, 203, 212–213, 229, 236–237, 241, 253, 262, 291, 313, 321, 331, 335, 344–345, 369, 379, 389, 391.

Application exercises: pages 26, 58, 90, 118, 150, 178, 214, 244, 282, 322, 350, 380, 402.

Most exercises throughout the textbook encourage problem-solving skills.

STANDARD 7 Reasoning and Proof

Instructional programs from pre-kindergarten through grade 12 should enable all students to:

- recognize reasoning and proof as fundamental aspects of mathematics;
- make and investigate mathematical conjectures;
- develop and evaluate mathematical arguments and proofs;
- select and use various types of reasoning and methods of proof.

Algebra

Reasoning skills/processes, conjectures, and argumentation are applied throughout in exercises at the end of each lesson, in *Problem Solving* and *Application exercises* under the previous standard, and in *Chapter Reviews* and *Chapter Tests.*

STANDARD 8 Communication

Instructional programs from pre-kindergarten through grade 12 should enable all students to:

- organize and consolidate their mathematical thinking through communication;
- communicate their mathematical thinking coherently and clearly to peers, teachers, and others;
- analyze and evaluate the mathematical thinking and strategies of others;
- use the language of mathematics to express mathematical ideas precisely.

Algebra

Helps students develop *mathematical communication skills* in a number of ways:

—Oral explanation and discussion: ***Problem Solving exercises*** throughout provide opportunities for oral language.

—***Learning Styles: Auditory/Verbal*** sidebars in the Teacher's Edition (examples on pages 15, 49, 51, 57, 77, 115)

—Graphical representations: pages 184–187, 254–260, 272–281, 288–297

—Definitions of topic-relevant terms are included in the first page of most lessons throughout.

—Notation is directly addressed on pages 4–5; and Scientific Notation is addressed on pages 129–133

STANDARD 9 Connections

Instructional programs from pre-kindergarten through grade 12 should enable all students to:

- recognize and use connections among mathematical ideas;
- understand how mathematical ideas interconnect and build on one another to produce a coherent whole;
- recognize and apply mathematics in contexts outside of mathematics.

Algebra

Relationships among diverse mathematical concepts such as arithmetic, linear equations, percentages, exponents, polynomials, data, fractions, inequalities, irrational numbers, geometry, and quadratic equations are explored throughout, and principles are presented as an integrated whole. The role of mathematics in history is explored in the Teacher's Edition on pages 3, 33, 73, 99, 128, 157, 187, 225, 274, 291, 329, 358, 387. In addition, the role of algebra in other areas is explored in the ***Problem Solving exercises*** on pages 5, 7, 11, 13, 35, 45, 49, 57, 67, 69, 73, 75, 83, 89, 99, 103, 105, 107, 109, 113, 115, 117, 137, 139, 141, 163, 167, 171, 177, 203, 212–213, 229, 236–237, 241, 253, 262, 291, 313, 321, 331, 335, 344–345, 369, 379, 389, 391; in ***Try This*** activities on pages 7, 37, 65, 115, 139, 141, 173, 205, 209, 229, 237, 255, 291, 293, 331, 337, 339, 369, 375, 391; in ***Writing About Mathematics*** activities on pages 15, 33, 47, 65, 104, 125, 127, 130, 161, 167, 171, 194, 209, 221, 223, 225, 229, 231, 241, 243, 252, 257, 261, 264, 267, 291, 293, 303, 308, 309, 312, 339, 359, 389; in ***Technology Connections*** on pages 19, 39, 71, 110, 133, 177, 199, 239, 271, 309, 333, 359, 395; in ***Algebra in Your Life*** activities on pages 15, 41, 77, 107, 128, 157, 187, 242, 262, 296, 331, 375, 394; and in ***Estimation Activities*** on pages 17, 52, 83, 106, 147, 176, 194, 233, 275, 301, 345, 367, 387.

STANDARD 10 Representation

Instructional programs from pre-kindergarten through grade 12 should enable all students to:

- create and use representations to organize, record, and communicate mathematical ideas;
- select, apply, and translate among mathematical representations to solve problems;
- use representations to model and interpret physical, social, and mathematical phenomena.

Algebra

Many different types of *representations* are used throughout the text in order to maximize *student understanding of concepts and relationships.* See the following examples:
Drawings (conceptual): pages 38–41, 78, 80, 256–258, 272–281.
Drawings (applied): pages 118, 167, 171, 178, 236, 377–379.
Charts/Tables: pages 85, 104–105, 134, 156, 185–186, 330.
Graphs: pages 101–102, 185–186, 272–274, 304–305, 322, 348–349.
Manipulative exercises: Teacher's Edition pages 125, 139, 145, 163, 173, 197, 205.

Learning Styles

The learning style activities in the *Algebra* Teacher's Edition provide activities to help students with special needs understand the lesson. These activities focus on the following learning styles: Visual/Spatial, Auditory/Verbal, Body/Kinesthetic, Logical/Mathematical, Interpersonal/Group Learning, LEP/ESL. These styles reflect Howard Gardner's theory of multiple intelligences. The writing activities suggested in this Student Text are appropriate for students who fit Gardner's description of Verbal/Linguistic Intelligence.

The activities are designed to help teachers capitalize on students' individual strengths and dominant learning styles. The activities reinforce the lesson by teaching or expanding upon the content in a different way.

Following are examples of activities featured in the *Algebra* Teacher's Edition:

Visual/Spatial

Students benefit from seeing illustrations or demonstrations beyond what is in the text.

LEARNING STYLES

Visual/Spatial

Have students copy the graphs shown in Exercise A. For each graph, ask students to apply the vertical line test. Have them attempt to draw a line that intersects the graph at more than one point. Have students post their efforts, indicating whether each graph passed or failed the vertical line test.

Interpersonal/Group Learning

Learners benefit from working with at least one other person on activities that involve a process and an end product.

LEARNING STYLES

Interpersonal Group Learning

Have students work in small groups to write, solve, and graph the inverse of the equations in problems 5–10 in Exercise B. For example, $y = 3x$ becomes $x = 3y$; $y = 2x + 1$ becomes $x = 2y + 1$. Ask the groups to describe the similarities and differences between their graphs and the graphs of the equations for Exercise B.

Auditory/Verbal

Students benefit from having someone read the text aloud or listening to the text on audiocassette. Musical activities appropriate for the lesson may help auditory learners.

LEARNING STYLES

Auditory/Verbal

Complete Exercise A orally in class. Ask volunteers to read aloud each sentence with their chosen word or phrase. Then ask them to explain why they chose that word or phrase to complete that sentence.

Body/Kinesthetic

Learners benefit from activities that include physical movement or tac tile experiences.

LEARNING STYLES

Body/Kinesthetic

Have students work in groups of four to play a game called "General Directions." Direct each group to use masking tape to create a −20 to +20 number line on the classroom floor. Have students take turns being "The General" and giving directions such as "The General says stand on +3," "The General says move to the opposite of −7," and "The General says give the absolute value of the number you're at."

LEP/ESL

Students benefit from activities that promote English language acquisition and interaction with English-speaking peers.

LEARNING STYLES

LEP/ESL

Have students work in pairs to write complete sentences describing the points in Exercise B. Using problem 11, provide a model sentence for students: "Point *Y* is 1 unit to the right of the *y*-axis and 2 units above the *x*-axis." For each problem, one student should write the sentence, and the partner should plot the point described. Encourage students to exchange roles after each problem.

Logical/Mathematical

Students learn by using logical/ mathematical thinking in relation to the lesson content.

LEARNING STYLES

Logical/Mathematical

Have each student pick four composite numbers between 100 and 1,000 and find the prime factorizations. For example,

$$121 = 11 \cdot 11$$
$$200 = 2 \cdot 2 \cdot 2 \cdot 5 \cdot 5$$
$$925 = 5 \cdot 5 \cdot 37$$
$$620 = 2 \cdot 2 \cdot 5 \cdot 31$$

Have students write the factored form on a piece of paper. Ask pairs of students to exchange papers and find the original numbers.

by
Siegfried Haenisch

AGS Publishing
Circle Pines, Minnesota 55014-1796
800-328-2560

About the Author

Siegfried Haenisch, Ed.D. has taught mathematics at every level, from elementary to graduate school, most recently as Professor in the Department of Mathematics and Statistics at the College of New Jersey. The Mathematical Association of America granted him the 1995 Award for Distinguished Teaching of Mathematics. Dr. Haenisch was the site director for the training of teachers in the New Jersey Algebra Project. He was a member of the National Science Foundation Institutes in Mathematics at Rutgers University, Oberlin College, and Princeton University. At Yale University, he was a member of the Seminar in the History of Mathematics, sponsored by the National Endowment in the Humanities. Dr. Haenisch currently serves as a mathematics curriculum consultant to school districts.

Photo credits for this textbook can be found on page 526.

The publisher wishes to thank the following educators for their helpful comments during the review process for *Algebra.* Their assistance has been invaluable.

Maria Antonopoulou, Algebra Teacher, Hastings Education Centre, Vancouver, B.C., Canada; **David Arnold,** SLD Teacher, Winter Park Ninth Grade Center, Winter Park, Florida; **Tamara Bell,** Special Education Teacher, Muncie Community Schools, Southside High School, Muncie, Indiana; **Jacqueline DeWitt,** Cooperative Consultant, Umatilla High School, Sorrento, Florida; **Tina Dobson,** Special Education Math Resource Specialist, Sandridge Junior High School; Roy, Utah; **Connie Eichhorn,** Career Center and Adult Education Program, Omaha Public Schools, Omaha, Nebraska; **Dr. Rita Giles,** Program Director, Fairfax County Public Schools, Alexandria, Virginia; **Anne Hobbs,** Special Education Secondary Coordinator, Hobbs Municipal Schools, Hobbs, New Mexico; **Deborah Horn,** Wayne City High School, Wayne City, Illinois; **Rosanne Hudok,** Learning Support Teacher, Keystone Oaks High School, Pittsburgh, Pennsylvania; **Robert Jones,** Mathematics Supervisor, Cleveland Public Schools, Cleveland, Ohio; **Lee Kucera,** Math Teacher, Capistrano Valley High School, Mission Viejo, California; **Anne Lally,** Algebra Teacher, Eli Whitney School, Chicago, Illinois; **Christine Lansford,** Coordinator of Special Education, Melville Comprehensive School, Melville, Saskatchewan, Canada; **Robert Maydak,** Math Specialist, Pittsburgh Mt. Oliver Intermediate Unit, Pittsburgh, Pennsylvania; **Kathe Neighbor,** Math Chair, Crawford High School, San Diego, California; **Rachelle Powell,** Department Chair, Dr. Ralph H. Poteet High School, Mesquite, Texas; **Jacqueline Smith,** Resource Department Chair, Sterling High School, Baytown, Texas; **Carol Warren,** Math Teacher, Crockett County High School, Alamo, Tennessee; **William Wible,** Math Resource Teacher, San Diego Unified, San Diego, California

Publisher's Project Staff

Vice President of Product Development, Kathleen T. Williams, Ph. D. NCSP; Associate Director, Product Development, Teri Mathews; Managing Editor: Patrick Keithahn; Editor: Jody Peterson; Development Assistant: Bev Johnson; Graphic Designer: Katie Sonmor; Creative Services Manager: Nancy Condon; Desktop Publishing Specialist: Linda Peterson; Purchasing Agent: Mary Kaye Kuzma; Senior Marketing Manager/Secondary Curriculum: Brian Holl

4201 Woodland Road
Circle Pines, MN 55014-1796
800-328-2560 • www.agsnet.com

Printed in the United States of America

ISBN 0-7854-3567-0

Product Number 93820

A 0 9 8 7 6 5 4 3 2 1

Contents

Algebra Contents **iii**

Chapter 3

Linear Equations with One Variable 62

Chapter 4

Applications of Algebra 94

iv Contents Algebra

Algebra Contents v

Chapter 7 Data, Statistics, and Probability 182

Chapter 8 Fractions and Algebra 218

vi *Contents Algebra*

Chapter 9 Linear Equations and Inequalities in the Coordinate Plane

Chapter 10 Systems of Linear Equations

Algebra Contents **vii**

viii *Contents Algebra*

Algebra Contents **ix**

Using This Section

How to Use This Book: A Study Guide

Overview

This section introduces *Algebra*, reviews study strategies, and identifies text features.

Objectives

- To introduce the structure and purpose of *Algebra*
- To review study skills
- To preview the student text

Student Pages x–xvii

Teacher's Resource Library 

How to Use This Book 1–7

Introduction to the Book

As a class, read the first three paragraphs of the introduction. Ask students to briefly summarize each paragraph and its purpose. After they read the introductory paragraphs, encourage students to list on the board situations in which they or family members use mathematics. Help them conclude that people use algebra daily.

How to Study

Ask a volunteer to read each bulleted study tip. Discuss how each suggestion can help students study more effectively.

Distribute copies of How to Use This Book 1, Study Habits Survey, pages 1 and 2. Students can complete the survey to assess their study and test-taking habits. Read the directions with students. Have them use the directions provided to score the completed survey. Encourage students to identify ways that they can improve their study and test-taking skills. Give them several weeks to improve their skills and then have them complete the survey again to assess their improvement. Advise students to review the survey occasionally to see whether they have improved their study and test-taking habits. Distribute How to Use This Book 2, Weekly Schedule, to show students one way to organize their time better.

How to Use This Book: A Study Guide

Welcome to *Algebra.* In this book, you will learn about the concepts of algebra. You will learn to use mathematical skills and algebra skills. Why do you need these skills? Many jobs use mathematics and algebra. People who work in banking, food service, printing, electronics, construction, surveying, insurance, and retail all use these skills on the job. Algebra skills are also useful in your everyday life, at home and in school.

As you read this book, notice how each lesson is organized. Information will appear at the beginning of each lesson. Read this information carefully. A sample problem with step-by-step instructions will follow. Use the instructions to learn how to solve a certain kind of problem. Once you know how to solve this kind of problem, you will have the chance to solve similar problems on your own. If you have trouble with a lesson, try reading it again.

Before you start to read this book, it is important that you understand how to use it. It is also important to know how to be successful in this course. This first section of the book is here to help you achieve these things.

How to Study

These tips can help you study more effectively:

- Plan a regular time to study.
- Choose a quiet desk or table where you will not be distracted. Find a spot that has good lighting.
- Gather all the books, pencils, paper, and other equipment you will need to complete your assignments.
- Decide on a goal. For example: "I will finish reading and taking notes on Chapter 1, Lesson 1, by 8:00."
- Take a five- to ten-minute break every hour to keep alert.
- If you start to feel sleepy, take a break and get some fresh air.

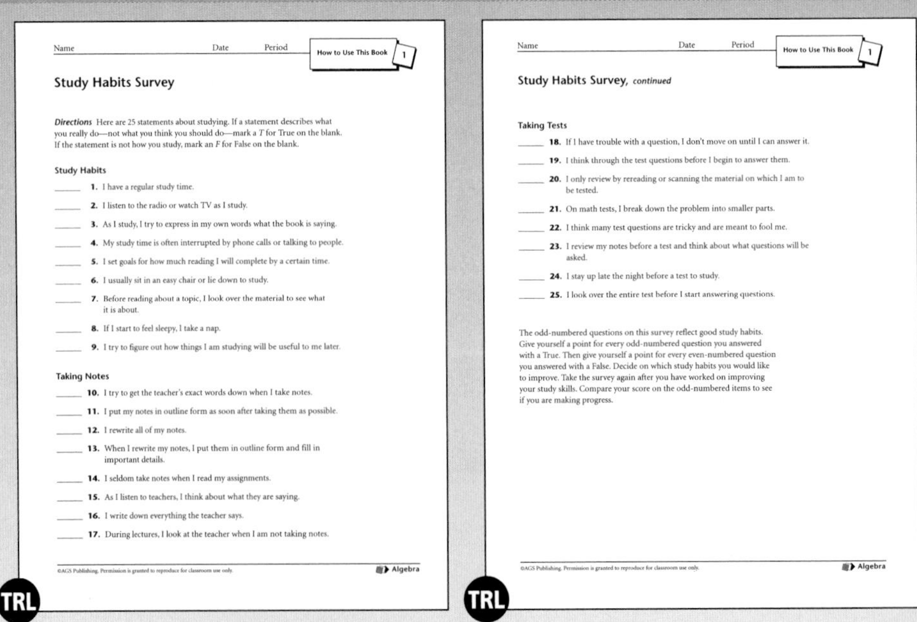

Name ______ Date ______ Period ______ How to Use This Book 1

Study Habits Survey

Directions Here are 25 statements about studying. If a statement describes what you really do—not what you think you should do—mark a *T* for True on the blank. If the statement is not how you study, mark an *F* for False on the blank.

Study Habits

_____ **1.** I have a regular study time.

_____ **2.** I listen to the radio or watch TV as I study.

_____ **3.** As I study, I try to express in my own words what the book is saying.

_____ **4.** My study time is often interrupted by phone calls or talking to people.

_____ **5.** I set goals for how much reading I will complete by a certain time.

_____ **6.** I usually sit in an easy chair or lie down to study.

_____ **7.** Before reading about a topic, I look over the material to see what it is about.

_____ **8.** If I start to feel sleepy, I take a nap.

_____ **9.** I try to figure out how things I am studying will be useful to me later.

Taking Notes

_____ **10.** I try to get the teacher's exact words down when I take notes.

_____ **11.** I put my notes in outline form as soon after taking them as possible.

_____ **12.** I rewrite all of my notes.

_____ **13.** When I rewrite my notes, I put them in outline form and fill in important details.

_____ **14.** I seldom take notes when I read my assignments.

_____ **15.** As I listen to teachers, I think about what they are saying.

_____ **16.** I write down everything the teacher says.

_____ **17.** During lectures, I look at the teacher when I am not taking notes.

 Algebra

Name ______ Date ______ Period ______ How to Use This Book 1

Study Habits Survey, *continued*

Taking Tests

_____ **18.** If I have trouble with a question, I don't move on until I can answer it.

_____ **19.** I think through the test questions before I begin to answer them.

_____ **20.** I only review by rereading or scanning the material on which I am to be tested.

_____ **21.** On math tests, I break down the problem into smaller parts.

_____ **22.** I think many test questions are tricky and are meant to fool me.

_____ **23.** I review my notes before a test and think about what questions will be asked.

_____ **24.** I stay up late the night before a test to study.

_____ **25.** I look over the entire test before I start answering questions.

The odd-numbered questions on this survey reflect good study habits. Give yourself a point for every odd-numbered question you answered with a True. Then give yourself a point for every even-numbered question you answered with a False. Decide on which study habits you would like to improve. Take the survey again after you have worked on improving your study skills. Compare your score on the odd-numbered items to see if you are making progress.

 Algebra

How to Use This Book 1, pages 1 and 2

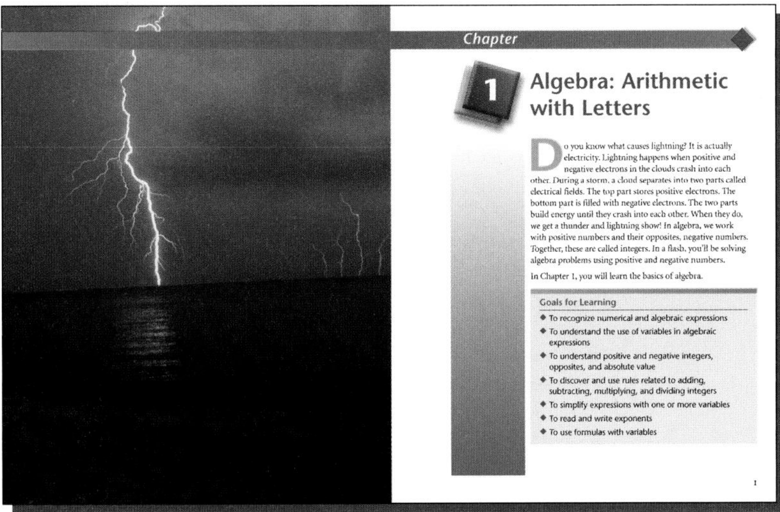

Chapter

1 Algebra: Arithmetic with Letters

Do you know what causes lightning? It is actually electricity. Lightning happens when positive and negative electrons in the clouds crash into each other. During a storm, a cloud separates into two parts called electrical fields. The top part stores positive electrons. The bottom part is filled with negative electrons. The two parts build energy until they crash into each other. When they do, we get a thunder and lightning show! In algebra, we work with positive numbers and their opposites, negative numbers. Together, these are called integers. In a flash, you'll be solving algebra problems using positive and negative numbers.

In Chapter 1, you will learn the basics of algebra.

Goals for Learning

- To recognize numerical and algebraic expressions
- To understand the use of variables in algebraic expressions
- To understand positive and negative integers, opposites, and absolute value
- To discover and use rules related to adding, subtracting, multiplying, and dividing integers
- To simplify expressions with one or more variables
- To read and write exponents
- To use formulas with variables

1

Before Beginning Each Chapter

- Read the chapter title and study the photograph. What does the photo tell you about the chapter title?
- Read the opening paragraphs.
- Study the Goals for Learning. The Chapter Review and tests will ask questions related to these goals.
- Look at the Chapter Review. The questions cover the most important information in the chapter.

Note the Chapter Features

Application
A look at how a topic in the chapter relates to real life

Application

Notes
Hints or reminders that point out important information

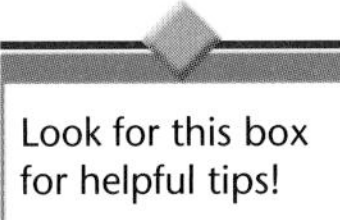
Look for this box for helpful tips!

The Chapter

Together with students, read Before Beginning Each Chapter and Note the Chapter Features on pages xi and xii. Tell students that you will preview a chapter to help them determine content and structure. On chart paper, write the heading Chapter Features. Then list the following features: chapter title, chapter-opening photographs, Goals for Learning, Notes, Technology Connection, Try This, Writing About Mathematics, Application, Calculator Practice, and Chapter Review. Ask small groups of students to examine one of the chapters in the text and identify each feature and its purpose. Write the purpose of each feature next to its name on the chart paper. Post the chart paper on a classroom wall for easy reference.

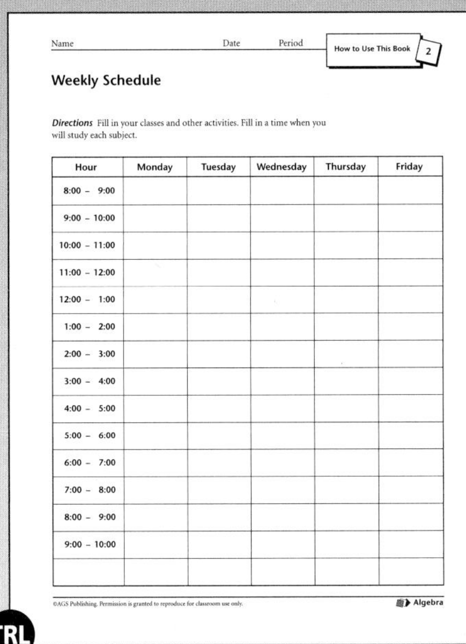

Name Date Period How to Use This Book 2

Weekly Schedule

Directions Fill in your classes and other activities. Fill in a time when you will study each subject.

Hour	Monday	Tuesday	Wednesday	Thursday	Friday
8:00 – 9:00					
9:00 – 10:00					
10:00 – 11:00					
11:00 – 12:00					
12:00 – 1:00					
1:00 – 2:00					
2:00 – 3:00					
3:00 – 4:00					
4:00 – 5:00					
5:00 – 6:00					
6:00 – 7:00					
7:00 – 8:00					
8:00 – 9:00					
9:00 – 10:00					

 Algebra

TRL

How to Use This Book 2

How to Use This Book: A Study Guide xi

The Chapter continued

Ask students to turn to page 15 of Chapter 1. Have them read the Writing About Mathematics feature. Discuss what the activity asks students to do. (*Write about ways to use division and multiplication in daily activities.*) Hand out copies of How to Use This Book 3, Writing About Mathematics. Explain that you will make copies of the page available for students to use for the writing activity in each chapter.

The Lesson

Read Before Beginning Each Lesson and As You Read the Lesson on pages xii and xiii together with students. On the board, draw a two-column chart, with one column labeled *Lesson Feature* and the other labeled *Purpose*. Help students complete the chart by identifying these features and their purposes: bold words, example boxes, practice exercises, and headings. Preview several lessons, helping students note the information given in paragraphs and the different kinds of practice exercises. Make sure students understand that the examples in the lessons provide models for performing basic operations and completing the practice exercises.

Technology Connection
Use technology to apply math skills

Try This
New ways to think about problems and solve them

Writing About Mathematics
Opportunities to write about problems and alternate solutions

Estimation Activity
Use estimation as a way to check reasonableness of an answer

Calculator Practice
How to solve problems using a calculator

Algebra in Your Life
Relates algebra to the "real world"

Before Beginning Each Lesson

Read the lesson title and restate it in the form of a question.

For example, write: *How are arithmetic and algebra related?*

Look over the entire lesson, noting the following:

- bold words
- text organization
- exercises
- notes in the margins
- photos

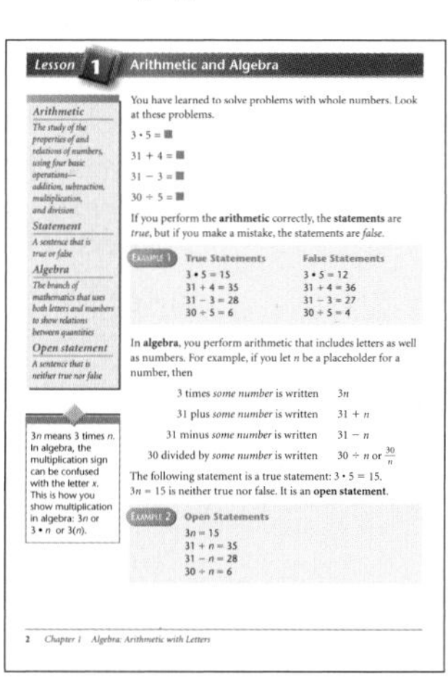

Lesson 1 Arithmetic and Algebra
Arithmetic
Statement
Algebra
Open statement
You have learned to solve problems with whole numbers. Look at these problems.
3 • 5 = ■
31 + 4 = ■
31 − 3 = ■
30 ÷ 5 = ■
If you perform the arithmetic correctly, the statements are true, but if you make a mistake, the statements are false.
True Statements
False Statements
In algebra, you perform arithmetic that includes letters as well as numbers.
Open Statements

Name Date Period How to Use This Book 3

Writing About Mathematics

Topic ______

 Algebra

TRL **How to Use This Book 3**

As You Read the Lesson

- Read the major headings.
- Read the subheads and paragraphs that follow.
- Read the content in the example boxes.
- Before moving on to the next lesson, see if you understand the concepts you read. If you do not, reread the lesson. If you are still unsure, ask for help.
- Practice what you have learned by doing the exercises in each lesson.

Using the Bold Words

> ***Bold type***
> *Words seen for the first time will appear in bold type*
>
> ***Glossary***
> *Words listed in this column are also found in the glossary*

Knowing the meaning of all the boxed words in the left column will help you understand what you read.

These words appear in **bold type** the first time they appear in the text and are often defined in the paragraph.

A **statement** is a sentence that is true or false.

All of the words in the left column are also defined in the **glossary**.

Statement (stāt´ mənt) a sentence that is true or false (p. 2)

What to Do with a Word You Do Not Know

When you come to a word you do not know, ask yourself:

- **Is the word a compound word?**
  Can you find two words within the word? This could help you understand the meaning. For example: *rainfall.*
- **Does the word have a prefix at the beginning?**
  For example: *improper*. The prefix *im-* means "not," so this word refers to something that is not proper.
- **Does the word have a suffix at the end?**
  For example: *variable, -able.* This means "able to vary."
- **Can you identify the root word? Can you sound it out in parts?** For example: *un known.*
- **Are there any clues in the sentence that will help you understand the word?**

Look for the word in the margin box, glossary, or dictionary. If you are still having trouble with a word, ask for help.

Vocabulary Strategy

Mathematics, like other curricula, has its own specialized vocabulary. It is essential that students know and understand the mathematics terms so that they can communicate in the discipline. *Algebra* highlights the important vocabulary by printing it in bold type and providing on-page definitions in the margins.

Have students read page xiii, which identifies the treatment of important mathematics terminology in the text and also provides a strategy for decoding words in context. On the board, write this sentence: *Read the directions carefully so that you do not make a mistake.* Ask students to use the strategy to help them decode the word *carefully*. Students should note that the word is *care* with two suffixes: *-ful* meaning "full of" and *-ly* meaning "in the manner." *Carefully* then means "in a manner full of care."

Distribute copies of How to Use This Book 4, Word Study. Tell students that they can use the sheet to help them determine meaning of words they do not know. Encourage students to use and keep a copy of each completed sheet. They can keep the copies in a notebook to build their own personal glossaries.

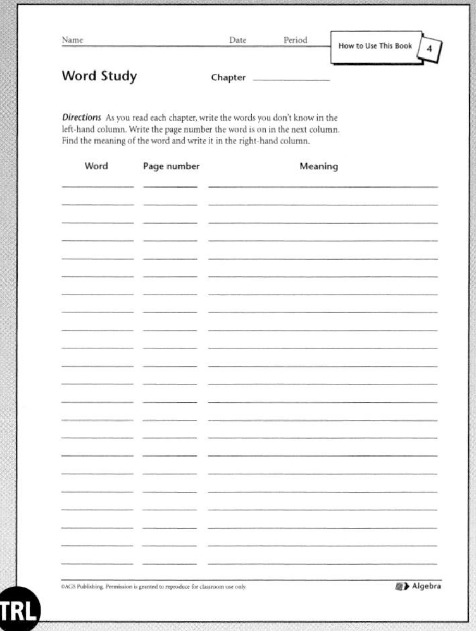

Name Date Period — How to Use This Book 4

Word Study Chapter

Directions As you read each chapter, write the words you don't know in the left-hand column. Write the page number the word is on in the next column. Find the meaning of the word and write it in the right-hand column.

Word	Page number	Meaning

 Algebra

TRL

How to Use This Book 4

Review and Test

After they read Using the Chapter Reviews and Preparing for Tests, remind students that the review will help prepare them for taking the test. Refer them once again to the chapter's Goals for Learning. The review and test focus on these major objectives.

With the class, read the Test-Taking Tip for Chapter 1. Explain that every tip provides a suggestion for preparing for or taking tests. Ask students if the tip for Chapter 1 provides a suggestion for taking a test or preparing for a test.

Remind students to read directions and the complete test or review item before they try to solve a problem or answer a question. Provide strategies for helping students complete the different kinds of review and test questions. For example, on multiple choice questions, students can first eliminate items they know are incorrect. For problems requiring computation, suggest that students use scratch paper to do the computation and then neatly transfer their work to the test or review paper.

Using the Chapter Reviews

- For each Chapter Review, answer the multiple choice questions first.
- Answer the questions under the other parts of the Chapter Review.
- To help you take tests, read the Test-Taking Tips at the end of each Chapter Review.

When learning math vocabulary, make flash cards with words and abbreviations on one side and definitions on the other side. Draw pictures next to the words, if possible. Then use the flash cards in a game to test your vocabulary skills.

Preparing for Tests

- Complete the exercises in each lesson. Make up similar problems to practice what you have learned. You may want to do this with a classmate and share your questions.
- Review your answers to lesson exercises and Chapter Reviews.
- Test yourself on vocabulary words and key ideas.
- Practice problem-solving strategies.

Using the Answer Key

Pages 432–464 of this book show answers and solutions to selected problems. The problems with black numbers show answers. The problems with red numbers also show step-by-step solutions. Use the answers and solutions to check your work.

Using a Calculator

An electronic calculator can help you with many algebra problems. There are many different kinds of calculators available. Some calculators have a few keys and perform only a few simple operations. Other calculators have many keys and do many advanced calculations. It is important to know what your calculator can do and how to use it. Here are some tips for using the keys on most calculators. To learn more about your own calculator, read the instructions that come with it.

The diagram shows an example of a scientific calculator. It describes the keys that you will most likely use in algebra.

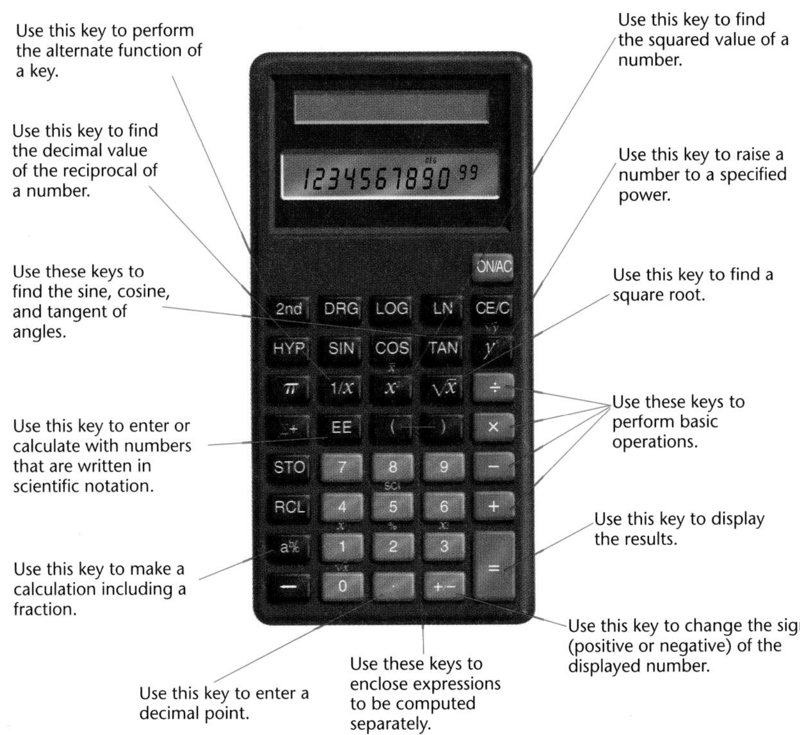
Use this key to perform the alternate function of a key.
Use this key to find the decimal value of the reciprocal of a number.
Use these keys to find the sine, cosine, and tangent of angles.
Use this key to enter or calculate with numbers that are written in scientific notation.
Use this key to make a calculation including a fraction.
Use this key to enter a decimal point.
Use these keys to enclose expressions to be computed separately.
Use this key to change the sign (positive or negative) of the displayed number.
Use this key to display the results.
Use these keys to perform basic operations.
Use this key to find a square root.
Use this key to raise a number to a specified power.
Use this key to find the squared value of a number.
1234567890 99
ON/AC
2nd DRG LOG LN CE/C
HYP SIN COS TAN
1/x
EE
STO 7 8 9
RCL 4 5 6 +
1 2 3 =
0

Using a Calculator

Have students read the calculator paragraphs and call-out descriptions on page xv. Demonstrate some of the calculator functions or ask student volunteers to show some of the calculator functions. Have students go to the Calculator Practice feature on page 9. Read the instructions out loud, then encourage students to complete Example 5.

Problem-Solving Strategies

Help students understand that a clear strategy for solving problems is one of the greatest math tools they can have. Emphasize that students will be better problem solvers if they follow strategic steps, such as Read, Plan, Solve, and Reflect.

After reading about the problem-solving strategy with students, write this sample problem on the board.

> Monday through Friday, Arturo works part-time at a card shop. This week he worked 18 hours. He worked 3 hours on both Monday and Wednesday. He worked 4 hours on both Tuesday and Thursday. How many hours did he work on Friday? (*4 hours*)

Distribute copies of How to Use This Book 5–6 to students. As a class, work through the questions on sheet 5 (Problem-Solving Strategies) and solve the problem. Help students note that different solution strategies will work on this problem. Tell students that their choice of a solution strategy may depend on the type of problem involved or on their personal preferences. Sheet 6, Problem Solving, can provide a visual for the problem-solving process. Encourage students to refer to and use these worksheets as they solve problems throughout the text. Students can also use How to Use This Book 7, Venn Diagram, to organize chapter concepts and to help solve problems.

Problem-Solving Strategies

The main reason for learning math skills is to help us use math to solve everyday problems. You will notice sets of problem-solving exercises throughout your text. When you learn a new math skill, you will have a chance to apply this skill to a real-life problem.

Following these steps will help you to solve the problems.

1 Read

Read the problem to discover what information you are to gather. Study the problem to decide if you have all the information you need or if you need more data. Also study the problem to decide if it includes information you do not need to solve the problem. Begin thinking about the steps needed to solve the problem.

Ask yourself:

- Am I looking for a part of a number?
- Am I looking for a larger number?
- Am I looking for more than one number?
- Will solving the problem require multiple steps?

For example, read this problem:

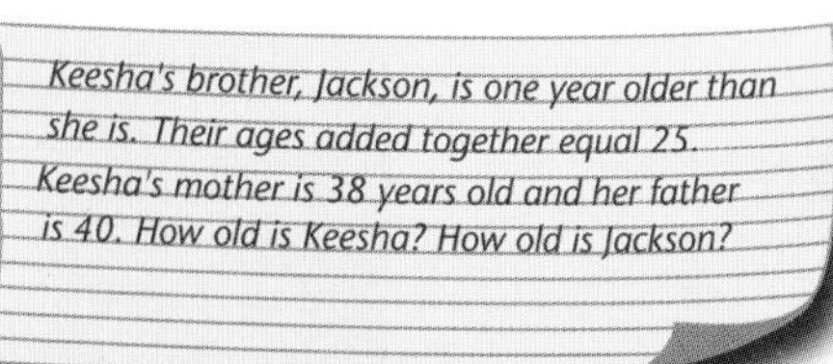

Keesha's brother, Jackson, is one year older than she is. Their ages added together equal 25. Keesha's mother is 38 years old and her father is 40. How old is Keesha? How old is Jackson?

This problem asks you to find out Keesha's and her brother's ages. It gives information about the difference in their ages and the sum of their ages. It also gives unnecessary information about their parents' ages.

In order to answer the questions, you see that you are looking for the part of 25 that is Keesha's age and the part that is Jackson's age. You will solve for two numbers.

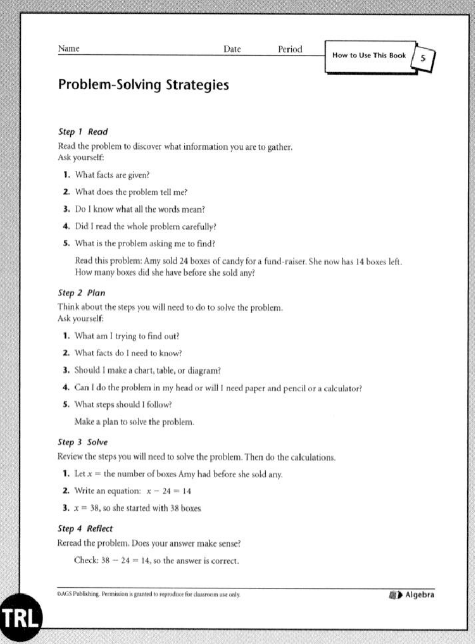

Name Date Period How to Use This Book 5

Problem-Solving Strategies

Step 1 Read

Read the problem to discover what information you are to gather.
Ask yourself:

1. What facts are given?
2. What does the problem tell me?
3. Do I know what all the words mean?
4. Did I read the whole problem carefully?
5. What is the problem asking me to find?

Read this problem: Amy sold 24 boxes of candy for a fund-raiser. She now has 14 boxes left. How many boxes did she have before she sold any?

Step 2 Plan

Think about the steps you will need to do to solve the problem.
Ask yourself:

1. What am I trying to find out?
2. What facts do I need to know?
3. Should I make a chart, table, or diagram?
4. Can I do the problem in my head or will I need paper and pencil or a calculator?
5. What steps should I follow?

Make a plan to solve the problem.

Step 3 Solve

Review the steps you will need to solve the problem. Then do the calculations.

1. Let x = the number of boxes Amy had before she sold any.
2. Write an equation: $x - 24 = 14$
3. $x = 38$, so she started with 38 boxes

Step 4 Reflect

Reread the problem. Does your answer make sense?

Check: $38 - 24 = 14$, so the answer is correct.

 Algebra

TRL

How to Use This Book 5

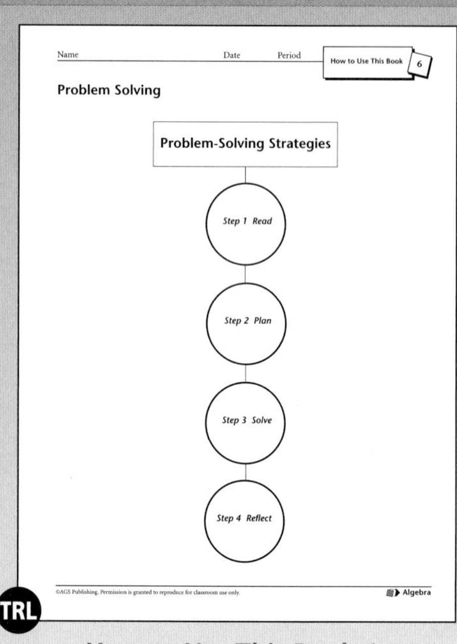

Name Date Period How to Use This Book 6

Problem Solving

 Algebra

TRL

How to Use This Book 6

2 Plan

Think about the steps you will need to do to solve the problem. Decide if you are going to calculate this mentally, on paper, or with a calculator. Will you need to add, subtract, multiply, or divide? Will you need to do more than one step? If possible, estimate your answer.

These strategies may help you to find a solution:

- ✔ Simplify or reword the problem
- ✔ Draw a picture
- ✔ Make a chart or graph to illustrate the problem
- ✔ Divide the problem into smaller parts
- ✔ Look for a pattern
- ✔ Use a formula or write an equation

In the example problem, you will need to subtract and divide. You can write an equation to solve the problem.

- ✔ Let x stand for Keesha's age.
- ✔ Let $x + 1$ stand for Jackson's age.
- ✔ Together their ages equal 25, so your equation is $x + (x + 1) = 25$ or $2x + 1 = 25$.

3 Solve

Follow your plan and do the calculations. Check your work. Make sure to label your answer correctly.

$2x + 1 = 25$
$2x + 1 - 1 = 25 - 1$
$2x = 24$
$2x \div 2 = 24 \div 2$
$x = 12$
x stands for Keesha's age, so Keesha is 12 years old.
$x + 1$ stands for her brother's age, so Jackson is 12 + 1 for 13 years old.

4 Reflect

Reread the problem and ask yourself if your answer makes sense. Did you answer the question? You can also check your work to see if your answer is correct.

Keesha and Jackson are one year apart. If Keesha is 12, then it makes sense to say that her older brother is 13. Their ages add up to 25. 12 + 13 = 25, so the answer is correct.

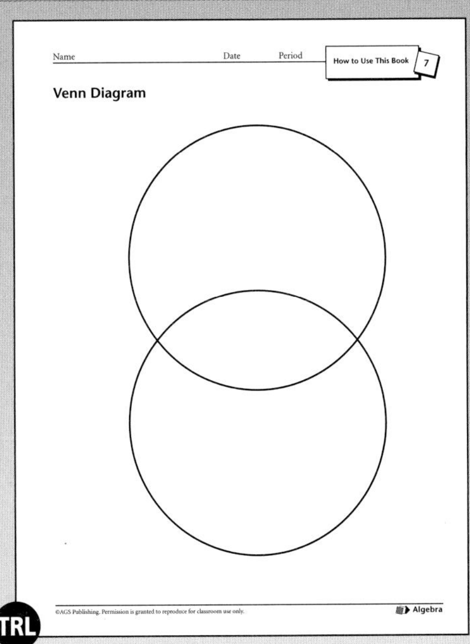
Name Date Period How to Use This Book 7

Venn Diagram

 Algebra

TRL

How to Use This Book 7

How to Use This Book: A Study Guide **xvii**

Chapter

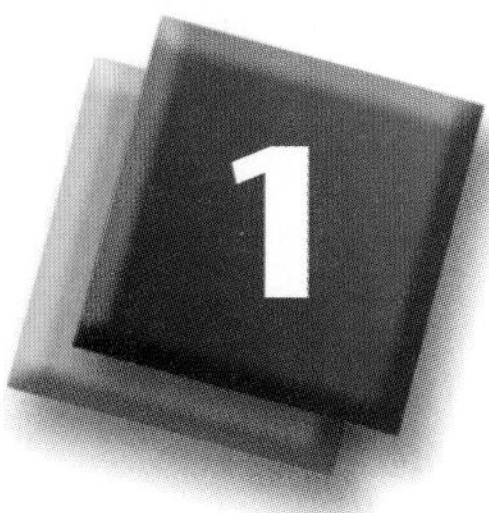

Planning Guide

Algebra: Arithmetic with Letters

		Student Text Lesson			
		Student Pages	Vocabulary	Practice Exercises	Solutions Key
Lesson 1	Arithmetic and Algebra	2–3	✔	✔	✔
Lesson 2	Representing Numbers Using Letters	4–5	✔	✔	✔
Lesson 3	Integers on the Number Line	6–7	✔	✔	✔
Lesson 4	Adding Integers	8–9	✔	✔	✔
Lesson 5	Subtracting Integers	10–11	✔	✔	✔
Lesson 6	Multiplying Integers	12–13	✔	✔	✔
Lesson 7	Dividing Positive and Negative Integers	14–15	✔	✔	✔
Lesson 8	Simplifying Expressions—One Variable	16–17	✔	✔	✔
Lesson 9	Simplifying Expressions—Several Variables	18–19	✔	✔	✔
Lesson 10	Positive Exponents	20–21	✔	✔	✔
Lesson 11	Formulas with Variables	22–25	✔	✔	✔
Application	Using a Formula	26		✔	✔

Chapter Activities

Teacher's Resource Library

Estimation Exercise 1: Estimating Answers to Operations on Positive and Negative Integers

Application Activity 1: Using a Formula

Everyday Algebra 1: Using Basic Operations

Community Connection 1: Landscaping

Teacher's Edition

Chapter 1 Project

Assessment Options

Student Text

Chapter 1 Review

Teacher's Resource Library

Chapter 1 Mastery Tests A and B

Student Text Features							Teaching Strategies							Learning Styles						Teacher's Resource Library			
Estimation Activity	Algebra in Your Life	Technology Connection	Writing About Mathematics	Try This	Problem Solving	Calculator Practice	Online Connection	Common Error	Applications (Home, Career, Community)	Mental Math	Manipulatives	Calculator	Group Problem Solving	Auditory/Verbal	Visual/Spatial	Logical/Mathematical	Body/Kinesthetic	Interpersonal/Group Learning	LEP/ESL	Activities	Alternative Activities	Workbook Activities	Self-Study Guide
								2		3								3		1	1	1	✔
					5				5		5		5							2	2	2	✔
				7	7			7			7		7				7			3	3	3	✔
						9					9	9				9				4–5	4–5	4	✔
					11			10			11		11						11	6	6	5	✔
					13								13		13					7	7	6–7	✔
	15		15				15					15		15						8	8	8	✔
17										17	17							17		9	9	9	✔
		19						18			19								19	10	10	10	✔
						21		21			21	21								11	11	11	✔
								22	23		23								24	12	12	12	✔
									24														✔

Software Options

Skill Track Software

Use the Skill Track Software for *Algebra* for additional reinforcement of this chapter. The software provides multiple-choice assessment items for students to access by computer.

Solutions Key

Use the Solutions Key with this chapter to help students who may need additional assistance. The Solutions Key CD provides solutions for every exercise in the student edition.

Other Resources

Alternative Activities

The Teacher's Resource Library (TRL) contains a set of worksheets written at a second-grade reading level called Alternative Activities. They cover the same content as the regular Activities.

Manipulatives

See the Manipulative activities in this chapter for hands-on modeling of the content. The following TRL pages can also be used:

Manipulatives Master 1 (Number Line)
Manipulatives Master 2 (Basic Mat)
Algebra Tiles; Unit Cubes; Pattern Blocks

Chapter at a Glance

Chapter 1: Algebra: Arithmetic with Letters
pages 1–29

Lessons

Skill Track for Algebra 

Teacher's Resource Library TRL

- Workbook Activities 1–12
- Activities 1–12
- Alternative Activities 1–12
- Application Activity 1
- Estimation Exercise 1
- Everyday Algebra 1
- Community Connection 1
- Chapter 1 Self-Study Guide
- Chapter 1 Mastery Tests A and B (Answer Keys for the Teacher's Resource Library begin on page 530 of this Teacher's Edition.)

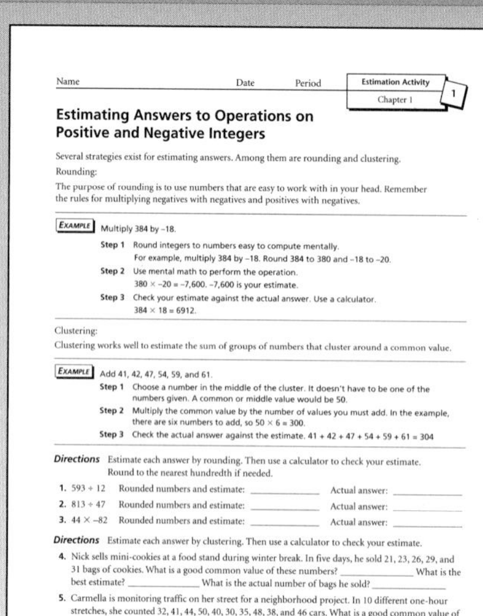

Name Date Period | **Estimation Activity** Chapter 1 | 1

Estimating Answers to Operations on Positive and Negative Integers

Several strategies exist for estimating answers. Among them are rounding and clustering.

Rounding:

The purpose of rounding is to use numbers that are easy to work with in your head. Remember the rules for multiplying negatives with negatives and positives with negatives.

EXAMPLE Multiply 384 by –18.

Step 1 Round integers to numbers easy to compute mentally. For example, multiply 384 by –18. Round 384 to 380 and –18 to –20.

Step 2 Use mental math to perform the operation. $380 \times -20 = -7{,}600$. –7,600 is your estimate.

Step 3 Check your estimate against the actual answer. Use a calculator. $384 \times 18 = 6912$.

Clustering:

Clustering works well to estimate the sum of groups of numbers that cluster around a common value.

EXAMPLE Add 41, 42, 47, 54, 59, and 61.

Step 1 Choose a number in the middle of the cluster. It doesn't have to be one of the numbers given. A common or middle value would be 50.

Step 2 Multiply the common value by the number of values you must add. In the example, there are six numbers to add, so $50 \times 6 = 300$.

Step 3 Check the actual answer against the estimate. $41 + 42 + 47 + 54 + 59 + 61 = 304$

Directions Estimate each answer by rounding. Then use a calculator to check your estimate. Round to the nearest hundredth if needed.

1. $593 \div 12$ Rounded numbers and estimate: ________ Actual answer: ________
2. $813 \div 47$ Rounded numbers and estimate: ________ Actual answer: ________
3. 44×-82 Rounded numbers and estimate: ________ Actual answer: ________

Directions Estimate each answer by clustering. Then use a calculator to check your estimate.

4. Nick sells mini-cookies at a food stand during winter break. In five days, he sold 21, 23, 26, 29, and 31 bags of cookies. What is a good common value of these numbers? ________ What is the best estimate? ________ What is the actual number of bags he sold? ________
5. Carmella is monitoring traffic on her street for a neighborhood project. In 10 different one-hour stretches, she counted 32, 41, 44, 50, 40, 30, 35, 48, 38, and 46 cars. What is a good common value of these numbers? ________ What is the best estimate? ________ How many cars did Carmella actually count? ________

 Algebra

TRL

Estimation Exercise 1

Name Date Period | **Community Connection** Chapter 1 | 1

Landscaping

Help beautify your community. Choose a concrete, asphalt, or gravel area in your community. Develop a plan to landscape the area. Suppose the concrete, asphalt, or gravel in that area is to be removed and grass planted in its place. Use this data to help answer the questions that follow.

- One pound of the variety of grass seed chosen for the area will cover 400 square feet.
- One pound of granular fertilizer will cover 250 square feet.
- The diameter of the circular area watered by a rotating sprinkler is 20 feet.

Step 1 What formula or formulas will you use to determine the area of the concrete, asphalt, or gravel region? (You may need to divide the region into smaller shapes such as rectangles and add the areas of those smaller shapes to find the total area of the region.)

Step 2 Find the area of the region.

Step 3 How much grass seed should be purchased to seed the area?

Step 4 Fertilizer is to be applied to the area one time. How much fertilizer should be purchased?

Step 5 What is the minimum number of times the sprinkler will have to be moved to water the entire area?

 Algebra

TRL

Community Connection 1

Chapter

Algebra: Arithmetic with Letters

Do you know what causes lightning? It is actually electricity. Lightning happens when positive and negative electrons in the clouds crash into each other. During a storm, a cloud separates into two parts called electrical fields. The top part stores positive electrons. The bottom part is filled with negative electrons. The two parts build energy until they crash into each other. When they do, we get a thunder and lightning show! In algebra, we work with positive numbers and their opposites, negative numbers. Together, these are called integers. In a flash, you'll be solving algebra problems using positive and negative numbers.

In Chapter 1, you will learn the basics of algebra.

Goals for Learning

- ◆ To recognize numerical and algebraic expressions
- ◆ To understand the use of variables in algebraic expressions
- ◆ To understand positive and negative integers, opposites, and absolute value
- ◆ To discover and use rules related to adding, subtracting, multiplying, and dividing integers
- ◆ To simplify expressions with one or more variables
- ◆ To read and write exponents
- ◆ To use formulas with variables

Name ______ Date ______ Period ______ **SELF-STUDY GUIDE**

CHAPTER 1: Algebra—Arithmetic with Letters

Goals 1.1 and 1.2 *To recognize numerical and algebraic expressions*
To understand the use of variables in algebraic expressions

Date	Assignment	Score
______	1: Read pages 2–3. Complete Exercises A–C on page 3.	______
______	2: Complete Workbook Activity 1.	______
______	3: Read page 4. Complete Exercises A–E on pages 4–5.	______
______	4: Complete Workbook Activity 2.	______

Comments:

Goal 1.3 *To understand positive and negative integers, opposites, and absolute value*

Date	Assignment	Score
______	5: Read pages 6–7. Complete Exercises A–C on page 7.	______
______	6: Complete Workbook Activity 3.	______

Comments:

Goal 1.4 *To discover and use rules related to adding, subtracting, multiplying, and dividing integers*

Date	Assignment	Score
______	7: Read page 8. Complete Exercises A–C on page 9.	______
______	8: Read and complete the Calculator Practice on page 9.	______
______	9: Complete Workbook Activity 4.	______
______	10: Read pages 10–11. Complete Exercises A–C on page 11.	______
______	11: Complete Workbook Activity 5.	______
______	12: Read pages 12–13. Complete Exercises A–C on page 13.	______
______	13: Complete Workbook Activities 6 and 7.	______
______	14: Read page 14. Complete Exercises A–C on page 15.	______
______	15: Complete Workbook Activity 8.	______

Comments:

 Algebra

TRL

Name ______ Date ______ Period ______ **SELF-STUDY GUIDE**

CHAPTER 1: Algebra—Arithmetic with Letters, continued

Goal 1.5 *To simplify expressions with one or more variables*

Date	Assignment	Score
______	16: Read page 16. Complete Exercises A–D on pages 16–17.	______
______	17: Complete Workbook Activity 9.	______
______	18: Read page 18. Complete Exercises A–C on pages 18–19.	______
______	19: Complete Workbook Activity 10.	______

Comments:

Goal 1.6 *To read and write exponents*

Date	Assignment	Score
______	20: Read page 20. Complete Exercises A–C on page 21.	______
______	21: Read and complete the Calculator Practice on page 21.	______
______	22: Complete Workbook Activity 11.	______

Comments:

Goal 1.7 *To use formulas with variables*

Date	Assignment	Score
______	23: Read page 22. Complete Exercises A–F on pages 22–25.	______
______	24: Complete Workbook Activity 12.	______
______	25: Read and complete the Application Exercise on page 26.	______
______	26: Complete the Chapter 1 Review on pages 27–29.	______

Comments:

Student's Signature ______ Date ______

Instructor's Signature ______ Date ______

 Algebra

TRL

Chapter 1 Self-Study Guide

Introducing the Chapter

Use the information in the chapter opener to help students understand that algebra was developed to help people—not just mathematicians—solve various types of numerical problems. Indicate to students that algebra is useful for finding the area of an athletic field as well as for finding the speed of a rocket. Ask students to speculate on the kinds of problems they might meet that can be solved with the help of algebra. Record students' responses and refer to them as students complete lessons and chapters in this text.

Chapter Project

Suggest students work in groups of four to create their own algebra booklet. Have them choose one of the following topics or a topic of their own.

- A temperature "flip book" that illustrates the temperature variations and the associated arithmetic expression for each variation
- A collection of math brain teasers or riddles and their arithmetic or algebraic solutions
- An illustrated algebra rule book that presents rules and examples for working with integers in students' own words and pictures.

Teacher's Resource

The AGS Publishing Teaching Strategies in Math Transparencies may be used with this chapter. They add an interactive dimension to expand and enhance the program content.

Career Interest Inventory

The AGS Publishing Harrington-O'Shea Career Decision-Making System-Revised (CDM) may be used with this chapter. Students can use the CDM to explore their interests and identify careers. The CDM defines career areas that are indicated by students' responses on the inventory.

Lesson at a Glance

Chapter 1 Lesson 1

Overview This lesson introduces true, false, and open statements.

Objective

- To identify arithmetic statements as *true, false,* or *open*

Student Pages 2–3

Teacher's Resource Library 

Workbook Activity 1

Activity 1

Alternative Activity 1

Mathematics Vocabulary

algebra **arithmetic** **open statement** **statement**

1 Warm-Up Activity

Review the four arithmetic operations—addition, subtraction, multiplication, and division. Write several arithmetic statements, some true and some false, on the board. For example, 4 + 5 = 9, 1 + 1 = 3, 5 − 3 = 4, and 4 − 3 = 2. Allow students time to recognize that some of the statements are not true. Use students' responses to introduce the concept of true and false statements in arithmetic.

2 Teaching the Lesson

Students will likely be familiar with the concepts of *true* and *false.* However, open statements may need additional explanation. Emphasize to students that until a value is assigned to a variable, algebraic statements are neither *true* nor *false.*

Common Error

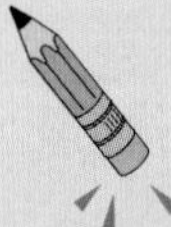

Help students avoid attaching any great significance to *n* as a placeholder for a number. Indicate that the choice of *n* is arbitrary. Explain that open statements can be written using *x, y, z,* or any other letter of the alphabet.

Lesson 1 Arithmetic and Algebra

Arithmetic
The study of the properties of and relations of numbers, using four basic operations—addition, subtraction, multiplication, and division

Statement
A sentence that is true or false

Algebra
The branch of mathematics that uses both letters and numbers to show relations between quantities

Open statement
A sentence that is neither true nor false

You have learned to solve problems with whole numbers. Look at these problems.

3 • 5 = ■

31 + 4 = ■

31 − 3 = ■

30 ÷ 5 = ■

If you perform the **arithmetic** correctly, the **statements** are *true*, but if you make a mistake, the statements are *false*.

Example 1

True Statements	False Statements
3 • 5 = 15	3 • 5 = 12
31 + 4 = 35	31 + 4 = 36
31 − 3 = 28	31 − 3 = 27
30 ÷ 5 = 6	30 ÷ 5 = 4

3*n* means 3 times *n*. In algebra, the multiplication sign can be confused with the letter *x*. This is how you show multiplication in algebra: 3*n* or 3 • *n* or 3(*n*).

In **algebra**, you perform arithmetic that includes letters as well as numbers. For example, if you let *n* be a placeholder for a number, then

3 times *some number* is written	$3n$
31 plus *some number* is written	$31 + n$
31 minus *some number* is written	$31 - n$
30 divided by *some number* is written	$30 \div n$ or $\frac{30}{n}$

The following statement is a true statement: 3 • 5 = 15. $3n = 15$ is neither true nor false. It is an **open statement**.

Example 2 **Open Statements**

$3n = 15$
$31 + n = 35$
$31 - n = 28$
$30 \div n = 6$

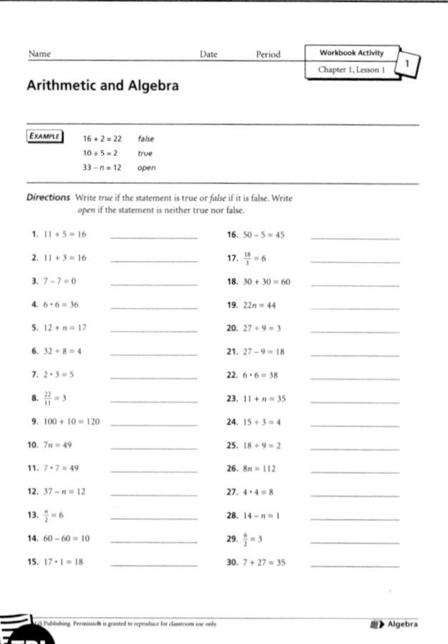

Name Date Period | Workbook Activity 1 | Chapter 1, Lesson 1

Arithmetic and Algebra

Example
16 + 2 = 22 *false*
10 ÷ 5 = 2 *true*
33 − *n* = 12 *open*

Directions Write *true* if the statement is true or *false* if it is false. Write *open* if the statement is neither true nor false.

1. 11 + 5 = 16 ______	16. 50 − 5 = 45 ______
2. 11 + 3 = 16 ______	17. $\frac{18}{3} = 6$ ______
3. 7 − 7 = 0 ______	18. 30 + 30 = 60 ______
4. 6 • 6 = 36 ______	19. 22*n* = 44 ______
5. 12 + *n* = 17 ______	20. 27 ÷ 9 = 3 ______
6. 32 ÷ 8 = 4 ______	21. 27 − 9 = 18 ______
7. 2 • 3 = 5 ______	22. 6 • 6 = 38 ______
8. $\frac{22}{11} = 3$ ______	23. 11 + *n* = 35 ______
9. 100 + 10 = 120 ______	24. 15 ÷ 3 = 4 ______
10. 7*n* = 49 ______	25. 18 ÷ 9 = 2 ______
11. 7 • 7 = 49 ______	26. 8*n* = 112 ______
12. 37 − *n* = 12 ______	27. 4 • 4 = 8 ______
13. $\frac{n}{2} = 6$ ______	28. 14 − *n* = 1 ______
14. 60 − 60 = 10 ______	29. $\frac{6}{2} = 3$ ______
15. 17 • 1 = 18 ______	30. 7 + 27 = 35 ______

 Algebra

Workbook Activity 1

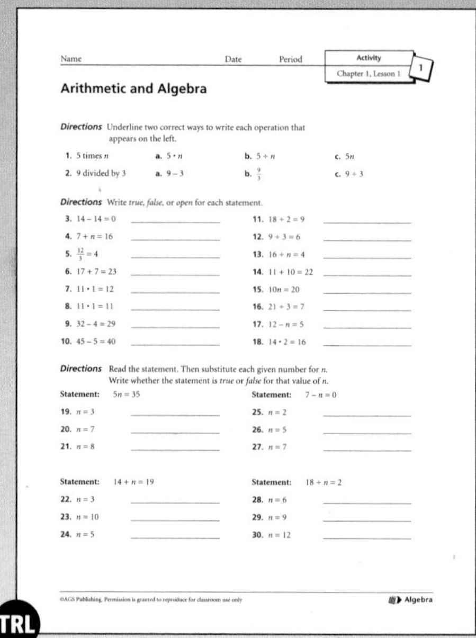

Name Date Period | Activity 1 | Chapter 1, Lesson 1

Arithmetic and Algebra

Directions Underline two correct ways to write each operation that appears on the left.

1. 5 times *n*	a. 5 • *n*	b. 5 ÷ *n*	c. 5*n*
2. 9 divided by 3	a. 9 − 3	b. $\frac{9}{3}$	c. 9 ÷ 3

Directions Write *true, false,* or *open* for each statement.

3. 14 − 14 = 0 ______	11. 18 ÷ 2 = 9 ______
4. 7 + *n* = 16 ______	12. 9 ÷ 3 = 6 ______
5. $\frac{12}{3} = 4$ ______	13. 16 ÷ *n* = 4 ______
6. 17 + 7 = 23 ______	14. 11 + 10 = 22 ______
7. 11 • 1 = 12 ______	15. 10*n* = 20 ______
8. 11 • 1 = 11 ______	16. 21 ÷ 3 = 7 ______
9. 32 − 4 = 29 ______	17. 12 − *n* = 5 ______
10. 45 − 5 = 40 ______	18. 14 • 2 = 16 ______

Directions Read the statement. Then substitute each given number for *n*. Write whether the statement is *true* or *false* for that value of *n*.

Statement: 5*n* = 35	**Statement:** 7 − *n* = 0
19. *n* = 3 ______	25. *n* = 2 ______
20. *n* = 7 ______	26. *n* = 5 ______
21. *n* = 8 ______	27. *n* = 7 ______
Statement: 14 + *n* = 19	**Statement:** 18 ÷ *n* = 2
22. *n* = 3 ______	28. *n* = 6 ______
23. *n* = 10 ______	29. *n* = 9 ______
24. *n* = 5 ______	30. *n* = 12 ______

 Algebra

Activity 1

Open statements become true or false statements when you substitute numbers for letters.

EXAMPLE 3 Is $3n = 15$ true or false when $n = 1, 2, 3, 4,$ or 5?

When $n = 1$, $3n = 15$ becomes $3 \bullet 1 = 15$ or $3 = 15$ False.
When $n = 2$, $3n = 15$ becomes $3 \bullet 2 = 15$ or $6 = 15$ False.
When $n = 3$, $3n = 15$ becomes $3 \bullet 3 = 15$ or $9 = 15$ False.
When $n = 4$, $3n = 15$ becomes $3 \bullet 4 = 15$ or $12 = 15$ False.
When $n = 5$, $3n = 15$ becomes $3 \bullet 5 = 15$ or $15 = 15$ True.

Exercise A Write true or false for each statement.

1. $3 \cdot 4 = 12$ true
2. $6 + 12 = 15$ false
3. $19 - 7 = 12$ true
4. $14 \div 7 = 2$ true
5. $\frac{42}{6} = 8$ false
6. $42 + 8 = 50$ true
7. $6 + 18 = 22$ false
8. $41 - 5 = 45$ false
9. $4 \cdot 9 = 36$ true
10. $84 - 44 = 50$ false

Exercise B Write true, false, or open for each statement.

11. $4 + 6 = 10$ true
12. $4n = 16$ open
13. $20 \div 5 = 5$ false
14. $60 - n = 50$ open
15. $60 - 10 = 50$ true
16. $60 + 17 = 67$ false
17. $\frac{3}{n} = 1$ open
18. $51 + n = 70$ open
19. $46 - 16 = 30$ true
20. $4 \cdot 6 = 24$ true

Exercise C Write true or false for each example.

Is $6 + n = 10$ true or false when

21. $n = 1$ false **22.** $n = 3$ false **23.** $n = 4$ true

Is $50 - n = 40$ true or false when

24. $n = 10$ true **25.** $n = 5$ false **26.** $n = 15$ false

Is $24 \div n = 4$ true or false when

27. $n = 12$ false **28.** $n = 4$ false **29.** $n = 6$ true

30. $n = 2$ false

3 Reinforce and Extend

LEARNING STYLES

Interpersonal/ Group Learning

Suggest students work in pairs to write four open statements. Have them write each statement on the front of an index card. Students should record the value of n for which the statement is true on the back of the card. Direct the partners to exchange sets of cards with another pair, and for each card, find the value of n for which each statement is true. Pairs can check their answers by reading the back of the cards.

MENTAL MATH

Ask students which arithmetic operations(s) will make each of the following open statements true.

3 ■ 2 = 5 (+)
3 ■ 2 = 6 (•)
3 ■ 1 = 2 (−)
3 ■ 1 = 3 (÷)
2 ■ 1 = 2 (• *or* ÷)
2 ■ 2 = 4 (+ *or* •)

MATH HISTORY

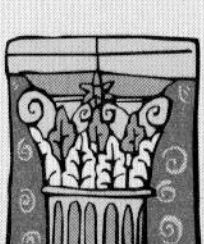

The origins of algebra date back over a thousand years. Muhammad Ibn Musa al-Khwarizmi, a mathematician and astronomer, lived in Baghdad during the golden age of science. He wrote a book about mathematics describing the Hindu-Arabic numeral system, the system we use today. The word *algebra* comes from the Arabic word *ab-jabr*, which was in the title of the book. In the 1200s, Europeans became interested in the book. They learned about the Hindu decimal system and Arabic notation of numerals, which is our present-day number system. And, of course, the book gave them the word *algebra*.

Lesson at a Glance

Chapter 1 Lesson 2

Overview This lesson introduces algebraic expressions.

Objective

- To identify numerical and algebraic expressions and their associated operations

Student Pages 4–5

Teacher's Resource Library TRL

- Workbook Activity 2
- Activity 2
- Alternative Activity 2

Mathematics Vocabulary

algebraic expression
coefficient
numerical expression
operation
variable

Warm-Up Activity

Have students count off to determine how many students are in class. Ask, "How many pairs of shoes are in this classroom?" Then ask, "How many shoes are in this classroom?" Invite a volunteer to explain how to find the answer to the second question. Help students arrive at the expression (number of students) • (2 shoes/student). Point out that they can rewrite this as the algebraic expression $2n$ where n = number of students.

Teaching the Lesson

Draw a 2 × 3 array of dots of squares on the board.

• • •

• • •

Point out that the array can be described by the expression 2 × 3 = 6. Ask students to write another expression that describes the array. *(2 + 2 + 2 = 6)* Next, make a 2 × 4 array of dots.

• • • •

• • • •

Ask students to identify two ways to describe the array and the total number of dots. *(2 + 2 + 2 + 2 = 8;*

Lesson 2 Representing Numbers Using Letters

Numerical expression
A mathematical sentence that includes operations and numbers

Operation
The mathematical processes of addition, subtraction, multiplication, and division

Algebraic expression
A mathematical sentence that includes at least one operation and a variable

Variable
A letter or symbol that stands for an unknown number

Coefficient
The number that multiplies the variable

A **numerical expression** includes only numbers and at least one **operation**.

$9 + 2$ $\qquad 15 - 11$

$7 \cdot 2$ $\qquad 64 \div 8$

An **algebraic expression** includes a **variable** with its **coefficient**, if it has one, and at least one operation.

$3y + 4$ $\qquad m - 17$

$3 + 2q$ $\qquad x \div 6$

EXAMPLE 1 Study the table.

5 + 11 is a numerical expression. Addition is the operation.

$6x + 1$ is an algebraic expression and x is the variable. The coefficient of x is 6. There are two operations in this expression—multiplication and addition.

	Numerical	Algebraic	Operation	Variable
$5 + 11$	Yes	No	Addition	None
$6x + 1$	No	Yes	Multiplication Addition	x
$c \div 4$	No	Yes	Division	c
$2 \cdot 8$	Yes	No	Multiplication	None

Exercise A Write numerical or algebraic for each expression. Identify the operations.

algebraic, division **1.** $m \div 8$

numerical, multiplication **2.** $9 \cdot 4.5$

algebraic, addition **3.** $x + 10$

numerical, addition **4.** $6 + 9$

numerical, subtraction **5.** $14 - 3$

6. $1.5 - 1.2$ numerical, subtraction

7. $4 + 6n$ algebraic, addition and multiplication

8. $13 \cdot 2$ numerical, multiplication

9. $2 \cdot 3n$ algebraic, multiplication

10. $\frac{n}{4}$ algebraic, division

Name Date Period **Workbook Activity** Chapter 1, Lesson 2 2

Representing Numbers Using Letters

EXAMPLE
Numerical expressions: 33 – 13 $\frac{36}{12}$
Algebraic expressions: $2m \div 5$ $8d + 2$
Variables: n in $7n + 7$ k in $k - 3$
Operations: Multiplication and addition in $2y + 3$ Division in $\frac{14}{2}$

Directions Name the variable in each algebraic expression.

1. $4y + 12$ ______
2. $k - 6$ ______
3. $2x + 7$ ______
4. $7n$ ______
5. $\frac{2m}{4}$ ______
6. $3(d)$ ______
7. $\frac{r}{4}$ ______
8. $14k - 10$ ______
9. $x - 100$ ______
10. $3 + p$ ______
11. $4 + y$ ______
12. $2m + 5$ ______

Directions Fill in the table. For each expression, write the expression type—*numerical* or *algebraic*—and list the operation or operations.

Expression	Expression Type	Operation(s)
$16 \div 2$	13.	14.
$8d$	15.	16.
$5 + 11$	17.	18.
$\frac{36}{12}$	19.	20.
$2p - 1$	21.	22.
$4k + 4$	23.	24.

Directions Solve the problem.

25. Only 17 members of Mr. Ricardo's class are going on the class trip. The class has a total of k students. Write an algebraic expression for the number of students who are *not* going on the trip. ______

 Algebra

TRL

Workbook Activity 2

Name Date Period **Activity** Chapter 1, Lesson 2 2

Representing Numbers Using Letters

Directions Write *true* or *false* for each question.

1. Is $2y = 10$ true or false when $y = 5$? ______
2. Is $d - 5 = 2$ true or false when $d = 8$? ______
3. Is $3k = 21$ true or false when $k = 7$? ______
4. Is $\frac{10}{w} = 2$ true or false when $w = 10$? ______

Directions Write *numerical* or *algebraic* for each expression.

5. $11 + n$ ______
6. $42 \div 7$ ______
7. $15 \cdot 7$ ______
8. $\frac{2}{w}$ ______

Directions List the operation or operations used in each expression.

9. $5n - 14$ ______
10. $\frac{72}{8}$ ______
11. $4d$ ______
12. $6y + 16$ ______

Directions Solve these problems.

13. Suppose a new computer can download 6 Web pages per second. Write a numerical expression for the number of pages it can download in 10 seconds. ______

14. Ben has a new box of a dozen golf balls. After he plays a round of golf, there are still 8 balls in the box. Write a numerical expression for the number of balls Ben used in one round of golf. ______

15. Let m represent the number of pages Amy can read in one hour. Write an algebraic expression for the number of pages she can read in 5 hours. ______

 Algebra

TRL

Activity 2

Exercise B Name the variable in each expression.

11. $6d + 8$ *d*
12. $5 + m$ *m*
13. $18 - e$ *e*
14. $4h$ *h*
15. $k - 7$ *k*
16. $5 + y$ *y*
17. $5y + 5$ *y*
18. $\frac{7}{x}$ *x*
19. $n \div 22$ *n*
20. $5c + 2$ *c*

Exercise C Identify the operation or operations in each expression.

21. $2x$ multiplication
22. $n \div 4$ division
23. $3d - 2$ multiplication and subtraction
24. $9 + s$ addition
25. $7v \div 3$ multiplication and division
26. $7 - 2p$ subtraction and multiplication
27. $6(n)$ multiplication
28. $\frac{r}{7}$ division
29. $4y$ multiplication
30. $6m + 1$ multiplication and addition

Exercise D Classify each expression, name the operation or operations, and identify any variables.

31. $3 + 6$ numerical, addition
32. $8 - 4$ numerical, subtraction
33. $3x$ algebraic, multiplication, *x*
34. $m \div 6$ algebraic, division, *m*
35. $2y + 7$ algebraic, multiplication and addition, *y*
36. $9 - n$ algebraic, subtraction, *n*
37. $11 \cdot 4$ numerical, multiplication
38. $9 + 3$ numerical, addition
39. $8m + 2$ algebraic, multiplication and addition, *m*
40. $9 \div 2$ numerical, division

PROBLEM SOLVING

Exercise E Solve each problem.

41. Write a numerical expression for the number of days in three weeks. $3 \cdot 7$

42. There are twenty years in a score. Write a numerical expression to represent the number of years in four scores. $4 \cdot 20$

43. Juan was born three years before his brother, who is now 18 years old. Write a numerical expression that represents Juan's age. $3 + 18$

44. Write an algebraic expression to represent how far a car travels at 50 mph in *d* hours. $50d$

45. Write an algebraic expression for the following pattern. Use *n* as the variable. $3 \cdot n$

$3 \cdot 1, 3 \cdot 2, 3 \cdot 3, 3 \cdot 4, 3 \cdot 5, 3 \cdot 6, \ldots$

$2 \cdot 4 = 8$) Continue with several other examples. Then ask students to name an algebraic expression that describes an array with two rows and *y* columns. *(2y)*

MANIPULATIVES

Modeling Expressions

Materials: Algebra Tiles

Group Practice: Identify the Algebra Tiles for students (see pages T8–T9). Use the Algebra Tiles to build models of algebraic expressions such as $2x - 3$ and $7 - 3y$. Ask students to guess what each model represents. Discuss the term symbolic equivalent and write the symbolic equivalent of each model. Give several examples in this manner.

Student Practice: Have students model expressions in Exercise B, Problems 11–17, sketch each model, and write its symbolic equivalent.

3 Reinforce and Extend

AT HOME

Encourage students to write an expression describing the loose change in their pockets or the amount in their savings bank. Have them use variables such as *p* for pennies, *d* for dimes, and *q* for quarters.

GROUP PROBLEM SOLVING

Suggest students work in groups of four to solve the following problem:

Rampert School students have an annual candy sale to raise funds for the school. The school gets 50¢ for every candy bar sold. The candy bars come 12 to a box. The organizers of the fundraiser hope that each student can raise $60. To meet that goal, how many boxes of candy bars must a student sell? *(10)*

Invite groups to record the steps they used to solve the problem. Then have the groups share their problem-solving approach with one another.

Lesson at a Glance

Chapter 1 Lesson 3

Overview This lesson presents integers on a number line.

Objective

- To recognize positive and negative integers and their opposites

Student Pages 6–7

Teacher's Resource Library TRL

Workbook Activity 3

Activity 3

Alternative Activity 3

Mathematics Vocabulary

absolute value	**opposites**
integers	**positive integers**
negative integers	**real numbers**

Warm-Up Activity

Ask students how they would draw a picture of the following action: Two people walked 5 steps forward, then 3 steps backward. They then walked 2 steps forward followed by 4 steps backward. Where were the people when they finished? *(where they started)* Indicate to students that they can use a number line to illustrate the path the people walked.

Teaching the Lesson

Draw an unlabeled number line on the board. Label the location of 1. Have students add labels to the number line by supplying answers to questions such as these:

- What number is neither positive or negative? *(0)*
- What number is the opposite of $+3$? *(-3)*
- What number(s) are 5 units from zero? *($+5$ and -5)*

Try This

Encourage students to solve the problem by visualizing a timeline and describing what occurs at $t = 0$.

Lesson 3 Integers on the Number Line

Real number
A number on the number line

Integer
A whole number or its opposite (…–2, –1, 0, 1, 2,…)

Negative integer
A whole number less than zero

Positive integer
A whole number greater than zero

Opposites
Numbers the same distance from zero but on different sides of zero on the number line

Numbers on the number line are examples of **real numbers.** Every point on the number line corresponds to a specific real number. The arrows at the end of the number line show that the pattern of numbers continues.

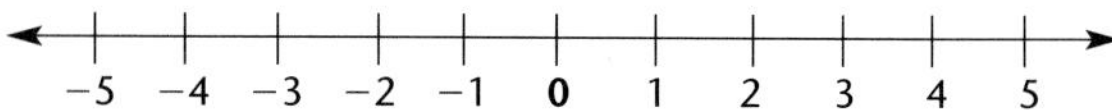

Positive and negative whole numbers and zero are called **integers**. Numbers to the left of zero are **negative integers** and are read as negative 1, negative 2, and so on.

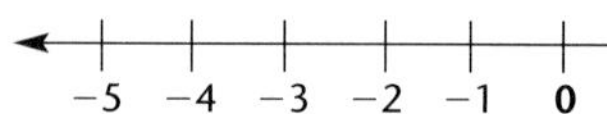

Numbers to the right of zero are **positive integers** and are read as positive 1 or 1, positive 2 or 2, and so on. Zero is neither negative or positive.

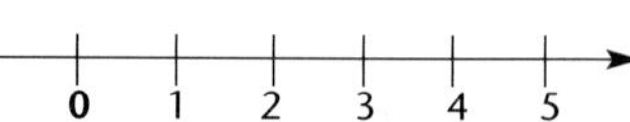

For every number other than **0**, there is an **opposite** number on the other side of zero. Opposites are the same distance from zero. When you add two opposites, their sum is zero.

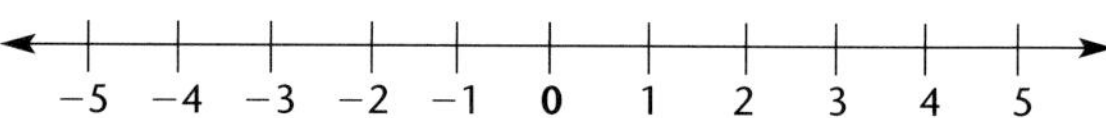

EXAMPLE 1

-5 is the opposite of 5.
5 is the opposite of -5.
5 is 5 units from 0.
-5 is also 5 units from 0.

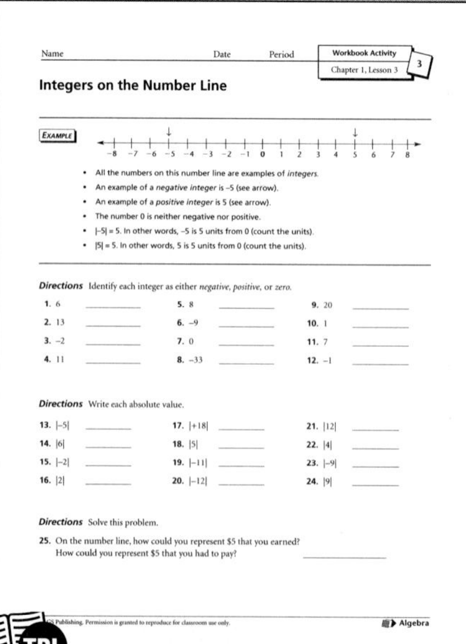

Name Date Period | Workbook Activity 3 | Chapter 1, Lesson 3

Integers on the Number Line

EXAMPLE

−8 −7 −6 −5 −4 −3 −2 −1 0 1 2 3 4 5 6 7 8

- All the numbers on this number line are examples of *integers.*
- An example of a *negative integer* is –5 (see arrow).
- An example of a *positive integer* is 5 (see arrow).
- The number 0 is neither negative nor positive.
- |–5| = 5. In other words, –5 is 5 units from 0 (count the units).
- |5| = 5. In other words, 5 is 5 units from 0 (count the units).

Directions Identify each integer as either *negative, positive,* or *zero.*

1. 6 ______ 5. 8 ______ 9. 20 ______
2. 13 ______ 6. –9 ______ 10. 1 ______
3. –2 ______ 7. 0 ______ 11. 7 ______
4. 11 ______ 8. –33 ______ 12. –1 ______

Directions Write each absolute value.

13. |–5| ______ 17. |+18| ______ 21. |12| ______
14. |6| ______ 18. |5| ______ 22. |4| ______
15. |–2| ______ 19. |–11| ______ 23. |–9| ______
16. |2| ______ 20. |–12| ______ 24. |9| ______

Directions Solve this problem.

25. On the number line, how could you represent \$5 that you earned? How could you represent \$5 that you had to pay? ______

 Algebra

TRL

Workbook Activity 3

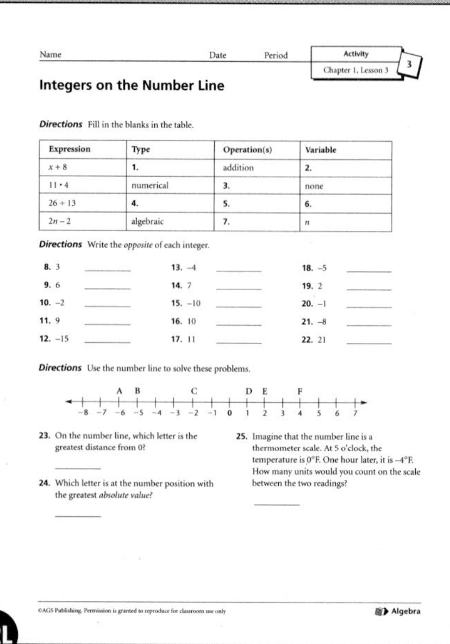

Name Date Period | Activity 3 | Chapter 1, Lesson 3

Integers on the Number Line

Directions Fill in the blanks in the table.

Expression	Type	Operation(s)	Variable
$x + 8$	1.	addition	2.
11 • 4	numerical	3.	none
26 ÷ 13	4.	5.	6.
$2n - 2$	algebraic	7.	n

Directions Write the *opposite* of each integer.

8. 3 ______ 13. –4 ______ 18. –5 ______
9. 6 ______ 14. 7 ______ 19. 2 ______
10. –2 ______ 15. –10 ______ 20. –1 ______
11. 9 ______ 16. 10 ______ 21. –8 ______
12. –15 ______ 17. 11 ______ 22. 21 ______

Directions Use the number line to solve these problems.

A B C D E F
−8 −7 −6 −5 −4 −3 −2 −1 0 1 2 3 4 5 6 7

23. On the number line, which letter is the greatest distance from 0? ______

24. Which letter is at the number position with the greatest *absolute value?* ______

25. Imagine that the number line is a thermometer scale. At 5 o'clock, the temperature is 0°F. One hour later, it is –4°F. How many units would you count on the scale between the two readings? ______

 Algebra

TRL

Activity 3

Absolute value
The distance a number on the number line is from zero

The distance an integer is from zero on the number line is called its **absolute value**.

EXAMPLE 2 In algebra,
| −5 | is read "the absolute value of negative 5."
| −5 | = 5, 5 units from 0.
| 5 | = 5, 5 units from 0.

21. +15 yards, −8 yards
22. 11° warmer
23. 4° warmer
24. opposites
25. Use a number line to indicate the time.

Try This... Answers will vary. Sample answer: −2 because a countdown usually begins with a negative real number and ends at zero.

Exercise A Find the opposite of each integer.

1. 4 −4
2. −1 1
3. 6 −6
4. −8 8
5. +11 −11
6. −17 17
7. −24 24
8. +14 −14
9. 9 −9
10. −3 3

Exercise B Find each absolute value.

11. | −2 | 2
12. | 13 | 13
13. | +4 | 4
14. | 5 | 5
15. | −6 | 6
16. | 10 | 10
17. | −3 | 3
18. | −11 | 11
19. | −8 | 8
20. | 0 | 0

PROBLEM SOLVING

Exercise C Solve each problem.

21. A football team gained 15 yards on the first play and lost 8 yards on the second. Use + and − numbers to show the team's progress.

22. How does a temperature of 4°F compare to −7°F?

23. How does a temperature of −2°F compare to −6°F?

24. Two different integers are the same distance apart on a number line. What word could you use to describe those integers?

25. Explain how you could use a number line to represent the time when an event happened in the past.

TRY THIS A bell will sound in exactly two minutes to signal the end of your class. Would you use −2 or +2 to describe the number of minutes until the bell rings? Explain.

Common Error

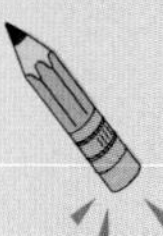

Because positive numbers are often written without signs, students sometimes assume that zero is positive. Using the number line, help students recognize that zero separates the positive and negative integers and that it is neither positive or negative.

Manipulatives

Opposites and Absolute Value

Materials: Unit Cubes (15 each of two opposite colors), Manipulatives Master 1 (Number Line)

Group Practice: Identify two colors of cubes to represent negative and positive integers, or opposites. Show how pairs of opposites such as +3 and −3 represent zero. Discuss the Zero Rule (see pages T8–T9). Introduce absolute value as the distance from zero on the number line. Use the number line to model examples of positive and negative integers. Write the symbolic equivalent for each.

Student Practice: Have students use the cubes with Exercise B, Problems 11–20 and Exercise C, Problems 21–23. Then have students sketch each model and write its symbolic equivalent.

Group Problem Solving

Discuss with students the part of the local weather report that describes the daily temperature as above or below normal (or average). You may wish to present students with a graph or other visual from a local forecaster that shows the variation from normal temperature. Invite students to work in groups of four. Have each group prepare its own number line that can be used to reflect the temperature's variation from normal every day for two weeks. Display the number lines around the classroom. Discuss the similarities and differences in the groups' number lines.

3 Reinforce and Extend

Learning Styles

Body/Kinesthetic

Have students work in groups of four to play a game called "General Directions." Direct each group to use masking tape to create a −20 to +20 number line on the classroom floor. Have students take turns being "The General" and giving directions such as "The General says stand on +3," "The General says move to the opposite of −7," and "The General says give the absolute value of the number you're at."

Lesson at a Glance

Chapter 1 Lesson 4

Overview This lesson shows how to add positive and negative integers.

Objective

- To find the sums of positive and negative integers

Student Pages 8–9

Teacher's Resource Library 

Workbook Activity 4

Activities 4–5

Alternative Activities 4–5

Mathematics Vocabulary

addend **sum**
addition

Warm-Up Activity

Offer the following as a class brain teaser. "I have a number, say, 5. I add a second number to it. The result of the addition is 1. What was the number I added to 5?" *(−4)*

Teaching the Lesson

Demonstrate the addition of a positive and negative number using the brain teaser from the Warm-Up Activity. Draw a number line on the board. Mark 5 as the starting number, and ask the class what is needed to reach the number 1. Help students decide that to reach 1, you must move four units to the left. Indicate that along a number line, movement to the left is described using a negative sign. Develop the statement

$$5 + (-4) = 1.$$

Use similar examples to demonstrate each of the possibilities for adding positive and negative numbers.

$$3 + 2 = 5$$

$$-4 + 1 = -3$$

$$-1 + (-2) = -3$$

Using a Calculator

Have students use Activity 5 to help them in purchasing a calculator. Also, you may

Adding Integers

Addition
The arithmetic operation of combining numbers to find their sum or total

Addend
A number that is added to one or more numbers

Sum
The answer to an addition problem

Addition is combining numbers to form a total. Each number being added is an **addend**. The answer is the **sum**.

Adding a positive to a positive makes the result more positive.

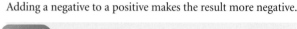

EXAMPLE 1 $3 + 4 = \blacksquare$
Start at 3, move 4 units to the right. Since you stopped at 7, $3 + 4 = 7$.

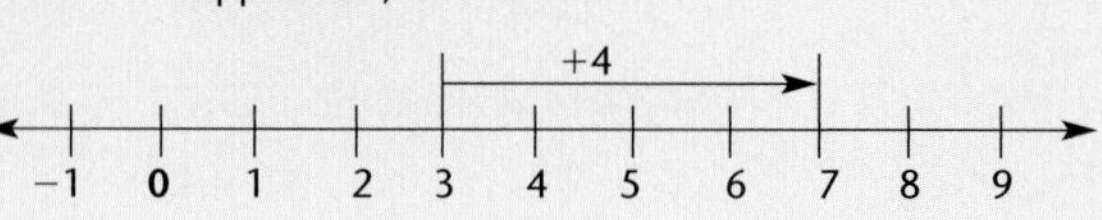

Adding a negative to a positive makes the result more negative.

EXAMPLE 2 $3 + (-4) = \blacksquare$
Start at 3, move 4 units to the left. Since you stopped at −1, $3 + (-4) = -1$.

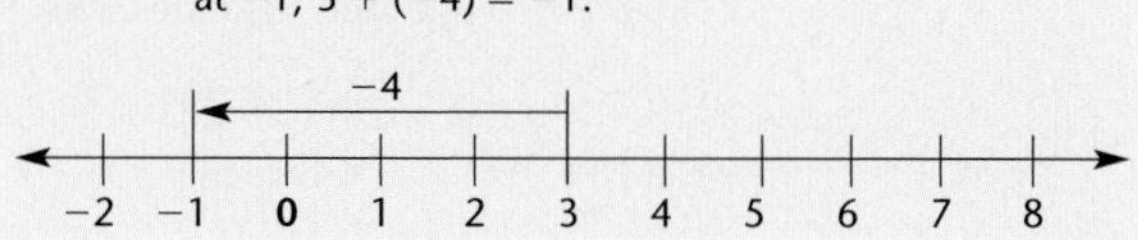

Adding a positive to a negative makes the result more positive.

EXAMPLE 3 $-3 + 4 = \blacksquare$
Start at −3, move 4 units to the right. Since you stopped at 1, $-3 + 4 = 1$.

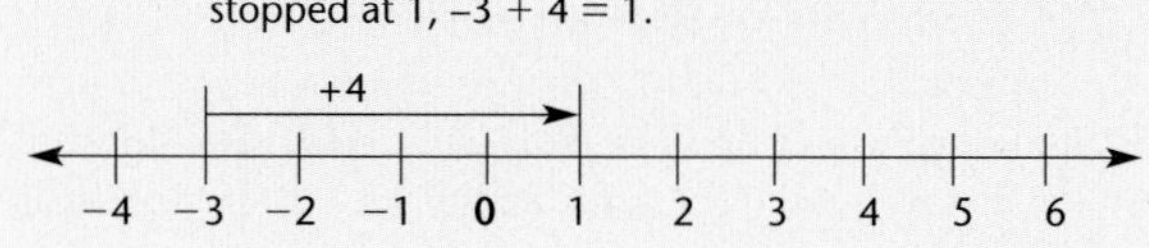

Adding a negative to a negative makes the result more negative.

EXAMPLE 4 $-3 + (-4) = \blacksquare$
Start at −3, move 4 units to the left. Since you stopped at −7, $-3 + (-4) = -7$.

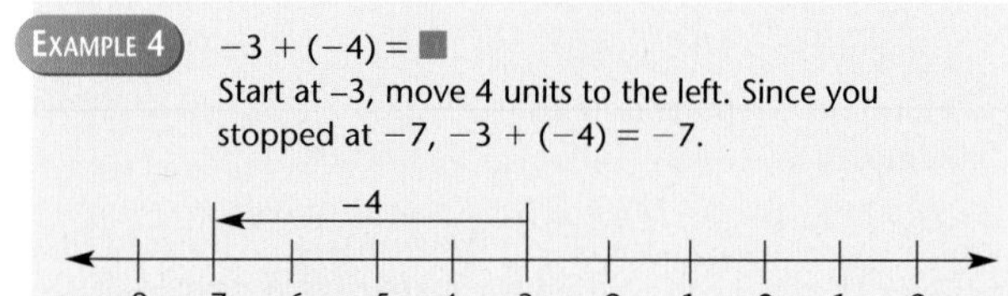

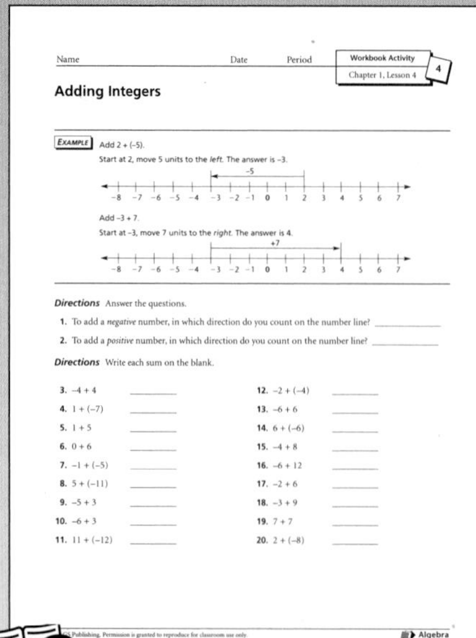

Name Date Period **Workbook Activity 4** Chapter 1, Lesson 4

Adding Integers

EXAMPLE Add 2 + (−5).
Start at 2, move 5 units to the *left*. The answer is −3.

Add −3 + 7.
Start at −3, move 7 units to the *right*. The answer is 4.

Directions Answer the questions.

1. To add a *negative* number, in which direction do you count on the number line? ________
2. To add a *positive* number, in which direction do you count on the number line? ________

Directions Write each sum on the blank.

3. −4 + 4 ____
4. 1 + (−7) ____
5. 1 + 5 ____
6. 0 + 6 ____
7. −1 + (−5) ____
8. 5 + (−11) ____
9. −5 + 3 ____
10. −6 + 3 ____
11. 11 + (−12) ____
12. −2 + (−4) ____
13. −6 + 6 ____
14. 6 + (−6) ____
15. −4 + 8 ____
16. −6 + 12 ____
17. −2 + 6 ____
18. −3 + 9 ____
19. 7 + 7 ____
20. 2 + (−8) ____

 Algebra

Workbook Activity 4

Name Date Period **Activity 4** Chapter 1, Lesson 4

Adding Integers

Directions Find each sum.

1. 16 + (−8) ____
2. −2 + 10 ____
3. 6 + (−3) ____
4. 0 + 5 ____
5. −2 + 4 ____
6. 2 + (−1) ____
7. 7 + (−7) ____
8. −9 + 10 ____
9. 8 + (−4) ____
10. −3 + 7 ____
11. 8 + 8 ____
12. 17 + (−5) ____

Directions Use a calculator to find each sum. Remember to use the +/− key for a negative number.

13. 8 + (−10) ____
14. −5 + 14 ____
15. −100 + 33 ____
16. −20 + (−4) ____
17. −5 + (−7) ____
18. −1 + 29 ____
19. −13 + (−7) ____
20. 16 + 55 ____
21. 11 + (−9) ____
22. 22 + (−22) ____

Directions Solve this problem. Answer the questions.

Cory spends $100 buying garden seeds to sell. He receives $80 from his sales by the end of the spring. Show how Cory can represent the money he paid out as a negative number and the money he took in as a positive number. Do not use dollar signs.

23. Paid out: ____
24. Took in: ____

Now add Cory's numbers to show the result of his seed business. Write the sum.

25. −100 + 80 = ____

 Algebra

Activity 4

Exercise A Find each sum.

1. $5 + 8$ 13	**6.** $-8 + (-6)$ -14	**11.** $-4 + (-2)$ -6
2. $-9 + (-3)$ -12	**7.** $-5 + 3$ -2	**12.** $3 + 2$ 5
3. $-4 + 8$ 4	**8.** $6 + 9$ 15	**13.** $5 + (-9)$ -4
4. $2 + 7$ 9	**9.** $-2 + (-2)$ -4	**14.** $-7 + (-4)$ -11
5. $-10 + 2$ -8	**10.** $6 + (-10)$ -4	**15.** $3 + (-3)$ 0

Exercise B Find each temperature.

16. -5°F + 4°F -1°F	**19.** 4°F + (-4)°F 0°F	**22.** 6°F + (-15)°F -9°F
17. -8°F + 6°F -2°F	**20.** -15°F + (-9)°F -24°F	**23.** -5°F + 15°F 10°F
18. 13°F + 7°F 20°F	**21.** -3°F + 11°F 8°F	**24.** 2°F + (-10)°F -8°F

Exercise C Find each temperature.

25. -5°C + (-5)°C -10°C	**27.** -4°C + 10°C 6°C	**29.** 7°C + -18°C -11°C
26. 9°C + 7°C 16°C	**28.** 3°C + (-3)°C 0°C	**30.** -2°C + (-9)°C -11°C

Calculator Practice

The [+/−] key on your calculator changes the sign of the number entered. You can use the [+/−] key to add integers.

EXAMPLE 5 $5 + -1$

Press 5 [+] 1 [+/−] [=] 4

$-4 + 8$

Press 4 [+/−] [+] 8 [=] 4

Exercise D Find each sum using a calculator.

31. $651 + -821$	**33.** $658 + -427$	**35.** $-951 + 458$
32. $-725 + -265$	**34.** $326 + 989$	

31. -170 32. -990 33. 231 34. 1,315 35. -493

wish to have students read the Using a Calculator on page xv of their textbook to familiarize themselves with how to use a calculator.

Manipulatives

Adding Integers

Materials: Unit Cubes (15 each of two opposite colors), Manipulatives Master 1 (Number Line)

Group Practice: Using the text examples, build models of the addends. To find the sum of same sign addends, place models end to end on the number line, with positive number models above the line and negative number models below the line. For opposite sign addends, place the positive number model above the number line and the negative number model below the line directly under the positive model. Pair the opposite-colored cubes one under the other. Discuss how each pair of opposites equals zero. The remaining cubes represent the sum.

Student Practice: Have students use cubes to find the sums in Exercise A, Problems 1–15. Instruct students to use the models to check their work.

3 Reinforce and Extend

Calculator

Have students predict the sign of the second number that will make each of the following statements true. Then have them confirm their prediction using calculators.

$789 + (\ )456 = 333$ $(-)$

$456 + (\ )321 = 777$ $(+)$

$789 + (\ )123 = 666$ $(-)$

$852 + (\ )147 = 999$ $(+)$

Challenge students to use their calculators to find two other similar statements using consecutive integers or consecutive calculator keys.

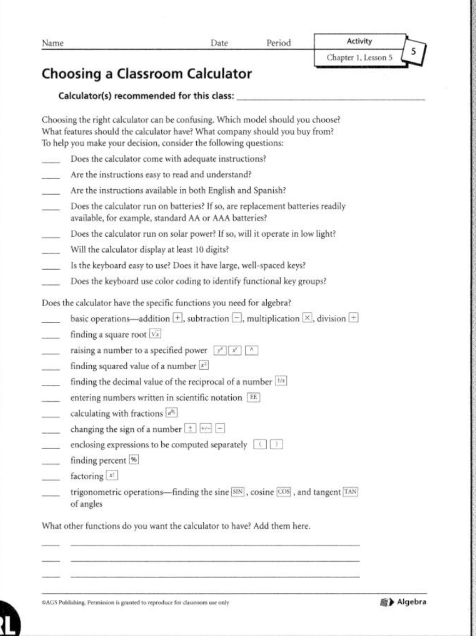

Name Date Period | Activity 5 | Chapter 1, Lesson 5

Choosing a Classroom Calculator

Calculator(s) recommended for this class: ____________

Choosing the right calculator can be confusing. Which model should you choose? What features should the calculator have? What company should you buy from? To help you make your decision, consider the following questions:

____ Does the calculator come with adequate instructions?
____ Are the instructions easy to read and understand?
____ Are the instructions available in both English and Spanish?
____ Does the calculator run on batteries? If so, are replacement batteries readily available, for example, standard AA or AAA batteries?
____ Does the calculator run on solar power? If so, will it operate in low light?
____ Will the calculator display at least 10 digits?
____ Is the keyboard easy to use? Does it have large, well-spaced keys?
____ Does the keyboard use color coding to identify functional key groups?

Does the calculator have the specific functions you need for algebra?

____ basic operations—addition [+], subtraction [−], multiplication [×], division [÷]
____ finding a square root [$\sqrt{x}$]
____ raising a number to a specified power [y^x] [x^y] [^]
____ finding squared value of a number [x^2]
____ finding the decimal value of the reciprocal of a number [1/x]
____ entering numbers written in scientific notation [EE]
____ calculating with fractions [$a^b/_c$]
____ changing the sign of a number [±] [+/−] [−]
____ enclosing expressions to be computed separately [(] [)]
____ finding percent [%]
____ factoring [x!]
____ trigonometric operations—finding the sine [SIN], cosine [COS], and tangent [TAN] of angles

What other functions do you want the calculator to have? Add them here.

____ ____________
____ ____________
____ ____________

 Algebra

TRL

Activity 5

Learning Styles

Logical/Mathematical

Tell students about a mathematical square puzzle. The puzzle is sometimes called a "magic square." In the square, the numbers in each row, column, and diagonal add up to the same sum. Have students complete the following squares. (Students are to fill in the numbers in parentheses.)

5	–9	(1)
(–5)	–1	(3)
–3	(7)	–7

2	(7)	(6)
9	5	(1)
4	(3)	(8)

Lesson at a Glance

Chapter 1 Lesson 5

Overview This lesson shows how to subtract positive and negative integers.

Objective

- To find the differences of positive and negative integers

Student Pages 10–11

Teacher's Resource Library 

Workbook Activity 5

Activity 6

Alternative Activity 6

Mathematics Vocabulary

difference **subtraction**

Warm-Up Activity

To emphasize the opposite relationship between addition and subtraction, begin this lesson with a brain teaser similar to the one used in the previous lesson. "I have a number, say, 5. I subtract a second number from it. The result of the subtraction is 9. What was the number I subtracted from 5?" *(−4)*

Teaching the Lesson

Invite a volunteer to draw a number line on the board and explain the brain teaser. Help the class develop the statement $5 - (-4) = 9$. Use similar examples to demonstrate each of the possibilities for subtracting positive and negative numbers.

$9 - 5 = 4$

$-4 - 2 = -6$

$-5 - (-3) = -2$

Common Error

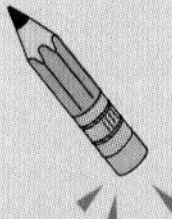

Students may confuse the operation signs—plus and minus—with the signs ascribed to integers—positive and negative. To help students recognize the differences, have them read problems aloud. For example, have them read $-5 - (+4)$ as *negative 5 minus positive four.*

Lesson 5 Subtracting Integers

> ***Subtraction***
> *The arithmetic operation of taking one number away from another to find the difference*
>
> ***Difference***
> *The answer to a subtraction problem*

Subtracting a positive from a positive makes the result less positive or more negative, so you move to the left.

Example 1 $3 - (+4) = ■$ Start at 3, move 4 units to the left. Since you stopped at −1, $3 - (+4) = -1$.
Note: $3 - (+4) = -1$ gives the same result as $3 + (-4) = -1$ because 4 and −4 are opposites.

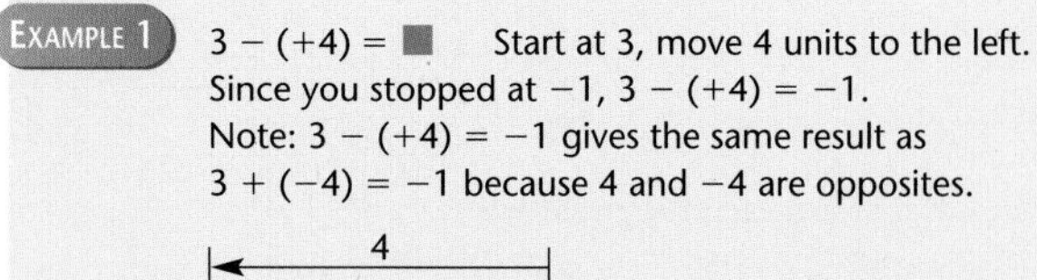

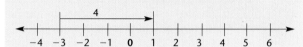

Subtracting a negative from a negative makes the result less negative or more positive, so you move to the right.

Example 2 $-3 - (-4) = ■$ Start at −3, move 4 units to the right. Since you stopped at +1, $-3 - (-4) = 1$.
Note: $-3 - (-4) = 1$ gives the same result as $-3 + 4 = 1$ because −4 and 4 are opposites.

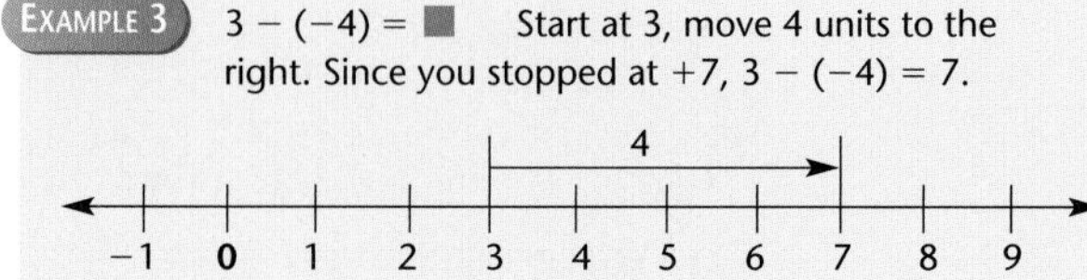

> **Subtraction** and addition are opposite arithmetic operations. In addition, two (or more) numbers are combined. In subtraction, one number is taken away from another number. The answer is the **difference**.

Subtracting a negative from a positive makes it less negative or more positive, so you move to the right.

Example 3 $3 - (-4) = ■$ Start at 3, move 4 units to the right. Since you stopped at +7, $3 - (-4) = 7$.

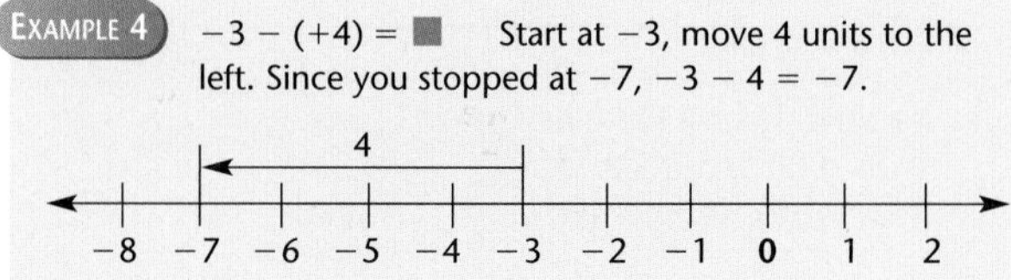

Subtracting a positive from a negative makes it less positive or more negative, so you move to the left.

Example 4 $-3 - (+4) = ■$ Start at −3, move 4 units to the left. Since you stopped at −7, $-3 - 4 = -7$.

4

−8 −7 −6 −5 −4 −3 −2 −1 0 1 2

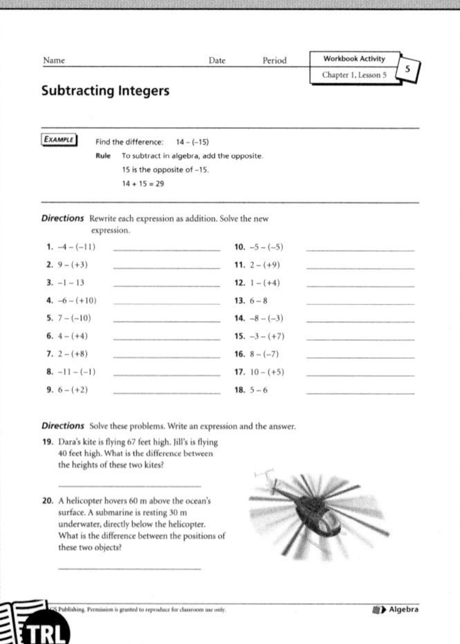

Name Date Period **Workbook Activity 5** Chapter 1, Lesson 5

Subtracting Integers

Example Find the difference: 14 − (−15)
Rule To subtract in algebra, add the opposite.
15 is the opposite of −15.
14 + 15 = 29

Directions Rewrite each expression as addition. Solve the new expression.

1. −4 − (−11) ______	**10.** −5 − (−5) ______
2. 9 − (+3) ______	**11.** 2 − (+9) ______
3. −1 − 13 ______	**12.** 1 − (+4) ______
4. −6 − (+10) ______	**13.** 6 − 8 ______
5. 7 − (−10) ______	**14.** −8 − (−3) ______
6. 4 − (+4) ______	**15.** −3 − (+7) ______
7. 2 − (+8) ______	**16.** 8 − (−7) ______
8. −11 − (−1) ______	**17.** 10 − (+5) ______
9. 6 − (+2) ______	**18.** 5 − 6 ______

Directions Solve these problems. Write an expression and the answer.

19. Dara's kite is flying 67 feet high. Jill's is flying 40 feet high. What is the difference between the heights of these two kites?

______

20. A helicopter hovers 60 m above the ocean's surface. A submarine is resting 30 m underwater, directly below the helicopter. What is the difference between the positions of these two objects?

______

 Algebra

TRL

Workbook Activity 5

Name Date Period **Activity 6** Chapter 1, Lesson 6

Subtracting Integers

Directions Find and write each sum.

1. 11 + 2 ______	**5.** 11 + (−2) ______
2. −5 + 8 ______	**6.** −17 + 17 ______
3. 3 + (−7) ______	**7.** 1 + (−13) ______
4. −7 + (−3) ______	**8.** −5 + (−9) ______

Directions Find and write each difference.

9. −9 − (−4) ______	**14.** −11 − (−11) ______
10. −2 − 8 ______	**15.** 4 − (+4) ______
11. 9 − 5 ______	**16.** −8 − (+2) ______
12. 7 − (+5) ______	**17.** 9 − 12 ______
13. 11 − (−2) ______	**18.** 5 − (+9) ______

Directions Solve these problems.

19. The highest temperature recorded in Centerville last year was 99°F on July 11. The lowest temperature was −13°F on January 16. What is the difference between the highest and lowest temperatures?

______

20. The Bigsby Building has 28 stories and three basement levels. Suppose you took the elevator from basement level 3 all the way to the 28th floor. Calculate the number of floors you would travel. (Hint: Use −3 to represent the basement level, and write a subtraction expression.)

______

 Algebra

TRL

Activity 6

IN SUMMARY:

$3 - (+4) = -1$	is the same as	$3 + (-4) = -1$
$-3 - (-4) = 1$	is the same as	$-3 + 4 = 1$
$3 - (-4) = 7$	is the same as	$3 + 4 = 7$
$-3 - (+4) = -7$	is the same as	$-3 + (-4) = -7$

Rule To subtract in algebra, add the opposite.
$3 - (+4) = 3 + (-4)$
$a - (b) = a + (-b)$

Exercise A Rewrite each subtraction expression as an addition expression. Solve the new expression.

1. $5 - (+4)$ $5 + -4$; 1
2. $8 - 2$ $8 + -2$; 6
3. $-5 - (-6)$ $-5 + 6$; 1
4. $-9 - (-8)$ $-9 + 8$; -1
5. $-7 - (+5)$ $-7 + -5$; -12
6. $-3 - 5$ $-3 + -5$; -8
7. $-3 - (-10)$ $-3 + 10$; 7
8. $11 - (+6)$ $11 + -6$; 5
9. $8 - (-1)$ $8 + 1$; 9
10. $4 - 3$ $4 + -3$; 1
11. $-6 - (+2)$ $-6 + -2$; -8
12. $7 - 3$ $7 + -3$; 4

Exercise B Find each difference.

13. $9 - 6$ 3
14. $-5 - (-8)$ 3
15. $8 - (-8)$ 16
16. $-5 - (+10)$ -15
17. $12 - (-3)$ 15
18. $-7 - (-3)$ -4
19. $7 - (+9)$ -2
20. $-6 - 6$ -12
21. $3 - 6$ -3
22. $-3 - (+5)$ -8
23. $5 - 8$ -3
24. $-7 - (+6)$ -13
25. $6 - (-9)$ 15
26. $-10 - (-7)$ -3
27. $8 - 2$ 6

PROBLEM SOLVING

Exercise C Solve each problem.

28. The record high temperature for Pennsylvania is 111°F. The record low is –42°F. What is the difference between the high and low? 153°F

29. What is the difference between Montana's record low of −70°F and New York's record low of −52°F? 18°F

30. Lake Eyre, Australia, has an elevation of −52 feet, while Lake Torrens, Australia, has an elevation of 92 feet. What is the difference between the elevations? 144 feet

LEARNING STYLES

LEP/ESL

Have students work in pairs. Direct the partners to make four flash cards, one with each of the following phrases:

a positive number
a negative number
added to
subtracted from

Ask students to take the first two cards, choose either the third or the fourth card that describes an operation, and place the operation card between the first two cards. Have the partners write a number sentence matching the description on the cards they chose.

MANIPULATIVES

Subtracting Integers

Materials: Unit Cubes (15 each of two opposite colors), Manipulatives Master 1 (Number Line)

Group Practice: Review how to change subtraction to addition of the opposite.

Student Practice: Have students use the cubes to build and solve Problems 1–12 in Exercise A. In Exercise B, remind students to change subtraction to addition of the opposite and to use cubes either to solve the problems or to check their answers.

3 Reinforce and Extend

GROUP PROBLEM SOLVING

Present the following situation to students.

Your class has been chosen to present a special program on the extremes of weather for the local access cable station. You need to find the greatest temperature ranges recorded in the world, compute the number of degrees involved, and report them on the program. You will also need to design a graphic to show these extremes. Divide the class into small groups. Suggest that the groups assign tasks such as researcher, producer, graphic artist, and announcer. Have the groups present their weather segments to the class. Remind students to name the source of their information.

The Guinness Book of Records lists the greatest temperature ranges (−90°F to 98°F in Verkhoyansk, Siberia); the greatest temperature variation in one day (44°F to −56°F in Browning, Montana, on January 23–24, 1916); and the most unusual rise in temperature (−4°F to 45°F between 7:30 A.M. and 7:32 A.M. on January 22, 1943, in Spearfish, South Dakota.)

Lesson at a Glance

Chapter 1 Lesson 6

Overview This lesson presents the rules for multiplying (positive) (positive), (negative) (negative) and (positive) (negative) integers.

Objectives

- To find the product of a positive integer times a positive integer
- To determine that the product of a negative integer times a negative integer is positive
- To identify the product of a negative integer times a positive integer as negative

Student Pages 12–13

Teacher's Resource Library 

Workbook Activities 6–7

Activity 7

Alternative Activity 7

Mathematics Vocabulary

factors **product**
multiplication

Warm-Up Activity

Ask students to describe the relationship between addition and multiplication. Prime their responses by writing the following expressions on the board: (3)(4) and (3) + (3) + (3) + (3). Ask students to tell how the two expressions are alike. *(Each describes 4 groups of 3 or 12.)*

Teaching the Lesson

Invite volunteers to use the examples as models for finding (2)(3), (4)(−5), and (−6)(3). Ask students to first describe each example: *two groups of three, four groups of negative five, and three groups of negative six.* Then have students indicate the multiplication (repeated addition) on a number line. Finally, have them supply the product for each.

Suggest to students they approach multiplication problems in two steps—always using both steps and always

Lesson 6 Multiplying Integers

Multiplication
The arithmetic operation of adding a number to itself many times

Factor
A number that is multiplied in a multiplication problem

Product
The answer to a multiplication problem

In **multiplication**, you simply add a number many times. The order in which you multiply two **factors** does not change the **product**.

In algebra, "3 times 3" is written as (3)(3) and "3 times n" is written as $3n$. You know that (3)(3) = 9. You can think of this as three groups of 3.

EXAMPLE 1 (3)(3) = 9

Start at zero and count by 3's on the number line.

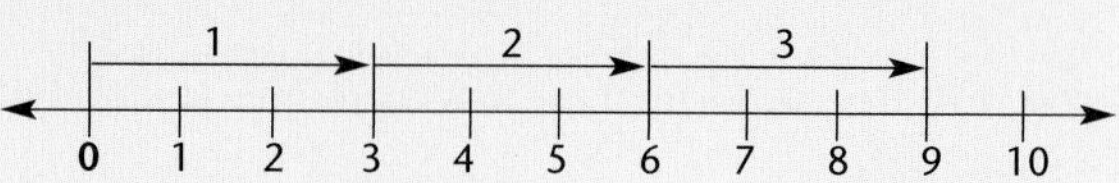

Rule (Positive) • (Positive) = (Positive)

EXAMPLE 2 (3)(−3) = ■

Start at zero and count by −3 on the number line.
(3)(−3) means three groups of −3.
(−3) + (−3) + (−3). Therefore, (3)(−3) = −9.

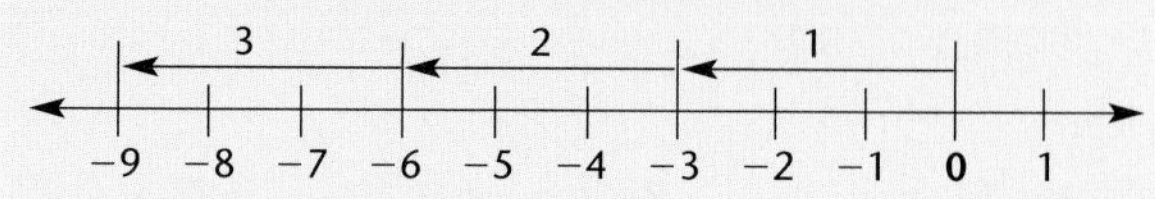

Rule (Positive) • (Negative) = (Negative)

EXAMPLE 3 (−3)(3) = ■

Treat this the same as (3)(−3).
(−3)(3) means three groups of (−3) or
(−3) + (−3) + (−3). Therefore, (−3)(3) = −9.

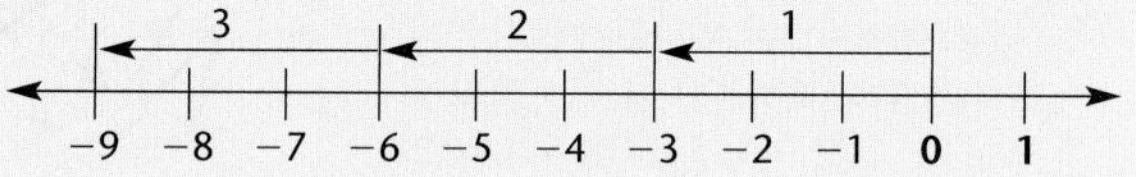

3 2 1
−9 −8 −7 −6 −5 −4 −3 −2 −1 0 1

Rule (Negative) • (Positive) = (Negative)

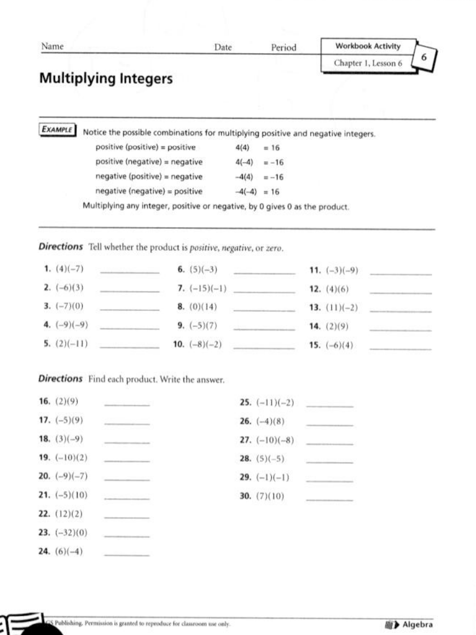

Name Date Period **Workbook Activity 6** Chapter 1, Lesson 6

Multiplying Integers

EXAMPLE Notice the possible combinations for multiplying positive and negative integers.

positive (positive) = positive 4(4) = 16
positive (negative) = negative 4(−4) = −16
negative (positive) = negative −4(4) = −16
negative (negative) = positive −4(−4) = 16

Multiplying any integer, positive or negative, by 0 gives 0 as the product.

Directions Tell whether the product is *positive, negative,* or *zero.*

1. (4)(−7) ______
2. (−6)(3) ______
3. (−7)(0) ______
4. (−9)(−9) ______
5. (2)(−11) ______
6. (5)(−3) ______
7. (−15)(−1) ______
8. (0)(14) ______
9. (−5)(7) ______
10. (−8)(−2) ______
11. (−3)(−9) ______
12. (4)(6) ______
13. (11)(−2) ______
14. (2)(9) ______
15. (−6)(4) ______

Directions Find each product. Write the answer.

16. (2)(9) ______
17. (−5)(9) ______
18. (3)(−9) ______
19. (−10)(2) ______
20. (−9)(−7) ______
21. (−5)(10) ______
22. (12)(2) ______
23. (−32)(0) ______
24. (6)(−4) ______
25. (−11)(−2) ______
26. (−4)(8) ______
27. (−10)(−8) ______
28. (5)(−5) ______
29. (−1)(−1) ______
30. (7)(10) ______

 Algebra

Workbook Activity 6

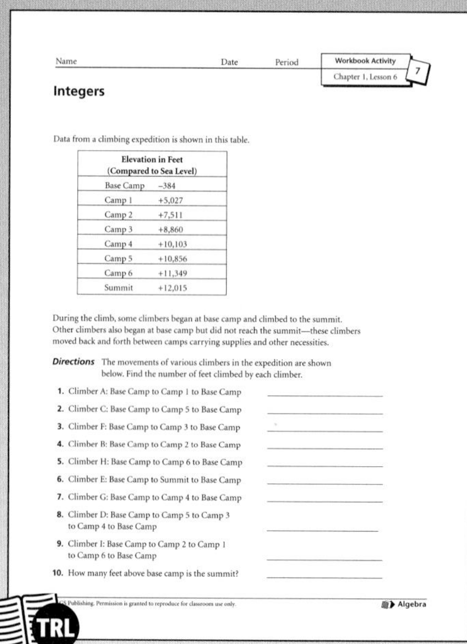

Name Date Period **Workbook Activity 7** Chapter 1, Lesson 6

Integers

Data from a climbing expedition is shown in this table.

Elevation in Feet (Compared to Sea Level)	
Base Camp	−384
Camp 1	+5,027
Camp 2	+7,511
Camp 3	+8,860
Camp 4	+10,103
Camp 5	+10,856
Camp 6	+11,349
Summit	+12,015

During the climb, some climbers began at base camp and climbed to the summit. Other climbers also began at base camp but did not reach the summit—these climbers moved back and forth between camps carrying supplies and other necessities.

Directions The movements of various climbers in the expedition are shown below. Find the number of feet climbed by each climber.

1. Climber A: Base Camp to Camp 1 to Base Camp ______
2. Climber C: Base Camp to Camp 5 to Base Camp ______
3. Climber F: Base Camp to Camp 3 to Base Camp ______
4. Climber B: Base Camp to Camp 2 to Base Camp ______
5. Climber H: Base Camp to Camp 6 to Base Camp ______
6. Climber E: Base Camp to Summit to Base Camp ______
7. Climber G: Base Camp to Camp 4 to Base Camp ______
8. Climber D: Base Camp to Camp 5 to Camp 3 to Camp 4 to Base Camp ______
9. Climber I: Base Camp to Camp 2 to Camp 1 to Camp 6 to Base Camp ______
10. How many feet above base camp is the summit? ______

 Algebra

Workbook Activity 7

EXAMPLE 4 This leaves only one other case, namely $(-3)(-3)$ or a (Negative) (Negative). This case cannot be shown on the number line. The product is 9. You need to solve exercises such as these using the following rule:

Rule (Negative) • (Negative) = (Positive)

So, $(-3)(-3) = 9$

Exercise A Find each product.

1. $(7)(8)$ 56	**8.** $(-4)(13)$ -52	**15.** $(-6)(-5)$ 30
2. $(-4)(-3)$ 12	**9.** $(6)(-10)$ -60	**16.** $(-8)(-2)$ 16
3. $(-5)(6)$ -30	**10.** $(3)(9)$ 27	**17.** $(5)(-10)$ -50
4. $(9)(-8)$ -72	**11.** $(-7)(-9)$ 63	**18.** $(15)(4)$ 60
5. $(9)(9)$ 81	**12.** $(-7)(3)$ -21	**19.** $(-4)(5)$ -20
6. $(-5)(-9)$ 45	**13.** $(8)(3)$ 24	**20.** $(-11)(-8)$ 88
7. $(5)(12)$ 60	**14.** $(-9)(2)$ -18	

Exercise B Tell whether each product is positive, negative, or zero.

21. $(-34)(-63)$ positive	**24.** $(-400)(205)$ negative	**27.** $(-771)(-522)$ positive
22. $(67)(-326)$ negative	**25.** $(0)(-345)$ zero	**28.** $(389)(399)$ positive
23. $(-487)(-351)$ positive	**26.** $(800)(-72)$ negative	

PROBLEM SOLVING

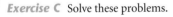

Exercise C Solve these problems.

29. One side of a ship has marks spaced three feet apart. Four marks are underwater. How many feet of the ship are underwater? 12 feet

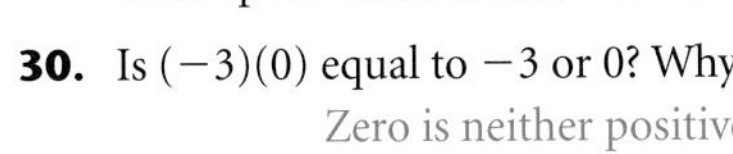

30. Is $(-3)(0)$ equal to -3 or 0? Why? Zero is neither positive or negative.

Multiplying Integers

Name Date Period Activity 7 Chapter 1, Lesson 7

Directions Find and write each difference.

1. $-2 - (+9)$ ______	**8.** $20 - (-11)$ ______
2. $5 - (+2)$ ______	**9.** $-4 - (+8)$ ______
3. $19 - 5$ ______	**10.** $7 - (-2)$ ______
4. $-11 - (-3)$ ______	**11.** $-1 - (+7)$ ______
5. $8 - (+7)$ ______	**12.** $23 - 13$ ______
6. $-6 - 16$ ______	**13.** $-3 - (+4)$ ______
7. $6 - (+2)$ ______	**14.** $-9 - (+10)$ ______

Directions Find and write each product.

15. $(-14)(1)$ ______	**22.** $(0)(-44)$ ______
16. $(6)(0)$ ______	**23.** $(-8)(2)$ ______
17. $(-7)(6)$ ______	**24.** $(-1)(-18)$ ______
18. $(5)(-9)$ ______	**25.** $(3)(-11)$ ______
19. $(3)(13)$ ______	**26.** $(-4)(-10)$ ______
20. $(-7)(-7)$ ______	**27.** $(7)(4)$ ______
21. $(-5)(-3)$ ______	**28.** $(12)(-3)$ ______

Directions Solve these problems.

29. One computer in Mrs. Wu's classroom has a connection to the Internet. Using this computer, each student can spend 5 minutes visiting Web sites. If the class has 10 students, how long (in minutes) is the Internet connection in use? ______

30. When Dee's pool is drained, she can see 3 depth marks below the water line. Each mark is labeled –3 to represent 3 feet under water. Write an expression to show how Dee can calculate the pool's depth. ______

 Algebra

TRL

Activity 7

performing the steps in the same order. First, determine the sign of the product; always performing the steps in the same order. First, determine the sign of the product; second, multiply the integers as if they had no signs. Ask students to determine the sign of the following products: $(4)(-73)$, $(-73)(4)$, $(-73)(-4)$, $(73)(4)$.second, multiply the integers as if they had no signs. Ask students to determine the sign of the following products: $(4)(-73)$, $(-73)(4)$, $(-73)(-4)$, $(73)(4)$.

3 Reinforce and Extend

LEARNING STYLES

Visual/Spatial

Write the following chart on the board, providing the information in the first two columns. Ask volunteers to supply the appropriate sign for the third column.

Factor	Factor	Product
(+)	(+)	(+)
(−)	(+)	(−)
(+)	(−)	(−)
(−)	(−)	(+)

Students might also make their own index cards using the information in the columns.

GROUP PROBLEM SOLVING

Pose the following problem for students.

The temperature on a winter day drops 2 degrees every hour for 9 hours. Write an expression that describes the total temperature drop, then find the total temperature drop. *[$(9)(-2) = -18$]*

Suggest students work in small groups. Have the groups share their solutions and their problem-solving strategies with one another.

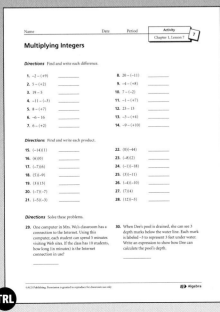

Lesson at a Glance

Chapter 1 Lesson 7

Overview This lesson presents the rules for dividing (positive) (positive), (negative) (negative), and (positive) (negative) integers.

Objectives

- To determine that the quotient of a positive integer times a positive integer is positive
- To identify the quotient of a negative integer times a negative integer as positive
- To describe the quotient of a negative integer times a positive integer as negative

Student Pages 14–15

Teacher's Resource Library 

Workbook Activity 8

Activity 8

Alternative Activity 8

Mathematics Vocabulary

dividend	**divisor**
division	**quotient**

1 Warm-Up Activity

Write a multiplication expression and its related division expression on the board. For example, $(4)(-5) = -20$ and $-20 \div 4 = -5$. Ask students to describe the relationship between multiplication and division. List their responses on the board. Help students recognize that division can be thought of as the opposite of multiplication.

2 Teaching the Lesson

Point out to students that they can predict or determine the sign of a quotient without completing the actual division. Offer the following examples and ask students to predict the sign of the quotient:
$(-39) \div (-13)$, $(+39) \div (-13)$,
$(-39) \div (+13)$, $(+39) \div (+13)$
Ask students to identify which rule they used to determine the sign of the quotient.

Lesson 7 Dividing Positive and Negative Integers

Division The arithmetic operation that finds how many times a number is contained in another number

Quotient The answer to a division problem

Dividend A number that is divided

Divisor The number by which you are dividing

Division is the arithmetic operation that finds how many times a number is contained in another number. The answer is the **quotient**.

EXAMPLE 1 $30 \div 6 = 5$

$6\overline{)30}$ = 5 — divisor: 6; dividend: 30; quotient: 5

Division and multiplication are opposite operations. Multiplying 3 by 4, then dividing the product by 4 gets you back to 3: $(3)(4) = 12$ and $12 \div 4 = 3$. You can use this information to discover the rules for division with negatives.

Division is the opposite of multiplication. A **dividend** is divided by a **divisor** to find a quotient.

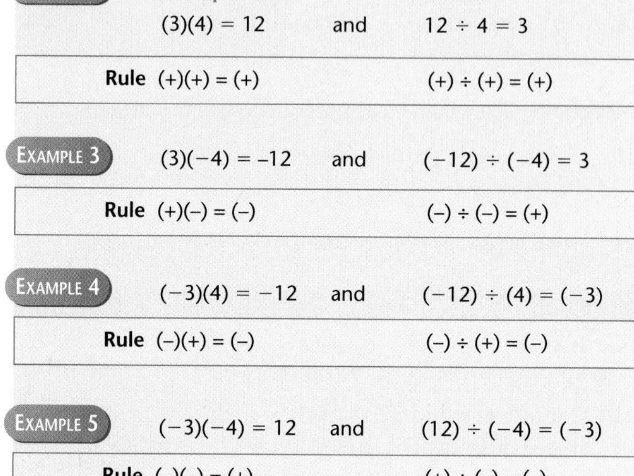

	Multiplication		Division
EXAMPLE 2	$(3)(4) = 12$	and	$12 \div 4 = 3$
Rule	$(+)(+) = (+)$		$(+) \div (+) = (+)$
EXAMPLE 3	$(3)(-4) = -12$	and	$(-12) \div (-4) = 3$
Rule	$(+)(-) = (-)$		$(-) \div (-) = (+)$
EXAMPLE 4	$(-3)(4) = -12$	and	$(-12) \div (4) = (-3)$
Rule	$(-)(+) = (-)$		$(-) \div (+) = (-)$
EXAMPLE 5	$(-3)(-4) = 12$	and	$(12) \div (-4) = (-3)$
Rule	$(-)(-) = (+)$		$(+) \div (-) = (-)$

Rules Like signs create positive products and quotients.
Unlike signs create negative products and quotients.

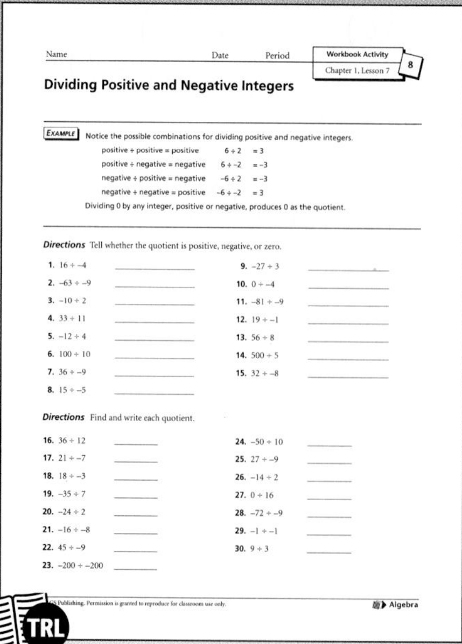

Name Date Period — Workbook Activity 8, Chapter 1, Lesson 7

Dividing Positive and Negative Integers

EXAMPLE Notice the possible combinations for dividing positive and negative integers.

positive ÷ positive = positive	6 ÷ 2	= 3
positive ÷ negative = negative	6 ÷ –2	= –3
negative ÷ positive = negative	–6 ÷ 2	= –3
negative ÷ negative = positive	–6 ÷ –2	= 3

Dividing 0 by any integer, positive or negative, produces 0 as the quotient.

Directions Tell whether the quotient is positive, negative, or zero.

1. 16 ÷ –4
2. –63 ÷ –9
3. –10 ÷ 2
4. 33 ÷ 11
5. –12 ÷ 4
6. 100 ÷ 10
7. 36 ÷ –9
8. 15 ÷ –5
9. –27 ÷ 3
10. 0 ÷ –4
11. –81 ÷ –9
12. 19 ÷ –1
13. 56 ÷ 8
14. 500 ÷ 5
15. 32 ÷ –8

Directions Find and write each quotient.

16. 36 ÷ 12
17. 21 ÷ –7
18. 18 ÷ –3
19. –35 ÷ 7
20. –24 ÷ 2
21. –16 ÷ –8
22. 45 ÷ –9
23. –200 ÷ –200
24. –50 ÷ 10
25. 27 ÷ –9
26. –14 ÷ 2
27. 0 ÷ 16
28. –72 ÷ –9
29. –1 ÷ –1
30. 9 ÷ 3

 Algebra

Workbook Activity 8

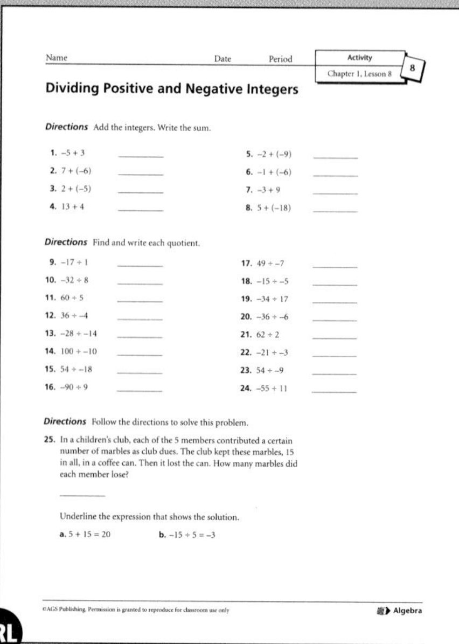

Name Date Period — Activity 8, Chapter 1, Lesson 8

Dividing Positive and Negative Integers

Directions Add the integers. Write the sum.

1. –5 + 3
2. 7 + (–6)
3. 2 + (–5)
4. 13 + 4
5. –2 + (–9)
6. –1 + (–6)
7. –3 + 9
8. 5 + (–18)

Directions Find and write each quotient.

9. –17 ÷ 1
10. –32 ÷ 8
11. 60 ÷ 5
12. 36 ÷ –4
13. –28 ÷ –14
14. 100 ÷ –10
15. 54 ÷ –18
16. –90 ÷ 9
17. 49 ÷ –7
18. –15 ÷ –5
19. –34 ÷ 17
20. –36 ÷ –6
21. 62 ÷ 2
22. –21 ÷ –3
23. 54 ÷ –9
24. –55 ÷ 11

Directions Follow the directions to solve this problem.

25. In a children's club, each of the 5 members contributed a certain number of marbles as club dues. The club kept these marbles, 15 in all, in a coffee can. Then it lost the can. How many marbles did each member lose?

Underline the expression that shows the solution.

a. 5 + 15 = 20 b. –15 ÷ 5 = –3

 Algebra

Activity 8

Writing About Mathematics

Explain how to check division problems using multiplication. Then write about ways you can use division and multiplication in daily activities.

Exercise A Find each quotient.

1. $42 \div 6$ 7

2. $-12 \div 4$ –3

3. $16 \div (-4)$ –4

4. $-25 \div (-5)$ 5

5. $81 \div 9$ 9

6. $-36 \div (-6)$ 6

7. $-54 \div (-9)$ 6

8. $48 \div 8$ 6

8. $-56 \div 7$ –8

10. $-8 \div (-4)$ 2

11. $0 \div (-1)$ 0

12. $40 \div (-5)$ –8

13. $50 \div 5$ 10

14. $-40 \div (-40)$ 1

15. $21 \div 3$ 7

16. $32 \div (-8)$ –4

17. $64 \div 8$ 8

18. $21 \div (-3)$ –7

19. $-18 \div (-6)$ 3

20. $-72 \div 9$ –8

Exercise B Tell whether each quotient is positive, negative, or zero.

21. $2226 \div (-42)$ negative

22. $-3458 \div 19$ negative

23. $676 \div (-26)$ negative

24. $5402 \div (73)$ positive

25. $-8514 \div (-33)$ positive

26. $121 \div (-11)$ negative

27. $-3563 \div 7$ negative

28. $0 \div (-21)$ zero

Exercise C Write + or − in each ■ to make each statement true.

29. ■ $21 \div 3 = 7$ +

30. ■ $30 \div 3 = -10$ –

Algebra in Your Life

Creating Color

Want to paint your room? You can choose from thousands of shades of color. To create each shade, a specified number of drops of one or more base colors is added to white paint. Want to work with color on your computer? Open a computer's drawing or paint program. Go to the "custom color" option where you'll see several cells with numbers. Experiment. If you add or subtract from the numbers in one or more of the cells, you'll see the new color you've created.

3 Reinforce and Extend

Learning Styles

Auditory/Verbal

Suggest that students work in pairs to determine the sign of a quotient. Have the partners make up their own division problems or use the problems in Exercise A. One partner reads the problem aloud, and the other indicates the sign of the quotient. Then they exchange roles. Listen to be sure that students are correctly reading the signs of the integers as *positive* and *negative.*

Calculator

Show students how to use the [+/–] key to find the quotient when either the divisor or the dividend is negative. For example, $39 \div (-3)$ requires the following steps:

Press 39 [÷] 3 [+/–] [=].

Read -13.

In the same manner, $-54 \div 3$ requires these steps:

Press 54 [+/–] [÷] 3 [=].

Read -18.

Have students practice using the calculator to find the quotients for the problems in Exercise B.

Online Connection

Have students visit www.ideafinder.com/history/timeline/the1900s.htm. Have students choose a time period that includes the past, present, and future and that extends for 50 years or so. Then have them make a number line representing those years. Use 0 to represent today's date. Have students put some important inventions from the past on their number lines. Also, have them include some inventions that they would like to see in the future and when they might occur (e.g., cars that don't need roads on which to travel, 30 years from now).

Lesson at a Glance

Chapter 1 Lesson 8

Overview This lesson shows how to simplify expressions with one variable.

Objective

- To simplify expressions with one variable by combining like terms

Student Pages 16–17

Teacher's Resource Library 

Workbook Activity 9

Activity 9

Alternative Activity 9

Mathematics Vocabulary

like terms **terms**
simplify

Warm-Up Activity

Ask students this question: "How many toes are in this classroom?" Encourage them to discuss the ways in which they can determine the number of toes. Help them recognize that number of toes = 10 times (number of students). Ask students how they can use the same information to describe the number of toes in any classroom, home, or movie theater. *[(10)(x) where x = number of people]* Note in particular those students who use a variable in their description. Record all suggestions.

Teaching the Lesson

Use red and blue algebra tiles to demonstrate combining like terms. Arrange 50 tiles in five groups: two containing only red tiles, three containing only blue tiles. Invite a volunteer to write an expression that represents all the tiles and all the groups. For example: 12 red + 13 red + 8 blue + 10 blue + 7 blue = 50 tiles. Next, have a second volunteer model combining like terms by combining tiles of like color and writing an expression to describe the tiles and the groups: 25 red tiles + 25 blue tiles = 50 tiles. Ask students to discuss whether or not the expression describing the tiles can be simplified further. Have them give reasons for their answers.

Lesson 8 Simplifying Expressions—One Variable

Term
Part of an expression separated by an addition or subtraction sign

Like terms
Terms that have the same variable

Simplify
Combine like terms

In algebra, you need to add, subtract, multiply, and divide using variables to stand for numbers.

In algebra $3n$ means $n + n + n$.
$2n$ means $n + n$.
n means $1n$ (the 1 is not written).

$3n$ and $2n$ and n are all called **terms**. $3n + 2n$ is an example of an algebraic expression that includes **like terms.**

To **simplify** an algebraic expression, combine the like terms.

EXAMPLE 1 $3n + 2n$

Combine the like terms, $3n$ and $2n$.

$3n + 2n$ means the same as

$$\underbrace{n + n + n}_{3n} + \underbrace{n + n}_{2n} = 5n$$

EXAMPLE 2 $3x - 15 - 10x$

Combine the like terms by subtracting the x's:

$3x - 10x$ (Think $3 - 10 = -7$)

$3x - 10x = -7x$

Since you cannot combine -15 with $-7x$, you are finished.

The simplified answer: $3x - 15 - 10x = -7x - 15$

Exercise A Simplify each expression.

1. $m + m$ $2m$
2. $s + s + s + s$ $4s$
3. $v + v + v$ $3v$
4. $b + b + b$ $3b$
5. $c + c + c + c$ $4c$

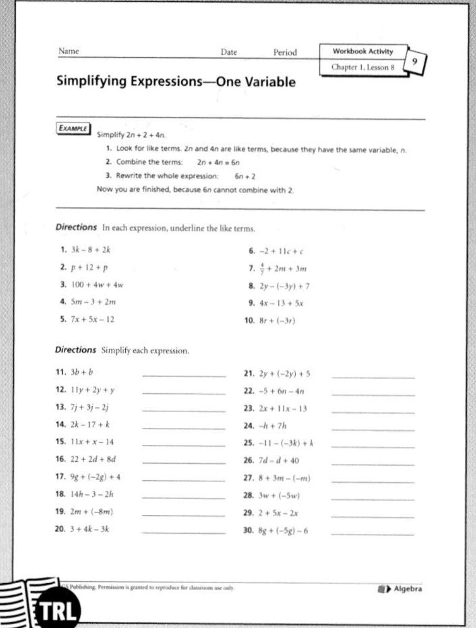

Name Date Period **Workbook Activity 9** Chapter 1, Lesson 8

Simplifying Expressions—One Variable

EXAMPLE Simplify $2n + 2 + 4n$.

1. Look for like terms. $2n$ and $4n$ are like terms, because they have the same variable, n.
2. Combine the terms: $2n + 4n = 6n$
3. Rewrite the whole expression: $6n + 2$

Now you are finished, because $6n$ cannot combine with 2.

Directions In each expression, underline the like terms.

1. $3k - 8 + 2k$
2. $p + 12 + p$
3. $100 + 4w + 4w$
4. $5m - 3 + 2m$
5. $7x + 5x - 12$
6. $-2 + 11c + c$
7. $\frac{4}{7} + 2m + 3m$
8. $2y - (-3y) + 7$
9. $4x - 13 + 5x$
10. $8r + (-3r)$

Directions Simplify each expression.

11. $3b + b$ ______
12. $11y + 2y + y$ ______
13. $7j + 3j - 2j$ ______
14. $2k - 17 + k$ ______
15. $11x + x - 14$ ______
16. $22 + 2d + 8d$ ______
17. $9g + (-2g) + 4$ ______
18. $14h - 3 - 2h$ ______
19. $2m + (-8m)$ ______
20. $3 + 4k - 3k$ ______
21. $2y + (-2y) + 5$ ______
22. $-5 + 6n - 4n$ ______
23. $2x + 11x - 13$ ______
24. $-h + 7h$ ______
25. $-11 - (-3k) + k$ ______
26. $7d - d + 40$ ______
27. $8 + 3m - (-m)$ ______
28. $3w + (-5w)$ ______
29. $2 + 5x - 2x$ ______
30. $8g + (-5g) - 6$ ______

 Algebra

TRL

Workbook Activity 9

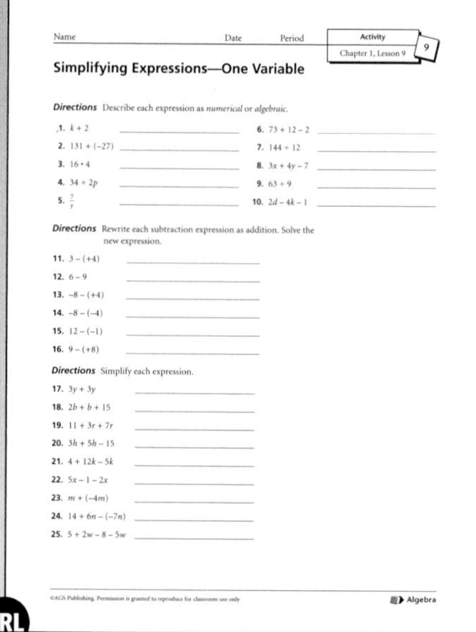

Name Date Period **Activity 9** Chapter 1, Lesson 9

Simplifying Expressions—One Variable

Directions Describe each expression as *numerical* or *algebraic.*

1. $k + 2$ ______
2. $131 + (-27)$ ______
3. $16 \cdot 4$ ______
4. $34 + 2p$ ______
5. $\frac{7}{y}$ ______
6. $73 + 12 - 2$ ______
7. $144 \div 12$ ______
8. $3x + 4y - 7$ ______
9. $63 \div 9$ ______
10. $2d - 4k - 1$ ______

Directions Rewrite each subtraction expression as addition. Solve the new expression.

11. $3 - (+4)$ ______
12. $6 - 9$ ______
13. $-8 - (+4)$ ______
14. $-8 - (-4)$ ______
15. $12 - (-1)$ ______
16. $9 - (+8)$ ______

Directions Simplify each expression.

17. $3y + 3y$ ______
18. $2b + b + 15$ ______
19. $11 + 3r + 7r$ ______
20. $3h + 5h - 15$ ______
21. $4 + 12k - 5k$ ______
22. $5x - 1 - 2x$ ______
23. $m + (-4m)$ ______
24. $14 + 6n - (-7n)$ ______
25. $5 + 2w - 8 - 5w$ ______

 Algebra

TRL

Activity 9

Exercise B Simplify each expression.

6. $2m + m$ $3m$
7. $6h + 4h$ $10h$
8. $3t + 6t$ $9t$
9. $k + 7k$ $8k$
10. $j + 3j + 6j$ $10j$
11. $5p + 6 + 8p$ $13p + 6$
12. $7 + 2i + 4i$ $7 + 6i$
13. $7y + 3y - 4$ $10y - 4$
14. $6z + 4z - 11$ $10z - 11$
15. $9 + 6c - 2c$ $9 + 4c$
16. $8x + 4 - 3x$ $5x + 4$
17. $6q - 3 - 2q$ $4q - 3$
18. $10p + 12 - 8p$ $2p + 12$
19. $20v + 9 + 9v$ $29v + 9$
20. $17w - 5 - 12w$ $5w - 5$
21. $-6g + g$ $-5g$
22. $k + (-12k)$ $-11k$
23. $6m + (-18m)$ $-12m$
24. $-5t + t + (-12t)$ $-16t$
25. $14x - (-14x)$ $28x$
26. $6 + j + (-15j)$ $6 + (-14j)$
27. $2r + 18 - 18r$ $-16r + 18$
28. $5f + (-3f) + 14$ $2f + 14$
29. $15u - 18 - 17u$ $-2u - 18$
30. $7 + 23m - (-14m)$ $7 + 37m$

Exercise C Find the missing term to make each statement true.

31. $c + ■ = 10c$ $9c$
32. $6j - ■ = 3j$ $3j$
33. $18e + ■ = 12e$ $-6e$
34. $■ - (-21x) = 21x$ 0
35. $90z + ■ = 80z$ $-10z$

Exercise D Write an expression for each statement.

36. The sum of four x and twenty. $4x + 20$
37. The difference between $2n$ and thirty. $2n - 30$ or $30 - 2n$
38. The sum of $5d$ and seventeen. $5d + 17$
39. Three subtracted from $4p$. $4p - 3$
40. Twenty-five added to $17q$. $17q + 25$

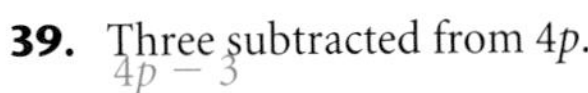

Estimation Activity

Estimate: Will the result of a multiplication or division problem be positive or negative?

$(37)(-0.12) = ?$ negative
$(37)(-0.12) \div 1.5 = ?$ negative
$(37)(-0.12) \div (-1.5) = ?$ positive
$(x)(-x^2)(-x) \div (x^3)(-x) = ?$ negative

Solution: For multiplication and division, an odd number of negative factors or divisors will give a negative result. An even number of negative factors or divisors will give a positive result.

Manipulatives

Combining Like Terms

Materials: Pattern Blocks, Unit Cubes, Manipulatives Master 2 (Basic Mat)

Group Practice: On an overhead projector, build models of the expressions in the examples. Use blocks to represent variables and cubes to represent constants. Compare with the symbolic equivalent. Show how shapes and cubes combine to make a new expression with a new simplified symbolic equivalent. For subtraction, remind students to change subtraction to addition of the opposite. Use the Basic Mat to differentiate positive and negative terms and apply the Zero Rule to simplify. Do several more examples using expressions students generate.

Student Practice: Have students use blocks and cubes for Exercise B, Problems 6–17, and Exercise C, Problems 31 and 32.

3 Reinforce and Extend

Learning Styles

Interpersonal/ Group Learning

Have students work in groups of four. Provide five index cards for each group. Ask the groups to compose five expressions that can be simplified. They should write each expression on the front of a card. On the back of the card, they should write the simplified expression. Have groups exchange cards and practice simplifying the expressions before checking the backs of the cards.

Mental Math

Write the following expressions on the board for students to simplify without using pencil and paper. Ask volunteers to explain their strategy for solving each problem.

$2x + 3x + 7$	*($5x + 7$)*
$3y + 4y + 9$	*($7y + 9$)*
$-25h + 22h + 4$	*($-3h + 4$)*
$k + k + k + 7k$	*($10k$)*
$9 - 3r - 10r$	*($9 - 13r$)*

Lesson at a Glance

Chapter 1 Lesson 9

Overview This lesson shows how to simplify expressions containing several variables.

Objective

- To simplify expressions containing several variables by combining like terms

Student Pages 18–19

Teacher's Resource Library TRL

Workbook Activity 10

Activity 10

Alternative Activity 10

Mathematics Vocabulary

unlike terms

1 Warm-Up Activity

By way of review, ask a volunteer to explain how to simplify an expression containing several terms but only one variable. Then ask if students have any ideas about how to simplify an expression with more than one variable, for example, $12x + 2x - 12b + 4b$. Encourage responses that combine like variables.

2 Teaching the Lesson

Present students with the following model.

Ahman has 2 apples and 3 oranges.

Point out to students that there is no way for Ahman to combine the apples and oranges, which are two different things. Indicate that $2x + 3y$ is a similar situation. Because x and y are unlike terms, they cannot be combined.

Common Error

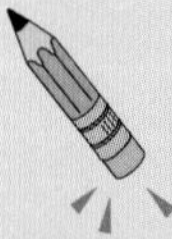

Students sometimes jump to conclusions concerning which terms may be like terms—confusing like *coefficients* with like *terms.* Impress upon students that in an expression, the variable, not the coefficient, determines which terms are like terms.

Lesson 9 Simplifying Expressions—Several Variables

Unlike terms
Terms that have different variables

You may have more than one variable in an expression.

Example 1

$3a + b$ — unlike terms

You cannot combine terms because a and b are unlike terms.

$3a + a$ — like terms

$3a + a$ are like terms and can be combined to create $4a$.

To simplify expressions, combine all like terms.

Example 2

$3x + 15 + 6x - 7 + y$

Combine x terms: $3x + 6x = 9x$

Combine integers: $15 - 7 = +8$

Note: You cannot combine unlike terms $9x$, y, and 8, so you are finished.

Rewrite $3x + 15 + 6x - 7 + y$ as $9x + y + 8$.

Exercise A Combine like terms. Simplify each expression.

1. $5x + 3x + 4 + 7b$
2. $14m + 7c + 4c + 4m$
3. $16 + 4a - 2a + 7u + 2u$
4. $5h - 3h + 14 + 15n$
5. $7y + 10p + 18 + 10p + 17y$
6. $13r + 25 - 8r + 14g + 5g$
7. $m + 10 + 2m + 7t$
8. $20p - 4 - 12p + 5q + 2q$
9. $8w - 13 - 4w + y$ — $4w - 13 + y$
10. $32j + 14 - 30j + 3h + 2h$ — $2j + 14 + 5h$
11. $8u + 7b + 17 + 2b - 4u$ — $4u + 9b + 17$
12. $25 + 16a - 22 + 7d - 15a + 7d$ — $3 + a + 14d$
13. $9g + 2 + 16r - 7g + 15 - 13r$ — $2g + 17 + 3r$
14. $8 + j - 3 + 4j + 17m$ — $5 + 5j + 17m$
15. $3m + 7y + 5 - m - 6y$ — $2m + y + 5$

1. $8x + 4 + 7b$　2. $18m + 11c$　3. $16 + 2a + 9u$　4. $2h + 14 + 15n$　5. $24y + 20p + 18$　6. $5r + 25 + 19g$　7. $3m + 10 + 7t$　8. $8p - 4 + 7q$

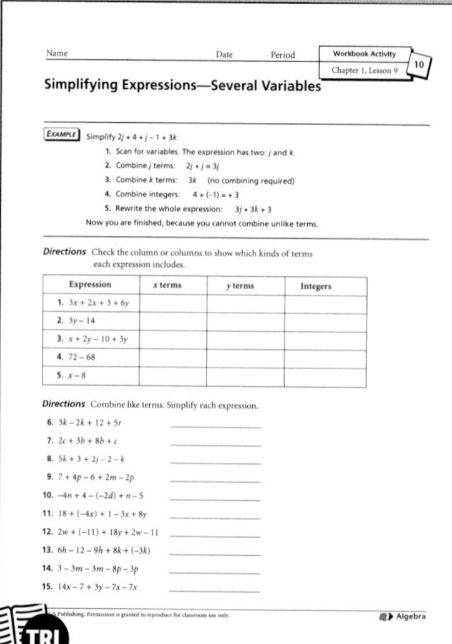

Name　Date　Period　Workbook Activity 10 Chapter 1, Lesson 9

Simplifying Expressions—Several Variables

EXAMPLE Simplify $2j + 4 + j - 1 + 3k$.

1. Scan for variables. The expression has two: j and k.
2. Combine j terms: $2j + j = 3j$
3. Combine k terms: $3k$ (no combining required)
4. Combine integers: $4 + (-1) = +3$
5. Rewrite the whole expression: $3j + 3k + 3$

Now you are finished, because you cannot combine unlike terms.

Directions Check the column or columns to show which kinds of terms each expression includes.

Expression	x terms	y terms	Integers
1. $3x + 2x + 3 + 6y$			
2. $3y - 14$			
3. $x + 2y - 10 + 3y$			
4. $72 - 68$			
5. $x - 8$			

Directions Combine like terms. Simplify each expression.

6. $3k - 2k + 12 + 5r$ ______
7. $2c + 3b + 8b + c$ ______
8. $5k + 3 + 2j - 2 - k$ ______
9. $7 + 4p - 6 + 2m - 2p$ ______
10. $-4n + 4 - (-2d) + n - 5$ ______
11. $18 + (-4x) + 1 - 3x + 8y$ ______
12. $2w + (-11) + 18y + 2w - 11$ ______
13. $6h - 12 - 9h + 8k + (-3k)$ ______
14. $3 - 3m - 3m - 8p - 3p$ ______
15. $14x - 7 + 3y - 7x - 7x$ ______

　Algebra

TRL **Workbook Activity 10**

Name　Date　Period　Activity 10 Chapter 1, Lesson 10

Simplifying Expressions—Several Variables

Directions Find and write each quotient.

1. $18 \div 3$ ______
2. $-49 \div 7$ ______
3. $24 \div -8$ ______
4. $-35 \div -7$ ______
5. $16 \div -4$ ______
6. $21 \div -7$ ______
7. $-19 \div -19$ ______
8. $-56 \div 8$ ______
9. $36 \div 4$ ______
10. $-11 \div 1$ ______

Directions Combine like terms. Simplify each expression.

11. $6x + 3 - 2y - x$ ______
12. $3k - 12 + y + k$ ______
13. $2h + 14 - 13 - 3w$ ______
14. $7n + 18 + 12p - 18 - n$ ______
15. $m + 4m + r + 3m$ ______
16. $15 + 3d + (-2j) + (-4d)$ ______
17. $22 + a - 17 - (-5b)$ ______
18. $-16 + 9x - 2y - 9x - y - y$ ______
19. $11r - 2 + (-2r) - (-5w)$ ______

Directions Solve the problem.

20. Everyone at the picnic contributed fruit to the picnic basket, as follows:
    Deana—2 oranges　Kim—1 peach
    Larry—3 apples　Dru—1 orange
    Write a simplified addition expression to represent the fruit contents of the picnic basket.
    ______

　Algebra

TRL **Activity 10**

16. $-9t - 14 + (-5c)$ or $-9t - 14 - 5c$

17. $8 + (-16c) + (-16b)$ or $8 - 16c - 16b$

18. $5n - 9 + 2c$

19. $6x + (-17) + 42f$

20. $-18m + 5 + (-6c)$ or $-18m + 5 - 6c$

21. $-y - 14 + 46c$

22. $20 + (-6g) - 8x$ or $20 - 6g - 8x$

23. $40j + (-32m) + 16$ or $40j - 32m + 16$

24. $-45d + 17s - 7$

25. $3m - 14 + 16r$

Exercise B Combine like terms. Simplify each expression.

16. $7t - 14 - 16t + 9c + (-14c)$

17. $8 - 8c - 8c - 4b - 12b$

18. $10n - 15 - 5n + 6 + 2c$

19. $3x + (-17) + 21f + 3x - (-21f)$

20. $-19m + 5 - (-m) + c - 7c$

21. $y - 14 + 30c - 2y + 16c$

22. $10 + (-4g) + 10 - 13x - 2g + 5x$

23. $20j + 20j - 16m - 16m + 16$

24. $-25d + 2s - 7 + 15s - 20d$

25. $9m - 14 - 6m + 4r + 12r$

Exercise C Tell whether each statement is true or false.

26. $m + 15c + (-3m) - 4$ simplifies to $8mc$ false

27. $30x + 9 + 9m + 14x - 3m$ simplifies to $34x + 9 + 6m$ false

28. $6 + 4m - 17g + 6m + 3g$ simplifies to $6 + 10m - 14g$ true

29. $17 + 6y - 10 + m + 7m$ simplifies to $27 + 6y + 8m$ false

30. $-j + 10s - j + 12 - 8s$ simplifies to $-2j + 2s + 12$ true

Technology Connection

Software Programs Use Formulas

Balancing your checkbook is easy when you use a software program. Just enter the dollar amounts of your checks and deposits in the right place. The software calculates your balance for you. In the same way, other software programs help businesses to do payroll. They also help insurance companies to figure out premiums, and scientists to calculate the growth of bacteria and viruses. These software programs have one thing in common—they all use formulas with variables!

Manipulatives

Simplifying Expressions with Several Variables

Materials: Pattern Blocks, Unit Cubes, Manipulatives Master 2 (Basic Mat)

Group Practice: On an overhead projector, build models of the expressions in the examples. Use blocks to represent two variables and cubes to represent two constants. Emphasize that unlike terms, like unlike shapes, cannot be combined. Discuss the meaning of *simplify.* For example, discuss how $8x + 4 + 7b$ is a simpler way to express $2x + 3 + 6x + 1 + 4b + 3b$.

Student Practice: Have students use manipulatives to solve or check their work in Exercises A, B, and C. Students should draw sketches of their models with the symbolic equivalent before and after simplifying.

3 Reinforce and Extend

Learning Styles

LEP/ESL

Have students make a dictionary of algebraic terms such as *terms, like terms, unlike terms,* and *simplify.* Suggest that they include a definition as well as several examples for each algebraic term they include in their dictionary. Encourage students to keep their algebraic dictionaries and to add terms, definitions, and examples as they progress through the chapter.

Lesson at a Glance

Chapter 1 Lesson 10

Overview This lesson shows how to multiply and divide with exponents.

Objectives

- To identify a number's exponent and base
- To simplify terms containing exponents

Student Pages 20–21

Teacher's Resource Library TRL

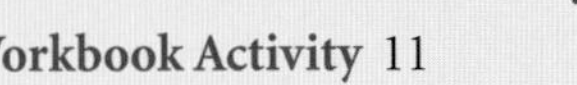

Workbook Activity 11

Activity 11

Alternative Activity 11

Mathematics Vocabulary

base **power**
exponent

1 Warm-Up Activity

Ask students if they are familiar with either of the following terms: *2 squared* or *2 to the second power.* Engage students in a discussion about the terms, allowing all students to present their views and opinions. Focus on those responses that indicate *2 squared* or *2 to the second power* is the same as *2 times 2.*

2 Teaching the Lesson

Tell students they can read 2^3 as "two to the third power" or "two cubed." Write other examples of bases and exponents on the board and have volunteers read the expressions. For example, 2^5, 2^{10}, and 4^8. *(two to the fifth power, two to the tenth power, and four to the eighth power)*

Lesson 10 Positive Exponents

Exponent
Number that tells the times another number is a factor

Base
The number being multiplied; a factor

Power
The product of multiplying any number by itself once or many times

2^3 is an example of a way to show a number (2) multiplied by itself three times.

2^3 The 3 is called the **exponent.** The 2 is called the **base.**

$a \cdot a \cdot a$ can be written as

$y \cdot y \cdot y \cdot y$ can be written as

You can multiply and divide by adding or subtracting exponents with the same base.

EXAMPLE 1 $y^2 \cdot y^3 = y \cdot y \cdot y \cdot y \cdot y = y^5$
or $y^2 \cdot y^3 = y^{2+3} = y^5$

Rule To multiply, add exponents with the same base.

EXAMPLE 2 $y^3 \div y^2 = \frac{y^3}{y^2} = \frac{y \cdot \not{y} \cdot \not{y}}{\not{y} \cdot \not{y}} = y$
or $y^3 \div y^2 = y^{3-2} = y^1 = y$

Rule To divide, subtract exponents with the same base.

Terms such as x^2 or x^3 have no numerical value until you substitute numbers for x.

EXAMPLE 3 If $x = 3$, $x^2 = 3 \cdot 3$ or 9 and $x^3 = 3 \cdot 3 \cdot 3$ or 27.
3 to the second **power** is 9.
3 to the third power is 27.

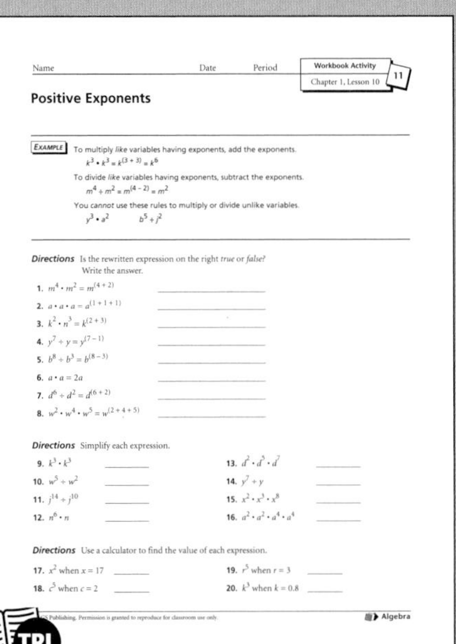

Name Date Period **Workbook Activity 11** Chapter 1, Lesson 10

Positive Exponents

EXAMPLE To multiply *like* variables having exponents, add the exponents.
$k^3 \cdot k^3 = k^{(3+3)} = k^6$
To divide *like* variables having exponents, subtract the exponents.
$m^4 \div m^2 = m^{(4-2)} = m^2$
You *cannot* use these rules to multiply or divide unlike variables.
$y^3 \cdot a^2$ $b^5 \div j^2$

Directions Is the rewritten expression on the right *true* or *false?* Write the answer.

1. $m^4 \cdot m^2 = m^{(4+2)}$ ________
2. $a \cdot a \cdot a = a^{(1+1+1)}$ ________
3. $k^2 \cdot n^3 = k^{(2+3)}$ ________
4. $y^7 \div y = y^{(7-1)}$ ________
5. $b^8 \div b^3 = b^{(8-3)}$ ________
6. $a \cdot a = 2a$ ________
7. $d^6 \div d^2 = d^{(6+2)}$ ________
8. $w^2 \cdot w^4 \cdot w^5 = w^{(2+4+5)}$ ________

Directions Simplify each expression.

9. $k^3 \cdot k^3$ ________
10. $w^5 \div w^2$ ________
11. $j^{14} \div j^{10}$ ________
12. $n^6 \cdot n$ ________
13. $d^2 \cdot d^5 \cdot d^7$ ________
14. $y^7 \div y$ ________
15. $x^2 \cdot x^3 \cdot x^8$ ________
16. $a^2 \cdot a^2 \cdot a^4 \cdot a^4$ ________

Directions Use a calculator to find the value of each expression.

17. x^2 when $x = 17$ ________
18. c^5 when $c = 2$ ________
19. r^5 when $r = 3$ ________
20. k^3 when $k = 0.8$ ________

 Algebra

TRL

Workbook Activity 11

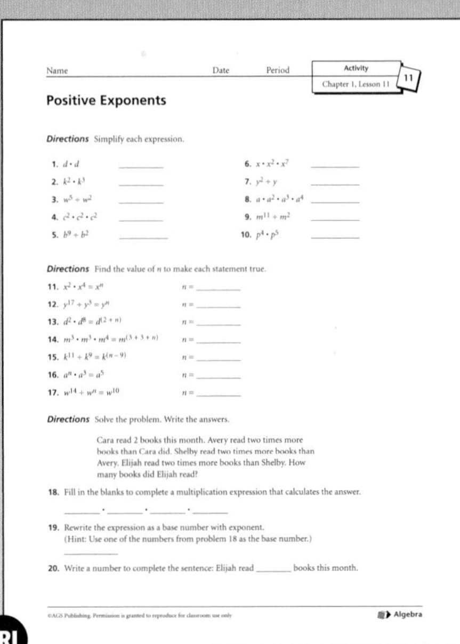

Name Date Period **Activity 11** Chapter 1, Lesson 11

Positive Exponents

Directions Simplify each expression.

1. $d \cdot d$ ________
2. $k^2 \cdot k^3$ ________
3. $w^5 \div w^2$ ________
4. $c^2 \cdot c^2 \cdot c^2$ ________
5. $b^9 \div b^2$ ________
6. $x \cdot x^2 \cdot x^7$ ________
7. $y^2 \div y$ ________
8. $a \cdot a^2 \cdot a^3 \cdot a^4$ ________
9. $m^{11} \div m^2$ ________
10. $p^4 \cdot p^5$ ________

Directions Find the value of n to make each statement true.

11. $x^2 \cdot x^4 = x^n$ $n =$ ________
12. $y^{17} \div y^3 = y^n$ $n =$ ________
13. $d^2 \cdot d^8 = d^{(2+n)}$ $n =$ ________
14. $m^3 \cdot m^3 \cdot m^4 = m^{(3+3+n)}$ $n =$ ________
15. $k^{11} \div k^9 = k^{(n-9)}$ $n =$ ________
16. $a^n \cdot a^3 = a^5$ $n =$ ________
17. $w^{14} \div w^n = w^{10}$ $n =$ ________

Directions Solve the problem. Write the answers.

Cara read 2 books this month. Avery read two times more books than Cara did. Shelby read two times more books than Avery. Elijah read two times more books than Shelby. How many books did Elijah read?

18. Fill in the blanks to complete a multiplication expression that calculates the answer.

________ • ________ • ________ • ________

19. Rewrite the expression as a base number with exponent.
(Hint: Use one of the numbers from problem 18 as the base number.)

____

20. Write a number to complete the sentence: Elijah read ________ books this month.

 Algebra

TRL

Activity 11

Exercise A Tell whether each statement is true or false. If the statement is false, write the correct solution.

1. $2^3 = 8$	true	**5.** $c^5 \cdot c^4 \cdot c^2 = c^{11}$	true	**8.** $\frac{b^{16}}{b^4} = b^{12}$	true
2. $x \cdot x \cdot x = x^3$	true	**6.** $y^3 \cdot y^3 = 6^y$	false; y^6	**9.** $a^{25} \div a^5 = a^5$	false; a^{20}
3. $m^2 \cdot m^5 = m^{10}$	false; m^7	**7.** $n^{10} \div n^2 = n^8$	true	**10.** $\frac{t^8}{t^5} = t^3$	true
4. $3^2 = 6$	false; 9				

Exercise B Simplify each expression.

11. $w^8 \cdot w^7$	w^{15}	**16.** $x^{11} \div x^5$	x^6	**21.** $x^3 \cdot x \cdot x^5 \cdot x^4$	x^{13}
12. $p^4 \div p^3$	p	**17.** $d^4 \cdot d^3 \cdot d$	d^8	**22.** $\frac{y^{16}}{y^{16}}$	1
13. $b^2 \cdot b$	b^3	**18.** $j^{18} \div j^6$	j^{12}	**23.** $\frac{g^{14}}{g^3}$	g^{11}
14. $c^{10} \div c^2$	c^8	**19.** $t \cdot t^8 \cdot t^{10}$	t^{19}	**24.** $r^4 \div r$	r^3
15. $v^7 \cdot v^7$	v^{14}	**20.** $m^{20} \div m^{18}$	m^2	**25.** $v^2 \cdot v^2 \cdot v^8 \cdot v^7$	v^{19}

Exercise C Find the value of n to make each statement true.

26. $y^3 \cdot b^4 \cdot y^6 = y^9 b^n$	4	**31.** $\frac{w^{12}}{w^6} = w^n$	6
27. $a^3 \cdot c^4 \cdot c^3 \cdot a^7 = a^{10}c^n$	7	**32.** $x^4 \cdot y^3 \cdot x^5 \cdot y^2 = x^n y^5$	9
28. $\frac{e^{14}}{e^n} = e^{10}$	4	**33.** $p^3 \cdot q^4 \cdot q^7 = p^n q^{11}$	3
29. $t \cdot v^6 \cdot t^2 = t^n v^6$	3	**34.** $z^n \div z^8 = z^6$	14
30. $i^n \div i^{10} = i^{35}$	45	**35.** $\frac{s^{20}}{s^n} = s^5$	15

Calculator Practice

Use the y^x or x^y key on your calculator to compute with exponents.

Example 4 Find 5^4.
Press 5 y^x 4 = .
The display will show 625.

Exercise D Use a calculator to find the value of each expression.

36. 25^4	390,625	**38.** $(\frac{1}{2})^3$	$\frac{1}{8}$	**40.** 3^{10}	59,049
37. $(4.1)^2$	16.81	**39.** $(0.01)^2$	0.0001		

Manipulatives

Simplifying Exponents

Materials: Pattern Blocks

Group Practice: On an overhead projector, use the introduction and examples to model variables with exponents. Stack one shape for each factor of the variable. For example, $y^3 = y \cdot y \cdot y =$ stack of three shapes. Stack the stacks and add shapes to find the product. To divide, place the denominator model directly below the numerator model. Pair up shapes from the numerator and denominator and remove, explaining that each pair represents 1. The quotient is represented by the remaining unpaired shapes. Do more examples of expressions with two or more variables. Emphasize that different shapes, like different variables, cannot be combined.

Student Practice: Have students use the shapes for all exercises, either to help with simplifying or to check their work.

3 Reinforce and Extend

Calculator

Point out to students that if their calculator does not have a y^x key, they can still find the value of expressions with exponents. Remind students that 24^4 is the same as $24 \cdot 24 \cdot 24 \cdot 24$. Have them predict which of the following have the same value and then confirm their predictions using a calculator.

25^2	*(625)*	4^4	*(256)*
5^4	*(625)*	2^9	*(512)*
9^2	*(81)*	16^2	*(256)*
36^2	*(1,296)*	6^4	*(1,296)*
2^{10}	*(1,024)*	4^5	*(1,024)*
3^4	*(81)*	8^3	*(512)*

Common Error

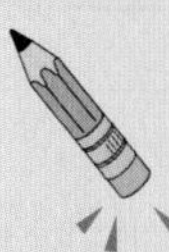

As some students write problems that have expressions with exponents, they may confuse exponents with ordinary coefficients. Indicate to students that they should take extra care when writing expressions with exponents, making sure they write the exponents slightly smaller than and above and to the right of the base. Students may benefit from practice writing base-and-exponent combinations on the board or on paper.

Lesson at a Glance

Chapter 1 Lesson 11

Overview The lesson introduces formulas for perimeter that include variables.

Objective

- To find the perimeters of regular polygons using formulas for perimeter

Student Pages 22–23

Teacher's Resource Library

Workbook Activity 12

Activity 12

Alternative Activity 12

Mathematics Vocabulary

equilateral triangle **perimeter**

Warm-Up Activity

Ask students to describe ways in which they could find the distance around—perimeter—of a classroom object such as a bulletin board, doorway, or computer screen. Record all responses on the board. Focus on responses that suggest measuring two sides and multiplying rather than measuring all four sides.

Teaching the Lesson

Draw a square on the board. Label each side of the square as *s*. Ask a volunteer to show that finding the perimeter of the square involves repeated addition. Ask a second volunteer to use the addition information to develop a formula for perimeter using multiplication.

Common Error

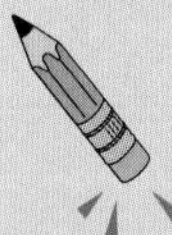

Some students may attempt to find the perimeter of a square, for instance, as $s + 4$. Help them recognize that the perimeter formulas rely on multiplication—$4s$ rather than $4 + s$.

Lesson 11 Formulas with Variables

Perimeter
The distance around the outside of a shape

Equilateral triangle
A triangle with three equal sides

In the formula for finding the **perimeter**, or distance around, any **equilateral triangle**, *s* stands for the length of a side of the triangle. The letter *s* represents an unknown quantity or variable. To find perimeter, add the length of each side of a figure.

EXAMPLE 1 **Perimeter** $= s + s + s = 3s$

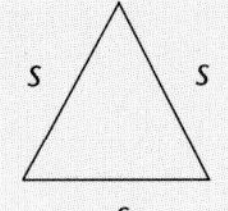

If $s = 2$, then $3s = (3)(2) = 6$
If $s = 15$, then $3s = (3)(15) = 45$

Square

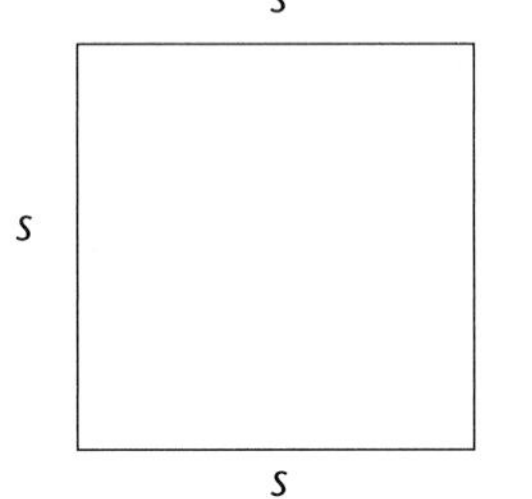

Exercise A Use the square for Problems 1–4.

1. What is the formula for finding the perimeter of this square? $P = 4$
2. Find the perimeter of a square, when $s = 4$ cm. 16 cm
3. Find the perimeter of a square, when $s = 10$ m. 40 m
4. What is the length of each side of a square when the perimeter is 36 meters? 9 met

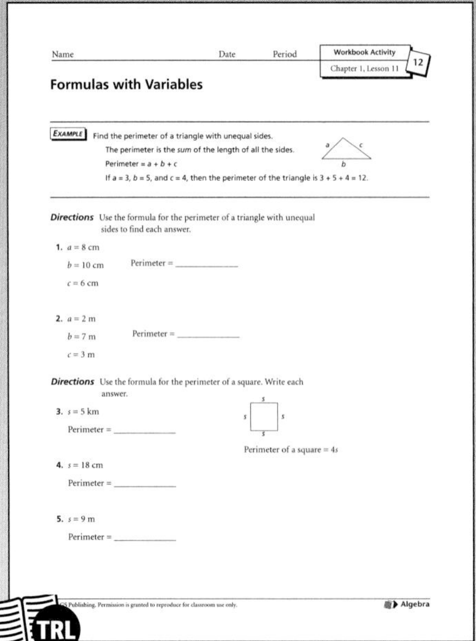

Name Date Period Workbook Activity 12 Chapter 1, Lesson 11

Formulas with Variables

EXAMPLE Find the perimeter of a triangle with unequal sides.
The perimeter is the *sum* of the length of all the sides.
Perimeter = $a + b + c$
If $a = 3$, $b = 5$, and $c = 4$, then the perimeter of the triangle is $3 + 5 + 4 = 12$.

Directions Use the formula for the perimeter of a triangle with unequal sides to find each answer.

1. $a = 8$ cm
   $b = 10$ cm Perimeter = ____________
   $c = 6$ cm
2. $a = 2$ m
   $b = 7$ m Perimeter = ____________
   $c = 3$ m

Directions Use the formula for the perimeter of a square. Write each answer.

Perimeter of a square = $4s$

3. $s = 5$ km
   Perimeter = ____________
4. $s = 18$ cm
   Perimeter = ____________
5. $s = 9$ m
   Perimeter = ____________

 Algebra

TRL

Workbook Activity 12

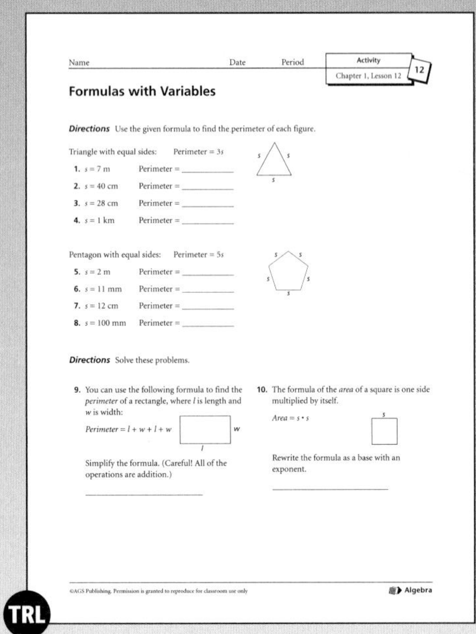

Name Date Period Activity 12 Chapter 1, Lesson 12

Formulas with Variables

Directions Use the given formula to find the perimeter of each figure.

Triangle with equal sides: Perimeter = $3s$

1. $s = 7$ m Perimeter = ____________
2. $s = 40$ cm Perimeter = ____________
3. $s = 28$ cm Perimeter = ____________
4. $s = 1$ km Perimeter = ____________

Pentagon with equal sides: Perimeter = $5s$

5. $s = 2$ m Perimeter = ____________
6. $s = 11$ mm Perimeter = ____________
7. $s = 12$ cm Perimeter = ____________
8. $s = 100$ mm Perimeter = ____________

Directions Solve these problems.

9. You can use the following formula to find the *perimeter* of a rectangle, where *l* is length and *w* is width:
   Perimeter = $l + w + l + w$
   Simplify the formula. (Careful! All of the operations are addition.)
   ____
10. The formula of the *area* of a square is one side multiplied by itself.
    Area = $s \cdot s$
    Rewrite the formula as a base with an exponent.
    ____

 Algebra

TRL

Activity 12

Triangle

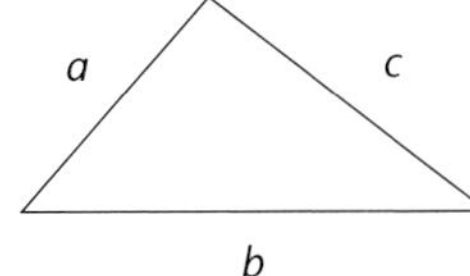

Exercise B Use the triangle for Problems 5–8.

5. What is the formula for finding the perimeter of this triangle? $P = a + b + c$

6. Find the perimeter, when a = 13 cm, b = 10 cm, and c = 20 cm. 43 cm

7. Find the perimeter, when a = 20 cm, b = 30 cm, and c = 40 cm. 90 cm

8. What is the length of side c when the perimeter is 100 m, b = 35 m, and a = 40 m? 25 m

Rectangle

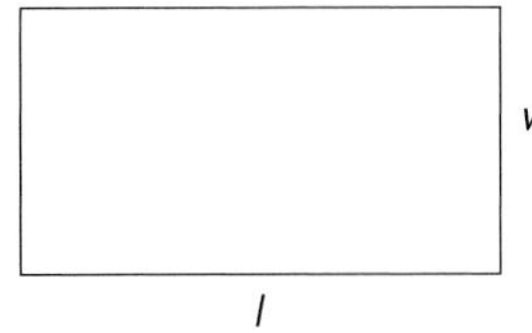

Exercise C Use the rectangle for Problems 9–12.

9. What is the formula for finding the perimeter of this rectangle? $P = l + w + l + w$ or $P = 2l + 2w$

10. Find the perimeter, when l = 15 mm and w = 8 mm. 46 mm

11. Find the perimeter, when l = 10 cm and w = 9 cm. 38 cm

12. What is the width of a rectangle when the perimeter is 14 m and the length is 4 m? 3 m

MANIPULATIVES

Modeling the Perimeter Formula

Materials: Pattern Blocks, Unit Cubes

Group Practice: Use shapes to model the perimeter formula. Replace each shape with a unit cube representing the variable's value that the shape represents. Count the cubes to find the perimeter.

Student Practice: Have students use the shapes and cubes to solve all of the problems in Exercises A–F. Instruct students to draw sketches of each step along with the corresponding symbolic equivalent.

3 Reinforce and Extend

IN THE COMMUNITY

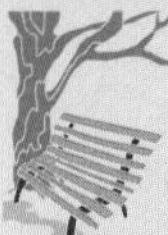

Assign groups of students the task of estimating how much fencing is needed to enclose an athletic field, garden, or parking lot belonging to the school. Suggest that students use any existing fences as models. Ask them to create a plan that shows how they would solve the problem, recording steps such as these:

- Decide whether the lot is a rectangle or a square.
- Measure the length of a side.
- Estimate the perimeter as if no gates or openings were needed.
- Draw a picture of the area to be fenced.

Have students execute their plans and estimate the size of the perimeter they propose to fence. Invite groups to explain their plans and results to the class.

Learning Styles

LEP/ESL

ESL students may have difficulty understanding how using formulas relates to making measurements. Provide students with a ruler, yardstick, or meter stick and a length of string greater than the perimeter of the classroom. Have groups of four students measure the length and width of the classroom using the ruler or other measuring device. Ask them to use their measurements and the formula for a perimeter of a rectangle to determine the perimeter of the classroom. Then have the groups place the string around the outside edge of the classroom, cutting the string once it has completely circled the room. Ask them to predict the length of the string. Have them confirm their prediction by measuring the string.

Pentagon

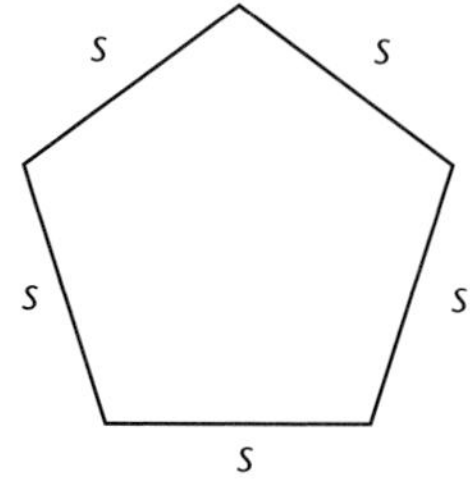

Exercise D Use the pentagon for Problems 13–16.

13. What is the formula for finding the perimeter of this regular pentagon? $P = 5s$

14. Find the perimeter, when $s = 6$ m. 30 m

15. Find the perimeter, when $s = 8$ cm. 40 cm

16. What is the length of each side of a regular pentagon when the perimeter is 100 km?

The Pentagon in Arlington, Virginia, has five wedge-shaped sections.

Rhombus

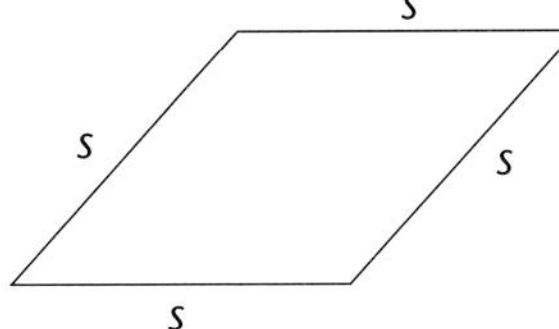

Exercise E Use the rhombus for Problems 17–21.

17. What is the formula for finding the perimeter of this rhombus? $P = 4s$

18. Find the perimeter, when $s = 15$ km. 60 km

19. Find the perimeter, when $s = 8$ km. 32 km

20. What is the length of each side of a rhombus when the perimeter is 28 km? 7 km

21. A rhombus has the same perimeter formula as what other polygon? square

Hexagon

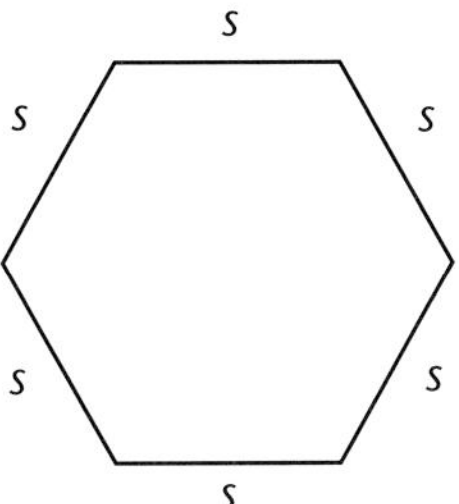

Exercise F Use the hexagon for Problems 22–25.

22. What is the formula for finding the perimeter of this hexagon? $P = 6s$

23. Find the perimeter, when $s = 10$ mm. 60 mm

24. Find the perimeter, when $s = 8$ km. 48 km

25. What is the length of each side of a regular hexagon when the perimeter is 72 m? 12 m

Algebra: Arithmetic with Letters **25**

Lesson at a Glance

Chapter 1 Application

Overview The lesson presents the formula for ground speed as an application of a formula with variables.

Objective

- To complete computations involving the formula $g = a - h$, where g is ground speed, a is air speed, and h is head wind speed

Student Page 24

Teacher's Resource Library

Application Activity 1

Everyday Algebra 1

Warm-Up Activity

Invite volunteers to share with the class what they know about tail winds and head winds in airplane travel. Have students discuss why knowing ground speed is important. *(to maintain schedules)*

Teaching the Lesson

Use a number line on the board to illustrate the effect of head wind on air speed. Ask a volunteer to plot the values from the example, 200, −67, and 133, on the number line. Then ask students to describe in their own words what effect head wind has on aircraft.

Reinforce and Extend

Career Connection

Invite an airline pilot or local television helicopter pilot to speak to the class. Ask the speaker to tell about instances in which he or she uses positive and negative numbers as well as instances in which he or she is concerned about head winds and tail winds.

Application $\pi^2 \Sigma + \Omega \sqrt{x^2}\ \% \neq y \geq n = \nabla 30^\circ \pi$

Using a Formula

The speed that an airplane travels is calculated by the formula $g = a - h$. Ground speed (g) equals air speed (a) minus head wind speed (h).

	Ground speed (g)	=	Air speed (a)	−	Head wind speed (h)
Example 1	g	=	200 mph	−	67 mph

$g = 200 - 67 = 133$ The ground speed (g) equals 133 mph.

Example 2	133 mph	=	a	−	67 mph

$133 = a - 67$
$a = 133 + 67 = 200$ The air speed (a) equals 200 mph.

Example 3	133 mph	=	200 mph	−	h

$133 = 200 - h$
$h = 200 - 133 = 67$ The head wind speed (h) equals 67 mph.

Exercise Copy the table. Find each missing value.

	Ground speed (g)	air speed (a)	head wind speed (h)	
1.	g	175 mph	53 mph	122 mph
2.	273 mph	293 mph	h	20 mph
3.	155 mph	a	15 mph	170 mph
4.	g	112 mph	27 mph	85 mph
5.	g	305 mph	41 mph	264 mph

You can find an airplane's speed by using an algebraic formula.

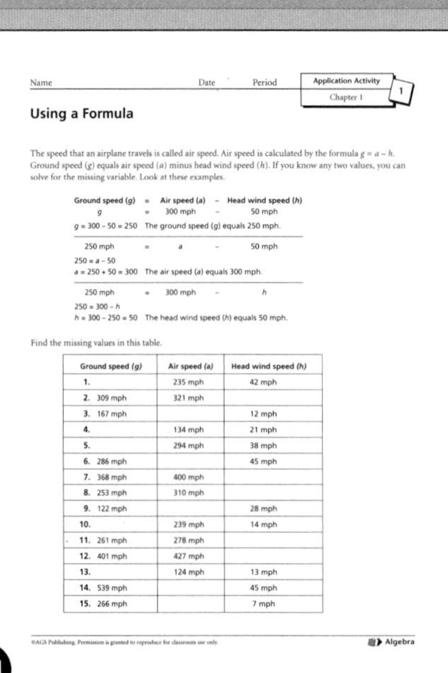

Name Date Period **Application Activity 1** Chapter 1

Using a Formula

The speed that an airplane travels is called air speed. Air speed is calculated by the formula $g = a - h$. Ground speed (g) equals air speed (a) minus head wind speed (h). If you know any two values, you can solve for the missing variable. Look at these examples.

Ground speed (g)	=	Air speed (a)	−	Head wind speed (h)
g	=	300 mph	−	50 mph

$g = 300 - 50 = 250$ The ground speed (g) equals 250 mph.

250 mph	=	a	−	50 mph

$250 = a - 50$
$a = 250 + 50 = 300$ The air speed (a) equals 300 mph.

250 mph	=	300 mph	−	h

$250 = 300 - h$
$h = 300 - 250 = 50$ The head wind speed (h) equals 50 mph.

Find the missing values in this table.

Ground speed (g)	Air speed (a)	Head wind speed (h)
1.	235 mph	42 mph
2. 309 mph	321 mph	
3. 167 mph		12 mph
4.	134 mph	21 mph
5.	294 mph	38 mph
6. 286 mph		45 mph
7. 368 mph	400 mph	
8. 253 mph	310 mph	
9. 122 mph		28 mph
10.	239 mph	14 mph
11. 261 mph	278 mph	
12. 401 mph	427 mph	
13.	124 mph	13 mph
14. 539 mph		45 mph
15. 266 mph		7 mph

 Algebra

TRL

Application Activity 1

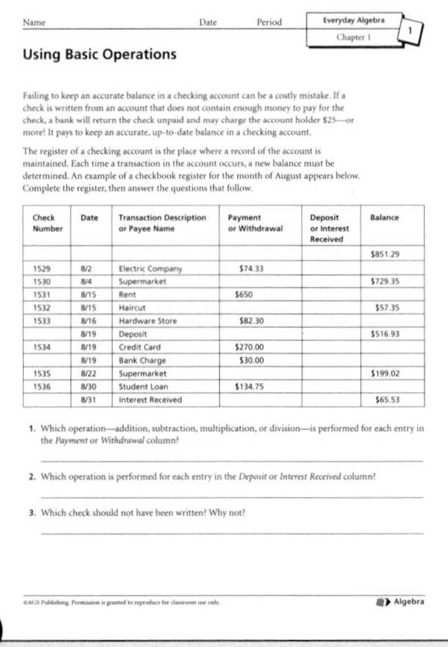

Name Date Period **Everyday Algebra 1** Chapter 1

Using Basic Operations

Failing to keep an accurate balance in a checking account can be a costly mistake. If a check is written from an account that does not contain enough money to pay for the check, a bank will return the check unpaid and may charge the account holder $25—or more! It pays to keep an accurate, up-to-date balance in a checking account.

The register of a checking account is the place where a record of the account is maintained. Each time a transaction in the account occurs, a new balance must be determined. An example of a checkbook register for the month of August appears below. Complete the register, then answer the questions that follow.

Check Number	Date	Transaction Description or Payee Name	Payment or Withdrawal	Deposit or Interest Received	Balance
					$851.29
1529	8/2	Electric Company	$74.33		
1530	8/4	Supermarket			$729.35
1531	8/15	Rent	$650		
1532	8/15	Haircut			$57.35
1533	8/16	Hardware Store	$82.30		
	8/19	Deposit			$516.93
1534	8/19	Credit Card	$270.00		
	8/19	Bank Charge	$30.00		
1535	8/22	Supermarket			$199.02
1536	8/30	Student Loan	$134.75		
	8/31	Interest Received			$65.53

1. Which operation—addition, subtraction, multiplication, or division—is performed for each entry in the *Payment* or *Withdrawal* column?

2. Which operation is performed for each entry in the *Deposit* or *Interest Received* column?

3. Which check should not have been written? Why not?

 Algebra

TRL

Everyday Algebra 1

Chapter 1 REVIEW

Write the letter of the correct answer.

1. Find the sum of $15 + (-13)$. B

A 28 **C** -2

B 2 **D** -28

2. Find the difference of $-6 - (-7)$. A

A 1 **C** 14

B -1 **D** -14

3. Find the quotient of $-25 \div (-5)$. A

A 5 **C** -5

B -20 **D** -30

4. Simplify the equation $8x + 14 + 14x$. C

A $28x + 8$ **C** $22x + 14$

B $22 + 14x$ **D** $28x + 8x$

5. Simplify the equation $a^3 \cdot b^4 \cdot a^6 \cdot b^2$. D

A a^{15} **C** $a^{36} \cdot b^8$

B b^{15} **D** a^9b^6

6. The perimeter of a regular hexagon is $6s$. Find the perimeter when $s = 9$ m. A

A 54 m **C** 45 m

B 36 m **D** 27 m

Chapter 1 Review

Each set of problems in the Chapter Review includes an example and solution to illustrate the concept. Use the given examples for reteaching the material in Chapter 1. For additional practice, refer to the Supplementary Problems for Chapter 1 (pages 406–407).

Chapter 1 Mastery Test

The Teacher's Resource Library includes two parallel forms of the Chapter 1 Mastery Test. The difficulty level of the two forms is equivalent. You may wish to use one form as a pretest and the other form as a posttest.

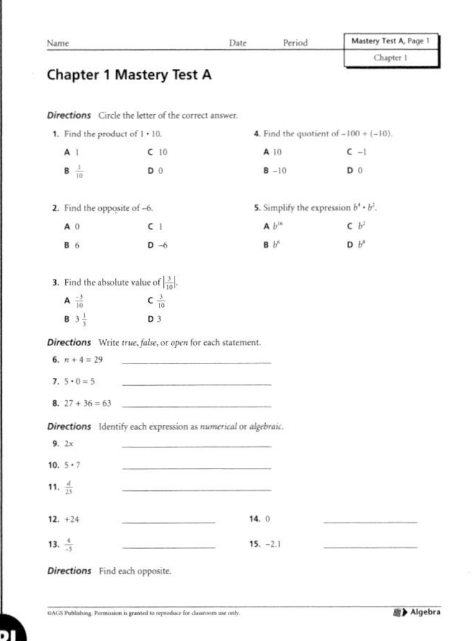

Name Date Period | Mastery Test A, Page 1 | Chapter 1

Chapter 1 Mastery Test A

Directions Circle the letter of the correct answer.

1. Find the product of $1 \cdot 10$.
A 1 **C** 10
B $\frac{1}{10}$ **D** 0

2. Find the opposite of -6.
A 0 **C** 1
B 6 **D** -6

3. Find the absolute value of $\left|\frac{3}{10}\right|$.
A $\frac{-3}{10}$ **C** $\frac{3}{10}$
B $3\frac{1}{3}$ **D** 3

4. Find the quotient of $-100 \div (-10)$.
A 10 **C** -1
B -10 **D** 0

5. Simplify the expression $b^4 \cdot b^2$.
A b^{16} **C** b^2
B b^6 **D** b^8

Directions Write *true*, *false*, or *open* for each statement.

6. $n + 4 = 29$ ______

7. $5 \cdot 0 = 5$ ______

8. $27 + 36 = 63$ ______

Directions Identify each expression as *numerical* or *algebraic*.

9. $2x$ ______

10. $5 \cdot 7$ ______

11. $\frac{d}{23}$ ______

12. $+24$ ______ **14.** 0 ______

13. $\frac{4}{-5}$ ______ **15.** -2.1 ______

Directions Find each opposite.

 Algebra

TRL

Name Date Period | Mastery Test A, Page 2 | Chapter 1

Chapter 1 Mastery Test A, continued

Directions Find the absolute value, or distance from zero.

16. $|8|$ ______ **18.** $\left|\frac{11}{-15}\right|$ ______

17. $|-4.09|$ ______ **19.** $|+1.7|$ ______

Directions Find each sum, difference, product, or quotient.

20. $(-25)(2)$ ______ **23.** $-41 + 13$ ______

21. $-5 + (-18)$ ______ **24.** $(-4)(-15)$ ______

22. $-22 - (-33)$ ______ **25.** $\frac{-32}{8}$ ______

Directions Simplify each expression.

26. $-9y + 18y$ ______

27. $m^{12} \div m^3$ ______

28. $(r^3)(r^5)(r^4)$ ______

29. $30a + 2 + (-5a)$ ______

30. $\frac{42n^5}{7n^2}$ ______

 Algebra

TRL

Chapter 1 Mastery Test A

Alternative Assessment

Alternative Assessment items correlate with student Goals for Learning at the beginning of this chapter.

■ **To recognize numerical and algebraic expressions**
Have students explain the only difference between numerical and algebraic expressions. Ask students to give an example of each kind of expression. *(Numerical expressions do not contain variables; algebraic expressions do.)*

■ **To understand the use of variables in algebraic expressions**
Have students describe how variables make algebra easier or harder than regular math (that doesn't use variables). Ask students to use examples to explain their answers. *(Students may say that using variables is confusing because they have always worked with numbers or that variables make it easier because you don't have to write out the entire number.)*

■ **To understand positive and negative integers, opposites, and absolute value**
Have students draw or use manipulatives (such as a thermometer) to show the importance of absolute value in problems about distance, temperature, or time. Example: The starting point is a city. Find distances to points east, west, north, and south of the city. *(Check that students' drawings or explanations demonstrate the concepts of positive and negative integers, opposites, and absolute value.)*

■ **To discover and use rules related to adding, subtracting, multiplying, and dividing integers**
Have students use manipulatives such as paper clips to demonstrate how adding and multiplying (or adding and subtraction) are related. Example: Use the paperclips to show how 3 + 3 + 3 = 3 × 3. *(Students should demonstrate the relationships between and among addition, subtraction, multiplication, and division.)*

Identify each expression as either a numerical or an algebraic expression.

Example: $s + 14$ Solution: algebraic expression

7. $5x - 3$ **8.** $9 + 6$ **9.** $4y$ **10.** $p \div 7$ **11.** $16 \div 4$

Find the absolute value, or distance from zero.

Example: $|-7|$ Solution: $|-7| = 7$

12. $|2|$ 2 **13.** $|-3|$ 3 **14.** $|6|$ 6 **15.** $|14|$ 14 **16.** $|-25|$ 25

Find each opposite.

Example: -8 Solution: $+8$ or 8

17. $+4$ -4 **18.** -6 6 **19.** -1.5 1.5 **20.** 0 0 **21.** $(\frac{3}{4})$ $-\frac{3}{4}$

Find each sum.

Example: $-8 + -8$ Solution: $-8 + -8 = -16$

22. $-8 + (-10)$ -18 **23.** $14 + 14$ 28 **24.** $7 + (-7)$ 0 **25.** $-12 + 20$ 8

Find each difference.

Example: $-4 - 2$ Solution: $-4 - 2 = -6$

26. $3 - 7$ -4 **27.** $-3 - (-2)$ -1 **28.** $10 - 4$ 6 **29.** $0 - 5$ -5

Find each product.

Example: $(-4)(4)$ Solution: $(-4)(4) = -16$

30. $(-5)(-8)$ 40 **31.** $(6)(-10)$ -60 **32.** $(-9)(6)$ -54 **33.** $(10)(0)$ 0

7. algebraic expression
8. numerical expression
9. algebraic expression
10. algebraic expression
11. numerical expression

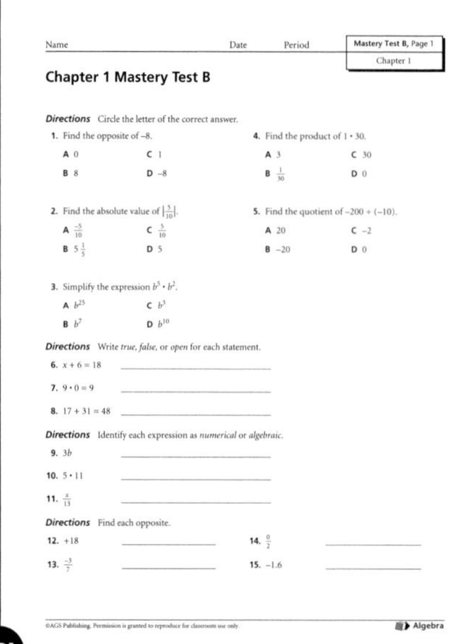

Name Date Period | Mastery Test B, Page 1 | Chapter 1

Chapter 1 Mastery Test B

Directions Circle the letter of the correct answer.

1. Find the opposite of –8.
A 0 C 1
B 8 D –8

4. Find the product of $1 \cdot 30$.
A 3 C 30
B $\frac{1}{30}$ D 0

2. Find the absolute value of $|\frac{5}{10}|$.
A $\frac{-5}{10}$ C $\frac{5}{10}$
B $5\frac{1}{5}$ D 5

5. Find the quotient of $-200 \div (-10)$.
A 20 C –2
B –20 D 0

3. Simplify the expression $b^5 \cdot b^2$.
A b^{25} C b^3
B b^7 D b^{10}

Directions Write *true*, *false*, or *open* for each statement.

6. $x + 6 = 18$ ________
7. $9 \cdot 0 = 9$ ________
8. $17 + 31 = 48$ ________

Directions Identify each expression as *numerical* or *algebraic*.

9. $3b$ ________
10. $5 \cdot 11$ ________
11. $\frac{x}{13}$ ________

Directions Find each opposite.

12. +18 ________ **14.** $\frac{0}{2}$ ________
13. $\frac{-3}{7}$ ________ **15.** –1.6 ________

 Algebra

TRL

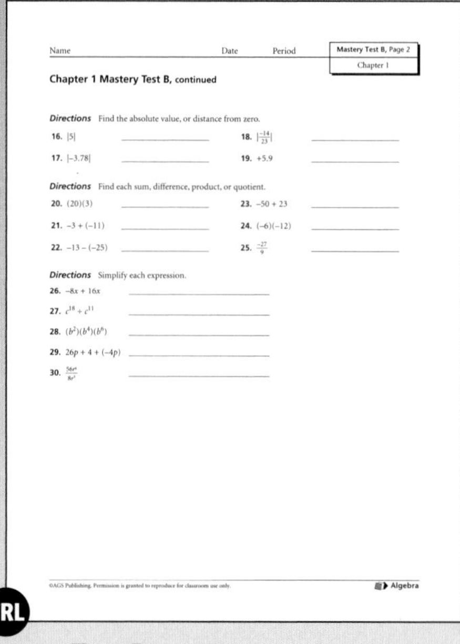

Name Date Period | Mastery Test B, Page 2 | Chapter 1

Chapter 1 Mastery Test B, continued

Directions Find the absolute value, or distance from zero.

16. $|5|$ ________ **18.** $|\frac{-14}{23}|$ ________
17. $|-3.78|$ ________ **19.** +5.9 ________

Directions Find each sum, difference, product, or quotient.

20. $(20)(3)$ ________ **23.** $-50 + 23$ ________
21. $-3 + (-11)$ ________ **24.** $(-6)(-12)$ ________
22. $-13 - (-25)$ ________ **25.** $\frac{-27}{9}$ ________

Directions Simplify each expression.

26. $-8x + 16x$ ________
27. $c^{18} + c^{11}$ ________
28. $(b^2)(b^4)(b^6)$ ________
29. $26p + 4 + (-4p)$ ________
30. $\frac{56r^4}{8r^3}$ ________

 Algebra

TRL

Chapter 1 Mastery Test B

Find each quotient.

Example: $8 \div -2$ Solution: $8 \div -2 = -4$

34. $16 \div (-4)$ -4 **35.** $-100 \div 10$ -10 **36.** $27 \div 9$ 3 **37.** $0 \div (-8)$ 0

Simplify each expression.

Example: $-12a + 5a$ Solution: $-12a + 5a = -7a$

38. $-3m + 16 - (-13m)$ $10m + 16$

39. $15y - 20y + 15$ $-5y + 15$

40. $-7n + 11 - 3x + 9x + 8n$ $n + 6x + 11$

41. $1.2k - 3.4k$ $-2.2k$

42. $9 + 4g - 5$ $4g + 4$

43. $128v + 11r - 150v - 3r$ $-22v + 8r$

44. $x^4 \cdot x^3 \cdot x$ x^8

45. $n^{10} \div n^2$ n^8

46. $v^{14} \div v^5$ v^9

47. $(e^2)(g)(g^4)(e^3)$ e^5g^5

48. $(d)(d^2)(d^3)$ d^6

49. $n^{10} \div n^4$ n^6

50. $(e)(e^7)(e)$ e^9

51. $j^7 \div j$ j^6

Use a formula to solve the problems.

Example: The width of a rectangle is x. Its length is twice the measure of its width. Write an expression in simplest form to represent the perimeter of the rectangle.

Solution: Let x = length

Let $2x$ = width

$p = x + x + 2x + 2x$

$p = 6x$

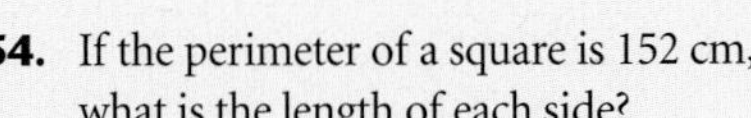

52. The perimeter of a square is $4s$. Find the perimeter when $s = 12$ mm.

53. The perimeter of an equilateral triangle is $3s$. Find the perimeter, when $s = 15$ km.

54. If the perimeter of a square is 152 cm, what is the length of each side?

55. If the perimeter of a regular hexagon is 96 m, what is the length of each side?

52. 48 mm 53. 45 km 54. 38 cm 55. 16 m

Test-Taking Tip

When studying for a test, write your own test problems with a partner. Then complete each other's test. Double-check your answers.

ALTERNATIVE ASSESSMENT, CONTINUED

- **To simplify expressions with one or more variables**

Provide students with several different groups of similar objects or shapes (for example, marbles, rubber bands, index cards, or pennies.) Have students use the manipulatives to demonstrate how like variables can be combined and unlike variables cannot be combined. *(The demonstration will show that like objects can be combined and unlike ones cannot. Example: You can multiply marbles with marbles, but you cannot mix marbles and index cards.)*

- **To read and write exponents**

Have students explain the difference between coefficients and exponents. Example: What is the difference between the coefficient 3 and the exponent 3? Are there any instances in which coefficients and exponents produce the same product? *(Students should explain that a coefficient is simply multiplied by the variable. With an exponent, the variable is multiplied by itself to the power of the exponent. Sometimes an exponent and a coefficient produce the same product. Example: 2(2) is the same as 2^2. x^1 is the same as 1x.)*

- **To use formulas with variables**

Ask students to explain the importance of knowing formulas when solving problems. Do formulas make it easier or harder to solve certain problems? *(Students should explain that knowing the formula for solving certain kinds of problems is very helpful. Without formulas, students would start from scratch each time a similar problem was encountered.)*

Chapter

Planning Guide

The Rules of Arithmetic

		Student Text Lesson: Student Pages	Vocabulary	Practice Exercises	Solutions Key
Lesson 1	Commutative Property of Addition	32–33	✔	✔	✔
Lesson 2	Commutative Property of Multiplication	34–35	✔	✔	✔
Lesson 3	Associative Property of Addition	36–37	✔	✔	✔
Lesson 4	Associative Property of Multiplication	38–41	✔	✔	✔
Lesson 5	The Distributive Property—Multiplication	42–43	✔	✔	✔
Lesson 6	The Distributive Property—Factoring	44–45	✔	✔	✔
Lesson 7	Properties of Zero	46–47	✔	✔	✔
Lesson 8	Properties of 1	48–49	✔	✔	✔
Lesson 9	Powers and Roots	50–53	✔	✔	✔
Lesson 10	More on Powers and Roots	54–55		✔	✔
Lesson 11	Order of Operations	56–57		✔	✔
Application	Using Square Root	58		✔	✔

Chapter Activities

Teacher's Resource Library

Estimation Exercise 2: Estimating Square Roots
Application Activity 2: Using Square Root
Everyday Algebra 2: Finding Volume
Community Connection 2: Transportation and Shipping

Teacher's Edition

Chapter 2 Project

Assessment Options

Student Text

Chapter 2 Review

Teacher's Resource Library

Chapter 2 Mastery Tests A and B

Student Text Features							Teaching Strategies							Learning Styles						Teacher's Resource Library			
Estimation Activity	Algebra in Your Life	Technology Connection	Writing About Mathematics	Try This	Problem Solving	Calculator Practice	Online Connection	Common Error	Applications (Home, Career, Community)	Mental Math	Manipulatives	Calculator	Group Problem Solving	Auditory/Verbal	Visual/Spatial	Logical/Mathematical	Body/Kinesthetic	Interpersonal/Group Learning	LEP/ESL	Activities	Alternative Activities	Workbook Activities	Self-Study Guide
			33						33								33			13	13	13	✔
					35		40						35		35	35				14	14	14	✔
				37						37									37	15	15	15	✔
	41	39							39									39		16	16	16	✔
								43										43		17	17	17	✔
					45			45					45							18	18	18	✔
			47					47		47									47	19	19	19	✔
					49								49	49						20	20	20	✔
52						53		50			51	52		51						21	21	21	✔
						55		54			55	55						49		22	22	22	✔
					57								57	57				57		23	23	23–24	✔
									58														✔

Software Options

Skill Track Software

Use the Skill Track Software for *Algebra* for additional reinforcement of this chapter. The software provides multiple-choice assessment items for students to access by computer.

Solutions Key

Use the Solutions Key with this chapter to help students who may need additional assistance. The Solutions Key CD provides solutions for every exercise in the student edition.

Other Resources

Alternative Activities

The Teacher's Resource Library (TRL) contains a set of worksheets written at a second-grade reading level called Alternative Activities. They cover the same content as the regular Activities.

Manipulatives

See the Manipulative activities in this chapter for hands-on modeling of the content.

Unit Cubes
Pattern Blocks

Chapter at a Glance

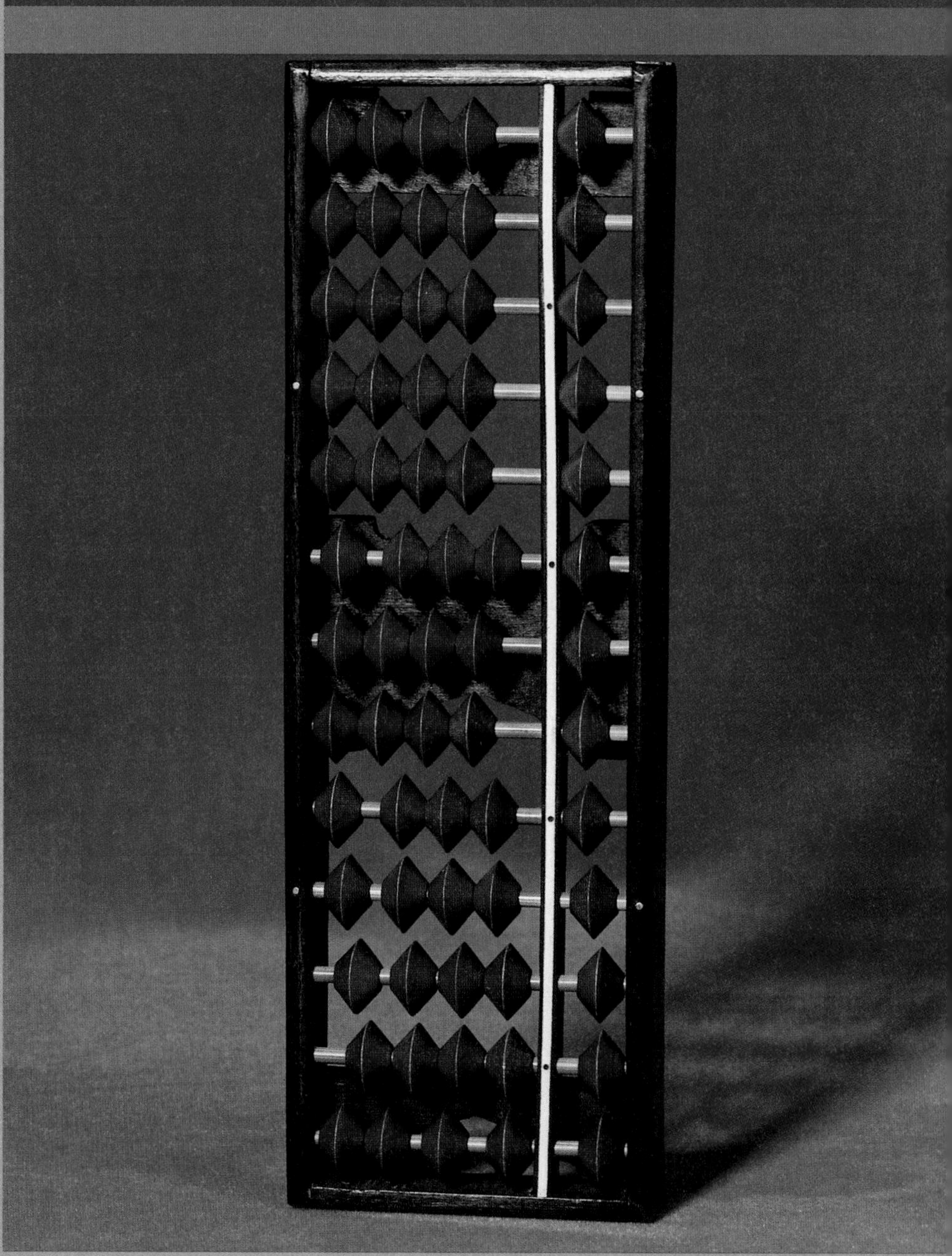

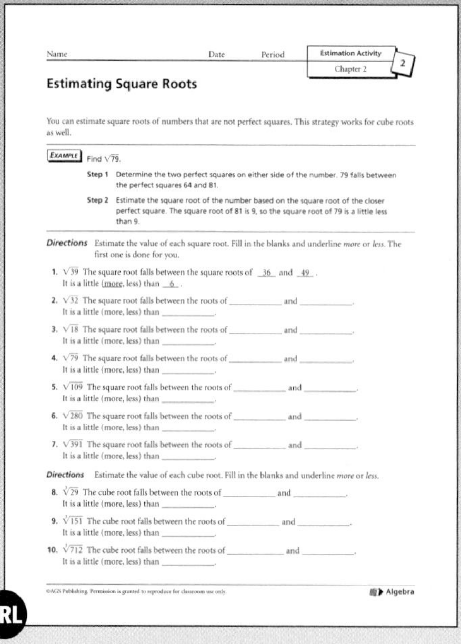

Name Date Period | Estimation Activity 2 | Chapter 2

Estimating Square Roots

You can estimate square roots of numbers that are not perfect squares. This strategy works for cube roots as well.

EXAMPLE Find $\sqrt{79}$.

Step 1 Determine the two perfect squares on either side of the number. 79 falls between the perfect squares 64 and 81.

Step 2 Estimate the square root of the number based on the square root of the closer perfect square. The square root of 81 is 9, so the square root of 79 is a little less than 9.

Directions Estimate the value of each square root. Fill in the blanks and underline *more* or *less*. The first one is done for you.

1. $\sqrt{39}$ The square root falls between the square roots of 36 and 49.
   It is a little (more, less) than 6.
2. $\sqrt{32}$ The square root falls between the roots of ________ and ________.
   It is a little (more, less) than ________.
3. $\sqrt{18}$ The square root falls between the roots of ________ and ________.
   It is a little (more, less) than ________.
4. $\sqrt{79}$ The square root falls between the roots of ________ and ________.
   It is a little (more, less) than ________.
5. $\sqrt{109}$ The square root falls between the roots of ________ and ________.
   It is a little (more, less) than ________.
6. $\sqrt{280}$ The square root falls between the roots of ________ and ________.
   It is a little (more, less) than ________.
7. $\sqrt{391}$ The square root falls between the roots of ________ and ________.
   It is a little (more, less) than ________.

Directions Estimate the value of each cube root. Fill in the blanks and underline *more* or *less*.

8. $\sqrt[3]{29}$ The cube root falls between the roots of ________ and ________.
   It is a little (more, less) than ________.
9. $\sqrt[3]{151}$ The cube root falls between the roots of ________ and ________.
   It is a little (more, less) than ________.
10. $\sqrt[3]{712}$ The cube root falls between the roots of ________ and ________.
   It is a little (more, less) than ________.

 Algebra

TRL

Estimation Exercise 2

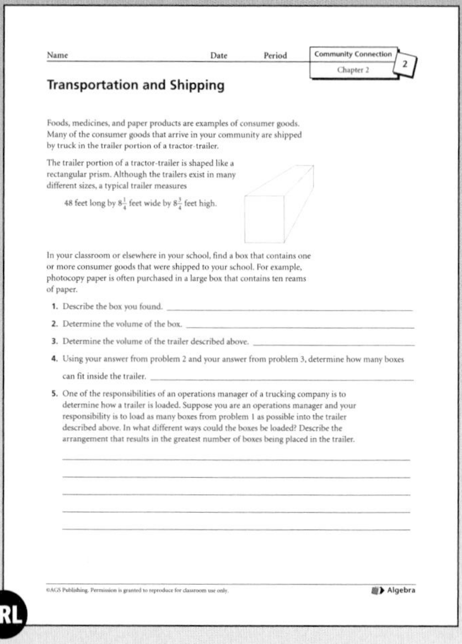

Name Date Period | Community Connection 2 | Chapter 2

Transportation and Shipping

Foods, medicines, and paper products are examples of consumer goods. Many of the consumer goods that arrive in your community are shipped by truck in the trailer portion of a tractor-trailer.

The trailer portion of a tractor-trailer is shaped like a rectangular prism. Although the trailers exist in many different sizes, a typical trailer measures

48 feet long by $8\frac{1}{4}$ feet wide by $8\frac{3}{4}$ feet high.

In your classroom or elsewhere in your school, find a box that contains one or more consumer goods that were shipped to your school. For example, photocopy paper is often purchased in a large box that contains ten reams of paper.

1. Describe the box you found. ________
2. Determine the volume of the box. ________
3. Determine the volume of the trailer described above. ________
4. Using your answer from problem 2 and your answer from problem 3, determine how many boxes can fit inside the trailer. ________
5. One of the responsibilities of an operations manager of a trucking company is to determine how a trailer is loaded. Suppose you are an operations manager and your responsibility is to load as many boxes from problem 1 as possible into the trailer described above. In what different ways could the boxes be loaded? Describe the arrangement that results in the greatest number of boxes being placed in the trailer.

 Algebra

TRL

Community Connection 2

Chapter

2 The Rules of Arithmetic

Have you ever tried using an abacus? If so, you know that an abacus is a simple kind of calculator. Ancient cultures in China, Japan, and Russia used abacuses to count money. People also used them to keep track of how much things weighed. The ancient Chinese based their arithmetic on the numbers 2 and 16. Our numbering system is based on the number 10. To use an abacus, you slide the beads up and down or left and right to add, subtract, multiply and divide. As you learn algebra, you will use your arithmetic skills to add, subtract, multiply, and divide in order to solve equations.

In Chapter 2, you will be introduced to basic rules of arithmetic as they apply to algebra.

Goals for Learning

- ◆ To recognize the commutative property of addition and multiplication
- ◆ To understand the associative property of addition and multiplication
- ◆ To understand the distributive property and factoring
- ◆ To recognize the properties of the numbers 0 and 1
- ◆ To identify and use powers and roots of numbers
- ◆ To discover and use the order of operations in making calculations

Introducing the Chapter

Use the information in this chapter to help students understand that ancient cultures in China, Japan, and Russia used abacuses. They used these simple manual calculators to add, subtract, multiply, and divide. Point out that students will use these same basic arithmetic skills in algebra.

Chapter Project

Suggest students work in groups of four to design a game as they work through this chapter. Have groups choose one of the following game ideas their own idea.

- An action-adventure game featuring the special powers of superheros Zero and One
- A board game in which advancing toward home depends on using the distributive property
- A target game that relies on the correct order of operations

Students should work together to decide the form of their game. Each team can assign team members tasks such as designer, sculptor, rule maker, and producer.

Teacher's Resource

The AGS Publishing Teaching Strategies in Math Transparencies may be used with this chapter. They add an interactive dimension to expand and enhance the program content.

Career Interest Inventory

The AGS Publishing Harrington-O'Shea Career Decision-Making System-Revised (CDM) may be used with this chapter. Students can use the CDM to explore their interests and identify careers. The CDM defines career areas that are indicated by students' responses on the inventory.

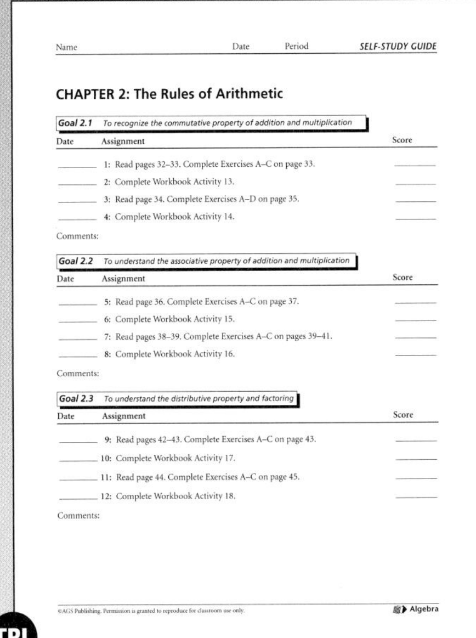

Name Date Period **SELF-STUDY GUIDE**

CHAPTER 2: The Rules of Arithmetic

Goal 2.1 *To recognize the commutative property of addition and multiplication*

Date	Assignment	Score
______	1: Read pages 32–33. Complete Exercises A–C on page 33.	______
______	2: Complete Workbook Activity 13.	______
______	3: Read page 34. Complete Exercises A–D on page 35.	______
______	4: Complete Workbook Activity 14.	______

Comments:

Goal 2.2 *To understand the associative property of addition and multiplication*

Date	Assignment	Score
______	5: Read page 36. Complete Exercises A–C on page 37.	______
______	6: Complete Workbook Activity 15.	______
______	7: Read pages 38–39. Complete Exercises A–C on pages 39–41.	______
______	8: Complete Workbook Activity 16.	______

Comments:

Goal 2.3 *To understand the distributive property and factoring*

Date	Assignment	Score
______	9: Read pages 42–43. Complete Exercises A–C on page 43.	______
______	10: Complete Workbook Activity 17.	______
______	11: Read page 44. Complete Exercises A–C on page 45.	______
______	12: Complete Workbook Activity 18.	______

Comments:

 Algebra

TRL

Name Date Period **SELF-STUDY GUIDE**

CHAPTER 2: The Rules of Arithmetic, continued

Goal 2.4 *To recognize the properties of the numbers 0 and 1*

Date	Assignment	Score
______	13: Read pages 46–47. Complete Exercises A–D on page 47.	______
______	14: Complete Workbook Activity 19.	______
______	15: Read pages 48–49. Complete Exercises A–C on page 49.	______
______	16: Complete Workbook Activity 20.	______

Comments:

Goal 2.5 *To identify and use powers and roots of numbers*

Date	Assignment	Score
______	17: Read pages 50–52. Complete Exercises A–B on pages 52–53.	______
______	18: Read and complete the Calculator Practice on page 53.	______
______	19: Complete Workbook Activity 21.	______
______	20: Read page 54. Complete Exercises A–B on page 55.	______
______	21: Read and complete the Calculator Practice on page 55.	______
______	22: Complete Workbook Activity 22.	______

Comments:

Goal 2.6 *To discover and use the order of operations in making calculations*

Date	Assignment	Score
______	23: Read page 56. Complete Exercises A–C on page 57.	______
______	24: Complete Workbook Activities 23 and 24.	______
______	25: Read and complete the Application Exercise on page 58.	______
______	26: Complete the Chapter 2 Review on pages 59–61.	______

Comments:

Student's Signature ______________________ Date __________

Instructor's Signature ______________________ Date __________

 Algebra

TRL

Chapter 2 Self-Study Guide

Lesson at a Glance

Chapter 2 Lesson 1

Overview This lesson uses a number line to demonstrate the commutative property of addition.

Objectives

- To recognize that the order of addition does not change the sum
- To use the commutative property of addition to rearrange terms in a sum

Student Pages 32–33

Teacher's Resource Library TRL

Workbook Activity 13

Activity 13

Alternative Activity 13

Mathematics Vocabulary

commutative property of addition

expanded notation

1 Warm-Up Activity

Open the discussion by offering an example in which order does make a difference. For example, putting on shoes before socks gives a result different from putting on socks first, then shoes. Ask students for additional examples in which order does make a difference. Close the discussion by indicating that addition of several numbers does *not* depend on the order in which they are added.

2 Teaching the Lesson

Draw a number line on the board. Invite a volunteer to represent an addition exercise, such as 5 + 4 on the number line. Invite a second volunteer to represent the sum 4 + 5. Indicate to students that the results are the same because the order of addition does not change the outcome.

Lesson 1 Commutative Property of Addition

Expanded notation
An algebraic expression written to show its smallest terms

Commutative property of addition
The order in which two numbers are added does not change their sum

Commutative is related to the word **commute**. Remember commute means to go from point A to point B and back from B to A. The distance between the two points is the same whether you go from A to B or B to A.

A number line can be used to show that the sum of 3 + 4 is equal to the sum of 4 + 3.

EXAMPLE 1 3 + 4 = ■

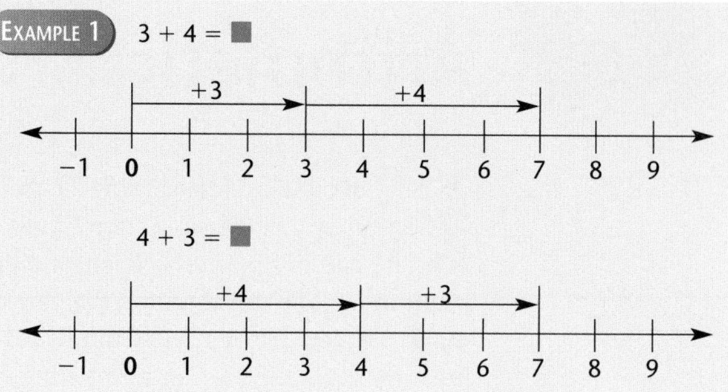

In algebra, you can use **expanded notation** to show that $3a + 4a$ and $4a + 3a$ both add to $7a$. Expanded notation means that the expression is written to show its smallest terms.

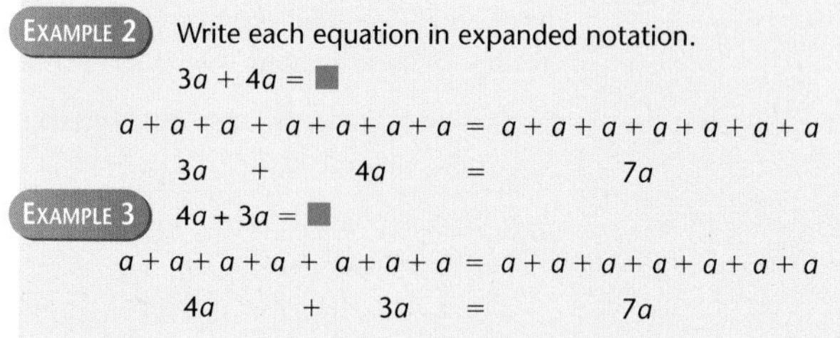

EXAMPLE 2 Write each equation in expanded notation.

$3a + 4a =$ ■

$a + a + a \;+\; a + a + a + a = a + a + a + a + a + a + a$

$3a \quad + \quad 4a \quad = \quad 7a$

EXAMPLE 3 $4a + 3a =$ ■

$a + a + a + a \;+\; a + a + a = a + a + a + a + a + a + a$

$4a \quad + \quad 3a \quad = \quad 7a$

The **commutative property of addition** states that you can rewrite any sum to change the order of the terms.

EXAMPLE 4 $6 + 4 = 4 + 6$

$m + n = n + m$

$10w + 12y = 12y + 10w$

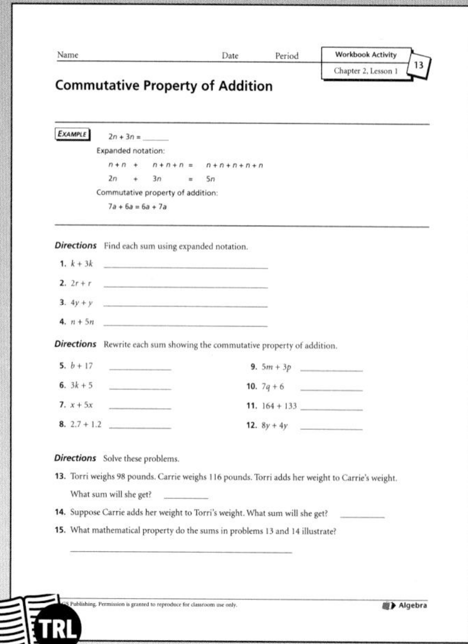

Name Date Period | Workbook Activity 13 | Chapter 2, Lesson 1

Commutative Property of Addition

EXAMPLE $2n + 3n =$ ______

Expanded notation:

$n + n \;+\; n + n + n = n + n + n + n + n$

$2n \;+\; 3n = 5n$

Commutative property of addition:

$7a + 6a = 6a + 7a$

Directions Find each sum using expanded notation.

1. $k + 3k$ ______
2. $2r + r$ ______
3. $4y + y$ ______
4. $n + 5n$ ______

Directions Rewrite each sum showing the commutative property of addition.

5. $b + 17$ ______
6. $3k + 5$ ______
7. $x + 5x$ ______
8. $2.7 + 1.2$ ______
9. $5m + 3p$ ______
10. $7q + 6$ ______
11. $164 + 133$ ______
12. $8y + 4y$ ______

Directions Solve these problems.

13. Torri weighs 98 pounds. Carrie weighs 116 pounds. Torri adds her weight to Carrie's weight. What sum will she get? ______
14. Suppose Carrie adds her weight to Torri's weight. What sum will she get? ______
15. What mathematical property do the sums in problems 13 and 14 illustrate? ______

 Algebra

TRL

Workbook Activity 13

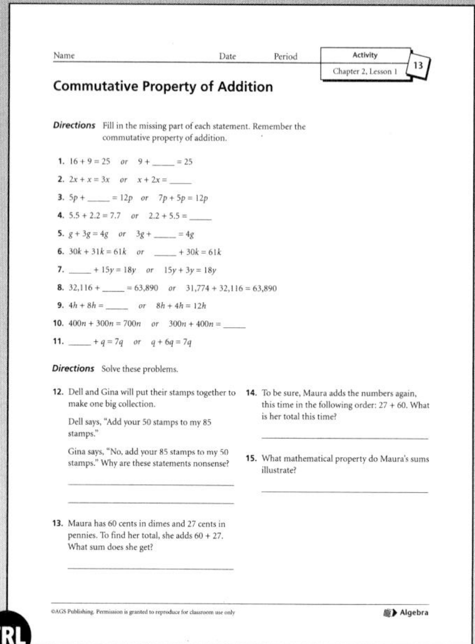

Name Date Period | Activity 13 | Chapter 2, Lesson 1

Commutative Property of Addition

Directions Fill in the missing part of each statement. Remember the commutative property of addition.

1. $16 + 9 = 25$ *or* $9 +$ ______ $= 25$
2. $2x + x = 3x$ *or* $x + 2x =$ ______
3. $5p +$ ______ $= 12p$ *or* $7p + 5p = 12p$
4. $5.5 + 2.2 = 7.7$ *or* $2.2 + 5.5 =$ ______
5. $g + 3g = 4g$ *or* $3g +$ ______ $= 4g$
6. $30k + 31k = 61k$ *or* ______ $+ 30k = 61k$
7. ______ $+ 15y = 18y$ *or* $15y + 3y = 18y$
8. $32{,}116 +$ ______ $= 63{,}890$ *or* $31{,}774 + 32{,}116 = 63{,}890$
9. $4h + 8h =$ ______ *or* $8h + 4h = 12h$
10. $400n + 300n = 700n$ *or* $300n + 400n =$ ______
11. ______ $+ q = 7q$ *or* $q + 6q = 7q$

Directions Solve these problems.

12. Dell and Gina will put their stamps together to make one big collection.

    Dell says, "Add your 50 stamps to my 85 stamps."

    Gina says, "No, add your 85 stamps to my 50 stamps." Why are these statements nonsense? ______

13. Maura has 60 cents in dimes and 27 cents in pennies. To find her total, she adds 60 + 27. What sum does she get? ______
14. To be sure, Maura adds the numbers again, this time in the following order: 27 + 60. What is her total this time? ______
15. What mathematical property do Maura's sums illustrate? ______

 Algebra

TRL

Activity 13

Answers to be shown on number lines:

1. $1 + 3, 3 + 1$
2. $2 + 3, 3 + 2$
3. $1 + 2, 2 + 1$
4. $5 + 2, 2 + 5$
5. $3 + 4, 4 + 3$
6. $3 + 6, 6 + 3$
7. $4 + 5, 5 + 4$
8. $1 + 6, 6 + 1$
9. $3 + 5, 5 + 3$
10. $7 + 2, 2 + 7$

Commutative Property of Addition

Two numbers may be added in either order without changing the sum. In general, for all terms or numbers a and b, $a + b = b + a$.

Exercise A Draw a number line to show that the sums are equal.

1. $1 + 3 = 3 + 1$
2. $2 + 3 = 3 + 2$
3. $1 + 2 = 2 + 1$
4. $5 + 2 = 2 + 5$
5. $3 + 4 = 4 + 3$
6. $3 + 6 = 6 + 3$
7. $4 + 5 = 5 + 4$
8. $1 + 6 = 6 + 1$
9. $3 + 5 = 5 + 3$
10. $7 + 2 = 2 + 7$

Exercise B Find each sum using expanded notation.

11. $2x + 4x$
$x + x + x + x + x + x = 6x$
12. $3c + c$
$c + c + c + c = 4c$
13. $4t + 2t$
$t + t + t + t + t + t = 6t$
14. $5j + 2j$
$j + j + j + j + j + j + j = 7j$
15. $6m + m$
$m + m + m + m + m + m + m = 7m$
16. $6v + 2v$
$v + v + v + v + v + v + v + v = 8v$
17. $y + 2y$
$y + y + y = 3y$
18. $3s + 5s$
$s + s + s + s + s + s + s + s = 8s$

Exercise C Rewrite each sum showing the commutative property of addition.

19. $a + 3$ $3 + a$
20. $a + b$ $b + a$
21. $x + y$ $y + x$
22. $2x + 6$ $6 + 2x$
23. $5g + 8g$ $8g + 5g$
24. $b + 9b$ $9b + b$
25. $4r + 7r$ $7r + 4r$
26. $2p + 6p$ $6p + 2p$
27. $2x + y$ $y + 2x$
28. $9k + 2k$ $2k + 9k$
29. $6p + 7p$ $7p + 6p$
30. $11 + 6$ $6 + 11$
31. $16q + 2q$ $2q + 16q$
32. $8i + i$ $i + 8i$
33. $x + 10$ $10 + x$
34. $2l + 3l$ $3l + 2l$
35. $5y + y$ $y + 5y$

Writing About Mathematics

Write about things you do in your day that are commutative. For example, does it matter whether you brush your teeth, then comb your hair, or if you reverse the order?

3 Reinforce and Extend

LEARNING STYLES

Body/Kinesthetic

Provide algebra tiles in two colors for students. Suggest that they work in pairs. One student should use the algebra tiles to represent an addition fact, for example, 21 red tiles + 13 blue tiles = 34 tiles. The second student should rearrange the tiles to make a similar addition fact: 13 blue tiles + 21 red tiles = 34 tiles.

AT HOME

Have students discuss a trip to a shopping mall to buy clothes. Encourage them to role-play a scene in which a customer buys a shirt and sweater. Ask students to identify how the commutative property of addition affects the amount of the purchase.

MATH HISTORY

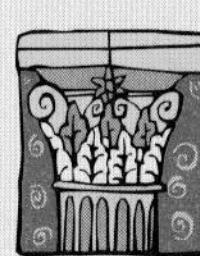

The concept of zero that we use in modern mathematics was invented in India by Hindu mathematicians during the Gupta Empire (A.D. 232 to A.D. 550). However, the Hindus were not the first people to come up with the concept of zero. The ancient Mayas of Central America were probably the first people to use zero in a mathematical system. Unlike the decimal system that we use today, the Mayas used a base 20 number system. The Mayan system only had three symbols: a shell-shaped symbol that represented zero, a dot for one, and a horizontal bar for five. Place value was shown by reading from bottom to top, with higher symbols standing for larger numbers. Each level increased the place value by 20.

Lesson at a Glance

Chapter 2 Lesson 2

Overview This lesson demonstrates the commutative property of multiplication using a number line.

Objectives

- To recognize that the order in which two terms are multiplied does not affect the product of the term
- To use the commutative property of multiplication to rearrange terms in a product

Student Pages 34–35

Teacher's Resource Library 

Workbook Activity 14

Activity 14

Alternative Activity 14

Mathematics Vocabulary

commutative property of multiplication
geometry

1 Warm-Up Activity

Present a portion of a multiplication table on an overhead projector, for example, the multiplication facts for 3 through 8.

	3	4	5	6	7	8
3	9					
4	12	16				
5	15	20	25			
6	18	24	30	36		
7	21	28	35	42	49	
8	24	32	40	48	56	64

Encourage students to supply the missing facts. Ask them to explain how they can use the completed part of the table to supply the products for the shaded part of the table.

2 Teaching the Lesson

Draw a number line on the board. Using strips of paper the same scale as the number line, make 5 groups of 3.

Lesson 2 Commutative Property of Multiplication

Geometry
The study of points, lines, angles, surfaces, and solids

Commutative property of multiplication
The order in which two numbers are multiplied does not change their product

A number line can be used to show that the product of $3 \cdot 4$ is equal to the product of $4 \cdot 3$.

EXAMPLE 1 $(3)(4) = 12$

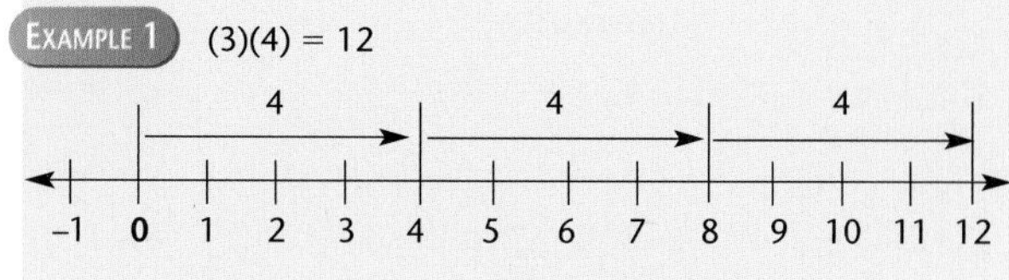

3 groups of 4 is the same as 12.

$(4)(3) = 12$

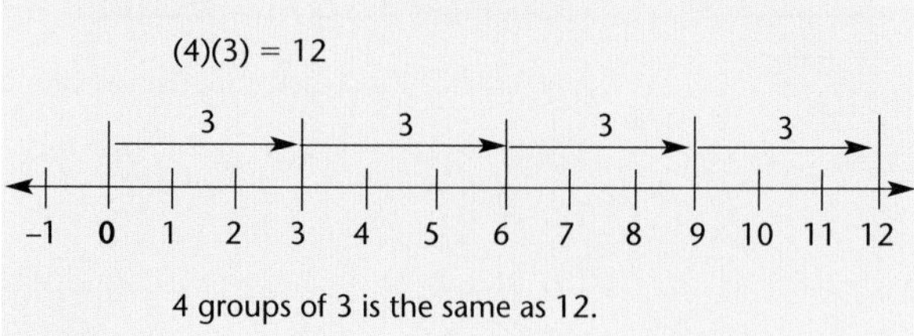

4 groups of 3 is the same as 12.

In **geometry**, you can find the area of a rectangle by multiplying its length (l) by its width (w).

Even though $3n$ is equal to $n3$, the number is usually written before the variable. Therefore, $3n$ is the preferred form.

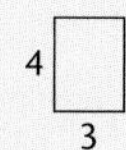

Because $(4)(3) = (3)(4)$, the area of each figure is 12 square units.

The **commutative property of multiplication** states that you can rewrite any product to change the order of the factors.

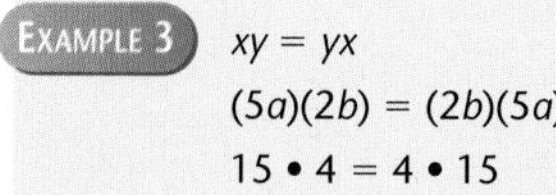

EXAMPLE 3 $xy = yx$

$(5a)(2b) = (2b)(5a)$

$15 \cdot 4 = 4 \cdot 15$

Commutative Property of Multiplication

Two numbers may be multiplied in either order without changing their product. In general, for all terms or numbers a and b, $ab = ba$.

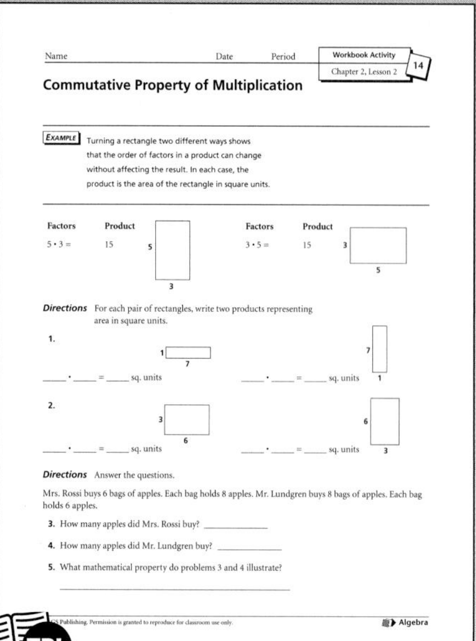

Name Date Period — Workbook Activity 14, Chapter 2, Lesson 2

Commutative Property of Multiplication

EXAMPLE Turning a rectangle two different ways shows that the order of factors in a product can change without affecting the result. In each case, the product is the area of the rectangle in square units.

Factors	Product		Factors	Product
$5 \cdot 3 =$	15		$3 \cdot 5 =$	15

Directions For each pair of rectangles, write two products representing area in square units.

1. ___ • ___ = ___ sq. units ___ • ___ = ___ sq. units

2. ___ • ___ = ___ sq. units ___ • ___ = ___ sq. units

Directions Answer the questions.

Mrs. Rossi buys 6 bags of apples. Each bag holds 8 apples. Mr. Lundgren buys 8 bags of apples. Each bag holds 6 apples.

3. How many apples did Mrs. Rossi buy? ________
4. How many apples did Mr. Lundgren buy? ________
5. What mathematical property do problems 3 and 4 illustrate?

 Algebra

Workbook Activity 14

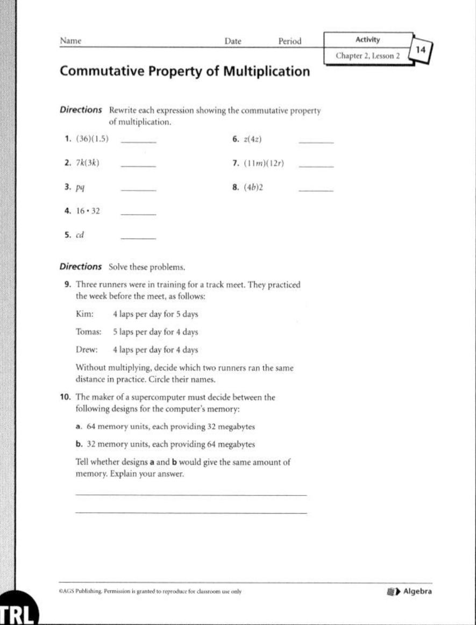

Name Date Period — Activity 14, Chapter 2, Lesson 2

Commutative Property of Multiplication

Directions Rewrite each expression showing the commutative property of multiplication.

1. $(36)(1.5)$ ____
2. $7k(3k)$ ____
3. pq ____
4. $16 \cdot 32$ ____
5. cd ____
6. $z(4z)$ ____
7. $(11m)(12r)$ ____
8. $(4b)2$ ____

Directions Solve these problems.

9. Three runners were in training for a track meet. They practiced the week before the meet, as follows:

   Kim: 4 laps per day for 5 days
   Tomas: 5 laps per day for 4 days
   Drew: 4 laps per day for 4 days

   Without multiplying, decide which two runners ran the same distance in practice. Circle their names.

10. The maker of a supercomputer must decide between the following designs for the computer's memory:

    a. 64 memory units, each providing 32 megabytes
    b. 32 memory units, each providing 64 megabytes

    Tell whether designs **a** and **b** would give the same amount of memory. Explain your answer.

 Algebra

Activity 14

Exercise A Draw a number line to show that each pair of products are equal.

1. $(2)(3) = (3)(2)$ **3.** $(5)(3) = (3)(5)$ **5.** $(4)(1) = (1)(4)$

2. $(4)(2) = (2)(4)$ **4.** $(2)(5) = (5)(2)$ **6.** $(1)(3) = (3)(1)$

Exercise B Write the factors and the product for the area of each rectangle.

7. 5 by 3; 3 by 5 **9.** 3 by 2; 2 by 3

8. 2 by 10; 10 by 2 **10.** 3 by 7; 7 by 3

7. Factors: 5 and 3. Product: 15.
8. Factors: 2 and 10. Product: 20.
9. Factors: 3 and 2. Product: 6.
10. Factors: 3 and 7. Product: 21.

Exercise C Rewrite each expression showing the commutative property of multiplication.

11. ab ba **14.** $z(2w)$ $(2w)z$ **17.** $h(9w)$ $(9w)h$

12. xy yx **15.** $(3z)(2)$ $(2)(3z)$ **18.** $(14k)(12y)$ $(12y)(14k)$

13. zw wz **16.** $5m(6b)$ $(6b)5m$

PROBLEM SOLVING

Exercise D Read each statement. If the commutative property can be used in the situation, write *yes*. If it cannot, write *no*.

19. Matt and Jenny order cheese, sausage, and onions on their pizza. yes

20. Juanita and Jose run inside the house, grab their game, and run back outside to play the game. no

21. To get ready, Yung washes his face and hands and combs his hair. yes

22. Violet first finishes her math homework; then she finishes her history reading. yes

23. Mike reads his literature assignment and answers the review questions. no

24. Rosalia cuts the lawn, pulls weeds out of the garden, and waters the plants. yes

25. Quentin reads the lesson on integers and then takes the mastery test. no

Answers to Problems 1–6

Answers to be shown on number lines:

1. top show 2 three times, bottom show 3 two times.
2. top show 4 two times, bottom show 2 four times.
3. top show 5 three times, bottom show 3 five times.
4. top show 2 five times, bottom show 5 two times.
5. top show 4 once, bottom show 1 four times.
6. top show 1 three times, bottom show 3 once.

Apply the strips to the number line to show that 5 groups of 3 equal 15. Invite a volunteer to continue the demonstration. Have the volunteer use paper strips representing 3 groups of 5 and show that 3 groups of 5 equal 15.

3 Reinforce and Extend

Learning Styles

Visual/Spatial

Have students work in pairs to create pictures that represent related multiplication facts. For example, one student might draw a 4 × 6 array of apples. The other student should then rearrange the array to represent the commutative property (a 6 × 4 array). Students should be prepared to explain why each array represents a product of 24.

Learning Styles

Logical/Mathematical

Direct students to draw a 3" by 5" rectangle on a sheet of paper. On a second sheet of paper, have them draw a 5" by 3" rectangle. Ask volunteers to use only the two drawings to show that the areas of the two rectangles are equal. (Cover one drawing with the other so that the sides align.)

Group Problem Solving

Have small groups of students develop a schedule for completing a presentation about the Mayan numbering system. Schedules should include steps such as library research, drafting, editing, rewriting, preparing presentation boards, and rehearsing presentation. Ask students to identify which, if any, steps are commutative.

Lesson at a Glance

Chapter 2 Lesson 3

Overview This lesson introduces the associative property of addition.

Objectives

- To demonstrate that the sum of several numbers is not affected by the order in which the numbers are added
- To use the associative property of addition to rearrange the terms in an addition expression

Student Pages 36–37

Teacher's Resource Library 

Workbook Activity 15

Activity 15

Alternative Activity 15

Mathematics Vocabulary

associative property of addition

1 Warm-Up Activity

Write the following sets of numbers on the board: 33, 55, 77 and 77, 33, 55. Ask students to discuss what they can predict about the sum of each group of numbers. Ask them to explain their prediction in their own words.

2 Teaching the Lesson

Use an overhead projector and algebra tiles to demonstrate the associative property of addition. Arrange several tiles in three groups, for example, 3, 7, and 8. Invite a volunteer to add the numbers, circling two numbers to be added first and then adding the remaining number. Have other volunteers show the same addition in different sequences. Have the class discuss why the sums are the same even though the addition sequences were different.

Try This

Point out to students that if they find just one instance in which changing the order of subtraction changes the difference, they will have shown there cannot be an associative property of subtraction.

Lesson 3 Associative Property of Addition

> ***Associative property of addition***
> *The same terms added in different groupings result in the same answer*

Add: $98 + 9 + 1$

You can add several numbers in the order in which they appear.

$$\begin{array}{r} 98 \\ +\ 9 \\ \hline 107 \end{array} \qquad \begin{array}{r} 107 \\ +\ 1 \\ \hline 108 \end{array}$$

Another way is to change the order of the numbers.

$$\begin{array}{r} 9 \\ +\ 1 \\ \hline 10 \end{array} \qquad \begin{array}{r} 10 \\ +\ 98 \\ \hline 108 \end{array}$$

You can use parentheses to show the order in which the numbers should be added.

$(98 + 9) + 1 = 108 \qquad 98 + (9 + 1) = 108$

$(98 + 9) + 1 = 108$ is the same as $98 + (9 + 1) = 108$.

The **associative property of addition** allows you to add terms in any order.

EXAMPLE 1 $7r + (2r + 3r) = (7r + 2r) + 3r$

EXAMPLE 2 $5x + (4x + 6x) = (5x + 4x) + 6x$

> **Associative Property of Addition**
> Numbers may be added with different groupings. The final answer does not change. In general, for all terms or numbers a, b, and c, $(a + b) + c = a + (b + c)$.

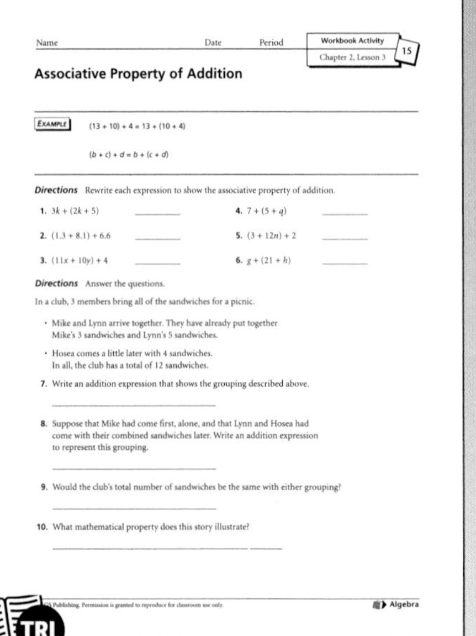

Name Date Period | Workbook Activity 15 | Chapter 2, Lesson 3

Associative Property of Addition

EXAMPLE $(13 + 10) + 4 = 13 + (10 + 4)$

$(b + c) + d = b + (c + d)$

Directions Rewrite each expression to show the associative property of addition.

1. $3k + (2k + 5)$ ______
2. $(1.3 + 8.1) + 6.6$ ______
3. $(11x + 10y) + 4$ ______
4. $7 + (5 + q)$ ______
5. $(3 + 12n) + 2$ ______
6. $g + (21 + h)$ ______

Directions Answer the questions.

In a club, 3 members bring all of the sandwiches for a picnic.

- Mike and Lynn arrive together. They have already put together Mike's 3 sandwiches and Lynn's 5 sandwiches.
- Hosea comes a little later with 4 sandwiches. In all, the club has a total of 12 sandwiches.

7. Write an addition expression that shows the grouping described above.
8. Suppose that Mike had come first, alone, and that Lynn and Hosea had come with their combined sandwiches later. Write an addition expression to represent this grouping.
9. Would the club's total number of sandwiches be the same with either grouping?
10. What mathematical property does this story illustrate?

 Algebra

Workbook Activity 15

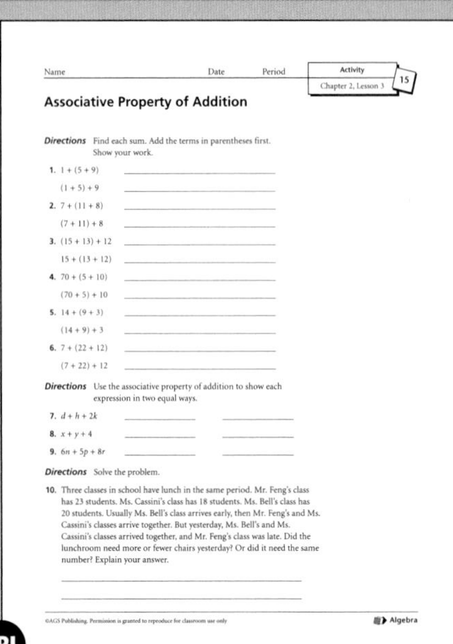

Name Date Period | Activity 15 | Chapter 2, Lesson 3

Associative Property of Addition

Directions Find each sum. Add the terms in parentheses first. Show your work.

1. $1 + (5 + 9)$ / $(1 + 5) + 9$
2. $7 + (11 + 8)$ / $(7 + 11) + 8$
3. $(15 + 13) + 12$ / $15 + (13 + 12)$
4. $70 + (5 + 10)$ / $(70 + 5) + 10$
5. $14 + (9 + 3)$ / $(14 + 9) + 3$
6. $7 + (22 + 12)$ / $(7 + 22) + 12$

Directions Use the associative property of addition to show each expression in two equal ways.

7. $d + h + 2k$
8. $x + y + 4$
9. $6n + 5p + 8r$

Directions Solve the problem.

10. Three classes in school have lunch in the same period. Mr. Feng's class has 23 students. Ms. Cassini's class has 18 students. Ms. Bell's class has 20 students. Usually Ms. Bell's class arrives early, then Mr. Feng's and Ms. Cassini's classes arrive together. But yesterday, Ms. Bell's and Ms. Cassini's classes arrived together, and Mr. Feng's class was late. Did the lunchroom need more or fewer chairs yesterday? Or did it need the same number? Explain your answer.

 Algebra

Activity 15

11. $(x + y) + z = x + (y + z)$
12. $(m + n) + o = m + (n + o)$
13. $(g + h) + j = g + (h + j)$
14. $(3t + f) + h = 3t + (f + h)$
15. $(w + 4c) + p = w + (4c + p)$
16. $(5r + x) + 7t = 5r + (x + 7t)$
17. $(4f + 9y) + 2x = 4f + (9y + 2x)$
18. $(13a + 8e) + 9f = 13a + (8e + 9f)$
19. $(21k + 13u) + 16s = 21k + (13u + 16s)$
20. $(33x + 41h) + 18k = 33x + (41h + 18k)$

21. $(3 + 6) + z$
22. $y + (13 + b)$
23. $(2b + 3c) + 8$
24. $(16 + 2x) + 9$
25. $5s + (3d + 28)$

Exercise A Find the sum for each pair of expressions. Add the terms in parentheses first.

1. $(4 + 6) + 15$ / $4 + (6 + 15)$ — $25 = 25$

2. $9 + (8 + 1)$ / $(9 + 8) + 1$ — $18 = 18$

3. $(15 + 5) + 7$ / $15 + (5 + 7)$ — $27 = 27$

4. $(12 + 8) + 5$ / $12 + (8 + 5)$ — $25 = 25$

5. $14 + (16 + 7)$ / $(14 + 16) + 7$ — $37 = 37$

6. $(4 + 6) + 14$ / $4 + (6 + 14)$ — $24 = 24$

7. $25 + (25 + 13)$ / $(25 + 25) + 13$ — $63 = 63$

8. $18 + (12 + 14)$ / $(18 + 12) + 14$ — $44 = 44$

9. $(33 + 17) + 22$ / $33 + (17 + 22)$ — $72 = 72$

10. $18 + (12 + 11)$ / $(18 + 12) + 11$ — $41 = 41$

Exercise B Use the associative property of addition to show each expression in two equal ways.

11. $x + y + z$

12. $m + n + o$

13. $g + h + j$

14. $3t + f + h$

15. $w + 4c + p$

16. $5r + x + 7t$

17. $4f + 9y + 2x$

18. $13a + 8e + 9f$

19. $21k + 13u + 16s$

20. $33x + 41h + 18k$

Exercise C Rewrite each expression showing the associative property of addition.

21. $3 + (6 + z)$

22. $(y + 13) + b$

23. $2b + (3c + 8)$

24. $16 + (2x + 9)$

25. $(5s + 3d) + 28$

TRY THIS Could there be an associative property of subtraction? Why or why not?

No. The order of the numbers cannot be changed in subtraction without changing the result.

3 Reinforce and Extend

Mental Math

Suggest students use the associative property of addition to rearrange these expressions so that they can find the sums without using pencil and paper.

$17 + 28 + 2$
[(28 + 2) + 17 = 30 + 17]

$39 + 43 + 11$
[43 + (39 + 11) = 43 + 50]

$26 + 24 + 47$
[(26 + 24) + 47 = 50 + 47]

$167 + 345 + 33$
[167 + 33) + 345 = 200 + 345]

Learning Styles

LEP/ESL

ESL students may have difficulty understanding the concept of the associative property of addition. Have students work in pairs. One student in each pair models the associative property of addition by adding three numbers in three different orders. The second student explains, in his or her own words, why the sum is the same, no matter what the order is. Encourage students to choose another set of three numbers and exchange roles.

Lesson at a Glance

Chapter 2 Lesson 4

Overview This lesson introduces the associative property of multiplication.

Objectives

- To demonstrate that the product of several numbers is not affected by the order in which the numbers are multiplied
- To use the associative property of addition to rearrange the terms in a multiplication expression
- To find the volumes of several rectangular solids

Student Pages 38–41

Teacher's Resource Library 

Workbook Activity 16

Activity 16

Alternative Activity 16

Mathematics Vocabulary

associative property of multiplication

1 Warm-Up Activity

Activate students' knowledge of the associative property of addition. Remind students that multiplication is repeated addition. Then ask them what they can predict about the product of 33, 55, and 77 and the product of 77, 33, and 55. Ask them to explain their prediction in their own words.

2 Teaching the Lesson

Use a cereal, shoe, or storage box to illustrate the associative property of multiplication. Label the height (h), width (w), and length (l) of the box with black marker or tape. Ask a volunteer to measure each dimension of the box and record the values for h, w, and l on the board. Encourage students to complete the chart for the demonstration box.

$(l \cdot w) \cdot h$	$l \cdot (w \cdot h)$

Lesson 4 Associative Property of Multiplication

Associative property of multiplication

The same terms multiplied in different groupings result in the same answer

The product of $3 \cdot 4 \cdot 10$ can be found in two different ways. One way is to perform the operations from left to right in the order they appear.

3 times 4 is 12.

12 times 10 is 120.

This is written as $(3 \cdot 4)10 = 12 \cdot 10 = 120$.

The second way is to change the order and multiply 4 by 10 to get 40, then multiply 3 times 40 to get 120.

This is written as $3(4 \cdot 10) = 3 \cdot 40 = 120$.

Both ways give the same product.

$(3 \cdot 4)10 = 3(4 \cdot 10)$

$12 \cdot 10 = 3 \cdot 40$

$120 = 120$

In geometry, you find the volume of a rectangular solid (such as a box) by multiplying its length (l) times its width (w) times its height (h), or volume $= lwh$.

Brackets are used as a second set of parentheses. For example, instead of writing $6((3 + 2) - 4)$, we can write $6[(3 + 2) - 4]$. This way it is easier to see what operation must be done first. In this case, add 3 and 2, subtract 4, and then multiply by 6.

Example 1

$h = 2 \quad w = 5 \quad l = 10$

The base of this solid figure measures 10 by 5.

Volume $= (10 \cdot 5) \cdot 2 = 50 \cdot 2 = 100$ cubic units
(l w h)

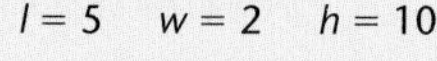

$l = 5 \quad w = 2 \quad h = 10$

The base of this solid figure measures 5 by 2.

Volume $= (5 \cdot 2)10 = 10 \cdot 10 = 100$ cubic units
(l w h)

The volumes are equal because it is the same box.

The **associative property of multiplication** states that you can place parentheses in any product of three factors, and the products will remain equal.

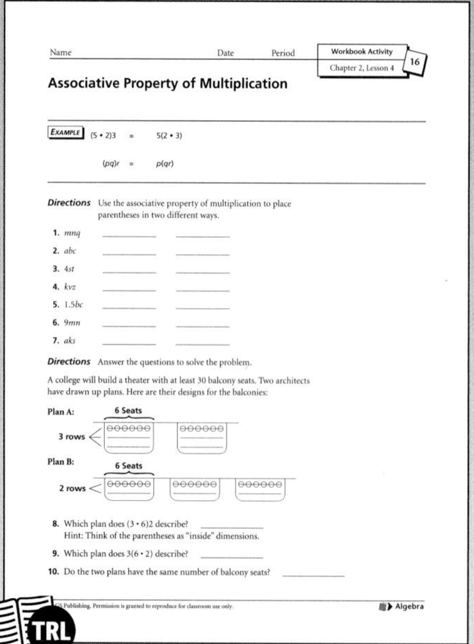

Name Date Period — Workbook Activity 16, Chapter 2, Lesson 4

Associative Property of Multiplication

Example $(5 \cdot 2)3 = 5(2 \cdot 3)$

$(pq)r = p(qr)$

Directions Use the associative property of multiplication to place parentheses in two different ways.

1. mnq ____ ____
2. abc ____ ____
3. $4st$ ____ ____
4. kvz ____ ____
5. $1.5bc$ ____ ____
6. $9mn$ ____ ____
7. aks ____ ____

Directions Answer the questions to solve the problem.

A college will build a theater with at least 30 balcony seats. Two architects have drawn up plans. Here are their designs for the balconies:

Plan A: 6 Seats, 3 rows

Plan B: 6 Seats, 2 rows

8. Which plan does $(3 \cdot 6)2$ describe? ____
Hint: Think of the parentheses as "inside" dimensions.
9. Which plan does $3(6 \cdot 2)$ describe? ____
10. Do the two plans have the same number of balcony seats? ____

 Algebra

Workbook Activity 16

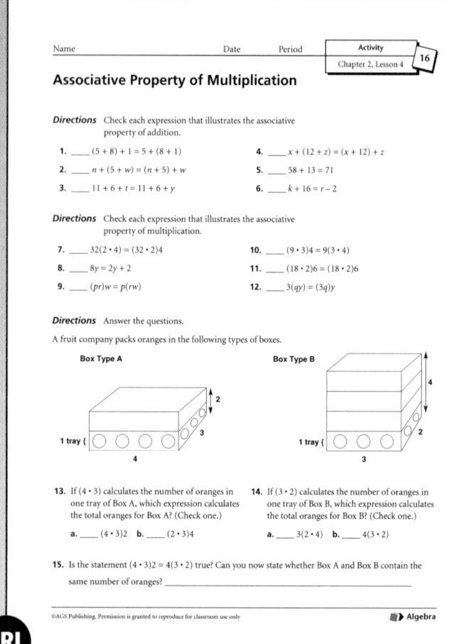

Name Date Period — Activity 16, Chapter 2, Lesson 4

Associative Property of Multiplication

Directions Check each expression that illustrates the associative property of addition.

1. ____ $(5 + 8) + 1 = 5 + (8 + 1)$
2. ____ $n + (5 + w) = (n + 5) + w$
3. ____ $11 + 6 + t = 11 + 6 + y$
4. ____ $x + (12 + z) = (x + 12) + z$
5. ____ $58 + 13 = 71$
6. ____ $k + 16 = r - 2$

Directions Check each expression that illustrates the associative property of multiplication.

7. ____ $32(2 \cdot 4) = (32 \cdot 2)4$
8. ____ $8y = 2y + 2$
9. ____ $(pr)w = p(rw)$
10. ____ $(9 \cdot 3)4 = 9(3 \cdot 4)$
11. ____ $(18 \cdot 2)6 = (18 \cdot 2)6$
12. ____ $3(qy) = (3q)y$

Directions Answer the questions.

A fruit company packs oranges in the following types of boxes.

13. If $(4 \cdot 3)$ calculates the number of oranges in one tray of Box A, which expression calculates the total oranges for Box A? (Check one.)
a. ____ $(4 \cdot 3)2$ b. ____ $(2 \cdot 3)4$
14. If $(3 \cdot 2)$ calculates the number of oranges in one tray of Box B, which expression calculates the total oranges for Box B? (Check one.)
a. ____ $3(2 \cdot 4)$ b. ____ $4(3 \cdot 2)$
15. Is the statement $(4 \cdot 3)2 = 4(3 \cdot 2)$ true? Can you now state whether Box A and Box B contain the same number of oranges? ____

 Algebra

Activity 16

Associative Property of Multiplication

All terms or numbers may be multiplied with different groupings. The final answer does not change. In general, for all terms or numbers a, b, and c, $(ab)c = a(bc)$.

EXAMPLE 2 Use the associative property of multiplication to place parentheses in two ways for the product xyz.
$(xy)z = x(yz)$

Exercise A Copy the problems. Find the products by multiplying the factors in parentheses first.

1. $(3 \cdot 5)20 = 3(5 \cdot 20)$ — 300 = 300
2. $4(6 \cdot 10) = (4 \cdot 6)10$ — 240 = 240
3. $[5(4 \cdot 13)] = [(5 \cdot 4)13]$ — 260 = 260
4. $8(2 \cdot 5) = (8 \cdot 2)5$ — 80 = 80
5. $[(15 \cdot 3)3] = [15(3 \cdot 3)]$ — 135 = 135
6. $(25 \cdot 4)9 = 25(4 \cdot 9)$ — 900 = 900
7. $17(5 \cdot 2) = (17 \cdot 5)2$ — 170 = 170
8. $[(14 \cdot 10)2] = [14(10 \cdot 2)]$ — 280 = 280
9. $[20(5 \cdot 4)] = [(20 \cdot 5)4]$ — 400 = 400
10. $8(15 \cdot 2) = (8 \cdot 15)2$ — 240 = 240

Technology Connection

Binary System

Computers process all information using a binary system. A binary system uses only two digits—0 and 1. A binary digit, called a "bit," is the smallest unit of information in the computer world. The 0 stands for "off," "no," or "false." The 1 stands for "on," "yes," or "true." Bits combine into large units called "bytes." A byte is 8 digits. In binary code, the byte for number 237 is 11101101. But computers aren't smarter than humans. After all, when we program them, we tell the computers what to do!

Have the class discuss the results. Ask them to explain how they could have predicted the results.

3 Reinforce and Extend

LEARNING STYLES

Interpersonal/ Group Learning

Have students work in small groups. Assign each group a multiplication expression with three terms, for example, $a \cdot b \cdot c$. Ask the groups to generate as many versions of their expression as they can. Students should identify how they used the commutative or associative property of multiplication to generate different versions of the same multiplication expression. Have the groups compare and discuss their results.

[$a \cdot (b \cdot c)$; $(a \cdot b) \cdot c$; $(b \cdot c) \cdot a$; $b \cdot (c \cdot a)$; $c \cdot (a \cdot b)$; $(c \cdot a) \cdot b$; $b \cdot (a \cdot c)$; $(b \cdot a) \cdot c$; $a \cdot (c \cdot b)$; $(a \cdot c) \cdot b$]

CAREER CONNECTION

Invite a carpenter or cabinet builder to speak to the class. Encourage the speaker to highlight his or her daily use of mathematics. You might ask the speaker to explain how he or she relies on multiplication to estimate the amount of time and materials needed for a job as well as the cost. Alert the speaker that students will have questions about the speaker's daily routine.

Online Connection

Have students visit www.cut-the-knot.org/SimpleGames/Calendar.shtml to play this game. It is a game of arithmetic progressions and averages. Ask students to try the game with their families or friends. (They do not need a computer at home to play the game, just a calendar and perhaps a calculator.) Ask them to read the explanation of how the game works and then write a short paragraph explaining it in their own words.

Exercise B Find the volume of each figure in two different ways.

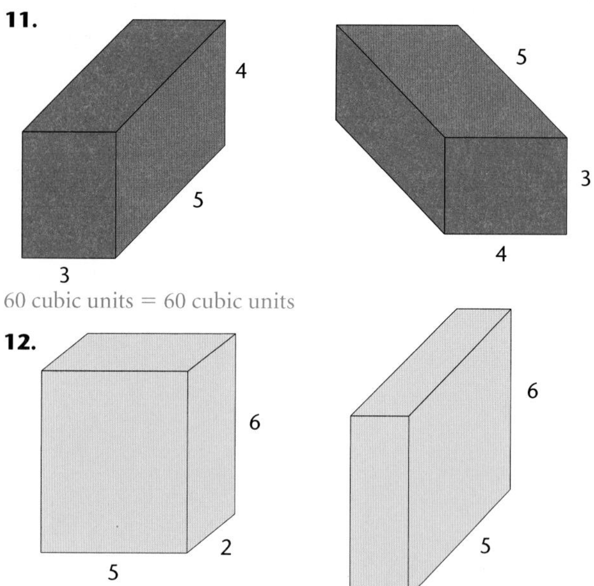

You can find the volume of rectangular solids by using the associative property of multiplication.

13.

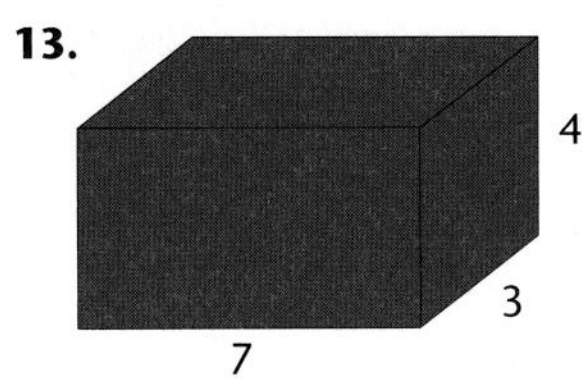

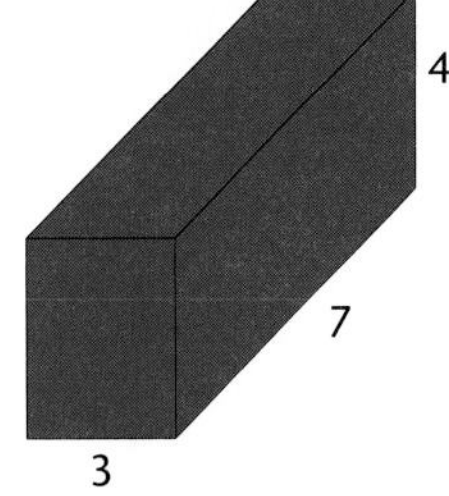

84 cubic units = 84 cubic units

14.

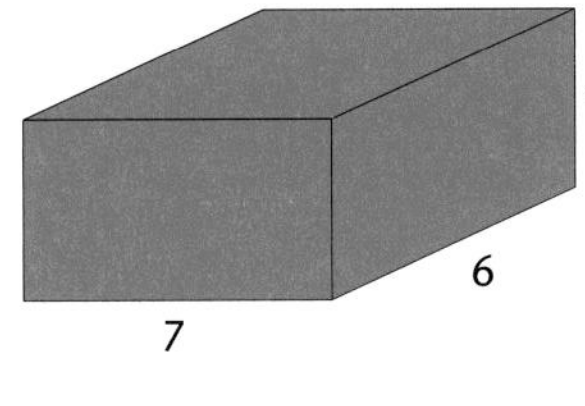

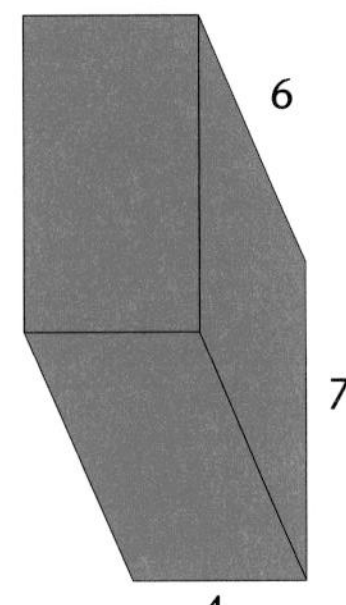

168 cubic units = 168 cubic units

Exercise C Use the associative property of multiplication to place parentheses in two different ways.

15. *lwh* $(lw)h = l(wh)$

16. *xyz* $(xy)z = x(yz)$

17. *fpn* $(fp)n = f(pn)$

18. *cdj* $(cd)j = c(dj)$

19. *mks* $(mk)s = m(ks)$

20. *ghy* $(gh)y = g(hy)$

Algebra in Your Life

Stepping through a Process

There are times when you need to do things in a certain order, and there are times when you don't. You follow step-by-step directions to build models from kits, bake cakes, or mix chemical formulas. Doing steps in the given order helps you get the results you want. The same is true of the order of operations in algebra. If you follow the steps in the right order, you end up with the correct answer.

Lesson at a Glance

Chapter 2 Lesson 5

Overview This lesson presents the distributive property of multiplication.

Objectives

- To identify the product of $a(b + c)$ as equal to the product $ab + ac$
- To use the distributive property of multiplication to find the area of rectangular shapes

Student Pages 42–43

Teacher's Resource Library 

Workbook Activity 17

Activity 17

Alternative Activity 17

Mathematics Vocabulary

distributive property

Warm-Up Activity

Present students with the following situation:

Every item at a secondhand music store costs 99¢. Ahmal chooses 3 tapes and 4 CDs.

Ask students to describe ways to write an expression showing how much Ahmal pays for his selections. Record students' suggestions on the board.

Teaching the Lesson

Use a number line, and an expression, such as 3(10 + 5), to illustrate the distributive property of multiplication. On one number line, mark off 10, then add 5 to reach 15. Then mark off three groups of 15 to reach 45. On a second number line, mark off three groups of ten, then three groups of five. Help students recognize that the end result is, again, 45.

Lesson 5 The Distributive Property—Multiplication

> ***Distributive property***
> *Numbers within parentheses can be multiplied by the same factor*

Three times the sum of 10 + 5 is written as 3(10 + 5).
You can find the result in two ways.
One way is to perform the operation inside parentheses first.

$3(10 + 5)$
$3(15)$
45

Another way is to use the **distributive property**.

$3(10 + 5) = 3(10 + 5)$
$3 \cdot 10 + 3 \cdot 5$
$30 + 15$
45

EXAMPLE 1 Simplify $3(a + b)$.
Since you cannot perform the operation inside parentheses first (because you do not know the values of a and b), use the distributive property.

$3(a + b) = a + b + a + b + a + b$
$= 3a + 3b$ *or*
$3(a + b)$
$(3 \bullet a) + (3 \bullet b)$
$3a + 3b$

$3 \bullet a$
$3\,(a + b) = 3a + 3b$
$3 \bullet b$

Use the distributive property to simplify these expressions.

EXAMPLE 2 $3(2x + 4y)$
$3(2x + 4y) = 2x + 4y + 2x + 4y + 2x + 4y$
$= 6x + 12y$ *or*
$3(2x + 4y) = (3)(2x) + (3)(4y) = 6x + 12y$

EXAMPLE 3 Let 10 be the height of two rectangles whose bases are 3 and 5. The areas of these rectangles represent the two products of the distributive property.

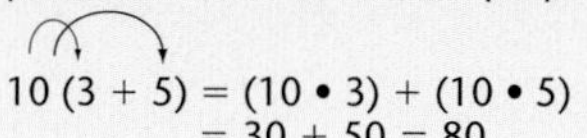
$10\,(3 + 5) = (10 \bullet 3) + (10 \bullet 5)$
$= 30 + 50 = 80$

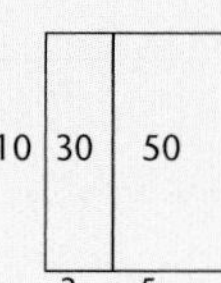

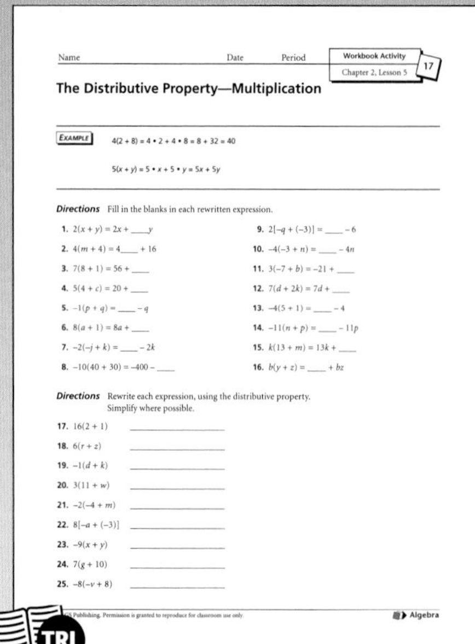

Name Date Period **Workbook Activity 17** Chapter 2, Lesson 5

The Distributive Property—Multiplication

EXAMPLE $4(2 + 8) = 4 \cdot 2 + 4 \cdot 8 = 8 + 32 = 40$
$5(x + y) = 5 \cdot x + 5 \cdot y = 5x + 5y$

Directions Fill in the blanks in each rewritten expression.

1. $2(x + y) = 2x +$ ____y
2. $4(m + 4) = 4$____ $+ 16$
3. $7(8 + 1) = 56 +$ ____
4. $5(4 + c) = 20 +$ ____
5. $-1(p + q) =$ ____ $- q$
6. $8(a + 1) = 8a +$ ____
7. $-2(-j + k) =$ ____ $- 2k$
8. $-10(40 + 30) = -400 -$ ____
9. $2[-q + (-3)] =$ ____ $- 6$
10. $-4(-3 + n) =$ ____ $- 4n$
11. $3(-7 + b) = -21 +$ ____
12. $7(d + 2k) = 7d +$ ____
13. $-4(5 + 1) =$ ____ $- 4$
14. $-11(n + p) =$ ____ $- 11p$
15. $k(13 + m) = 13k +$ ____
16. $b(y + z) =$ ____ $+ bz$

Directions Rewrite each expression, using the distributive property. Simplify where possible.

17. $16(2 + 1)$ ________
18. $6(r + z)$ ________
19. $-1(d + k)$ ________
20. $3(11 + w)$ ________
21. $-2(-4 + m)$ ________
22. $8[-a + (-3)]$ ________
23. $-9(x + y)$ ________
24. $7(g + 10)$ ________
25. $-8(-v + 8)$ ________

 Algebra

Workbook Activity 17

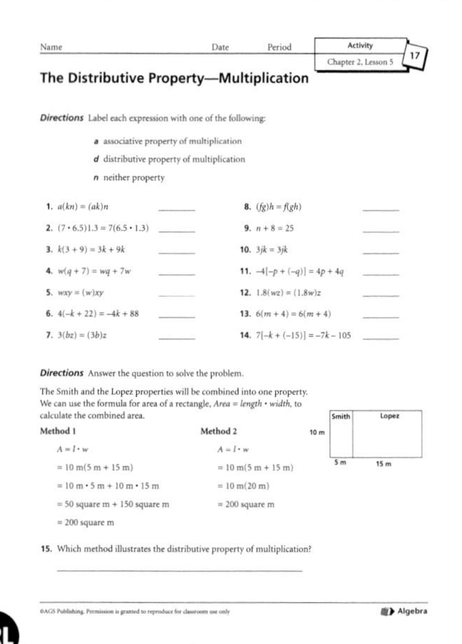

Name Date Period **Activity 17** Chapter 2, Lesson 5

The Distributive Property—Multiplication

Directions Label each expression with one of the following:

a associative property of multiplication
d distributive property of multiplication
n neither property

1. $a(kn) = (ak)n$ ____
2. $(7 \cdot 6.5)1.3 = 7(6.5 \cdot 1.3)$ ____
3. $k(3 + 9) = 3k + 9k$ ____
4. $w(q + 7) = wq + 7w$ ____
5. $wxy = (w)xy$ ____
6. $4(-k + 22) = -4k + 88$ ____
7. $3(bz) = (3b)z$ ____
8. $(fg)h = f(gh)$ ____
9. $n + 8 = 25$ ____
10. $3jk = 3jk$ ____
11. $-4[-p + (-q)] = 4p + 4q$ ____
12. $1.8(wz) = (1.8w)z$ ____
13. $6(m + 4) = 6(m + 4)$ ____
14. $7[-k + (-15)] = -7k - 105$ ____

Directions Answer the question to solve the problem.

The Smith and the Lopez properties will be combined into one property. We can use the formula for area of a rectangle, *Area = length • width*, to calculate the combined area.

Smith | Lopez | 10 m | 5 m | 15 m

Method 1
$A = l \cdot w$
$= 10\text{ m}(5\text{ m} + 15\text{ m})$
$= 10\text{ m} \cdot 5\text{ m} + 10\text{ m} \cdot 15\text{ m}$
$= 50$ square m $+ 150$ square m
$= 200$ square m

Method 2
$A = l \cdot w$
$= 10\text{ m}(5\text{ m} + 15\text{ m})$
$= 10\text{ m}(20\text{ m})$
$= 200$ square m

15. Which method illustrates the distributive property of multiplication?

____

 Algebra

Activity 17

Distributive Property of Multiplication

In a problem that mixes multiplication with addition or subtraction, you can multiply each term in parentheses by a single factor. In general, for all terms or numbers a, b, and c, $a(b + c) = ab + ac$.

Exercise A Copy and complete using the distributive property.

1. $4(10 + 5) = 4 \cdot ■ + 4 \cdot ■$ 10; 5

2. $18(9 + 8) = 18 \cdot ■ + 18 \cdot ■$ 9; 8

3. $4(b + 14) = 4 \cdot ■ + 4 \cdot ■$ b; 14

4. $8(m + b) = 8 \cdot ■ + 8 \cdot ■$ m; b

5. $-2(6 + 7) = -2 \cdot ■ + -2 \cdot ■$ 6; 7

6. $7(22 + -6) = 7 \cdot ■ + 7 \cdot ■$ 22; -6

7. $-3(-9 + n) = -3 \cdot ■ + -3 \cdot ■$ -9; n

8. $-9(31 + 16) = -9 \cdot ■ + -9 \cdot ■$ 31; 16

Exercise B Use the distributive property to simplify each expression.

9. $4(a + b)$ $4a + 4b$

10. $6(8 + c)$ $48 + 6c$

11. $-2(d + k)$ $-2d + -2k$

12. $3(-x + y)$ $-3x + 3y$

13. $-4(a + b)$ $-4a + -4b$

14. $7[-c + (-x)]$ $-7c + -7x$

15. $-9(-v + 9)$ $9v + -81$

16. $-5(-z + 10)$ $5z + -50$

17. $8(z + 4)$ $8z + 32$

18. $2(-b + m)$ $-2b + 2m$

19. $3[-x + (-4)]$ $-3x + -12$

Exercise C Use the distributive property to find the area of each figure.

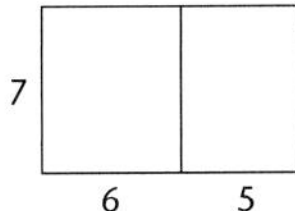

20. $7(6 + 5)$

77 square units

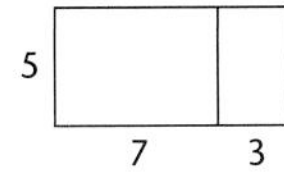

22. $5(7 + 3)$

50 square units

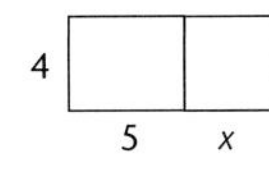

24. $4(5 + x)$

$20 + 4x$ square units

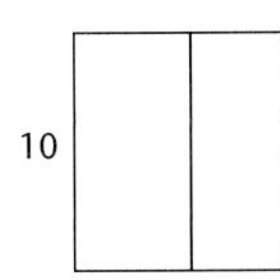

21. $10(5 + 4)$

90 square units

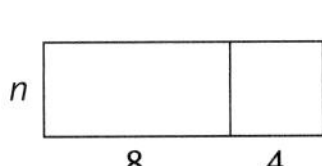

23. $n(8 + 4)$

$12n$ square units

x
y z

25. $x(y + z)$

$xy + xz$ square units

Common Error

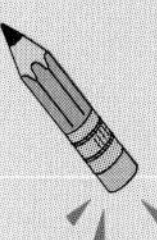

Students beginning to use the distributive property sometimes multiply only one of the terms within the parentheses. For example, they may simplify $3(x + y)$ as $3x + y$. Stress to students that it is important that they remember to multiply each term within the parentheses by the single factor.

3 Reinforce and Extend

Learning Styles

Interpersonal/ Group Learning

Suggest students work in groups of four. Each group will need three number cubes. One student rolls the number cubes, and the others use the numbers to write an expression in the form $a(b + c)$ or $ab + ac$. The group that writes an expression that has the highest value wins a point. Allow each student two turns at rolling the cubes. Ask students how they arranged the numbers to get the greatest product. (a should be the greatest of the three numbers.)

Lesson at a Glance

Chapter 2 Lesson 6

Overview This lesson discusses the use of the distributive property of multiplication to find the factors of an expression.

Objectives

- To identify common factors using the distributive property of multiplication
- To factor expressions using the distributive property of multiplication

Student Pages 44–45

Teacher's Resource Library 

Workbook Activity 18

Activity 18

Alternative Activity 18

Mathematics Vocabulary

common factor
factoring

Warm-Up Activity

Ask students if they are familiar with the term *factor.* For example, do they know that 3 and 8 are factors of 24? Write $3 \times 8 = 24$ on the board and identify 3 and 8 as factors. Remind students that *factor* is another term for *multiplier.*

Teaching the Lesson

List the following terms on the board and ask students which can be combined with one another: 3, 6, 9, $2a$, $3b$, $7c$, $6a$, $4c$, and $9b$. Have students discuss how they chose which terms could be combined. *(Only those with common terms can be combined.)*

Lesson 6 The Distributive Property—Factoring

Common factor
A multiplier shared by the terms in an expression

Factoring
Using the distributive property to separate the common factor from the terms in the expression

Recall that like terms in an expression can be combined.

$$2a + 3a = (a + a) + (a + a + a) = 5a$$

In the expression $2a + 3a$, a is common to both terms, so a is a **common factor** of $2a + 3a$. Therefore, $2a + 3a = a(2 + 3) = 5a$.

Common factors and the distributive property can be used to factor, or rewrite, expressions.

EXAMPLE 1 Factor the expression $ab + ax$.

Since a is common to both terms, a is a common factor, and using the distributive property, you can rewrite $ab + ax$ as $a(b + x)$. So the expression $ab + ax$ factored is $a(b + x)$.

Since $a(b + x)$ is the product of two factors, this use of the distributive property is called **factoring**.

EXAMPLE 2 $-3x - 3y = -3(x + y)$

(-3) is the common factor.

You can always check by multiplying:

Since $-3(x + y) = -3x + (-3y) = -3x - 3y$, the factoring is correct.

Remember:
subtracting means adding the opposite.
$6 - (-2) =$
$6 + 2 = 8$
$-4 - 2 =$
$-4 + (-2) = -6$

EXAMPLE 3 $ax^2 - ay^2 = a(x^2 - y^2)$

a is the common factor.

Check: $a(x^2 - y^2) = a[x^2 + (-y^2)] = ax^2 + a(-y^2)$
$= ax^2 - ay^2$

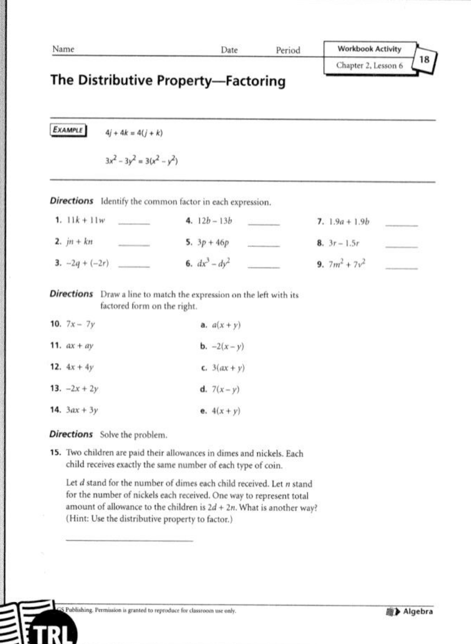

Name Date Period **Workbook Activity 18** Chapter 2, Lesson 6

The Distributive Property—Factoring

EXAMPLE $4j + 4k = 4(j + k)$
$3x^2 - 3y^2 = 3(x^2 - y^2)$

Directions Identify the common factor in each expression.

1. $11k + 11w$ ______
2. $jn + kn$ ______
3. $-2q + (-2r)$ ______
4. $12b - 13b$ ______
5. $3p + 46p$ ______
6. $dx^3 - dy^2$ ______
7. $1.9a + 1.9b$ ______
8. $3r - 1.5r$ ______
9. $7m^2 + 7v^2$ ______

Directions Draw a line to match the expression on the left with its factored form on the right.

10. $7x - 7y$ a. $a(x + y)$
11. $ax + ay$ b. $-2(x - y)$
12. $4x + 4y$ c. $3(ax + y)$
13. $-2x + 2y$ d. $7(x - y)$
14. $3ax + 3y$ e. $4(x + y)$

Directions Solve the problem.

15. Two children are paid their allowances in dimes and nickels. Each child receives exactly the same number of each type of coin.

Let d stand for the number of dimes each child received. Let n stand for the number of nickels each received. One way to represent total amount of allowance to the children is $2d + 2n$. What is another way? (Hint: Use the distributive property to factor.)

______

 Algebra

Workbook Activity 18

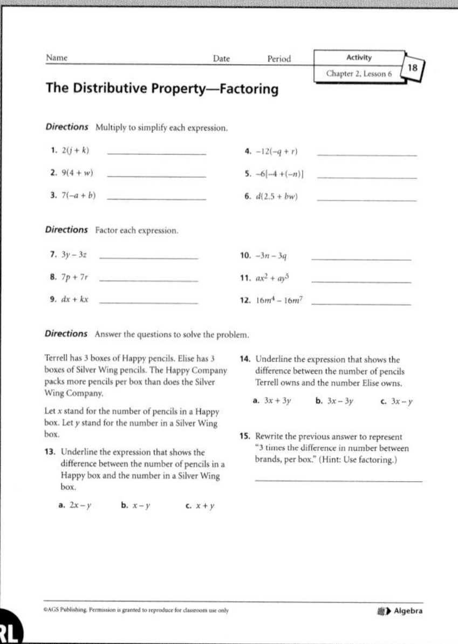

Name Date Period **Activity 18** Chapter 2, Lesson 6

The Distributive Property—Factoring

Directions Multiply to simplify each expression.

1. $2(j + k)$ ______
2. $9(4 + w)$ ______
3. $7(-a + b)$ ______
4. $-12(-q + r)$ ______
5. $-6[-4 + (-n)]$ ______
6. $d(2.5 + bw)$ ______

Directions Factor each expression.

7. $3y - 3z$ ______
8. $7p + 7r$ ______
9. $dx + kx$ ______
10. $-3n - 3q$ ______
11. $ax^2 + ay^5$ ______
12. $16m^4 - 16m^7$ ______

Directions Answer the questions to solve the problem.

Terrell has 3 boxes of Happy pencils. Elise has 3 boxes of Silver Wing pencils. The Happy Company packs more pencils per box than does the Silver Wing Company.

Let x stand for the number of pencils in a Happy box. Let y stand for the number in a Silver Wing box.

13. Underline the expression that shows the difference between the number of pencils in a Happy box and the number in a Silver Wing box.
 a. $2x - y$ b. $x - y$ c. $x + y$

14. Underline the expression that shows the difference between the number of pencils Terrell owns and the number Elise owns.
 a. $3x + 3y$ b. $3x - 3y$ c. $3x - y$

15. Rewrite the previous answer to represent "3 times the difference in number between brands, per box." (Hint: Use factoring.)

______

 Algebra

Activity 18

Exercise A Identify the common factor in each expression.

1. $2a + 3a$ a
2. $5w + 7w$ w
3. $4x + 5x$ x
4. $-8e + 9e$ e
5. $6b - 2b$ $2b$
6. $-10e - 4e$ $-2e$
7. $-3z - 2z$ $-z$
8. $7w - 2w$ w
9. $3a - 2a$ a
10. $-2x + 3x$ x

Exercise B Use the distributive property to factor each expression.

11. $4x + 4y$ $4(x + y)$
12. $5y + 5w$ $5(y + w)$
13. $3j - 3p$ $3(j - p)$
14. $-8k - 8g$ $-8(k + g)$
15. $6y + 6z$ $6(y + z)$
16. $15s - 15t$ $15(s - t)$
17. $-4m - 4y$ $-4(m + y)$
18. $fp + fg$ $f(p + g)$
19. $ax - ay$ $a(x - y)$
20. $mi - mb$ $m(i - b)$
21. $-as + aj$ $a(-s + j)$
22. $ky - kx$ $k(y - x)$
23. $-uv - um$ $-u(v + m)$
24. $tj - tr$ $t(j - r)$
25. $bx^2 + by^2$ $b(x^2 + y^2)$
26. $cw^3 - cx^2$ $c(w^3 - x^2)$
27. $wx^4 + wm^2$ $w(x^4 + m^2)$
28. $-ha - hx^2$ $-h(a + x^2)$

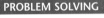

PROBLEM SOLVING

Exercise C Solve each problem.

29. Sylvia is in grade 9 homeroom b, and her friend Mai is in grade 9 homeroom c. What do they have in common? Use the distributive property to write an expression that shows the common factor. $9(b + c)$

30. Mai's class schedule has her taking 4 classes before lunch and 3 classes after lunch. Allow c to represent classes. Use the distributive property to write an expression that shows the number of classes Mai takes. $c(4 + 3)$

Common Error

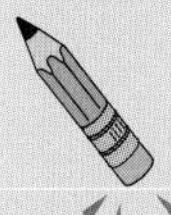

Students sometimes fail to use parentheses properly when factoring an expression. They correctly identify the common factor but do not effectively use the distributive property. For example, factoring $4x - 4y$ as $4x - y$. Emphasize to students that factoring relies on the distributive property. Stress that the best method for checking that they have accurately factored an expression is to multiply the factors. The product should be the same as the original expression.

3 Reinforce and Extend

Group Problem Solving

Have small groups of students write and then factor an expression describing each of the following:

- Every boy and girl is allowed 3 hours of computer time a week.
- Teachers and parents volunteer for 2 hours of tutoring a month.
- Pet licenses cost $4 a year for each dog and cat.

Have students present their results to the class as a TV mini-news minute. One group member might design the presentation, another member draw and letter the actual designs, a third act as announcer, and the fourth act as producer, gathering the needed materials and coordinating the group's efforts.

Lesson at a Glance

Chapter 2 Lesson 7

Overview This lesson presents the addition and multiplication properties of zero: $0 + a = a$; $0 \cdot a = 0$

Objectives

- To indicate that the sum of opposite numbers is zero
- To recognize that adding zero to a number does not change the number
- To determine that zero times any number is zero

Student Pages 46–47

Teacher's Resource Library 

Workbook Activity 19

Activity 19

Alternative Activity 19

Mathematics Vocabulary

addition property of zero
additive inverses
multiplication property of zero

Warm-Up Activity

Generate interest in the lesson by posing the following problems:

- "I'm thinking of a number. No matter what number I add to it, the sum is always the same as the number I added. What is the number?"
- "I'm thinking of a number. No matter what number I multiply it by, the product is always the number I started with. What is the number?"

(The answer to both questions is zero.)

Teaching the Lesson

Draw a number line on a transparent medium such as acetate or on tracing paper. Fold the number line along the zero mark so that each number and its opposite are overlapping. Help students recognize that the folded number line shows that opposite numbers add to zero.

Lesson 7 Properties of Zero

Addition property of zero
A number does not change if 0 is added or subtracted

Additive inverses
Numbers that equal 0 when added together; also called opposites

If you add zero to any number, that number does not change. If you subtract zero from any number, that number does not change.

EXAMPLE 1 $3 + 0 = 3$ and $0 + 3 = 3$
$-1 + 0 = -1$ and $-1 - 0 = -1$

Addition Property of Zero
Adding zero to a number does not change the number.
$4 + 0 = 4$ $0 + 4 = 4$ $a + 0 = a$ $0 + a = a$

Any two numbers whose sum is 0 are opposites of each other.

EXAMPLE 2 $3 + (-3) = 0$

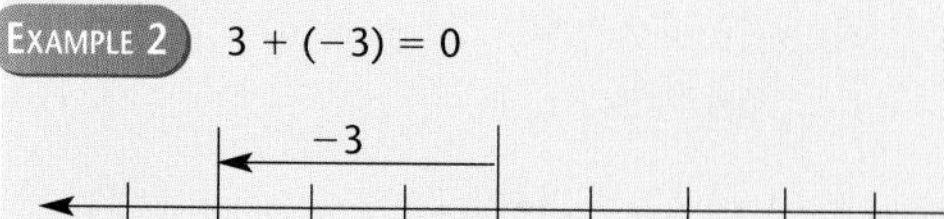

EXAMPLE 3 $a + (-a) = 0$

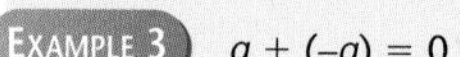

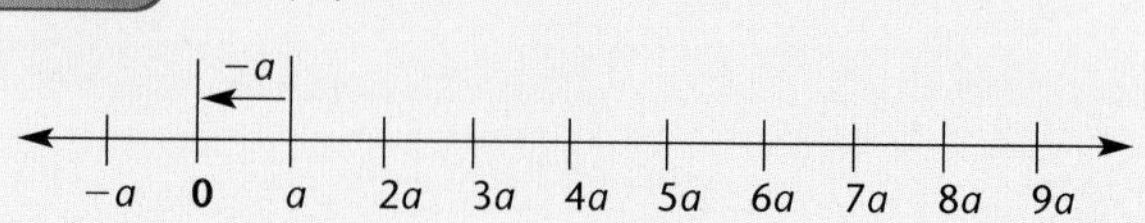

Additive Inverse Property
Any two numbers whose sum is 0 are **additive inverses**, or *opposites*, of each other.

Because there is only one point for 0 on the number line, zero is its own opposite.

EXAMPLE 4 $5 + \blacksquare = 0$
Since the opposite of 5 is -5, $5 + (-5) = 0$.
$-x + \blacksquare = 0$
Since the opposite of $-x$ is x, $-x + x = 0$.

Name Date Period **Workbook Activity 19** Chapter 2, Lesson 7

Properties of Zero

EXAMPLE

Additive Property of Zero:	$4 + 0 = 4$	$-2 + 0 = -2$
Additive Inverse Property:	$-3 + 3 = 0$	$5 + (-5) = 0$
Multiplication Property of Zero:	$0(6) = 0$	$-4(0) = 0$

Directions If the two numbers are additive inverses, write *true*. Otherwise, write *false*.

1. -12 12 ________ 4. -75 75 ________
2. 7 -7 ________ 5. -8 -8 ________
3. -5 0 ________ 6. x $-x$ ________

Directions Write each sum.

7. $9 + 0$ ________ 10. $k + 0$ ________ 13. $0 - 37$ ________
8. $0 + 27$ ________ 11. $-16 + 0$ ________ 14. $k^5 + 0$ ________
9. $0 - 14$ ________ 12. $0 + m^2$ ________ 15. $0 - y^2$ ________

Directions Write each product.

16. $0(112)$ ________ 19. $(xy)(0)$ ________ 22. $(-jk)(0)$ ________
17. $(-17)(0)$ ________ 20. $(0)(-9)$ ________ 23. $n^7 \cdot 0$ ________
18. $0 \cdot q$ ________ 21. $(cde)(0)$ ________ 24. $(0)(ab^3)$ ________

Directions Solve the problem.

25. Jenna said to Brett, "I'll give you double the number of marbles you have in your pocket."
Brett replied, "But I don't have *any* marbles in my pocket."
Jenna responded, "So I'll give you double nothing, which is nothing."

How could Jenna say the same thing in a mathematical expression? Underline one.

a. $1 + 2 = 3$ b. $0 + 2 = 2$ c. $2(0) = 0$

 Algebra

TRL Workbook Activity 19

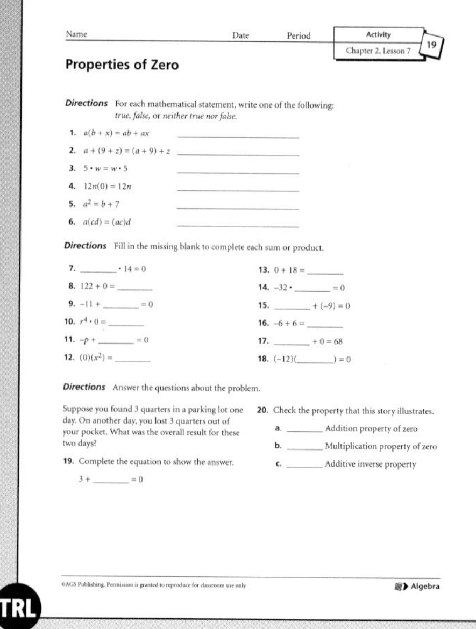

Name Date Period **Activity 19** Chapter 2, Lesson 7

Properties of Zero

Directions For each mathematical statement, write one of the following: *true, false,* or *neither true nor false.*

1. $a(b + x) = ab + ax$ ________
2. $a + (9 + z) = (a + 9) + z$ ________
3. $5 \cdot w = w \cdot 5$ ________
4. $12n(0) = 12n$ ________
5. $a^2 = b + 7$ ________
6. $a(cd) = (ac)d$ ________

Directions Fill in the missing blank to complete each sum or product.

7. ________ $\cdot 14 = 0$ 13. $0 + 18 =$ ________
8. $122 + 0 =$ ________ 14. $-32 \cdot$ ________ $= 0$
9. $-11 +$ ________ $= 0$ 15. ________ $+ (-9) = 0$
10. $r^4 \cdot 0 =$ ________ 16. $-6 + 6 =$ ________
11. $-p +$ ________ $= 0$ 17. ________ $+ 0 = 68$
12. $(0)(x^2) =$ ________ 18. $(-12)($________$) = 0$

Directions Answer the questions about the problem.

Suppose you found 3 quarters in a parking lot one day. On another day, you lost 3 quarters out of your pocket. What was the overall result for these two days?

19. Complete the equation to show the answer.
$3 +$ ________ $= 0$

20. Check the property that this story illustrates.
a. ________ Addition property of zero
b. ________ Multiplication property of zero
c. ________ Additive inverse property

 Algebra

TRL Activity 19

Multiplication property of zero
Zero times any number is zero

Writing About Mathematics

Explain what the opposite of a positive integer is and what the opposite of a negative integer is.

If you add or subtract zero with any number, that number does not change.

EXAMPLE 5 Counting by 2's

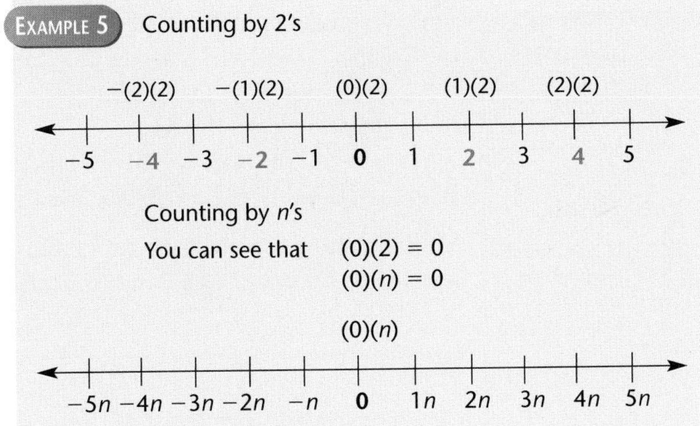

Multiplication Property of Zero
Zero times any number is zero.
$(0)(n) = 0$ where n is any number.
$0(a + b) = 0$ because $0(a + b) = (0)(a) + 0(b) = 0 + 0$.

Exercise A Write each sum.

1. $3 + 0$ 3 **2.** $0 - 7$ -7 **3.** $x^2 + 0$ x^2 **4.** $0 - y^3$ $-y^3$

Exercise B Copy and fill in the missing number or letter.

5. $-5 + n = 0$ 5 **6.** $4 - n = 0$ 4 **7.** $a + n = 0$ $-a$ **8.** $-x^2 + n = 0$ x^2

Exercise C Write each product.

9. $0(5)$ 0 **10.** $(0)(y)$ 0 **11.** $(-8)(0)$ 0 **12.** $(ax)(0)$ 0 **13.** $(a + b)(0)$ 0

Exercise D Write your answer to each question.

14. How are 23 meters below sea level and 23 meters above sea level related to each other? They are opposites.

15. Explain why 5° Fahrenheit is 10 degrees warmer than −5° Fahrenheit.
5°F − (−5°F) = 10°F

COMMON ERROR

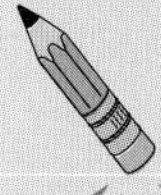

Students sometimes suggest that the opposite of 0 is −0. Use the number line to stress that zero is a number that separates the positive and negative numbers. Zero itself is neither positive or negative.

3 Reinforce and Extend

LEARNING STYLES

LEP/ESL

Pair less proficient students with those of greater language ability. Direct the partners to prepare a set of flash cards showing the addition and multiplication properties of zero. One side of each card should have an example, such as $n + 0 = n$, or $3 + (-3) = 0$. On the back of the card, students should write, in their own words, what the example represents. Post all the flash cards in the classroom and invite students to choose which cards they think would be the most useful study aids.

MENTAL MATH

Have students identify the operation or variable indicated by the ■.

3 ■ 0 = 0	(•)
3 ■ 0 = 3	(+)
n ■ 0 = 0	(•)
n ■ 0 = n	(+)
a + ■ = 0	($-a$)
$-a$ + ■ = 0	(a)
($a + b$) ■ 0 = ($a + b$)	(+)
($a + b$) ■ 0 = 0	(•)

Lesson at a Glance

Chapter 2 Lesson 8

Overview This lesson presents the multiplication properties of one and defines multiplicative inverses.

Objectives

- To recognize that a number or term does not change if multiplied by 1
- To identify as multiplicative inverses, or reciprocals, any two numbers whose product equals 1

Student Pages 48–49

Teacher's Resource Library TRL

Workbook Activity 20

Activity 20

Alternative Activity 20

Mathematics Vocabulary

multiplication property of 1
multiplicative inverses
reciprocals

1 Warm-Up Activity

Pose the following question:

"I'm thinking of a number. No matter what number I multiply it by, the product is always the same as the multiplier. What is the number?"

Ask students to provide several examples, both arithmetic and algebraic, to support their response.

2 Teaching the Lesson

Draw a number line on the board. Divide the distance from 0 to 1 into two equal parts, labeling the $\frac{1}{2}$ point. Ask a volunteer to use the number line to show that $\frac{1}{2} + \frac{1}{2} = 2(\frac{1}{2}) = 1$. Have another volunteer draw and divide a number line to show that $\frac{1}{4}(4) = 1$. Have students identify the multiplicative inverses used in the demonstration.

Lesson 8 Properties of 1

Multiplication property of 1
A number or term does not change when multiplied by 1

Multiplicative inverses
Any two numbers or terms whose product equals 1

Reciprocals
Multiplicative inverses

One is a special number. It is a factor of any number or variable.

3 means one 3 or (1)(3).
x means one x or $(1)(x)$.
$(a + b)$ means one $(a + b)$ or $(1)(a + b)$.

In each of these cases, 1 is a factor, even when it is not written.

Multiplying any number or term by 1 does not change the number or term. This is the **multiplication property of 1.**

$(1)(n) = n = (n)(1)$ for any number n.

> **Multiplication Property of 1**
> A number or term does not change when multiplied by 1.

Knowing that multiplying by 1 does not change the value of a term is very helpful in arithmetic and algebra.

Important note:
0 does not have an inverse, or reciprocal.
$\frac{1}{0}$ is not a number or symbol for a number.

EXAMPLE 1 Arithmetic:

$\frac{1}{2} \bullet 1 = \frac{1}{2};\ 1 = \frac{3}{3}$, so $\frac{1}{2} \bullet \frac{3}{3} = \frac{3}{6} = \frac{1}{2}$

Algebra:

$(a)(1) = a;\ 1 = \frac{b}{b}$ so $(a)(\frac{b}{b}) = \frac{ab}{b} = a$

$\frac{b}{b}$ is the same as $b \div b = 1$; any number divided by itself equals 1. You also know that $(\frac{1}{2})(2) = 1$ and $a(\frac{1}{a}) = \frac{a}{a} = 1$.

When two numbers or terms are multiplied and their product is 1, they are called **multiplicative inverses**, or **reciprocals**, of each other.

$\frac{1}{2}$ and $\frac{2}{1}$ or 2 are reciprocals of each other.

a and $\frac{1}{a}$ are reciprocals of each other.

> **Multiplicative Inverses (Reciprocals)**
> Any two numbers or terms whose product equals 1 are multiplicative inverses, or reciprocals, of each other.

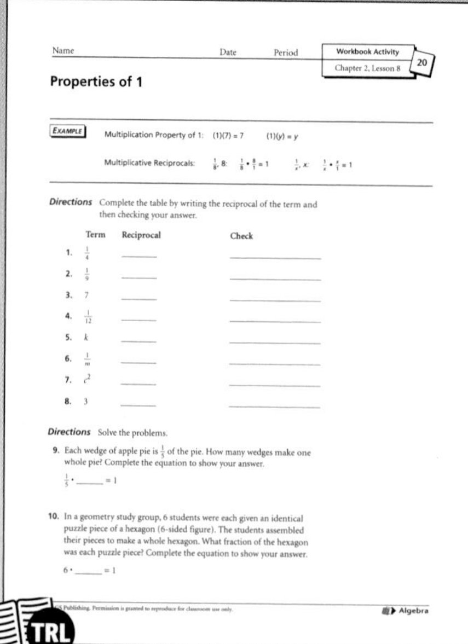

Name Date Period **Workbook Activity 20** Chapter 2, Lesson 8

Properties of 1

EXAMPLE Multiplication Property of 1: (1)(7) = 7 (1)(y) = y

Multiplicative Reciprocals: $\frac{1}{8}$, 8: $\frac{1}{8} \bullet \frac{8}{1} = 1$ $\frac{1}{x}$, x: $\frac{1}{x} \bullet \frac{x}{1} = 1$

Directions Complete the table by writing the reciprocal of the term and then checking your answer.

	Term	Reciprocal	Check
1.	$\frac{1}{4}$	______	______
2.	$\frac{1}{9}$	______	______
3.	7	______	______
4.	$\frac{1}{12}$	______	______
5.	k	______	______
6.	$\frac{1}{m}$	______	______
7.	c^2	______	______
8.	3	______	______

Directions Solve the problems.

9. Each wedge of apple pie is $\frac{1}{5}$ of the pie. How many wedges make one whole pie? Complete the equation to show your answer.
$\frac{1}{5} \bullet$ ______ = 1

10. In a geometry study group, 6 students were each given an identical puzzle piece of a hexagon (6-sided figure). The students assembled their pieces to make a whole hexagon. What fraction of the hexagon was each puzzle piece? Complete the equation to show your answer.
$6 \bullet$ ______ = 1

 Algebra

TRL

Workbook Activity 20

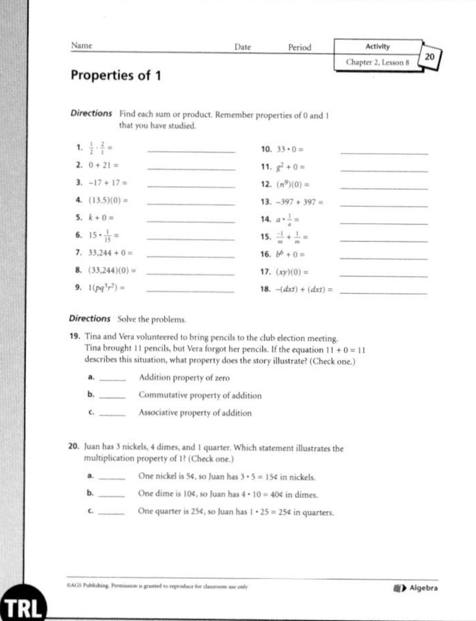

Name Date Period **Activity 20** Chapter 2, Lesson 8

Properties of 1

Directions Find each sum or product. Remember properties of 0 and 1 that you have studied.

1. $\frac{1}{2} \cdot \frac{2}{1} =$ ______
2. $0 + 21 =$ ______
3. $-17 + 17 =$ ______
4. $(13.5)(0) =$ ______
5. $k + 0 =$ ______
6. $15 \bullet \frac{1}{15} =$ ______
7. $33{,}244 + 0 =$ ______
8. $(33{,}244)(0) =$ ______
9. $1(pq^3r^2) =$ ______
10. $33 \bullet 0 =$ ______
11. $g^2 + 0 =$ ______
12. $(n^9)(0) =$ ______
13. $-397 + 397 =$ ______
14. $a \bullet \frac{1}{a} =$ ______
15. $\frac{-1}{m} + \frac{1}{m} =$ ______
16. $b^6 + 0 =$ ______
17. $(xy)(0) =$ ______
18. $-(dxt) + (dxt) =$ ______

Directions Solve the problems.

19. Tina and Vera volunteered to bring pencils to the club election meeting. Tina brought 11 pencils, but Vera forgot her pencils. If the equation 11 + 0 = 11 describes this situation, what property does the story illustrate? (Check one.)
    a. ______ Addition property of zero
    b. ______ Commutative property of addition
    c. ______ Associative property of addition

20. Juan has 3 nickels, 4 dimes, and 1 quarter. Which statement illustrates the multiplication property of 1? (Check one.)
    a. ______ One nickel is 5¢, so Juan has 3 • 5 = 15¢ in nickels.
    b. ______ One dime is 10¢, so Juan has 4 • 10 = 40¢ in dimes.
    c. ______ One quarter is 25¢, so Juan has 1 • 25 = 25¢ in quarters.

 Algebra

TRL

Activity 20

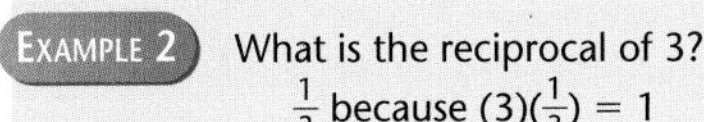

Example 2 What is the reciprocal of 3?
$\frac{1}{3}$ because $(3)(\frac{1}{3}) = 1$

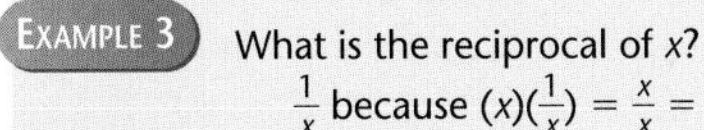

Example 3 What is the reciprocal of x?
$\frac{1}{x}$ because $(x)(\frac{1}{x}) = \frac{x}{x} = 1$

Example 4 What is the reciprocal of $\frac{1}{y}$?
y because $(y)(\frac{1}{y}) = \frac{y}{y} = 1$

Exercise A Copy and write the missing factor.

1. $\frac{1}{2}■ = \frac{5}{10}$ $\frac{5}{5}$
2. $\frac{3}{4}■ = \frac{18}{24}$ $\frac{6}{6}$
3. $\frac{7}{8}■ = \frac{14}{16}$ $\frac{2}{2}$
4. $\frac{1}{3}■ = \frac{7}{21}$ $\frac{7}{7}$
5. $\frac{3}{8}■ = \frac{12}{32}$ $\frac{4}{4}$
6. $a■ = \frac{ab}{b}$ $\frac{b}{b}$
7. $m■ = \frac{mk}{k}$ $\frac{k}{k}$
8. $w■ = \frac{wp}{p}$ $\frac{p}{p}$
9. $x■ = \frac{3x}{3}$ $\frac{3}{3}$
10. $t■ = \frac{6t}{6}$ $\frac{6}{6}$

Exercise B What is the reciprocal of each term? Check by multiplying.

11. $\frac{1}{3}$ $3; (\frac{1}{3})(\frac{3}{1}) = 1$
12. 7 $\frac{1}{7}; (7)(\frac{1}{7}) = 1$
13. c $\frac{1}{c}; (c)(\frac{1}{c}) = 1$
14. $\frac{1}{x^3}$ $x^3; (\frac{1}{x^3})(x^3) = 1$
15. n^2 $\frac{1}{n^2}; (n^2)(\frac{1}{n^2}) = 1$
16. 12 $\frac{1}{12}; (12)(\frac{1}{12}) = 1$
17. $\frac{1}{d}$ $d; (\frac{1}{d})(d) = 1$
18. $\frac{1}{y}$ $y; (\frac{1}{y})(y) = 1$

PROBLEM SOLVING

Exercise C Solve each problem.

19. An apple is cut into 4 equal slices. How many fourths are in the apple?
20. If today's temperature of 1° F is the multiplicative inverse of yesterday's temperature, what was yesterday's temperature?

19. 4; $4(\frac{1}{4}) = 1$

20. 1°F

3 Reinforce and Extend

Learning Styles

Auditory/Verbal

Write the following list on the board: *Multiplication Property of 1, Multiplicative Inverses, Multiplication Property of Zero, Addition Property of Zero, Adding Opposites,* and *Multiplying Reciprocals.* Ask students to sit in a circle of six and to snap their fingers to create a beat. The first student must give an example of the first item on the list (e.g., $1 \cdot x = x$). The second student must give an example of the next item on the list (e.g., $y + 0 = y$), and so on. Have students continue around the circle until everyone has a turn.

Group Problem Solving

Have small groups of students plot the rise and fall of individual stocks for 20 days. Students can follow fast-food, footwear, or computer stocks, choosing the stocks they wish to follow by reading the stock market listings in the newspaper. Indicate that all changes in stock prices should be recorded in eighths.

At the end of the time period, groups should present their data to the class as a Stock Market Update. The update should include a graph of the stock's performance, examples of opposite or inverse numbers, and an indication of how the multiplication property of 1 was used in their calculations. Groups can assign tasks to members such as researcher, recorder, grapher, and interpreter or narrator.

Lesson at a Glance

Chapter 2 Lesson 9

Overview This lesson defines the root of a number.

Objectives

- To identify the root of a number as an equal factor of the number
- To find the square root of a number using a calculator

Student Pages 50–53

Teacher's Resource Library 

Workbook Activity 21

Activity 21

Alternative Activity 21

Mathematics Vocabulary

root

Warm-Up Activity

Briefly review with students the meaning of expressions such as 2^2, 3^4, and a^n. Write these expressions on the board and ask students to identify the power, the exponent, and the base of each expression.

Teaching the Lesson

Use unit cubes from a set of base ten blocks or sugar cubes to make a 5×5 square. Have students count the number of cubes in the square. *(25)* Next, ask volunteers to build a block that is 5 cubes tall, 5 cubes wide, and 5 cubes long. Then have students count the number of smaller cubes contained in the large block. *(125)*

Common Error

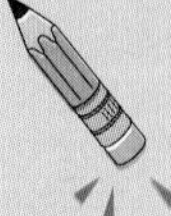

Some students may read 5^4 as "5 to the fourth power" but calculate the value as $5 \cdot 4$. They may read $\sqrt[3]{81}$ as "cube root of 81" but calculate the value as $81 \div 3$. Encourage students to think of 5^4 as $5 \cdot 5 \cdot 5 \cdot 5$ and stress the difference between the long division sign ($\overline{)\quad}$) and the sign used to indicate roots ($\sqrt{\quad}$).

Lesson  Powers and Roots

Root
An equal factor of a number

Recall what you have learned about powers and positive exponents such as 2^3, 4^2, a^3, and x^5. The opposite of taking a power of a number is called taking a **root** of a number.

Example 1

Area $= s^2$

$5^2 = (5)(5) = 25$

5 squared equals 25.

Area of square $= 25$

$s = \sqrt{\text{Area}}$

$\sqrt{25} =$

The square root of 25 equals 5.

Side of square $= \sqrt{25} = 5$

Example 2

Volume $= s^3$

$5^3 = (5)(5)(5) = 125$

5 cubed equals 125.

Volume of cube $= 125$

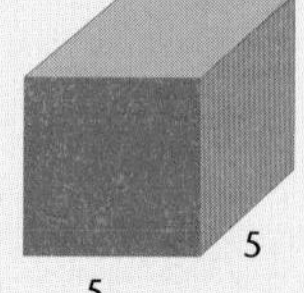

$s = \sqrt[3]{\text{Volume}}$

$\sqrt[3]{125} = 5$

The cube or third root of 125 equals 5.

Side of cube $= \sqrt[3]{125} = 5$

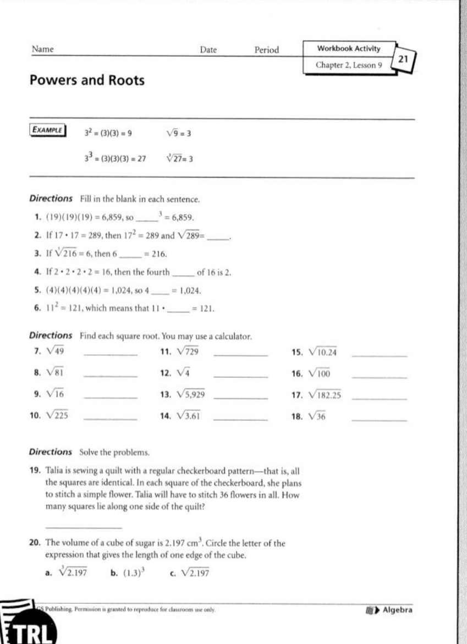

Name Date Period | Workbook Activity 21 | Chapter 2, Lesson 9

Powers and Roots

Example $3^2 = (3)(3) = 9$ $\sqrt{9} = 3$

$3^3 = (3)(3)(3) = 27$ $\sqrt[3]{27} = 3$

Directions Fill in the blank in each sentence.

1. $(19)(19)(19) = 6{,}859$, so $\_\_\_\_^3 = 6{,}859$.
2. If $17 \cdot 17 = 289$, then $17^2 = 289$ and $\sqrt{289} = \_\_\_\_$.
3. If $\sqrt[3]{216} = 6$, then $6\_\_\_\_ = 216$.
4. If $2 \cdot 2 \cdot 2 \cdot 2 = 16$, then the fourth ____ of 16 is 2.
5. $(4)(4)(4)(4)(4) = 1{,}024$, so $4\_\_\_\_ = 1{,}024$.
6. $11^2 = 121$, which means that $11 \cdot \_\_\_\_ = 121$.

Directions Find each square root. You may use a calculator.

7. $\sqrt{49}$ ____
8. $\sqrt{81}$ ____
9. $\sqrt{16}$ ____
10. $\sqrt{225}$ ____
11. $\sqrt{729}$ ____
12. $\sqrt{4}$ ____
13. $\sqrt{5{,}929}$ ____
14. $\sqrt{3.61}$ ____
15. $\sqrt{10.24}$ ____
16. $\sqrt{100}$ ____
17. $\sqrt{182.25}$ ____
18. $\sqrt{36}$ ____

Directions Solve the problems.

19. Talia is sewing a quilt with a regular checkerboard pattern—that is, all the squares are identical. In each square of the checkerboard, she plans to stitch a simple flower. Talia will have to stitch 36 flowers in all. How many squares lie along one side of the quilt?

____

20. The volume of a cube of sugar is $2.197\ \text{cm}^3$. Circle the letter of the expression that gives the length of one edge of the cube.

a. $\sqrt[3]{2.197}$ **b.** $(1.3)^3$ **c.** $\sqrt{2.197}$

Algebra

TRL

Workbook Activity 21

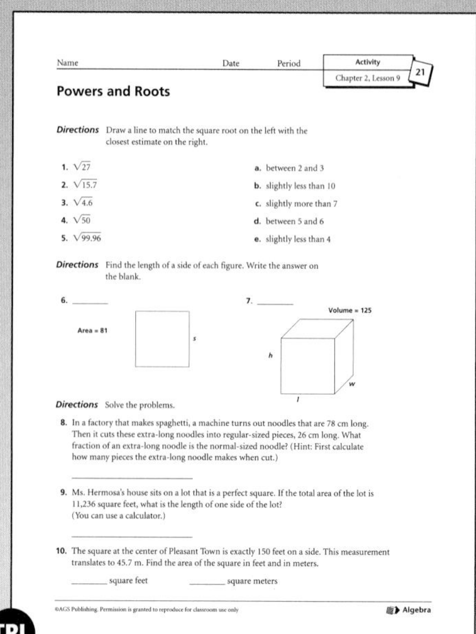

Name Date Period | Activity 21 | Chapter 2, Lesson 9

Powers and Roots

Directions Draw a line to match the square root on the left with the closest estimate on the right.

1. $\sqrt{27}$ — **a.** between 2 and 3
2. $\sqrt{15.7}$ — **b.** slightly less than 10
3. $\sqrt{4.6}$ — **c.** slightly more than 7
4. $\sqrt{50}$ — **d.** between 5 and 6
5. $\sqrt{99.96}$ — **e.** slightly less than 4

Directions Find the length of a side of each figure. Write the answer on the blank.

6. ____ Area = 81, s

7. ____ Volume = 125, h, w, l

Directions Solve the problems.

8. In a factory that makes spaghetti, a machine turns out noodles that are 78 cm long. Then it cuts these extra-long noodles into regular-sized pieces, 26 cm long. What fraction of an extra-long noodle is the normal-sized noodle? (Hint: First calculate how many pieces the extra-long noodle makes when cut.)

____

9. Ms. Hermosa's house sits on a lot that is a perfect square. If the total area of the lot is 11,236 square feet, what is the length of one side of the lot? (You can use a calculator.)

____

10. The square at the center of Pleasant Town is exactly 150 feet on a side. This measurement translates to 45.7 m. Find the area of the square in feet and in meters.

____ square feet ____ square meters

Algebra

TRL

Activity 21

Example 3 $5^4 = (5)(5)(5)(5) = 625$ 5 to the fourth power equals 625. $\sqrt[4]{625} = 5$ The fourth root of 625 equals 5.

$5^n = \underbrace{(5)(5)\ldots(5)}$ 5 to the nth power equals 5^n. $\sqrt[n]{5^n} = 5$ The nth root of 5^n is 5.

Example 4 $A = (2x)(2x) = (2 \bullet 2 \bullet x \bullet x) = 4x^2$
$\sqrt{4x^2} = 2x = \text{side}$

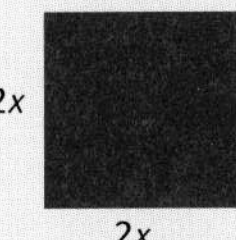

$V = (2x)(2x)(2x) =$
$(2 \bullet 2 \bullet 2 \bullet x \bullet x \bullet x) = 8x^3$
$\sqrt[3]{8x^3} = 2x = \text{side}$

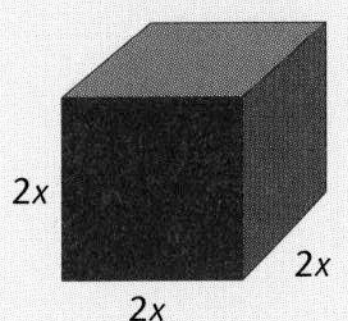

Rule For any number x,
$\sqrt[n]{x} = a$ if and only if $a^n = x$.
The nth root of x is a number a if and only if an gives you x.

By the examples you just did,

$\sqrt{25} = 5$ because $5^2 = 25$
$\sqrt[3]{125} = 5$ because $5^3 = 125$
$\sqrt[4]{625} = 5$ because $5^4 = 625$

To find roots that are not whole numbers, you can estimate the whole number that is less than the root and the whole number that is greater than the root.

Manipulatives

Powers and Roots

Materials: Unit Cubes

Group Practice: Build models of squares and cubes of numbers and discuss how area equals the number of cubes in the model. To illustrate roots, have several models of squares and cubes preassembled and discuss how to determine the root. Write the symbolic equivalent for each model.

Student Practice: Students can build additional models to investigate these concepts on their own.

3 Reinforce and Extend

Learning Styles

Auditory/Verbal

Have students work in pairs. Direct one member of the pair to choose an item from Exercise B and give directions on how to estimate the value of the square root. The second student follows these directions, thinking aloud and orally estimating the value of the square root. Then have the second student choose an item from Exercise B and give directions for the first student.

Calculator

Calculators that find roots higher than 2 often use a [2nd] key, which acts a bit like a shift key. The sequence below indicates how to use the [2nd] key to find the $\sqrt[4]{16}$ with a calculator that offers a $\sqrt[x]{y}$ function.

Enter 16.

Press [2nd].

Press [$\sqrt[x]{y}$].

Enter 4.

Press [=].

Read 2.

Have students practice finding higher roots using these examples.

$\sqrt[3]{125}$	*(5)*	$\sqrt[10]{1024}$	*(2)*
$\sqrt[4]{256}$	*(4)*	$\sqrt[4]{630}$	*(5.01)*
$\sqrt[3]{28}$	*(3.04)*	$\sqrt[8]{256}$	*(2)*
$\sqrt[5]{32}$	*(2)*	$\sqrt[3]{729}$	*(9)*

Remember what the signs mean:
< is read as "is less than."
> is read as "is greater than."

Example 5 $\sqrt{14}$ is between which two integers?

Study the list of square roots:

$$\underset{1}{\sqrt{1}} < \sqrt{2} < \sqrt{3} < \underset{2}{\sqrt{4}} < \sqrt{5} < \sqrt{6} < \sqrt{7} < \sqrt{8} < \underset{3}{\sqrt{9}} <$$

$$\sqrt{10} < \sqrt{11} < \sqrt{12} < \sqrt{13} < \sqrt{14} < \sqrt{15} < \underset{4}{\sqrt{16}}$$

So $\sqrt{14}$ is between 3 and 4.

You can write this in algebra as $3 < \sqrt{14} < 4$.

Exercise A Find the length of a side of each figure.

1.

Area = 36 6

2.

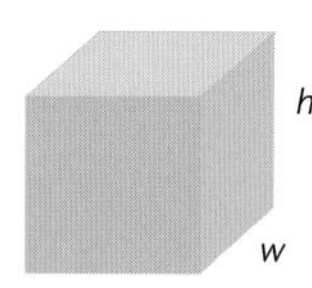

Volume = 27 3

Estimation Activity

Estimate: Find the square root of a number that is not a perfect square.

What is $\sqrt{45}$?

Solution: To estimate a square root, put the square root between the closest perfect square integers above and below the given number.

$6^2 = 36$ and $7^2 = 49$
$\sqrt{36} < \sqrt{45} < \sqrt{49}$ or $6 < \sqrt{45} < 7$
The square root of 49 is closer to 6 than 7.

Exercise B Estimate the value of each square root by finding a whole number greater than and a whole number less than the square root.

3. $\sqrt{15}$ $3 < \sqrt{15} < 4$

4. $\sqrt{24}$ $4 < \sqrt{24} < 5$

5. $\sqrt{7}$ $2 < \sqrt{7} < 3$

6. $\sqrt{48}$ $6 < \sqrt{48} < 7$

7. $\sqrt{83}$ $9 < \sqrt{83} < 10$

8. $\sqrt{105}$ $10 < \sqrt{105} < 11$

Calculator Practice

To find a value of a root more precisely and quickly, use a calculator.

EXAMPLE 6 Find $\sqrt{14}$.

Enter 14
Press $\boxed{\sqrt{\ }}$
Read 3.74166
$\sqrt{14} = 3.74166$

Use the calculator to find 3.74166^2. Because $3.74166^2 = 14.00002$, you know that 3.74166 is a very precise approximation of the square root of 14.

Exercise C Use your calculator to find the square root of each term.

9. $\sqrt{655.36}$ 25.6

10. $\sqrt{103426.56}$ 321.6

11. $\sqrt{3.0625}$ 1.75

12. $\sqrt{6593.44}$ 81.2

Lesson at a Glance

Chapter 2 Lesson 10

Overview This lesson introduces roots and powers in algebraic terms.

Objective

- To simplify expressions containing roots and powers using the associative property of multiplication

Student Pages 54–55

Teacher's Resource Library 

Workbook Activity 22

Activity 22

Alternative Activity 22

1 Warm-Up Activity

Write $\sqrt{x}$, $\sqrt{ab}$, $\sqrt{4}$ and $\sqrt{29}$ on the board. Ask students what is the value of each term. Lead them to conclude that they cannot find a value for the terms that contain variables.

2 Teaching the Lesson

Stress to students that each square has a negative as well as a positive square root. Point out that this is possible because a negative number times a negative number is always a positive number.

Common Error

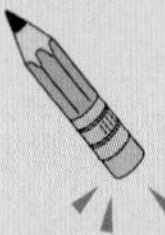

Students may confuse finding the square root of a negative number with a negative square root. Be sure to stress the differences between $\sqrt{16}$, which is not a real number, and -4, which is a square root of 16 and a real number. Encourage students to use multiplication to check powers and roots. $(-4)(-4) = 16$. Remind them that although $(4)(-4) = -16$, the numbers have different signs and therefore do not satisfy the definition of *a number multiplied by itself.*

Lesson 10 More on Powers and Roots

When you use letters as variables, you cannot find roots and powers. You can only write their symbols. Only after you substitute numbers for variables can you evaluate the terms and expressions.

Example 1 y to the fourth power y^4
the fourth root of y $\sqrt[4]{y}$

Example 2 x to the tenth x^{10}
the fifth root of x $\sqrt[5]{x}$

What is the value of y^4 when $y = 2$?
$y^4 = 2^4 = (2)(2)(2)(2) = 16$

What is the value of $\sqrt[4]{y}$ when $y = 16$?
$\sqrt[4]{y} = \sqrt[4]{16} = 2$

Square roots can be negative as well as positive.

$(5)(5) = 25$ $(-5)(-5) = 25$
$\sqrt{25} = 5$ $\sqrt{25} = -5$

Note: $\sqrt{-25}$ is not an integer, because
$5^2 = 25$ and $(-5)^2 = 25$,
so neither 5 nor -5 is a root of $\sqrt{-25}$.

The square root of a negative number is not a real number.

Example 3 $\sqrt{36} = 6$ or -6 because $6^2 = 36$ and $(-6)^2 = 36$

Example 4 $\sqrt{a^2} = a$ or $-a$ because $(a)(a) = a^2$ and $(-a)(-a) = a^2$
Because $(-2)(-2)(-2) = -8$, $\sqrt[3]{-8} = -2$.
It is possible to find cube roots of negative numbers.

Powers	Roots
$(-2a)^2 = (-2a)(-2a) = 4a^2$	$\sqrt[3]{-27} = -3$ because $(-3)(-3)(-3) = -27$
$(-2a)^3 = (-2a)(-2a)(-2a) = -8a^3$	$\sqrt[3]{-x^3} = -x$ because $(-x)(-x)(-x) = -x^3$
$(-5x)^3 = (-5x)(-5x)(-5x) = -125x^3$	$\sqrt[3]{-x^6} = -x^2$ because $(-x^2)(-x^2)(-x^2) = -x^6$

Name Date Period **Workbook Activity 22** Chapter 2, Lesson 10

More on Powers and Roots

Example Simplify the expression: $(-2x)^3$
Step 1 $(-2x)^3 = (-2x)(-2x)(-2x)$
Step 2 Multiply (-2) three times: $(-2)(-2)(-2) = -8$
Step 3 Multiply x three times: $(x)(x)(x) = x^3$
Step 4 Multiply the expanded number and variable: $-8x^3$
Note: $\sqrt{x^2} = x$ or $-x$ $\sqrt[3]{x^3} = x$ $\sqrt[3]{-x^3} = -x$

Directions Simplify each term. You can use a calculator.

1. $(8d)^2$ ______
2. $(-10n)^2$ ______
3. $(-2y)^3$ ______
4. $(3m)^4$ ______

Directions Find each value. Write all the possible roots.

5. $\sqrt{16}$ ______
6. $\sqrt{9}$ ______
7. $\sqrt[3]{8}$ ______
8. $\sqrt[3]{-8}$ ______
9. $\sqrt{k^2}$ ______
10. $\sqrt{100}$ ______
11. $\sqrt[3]{-27}$ ______
12. $\sqrt[3]{-216}$ ______
13. $\sqrt{216}$ ______

Directions Answer the questions to solve the problem.

If a scientist built a machine that could transport people backward in time, then normal time might be represented as a positive number and backward time as a negative number. Suppose you could square or cube backward time.

14. What would be the square of −10 units of backward time? ______
15. What would be the cube of −10 units of backward time? ______

 Algebra

Workbook Activity 22

Name Date Period **Activity 22** Chapter 2, Lesson 10

More on Powers and Roots

Directions Find the value of each expression when $w = 36$, $x = -64$, $y = 5$, and $z = -3$.

1. y^2 ______
2. z^3 ______
3. $\sqrt[3]{x}$ ______
4. $\sqrt{w}$ ______
5. $\sqrt[3]{-x}$ ______
6. $-y^2$ ______
7. z^2 ______
8. y^3 ______
9. $-y^3$ ______

Directions Find the value of each expression when $a = 25$, $b = -27$, $c = 64$, and $d = -2$.

10. d^2 ______
11. $\sqrt{a}$ ______
12. $\sqrt[3]{b}$ ______
13. $\sqrt{c}$ ______
14. d^3 ______
15. $\sqrt[3]{c}$ ______
16. $\sqrt[3]{-c}$ ______
17. d^4 ______
18. d^5 ______

Directions Solve the problems.

19. An exploration team on Mars maps an Earth colony as a perfect square on the Martian surface. Its area is 64 square km or 24.7 square miles. Find the approximate length of one side of the square in miles by estimating whole number roots from the number line. Then fill in the blanks.

$\overset{3}{\sqrt{9}} < \sqrt{10} < \sqrt{11} < \sqrt{12} < \sqrt{13} < \sqrt{14} < \sqrt{15} < \overset{4}{\sqrt{16}} < \sqrt{17} < \sqrt{18} < \sqrt{19} < \sqrt{20} < \sqrt{21} < \sqrt{22} < \sqrt{23} < \sqrt{24} < \overset{5}{\sqrt{25}} < \sqrt{26}$

One side of the square is between ______ and ______ miles long.

20. Tara has 10 building blocks of equal size. She lines them up, single file and touching, on a shelf that is 31 cm long. If the volume of a block is 27 cm^3, will she have enough room on the shelf to add an eleventh block? Explain your answer.

______

 Algebra

Activity 22

Exercise A Find each value.

1. $\sqrt{49}$ 7 and −7
2. $\sqrt{a^4}$ a^2 or $-a^2$
3. $\sqrt{b^6}$ b^3 or $-b^3$
4. $\sqrt{81}$ 9 and −9
5. $\sqrt[3]{-8}$ −2
6. $\sqrt[3]{64}$ 4
7. $\sqrt[3]{-x^6}$ $-x^2$
8. $\sqrt[3]{-y^9}$ y^3

Exercise B Find the value of each expression when $a = 8, b = 16$, and $c = 64$.

9. $\sqrt{c}$ 8 and −8
10. $\sqrt[3]{a}$ 2
11. $\sqrt[4]{b}$ 2 and −2
12. $\sqrt[3]{c}$ 4
13. $\sqrt{b}$ 4 and −4
14. $\sqrt[5]{c}$ 2.29739671

Use your calculator to simplify $(-3m)^4$.
First, think of this problem in terms of expanded notation:

$$(-3m)^4 = (-3m)(-3m)(-3m)(-3m)$$

Notice we're multiplying −3 four times. Then use your calculator.

EXAMPLE 5 Simplify $(-3m)^4$.

Enter 3 [+/−] [×] 3 [+/−] [×] 3 [+/−] [×] 3 [+/−]

Press [=]

The display reads 81.

You know that $(m)(m)(m)(m) = m^4$

Therefore, $(-3m)^4 = 81m^4$

Exercise C Use your calculator to simplify each term.

15. $(-5x)^3$
16. $(2y)^5$
17. $(-4m)^4$
18. $(-8g)^3$
19. $(16w)^2$
20. $(5z)^4$
21. $(-3n)^5$
22. $(4t)^2$
23. $(-3v)^6$
24. $(-2x)^3$
25. $(-6a)^4$

15. $-125x^3$
16. $32y^5$
17. $256m^4$
18. $-512g^3$
19. $256w^2$
20. $625z^4$
21. $-243n^5$
22. $16t^2$
23. $729v^6$
24. $-8x^3$
25. $1{,}296a^4$

MANIPULATIVES

M Simplifying Roots

Materials: Pattern Blocks

Group Practice: Stack shapes to build powers. Remind students that $\sqrt{\ }$ means 2 equal factors, $\sqrt[3]{\ }$ means 3 equal factors, etc. To simplify $\sqrt{b^6}$, b^6 must be split into 2 equal factors, i.e., 2 stacks of 3 b shapes. Thus, each equal factor, b^3, is a root. Do several more examples having students use shapes to build models and find roots.

Student Practice: Have students solve Exercise A, Problems 2, 3, and 8 using shapes. Provide students with several more examples to practice on their own.

3 Reinforce and Extend

LEARNING STYLES

Interpersonal/ Group Learning

Ask pairs of students to decide on an answer to the following:

What is the sign of $(-a)^n$ when n is an odd number? when n is an even number?

Invite volunteers to share their reasoning with the class.

CALCULATOR

Calculators that find powers higher than 2 often have a [y^x] key, which eliminates the need for repeated multiplication. The sequence below indicates how to use the [y^x] key to find 23^3.

Enter 23.

Press [y^x].

Press 3.

Press [=].

Read 12,167.

Have students practice finding higher powers using these examples.

-6^3	*(−216)*	21^4	*(194481)*
4^5	*(1024)*	12^3	*(1728)*
7^3	*(343)*	2^{13}	*(8192)*

Lesson at a Glance

Chapter 2 Lesson 11

Overview This lesson presents the order of operations to be used in expressions.

Objectives

- To evaluate complex expressions following the order of operations
- To use the order of operations to simplify complex expressions

Student Pages 56–57

Teacher's Resource Library 

Workbook Activities 23–24

Activity 23

Alternative Activity 23

1 Warm-Up Activity

Ask students to calculate the value of $3 \cdot 6 + 2$. Record their responses on the board. Ask them to explain how they evaluated the expression. Lead students to recognize the order in which terms are added or multiplied makes a difference in the result.
[$(3 \cdot 6) + 2 = 20$; $3 \cdot (6 + 2) = 24$]

2 Teaching the Lesson

Ask a volunteer to review for the class the commutative and associative properties of addition and multiplication. Remind students that with these operations, order does *not* make a difference. Make sure students understand that when several operations are involved, the order of operations *does* make a difference.

Lesson 11 Order of Operations

If you have an expression with a number of different operations, there are rules to help you decide the order in which the operations must be performed.

Example 1 $3 + (4)(5) = ■$

Should you add or multiply first?

If you add first:	If you multiply first:
$3 + (4)(5)$	$3 + (4)(5)$
$7 \quad (5)$	$3 + 20$
35	23

The correct answer is 23. The only way to get 23 from $3 + (4)(5)$ is to multiply first, and then add 3; $3 + 20 = 23$.

Order of Operations

1. If grouping symbols such as parentheses are used, perform the operations inside the grouping symbols first.
2. Evaluate powers.
3. Multiply and divide in order from left to right.
4. Add and subtract in order from left to right.

Example 2 $3^2 \bullet 2$

Step 1 Square 3.
$3^2 = (3)(3) = 9$

Step 2 Multiply by 2.
$9 \bullet 2 = 18$
$3^2 \bullet 2 = 18$

Example 3 $(2^2 \div 2) \bullet x$

Step 1 Square 2.
$2^2 = (2)(2) = 4$

Step 2 Divide by 2.
$4 \div 2 = 2$

Step 3 Multiply by x.
$2 \bullet x = 2x$
$(2^2 \div 2) \bullet x = 2x$

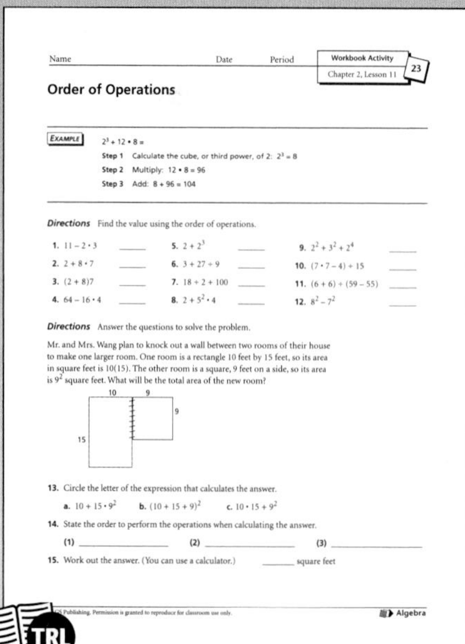

Name Date Period | Workbook Activity 23 | Chapter 2, Lesson 11

Order of Operations

Example $2^3 + 12 \bullet 8 =$

Step 1 Calculate the cube, or third power, of 2: $2^3 = 8$
Step 2 Multiply: $12 \bullet 8 = 96$
Step 3 Add: $8 + 96 = 104$

Directions Find the value using the order of operations.

1. $11 - 2 \cdot 3$ ____	5. $2 + 2^3$ ____	9. $2^2 + 3^2 + 2^4$ ____
2. $2 + 8 \cdot 7$ ____	6. $3 + 27 \div 9$ ____	10. $(7 \cdot 7 - 4) \div 15$ ____
3. $(2 + 8)7$ ____	7. $18 \div 2 + 100$ ____	11. $(6 + 6) \div (59 - 55)$ ____
4. $64 - 16 \cdot 4$ ____	8. $2 + 5^2 \cdot 4$ ____	12. $8^2 - 7^2$ ____

Directions Answer the questions to solve the problem.

Mr. and Mrs. Wang plan to knock out a wall between two rooms of their house to make one larger room. One room is a rectangle 10 feet by 15 feet, so its area in square feet is 10(15). The other room is a square, 9 feet on a side, so its area is 9^2 square feet. What will be the total area of the new room?

13. Circle the letter of the expression that calculates the answer.
 a. $10 + 15 \cdot 9^2$ b. $(10 + 15 + 9)^2$ c. $10 \cdot 15 + 9^2$
14. State the order to perform the operations when calculating the answer.
 (1) ________ (2) ________ (3) ________
15. Work out the answer. (You can use a calculator.) ______ square feet

 Algebra

Workbook Activity 23

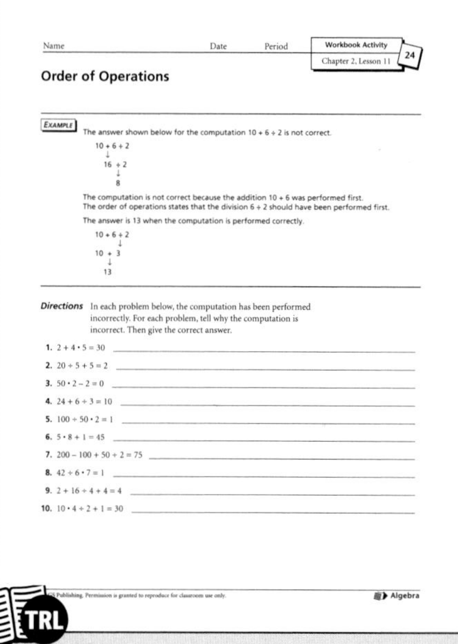

Name Date Period | Workbook Activity 24 | Chapter 2, Lesson 11

Order of Operations

Example The answer shown below for the computation $10 + 6 \div 2$ is not correct.

$10 + 6 \div 2$
↓
$16 \div 2$
↓
8

The computation is not correct because the addition $10 + 6$ was performed first.
The order of operations states that the division $6 \div 2$ should have been performed first.

The answer is 13 when the computation is performed correctly.

$10 + 6 \div 2$
↓
$10 + 3$
↓
13

Directions In each problem below, the computation has been performed incorrectly. For each problem, tell why the computation is incorrect. Then give the correct answer.

1. $2 + 4 \cdot 5 = 30$ ________
2. $20 \div 5 + 5 = 2$ ________
3. $50 \cdot 2 - 2 = 0$ ________
4. $24 + 6 \div 3 = 10$ ________
5. $100 \div 50 \cdot 2 = 1$ ________
6. $5 \cdot 8 + 1 = 45$ ________
7. $200 - 100 + 50 \div 2 = 75$ ________
8. $42 \div 6 \cdot 7 = 1$ ________
9. $2 + 16 \div 4 + 4 = 4$ ________
10. $10 \cdot 4 \div 2 + 1 = 30$ ________

 Algebra

Workbook Activity 24

Exercise A Find the value using the order of operations.

1. $3 - (2)(5)$	-7	**5.** $10 \div (5)(2)$	4	**9.** $10 - (15)(2)$	-20
2. $(3 + 4) \cdot 5$	35	**6.** $82 - 3 \cdot 5$	67	**10.** $6 + (-82) - 3$	-79
3. $5 + 16 \div 4$	9	**7.** $43 - 82 + (-3)$	-42	**11.** $8 + 6 \div 2$	11
4. $(4 + 12) \div 22$	$\frac{8}{11}$	**8.** $6(2 + 4)$	36	**12.** $52 + (6)(2)$	64

Exercise B Use the order of operations to simplify.

13. $10c - 3c(2)$	$4c$	**17.** $25y + (-15y - 3y)$	$7y$	**20.** $5s^3 + 3s^3 + 2s^3$	$10s^3$
14. $(5x + 4x) \div 3$	$3x$	**18.** $(6)(2t) - 4t$	$8t$	**21.** $3z^2 + 2z^2 - z^2$	$4z^2$
15. $8k + 6(k + 2k)$	$26k$	**19.** $4b^2 + (3b)(b)$	$7b^2$	**22.** $7d^2 - (d^2 + 2d^2)$	$4d^2$
16. $8n - 6n + (2n - n)$	$3n$				

PROBLEM SOLVING

Exercise C Solve each problem.

23. Corinne pays \$5.00 for materials to make pillows. She makes 3 pillows and sells 2 for \$10.00 each and 1 for \$5.00. What is Corinne's profit? \$20

24. Martha buys three sets of earrings for \$2.99 each, four bracelets for \$5.99 each, and a bottle of nail polish for \$2.79. How much does she spend? \$35.72

25. John buys a poster for \$5.00. He also buys 3 CDs for \$8.00 each. How much does he spend? \$29.00

Name Date Period **Activity 23** Chapter 2, Lesson 11

Order of Operations

Directions Find the value using the order of operations.

1. $3 \cdot 2 \cdot 4 \cdot 1 + 6$	______	**7.** $8^2 + 0 \cdot 8$	______
2. $60 \div 5 \div 12$	______	**8.** $6^2 - 35$	______
3. $5 + (-13) - 1$	______	**9.** $24 \div 8 - 6$	______
4. $3 \cdot 9 + 2 \cdot 7$	______	**10.** $7 - (8)(5)$	______
5. $36 \div 9 \cdot 2$	______	**11.** $(3^3 - 5 \cdot 3 + 2^2)0$	______
6. $13 + 33 \div 11$	______	**12.** $(7 + 16 - 2)3$	______

Directions Use the order of operations to simplify.

13. $16a - 5a \cdot 3$	______	**18.** $7(3n) - 12n$	______
14. $12k + 5k - 18k \div 6$	______	**19.** $d^2(11 + 2 - 5)$	______
15. $y - (4y + 2 \cdot 2y)$	______	**20.** $d^2 + (17d^2 - 5 \cdot 2d^2)$	______
16. $6(4y + 2 \cdot 2y)$	______	**21.** $16 \cdot 2x + 2 \cdot 5^2(-x)$	______
17. $(21r \div -7 - 2r \cdot 3 \cdot 5)0$	______	**22.** $(y^2 + 2y^2) - 3y^2$	______

Directions Answer the questions to solve the problem.

Dellise has 5 identical boxes to store. Each box is a perfect cube having an edge 4 inches long. How much volume will the 5 boxes take up?

23. Circle the letter of the expression that calculates the answer.

a. $4 \cdot 3 + 5$ **b.** $5 \cdot 4^3$ **c.** $5 \cdot 4^2$

24. State the order to perform the operations when calculating the answer.

a. ______________________

b. ______________________

25. Work out the answer. (You can use a calculator.)

__________ cubic inches

Algebra

TRL

Activity 23

3 Reinforce and Extend

LEARNING STYLES

Interpersonal/ Group Learning

Have students work in small groups. Assign each group a different integer. Direct the groups to write several expressions that meet these requirements:

- Each uses the integer four times.
- Each has a different value.

For example, $2 + 2 - 2 - 2 = 0$, $(2 \div 2) \cdot (2 \div 2) = 1$, and so on. Indicate that students can use any or all of the operations, exponents, parentheses, and brackets. The group that generates the greatest number of expressions, without repeating any values, wins.

LEARNING STYLES

Auditory/Verbal

Invite students to write a verse, rhyme, rap, or anagram to help them remember the order of operations. Two examples are EPMDAS, from the first letters of "exponents, parentheses, multiply, divide, add, subtract," and "Every Person Must Dance At Sunset," which uses the initial letters to make a mnemonic, or memory device.

GROUP PROBLEM SOLVING

Invite students to plan a Fall Festival party for the class. Tell them they have a budget of \$200. Have small groups develop plans for the party, including purchasing refreshments, decorations, and entertainment. Each group should present a formal plan indicating what items they intend to purchase, how many of each item they will buy, and how much each item will cost. Plans should also indicate date, time, and location of the party. Have groups present their plans. Then have the class vote on which plan is the most complete and reasonable.

Lesson at a Glance

Chapter 2 Application

Overview This lesson uses an application of square roots in finding area.

Objective

- To use square roots to find the dimensions of a given area

Student Page 58

Teacher's Resource Library 

Application Activity 2

Everyday Algebra 2

Warm-Up Activity

Hold a class discussion about earthquakes. Ask students to offer any information they know about earthquakes. Invite any student who has experienced an earthquake to share the experience with the class.

Teaching the Lesson

Draw a series of squares on the board:

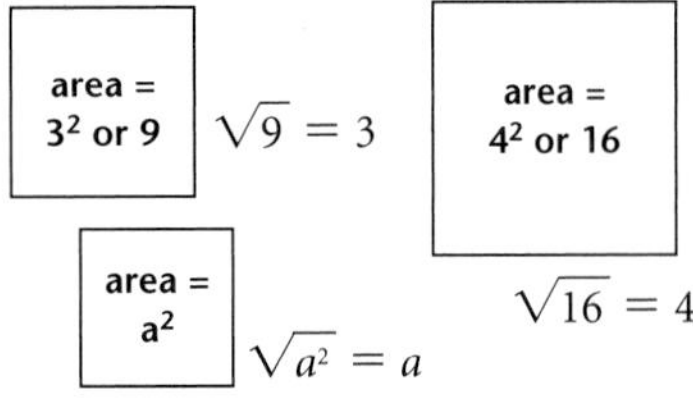

Point out that in each case, the side of the square is equivalent to the square root of the area.

Application 

Using Square Root

A square root is a tool that can be used when exploring the area of a square.

Example 1 Suppose the damage caused by an earthquake is enclosed by an imaginary square that has an area of 10,000 square blocks. In blocks, what is the measure of one side of the square?

Step 1 Write the formula for finding the area of a square. $A = s^2$

Step 2 Substitute 10,000 into the formula. $10{,}000 = s^2$

Step 3 Find the square root to find the length of one side of the square. $\sqrt{10{,}000} = \sqrt{s^2}$

$100 = s$ One side of the square measured 100 blocks.

Exercise Use the information about the damage caused by different earthquakes to answer the following questions.

Earthquake	Area
Earthquake A	100 square blocks
Earthquake B	625 square blocks
Earthquake C	324 square blocks
Earthquake D	1,369 square blocks
Earthquake E	1,024 square blocks

1. If the damage caused by Earthquake A is measured in the shape of a square, what is the measure in blocks of one side of the damaged area? 10 blocks
2. If the damage caused by Earthquake B is measured in the shape of a square, what is the measure in blocks of one side of the damaged area? 25 blocks
3. If the damage caused by Earthquake C is measured in the shape of a square, what is the measure in blocks of one side of the damaged area? 18 blocks
4. If the damage caused by Earthquake D is measured in the shape of a square, what is the measure in blocks of one side of the damaged area? 37 blocks
5. If the damage caused by Earthquake E is measured in the shape of a square, what is the measure in blocks of one side of the damaged area? 32 blocks

58 *Chapter 2 The Rules of Arithmetic*

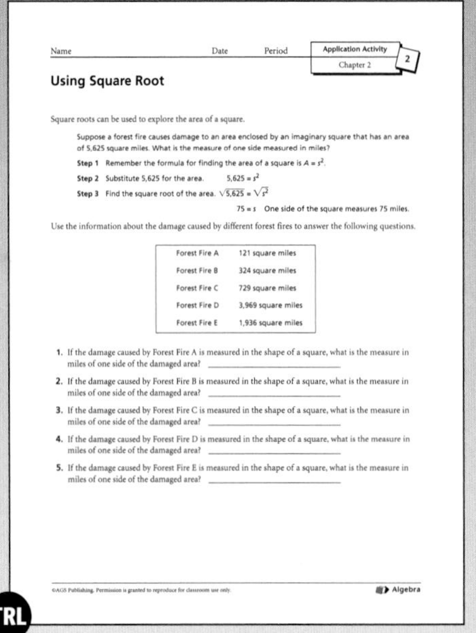

Name Date Period Application Activity 2 Chapter 2

Using Square Root

Square roots can be used to explore the area of a square.

Suppose a forest fire causes damage to an area enclosed by an imaginary square that has an area of 5,625 square miles. What is the measure of one side measured in miles?

Step 1 Remember the formula for finding the area of a square is $A = s^2$.

Step 2 Substitute 5,625 for the area. $5{,}625 = s^2$

Step 3 Find the square root of the area. $\sqrt{5{,}625} = \sqrt{s^2}$

$75 = s$ One side of the square measures 75 miles.

Use the information about the damage caused by different forest fires to answer the following questions.

Forest Fire	Area
Forest Fire A	121 square miles
Forest Fire B	324 square miles
Forest Fire C	729 square miles
Forest Fire D	3,969 square miles
Forest Fire E	1,936 square miles

1. If the damage caused by Forest Fire A is measured in the shape of a square, what is the measure in miles of one side of the damaged area? ______
2. If the damage caused by Forest Fire B is measured in the shape of a square, what is the measure in miles of one side of the damaged area? ______
3. If the damage caused by Forest Fire C is measured in the shape of a square, what is the measure in miles of one side of the damaged area? ______
4. If the damage caused by Forest Fire D is measured in the shape of a square, what is the measure in miles of one side of the damaged area? ______
5. If the damage caused by Forest Fire E is measured in the shape of a square, what is the measure in miles of one side of the damaged area? ______

 Algebra

TRL

Application Activity 2

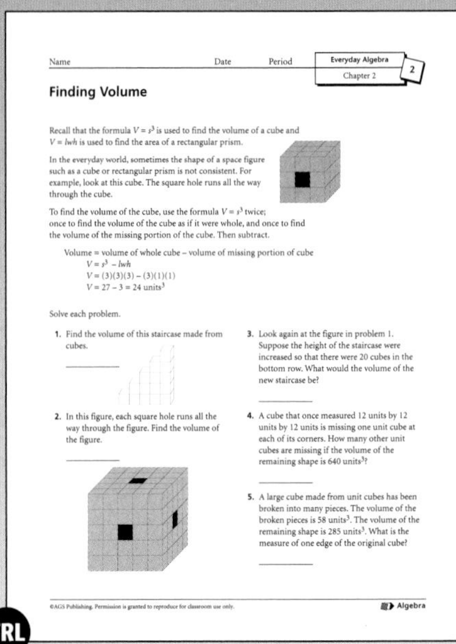

Name Date Period Everyday Algebra 2 Chapter 2

Finding Volume

Recall that the formula $V = s^3$ is used to find the volume of a cube and $V = lwh$ is used to find the area of a rectangular prism.

In the everyday world, sometimes the shape of a space figure such as a cube or rectangular prism is not consistent. For example, look at this cube. The square hole runs all the way through the cube.

To find the volume of the cube, use the formula $V = s^3$ twice; once to find the volume of the cube as if it were whole, and once to find the volume of the missing portion of the cube. Then subtract.

Volume = volume of whole cube – volume of missing portion of cube

$V = s^3 - lwh$

$V = (3)(3)(3) - (3)(1)(1)$

$V = 27 - 3 = 24$ units^3

Solve each problem.

1. Find the volume of this staircase made from cubes. ______
2. In this figure, each square hole runs all the way through the figure. Find the volume of the figure. ______
3. Look again at the figure in problem 1. Suppose the height of the staircase were increased so that there were 20 cubes in the bottom row. What would the volume of the new staircase be? ______
4. A cube that once measured 12 units by 12 units by 12 units is missing one unit cube at each of its corners. How many other unit cubes are missing if the volume of the remaining shape is 640 units^3? ______
5. A large cube made from unit cubes has been broken into many pieces. The volume of the broken pieces is 58 units^3. The volume of the remaining shape is 285 units^3. What is the measure of one edge of the original cube? ______

 Algebra

TRL

Everyday Algebra 2

Chapter 2 REVIEW

Write the letter of the correct answer.

1. How would the product of $(5n)(3y)$ be rewritten using the commutative property of multiplication? A

A $(3y)(5n)$ **C** $(8y)(8n)$
B $8yn$ **D** $3yn$

2. Using the associative property of addition, what would be two equal ways to write the expression $3x + 4w + z$ with parentheses? D

A $z(3x + 4w) = 3x + (4w + z)$
C $3(x + 4)w + 4z = 7x + (7w + 7z)$
B $3x + 4(w + z) = (3x + 4)(w + z)$
D $(3x + 4w) + z = 3x + (4w + z)$

3. Find the product of $7(4 \cdot 5) = (7 \cdot 4)5$. Remember to multiply the factors in the parentheses first. C

A $120 = 120$ **C** $140 = 140$
B $140 = 120$ **D** $160 = 140$

4. Find the value of $\sqrt[3]{-27}$. C

A 3 **C** -3
B 9 **D** 18

5. Find the value of 7^2. B

A 2^7 **C** -49
B 49 **D** 14

6. Simplify the expression $6 + (-5)^2 - 4$. C

A -8 **C** 27
B 12 **D** -27

7. Simplify the expression $3(9n + 3n) + n$ using the order of operations. A

A $37n$ **C** $13n$
B $27n$ **D** $16n$

3 Reinforce and Extend

IN THE COMMUNITY

Have small groups of students find out whether earthquakes have occurred in or near their community. Suggest they check with local historical societies, weather forecasting stations, and state departments of conservation or geology. Have the groups prepare an "Earthquake Report" for the evening news. Reports should identify the location of the closest earthquakes and show their date, location, and magnitude.

Chapter 2 Review

Each set of problems in the Chapter Review includes an example and solution to illustrate the concept. Use the given examples for reteaching the material in Chapter 2. For additional practice, refer to the Supplementary Problems for Chapter 2 (pages 408–409).

Chapter 2 Mastery Test 

The Teacher's Resource Library includes parallel forms of the Chapter 2 Mastery Test. The difficulty level of the two forms is equivalent. You may wish to use one form as a pretest and the other form as a posttest.

Name Date Period **Mastery Test A, Page 1** Chapter 2

Chapter 2 Mastery Test A

Directions Circle the letter of the correct answer.

1. Find the equivalent of $p(q - r)$.
A $(p)(q) - (r)$ **C** $(p)(q)(r)$
B $(pq)(-r)$ **D** $(p)(q) - (p)(r)$

2. Solve for m. $9 + m = 0$
A -9 **C** 9
B 0 **D** $\frac{1}{9}$

3. Find the reciprocal of $\frac{x}{3}$.
A $\frac{3}{x}$ **C** $\frac{x}{1}$
B $\frac{1}{x}$ **D** $\frac{1n}{3}$

4. Simplify $(2r)^2$.
A $2^2 + r^2$ **C** $4r^2$
B $4r$ **D** 16

5. Simplify $2 + (-4)^2 - 10$.
A -6 **C** 258
B 8 **D** 28

Directions Each expression is an example of a property. Choose the letter of the most correct response. A response may be used more than once.

6. $(1 + 9) + 4 = 1 + (9 + 4)$ ____
7. $3 + (-7) = -7 + (+3)$ ____
8. $12(3 \cdot 4) = (12 \cdot 3)4$ ____
9. $8m + 5n = 5n + 8m$ ____
10. $[(25 \cdot 20)50] = [25(20 \cdot 50)]$ ____

a. commutative property of addition
b. associative property of multiplication
c. commutative property of multiplication
d. distributive property of multiplication
e. associative property of addition

 Algebra

Name Date Period **Mastery Test A, Page 2** Chapter 2

Chapter 2 Mastery Test A, continued

Directions Find each product.

11. $4(2 \cdot 8)$ ____________ **12.** $12[-p + (-r)]$ ____________

Directions Factor each expression.

13. $6c + 6d$ ____________ **14.** $g^2h + j^3h$ ____________

Directions What missing number or variable makes each statement true?

15. $0 = 5 - ■$ ______ **17.** $(1)(g) = (■)$ ______
16. $(-1)(■) = -1$ ______

Directions Write the reciprocal of each term.

18. -2 ________
19. b^4 ________
20. $-m$ ________

Directions Simplify.

21. $(-2m)^3$ ________
22. $(100z)^2$ ________

Directions Simplify each expression using the order of operations.

23. $12e - 6e(3)$ ________
24. $5(a - 3a) + a$ ________
25. $(280z) + (120z)(2)$ ________

 Algebra

TRL TRL

Chapter 2 Mastery Test A

ALTERNATIVE ASSESSMENT

Alternative Assessment items correlate with student Goals for Learning at the beginning of this chapter.

■ **To recognize the commutative property of addition and multiplication**
Have students decide if the following problems are examples of the commutative property of addition or multiplication by answering yes or no.

$3x + 3y = 3y + 2x$ *(no)*

$15x \cdot 4y = 4y \cdot 15x$ *(yes)*

$7 + 8 + 9 + 10 = 8 + 10 + 7 + 9$ *(yes)*

$n + 4 + m + p = 4mnp$ *(no)*

$2s \cdot 4s = 4s \cdot 2s$ *(yes)*

■ **To understand the associative property of addition and multiplication**
Have students decide if the following problems are examples of the associative property of addition or multiplication by answering *yes* or *no*.

$2x + (3y + 4z) = (2x + 3y) + 4z$ *(yes)*

$(5x \cdot 4y)(9 \cdot 15) = 5x(4y\, 9 \cdot 15)$ *(yes)*

$(10 + 12) + (15 + 21) = (10 + 15) + (12 + 21)$ *(yes)*

$9(s \cdot t \cdot u \cdot v) = s(9t \cdot u \cdot v)$ *(yes)*

$1005 \cdot 959 \cdot x \cdot y \cdot z = 959(x \cdot y \cdot z) + 1005$ *(no)*

■ **To understand the distributive property and factoring**
Have students work in groups to make their own problems illustrating the distributive property and factoring. Have groups present their problems to the class and explain how they came up with the problems.

■ **To recognize the properties of the numbers 0 and 1**
Have students use simple manipulatives such as toothpicks to explain what happens to any number multiplied by 0 and what happens to any number multiplied by 1. *(Manipulatives should "disappear" when multiplied by 0. Manipulatives should show no change when multiplied by 1.)*

Chapter 2 REVIEW - continued

Rewrite each sum using the commutative property of addition.

Example: $s + 14$ Solution: $14 + s$

8. $m + 8$ $8 + m$
9. $3x + b$ $b + 3x$
10. $2p + 11$ $11 + 2p$
11. $14g + 8a$ $8a + 14g$

Write each expression with parentheses in two equal ways, using the associative property of addition.

Example: $a + b + c$ Solution: $(a + b) + c = a + (b + c)$

12. $x + y + z$
13. $h + t + s$
14. $7r + f + 3c$
15. $2m + 6n + s$
16. $d + 6c + p$
17. $4b + x + 2$

12. $(x + y) + z = x + (y + z)$
13. $(h + t) + s = h + (t + s)$
14. $(7r + f) + 3c = 7r + (f + 3c)$
15. $(2m + 6n) + s = 2m + (6n + s)$
16. $(d + 6c) + p = d + (6c + p)$
17. $(4b + x) + 2 = 4b + (x + 2)$
18. $120 = 120$
19. $100 = 100$
20. $1{,}000 = 1{,}000$

Copy the problems. Find each product. Remember to multiply the factors in the parentheses first.

Example: $4(3 \cdot 2) = (4 \cdot 3)2$ Solution: $4(6) = 12(2)$
$24 = 24$

18. $4(6 \cdot 5) = (4 \cdot 6)5$
19. $25(2 \cdot 2) = (25 \cdot 2)2$
20. $(10 \cdot 4)25 = 10(4 \cdot 25)$

Use the distributive property to multiply.

Example: $3(a + b)$ Solution: $3a + 3b$

21. $6(m + n)$ $6m + 6n$
22. $-5(d + e)$ $-5d + (-5e)$
23. $2(-x + z)$ $-2x + 2z$
24. $-4(r + b)$ $-4r + (-4b)$
25. $7[-h + (-p)]$ $-7h + (-7p)$
26. $4[-p + (-r)]$ $-4p + (-4r)$

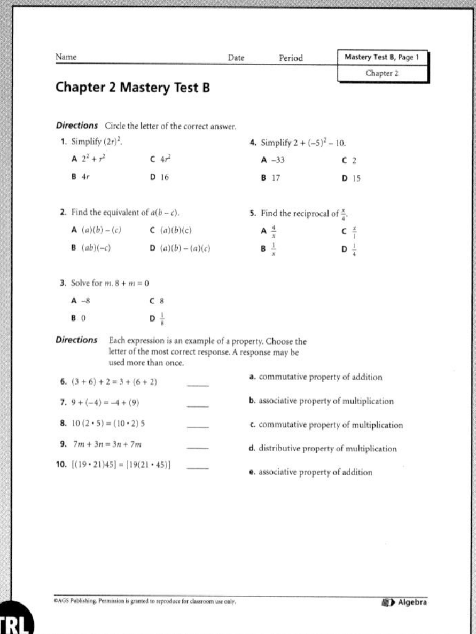

Name Date Period | Mastery Test B, Page 1 | Chapter 2

Chapter 2 Mastery Test B

Directions Circle the letter of the correct answer.

1. Simplify $(2r)^2$.
   A $2^2 + r^2$ C $4r^2$
   B $4r$ D 16

2. Find the equivalent of $a(b - c)$.
   A $(a)(b) - (c)$ C $(a)(b)(c)$
   B $(ab)(-c)$ D $(a)(b) - (a)(c)$

3. Solve for m. $8 + m = 0$
   A -8 C 8
   B 0 D $\frac{1}{8}$

4. Simplify $2 + (-5)^2 - 10$.
   A -33 C 2
   B 17 D 15

5. Find the reciprocal of $\frac{x}{4}$.
   A $\frac{4}{x}$ C $\frac{x}{1}$
   B $\frac{1}{x}$ D $\frac{1}{4}$

Directions Each expression is an example of a property. Choose the letter of the most correct response. A response may be used more than once.

6. $(3 + 6) + 2 = 3 + (6 + 2)$ ____
7. $9 + (-4) = -4 + (9)$ ____
8. $10\,(2 \cdot 5) = (10 \cdot 2)\,5$ ____
9. $7m + 3n = 3n + 7m$ ____
10. $[(19 \cdot 21)45] = [19(21 \cdot 45)]$ ____

a. commutative property of addition
b. associative property of multiplication
c. commutative property of multiplication
d. distributive property of multiplication
e. associative property of addition

 Algebra

TRL

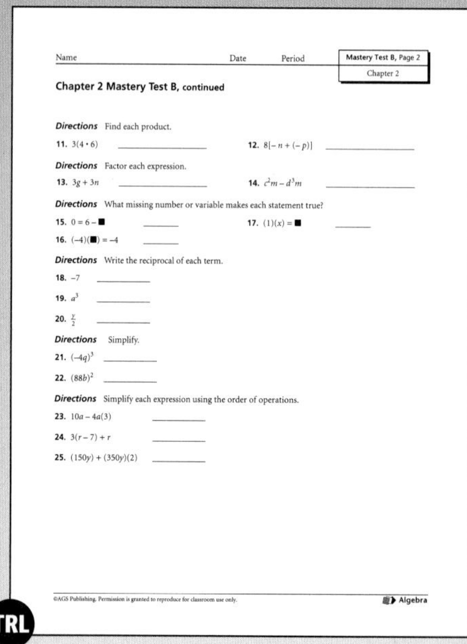

Name Date Period | Mastery Test B, Page 2 | Chapter 2

Chapter 2 Mastery Test B, continued

Directions Find each product.

11. $3(4 \cdot 6)$ ________
12. $8[-n + (-p)]$ ________

Directions Factor each expression.

13. $3g + 3n$ ________
14. $c^2m - d^3m$ ________

Directions What missing number or variable makes each statement true?

15. $0 = 6 - ■$ ____
16. $(-4)(■) = -4$ ____
17. $(1)(x) = ■$ ____

Directions Write the reciprocal of each term.

18. -7 ____
19. a^3 ____
20. $\frac{y}{2}$ ____

Directions Simplify.

21. $(-4q)^3$ ____
22. $(88b)^2$ ____

Directions Simplify each expression using the order of operations.

23. $10a - 4a(3)$ ____
24. $3(r - 7) + r$ ____
25. $(150y) + (350y)(2)$ ____

 Algebra

TRL

Chapter 2 Mastery Test B

Use the distributive property to factor each expression.

Example: $3x + 3y$ Solution: $3(x + y)$

27. $5n + 5s$ $5(n + s)$

28. $4x - 4v$ $4(x - v)$

29. $2b + 3b$ $b(2 + 3)$

30. $xg^3 - xr^2$ $x(g^3 - r^2)$

Copy and fill in the missing number or letter.

Example: $6 + ■ = 0$ Solution: $6 + (-6) = 0$

31. $8 + ■ = 0$ -8

32. $6 - ■ = 0$ 6

33. $w + ■ = 0$ $-w$

34. $-y^3 + ■ = 0$ y^3

35. $-5 + ■ = 0$ 5

36. $n^2 + ■ = 0$ $-n^2$

What is the reciprocal of each term?

Example: 4 Solution: $\frac{1}{4}$

37. $\frac{1}{8}$ 8

38. x^3 $\frac{1}{x^3}$

39. $\frac{1}{c}$ c

40. a^2 $\frac{1}{a^2}$

Find each value.

Example: 5^2 Solution: $(5)(5) = 25$

41. $\sqrt{64}$ 8 and -8

42. $\sqrt[3]{x^3}$ x

43. 6^3 216

44. 10^3 1,000

Simplify each term.

Example: $(-4x)^2$ Solution: $(-4x)(-4x) = 16x^2$

45. $(-3y)^3$ $-27y^3$

46. $(2c)^5$ $32c^5$

47. $(-2m)^4$ $16m^4$

48. $(4g)^3$ $64g^3$

49. $(7j)^2$ $49j^2$

50. $(-5z)^5$ $-3{,}125z^5$

Test-Taking Tip

When you review your notes to prepare for an exam, use a marker to highlight key words and example problems.

Alternative Assessment, continued

- **To identify and use powers and roots of numbers**
Have students show mathematically the difference between "6 to the third power" and "6 times 3" and also the difference between the "cube root of 729" and "729 divided by 3" *($6 \cdot 6 \cdot 6$ (or 6^3) = 216 vs. $6 \cdot 3 = 18$; $\sqrt[3]{729} = 9$ vs. $729 \div 3 = 243$)*

- **To discover and use the order of operations making calculations**
Have students create a jingle, rhyme, or other memory jogger to help them remember the rules of order of operations. *(A common mnemonic device is, "Please excuse my dear Aunt Sally," where please = parentheses; excuse = exponents; my = multiplication; dear = division; aunt = addition; and Sally = subtraction.)*

Chapter

Planning Guide

Linear Equations with One Variable

		Student Text Lesson: Student Pages	Vocabulary	Practice Exercises	Solutions Key
Lesson 1	Writing Equations	64–65	✔	✔	✔
Lesson 2	Solving Equations: $x - b = c$	66–67		✔	✔
Lesson 3	Solving Equations: $x + b = c$	68–69		✔	✔
Lesson 4	Solving Multiplication Equations	70–71		✔	✔
Lesson 5	Solving Equations with Fractions	72–73		✔	✔
Lesson 6	Solving Equations—More Than One Step	74–75		✔	✔
Lesson 7	Equations Without Numbers	76–77	✔	✔	✔
Lesson 8	Formulas	78–79		✔	✔
Lesson 9	The Pythagorean Theorem	80–83	✔	✔	✔
Lesson 10	Inequalities on the Number Line	84–87	✔	✔	✔
Lesson 11	Solving Inequalities with One Variable	88–89		✔	✔
Application	Using Equations	90		✔	✔

Chapter Activities

Teacher's Resource Library

Estimation Exercise 3: Estimating the Value of a Variable in an Equation
Application Activity 3: Using Equations
Everyday Algebra 3: Calculating Distances
Community Connection 3: Understanding Pricing

Teacher's Edition

Chapter 3 Project

Assessment Options

Student Text

Chapter 3 Review

Teacher's Resource Library

Chapter 3 Mastery Tests A and B

Student Text Features							Teaching Strategies							Learning Styles						Teacher's Resource Library			
Estimation Activity	Algebra in Your Life	Technology Connection	Writing About Mathematics	Try This	Problem Solving	Calculator Practice	Online Connection	Common Error	Applications Home, Career, Community	Mental Math	Manipulatives	Calculator	Group Problem Solving	Auditory/Verbal	Visual/Spatial	Logical/Mathematical	Body/Kinesthetic	Interpersonal/Group Learning	LEP/ESL	Activities	Alternate Activities	Workbook Activities	Self-Study Guide
			65	65							65				65				65	24	24	25	✔
					67			67			67		67							25	25	26	✔
					69				69		69		69				69			26	26	27	✔
			71					71			71							71	71	27	27	28	✔
					73							73	73							28	28	29	✔
					75			75			75		75							29	29	30	✔
	77							77						77						30	30	31	✔
									79									79		31	31	32	✔
					83	82	83	81			81	82	83				81			32	32	33–34	✔
										85					85			86, 87	87	33	33	35	✔
					89								89		89					34	34	36	✔
									90														✔

Software Options

Skill Track Software

Use the Skill Track Software for *Algebra* for additional reinforcement of this chapter. The software provides multiple-choice assessment items for students to access by computer.

Solutions Key

Use the Solutions Key with this chapter to help students who may need additional assistance. The Solutions Key CD provides solutions for every exercise in the student edition.

Other Resources

Alternative Activities

The Teacher's Resource Library (TRL) contains a set of worksheets written at a second-grade reading level called Alternative Activities. They cover the same content as the regular Activities.

Manipulatives

See the Manipulative activities in this chapter for hands-on modeling of the content. The following TRL pages can also be used:

Manipulatives Master 3 (Sentence Mat)
Algebra Tiles; Unit Cubes

Chapter at a Glance

Chapter 3: Linear Equations with One Variable

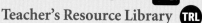

pages 64–93

Lessons

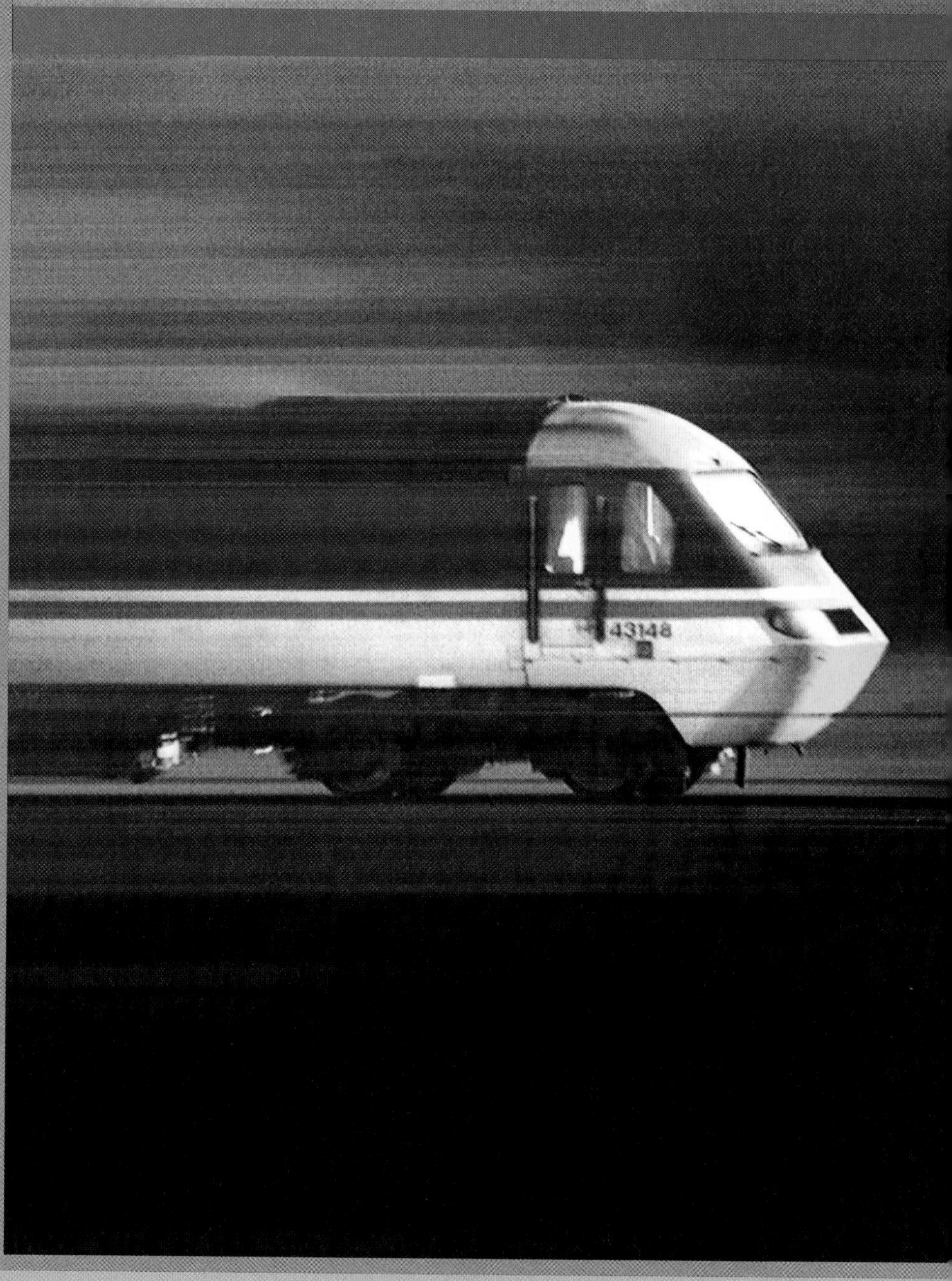

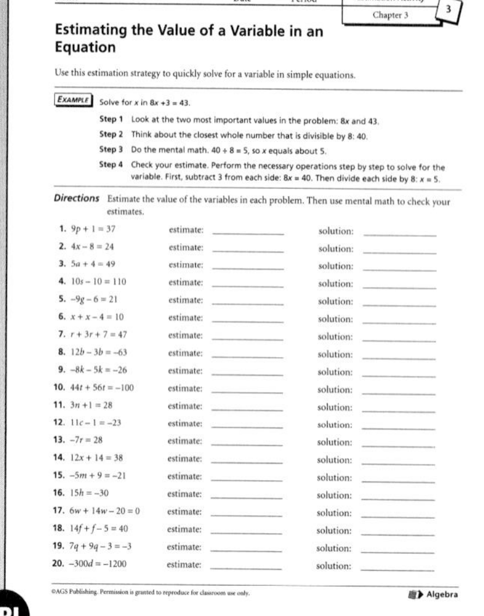

Name Date Period | Estimation Activity Chapter 3 | 3

Estimating the Value of a Variable in an Equation

Use this estimation strategy to quickly solve for a variable in simple equations.

EXAMPLE Solve for x in $8x + 3 = 43$.

Step 1 Look at the two most important values in the problem: $8x$ and 43.

Step 2 Think about the closest whole number that is divisible by 8: 40.

Step 3 Do the mental math. $40 \div 8 = 5$, so x equals about 5.

Step 4 Check your estimate. Perform the necessary operations step by step to solve for the variable. First, subtract 3 from each side: $8x = 40$. Then divide each side by 8: $x = 5$.

Directions Estimate the value of the variables in each problem. Then use mental math to check your estimates.

1. $9p + 1 = 37$ estimate: ______ solution: ______
2. $4x - 8 = 24$ estimate: ______ solution: ______
3. $5a + 4 = 49$ estimate: ______ solution: ______
4. $10s - 10 = 110$ estimate: ______ solution: ______
5. $-9g - 6 = 21$ estimate: ______ solution: ______
6. $x + x - 4 = 10$ estimate: ______ solution: ______
7. $r + 3r + 7 = 47$ estimate: ______ solution: ______
8. $12b - 3b = -63$ estimate: ______ solution: ______
9. $-8k - 5k = -26$ estimate: ______ solution: ______
10. $44t + 56t = -100$ estimate: ______ solution: ______
11. $3n + 1 = 28$ estimate: ______ solution: ______
12. $11c - 1 = -23$ estimate: ______ solution: ______
13. $-7r = 28$ estimate: ______ solution: ______
14. $12x + 14 = 38$ estimate: ______ solution: ______
15. $-5m + 9 = -21$ estimate: ______ solution: ______
16. $15h = -30$ estimate: ______ solution: ______
17. $6w + 14w - 20 = 0$ estimate: ______ solution: ______
18. $14f + f - 5 = 40$ estimate: ______ solution: ______
19. $7q + 9q - 3 = -3$ estimate: ______ solution: ______
20. $-300d = -1200$ estimate: ______ solution: ______

Algebra

TRL

Estimation Exercise 3

Name Date Period | Community Connection Chapter 3 | 3

Understanding Pricing

You can write and use an equation to find the unit price of many different things you buy. For example, in a grocery store or supermarket, one bag of white potatoes may be marked 5 pounds for \$1.00 while another bag may be marked 10 pounds for \$1.75. To determine which bag of potatoes represents the better buy, find the unit price, or cost for 1 pound, of each.

\$1.00 ÷ 5 = \$0.20 The unit price is 20¢ for 1 pound.

\$1.75 ÷ 10 = \$0.175 The unit price is 17.5¢ for 1 pound.

If the potatoes are similar, 10 pounds of potatoes for \$1.75 is a better buy than 5 pounds of potatoes for \$1.00.

Collect data from a supermarket or grocery store to complete items 1–9. For each item, choose two sizes of the same food. For example, you might choose a 16-ounce jar and a 28-ounce jar of *Brand X* peanut butter for item 1.

Type of Food	Brand	Size	Unit Price
1.			
2.			
3.			
4.			
5.			
6.			
7.			
8.			
9.			

10. What would you say to someone who says "The better buy is always the larger size"?

______

Algebra

TRL

Community Connection 3

Chapter

Linear Equations with One Variable

Before the telegraph was invented, train brakemen sometimes walked the tracks to a point ahead of waiting trains. Why? They were looking for trains coming from the other direction that were behind schedule. When the brakeman spotted a late train coming his way, he waved a red flag. The train would then stop and wait at the nearest town until the other train could pass. This prevented speeding trains from crashing into each other. Using algebra, you can calculate the answer to problems involving distance, speed, and time using the formula *distance* = *rate* × *time*. If you know any two of the variables, you can easily solve for the third.

In Chapter 3, you will explore how to write and solve linear equations.

Goals for Learning

- ◆ To write and solve equations
- ◆ To use formulas for perimeter and area to solve problems
- ◆ To use the Pythagorean theorem to solve problems
- ◆ To graph inequalities on the number line
- ◆ To solve inequalities

Introducing the Chapter

Use the information in the chapter opener to help students understand the widespread usefulness of linear equations. One example is solving problems using distance, speed, and time. Another example is the Pythagorean theorem, which can be used to calculate the distance from home plate to second base in baseball.

Chapter Project

Suggest students work in small groups to create a Right Triangle Scrapbook. Have the groups choose one of the following scrapbook themes or an idea of their own.

- A theme of right triangles at play in sports: baseball, kite flying, skateboarding, sailing, etc.
- A ladder theme, showing right triangles formed by ladders, construction cranes, and ladders mounted on fire trucks

Students should work together to identify the right triangle involved and develop problems and data describing the lengths of the sides of the triangle involved. Each team can assign tasks to group members such as researcher, compiler, artist, and recorder.

Teacher's Resource

The AGS Publishing Teaching Strategies in Math Transparencies may be used with this chapter. They add an interactive dimension to expand and enhance the program content.

Career Interest Inventory

The AGS Publishing Harrington-O'Shea Career Decision-Making System-Revised (CDM) may be used with this chapter. Students can use the CDM to explore their interests and identify careers. The CDM defines career areas that are indicated by students' responses on the inventory.

Name ______ Date ______ Period ______ *SELF-STUDY GUIDE*

CHAPTER 3: Linear Equations with One Variable

Goal 3.1 *To write and solve equations*

Date	Assignment	Score
______	1: Read page 64. Complete Exercises A–B on pages 64–65.	______
______	2: Complete Workbook Activity 25.	______
______	3: Read pages 66–67. Complete Exercises A–C on page 67.	______
______	4: Complete Workbook Activity 26.	______
______	5: Read pages 68–69. Complete Exercises A–C on page 69.	______
______	6: Complete Workbook Activity 27.	______
______	7: Read page 70. Complete Exercises A–B on page 71.	______
______	8: Complete Workbook Activity 28.	______
______	9: Read page 72. Complete Exercises A–B on page 73.	______
______	10: Complete Workbook Activity 29.	______
______	11: Read pages 74–75. Complete Exercises A–C on page 74.	______
______	12: Complete Workbook Activity 30.	______
______	13: Read page 76. Complete Exercise A on page 77.	______
______	14: Complete Workbook Activity 31.	______

Comments:

Goal 3.2 *To use formulas for perimeter and area to solve problems*

Date	Assignment	Score
______	15: Read pages 78–79. Complete Exercise A on page 79.	______
______	16: Complete Workbook Activity 32.	______

Comments:

 Algebra

TRL

Name ______ Date ______ Period ______ *SELF-STUDY GUIDE*

CHAPTER 3: Linear Equations with One Variable, continued

Goal 3.3 *To use the Pythagorean theorem to solve problems*

Date	Assignment	Score
______	17: Read pages 80–81. Complete Exercise A on page 81.	______
______	18: Complete Exercise C on page 83.	______
______	19: Read and complete the Calculator Practice on pages 82–83.	______
______	20: Complete Workbook Activities 33 and 34.	______

Goal 3.4 *To graph inequalities on the number line*

Comments:

Date	Assignment	Score
		______

Goal 3.5 *To solve inequalities* 21: Read pages

84–86. Complete Exercises A–C on pages 86–87. ______

______ 22: Complete Workbook Activity 35. ______

Comments:

Date	Assignment	Score
______	23: Read pages 88–89. Complete Exercises A–C on page 89.	______
______	24: Complete Workbook Activity 36.	______
______	25: Read and complete the Application Exercise on page 90.	______
______	26: Complete the Chapter 3 Review on pages 91–93.	______

 Algebra

TRL

Chapter 3 Self-Study Guide

Lesson at a Glance

Chapter 3 Lesson 1

Overview This lesson demonstrates how statements of equality can be written as equations.

Objectives

- To write statements of equality in the form of equations
- To determine whether equations are true for specified values of the variable

Student Pages 64–65

Teacher's Resource Library 

Workbook Activity 25

Activity 24

Alternative Activity 24

Mathematics Vocabulary

equation

1 Warm-Up Activity

Introduce the concept of equations by sharing the following with students: "I'm thinking of a number. Two times this number is 4. What is the number?" Encourage respondents to explain how they found their answer.

2 Teaching the Lesson

Write a statement of equality on the board. Using a "think-aloud" technique, help students translate the statement into an equation. For example:

8 times some number equals 24.
Let some number = x.
8 times x equals 24
Substitute an = sign for "equals."
8 times $x = 24$
Replace "times" with a •.
$8 \cdot x = 24$

Present additional examples, using the statements in Exercise B as guides, and ask volunteers to show the think-aloud process for writing equations.

Lesson 1 Writing Equations

Equation

A mathematical sentence stating that two quantities are equal and written as two expressions separated by an equal sign $(4n + 4n = 8n)$

An algebraic **equation** such as $3n = 15$ is read "3 times some number equals 15." The equation $3n = 15$ is neither true nor false—it is an open statement because the value of the variable n is unknown.

$3n = 15$ is a true statement when $n = 5$;
5 is called the root of the equation.

$3n = 15$ is a false statement when $n \neq 5$,
which is read "n is not equal to 5."

Statements of equality can be written as equations.

EXAMPLE 1 6 times some number equals 18.
Let x be that number.
Solution: $6x = 18$

When working with algebraic equations, remember that any letter of the alphabet can be used to represent a variable

The root of an equation can be found by substituting different numbers for the variable. If the number is the root, the statement is true. If the number is not the root, the statement is false.

EXAMPLE 2 $4x = 20$ $\quad x = 1, 4, 5$
$(4)(1) = 20$ False
$(4)(4) = 20$ False
$(4)(5) = 20$ True

Exercise A Write an equation for each statement. Let x be the variable in the equation.

1. 9 times some number equals 36. $9x = 36$
2. Sixteen times some number plus 3 equals 51. $16x + 3 = 51$
3. Nine times some number minus 18 equals zero. $9x - 18 = 0$

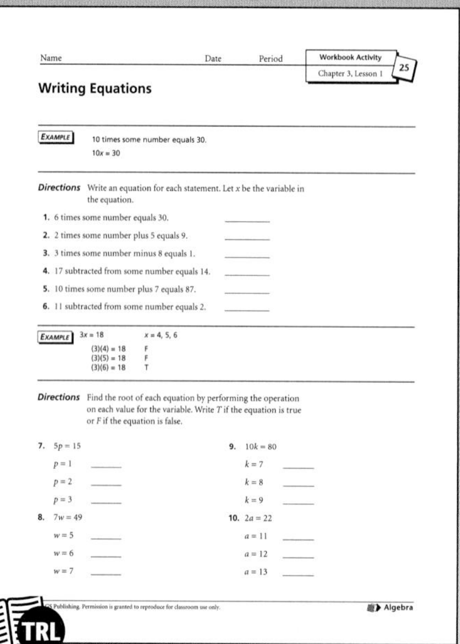

Name Date Period **Workbook Activity 25** Chapter 3, Lesson 1

Writing Equations

EXAMPLE 10 times some number equals 30.
$10x = 30$

Directions Write an equation for each statement. Let x be the variable in the equation.

1. 6 times some number equals 30. ______
2. 2 times some number plus 5 equals 9. ______
3. 3 times some number minus 8 equals 1. ______
4. 17 subtracted from some number equals 14. ______
5. 10 times some number plus 7 equals 87. ______
6. 11 subtracted from some number equals 2. ______

EXAMPLE $3x = 18$ $\quad x = 4, 5, 6$
$(3)(4) = 18$ F
$(3)(5) = 18$ F
$(3)(6) = 18$ T

Directions Find the root of each equation by performing the operation on each value for the variable. Write *T* if the equation is true or *F* if the equation is false.

7. $5p = 15$
   $p = 1$ ______
   $p = 2$ ______
   $p = 3$ ______
8. $7w = 49$
   $w = 5$ ______
   $w = 6$ ______
   $w = 7$ ______
9. $10k = 80$
   $k = 7$ ______
   $k = 8$ ______
   $k = 9$ ______
10. $2a = 22$
   $a = 11$ ______
   $a = 12$ ______
   $a = 13$ ______

 Algebra

Workbook Activity 25

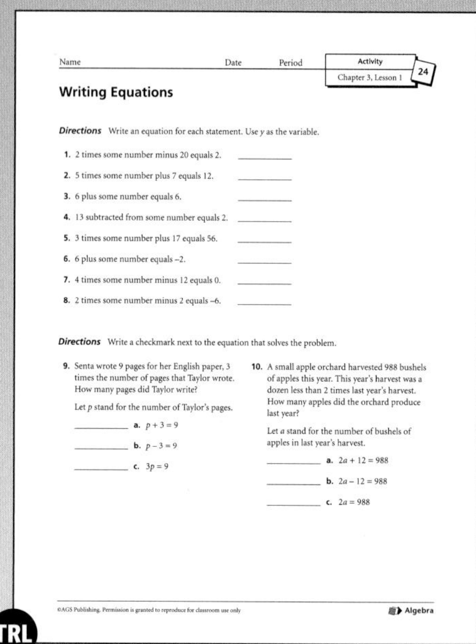

Name Date Period **Activity 24** Chapter 3, Lesson 1

Writing Equations

Directions Write an equation for each statement. Use y as the variable.

1. 2 times some number minus 20 equals 2. ______
2. 5 times some number plus 7 equals 12. ______
3. 6 plus some number equals 6. ______
4. 13 subtracted from some number equals 2. ______
5. 3 times some number plus 17 equals 56. ______
6. 6 plus some number equals –2. ______
7. 4 times some number minus 12 equals 0. ______
8. 2 times some number minus 2 equals –6. ______

Directions Write a checkmark next to the equation that solves the problem.

9. Senta wrote 9 pages for her English paper, 3 times the number of pages that Taylor wrote. How many pages did Taylor write?

   Let p stand for the number of Taylor's pages.

   ______ **a.** $p + 3 = 9$
   ______ **b.** $p - 3 = 9$
   ______ **c.** $3p = 9$

10. A small apple orchard harvested 988 bushels of apples this year. This year's harvest was a dozen less than 2 times last year's harvest. How many apples did the orchard produce last year?

   Let a stand for the number of bushels of apples in last year's harvest.

   ______ **a.** $2a + 12 = 988$
   ______ **b.** $2a - 12 = 988$
   ______ **c.** $2a = 988$

 Algebra

Activity 24

Remember that *equals, is,* and *is equal to* are all terms used for the equal sign.

4. 8 times some number equals 40. $8x = 40$
5. 5 times some number plus three equals 28. $5x + 3 = 28$
6. 2 times some number minus 3 equals 3. $2x - 3 = 3$
7. 3 multiplied by some number is equal to 27. $3x = 27$
8. 7 times some number equals 49. $7x = 49$
9. Ten times some number minus 13 equals 47. $10x - 13 = 47$
10. 8 times some number plus 7 equals 71. $8x + 7 = 71$
11. 6 subtracted from some number is 25. $x - 6 = 25$
12. 14 times some number minus 28 equals 14. $14x - 28 = 14$
13. 4 subtracted from some number is 10. $x - 4 = 10$
14. Four multiplied by some number plus six equals 46. $4x + 6 = 46$

Writing About Mathematics

Write a comparison of a sentence and an equation explaining the parts of each and how they are similar. Then create several sentence problems with their related equations.

Exercise B Find the root of each equation by writing T (true) or F (false) for each value.

15. $2s = 14$ $s = 5, 6, 7, 8$ F, F, T, F
16. $3p = 15$ $p = 2, 3, 4, 5$ F, F, F, T
17. $9m = 63$ $m = 1, 3, 6, 7$ F, F, F, T
18. $8w = 72$ $w = 9, 10, 11, 12$ T, F, F, F
19. $6n = 18$ $n = 1, 2, 3, 4$ F, F, T, F
20. $2s = 30$ $s = 10, 15, 20, 25$ F, T, F, F
21. $5a = 10$ $a = 2, 4, 6, 8$ T, F, F, F
22. $7e = 21$ $e = 1, 3, 5, 7$ F, T, F, F
23. $4y = 16$ $y = 4, 5, 6, 7$ T, F, F, F
24. $3j = 9$ $j = 2, 3, 6, 9$ F, T, F, F
25. $8g = 32$ $g = 2, 3, 4, 5$ F, F, T, F

TRY THIS Use mental math to find a solution to the equation $19 = y - 20$.

Methods will vary; $y = 39$

NOTE: As students complete the items in Exercise A, tell them to assume that any multiplication takes place before addition or subtraction. This will help students avoid misinterpreting statements. For example, item 2 is $16x + 3$, rather than $16(x + 3)$.

Try This

Students may find it easier to solve the problem if they think of the equation in sentence form: "20 subtracted from some number equals 19."

MANIPULATIVES

Modeling Equations

Materials: Algebra Tiles, Unit Cubes, Manipulatives Master 3 (Sentence Mat)

Group Practice: Model equations on the Sentence Mat, changing subtraction to addition of the opposite when necessary. Have students write the symbolic equivalent of each model. To find the root of an equation of the form $ax = b$, model the equation with Algebra Tiles, then replace the unknown pieces with Unit Cube models of the given value of the variable. Show how to evaluate the expression to determine the root.

Student Practice: Instruct students to use Algebra Tiles to model equations in Exercise A, Problems 3, 5, 6, 11, and 13. Have students use Algebra Tiles and Unit Cubes in Exercise B, Problems 15, 16, 19, 21, 23, and 24.

LEARNING STYLES

Visual/Spatial

Distribute multiplication tables 1–10 to students. Have them work in pairs to find the root of each equation in Exercise B. Ask students to write directions explaining how they found the roots using the multiplication table.

3 Reinforce and Extend

LEARNING STYLES

LEP/ESL

ESL students might benefit from writing the items in Exercise B as word statements. Have students work in pairs, one student writing the statement in words, the other reading the statement aloud. Direct partners to change roles once they have written five statements.

Lesson at a Glance

Chapter 3 Lesson 2

Overview This lesson presents the steps necessary for solving equations of the form $x - b = c$.

Objectives

- To solve equations of the form $x - b = c$
- To employ adding opposites as a strategy for solving equations

Student Pages 66–67

Teacher's Resource Library 

Workbook Activity 26

Activity 25

Alternative Activity 25

1 Warm-Up Activity

Write the following on the board:

$$2 + 3 = 5$$
$$4 + 2 + 3 \;\blacksquare\; 5 + 4$$
$$6 + 2 + 3 \;\blacksquare\; 5 + 6$$
$$7 + 2 + 3 \;\blacksquare\; 5 + 7$$

Circle the common element, $2 + 3 \;\blacksquare\; 5$, in the last three statements. Ask students what mathematical sign can replace the ■ in those statements. Have them explain their reasons in their own words.

2 Teaching the Lesson

Review with students the relationship between opposite numbers. Impress upon them that the sum of opposites, such as $3 + (-3)$, is always zero. Write the first example, $n - 17 = 81$, on the overhead projector. Point out that students will have the value of n if they "remove" the "minus 17" from the left side of the equation. Indicate that adding the opposite of -17, $+17$, to the left side of the equation will "remove" the -17 from the left side. Stress to students, however, that to keep the equation true, they will need to add $+17$ to the right side of the equation as well. Show the steps:

$$\begin{aligned} n - 17 &= 81 \\ n - 17 + 17 &= 81 + 17 \\ n + 0 &= 81 + 17 \\ n &= 98 \end{aligned}$$

Lesson 2 Solving Equations: $x - b = c$

Whenever you find the root of an equation, you are solving the equation. Some equations can be solved mentally. For example, to solve $n - 1 = 4$, think "If you subtract 1 from a number, you get 4. What is the number?" Since $5 - 1 = 4$, $n = 5$.

When equations cannot be solved mentally, you can add equal amounts to both sides of an equation to find the root, or value, of the variable.

EXAMPLE 1 Solve $n - 17 = 81$ for n.

Step 1	Write the equation.	$n - 17 = 81$
Step 2	Add 17 to both sides of the equation.	$n - 17 = 81$ $+ 17 = + 17$
Step 3	Simplify.	$n - 17 = 81$ $+ 17 = + 17$ $n = 98$
Step 4	Check.	$98 - 17 = 81$

EXAMPLE 2 Solve $x - 29 = 43$ for x.

Step 1	Write the equation.	$x - 29 = 43$
Step 2	Add 29 to both sides of the equation.	$x - 29 = 43$ $+ 29 = + 29$
Step 3	Simplify.	$x - 29 = 43$ $+ 29 = + 29$ $x = 72$
Step 4	Check.	$72 - 29 = 43$

Subtracting a negative is the same as adding the opposite.

EXAMPLE 3 Solve $g - (-2) = 7$ for x.

Step 1	Rewrite the equation.	$g + 2 = 7$
Step 2	Add (-2) to both sides of the equation.	$g + 2 = 7$ $+ (-2) = + (-2)$
Step 3	Simplify.	$g + 2 = 7$ $+ (-2) = + (-2)$ $g = 5$
Step 4	Check.	$5 - (-2) = 7$

Name Date Period **Workbook Activity 26** Chapter 3, Lesson 2

Solving Equations: $x - b = c$

EXAMPLE Solve $m - 2 = 8$ for m.

Step 1	Write the equation.	$m - 2 = 8$
Step 2	Add 2 to both sides of the equation.	$m - 2 + 2 = 8 + 2$
Step 3	Simplify.	$m = 10$
Step 4	Check.	$10 - 2 = 8$

Directions Solve each equation. Check your answer.

1. $x - 4 = 20$ _____
2. $b - 7 = 1$ _____
3. $n - 2 = 7$ _____
4. $k - 13 = 3$ _____
5. $d - 100 = 100$ _____
6. $c - 11 = 0$ _____
7. $y - 4 = 14$ _____
8. $r - 80 = 20$ _____
9. $w - 8 = 0$ _____

Directions Read the problem and follow the directions.

10. A sports store buys a shipment of catcher's mitts at the beginning of the year. By year's end, the store has sold 100 mitts and has 150 left. How many mitts did the store have at the first of the year?

    Let x stand for the number of catcher's mitts the store had at the beginning of the year: $x - 100 = 150$

    How would you solve this equation? Circle the answer.

    a. Subtract 100 from both sides.
    b. Add 100 to both sides.
    c. Subtract 150 from both sides.

 Algebra

TRL

Workbook Activity 26

Name Date Period **Activity 25** Chapter 3, Lesson 2

Solving Equations: $x - b = c$

Directions Find the integer solution to each equation. Check your answer.

1. $k - (-4) = 6$ _____
2. $x - (-1) = 3$ _____
3. $w - (-11) = 11$ _____
4. $n - (-5) = 9$ _____
5. $d - (-7) = 15$ _____

Directions Find the error in the solution to each equation. Write a sentence or two telling what is wrong and how to correct the error.

6. $a - 5 = 19$
$a - 5 + 5 = 19$
$a = 19$
7. $a - 8 = 3$
$a - 8 + 8 = 3 + 7$
$a = 10$

Directions Solve the problems.

8. Ken counts 6 bus tokens in his desk drawer. If he used 9 tokens for rides this week and bought no new tokens, how many tokens did he have at the beginning of the week?
9. The temperature fell 36°F today. By midnight, it was 20°F. What was the temperature at the start of the day?
10. Chenille is a great golfer, but she loses lots of golf balls. At the end of an 18-hole course, she still had 2 balls after losing 11. How many balls did Chenille have when she started playing?

 Algebra

TRL

Activity 25

Remember b and $-b$ are opposites because they add to zero.

In these examples, each equation was solved by adding the opposite. Whenever you add an opposite, remember to add the opposite to both sides of the equation.

Rule To solve equations of the form $x - b = c$, add b to both sides of the equation.

Exercise A Find the solution for each equation. Check your answer.

1. $x - 7 = 9$ 16
2. $m - 6 = 1$ 7
3. $e - 5 = 6$ 11
4. $y - 2 = 3$ 5
5. $j - 8 = 15$ 23
6. $u - 3 = 0$ 3
7. $p - 12 = 25$ 37
8. $w - 20 = 29$ 49
9. $t - 32 = 15$ 47
10. $a - 14 = 9$ 23
11. $h - 20 = 35$ 55
12. $n - 17 = 19$ 36
13. $d - 22 = 70$ 92
14. $z - 11 = 2$ 13

Exercise B Find the solution for each equation by rewriting the subtraction as addition. Check your answer.

15. $m-(-2)=9$ 7
16. $x-(-3)=2$ −1
17. $m-(-4)=4$ 0
18. $f-(-6)=9$ 3
19. $z-(-8)=2$ −6
20. $j-(-2)=3$ 1

PROBLEM SOLVING

Exercise C Write an equation for each problem. Solve the equation.

21. The price of a CD is reduced by $4.50. If Juanita pays $5.00 for the CD, what was its original price? $9.50
22. Phil pays $16.97 for a computer game. The price was reduced by $4.99. What was the original price? $21.96
23. The price of a shirt is reduced by $11.50. If Jenny pays $9.83 for the shirt, what was its original price? $21.33
24. Melvin pays $2.97 for a paperback book. The price was reduced by $1.50. What was the original price? $4.47
25. Adam wants to know the original price of a bag of popcorn. He could only remember he paid $3.73, which was $2.51 less than the original price. What was the original price? $6.24

COMMON ERROR

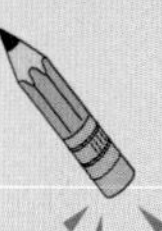

As students begin solving equations of the form $x - b = c$, they may add b to the side of the equation containing the variable but fail to add b to the second side as well. Suggest students follow the steps shown in the text, adding b to both sides of the equation, then complete any addition or subtraction necessary.

MANIPULATIVES

M **Solving Equations: $x - b = c$**

Materials: Algebra Tiles, Manipulatives Master 3 (Sentence Mat)

Group Practice: Model $x - 5 = 3$ and evaluate x mentally. Discuss the Addition Property of Equality. Add +5 to both sides and simplify. Evaluate x again and discuss results. Next, explain that to solve an equation, isolate the variable. To isolate x, use the Zero Rule to remove −5 by adding +5 to both sides of the equation. x equals 8. Check work by rebuilding the original equation, replacing the x piece with 8 positive shapes and evaluating. Repeat with several more equations students generate.

Student Practice: Instruct students to use manipulatives in Exercise A, skipping 8, 9, 11, and 13. Have them use manipulatives to check their work.

3 Reinforce and Extend

GROUP PROBLEM SOLVING

Pose the following situation to students:

Alcott School allows each class a monthly budget of $50 for miscellaneous supplies. The current budget balance for Ms. Limon's class is $24.20. The receipt for the purchases was lost. However, the treasurer remembers buying 20 notebooks to use as math journals and that the notebooks were either $1.29, $1.39, or $1.49. How much did each notebook cost? *($1.29)*

Have students work in small groups to solve the problem and prepare a storyboard or comic strip showing how they found the cost of one notebook. Indicate that the presentation should use equations to describe the problem. Encourage students to assign jobs such as storyboard designer, artist, and writer. One student can be responsible for obtaining the materials needed to produce the storyboard.

Lesson at a Glance

Chapter 3 Lesson 3

Overview This lesson presents the steps necessary for solving equations of the form $x + b = c$.

Objectives

- To solve equations of the form $x + b = c$
- To use the addition of opposites as a strategy for solving equations

Student Pages 68–69

Teacher's Resource Library 

Workbook Activity 27

Activity 26

Alternative Activity 26

1 Warm-Up Activity

Use a number riddle to spark student interest in the topic. For example: "If I add 22 to a number, the result is 33. What is the number?" Record students' responses on the board, acknowledging the correct response.

2 Teaching the Lesson

Remind students that the operation of subtraction is the same as addition of the opposite. Offer the following example:

$$10 - 4 = 10 + (-4) = 6$$

Using the first example as a demonstration, write $a + 24 = 51$ on the overhead projector. Explain step 2 in terms of adding opposites.

$$\begin{aligned} a + 24 &= 51 \\ a + 24 + (-24) &= 51 + (-24) \\ a + 24 - 24 &= 51 - 24 \end{aligned}$$

Ask a volunteer to use the overhead projector and show that $r + 1.4 = 3.7$ can be solved by adding opposites to both sides of the equation.

Lesson 3 Solving Equations: $x + b = c$

Recall that you used the idea of opposites to solve equations of the form $x - b = c$. The same idea of opposites can be used to solve equations of the form $x + b = c$.

Example 1 Solve $a + 24 = 51$ for a.

Step 1 Write the equation. $\quad a + 24 = 51$

Step 2 Subtract 24 from both sides of the equation. This is the same as adding -24 to both sides.

$$\begin{aligned} a + 24 &= 51 \\ -24 &= -24 \end{aligned}$$

Step 3 Simplify.

$$\begin{aligned} a + 24 &= 51 \\ -24 &= -24 \\ a &= 27 \end{aligned}$$

Step 4 Check. $\quad 27 + 24 = 51$

Example 2 Solve $r + 1.4 = 3.7$ for r.

Step 1 Write the equation. $\quad r + 1.4 = 3.7$

Step 2 Subtract 1.4 from both sides of the equation.

$$\begin{aligned} r + 1.4 &= 3.7 \\ -\ 1.4 &= -1.4 \end{aligned}$$

Step 3 Simplify.

$$\begin{aligned} r + 1.4 &= 3.7 \\ -\ 1.4 &= -1.4 \\ r &= 2.3 \end{aligned}$$

Step 4 Check. $\quad 2.3 + 1.4 = 3.7$

> Remember that subtraction is the same as adding the opposite.

Example 3 Solve $k + (-2) = 7$ for k.

Step 1 Rewrite the equation. $\quad k - 2 = 7$

Step 2 Add 2 to both sides of the equation.

$$\begin{aligned} k - 2 &= 7 \\ +2 &= +2 \end{aligned}$$

Step 3 Simplify.

$$\begin{aligned} k - 2 &= 7 \\ +2 &= +2 \\ k &= 9 \end{aligned}$$

Step 4 Check. $\quad 9 + (-2) = 7$

Again, each equation was solved by adding the opposite. Whenever you add an opposite, remember to add the opposite to both sides of the equation.

Name Date Period | Workbook Activity 27 | Chapter 3, Lesson 3

Solving Equations: $x + b = c$

Example Solve $k + 5 = 9$ for k.

Step 1 Write the equation. $\quad k + 5 = 9$

Step 2 Subtract 5 from both sides of the equation. $\quad k + 5 - 5 = 9 - 5$

Step 3 Simplify. $\quad k = 4$

Step 4 Check. $\quad 4 + 5 = 9$

Directions Solve each equation. Check your answer.

1. $w + 3 = 4$
2. $r + 8 = 12$
3. $y + 2 = 7$
4. $c + 1.5 = 4.5$
5. $k + 22 = 60$
6. $d + 9 = 18$
7. $n + 5 = 40$
8. $b + 7 = 14$
9. $x + 32 = 38$

Directions Read the problem and follow the directions.

10. Amy read 17 books over the summer, 11 more than Tim. How many books did Tim read?

    Let r stand for the number of books Tim read over the summer: $r + 11 = 17$

    How would you solve this equation? Circle the answer.

    a. Add 11 to both sides.

    b. Subtract 11 from both sides.

    c. Subtract 17 from both sides.

 Algebra

TRL

Workbook Activity 27

Name Date Period | Activity 26 | Chapter 3, Lesson 3

Solving Equations: $x + b = c$

Directions Find the integer solution to each equation. Check your answer.

1. $a + (-1) = 1$
2. $x + (-9) = 3$
3. $d + (-3) = 0$
4. $n + (-5) = 10$
5. $q + (-4) = 10$
6. $b + (-18) = 40$
7. $m + (-3) = 15$
8. $y + (-14) = 14$
9. $c + (-11) = 6$
10. $j + (-99) = 1$
11. $x + (-999) = 1$

Directions Solve the problems.

12. The Anderson family travels 835 miles on their vacation, 245 miles farther than the Merida family travels on theirs. How far do the Meridas travel on vacation?

13. In a sale, Teresa buys a modem for her computer. The original price was \$189.99 and the discount is \$29.49. How much does Teresa pay?

14. At the trading card fair, Zack trades 9 basketball cards. He trades 5 more cards than Paulo does. How many cards does Paulo trade?

15. Hussein has a camera with a roll of film that takes 36 pictures. He knows that the roll still has 14 pictures left to take. How many photos has Hussein already taken on this roll?

 Algebra

TRL

Activity 26

Remember b and $-b$ are opposites because they add to zero.

Rule To solve equations of the form $x + b = c$, add $-b$ to both sides of the equation.

Exercise A Find the solution for each equation. Check your answer.

1. $x + 4 = 10$ 6
2. $y + 3 = 7$ 4
3. $g + 6 = 9$ 3
4. $j + 2 = 3$ 1
5. $k + 1 = 6$ 5
6. $c + 10 = 15$ 5
7. $e + 12 = 25$ 13
8. $i + 23 = 27$ 4
9. $m + 16 = 30$ 14
10. $v + 32 = 50$ 18
11. $t + 80 = 89$ 9
12. $w + 51 = 67$ 16
13. $b + 17 = 17$ 0
14. $f + 10 = 58$ 48
15. $h + 30 = 37$ 7
16. $s + 3.5 = 3.7$ 0.2
17. $y + 1.6 = 4$ 2.4
18. $t + 9.2 = 15.6$ 6.4
19. $r + 6.9 = 11.3$ 4.4
20. $a + 31.5 = 40$ 8.5

Exercise B Find the solution for each equation. Check your answer.

21. $c + (-3) = 9$ 12
22. $d + (-4) = 2$ 6
23. $a + (-7) = 7$ 14
24. $t + (-5) = 15$ 20
25. $y + (-16) = 29$ 45
26. $p + (-11) = 13$ 24

PROBLEM SOLVING

Exercise C Write an equation for each problem. Solve the equation.

27. Marsha notices the original price of a calculator is \$13.99. The discount is \$5.22. How much does she pay? \$8.77

28. Amphone wants to buy a pair of jeans, which were originally \$29.99. The discount is \$4.75. How much do the jeans cost? \$25.24

29. Gary buys a CD player that was originally \$99.99. The discount is \$27.99. What is the sale price? \$72.00

30. Karim notices the original price of a computer is \$1,300.00. The discount is \$275.00. How much does he pay? \$1,025.00

MANIPULATIVES

Solving Equations: $x + b = c$

Materials: Algebra Tiles, Manipulatives Master 3 (Sentence Mat)

Group Practice: Model $x + 5 = 3$ and evaluate x mentally. Explain that to solve an equation, isolate the variable. To isolate x, use the Zero Rule to remove $+5$ by subtracting it from both sides of the equation. x equals -2. Check work by rebuilding the original equation, replacing the x piece with shapes and evaluating. Repeat with equations students generate.

Student Practice: Instruct students to use manipulatives in Exercise A, Problems 1–7 and Exercise B, Problems 21–24.

3 Reinforce and Extend

LEARNING STYLES

Body/Kinesthetic

Have pairs of students use graph paper to develop a number line from 0 to 50. Then have students take turns using the number line to demonstrate the solutions for equations 1–10 in Exercise A. For example, to demonstrate $x + 4 = 10$, students can place a mark at 10, then count out -4 along the number line, finishing at 6.

GROUP PROBLEM SOLVING

Suggest students work in small groups to show that each of the problems in Exercise C can be written in two forms: $x + b = c$ and $c - b = x$. Have students discuss why this should be so, asking each group to present its conclusions to the class.

AT HOME

Suggest students collect newspaper advertisements, concentrating on ads of this form: Originally \$A, Now only \$C, Save \$B. Ask students to use the information in the advertisements to write equations of the form $x + b = c$, solving for x when necessary. Students can determine the percent discount represented by each advertisement [(amount saved ÷ original cost) 100% = percent saved] and then rank the ads in order of increasing discount.

Lesson at a Glance

Chapter 3 Lesson 4

Overview This lesson introduces equations of the form $ax = b$.

Objective

- To use multiplication by reciprocals to solve multiplication equations

Student Pages 70–71

Teacher's Resource Library 

Workbook Activity 28

Activity 27

Alternative Activity 27

Warm-Up Activity

Offer the following puzzles to students:

3 times what number = 1 $(\frac{1}{3})$

5 times what number = 1 $(\frac{1}{5})$

n times what number = 1 $(\frac{1}{n})$

Use this opportunity to remind students that any number times its reciprocal equals one.

Teaching the Lesson

Write the first example, $3w = 57$, on the overhead projector. Point out that students will have the value of w if they can somehow change the coefficient of w from 3 to 1. Indicate that multiplying the left side of the equation by $\frac{1}{3}$ will give w a coefficient of 1. Stress to students, however, that to keep the equation true, they will need to multiply the right side of the equation by $\frac{1}{3}$ as well. Show the steps indicated in the first example. Once the problem is solved, draw students' attention to the following step:

$$\frac{3}{3}w = \frac{57}{3}$$

Indicate to students that this step shows that multiplying both sides of the equation by $\frac{1}{3}$ is the same as dividing both sides of the equation by 3.

Lesson 4 Solving Multiplication Equations

Some equations that include multiplication can be solved mentally. For example, to solve $9q = 36$, think "Nine times what number is 36?" Since $9 \cdot 4 = 36$, $q = 4$.

When equations that include multiplication cannot be solved mentally, you can find the value of the variable by multiplying both sides of the equation by the reciprocal of the coefficient.

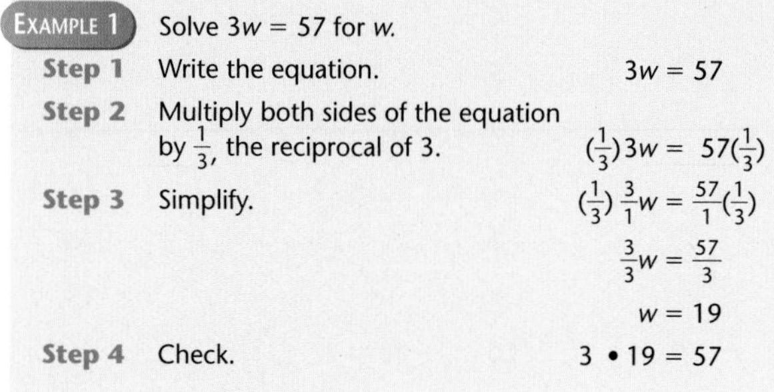

Example 1 Solve $3w = 57$ for w.

Step 1 Write the equation. $3w = 57$

Step 2 Multiply both sides of the equation by $\frac{1}{3}$, the reciprocal of 3. $(\frac{1}{3})3w = 57(\frac{1}{3})$

Step 3 Simplify. $(\frac{1}{3})\frac{3}{1}w = \frac{57}{1}(\frac{1}{3})$

$\frac{3}{3}w = \frac{57}{3}$

$w = 19$

Step 4 Check. $3 \cdot 19 = 57$

Multiplying by $\frac{1}{3}$ is the same as dividing by 3. In general, dividing by a number n is the same as multiplying by $\frac{1}{n}$. This fact gives you a choice—you can solve equations that include multiplication by dividing or by multiplying by the reciprocal of the coefficient.

Example 2 Find the value of the variable in the expression $5c = 125$.

Divide each side by 5.	Multiply each side by $\frac{1}{5}$.
$5c = 125$	$5c = 125$
$\frac{5}{5}c = \frac{125}{5}$	$(\frac{1}{5})5c = 125(\frac{1}{5})$
$c = 25$	$\frac{5}{5}c = \frac{125}{5}$
	$c = 25$
Check. $5 \cdot 25 = 125$	Check. $5 \cdot 25 = 125$

Name Date Period **Workbook Activity 28** Chapter 3, Lesson 4

Solving Multiplication Equations

Example Solve $4y = 16$ for y.

Step 1 Write the equation. $4y = 16$

Step 2 Multiply both sides of the equation by $\frac{1}{4}$, the reciprocal of 4. $(\frac{1}{4})4y = 16(\frac{1}{4})$

Step 3 Simplify. $y = 4$

Step 4 Check. $4 \cdot 4 = 16$

Note: Another way to do Step 2 is to *divide* both sides of the equation by 4. $\frac{4y}{4} = \frac{16}{4}$

Directions Solve each equation. Check your answer.

1. $2q = 14$ ______
2. $10k = 30$ ______
3. $7x = 28$ ______
4. $3d = 18$ ______
5. $6w = 66$ ______
6. $4j = -16$ ______
7. $8y = 48$ ______
8. $-5n = -20$ ______
9. $3.2p = 12.8$ ______

Directions Read the problem and follow the directions.

10. Juanita is 15, five times the age of her brother, Frank. How old is Frank?

    Let a stand for Frank's age: $5a = 15$

    How would you solve this equation? Circle the answer.

    a. Subtract 5 from both sides of the equation.
    b. Multiply both sides of the equation by 5.
    c. Multiply both sides of the equation by $\frac{1}{5}$.

 Algebra

TRL

Workbook Activity 28

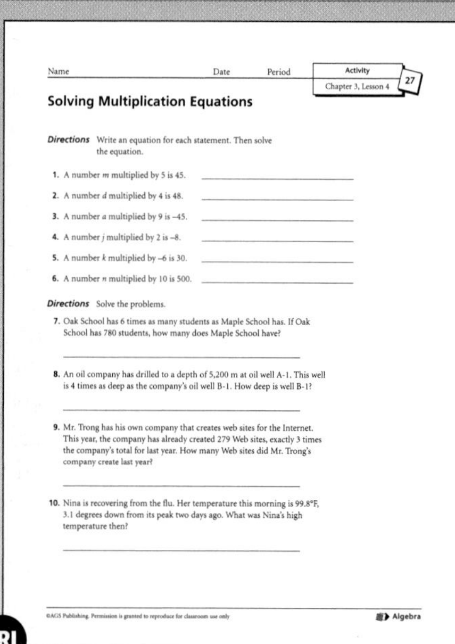

Name Date Period **Activity 27** Chapter 3, Lesson 4

Solving Multiplication Equations

Directions Write an equation for each statement. Then solve the equation.

1. A number m multiplied by 5 is 45. ______
2. A number d multiplied by 4 is 48. ______
3. A number a multiplied by 9 is –45. ______
4. A number j multiplied by 2 is –8. ______
5. A number k multiplied by –6 is 30. ______
6. A number n multiplied by 10 is 500. ______

Directions Solve the problems.

7. Oak School has 6 times as many students as Maple School has. If Oak School has 780 students, how many does Maple School have?
8. An oil company has drilled to a depth of 5,200 m at oil well A-1. This well is 4 times as deep as the company's oil well B-1. How deep is well B-1?
9. Mr. Trong has his own company that creates web sites for the Internet. This year, the company has already created 279 Web sites, exactly 3 times the company's total for last year. How many Web sites did Mr. Trong's company create last year?
10. Nina is recovering from the flu. Her temperature this morning is 99.8°F, 3.1 degrees down from its peak two days ago. What was Nina's high temperature then?

 Algebra

TRL

Activity 27

Exercise A Find the solution for each equation.

1.	$5x = 25$	5	**14.**	$8.8f = 17.6$	2
2.	$2z = 8$	4	**15.**	$7.5p = 45$	6
3.	$8m = 32$	4	**16.**	$1.9t = -19$	-10
4.	$6b = 54$	9	**17.**	$-0.5z = 25$	-50
5.	$4x = 40$	10	**18.**	$-2.3u = -18.4$	8
6.	$3v = 24$	8	**19.**	$5.3a = 31.8$	6
7.	$7a = 63$	9	**20.**	$11.1w = -44.4$	-4
8.	$4c = 12$	3	**21.**	$25.2e = -50.4$	-2
9.	$7n = 14$	2	**22.**	$-35.5x = 248.5$	-7
10.	$5y = 35$	7	**23.**	$0.9c = 8.1$	9
11.	$6.2x = 12.4$	2	**24.**	$-22.7b = -204.3$	9
12.	$3.7h = 11.1$	3	**25.**	$-4.4t = 48.4$	-11
13.	$4.5d = 18$	4	**26.**	$8.6i = -137.6$	-16

Exercise B Write an equation for each statement. Solve the equation.

$x = 4$ **27.** A number x multiplied by 13 is 52. What is the value of x?

$f = 6$ **28.** A number f multiplied by 32 is 192. What is the value of f?

$g = -11$ **29.** A number g multiplied by -6 is 66. What is the value of g?

$n = -6$ **30.** A number n multiplied by 5.5 is -33. What is the value of n?

Technology Connection

Let the Spreadsheet Do the Work

Software spreadsheet programs allow you to calculate totals in columns and rows. You simply type in the equation you need. Suppose you want the total of the numbers in column A, rows 1 through 10. Just write the correct equation in column A, row 11 to show the total. Every time you change a number in any one of the rows, the total will change in row 11. Imagine what it was like when people had to do all that with just a pencil and paper!

Common Error

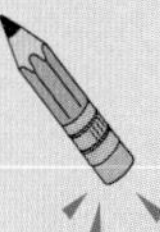

As with previous strategies for solving equations, students learning this strategy occasionally forget they must multiply (or divide) both sides of the equation to keep the equation a true statement. Encourage students to follow the steps shown in the text, writing the reciprocal (or divisor) on both sides of the equation, before simplifying the side with the variable.

Manipulatives

Isolating the Variable Using Division

Materials: Algebra Tiles

Group Practice: Model $3x = 12$. Explain that you want to know what one x equals, so x pieces must be divided into 3 groups. You must do the same to the other side of the equation, so divide 12 into 3 equal groups also. Show how one x equals 4 units. Check work by modeling the original equation, then replacing each x piece with 4 units.

Student Practice: Have students use Algebra Tiles to find solutions in Exercise A, Problems 1–3, 6, and 8–10.

Learning Styles

LEP/ESL

Have pairs of students write equations 1–10 from Exercise A in the form of statements. (They can use the statements in Exercise B as models.) For each equation, one partner writes the statement, and the other partner reads the statement aloud. Partners then work together to find the value of the variable. Have partners exchange roles after completing each statement and solution.

3 Reinforce and Extend

Learning Styles

Interpersonal/ Group Learning

Suggest students work in small groups to produce a five-minute "How To" segment for a *Math Improvement* television show. Encourage students to present step-by-step directions for solving multiplication equations using either multiplication by reciprocals or division. Encourage students to assign tasks to group members such as scriptwriter, artist, director, and announcer.

Lesson at a Glance

Chapter 3 Lesson 5

Overview This lesson applies the strategies for solving multiplication equations to equations with a fraction as the coefficient of the variable.

Objective

- To use multiplication by reciprocals to solve multiplication equations in which the coefficient of the variable is a fraction

Student Pages 72–73

Teacher's Resource Library 

Workbook Activity 29

Activity 28

Alternative Activity 28

Warm-Up Activity

Ask students to identify the reciprocals of the following numbers: $\frac{1}{4}$, $\frac{3}{5}$, $\frac{7}{8}$, and $\frac{1}{n}$. Encourage students to describe what they know about the product of these numbers and their reciprocals. *(The product equals 1.)*

Teaching the Lesson

Write the first example, $\frac{1}{4}h = 6$, on the overhead projector. Ask students how they can change the coefficient of h from $\frac{1}{4}$ to 1. Lead students to conclude that multiplying the left side of the equation by $\frac{4}{1}$ will give h a coefficient of 1. Remind students that to keep the equation true, they will need to multiply the right side of the equation by $\frac{4}{1}$ as well. Solve the example, showing each of the steps indicated. If feasible, have a volunteer use the overhead projector to explain the second example. Make certain the step of multiplying by the reciprocal is highlighted by the volunteer.

Lesson 5 Solving Equations with Fractions

Some algebra equations involve multiplication with fractions. To solve these equations, multiply both sides of the equation by the reciprocal of the fraction.

> Always check your work. Replace the variable with your answer and solve the problem.

EXAMPLE 1 Solve $\frac{1}{4}h = 6$ for h.

Step 1 Write the equation. $\frac{1}{4}h = 6$

Step 2 Multiply both sides of the equation by $\frac{4}{1}$, the reciprocal of $\frac{1}{4}$. $\left(\frac{4}{1}\right)\frac{1}{4}h = 6\left(\frac{4}{1}\right)$

Step 3 Simplify.

$$\left(\frac{4}{1}\right)\frac{1}{4}h = \frac{6}{1}\left(\frac{4}{1}\right)$$
$$\left(\frac{4}{1}\right)\frac{1}{4}h = \frac{6}{1}\left(\frac{4}{1}\right)$$
$$\frac{4}{4}h = \frac{24}{1}$$
$$h = 24$$

Step 4 Check. $\frac{1}{4}(24) = 6$

EXAMPLE 2 Solve $-\frac{2}{3}m = 12$ for m.

Step 1 Write the equation. $-\frac{2}{3}m = 12$

Step 2 Multiply both sides of the equation by $-\frac{3}{2}$, the reciprocal of $-\frac{2}{3}$.

$$(-\tfrac{3}{2})\ -\tfrac{2}{3}m = 12(-\tfrac{3}{2})$$

Step 3 Simplify.

$$(-\tfrac{3}{2})\ -\tfrac{2}{3}m = 12(-\tfrac{3}{2})$$
$$(-\tfrac{3}{2})\ -\tfrac{2}{3}m = \tfrac{12}{1}(-\tfrac{3}{2})$$
$$\frac{6}{6}m = -\frac{36}{2}$$
$$m = -18$$

Step 4 Check.

$$(-\tfrac{2}{3})(-18) = 12$$
$$\frac{36}{3} = 12$$

> **Rule** To solve an equation that involves multiplication with fractions, multiply both sides of the equation by the reciprocal of the fraction.

Name Date Period **Workbook Activity** Chapter 3, Lesson 5 **29**

Solving Equations with Fractions

EXAMPLE Solve $\frac{1}{3}y = 5$ for y.

Step 1 Write the equation. $\frac{1}{3}y = 5$

Step 2 Multiply both sides of the equation by the reciprocal of the fraction. $(\frac{3}{1})\frac{1}{3}y = (\frac{3}{1})5$

Step 3 Simplify. $y = 15$

Step 4 Check. $\frac{1}{3}(15) = 5$

Directions Solve each equation. Check your answer.

1. $\frac{1}{4}x = 1$ ________
2. $\frac{1}{8}w = 3$ ________
3. $\frac{1}{7}q = 2$ ________
4. $\frac{2}{5}r = 6$ ________
5. $\frac{4}{5}m = 20$ ________
6. $\frac{7}{8}k = 42$ ________
7. $\frac{2}{3}d = -10$ ________
8. $\frac{11}{16}y = 33$ ________
9. $\frac{1}{-5a} = -4$ ________

Directions Read the problem and follow the directions.

10. Spruceville received 35 inches of snow last winter, or $\frac{5}{8}$ of its average annual snowfall. What is Spruceville's average annual snowfall?

Let n stand for Spruceville's average annual snowfall:

$\frac{5}{8}n = 35$

How would you solve this equation? Circle the answer.

a. Subtract 35 and then multiply by $\frac{5}{8}$.
b. Multiply both sides by $\frac{8}{5}$.
c. Subtract $\frac{5}{8}$ from both sides.

 Algebra

TRL

Workbook Activity 29

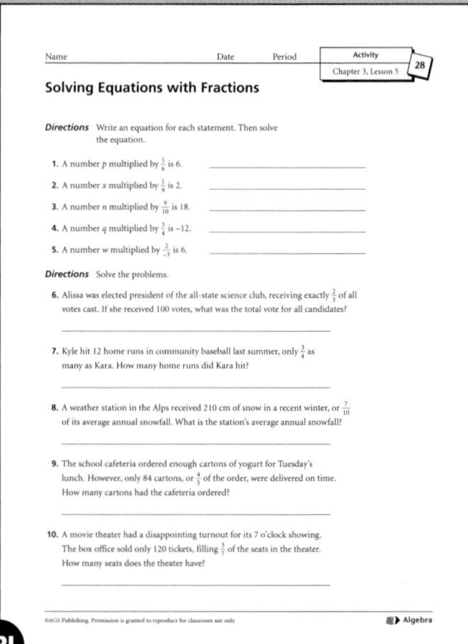

Name Date Period **Activity** Chapter 3, Lesson 5 **28**

Solving Equations with Fractions

Directions Write an equation for each statement. Then solve the equation.

1. A number p multiplied by $\frac{1}{6}$ is 6. ________
2. A number x multiplied by $\frac{1}{9}$ is 2. ________
3. A number n multiplied by $\frac{9}{10}$ is 18. ________
4. A number q multiplied by $\frac{3}{4}$ is −12. ________
5. A number w multiplied by $\frac{2}{-3}$ is 6. ________

Directions Solve the problems.

6. Alissa was elected president of the all-state science club, receiving exactly $\frac{2}{3}$ of all votes cast. If she received 100 votes, what was the total vote for all candidates?
7. Kyle hit 12 home runs in community baseball last summer, only $\frac{3}{4}$ as many as Kara. How many home runs did Kara hit?
8. A weather station in the Alps received 210 cm of snow in a recent winter, or $\frac{7}{10}$ of its average annual snowfall. What is the station's average annual snowfall?
9. The school cafeteria ordered enough cartons of yogurt for Tuesday's lunch. However, only 84 cartons, or $\frac{4}{5}$ of the order, were delivered on time. How many cartons had the cafeteria ordered?
10. A movie theater had a disappointing turnout for its 7 o'clock showing. The box office sold only 120 tickets, filling $\frac{3}{7}$ of the seats in the theater. How many seats does the theater have?

 Algebra

TRL

Activity 28

Exercise A Find the solution for each equation.

1. $\frac{1}{2}x = 3$ 6
2. $\frac{1}{3}y = 4$ 12
3. $\frac{1}{5}c = 7$ 35
4. $\frac{1}{8}d = 2$ 16
5. $\frac{1}{4}a = 5$ 20
6. $\frac{2}{3}f = 6$ 9
7. $\frac{3}{5}g = 9$ 15
8. $\frac{7}{8}h = 14$ 16
9. $\frac{5}{7}m = 5$ 7
10. $\frac{8}{9}p = 16$ 18
11. $\frac{5}{8}y = 20$ 32
12. $\frac{3}{4}x = 12$ 16
13. $\frac{1}{2}w = 8$ 16
14. $\frac{6}{10}e = 18$ 30
15. $\frac{5}{8}r = 25$ 40
16. $\frac{8}{16}s = -8$ −16
17. $-\frac{3}{5}d = 24$ −40
18. $-\frac{9}{10}g = 18$ −20
19. $-\frac{2}{5}x = -20$ 50
20. $\frac{15}{16}c = 30$ 32
21. $\frac{9}{10}v = -18$ −20
22. $-\frac{6}{7}b = 12$ −14
23. $\frac{10}{15}n = 40$ 60
24. $-\frac{1}{8}j = -8$ 64
25. $\frac{3}{4}i = 27$ 36
26. $\frac{1}{2}u = -10$ −20

PROBLEM SOLVING

Exercise B Write an equation for each problem. Solve the equation.

27. Two-thirds of Mrs. Minsinski's class are football fans. How many students are in the class if there are 16 football fans altogether? 24 students
28. A box contains eight calculators. It is one-sixth full. If the box were full, how many calculators would be in the box? 48 calculators
29. Jon answers nine questions on a test. He is only finished with one-half of the test. How many questions are on the test? 18 questions
30. Maggie ordered three-fifths of a truckload of mulch for her garden. She receives eight cubic yards of mulch. How much mulch is in a full truckload? $13\frac{1}{3}$ cubic yards of mulch

3 Reinforce and Extend

Group Problem Solving

Have small groups of students consider the following situation.

Havermill School needs to increase its students' reading and math scores. Currently $\frac{1}{7}$ of the school, 30 students, score above average in reading and math. By the end of the year, the school would like $\frac{1}{5}$ of its students to score above average. If the school meets its goal, how many students will score above average? *[$(\frac{1}{7})x = 30$; $x = 210$; $(\frac{1}{5})210 = 42$]*

Suggest students use the examples as models, first finding how many students are in the school, then finding $\frac{1}{5}$ of that number. Invite students to present their solutions in poster form.

Calculator

Remind students that a fraction implies division—numerator divided by denominator. Demonstrate how they can multiply by a fraction using the calculator.

For example, for $(\frac{9}{8})16$:

Press 9 ÷ 8 × 16 =.

The display reads 18.

Have students find the following products using a calculator.

$(\frac{5}{8})40$	*(25)*
$(\frac{6}{8})56$	*(42)*
$(\frac{13}{15})225$	*(195)*
$(\frac{7}{6})18$	*(21)*
$(\frac{5}{11})121$	*(55)*
$(\frac{9}{4})36$	*(81)*

Math History

Every student of mathematics is familiar with the Greek mathematician Pythagoras, who lived in the sixth century B.C. The formula we use for determining the length of the hypotenuse of a triangle—$c^2 = a^2 + b^2$—is named after Pythagoras. The Pythagorean theorem allows us to find the length of one side of a right triangle when the other two sides are known. Although the formula for finding the length of a triangle's side was named for a Greek, the Chinese also discovered and used the same theorem. The classic Chinese mathematics book, *Arithmetic in Nine Sections*, was written during the Han Dynasty (202 B.C. to A.D. 220). One section of the book includes a problem and a solution that mirror the Pythagorean theorem.

Lesson at a Glance

Chapter 3 Lesson 6

Overview This lesson introduces equations whose solutions require more than one operation.

Objectives

- To solve equations requiring more than one step
- To use both opposites and reciprocals, as necessary, to solve an equation

Student Pages 74–75

Teacher's Resource Library 

Workbook Activity 30

Activity 29

Alternative Activity 29

1 Warm-Up Activity

Open the lesson by presenting the following brain teaser to students: "I'm thinking of a number. Three times that number minus 7 equals 20. What is the number?" *(9)* Invite volunteers to name the mystery number and to describe how they found it. Record all reasonable responses on the board.

2 Teaching the Lesson

Write the first example, $3x - 7$, on the board or overhead projector. Help students recognize that to find the value of x, they need to complete two steps: remove -7 from the left side of the equation and change the coefficient of x from 3 to 1. Point out to students that they already have experience in accomplishing each of these steps. Also point out that they can choose which step to complete first: removing the -7 or changing the coefficient. Demonstrate each step in each of the solution methods given for the example.

Lesson 6 Solving Equations—More Than One Step

Some equations have more than one operation. You may need to combine two or more solutions to find the value of the variable.

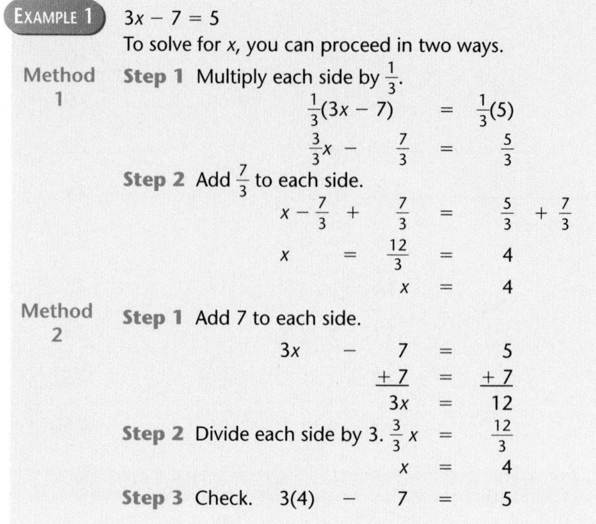

EXAMPLE 1 $3x - 7 = 5$

To solve for x, you can proceed in two ways.

Method 1

Step 1 Multiply each side by $\frac{1}{3}$.

$$\frac{1}{3}(3x - 7) = \frac{1}{3}(5)$$

$$\frac{3}{3}x - \frac{7}{3} = \frac{5}{3}$$

Step 2 Add $\frac{7}{3}$ to each side.

$$x - \frac{7}{3} + \frac{7}{3} = \frac{5}{3} + \frac{7}{3}$$

$$x = \frac{12}{3} = 4$$

$$x = 4$$

Method 2

Step 1 Add 7 to each side.

$$3x - 7 = 5$$

$$+7 = +7$$

$$3x = 12$$

Step 2 Divide each side by 3. $\frac{3}{3}x = \frac{12}{3}$

$$x = 4$$

Step 3 Check. $3(4) - 7 = 5$

You might try performing some steps mentally.

$2c = 18$ Think: 2 times what number is 18? $c = 9$

$4e + 1 = 21$ Think: Subtract 1 from each side.
4 times what number is 20? $e = 5$

To solve equations with more than one operation, you should always complete one operation before beginning the other.

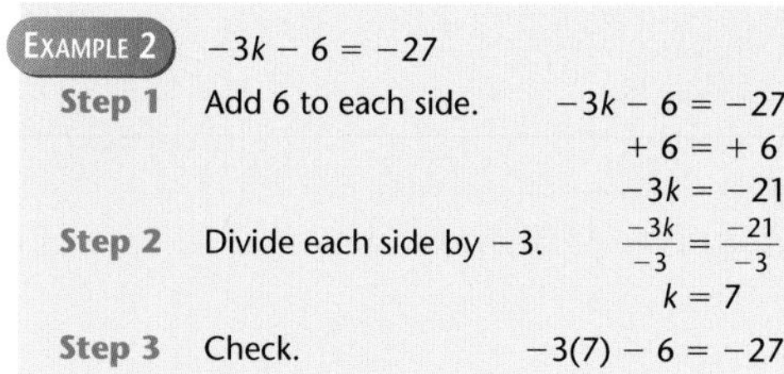

EXAMPLE 2 $-3k - 6 = -27$

Step 1 Add 6 to each side. $-3k - 6 = -27$
$+6 = +6$
$-3k = -21$

Step 2 Divide each side by -3. $\frac{-3k}{-3} = \frac{-21}{-3}$
$k = 7$

Step 3 Check. $-3(7) - 6 = -27$

Name Date Period **Workbook Activity 30** Chapter 3, Lesson 6

Solving Equations—More Than One Step

EXAMPLE Solve $2m - 7 = 1$ for m.

Step 1 Add 7 to both sides. $2m - 7 + (7) = 1 + (7)$ Simplify: $2m = 8$

Step 2 Divide both sides by 2. $\frac{2m}{2} = \frac{8}{2}$ Simplify: $m = 4$

Step 3 Check. $2(4) - 7 = 1$ Simplify: $1 = 1$

Directions Solve each equation. Check your answer.

1. $4b + 1 = 17$ ________
2. $2c + 18 = 24$ ________
3. $7x - 2 = 5$ ________
4. $3p + 8 = 38$ ________
5. $8v - 1 = 39$ ________
6. $2w - 16 = 0$ ________
7. $5g + 5 = 35$ ________

Directions One step is missing in the solution to each equation. In a complete sentence, write the missing step.

8. $7y - 4 = 10$
   Step 1 Add 4 to both sides of the equation.
   Step 2 ________
9. $2d + 1 = 19$
   Step 1 ________
   Step 2 Divide both sides of the equation by 2.
10. $3k + 3 = 12$
    Step 1 Subtract 3 from both sides of the equation.
    Step 2 ________

 Algebra

TRL **Workbook Activity 30**

Name Date Period **Activity 29** Chapter 3, Lesson 6

Solving Equations—More Than One Step

Directions Study the solution for each equation and tell whether it is *correct* or *incorrect*. If the solution is incorrect, explain why.

1. $3n + 1 = 28$
   Step 1 $3n + 1 - 1 = 28 - 1$
   Simplify: $3n = 27$
   Step 2 $\frac{3n}{3} = \frac{27}{3}$
   Simplify: $n = 9$
2. $4k - 1 = 15$
   Step 1 $4k - 1 + 1 = 15$
   Simplify: $4k = 15$
   Step 2 $\frac{4k}{4} = \frac{15}{4}$
   Simplify: $k = \frac{15}{4}$ (or $3\frac{3}{4}$)
3. $\frac{2}{3}r - 2 = 20$
   Step 1 $\frac{2}{3}r - 2 + 2 = 20 + 2$
   Simplify: $\frac{2}{3}r = 22$
   Step 2 $(\frac{3}{2})\frac{2}{3}r = \frac{22}{1}(\frac{3}{2})$
   Simplify: $r = 33$

Directions Solve the problems.

4. Terry says, "I have 8 cousins."
   Rita says, "Then you have one less than three times as many as I do." How many cousins does Rita have?
5. Yesterday at the museum, 602 people viewed the dinosaur exhibit. This attendance was 10 less than 3 times the number of people who viewed the wetlands exhibit. How many people viewed the wetlands exhibit yesterday?

 Algebra

TRL **Activity 29**

EXAMPLE 3 $\frac{3}{4}p + 12 = 0$

Step 1	Subtract 12 from each side.	$\frac{3}{4}p + 12 = 0$ $-12 = -12$ $\frac{3}{4}p = -12$
Step 2	Multiply each side by $\frac{4}{3}$, the reciprocal of $\frac{3}{4}$.	$\left(\frac{4}{3}\right)\frac{3}{4}p = -\frac{12}{1}\left(\frac{4}{3}\right)$ $p = -\frac{48}{3}$ or -16
Step 3	Check.	$\frac{3}{4}(-16) + 12 = 0$

Exercise A Solve each equation.

1. $3x - 6 = 6$ 4
2. $3y + 1 = 7$ 2
3. $2m - 3 = 7$ 5
4. $5b - 2 = 13$ 3
5. $2g + 4 = 16$ 6
6. $7a + 2 = 16$ 2
7. $4e - 3 = 1$ 1
8. $2k + 3 = 17$ 7
9. $2w - 8 = 8$ 8
10. $9d - 25 = 2$ 3
11. $4t + 5 = 25$ 5
12. $6s - 10 = 10$ $3\frac{1}{3}$
13. $3p + 20 = 50$ 10
14. $3i - 4 = 23$ 9
15. $5p + 0 = 0$ 0
16. $2t - 4 = 8$ 6

Exercise B Solve each equation.

17. $-6b + 20 = -16$ 6
18. $-4m + 2 = 14$ -3
19. $-9c - 4 = -4$ 0
20. $2y - (-10) = 18$ 4
21. $-\frac{1}{2}g + 2 = 6$ -8
22. $3r - 25 = 5$ 10
23. $\frac{2}{3}s - (-4) = 8$ 6
24. $\frac{4}{5}a + (-5) = 0$ $6\frac{1}{4}$
25. $-\frac{2}{7}w - 6 = -4$ -7

PROBLEM SOLVING

Exercise C Solve each problem by using an equation.

26. To find the number of square miles in Adair County, Kentucky, solve $s = 57 + (77)(5)$. 442 square miles
27. By solving $s + 27 = (20)(30)$, you will find the number of square miles in Clay County, Iowa. 573 square miles
28. To calculate the number of square miles in Dane County, Wisconsin, solve $s = 35^2 - 28$. 1,197 square miles
29. Solve the equation $s - 26 = (9)(5)$ to find the number of square miles in Kings County, New York. 71 square miles
30. You will find the number of square miles in Los Angeles County, California, by solving $s = (4 \cdot 10^3) + 71$. 4,071 square miles

COMMON ERROR

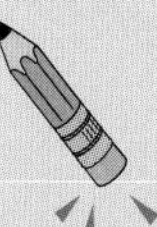

Students who choose to use multiplication as the first step in solving multistep equations often forget to multiply *each* term on both sides of the equation. For example, in $3x - 7 = 5$, they may multiply $3x$ by $\frac{1}{3}$ but forget to also multiply 7 by $\frac{1}{3}$. Suggest students write out each step of their solution, watching carefully to ensure that they have multiplied each term on both sides of the equation.

MANIPULATIVES

Solving Two-Step Equations

Materials: Algebra Tiles, Manipulatives Master 3 (Sentence Mat)

Group Practice: Model the equation in the example to illustrate Method 2. If necessary, review the Algebra Tiles activities in Lessons 2 and 3. Use the procedures in those lessons to solve these two-step equations.

Student Practice: Have students use Algebra Tiles to solve Problems 1–10 in Exercise A.

3 Reinforce and Extend

GROUP PROBLEM SOLVING

Suggest students work in pairs to solve the following problem.

The following is information about the student lunch program at Marquette School.

Tuesday, October 14	
cost per lunch	$0.40
uneaten lunches	43
total spent on lunches	$62.80

The school orders enough lunches for all students but does not pay for any uneaten lunches. How many students are in Marquette School? *[0.40(x) − 0.40(43) = $62.80; x = 200]*

Invite groups to present their solutions, including any equations they may have used, as a "Just the Facts" segment of the lunchtime news. Students can assign roles to group members such as writer, announcer, designer, and coordinator.

Lesson at a Glance

Chapter 3 Lesson 7

Overview This lesson presents literal equations for solution.

Objective

- To use the strategies of reciprocals and opposites to solve equations involving letters only

Student Pages 76–77

Teacher's Resource Library 

Workbook Activity 31

Activity 30

Alternative Activity 30

Mathematics Vocabulary

constant
literal equation

Warm-Up Activity

Remind students that they are now familiar with solving equations of the forms $x - b = c$ and $x + b = c$ when b and c are replaced by numbers. Indicate that now students will learn how to solve these equations for x, without using numbers. Ask students how this might be done and record their suggestions on the board.

Teaching the Lesson

Use the numerical and literal examples given in the text to help students understand that the steps involved in solving a literal equation are the same as those used to solve numerical equations.

Lesson 7 Equations Without Numbers

Literal equation
An equation that has only letters

Constant
Specific real number

In algebra, it is possible to have no numbers at all in an equation, only letters. These are called **literal equations.** Here is an example:

$ax + b = c$

In the equation, a, b, and c represent real numbers, and x represents the variable. The letters x, y, and z usually represent variables, while a, b, and c usually represent **constants,** or specific real numbers.

You can solve literal equations using the same methods you have learned for numbers.

EXAMPLE 1 Solve the equation for x.

Step 1	Write the equation.	$3x + 4 = 13$
Step 2	Subtract 4 from both sides.	$3x + 4 = 13$ $-4 = -4$ $3x = 9$
Step 3	Divide each side by 3.	$\frac{3x}{3} = \frac{9}{3}$ $x = 3$
Step 4	Check.	$(3)(3) + 4 = 13$ $13 = 13$ True

EXAMPLE 2 Solve for x.

Step 1	Write the equation.	$ax + b = c$
Step 2	Subtract b from both sides.	$ax + b = c$ $-b = -b$ $ax = (c - b)$
Step 3	Divide each side by a.	$\frac{ax}{a} = \frac{(c - b)}{a}$ $x = \frac{c - b}{a}$
Step 4	Check.	$a\frac{(c - b)}{a} + b = c$ $(c - b) + b = c$ $c = c$ True

Name Date Period **Workbook Activity 31** Chapter 3, Lesson 7

Equations Without Numbers

EXAMPLE $ax - b = c$ Solve for x.

Step 1	Write the equation.	$2x - 5 = 7$	$ax - b = c$
Step 2	Add 5 or b to both sides.	$2x - 5 + 5 = 7 + 5$ $2x = 12$	$ax - b + b = c + b$ $ax = b + c$
Step 3	Divide each side by 2 or a.	$\frac{2x}{2} = \frac{12}{2}$	$\frac{ax}{a} = \frac{b + c}{a}$
Step 4	Check.	$x = 6$ $2(6) - 5 = 7$ $7 = 7$	$x = \frac{b + c}{a}$ $a(\frac{b + c}{a}) - b = c$ $(b + c) - b = c$ $c = c$

Directions Solve each equation for x. Check your answer.

1. $ax - c = b$ ________
2. $bc = ax$ ________
3. $x - b + a = c$ ________
4. $abx = -c$ ________

Directions Follow the directions to solve the problem.

5. Center School has won two more soccer games than the combined wins of River School and Bluff School.

   This statement can be turned into a mathematical equation.
   - Let x stand for the number of games Center School has won.
   - Let y stand for the number of games River School has won.
   - Let z stand for the number of games Bluff School has won.

   $x = y + z + 2$

   Solve the equation for z to show the number of soccer games Bluff School has won.

 Algebra

Workbook Activity 31

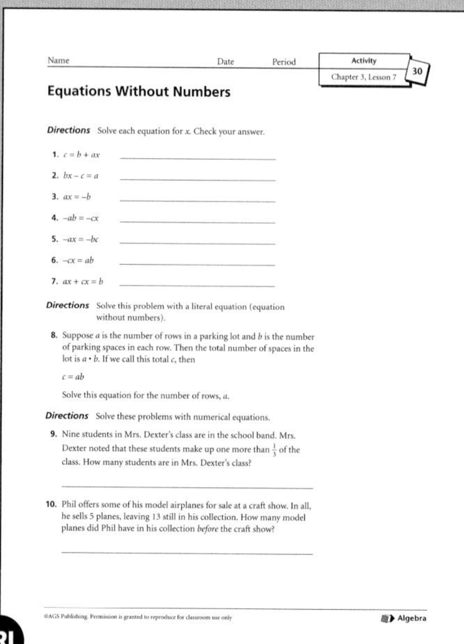

Name Date Period **Activity** Chapter 3, Lesson 7 30

Equations Without Numbers

Directions Solve each equation for x. Check your answer.

1. $c = b + ax$ ________
2. $bx - c = a$ ________
3. $ax = -b$ ________
4. $-ab = -cx$ ________
5. $-ax = -bc$ ________
6. $-cx = ab$ ________
7. $ax + cx = b$ ________

Directions Solve this problem with a literal equation (equation without numbers).

8. Suppose a is the number of rows in a parking lot and b is the number of parking spaces in each row. Then the total number of spaces in the lot is $a \cdot b$. If we call this total c, then

   $c = ab$

   Solve this equation for the number of rows, a.

Directions Solve these problems with numerical equations.

9. Nine students in Mrs. Dexter's class are in the school band. Mrs. Dexter noted that these students make up one more than $\frac{1}{3}$ of the class. How many students are in Mrs. Dexter's class?

10. Phil offers some of his model airplanes for sale at a craft show. In all, he sells 5 planes, leaving 13 still in his collection. How many model planes did Phil have in his collection *before* the craft show?

 Algebra

Activity 30

EXAMPLE 3 Solve for x.

$$3x = 12$$
$$\frac{3x}{3} = \frac{12}{3}$$
$$x = 4$$

Check. $3(4) = 12$

True

EXAMPLE 4 Solve for x.

$$ax = b$$
$$\frac{ax}{a} = \frac{b}{a}$$
$$x = \frac{b}{a}$$

Check. $a(\frac{b}{a}) = b$

$b = b$

True

These examples show that literal equations can be solved in the same way as equations with numbers.

Exercise A Solve for x.

1. $-ax = b$ $x = \frac{b}{-a}$
2. $cx + ax = b$ $x = \frac{b}{(c + a)}$
3. $-b = -ax$ $x = \frac{b}{a}$
4. $cx - bx = a$ $x = \frac{a}{(c - b)}$
5. $-a = bx$ $x = \frac{-a}{b}$
6. $ax + bx = c$ $x = \frac{c}{(a + b)}$
7. $-c = bx + ax$ $x = \frac{-c}{(b + a)}$
8. $ax - bx = c$ $x = \frac{c}{(a - b)}$
9. $cx = -b$ $x = \frac{-b}{c}$
10. $cx + bx = a$ $x = \frac{a}{(c + b)}$
11. $bx - ax = c$ $x = \frac{c}{(b - a)}$
12. $-bx = c$ $x = \frac{c}{-b}$
13. $cx - bx = a$ $x = \frac{a}{(c - b)}$
14. $ax + bx = -c$ $x = \frac{-c}{(a + b)}$
15. $-a = cx + bx$ $x = \frac{-a}{(c + b)}$
16. $cx - bx = -a$ $x = \frac{-a}{(c - b)}$
17. $bx + ax = c$ $x = \frac{c}{(b + a)}$
18. $-c = ax - bx$ $x = \frac{-c}{(a - b)}$
19. $cx + ax = -b$ $x = \frac{-b}{(c + a)}$
20. $cx + ax = b$ $x = \frac{b}{(c + a)}$

Algebra in Your Life **Packaging a Product**

When you're at the store, do you ever think about why a package or can is the size it is? Package designers use volume formulas to determine how much of a product will fit into a container. Designers know that two differently shaped containers with the same volume may not hold the same amount. However, the package that holds the most isn't always the best design. Designers must also think about how the product will look to customers and how it will fit on a shelf.

COMMON ERROR

As with most equations, the greatest danger in solving literal equations is failing to treat each side of the equation in the same manner—multiplying each side by a reciprocal, dividing each side by a number, or adding an opposite to each side of the equation. Stress to students that all operations to solve an equation must be applied to each side of the equation. Encourage students to check their work as a way of making certain they have applied operations to both sides of the equation.

3 Reinforce and Extend

LEARNING STYLES

Auditory/Verbal

Suggest students work in pairs. Ask the partners to solve the even-numbered items in Exercise A orally. One partner explains each of the steps involved in solving the equation. The other partner listens and writes the steps, then checks the results. Students should change roles of speaker and listener after solving each equation.

Lesson at a Glance

Chapter 3 Lesson 8

Overview This lesson introduces a special form of the literal equation, the formula.

Objective

- To solve standard formulas for given variables

Student Pages 78–79

Teacher's Resource Library TRL

Workbook Activity 32

Activity 31

Alternative Activity 31

1 Warm-Up Activity

Point out to students that one of the most common applications of literal equations is in formulas, for example, formulas to find area, volume, perimeter, and distance. Ask students to identify any formulas with which they are familiar. List their responses on the board.

2 Teaching the Lesson

Use the examples to introduce formulas to students. Draw a triangle on the board or overhead projector. Trace the perimeter of the figure, helping students to understand the relationship between the perimeter of the triangle and the formula to find the perimeter. Draw the other three shapes and relate the appropriate formula for perimeter or area to each.

Lesson 8 Formulas

Formulas are examples of literal equations. Most formulas you have learned are found in geometry. Sometimes you will need to rearrange a formula to solve a problem.

EXAMPLE 1 Perimeter of a triangle

$P = a + b + c$

Solve the formula for side a.

$$a + (b + c) = P$$
$$a + (b + c) - (b + c) = P - (b + c)$$
$$a = P - (b + c)$$

EXAMPLE 2 Perimeter of a square

$P = 4s$

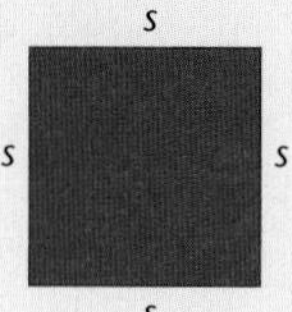

Solve for s.

$$4s = P$$
$$\frac{4s}{4} = \frac{P}{4}$$
$$s = \frac{P}{4}$$

EXAMPLE 3 Area of a triangle

$A = \frac{1}{2}bh$

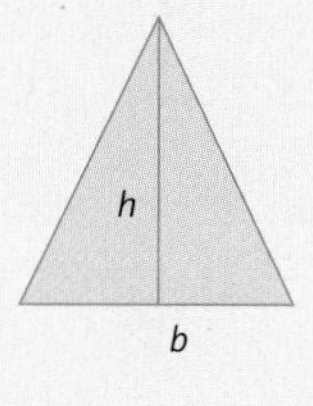

Solve for h.

$$\frac{1}{2}bh = A$$
$$2(\frac{1}{2}bh) = 2(A)$$
$$\frac{bh}{b} = \frac{2A}{b}$$
$$h = \frac{2A}{b}$$

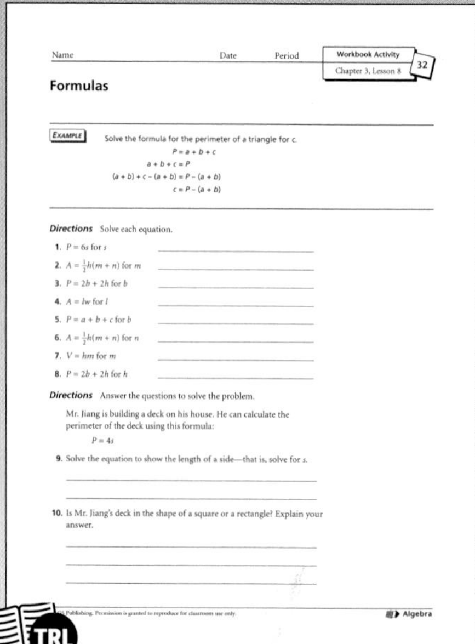

Name Date Period — Workbook Activity 32, Chapter 3, Lesson 8

Formulas

EXAMPLE Solve the formula for the perimeter of a triangle for c.

$$P = a + b + c$$
$$a + b + c = P$$
$$(a + b) + c - (a + b) = P - (a + b)$$
$$c = P - (a + b)$$

Directions Solve each equation.

1. $P = 6s$ for s
2. $A = \frac{1}{2}h(m + n)$ for m
3. $P = 2b + 2h$ for b
4. $A = lw$ for l
5. $P = a + b + c$ for b
6. $A = \frac{1}{2}h(m + n)$ for n
7. $V = hm$ for m
8. $P = 2b + 2h$ for h

Directions Answer the questions to solve the problem.

Mr. Jiang is building a deck on his house. He can calculate the perimeter of the deck using this formula:

$P = 4s$

9. Solve the equation to show the length of a side—that is, solve for s.

10. Is Mr. Jiang's deck in the shape of a square or a rectangle? Explain your answer.

 Algebra

Workbook Activity 32

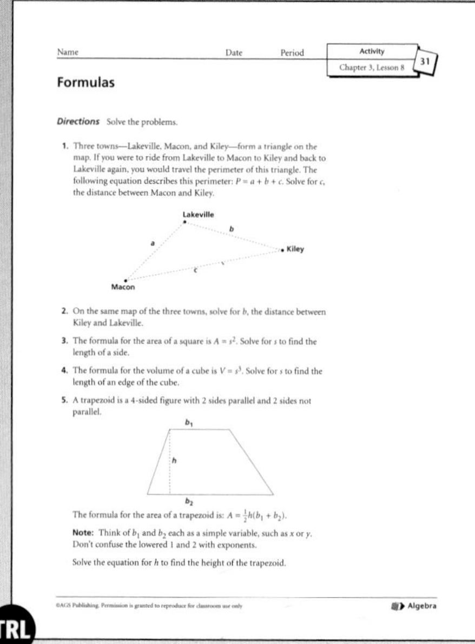

Name Date Period — Activity 31, Chapter 3, Lesson 8

Formulas

Directions Solve the problems.

1. Three towns—Lakeville, Macon, and Kiley—form a triangle on the map. If you were to ride from Lakeville to Macon to Kiley and back to Lakeville again, you would travel the perimeter of this triangle. The following equation describes this perimeter: $P = a + b + c$. Solve for c, the distance between Macon and Kiley.

2. On the same map of the three towns, solve for b, the distance between Kiley and Lakeville.
3. The formula for the area of a square is $A = s^2$. Solve for s to find the length of a side.
4. The formula for the volume of a cube is $V = s^3$. Solve for s to find the length of an edge of the cube.
5. A trapezoid is a 4-sided figure with 2 sides parallel and 2 sides not parallel.

The formula for the area of a trapezoid is: $A = \frac{1}{2}h(b_1 + b_2)$.

Note: Think of b_1 and b_2 each as a simple variable, such as x or y. Don't confuse the lowered 1 and 2 with exponents.

Solve the equation for h to find the height of the trapezoid.

 Algebra

Activity 31

EXAMPLE 4 Area of a rectangle

$A = bh$

Solve for b. $bh = A$

$\frac{bh}{h} = \frac{A}{h}$

$b = \frac{A}{h}$

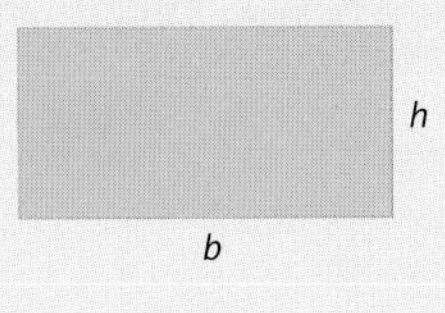

Exercise A Solve each equation.

1. $A = bh$ for h. $h = \frac{A}{b}$
2. $A = lw$ for w. $w = \frac{A}{l}$
3. $P = 3s$ for s. $s = \frac{P}{3}$
4. $A = \frac{1}{2}bh$ for h. $h = \frac{2A}{b}$
5. $W = fd$ for d. $d = \frac{W}{f}$
6. $A = \frac{1}{2}bh$ for b. $b = \frac{2A}{h}$
7. $A = bh$ for b. $b = \frac{A}{h}$
8. $d = rt$ for t. $t = \frac{d}{r}$
9. $P = 5s$ for s. $s = \frac{P}{5}$
10. $P = a + b + c$ for a. $a = P - (b + c)$
11. $d = rt$ for r. $r = \frac{d}{t}$
12. $P = a + b + c$ for b. $b = P - (a + c)$
13. $W = fd$ for f. $f = \frac{W}{d}$
14. $P = 2\pi r$ for r. $r = \frac{P}{(2\pi)}$
15. $A = \frac{1}{2}(b_1 + b_2)h$ for h. $h = \frac{2A}{(b_1 + b_2)}$
16. $A = sd$ for d. $d = \frac{A}{s}$
17. $P = a + c$ for a. $a = P - c$
18. $A = yz$ for z. $z = \frac{A}{y}$
19. $A = \frac{d}{n}$ for d. $d = An$
20. $P = c - d$ for c. $c = P + d$
21. $A = \frac{1}{2s}$ for s. $s = \frac{1}{2A}$
22. $V = hm$ for h. $h = \frac{V}{m}$
23. $\frac{a}{P} = s$ for a. $a = sP$
24. $P = c + d - e$ for c. $c = P - (d - e)$
25. $\frac{c}{d} = A + b$ for A. $A = (\frac{c}{d}) - b$

3 Reinforce and Extend

CAREER CONNECTION

Invite an architect or interior designer to speak to the class. Encourage the speaker to concentrate on those aspects of his or her daily work that require the knowledge and use of formulas such as those for finding the area, perimeter, and volume of various shapes. Alert the speaker that students may have additional questions about the educational background and job requirements needed for the profession.

LEARNING STYLES

Interpersonal/ Group Learning

Have students work in groups of four. Suggest groups compete, trying to match items 1–15 in Exercise A with real-life applications. For example,

$A = bh$	area of a rectangle equals base times height
$W = fd$	work equals force times distance

and so on. Indicate that students may want to look in science textbooks and other sources to identify the formulas. The group that identifies the most formulas wins.

Lesson at a Glance

Chapter 3 Lesson 9

Overview This lesson presents the Pythagorean theorem.

Objective

- To use the Pythagorean theorem to solve for the value of the third side of a right triangle

Student Pages 80–83

Teacher's Resource Library 

Workbook Activity 33–34

Activity 32

Alternative Activity 32

Mathematics Vocabulary

hypotenuse
Pythagorean theorem
right triangle

1 Warm-Up Activity

Draw several different sizes of right triangles on the board. Indicate to students that this lesson deals exclusively with triangles that have a 90°, or right, angle. Have volunteers identify the right angle in each triangle on the board.

2 Teaching the Lesson

Work though the example with students. Indicate that $a^2 + 2ab + b^2$ represents the area of the square on the left. Then indicate that $c^2 + 4(\frac{1}{2}ab)$ represents the area of the square on the right. Be sure students understand the algebraic step that leads to $a^2 + b^2 = c^2$.

Lesson 9 The Pythagorean Theorem

Pythagorean theorem
A formula that states that in a right triangle, the length of the hypotenuse squared is equal to the length of side b squared and the length of side a squared

Right triangle
A three-sided figure, or triangle, with one right, or 90°, angle

Hypotenuse
The longest side in a right triangle

The Pythagorean Theorem

The **Pythagorean theorem** is an important formula. It states that in any **right triangle,** c is the longest side known as the **hypotenuse,** and a and b are the other sides: $c^2 = a^2 + b^2$.

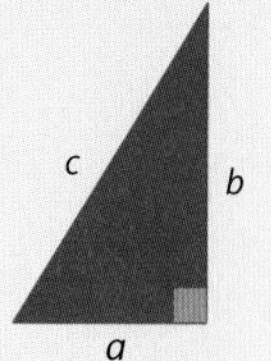

A proof of this can be shown algebraically.

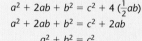

EXAMPLE 1

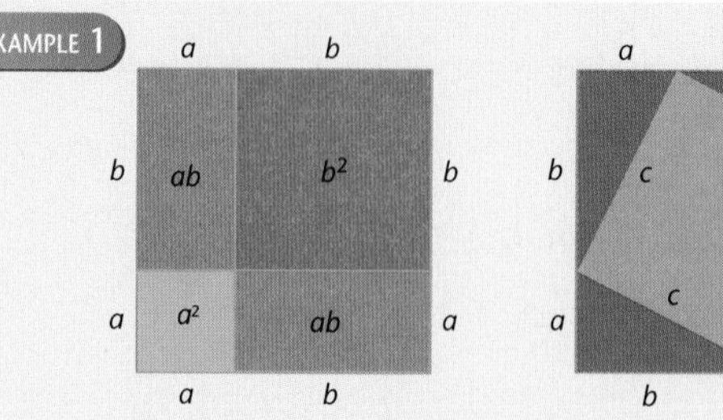

Add the areas in each of the equal squares.

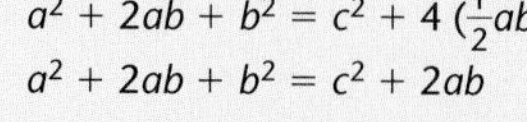

$a^2 + 2ab + b^2 = c^2 + 4\,(\frac{1}{2}ab)$

$a^2 + 2ab + b^2 = c^2 + 2ab$ Subtract $2ab$ from both sides.

$a^2 + b^2 = c^2$

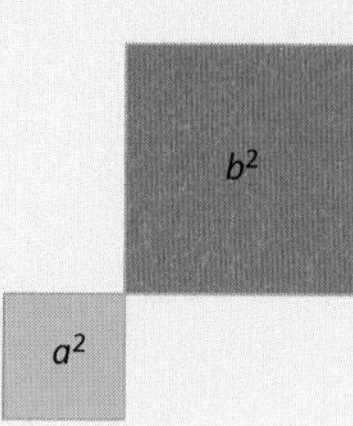

The area $a^2 + b^2$ is equal to the area c^2.

The Pythagorean theorem was named for Pythagoras, a Greek who lived in the sixth century B.C.

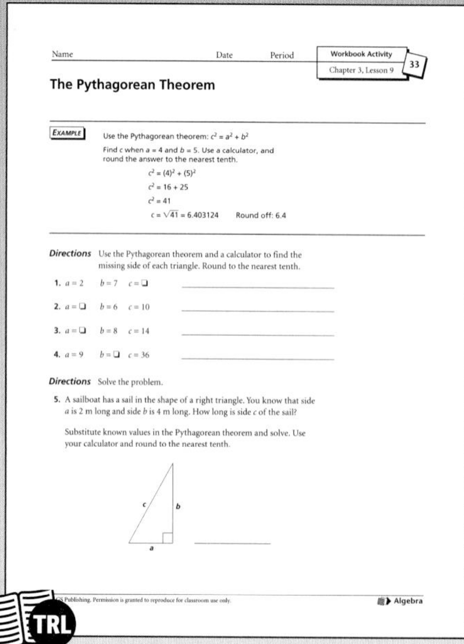

Name Date Period

Workbook Activity 33
Chapter 3, Lesson 9

The Pythagorean Theorem

EXAMPLE Use the Pythagorean theorem: $c^2 = a^2 + b^2$

Find c when $a = 4$ and $b = 5$. Use a calculator, and round the answer to the nearest tenth.

$c^2 = (4)^2 + (5)^2$

$c^2 = 16 + 25$

$c^2 = 41$

$c = \sqrt{41} = 6.403124$ Round off: 6.4

Directions Use the Pythagorean theorem and a calculator to find the missing side of each triangle. Round to the nearest tenth.

1. $a = 2$ $b = 7$ $c = ❑$ ______
2. $a = ❑$ $b = 6$ $c = 10$ ______
3. $a = ❑$ $b = 8$ $c = 14$ ______
4. $a = 9$ $b = ❑$ $c = 36$ ______

Directions Solve the problem.

5. A sailboat has a sail in the shape of a right triangle. You know that side a is 2 m long and side b is 4 m long. How long is side c of the sail?

Substitute known values in the Pythagorean theorem and solve. Use your calculator and round to the nearest tenth.

c b a ______

 Algebra

Workbook Activity 33

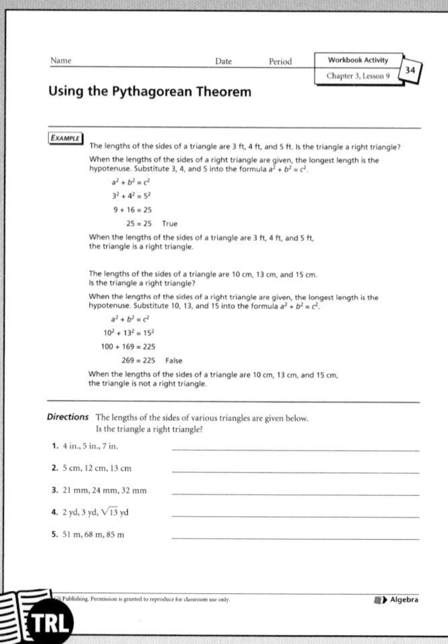

Name Date Period

Workbook Activity 34
Chapter 3, Lesson 9

Using the Pythagorean Theorem

EXAMPLE The lengths of the sides of a triangle are 3 ft, 4 ft, and 5 ft. Is the triangle a right triangle?

When the lengths of the sides of a right triangle are given, the longest length is the hypotenuse. Substitute 3, 4, and 5 into the formula $a^2 + b^2 = c^2$.

$a^2 + b^2 = c^2$

$3^2 + 4^2 = 5^2$

$9 + 16 = 25$

$25 = 25$ True

When the lengths of the sides of a triangle are 3 ft, 4 ft, and 5 ft, the triangle is a right triangle.

The lengths of the sides of a triangle are 10 cm, 13 cm, and 15 cm. Is the triangle a right triangle?

When the lengths of the sides of a right triangle are given, the longest length is the hypotenuse. Substitute 10, 13, and 15 into the formula $a^2 + b^2 = c^2$.

$a^2 + b^2 = c^2$

$10^2 + 13^2 = 15^2$

$100 + 169 = 225$

$269 = 225$ False

When the lengths of the sides of a triangle are 10 cm, 13 cm, and 15 cm, the triangle is not a right triangle.

Directions The lengths of the sides of various triangles are given below. Is the triangle a right triangle?

1. 4 in., 5 in., 7 in. ______
2. 5 cm, 12 cm, 13 cm ______
3. 21 mm, 24 mm, 32 mm ______
4. 2 yd, 3 yd, $\sqrt{13}$ yd ______
5. 51 m, 68 m, 85 m ______

 Algebra

Workbook Activity 34

EXAMPLE 2 Using the Pythagorean theorem: $c^2 = a^2 + b^2$

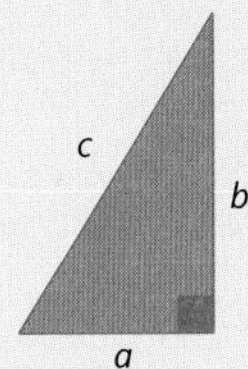

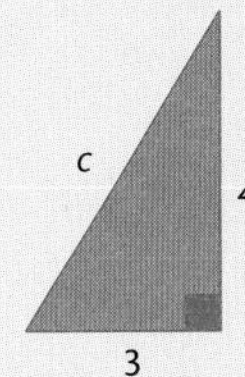

Suppose you know $a = 3$, $b = 4$, and c is unknown. Solve for c.

$c^2 = a^2 + b^2$

$c^2 = 3^2 + 4^2$

$c^2 = 9 + 16$

$c^2 = 25$ Find the square root of 25.

$c = 5$

Check. $5^2 = 3^2 + 4^2$

$25 = 25$ True

Solve for a. $c^2 = a^2 + b^2$

$c^2 - b^2 = a^2$

$\sqrt{c^2 - b^2} = a$ Find the square root of both sides of the equation.

Exercise A Use the Pythagorean theorem to find the missing value.

1.	$a^2 = ■$	$b^2 = 50$	$c^2 = 100$	50
2.	$a^2 = 36$	$b^2 = 75$	$c^2 = ■$	111
3.	$a^2 = 64$	$b^2 = ■$	$c^2 = 90$	26
4.	$a^2 = 10$	$b^2 = ■$	$c^2 = 55$	45
5.	$a^2 = ■$	$b^2 = 27$	$c^2 = 78$	51

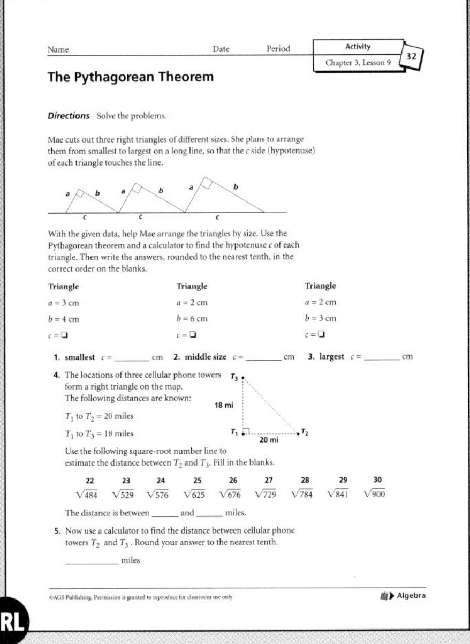

Name Date Period — Activity 32, Chapter 3, Lesson 9

The Pythagorean Theorem

Directions Solve the problems.

Mae cuts out three right triangles of different sizes. She plans to arrange them from smallest to largest on a long line, so that the c side (hypotenuse) of each triangle touches the line.

With the given data, help Mae arrange the triangles by size. Use the Pythagorean theorem and a calculator to find the hypotenuse c of each triangle. Then write the answers, rounded to the nearest tenth, in the correct order on the blanks.

Triangle	Triangle	Triangle
$a = 3$ cm	$a = 2$ cm	$a = 2$ cm
$b = 4$ cm	$b = 6$ cm	$b = 3$ cm
$c = ❑$	$c = ❑$	$c = ❑$

1. **smallest** $c =$ ______ cm 2. **middle size** $c =$ ______ cm 3. **largest** $c =$ ______ cm

4. The locations of three cellular phone towers form a right triangle on the map. The following distances are known:

   T_1 to T_2 = 20 miles

   T_1 to T_3 = 18 miles

   Use the following square-root number line to estimate the distance between T_2 and T_3. Fill in the blanks.

22	23	24	25	26	27	28	29	30
$\sqrt{484}$	$\sqrt{529}$	$\sqrt{576}$	$\sqrt{625}$	$\sqrt{676}$	$\sqrt{729}$	$\sqrt{784}$	$\sqrt{841}$	$\sqrt{900}$

   The distance is between ______ and ______ miles.

5. Now use a calculator to find the distance between cellular phone towers T_2 and T_3. Round your answer to the nearest tenth.

   ______ miles

Algebra

TRL

Activity 32

COMMON ERROR

Students occasionally skip steps as they apply the Pythagorean theorem. Often skipped is the step that squares the values for a and b, leading students to solve the equation $a + b = \sqrt{c}$. Another common error is failing to take the square root of c^2, leading students to solve the equation $a^2 + b^2 = c$. Stress the two variations of the Pythagorean theorem: $a^2 + b^2 = c^2$ and $\sqrt{(a^2 + b^2)} = \sqrt{c^2}$.

MANIPULATIVES

Solving $a^2 + b^2 = c^2$

Materials: Unit Cubes

Group Practice: Write the equation $3^2 + 4^2 = 5^2$ and draw and label the corresponding right triangle. Discuss the equation in terms of the Pythagorean theorem. To prove the theorem, build a model of the square of each number, combine the cubes in 3^2 and 4^2, and compare to the number of cubes in 5^2. Repeat for a 6, 8, 10 triangle, if necessary. Next, draw a right triangle and label one leg *8*, one leg a, and the hypotenuse *10*. Write the equation $a^2 + 8^2 = 10^2$. Build models of 8^2 and 10^2. Ask students how to find a^2. Then discuss how to find the length of leg a.

Student Practice: Have students use cubes for Exercise A.

Reinforce and Extend

LEARNING STYLES

Body/Kinesthetic

Have pairs of students discuss the Pythagorean theorem. Ask each student to draw a series of right triangles, labeling the legs a and b and the hypotenuse c. Then have students take turns explaining the relationship between a^2, b^2, and c^2 to his or her partner.

CALCULATOR

On some calculators, the $\sqrt{x}$ key is accessed by using a 2nd key. Explain to students that the 2nd key acts a bit like a shift key on a keyboard. Demonstrate how to use the 2nd key to access the $\sqrt{x}$ key to solve the following problem: For $c^2 = a^2 + b^2$, if $c = 29$ and $b = 21$, find a. $29^2 = 21^2 + a^2$

Press 29 x^2 =.
Read 841.
Press 21 x^2 =.
Read 441.
Solve for b^2: $841 - 441 = 400$
Press 400 2nd $\sqrt{x}$.
Read 200.

Have students use the 2nd key and the $\sqrt{x}$ key to find the missing values (the ones shown in parentheses).

$a = (7)$ $b = 24$ $c = 25$
$a = 9$ $b = 40$ $c = (41)$
$a = 8$ $b = (15)$ $c = 17$
$a = 10$ $b = (24)$ $c = 26$

Calculator Practice

The *square key* x^2 and the *square root key* $\sqrt{\ }$ on your calculator can be used to find the missing side of a right triangle, using the Pythagorean theorem.

$a = 32$ $b = ■$ $c = 40$

Step 1 Set up the problem using the Pythagorean theorem.
$c^2 = a^2 + b^2$
$40^2 = 32^2 + b^2$

Step 2 Use the calculator square key x^2 to simplify.

Press 40 x^2 = . The display reads 1600.

Press 32 x^2 = . The display reads 1024.

Now $40^2 = 32^2 + b^2$

becomes $1600 = 1024 + b^2$.

Step 3 Solve for b^2.
$1600 - 1024 = 1024 + b^2 - 1024$
$576 = b^2$

Step 4 Solve by finding the square root of each side of the equation. Use the *square root key* $\sqrt{\ }$ to find the value of b.

$\sqrt{576} = b^2$

Press 576 $\sqrt{\ }$ =. The display reads 24.

$\sqrt{576} = 24$

Therefore, $b = 24$.

Exercise B Use a calculator to find the missing side of each right triangle. Round your answer to the nearest tenth.

6. $a = 9$ $b = 40$ $c = ■$ 41
7. $a = ■$ $b = 6$ $c = 10$ 8
8. $a = 18$ $b = ■$ $c = 30$ 24
9. $a = 39$ $b = 36$ $c = ■$ 53.1
10. $a = 12$ $b = ■$ $c = 20$ 16
11. $a = 25$ $b = 9$ $c = ■$ 26.6

PROBLEM SOLVING

Exercise C Use the Pythagorean theorem to solve each problem.

blocks **12.** Martin leaves school and walks four blocks north and then three blocks east. How far is Martin from school?

8 feet **13.** A 10-foot ladder is leaning against a pole. The base of the ladder is six feet away from the pole. How high up the pole does the ladder reach?

blocks **14.** To get to the grocery store from her house, Francine walks 12 blocks east and then 5 blocks south. Using a straight line, how far is the grocery store from Francine's house?

26 feet **15.** A 10-foot telephone pole has a support wire attached to the top of the pole and the ground. It is attached 24 feet away from the bottom of the pole. How long is the support wire?

Estimation Activity

Estimate: The area of a triangle when you only know the length of one side.

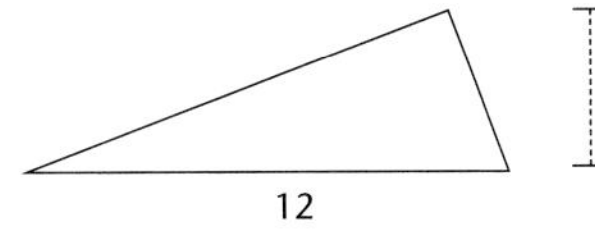

Solution: Estimate the height based on the length of the known side. Then calculate the area.

Height = about $\frac{1}{3}$ of the base.

Area $\approx \frac{1}{2}(12)(\frac{12}{3})$ or $(6)(4) = 24$ units^2

Group Problem Solving

Offer students the following problem. Suggest that they work in small groups to find a solution. Have each group present its solution as a sequence of frames in a storyboard. Presentations should include a diagram of the problem.

Students at Hilmann School plan to plant 22 oak trees around the perimeter of the school. Each tree needs to be braced with three wires. Each wire is attached $3\frac{1}{2}$ feet from the ground and $2\frac{1}{2}$ feet from the base of the trunk. What is the minimum amount of wire the students will need?

($\sqrt{3.5^2 + 2.5^2} = 4.3$ ft per wire, $3 \times 4.3 = 12.9$ ft/tree, 13 ft/tree $\times$ 22 trees $= 286$ ft)

Online Connection

This Internet site provides 40 different proofs of the Pythagorean theorem: www.cut-the-knot.org/pythagoras/index.shtml. Proof #5 was discovered by President James Garfield in 1876. Proof #16 is ascribed to Leonardo da Vinci (1452–1519). Some proofs may be difficult for students at this level to understand, but proof #36 is recommended for solving by middle school and high school students.

Lesson at a Glance

Chapter 3 Lesson 10

Overview This lesson explores equalities, inequalities, and disjunctions.

Objectives

- To write statements of equality or inequality based on information on a number line
- To graph statements of equality or inequality on a number line

Student Pages 84–87

Teacher's Resource Library 

Workbook Activity 35

Activity 33

Alternative Activity 33

Mathematics Vocabulary

disjunction
equality
graphing
inequality
truth table

Warm-Up Activity

Write the following on the board:

$2 + 3 > 4$

$4 + 2 + 3$ ■ $4 + 4$

$6 + 2 + 3$ ■ $4 + 6$

$7 + 2 + 3$ ■ $4 + 7$

Circle the common element, $2 + 3$ ■ 4, in the last three statements. Ask students what mathematical sign can replace the ■ in those statements. Have them explain their reasons in their own words.

Teaching the Lesson

Graph the first two examples on a number line on the board or on an overhead projector. Make certain students understand the difference between a closed dot (the value is included) and an open dot (the value is excluded).

Lesson 10 Inequalities on the Number Line

> ***Graphing***
> *Showing on a number line the relationship of a set of numbers*
>
> ***Equality***
> *The state of being equal; shown by the equal sign*
>
> ***Inequality***
> *The state of being unequal; shown by the less than, greater than, and unequal to signs*
>
> ***Disjunction***
> *A compound statement that uses the word or to connect two simple statements*

Recall that a number line can be used to display positive and negative integers. A number line can also help give you a *picture* of number sets. This *picturing* is called **graphing.**

The statement $x = 3$ is an **equality.**

When $x \neq 3$ (read as "x is not equal to 3"), the statement is an **inequality.**

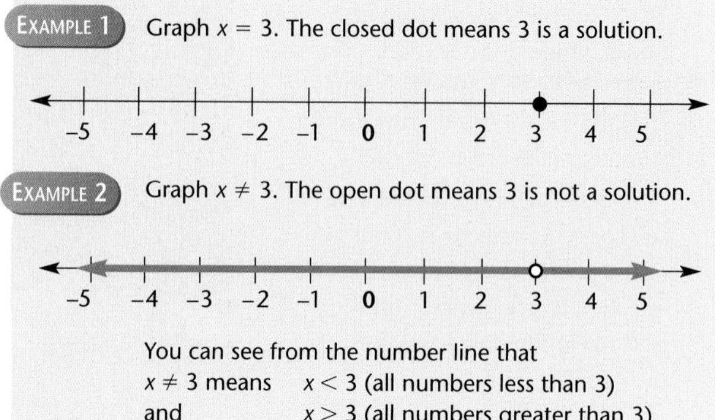

EXAMPLE 1 Graph $x = 3$. The closed dot means 3 is a solution.
−5 −4 −3 −2 −1 0 1 2 3 4 5
EXAMPLE 2 Graph $x \neq 3$. The open dot means 3 is not a solution.
−5 −4 −3 −2 −1 0 1 2 3 4 5
You can see from the number line that
$x \neq 3$ means $x < 3$ (all numbers less than 3)
and $x > 3$ (all numbers greater than 3)

The inequality $3 \leq 5$ is read "$3 < 5$ or $3 = 5$." This is an example of an *or* statement called a **disjunction.**

A disjunction is a compound statement using the word *or* to connect two simple statements. There is a rule that tells you when a disjunction is True (T) or False (F).

> **Rule for Disjunctions**
> A disjunction is always true except when both parts of the disjunction are false.

So "$3 < 5$ or $3 = 5$" is a true disjunction

(T) or F

and $3 \leq 5$ is a True statement.

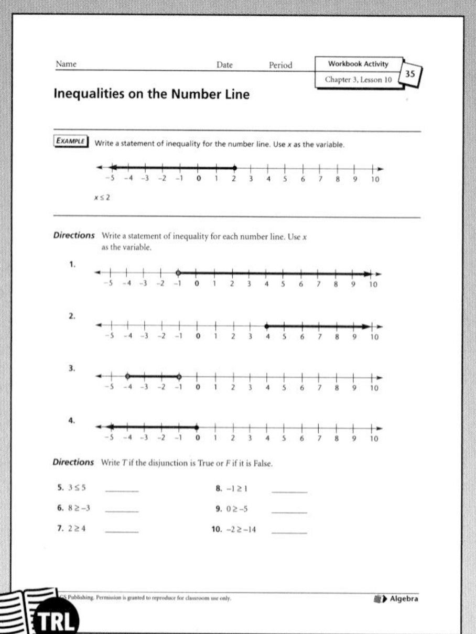

Name Date Period | Workbook Activity 35 | Chapter 3, Lesson 10

Inequalities on the Number Line

EXAMPLE Write a statement of inequality for the number line. Use x as the variable.

−5 −4 −3 −2 −1 0 1 2 3 4 5 6 7 8 9 10

$x \leq 2$

Directions Write a statement of inequality for each number line. Use x as the variable.

1. −5 −4 −3 −2 −1 0 1 2 3 4 5 6 7 8 9 10
2. −5 −4 −3 −2 −1 0 1 2 3 4 5 6 7 8 9 10
3. −5 −4 −3 −2 −1 0 1 2 3 4 5 6 7 8 9 10
4. −5 −4 −3 −2 −1 0 1 2 3 4 5 6 7 8 9 10

Directions Write *T* if the disjunction is True or *F* if it is False.

5. $3 \leq 5$ ______
6. $8 \geq -3$ ______
7. $2 \geq 4$ ______
8. $-1 \geq 1$ ______
9. $0 \geq -5$ ______
10. $-2 \geq -14$ ______

 Algebra

Workbook Activity 35

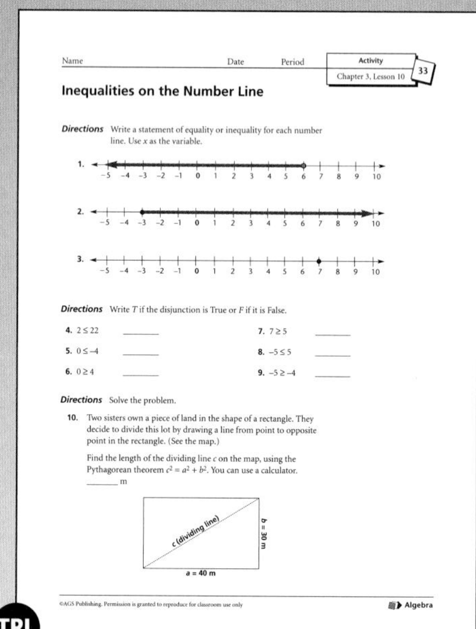

Name Date Period | Activity 33 | Chapter 3, Lesson 10

Inequalities on the Number Line

Directions Write a statement of equality or inequality for each number line. Use x as the variable.

1. −5 −4 −3 −2 −1 0 1 2 3 4 5 6 7 8 9 10
2. −5 −4 −3 −2 −1 0 1 2 3 4 5 6 7 8 9 10
3. −5 −4 −3 −2 −1 0 1 2 3 4 5 6 7 8 9 10

Directions Write *T* if the disjunction is True or *F* if it is False.

4. $2 \leq 22$ ______
5. $0 \leq -4$ ______
6. $0 \geq 4$ ______
7. $7 \geq 5$ ______
8. $-5 \leq 5$ ______
9. $-5 \geq -4$ ______

Directions Solve the problem.

10. Two sisters own a piece of land in the shape of a rectangle. They decide to divide this lot by drawing a line from point to opposite point in the rectangle. (See the map.)

    Find the length of the dividing line c on the map, using the Pythagorean theorem $c^2 = a^2 + b^2$. You can use a calculator.
    ______ m

    c (dividing line) — $b = 30$ m — $a = 40$ m

 Algebra

Activity 33

Truth table
A table of true and false values

If p is any statement, p can be T or F (2 possibilities).
If q is any statement, q can be T or F (2 possibilities).
p and q together have $2 \cdot 2 = 4$ possible combinations.

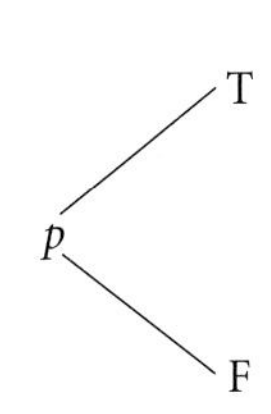
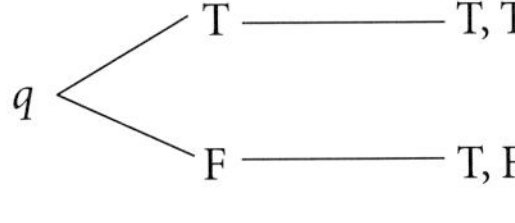
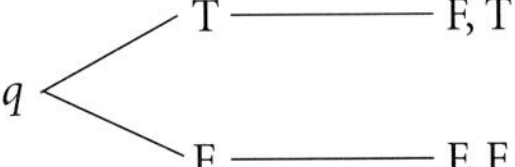

The rule for disjunctions can be summarized by a **truth table,** a table of T and F values like this:

p	q	Disjunction p or q
T	T	T
T	F	T
F	T	T
F	F	F

Use the rule for disjunctions to give the truth-value of each inequality.

$4 \le 10$

$4 \le 10$ means $4 < 10$ or $4 = 10$
T F — T or F means the statement is T.

Conclusion: $4 \le 10$ is T.

EXAMPLE 4

$-2 \ge 2$

$-2 \ge 2$ means $-2 > 2$ or $-2 = 2$.
F F — F or F means the statement is F.

Conclusion: $-2 \ge 2$ is F.

To graph the inequality $x \le 3$, you want to graph all points for which $x \le 3$ is true.

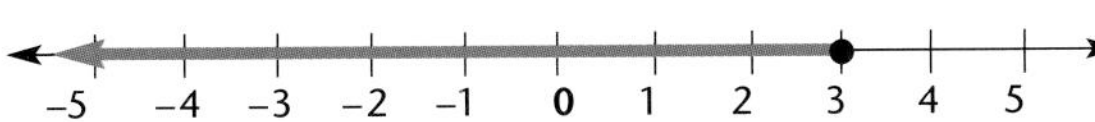

$x \le 3$ means $x < 3$ or $x = 3$
T T

Reinforce and Extend

LEARNING STYLES

Visual/Spatial

Have pairs of students prepare five cards, each showing one of the signs =, <, >, ≥, and ≤, and place the cards face down in a pile. One partner rolls two number cubes and chooses one card. That partner then writes a statement using the numbers on the cubes and the symbol on the card. The other partner reads the statement aloud and determines whether it is true or false. Partners change roles after each turn.

MENTAL MATH

Present students with the following pairs of numbers. Ask them to use =, <, or > to make the numbers into a statement that is true or false as indicated.

4, 3	True	*(4 > 3)*
4, 3	False	*(4 = 3 or 4 < 3)*
17, 15	True	*(17 > 15)*
32, 0	False	*(32 = 0 or 32 < 0)*
5, 9	True	*(5 < 9)*

Learning Styles

Interpersonal/ Group Learning

Have small groups of students prepare a truth table for the following statements. The table should give the truth-values for p, q, and the disjunction "p or q."

p = all birds have feathers
q = most birds can fly

p = the sun rises in the east
q = fish can sing

p = baseball is played on ice
q = hockey is played with a puck

p = bowling balls are light
q = Ping-Pong balls are heavy

Example truth table:

p	*q*	*p or q*
T	T	T
T	F	F
F	T	F
F	F	F

Example 5 Graph the inequality $x \geq 3$.

Graph the inequality $x \geq 3$ by darkening a circle around 3 and drawing a line segment and an arrow to the right.

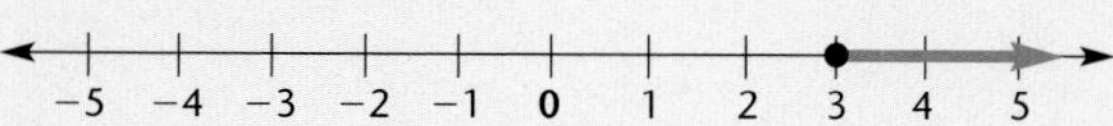

This graph shows all numbers between −1 and 1.

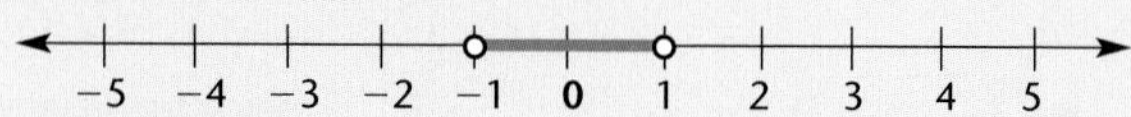

In algebra, the data displayed by the graph are $-1 < x < 1$ or −1 is less than x, which is less than 1.
(This also can be read as x is between −1 and 1.)

This graph shows all numbers between −1 and 1 *including* the points −1 and 1.

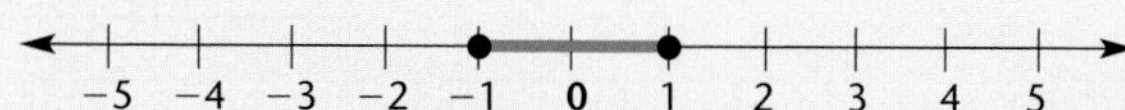

The data displayed by the graph can be written as $-1 \leq x \leq 1$.

Exercise A Write a statement of equality or inequality for each graph on the number line. Use x as the variable.

1.  $x = 6$

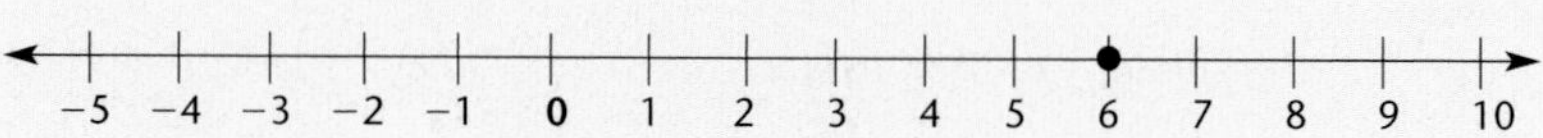

2. $x = -3$

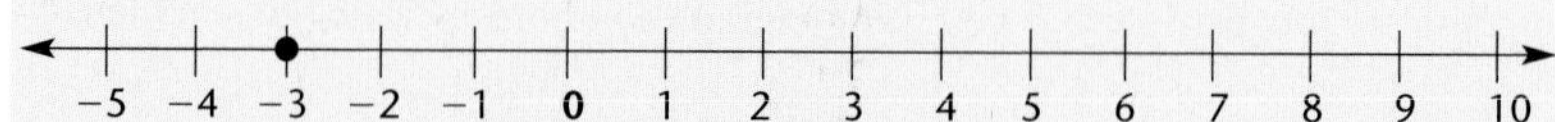

3. $x \neq 9$

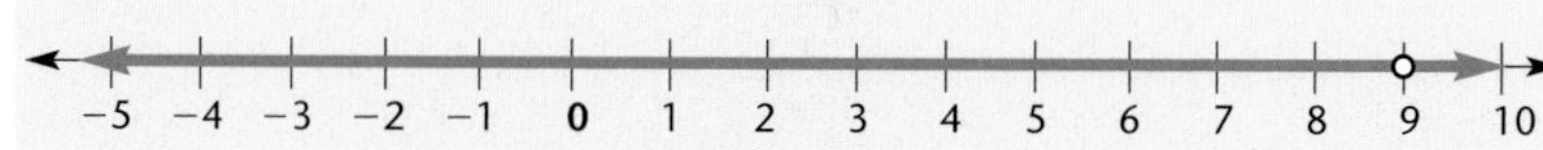

4. $x \le 2$

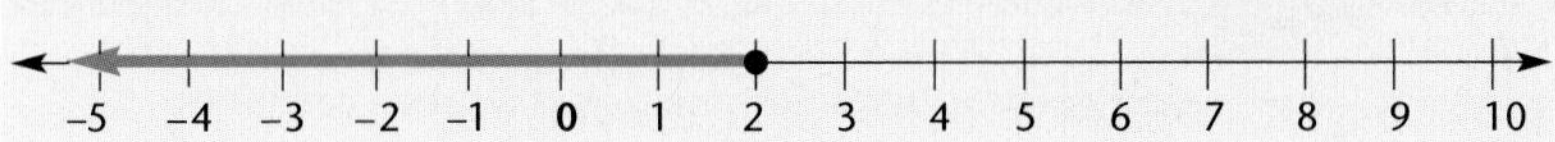

5. $x \ne -5$

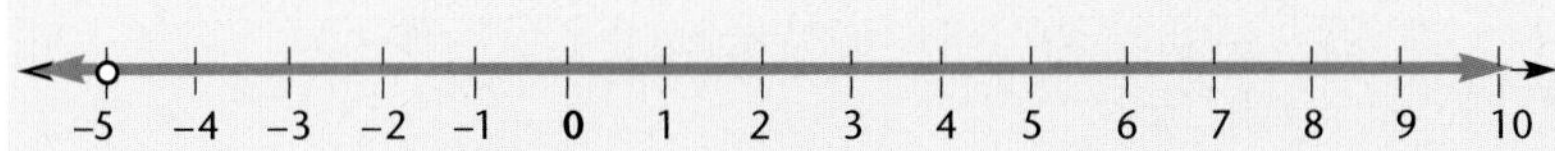

6. $x \ge -4$

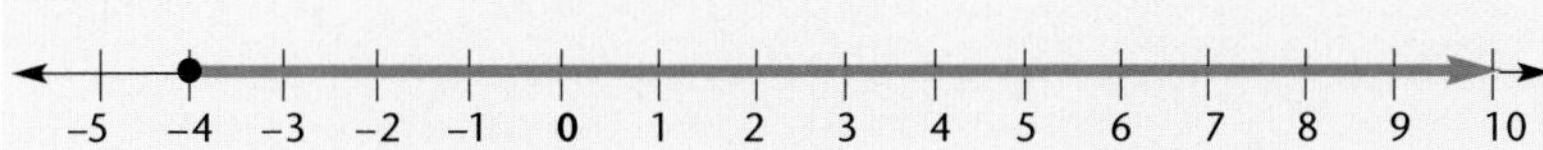

7. $x > 1$

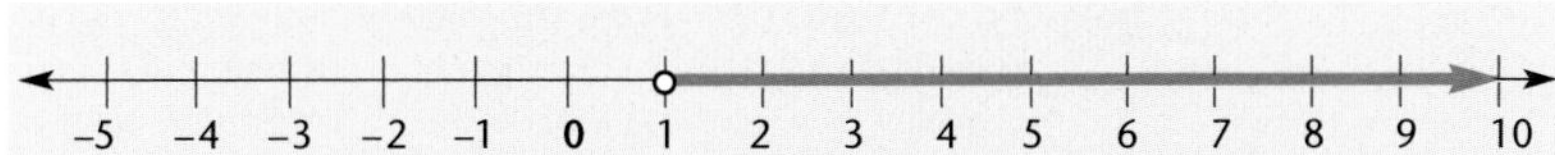

Exercise B Graph each of the equalities or inequalities on a number line.

8. $x < 2$	open dot on 2, arrow left	**14.** $x \ne 6$	open dot on 6, arrow right, arrow left
9. $x = 2$	closed dot on 2	**15.** $1 < x < 4$	opendots on 1 and 4, line connecting 1 and 4
10. $x \ge -5$	closed dot on −5, arrow right	**16.** $-2 < x < 0$	open dots on −2 and 0, line connecting −2 and 0
11. $x \le -3$	closed dot on −3, arrow left	**17.** $-8 \le x \le 8$	closed dots on −8 and 8, line connecting −8 and 8
12. $x = -10$	closed dot on −10	**18.** $7 \le x \le 10$	closed dots on 7 and 10, line connecting 7 and 10
13. $x > -4$	open dot on −4, arrow right	**19.** $x \ne 3$	open dot on 3, arrow right, arrow left

Exercise C Write T if the disjunction is True or F if the disjunction is False.

20. $1 \le 10$	T	**23.** $-2 \ge -2$	T
21. $10 \le 10$	T	**24.** $7 \le 10$	T
22. $-2 \ge 1$	F	**25.** $x \le -1$ when $x = 0$	F

Learning Styles

LEP/ESL

ESL students may benefit from additional practice reading equality and inequality statements. Have students work in pairs. As one partner reads aloud an item from Exercise B, the other partner writes the statement without using symbols. Be certain students change roles frequently.

Learning Styles

Interpersonal/ Group Learning

Have students work in groups of four. Each group will need two number cubes. Two students roll the number cubes and then use either the ≥ or the ≤ symbol to write statements using the numbers from a single toss. Remaining group members identify the statements as either true or false. Groups might try to form only true or only false statements.

Lesson at a Glance

Chapter 3 Lesson 11

Overview This lesson shows how to solve inequalities with one variable.

Objectives

- To solve inequalities with one variable
- To use strategies including opposites and reciprocals to solve inequalities with one variable

Student Pages 88–89

Teacher's Resource Library 

Workbook Activity 36

Activity 34

Alternative Activity 34

1 Warm-Up Activity

Write the following on the board:

5	>	4
4 + 5	■	5 + 4
6(5)	■	(4)6
−6(5)	■	(4)(−6)

Circle the common element, 5 ■ 4, in the last three statements. Ask students what mathematical sign can replace the ■ in those statements. Have them describe their observations in their own words.

 2 Teaching the Lesson

Demonstrate the second set of examples on the board or overhead projector. Help students recognize that dividing or multiplying an equality by a negative number changes the direction of the inequality.

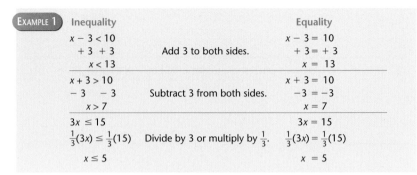

Lesson 11 Solving Inequalities with One Variable

Solve inequalities the same way you solved equalities.

EXAMPLE 1

Inequality		Equality
$x - 3 < 10$		$x - 3 = 10$
$+3 \quad +3$	Add 3 to both sides.	$+3 = +3$
$x < 13$		$x = 13$
$x + 3 > 10$		$x + 3 = 10$
$-3 \quad -3$	Subtract 3 from both sides.	$-3 = -3$
$x > 7$		$x = 7$
$3x \le 15$		$3x = 15$
$\frac{1}{3}(3x) \le \frac{1}{3}(15)$	Divide by 3 or multiply by $\frac{1}{3}$.	$\frac{1}{3}(3x) = \frac{1}{3}(15)$
$x \le 5$		$x = 5$

Rule You can add or subtract the same number from both sides of an inequality, and you can multiply or divide both sides of an inequality by a *positive* number without changing the value of the inequality.

The reason you *cannot* divide or multiply by a negative number without changing the direction of the inequality sign is as follows:

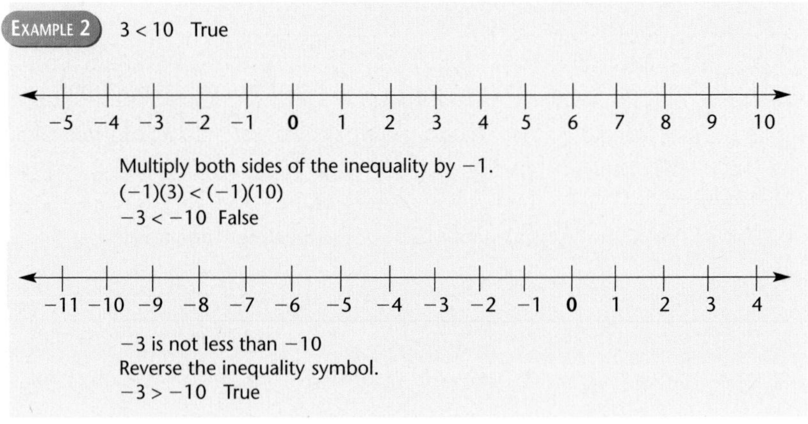

EXAMPLE 2 $3 < 10$ True

Multiply both sides of the inequality by −1.
$(-1)(3) < (-1)(10)$
$-3 < -10$ False

−3 is not less than −10
Reverse the inequality symbol.
$-3 > -10$ True

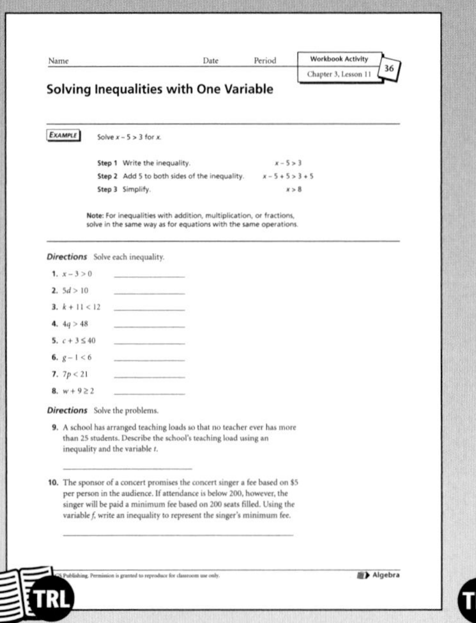

Name Date Period **Workbook Activity 36** Chapter 3, Lesson 11

Solving Inequalities with One Variable

EXAMPLE Solve $x - 5 > 3$ for x.

Step 1 Write the inequality. $x - 5 > 3$
Step 2 Add 5 to both sides of the inequality. $x - 5 + 5 > 3 + 5$
Step 3 Simplify. $x > 8$

Note: For inequalities with addition, multiplication, or fractions, solve in the same way as for equations with the same operations.

Directions Solve each inequality.

1. $x - 3 > 0$ ______
2. $5d > 10$ ______
3. $k + 11 < 12$ ______
4. $4q > 48$ ______
5. $c + 3 \le 40$ ______
6. $g - 1 < 6$ ______
7. $7p < 21$ ______
8. $w + 9 \ge 2$ ______

Directions Solve the problems.

9. A school has arranged teaching loads so that no teacher ever has more than 25 students. Describe the school's teaching load using an inequality and the variable *t*.

______

10. The sponsor of a concert promises the concert singer a fee based on $5 per person in the audience. If attendance is below 200, however, the singer will be paid a minimum fee based on 200 seats filled. Using the variable *f*, write an inequality to represent the singer's minimum fee.

______

 Algebra

Workbook Activity 36

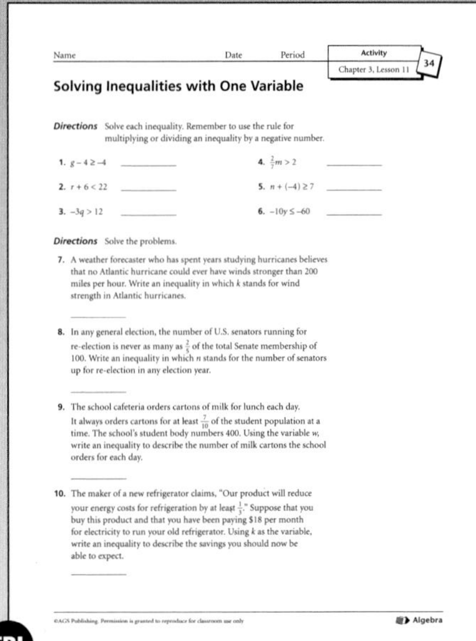

Name Date Period **Activity 34** Chapter 3, Lesson 11

Solving Inequalities with One Variable

Directions Solve each inequality. Remember to use the rule for multiplying or dividing an inequality by a negative number.

1. $g - 4 \ge -4$ ______
2. $r + 6 < 22$ ______
3. $-3q > 12$ ______
4. $\frac{2}{7}m > 2$ ______
5. $n + (-4) \ge 7$ ______
6. $-10y \le -60$ ______

Directions Solve the problems.

7. A weather forecaster who has spent years studying hurricanes believes that no Atlantic hurricane could ever have winds stronger than 200 miles per hour. Write an inequality in which *k* stands for wind strength in Atlantic hurricanes.

______

8. In any general election, the number of U.S. senators running for re-election is never as many as $\frac{2}{5}$ of the total Senate membership of 100. Write an inequality in which *n* stands for the number of senators up for re-election in any election year.

______

9. The school cafeteria orders cartons of milk for lunch each day. It always orders cartons for at least $\frac{7}{10}$ of the student population at a time. The school's student body numbers 400. Using the variable *w*, write an inequality to describe the number of milk cartons the school orders for each day.

______

10. The maker of a new refrigerator claims, "Our product will reduce your energy costs for refrigeration by at least $\frac{1}{3}$." Suppose that you buy this product and that you have been paying $18 per month for electricity to run your old refrigerator. Using *k* as the variable, write an inequality to describe the savings you should now be able to expect.

______

 Algebra

Activity 34

EXAMPLE 3 Divide both sides of $6 > 4$ by -2.

Divide both sides by -2.	$\frac{6}{-2} > \frac{4}{-2}$	
	$-3 > -2$	False
Reverse the inequality sign.	$-3 < -2$	True

Rule When you multiply or divide an inequality by a negative number, you must reverse the direction of the inequality sign to keep the statement true.

Exercise A Solve each inequality.

1. $x + 4 > 10$ $x > 6$
2. $\frac{7}{8}b < -21$ $b < -24$
3. $w + 8 > 15$ $w > 7$
4. $6s \le 42$ $s \le 7$
5. $g + (-5) \le 15$ $g \le 20$
6. $4f < 44$ $f < 11$
7. $\frac{1}{2}m < -7$ $m < -14$
8. $p - 4 \le 5$ $p \le 9$

Exercise B Solve each inequality. Remember to use the rule for multiplying or dividing an inequality by a negative number.

9. $-5c < 20$ $c > -4$
10. $-\frac{1}{3}y \ge 3$ $y \le -9$
11. $-2t \ge -20$ $t \le 10$
12. $-\frac{1}{6}k \le -3$ $k \ge 18$
13. $-4x > 16$ $x < -4$
14. $-\frac{3}{8}c > -9$ $c < 24$
15. $-11m \le 33$ $m \ge -3$
16. $-\frac{2}{3}n > -14$ $n < 21$

PROBLEM SOLVING

Exercise C Write an inequality to solve each problem.

17. Juan finds the growth rate of snow peas is always less than 95 mm per day. Describe the growth rate of peas using an inequality and the letter *p*.
18. At the county agricultural center, Young finds that the germination temperature for Kentucky bluegrass has to be greater than 58°F. Write an inequality that uses the letter *g* to describe the temperature.
19. Kim learns the number of grubs in a city lawn is always less than 2,500. Show the number of grubs as an inequality that includes the letter *i*.
20. During a pumpkin-growing contest, John finds the number of Connecticut field pumpkins entered is never more than $\frac{1}{3}$ the number of people attending the contest. One hundred fifty people are registered. Use the letter *c* and an inequality to show the number of Connecticut field pumpkins entered in the contest.

17. $p < 95$ 18. $g > 58$
19. $i < 2{,}500$ 20. $c \le \frac{1}{3}(150)$ or $c \le 50$

3 Reinforce and Extend

LEARNING STYLES

Logical/Mathematical

Have students solve the even-numbered items in Exercise A. For each item, students should graph the inequality on a number line, then add, subtract, multiply, or divide to solve the inequality.

GROUP PROBLEM SOLVING

Direct students to work in groups of four to develop equality and inequality statements that can be used to identify the families to which wildflowers belong. Students can develop statements such as

rose — petals = 5
daisy — rays < 30
aster — rays > 40
lily — petals = 6.

Allow students to decide which characteristic—leaves, petals, rays, stamens, sepals, or height—they will use. Suggest they use sources such as wildflower field guides. Have groups prepare posters to present their information.

Lesson at a Glance

Chapter 3 Application

Overview This lesson presents an application of equations: comparing the unknown to the known.

Objective

- To use known data to develop and solve equations to find unknown data

Student Page 90

Teacher's Resource Library 

Application Activity 3

Everyday Algebra 3

Warm-Up Activity

Ask students to describe, and name, if possible, the tallest building they have seen or visited.

Teaching the Lesson

Point out to students that the key to many word problems is to (1) correctly identify the unknown, (2) use the given information to write an equation that describes the unknown, and (3) solve for the unknown. Review the example.

Reinforce and Extend

IN THE COMMUNITY

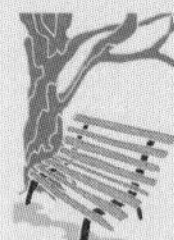

Have small groups of students choose their community, a large city, or their state as their subject and use local resources such as libraries and historical societies to find the heights of the three tallest buildings in those places. They may gather data in feet, meters, or number of stories. Have the groups develop a class graph showing the locations and relative heights of the tallest buildings. Each group can use the graph to write three equations. Groups can then exchange and solve each other's equations.

Application $\pi^2 \Sigma + \Omega \sqrt{x^2} \% \neq y \geq n = \nabla 30^\circ \pi$

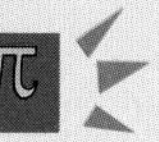

Using Equations Set up equations to solve problems. First identify the unknown. Assign a letter to represent the unknown. Create an equation that relates the unknown to the known. Then solve the equation.

EXAMPLE 1 The Osborn Building in St. Paul has two-thirds as many stories as the Xerox Tower in Rochester, Minnesota. The Osborn Building has 20 stories. How many stories does the Xerox Tower have?

Step 1 Read the problem carefully to set up the equation.

j = number of stories in the Xerox Tower

$\frac{2}{3}j = 20$

Step 2 Solve the equation.

$\frac{2}{3}j = 20$

$\frac{2}{3}j \bullet \frac{3}{2} = 20 \bullet \frac{3}{2}$ (multiply each side by $\frac{3}{2}$, the reciprocal of $\frac{2}{3}$)

$j = 30$

Step 3 Write your answer in sentence form. The Xerox Tower has 30 stories.

Exercise Use equations to solve the following problems about buildings around the country.

1. One Liberty Place is the tallest building in Philadelphia, measuring 945 feet, which is 397 feet taller than Philadelphia's City Hall Tower. How tall is the City Hall Tower? 548 feet
2. One Liberty Place is 585 feet taller than Philadelphia's City Hall Tower, not including the statue of William Penn. How tall is the statue of William Penn on top of City Hall Tower? 188 feet
3. The 333 Market Building in San Francisco is only half the size of Society Center in Cleveland. The 333 Market Building is 474 feet tall. How tall is Society Center? 948 feet
4. The John Hancock Tower in Boston has triple the number of stories as the Southern National Finance Center building in Winston-Salem. The John Hancock Tower has 60 stories. How many stories does the Southern National Finance Center building have? 20 stories
5. Chicago's Amoco Building is 1,136 feet tall, which is 688 feet taller than Denver's Amoco Building. How tall is Denver's Amoco Building? 448 feet

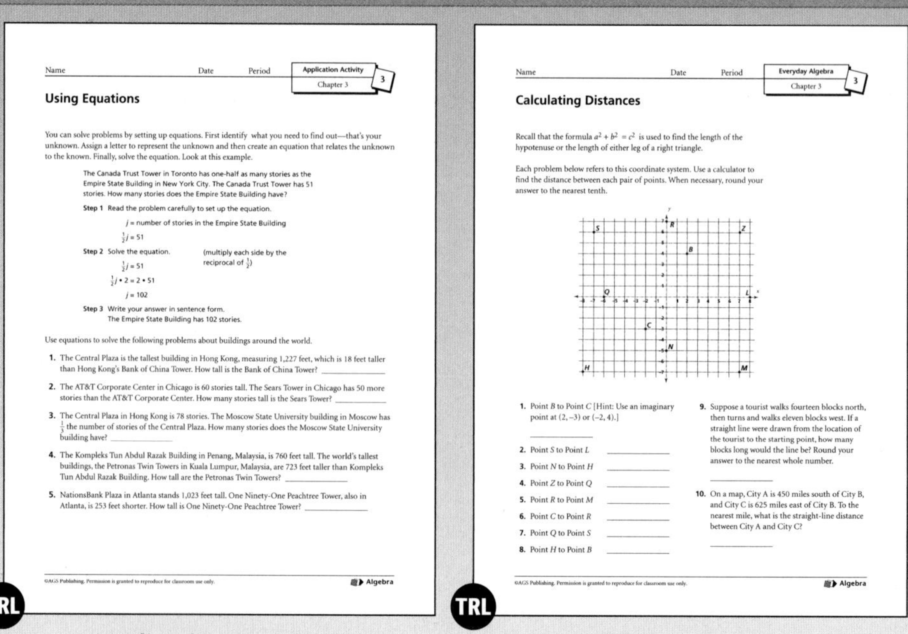

Name Date Period **Application Activity 3** Chapter 3

Using Equations

You can solve problems by setting up equations. First identify what you need to find out—that's your unknown. Assign a letter to represent the unknown and then create an equation that relates the unknown to the known. Finally, solve the equation. Look at this example.

The Canada Trust Tower in Toronto has one-half as many stories as the Empire State Building in New York City. The Canada Trust Tower has 51 stories. How many stories does the Empire State Building have?

Step 1 Read the problem carefully to set up the equation.

j = number of stories in the Empire State Building

$\frac{1}{2}j = 51$

Step 2 Solve the equation. (multiply each side by the reciprocal of $\frac{1}{2}$)

$\frac{1}{2}j = 51$

$\frac{1}{2}j \bullet 2 = 2 \bullet 51$

$j = 102$

Step 3 Write your answer in sentence form. The Empire State Building has 102 stories.

Use equations to solve the following problems about buildings around the world.

1. The Central Plaza is the tallest building in Hong Kong, measuring 1,227 feet, which is 18 feet taller than Hong Kong's Bank of China Tower. How tall is the Bank of China Tower? ________
2. The AT&T Corporate Center in Chicago is 60 stories tall. The Sears Tower in Chicago has 50 more stories than the AT&T Corporate Center. How many stories tall is the Sears Tower? ________
3. The Central Plaza in Hong Kong is 78 stories. The Moscow State University building in Moscow has $\frac{1}{3}$ the number of stories of the Central Plaza. How many stories does the Moscow State University building have? ________
4. The Kompleks Tun Abdul Razak Building in Penang, Malaysia, is 760 feet tall. The world's tallest buildings, the Petronas Twin Towers in Kuala Lumpur, Malaysia, are 723 feet taller than Kompleks Tun Abdul Razak Building. How tall are the Petronas Twin Towers? ________
5. NationsBank Plaza in Atlanta stands 1,023 feet tall. One Ninety-One Peachtree Tower, also in Atlanta, is 253 feet shorter. How tall is One Ninety-One Peachtree Tower? ________

 Algebra

TRL

Application Activity 3

Name Date Period **Everyday Algebra 3** Chapter 3

Calculating Distances

Recall that the formula $a^2 + b^2 = c^2$ is used to find the length of the hypotenuse or the length of either leg of a right triangle.

Each problem below refers to this coordinate system. Use a calculator to find the distance between each pair of points. When necessary, round your answer to the nearest tenth.

1. Point B to Point C [Hint: Use an imaginary point at (2, –3) or (–2, 4).] ________
2. Point S to Point L ________
3. Point N to Point H ________
4. Point Z to Point Q ________
5. Point R to Point M ________
6. Point C to Point R ________
7. Point Q to Point S ________
8. Point H to Point B ________
9. Suppose a tourist walks fourteen blocks north, then turns and walks eleven blocks west. If a straight line were drawn from the location of the tourist to the starting point, how many blocks long would the line be? Round your answer to the nearest whole number. ________
10. On a map, City A is 450 miles south of City B, and City C is 625 miles east of City B. To the nearest mile, what is the straight-line distance between City A and City C? ________

 Algebra

TRL

Everyday Algebra 3

Chapter 3 REVIEW

Find the solution for the equation.
Write the letter of the correct answer.

1. $m - 3 = 4$ C

A $m = 1$ **C** $m = 7$

B $m = -7$ **D** $m = -1$

2. $j + 2 = -8$ A

A $j = -10$ **C** $j = -6$

B $j = 6$ **D** $j = -8$

3. $\frac{1}{4}x = 8$ C

A $x = 2$ **C** $x = 32$

B $x = 12$ **D** $x = 16$

4. $-6x = 24$ B

A 4 **C** 18

B -4 **D** -30

5. $3.2h = -6.4$ D

A $h = 2$ **C** $h = 9.6$

B $h = -3.2$ **D** $h = -2$

Solve for x. Write the letter of the correct answer.

6. $-a = bx$ B

A $b = \frac{-a}{x}$ **C** $x = \frac{-b}{a}$

B $x = \frac{-a}{b}$ **D** $x = \frac{a}{b}$

7. $cx + ax = b$ A

A $x = \frac{b}{(c + a)}$ **C** $x = b(a + c)$

B $x = \frac{(c + a)}{b}$ **D** $x = \frac{b}{2ac}$

Chapter 3 Review

Each set of problems in the Chapter Review includes an example and solution to illustrate the concept. Use the given examples for reteaching the materials in Chapter 3. For additional practice, refer to the Supplementary Problems for Chapter 3 (pages 410–411).

Chapter 3 Mastery Test 

The Teacher's Resource Library includes parallel forms of the Chapter 3 Mastery Test. The difficulty level of the two forms is equivalent. You may wish to use one form as a pretest and the other form as a posttest.

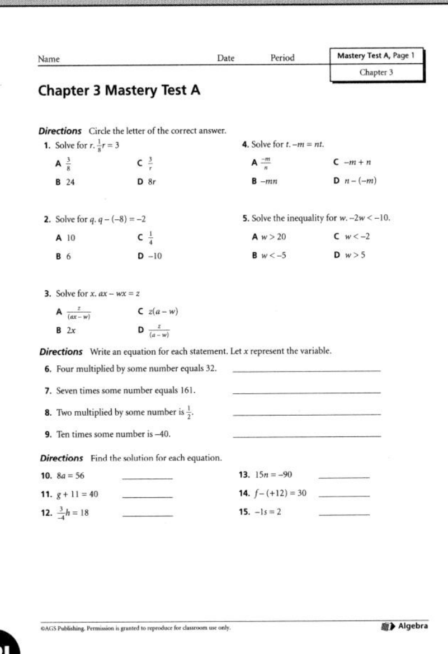

Name Date Period | Mastery Test A, Page 1 | Chapter 3

Chapter 3 Mastery Test A

Directions Circle the letter of the correct answer.

1. Solve for r. $\frac{1}{8}r = 3$

A $\frac{3}{8}$ **C** $\frac{3}{r}$ **B** 24 **D** $8r$

2. Solve for q. $q - (-8) = -2$

A 10 **C** $\frac{1}{4}$ **B** 6 **D** -10

3. Solve for x. $ax - wx = z$

A $\frac{z}{(ax - w)}$ **C** $z(a - w)$ **B** $2x$ **D** $\frac{z}{(a - w)}$

4. Solve for t. $-m = nt$.

A $\frac{-m}{n}$ **C** $-m + n$ **B** $-mn$ **D** $n - (-m)$

5. Solve the inequality for w. $-2w < -10$.

A $w > 20$ **C** $w < -2$ **B** $w < -5$ **D** $w > 5$

Directions Write an equation for each statement. Let x represent the variable.

6. Four multiplied by some number equals 32. ____________

7. Seven times some number equals 161. ____________

8. Two multiplied by some number is $\frac{1}{2}$. ____________

9. Ten times some number is –40. ____________

Directions Find the solution for each equation.

10. $8a = 56$ ________ **13.** $15n = -90$ ________

11. $g + 11 = 40$ ________ **14.** $f - (+12) = 30$ ________

12. $\frac{3}{-4}h = 18$ ________ **15.** $-1s = 2$ ________

 Algebra

TRL

Name Date Period | Mastery Test A, Page 2 | Chapter 3

Chapter 3 Mastery Test A, continued

Directions Solve.

16. The formula for finding the area of a triangle is $A = \frac{1}{2}bh$ where b represents the length of the base of the triangle and h represents the height. Solve the formula for b. $b =$ ______

17. The formula for finding the one side of a right triangle is $a^2 + b^2 = c^2$ where a and b represent the lengths of the legs of the triangle and c represents the length of the hypotenuse. Suppose the hypotenuse of a right triangle measures 13 cm and one leg measures 5 cm. What is the length of the other leg? ______ cm

Directions Write a statement of equality or inequality for each graph on the number line. Use x as the variable.

18. −5 −4 −3 −2 −1 0 1 2 3 4 5 ____________

19. −3 −2 −1 0 1 2 3 4 5 6 7 ____________

20. −8 −7 −6 −5 −4 −3 −2 −1 0 1 2 ____________

 Algebra

TRL

Chapter 3 Mastery Test A

Alternative Assessment

Alternative Assessment items correlate with student Goals for Learning at the beginning of this chapter.

■ **To write and solve equations**
Have students write an equation for the following problem, then have them solve it: Heidi and Ming each buy 3 CDs totaling $63.00. What is the average cost per CD? Let p equal the price of 1 CD. *($2 \cdot 3p = 63$; $p = 10.50$)*

■ **To use formulas for perimeter and area to solve problems**
Have students solve the following problem using the formula for the area of a circle: The area of a circle is $A = \pi r^2$ where A equals the area and r equals the radius. Find the radius of a circle whose area equals 113.04. Let $\pi = 3.14$. *($r = 6$)*

■ **To use the Pythagorean theorem to solve problems**
Have students solve the following problem using the Pythagorean theorem: The park department is planting 20 new trees. Each tree needs a support wire, which is attached 2 feet from the base of the tree and 3 feet up from the ground. About how long will each support wire need to be (excluding the amount needed for wrapping around the tree and the ground stake)? Round to the nearest hundredth. Extra points: Assume 1 extra foot for wrapping around each tree and 0.5 feet extra for each ground stake. How much wire must the park department buy? Round upwards to the nearest foot. *(Answer: $c = \sqrt{13}$ or 3.61 ft. Extra points: $20(3.61 + 1.5) = 102.2$ ft of wire needed, so 103 ft of wire must be purchased.)*

■ **To graph inequalities on the number line**
Have students describe the significance of open dots and closed dots on a number line. *(An open dot means that a number is not included in the solution. Example: An open dot on the number five would mean that $x \neq 5$. A closed means that the number is included. Example: A closed dot on the number 7 means $x = 7$.)*

Write an equation for each statement. Let x be the variable in each equation.

Example: 4 times some number equals 32. Solution: $4x = 32$

8. 3 times some number equals 36. $3x = 36$

9. 14 times some number plus 5 equals 33. $14x + 5 = 33$

10. 6 times some number minus 18 equals 24. $6x - 18 = 24$

11. 8 times some number equals 24. $8x = 24$

Solve each problem using a formula for perimeter or area.

Example: $P = 3s$ Solve for s. Solution: $P = 3s$ (divide each side by 3)

$$\frac{P}{3} = \frac{3s}{3}$$

$$\frac{P}{3} = s$$

12. $P = 5s$ Solve for s. $s = \frac{P}{5}$

13. $\frac{A}{h} = w$ Solve for A. $A = wh$

14. $P - c = a + b$ Solve for P. $P = a + b + c$

15. $2A = bh$ Solve for A. $A = \frac{(bh)}{2}$

16. $P = a + b + c$ Solve for a. $a = P - b - c$

Use the Pythagorean theorem and a calculator to find the missing side of each right triangle.

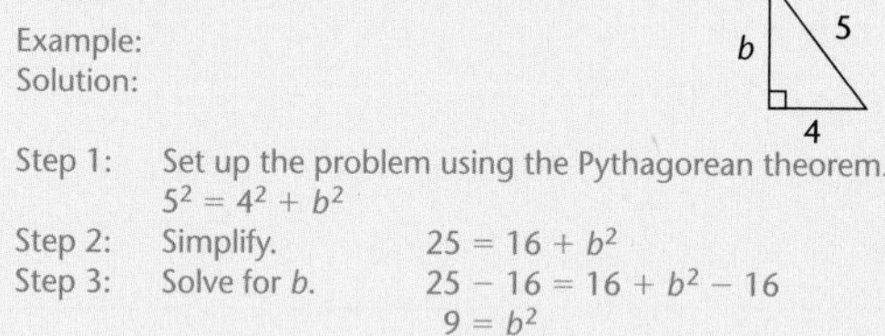

Example:
Solution:

Step 1: Set up the problem using the Pythagorean theorem.
$5^2 = 4^2 + b^2$

Step 2: Simplify. $25 = 16 + b^2$

Step 3: Solve for b. $25 - 16 = 16 + b^2 - 16$
$9 = b^2$
$3 = b$

Name Date Period | Mastery Test B, Page 1 | Chapter 3

Chapter 3 Mastery Test B

Directions Circle the letter of the correct answer.

1. Solve for b. $-r = sb$
   A $-\frac{r}{s}$ B $-rs$ C $-r + s$ D $s - (-r)$
2. Solve for r. $\frac{1}{8}r = 4$
   A $\frac{4}{8}$ B 32 C $\frac{4}{r}$ D $8r$
3. Solve for y. $ay - xy = z$
   A $\frac{z}{(ay - x)}$ B $2y$ C $z(a - x)$ D $\frac{z}{(a - x)}$
4. Solve the inequality for w. $-3w > -15$
   A $w > 45$ B $w < -5$ C $w < -3$ D $w > 5$
5. Solve for q. $q - (-8) = -3$
   A 11 B 5 C $\frac{-3}{8}$ D -11

Directions Write an equation for each statement. Let x represent the variable.

6. Three multiplied by some number equals 27. ______
7. Nine times some number equals 210. ______
8. Five multiplied by some number is $\frac{1}{5}$. ______
9. Twelve times some number is -36. ______

Directions Find the solution for each equation.

10. $6a = 48$ ______
11. $w - 23 = 31$ ______
12. $\frac{1}{-3}z =$ ______
13. $12r = -72$ ______
14. $m - (+8) = 43$ ______
15. $-3q = 6$ ______

 Algebra

TRL

Name Date Period | Mastery Test B, Page 2 | Chapter 3

Chapter 3 Mastery Test B, continued

Directions Solve

16. The formula for finding the area of a triangle is $A = \frac{1}{2}bh$ where b represents the length of the base of the triangle and h represents the height. Solve the formula for b. $b =$ ______
17. The formula for finding the one side of a right triangle is $a^2 + b^2 = c^2$ where a and b represent the lengths of the legs of the triangle and c represents the length of the hypotenuse. Suppose the hypotenuse of a right triangle measures 13 cm and one leg measures 5 cm. What is the length of the other leg? ______ cm

Directions Write a statement of equality or inequality for each graph on the number line. Use x as the variable.

18. −5 −4 −3 −2 −1 0 1 2 3 4 5 ______
19. −3 −2 −1 0 1 2 3 4 5 6 7 ______
20. −8 −7 −6 −5 −4 −3 −2 −1 0 1 2 ______

 Algebra

TRL

Chapter 3 Mastery Test B

Find the length of the missing side of each triangle.

17. $c = 10$

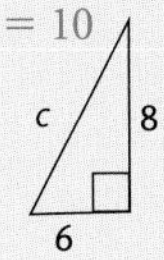

19. $a = 9$

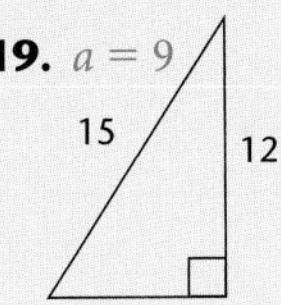

18. $c = 20$

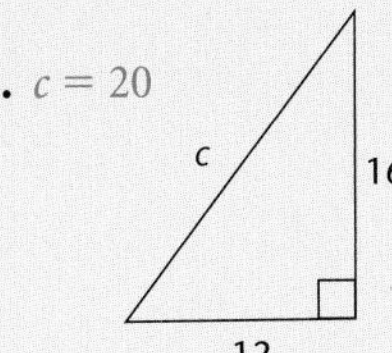

20.

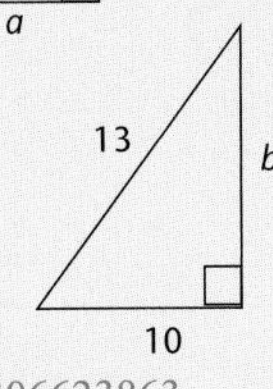

$b = 8.306623863$

Graph each equality or inequality using a number line.

Example: $x \leq 3$ Solution:

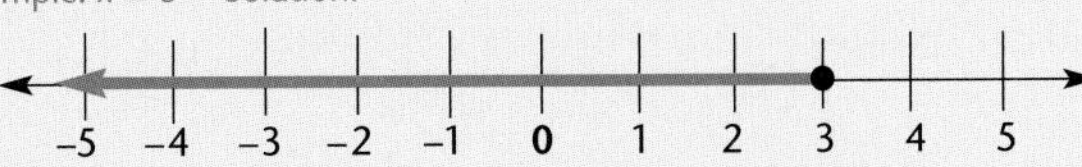

21. $x = -2$

22. $x < 5$

23. $x \neq 6$

24. $1 < x \leq 4$

25. $-9 \leq x \leq 2$

26. $x + 8 < 10$

21. closed circle at -2

22. open circle at 5, darkened arrow left

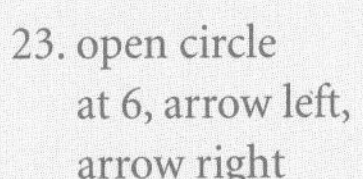

23. open circle at 6, arrow left, arrow right

24. open circle at 1, closed circle at 4, connected by darkened line segment

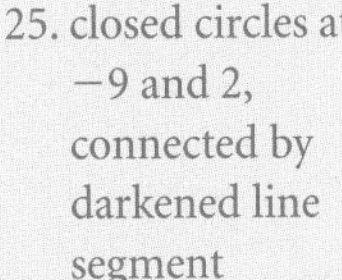

25. closed circles at -9 and 2, connected by darkened line segment

26. open circle on 2, darkened arrow left

Solve each inequality.

Example: $3s < 27$

Solution: $3s < 27$
(divide each side by 3)

$\frac{3s}{3} < \frac{27}{3}$

$s < 9$

27. $b + (-5) \geq 13$ $b \geq 18$

28. $-6d \leq 48$ $d \geq -8$

29. $v - 4 \leq 5$ $v < 9$

30. $3x > -21$ $x > -7$

Test-Taking Tip

When taking a mathematics test, complete the answers that you know before tackling more difficult problems.

Alternative Assessment, continued

■ **To solve inequalities**
Have students explain why you must reverse the direction of the inequality sign when you multiply or divide by a negative number. *(A negative multiplied or divided by a positive is always negative, or a positive multiplied or divided by a negative is also always negative.)*

Chapter

Planning Guide

Applications of Algebra

		Student Text Lesson			
		Student Pages	Vocabulary	Practice Exercises	Solutions Key
Lesson 1	Writing Equations—Odd and Even Integers	96–97	✔	✔	✔
Lesson 2	Using the 1% Solution to Solve Problems	98–99	✔	✔	✔
Lesson 3	Using the Percent Equation	100–103	✔	✔	✔
Lesson 4	Solving Distance, Rate, and Time Problems	104–107		✔	✔
Lesson 5	Using a Common Unit—Cents	108–110		✔	✔
Lesson 6	Calculating Simple Interest	111–113	✔	✔	✔
Lesson 7	Deriving a Formula for Mixture Problems	114–115		✔	✔
Lesson 8	Ratio and Proportion	116–117	✔	✔	✔
Application	Using Proportions	118		✔	✔

Chapter Activities

Teacher's Resource Library

Estimation Exercise 4: Estimating Distance, Rate, and Time
Application Activity 4: Using Proportions
Everyday Algebra 4: Using Proportions
Community Connection 4: Automobile Leasing

Teacher's Edition

Chapter 4 Project

Assessment Options

Student Text

Chapter 4 Review

Teacher's Resource Library

Chapter 4 Mastery Tests A and B

Student Text Features							Teaching Strategies							Learning Styles						Teacher's Resource Library			
Estimation Activity	Algebra in Your Life	Technology Connection	Writing About Mathematics	Try This	Problem Solving	Calculator Practice	Online Connection	Common Error	Applications Home, Career, Community	Mental Math	Manipulatives	Calculator	Group Problem Solving	Auditory/Verbal	Visual/Spatial	Logical/Mathematical	Body/Kinesthetic	Interpersonal/Group Learning	LEP/ESL	Activities	Alternate Activities	Workbook Activities	Self-Study Guide
								97								97				35	35	37	✔
					99					99			99							36	36	38	✔
					103				102				103					102		37	37	39–40	✔
106	107		104		105		106		105				104				105			38	38	41	✔
		110			109	110						110	109						109	39	39	42	✔
					113			112	112				112							40	40	43	✔
				115	115								115	115						41	41	44	✔
					117								117		117					42	42	45	✔
															118								✔

Software Options

Skill Track Software

Use the Skill Track Software for *Algebra* for additional reinforcement of this chapter. The software provides multiple-choice assessment items for students to access by computer.

Solutions Key

Use the Solutions Key with this chapter to help students who may need additional assistance. The Solutions Key CD provides solutions for every exercise in the student edition.

Other Resources

Alternative Activities

The Teacher's Resource Library (TRL) contains a set of worksheets written at a second-grade reading level called Alternative Activities. They cover the same content as the regular Activities.

Manipulatives

See the Manipulative activities in this chapter for hands-on modeling of the content.

Chapter at a Glance

Chapter 4: Applications of Algebra
pages 94–121

Skill Track for Algebra 

Teacher's Resource Library TRL

- Workbook Activities 37–45
- Activities 35–42
- Alternative Activities 35–42
- Application Activity 4
- Estimation Exercise 4
- Everyday Algebra 4
- Community Connection 4
- Chapter 4 Self-Study Guide
- Chapter 4 Mastery Tests A and B

(Answer Keys for the Teacher's Resource Library begin on page 530 of this Teacher's Edition.)

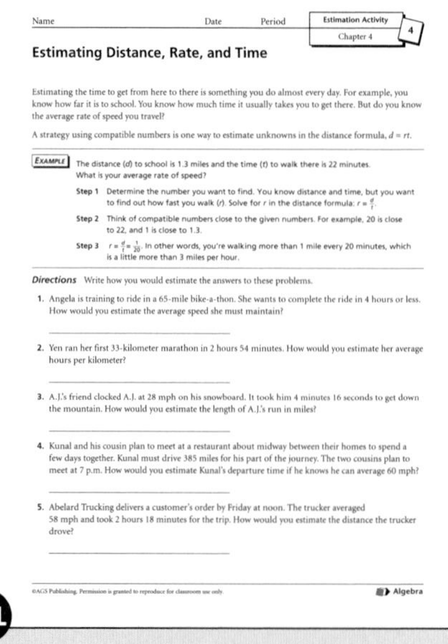

Name Date Period | Estimation Activity 4 | Chapter 4

Estimating Distance, Rate, and Time

Estimating the time to get from here to there is something you do almost every day. For example, you know how far it is to school. You know how much time it usually takes you to get there. But do you know the average rate of speed you travel?

A strategy using compatible numbers is one way to estimate unknowns in the distance formula, $d = rt$.

EXAMPLE The distance (d) to school is 1.3 miles and the time (t) to walk there is 22 minutes. What is your average rate of speed?

Step 1 Determine the number you want to find. You know distance and time, but you want to find out how fast you walk (r). Solve for r in the distance formula: $r = \frac{d}{t}$.

Step 2 Think of compatible numbers close to the given numbers. For example, 20 is close to 22, and 1 is close to 1.3.

Step 3 $r = \frac{d}{t} = \frac{1}{20}$. In other words, you're walking more than 1 mile every 20 minutes, which is a little more than 3 miles per hour.

Directions Write how you would estimate the answers to these problems.

1. Angela is training to ride in a 65-mile bike-a-thon. She wants to complete the ride in 4 hours or less. How would you estimate the average speed she must maintain?

2. Yen ran her first 33-kilometer marathon in 2 hours 54 minutes. How would you estimate her average hours per kilometer?

3. A.J.'s friend clocked A.J. at 28 mph on his snowboard. It took him 4 minutes 16 seconds to get down the mountain. How would you estimate the length of A.J.'s run in miles?

4. Kunal and his cousin plan to meet at a restaurant about midway between their homes to spend a few days together. Kunal must drive 385 miles for his part of the journey. The two cousins plan to meet at 7 p.m. How would you estimate Kunal's departure time if he knows he can average 60 mph?

5. Abelard Trucking delivers a customer's order by Friday at noon. The trucker averaged 58 mph and took 2 hours 18 minutes for the trip. How would you estimate the distance the trucker drove?

 Algebra

TRL

Estimation Exercise 4

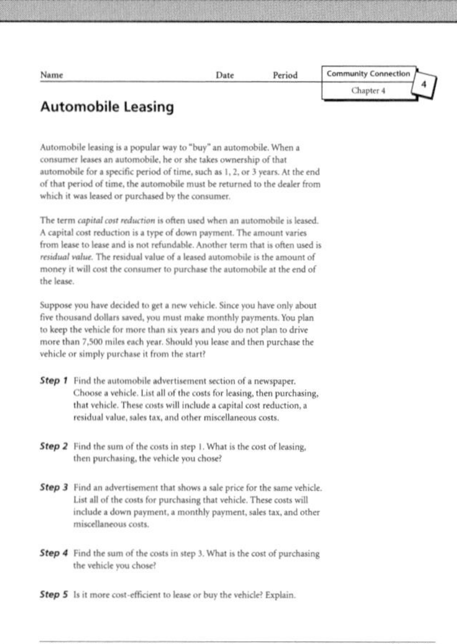

Name Date Period | Community Connection 4 | Chapter 4

Automobile Leasing

Automobile leasing is a popular way to "buy" an automobile. When a consumer leases an automobile, he or she takes ownership of that automobile for a specific period of time, such as 1, 2, or 3 years. At the end of that period of time, the automobile must be returned to the dealer from which it was leased or purchased by the consumer.

The term *capital cost reduction* is often used when an automobile is leased. A capital cost reduction is a type of down payment. The amount varies from lease to lease and is not refundable. Another term that is often used is *residual value.* The residual value of a leased automobile is the amount of money it will cost the consumer to purchase the automobile at the end of the lease.

Suppose you have decided to get a new vehicle. Since you have only about five thousand dollars saved, you must make monthly payments. You plan to keep the vehicle for more than six years and you do not plan to drive more than 7,500 miles each year. Should you lease and then purchase the vehicle or simply purchase it from the start?

Step 1 Find the automobile advertisement section of a newspaper. Choose a vehicle. List all of the costs for leasing, then purchasing, that vehicle. These costs will include a capital cost reduction, a residual value, sales tax, and other miscellaneous costs.

Step 2 Find the sum of the costs in step 1. What is the cost of leasing, then purchasing, the vehicle you chose?

Step 3 Find an advertisement that shows a sale price for the same vehicle. List all of the costs for purchasing that vehicle. These costs will include a down payment, a monthly payment, sales tax, and other miscellaneous costs.

Step 4 Find the sum of the costs in step 3. What is the cost of purchasing the vehicle you chose?

Step 5 Is it more cost-efficient to lease or buy the vehicle? Explain.

 Algebra

TRL

Community Connection 4

Chapter

Applications of Algebra

Scientists create and test formulas to search for cures to diseases or to prove new theories. Equations and formulas have many common uses in daily life. For example, recipes are formulas. Leave out an ingredient and you get a flat cake! There are formulas for every kind of mixture problem. The correct antifreeze-to-water ratio is important for a car radiator. Even artists use formulas to mix just the right color or to cast a metal sculpture. If you think about it, you probably use formulas almost every day of the week.

In Chapter 4, you will write and apply algebraic equations and formulas.

Goals for Learning

- To write an algebraic equation for a number sentence
- To identify formulas to use in specific types of problems
- To write problems using algebraic formulas
- To solve problems by applying algebraic equations

Name Date Period *SELF-STUDY GUIDE*

CHAPTER 4: Applications of Algebra

Goal 4.1 *To write an algebraic equation for a number sentence*

Date	Assignment	Score
______	1: Read pages 96–97. Complete Exercises A–C on page 97.	______
______	2: Complete Workbook Activity 37.	______

Goals 4.2 and 4.3 *To identify formulas to use in specific types of problems*
To write problems using algebraic formulas

Comments:

Date	Assignment	Score
______	3: Read pages 98–99. Complete Exercise A on page 99.	______
______	4: Complete Workbook Activity 38.	______
______	5: Read pages 100–102. Complete Exercises A–C on pages 102–103.	______
______	6: Complete Workbook Activities 39 and 40.	______
______	7: Read pages 104–106. Complete Exercises A–B on pages 105 and 107.	______
______	8: Complete Workbook Activity 41.	______
______	9: Read page 108. Complete Exercise A on page 109.	______
______	10: Read and complete the Calculator Practice on page 110.	______
______	11: Complete Workbook Activity 42.	______
______	12: Read pages 111–112. Complete Exercises A–C on pages 112–113.	______
______	13: Complete Workbook Activity 43.	______
______	14: Read pages 114–115. Complete Exercise A on page 115.	______
______	15: Complete Workbook Activity 44.	______

Comments:

 Algebra

TRL

Name Date Period *SELF-STUDY GUIDE*

CHAPTER 4: Applications of Algebra, continued

Goal 4.4 *To solve problems by applying algebraic equations*

Date	Assignment	Score
______	16: Read pages 116–117. Complete Exercises A–B on page 117.	______
______	17: Complete Workbook Activity 45.	______
______	18: Read and complete the Application Exercise on page 118.	______
______	19: Complete the Chapter 4 Review on pages 119–121.	______

Comments:

Student's Signature ______________ Date ______

Instructor's Signature ______________ Date ______

 Algebra

TRL

Chapter 4 Self-Study Guide

Introducing the Chapter

Use the information in the chapter opener to help students understand that algebraic equations and formulas have many common uses in everyday life. Point out that formulas are used to develop new medications, make and bake a cake, or determine the correct antifreeze-to-water ratio for a vehicle's radiator.

Chapter Project

Suggest students work in pairs. After completing each lesson, have students list on a sheet of paper the different applications of algebra presented in the lesson. Upon completing the chapter, have students present their lists to their classmates and compare entries. At this time, present the list that was recorded during the chapter introduction. Then encourage a discussion of each unique entry on the lists by asking students to name one or more vocations in everyday life that may require each particular skill.

Teacher's Resource

The AGS Publishing Teaching Strategies in Math Transparencies may be used with this chapter. They add an interactive dimension to expand and enhance the program content.

Career Interest Inventory

The AGS Publishing Harrington-O'Shea Career Decision-Making System-Revised (CDM) may be used with this chapter. Students can use the CDM to explore their interests and identify careers. The CDM defines career areas that are indicated by students' responses on the inventory.

Lesson at a Glance

Chapter 4 Lesson 1

Overview This lesson introduces algebraic equations.

Objective

- To write and solve algebraic equations

Student Pages 96–97

Teacher's Resource Library 

Workbook Activity 37

Activity 35

Alternative Activity 35

Mathematics Vocabulary

consecutive

Warm-Up Activity

Using ■ as a placeholder for the variable, write several basic number sentences on the board and invite volunteers to identify the solution for each number sentence.

■ + 6 = 10	*(4)*
15 − ■ = 7	*(8)*
4 + (■ • 2) = 14	*(5)*
■ − (6 + 5) = 9	*(20)*

Remind students that ■ functions as a placeholder for an unknown quantity. Then ask students to describe how unknown quantities are represented algebraically. Lead them to understand that in algebra, letters of the alphabet are used as variables—placeholders for unknown quantities. Remind students that any letter of the alphabet can be used to algebraically represent a variable.

Teaching the Lesson

Remind students that when they write equations, the order in which the terms of the equation are written is very important. For example, point out that $n - 2$ (two less than n) is different than $2 - n$ (n less than 2).

Lesson 1 Writing Equations—Odd and Even Integers

Consecutive
Following one after the other in order

A number sentence gives information about an unknown number or numbers. A number sentence can be written as an algebraic equation. Then the equation can be solved to identify the number.

EXAMPLE 1 Six times a number added to 15 is 27. What is the number?

Step 1 First, make a "model" of the problem.
Choose a letter to represent the number.
Decide if the letter has a coefficient.
Let n = the number.
Let $6n$ represent six times the number.

Step 2 Write and solve the algebraic equation.

$$15 + 6n = 27$$
$$15 - 15 + 6n = 27 - 15$$
$$6n = 12$$
$$n = 2$$

Step 3 Check. $15 + (6)(2) = 27 \quad 15 + 12 = 27$ True
The number is 2.

A number sentence may describe **consecutive** integers. Algebraic equations can be used to find the consecutive numbers.

EXAMPLE 2 The sum of two consecutive integers is 31. What are the integers?
Think of the integers on the number line.

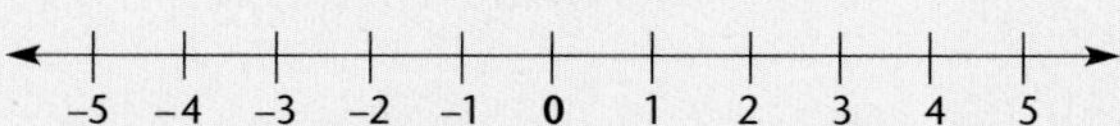

The common difference between consecutive integers is 1.

Step 1 Let n = one of the integers.
Let $n + 1$ = the consecutive integer.

Step 2 Write and solve the equation. $n + (n + 1) = 31$

$$2n + 1 = 31$$
$$2n = 30$$
$$n = 15 \text{ and } n + 1 = 16$$

Step 3 Check. $15 + 16 = 31$ True
The two consecutive integers are 15 and 16.

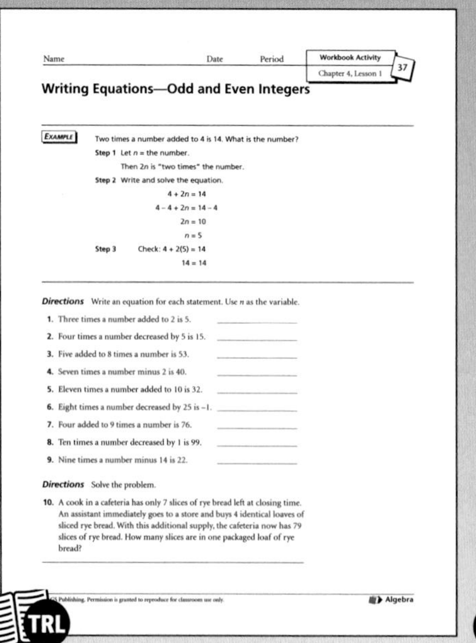

Name Date Period | Workbook Activity 37 | Chapter 4, Lesson 1

Writing Equations—Odd and Even Integers

EXAMPLE Two times a number added to 4 is 14. What is the number?

Step 1 Let n = the number.
Then $2n$ is "two times" the number.

Step 2 Write and solve the equation.

$$4 + 2n = 14$$
$$4 - 4 + 2n = 14 - 4$$
$$2n = 10$$
$$n = 5$$

Step 3 Check: $4 + 2(5) = 14$
$14 = 14$

Directions Write an equation for each statement. Use n as the variable.

1. Three times a number added to 2 is 5. ________
2. Four times a number decreased by 5 is 15. ________
3. Five added to 8 times a number is 53. ________
4. Seven times a number minus 2 is 40. ________
5. Eleven times a number added to 10 is 32. ________
6. Eight times a number decreased by 25 is –1. ________
7. Four added to 9 times a number is 76. ________
8. Ten times a number decreased by 1 is 99. ________
9. Nine times a number minus 14 is 22. ________

Directions Solve the problem.

10. A cook in a cafeteria has only 7 slices of rye bread left at closing time. An assistant immediately goes to a store and buys 4 identical loaves of sliced rye bread. With this additional supply, the cafeteria now has 79 slices of rye bread. How many slices are in one packaged loaf of rye bread?

 Algebra

TRL

Workbook Activity 37

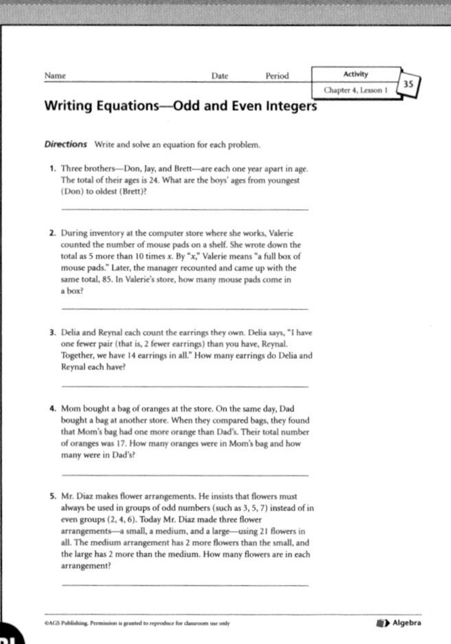

Name Date Period | Activity 35 | Chapter 4, Lesson 1

Writing Equations—Odd and Even Integers

Directions Write and solve an equation for each problem.

1. Three brothers—Don, Jay, and Brett—are each one year apart in age. The total of their ages is 24. What are the boys' ages from youngest (Don) to oldest (Brett)?

2. During inventory at the computer store where she works, Valerie counted the number of mouse pads on a shelf. She wrote down the total as 5 more than 10 times x. By "x," Valerie means "a full box of mouse pads." Later, the manager recounted and came up with the same total, 85. In Valerie's store, how many mouse pads come in a box?

3. Delia and Reynal each count the earrings they own. Delia says, "I have one fewer pair (that is, 2 fewer earrings) than you have, Reynal. Together, we have 14 earrings in all." How many earrings do Delia and Reynal each have?

4. Mom bought a bag of oranges at the store. On the same day, Dad bought a bag at another store. When they compared bags, they found that Mom's bag had one more orange than Dad's. Their total number of oranges was 17. How many oranges were in Mom's bag and how many were in Dad's?

5. Mr. Diaz makes flower arrangements. He insists that flowers must always be used in groups of odd numbers (such as 3, 5, 7) instead of in even groups (2, 4, 6). Today Mr. Diaz made three flower arrangements—a small, a medium, and a large—using 21 flowers in all. The medium arrangement has 2 more flowers than the small, and the large has 2 more than the medium. How many flowers are in each arrangement?

 Algebra

TRL

Activity 35

EXAMPLE 3 The sum of three consecutive *odd* integers is 33. What are the integers? Think of the set of odd integers on the number line.

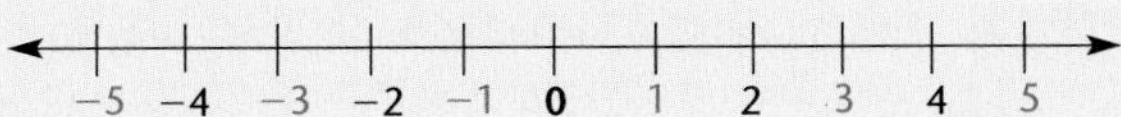

The common difference between consecutive odd numbers is 2.

Step 1 Let n = the smallest odd integer.
Let $n + 2$ = the next odd integer.
Let $n + 4$ = the greatest odd integer.

$n \underbrace{\quad}_{2} n+2 \underbrace{\quad}_{2} n+4$

Step 2 Write the equation. $n + (n + 2) + (n + 4) = 33$

$3n + 6 = 33$

$3n = 27$

$n = 9 \quad n + 2 = 11 \quad n + 4 = 13$

Step 3 Check. $9 + 11 + 13 = 33$ True

The three consecutive odd integers are 9, 11, and 13.

Exercise A Let n represent an even integer. Write an expression for each of the following.

1. the next consecutive integer $n + 1$
2. the next even integer $n + 2$
3. the previous even integer $n - 2$

Exercise B Write the equation and solve to answer each question.

4. Seven times a number decreased by 2 is 19. What is the number? 3
5. An integer added to 24 equals 16. What is the integer? −8
6. The sum of two consecutive odd integers is −8. What are the integers? −5, −3
7. The sum of three consecutive even integers is 36. What are the integers? 10, 12, 14
8. The sum of two consecutive integers is −13. What are the integers? −7, −6

Exercise C Show that the following equations are true. Express your answers in terms of variables.

9. even integer + even integer = even integer $2n + 2m = 2(n + m)$
10. odd integer + odd integer = even integer $2n + 1 + 2m + 1 = 2(n + m) + 2$

COMMON ERROR

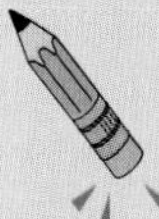

Remind students that the value of a variable will change from one problem to another. For example, point out that the value of n in the equation $n + 1 = 5$ is different from the value of n in the equation $n - 10 = 20$.

3 Reinforce and Extend

LEARNING STYLES

Logical/Mathematical

Draw a number line from −10 to +10 on the board. Invite volunteers to go to the board and demonstrate how the number line can be used to answer these questions:

- An integer added to +4 creates a sum of +7. What is the integer? *(+3)*
- An integer added to +1 creates a sum of −8. What is the integer? *(−9)*
- The product of two consecutive integers is +30. What are the integers? *(+5, +6 and −6, −5)*

Encourage volunteers to generate other questions and demonstrate how to use the number line to answer each question.

Lesson at a Glance

Chapter 4 Lesson 2

Overview This lesson introduces the 1% method of solving percent problems.

Objective

- To solve percent problems by first finding 1% of the solution

Student Pages 98–99

Teacher's Resource Library 

Workbook Activity 38

Activity 36

Alternative Activity 36

Mathematics Vocabulary

percent

Warm-Up Activity

Review percents by reminding students that a percent is a ratio of a number to 100. On the board, write "23% means 23 out of 100 or $\frac{23}{100}$." Choose other percents and invite volunteers to describe the percents in the same way. Encourage them to name the fractions in simplest form. Culminate the activity by reminding students that a percent of a number does not always have to be less than 100%. It may be exactly 100% or more than 100%. For example, point out that 10 is 100% of 10, and 10 is 200% of 5.

Teaching the Lesson

Explain that once 1% of a correct answer is known, 100% or all of the correct answer can be found by moving the decimal point in the 1% answer two places to the right. For example, if 1% of a correct answer is 50, 100% of the correct answer will be 50 with the decimal point moved two places to the right, or 5,000. Encourage students to use pencil and paper to find 1% of a correct answer, then find 100% using mental math.

Lesson 2 Using the 1% Solution to Solve Problems

Percent
Part per one hundred

The 1% solution method is a way of solving percent problems. Solve first for 1%, then use that information to answer the question.

Recall that **percent** means "part per one hundred."

For example, $20\% = \frac{20}{100} = 0.20 = \frac{1}{5}$, and $100\% = \frac{100}{100} = 1$.

The 1% solution method can be used to find the total number from a percentage.

EXAMPLE 1 There are 120 seniors at Belmont High. If 20% of the students in the school are seniors, how many students attend Belmont High?

20% of population = 120	Given.
20% ÷ 20 = 120 ÷ 20	Divide both sides by 20 to solve for 1%.
1% of population = 6	
100% of population = 600	Multiply both sides by 100 to find the total population.

600 students attend Belmont High.

The 1% solution method can be used to find a portion of the total number from a percentage.

EXAMPLE 2 A city has a population of 100,000. If 23% of the population are 18 years old or younger, how many people are 18 or younger?

100% of population = 100,000	Given.
1% of population = 1,000	Divide both sides by 100 to solve for 1%.
23% of population = (1,000)(23) = 23,000	Multiply both sides by 23 to find the total youth population that is 18 years old or younger.

23,000 people are 18 years old or younger.

The 1% solution method can be used to find what percentage a portion is of the total number.

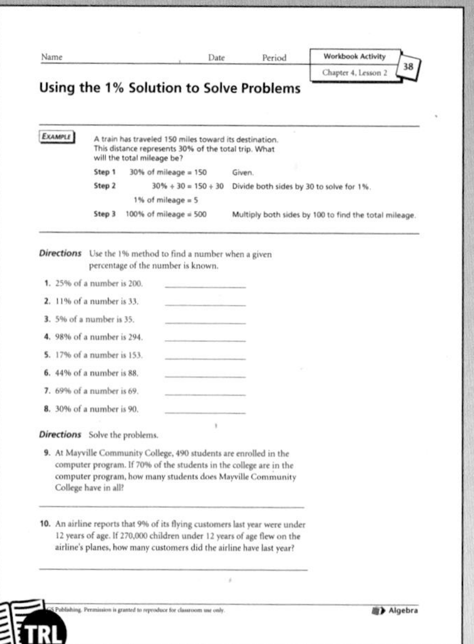

Name Date Period — Workbook Activity 38, Chapter 4, Lesson 2

Using the 1% Solution to Solve Problems

EXAMPLE A train has traveled 150 miles toward its destination. This distance represents 30% of the total trip. What will the total mileage be?

Step 1	30% of mileage = 150	Given.
Step 2	30% ÷ 30 = 150 ÷ 30	Divide both sides by 30 to solve for 1%.
	1% of mileage = 5	
Step 3	100% of mileage = 500	Multiply both sides by 100 to find the total mileage.

Directions Use the 1% method to find a number when a given percentage of the number is known.

1. 25% of a number is 200. ______
2. 11% of a number is 33. ______
3. 5% of a number is 35. ______
4. 98% of a number is 294. ______
5. 17% of a number is 153. ______
6. 44% of a number is 88. ______
7. 69% of a number is 69. ______
8. 30% of a number is 90. ______

Directions Solve the problems.

9. At Mayville Community College, 490 students are enrolled in the computer program. If 70% of the students in the college are in the computer program, how many students does Mayville Community College have in all? ______
10. An airline reports that 9% of its flying customers last year were under 12 years of age. If 270,000 children under 12 years of age flew on the airline's planes, how many customers did the airline have last year? ______

 Algebra

Workbook Activity 38

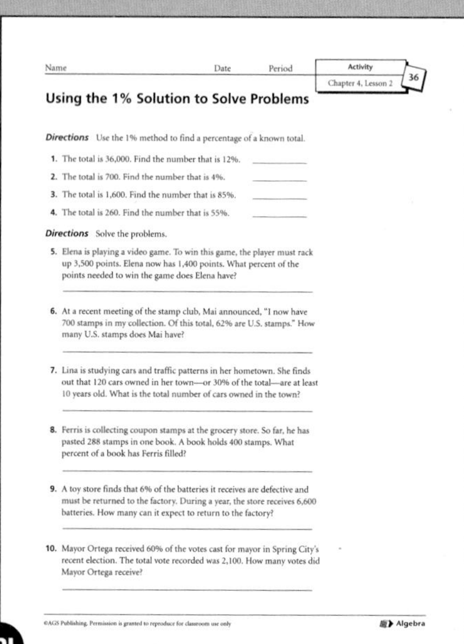

Name Date Period — Activity 36, Chapter 4, Lesson 2

Using the 1% Solution to Solve Problems

Directions Use the 1% method to find a percentage of a known total.

1. The total is 36,000. Find the number that is 12%. ______
2. The total is 700. Find the number that is 4%. ______
3. The total is 1,600. Find the number that is 85%. ______
4. The total is 260. Find the number that is 55%. ______

Directions Solve the problems.

5. Elena is playing a video game. To win this game, the player must rack up 3,500 points. Elena now has 1,400 points. What percent of the points needed to win the game does Elena have? ______
6. At a recent meeting of the stamp club, Mai announced, "I now have 700 stamps in my collection. Of this total, 62% are U.S. stamps." How many U.S. stamps does Mai have? ______
7. Lina is studying cars and traffic patterns in her hometown. She finds out that 120 cars owned in her town—or 30% of the total—are at least 10 years old. What is the total number of cars owned in the town? ______
8. Ferris is collecting coupon stamps at the grocery store. So far, he has pasted 288 stamps in one book. A book holds 400 stamps. What percent of a book has Ferris filled? ______
9. A toy store finds that 6% of the batteries it receives are defective and must be returned to the factory. During a year, the store receives 6,600 batteries. How many can it expect to return to the factory? ______
10. Mayor Ortega received 60% of the votes cast for mayor in Spring City's recent election. The total vote recorded was 2,100. How many votes did Mayor Ortega receive? ______

 Algebra

Activity 36

EXAMPLE 3 You want to raise $1,000 for charity. You have raised $550. What percent of the total did you raise?

100% of the total = $1,000	Given.
1% = $10	Divide both sides by 100.
55% = $550	Multiply both sides by 55 to find the percent of the total raised.

55% of the total was raised.

PROBLEM SOLVING

Exercise A Use the 1% solution to solve each problem.

1. Jay earns $2,500 a month. He pays $850 a month to rent an apartment. What percent of Jay's income does he pay for rent? 34%
2. A tennis resort has 1,200 guests. If 65% of the guests play doubles and singles, how many guests will play both games?) guests
3. 24,600 people attend a baseball game. If 75% of the seats are filled, how many seats are in the ball park?)0 seats
4. Jeremy wants to buy a computer that costs $1,600. He has already saved $1,280. What percent of the total has he saved? 80%
5. Suppose 40 people come to your party. If 15% of your guests arrive early, how many people arrive early? people
6. Maria has an annual income of $32,000. If she saves 8% of her income, how much money does she save? $2,560
7. There are 30 mystery books in Chin's book collection. If 6% of his books are mysteries, how many books does Chin have in his collection? 500 books
8. There are 10,000 people at a concert. Of those people, 6,250 are adults. What percent of the people at the concert are adults? $62\frac{1}{2}\%$
9. A cable television provider offers six different news stations. If 25% of the stations offered are news, how many stations are offered by the provider? 24 stations
10. In an apartment building, 45% of the families have pets. If 27 families have pets, how many families live in the building? 60 families

3 Reinforce and Extend

MENTAL MATH

Invite ten volunteers to each write a positive integer on the board. The integers may be large or small. Then explain that each integer represents 1% of a number. Invite students to find 100% of the number mentally by moving the decimal point in each integer two places to the right. Substitute 10% for 1% and repeat the activity using different integers.

GROUP PROBLEM SOLVING

Encourage students to work in groups of four to discuss and solve the following problem:

Tara earns a salary of $2,500 each month. Last month, she spent $2\frac{1}{2}\%$ of her salary on gifts for her family. Use the 1% solution method to find the amount of money Tara spent on gifts for her family. *(Since 1% of $2,500 = $25, $\frac{1}{2}\%$ of $2,500 is $\frac{1}{2}$ of $25 or $12.50; $25 + $25 + $12.50 = $62.50)*

Invite groups to record the steps they used to solve the problem. Then have them share their problem-solving approach with one another.

MATH HISTORY

No single individual or civilization was responsible for the development of algebra. Almost every ancient culture was fascinated by mathematics. Some used mathematics and geometry to create monumental structures such as the Egyptian pyramids in Africa and the Mayan pyramids on the Yucatan Peninsula of Central America. In ancient China, scholars of the Han Dynasty extended the knowledge of theoretical mathematics. Both ancient India and the Mayan civilizations gave us the concept of zero. And the ancient Indians also gave us the basis for the decimal system. Ancient Arabia created the numbers we write today—Arabic numerals. The Greeks also came up with many of the mathematical concepts that we use today, including Euclidian geometry. The accomplishments of many cultures around the globe are based on modern mathematical theory and practice.

Lesson at a Glance

Chapter 4 Lesson 3

Overview This lesson introduces the percent equation.

Objective

- To use the percent equation to find a percent of a number

Student Pages 100–103

Teacher's Resource Library TRL

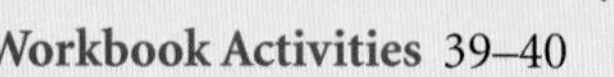

Workbook Activities 39–40

Activity 37

Alternative Activity 37

Mathematics Vocabulary

circle graph

1 Warm-Up Activity

Draw a large circle on the board. Draw a diameter of the circle and label one part of the circle $\frac{1}{2}$. In the unlabeled portion of the circle, draw a radius perpendicular to the diameter and label one part of the circle $\frac{1}{4}$. Divide the remaining unlabeled portion of the circle into two equal parts and label each part $\frac{1}{8}$. Ask students to compute the sum of the fractions in the circle. *($\frac{8}{8}$ or 1)* Explain that if a circle graph displays fractions, the sum of the fractions must be one whole, or 1.

Ask students to change each fraction to a percent and compute the sum of the percents in the circle. *(100%)* Explain that if a circle graph displays percents, the sum of the percents must also be one whole or 1, which is the same as 100%. Point out that the sum of the fractions or percents in a circle graph can never be less than or greater than 1.

2 Teaching the Lesson

Write the percent equation on the board. Explain that even though the percent equation contains three variables (p, n, and r), two variables will always be given in a percent problem. The third variable represents the solution. In some problems, the variable p may represent the solution. In other problems, the variable n or the variable r will represent the solution.

Lesson 3 Using the Percent Equation

Another way to solve a percent problem is to find a fraction of a number. First, you change the percent into a fraction. Use the percent equation.

> Remember that percent means part of 100. For example, 20% is equal to $\frac{20}{100}$.

Percent Equation

Fraction	•	Number	=	Result	where
$(\frac{p}{100})$	•	(n)	=	r	p = the number that is the percent n = the total number r = result

In percent problems, you will be given two variables. You can solve for a third one using algebra.

You can use the percent equation to find out what the percent number is when the percent and the total are known.

EXAMPLE 1 25% of the 20 students in the class have seen the latest hit movie. How many of the students have seen the movie?

Substitute the values into the percent equation. Then solve for r.

25% of 20 is what number?

Step 1 Write the percent equation. $(\frac{p}{100})(n) = r$

Step 2 Change the percent into a fraction. $p = 25$ $(\frac{25}{100})(n) = r$

Step 3 Write the total number. $n = 20$ $(\frac{25}{100})(20) = r$

Step 4 Simplify the fraction. $(\frac{1}{4})(20) = r$

Step 5 Solve the equation. $(\frac{1}{4})(20) = 5$

25% of 20 is 5. Five students have seen the movie.

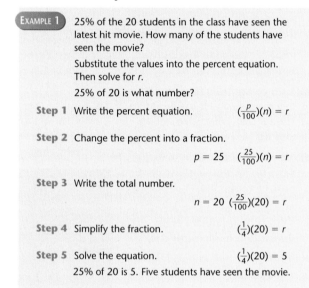

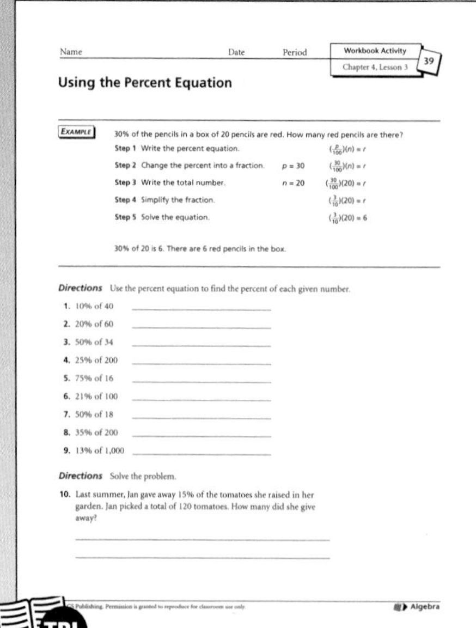

Name Date Period | Workbook Activity 39 | Chapter 4, Lesson 3

Using the Percent Equation

EXAMPLE 30% of the pencils in a box of 20 pencils are red. How many red pencils are there?

Step 1 Write the percent equation. $(\frac{p}{100})(n) = r$

Step 2 Change the percent into a fraction. $p = 30$ $(\frac{30}{100})(n) = r$

Step 3 Write the total number. $n = 20$ $(\frac{30}{100})(20) = r$

Step 4 Simplify the fraction. $(\frac{3}{10})(20) = r$

Step 5 Solve the equation. $(\frac{3}{10})(20) = 6$

30% of 20 is 6. There are 6 red pencils in the box.

Directions Use the percent equation to find the percent of each given number.

1. 10% of 40 ____
2. 20% of 60 ____
3. 50% of 34 ____
4. 25% of 200 ____
5. 75% of 16 ____
6. 21% of 100 ____
7. 50% of 18 ____
8. 35% of 200 ____
9. 13% of 1,000 ____

Directions Solve the problem.

10. Last summer, Jan gave away 15% of the tomatoes she raised in her garden. Jan picked a total of 120 tomatoes. How many did she give away?

 Algebra

Workbook Activity 39

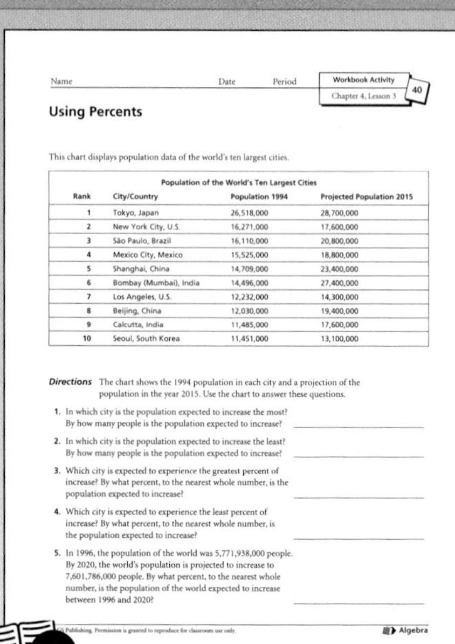

Name Date Period | Workbook Activity 40 | Chapter 4, Lesson 3

Using Percents

This chart displays population data of the world's ten largest cities.

Population of the World's Ten Largest Cities

Rank	City/Country	Population 1994	Projected Population 2015
1	Tokyo, Japan	26,518,000	28,700,000
2	New York City, U.S.	16,271,000	17,600,000
3	São Paulo, Brazil	16,110,000	20,800,000
4	Mexico City, Mexico	15,525,000	18,800,000
5	Shanghai, China	14,709,000	23,400,000
6	Bombay (Mumbai), India	14,496,000	27,400,000
7	Los Angeles, U.S.	12,232,000	14,300,000
8	Beijing, China	12,030,000	19,400,000
9	Calcutta, India	11,485,000	17,600,000
10	Seoul, South Korea	11,451,000	13,100,000

Directions The chart shows the 1994 population in each city and a projection of the population in the year 2015. Use the chart to answer these questions.

1. In which city is the population expected to increase the most? By how many people is the population expected to increase? ____
2. In which city is the population expected to increase the least? By how many people is the population expected to increase? ____
3. Which city is expected to experience the greatest percent of increase? By what percent, to the nearest whole number, is the population expected to increase? ____
4. Which city is expected to experience the least percent of increase? By what percent, to the nearest whole number, is the population expected to increase? ____
5. In 1996, the population of the world was 5,771,938,000 people. By 2020, the world's population is projected to increase to 7,601,786,000 people. By what percent, to the nearest whole number, is the population of the world expected to increase between 1996 and 2020? ____

 Algebra

Workbook Activity 40

Circle graph

A graphic way to present information using the parts of a circle

You can use the percent equation to find percent when the percent number and the total are known.

EXAMPLE 2 4 of the 5 students who saw the movie would like to see it again. What percent of students would like to see the movie again?

4 is what percent of 5?

Substitute the values into the percent equation. Then solve for p.

$$\left(\frac{p}{100}\right)(n) = r$$

$n = 5 \quad r = 4 \quad \left(\frac{p}{100}\right)(5) = 4$

$$5p = 400$$

$$p = 80$$

4 is 80% of 5.

You can use the equation to find the total when the percent and the percent number are known.

EXAMPLE 3 15 is 25% of what number?

Substitute the values into the percent equation. Then solve for n.

$$\left(\frac{p}{100}\right)(n) = r$$

$p = 25 \quad r = 15 \quad \left(\frac{25}{100}\right)(n) = 15$

$25n = 1500 \quad n = 60$

15 is 25% of 60.

The percent equation can also be used to solve percent problems that are displayed by a circle graph. A **circle graph** shows the different parts into which a whole is divided. For example, the circle graph below shows that 60% of 30 students attended a school sports event last week, while 40% of 30 students did not.

Did You Attend a School Sports Event Last Week?

(30 students surveyed)

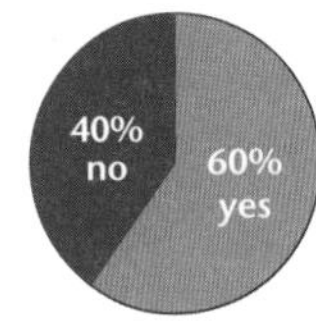

After students discuss and complete the circle graph example on page 101, ask them to find the sum of the percents displayed by the graph. *(100%)* Remind students that the sum of the percents displayed by any circle graph must always be 100. You may wish to point out that the only exception to this rule occurs when the percents displayed by a circle graph are rounded, such as to the nearest whole number. When percent data is rounded, the sum of the percents displayed by a circle graph may be less than or greater than 100.

After students discuss and complete the circle graph on page 102, ask them to find the sum of the revenues displayed by the completed graph *($40 million)* and compare it to the total revenues that were given in the problem. *($40 million)* Point out that comparing the data displayed by a circle graph to the data that has een given in a problem is one way to check that the circle graph has been completed correctly.

After all of the examples on pages 101–102 have been discussed, invite volunteers to describe strategies that can be used to help identify which data in a problem is represented by the variable p, which data in a problem is represented by the variable n, and which data in a problem is represented by the variable r. As volunteers share strategies, encourage the remaining class members to record those strategies they feel to be most useful and refer to the strategies as they complete problems 1–20.

Name ____ Date ____ Period ____ Activity 37, Chapter 4, Lesson 3

Using the Percent Equation

Directions Use the percent equation to find the total.

1. 7 is 25% of what number? ________
2. 40 is 80% of what number? ________
3. 13 is 50% of what number? ________
4. 22 is 20% of what number? ________
5. 36 is 75% of what number? ________

Directions Solve the problems.

6. Crystal's soccer team won 14 of the 20 games they played last season. What percent of games played did they win? ________
7. At Liberty School, 168 students—or 56% of the total student body—are taking a foreign language course. How many students does Liberty School have in all? ________
8. Last year at a state driver's license office, 16% of all the drivers seeking to renew their licenses had let their old licenses expire. In all, 23,400 people renewed licenses at this office. How many of their licenses had expired? ________
9. The park near a museum has a brick wall around it. The north wall of the park contains 6,230 bricks, which is only 70% of the bricks in the west wall. How many bricks does the west wall contain? ________
10. Mr. Kelly took an opinion poll of his class of 25 students. He asked how many were in favor of writing a term paper in place of a final exam. Only 4 were in favor of this idea. What percent of the class is this group of students who favor a term paper? ________

Algebra

TRL

Activity 37

3 Reinforce and Extend

Learning Styles

Interpersonal/ Group Learning

Suggest students work in groups of three. Ask one group member to write a fraction exercise that involves finding a percent of a number. Ask the second group member to estimate the answer. Ask the third group member to compute the exact answer. Have students switch roles several times, then discuss the value of taking the time to make an estimate each time a computation is performed.

At Home

Invite students to consult with family members and determine how the income their family receives each month is spent. Have students compile their data in the form of a circle graph. Each graph should include expenses such as mortgage/rent, utilities, taxes, food, recreation, transportation, savings, etc.

You can also use percents to make a circle graph.

Example 4 A professional sports team earns $40 million of revenue annually. Of that amount, 30% is from ticket sales and 70% is from other sources. Represent the information in a circle graph.

Step 1 Write a title for the circle graph and draw a circle to represent the whole.

Annual Team Revenue

Step 2 The circle graph will be made up of two parts (70% of the whole and 30% of the whole). Since a circle measures 360°, divide the circle into two parts by finding 70% of 360° and 30% of 360°.

Annual Team Revenue

70% of 360° = 252°

30% of 360° = 108°

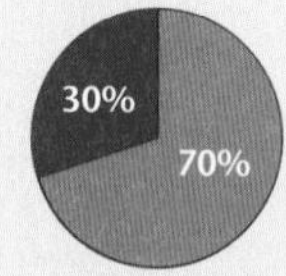

Step 3 Determine the information that the circle graph is supposed to display by finding 70% of $40 million and 30% of 40 million. Then write the answers on the graph. Add labels identifying each part.

Annual Team Revenue

70% of $40 million = $28 million

30% of $40 million = $12 million

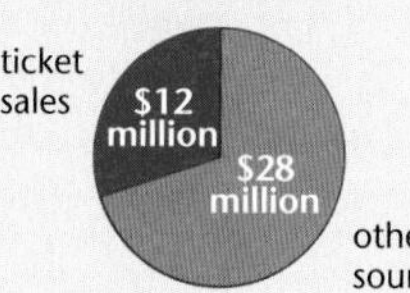

Exercise A Find the percent of each number.

1. 25% of 40 10

2. 42% of 720 $302\frac{2}{5}$

3. 50% of 82 41

4. 80% of 200 160

5. 65% of 510 $331\frac{1}{2}$

6. 70% of 90 63

7. 30% of 450 135

8. 92% of 800 736

9. 18% of 75 $13\frac{1}{2}$

10. 45% of 60 27

PROBLEM SOLVING

Exercise B Solve each problem using the percent equation.

11. All of the students in Ms. Elgin's science class are going on the class field trip to the planetarium. There are 20 students in the class. What percentage of students in Ms. Elgin's class are going on the field trip?

12. Of the 450 students in the school, 75 students take biology classes. What percentage of students in the school are taking biology classes?

11. 100%
12. $16\frac{2}{3}\%$
13. $37\frac{1}{2}\%$
14. 2 students
15. 100 freshmen

13. Every day, school bus 101 carries 40 students to and from school. Fifteen of the students live more than 10 miles from school. What percent of the students live more than 10 miles from school?

14. Of the 16 students in the school orchestra, 12.5% play the violin. How many students play the violin?

15. This room is the homeroom for 25 freshmen. That is 25% of all the freshmen in the school. How many freshmen does the school have?

Exercise C Use the information on calculating with percents to explore information about sports teams earnings. Compute the dollar values for each percent and make a circle graph to show the information.

16. Major League Baseball Teams—Average Earnings: $66 million

Ticket Sales	40%
Television and Radio	35%
Stadium Revenue	18%
Licensing and Other Sources	7%

17. National Basketball Association Teams—Average Earnings: $50 million

Ticket Sales	41%
Television and Radio	40%
Arena Revenue	12%
Licensing and Other Sources	7%

See Teacher's Edition page for answers to problems 16–19.

20. a. baseball b. football

18. National Football League Teams—Average Earnings: $64 million

Ticket Sales	24%
Television and Radio	63%
Arena Revenue	9%
Licensing and Other Sources	4%

19. National Hockey League Teams—Average Earnings: $35 million

Ticket Sales	63%
Television and Radio	17%
Arena Revenue	16%
Licensing and Other Sources	4%

20. Identify the sport that makes the most money from
a. Ticket Sales
b. Television and Radio

Group Problem Solving

Have pairs of students discuss and solve the following problem:

Rent represents 30% of a family's expenses for one month. If $1,680 represents the remainder of the family's expenses for that month, how much did the family pay for rent that month? *($720)*

Invite groups to record the steps they used to solve the problem. Then have them share their problem-solving approach with one another and describe different strategies that might be used to check whether an answer is correct.

Answers to Problems 16–19

16.

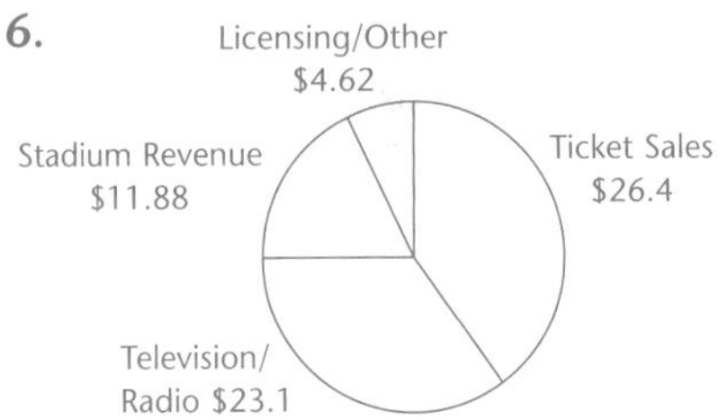

17.

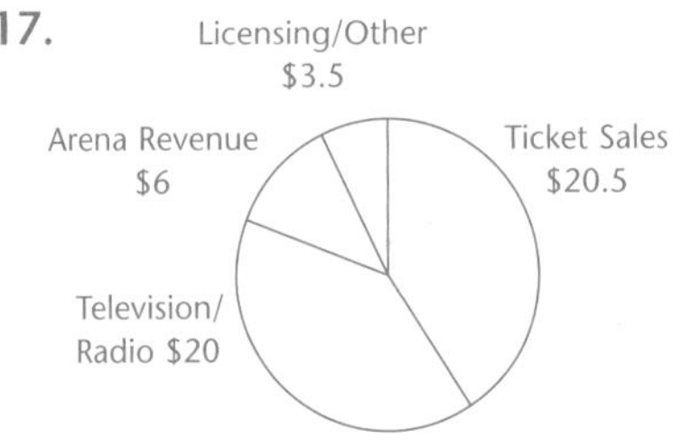

18.

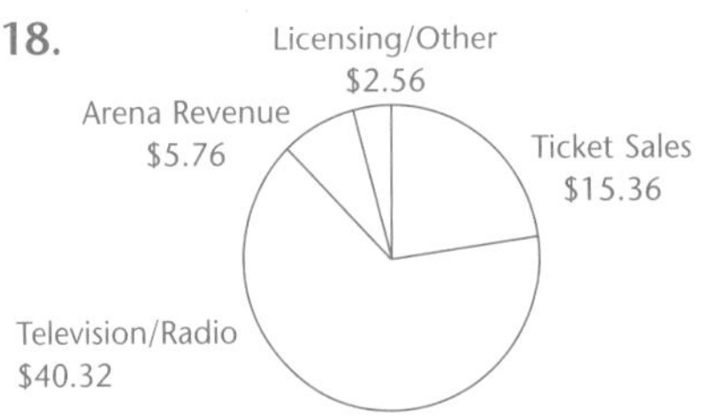

19.

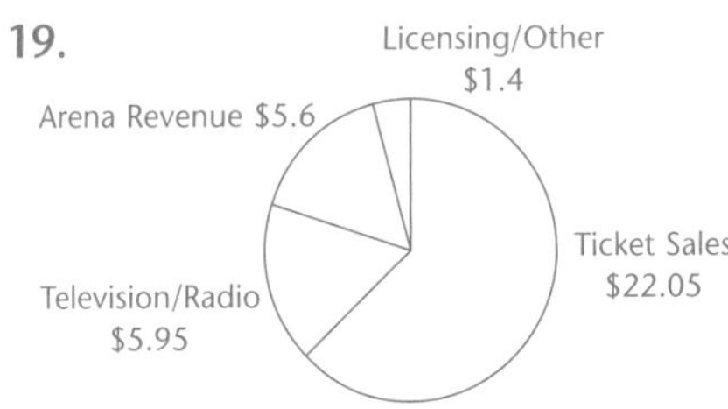

Lesson at a Glance

Chapter 4 Lesson 4

Overview This lesson introduces formulas for distance, rate, and time.

Objectives

- To apply formulas to determine distance, rate, or time

Student Pages 104–107

Teacher's Resource Library TRL

Workbook Activity 41

Activity 38

Alternative Activity 38

Warm-Up Activity

Have students name various modes of transportation (walking, driving, flying, etc.), name the city or community in which they live, and name another city in their state. For each mode of transportation, ask students to estimate the time it would take to travel from one city to the other.

Teaching the Lesson

Write the formulas $d = rt$, $r = \frac{d}{t}$, and $t = \frac{d}{r}$ on the board. Point out that multiplication is used to solve for d and division is used to solve for r or t.

Reinforce and Extend

Group Problem Solving

Suggest students work in small groups. Ask each group member to estimate how long it takes to travel to school in the morning and the distance that is traveled to get to school. Ask the group to then work cooperatively and determine the average speed in miles per hour for each student's morning commute.

Lesson 4 Solving Distance, Rate, and Time Problems

Writing About Mathematics

What property of equality was used to transform $d = rt$ into $r = \frac{d}{t}$? Explain.

The total distance traveled is equal to the average rate of speed multiplied by the total time.

Formulas for Distance, Rate, and Time

Total distance = Average rate of speed • Total time $d = rt$

Average rate of speed $= \frac{\text{total distance}}{\text{total time}}$ $r = \frac{d}{t}$

Total time $= \frac{\text{total distance}}{\text{average rate of speed}}$ $t = \frac{d}{r}$

Average rate of speed is expressed as miles per (one) hour or kilometers per (one) hour.

Example 1 Suppose you drive for $3\frac{1}{2}$ hours at 50 miles per hour (mph).
How many miles have you driven?
50 mph means 50 miles in one hour.

50 miles	50 miles	50 miles	25 miles
1 hour	2 hours	3 hours	$3\frac{1}{2}$ hours

= 175 miles

This diagram shows that you drove 50 miles in 1 hour, 100 miles in 2 hours, 150 miles in 3 hours, and 175 miles in $3\frac{1}{2}$ hours.

Or, you can use the formula $d = rt$ to find out how many miles, or the distance, you drove.

$d = rt$

$d = (50)(3\frac{1}{2}) = 175$ miles

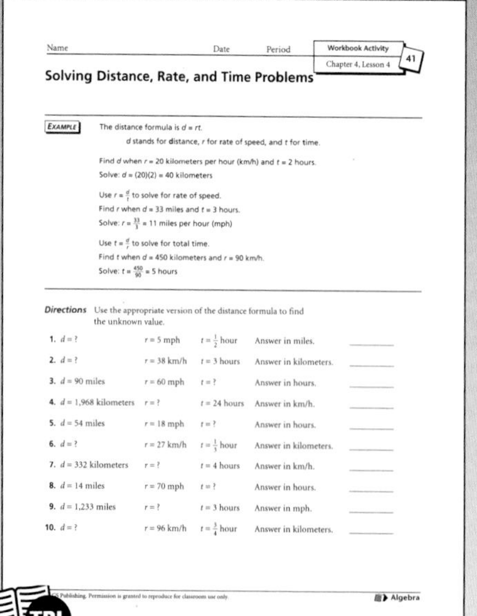

Name Date Period — Workbook Activity 41, Chapter 4, Lesson 4

Solving Distance, Rate, and Time Problems

Example The distance formula is $d = rt$.
d stands for distance, r for rate of speed, and t for time.

Find d when $r = 20$ kilometers per hour (km/h) and $t = 2$ hours.
Solve: $d = (20)(2) = 40$ kilometers

Use $r = \frac{d}{t}$ to solve for rate of speed.
Find r when $d = 33$ miles and $t = 3$ hours.
Solve: $r = \frac{33}{3} = 11$ miles per hour (mph)

Use $t = \frac{d}{r}$ to solve for total time.
Find t when $d = 450$ kilometers and $r = 90$ km/h.
Solve: $t = \frac{450}{90} = 5$ hours

Directions Use the appropriate version of the distance formula to find the unknown value.

1. $d = ?$	$r = 5$ mph	$t = \frac{1}{2}$ hour	Answer in miles.	____
2. $d = ?$	$r = 38$ km/h	$t = 3$ hours	Answer in kilometers.	____
3. $d = 90$ miles	$r = 60$ mph	$t = ?$	Answer in hours.	____
4. $d = 1{,}968$ kilometers	$r = ?$	$t = 24$ hours	Answer in km/h.	____
5. $d = 54$ miles	$r = 18$ mph	$t = ?$	Answer in hours.	____
6. $d = ?$	$r = 27$ km/h	$t = \frac{1}{3}$ hour	Answer in kilometers.	____
7. $d = 332$ kilometers	$r = ?$	$t = 4$ hours	Answer in km/h.	____
8. $d = 14$ miles	$r = 70$ mph	$t = ?$	Answer in hours.	____
9. $d = 1{,}233$ miles	$r = ?$	$t = 3$ hours	Answer in mph.	____
10. $d = ?$	$r = 96$ km/h	$t = \frac{3}{4}$ hour	Answer in kilometers.	____

 Algebra

Workbook Activity 41

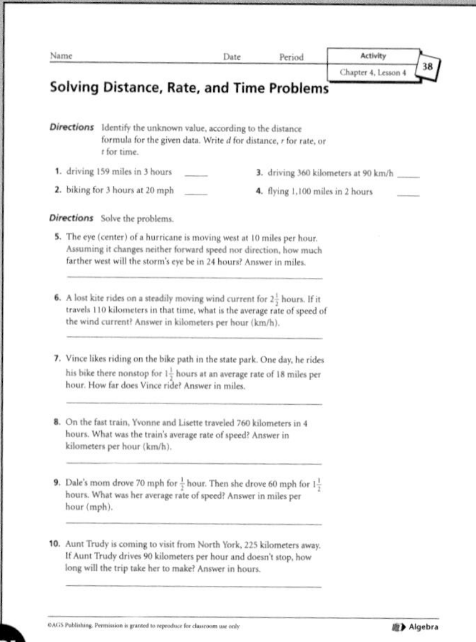

Name Date Period — Activity 38, Chapter 4, Lesson 4

Solving Distance, Rate, and Time Problems

Directions Identify the unknown value, according to the distance formula for the given data. Write d for distance, r for rate, or t for time.

1. driving 159 miles in 3 hours ____
2. biking for 3 hours at 20 mph ____
3. driving 360 kilometers at 90 km/h ____
4. flying 1,100 miles in 2 hours ____

Directions Solve the problems.

5. The eye (center) of a hurricane is moving west at 10 miles per hour. Assuming it changes neither forward speed nor direction, how much farther west will the storm's eye be in 24 hours? Answer in miles. ____
6. A lost kite rides on a steadily moving wind current for $2\frac{1}{2}$ hours. If it travels 110 kilometers in that time, what is the average rate of speed of the wind current? Answer in kilometers per hour (km/h). ____
7. Vince likes riding on the bike path in the state park. One day, he rides his bike there nonstop for $1\frac{1}{2}$ hours at an average rate of 18 miles per hour. How far does Vince ride? Answer in miles. ____
8. On the fast train, Yvonne and Lisette traveled 760 kilometers in 4 hours. What was the train's average rate of speed? Answer in kilometers per hour (km/h). ____
9. Dale's mom drove 70 mph for $\frac{1}{2}$ hour. Then she drove 60 mph for $1\frac{1}{2}$ hours. What was her average rate of speed? Answer in miles per hour (mph). ____
10. Aunt Trudy is coming to visit from North York, 225 kilometers away. If Aunt Trudy drives 90 kilometers per hour and doesn't stop, how long will the trip take her to make? Answer in hours. ____

 Algebra

Activity 38

EXAMPLE 2 Suppose you travel 378 miles in 7 hours.
What is your average rate of speed?
(Hint: How many miles did you travel in one hour?)

1 hour	2 hours	3 hours	4 hours	5 hours	6 hours	7 hours	378 miles

Divide the total number of miles driven (378 miles) by the number of hours (7 hours) to find average speed.

$\frac{378}{7}$ = 54 miles per (one) hour.

The formula $r = \frac{d}{t}$ uses the same steps to find average rate of speed.

$r = \frac{d}{t}$ $\quad r = \frac{378}{7}$ = 54 miles per hour

PROBLEM SOLVING

Exercise A Solve each problem using miles.

1. Fernando drives 165 miles at a constant speed of 55 miles per hour. How many hours does he drive? 3 hours

2. Maria and Julia live 690 miles apart. They decide to meet. Maria drives toward Julia at 60 miles per hour and Julia drives toward Maria at 55 miles per hour. How long will it take for them to meet? 6 hours

LEARNING STYLES

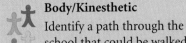

Body/Kinesthetic

Identify a path through the school that could be walked by a group of students. The path should begin and end at the door to the classroom. Divide the class into three groups. Ask one group to measure the length of the path. Ask the second group to walk the path at a normal walking speed. Ask the third group to determine the length of time it takes the group of walkers to walk the path. After the activity, invite students to work cooperatively and determine the walking speed of the walkers in feet per second. You might choose to challenge the students to convert the feet per second measure to miles per hour.

IN THE COMMUNITY

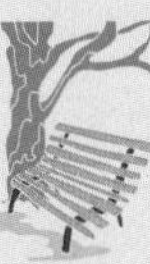

In many communities, traffic signals are timed so that motor vehicles can efficiently move from one location to another. Have students work in three groups with the goal of finding out how their community (or a nearby community) uses traffic signals to manage the movement of motor vehicles. Ask one group to find out where the information can be obtained, ask another group to get the information, and ask the remaining group to present the information to the class using some type of visual aid.

Online Connection

Have students visit www.kent.net/home-hardware/tips/concretemixing.html to learn about mixing concrete. First have them read the article about the kinds of concrete and the proportions in which it is mixed. Then have them use the information to figure out which kind and how much concrete they will need for a sidewalk 15 feet long, 4 feet wide, and 4 inches thick.

Example 3 Suppose you drive 80 kilometers per hour for $1\frac{1}{2}$ hours and 90 kilometers per hour for $\frac{1}{2}$ hour. What is your average rate of speed?

80 km/h means 80 kilometers in one hour, or 120 kilometers in $1\frac{1}{2}$ hours.

90 km/h means 90 kilometers in one hour, or 45 kilometers in $\frac{1}{2}$ hour.

  120 kilometers in $1\frac{1}{2}$ hours
+ 45 kilometers in $\frac{1}{2}$ hour

  165 kilometers in 2 hours, or $165 \div 2 = 82.5$ kilometers in 1 hour

Use the formula Average rate $= \frac{\text{Total distance}}{\text{Total time}}$ and solve for r.

$$r = \frac{d}{t}$$

$$= \frac{(80)(1\frac{1}{2}) + 90(\frac{1}{2})}{1\frac{1}{2} + \frac{1}{2}}$$

$$= \frac{120 + 45}{2}$$

$$= \frac{165}{2}$$

$$= 82.5 \text{ km/h}$$

Estimation Activity

Estimate: Sammi buys a sweater that costs $29.67. If the sales tax is 6%, how much sales tax will Sammi pay?

Solution:
Round $29.67 to $30.00.
Figure 1% of $30.00 = $0.30 or 30%
Multiply $0.30 by 6 $0.30 x 6 = $1.80

Sammi will pay $1.80 in sales tax.

PROBLEM SOLVING

Exercise B Solve each problem using kilometers.

3. Jessica rides her bicycle for $2\frac{3}{4}$ hours at an average rate of speed of $14\frac{1}{2}$ kilometers per hour. How many kilometers does she ride? $39\frac{7}{8}$ km

4. On Saturday, Erica and Bianca travel 324 kilometers. They reach their destination in 4 hours. What is their average speed? 81 km per hour

5. Jake and Lisa walk at a rate of 9 kilometers per hour for $1\frac{1}{4}$ hours and 6 kilometers per hour for 15 minutes. What is their average speed? $8\frac{1}{2}$ km per hour

Algebra in Your Life

Building, Baking, Candlestick Making . . .

Everything we build, cook, and mix uses ratio and proportion. We build houses from plans drawn to scale. We bake cookies by mixing specific proportions of ingredients. A one-to-one ratio of blue and yellow paint makes green. Changing the ratio produces different shades of blue-greens and yellow-greens. A two-to-one ratio of hydrogen and oxygen atoms produces water. Let's face it—we just can't get away from ratios and proportions!

Lesson at a Glance

Chapter 4 Lesson 5

Overview This lesson introduces writing and solving equations for cents.

Objective

- To write and solve equations for cents

Student Pages 108–110

Teacher's Resource Library 

Workbook Activity 42

Activity 39

Alternative Activity 39

Warm-Up Activity

Choose a coin and ask students to describe that coin as many different ways as they can. For example, you might choose a dime, and students might describe the dime as twice the value of a nickel, $\frac{1}{10}$ the value of a dollar, $\frac{2}{5}$ the value of a quarter, and so on. Repeat the activity several times by naming a different coin each time.

Teaching the Lesson

After discussing the examples on pages 108–109, you might choose to have students work in small groups. Supply each group with coin sets or a variety of real coins. Choose a handful of coins and describe those coins to each group. Your description should not include the exact number of each coin. Instead, it should include the exact value of the coins, the names of the coins, and the number of each coin with respect to the other coins, such as "I have 93¢ in pennies, nickels, dimes, and quarters. I have twice as many nickels as pennies and twice as many quarters as dimes." Ask each group to arrange their coins in different ways until they duplicate the arrangement you described. Repeat the activity several times.

Lesson 5 Using a Common Unit—Cents

American money is made up of coins and bills. Each coin and bill is a specific amount of money.

1 penny = 1 cent
1 nickel = 5 cents
1 dime = 10 cents
1 quarter = 25 cents
1 half-dollar = 50 cents
1 dollar = 100 cents

To solve problems dealing with money, you can write and solve algebraic equations.

EXAMPLE 1 John has $5.00 in nickels and dimes. If he has twice as many dimes as nickels, how many of each coin does he have?

Let x = number of nickels. Let $2x$ = number of dimes since there are twice as many dimes as nickels.

Write an equation. To eliminate the decimal point, multiply dollar amounts by 100. $5.00 is the same as 500 cents.

nickels + dimes = total amount

$x(5¢) + 2x(10¢) = 500$

$25x = 500$

$x = 20$ and $2x = 40$

John has 20 nickels and 40 dimes.

Check. $20(5¢) + 40(10¢) = 100¢ + 400¢ = 500¢$

Divide cents by 100 to get dollars.

$500¢ \div 100 = \$5.00$

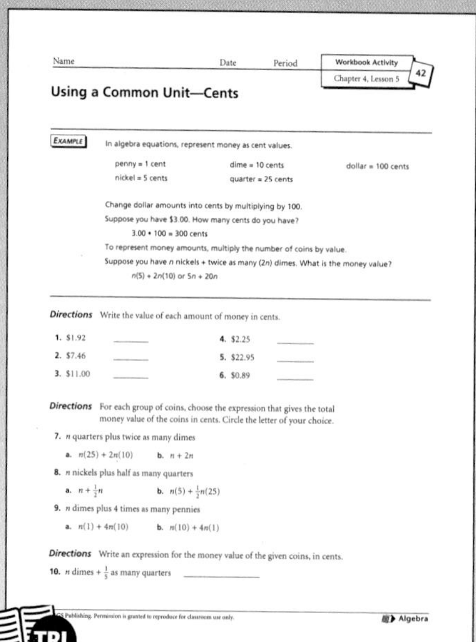

Name Date Period | Workbook Activity 42 | Chapter 4, Lesson 5

Using a Common Unit—Cents

EXAMPLE In algebra equations, represent money as cent values.

penny = 1 cent   dime = 10 cents   dollar = 100 cents
nickel = 5 cents   quarter = 25 cents

Change dollar amounts into cents by multiplying by 100.
Suppose you have $3.00. How many cents do you have?
3.00 • 100 = 300 cents
To represent money amounts, multiply the number of coins by value.
Suppose you have n nickels + twice as many ($2n$) dimes. What is the money value?
$n(5) + 2n(10)$ or $5n + 20n$

Directions Write the value of each amount of money in cents.

1. $1.92 ______
2. $7.46 ______
3. $11.00 ______
4. $2.25 ______
5. $22.95 ______
6. $0.89 ______

Directions For each group of coins, choose the expression that gives the total money value of the coins in cents. Circle the letter of your choice.

7. n quarters plus twice as many dimes
   a. $n(25) + 2n(10)$ b. $n + 2n$
8. n nickels plus half as many quarters
   a. $n + \frac{1}{2}n$ b. $n(5) + \frac{1}{2}n(25)$
9. n dimes plus 4 times as many pennies
   a. $n(1) + 4n(10)$ b. $n(10) + 4n(1)$

Directions Write an expression for the money value of the given coins, in cents.

10. n dimes + $\frac{1}{5}$ as many quarters ______

 Algebra

Workbook Activity 42

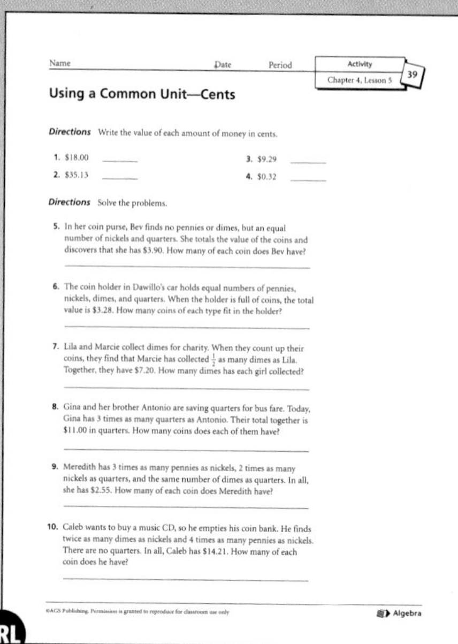

Name Date Period | Activity 39 | Chapter 4, Lesson 5

Using a Common Unit—Cents

Directions Write the value of each amount of money in cents.

1. $18.00 ______
2. $35.13 ______
3. $9.29 ______
4. $0.32 ______

Directions Solve the problems.

5. In her coin purse, Bev finds no pennies or dimes, but an equal number of nickels and quarters. She totals the value of the coins and discovers that she has $3.90. How many of each coin does Bev have?
6. The coin holder in Dawillo's car holds equal numbers of pennies, nickels, dimes, and quarters. When the holder is full of coins, the total value is $3.28. How many coins of each type fit in the holder?
7. Lila and Marcie collect dimes for charity. When they count up their coins, they find that Marcie has collected $\frac{1}{2}$ as many dimes as Lila. Together, they have $7.20. How many dimes has each girl collected?
8. Gina and her brother Antonio are saving quarters for bus fare. Today, Gina has 3 times as many quarters as Antonio. Their total together is $11.00 in quarters. How many coins does each of them have?
9. Meredith has 3 times as many pennies as nickels, 2 times as many nickels as quarters, and the same number of dimes as quarters. In all, she has $2.55. How many of each coin does Meredith have?
10. Caleb wants to buy a music CD, so he empties his coin bank. He finds twice as many dimes as nickels and 4 times as many pennies as nickels. There are no quarters. In all, Caleb has $14.21. How many of each coin does he have?

 Algebra

Activity 39

EXAMPLE 2 Andrea has six times as many dimes as quarters. If her dimes and quarters total $12.75, how many of each coin does she have?

Let x = number of quarters.

Let $6x$ = number of dimes since there are six times as many dimes as quarters.

$$6x(10) + (25)x = 1{,}275$$
$$60x + 25x = 1{,}275$$
$$85x = 1{,}275$$
$$x = 15 \text{ and } 6x = 90$$

Andrea has 15 quarters and 90 dimes.

Check. 15(25¢) + 90(10¢) = 375¢ + 900¢ = 1,275¢, or $12.75

PROBLEM SOLVING

Exercise A Solve the problems by answering the questions.

1. Tricia has the same number of nickels and dimes in her pocket. The coins total $3.60.
   - **a.** How many of each coin does she have? 24 of each coin
   - **b.** How many coins are in Tricia's pocket? 48 coins
2. Gilberto has three times as many quarters as half-dollars. The coins total $13.75.
   - **a.** How many of each coin does he have? 33 quarters, 11 half-dollars
   - **b.** How many coins does Gilberto have? 44 coins
3. Kristi has $13.20 in dimes and half-dollars. She has one-half as many dimes as half-dollars.
   - **a.** How many of each coin does she have? 12 dimes and 24 half-dollars
   - **b.** How many coins does Kristi have? 36 coins
4. Latisha noticed that she has the same number of nickels, dimes, quarters, and half-dollars in her drawer. The coins total $12.60.
   - **a.** How many of each coin does she have? 14 coins
   - **b.** The nickels and dimes total what amount? $2.10
   - **c.** The quarters and half-dollars total what amount? $10.50

Reinforce and Extend

LEARNING STYLES

LEP/ESL

Explain that coins and currencies vary from one country to another. Invite volunteers with a knowledge of the monetary systems of other countries to explain how those monetary systems function. They might bring in coins and currencies from the other countries to show in class.

GROUP PROBLEM SOLVING

Have small groups of students discuss and solve the following problem:

Suppose a child visits a supermarket with $1.00 in coins. Although none of the coins are half-dollars, the child has at least one penny, one nickel, one dime, and one quarter. What is the greatest number of coins the child could have? *(63)* What is the least number? *(11)*

Calculator

Use the board to demonstrate this alternative method for solving the Calculator example on page 110:

$$3x(0.10) + x(0.05) = 3.50$$
$$0.30x + 0.05x = 3.50$$
$$0.35x = 3.5$$
$$x = 10$$
$$3x = 30$$

Explain that the method represents each amount of money as a decimal: a dime is represented as $0.10 or 0.10, a nickel is represented as $0.05 or 0.05, and 350¢ is represented as $3.50 or 3.50. Have students use this method and a calculator to check their answers to problems 5–10.

Calculator Practice

You can use a calculator to solve problems involving money.

Example 3 $3.50, three times more dimes than nickels

Set up your equation: $3x(10¢) + x(5¢) = 350¢$

Press: 3 [×] 10 [+] 5 [=]. Your calculator will read 35.

Clear, and then press: 350 [÷] 35 [=] 10, the number of nickels.

Press: [×] 3 [=] 30, the number of dimes.

Exercise B Use a calculator to tell how many nickels and how many dimes in each problem.

Answer	Problem
24 nickels and 12 dimes	**5.** $2.40, two times more nickels than dimes
20 nickels and 20 dimes	**6.** $3.00, the same number of nickels as dimes
20 nickels and 80 dimes	**7.** 900¢, 4 times more dimes than nickels
50 nickels and 10 dimes	**8.** 350¢, 5 times more nickels than dimes
2 nickels and 16 dimes	**9.** $1.70, 8 times more dimes than nickels
78 nickels and 13 dimes	**10.** 520¢, 6 times more nickels than dimes

Technology Connection

Internet Calculators

There's a calculator on the Internet for just about any type of number you want to know. There are calculators that compute interest for a loan. There are calculators to figure the distance from one place to another and how much gas you'll use. Other calculators figure the cost of living in different cities. You can also find what your car is worth, or how long it will take to build a house. And that's just for starters. Type "online calculator" into a search engine, and see what you can find!

Name Date Period **Workbook Activity 43** Chapter 4, Lesson 6

Calculating Simple Interest

Example

- Use the formula $I = prt$ to calculate simple interest.
  How much interest will $300 at 6% interest earn in 1 year?
  $I = \$300(0.06)(1) = \$18$
- Use the formula $p = \frac{I}{rt}$ to solve for p and calculate principal.
  Find the principal in an account that has a rate of 5% and earns $75 interest in 2 years.
  $p = \frac{\$75}{(0.05)(2)} = \$750$
- Use the formula $r = \frac{I}{pt}$ to solve for r and calculate rate of interest.
  What is the rate of interest if $1,000 earns $240 interest in 3 years?
  $r = \frac{\$240}{(\$1,000)(3)} = 0.08$, or 8%

Directions Calculate interest on the given principal, rate, and time.

1. $p = \$200$ $r = 3\%$ $t = 1$ year ______
2. $p = \$720$ $r = 4\%$ $t = 1$ year ______
3. $p = \$1,400$ $r = 7\%$ $t = 2$ years ______

Directions Calculate principal from the given interest, rate, and time.

4. $I = \$90$ $r = 6\%$ $t = 3$ years ______
5. $I = \$27$ $r = 3\%$ $t = 1$ year ______
6. $I = \$256$ $r = 8\%$ $t = 1$ year ______

Directions Calculate rate from the given interest, principal, and time.

7. $I = \$63$ $p = \$700$ $t = 1$ year ______
8. $I = \$24$ $p = \$150$ $t = 4$ years ______
9. $I = \$48$ $p = \$960$ $t = 1$ year ______

Directions Solve the problem.

10. For 2 years, Will kept $655 in a savings account that earned 4% annual interest. How much interest did Will earn?

 Algebra

TRL

Workbook Activity 43

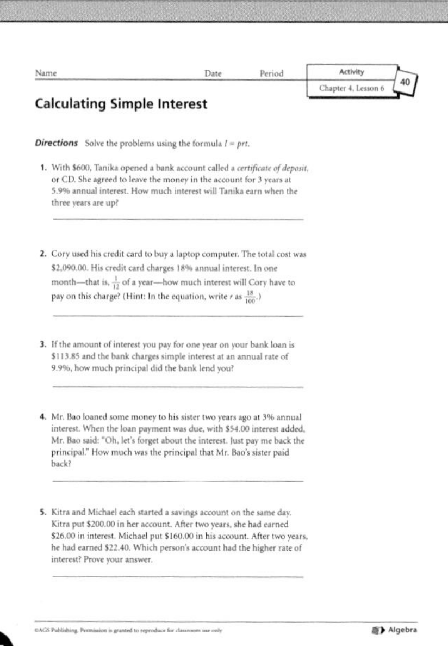

Name Date Period **Activity 40** Chapter 4, Lesson 6

Calculating Simple Interest

Directions Solve the problems using the formula $I = prt$.

1. With $600, Tanika opened a bank account called a *certificate of deposit*, or CD. She agreed to leave the money in the account for 3 years at 5.9% annual interest. How much interest will Tanika earn when the three years are up?
2. Cory used his credit card to buy a laptop computer. The total cost was $2,090.00. His credit card charges 18% annual interest. In one month—that is, $\frac{1}{12}$ of a year—how much interest will Cory have to pay on this charge? (Hint: In the equation, write r as $\frac{18}{100}$.)
3. If the amount of interest you pay for one year on your bank loan is $113.85 and the bank charges simple interest at an annual rate of 9.9%, how much principal did the bank lend you?
4. Mr. Bao loaned some money to his sister two years ago at 3% annual interest. When the loan payment was due, with $54.00 interest added, Mr. Bao said: "Oh, let's forget about the interest. Just pay me back the principal." How much was the principal that Mr. Bao's sister paid back?
5. Kitra and Michael each started a savings account on the same day. Kitra put $200.00 in her account. After two years, she had earned $26.00 in interest. Michael put $160.00 in his account. After two years, he had earned $22.40. Which person's account had the higher rate of interest? Prove your answer.

 Algebra

TRL

Activity 40

Lesson 6 Calculating Simple Interest

Interest
The amount of money paid or received for the use of borrowed money

Principal
The amount of money deposited, borrowed, or loaned

When you deposit money in a bank, your money earns **interest** because the bank is using (borrowing) your money to make investments. The rate of interest is applied to your money for 1 year at a time. The money you earn is simple annual interest.

Simple Interest Formula

$I = p \bullet r \bullet t$ or $I = prt$

where I is the interest in dollars, p is the **principal** in dollars, r is the rate in percent, and t is the time in years.

EXAMPLE 1

If you deposit $500 at a rate of 6% for 2 years, how much interest will you earn?

Substitute the values into the formula $I = prt$ to solve.

$p = \$500$	$I = prt$
$r = 6\% = 0.06$	$= (\$500)(6\%)(2 \text{ years})$
$t = 2$ years	$= (500)(0.06)(2)$
$I =$ interest	$I = 60$

The interest earned is $60.

EXAMPLE 2

Find the principal in an account that has a rate of 7.5% for 1 year and earns $900 in interest.

Use the formula $I = prt$ to solve for p.

$I = prt \quad \frac{I}{rt} = \frac{prt}{rt} \quad \frac{I}{rt} = p$

Substitute the values into the formula to solve.

$p = \frac{I}{rt}$

$r = 7.5\% = 0.075 \quad p = \frac{\$900}{(0.075)}$

$t = 1$ year

$I = \$900$

$p =$ principal $\quad p = \$12{,}000$

The principal is $12,000.

Lesson at a Glance

Chapter 4 Lesson 6

Overview This lesson introduces the simple interest formula.

Objectives

- To compute interest by applying the simple interest formula

Student Pages 111–113

Teacher's Resource Library 

Workbook Activity 43

Activity 40

Alternative Activity 40

Mathematics Vocabulary

interest
principal

1 Warm-Up Activity

Explain that interest is the amount of money paid or received for the use of borrowed money. Then ask students to name as many situations as they can in which interest is earned and as many situations as they can in which interest is paid. Initiate the discussion by pointing out that interest is earned if money is deposited into a savings account, and interest is paid if money is borrowed to purchase an automobile.

2 Teaching the Lesson

Discuss with students the changes that may need to be made to the values r and t before simple interest can be computed. Have students note that r will almost always be expressed in a problem as a percent and will need to be changed to a decimal, and t will sometimes, but not always, be expressed in a problem as years. When it is not expressed as years, it too must be changed.

Common Error

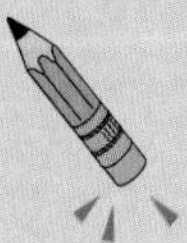

When changing a percent to a decimal, students sometimes move the decimal point the wrong direction and/or an incorrect number of places. Remind them that when a percent is changed to a decimal, the decimal point is moved two places to the left, and the percent sign is deleted.

3 Reinforce and Extend

Group Problem Solving

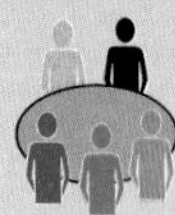

Have pairs of students discuss and solve the following problem:

Suppose $900 is deposited into a money-market account that earns a simple interest rate of 3%. Find the value of the account after 5 months if no deposits to that account or withdrawals from that account are made during that time. *($11.25)*

Invite groups to share their problem-solving approach with one another.

Career Connection

Invite a volunteer from a local lending institution to visit the class and explain the movement of money within the banking system. Also, ask the representative to describe different things consumers should be aware of when they borrow money, and different strategies consumers might use to recognize why one loan represents a "better buy" than another.

Example 3 Keesha borrows $3,000 for 1 year. At the end of the year, she has paid $210 in interest. Find the rate of interest.

Use the formula $I = prt$ to solve for r.

$r = \frac{I}{pt}$

Substitute the values into the formula to solve.

$p = \$3,000$ $\quad r = \frac{\$210}{\$3,000}$

$t = 1$ year

$I = \$210$

$r =$ rate of interest $\quad r = 0.07 = 7\%$

The rate of interest is 7%.

Exercise A Find the interest.

1. Principal: $3,000
Rate: 5.5%
Time: 1 year $165

2. Principal: $8,000
Rate: 8%
Time: 2 years $1,280

3. Principal: $5,000
Rate: 11.5%
Time: 4 years $2,300

Exercise B Find the principal or rate of interest.

4. Interest: $640
Rate: 4%
Time: 1 year $16,000

5. Interest: $2,016
Rate: 12%
Time: 3 years $5,600

6. Principal: $4,000
Interest: $720
Time: 2 years 9%

PROBLEM SOLVING

Exercise C Solve each problem.

7. Find the interest earned on $4,200 at a 6.25% annual interest rate for 5 years. $1,312.50

8. Terence opens a savings account with a deposit of $1,000. After 1 year, he receives $50 in interest. What is the annual interest rate? 5%

9. Suppose you lend a friend $400 for 2 years. You loan the money at a rate of 6%. How much should your friend pay you in interest at the end of 2 years? $48

10. Credit cards usually have high interest rates. Jennifer has a credit card bill of $1,350. The interest rate is 18% per year. How much interest will Jennifer pay at the end of 1 month? (Hint: 1 month $= \frac{1}{12}$ of a year) $20.25

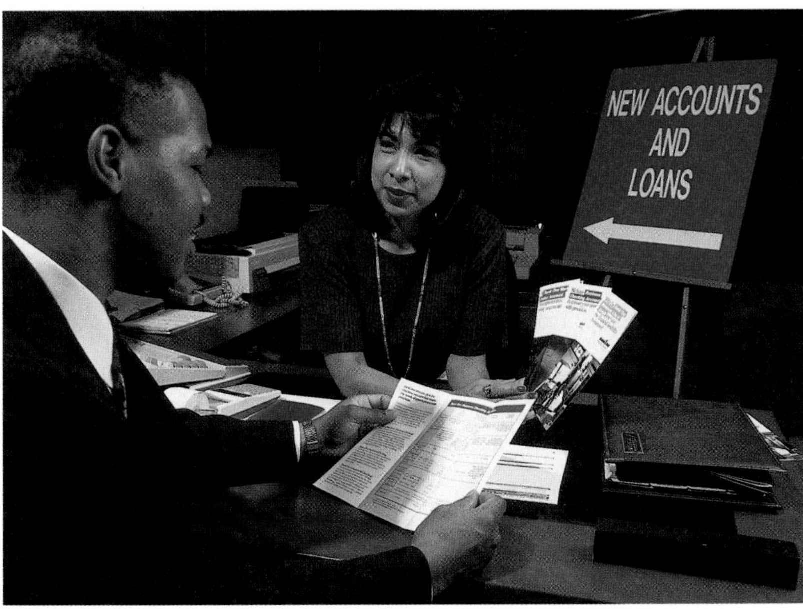

Lesson at a Glance

Chapter 4 Lesson 7

Overview This lesson introduces mixture problems.

Objective

- To derive and apply formulas to solve mixture problems

Student Pages 114–115

Teacher's Resource Library 

Workbook Activity 44

Activity 41

Alternative Activity 41

1 Warm-Up Activity

Write the following sentences on the board:

A 5-pound bag of flour costs $2.00.
A 5-pound bag of sugar costs $2.50.

Then ask:

- What is the unit cost, or cost per pound, of the flour? *($0.40)*
- What is the unit cost, or cost per pound, of the sugar? *($0.50)*
- Suppose that in a container, one pound of flour is mixed with one pound of sugar. How many pounds altogether would be in the container? *(2 pounds)*
- What is the cost of the mixture? *($0.40 + $0.50 = $0.90)*
- What is the *average* cost per pound of the mixture in the container? *($0.90 ÷ 2 = $0.45)*

Explain that the study of algebra sometimes includes mixture problems. Invite volunteers to describe other mixtures of flour and sugar. Challenge the class to determine the cost per pound of each mixture.

2 Teaching the Lesson

Explain the relationship shared by a mixture and a mean. Remind students that the mean of a set of data is determined by finding the sum of the values in the set and dividing by the number of values in the set. Point out that, in some mixture problems, such as the first example on page 114, the mean must be found; in other mixture problems, such as the second example on page 114, the mean is known.

Lesson 7 Deriving a Formula for Mixture Problems

Mixture problems can be solved in different ways.

EXAMPLE 1 Peanuts cost $3.00 per pound and walnuts cost $5.00 per pound. If you mix three pounds of peanuts with two pounds of walnuts, what is the cost for one pound of the mixture?

Peanuts cost	$3.00 for 1 pound
	$9.00 for 3 pounds
Walnuts cost	$5.00 for 1 pound
	$10.00 for 2 pounds

Add the amounts to get the total price and the total weight.

Peanuts	$ 9.00 for 3 pounds
Walnuts	$10.00 for 2 pounds
Mixture:	$19.00 for 5 pounds

One pound of the mixture costs $19.00 ÷ 5 or $3.80.

In algebra, the following formula copies the steps used above.

$$\text{Price per pound} = \frac{\text{cost of total mixture}}{\text{number of pounds}}$$

$$\text{Price per pound} = \frac{(3)(\$3) + (2)(\$5)}{3+2}$$

$$= \frac{\$19}{5} = \$3.80$$

EXAMPLE 2 A grocer wants to mix peanuts and walnuts. Peanuts cost $3.00 per pound and walnuts cost $5 per pound. If she wants 100 pounds of a mixture to sell for $3.50 a pound, how much of each kind of nut should she use?

Let x represent the number of pounds of peanuts and $100 - x$ represent the number of pounds of walnuts.

You know that 100 pounds at $3.50 per pound is $350.00 for the total mixture.

Cost of peanuts + cost of walnuts = $350

$$\$3x + \$5(100 - x) = \$350$$

Write the equation and solve for x.

$$3x + 5(100 - x) = 350$$
$$3x + 500 - 5x = 350$$
$$500 - 2x = 350$$
$$-2x = -150$$
$$2x = 150$$
$$x = 75 \text{ and } 100 - x = 25$$

The grocer should use 75 pounds of peanuts and 25 pounds of walnuts.

Check. $(\$3)(75) + (\$5)(25) = \$225 + \$125 = \$350$

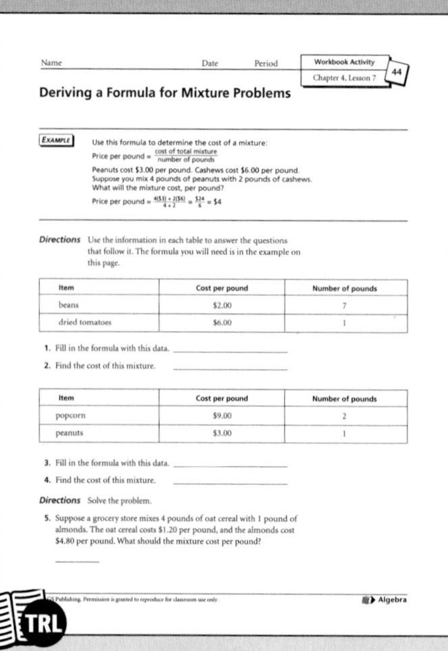

Name Date Period — Workbook Activity 44 — Chapter 4, Lesson 7

Deriving a Formula for Mixture Problems

EXAMPLE Use this formula to determine the cost of a mixture:
Price per pound = $\frac{\text{cost of total mixture}}{\text{number of pounds}}$
Peanuts cost $3.00 per pound. Cashews cost $6.00 per pound. Suppose you mix 4 pounds of peanuts with 2 pounds of cashews. What will the mixture cost, per pound?
Price per pound = $\frac{4(\$3) + 2(\$6)}{4+2} = \frac{\$24}{6} = \$4$

Directions Use the information in each table to answer the questions that follow it. The formula you will need is in the example on this page.

Item	Cost per pound	Number of pounds
beans	$2.00	7
dried tomatoes	$6.00	1

1. Fill in the formula with this data. ______
2. Find the cost of this mixture. ______

Item	Cost per pound	Number of pounds
popcorn	$9.00	2
peanuts	$3.00	1

3. Fill in the formula with this data. ______
4. Find the cost of this mixture. ______

Directions Solve the problem.

5. Suppose a grocery store mixes 4 pounds of oat cereal with 1 pound of almonds. The oat cereal costs $1.20 per pound, and the almonds cost $4.80 per pound. What should the mixture cost per pound?

Algebra

Workbook Activity 44

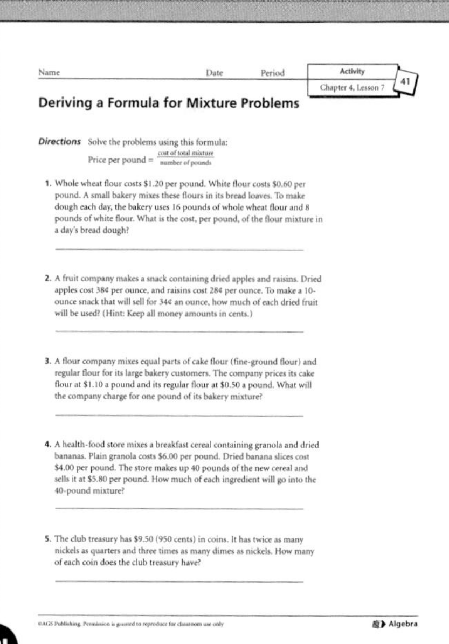

Name Date Period — Activity 41 — Chapter 4, Lesson 7

Deriving a Formula for Mixture Problems

Directions Solve the problems using this formula:
Price per pound = $\frac{\text{cost of total mixture}}{\text{number of pounds}}$

1. Whole wheat flour costs $1.20 per pound. White flour costs $0.60 per pound. A small bakery mixes these flours in its bread loaves. To make dough each day, the bakery uses 16 pounds of whole wheat flour and 8 pounds of white flour. What is the cost, per pound, of the flour mixture in a day's bread dough?
2. A fruit company makes a snack containing dried apples and raisins. Dried apples cost 38¢ per ounce, and raisins cost 28¢ per ounce. To make a 10-ounce snack that will sell for 34¢ an ounce, how much of each dried fruit will be used? (Hint: Keep all money amounts in cents.)
3. A flour company mixes equal parts of cake flour (fine-ground flour) and regular flour for its large bakery customers. The company prices its cake flour at $1.10 a pound and its regular flour at $0.50 a pound. What will the company charge for one pound of its bakery mixture?
4. A health-food store mixes a breakfast cereal containing granola and dried bananas. Plain granola costs $6.00 per pound. Dried banana slices cost $4.00 per pound. The store makes up 40 pounds of the new cereal and sells it at $5.80 per pound. How much of each ingredient will go into the 40-pound mixture?
5. The club treasury has $9.50 (950 cents) in coins. It has twice as many nickels as quarters and three times as many dimes as nickels. How many of each coin does the club treasury have?

Algebra

Activity 41

PROBLEM SOLVING

Exercise A Solve each problem.

1. Cashews cost $4 per pound and peanuts cost $2.50 per pound. If you mix 4 pounds of cashews and 4 pounds of peanuts, what is the cost of one pound of the mixture?
2. The price for one pound of a mixture of cashews and walnuts is $6.25. The total cost of the mixture is $27. What is the total number of pounds in the mixture?
3. Peanuts cost $4 per pound and walnuts cost $5.50 per pound. A 40-pound mixture sells for $184. How many pounds of each kind of nut are in the mixture?
4. Suppose you want to make a mixture of peanuts and walnuts that costs $2.70 per pound. How many pounds of peanuts at $1.50 per pound should be mixed with 24 pounds of walnuts at $3.50 per pound?
5. A grocer purchased a 100-pound mixture of nuts for $150. The mixture contains 40 pounds of walnuts that cost $2.25 per pound. What is the average cost per pound of the other nuts in the mixture?

1. $3.25
2. 4.32 pounds
3. 24 pounds of peanuts, 16 pounds of walnuts
4. 16 pounds
5. $1.00

Possible response: $V = \frac{C}{A}$

TRY THIS Create a formula for solving mixture problems. Use *C* for total cost, *V* for value (price per pound), and *A* for amount (number of pounds).

Try This

Invite students to write the formula they create on the board. Then ask them to test whether their formula is correct by using it to solve mixture problems that have known correct answers, as in the examples on page 114. A formula is likely to be correct if it can provide correct answer to both examples.

3 Reinforce and Extend

LEARNING STYLES

Auditory/Verbal

Divide the class into two groups. Read the following scenario. "Ten boxes are being transported on a freight elevator. Five of the boxes weigh 100 pounds each. The other five boxes weigh 200 pounds each. What is the average weight of a box being transported by the freight elevator?" *[5(100) + 5(200) = 1,500; 1,500 ÷ 10 = 150 lb]* Do not read the scenario a second time. Instruct each group to exchange information and ideas, then solve the problem mentally.

GROUP PROBLEM SOLVING

Have small groups of students discuss and solve the following problem:

Jorge makes a snack food that is a mixture of peanuts, raisins, and dried bananas. Peanuts cost $2.50 per pound, raisins $3.00 per pound, and dried bananas $4.00 per pound. If the cost per pound of the mixture is $3.00, how many pounds of each ingredient are in the mixture? *(4 pounds of peanuts, 1 pound of raisins, 2 pounds of dried bananas)*

Invite groups to share their problem-solving approach with one another.

Lesson at a Glance

Chapter 4 Lesson 8

Overview This lesson introduces ratios and proportions.

Objective

- To express a ratio in simplest form and find a missing term in a proportion

Student Pages 116–117

Teacher's Resource Library 

Workbook Activity 45

Activity 42

Alternative Activity 42

Mathematics Vocabulary

cross products
proportion
ratio

 Warm-Up Activity

Challenge students to solve the following problem:

If $\frac{1}{2}$ of the students in one classroom are female, and $\frac{1}{2}$ of the students in another classroom are female, are there the same number of females in both classrooms? Give an argument for both cases—yes and no. *(Yes: If each classroom contains the same number of students, then each classroom contains the same number of females; No: If each classroom contains a different number of students, then each classroom contains a different number of females.)*

Help students recall that fractions are examples of ratios. In the example problem, the fraction $\frac{1}{2}$ describes the ratio of the number of females to the total number of students in each classroom.

 Teaching the Lesson

You might choose to introduce students to the terms *means* and *extremes*. Point out that in a proportion, two values represent the means and two values represent the extremes. On the board, write the proportion $\frac{a}{b} = \frac{c}{d}$. Explain that b and c represent the means of the proportion, and a and d represent the

Lesson 8 Ratio and Proportion

Ratio
A comparison of two quantities using division

Proportion
An equation made up of two equal ratios

Cross products
The result of multiplying the denominator of one fraction with the numerator of another

A **ratio** is a comparison between two like quantities or numbers. Examples of ratios include

$\frac{3}{5}$ $\frac{3\text{ ft}}{5\text{ ft}}$ $\frac{3\text{ min}}{5\text{ min}}$

In algebra, the ratio of a to b is written as $a{:}b$, or $\frac{a}{b}$.

EXAMPLE 1 An algebra class has 32 students. What is the ratio of males to females if there are 15 boys and 17 girls in the class?

The ratio of males to females is $\frac{15}{17}$.
You can also write 15:17 or 15 to 17.

Note that $15 + 17 = 32$, the total number of students.

What is the ratio of girls to boys?
$\frac{17}{15}$, 17:15, or 17 to 15.
Both ratios contain the same information, but have different values since $\frac{15}{17} \neq \frac{17}{15}$.

Two equal ratios make up a **proportion**.

For example, $\frac{2}{4} = \frac{1}{2}$ are equal ratios that form a proportion.

In any true proportion, the **cross products** of the proportion are equal to one another.

EXAMPLE 2 Is $\frac{1}{3} = \frac{3}{9}$ a proportion?

Step 1 Find the cross products of the proportion.

$\frac{1}{3} \times \frac{3}{9}$

The cross products are $1 \bullet 9 = 9$ and $3 \bullet 3 = 9$.

Step 2 Compare the cross products.
Since $1 \bullet 9 = 9$ and $3 \bullet 3 = 9$, the cross products are equal and $\frac{1}{3} = \frac{3}{9}$ is a proportion.

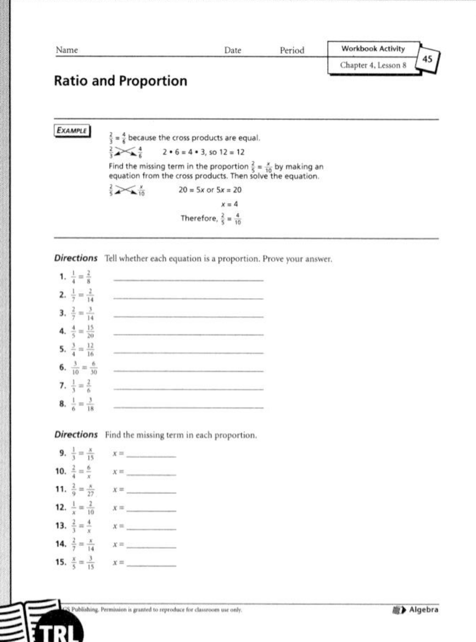

Name Date Period **Workbook Activity 45** Chapter 4, Lesson 8

Ratio and Proportion

EXAMPLE

$\frac{2}{3} = \frac{4}{6}$ because the cross products are equal.

$\frac{2}{3} \times \frac{4}{6}$ $2 \bullet 6 = 4 \bullet 3$, so $12 = 12$

Find the missing term in the proportion $\frac{2}{5} = \frac{x}{10}$ by making an equation from the cross products. Then solve the equation.

$\frac{2}{5} \times \frac{x}{10}$ $20 = 5x$ or $5x = 20$

$x = 4$

Therefore, $\frac{2}{5} = \frac{4}{10}$

Directions Tell whether each equation is a proportion. Prove your answer.

1. $\frac{1}{4} = \frac{2}{8}$ ______
2. $\frac{1}{7} = \frac{2}{14}$ ______
3. $\frac{2}{7} = \frac{3}{14}$ ______
4. $\frac{4}{5} = \frac{15}{20}$ ______
5. $\frac{3}{4} = \frac{12}{16}$ ______
6. $\frac{3}{10} = \frac{6}{30}$ ______
7. $\frac{1}{3} = \frac{2}{6}$ ______
8. $\frac{1}{6} = \frac{3}{18}$ ______

Directions Find the missing term in each proportion.

9. $\frac{1}{3} = \frac{x}{15}$ $x =$ ______
10. $\frac{2}{4} = \frac{6}{x}$ $x =$ ______
11. $\frac{2}{9} = \frac{x}{27}$ $x =$ ______
12. $\frac{1}{x} = \frac{2}{10}$ $x =$ ______
13. $\frac{2}{3} = \frac{4}{x}$ $x =$ ______
14. $\frac{2}{7} = \frac{x}{14}$ $x =$ ______
15. $\frac{x}{5} = \frac{3}{15}$ $x =$ ______

 Algebra

Workbook Activity 45

Name Date Period **Activity 42** Chapter 4, Lesson 8

Ratio and Proportion

Directions Write each ratio. Use the format *a:b*.

1. A company has 100 female and 50 male employees. Write the ratio of female to male employees. ______
2. For the same company, write the ratio of male to female employees. ______
3. In a box of colored light bulbs, 12 bulbs are green and 36 are silver. Write the ratio of green to silver bulbs. ______
4. For the same box, write the ratio of silver to green bulbs. ______

Directions Write each ratio. Use the format $\frac{a}{b}$.

5. A computer company has two laptop models. Model A-100 has 8 MB of memory. Model A-200 has 16 MB of memory. Write the ratio of A-200 memory to A-100 memory. ______
6. Burr Ridge has a population of 3,800. Deerfield has a population of 38,000. Write the ratio of Burr Ridge's population to that of Deerfield. ______
7. A bookstore has 80 copies of a cookbook and 240 copies of a popular novel. Write the ratio of cookbook copies to novel copies. ______
8. A particular dinosaur is estimated to have weighed 20,000 pounds when alive. The average adult human male weighs 150 pounds. Write the ratio of the human's weight to the dinosaur's weight. ______

Directions Solve each problem.

9. Mrs. Ray's class has 18 girls and 9 boys. Mr. Li's class has 16 girls and 8 boys. Is the girl-boy ratio the same in each class? Explain.
______
______
10. Sky Blue paint is made by mixing 7 pints blue to 3 pints white. How much blue should be mixed with 9 pints of white? Hint: Set up a proportion and find the missing term.
______
______

 Algebra

TRL

Activity 42

To find the missing term in any proportion, set the cross products equal to each other. Then solve for the variable.

EXAMPLE 3 Find the missing term in the proportion $\frac{3}{4} = \frac{9}{x}$.

Step 1 Set the cross products equal to each other.

$\frac{3}{4} \times \frac{9}{x}$ $\quad (3)(x) = (9)(4)$

$3x = 36$

Step 2 Solve for x. $\quad 3x = 36$

$\frac{3x}{3} = \frac{36}{3}$

$x = 12$

Step 3 $\frac{3}{4} = \frac{9}{12}$ $\quad 3 \bullet 12 = 4 \bullet 9$

$36 = 36$

PROBLEM SOLVING

Exercise A Solve each problem. Your answer will be a ratio. Write the ratio as a fraction in lowest terms.

1. a. $\frac{8}{5}$ b. $\frac{5}{8}$ c. $\frac{5}{13}$ d. $\frac{8}{13}$

1. In a small business, 64 of the employees are women and 40 of the employees are men. What is the ratio of
   a. women to men?
   b. men to women?
   c. men to the total number of employees?
   d. women to the total number of employees?

2. $\frac{3}{7}$

2. An algebra test of 50 questions included 15 questions on Chapter 4. What is the ratio of questions from Chapter 4 to the other questions on the test?

3. a. $\frac{3}{2}$ b. $\frac{2}{3}$ c. $\frac{1}{8}$ d. $\frac{1}{12}$

3. A rectangular garden measures 12 feet (length) by 8 feet (width). What is the ratio of
   a. length to width?
   b. width to length?
   c. length to area?
   d. width to area?

Exercise B Find the missing term in each proportion.

4. $\frac{2}{3} = \frac{n}{9}$ $\quad n = 6$ **7.** $\frac{2}{4} = \frac{n}{18}$ $\quad n = 9$ **10.** $\frac{8}{n} = \frac{5}{10}$ $\quad n = 16$ **13.** $\frac{3}{5} = \frac{24}{n}$ $\quad n = 40$

5. $\frac{6}{8} = \frac{y}{4}$ $\quad y = 3$ **8.** $\frac{x}{15} = \frac{3}{5}$ $\quad x = 9$ **11.** $\frac{9}{27} = \frac{y}{9}$ $\quad y = 3$ **14.** $\frac{12}{15} = \frac{x}{50}$ $\quad x = 40$

6. $\frac{4}{11} = \frac{20}{x}$ $\quad x = 55$ **9.** $\frac{6}{x} = \frac{48}{40}$ $\quad x = 5$ **12.** $\frac{1}{4} = \frac{x}{32}$ $\quad x = 8$ **15.** $\frac{18}{24} = \frac{30}{x}$ $\quad x = 40$

extremes. Explain that in any true proportion, $bc = ad$. Encourage students to check their answers to problems 4–15 by comparing the product of the means to the product of the extremes in each proportion: if the product of the means is equal to the product of the extremes, the answer is correct.

3 Reinforce and Extend

LEARNING STYLES

Visual/Spatial

Draw this proportion on the board. Invite students to find, and explain how to find, the correct answer.

$$\frac{\downarrow\downarrow\downarrow}{\uparrow\uparrow\uparrow\uparrow\uparrow\uparrow} = \frac{\downarrow}{?}$$

($\frac{\downarrow\downarrow\downarrow}{\uparrow\uparrow\uparrow\uparrow\uparrow\uparrow} = \frac{\downarrow}{\uparrow\uparrow}$; *Explanations will vary.*)

GROUP PROBLEM SOLVING

Encourage students to work in groups of three to discuss the following proportions and supply more than one correct answer for each:

$$\frac{■}{■} = \frac{1}{2}$$

$$\frac{2}{■} = \frac{■}{10}$$

Invite groups to share and compare answers, then explain why there is an infinite number of correct answers for each proportion. *(In a true proportion, one fraction is simply an equivalent fraction of the other. For any fraction, there is an infinite number of equivalent fractions.)*

Lesson at a Glance

Chapter 4 Application

Overview This lesson introduces applications of proportions.

Objective

- To form and solve proportions using real-life data

Student Page 118

Teacher's Resource Library 

Application Activity 4

Everyday Algebra 4

Warm-Up Activity

Invite students to solve this problem:

There are 3 males and 1 female in Room A, 12 males and 4 females in Room B, and 6 males and 2 females in Room C. If all of the people in Rooms A and B move to Room C, what will be the ratio of males to females in Room C? *(21 to 7 or 3 to 1)*

Teaching the Lesson

Write the fraction $\frac{\text{inches}}{\text{feet}}$ on the board and point out the need to be consistent when setting up proportions. Explain that being *consistent* means that if you choose to write the first fraction in a proportion as inches over feet, the second fraction in the proportion must also be written as inches over feet. Complete a proportion on the board by writing $= \frac{\text{inches}}{\text{feet}}$.

Encourage students to label each value of a proportion with labels such as inches, feet, miles, and so on. Point out that the labels will help them make sure a proportion is set up or written in a consistent way.

Reinforce and Extend

Learning Styles

Visual/Spatial

Several different proportions can be used to generate correct answers for problems 1–5. Invite volunteers to use the board and demonstrate as many different proportions as possible for each problem.

Application

Using Proportions

Many answers can be found by writing and solving proportions.

Example 1 If the large gear turns 5 times, how many times will the small gear turn?

Step 1 Find how many times the small gear turns for one turn of the large gear.

$\frac{\text{Large gear}}{\text{Small gear}} = \frac{20}{12} = \frac{5}{3} = 1\frac{2}{3}$

For one turn of the large gear, the small one turns $\frac{5}{3}$ or $1\frac{2}{3}$ times.

Step 2 Write the proportion. $\frac{\text{1 turn of large gear}}{\text{5 turns of large gear}} = \frac{\frac{5}{3}\text{turns of small gear}}{x}$

Step 3 Rewrite the proportion algebraically. Then solve for x.

$\frac{1}{5} = \frac{5}{3} \div x \qquad x = (5)(\frac{5}{3}) \qquad x = \frac{25}{3} = 8\frac{1}{3}$

For five turns of the large gear, the small one turns $8\frac{1}{3}$ times.

Exercise Solve each problem.

1. Jody can swim 18 laps in 25 minutes. At that rate, how many laps can she swim in 125 minutes?
2. Darrell drives 147 miles in 3 hours. If he drives at the same speed, how many miles can he drive in 7 hours?
3. If 5 gallons of gasoline cost $6.60, how much do 9 gallons of gasoline cost?

The scale on a map reads 2 inches = 60 miles.

4. If two cities measure $5\frac{1}{2}$ inches apart, how far apart are they in actual miles?
5. If the actual distance between two cities is 280 miles, what is the distance on the map?

1. 90 laps
2. 343 miles
3. $11.88
4. 165 miles
5. $9\frac{1}{3}$ inches

Name Date Period | Application Activity 4 | Chapter 4

Using Proportions

Many problems can be solved using proportions. Look at the following example.

If the large gear on a bicycle turns 3 times, how many times will the small gear turn?

Large gear — Small gear

Step 1 Find how many times the small gear turns for one turn of the large gear.

$\frac{\text{Large gear}}{\text{Small gear}} = \frac{18}{8} = \frac{9}{4} = 2\frac{1}{4}$

For one turn of the large gear, the small one turns $\frac{9}{4}$ or $2\frac{1}{4}$ times.

Step 2 Write the proportion. $\frac{\text{1 turn of large gear}}{\text{3 turns of large gear}} = \frac{\frac{9}{4}\text{ turns of small gear}}{x}$

Step 3 Rewrite the proportion algebraically. Then solve for x.

$\frac{1}{3} = \frac{9}{4} \div x \qquad x = (3)(\frac{9}{4}) \qquad x = \frac{27}{4} = 6\frac{3}{4}$

For three turns of the large gear, the small one turns $6\frac{3}{4}$ times.

Solve each problem.

1. Lara can run 8 laps in 20 minutes. At that rate, how many laps can she run in 80 minutes? ______
2. Colin rides his bike 39 miles in 3 hours. If he rides at the same speed, how many miles can he ride in 5 hours? ______
3. If 4 gallons of gas cost $5.44, how much do 11 gallons cost? ______
4. A recipe that makes 2 dozen cookies calls for $4\frac{1}{2}$ cups of flour. How much flour would be needed to make 7 dozen cookies? ______
5. The indoor track at Sylvia's gym is short, and she has to run 14 laps to go one mile. How many laps must Sylvia run to go $2\frac{1}{2}$ miles? ______
6. Juan can swim 16 laps at the pool in 24 minutes. If he keeps swimming at the same rate, about how many laps can he swim in one hour? ______
7. The scale on a map reads 3 inches = 100 miles. If two cities measure $4\frac{1}{2}$ inches apart, how far apart are they in actual miles? ______
8. The scale on a map reads 3 inches = 100 miles. If the actual distance between two cities is 320 miles, what is the distance on the map? ______
9. The scale on a map reads 2 inches = 5 miles. If two towns measure $7\frac{3}{8}$ inches apart, how far apart are they in actual miles? ______
10. The scale on a map reads 4 cm = 30 miles. If the actual distance between two towns is 120 miles, how far apart are they on the map? ______

 Algebra

TRL

Application Activity 4

Name Date Period | Everyday Algebra 4 | Chapter 4

Using Proportions

Exercises involving direct variation are one example of the application of proportions. The lightning and thunder of a thunderstorm provide an example of direct variation. During a thunderstorm, the time it takes you to hear the sound of thunder varies directly with your distance from the lightning that caused the thunder. For example, you will hear the sound of thunder 5 seconds after the flash of lightning for every 1 mile you are from the lightning.

The equation $y = 5x$ can be used to model this direct variation. In the equation, x = your distance in miles from the lightning and y = the number of seconds between seeing the flash of lightning and hearing the sound of thunder.

Suppose that you are 2 miles from a flash of lightning. To find how long the sound of thunder will take to reach you, substitute 2 for x in the formula $y = 5x$ and solve for y.

$y = 5x$

$y = 5(2)$

$y = 10$ The sound of thunder will take 10 seconds to reach you.

In the diagram, the 25 pounds of force applied at one end of the lever will lift a 100-pound weight placed at the opposite end.

25 pounds — 100 pounds

Write an equation that describes the direct variation. Then use your equation to find the answer to each question.

1. How much force would be required to lift a 50-pound weight? ______
2. How much force would be required to lift a 1,000-pound weight? ______
3. What is the maximum amount of weight that could be lifted by applying 1 pound of force? ______
4. What is the maximum amount of weight that could be lifted by applying 500 pounds of force? ______
5. Suppose the pivot point of the lever were moved and the result is that it now takes 15 pounds of force to lift a 40-pound weight. Write an equation that describes the direct variation. ______

 Algebra

TRL

Everyday Algebra 4

Chapter 4 REVIEW

Write the letter of the correct answer.

1. What is 30% of 150? D

A 40 **C** 120

B 90 **D** 45

2. 63 is what percent of 90? A

A 70% **C** 30%

B 63% **D** 143%

3. 135 is 30% of what number? B

A 105 **C** 165

B 450 **D** 45

4. Louis drives for $5\frac{1}{2}$ hours at an average rate of 65 miles per hour. How many miles does he drive? A

A $357\frac{1}{2}$ mi **C** 455 mi

B 325 mi **D** 330 mi

5. Peanuts cost $2.50 per pound and walnuts cost $5.00 per pound. If you mix 4 pounds of peanuts with 4 pounds of walnuts, what is the cost of one pound of the mixture? C

A $7.50 **C** $3.75

B $30.00 **D** $15.00

6. Peanuts cost $2 per pound and cashews cost $4 per pound. A 50-pound mixture cost $164. How many pounds of each kind of nut are in the mixture? B

A 12 pounds of peanuts, 24 pounds of cashews **C** 32 pounds of peanuts, 18 pounds of cashews

B 18 pounds of peanuts, 32 pounds of cashews **D** 38 pounds of peanuts, 12 pounds of cashews

Chapter 4 Review

Each set of problems in the Chapter Review includes an example and solution to illustrate the concept. Use the given examples for reteaching the materials in Chapter 4. For additional practice, refer to the Supplementary Problems for Chapter 4 (pages 412–413).

Chapter 4 Mastery Test 

The Teacher's Resource Library includes parallel forms of the Chapter 4 Mastery Test. The difficulty level of the two forms is equivalent. You may wish to use one form as a pretest and the other form as a posttest.

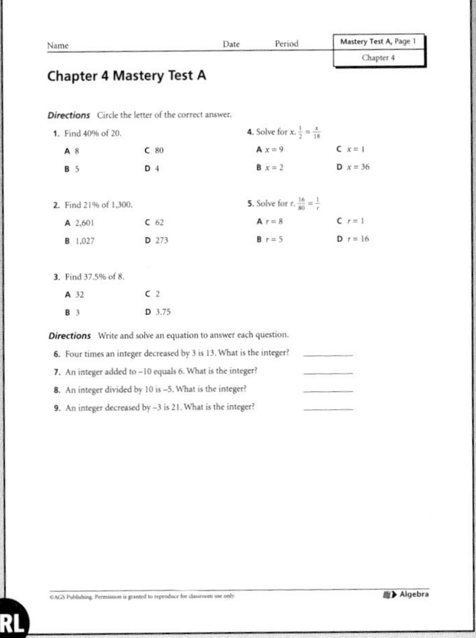

Name Date Period | Mastery Test A, Page 1 | Chapter 4

Chapter 4 Mastery Test A

Directions Circle the letter of the correct answer.

1. Find 40% of 20.

A 8 **C** 80

B 5 **D** 4

2. Find 21% of 1,300.

A 2,601 **C** 62

B 1,027 **D** 273

3. Find 37.5% of 8.

A 32 **C** 2

B 3 **D** 3.75

4. Solve for x. $\frac{1}{2} = \frac{x}{18}$

A $x = 9$ **C** $x = 1$

B $x = 2$ **D** $x = 36$

5. Solve for r. $\frac{16}{80} = \frac{1}{r}$

A $r = 8$ **C** $r = 1$

B $r = 5$ **D** $r = 16$

Directions Write and solve an equation to answer each question.

6. Four times an integer decreased by 3 is 13. What is the integer? ________

7. An integer added to –10 equals 6. What is the integer? ________

8. An integer divided by 10 is –5. What is the integer? ________

9. An integer decreased by –3 is 21. What is the integer? ________

 Algebra

TRL

Name Date Period | Mastery Test A, Page 2 | Chapter 4

Chapter 4 Mastery Test A, continued

Directions Solve.

10. JoAnne earns a monthly salary of $2,800. What percent of JoAnne's monthly income is spent for rent if her rent is $700 each month? ________

11. A bicyclist pedals at an average speed of 18 miles per hour for $2\frac{1}{2}$ hours. In that time, how many miles did the bicyclist travel? (Hint: Use $d = rt$.) ________

12. Of the 24 students enrolled in a mathematics class, 3 students are members of the Math Club. These 3 students represent what percent of all of the students in the class? ________

13. A deposit of $500 is made in a savings account that pays 6% interest compounded annually. If no withdrawals or additional deposits are made, what will be the value of the account after 1 year? (Hint: Use $I = prt$.) ________

14. Elaine scored 16 questions correct on a 20-question mathematics quiz. In simplest form, what is Elaine's ratio of correct answers to incorrect answers? ________

15. In a sophomore class of 350 students, 42 students are not taking a mathematics class of any kind. What percent of the sophomore class is not taking a mathematics class of any kind? ________

16. A coin bank contains twice as many nickels as dimes and five times as many pennies as dimes. The value of the collection is $2.00 or 200¢. How many pennies, nickels, and dimes are in the collection? ________

17. Five pounds of cashews are mixed with five pounds of walnuts. If walnuts cost $8.50 per pound and cashews cost $6.00 per pound, what is the cost of one pound of the mixture? ________

18. On Saturday, Jamaal drove 286 miles in $5\frac{1}{2}$ hours. What was Jamaal's average speed in miles per hour? (Hint: Use $r = \frac{d}{t}$.) ________

19. The ratio of the length to the width of a rectangle is 7 to 2. If the perimeter of the rectangle is 54 inches, what are the measures of the length and width of the rectangle? ________

20. A grocer purchased a 100-pound mixture of nuts for $515. The mixture contains 70 pounds of peanuts that cost $3.50 per pound. The remaining nuts in the mixture are almonds. What is the cost per pound of the almonds in the mixture? ________

 Algebra

TRL

Chapter 4 Mastery Test A

ALTERNATIVE ASSESSMENT

Alternative Assessment items correlate with student Goals for Learning at the beginning of this chapter.

■ **To write an algebraic equation for a number sentence**
Have students list advantages of using algebraic equations over number sentences. *(Reduce possibility of errors, less time, easier to read and interpret, more precise.)*

■ **To identify formulas to use in specific types of problems**
Have students identify the formula they would use to solve the following problems: Write the proportion of 1 pint of oil to 6 gallons of gasoline. *(proportion: students need to remember that there are 8 pints in 1 gallon: 1:48)*

Find the amount of interest on a loan of $1,000 at 5% for 2 years. (simple interest: $I = 0.05 \cdot 1000 \cdot 2$)

How long would it take to drive 240 miles at an average speed of 50 miles per hour? *(distance, rate and time: $t = 240/50$)*

What is the number of square feet in a garden measuring 12 feet × 8 feet? *(area of a rectangle: $A = 12 \cdot 8$)*

How would you double a recipe that yields 36 cookies? *(proportion: 2 times each ingredient, that is, 2 times the amount of flour, sugar, etc.)*

■ **To write problems using algebraic formulas**
Have students work in groups of two or three to choose a formula. The formula can be from their *Algebra* book, science textbook, etc. Then the group should write two real-life problems using that formula. You may want to choose a number of formulas and provide them to the groups so that no groups use the same formula. After groups have completed their problems, they can trade problems with another group and solve that group's problems.

Solve each problem.

Example: The sum of two consecutive numbers is 13. What are the numbers? Solution: $n + (n + 1) = 13$ $2n = 12$ $n = 6, n + 1 = 7$

7. The sum of three consecutive integers is 114. What are the integers? 37, 38, 39

8. The sum of two consecutive odd integers is 36. What are the integers? 17, 19

Solve each problem using the 1% solution method.

Example: Shari has 6 cousins who are boys. If 60 percent of her cousins are boys, how many cousins does Shari have?
Solution: 60% of cousins = 6

$$60\% \div 60 = 6 \div 60$$
$$1\% = \frac{1}{10}$$
$$1\% \bullet 100 = \frac{1}{10} \bullet 100$$
$$100\% = 10 \text{ cousins}$$

9. There are 40 oak trees in the park. If 10% of the trees in the park are oak trees, how many trees are in the park? 400

10. Jason wants to buy a mountain bike that costs $350. He has already saved $105. What percent of the total cost has he saved? 30%

11. A town has a population of 4,800 people. If 25% of the population are senior citizens, how many people are senior citizens? 1,200

Solve each problem.

Example: Marisa rides her bicycle for two hours at an average rate of speed of 15 km/h. How far does she ride? Solution: $d = 15(2)$ $d = 30$

12. $65\frac{5}{8}$ mph
13. 19 nickles, 38 dimes

12. Bette drives at 60 miles per hour for $2\frac{1}{2}$ hours and at 75 miles per hour for $1\frac{1}{2}$ hours. What is her average rate of speed?

13. Kim has $4.75 in nickels and dimes. If she has twice as many dimes as nickels, how many of each coin does she have?

120 Chapter 4 Applications of Algebra

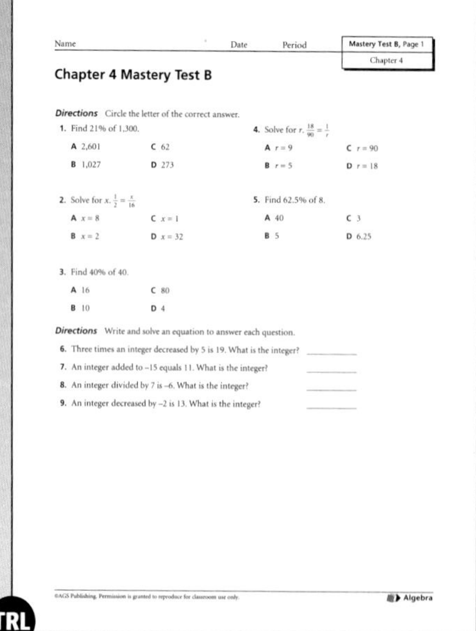

Name Date Period | Mastery Test B, Page 1 | Chapter 4

Chapter 4 Mastery Test B

Directions Circle the letter of the correct answer.

1. Find 21% of 1,300.
 A 2,601 C 62
 B 1,027 D 273

2. Solve for x. $\frac{1}{2} = \frac{x}{16}$
 A $x = 8$ C $x = 1$
 B $x = 2$ D $x = 32$

3. Find 40% of 40.
 A 16 C 80
 B 10 D 4

4. Solve for r. $\frac{18}{90} = \frac{1}{r}$
 A $r = 9$ C $r = 90$
 B $r = 5$ D $r = 18$

5. Find 62.5% of 8.
 A 40 C 3
 B 5 D 6.25

Directions Write and solve an equation to answer each question.

6. Three times an integer decreased by 5 is 19. What is the integer? ______
7. An integer added to –15 equals 11. What is the integer? ______
8. An integer divided by 7 is –6. What is the integer? ______
9. An integer decreased by –2 is 13. What is the integer? ______

 Algebra

TRL

Name Date Period | Mastery Test B, Page 2 | Chapter 4

Chapter 4 Mastery Test B, continued

Directions Solve.

10. JoAnne earns a monthly salary of $3,000. What percent of JoAnne's monthly income is spent for rent if her rent is $600 each month? ______
11. A bicyclist pedals at an average speed of 16 miles per hour for 3 hours. In that time, how many miles did the bicyclist travel? (Hint: Use $d = rt$.) ______
12. Of the 25 students enrolled in a mathematics class, 2 students are members of the Math Club. These 2 students represent what percent of all of the students in the class? ______
13. A deposit of $400 is made in a savings account that pays 8% interest compounded annually. If no withdrawals or additional deposits are made, what will be the value of the account after 1 year? (Hint: Use $I = prt$.) ______
14. Elaine scored 15 questions correct on a 20-question mathematics quiz. In simplest form, what is Elaine's ratio of correct answers to incorrect answers? ______
15. In a sophomore class of 275 students, 44 students are not taking a mathematics class of any kind. What percent of the sophomore class is not taking a mathematics class of any kind? ______
16. A coin bank contains three as many nickels as dimes and five times as many pennies as dimes. The value of the collection is $3.00 or 300¢. How many pennies, nickels, and dimes are in the collection? ______
17. Five pounds of cashews are mixed with five pounds of walnuts. If walnuts cost $8.00 per pound and cashews cost $5.00 per pound, what is the cost of one pound of the mixture? ______
18. On Saturday, Jamaal drove 264 miles in 6 hours. What was Jamaal's average speed in miles per hour? (Hint: Use $r = \frac{d}{t}$.) ______
19. The ratio of the length to the width of a rectangle is 8 to 3. If the perimeter of the rectangle is 66 inches, what are the measures of the length and width of the rectangle? ______
20. A grocer purchased a 100-pound mixture of nuts for $540. The mixture contains 60 pounds of peanuts that cost $4.00 per pound. The remaining nuts in the mixture are almonds. What is the cost per pound of the almonds in the mixture? ______

 Algebra

TRL

Chapter 4 Mastery Test B

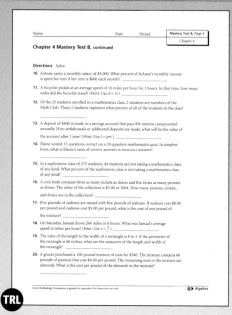

14. $132

15. 8 nickles, 2 dimes, 6 quarters

16. 9%

14. Find the interest earned on a deposit of $800 at 5.5% annual interest rate for 3 years. (Hint: Use the formula $I = prt$.)

15. Chen has $2.10 in nickels, dimes, and quarters. He has three times as many quarters as dimes and four times as many nickels as dimes. How many of each coin does Chen have?

16. Miwa borrows $1,250 for 1 year. At the end of the year, she pays $112.50 in interest. Find the rate of interest she was charged. (Hint: Use the formula $I = prt$.)

Find the missing term in each proportion.

Example: $\frac{1}{2} = \frac{4}{x}$ Solution: $1x = 2(4)$ $x = 8$

17. $\frac{x}{21} = \frac{5}{35}$ $x = 3$

18. $\frac{12}{15} = \frac{x}{20}$ $x = 16$

Solve using a proportion.

Example: If 2 gallons of milk cost $3.50, how much would 3 gallons cost?

Solution: $\frac{3.50}{2} = \frac{x}{3}$ $3.50(3) = 2x$ $10.50 = 2x$ $\$5.25 = x$

$26\frac{2}{3}$ mph

19. A bicyclist completes a 120-mile race in 4 hours 30 minutes. What is the average speed, in miles per hour, of the bicyclist?

20. If 8 feet of fencing costs $12.40, how much does 36 feet of fencing cost? $55.80

Test-Taking Tip

Read a problem thoroughly before you begin to solve it. After you have completed your answer, read the problem again to be sure your answer makes sense.

Alternative Assessment, Continued

■ **To solve problems by applying algebraic equations**

Have students explain why solving problems with algebraic equations makes math easier. Ask if students can list any reasons why using equations might make math more difficult. *(Algebraic equations provide an organized way to solve for unknown quantities.)*

Chapter

Planning Guide

Exponents and Polynomials

		Student Text Lesson: Student Pages	Vocabulary	Practice Exercises	Solutions Key
Lesson 1	**Exponents**	124–125		✔	✔
Lesson 2	**Negative Exponents**	126–128	✔	✔	✔
Lesson 3	**Exponents and Scientific Notation**	129–130	✔	✔	✔
Lesson 4	**Computing in Scientific Notation**	131–133		✔	✔
Lesson 5	**Defining and Naming Polynomials**	134–135	✔	✔	✔
Lesson 6	**Adding and Subtracting Polynomials**	136–137		✔	✔
Lesson 7	**Multiplying Polynomials**	138–139		✔	✔
Lesson 8	**Special Polynomial Products**	140–141		✔	✔
Lesson 9	**Dividing a Polynomial by a Monomial**	142–143		✔	✔
Lesson 10	**Dividing a Polynomial by a Binomial**	144–147		✔	✔
Lesson 11	**Polynomials in Two or More Variables**	148–149		✔	✔
Application	**Polynomial Interest**	150		✔	✔

Chapter Activities

Teacher's Resource Library

Estimation Exercise 5: Estimating Quotients of Polynomials Divided by Monomials
Application Activity 5: Polynomial Interest
Everyday Algebra 5: Using Scientific Notation
Community Connection 5: Careers and Scientific Notation

Teacher's Edition

Chapter 5 Project

Assessment Options

Student Text

Chapter 5 Review

Teacher's Resource Library

Chapter 5 Mastery Tests A and B

Student Text Features							Teaching Strategies							Learning Styles						Teacher's Resource Library			
Estimation Activity	Algebra in Your Life	Technology Connection	Writing About Mathematics	Try This	Problem Solving	Calculator Practice	Online Connection	Common Error	Applications Home, Career, Community	Mental Math	Manipulatives	Calculator	Group Problem Solving	Auditory/Verbal	Visual/Spatial	Logical/Mathematical	Body/Kinesthetic	Interpersonal/Group Learning	LEP/ESL	Activities	Alternate Activities	Workbook Activities	Self-Study Guide
			125					124			125	125						125		43	43	46	✔
	128		127					127		127								127		44	44	47	✔
			130			130						130	130		130					45	45	48	✔
		133								132							132			46	46	49	✔
													135						135	47	47	50	✔
					137			136				137	137	137						48	48	51	✔
				139	139					139	139		139					139		49	49	52	✔
				141	141			141			141		141							50	50	53–54	✔
								142				143		143						51	51	55	✔
147								144	146, 147		145		147			146		147	145	52	52	56	✔
							149	149				149						149		53	53	57	✔
								150	151						151								✔

Software Options

Skill Track Software

Use the Skill Track Software for *Algebra* for additional reinforcement of this chapter. The software provides multiple-choice assessment items for students to access by computer.

Solutions Key

Use the Solutions Key with this chapter to help students who may need additional assistance. The Solutions Key CD provides solutions for every exercise in the student edition.

Other Resources

Alternative Activities

The Teacher's Resource Library (TRL) contains a set of worksheets written at a second-grade reading level called Alternative Activities. They cover the same content as the regular Activities.

Manipulatives

See the Manipulative activities in this chapter for hands-on modeling of the content. The following TRL pages can also be used:

Manipulatives Master 4 (Factor Frame)
Algebra Tiles
Pattern Blocks

Chapter at a Glance

Chapter 5: Exponents and Polynomials
pages 122–153

Lessons

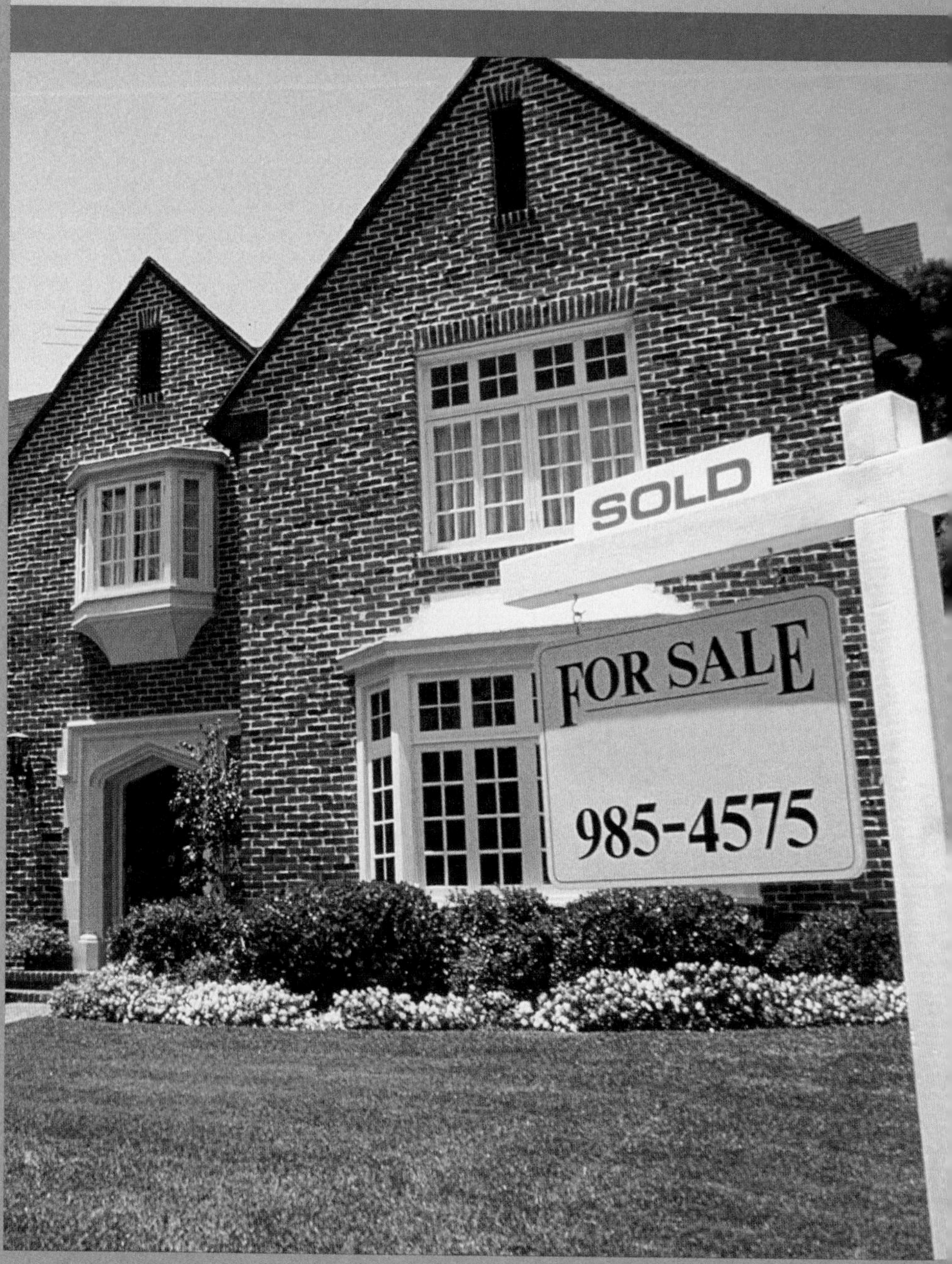

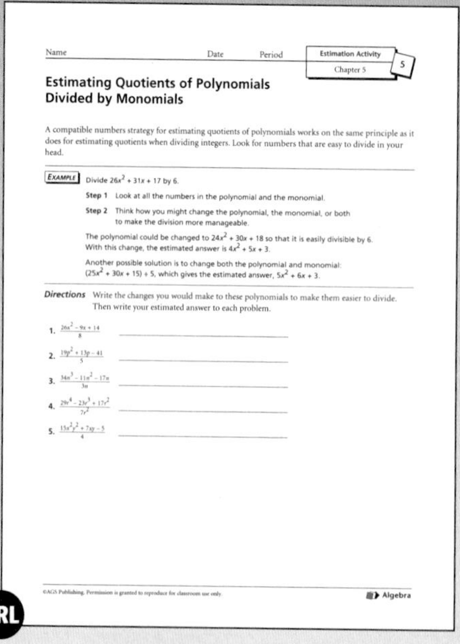

Name Date Period | Estimation Activity 5 | Chapter 5

Estimating Quotients of Polynomials Divided by Monomials

A compatible numbers strategy for estimating quotients of polynomials works on the same principle as it does for estimating quotients when dividing integers. Look for numbers that are easy to divide in your head.

EXAMPLE Divide $26x^2 + 31x + 17$ by 6.

Step 1 Look at all the numbers in the polynomial and the monomial.

Step 2 Think how you might change the polynomial, the monomial, or both to make the division more manageable.

The polynomial could be changed to $24x^2 + 30x + 18$ so that it is easily divisible by 6. With this change, the estimated answer is $4x^2 + 5x + 3$.

Another possible solution is to change both the polynomial and monomial: $(25x^2 + 30x + 15) \div 5$, which gives the estimated answer, $5x^2 + 6x + 3$.

Directions Write the changes you would make to these polynomials to make them easier to divide. Then write your estimated answer to each problem.

1. $\frac{26x^2 - 9x + 14}{8}$ ________
2. $\frac{19p^2 + 13p - 41}{5}$ ________
3. $\frac{34n^3 - 11n^2 - 17n}{3n}$ ________
4. $\frac{29r^4 - 23r^3 + 17r^2}{7r^2}$ ________
5. $\frac{15x^2y^2 + 7xy - 5}{4}$ ________

 Algebra

TRL

Estimation Exercise 5

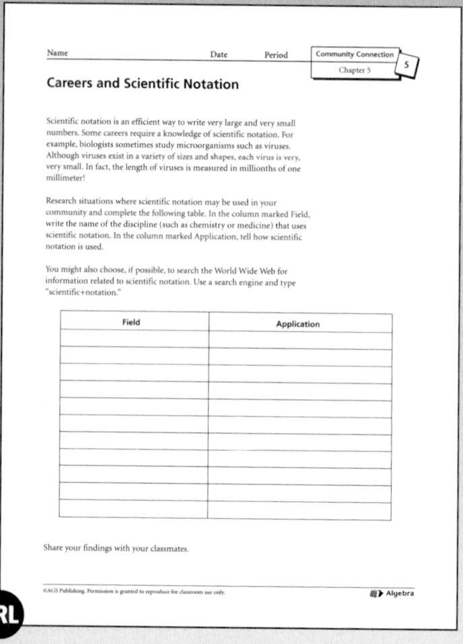

Name Date Period | Community Connection 5 | Chapter 5

Careers and Scientific Notation

Scientific notation is an efficient way to write very large and very small numbers. Some careers require a knowledge of scientific notation. For example, biologists sometimes study microorganisms such as viruses. Although viruses exist in a variety of sizes and shapes, each virus is very, very small. In fact, the length of viruses is measured in millionths of one millimeter!

Research situations where scientific notation may be used in your community and complete the following table. In the column marked Field, write the name of the discipline (such as chemistry or medicine) that uses scientific notation. In the column marked Application, tell how scientific notation is used.

You might also choose, if possible, to search the World Wide Web for information related to scientific notation. Use a search engine and type "scientific+notation."

Field	Application

Share your findings with your classmates.

 Algebra

TRL

Community Connection 5

Chapter

Exponents and Polynomials

Most people don't have thousands of dollars to buy expensive things like houses or cars. To buy a house, you go to a bank and apply for a loan called a mortgage. You need to borrow enough money to pay for the cost of the house. That is called the "principal." Along with the principal, you pay the bank extra money, or interest. Bankers use an algebraic formula to divide the total mortgage into monthly payments. Each month, the interest you owe decreases and the principal you're paying off increases. This kind of calculation is a polynomial. Polynomials involve doing several arithmetic functions using exponents.

In Chapter 5, you will examine exponents and polynomials.

Goals for Learning

- ◆ To recognize and use exponents in computations
- ◆ To identify the benefit of using scientific notation in some calculations
- ◆ To define, name, and solve polynomials

123

Introducing the Chapter

Use the information in the chapter opener to help students understand that many people in a wide variety of occupations use algebra regularly. Exponents and polynomials, for example, are essential in science, business, medicine, education, law, and so on. They provide a simpler way to use formulas, such as computing monthly payments on a loan.

Chapter Project

Have students create a poster of formulas with exponents or polynomials. Suggest that they choose one of the following areas of study:

Biology	Geometry
Business	Industrial Arts
Chemistry	Law
Earth Science	Physics

Students should choose at least four formulas from one area, write each formula's use, give an example for each formula, and illustrate the example.

Teacher's Resource

The AGS Publishing Teaching Strategies in Math Transparencies may be used with this chapter. They add an interactive dimension to expand and enhance the program content.

Career Interest Inventory

The AGS Publishing Harrington-O'Shea Career Decision-Making System-Revised (CDM) may be used with this chapter. Students can use the CDM to explore their interests and identify careers. The CDM defines career areas that are indicated by students' responses on the inventory.

Name ______ Date ______ Period ______ *SELF-STUDY GUIDE*

CHAPTER 5: Exponents and Polynomials

Goal 5.1 *To recognize and use exponents in computations*

Date	Assignment	Score
______	1: Read pages 124–125. Complete Exercises A–C on page 125.	______
______	2: Complete Workbook Activity 46.	______
______	3: Read pages 126–127. Complete Exercises A–C on pages 127–128.	______
______	4: Complete Workbook 47.	______

Comments:

Goal 5.2 *To identify the benefit of using scientific notation in some calculations*

Date	Assignment	Score
______	5: Read page 129. Complete Exercises A–B on page 130.	______
______	6: Read and complete the Calculator Practice on page 130.	______
______	7: Complete Workbook Activity 48.	______
______	8: Read pages 131–132. Complete Exercises A–C on pages 132–133.	______
______	9: Complete Workbook Activity 49.	______

Comments:

 Algebra

TRL

Name ______ Date ______ Period ______ *SELF-STUDY GUIDE*

CHAPTER 5: Exponents and Polynomials, continued

Goal 5.3 *To define, name, and solve polynomials*

Date	Assignment	Score
______	10: Read pages 134–135. Complete Exercises A–D on page 135.	______
______	11: Complete Workbook Activity 50.	______
______	12: Read page 136. Complete Exercises A–C on page 137.	______
______	13: Complete Workbook Activity 51.	______
______	14: Read pages 138–139. Complete Exercises A–B on page 139.	______
______	15: Complete Workbook Activity 52.	______
______	16: Read page 140. Complete Exercises A–B on page 141.	______
______	17: Complete Workbook Activities 53–54.	______
______	18: Read pages 142–143. Complete Exercises A–C on page 143.	______
______	19: Complete Workbook Activity 55.	______
______	20: Read pages 144–146. Complete Exercises A–D on pages 146–147.	______
______	21: Complete Workbook Activity 56.	______
______	22: Read page 148. Complete Exercises A–C on page 149.	______
______	23: Complete Workbook Activity 57.	______
______	24: Read and complete the Application Exercise on page 150.	______
______	25: Complete the Chapter 5 Review on pages 151–153.	______

Comments:

Student's Signature ______ Date ______

Instructor's Signature ______ Date ______

 Algebra

TRL

Chapter 5 Self-Study Guide

Lesson at a Glance

Chapter 5 Lesson 1

Overview This lesson introduces exponent rules.

Objective

- To multiply and divide with exponents

Student Pages 124–125

Teacher's Resource Library 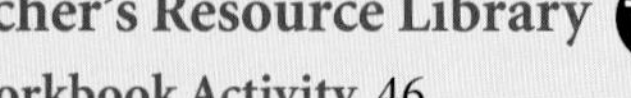

Workbook Activity 46

Activity 43

Alternative Activity 43

Warm-Up Activity

Have students write expanded notation. For example, $x^3 = x \cdot x \cdot x$. Ask, "What does $(x^3)^2$ mean and how can it be simplified?" Allow students time to realize that this means x^3 squared or x^3 multiplied by itself. Use student responses to introduce the general rules for multiplying and dividing exponents.

Teaching the Lesson

Go over the examples on pages 124 and 125 on the board as students follow along.

Common Error

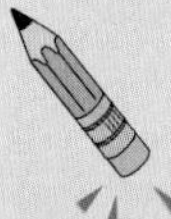

Some students will confuse the rule $(x^n)(x^m) = x^{n+m}$ with $(x^n)^m = x^{n \cdot m}$. Go over several examples in which the wrong rule has been applied and ask students why the simplification is incorrect. For example, have them explain why $(x^5)(x^2) \neq x^{10}$ or $(x^3)^7 \neq x^{10}$.

Lesson 1 Exponents

In Chapter 1, you learned how to multiply $(x^3)(x^4)$:

$$(x^3)(x^4) = (x \cdot x \cdot x)\ (x \cdot x \cdot x \cdot x) = x^7.$$

In other words, $(x^3)(x^4) = x^{3+4} = x^7$.

> **Rule** The general rule is $(x^n)(x^m) = x^{n+m}$. To multiply terms with exponents, add the exponents.

You can use what you know about exponents to find the value of $(x^2)^4$:

$$(x^2)^4 \text{ can be written as } \overbrace{(x^2)(x^2)(x^2)(x^2)}^{4 \text{ times}} = x^8.$$

In other words, $(x^2)^4 = x^{2 \cdot 4} = x^8$.

> **Rule** The general rule is $(x^n)^m = x^{n \cdot m}$.
> To raise a power to a power, multiply the exponents.

Suppose you need to simplify $x^7 \div x^3$.
You can rewrite the problem as

$$\frac{x^7}{x^3} = \frac{\cancel{x} \cdot \cancel{x} \cdot \cancel{x} \cdot x \cdot x \cdot x \cdot x}{\cancel{x} \cdot \cancel{x} \cdot \cancel{x}} = \frac{x \cdot x \cdot x \cdot x}{1} = x^4.$$

In other words, $\frac{x^7}{x^3} = x^{7-3} = x^4$.

> **Rule** The general rule is $x^n \div x^m = x^{n-m}$.
> To divide terms with exponents, subtract the exponents.
>
> **Important note** This is only true when $x \neq 0$. $\frac{0}{0}$ is undefined.

Example 1 $x^5 \div x^2 = \frac{x^5}{x^2} = \frac{\cancel{x} \cdot \cancel{x} \cdot x \cdot x \cdot x}{\cancel{x} \cdot \cancel{x}} = \frac{x \cdot x \cdot x}{1} = x^3,\ x \neq 0$

Example 2 $\frac{m^7}{m^2} = m^{7-2} = m^5,\ m \neq 0$

Example 3 $(y^3)^2 = (y^3)(y^3) = y^{2 \cdot 3} = y^6$

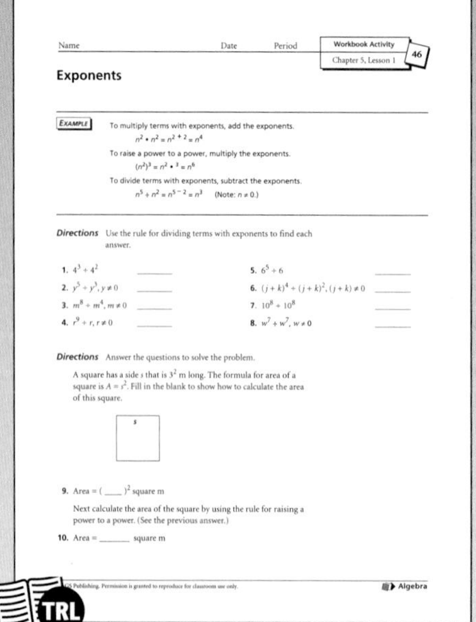

Name Date Period | Workbook Activity 46 | Chapter 5, Lesson 1

Exponents

Example To multiply terms with exponents, add the exponents.
$n^2 \cdot n^2 = n^{2+2} = n^4$
To raise a power to a power, multiply the exponents.
$(n^2)^3 = n^{2 \cdot 3} = n^6$
To divide terms with exponents, subtract the exponents.
$n^5 \div n^2 = n^{5-2} = n^3$ (Note: $n \neq 0$.)

Directions Use the rule for dividing terms with exponents to find each answer.

1. $4^3 \div 4^2$ ______
2. $y^5 \div y^3, y \neq 0$ ______
3. $m^8 \div m^4, m \neq 0$ ______
4. $r^9 \div r, r \neq 0$ ______
5. $6^5 \div 6$ ______
6. $(j+k)^4 \div (j+k)^2, (j+k) \neq 0$ ______
7. $10^8 \div 10^8$ ______
8. $w^7 \div w^7, w \neq 0$ ______

Directions Answer the questions to solve the problem.

A square has a side s that is 3^2 m long. The formula for area of a square is $A = s^2$. Fill in the blank to show how to calculate the area of this square.

9. Area = (____)^2 square m

Next calculate the area of the square by using the rule for raising a power to a power. (See the previous answer.)

10. Area = ______ square m

 Algebra

Workbook Activity 46

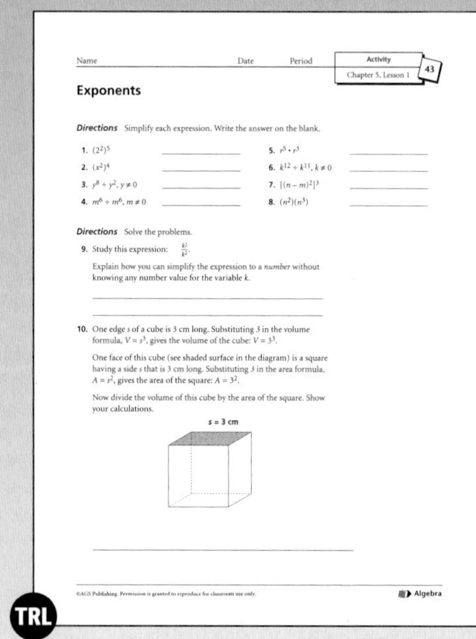

Name Date Period | Activity 43 | Chapter 5, Lesson 1

Exponents

Directions Simplify each expression. Write the answer on the blank.

1. $(2^2)^5$ ______
2. $(x^2)^4$ ______
3. $y^8 \div y^2, y \neq 0$ ______
4. $m^6 \div m^6, m \neq 0$ ______
5. $r^5 \cdot r^3$ ______
6. $k^{12} \div k^{11}, k \neq 0$ ______
7. $[(n-m)^2]^3$ ______
8. $(n^2)(n^3)$ ______

Directions Solve the problems.

9. Study this expression: $\frac{k^2}{k^2}$.
Explain how you can simplify the expression to a *number* without knowing any number value for the variable k.

10. One edge s of a cube is 3 cm long. Substituting 3 in the volume formula, $V = s^3$, gives the volume of the cube: $V = 3^3$.
One face of this cube (see shaded surface in the diagram) is a square having a side s that is 3 cm long. Substituting 3 in the area formula, $A = s^2$, gives the area of the square: $A = 3^2$.
Now divide the volume of this cube by the area of the square. Show your calculations.

 Algebra

Activity 43

Writing About Mathematics

Any number (except zero) raised to the power of zero is 1. For example, $3^0 = 1$. Tell why.

Raising a number to the zero power is a special case.

Example 4 $\frac{32}{32} = \frac{2^5}{2^5} = 2^{5-5} = 2^0 = 1$

or $\frac{2^5}{2^5} = \frac{2 \cdot 2 \cdot 2 \cdot 2 \cdot 2}{2 \cdot 2 \cdot 2 \cdot 2 \cdot 2} = 1$

What is the value of x^0, when $x \neq 0$?

You already know that $1 = \frac{x^2}{x^2}$

and that $\frac{x^2}{x^2} = x^{2-2} = x^0$.

You can put these two statements together:

$1 = \frac{x^2}{x^2} = x^{2-2} = x^0$, so $1 = x^0$.

Rule	$x^0 = 1$ when $x \neq 0$.

You can use what you know about multiplying and dividing exponents to find solutions to problems.

$(2^2)^2 = 2^{2 \cdot 2} = 2^4 = 2 \cdot 2 \cdot 2 \cdot 2 = 16$

Exercise A Show why these statements are true.

1. $(3^2)^3 = 729$ $3^6 = 729$
2. $(2^2)^5 = 1{,}024$ $2^{10} = 1{,}024$
3. $(x^3)^4 = x^{12}$ $x^{3 \cdot 4} = x^{12}$
4. $(y^5)^3 = y^{15}$ $y^{5 \cdot 3} = y^{15}$
5. $(m^4)^4 = m^{16}$ $m^{4 \cdot 4} = m^{16}$
6. $[(x + y)^2]^3 = (x + y)^6$ $(x + y)^{2 \cdot 3} = (x + y)^6$
7. $[(2x + 3y)^4]^2 = (2x + 3y)^8$ $(2x + 3y)^{4 \cdot 2} = (2x + 3y)^8$

Exercise B Simplify each expression.

8. $(3^5) \div (3^3)$ 9
9. $\frac{4^4}{4^3}$ 4
10. $\frac{x^5}{x^4}, x \neq 0$ x
11. $y^5 \div y^3, y \neq 0$ y^2
12. $\frac{m^7}{m^3}, m \neq 0$ m^4
13. $(x + y)^5 \div (x + y)^2, (x + y) \neq 0$ $(x + y)^3$
14. $\frac{(2p + 3q)^6}{(2p + 3q)^2}, (2p + 3q) \neq 0$ $(2p + 3q)^4$

Exercise C Show two ways to simplify each expression.

15. $(3^5) \div (3^5)$ $3^{5-5} = 1$ $243 \div 243 = 1$
16. $\frac{2^{10}}{2^{10}}$ $2^{10-10} = 1$ $1{,}024 \div 1{,}024 = 1$
17. $\frac{x^7}{x^7}, x \neq 0$ $x^{7-7} = 1$ $\frac{1}{1} = 1$
18. $(4x + 2y)5 \div (4x + 2y)^5, (4x + 2y) \neq 0$ $(4x + 2y)^{5-5} = 1$ $\frac{1}{1} = 1$
19. $\frac{(p + q)^3}{(p + q)^3}, (p + q) \neq 0$ $(p + q)^{3-3} = 1$ $\frac{1}{1} = 1$
20. $\frac{p^4}{p^4}, p \neq 0$ $p^{4-4} = 1$ $\frac{1}{1} = 1$

Manipulatives

Simplifying Variables with Exponents

Materials: Pattern Blocks

Group Practice: Make 4 models of x^2 to model the example in the text, $(x^2)^4$. Since powers of a number can be modeled by stacking, stack the 4 models of x^2. Count the blocks to simplify.

Student Practice: Have students use the blocks to complete Exercises A and B. Remind them that a block can represent a variable, number, or quantity, such as $(x + y)$, as in Exercise A, Problem 6. Students should write on their paper what the block represents in each problem. Have them sketch each model and write its symbolic equivalent.

3 Reinforce and Extend

Learning Styles

Interpersonal/ Group Learning

Have each student write four examples of the exponent rules for multiplying and dividing. Three examples must be correct, but the fourth is incorrect. Then have students check other students' problems to see if they can find the error. Ask students to tally the number of problems they correctly answered. Collect the problems and review them with the class.

Calculator

Have students find the value of *n*.

$(x^{15})^9 = x^n$ (135)

$(x^{18})^{22} = x^n$ (396)

$(x^{23})^{13} = x^n$ (299)

$(x^{46})^{11} = x^n$ (506)

$(x^{73})^{29} = x^n$ (2117)

$(x^{34})^{61} = x^n$ (2074)

$(x^{34})^{34} = x^n$ (1156)

$(x^{81})^{27} = x^n$ (2187)

$(x^{55})^{63} = x^n$ (3465)

$(x^{99})^{24} = x^n$ (2376)

Lesson at a Glance

Chapter 5 Lesson 2

Overview This lesson introduces negative exponents.

Objective

- To rewrite expressions as positive and negative exponents

Student Pages 126–128

Teacher's Resource Library

Workbook Activity 47

Activity 44

Alternative Activity 44

Mathematics Vocabulary

negative exponent

Warm-Up Activity

Review the general rule $x^n \div x^m = x^{n-m}$. Apply the rule using whole numbers that have the same base and the numerator is less than the denominator. For example, $\frac{2^2}{2^5} = 2^{-3}$. Have students use their scientific calculators to find the value of 2^{-3}. Now compare this value to $\frac{1}{2^3}$. Students will find it is the same value for both expressions. *(0.125)* Use this example to explain negative and positive exponents.

Teaching the Lesson

Have students study the two columns of problems on page 126 and explain the pattern. Go over the examples on pages 126 and 127.

Lesson 2 Negative Exponents

Negative exponent

For any nonzero integers a and n, $a^{-n} = \frac{1}{a^n}$

The number patterns below show how to use **negative exponents** to show numbers less than 1.

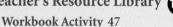

$10^3 = 1{,}000$		$2^3 = 8$	
	$\div$ 10 gives		$\div$ 2 gives
$10^2 = 100$		$2^2 = 4$	
	$\div$ 10 gives		$\div$ 2 gives
$10^1 = 10$		$2^1 = 2$	
	$\div$ 10 gives		$\div$ 2 gives
$10^0 = 1$		$2^0 = 1$	
	$\div$ 10 gives		$\div$ 2 gives
$10^{-1} = \frac{1}{10} = \frac{1}{10^1}$		$2^{-1} = \frac{1}{2} = \frac{1}{2^1}$	
	$\div$ 10 gives		$\div$ 2 gives
$10^{-2} = \frac{1}{100} = \frac{1}{10^2}$		$2^{-2} = \frac{1}{4} = \frac{1}{2^2}$	
	$\div$ 10 gives		$\div$ 2 gives
$10^{-3} = \frac{1}{1{,}000} = \frac{1}{10^3}$		$2^{-3} = \frac{1}{8} = \frac{1}{2^3}$	
and so on		and so on	

Rewrite $\frac{1}{10^4}$ with a negative exponent: $\frac{1}{10^4} = 10^{-4}$

Rewrite $\frac{1}{(x+y)^5}$ with a negative exponent, $(x + y) \neq 0$:

$$\frac{1}{(x+y)^5} = (x+y)^{-5}$$

You can also use the rule for exponents in division to find negative exponents. Remember $3^0 = 1$.

$$\frac{1}{3^2} = \frac{3^0}{3^2} = 3^{0-2} = 3^{-2}$$

$$\frac{1}{x^3} = \frac{x^0}{x^3} = x^{0-3} = x^{-3}$$

Name Date Period **Workbook Activity 47** Chapter 5, Lesson 2

Negative Exponents

EXAMPLE Rewrite $\frac{1}{10^2}$ with a negative exponent: 10^{-2}.
Rewrite $\frac{1}{x^3}$ with a negative exponent, $x \neq 0$: x^{-3}.
Rewrite 2^{-5} with a positive exponent: $\frac{1}{2^5}$.
Rewrite n^{-2} with a positive exponent, $n \neq 0$: $\frac{1}{n^2}$.

Directions Rewrite using a negative exponent.

1. $\frac{1}{8^2}$ ______
2. $\frac{1}{2}$ ______
3. 3^2 [illegible] ______
4. $\frac{1}{10^3}$ ______
5. 10^3 [illegible] ______
6. $\frac{1}{c^2}, c \neq 0$ ______
7. $8^2 \div 8^5$ ______
8. $\frac{1}{y^7}, y \neq 0$ ______
9. $\frac{1}{18^3}$ ______
10. $\frac{1}{(3j-2k)^4}$ ______

Directions Rewrite using a positive exponent.

11. 5^{-3} ______
12. 10^{-3} ______
13. x^{-5} ______
14. 8^{-5} ______
15. y^{-7} ______
16. 10^{-7} ______
17. $(2d + 3k)^{-3}$ ______
18. n^{-4} ______
19. 7^{-2} ______
20. $(m - 3n)^{-2}$ ______

Directions Simplify each power of 2.

21. $2^2 =$ ______
22. $2^1 =$ ______
23. $2^0 =$ ______
24. $2^{-1} =$ ______
25. $2^{-2} =$ ______

 Algebra

Workbook Activity 47

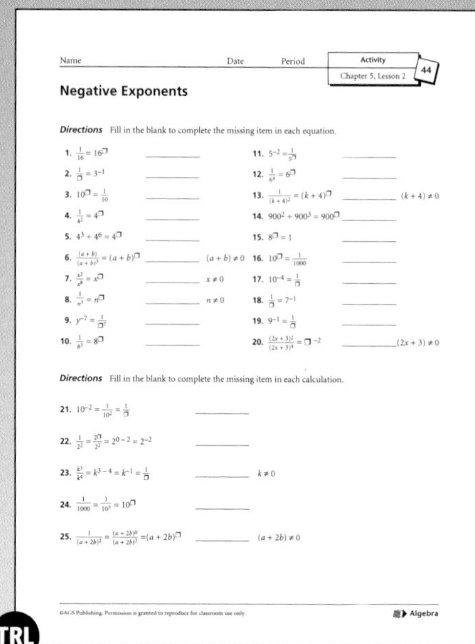

Name Date Period **Activity 44** Chapter 5, Lesson 2

Negative Exponents

Directions Fill in the blank to complete the missing item in each equation.

1. $\frac{1}{16} = 16^{\square}$ ______
2. $\frac{1}{\square} = 3^{-1}$ ______
3. $10^{\square} = \frac{1}{10}$ ______
4. $\frac{1}{4^2} = 4^{\square}$ ______
5. $4^3 \div 4^6 = 4^{\square}$ ______
6. $\frac{(a+b)}{(a+b)^3} = (a+b)^{\square}$ ______ $(a + b) \neq 0$
7. $\frac{x^2}{x^8} = x^{\square}$ ______ $x \neq 0$
8. $\frac{1}{n^3} = n^{\square}$ ______ $n \neq 0$
9. $y^{-7} = \frac{1}{\square^7}$ ______
10. $\frac{1}{8^3} = 8^{\square}$ ______
11. $5^{-2} = \frac{1}{5^{\square}}$ ______
12. $\frac{1}{6^4} = 6^{\square}$ ______
13. $\frac{1}{(k+4)^2} = (k+4)^{\square}$ ______ $(k + 4) \neq 0$
14. $900^2 \div 900^3 = 900^{\square}$ ______
15. $8^{\square} = 1$ ______
16. $10^{\square} = \frac{1}{1000}$ ______
17. $10^{-4} = \frac{1}{\square}$ ______
18. $\frac{1}{\square} = 7^{-1}$ ______
19. $9^{-1} = \frac{1}{\square}$ ______
20. $\frac{(2x+3)^2}{(2x+3)^4} = \square^{-2}$ ______ $(2x + 3) \neq 0$

Directions Fill in the blank to complete the missing item in each calculation.

21. $10^{-2} = \frac{1}{10^2} = \frac{1}{\square}$ ______
22. $\frac{1}{2^2} = \frac{2^{\square}}{2^2} = 2^{0-2} = 2^{-2}$ ______
23. $\frac{k^3}{k^4} = k^{3-4} = k^{-1} = \frac{1}{\square}$ ______ $k \neq 0$
24. $\frac{1}{1000} = \frac{1}{10^3} = 10^{\square}$ ______
25. $\frac{1}{(a+2b)^2} = \frac{(a+2b)^0}{(a+2b)^2} = (a+2b)^{\square}$ ______ $(a + 2b) \neq 0$

 Algebra

Activity 44

Writing About Mathematics

Explain why $\frac{1}{3^2}$ can be rewritten as 3^{-2}.

EXAMPLE 1 $\frac{x^5}{x^7} = \frac{\cancel{x} \cdot \cancel{x} \cdot \cancel{x} \cdot \cancel{x} \cdot \cancel{x}}{\cancel{x} \cdot \cancel{x} \cdot \cancel{x} \cdot \cancel{x} \cdot \cancel{x} \cdot x \cdot x} = \frac{1}{x^2} = x^{-2}$

or $\frac{x^5}{x^7} = x^{5-7} = x^{-2}$

EXAMPLE 2 $\frac{(2x+3y)^8}{(2x+3y)^{11}} = (2x+3y)^{8-11} = (2x+3y)^{-3}$

EXAMPLE 3 Write $(2x+3y)^{-3}$ with a positive exponent:

$$(2x+3y)^{-3} = (2x+3y)^{-3} \bullet 1 = (2x+3y)^{-3} \bullet \frac{(2x+3y)^3}{(2x+3y)^3}$$

$$= \frac{(2x+3y)^{-3} \bullet (2x+3y)^3}{(2x+3y)^3} = \frac{(2x+3y)^{-3+3}}{(2x+3y)^3}$$

$$= \frac{(2x+3y)^0}{(2x+3y)^3} = \frac{1}{(2x+3y)^3}$$

Exercise A Rewrite using a negative exponent.

1. $\frac{4^5}{4^9}$ 4^{-4}
2. $\frac{1}{5^3}$ 5^{-3}
3. $\frac{1}{10^5}$ 10^{-5}
4. $2^5 \div 2^{10}$ 2^{-5}
5. $10^{10} \div 10^{20}$ 10^{-10}
6. $\frac{1}{10^{23}}$ 10^{-23}
7. $\frac{1}{15^2}$ 15^{-2}
8. $14^3 \div 14^5$ 14^{-2}
9. $\frac{203^3}{203^7}$ 203^{-4}
10. $5{,}280^2 \div 5{,}280^3$ $5{,}280^{-1}$

COMMON ERROR

Emphasize that the rule clearly states $a^{-n} = \frac{1}{a^n}$. Students may write $a^{-n} = \frac{1}{a^{-n}}$. Try to prevent this by asking students to explain why the following problems are incorrect:

$6^{-3} = \frac{1}{6^{-3}}$

$x^4 = \frac{1}{x^4}$

$\frac{1}{5^{-4}} = 5^{-4}$

$\frac{1}{8^{-n}} = 8^{-n}$

$4^{-9} = \frac{1}{9^{-4}}$

(All of these problems have incorrect exponents.)

3 Reinforce and Extend

LEARNING STYLES

Interpersonal/ Group Learning

Have students individually complete problems 1–25. Then have groups of students check for errors. When an error is found, have students discuss the correct process and make appropriate changes to their papers.

MENTAL MATH

Ask students to mentally find the value of *x*.

$\frac{4^5}{4^x} = 4^{-5}$ $(x = 10)$

$(z+1)^x \div (z+1)^8 = (z+1)^{-2}$ $(x = 6)$

$\frac{j^x}{j^2} = j^{-1}$ $(x = 1)$

$\frac{v^{10}}{v^2} = v^x$ $(x = 8)$

$(y^2)^x = y^{10}$ $(x = 5)$

Math History

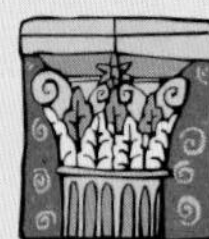

François Viète (1540-1603) was an influential French mathematician, although he claimed mathematics was more of a hobby than a vocation. He practiced law and held various political appointments before turning his mind toward mathematics. Viète made many important contributions to the field of algebraic notation. In 1591 his book *In Artem Analyticam Isagoge* was published in which Viète introduced the first systematic algebraic notation. Among his contributions to the field of algebra are the introduction of letters for variables, a new method of notation for exponents, a substitution method for solving polynomials (named for him), and the introduction of the term "coefficient."

Exercise B Rewrite using a negative exponent.

11. $\frac{x^5}{x^7}, x \neq 0$ — x^{-2}

12. $\frac{1}{m^3}, m \neq 0$ — m^{-3}

13. $\frac{1}{(x + 2y)^4}, (x + 2y) \neq 0$ — $(x + 2y)^{-4}$

14. $(x + 3y)^3 \div (x + 3y)^5$, $(x + 3y) \neq 0$ — $(x + 3y)^{-2}$

15. $\frac{(x + y)^3}{(x + y)^6}, (x + y) \neq 0$ — $(x + y)^{-3}$

16. $(2x + 3y)^2 \div (2x + 3y)^8$, $(2x + 3y) \neq 0$ — $(2x + 3y)^{-6}$

17. $(-3m - 9)^3 \div (-3m - 9)^6$, $(-3m - 9) \neq 0$ — $(-3m - 9)^{-3}$

18. $\frac{x^3}{x^7}, x \neq 0$ — x^{-4}

Exercise C Rewrite using a positive exponent.

19. 3^{-2} — $\frac{1}{3^2}$

20. 10^{-2} — $\frac{1}{10^2}$

21. 10^{-23} — $\frac{1}{10^{23}}$

22. x^{-4} — $\frac{1}{x^4}$

23. $2y^{-6}$ — $\frac{2}{y^6}$

24. $(4p + 3q)^{-3}$ — $\frac{1}{(4p + 3q)^3}$

25. 4^{-2} — $\frac{1}{4^2}$

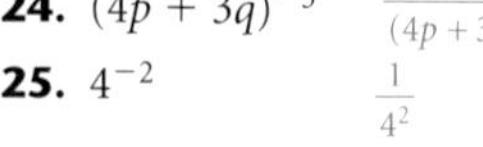

Algebra in Your Life

On Opposite Ends of the Ruler

Particle physicists are scientists who study things smaller than atoms—particles measuring as small as 10^{-16} meters! They have found quarks and leptons, and they suspect even smaller particles exist. Astrophysicists study things in the largest scale you can imagine—the universe. They have found that less than 10 percent of the mass of the universe consists of the kind of matter we can see. The last century revealed much about our universe. Just imagine what this one will bring!

Lesson 3 Exponents and Scientific Notation

> ***Scientific notation***
> *A number written as the product of a number between 1 and 10 and a power of ten.*
> *Any number in scientific notation* $= (1 \le x < 10)(10^n)$

Scientists and researchers often need to record and work with very large or very small numbers. To make writing these numbers easier, they have developed a way of writing these numbers called **scientific notation.**

EXAMPLE 1 Write 394.74 in scientific notation.

$394.74 = 3.9474(10^2)$

Step 1 Move the decimal point so the number is between 1 and 10.

394.74

Step 2 Write the new number and then count the number of places the decimal point moved. In this example, the decimal point moved 2 places to the *left*.

3.9474

Step 3 Multiply the number from Step 2 times 10 raised to the number of places the decimal point moved.

$3.9474(10^2)$

> Use a positive exponent if the decimal point moved to the left.
>
> Use a negative exponent if the decimal point moved to the right.

EXAMPLE 2 Write 0.0003947 in scientific notation.

Step 1 Move the decimal point so the number is between 1 and 10.

0.0003947

Step 2 Write the new number, and then count the number of places the decimal point moved. In this example, the decimal point moved 4 places to the *right*.

3.947

Step 3 Multiply the number from Step 2 times 10 raised to the number of places the decimal point moved.

$3.947 \cdot 10^{-4}$

Name Date Period **Workbook Activity 48** Chapter 5, Lesson 3

Exponents and Scientific Notation

EXAMPLE Write 500.37 and 0.0041 in scientific notation.

Step 1	500.37	0.0041
Step 2	Count decimal places: 2 to the left.	Count decimal places: 3 to the right.
Step 3	$5.0037 \cdot 10^2$	$4.1 \cdot 10^{-3}$
	(Rule: Use a positive exponent if the decimal point moved left.)	(Rule: Use a negative exponent if the decimal point moved right.)

Directions Write each number in scientific notation.

1. 29,900 ______
2. 0.0016 ______
3. 0.0199 ______
4. 883 ______
5. 11,000 ______
6. 2,230,000 ______
7. 0.001 ______
8. 0.0000314 ______
9. 0.0009999 ______
10. 304,922 ______
11. 17,250 ______
12. 29,839,250 ______
13. 0.0000000033 ______
14. 3,000,000,000 ______
15. 222.6 ______
16. 0.0000002 ______
17. 260,000,000 ______
18. 0.00007 ______

Directions Solve the problems.

19. A certain bacteria cell is 0.0008 mm thick. Write this measurement in scientific notation. ______
20. Dinosaurs became extinct (that is, died out) about 65 million years ago. This number is written out as 65,000,000. Rewrite it in scientific notation. ______

 Algebra

TRL

Workbook Activity 48

Name Date Period **Activity 45** Chapter 5, Lesson 3

Exponents and Scientific Notation

Directions Rewrite these numbers so they are no longer in scientific notation.

1. $2.27 \cdot 10^{-2}$ ______
2. $3.772 \cdot 10^4$ ______
3. $5.6 \cdot 10^{-1}$ ______
4. $9.7 \cdot 10^7$ ______
5. $1.33586(10^5)$ ______
6. $1.33586(10^{-5})$ ______
7. $4.22 \cdot 10^2$ ______
8. $8.96 \cdot 10^3$ ______

Directions Solve the problems.

9. The last ice age ended about 10,000 years ago. Write this length of time in scientific notation. ______
10. The distance between the earth and the sun is about 93 million miles. This number is written out as 93,000,000. Rewrite it in scientific notation. ______
11. A certain virus is 0.0000050 mm long. Write this measurement in scientific notation. ______
12. Many scientists believe that the earth is more than 4 billion years old. This number is written out as 4,000,000,000. Rewrite it in scientific notation. ______
13. An adult blue whale can weigh as much as 300,000 pounds. Write this weight in scientific notation. ______
14. A certain kind of bat (a flying animal) weighs between 0.001 and 0.01 pounds. Rewrite this weight range in scientific notation. ______
15. The population of the planet earth has been estimated at 6 billion people. This number is written out as 6,000,000,000. Rewrite it in scientific notation. ______

 Algebra

TRL

Activity 45

Lesson at a Glance

Chapter 5 Lesson 3

Overview This lesson demonstrates how to write numbers using scientific notation.

Objective

- To use scientific notation to write very large or very small numbers

Student Pages 129–130

Teacher's Resource Library 

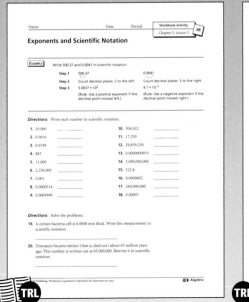

Workbook Activity 48

Activity 45

Alternative Activity 45

Mathematics Vocabulary

scientific notation

1 Warm-Up Activity

Have students factor out as many tens as possible from a list of whole numbers that are multiples of ten. Give them some examples.

$400 = 4 \cdot 10 \cdot 10$
$800 = 8 \cdot 10 \cdot 10$
$2{,}300 = 23 \cdot 10 \cdot 10$
$32{,}000 = 32 \cdot 10 \cdot 10 \cdot 10$
$5{,}000 = 5 \cdot 10 \cdot 10 \cdot 10$

Ask students to look for a shortcut. (Counting the number of zeros will tell you how many tens can be factored out.) Use this to introduce scientific notation as counting digits to determine the exponent.

2 Teaching the Lesson

Write several large numbers on the board. Then write them in scientific notation. Have students look for the rule for writing numbers in scientific notation. Go over the examples on page 129.

Have students explain why the following list of numbers will all have negative exponents in scientific notation:

0.00125	0.0898
0.00789	0.5413
0.025	

(All the numbers are less than zero; so they will have negative exponents in scientific notation.)

Have students explain why the following list of numbers will all have positive exponents in scientific notation:

2356	7,250,000,000
165	5,880,000
568,588	

(All the numbers are greater than zero; so they will all have positive exponents in scientific notation.)

3 Reinforce and Extend

Learning Styles

Visual/Spatial

Have students use an encyclopedia or a science textbook to make a poster of our solar system showing all nine planets and the sun. Ask students to indicate on their posters the distances between the sun and the individual planets using scientific notation.

Calculator

Have students use a scientific calculator to translate each number into scientific notation.

68,000	*(6.8⁰⁴)*
132	*(1.32⁰²)*
8,000,000	*(8.⁰⁶)*
9,614	*(9.614⁰³)*
81	*(8.1⁰¹)*
500.32	*(5.0032⁰²)*
1,000,000	*(1.⁰⁶)*
0.000004	*(4.⁻⁰⁶)*
0.00325	*(3.25⁻⁰³)*
0.000076	*(7.6⁻⁰⁵)*

Writing About Mathematics

Find a use of scientific notation in a science book or an encyclopedia. Write a sentence about what you found and share your findings with other students.

Exercise A Write each number in scientific notation.

1. 186,000 — $1.86 \cdot 10^5$
2. 0.00563 — $5.63 \cdot 10^{-3}$
3. 276,000,000,000 — $2.76 \cdot 10^{11}$
4. 0.0156 — $1.56 \cdot 10^{-2}$
5. 1,342.54 — $1.34254 \cdot 10^3$
6. 0.002010 — $2.01 \cdot 10^{-3}$
7. 0.0000000001 — $1.0 \cdot 10^{-10}$
8. 1,000,000,000 — $1.0 \cdot 10^9$
9. 935,420,000 — $9.3542 \cdot 10^8$
10. 0.00000305 — $3.05 \cdot 10^{-6}$

Exercise B Rewrite these numbers so they are no longer in scientific notation.

11. $3.28 \cdot 10^{-3}$ — 0.00328
12. $5.42 \cdot 10^6$ — 5,420,000
13. $1.86(10^2)$ — 186
14. $2.71(10^{-8})$ — 0.0000000271
15. $5.280(10^3)$ — 5,280
16. $5.42 \cdot 10^{-6}$ — 0.00000542
17. $1.6 \cdot 10^{-27}$ — see left
18. $1.1122(10^{-4})$ — 0.00011122
19. $1.1122(10^4)$ — 11,122
20. $3.1 \cdot 10^{-4}$ — 0.00031

17. 0.0000000000000000000000000016

Calculator Practice

You can use a calculator to translate numbers into scientific notation. Some calculators have a *function* or *mode* that will translate the number immediately.

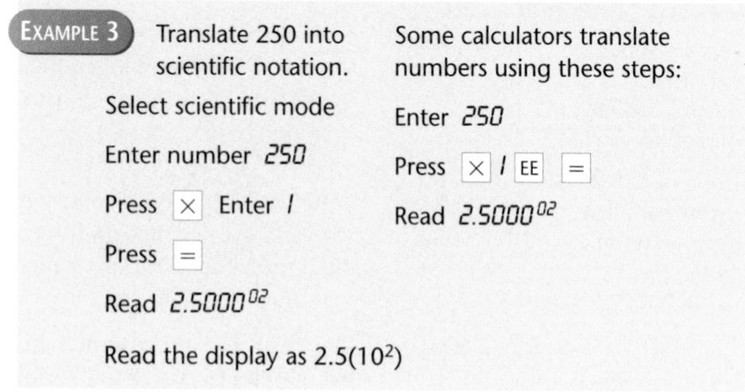

Example 3 Translate 250 into scientific notation.

Select scientific mode

Enter number 250

Press [×] Enter 1

Press [=]

Read 2.5000⁰²

Read the display as $2.5(10^2)$

Some calculators translate numbers using these steps:

Enter 250

Press [×] 1 [EE] [=]

Read 2.5000⁰²

Exercise C Use a calculator to check your answers in Exercise A.

Group Problem Solving

Students act as math detectives to discover what is wrong with each of the following problems:

$0.00025 = 25 \cdot 10^{-3}$

(The first number must be less than 10 but no less than 1, then adjust the exponent.)

$0.000045 = 4.5 \cdot 10^5$

(The exponent needs to be negative.)

$68{,}000{,}000 = 68 \cdot 10^6$

(The first number must be less than 10 but no less than 1, then adjust the exponent.)

$52{,}000 = 5.2 \cdot 10^{-4}$

(The exponent needs to be positive.)

$0.0058 = 5.8^{-3}$

(The base of 10 needs to be written.)

Lesson 4 Computing in Scientific Notation

Scientific notation is useful for multiplying or dividing very large or very small numbers.

EXAMPLE 1 Find $(13{,}000{,}000)^2$.

Step 1 Write the number in scientific notation.

$13{,}000{,}000 = 1.3 \bullet 10^7$

$(13{,}000{,}000)^2 = (1.3 \bullet 10^7)^2$

Step 2 Change the order of the factors to make the multiplication easier.

$(1.3 \bullet 10^7)^2 = (1.3 \bullet 10^7)(1.3 \bullet 10^7)$

$= 1.3 \bullet 1.3 \bullet 10^7 \bullet 10^7$

$= (1.3)^2(10^7)^2$

Step 3 Complete the multiplication, using the rule for raising exponents to a power.

$(1.69)(10^{7 \bullet 2}) = (1.69)(10^{14})$

Step 4 Check that the product is written in scientific notation.

The answer is $1.69(10^{14})$.

EXAMPLE 2 Find the product of $0.0000006 \bullet 32{,}000{,}000 \bullet 0.0043$.

Step 1 Write each number in scientific notation.

$(6.0 \bullet 10^{-7})(3.2 \bullet 10^7)(4.3 \bullet 10^{-3})$

Step 2 Use the commutative property to change the order of the factors.

$(6.0 \bullet 3.2 \bullet 4.3)(10^{-7} \bullet 10^7 \bullet 10^{-3})$

Step 3 Complete the multiplication, using the rule for multiplying with exponents.

$(82.56)(10^{-7+7-3}) = (82.56)(10^{-3})$

Step 4 Write the product in scientific notation.

$(8.256)(10)(10^{-3}) = 8.256(10^{-2})$

Lesson at a Glance

Chapter 5 Lesson 4

Overview This lesson shows how to multiply and divide in scientific notation.

Objective

- To find products and quotients in scientific notation

Student Pages 131–133

Teacher's Resource Library 

Workbook Activity 49

Activity 46

Alternative Activity 46

1 Warm-Up Activity

Review the general rule $(x^n)(x^m) = x^{n+m}$. Have students find the products in these problems:

$(10^4)(10^2)$ *(10^6)*

$(10^{-2})(10^{-5})$ *(10^{-7})*

$(10^3)(10^{-5})$ *(10^{-2})*

$(10^7)(10^{-4})$ *(10^3)*

$(10^{-8})(10^9)$ *(10)*

Review the general rule $x^n \div x^m = x^{n-m}$. Have students find the quotients in these problems:

$10^4 \div 10^2$ *(10^2)*

$10^{-2} \div 10^{-5}$ *(10^3)*

$10^3 \div 10^{-5}$ *(10^8)*

$10^7 \div 10^{-4}$ *(10^{11})*

$10^{-8} \div 10^9$ *$(10^1$ or $10)$*

2 Teaching the Lesson

Go over several examples using the rules from the Warm-Up activity.

$(1.3)(2.3)(10^7)(10^{-4})$

$(2.99 \bullet 10^3)$

$(6.25)(10^{-2}) \div (5)(10^{-5})$

$(1.25 \bullet 10^3)$

$(3.2)(10^3)(2.5)(10^{-5})$

$(8 \bullet 10^{-2})$

$(8.2)(10^7) \div (4.1)(10^{-4})$

$(2 \bullet 10^{11})$

$(18.6)(10^{-8}) \div (6.2)(10^9)$

$(3 \bullet 10^{-17})$

Name Date Period | Workbook Activity 49 | Chapter 5, Lesson 4

Computing in Scientific Notation

EXAMPLE Multiply: $0.005 \bullet 7{,}150{,}000$

Step 1 $0.005 = 5.0 \bullet 10^{-3}$ $7{,}150{,}000 = 7.15 \bullet 10^6$

Step 2 $(5.0 \bullet 10^{-3})(7.15 \bullet 10^6) = (5.0 \bullet 7.15)(10^{-3} \bullet 10^6)$

Step 3 $(35.75)(10^{-3+6}) = (35.75)(10^3)$

Step 4 $(3.575)(10)(10^3) = (3.575)(10^{1+3}) = (3.575)(10^4)$

Directions Find each product. Write the answer in scientific notation.

1. $0.0007 \cdot 190$ ________
2. $2{,}400{,}000 \cdot 0.006$ ________
3. $0.0018 \cdot 0.054$ ________
4. $18{,}500 \cdot 2{,}250$ ________
5. $3{,}600 \cdot 0.00000005$ ________

EXAMPLE Divide: $110{,}000{,}000 \div 250$

Step 1 $110{,}000{,}000 = 1.1 \bullet 10^8$ $250 = 2.5 \bullet 10^2$

Step 2 $\frac{1.1 \bullet 10^8}{2.5 \bullet 10^2} = (1.1 \div 2.5)(10^8 \div 10^2)$

Step 3 $(0.44)(10^{8-2}) = 0.44(10$

Step 4 $4.4(10^{-1})(10^6) = (4.4)(10^{-1+6}) = (4.4)(10^5)$

Directions Find each quotient. Write the answer in scientific notation.

6. $93{,}000{,}000 \div 3{,}100$ ________
7. $7{,}700 \div 0.0025$ ________
8. $1{,}008 \div 900{,}000$ ________
9. $0.00086 \div 0.025$ ________
10. $19.8 \div 0.0003$ ________

 Algebra

TRL

Workbook Activity 49

Name Date Period | Activity 46 | Chapter 5, Lesson 4

Computing in Scientific Notation

Directions Use scientific notation to solve these problems. Write all answers in scientific notation.

1. A magazine has 6,270,000 subscribers (people who take the magazine regularly). The company that publishes the magazine will divide its list of subscribers into 100 equal groups to conduct a special study. Find the size of each group. ________
2. A cereal company is sending a shipment of its top-selling breakfast cereal to warehouses all over the United States. The cereal has been loaded onto 48 trucks. Each truck holds 8,000 packages of cereal. How many packages are in the total shipment? ________
3. A biologist (scientist who studies living things) estimates that 40,000,000,000 (40 billion) cells of a bacteria are living on corn in a field. If the field contains 1,000 corn plants, how many cells of bacteria, on average, are on each corn plant? ________
4. You are on a spaceship traveling to a distant planet. The total distance you will travel from earth is 3,300,000,000 miles. If you travel 1,100,000 miles in one day, how many days will the trip take, one way? ________
5. In a software company, computer programmers are trying to find a tiny but difficult error in lines of a computer code. If 100 programmers are looking for the error, and each programmer is assigned 10,000 lines of code to examine, how many lines of code are being examined in total? ________

 Algebra

TRL

Activity 46

Reinforce and Extend

LEARNING STYLES

Body/Kinesthetic

Have pairs of students make a number line from -15 to 15 that is wide enough for a paper token to mark a point on the number line. Ask them to begin by putting the token on zero. Then have students do Exercises A and B using the number line. For example, for problem 1, they must first multiply 1.4 and 6.3. To calculate the exponent, they begin at zero, move three positive and then four negative. Therefore, the exponential part of the answer is 10^{-1}.

MENTAL MATH

Have students calculate the following problems mentally.

$(8)(10^{20}) \div (2)(10^{10})$
($4 \cdot 10^{10}$)

$(5)(10^{15})(5)(10^{-5})$
($2.5 \cdot 10^{11}$)

$(6 \cdot 10^2)^2$
($3.6 \cdot 10^5$)

$(4)(2)(10^{10})(10^5)$
($8 \cdot 10^{15}$)

$(16)(10^{20}) \div (4)(10^3)$
($4 \cdot 10^{17}$)

EXAMPLE 3 Find the quotient of $9{,}250{,}000 \div 25{,}000$.

Step 1 Write each number in scientific notation.
$9.25 \cdot 10^6 \div 2.5 \cdot 10^4$

Step 2 Rewrite the division as a fraction.
$\frac{9.25 \cdot 10^6}{2.5 \cdot 10^4} = \frac{9.25}{2.5} \cdot \frac{10^6}{10^4} = (9.25 \div 2.5)(10^6 \div 10^4)$

Step 3 Complete the division, using the rule for dividing with exponents.
$(3.7)(10^{6-4}) = (3.7)(10^2)$

Step 4 Check that the product is written in scientific notation.
The answer is $3.7(10^2)$.

Exercise A Find the products. Write your answer in scientific notation.

Problem	Answer
1. $1.4(10^3) \cdot 6.3(10^{-4})$	$8.82 \cdot 10^{-1}$
2. $8.1(10^{14}) \cdot 9.0(10^{-6})$	$7.29 \cdot 10^9$
3. $(4.01 \cdot 10^2)^3$	$6.4481201 \cdot 10^7$
4. $(3.4 \cdot 10^2)(1.3 \cdot 10^5)(2.54 \cdot 10^{-6})$	$1.12268 \cdot 10^2$
5. $52{,}000{,}000 \cdot 706{,}000$	$3.6712 \cdot 10^{13}$
6. $(11{,}000{,}000)^2$	$1.21 \cdot 10^{14}$
7. $(0.00008) \cdot (640{,}000{,}000)$	$5.12 \cdot 10^4$
8. $(350{,}000) \cdot (1{,}200) \cdot (16{,}000{,}000)$	$6.72 \cdot 10^{15}$
9. $(0.00645) \cdot (0.00004302 \cdot (0.000000035)$	$9.711765 \cdot 10^{-15}$
10. $[(2000)^3 \cdot (50{,}000)^2]^2$	$4.0 \cdot 10^{38}$

Exercise B Find each quotient. Write your answer in scientific notation.

11. $(6.8 \cdot 10^2) \div (3.4 \cdot 10^6)$ $2.0 \cdot 10^{-4}$

12. $(7.62 \cdot 10^{-2}) \div (2.54 \cdot 10^6)$ $3.0 \cdot 10^{-8}$

13. $1.6(10^6) \div 4.0(10^{-2})$ $4.0 \cdot 10^7$

14. $4.1(10^9) \div 8.2(10^{-2})$ $5.0 \cdot 10^{10}$

15. $545{,}000{,}000 \div 100{,}000$ $5.45 \cdot 10^3$

16. $350{,}000 \div 1{,}400{,}000$ $2.5 \cdot 10^{-1}$

17. $\frac{0.00008}{640{,}000{,}000}$ $1.25 \cdot 10^{-13}$

18. $\frac{1{,}200}{240{,}000{,}000}$ $5.0 \cdot 10^{-6}$

19. $\frac{0.000645}{0.005}$ $1.29 \cdot 10^{-1}$

20. $\frac{50{,}000^2}{0.00001}$ $2.5 \cdot 10^{14}$

Exercise C Use a calculator with a scientific mode to check your answers to Exercises A and B.

Technology Connection

Smashing Atoms

Scientists use accelerators—atom smashers—to release the parts of atoms called quarks and leptons. One accelerator in the United States uses 1,000 superconducting magnets. Each magnet weighs about 20 tons. The magnets steer bunches of protons—parts of atoms—around the accelerator, or ring, as the scientists call it. Each bunch contains more than one trillion protons. No wonder scientific notation was invented! How else could scientists work with such huge numbers?

Exponents and Polynomials **133**

Lesson at a Glance

Chapter 5 Lesson 5

Overview This lesson introduces polynomials.

Objectives

- To classify polynomials as monomials, binomials, trinomials, or polynomials
- To identify the degree of a polynomial
- To write a polynomial from a description

Student Pages 134–135

Teacher's Resource Library 

Workbook Activity 50

Activity 47

Alternative Activity 47

Mathematics Vocabulary

degree of a polynomial
monomial
polynomial
standard form

Warm-Up Activity

Have students organize a list of numbers in exponential form from least to greatest. For example, $2^3, 2^2, 2^{13}, 2^7, 2^6, 2^{12}, 2^{20}, 2^{10}$. *($2^2, 2^3, 2^6, 2^7, 2^{10}, 2^{12}, 2^{13}, 2^{20}$)* This will help to develop the concept of the standard form of polynomials.

Teaching the Lesson

Go over the table on page 134. Have students write and classify ten different polynomials.

To help students recognize standard form, make a list of polynomials and have students put them in standard form. For example,

$8x + 3x^6 + 9x^2 - 9$
($3x^6 + 9x^2 + 8x - 9$)
$5y + 2y^3 + 4y^2 - 20$
($2y^3 + 4y^2 + 5y - 20$)
$3q^3 + q + 5 + 8q^9$
($8q^9 + 3q^3 + q + 5$)
$5v + 3v^2 - 14$
($3v^2 + 5v - 14$)
$6b + 3b^7 + 9b^2 - 1$
($3b^7 + 9b^2 + 6b - 1$)

Lesson 5 Defining and Naming Polynomials

Polynomial
An algebraic expression made up of one term or the sum or difference of two or more terms in the same variable

Monomial
A term that is a number, a variable, or the product of a number and one or more variables

Degree of a polynomial
Greatest power of the variable

You have already worked with algebraic expressions such as $3a - b + 5 - 2a$. In this lesson, you will be introduced to algebraic expressions known as **polynomials.**

EXAMPLE 1 These expressions are polynomials in one variable.

Polynomial	Number of Terms	Name of Polynomial
$3x^2$	one term	*monomial*
$3x^2 + x$	two terms	*binomial*
$3x^2 + x + 1$	three terms	*trinomial*
$x^3 + 2x^2 - x + 5$	many terms	*polynomial*

Some algebraic expressions are *not* polynomials.

$x^{-4} + x^2 + 3$	has a negative exponent
$\frac{1}{x^2 + 3}$	is not a sum or difference
$\frac{5}{x^{-3}}$	is not a sum, has a negative exponent
$2y^3 + x^2 + x + 1$	has more than one variable
$\frac{3}{x^2}$	has a variable in the denominator

Polynomials can be named by their terms.

EXAMPLE 2

binomial (or polynomial) in x	$x^2 + 1$
trinomial (or polynomial) in x	$x^2 + x + 1$
trinomial (or polynomial) in y	$y^2 + y + 1$
polynomial in z	$2z^3 + z^2 + z + 1$

The greatest power of the variable is called the **degree of a polynomial.**

EXAMPLE 3

6	degree 0 (The degree of a constant is 0.)
$x - 3$	degree 1
$x^2 + x + 1$	degree 2
$x^3 + 4x^2 + 1$	degree 3

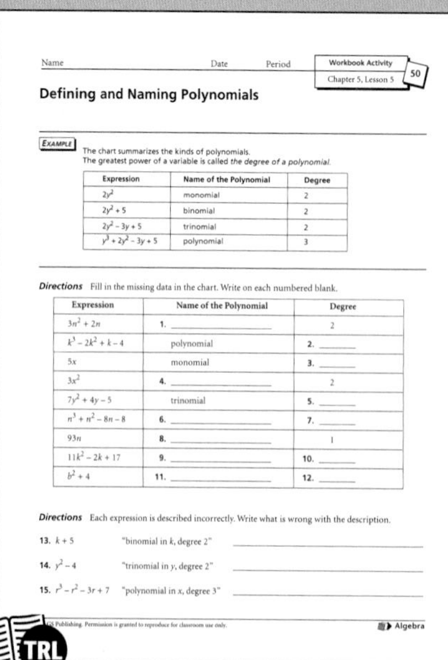

Name Date Period — Workbook Activity 50, Chapter 5, Lesson 5

Defining and Naming Polynomials

EXAMPLE The chart summarizes the kinds of polynomials.
The greatest power of a variable is called *the degree of a polynomial.*

Expression	Name of the Polynomial	Degree
$2y^2$	monomial	2
$2y^2 + 5$	binomial	2
$2y^2 - 3y + 5$	trinomial	2
$y^3 + 2y^2 - 3y + 5$	polynomial	3

Directions Fill in the missing data in the chart. Write on each numbered blank.

Expression	Name of the Polynomial	Degree
$3n^2 + 2n$	1. ______	2
$k^3 - 2k^2 + k - 4$	polynomial	2. ______
$5x$	monomial	3. ______
$3x^2$	4. ______	2
$7y^2 + 4y - 5$	trinomial	5. ______
$n^3 + n^2 - 8n - 8$	6. ______	7. ______
$93n$	8. ______	1
$11k^2 - 2k + 17$	9. ______	10. ______
$b^2 + 4$	11. ______	12. ______

Directions Each expression is described incorrectly. Write what is wrong with the description.

13. $k + 5$ "binomial in k, degree 2" ______
14. $y^2 - 4$ "trinomial in y, degree 2" ______
15. $r^3 - r^2 - 3r + 7$ "polynomial in x, degree 3" ______

 Algebra

Workbook Activity 50

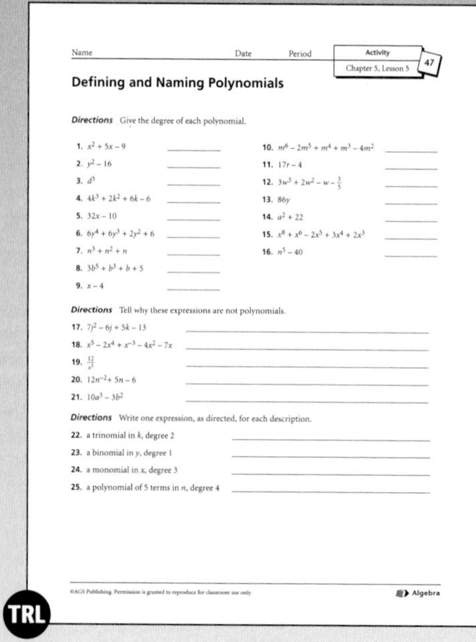

Name Date Period — Activity 47, Chapter 5, Lesson 5

Defining and Naming Polynomials

Directions Give the degree of each polynomial.

1. $x^2 + 5x - 9$ ______
2. $y^2 - 16$ ______
3. d^3 ______
4. $4k^3 + 2k^2 + 6k - 6$ ______
5. $32x - 10$ ______
6. $6y^4 + 6y^3 + 2y^2 + 6$ ______
7. $n^3 + n^2 + n$ ______
8. $3b^5 + b^3 + b + 5$ ______
9. $x - 4$ ______
10. $m^6 - 2m^5 + m^4 + m^3 - 4m^2$ ______
11. $17r - 4$ ______
12. $3w^3 + 2w^2 - w - \frac{3}{5}$ ______
13. $86y$ ______
14. $a^2 + 22$ ______
15. $x^8 + x^6 - 2x^5 + 3x^4 + 2x^3$ ______
16. $n^5 - 40$ ______

Directions Tell why these expressions are not polynomials.

17. $7j^2 - 6j + 5k - 13$ ______
18. $x^5 - 2x^4 + x^{-3} - 4x^2 - 7x$ ______
19. $\frac{12}{x^3}$ ______
20. $12n^{-2} + 5n - 6$ ______
21. $10a^3 - 3b^2$ ______

Directions Write one expression, as directed, for each description.

22. a trinomial in k, degree 2 ______
23. a binomial in y, degree 1 ______
24. a monomial in x, degree 3 ______
25. a polynomial of 5 terms in n, degree 4 ______

 Algebra

Activity 47

Standard form
Arrangement of variables from left to right, from greatest to least degree of power

The terms in a polynomial can be arranged in any order. However, in **standard form,** they are arranged left to right, from greatest to least degree of power. Always place the terms in standard form before using a polynomial in a computation.

EXAMPLE 4 $x^5 - x^3 + 7x$

Exercise A Name each expression by the number of its terms. Use monomial, binomial, trinomial, and polynomial.

1. $y^2 + 1$ binomial in y
2. $n^2 + n + 1$ trinomial in n
3. $5x^2 + 2x - 4$ trinomial in x
4. $5z^4 + z^3 + z + 1$ polynomial in z
5. $2p^3 + p^2 + p - \frac{1}{3}$ polynomial in p
6. $2x^5 + x^3 + x + 23$ polynomial in x
7. $7y^4 + 4y + 8$ trinomial in y
8. $7a^3 + a^2$ binomial in a
9. $b^7 + b^6 + b^5 + b^4 + b^3 + b^2 + b$ polynomial in b
10. b^{10} monomial in b

Exercise B Give the degree of each polynomial.

11. $3n^2 + 2n + 1$ 2
12. $3w^2 + 2w + w - 31$ 2
13. $5x^4 + 2x^3 + 54$ 4
14. $5a^5 + a^3 + a + 1$ 5
15. $2s^3 + s^2 + s - \frac{1}{2}$ 3
16. $2x^5 + x^4 + x^3 + x + 23$ 5
17. $z^7 + 5z^4 + z^3 + z + 432$ 7
18. $7b^4 + 7b^3 + 4b^2 + 8$ 4
19. $a^3 + a^2 + a$ 3
20. $b^7 + 2b^6 + 3b^5 + 4b^4 + 5b^3 + 6b^2 + 7b$ 7

Exercise C Write one polynomial for each description.

21. a trinomial in x, degree 3 $x^3 + x + 1$
22. a polynomial in y, degree 4 $y^4 - 2y^3 + y - 3$
23. a binomial in b, degree 5 $b^5 + 1$
24. a polynomial in z, degree 3 $z^3 + z^2 + z + 1$
25. a monomial in r, degree n $4r^n$

Exercise D Tell why these expressions are not polynomials.

26. $3n^{-2} + 2n + 23$ negative exponent
27. $3w^2 \div 2w$ is not a sum or difference
28. $5x^4 + \frac{1}{3x^3}$ has a variable in the denominator
29. $\frac{5}{x^n}$ is not a sum or difference
30. $x^3 + 5y^2 + x - 5$ has more than one variable

Reinforce and Extend

LEARNING STYLES

LEP/ESL

Have students form groups of two or three according to their native language. Have one student role-play the teacher and explain the lesson again in his or her native language. The other member(s) of the group role-play the student(s). Have students switch roles when they are finished.

GROUP PROBLEM SOLVING

At the conclusion of the lesson, have students form groups of two or three. Explain that the purpose of working in a group is to help each other. Assign the groups five problems at a time from page 135. Call on the groups to give the answers to their problems and to explain their reasoning.

Lesson at a Glance

Chapter 5 Lesson 6

Overview This lesson demonstrates how to add and subtract polynomials.

Objective

- To add or subtract polynomials

Student Pages 136–137

Teacher's Resource Library 

Workbook Activity 51

Activity 48

Alternative Activity 48

Warm-Up Activity

Offer the class the following brain teaser: "I can evaluate the expression $4x + 2x + x + 3x$, when x is any value, before you can with a pencil, paper, and a calculator. For example, when $x = 8.4$, the solution is 84. Look for a shortcut. How am I able to do this so fast?" *(The expression can be simplified to 10x.)*

Teaching the Lesson

Demonstrate the sums and differences of polynomials by doing the examples on page 136.

Common Error

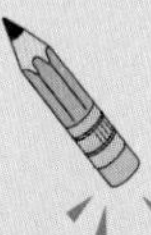

Emphasize the importance of writing clearly and lining up like terms when you are adding or subtracting polynomials. Some students may line up unlike terms to add or subtract. For example, ask students what is wrong with the following setup:

$$\begin{array}{r} 5x^4 + 3x^3 + 8x - 11 \\ + \; 7x^4 + 2x^2 + 4x + 20 \\ \hline \end{array}$$

($3x^3$ and $2x^2$ each needs to be in its own column.)

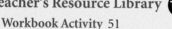

Lesson 6 Adding and Subtracting Polynomials

You can find the sum of two or more polynomials by adding like terms.

Example 1 Add $(5x^4 + x^3 - 2x^2 + 7x - 5)$ and $(-2x^3 + x^2 - 5x + 3)$.

Step 1 Rewrite the expression and line up like terms.

$$\begin{array}{rrrrrr} & 5x^4 & + \; x^3 & - \; 2x^2 & + \; 7x & - \; 5 \\ + & & - \; 2x^3 & + \; x^2 & - \; 5x & + \; 3 \\ \hline \end{array}$$

Step 2 Add like terms.

$$\begin{array}{rrrrrr} & 5x^4 & + \; x^3 & - \; 2x^2 & + \; 7x & - \; 5 \\ + & & - \; 2x^3 & + \; x^2 & - \; 5x & + \; 3 \\ \hline & 5x^4 & - \; x^3 & - \; x^2 & + \; 2x & - \; 2 \end{array}$$

You can find the difference of two or more polynomials by subtracting like terms.

Example 2 Subtract $(-2x^3 + x^2 - 5x + 3)$ from $(5x^4 + x^3 - 2x^2 + 7x - 5)$.

Step 1 Remember that to subtract, you add the opposite.

$-(-2x^3 + x^2 - 5x + 3)$ is equal to

$(-1)(-2x^3 + x^2 - 5x + 3) = 2x^3 - x^2 + 5x - 3$

Step 2 Rewrite the expression and line up like terms.

$$\begin{array}{rrrrrr} & 5x^4 & + \; x^3 & - \; 2x^2 & + \; 7x & - \; 5 \\ + & & 2x^3 & - \; x^2 & + \; 5x & - \; 3 \\ \hline \end{array}$$

Step 3 Add like terms.

$$\begin{array}{rrrrrr} & 5x^4 & + \; x^3 & - \; 2x^2 & + \; 7x & - \; 5 \\ + & & 2x^3 & - \; x^2 & + \; 5x & - \; 3 \\ \hline & 5x^4 & + \; 3x^3 & - \; 3x^2 & + \; 12x & - \; 8 \end{array}$$

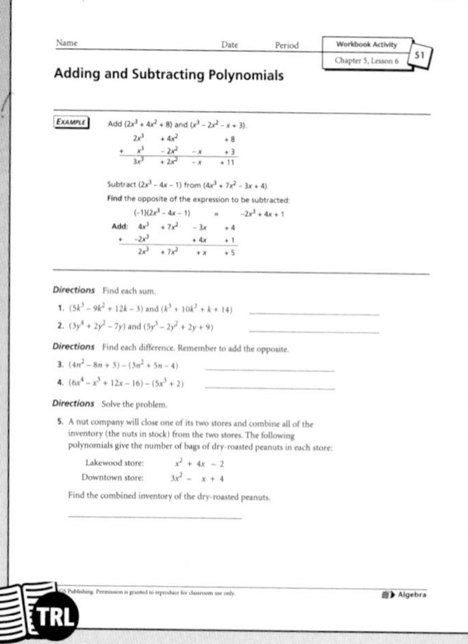

Name Date Period — Workbook Activity 51, Chapter 5, Lesson 6

Adding and Subtracting Polynomials

Example Add $(2x^3 + 4x^2 + 8)$ and $(x^3 - 2x^2 - x + 3)$.

$$\begin{array}{rrrrr} & 2x^3 & + \; 4x^2 & & + \; 8 \\ + & x^3 & - \; 2x^2 & - \; x & + \; 3 \\ \hline & 3x^3 & + \; 2x^2 & - \; x & + \; 11 \end{array}$$

Subtract $(2x^3 - 4x - 1)$ from $(4x^3 + 7x^2 - 3x + 4)$.

Find the opposite of the expression to be subtracted:

$(-1)(2x^3 - 4x - 1) = -2x^3 + 4x + 1$

$$\begin{array}{rrrrr} \textbf{Add:} & 4x^3 & + \; 7x^2 & - \; 3x & + \; 4 \\ + & -2x^3 & & + \; 4x & + \; 1 \\ \hline & 2x^3 & + \; 7x^2 & + \; x & + \; 5 \end{array}$$

Directions Find each sum.

1. $(5k^3 - 9k^2 + 12k - 3)$ and $(k^3 + 10k^2 + k + 14)$ ______
2. $(3y^4 + 2y^2 - 7y)$ and $(5y^3 - 2y^2 + 2y + 9)$ ______

Directions Find each difference. Remember to add the opposite.

3. $(4n^2 - 8n + 3) - (3n^2 + 5n - 4)$ ______
4. $(6x^4 - x^3 + 12x - 16) - (5x^3 + 2)$ ______

Directions Solve the problem.

5. A nut company will close one of its two stores and combine all of the inventory (the nuts in stock) from the two stores. The following polynomials give the number of bags of dry-roasted peanuts in each store:

   Lakewood store: $x^2 + 4x - 2$

   Downtown store: $3x^2 - x + 4$

   Find the combined inventory of the dry-roasted peanuts.

   ______

Algebra

Workbook Activity 51

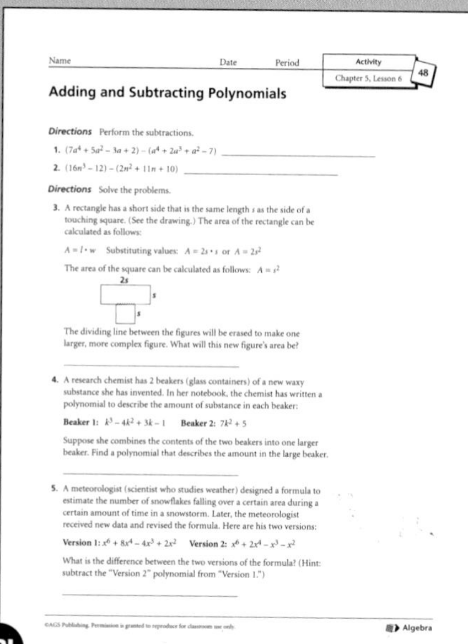

Name Date Period — Activity 48, Chapter 5, Lesson 6

Adding and Subtracting Polynomials

Directions Perform the subtractions.

1. $(7a^4 + 5a^2 - 3a + 2) - (a^4 + 2a^3 + a^2 - 7)$ ______
2. $(16n^3 - 12) - (2n^2 + 11n + 10)$ ______

Directions Solve the problems.

3. A rectangle has a short side that is the same length s as the side of a touching square. (See the drawing.) The area of the rectangle can be calculated as follows:

   $A = l \cdot w$ Substituting values: $A = 2s \cdot s$ or $A = 2s^2$

   The area of the square can be calculated as follows: $A = s^2$

   The dividing line between the figures will be erased to make one larger, more complex figure. What will this new figure's area be?

   ______

4. A research chemist has 2 beakers (glass containers) of a new waxy substance she has invented. In her notebook, the chemist has written a polynomial to describe the amount of substance in each beaker:

   Beaker 1: $k^3 - 4k^2 + 3k - 1$ **Beaker 2:** $7k^2 + 5$

   Suppose she combines the contents of the two beakers into one larger beaker. Find a polynomial that describes the amount in the large beaker.

   ______

5. A meteorologist (scientist who studies weather) designed a formula to estimate the number of snowflakes falling over a certain area during a certain amount of time in a snowstorm. Later, the meteorologist received new data and revised the formula. Here are his two versions:

   Version 1: $x^6 + 8x^4 - 4x^3 + 2x^2$ **Version 2:** $x^6 + 2x^4 - x^3 - x^2$

   What is the difference between the two versions of the formula? (Hint: subtract the "Version 2" polynomial from "Version 1.")

   ______

Algebra

Activity 48

Exercise A Find each sum.

1. $(2y^5 + y^3 + 7y + 33)$ and $(4y^6 + y^3 - 4y^2 - 7y - 5)$ $4y^6 + 2y^5 + 2y^3 - 4y^2 + 28$
2. $(2x^4 - 4x^3 - 15x^2 + 21x + 4)$ and $(4x^4 + 2x^3 + 17)$ $6x^4 - 2x^3 - 15x^2 + 21x + 21$
3. $(b^4 + b^3 - 2b^2 + 7b - 5)$ and $(-3b^4 - b^3 - 2b^2 - 2b)$ $-2b^4 - 4b^2 + 5b - 5$
4. $(m^4 + m^2 - 5)$ and $(m^3 + m + 5)$ $m^4 + m^3 + m^2 + m$
5. $(4x^4 + 7x^3 + 15x^2 + 4)$ and $(4x^3 + 2x^2 + 17x)$ $4x^4 + 11x^3 + 17x^2 + 17x + 4$
6. $(2b^5 + 3b^4 - 4b^3 + 7b^2)$ and $(-2b - 12)$ $2b^5 + 3b^4 - 4b^3 + 7b^2 - 2b - 12$
7. $(-4x^7 - 6x^5 - 7x^3 - 9x - 2) + (-x^7 + 6x^6 + 2x^2 + 8)$ see left
8. $(5m^4 + 2m^2 - 5m)$ and $(5m^3 + 2m + 10)$ $5m^4 + 5m^3 + 2m^2 - 3m + 10$
9. $(x^7 + x^5 - 3x^3) + (x^7 - 6x^6 + 8x - 2) + (-2x^2 + 8x - 14)$ see left
10. $(7y^5 + 8y^2 + 3) + (7y^5 + y^3) + (-4y^2 - y - 3)$ $14y^5 + y^3 + 4y^2 - y$

Exercise B Find each difference. Remember to add the opposite.

11. $(2y^5 + y^3 + 7y + 33) - (4y^6 + y^3 - 4y^2 - 7y - 5)$ $-4y^6 + 2y^5 + 4y^2 + 14y + 38$
12. $(2x^4 - 4x^3 - 15x^2 + 21x + 4) - (4x^4 + 2x^3 + 17)$ $-2x^4 - 6x^3 - 15x^2 + 21x - 13$
13. $(b^4 + b^3 - 2b^2 + 7b - 5) - (-3b^4 - b^3 - 2b^2 - 2b)$ $4b^4 + 2b^3 + 9b - 5$
14. $(m^4 + m^2 - 5) - (m^3 + m - 5)$ $m^4 - m^3 + m^2 - m$
15. $(x^7 + x^5 - 3x^3 + 8x - 2) - (x^7 - 6x^6 - 3x^3 + 8x - 14)$ $6x^6 + x^5 + 12$
16. Subtract $(7y^5 + y^3 - 4y^2 - y - 3)$ from $(7y^5 + 8y^2 + 3)$ $-y^3 + 12y^2 + y + 6$
17. Subtract $(4x^3 + 2x^2 + 17x)$ from $(4x^4 + 7x^3 + 15x^2 + 4)$ $4x^4 + 3x^3 + 13x^2 - 17x + 4$
18. Subtract $(-2b - 12)$ from $(2b^5 + 3b^4 - 4b^3 + 7b^2)$ $2b^5 + 3b^4 - 4b^3 + 7b^2 + 2b + 12$

PROBLEM SOLVING

Exercise C Follow the directions.

19. Franco is remodeling his kitchen. He is going to put baseboards around the perimeter of the room. Write an expression that shows the perimeter of Franco's kitchen. $2x^2 + 2x + 10$

20. For an art project, Clarissa is decorating the lid of a box shaped like a triangle. She is gluing lace to the perimeter of the triangle-shaped lid. She wants to know what the perimeter of the lid is so that she can cut the right amount of lace. Write an expression to help her find the perimeter of the lid. $x^2 + 2x - 3$

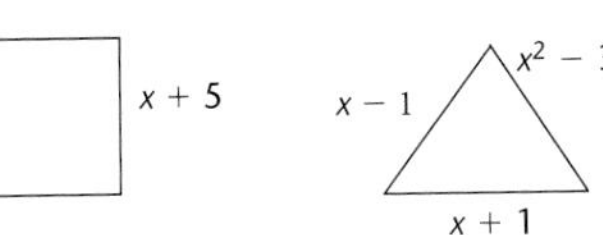

3 Reinforce and Extend

LEARNING STYLES

Auditory/Verbal

Have pairs of students take turns orally setting up problems 11–18 on page 137. As one student speaks, the other student checks to make sure the integer rule for subtraction is used correctly.

CALCULATOR

Have students use a calculator to solve these problems:

$(527x^4 + 651x^3 + 845x) + (687x^4 + 321x^3 + 899x)$

$(1{,}214x^4 + 972x^3 + 1{,}744x)$

$(8.411y^5 + 2.752y^2 + 4.973y + 20.665) - (-2.59y^5 + 2.72y^2 + 4.97)$

$(11.001y^5 + 0.032y^2 + 4.973y + 15.695)$

$(5789c^2 + 3651c) + (2575c^2 + 267c)$

$(8364c^2 + 3918c)$

$(68.875x^9 - 57.598x) - (45.5x^3 - 5.578x)$

$(68.875x^9 - 45.5x^3 - 52.02x)$

$(0.257y^3 + 0.52y^2 + 0.65) + (0.652y^3 + 0.502y^2 + 0.657)$

$(0.909y^3 + 1.022y^2 + 1.307)$

GROUP PROBLEM SOLVING

To help students demonstrate an understanding of the addition and subtraction of polynomials, have them design a city zoo. First, ask students to decide what features the zoo will have. Second, assign pairs of students one of the features of the zoo. Each group draws a detailed polygon of its feature and calculates the perimeter. Third, have students assemble their polygons to show the whole zoo.

Lesson at a Glance

Chapter 5 Lesson 7

Overview This lesson shows how to multiply monomials and polynomials.

Objective

- To multiply monomials and polynomials

Student Pages 138–139

Teacher's Resource Library TRL

Workbook Activity 52

Activity 49

Alternative Activity 49

1 Warm-Up Activity

Have students recall the distributive property by simplifying the following problems:

$3(x + 1)$	*$(3x + 3)$*
$4(3b + 6)$	*$(12b + 24)$*
$2(6x - 5)$	*$(12x - 10)$*
$7(2d + 3g)$	*$(14d + 21g)$*
$6(3s - 7)$	*$(18s - 42)$*

This will help students multiply with monomials and polynomials because they will be using the distributive property.

2 Teaching the Lesson

Demonstrate that the multiplication of monomials and polynomials can be solved using the same algorithms as multiplying whole numbers. For example, $(2x^2 + x)(2x)$ can be written as

$$\begin{array}{r} (2x^2 + x) \\ \times \quad (2x) \\ \hline 4x^3 + 2x^2 \end{array}$$

Try This

Have students work easier problems first to look for a pattern.

First, solve $a(x + y + z)$.

Then solve $(a + b)(x + y + z)$.

Finally, solve $(a + b + c)(x + y + z)$.

Lesson 7 Multiplying Polynomials

You can use the distributive property to multiply monomials and polynomials.

Example 1

$$x^2(2x^2 + 1) = (x^2 \bullet 2x^2) + x^2 = 2x^4 + x^2$$

Example 2

$$x^2(3x^3 + x + 1) = (x^2 \bullet 3x^3) + (x^2 \bullet x) + x^2 = 3x^5 + x^3 + x^2$$

Example 3

$$x^2(4x^5 + x^3 - 2x^2 + x - 5) =$$
$$(x^2 \bullet 4x^5) + (x^2 \bullet x^3) - (x^2 \bullet 2x^2) + (x^2 \bullet x) - 5x^2 =$$
$$4x^7 + x^5 - 2x^4 + x^3 - 5x^2$$

Suppose you must simplify the following expression: $3(a + b) + 2(a + b)$. You can use the distributive property and simplify this sum in two ways. **Hint:** Think of $(a + b)$ as a single variable as in $3x + 2x = 5x$.

$$3(a + b) + 2(a + b) \quad = \quad (3 + 2)(a + b)$$

$3a + 3b + 2a + 2b$	$5(a + b)$
$5a + 5b$	$5a + 5b$

You can use the distributive property to multiply two binomials.

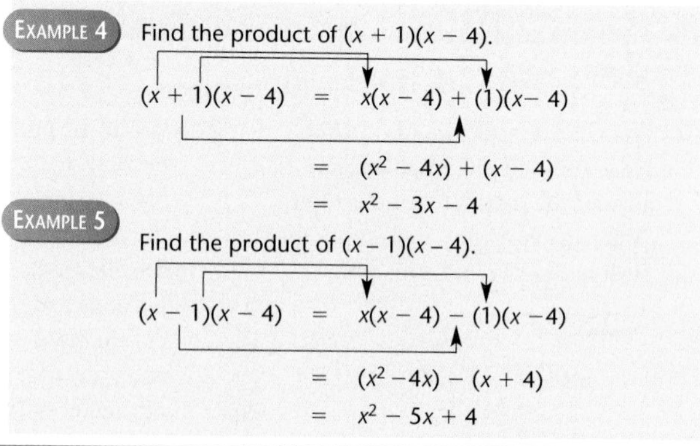

Example 4 Find the product of $(x + 1)(x - 4)$.

$$(x + 1)(x - 4) = x(x - 4) + (1)(x - 4)$$
$$= (x^2 - 4x) + (x - 4)$$
$$= x^2 - 3x - 4$$

Example 5 Find the product of $(x - 1)(x - 4)$.

$$(x - 1)(x - 4) = x(x - 4) - (1)(x - 4)$$
$$= (x^2 - 4x) - (x + 4)$$
$$= x^2 - 5x + 4$$

Name Date Period | Workbook Activity 52 | Chapter 5, Lesson 7

Multiplying Polynomials

Example Multiply $(n + 2)(n - 3)$. Use the distributive property.

$$(n + 2)(n - 3) = n(n - 3) + 2(n - 3)$$
$$= n^2 - 3n + 2n - 6$$
$$= n^2 - n - 6$$

Directions Find each product.

1. $(k + 4)(3k - 6)$
2. $(-2x + 5)(-x - 10)$
3. $(c^2 + c)^2$
4. $(d^2)(d + 5)$
5. $(y + 9)(y^2 - 2y + 6)$
6. $(n - 3)(n^3 + 6n - 3)$
7. $(w^3 + 1)(w^2 - 4)$
8. $(-2x - 5)(3x^5 + x^4 - 4x^3 + 6x^2)$
9. $(c^3)(c^2 - 3c + 9)$
10. $(2k + 7)(2k - 5)$
11. $(m - 3)(m^4 - 3m^3 - 7m - 1)$
12. $(8b + 3)(2b - 9)$
13. $(k^3)(k^6 + 2k^5 - 3k^4 - 8k^3 + 4k^2 - 9k - 9)$
14. $(7n - 4)(3n^3 - 8n^2 - 5n + 8)$

Directions Solve the problem.

15. A machine in a factory turns out a large metal grid (a crisscross or checkerboard pattern), which later gets cut into small pieces for computer parts. The measurements of this large grid are as follows:

    length: $(3x + 12)$ width: $(2x - 3)$

    Find the area of this grid, using the formula: Area = length • width.

 Algebra

TRL

Workbook Activity 52

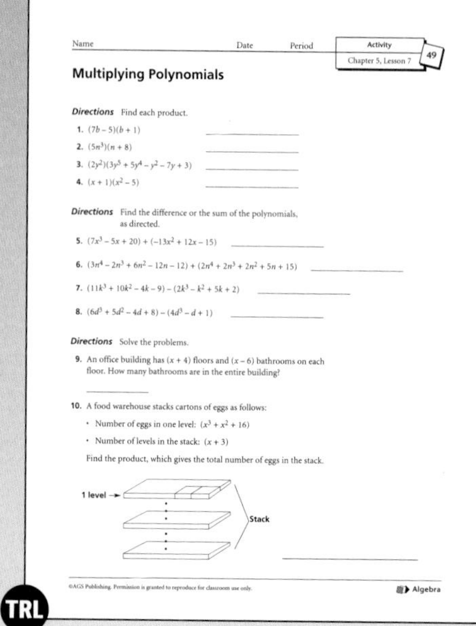

Name Date Period | Activity 49 | Chapter 5, Lesson 7

Multiplying Polynomials

Directions Find each product.

1. $(7b - 5)(b + 1)$
2. $(5n^3)(n + 8)$
3. $(2y^2)(3y^5 + 5y^4 - y^2 - 7y + 3)$
4. $(x + 1)(x^2 - 5)$

Directions Find the difference or the sum of the polynomials, as directed.

5. $(7x^3 - 5x + 20) + (-13x^2 + 12x - 15)$
6. $(3n^4 - 2n^3 + 6n^2 - 12n - 12) + (2n^4 + 2n^3 + 2n^2 + 5n + 15)$
7. $(11k^3 + 10k^2 - 4k - 9) - (2k^3 - k^2 + 5k + 2)$
8. $(6d^3 + 5d^2 - 4d + 8) - (4d^3 - d + 1)$

Directions Solve the problems.

9. An office building has $(x + 4)$ floors and $(x - 6)$ bathrooms on each floor. How many bathrooms are in the entire building?

10. A food warehouse stacks cartons of eggs as follows:
    - Number of eggs in one level: $(x^3 + x^2 + 16)$
    - Number of levels in the stack: $(x + 3)$

    Find the product, which gives the total number of eggs in the stack.

 Algebra

TRL

Activity 49

TRY THIS

Explain in words or draw a diagram showing how you would multiply $(a+b+c)(x+y+z)$.

Answer for "Try This…"

$(ax + ay + az) + (bx + by + bz) + (cx + cy + cz)$

You can use the distributive property to find the product of a binomial and a trinomial.

EXAMPLE 6 Find the product of $(x + 4)(x^2 + 3x + 1)$.

$$\begin{aligned}(x + 4)(x^2 + 3x + 1) &= x(x^2 + 3x + 1) + (4)(x^2 + 3x + 1)\\ &= (x^3 + 3x^2 + x) + (4x^2 + 12x + 4)\\ &= x^3 + 7x^2 + 13x + 4\end{aligned}$$

Exercise A Find each product.

1. $(x + 2)(8x - 2)$
   $8x^2 + 14x - 4$
2. $(-8y^2 + 3)(-4y - 3)$
   $32y^3 + 24y^2 - 12y - 9$
3. $(b^4 + b^3)^2$
   $b^8 + 2b^7 + b^6$
4. $(m^4 + 5)(m^3 + m^2 + 1)$
   $m^7 + m^6 + m^4 + 5m^3 + 5m^2 + 5$
5. $(15x^2 + 4)(4x^3 - 17x)$
   $60x^5 - 239x^3 - 68x$
6. $(2y + 3)(4y^3 - 7y - 2)$
   $8y^4 + 12y^3 - 14y^2 - 25y - 6$
7. $(2x^4 - x)(x^2 + 2x + 1)$
   $2x^6 + 4x^5 + 2x^4 - x^3 - 2x^2 - x$
8. $(-9x - 2)(-x^6 + 2x^2 + 8)$
   $9x^7 + 2x^6 - 18x^3 - 4x^2 - 72x - 16$
9. $(5m^4 + 2m^2 - 5m)(2m + 10)$
   $10m^5 + 50m^4 + 4m^3 + 10m^2 - 50m$
10. $(-2b - 12)(2b^5 + 3b^4 - 4b^3 + 7b^2)$
    $-4b^6 - 30b^5 - 28b^4 + 34b^3 - 84b^2$

PROBLEM SOLVING

Exercise B Write a polynomial for each problem.

11. Ellie and Terrell are carpeting their square living room. They need to know the area of the room to buy the carpeting. What is the area of the room with each side measuring $a + 2b$?

    $a + 2b$

12. Before the carpeting is put down in the living room, Ellie is going to paint the baseboards. She needs to know the perimeter of the room to help her estimate how much paint she will need. What is the perimeter of the room?

13. Ellie and Terrell are also putting new carpeting in their family room, which is a rectangle having length $= x + 3$ and width $= x + 1$. What is the area of the family room?

14. If their family room had a length twice that of its actual length, what would the area of the room be?

15. The kitchen has a width that is three times the width of the family room but the same length. What is the area of the kitchen?

11. $a^2 + 4ab + 4b^2$
12. $4a + 8b$
13. $x^2 + 4x + 3$
14. $2x^2 + 8x + 6$
15. $3x^2 + 12x + 9$

MANIPULATIVES

M Modeling Polynomials

Materials: Algebra Tiles, Manipulatives Master 4 (Factor Frame)

Group Practice: Using the expression $x^2(2x^2 + 1)$ from the first example, build models of the multiplicand and the multiplier and place them on the outside of the Factor Frame. To find the product, use the distributive property to multiply the factors. Place the Algebra Tiles that represent the products of the factors in the rectangle. (See page T9, "Using the Factor Frame," for more detailed instructions.) Write the symbolic equivalent of the factors and the products on the outside of the Factor Frame. Use the same procedure for multiplying two binomials.

Student Practice: Have students use models to solve problems or check their work for Exercise A, Problems 1 and 2; Exercise B; and Supplementary Problems 26 and 31 on page 415.

3 Reinforce and Extend

MENTAL MATH

Have students mentally find the value of n.

$(x + 4)(2x + 8) = 2x^2 + n + 32$
$(n = 16x)$

$(3x^2 + 5x + 9)(9x) = n + 45x^2 + 81x$
$(n = 27x^3)$

$(6x - 4)(3x - 5) = 18x^2 + n + 20$
$(n = -42x)$

$(8y + 6)(3y - 4) = n - 14y - 24$
$(n = 24y^2)$

$(b + 6c)(b + 3c) = b^2 + 9bc + n$
$(n = 18c^2)$

GROUP PROBLEM SOLVING

Encourage students to demonstrate an understanding of multiplying polynomials by designing a mall. First, have students decide what features the mall will have. Second, assign pairs of students one of the features of the mall. Each group draws a detailed polygon of its feature and calculates the area. Third, have students assemble their polygons to show the whole mall.

LEARNING STYLES

Interpersonal/ Group Learning

Have each student write a ten-problem quiz on multiplying with monomials and polynomials. The quiz must include an answer key on a separate paper. Have students exchange quizzes. Give them time to take the quizzes. Then have them check each other's work.

Lesson at a Glance

Chapter 5 Lesson 8

Overview This lesson shows the pattern of some polynomial products.

Objective

- To recognize patterns in polynomial products

Student Pages 140–141

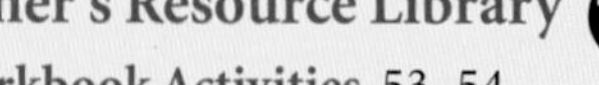

Teacher's Resource Library TRL

Workbook Activities 53–54

Activity 50

Alternative Activity 50

Warm-Up Activity

Propose this brain teaser to students: "I can multiply $(x + y)(x + y)$, $(b + c)(b + c)$, $(b + 2)(b - 2)$, $(a + 4)(a - 4)$, $(s + 6)(s + 6)$, and $(c + 3)(c + 3)$ in my head faster than it can be done on paper. I do not have the answers memorized."

$(x + y)(x + y) = x^2 + 2xy + y^2$

$(b + c)(b + c) = b^2 + 2bc + c^2$

$(a + 4)(a - 4) = a^2 - 16$

$(b + 2)(b - 2) = b^2 - 4$

$(s + 6)(s + 6) = s^2 + 12s + 36$

$(c + 3)(c + 3) = c^2 + 6c + 9$

"How can I calculate these problems in my head faster than with paper and pencil? Look for a pattern."

Teaching the Lesson

Go over the examples of special polynomial products on page 140 with students. Change the variables in $(a + b)^2$ to $(c + d)^2$ and demonstrate that the product has the same pattern.

Try This

Have students work easier problems first to look for a pattern.

First, solve $(a + b)^2$.

Then solve $(a + b)^3$.

Finally, solve $(a + b)^4$.

Lesson 8 Special Polynomial Products

The products of some polynomials form a pattern.

EXAMPLE 1 Find $(a + b)^2$.

$$\begin{aligned}(a + b)^2 = (a + b)(a + b) &= a(a + b) + b(a + b)\\ &\quad a^2 + ab + ba + b^2\\ &\quad a^2 + ab + ab + b^2\\ (a + b)^2 &= a^2 + 2ab + b^2\end{aligned}$$

EXAMPLE 2 Find $(a - b)^2$.

$$\begin{aligned}(a - b)^2 = (a - b)(a - b) &= a(a - b) - b(a - b)\\ &\quad a^2 - ab - ba + b^2\\ &\quad a^2 - ab - ab + b^2\\ (a - b)^2 &= a^2 - 2ab + b^2\end{aligned}$$

EXAMPLE 3 Find $(a + b)(a - b)$.

$$\begin{aligned}(a + b)(a - b) &= a(a - b) + b(a - b)\\ &\quad a^2 - ab + ba - b^2\\ &\quad a^2 - ab + ab - b^2\\ (a + b)(a - b) &= a^2 - b^2\end{aligned}$$

EXAMPLE 4 Find $(a + b)^3$.

$$\begin{aligned}(a + b)^3 &= (a + b)(a + b)(a + b)\\ &\quad (a + b)[(a + b)(a + b)]\\ &\quad (a + b)(a^2 + 2ab + b^2)\\ &\quad a^3 + 2a^2b + ab^2 + a^2b + 2ab^2 + b^3\end{aligned}$$

$$(a + b)^3 = a^3 + 3a^2b + 3ab^2 + b^3$$

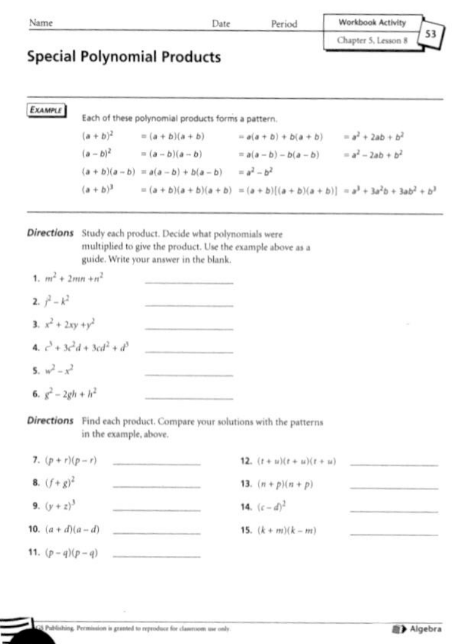

Name Date Period Workbook Activity 53 Chapter 5, Lesson 8

Special Polynomial Products

EXAMPLE Each of these polynomial products forms a pattern.

$(a + b)^2 = (a + b)(a + b) = a(a + b) + b(a + b) = a^2 + 2ab + b^2$

$(a - b)^2 = (a - b)(a - b) = a(a - b) - b(a - b) = a^2 - 2ab + b^2$

$(a + b)(a - b) = a(a - b) + b(a - b) = a^2 - b^2$

$(a + b)^3 = (a + b)(a + b)(a + b) = (a + b)[(a + b)(a + b)] = a^3 + 3a^2b + 3ab^2 + b^3$

Directions Study each product. Decide what polynomials were multiplied to give the product. Use the example above as a guide. Write your answer in the blank.

1. $m^2 + 2mn + n^2$ ________
2. $j^2 - k^2$ ________
3. $x^2 + 2xy + y^2$ ________
4. $c^3 + 3c^2d + 3cd^2 + d^3$ ________
5. $w^2 - x^2$ ________
6. $g^2 - 2gh + h^2$ ________

Directions Find each product. Compare your solutions with the patterns in the example, above.

7. $(p + r)(p - r)$ ________
8. $(f + g)^2$ ________
9. $(y + z)^3$ ________
10. $(a + d)(a - d)$ ________
11. $(p - q)(p - q)$ ________
12. $(t + u)(t + u)(t + u)$ ________
13. $(n + p)(n + p)$ ________
14. $(c - d)^2$ ________
15. $(k + m)(k - m)$ ________

Algebra

TRL

Workbook Activity 53

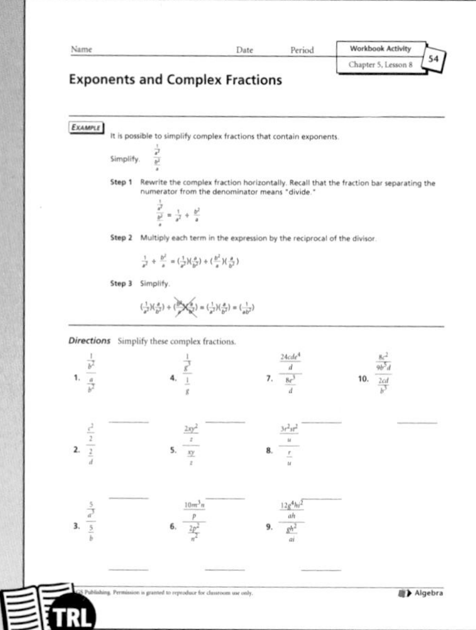

Name Date Period Workbook Activity 54 Chapter 5, Lesson 8

Exponents and Complex Fractions

EXAMPLE It is possible to simplify complex fractions that contain exponents.

Simplify. $\frac{\frac{1}{a^2}}{\frac{b^2}{a}}$

Step 1 Rewrite the complex fraction horizontally. Recall that the fraction bar separating the numerator from the denominator means "divide."

$\frac{\frac{1}{a^2}}{\frac{b^2}{a}} = \frac{1}{a^2} \div \frac{b^2}{a}$

Step 2 Multiply each term in the expression by the reciprocal of the divisor.

$\frac{1}{a^2} \div \frac{b^2}{a} = (\frac{1}{a^2})(\frac{a}{b^2}) \div (\frac{b^2}{a})(\frac{a}{b^2})$

Step 3 Simplify.

$(\frac{1}{a^2})(\frac{a}{b^2}) \div (\frac{b^2}{a})(\frac{a}{b^2}) = (\frac{1}{a^2})(\frac{a}{b^2}) = (\frac{1}{ab^2})$

Directions Simplify these complex fractions.

1. $\frac{\frac{1}{b^2}}{\frac{a}{b^2}}$ ________
2. $\frac{\frac{c^2}{2}}{\frac{2}{d}}$ ________
3. $\frac{\frac{5}{a^3}}{\frac{5}{b}}$ ________
4. $\frac{\frac{1}{g^3}}{\frac{1}{g}}$ ________
5. $\frac{\frac{2xy^2}{z}}{\frac{xy}{z}}$ ________
6. $\frac{\frac{10m^3n}{p}}{\frac{2p^2}{n^2}}$ ________
7. $\frac{\frac{24cde^4}{d}}{\frac{8e^3}{d}}$ ________
8. $\frac{\frac{3r^2st^2}{u}}{\frac{r}{u}}$ ________
9. $\frac{\frac{12g^4hi^2}{ah}}{\frac{gh^2}{ai}}$ ________
10. $\frac{\frac{8c^2}{9b^5d}}{\frac{2cd}{b^3}}$ ________

Algebra

TRL

Workbook Activity 54

TRY THIS

What polynomial represents $(a + b)^4$?

$a^4 + 4a^3b + 6a^2b^2 + 4ab^3 + b^4$

Students' intermediate steps should reflect patterns shown in examples.

Exercise A Find each product. Compare your solutions with the patterns on page 138.

1. $(x + y)^2$ $x^2 + 2xy + y^2$
2. $(p - q)^2$ $p^2 - 2pq + q^2$
3. $(m - n)(m + n)$ $m^2 - n^2$
4. $(x + y)^3$ $x^3 + 3x^2y + 3xy^2 + y^3$
5. $(x + 2)^2$ $x^2 + 4x + 4$
6. $(y + 3)^3$ $y^3 + 9y^2 + 27y + 27$
7. $(z - 3)(z + 3)$ $z^2 - 9$
8. $(m - 4)^2$ $m^2 - 8m + 16$
9. $(x + 5)(x - 5)$ $x^2 - 25$
10. $(n + 2)^3$ $n^3 + 6n^2 + 12n + 8$
11. $(x + 3)^2$ $x^2 + 6x + 9$

PROBLEM SOLVING

Exercise B Find the product for each problem.

12. Tanyika is going to buy potting soil for a flowerpot shaped like a cube. Knowing the volume of the flowerpot will help Tanyika choose the size of package of dirt to buy. The flowerpot has a side length of $z + 4$. What is its volume?
$z^3 + 12z^2 + 48z + 64$

13. Maura's flower box has a length of $x + 3$, a width of $x + 1$, and a height of $x + 2$. What is its volume?

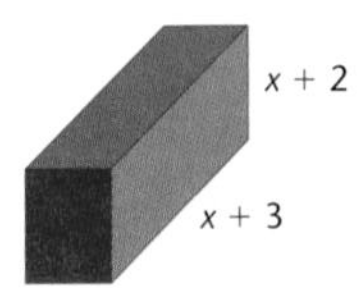

$x^3 + 6x^2 + 11x + 6$

14. Maura also wants to line the bottom of her flower box with plastic sheeting. She needs to determine the area of the box bottom to know how much sheeting she will need. What is the area? $x^2 + 4x + 3$

15. Aaron is packing groceries in a rectangular grocery bag. He wants to know the volume of the bag. The bag's dimensions are $m - n$, $m - n$, and $m + n$. What is its volume?
$m^3 - m^2n - mn^2 + n^3$

COMMON ERROR

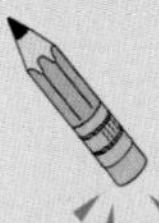

Help students avoid confusing the pattern for $(a + b)(a - b)$ with the other patterns by having them correct the following errors:

$(a + b)(a - b) = a^2 - 2ab + b^2$
$[(a + b)(a - b) = a^2 - b^2]$

$(x + 2)(x - 2) = x^2 + 4$
$[(x + 2)(x - 2) = x^2 - 4]$

$(m - 4)(m + 4) = m^2 - 4m + 16$
$[(m - 4)(m + 4) = m^2 - 16]$

$(n - 3)(n + 3) = n^3 + 3n^2 + 3n - 9$
$[(n - 3)(n + 3) = n^2 - 9]$

$(z - 4)(z + 4) = 2z + 8$
$[(z - 4)(z + 4) = z^2 - 16]$

MANIPULATIVES

Multiplying Polynomials

Materials: Algebra Tiles, Manipulatives Master 4 (Factor Frame)

Group Practice: Review procedures for using Algebra Tiles and the Factor Frame to multiply binomials. Choose an expression. Build models of the multiplicand and the multiplier and place them on the outside of the Factor Frame. To find the product, use the distributive property to multiply the factors and place the Algebra Tiles that represent the products of the factors in the rectangle. (See page T9, "Using the Factor Frame.")

Student Practice: Have students use models to complete Exercise A (but skip Problems 4, 6, and 10); Exercise B, Problem 14; and Supplementary Problem 27 on page 415.

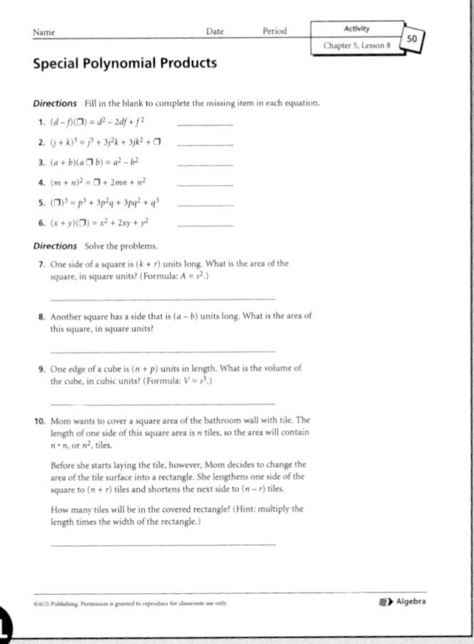

Name Date Period | Activity 50 | Chapter 5, Lesson 8

Special Polynomial Products

Directions Fill in the blank to complete the missing item in each equation.

1. $(d - f)(\square) = d^2 - 2df + f^2$ ______
2. $(j + k)^3 = j^3 + 3j^2k + 3jk^2 + \square$ ______
3. $(a + b)(a \square b) = a^2 - b^2$ ______
4. $(m + n)^2 = \square + 2mn + n^2$ ______
5. $(\square)^3 = p^3 + 3p^2q + 3pq^2 + q^3$ ______
6. $(x + y)(\square) = x^2 + 2xy + y^2$ ______

Directions Solve the problems.

7. One side of a square is $(k + r)$ units long. What is the area of the square, in square units? (Formula: $A = s^2$.)
______
8. Another square has a side that is $(a - b)$ units long. What is the area of this square, in square units?
______
9. One edge of a cube is $(n + p)$ units in length. What is the volume of the cube, in cubic units? (Formula: $V = s^3$.)
______
10. Mom wants to cover a square area of the bathroom wall with tile. The length of one side of this square area is n tiles, so the area will contain $n \cdot n$, or n^2, tiles.

Before she starts laying the tile, however, Mom decides to change the area of the tile surface into a rectangle. She lengthens one side of the square to $(n + r)$ tiles and shortens the next side to $(n - r)$ tiles.

How many tiles will be in the covered rectangle? (Hint: multiply the length times the width of the rectangle.)
______

 Algebra

TRL

Activity 50

Reinforce and Extend

GROUP PROBLEM SOLVING

Have small groups of students create three word problems in which polynomial products must be used to solve the problem. Encourage students to write problems about a topic that interests them, for example, basketball, cooking, science, music, and so on. Have them write the solutions on a separate sheet of paper. Ask the groups to exchange and solve each other's problems.

Lesson at a Glance

Chapter 5 Lesson 9

Overview This lesson shows how to divide a polynomial by a monomial.

Objective

- To divide a polynomial by a monomial

Student Pages 142–143

Teacher's Resource Library 

Workbook Activity 55

Activity 51

Alternative Activity 51

Warm-Up Activity

Have students intuitively solve for n.

$(3x^2 + 7x) = n(3x + 7)$

$(n = x)$

$(24y^2 + 16y - 32) = n(3y^2 + 2y - 4)$

$(n = 8)$

$(25a^3 + 45a^2) = n(5a + 9)$

$(n = 5a^2)$

$(6b^2 + 120b) = 6b(n)$

$[n = (b + 20)]$

$(12z^2 + 24z) = 6z(n)$

$[n = (2z + 4)]$

Teaching the Lesson

Demonstrate on the board the examples on pages 142 and 143. After the first example, call on students to complete each step in the second and third examples.

Common Error

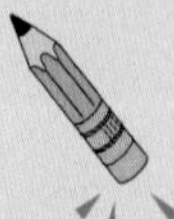

Help students avoid the common error of not dividing all the terms of the quotient by the divisor. Suggest that students create four problems and solutions, with one solution that is incorrect. Then have students exchange problems to see whether they can detect the error.

Lesson 9 Dividing a Polynomial by a Monomial

The distributive property can be used to divide a polynomial by a monomial.

Example 1 Find the quotient of $(12x^4 - 8x^3 + 4x^2) \div 4$.

Step 1 Rewrite the problem.

$$\frac{12x^4 - 8x^3 + 4x^2}{4} \quad \frac{\text{(dividend)}}{\text{(divisor)}}$$

Step 2 Divide each term of the numerator by the term in the denominator.

$$\frac{12x^4}{4} - \frac{8x^3}{4} + \frac{4x^2}{4} = \frac{12}{4}x^4 - \frac{8}{4}x^3 + \frac{4}{4}x^2 = 3x^4 - 2x^3 + x^2$$

Step 3 Check the answer. In this example, because there is no remainder (or a remainder of 0), you can check the answer by multiplying:

$$\text{(quotient)} \bullet \text{(divisor)} = \text{(dividend)}$$
$$(3x^4 - 2x^3 + x^2) \bullet (4) = 12x^4 - 8x^3 + 4x^2$$

Example 2 Find the quotient of $(3x^3 - 5x^2 + 4x) \div x$.

Step 1 Rewrite the problem.

$$\frac{3x^3 - 5x^2 + 4x}{x} \quad \frac{\text{(dividend)}}{\text{(divisor)}}$$

Step 2 Divide each term of the numerator by the term in the denominator.

$$\frac{3x^3}{x} - \frac{5x^2}{x} + \frac{4x}{x} = 3x^{3-1} - 5x^{2-1} + 4x^{1-1}$$
$$= 3x^2 - 5x + 4$$

Step 3 Check the answer by multiplying.

$$\text{(quotient)} \bullet \text{(divisor)} = \text{(dividend)}$$
$$(3x^2 - 5x + 4) \bullet (x) = 3x^3 - 5x^2 + 4x$$

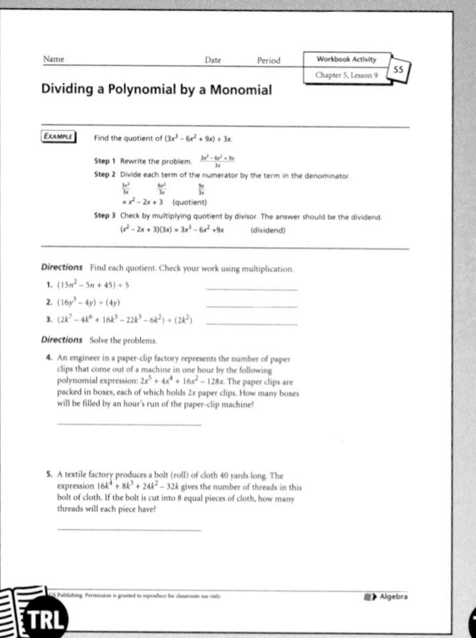

Name Date Period Workbook Activity 55 Chapter 5, Lesson 9

Dividing a Polynomial by a Monomial

Workbook Activity 55

Name Date Period Activity 51 Chapter 5, Lesson 9

Dividing a Polynomial by a Monomial

Activity 51

Be sure to watch for + and – signs when dividing polynomials.

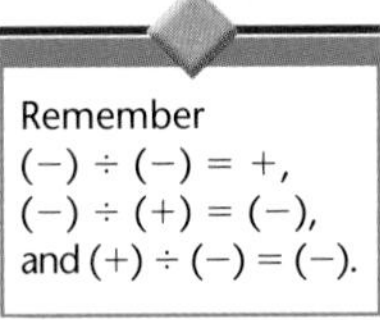

Remember
$(-) \div (-) = +$,
$(-) \div (+) = (-)$,
and $(+) \div (-) = (-)$.

EXAMPLE 3 $\frac{-3y^4}{-y^2} = 3y^2$; check: $(3y^2)(-y^2) = -3y^4$

while $\frac{-3y^4}{y^2} = -3y^2$; check: $(-3y^2)(y^2) = -3y^4$

and $\frac{3y^4}{-y^2} = -3y^2$; check: $(-3y^2)(-y^2) = 3y^4$

Students' answers should be supported by multiplication checks.

Exercise A Find each quotient. Check your work using multiplication.

1. $\frac{(16x^2 + 4)}{4}$ $4x^2 + 1$
2. $\frac{(9y^3 + 6y - 3)}{3}$ $3y^3 + 2y - 1$
3. $\frac{(-32x^3 + 24x^2 - 16x + 8)}{8}$ $-4x^3 + 3x^2 - 2x + 1$
4. $\frac{(-32a^3 + 24a^2 - 16a + 8)}{-4}$ $8a^3 - 6a^2 + 4a - 2$
5. $(7m^2 - 7m + 7) \div 7$ $m^2 - m + 1$
6. $(-18p^3 + 36p^2 + 9p) \div 9$ $-2p^3 + 4p^2 + p$

Exercise B Find each quotient. Check your work using multiplication.

7. $\frac{(26x^3 + 4x^2)}{x}$ $26x^2 + 4x$
8. $\frac{(-21y^9 - 6y^4 - 21y}{y}$ $-21y^8 - 6y^3 - 21$
9. $\frac{(23x^6 - 41m^4 + 31x^2)}{x^2}$ $23x^4 - 41x^2 + 31$
10. $(-5m^7 - 7m^2 + 7m) \div m$ $-5m^6 - 7m + 7$
11. $(-25x^6 + 14x^2 + 9x) \div -x$ $25x^5 - 14x - 9$
12. $\frac{(-32a^3 + 24a^2 - 16a)}{-4a}$ $8a^2 - 6a + 4$

Exercise C Find each quotient. Check your work using multiplication.

13. $\frac{(15y^5 + y^4 + 5y^3 - 17y^2 + y)}{y}$ $15y^4 + y^3 + 5y^2 - 17y + 1$
14. $\frac{(x^6 + 6x^5 - 15x^4 + 20x^3 - 15x^2)}{x^2}$ $x^4 + 6x^3 - 15x^2 + 20x - 15$
15. $\frac{(a^7 - 12a^6 - 18a^5 - 20a^3)}{-a^3}$ $-a^4 + 12a^3 + 18a^2 + 20$

3 Reinforce and Extend

LEARNING STYLES

Auditory/Verbal

Have students form groups of two or three. One student thinks "out loud" the process of dividing a polynomial by a monomial. A second student writes down the first student's solution. Group members check the answer together. All group members take turns thinking "out loud."

CALCULATOR

Have students use a calculator to solve the following problems:

$(784x^2 + 976x - 336) \div 16$
$(49x^2 + 61x - 21)$

$(42.201y^2 + 32.9793y + 3.126) \div 5.21$
$(8.1y^2 + 6.33y + 0.6)$

$(2.144x^3 - 5.36x) \div 0.67x$
$(3.2x^2 - 8)$

$(-16.47r^5 - 5.13r^4 + 9.45r^2) \div -2.7r^2$
$(6.1r^3 + 1.9r^2 - 3.5)$

$(10.962t^2 + 0.4176t + 1.131) \div -1.74$
$(-6.3t^2 - 0.24t - 0.65)$

Lesson at a Glance

Chapter 5 Lesson 10

Overview This lesson demonstrates how to divide a polynomial by a binomial.

Objective

- To divide a polynomial by a binomial

Student Pages 144–147

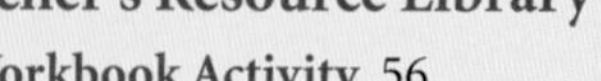

Teacher's Resource Library TRL

Workbook Activity 56

Activity 52

Alternative Activity 52

1 Warm-Up Activity

Have students write out the division steps for the following problems to prepare them for dividing a polynomial by a binomial.

$5768 \div 8$	*(721)*
$3110 \div 5$	*(622)*
$1300 \div 25$	*(52)*
$4565 \div 27$	*(169 r2)*
$466 \div 15$	*(31 r1)*

2 Teaching the Lesson

In order to help students make the connection between arithmetic division and algebraic division, make columns on the board to demonstrate the examples on pages 144 and 145.

Common Error

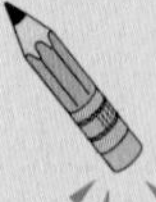

Stress the importance of keeping columns aligned when dividing. Some students may make crooked columns and become confused.

Lesson 10 Dividing a Polynomial by a Binomial

Dividing a polynomial by a binomial is similar to the long division you learned in arithmetic. As in arithmetic, division can result in a quotient and no remainder or a quotient and a remainder that is not zero.

Case I Remainder = 0

Example 1 Find the quotient of $345 \div 15$.

Step 1 Divide 15 into 34.

$$15\overline{)345} \text{ quotient } 2 \qquad 15\overline{)34} \text{ quotient } 2$$

Step 2 Multiply and subtract product.

$$\begin{array}{r} 2 \\ 15\overline{)345} \\ -\underline{30} \\ 4 \end{array} \qquad (2)(15) = 30 \qquad 34 - 30 = 4$$

Step 3 Bring down 5 and divide 15 into 45.

$$\begin{array}{r} 23 \\ 15\overline{)345} \\ -\underline{30} \\ 45 \end{array} \qquad 15\overline{)45} \text{ quotient } 3$$

Step 4 Multiply and subtract product.

$$\begin{array}{r} 23 \\ 15\overline{)345} \\ -\underline{30} \\ 45 \\ -\underline{45} \\ 0 \end{array} \qquad (3)(15) = 45 \qquad 45 - 45 = 0$$

Step 5 Check by multiplication.

$(23)(15) = 345$

Example 2 Find the quotient of $(x^2 - x - 6) \div (x + 2)$.

Step 1 Divide x into x^2.

$$\begin{array}{r} x \\ x + 2\overline{)x^2 - x - 6} \end{array} \qquad \begin{array}{r} x \\ x\overline{)x^2} \end{array}$$

Step 2 Multiply and subtract product.

$$\begin{array}{r} x \\ x + 2\overline{)x^2 - x - 6} \\ \underline{-(x^2 + 2x)} \\ -3x \end{array} \qquad \begin{array}{r} (x)(x + 2) = x^2 + 2x \\ x^2 - x \\ \underline{-x^2 - 2x} \\ 0 - 3x \end{array}$$

Step 3 Bring down -6 and divide x into $-3x$.

$$\begin{array}{r} x - 3 \\ x + 2\overline{)x^2 - x - 6} \\ \underline{-(x^2 + 2x)} \\ -3x - 6 \end{array} \qquad \begin{array}{r} -3 \\ x\overline{)-3x} \end{array}$$

Step 4 Multiply and subtract product.

$$\begin{array}{r} x - 3 \\ x + 2\overline{)x^2 - x - 6} \\ \underline{-(x^2 + 2x)} \\ -3x - 6 \\ \underline{-(-3x - 6)} \\ 0 \end{array} \qquad (-3)(x+2) = -3x-6$$

Step 5 Check by multiplication.

$(x - 3)(x + 2) = x^2 - x - 6$

Name Date Period — Workbook Activity 56, Chapter 5, Lesson 10

Dividing a Polynomial by a Binomial

Example Find the quotient of $(x^2 - 3x - 5) \div (x + 1)$.

$$\begin{array}{r} x - 4 \\ x + 1\overline{)x^2 - 3x - 5} \\ \underline{-(x^2 + x)} \\ -4x - 5 \\ \underline{-(-4x - 4)} \\ -1 \end{array} \text{ remainder}$$

Check by multiplication: $(x + 1)(x - 4) - 1 = x^2 - 3x - 5$

Directions Find each quotient. Identify any remainder.

1. $(2x^2 - x - 15) \div (2x + 5)$ ________
2. $(14a^2 - 26a - 4) \div (7a + 1)$ ________
3. $(5y^2 + 4y - 12) \div (y + 2)$ ________
4. $(3d^2 - 3d - 5) \div (d + 2)$ ________

Directions Tell what is wrong with the following division work. Show how to correct the error.

5. $$\begin{array}{r} x^4 \\ x + 3\overline{)x^5 + 3x - 9} \\ \underline{x^5 + 3x^4} \\ ? \end{array}$$

 Algebra

Workbook Activity 56

Name Date Period — Activity 52, Chapter 5, Lesson 10

Dividing a Polynomial by a Binomial

Directions Give the degree of each polynomial. Remember that monomials and binomials are types of polynomials.

1. $k^5 + 2k^4 - 8k^3 + 5k^2 - 4k - 16$ ________
2. $n^7 - 9$ ________
3. $b^2 + 15$ ________
4. $y^3 - 10y^2 - y + 8$ ________
5. $d - 11$ ________
6. $x^4 - 2x^2$ ________
7. $2n^3 - n^2 + 4$ ________
8. $m + 4$ ________
9. $y^9 - 3y^5 - 8y$ ________
10. $9k^2$ ________

Directions Find each quotient. Then check your work using multiplication.

$(a^2 + 6a + 9) \div (a + 3)$ **11.** Quotient: ________	**12.** Show checking. ________
$(x^2 - x - 10) \div (x + 2)$ **13.** Quotient: ________	**14.** Show checking. ________
$(x^3 + 6x^2 + 12x + 8) \div (x + 2)$ **15.** Quotient: ________	**16.** Show checking. ________
$(n^2 - 8n + 19) \div (n - 4)$ **17.** Quotient: ________	**18.** Show checking. ________
$(k^2 - 49) \div (k - 7)$ **19.** Quotient: ________	**20.** Show checking. ________

 Algebra

Activity 52

Case II Remainder $\neq 0$

Example 3 Find the quotient of $346 \div 15$.

Step 1 Divide 15 into 34.

$$15\overline{)346}\ \text{quotient } 2 \qquad 15\overline{)34}\ \text{quotient } 2$$

Step 2 Multiply and subtract product.

$(2)(15) = 30$

$$\begin{array}{r} 2 \\ 15\overline{)346} \\ -\underline{30} \\ 4 \end{array} \qquad 34 - 30 = 4$$

Step 3 Bring down 6 and divide 15 into 46.

$$\begin{array}{r} 23 \\ 15\overline{)346} \\ -\underline{30} \\ 46 \end{array} \qquad \begin{array}{r} 3 \\ 15\overline{)46} \end{array}$$

Step 4 Multiply and subtract product.

$(3)(15) = 45$

$$\begin{array}{r} 23 \\ 15\overline{)346} \\ -\underline{30} \\ 46 \\ -\underline{45} \\ 1 \text{ remainder} \end{array} \qquad 46 - 45 = 1$$

Step 5 Check by multiplication.

$(23)(15) + 1 = 346$

Example 4 Find the quotient of $(x^2 - x - 7) \div (x + 2)$.

Step 1 Divide x into x^2.

$$\begin{array}{r} x \\ (x + 2)\overline{)x^2 - x - 7} \end{array} \qquad \begin{array}{r} x \\ x\overline{)x^2} \end{array}$$

Step 2 Multiply and subtract product.

$(x)(x + 2) = x^2 + 2x$

$$\begin{array}{r} x \\ x + 2\overline{)x^2 - x - 7} \\ \underline{-(x^2 + 2x)} \\ -3x \end{array} \qquad \begin{array}{r} x^2 - x \\ \underline{-x^2 - 2x} \\ 0 - 3x \end{array}$$

Step 3 Bring down -7 and divide x into $-3x$.

$$\begin{array}{r} x - 3 \\ x + 2\overline{)x^2 - x - 7} \\ \underline{-(x^2 + 2x)} \\ -3x - 7 \end{array} \qquad \begin{array}{r} -3 \\ x\overline{)-3x} \end{array}$$

Step 4 Multiply and subtract product.

$(-3)(x+2) = -3x - 6$

$$\begin{array}{r} x - 3 \\ x + 2\overline{)x^2 - x - 7} \\ \underline{-(x^2 + 2x)} \\ -3x - 7 \\ \underline{-(-3x - 6)} \\ 0 - 1 \text{ remainder} \end{array}$$

Step 5 Check by multiplication.

$(x + 2)(x - 3) - 1 = x^2 - x - 6 - 1$
$= x^2 - x - 7$

Manipulatives

Dividing with Binomials

Materials: Algebra Tiles, Manipulatives Master 4 (Factor Frame)

Group Practice: Using the example $(2x^2 + 3x + 1) \div (x + 1)$ and the examples in the text, build models of the divisor and the dividend. Place the divisor on the left side of the Factor Frame. Arrange the dividend model pieces inside the Factor Frame so that they meet the two conditions, applying the Zero Rule if necessary. (See page T9, "Using the Factor Frame.") Explain that if after adding pairs of opposites to complete the rectangle there are extra pieces, these pieces represent the remainder. To find the quotient, fill in the top of the Factor Frame with the appropriate pieces to complete the arrangement. (Note: Learning how to arrange the pieces in the rectangle to meet the two conditions takes practice, especially when applying the Zero Rule. Spend as much time as necessary on guided practice for students to fully understand the process before assigning independent work.)

Student Practice: Have students use models for Exercise A, Problems 1–4, 6, 7 and 9, and Exercise B, Problems 11–15 and 18. Have them find the quotient or check answers obtained by using the division algorithm in the text.

Reinforce and Extend

Learning Styles

LEP/ESL

Even though ESL students may know how to divide a polynomial by a binomial, they may not know the English terms involved in the process. Before doing this lesson, have students use each term to label the example problems on pages 131 and 132. The terms to be used are *polynomial, binomial, quotient, dividend, divisor,* and *remainder.*

Learning Styles

Logical/Mathematical

Have students calculate these problems and explain the pattern that develops.

$(24x^2 + 216x + 480) \div (x + 5)$
$[(24)(x + 4)]$

$(24x^2 + 216x + 480) \div (2x + 10)$
$[(12)(x + 4)]$

$(24x^2 + 216x + 480) \div (3x + 15)$
$[(8)(x + 4)]$

$(24x^2 + 216x + 480) \div (4x + 20)$
$[(6)(x + 4)]$

$(24x^2 + 216x + 480) \div (6x + 30)$
$[(4)(x + 4)]$

(The pattern: the coefficient in the divisor and the coefficient in the quotient multiply to 24.)

Career Connection

Company accountants must figure out a company's annual budget. There are numerous restrictions they must consider. One restriction in creating a budget is a limited amount of money. Another restriction is that the amount that can be spent in each area is limited by an expression. Calculate the amount to be spent in each area.

Budget in dollars: $3x^2 + 15x + 18$

Area/limit

Advertising/3
Imports/$(x + 3)$
Milling/$(x + 2)$
Taxes/2
Labor/9

Amount Budgeted

$(x^2 + 5x + 6)$
$(3)(x + 2)$
$(3)(x + 3)$
$(1\frac{1}{2}x^2 + 7\frac{1}{2}x + 9)$
$(\frac{1}{3}x^2 + 1\frac{2}{3}x + 2)$

Check to be sure the powers are in descending order before dividing a polynomial.

If the coefficient of one power of the variable is zero, then mark its place with a zero. Be sure to keep terms with the same power aligned in the same column.

Example 5 Find the quotient of $\frac{(8p^3 - 125)}{2p - 5}$.

$$\begin{array}{r} 4p^2 + 10p + 25 \\ 2p - 5 \enclose{longdiv}{8p^3 + 0 + 0 - 125} \\ -(8p^3 - 20p^2) \\ \hline +20p^2 + 0 \\ -(20p^2 - 50p) \\ \hline +50p - 125 \\ -(50p - 125) \\ \hline 0 \quad 0 \end{array}$$

Check. $(4p^2 + 10p + 25)(2p - 5)$

$$\begin{array}{r} 8p^3 + 20p^2 + 50p \\ -20p^2 - 50p - 125 \\ 8p^3 - 125 \end{array}$$ True

Exercise A Find each quotient.

1. $\frac{x^2 - 2x - 8}{(x + 2)}$ $x - 4$
2. $\frac{x^2 + 8x + 15}{(x + 5)}$ $x + 3$
3. $\frac{x^2 - 5x + 6}{(x - 3)}$ $x - 2$
4. $\frac{x^2 - 3x + 2}{(x - 1)}$ $x - 2$
5. $\frac{x^2 + 5x - 50}{(x - 5)}$ $x + 10$
6. $\frac{x^2 - 11x + 28}{(x - 4)}$ $x - 7$
7. $\frac{x^2 + 10x + 24}{(x + 6)}$ $x + 4$
8. $\frac{x^2 - 36}{(x - 6)}$ $x + 6$
9. $\frac{x^2 - 4}{(x + 2)}$ $x - 2$
10. $\frac{x^2 - 100}{(x - 10)}$ $x + 10$

Exercise B Find each quotient. Identify any remainder.

11. $\frac{x^2 - 7x + 11}{(x - 2)}$ $x - 5$ r1

12. $\frac{x^2 + x - 15}{(x + 4)}$ $x - 3$ r -3

13. $\frac{x^2 + 9x + 9}{(x + 7)}$ $x + 2$ r -5

14. $\frac{x^2 - 8x + 15}{(x - 4)}$ $x - 4$ r -1

15. $\frac{x^2 - 2x - 22}{(x + 4)}$ $x - 6$ r2

Exercise C Find each quotient.

16. $\frac{15m^3 - 5m^2 - 6m + 2}{(3m - 1)}$

17. $\frac{-8m^2 - 14m - 16}{(2m + 5)}$

18. $\frac{a^2 - 16}{(a - 4)}$

19. $\frac{12y^3 - 3y^2 - 20y + 5}{(4y - 1)}$

20. $\frac{3x^3 + 7x^2 - 7x - 9}{(3x + 1)}$

21. $\frac{x^3 + x^2 - 22x + 8}{(x - 4)}$

22. $\frac{27p^3 - 8}{(3p - 2)}$

23. $\frac{2y^3 - 5y^2 + 39}{(2y + 3)}$

24. $\frac{8p^3 - 125}{(2p - 5)}$

25. $\frac{15z^4 - 15z + 1}{(3z^3 - 3)}$

16. $5m^2 - 2$
17. $-4m + 3$ r -31
18. $a + 4$
19. $3y^2 - 5$
20. $x^2 + 2x - 3$ r -6
21. $x^2 + 5x - 2$
22. $9p^2 + 6p + 4$
23. $y^2 - 4y + 6$ r21
24. $4p^2 + 10p + 25$
25. $5z$ r1

Exercise D Check your answers to Exercises A, B, and C by multiplying (quotient • divisor) and adding any remainder.

Estimation Activity

Estimate: Find the graphed relationship between x^3 and x^2.

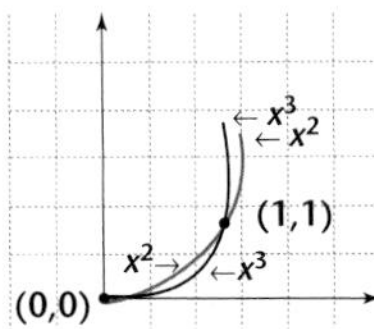

Solution: Look at the graph. Is $x^3 > x^2$ for all positive values of x? $x^3 = x^2$ when $x = 0$ or 1.

$x^3 < x^2$ when $0 < x < x^3 > x^2$ when $x > 1$ x^3 is $\leq x^2$ for all positive values of x.

Learning Styles

Interpersonal/ Group Learning

Have students work in small groups. Each student has his or her own paper, pencil, and book. Assign students problems to do from pages 146–147. Each student answers the problems and checks his or her answers with the other members of the group. Encourage students to show all their work.

Group Problem Solving

Have students work in small groups to create four word problems in which a polynomial is divided by a binomial. For example, "Some equation multiplied by the expression $(y + 2)$ is $(y^2 - y - 6)$. What is the equation?" Have groups exchange word problems to see whether they can solve them. As a class, review some of the word problems.

At Home

Have students make a table that shows a budget for running a household. They must include the following items in their household budget: mortgage/rent, food, electricity, other utilities, taxes, clothes, transportation, and entertainment. You may want them to include more areas. Limit the total amount of money they have each month by a polynomial. Have students limit the amount they spend on each item to a binomial.

Lesson at a Glance

Chapter 5 Lesson 11

Overview This lesson shows how to evaluate polynomial expressions when the values of two or more variables are given.

Objectives

- To evaluate polynomials with two or more variables
- To recognize the notation $P(x, y)$

Student Pages 148–149

Teacher's Resource Library 

Workbook Activity 57

Activity 53

Alternative Activity 53

Warm-Up Activity

Have students evaluate some increasingly complex algebraic expressions to prepare them for evaluating polynomial expressions.

$x - 4$ for $x = 10$ *(6)*

$7x$ for $x = 3$ *(21)*

$3x + 10$ for $x = 12$ *(46)*

$x^2 - 4$ for $x = 6$ *(32)*

$x^2 + 2x + 7$ for $x = 5$ *(42)*

$3x^2 - 2x + 23$ for $x = 0$ *(23)*

$x^3 + 10$ for $x = -5$ *(−115)*

Review that a negative number squared is positive and a negative number cubed is negative.

Teaching the Lesson

Explain that evaluating polynomials with two variables is very similar to evaluating the expressions in the Warm-Up Activity. Go through the first example in the textbook, paying special attention to the notation $P(x, y)$. Then choose two other values, such as $P(2, 3)$ and substitute them for the variables in the first example. Work through the steps on the board with the class. Discuss the other examples in the textbook with students. Have each student do problem 1 of Exercise A, then discuss their solutions as a class before assigning the other problems.

Lesson 11 Polynomials in Two or More Variables

The expression $(x + y)^2 = x^2 + 2xy + y^2$ is an example of a polynomial in two variables. The variables are x and y. The notation for "P of x and y equals $x^2 + 2xy + y^2$" is

$$P(x, y) = x^2 + 2xy + y^2.$$

The variables x and y are placeholders for numbers and are called independent variables. By replacing x and y with numbers, you evaluate the polynomial.

Example 1 Given: $P(x, y) = x^2 + 2xy + y^2$

Evaluate $P(x, y)$ for $x = 2$ and $y = -1$.

$$P(x, y) = P(2, -1) = (2)^2 + 2(2)(-1) + (-1)^2$$
$$= 4 - 4 + 1 = 1$$
$$P(2, -1) = 1$$

Example 2 Given: $P(x, y) = x^3 + 2x^2y + xy^2 + y^3$

Evaluate $P(x, y)$ for $x = 1$ and $y = -2$.

$$P(x, y) = P(1, -2) = 1^3 + 2(1)^2(-2) + (1)(-2)^2 + (-2)^3$$
$$= 1 - 4 + 4 - 8 = -7$$
$$P(1, -2) = -7$$

Example 3 Given: $P(x, y, z) = x^2y + xy^2z + y^2z^2$

Evaluate $P(x, y, z)$ for $x = -1$, $y = 2$, $z = 3$.

$$P(x, y, z) = P(-1, 2, 3) = (-1)^2(2) + (-1)(2^2)(3) + (2^2)(3^2)$$
$$= 2 - 12 + 36 = 26$$
$$P(-1, 2, 3) = 26$$

Name Date Period — Workbook Activity 57, Chapter 5, Lesson 11

Polynomials in Two or More Variables

Example Evaluate $P(x, y) = x^2 + xy + y^2$ for $x = 2$ and $y = -2$

Step 1 Substitute the variables with their values.

$P(2, -2) = (2)^2 + (2)(-2) + (-2)^2$

Step 2 Follow the order of operations.

$4 + -4 + 4$

Step 3 Add.

$4 + -4 + 4 = 4$

$P(x, y) = 4$

Directions Evaluate $P(x, y) = x^2 + xy + y^2$ for each set of values.

1. $x = 1, y = -2$ ______
2. $x = -1, y = 6$ ______
3. $x = \frac{1}{3}, y = -3$ ______
4. $x = -6, y = 5$ ______
5. $x = \frac{1}{2}, y = 8$ ______

Directions Evaluate $P(x, y) = x^3y^2 + x^2y + xy^3$ at

6. $P(1, 2)$ ______
7. $P(-3, -2)$ ______
8. $P(7, 0)$ ______
9. $P(8, 2)$ ______
10. $P(-1, -5)$ ______

Directions Evaluate $P(x, y, z) = x^3yz^2 + x^2y^2z^2 + xy^3 + yz$ for

11. $x = 1, y = 2, z = 1$ ______
12. $x = 1, y = 0, z = 4$ ______
13. $x = 2, y = -1, z = 3$ ______
14. $x = 0, y = 5, z = -1$ ______
15. $x = 2, y = -4, z = 0$ ______

 Algebra

Workbook Activity 57

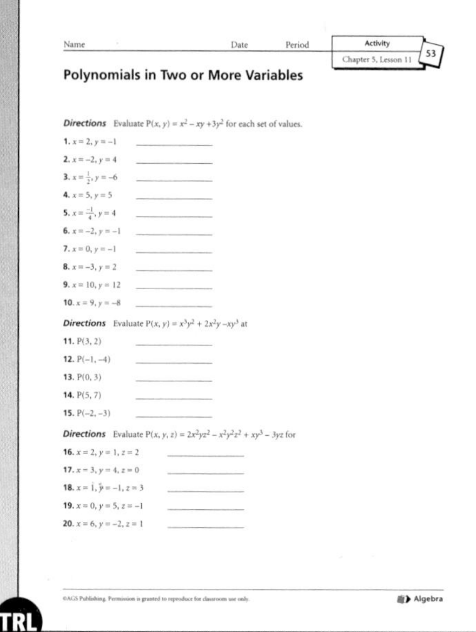

Name Date Period — Activity 53, Chapter 5, Lesson 11

Polynomials in Two or More Variables

Directions Evaluate $P(x, y) = x^2 - xy + 3y^2$ for each set of values.

1. $x = 2, y = -1$ ______
2. $x = -2, y = 4$ ______
3. $x = \frac{1}{2}, y = -6$ ______
4. $x = 5, y = 5$ ______
5. $x = \frac{-1}{4}, y = 4$ ______
6. $x = -2, y = -1$ ______
7. $x = 0, y = -1$ ______
8. $x = -3, y = 2$ ______
9. $x = 10, y = 12$ ______
10. $x = 9, y = -8$ ______

Directions Evaluate $P(x, y) = x^3y^2 + 2x^2y - xy^3$ at

11. $P(3, 2)$ ______
12. $P(-1, -4)$ ______
13. $P(0, 3)$ ______
14. $P(5, 7)$ ______
15. $P(-2, -3)$ ______

Directions Evaluate $P(x, y, z) = 2x^2yz^2 - x^2y^2z^2 + xy^3 - 3yz$ for

16. $x = 2, y = 1, z = 2$ ______
17. $x = 3, y = 4, z = 0$ ______
18. $x = 1, y = -1, z = 3$ ______
19. $x = 0, y = 5, z = -1$ ______
20. $x = 6, y = -2, z = 1$ ______

 Algebra

Activity 53

Exercise A Evaluate $P(x, y) = x^2 + xy + y^2$ for

1. $P(0, -1) = 1$	**1.** $x = 0, y = -1$
2. $P(-2, 5) = 19$	**2.** $x = -2, y = 5$
3. $P(\frac{1}{2}, -4) = 14\frac{1}{4}$	**3.** $x = \frac{1}{2}, y = -4$
4. $P(-3, 5) = 19$	**4.** $x = -3, y = 5$
5. $P(\frac{1}{3}, 9) = 84\frac{1}{9}$	**5.** $x = \frac{1}{3}, y = 9$

Exercise B Evaluate $P(x, y) = x^3y^2 + x^2y + xy^3$ at

6. $P(2, 1) = 14$	**6.** $P(2, 1)$
7. $P(-1, -1) = -1$	**7.** $P(-1, -1)$
8. $P(5, 0) = 0$	**8.** $P(5, 0)$
9. $P(9, 1) = 819$	**9.** $P(9, 1)$
10. $P(-2, -3) = -30$	**10.** $P(-2, -3)$

Exercise C Evaluate $P(x, y, z) = x^3yz^2 + x^2y^2z^2 + xy^3 + yz$ for

11. $P(1, 1, 1) = 4$	**11.** $x = 1, y = 1, z = 1$
12. $P(-1, 0, 5) = 0$	**12.** $x = -1, y = 0, z = 5$
13. $P(2, -1, 2) = -20$	**13.** $x = 2, y = -1, z = 2$
14. $P(0, 5, -2) = -10$	**14.** $x = 0, y = 5, z = -2$
15. $P(1, -2, -3) = 25$	**15.** $x = 1, y = -2, z = -3$

Common Error

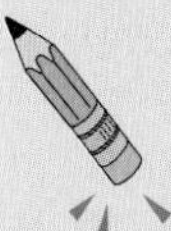

Explain that with more complex polynomials, it is important to use parentheses to separate the evaluated elements of the expression. Parentheses help students to follow the order of operations.

3 Reinforce and Extend

Learning Styles

Interpersonal/ Group Learning

After students have worked through the exercises, separate the class into pairs. Direct each partner to come up with new sets of values for x and y and trade those values with their partner. Each partner can evaluate the polynomial for Exercise A and the polynomial for Exercise B. Partners can then check each other's work.

Calculator

Have students use their calculators to evaluate the polynomial expressions in Exercise A, Exercise B, and Exercise C, using the following values:

Exercise A for $x = 17$ and $y = -31$ *(723)*

Exercise B for $x = 13$ and $y = -20$ *(771,420)*

Exercise C for $x = 17, y = 18$, and $z = -13$ *(30,730,284)*

Online Connection

Students can visit tcaep.co.uk/astro/planets/index.htm to practice using scientific notation. The Internet site includes many statistics on each planet and its satellites. Ask students to choose two planets to compare volumes and masses. For example, Earth's mass is listed as 5.9736×10^{24} kg, and Jupiter's mass is $1{,}896.6 \times 10^{24}$ kg. Ask students to calculate the difference and then to put the answer in proper scientific notation form.

Lesson at a Glance

Chapter 5 Application

Overview This lesson shows an application of polynomials—calculating compound interest.

Objective

- To use a formula to calculate compound interest

Student Page 150

Teacher's Resource Library 

Application Activity 5

Everyday Algebra 5

Warm-Up Activity

Introduce the idea of simple interest by telling students that a five-percent return gives you $5 for every $100 you have in an account per year. Ask, "How much interest will I have in two years?" *($10)* "How much will I have in three years?" *($15)* Now propose the situation in which you receive your interest every six months instead of at the end of every one, two, or three years. Ask, "At the end of the first year will I have more or less than $5 interest?" *(More, because your interest was compounded)*

Teaching the Lesson

Show students how to use the formula by going over the example on page 150. Create several other examples.

Common Error

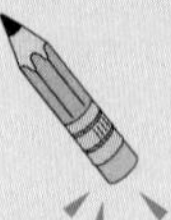

Review the order of operations with the class to prevent confusion over which operations need to be performed first.

Order of Operations

First, do all operations inside parentheses.

Second, do exponents.

Third, do multiplication and division from left to right.

Fourth, do addition and subtraction from left to right.

Application

Polynomial Interest

One type of savings account is a simple savings account. If you invest an amount, P, called the principal, at an annual interest rate of r, you will have $P + (P \cdot r)$ dollars at the end of one year. If you let S stand for savings, you can write this as

$$S = P + (P \cdot r) \text{ or } S = P(1 + r).$$

How much savings will you have if you place $100 for one year in an account that pays 5 percent interest?

$$S = P(1 + r)$$
$$S = \$100(1 + .05) = \$105$$

If you leave your savings in the account for a second year, the new principal is $105. The amount of savings becomes

$$S = [P(1 + r)](1 + r) \text{ or } S = P(1 + r)^2$$

If a principal, P, is invested at an interest rate, r, and interest is compounded annually for t years, the total savings will be $S = P(1 + r)^t$.

In some savings accounts, interest is computed (or compounded) more frequently than once a year. Some accounts compound interest quarterly (four times a year); some compound interest daily!

Example 1 You place $100 in a savings account. The annual interest rate is 5 percent and is compounded quarterly. What is your total savings after one year? In this example, $P = \$100$; $r = 5$ percent; $n = 4$, the number of times the interest is compounded in a year; and $t = 1$, the number of years.

$$S = P(1 + \tfrac{r}{n})^{nt}$$
$$S = 100(1 + \tfrac{.05}{4})^{4 \cdot 1}$$
$$S = 100(1 + 0.0125)^4$$
$$S = 100(1.0509453) = \$105.09$$

Exercise Find the amount of savings in each instance.

1. $1,000 deposited for one year at 5 percent annual interest, compounded every six months. $1,050.63
2. $1,000 deposited for one year at 5 percent annual interest, compounded quarterly. $1,050.95
3. $1,000 deposited for two years at 5 percent annual interest, compounded quarterly. $1,104.49
4. $1,000 deposited for three years at 8 percent annual interest, compounded annually. $1,259.71
5. $1,000 deposited for three years at 8 percent annual interest, compounded quarterly. $1,268.24

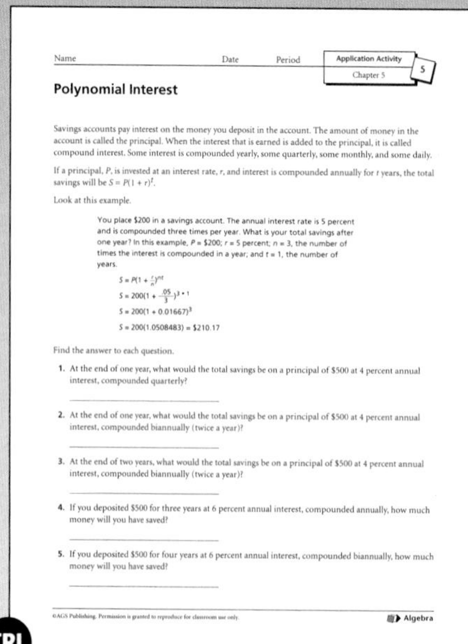

Name Date Period | Application Activity 5 | Chapter 5

Polynomial Interest

Savings accounts pay interest on the money you deposit in the account. The amount of money in the account is called the principal. When the interest that is earned is added to the principal, it is called compound interest. Some interest is compounded yearly, some quarterly, some monthly, and some daily.

If a principal, P, is invested at an interest rate, r, and interest is compounded annually for t years, the total savings will be $S = P(1 + r)^t$.

Look at this example.

You place $200 in a savings account. The annual interest rate is 5 percent and is compounded three times per year. What is your total savings after one year? In this example, $P = \$200$; $r = 5$ percent; $n = 3$, the number of times the interest is compounded in a year; and $t = 1$, the number of years.

$$S = P(1 + \tfrac{r}{n})^{nt}$$
$$S = 200(1 + \tfrac{.05}{3})^{3 \cdot 1}$$
$$S = 200(1 + 0.01667)^3$$
$$S = 200(1.0508483) = \$210.17$$

Find the answer to each question.

1. At the end of one year, what would the total savings be on a principal of $500 at 4 percent annual interest, compounded quarterly? ______
2. At the end of one year, what would the total savings be on a principal of $500 at 4 percent annual interest, compounded biannually (twice a year)? ______
3. At the end of two years, what would the total savings be on a principal of $500 at 4 percent annual interest, compounded biannually (twice a year)? ______
4. If you deposited $500 for three years at 6 percent annual interest, compounded annually, how much money will you have saved? ______
5. If you deposited $500 for four years at 6 percent annual interest, compounded biannually, how much money will you have saved? ______

 Algebra

TRL Application Activity 5

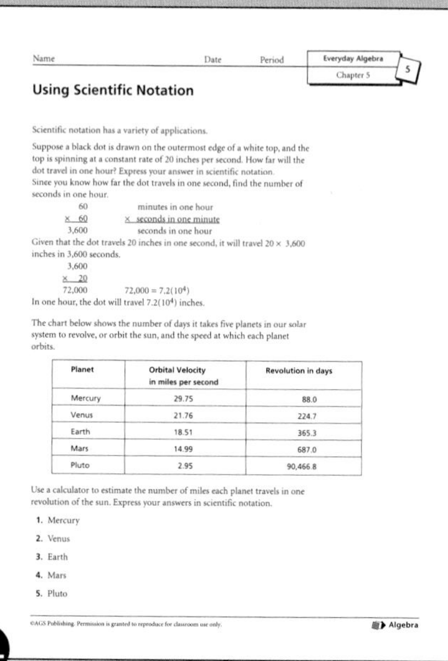

Name Date Period | Everyday Algebra 5 | Chapter 5

Using Scientific Notation

Scientific notation has a variety of applications.

Suppose a black dot is drawn on the outermost edge of a white top, and the top is spinning at a constant rate of 20 inches per second. How far will the dot travel in one hour? Express your answer in scientific notation.
Since you know how far the dot travels in one second, find the number of seconds in one hour.

60	minutes in one hour
× 60	× seconds in one minute
3,600	seconds in one hour

Given that the dot travels 20 inches in one second, it will travel 20 × 3,600 inches in 3,600 seconds.

3,600
× 20
72,000 $\quad 72{,}000 = 7.2(10^4)$

In one hour, the dot will travel $7.2(10^4)$ inches.

The chart below shows the number of days it takes five planets in our solar system to revolve, or orbit the sun, and the speed at which each planet orbits.

Planet	Orbital Velocity in miles per second	Revolution in days
Mercury	29.75	88.0
Venus	21.76	224.7
Earth	18.51	365.3
Mars	14.99	687.0
Pluto	2.95	90,466.8

Use a calculator to estimate the number of miles each planet travels in one revolution of the sun. Express your answers in scientific notation.

1. Mercury
2. Venus
3. Earth
4. Mars
5. Pluto

 Algebra

TRL Everyday Algebra 5

Chapter 5 REVIEW

Write the letter of the correct answer.

1. Simplify $(x^6)^3$. C

A x^9 | C x^{18}
B x^3 | D x^2

2. Simplify $[(a + b)^3]^2$. D

A $(a + b)^{\frac{3}{2}}$ | C $(a + b)^1$
B $(a + b)^5$ | D $(a + b)^6$

3. Find the quotient of $\frac{4^5}{4^4}$. A

A 4 | C 1
B $1\frac{1}{4}$ | D 64

4. Find the quotient of $(4x + 2y)^5 \div (4x + 2y)^7$, $4x + 2y \neq 0$. C

A $(4x + 2y)^2$ | C $(4x + 2y)^{-2}$
B $(4x + 2y)^{12}$ | D $(4x + 2y)^{\frac{5}{7}}$

5. What is 4,000,000,000 in scientific notation? B

A $4.0 \cdot 10^8$ | C 40^9
B $4.0 \cdot 10^9$ | D $4.0 \cdot 10^{10}$

6. What is $3.14(10^{-4})$ in standard notation? B

A 31,400 | C 0.00314
B 0.000314 | D 3.000014

Name Date Period | Mastery Test A, Page 1 | Chapter 5

Chapter 5 Mastery Test A

Directions Circle the letter of the correct answer.

1. Simplify $(x^5)^6$.
   A x^{-1} C x^{15}
   B x^{11} D x^{30}
2. Rewrite $\frac{1}{(4^3)}$ using a negative exponent.
   A 12^{-3} C 4^{-3}
   B $\frac{1}{(4^{-3})}$ D 3^4
3. What is 0.0078 in scientific notation?
   A $7.8(10^3)$ C $78(10^{-4})$
   B $0.78(10^{-2})$ D $7.8(10^{-3})$
4. What is $3.5(10^4)$ in standard form?
   A 14 C 0.00035
   B 35,000 D 350,000
5. Simplify $\frac{5^3}{5^2}$.
   A 5 C 15
   B $1\frac{1}{2}$ D 225

Directions Rewrite using a negative exponent.

6. $\frac{1}{p^7}$, $p \neq 0$ ____________
7. $\frac{1}{(r + 2s)^4}$, $r + 2s \neq 0$ ____________

Directions Find each sum, difference, product, or quotient. Express your answer in scientific notation.

8. $1.2(10^{-2}) + 4.1(10^{-2})$ ____________
9. $9.7(10^{-3}) - 5.6(10^{-3})$ ____________
10. $5.6(10^3) \div 1.4(10^{-2})$ ____________

 Algebra

TRL

Name Date Period | Mastery Test A, Page 2 | Chapter 5

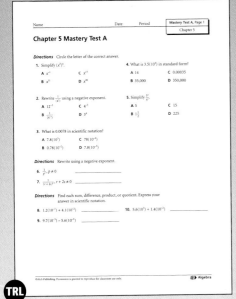

Chapter 5 Mastery Test A, continued

Directions Find each sum or difference.

11. $(2y^5 + 3y^4 + y + 1) + (8y^5 - 3y^4 + 4y - 7)$ ____________
12. $(w^7 - w^2 + w) - (w^6 + w^3 - w)$ ____________
13. $(10p^4 + p^3 - 4p^2 - 8) - (-12p^4 + 5p^3 - 2p + 3)$ ____________

Directions Multiply.

14. $3y^2(y - 4)$ ____________
15. $(-7h - 3)(2h - 2)$ ____________
16. $(c - 1)(-8c^2 + c - 5)$ ____________

Directions Divide.

17. $\frac{-30d^8 + 50}{-5}$ ____________
18. $22z^4 - 14z^2 \div -2z^2$ ____________
19. $\frac{2w^2 + 7w + 6}{(w + 2)}$ ____________
20. $\frac{30a^3 - 26a^2 - 36a + 8}{(10a - 2)}$ ____________

 Algebra

TRL

Chapter 5 Mastery Test A

3 Reinforce and Extend

IN THE COMMUNITY

Have students bring in a local newspaper to use to find the local interest rate on car loans, home mortgages, and personal loans. Have students calculate the compound interest on cars, homes, and personal mortgages.

LEARNING STYLES

Visual/Spatial

Have students calculate the simple interest and the compound interest for the problems on page 150. To compare the different answers, have students construct bar graphs for each problem, using graph paper and colored pencils or markers.

Chapter 5 Review

Each set of problems in the Chapter Review includes an example and solution to illustrate the concept. Use the given examples for reteaching the materials in Chapter 5. For additional practice, refer to the Supplementary Problems for Chapter 5 (pages 414–415).

Chapter 5 Mastery Test 

The Teacher's Resource Library includes parallel forms of the Chapter 5 Mastery Test. The difficulty level of the two forms is equivalent. You may wish to use one form as a pretest and the other form as a posttest.

ALTERNATIVE ASSESSMENT

Alternative Assessment items correlate with student Goals for Learning at the beginning of this chapter.

■ **To recognize and use exponents in computations**

Have students show the difference between several groups of exponential expressions such as the following:

$(x^2)(x^3)$ and $(x^2)^3$
$[(1^2) \cdot (x^3) = x^5; (x^2)^3 = x^6]$

$(n^5)(n^2)$ and $(x^5)^2$
$[(n^5) \cdot (n^2) = n^7; (n^5)^2 = x^{10}]$

$(y^4)(x^9)$ and $(y^4)^9$
$[(y^4) \cdot (y^9) = y^{13}; (y^4)^9 = y^{36}]$

(Note: Students may decide to show their answers by writing out the number of variables—for example, 6 x's instead of x^6—rather than using exponents. Explain how using exponents reduces the chance of error.)

■ **To identify the benefit of using scientific notation in some calculations**

Have students identify and explain why some professions use scientific notation. Have a student write out a very large number and a very small number, such as x^{36} or y^{-41}. *(Examples should include professions that deal in very large and very small numbers—microbiologists, atomic scientists, astronomers, astronauts, etc. Scientific notation is beneficial because it's less likely you'll make calculation errors. It is also less cumbersome to write out very large or very small numbers.)*

■ **To define, name, and solve polynomials**

On a piece of paper, have students draw a table with ten wide rows and four columns. Label the first column *Polynomial*, the second column *Degree*, the third column *Not*, and the fourth column *Why Not*. Then have students make up several polynomials, and write the degree of each. In the third column have them write several expressions that are not polynomials. In the fourth column, have them explain why the expressions are not polynomials. Lastly, ask students to multiply the 5 pairs of polynomials in rows 1 and 2, 3 and 4, and so on.

Find the sum, difference, product, or quotient.
Write your answer in scientific notation.

Example: $2(10^3) + 2(10^3)$ Solution: $2(10^3) + 2(10^3) = 4(10^3)$

7. $3.1(10^{-4}) + 4.2(10^{-4})$ $7.3(10^{-4})$

8. $4.7(10^{-2}) - 3.6(10^{-2})$ $1.1(10^{-2})$

9. $1.3(10^{-6}) \cdot 4.2(10^{-4}) \cdot 1.9(10^{2})$ $1.0374(10^{-7})$

10. $8.58(10^{-4}) \div 4.29(10^{-4})$ 2.0

11. $0.2825(10^{-6}) \div 1.13(10^{2})$ $2.5(10^{-9})$

Find the sum and the difference for each pair of polynomials.

Example: $x^2 + 2y + 2$, $x^2 - y + 1$ Solution: Add
$$\begin{array}{r} x^2 + 2y + 2 \\ + \; x^2 - y + 1 \\ \hline 2x^2 + y + 3 \end{array}$$

Subtract
$$\begin{array}{r} x^2 + 2y + 2 \\ - \; (x^2 - y + 1) \\ \hline \end{array} = \begin{array}{r} x^2 + 2y + 2 \\ (-1)(x^2 - y + 1) \\ \hline \end{array} = \begin{array}{r} x^2 + 2y + 2 \\ - \; x^2 + y - 1 \\ \hline 3y + 1 \end{array}$$

12. $3y^5 + 2y^3 + 1y + 3$
$4y^5 + 5y^3 - 7y - 8$

13. $2x^4 - 4x^3 - 6x^2 + 8x + 10$
$3x^4 + 5x^3 + 7$

14. $b^4 + 4b^3 - 6b^2 + 4b - 1$
$-3b^4 - 3b^3 - 5b^2 - 4b$

15. $m^5 + m^3 - 5$
$m^4 + m^2 + 5$

16. $4x^4 + 8x^3 + 16x^2 + 4$
$4x^3 + 2x^2 + 16x$

12. $7y^5 + 7y^3 - 6y - 5; -y^5 - 3y^3 + 8y + 11$
13. $5x^4 + x^3 - 6x^2 + 8x + 17; -x^4 - 9x^3 - 6x^2 + 8x + 3$
14. $-2b^4 + b^3 - 11b^2 - 1; 4b^4 + 7b^3 - b^2 + 8b - 1$
15. $m^5 + m^4 + m^3 + m^2; m^5 - m^4 + m^3 - m^2 - 10$
16. $4x^4 + 12x^3 + 18x^2 + 16x + 4; 4x^4 + 4x^3 + 14x^2 - 16x + 4$

Name Date Period **Mastery Test B, Page 1** Chapter 5

Chapter 5 Mastery Test B

Directions Circle the letter of the correct answer.

1. What is $4.5(10^4)$ in standard form?
A 18 **C** 0.00045
B 45,000 **D** 450,000

2. Simplify $(x^4)^5$.
A x^{-1} **C** x^{10}
B x^9 **D** x^{20}

3. Rewrite $\frac{1}{(4^4)}$ using a negative exponent.
A 16^{-4} **C** 4^{-4}
B $\frac{1}{(4^{-4})}$ **D** 4^4

4. Simplify $\frac{(6^3)}{(6^2)}$.
A 6 **C** 18
B $1\frac{1}{2}$ **D** 256

5. What is 0.0068 in scientific notation?
A $6.8(10^3)$ **C** $68(10^{-4})$
B $0.68(10^{-2})$ **D** $6.8(10^{-3})$

Directions Rewrite using a negative exponent.

6. $\frac{1}{x^3}, x \neq 0$ ________

7. $\frac{1}{(n + 3m)^2}, n + 3m \neq 0$ ________

Directions Find each sum, difference, product, or quotient. Express your answer in scientific notation.

8. $3.4(10^{-4}) + 0.8(10^{-4})$ ________

9. $8.7(10^{-2}) - 2.3(10^{-2})$ ________

10. $6.3(10^5) \div 1.5(10^{-3})$ ________

 Algebra

TRL

Name Date Period **Mastery Test B, Page 2** Chapter 5

Chapter 5 Mastery Test B, continued

Directions Find each sum or difference.

11. $(4y^3 + 3y^2 + y + 1) + (10y^6 - 4y^5 + 6y - 3)$ ________

12. $(n^5 - n^3 + n) + (n^8 + n^4 - n)$ ________

13. $(7z^7 + z^4 + 5z^2) - (-10z^6 + 3z^4 - 2z + 8)$ ________

Directions Multiply.

14. $2r^3(r - 2)$ ________

15. $(-3d - 7)(6d - 1)$ ________

16. $(m - 2)(-6m^2 + 2m - 9)$ ________

Directions Divide.

17. $\frac{-25q^2 + 75}{-25}$ ________

18. $12a^3 - 18a^2 \div -3a$ ________

19. $\frac{4z^2 + 12z + 8}{(z + 1)}$ ________

20. $\frac{24ac^3 - 4c^3 + -40c^2 + 12}{(12c + -4)}$ ________

 Algebra

TRL

Chapter 5 Mastery Test B

17. $18x^4 + 2x^3 - 14x^2$

18. $9x^5 + 27x^4$

19. $-12y^3 - 12y^2 - 12y - 12$

20. $x^2 + 9x + 20$

21. $4x^2 - 5x - 6$

22. $m^6 + 2m^5 + m^4$

23. $2m^7 + 3m^6 + 2m^4 + 10m^3 + 15m^2 + 10$

Find the product.

Example: $(x + 2)(x + 2)$ Solution: $(x + 2)(x + 2) = x(x + 2) + 2(x + 2)$
$= x^2 + 4x + 4$

17. $2x^2(9x^2 + x - 7)$

18. $(x + 3)(9x^4)$

19. $(4y^2 + 4)(-3y - 3)$

20. $(x + 5)(x + 4)$

21. $(4x + 3)(x - 2)$

22. $(m^3 + m^2)^2$

23. $(m^4 + 5)(2m^3 + 3m^2 + 2)$

Find the quotients. Identify any remainder. Use multiplication to check your answer.

Example: $\frac{10x^2 + 20x + 5}{5}$ Solution: $\frac{10x^2 + 20x + 5}{5} = 2x^2 + 4x + 1$

24. $\frac{(12y^3 - 18y - 36)}{6}$ $2y^3 - 3y - 6$

25. $\frac{(-30x^3 + 25x^2 - 20x + 10)}{-5}$ $6x^3 - 5x^2 + 4x - 2$

26. $\frac{(p^2 - 2p)^2}{(p^2 - 2p)}$ $p^2 - 2p$

27. $\frac{(3x^2 - 6x)}{x(x - 2)}$ 3

28. $(33x^3 + 24x^2 + 18x - 12) \div 3x$ $11x^2 + 8x + 6$ r–12

29. $(x^3 - 49x) \div (x + 7)$ $(x^2 - 7x)$ or $x(x - 7)$

30. $(5x - 1)\overline{)15x^3 - 13x^2 - 18x + 4}$ $3x^2 - 2x - 4$

Test-Taking Tip

When you study for chapter tests, practice the step-by-step formulas and procedures.

Chapter

Planning Guide
Factoring

		Student Text Lesson			
		Student Pages	Vocabulary	Practice Exercises	Solutions Key
Lesson 1	Greatest Common Factor	156–159	✔	✔	✔
Lesson 2	Factoring Polynomials	160–161		✔	✔
Lesson 3	Factoring Trinomials: $x^2 + bx + c$	162–163		✔	✔
Lesson 4	Factoring Trinomials: $ax^2 + bx + c$	164–165		✔	✔
Lesson 5	Factoring Expressions: $a^2 - b^2$	166–167	✔	✔	✔
Lesson 6	Factoring Expressions: $a^2 + 2ab + b^2$	168–171	✔	✔	✔
Lesson 7	Zero as a Factor	172–173		✔	✔
Lesson 8	Solving Quadratic Equations—Factoring	174–177	✔	✔	✔
Application	Frame Factor	178		✔	✔

Chapter Activities

Teacher's Resource Library

Estimation Exercise 6: Estimating Factors
Application Activity 6: Frame Factor
Everyday Algebra 6: Using Formulas
Community Connection 6: Exact or Estimated Measurements

Teacher's Edition

Chapter 6 Project

Assessment Options

Student Text

Chapter 6 Review

Teacher's Resource Library

Chapter 6 Mastery Tests A and B

Student Text Features							Teaching Strategies							Learning Styles						Teacher's Resource Library			
Estimation Activity	Algebra in Your Life	Technology Connection	Writing About Mathematics	Try This	Problem Solving	Calculator Practice	Online Connection	Common Error	Applications Home, Career, Community	Mental Math	Manipulatives	Calculator	Group Problem Solving	Auditory/Verbal	Visual/Spatial	Logical/Mathematical	Body/Kinesthetic	Interpersonal/Group Learning	LEP/ESL	Activities	Alternate Activities	Workbook Activities	Self-Study Guide
	157					159		159		158		159			157				158	54	54	58	✔
			161					161								161				55	55	59	✔
					163				163		163		163	163						56	56	60	✔
								165	165		165									57	57	61	✔
			167		167				167				167		167					58	58	62	✔
			171		171		171	169					171	170	170		169		169	59	59	63	✔
				173						173	173				173					60	60	64	✔
176		177			177					176	175		177	177				176	175	61	61	65	✔
									178								179						✔

Software Options

Skill Track Software

Use the Skill Track Software for *Algebra* for additional reinforcement of this chapter. The software provides multiple-choice assessment items for students to access by computer.

Solutions Key

Use the Solutions Key with this chapter to help students who may need additional assistance. The Solutions Key CD provides solutions for every exercise in the student edition.

Other Resources

Alternative Activities

The Teacher's Resource Library (TRL) contains a set of worksheets written at a second-grade reading level called Alternative Activities. They cover the same content as the regular Activities.

Manipulatives

See the Manipulative activities in this chapter for hands-on modeling of the content. The following TRL pages can also be used:

Manipulatives Master 4 (Factor Frame)
Algebra Tiles

Chapter at a Glance

Chapter 6: Factoring

pages 154–181

Lessons

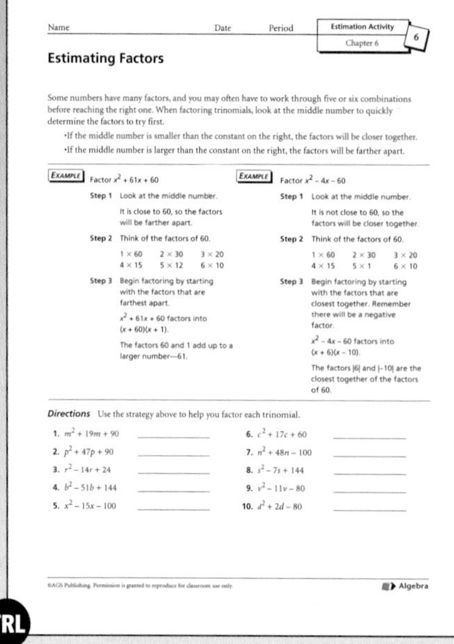

Name ____ Date ____ Period ____ Estimation Activity 6 Chapter 6

Estimating Factors

Some numbers have many factors, and you may often have to work through five or six combinations before reaching the right one. When factoring trinomials, look at the middle number to quickly determine the factors to try first.

- If the middle number is smaller than the constant on the right, the factors will be closer together.
- If the middle number is larger than the constant on the right, the factors will be farther apart.

EXAMPLE Factor $x^2 + 61x + 60$

Step 1 Look at the middle number.
It is close to 60, so the factors will be farther apart.

Step 2 Think of the factors of 60.
1×60 2×30 3×20
4×15 5×12 6×10

Step 3 Begin factoring by starting with the factors that are farthest apart.
$x^2 + 61x + 60$ factors into $(x + 60)(x + 1)$.
The factors 60 and 1 add up to a larger number—61.

EXAMPLE Factor $x^2 - 4x - 60$

Step 1 Look at the middle number.
It is not close to 60, so the factors will be closer together.

Step 2 Think of the factors of 60.
1×60 2×30 3×20
4×15 5×1 6×10

Step 3 Begin factoring by starting with the factors that are closest together. Remember there will be a negative factor.
$x^2 - 4x - 60$ factors into $(x + 6)(x - 10)$.
The factors $|6|$ and $|-10|$ are the closest together of the factors of 60.

Directions Use the strategy above to help you factor each trinomial.

1. $m^2 + 19m + 90$ ____
2. $p^2 + 47p + 90$ ____
3. $r^2 - 14r + 24$ ____
4. $b^2 - 51b + 144$ ____
5. $x^2 - 15x - 100$ ____
6. $c^2 + 17c + 60$ ____
7. $n^2 + 48n - 100$ ____
8. $s^2 - 7s + 144$ ____
9. $v^2 - 11v - 80$ ____
10. $d^2 + 2d - 80$ ____

 Algebra

TRL

Estimation Exercise 6

Name ____ Date ____ Period ____ Community Connection 6 Chapter 6

Exact or Estimated Measurements

Recall that *perimeter* describes the distance around a polygon and *circumference* describes the distance around a circle. In some situations, an estimate of perimeter or circumference is useful. For example, if you exercise by jogging the same route each day, you might describe the length of that route as *about 3 miles* or *about 5 kilometers*.

In other situations, an exact measure of perimeter or circumference is necessary. For example, the speedometer and odometer of a motor vehicle are calibrated for tires of a known circumference. If you install tires of a different circumference on a motor vehicle, the accuracy of the speedometer and odometer will be affected.

Find other examples in your school, home, and community in which estimates and exact measures of perimeter or circumference are required. Record your examples in this chart. One entry has been completed for you. After your chart is complete, share your findings with your classmates.

Application and Description	Perimeter or Circumference	Exact or Estimate
carpentry/woodworking: moldings used to trim a window or door	perimeter	exact

 Algebra

TRL

Community Connection 6

Chapter

Factoring

If there are eight cars parked in a row and there are four rows, how many cars are in the parking lot? The quickest way to the answer is by multiplying eight by four to get 32. You can also do it the other way around. Suppose you know that the parking lot has 32 spaces and you know there are four rows. How many cars are in each row? You divide 32 by four and get eight. To simplify algebraic expressions, you must divide, or factor. Knowing the multiplication tables makes factoring easy.

In Chapter 6, you will factor integers and algebraic expressions.

Goals for Learning

- ◆ To completely factor integers
- ◆ To find the greatest common factor of polynomials
- ◆ To factor trinomials
- ◆ To factor algebraic expressions
- ◆ To identify zero as a factor
- ◆ To use factoring as a means of solving equations

TRL

Name Date Period *SELF-STUDY GUIDE*

CHAPTER 6: Factoring

Goal 6.1 *To completely factor integers*

Date	Assignment	Score
______	1: Read pages 156–158. Complete Exercises A–C on pages 158–159.	______
______	2: Read and complete the Calculator Practice on page 159.	______
______	3: Complete Workbook Activity 58.	______

Comments:

Goal 6.2 *To find the greatest common factor of polynomials*

Date	Assignment	Score
______	4: Read pages 160–161. Complete Exercise A on page 161.	______
______	5: Complete Workbook Activity 59.	______

Comments:

Goal 6.3 *To factor trinomials*

Date	Assignment	Score
______	6: Read pages 162–163. Complete Exercises A–C on page 163.	______
______	7: Complete Workbook Activity 60.	______
______	8: Read pages 164–165. Complete Exercises A–C on page 165.	______
______	9: Complete Workbook Activity 61.	______

Comments:

 Algebra

TRL

Name Date Period *SELF-STUDY GUIDE*

CHAPTER 6: Factoring, continued

Goal 6.4 *To factor algebraic expressions*

Date	Assignment	Score
______	10: Read pages 166–167. Complete Exercises A–E on page 167.	______
______	11: Complete Workbook Activity 62.	______
______	12: Read pages 168–169. Complete Exercises A–D on pages 169–171.	______
______	13: Complete Workbook Activity 63.	______

Comments:

Goal 6.5 *To identify zero as a factor*

Date	Assignment	Score
______	14: Read page 172. Complete Exercises A–B on page 173.	______
______	15: Complete Workbook Activity 64.	______

Comments:

Goal 6.6 *To use factoring as a means of solving equations*

Date	Assignment	Score
______	16: Read pages 174–175. Complete Exercises A–D on pages 176–177.	______
______	17: Complete Workbook Activity 65.	______
______	18: Read and complete the Application Exercise on page 178.	______
______	19: Complete the Chapter 6 Review on pages 179–181.	______

Comments:

Student's Signature ______________ Date ________

Instructor's Signature ______________ Date ________

 Algebra

Chapter 6 Self-Study Guide

Introducing the Chapter

Use the information in the chapter opener to emphasize that algebra has many applications in life. For example, city planners use algebraic expressions to plan parking lots. Factoring a polynomial can help you model dimensions for a room or garden. Factoring is one way to solve quadratic equations. The solutions from your quadratic equations, for example, can be used to frame pictures or model the motion of a projectile.

Chapter Project

Have students keep a math journal for the chapter. Write in their own words explanations for the concepts presented in each lesson and illustrated definitions. Suggest they also make diagrams or charts to show the steps in factoring different types of polynomials.

When the class has completed the chapter, divide them into one group per lesson. To share their journals, each group can create a poster, model, or demonstration to illustrate one or more concepts from the chapter.

Teacher's Resource

The AGS Publishing Teaching Strategies in Math Transparencies may be used with this chapter. They add an interactive dimension to expand and enhance the program content.

Career Interest Inventory

The AGS Publishing Harrington-O'Shea Career Decision-Making System-Revised (CDM) may be used with this chapter. Students can use the CDM to explore their interests and identify careers. The CDM defines career areas that are indicated by students' responses on the inventory.

Lesson at a Glance

Chapter 6 Lesson 1

Overview This lesson demonstrates how to factor composite numbers into prime numbers and defines greatest common factor (GCF).

Objectives

- To identify prime numbers whose product is a composite number
- To identify the greatest common factor (GCF) of a term or number

Student Pages 156–159

Teacher's Resource Library TRL

Workbook Activity 58

Activity 54

Alternative Activity 54

Mathematics Vocabulary

composite number
factoring completely
greatest common factor (GCF)
prime number

1 Warm-Up Activity

Discuss various ways things can be divided into smaller building blocks (a chain into links, a book into folios or pages, etc.). Ask, "How could you divide a number into smaller building blocks?" After students offer their answers, inform them that in this lesson, they will practice breaking a number into the smaller numbers multiplied to produce it.

2 Teaching the Lesson

Review exponential forms of numbers with students. Use the Prime Factorization table to assess student understanding of prime numbers and factorization. Call on students to explain in their own words the meaning of specific entries, e.g., "29 is a prime number because it can be divided only by itself and 1. Therefore, it cannot be factored."

Be sure students grasp the concept of factoring before introducing the GCF. In finding the GCF, they compare the factors of different expressions in order to

Lesson 1 Greatest Common Factor

Prime number
An integer that can be divided only by itself and 1

Composite number
An integer that is not a prime number

Factoring completely
Expressing an integer as a product of only prime numbers

An integer that can be divided only by itself and 1 is a **prime number.** Integers that are not prime numbers are called **composite numbers.** Composite numbers can be written as a product of two or more prime numbers.

EXAMPLE 1

$17 = 17 \cdot 1$	17 is a prime number.
$18 = 2 \cdot 3 \cdot 3$	2 and 3 are prime factors of 18.
	18 is a composite number.

Expressing an integer as a product of only prime numbers is called **factoring completely.**

Study the chart showing the prime factorization for the integers 1 to 50. Note that 1 is not a prime number.

Remember factors are numbers that are multiplied in a multiplication problem.

Prime Factorization for Integers 1–50

1		**18**	$2 \cdot 3^2$	**35**	$5 \cdot 7$
2	prime	**19**	prime	**36**	$2^2 \cdot 3^2$
3	prime	**20**	$2^2 \cdot 5$	**37**	prime
4	2^2	**21**	$3 \cdot 7$	**38**	$2 \cdot 19$
5	prime	**22**	$2 \cdot 11$	**39**	$3 \cdot 13$
6	$2 \cdot 3$	**23**	prime	**40**	$2^3 \cdot 5$
7	prime	**24**	$2^3 \cdot 3$	**41**	prime
8	2^3	**25**	5^2	**42**	$2 \cdot 3 \cdot 7$
9	3^2	**26**	$2 \cdot 13$	**43**	prime
10	$2 \cdot 5$	**27**	3^3	**44**	$2^2 \cdot 11$
11	prime	**28**	$2^2 \cdot 7$	**45**	$3^2 \cdot 5$
12	$2^2 \cdot 3$	**29**	prime	**46**	$2 \cdot 23$
13	prime	**30**	$2 \cdot 3 \cdot 5$	**47**	prime
14	$2 \cdot 7$	**31**	prime	**48**	$2^4 \cdot 3$
15	$3 \cdot 5$	**32**	2^5	**49**	7
16	2^4	**33**	$3 \cdot 11$	**50**	$2 \cdot 5^2$
17	prime	**34**	$2 \cdot 17$		

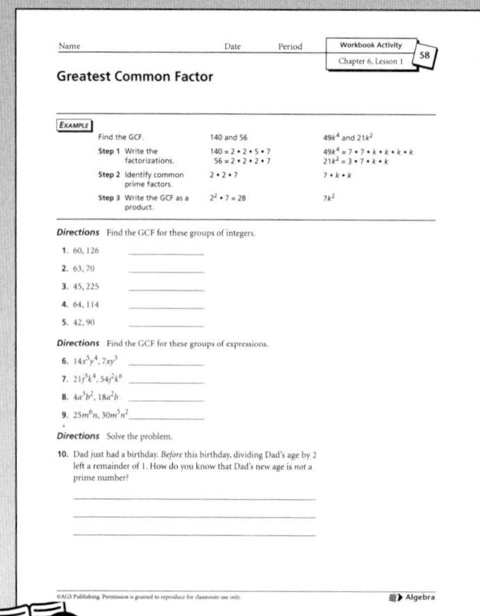

Name Date Period — Workbook Activity 58, Chapter 6, Lesson 1

Greatest Common Factor

EXAMPLE

		140 and 56	$49k^4$ and $21k^2$
Find the GCF.			
Step 1	Write the factorizations.	$140 = 2 \cdot 2 \cdot 5 \cdot 7$ $56 = 2 \cdot 2 \cdot 2 \cdot 7$	$49k^4 = 7 \cdot 7 \cdot k \cdot k \cdot k \cdot k$ $21k^2 = 3 \cdot 7 \cdot k \cdot k$
Step 2	Identify common prime factors.	$2 \cdot 2 \cdot 7$	$7 \cdot k \cdot k$
Step 3	Write the GCF as a product.	$2^2 \cdot 7 = 28$	$7k^2$

Directions Find the GCF for these groups of integers.

1. 60, 126 ______
2. 63, 70 ______
3. 45, 225 ______
4. 64, 114 ______
5. 42, 90 ______

Directions Find the GCF for these groups of expressions.

6. $14x^5y^4, 7xy^3$ ______
7. $21j^3k^4, 54j^2k^6$ ______
8. $4a^3b^2, 18a^2b$ ______
9. $25m^6n, 30m^5n^2$ ______

Directions Solve the problem.

10. Dad just had a birthday. *Before* this birthday, dividing Dad's age by 2 left a remainder of 1. How do you know that Dad's new age is *not* a prime number?

 Algebra

TRL

Workbook Activity 58

Name Date Period — Activity 54, Chapter 6, Lesson 1

Greatest Common Factor

Directions Find the GCF for these groups of integers.

1. 48, 84 ______
2. 44, 60 ______
3. 80, 175 ______

Directions Find the GCF for these groups of expressions.

4. $54p, 21p^3$ ______
5. $11c^3d^4, 22c^2$ ______
6. $15a^3b^2, 20a^5b^4, 5a^2b^2$ ______
7. $12m^5n^2, 21m^3n^2, 33m^3n^2$ ______

Directions Use a scientific calculator to find the number represented by each prime factorization.

8. $2^4 \cdot 5^2$ ______
9. $2^3 \cdot 3^2 \cdot 7^2$ ______
10. $2^2 \cdot 7^2 \cdot 10^2$ ______
11. $4^2 \cdot 6^2$ ______
12. $2^6 \cdot 3^2 \cdot 4^3$ ______
13. $2^5 \cdot 3^3$ ______
14. $2^2 \cdot 8^2$ ______
15. $3^2 \cdot 4^2$ ______
16. $2^2 \cdot 5^2 \cdot 9^2$ ______
17. $5^3 \cdot 7^2$ ______
18. $4^3 \cdot 5^2$ ______
19. $3^4 \cdot 4^2$ ______

Directions Solve the problem.

20. At the doctor's office, the medical assistant weighed Ted. "My weight is a prime number!" exclaimed Ted. Ted's weight always stays between 145 and 155 pounds. Tell what numbers you can easily rule out from being prime in the range of 145–155 and explain why. Then list the remaining possibilities for prime numbers.

 Algebra

TRL

Activity 54

EXAMPLE 2 Factor 120 completely.

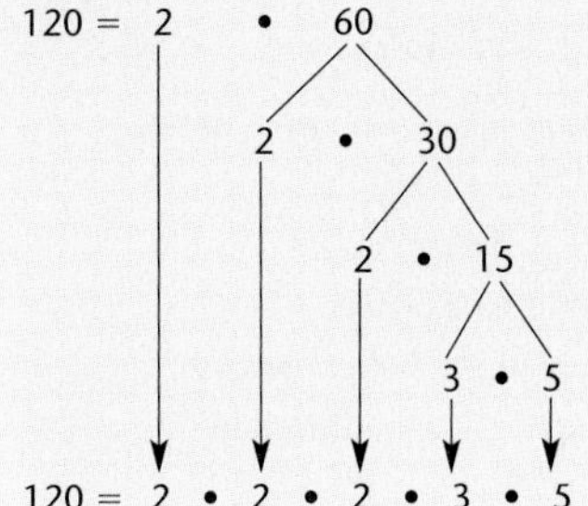

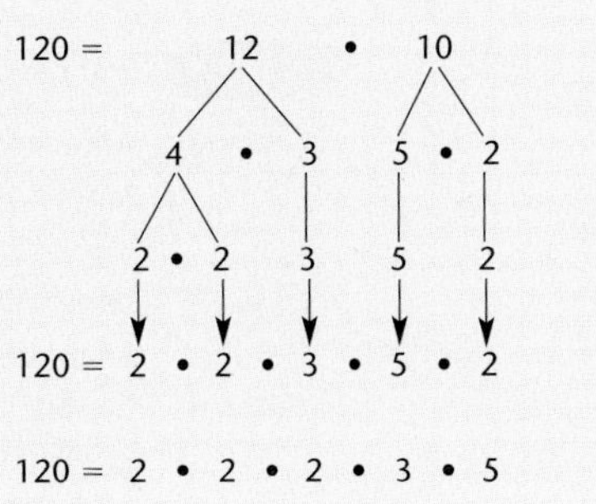

Greatest common factor (GCF)

The largest factor of two or more numbers or terms

The **greatest common factor** is the greatest factor that divides into each term or number. The greatest common factor is often abbreviated as GCF.

EXAMPLE 3 Find the GCF of 120 and 28.

Step 1 Write the complete factorization of each number.

120 = 2 • 2 • 2 • 3 • 5

28 = 2 • 2 • 7

Step 2 Identify the common prime factors.

2 • 2 is common to both numbers.

Step 3 The GCF is the product of all the common prime factors.

2^2 is the GCF of 120 and 28.

Algebra in Your Life **Turning a Big Decision into Smaller Ones**

You have probably needed to make a big decision in your life. Maybe you will soon need to decide what you are going to do after graduation. You can make this big decision easier by breaking it into several smaller decisions. In other words, you use factoring. Some of the factors you might list are your interests, education, living situation, and job. List all the factors you can, and your decision gets easier—just as factoring an equation can make finding its solution easier.

separate out numbers or elements that are *shared in common.*

Exercise C on page 159 requires students to explore the table on page 156 and explain their understanding of it. You may choose to complete this exercise together in class and assign Exercises A and B afterwards.

After students complete the exercises, assess understanding by asking:

- Why is factoring the reverse of multiplication? *(It requires you to divide out common factors.)*
- Circle the expression in each group that does not share a factor with the other three:

$3a^5, 10a^3, 6b^2, a^2b$ $(6b^2)$

$2x^3, 4a^3, x^2y^2, 8xa$ $(4a^3)$

$28m^2, 14n^3, 7mn, 49n^5$ $(28m^2)$

3 Reinforce and Extend

LEARNING STYLES

Visual/Spatial

Some students will benefit by diagramming the factorization of larger numbers. After they study the diagrams on page 157, ask volunteers to create similar diagrams on the board for composite numbers in the third column of the table on page 156 (36, 38, . . . 50). Use a similar approach in having students explain how they find the GCF of numbers and algebraic expressions on pages 158–159.

MATH HISTORY

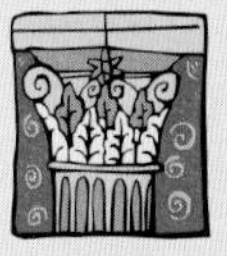

In 1536, the Spanish brought a printing press to New Spain, now Mexico. This press was used to print the first mathematics text written and published in the Americas.

Summario compendiso de las quentas de plata y re by Juan Diez Freyle was published in 1556. The main part of the book concerned the conversion of gold ore into the value equivalents of different kinds of coins used in New Spain.

A section of the book was devoted to algebra and included problems that required people to solve the quadratic equation. An example of one of these problems is, "A man traveling on a road asks another how many leagues it is to a certain place. The other replies, 'There are so many leagues that, squaring the number and dividing the product by 5, the quotient will be 80.'" Freyle's book is believed to be the first non-religious book published in the Americas.

Learning Styles

LEP/ESL

ESL students may have difficulty with the concept of factorization. Have them think of it as "undoing" a multiplication problem. Present a composite number (e.g., 20) and ask, "What whole numbers could you multiply to get this product?" *(2 • 10, 4 • 5, 2 • 2 • 5)* Have students write these number sets on the board and use them to determine whether a number is prime (only 1 and the number itself appear in the set) or what the prime factors of the number are. *(for 20, 2 • 2 • 5 or 22 • 5)*

Mental Math

To help students gain facility in dealing with exponential forms, write such forms on the board and have students respond orally by

- Identifying the term: e.g., "two cubed" or "two to the third power"
- Expanding the term as a number sentence: e.g., "2 times 2 times 2"
- Giving the number the term represents: e.g., "8"

You can find the GCF of algebraic expressions using these same steps.

Example 4 Find the GCF of $21a^3$ and $18a^5$.

Step 1 Write the complete factorization of each number.

$21a^3 = 3 \cdot 7 \cdot a \cdot a \cdot a$

$18a^5 = 2 \cdot 3 \cdot 3 \cdot a \cdot a \cdot a \cdot a \cdot a$

Step 2 Identify the common prime factors.

$3 \cdot a \cdot a \cdot a$ are common to both numbers.

Step 3 The GCF is the product of all the common prime factors.

$3a^3$ is the GCF of $21a^3$ and $18a^5$.

Example 5 Find the GCF of $24a^3b^3$ and $28a^5b$.

Step 1 Write the complete factorization of each number.

$24a^3b^3 = 2 \cdot 2 \cdot 2 \cdot 3 \cdot a \cdot a \cdot a \cdot b \cdot b \cdot b$

$28a^5b = 2 \cdot 2 \cdot 7 \cdot a \cdot a \cdot a \cdot a \cdot a \cdot b$

Step 2 Identify the common prime factors.

$2 \cdot 2 \cdot a \cdot a \cdot a \cdot b$ are common to both numbers.

Step 3 The GCF is the product of all the common prime factors.

2^2a^3b is the GCF of $24a^3b^3$ and $28a^5b$.

Exercise A Find the GCF for these groups of integers.

1. 72, 36 $2^2 \cdot 3^2$
2. 24, 48 $2^3 \cdot 3$
3. 27, 24 3
4. 72, 24 $2^3 \cdot 3$
5. 72, 36, 24 $2^2 \cdot 3$
6. 78, 26 $2 \cdot 13$
7. 66, 99 $3 \cdot 11$
8. 39, 169 13
9. 25, 225 5^2
10. 132, 512 2^2

Exercise B Find the GCF for these groups of expressions.

11. $3x^2, 3x$	$3x$	**16.** $33a^3b^5, 66a^2b^3$	$33a^2b^3$
12. $18y^2, 3y^2$	$3y^2$	**17.** $21x^3y^2, 7x^2y, 42xy$	$7xy$
13. $m^2n^2, 3m^2$	m^2	**18.** $3a^6, 4a^5, a^4$	a^4
14. $27p^3, 9p$	$9p$	**19.** $24x^2y, 36x^2y^2, 20xy^2$	$4xy$
15. $12x^2, 8x$	$4x$	**20.** $42ab^2, 42$	42

Exercise C Answer these questions using the table of prime numbers 1–50 on page 156.

21. What is the largest prime integer less than 50?

22. Why is 2 the only even prime number?

23. How many composite integers are less than 50?

24. How many prime numbers are less than 50?

25. How can you use the table to factor 180 completely?

21. 47
22. Because 2 is divisible only by itself and 1; all other even numbers are divisible by 2.
23. 33
24. 15
25. sample answer: Since 180 = 20 • 9, 180 = $(2^2 \cdot 5)(3^2)$ or $2^2 \cdot 3^2 \cdot 5$.

Calculator Practice

Use the exponent key on a scientific calculator to check the prime factorization of any number. This key raises a number to a power. On some calculators, it is [y^x] and on others it is [^].

EXAMPLE 6 Does $2^4 \cdot 7^2 = 784$?

Clear your calculator display, then enter:

2 [y^x] 4 [×] 7 [y^x] 2 [=]

2 [^] 4 [×] 7 [^] 2 [=]

Your display will show 784.

Exercise D Use a scientific calculator to find the number represented by these prime factorizations.

26. $2^3 \cdot 3^2$

27. $3^2 \cdot 5^3$

28. $2^5 \cdot 5^2 \cdot 7^3$

29. $5^4 \cdot 7^2 \cdot 11^2$

30. $2^6 \cdot 3^3 \cdot 5^2 \cdot 7^2$

26. 72
27. 1,125
28. 274,400
29. 3,705,625
30. 2,116,800

Common Error

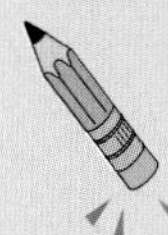

When students complete step 1 of finding the GCF, they may think they have to multiply the common elements in each row. Explain that they are simply identifying and recording elements that are shared. In a sense, they are crossing them off (setting them aside) temporarily. For clarity, have them write the two parts of each expression after factoring:

$21a^3 = 3a^3 \cdot 7$

$18a^5 = 3a^3 \cdot 6a^2$

Calculator

Be sure students are aware of their individual calculator's requirements for entering expressions involving powers. For example, the TI-82 and TI-83 require that powers of negative values be entered using parentheses and the negation key (bottom row)—*not the minus key.*

To calculate $(-3)^6$,

press [(] [(−)] 3 [)] [^] 6 [=].

The display reads 729.

However, if you press [−] 3 [^] 6, you will get −729.

Lesson at a Glance

Chapter 6 Lesson 2

Overview This lesson applies understanding of the GCF to factoring algebraic sums and differences.

Objective

- To find the GCF of two and three algebraic terms in a sum or difference

Student Pages 160–161

Teacher's Resource Library 

Workbook Activity 59

Activity 55

Alternative Activity 55

Warm-Up Activity

You may wish to begin with a review of "Multiplying Polynomials" (Chapter 5, Lesson 7).

Write the equation illustrating the distributive property on the board.

$a(b + c) = ab + ac$

Ask students to explain this property in their own words. Then have a volunteer explain how factoring is the reverse of this process.

Ask, "Why might it be helpful in solving an equation to factor out the terms that its elements have in common?" *(To simplify, to make solution clearer)* Inform students that Lesson 2 will help them apply the GCF to simplifying algebraic equations.

Teaching the Lesson

Among the real-world applications of factoring polynomials are area and dimension problems. Use algebra tiles (or drawings on the board or an overhead projector) to model an area problem. Demonstrate that the dimensions of the shape formed are the factors of the expression.

Lesson 2 Factoring Polynomials

You can use what you know about finding a GCF to factor an algebraic sum or difference.

EXAMPLE 1 Factor $a^3b^2 + a^2b$.

Step 1 Find the GCF.

$a^3b^2 = \boxed{a \bullet a} \bullet a \bullet \boxed{b} \bullet b$

$a^2b = \boxed{a \bullet a} \bullet \boxed{b}$

The GCF is $a \bullet a \bullet b = a^2b$.

Step 2 Write the expression using the GCF.

$a^3b^2 + a^2b = a^2b(ab) + a^2b(1)$

$= a^2b(ab + 1)$

(using the distributive property)

Step 3 Check. $a^2b(ab + 1) = a^3b^2 + a^2b$

EXAMPLE 2 Factor $5x^4 + 10x^2$.

Step 1 Find the GCF.

$5x^4 = \boxed{5} \bullet \boxed{x \bullet x} \bullet x \bullet x$

$10x^2 = 2 \bullet \boxed{5} \bullet \boxed{x \bullet x}$

The GCF is $5 \bullet x \bullet x = 5x^2$.

Step 2 Write the expression using the GCF.

$5x^4 + 10x^2 = 5x^2(x^2) + 5x^2(2)$

$= 5x^2(x^2 + 2)$

(using the distributive property)

Step 3 Check. $5x^2(x^2 + 2) = 5x^4 + 10x^2$

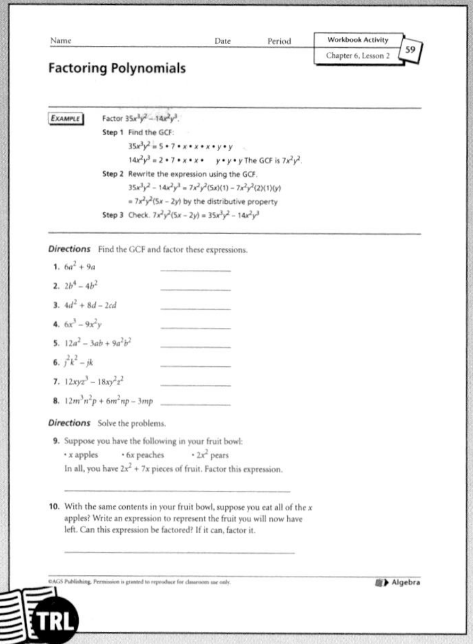

Name Date Period | Workbook Activity 59 | Chapter 6, Lesson 2

Factoring Polynomials

EXAMPLE Factor $35x^3y^2 - 14x^2y^3$.

Step 1 Find the GCF:

$35x^3y^2 = 5 \bullet 7 \bullet x \bullet x \bullet x \bullet y \bullet y$

$14x^2y^3 = 2 \bullet 7 \bullet x \bullet x \bullet y \bullet y \bullet y$ The GCF is $7x^2y^2$.

Step 2 Rewrite the expression using the GCF.

$35x^3y^2 - 14x^2y^3 = 7x^2y^2(5x)(1) - 7x^2y^2(2)(1)(y)$

$= 7x^2y^2(5x - 2y)$ by the distributive property

Step 3 Check. $7x^2y^2(5x - 2y) = 35x^3y^2 - 14x^2y^3$

Directions Find the GCF and factor these expressions.

1. $6a^2 + 9a$ ____
2. $2b^4 - 4b^2$ ____
3. $4d^2 + 8d - 2cd$ ____
4. $6x^3 - 9x^2y$ ____
5. $12a^2 - 3ab + 9a^2b^2$ ____
6. $j^2k^2 - jk$ ____
7. $12xyz^3 - 18xy^2z^2$ ____
8. $12m^3n^2p + 6m^2np - 3mp$ ____

Directions Solve the problems.

9. Suppose you have the following in your fruit bowl:
   • x apples • $6x$ peaches • $2x^2$ pears
   In all, you have $2x^2 + 7x$ pieces of fruit. Factor this expression.
   ____
10. With the same contents in your fruit bowl, suppose you eat all of the x apples? Write an expression to represent the fruit you will now have left. Can this expression be factored? If it can, factor it.
   ____

 Algebra

Workbook Activity 59

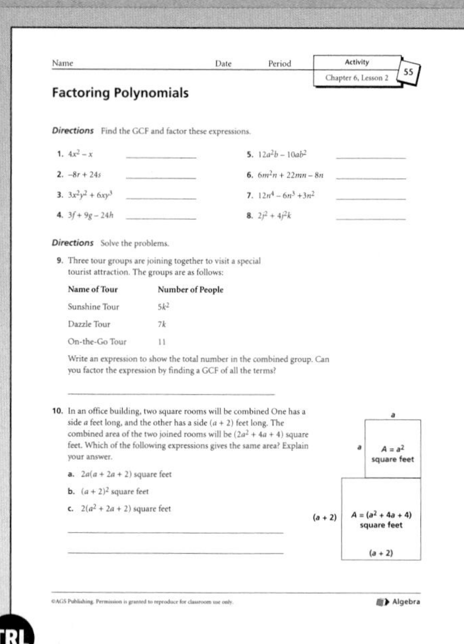

Name Date Period | Activity 55 | Chapter 6, Lesson 2

Factoring Polynomials

Directions Find the GCF and factor these expressions.

1. $4x^2 - x$ ____
2. $-8r + 24s$ ____
3. $3x^2y^2 + 6xy^3$ ____
4. $3f + 9g - 24h$ ____
5. $12a^2b - 10ab^2$ ____
6. $6m^2n + 22mn - 8n$ ____
7. $12n^4 - 6n^3 + 3n^2$ ____
8. $2j^2 + 4j^2k$ ____

Directions Solve the problems.

9. Three tour groups are joining together to visit a special tourist attraction. The groups are as follows:

Name of Tour	Number of People
Sunshine Tour	$5k^2$
Dazzle Tour	$7k$
On-the-Go Tour	11

   Write an expression to show the total number in the combined group. Can you factor the expression by finding a GCF of all the terms?
   ____

10. In an office building, two square rooms will be combined One has a side a feet long, and the other has a side $(a + 2)$ feet long. The combined area of the two joined rooms will be $(2a^2 + 4a + 4)$ square feet. Which of the following expressions gives the same area? Explain your answer.
   a. $2a(a + 2a + 2)$ square feet
   b. $(a + 2)^2$ square feet
   c. $2(a^2 + 2a + 2)$ square feet
   ____

 Algebra

Activity 55

Writing About Mathematics

How is a common factor different from the greatest common factor? Give an example.

When you factor algebraic expressions, there may be more than two terms to factor, and the factors may be numbers as well as variables.

EXAMPLE 3 Factor $6t^3 - 3t^2 + 9$.

Because 9 is a constant and not a coefficient of t, you know that t cannot be a factor of each term in the expression. Therefore, you need only find the GCF for the coefficients of 9, 6, and -3. The GCF of these numbers is 3.

$6t^3 - 3t^2 + 9 = 3(2t^3 - t^2 + 3)$

Exercise A Find the GCF, then factor these expressions.

1. $3x^2 + 3$
2. $18y^2 - 6$
3. $m^2n^2 + 3m^2$
4. $6x^3 + 18$
5. $6x^3 + 18x^2 + 24$
6. $5a^3 + 25a^2 - 35a + 20$
7. $16m^3 + 24m^2 + 16$
8. $25x^2y + 15xy^2 + 30$
9. $32x^5 + 64x^4 + 16x$
10. $21x^3y^2 - 7x^2y + 42xy$
11. $-3a^6 - 4a^5 - a^4$
12. $4x^2y - 16x^2y^2 + 20xy^2$
13. $-24x^2y + 6x^2y^2 + 30y^2$
14. $18a^2 - 36a^2b^2 + 44b^2$
15. $-15x^3y^2 - 45x^2y^2 - 33xy^2$
16. $4a^2b^7 - 32a^2b^6 + 8ab^2$
17. $17x^2y - 34xy$
18. $3m^2n - 39m^2n^2 - 13n$
19. $-40t^2 + 5t^2s + 20ts^2$
20. $6p^4q + pqr - 3pr$

1. $3(x^2 + 1)$
2. $6(3y^2 - 1)$
3. $m^2(n^2 + 3)$
4. $6(x^3 + 3)$
5. $6(x^3 + 3x^2 + 4)$
6. $5(a^3 + 5a^2 - 7a + 4)$
7. $8(2m^3 + 3m^2 + 2)$
8. $5(5x^2y + 3xy^2 + 6)$
9. $16x(2x^4 + 4x^3 + 1)$
10. $7xy(3x^2y - x + 6)$
11. $a^4(-3a^2 - 4a - 1)$ or $-a^4(3a^2 + 4a + 1)$
12. $4xy(x - 4xy + 5y)$
13. $6y(-4x^2 + x^2y + 5y)$
14. $2(9a^2 - 18a^2b^2 + 22b^2)$
15. $3xy^2(-5x^2 - 15x - 11)$ or $-3xy^2(5x^2 + 15x + 11)$
16. $4ab^2(ab^5 - 8ab^4 + 2)$
17. $17xy(x - 2)$
18. $n(3m^2 - 39m^2n - 13)$
19. $5t(-8t + ts + 4s^2)$
20. $p(6p^3q + qr - 3r)$

For example, using

$x^2 + 2x$ (area)

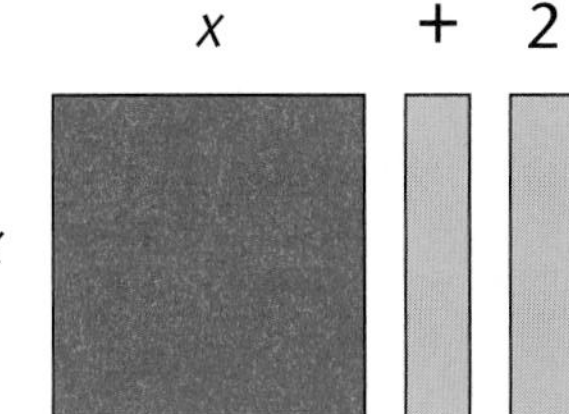

When students complete Exercise A, remind them that they can only factor out elements that are shared in all the terms of the expression.

COMMON ERROR

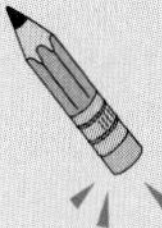

Students may make errors in factoring polynomials because they fail to keep track of all the terms' components. Remind them that the factored element must share a common strand with *all* items in the polynomial. Require students to check their factors by multiplying them. If the product is not the original polynomial, they must try again.

3 Reinforce and Extend

LEARNING STYLES

Logical/Mathematical

As students offer their answers to Exercise A, have them explain in their own words how they found the GCF. For additional practice, use the following polynomials. Write each on the board, along with an incorrect GCF. As volunteers correct the answers on the board, have them explain what was wrong with the original solution.

$12a^4 + 16a^3x + 4a + 4$
(incorrect: 4a; correct: 4)

$21b^2c^2 - 7b^2c + 14c$
(incorrect: 7bc; correct: 7c)

$4x^2y + 10xy + 20y$
(incorrect: 2xy; correct: 2y)

$18a^3b^2c^5 + 12ac^5 + 24b$
(incorrect: 6abc; correct: 6)

Lesson at a Glance

Chapter 6 Lesson 3

Overview This lesson demonstrates how a trinomial is derived by multiplying two binomials and shows how to factor a trinomial.

Objectives

- To comprehend a model for deriving trinomials
- To learn a four-step process for factoring a trinomial

Student Pages 162–163

Teacher's Resource Library 

Workbook Activity 60

Activity 56

Alternative Activity 56

1 Warm-Up Activity

Write the following symbols on the board, using different colored chalk for each square.

Ask students to work in pairs and use colors to draw the model for this multiplication problem. Have them check to be sure they have distributed each color in the first element over both colors in the second element. Repeat the process, using red and blue in both elements, and compare the results. Ask, "Which model illustrates a trinomial function?" *(the red and blue one)* Tell students that they will study the structure of binomial factors that give a trinomial in this lesson and the following one.

2 Teaching the Lesson

Because factoring is the reversing of the multiplication process, a brief review of multiplication of polynomials is advisable. Be sure students understand that the middle term of a trinomial is created by adding together two like terms. Demonstrate this combination with diagrams such as the following:

$(x + b)(x + c)$

Lesson 3 Factoring Trinomials: $x^2 + bx + c$

A trinomial is a polynomial that is made up of three terms. There are several different forms of trinomials. This lesson explores trinomials of the form $x^2 + bx + c$. Examples of these trinomials include $x^2 + 8x + 12$ and $x^2 - 3x - 10$.

A trinomial is the product of two factors. For example, if the factors of a trinomial were $(x + 2)$ and $(x - 1)$, the trinomial would be

$$\begin{aligned}(x + 2)(x - 1) &= x(x - 1) + 2(x - 1)\\ &= x^2 - x + 2x - 2\\ &= x^2 + x - 2\end{aligned}$$

This shows that $x^2 + x - 2 = (x + 2)(x - 1)$

a trinomial = product of 2 factors

If you start with the trinomial and try to find the factors, you might think of the model in this way:

$x^2 + x - 2 = (■ + ■)(■ - ■)$ You know each factor contains an x because the product contains x^2.

$x^2 + x - 2 = (x + ■)(x - ■)$ The factors of -2 must be either $(2)(-1)$ or $(-2)(1)$.

The middle term tells you that the sum of the factors of -2 must be 1 (because $1x = x$).

Possible factors include $(2) + (-1) = 1$ and $(-2) + (1) = -1$. The factors must then be $(2) + (-1)$. $x^2 + x - 2 = (x + 2)(x - 1)$

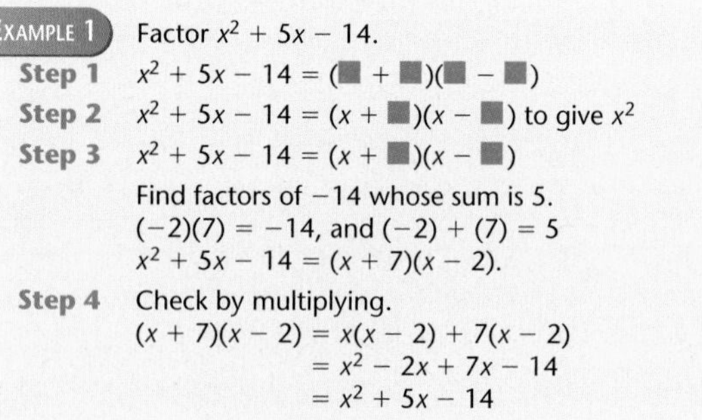

Example 1 Factor $x^2 + 5x - 14$.

Step 1 $x^2 + 5x - 14 = (■ + ■)(■ - ■)$

Step 2 $x^2 + 5x - 14 = (x + ■)(x - ■)$ to give x^2

Step 3 $x^2 + 5x - 14 = (x + ■)(x - ■)$

Find factors of -14 whose sum is 5.

$(-2)(7) = -14$, and $(-2) + (7) = 5$

$x^2 + 5x - 14 = (x + 7)(x - 2)$.

Step 4 Check by multiplying.

$$\begin{aligned}(x + 7)(x - 2) &= x(x - 2) + 7(x - 2)\\ &= x^2 - 2x + 7x - 14\\ &= x^2 + 5x - 14\end{aligned}$$

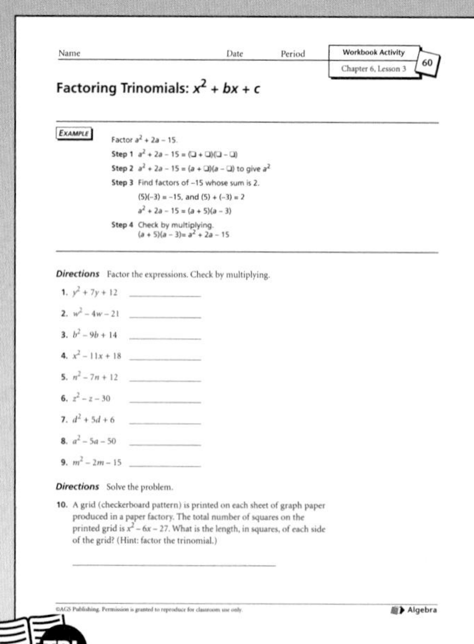

Name Date Period | Workbook Activity 60 | Chapter 6, Lesson 3

Factoring Trinomials: $x^2 + bx + c$

Example Factor $a^2 + 2a - 15$.

Step 1 $a^2 + 2a - 15 = (□ + □)(□ - □)$

Step 2 $a^2 + 2a - 15 = (a + □)(a - □)$ to give a^2

Step 3 Find factors of -15 whose sum is 2.

$(5)(-3) = -15$, and $(5) + (-3) = 2$

$a^2 + 2a - 15 = (a + 5)(a - 3)$

Step 4 Check by multiplying.

$(a + 5)(a - 3) = a^2 + 2a - 15$

Directions Factor the expressions. Check by multiplying.

1. $y^2 + 7y + 12$ ______
2. $w^2 - 4w - 21$ ______
3. $b^2 - 9b + 14$ ______
4. $x^2 - 11x + 18$ ______
5. $n^2 - 7n + 12$ ______
6. $z^2 - z - 30$ ______
7. $d^2 + 5d + 6$ ______
8. $a^2 - 5a - 50$ ______
9. $m^2 - 2m - 15$ ______

Directions Solve the problem.

10. A grid (checkerboard pattern) is printed on each sheet of graph paper produced in a paper factory. The total number of squares on the printed grid is $x^2 - 6x - 27$. What is the length, in squares, of each side of the grid? (Hint: factor the trinomial.)

______

 Algebra

Workbook Activity 60

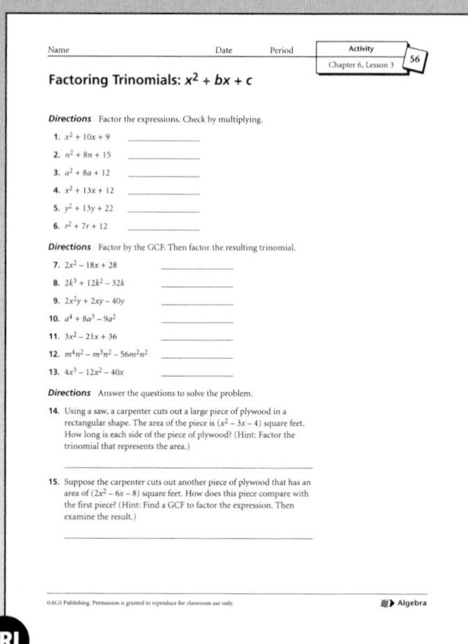

Name Date Period | Activity 56 | Chapter 6, Lesson 3

Factoring Trinomials: $x^2 + bx + c$

Directions Factor the expressions. Check by multiplying.

1. $x^2 + 10x + 9$ ______
2. $n^2 + 8n + 15$ ______
3. $a^2 + 8a + 12$ ______
4. $x^2 + 13x + 12$ ______
5. $y^2 + 13y + 22$ ______
6. $r^2 + 7r + 12$ ______

Directions Factor by the GCF. Then factor the resulting trinomial.

7. $2x^2 - 18x + 28$ ______
8. $2k^3 + 12k^2 - 32k$ ______
9. $2x^2y + 2xy - 40y$ ______
10. $a^4 + 8a^3 - 9a^2$ ______
11. $3x^2 - 21x + 36$ ______
12. $m^4n^2 - m^3n^2 - 56m^2n^2$ ______
13. $4x^3 - 12x^2 - 40x$ ______

Directions Answer the questions to solve the problem.

14. Using a saw, a carpenter cuts out a large piece of plywood in a rectangular shape. The area of the piece is $(x^2 - 3x - 4)$ square feet. How long is each side of the piece of plywood? (Hint: Factor the trinomial that represents the area.)

______

15. Suppose the carpenter cuts out another piece of plywood that has an area of $(2x^2 - 6x - 8)$ square feet. How does this piece compare with the first piece? (Hint: Find a GCF to factor the expression. Then examine the result.)

______

 Algebra

Activity 56

1. $(x + 2)(x + 3)$
2. $(m - 6)(m + 2)$
3. $(a - 2)(a - 4)$
4. $(x - 3)(x + 8)$
5. $(y + 6)(y - 3)$
6. $(m - 10)(m + 2)$
7. $(t - 5)(t + 4)$
8. $(y - 5)(y + 1)$
9. $(x - 1)(x + 17)$
10. $x^2(x + 4)(x + 3)$
11. $2b(b^2 + 5b + 4) = 2b(b + 4)(b + 1)$

Not every trinomial can be factored in this way. For example, in $x^2 + x - 3$, the factors of -3 are $(-3)(1)$ or $(3)(-1)$.

The coefficient of the middle term is (1), so you know the sum of the factors of -3 must be 1. But $(-3) + (1) = -2$, and $(3) + (-1) = 2$. Neither combination of factors gives the correct middle term.

Some trinomials may have a common factor. In these cases, you will need to find the GCF first.

EXAMPLE 2 Factor $2x^4 + 10x^3 - 28x^2$.

Step 1 Find the common factors.
$2x^4 + 10x^3 - 28x^2 = 2x^2(x^2 + 5x - 14)$

Step 2 Factor the polynomial.
$2x^2(x^2 + 5x - 14) = 2x^2(x + 7)(x - 2)$
from previous example
so $2x^4 + 10x^3 - 28x^2 = 2x^2(x + 7)(x - 2)$.

Exercise A Factor the following expressions. Check by multiplying.

1. $x^2 + 5x + 6$
2. $m^2 - 4m - 12$
3. $a^2 - 6a + 8$
4. $x^2 + 5x - 24$
5. $y^2 + 3y - 18$
6. $m^2 - 8m - 20$
7. $t^2 - t - 20$
8. $y^2 - 4y - 5$
9. $x^2 + 16x - 17$

Exercise B Factor these expressions. Be sure to find any common factors.

10. $x^4 + 7x^3 + 12x^2$
11. $2b^3 + 10b^2 + 8b$
12. $3p^4 - 24p^3 + 45p^2$
13. $a^4 + 7a^2 + 12$

12. $3p^2(p^2 - 8p + 15) = 3p^2(p - 5)(p - 3)$
13. $(a^2 + 3)(a^2 + 4)$

PROBLEM SOLVING

Exercise C Solve these problems.

14. Suppose the trinomial $x^2 - x - 2$ represents the area of a rectangle. What factors represent the length and width of that rectangle?

$(x + 1)(x - 2)$

15. Suppose the trinomial $x^2 + 4x + 3$ represents the area of a rectangle. What is the perimeter of that rectangle?

$2(x + 1) + 2(x + 3) = 4x + 8$

MANIPULATIVES

Factoring Polynomials

Materials: Algebra Tiles, Manipulatives Master 4 (Factor Frame)

Group Practice: Build a model of the polynomial to be factored using the Algebra Tiles. Arrange the pieces inside the Factor Frame so that they meet the two conditions, applying the Zero Rule when necessary. (See page T9, "Using the Factor Frame.") Arrange pieces on the outside of the Factor Frame to find the factors of the polynomial represented inside the Factor Frame.

Student Practice: Have students use models for Exercises A and C and Supplementary Problems 11–13 on page 416. Instruct them to factor the expressions or check their answers obtained by using the method in the example.

3 Reinforce and Extend

GROUP PROBLEM SOLVING

Suggest that students work in groups of four to solve the following problem, which requires creative critical thinking:

The area of a circle is πr^2. You want to mark off a circular game area. The area of the circle cannot be smaller than $A = \pi(4x^2 + 12x + 9)$.

Find the expression for the smallest radius your playing field can have. *[r = (2x + 3)]*

Remind students that a square results from multiplying a number times itself. Therefore, a polynomial that is a square must result from a binomial times itself. (Note: This problem anticipates trinomial perfect squares (discussed in Lesson 6). If some students are unable to solve the problem at this time, pose it again as they study Lesson 6.)

CAREER CONNECTION

Invite an investment adviser to talk to the class about the use of polynomials to figure returns on investments and to demonstrate other uses of polynomial expressions and factoring in the world of finance. Encourage students to think of questions they would like to ask the speaker prior to his or her visit.

LEARNING STYLES

Auditory/Verbal

Factoring a polynomial requires a number of complex steps. Have students work through problems aloud, explaining to a partner how they discover the elements making up each component binomial factor. Students should also explain how they determine whether a GCF exists in the trinomial (see problems 10, 11, and 12) and the extra step involved in factoring it out.

Lesson at a Glance

Chapter 6 Lesson 4

Overview This lesson introduces and explains how to factor trinomials in which the x^2 element possesses a coefficient greater than 1.

Objectives

- To factor expressions of the type $ax^2 + bx + c$
- To use trial and error to find all possible combinations that can give the quantity b in this form of trinomial

Student Pages 164–165

Teacher's Resource Library 

Workbook Activity 61

Activity 57

Alternative Activity 57

Warm-Up Activity

Remind students that there are several forms of polynomials. Write the following on the board:

$x^2 + bx + c$

$ax^2 + bx + c$

Ask, "What is the difference between these two polynomials?" *(The first term of the second polynomial has added a number a to the x^2.)* Have students explain how their approach to factoring this new type of polynomial might differ. *(They will have to find the factors of the coefficient a. There will be more combinations to consider.)*

Teaching the Lesson

Have students study the makeup of the trinomials in the exercises and in Exercise A identify the a, b, and c numbers in each expression. Ask them to explain why the a number cannot be factored out in these trinomials. *(There is no GCF for the a, b, and c numbers.)* Be sure students understand that they must find factors of c whose sum is b.

Lesson 4 Factoring Trinomials: $ax^2 + bx + c$

Another form of a trinomial is $ax^2 + bx + c$. Examples of these trinomials include $4x^2 + 8x + 3$ and $20x^2 - 29x + 6$. In these trinomials, the coefficient of the x^2 term is some number other than 1.

$4x^2 + 8x + 3$	$20x^2 - 29x + 6$
The coefficient of x^2 is 4.	The coefficient of x^2 is 20.

When the coefficient of the x^2 term is some number other than 1, you must find the factors of this coefficient in order to factor the trinomial.

Example 1 Factor $6x^2 + 13x + 5$.

Step 1 $6x^2 + 13x + 5 = (\blacksquare x + \blacksquare)(\blacksquare x + \blacksquare)$
to give x^2

Step 2 Find factors of 6 and 5 whose sum is 13.

Factors of 6 = (6)(1) or (2)(3)

Factors of 5 = (5)(1)

Try different combinations using trial and error.

There are four possible combinations:

$(1x + 1)(6x + 5) = 1x(6x + 5) + 1(6x + 5) = 6x^2 + 5x + 6x + 5$
$= 6x^2 + 11x + 5$

$(1x + 5)(6x + 1) = 1x(6x + 1) + 5(6x + 1) = 6x^2 + x + 30x + 5$
$= 6x^2 + 31x + 5$

$(2x + 5)(3x + 1) = 2x(3x + 1) + 5(3x + 1) = 6x^2 + 2x + 15x + 5$
$= 6x^2 + 17x + 5$

$(2x + 1)(3x + 5) = 2x(3x + 5) + 1(3x + 5) = 6x^2 + 10x + 3x + 5$
$= 6x^2 + 13x + 5$

The last combination gives us the desired product.

The factors of $6x^2 + 13x + 5$ are $(2x + 1)(3x + 5)$.

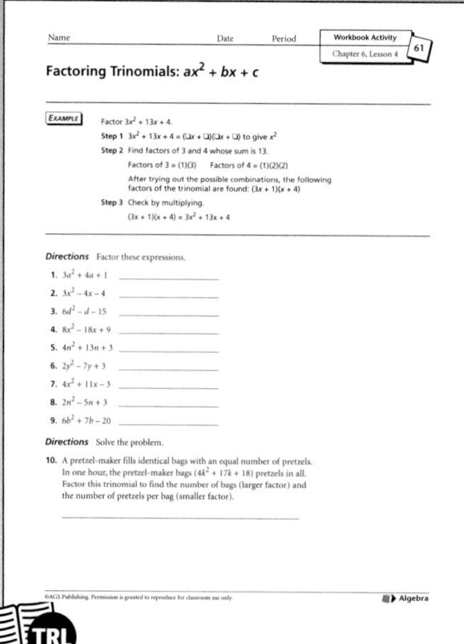

Name Date Period **Workbook Activity 61** Chapter 6, Lesson 4

Factoring Trinomials: $ax^2 + bx + c$

Example Factor $3x^2 + 13x + 4$.

Step 1 $3x^2 + 13x + 4 = (\square x + \square)(\square x + \square)$ to give x^2

Step 2 Find factors of 3 and 4 whose sum is 13.

Factors of 3 = (1)(3) Factors of 4 = (1)(2)(2)

After trying out the possible combinations, the following factors of the trinomial are found: $(3x + 1)(x + 4)$

Step 3 Check by multiplying.

$(3x + 1)(x + 4) = 3x^2 + 13x + 4$

Directions Factor these expressions.

1. $3a^2 + 4a + 1$ ______
2. $3x^2 - 4x - 4$ ______
3. $6d^2 - d - 15$ ______
4. $8x^2 - 18x + 9$ ______
5. $4n^2 + 13n + 3$ ______
6. $2y^2 - 7y + 3$ ______
7. $4x^2 + 11x - 3$ ______
8. $2n^2 - 5n + 3$ ______
9. $6b^2 + 7b - 20$ ______

Directions Solve the problem.

10. A pretzel-maker fills identical bags with an equal number of pretzels. In one hour, the pretzel-maker bags $(4k^2 + 17k + 18)$ pretzels in all. Factor this trinomial to find the number of bags (larger factor) and the number of pretzels per bag (smaller factor).

______

 Algebra

Workbook Activity 61

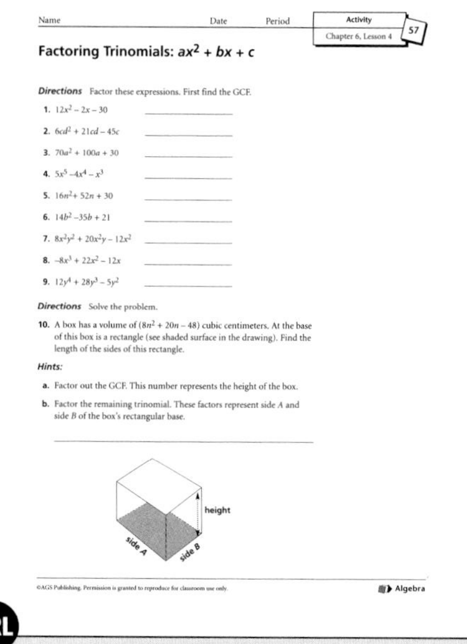

Name Date Period **Activity 57** Chapter 6, Lesson 4

Factoring Trinomials: $ax^2 + bx + c$

Directions Factor these expressions. First find the GCF.

1. $12x^2 - 2x - 30$ ______
2. $6cd^2 + 21cd - 45c$ ______
3. $70a^2 + 100a + 30$ ______
4. $5x^5 - 4x^4 - x^3$ ______
5. $16n^2 + 52n + 30$ ______
6. $14b^2 - 35b + 21$ ______
7. $8x^2y^2 + 20x^2y - 12x^2$ ______
8. $-8x^3 + 22x^2 - 12x$ ______
9. $12y^4 + 28y^3 - 5y^2$ ______

Directions Solve the problem.

10. A box has a volume of $(8n^2 + 20n - 48)$ cubic centimeters. At the base of this box is a rectangle (see shaded surface in the drawing). Find the length of the sides of this rectangle.

Hints:

a. Factor out the GCF. This number represents the height of the box.

b. Factor the remaining trinomial. These factors represent side A and side B of the box's rectangular base.

______

 Algebra

Activity 57

EXAMPLE 2 Factor $3x^2 + 14x - 5$.

Note that in this expression the constant is a negative. In this case, you will need to test for proper signs as well as correct factors.

Step 1 $3x^2 + 14x - 5 = (\blacksquare x + \blacksquare)(\blacksquare x - \blacksquare)$
to give x^2

Step 2 Find factors of 3 and -5 whose sum is $+14$.

Factors of $-5 = (5)(-1)$ or $(-5)(1)$
Factors of $3 = (3)(1)$

Try different combinations using trial and error.
There are four possible combinations:

$(1x + 1)(3x - 5) = x(3x - 5) + 1(3x - 5) = 3x^2 - 5x + 3x - 5$
$= 3x^2 - 2x - 5$

$(3x + 1)(1x - 5) = 3x(x - 5) + 1(x - 5) = 3x^2 - 15x + x - 5$
$= 3x^2 - 14x + 5$

$(1x - 1)(3x + 5) = x(3x + 5) - 1(3x + 5) = 3x^2 + 5x - 3x - 5$
$= 3x^2 + 2x - 5$

$(3x - 1)(1x + 5) = 3x(x + 5) - 1(x + 5) = 3x^2 + 15x - x - 5$
$= 3x^2 + 14x - 5$

The last combination gives us the desired product.
The factors of $3x^2 + 14x - 5$ are $(3x - 1)(1x + 5)$.

Exercise A Factor these expressions.

1. $3y^2 + 14y + 8$ — $(3y + 2)(y + 4)$
2. $12b^2 + 17b + 6$ — $(3b + 2)(4b + 3)$
3. $6c^2 + 19c + 15$ — $(2c + 3)(3c + 5)$
4. $20r^2 + 104r + 20$ — $(2r + 10)(10r + 2)$
5. $20m^2 + 50m + 20$ — $(2m + 4)(10m + 5)$
6. $20x^2 + 40x + 20$ — $(4x + 4)(5x + 5)$
7. $20y^2 + 401y + 20$ — $(20y + 1)(y + 20)$
8. $42x^2 + 84x + 42$ — $(7x + 7)(6x + 6)$

Exercise B Factor these expressions. Don't forget about positive and negative signs.

9. $7x^2 + 4x - 3$ — $(7x - 3)(x + 1)$
10. $8a^2 - 26a + 15$ — $(4a - 3)(2a - 5)$
11. $49x^2 + 7x - 6$ — $(7x - 2)(7x + 3)$
12. $7a^2 + 19a - 6$ — $(7a - 2)(a + 3)$
13. $6y^2 - 10y - 24$ — $(3y + 4)(2y - 6)$
14. $11x^2 - 41x - 12$ — $(11x + 3)(x - 4)$
15. $6x^2 - 26x + 28$ — $(3x - 7)(2x - 4)$
16. $2x^2 - 14x + 12$ — $(2x - 2)(x - 6)$
17. $3x^2 - 2x - 16$ — $(3x - 8)(x + 2)$

Exercise C Factor these expressions. First find the GCF.

18. $4x^3 + 20x^2 + 16x$ — $4x(x + 4)(x + 1)$
19. $12x^4 + 26x^3 - 16x^2$ — $2x^2(3x + 8)(2x - 1)$
20. $10x^2 + 48x - 10$ — $2(5x - 1)(x + 5)$

Introduce the FOIL method: first, outside, inside, last.

Steps:

1. Multiply first terms of each binomial.
2. Multiply outer terms.
3. Multiply inner terms.
4. Multiply last terms.
5. Add like terms to simplify.

MANIPULATIVES

Factoring Trinomials

Materials: Algebra Tiles, Manipulatives Master 4 (Factor Frame)

Group Practice: Review procedures for factoring using the Algebra Tiles and the Factor Frame. Build a model of a trinomial to be factored. Arrange the pieces inside the Factor Frame so that they meet the two conditions. Apply the Zero Rule when necessary. (See page T9, "Using the Factor Frame.") Arrange pieces on the outside of the Factor Frame to find the factors of the trinomial represented inside the Factor Frame.

Student Practice: Have students use models for Exercise B, Problems 9, 13, and 17 to factor the expressions or to check their answers.

3 Reinforce and Extend

COMMON ERROR

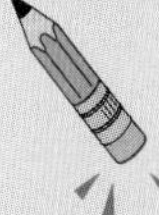

Because there are so many steps with substeps, students may make errors of several kinds: sign errors, exponent errors, errors in combining like terms. Use student work to illustrate and correct errors.

AT HOME

Find a quilt or other object at home that has a pattern of squares within a larger square, like this:

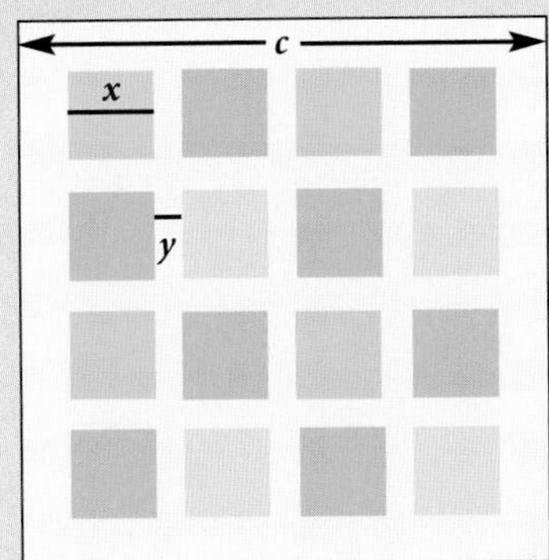

Draw a model of the object, labeling the dimensions of the geometric shapes and the overall piece. Bring in the drawing and use it to create algebraic expressions representing the perimeter and area of the piece. (Hint: Let x = width of each square, y = width of ("lattice") fabric between squares, and c = width of the outside border.)

- Show an expression that represents the perimeter of the quilt. Calculate the actual perimeter.
- Show an expression that represents the area of the quilt. Calculate the actual area.

Lesson at a Glance

Chapter 6 Lesson 5

Overview This lesson explains how the polynomial $a^2 - b^2$ models the difference of two perfect squares.

Objectives

- To define perfect squares
- To factor polynomials of the type $a^2 - b^2$, which represent the difference of two perfect squares

Student Pages 166–167

Teacher's Resource Library 

Workbook Activity 62

Activity 58

Alternative Activity 58

Mathematics Vocabulary

perfect squares

Warm-Up Activity

Write the following on the board and ask, "What is the relationship between these numbers?" *(The first number squared equals the second number.)*

5, 25	8, 64
6, 36	9, 81
7, 49	10, 100

Build on student responses to review the terms *square* and *square root* and the square root symbol.

Use tiles or squares drawn on the board to model *a* and a^2 for the number 3 to demonstrate visually the relationship between square and square root. Then ask students to read this lesson to learn about a special polynomial built from perfect squares.

Teaching the Lesson

When discussing the concept of perfect squares, it may be helpful to display the following pattern: $(0^2, 1^2, 2^2, 3^2, 4^2, 5^2, \ldots) = 0, 1, 4, 9, 16, 25, \ldots)$ Have students refer to the pattern to define the concept in their own words. Demonstrate that not all integers are perfect squares by having students find the square roots of 2, 3, and 5.

Lesson 5 Factoring Expressions: $a^2 - b^2$

Perfect square
The square of an integer

The squares of integers are called **perfect squares**. Examples of perfect squares include a^2 (because $a \cdot a = a^2$) and b^2 (because $b \cdot b = b^2$). Since a^2 is a perfect square and b^2 is a perfect square, $a^2 - b^2$ represents the difference of two perfect squares.

You can check this fact using multiplication:

$$(a + b)(a - b) = a(a - b) + b(a - b)$$
$$= a^2 - ab + ba - b^2$$

Using the commutative property of multiplication:

$$= a^2 - ab + ab - b^2$$
$$= a^2 - b^2$$

You can use geometry to visualize this process.

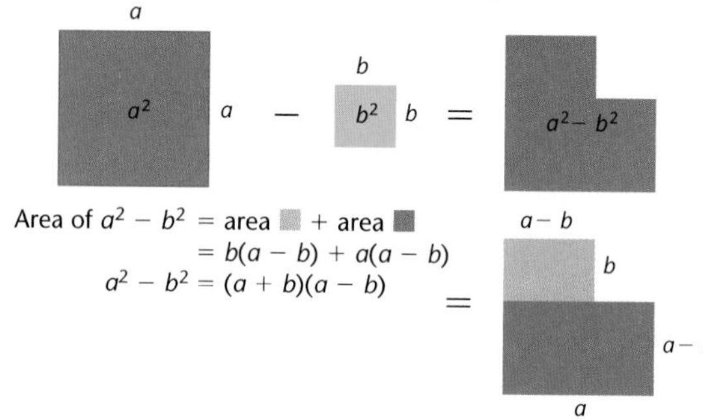

Rule The difference of two perfect squares can be factored using the model: $a^2 - b^2 = (a + b)(a - b)$, where $a = \sqrt{a^2}$ and $b = \sqrt{b^2}$.

EXAMPLE 1 You know that $25 = 5^2$, $9 = 3^2$, $25 - 9 = 16$.

You can use these facts to test the model:

Let $a = 5$ and $b = 3$. Then $a^2 - b^2 = 25 - 9 = 16$ True

and $(5 - 3)(5 + 3) = (2)(8) = 16$ True

Use the model to find the factors of $x^2 - 9$.

Step 1 Find the square roots of *a* and *b*:
$\sqrt{x^2} = x$ and $\sqrt{9} = 3$

Step 2 Place the values in the model.
$x^2 - 9 = (x + 3)(x - 3)$

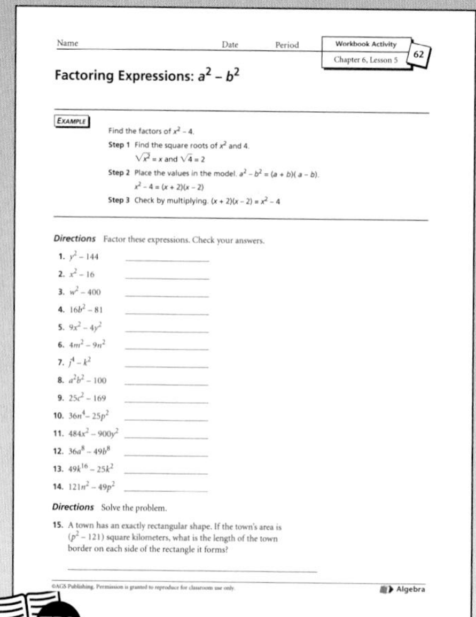

Name Date Period **Workbook Activity 62** Chapter 6, Lesson 5

Factoring Expressions: $a^2 - b^2$

EXAMPLE Find the factors of $x^2 - 4$.

Step 1 Find the square roots of x^2 and 4.
$\sqrt{x^2} = x$ and $\sqrt{4} = 2$

Step 2 Place the values in the model. $a^2 - b^2 = (a + b)(a - b)$.
$x^2 - 4 = (x + 2)(x - 2)$

Step 3 Check by multiplying. $(x + 2)(x - 2) = x^2 - 4$

Directions Factor these expressions. Check your answers.

1. $y^2 - 144$ ______
2. $x^2 - 16$ ______
3. $w^2 - 400$ ______
4. $16b^2 - 81$ ______
5. $9x^2 - 4y^2$ ______
6. $4m^2 - 9n^2$ ______
7. $j^4 - k^2$ ______
8. $a^2b^2 - 100$ ______
9. $25c^2 - 169$ ______
10. $36n^4 - 25p^2$ ______
11. $484x^2 - 900y^2$ ______
12. $36a^8 - 49b^8$ ______
13. $49k^{16} - 25k^2$ ______
14. $121n^2 - 49p^2$ ______

Directions Solve the problem.

15. A town has an exactly rectangular shape. If the town's area is $(p^2 - 121)$ square kilometers, what is the length of the town border on each side of the rectangle it forms?

______

 Algebra

TRL

Workbook Activity 62

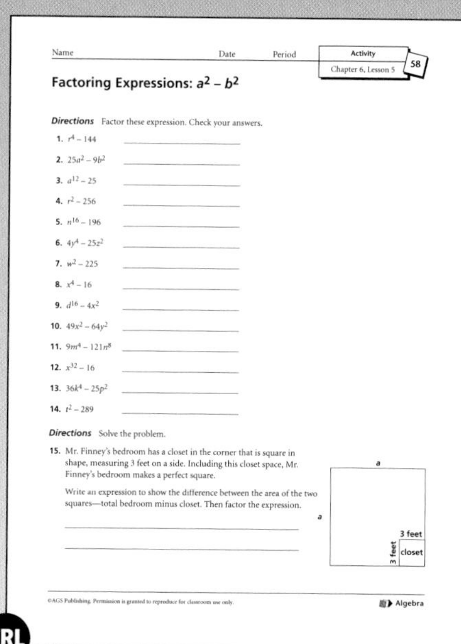

Name Date Period **Activity 58** Chapter 6, Lesson 5

Factoring Expressions: $a^2 - b^2$

Directions Factor these expression. Check your answers.

1. $r^4 - 144$ ______
2. $25a^2 - 9b^2$ ______
3. $a^{12} - 25$ ______
4. $r^2 - 256$ ______
5. $n^{16} - 196$ ______
6. $4y^4 - 25z^2$ ______
7. $w^2 - 225$ ______
8. $x^4 - 16$ ______
9. $d^{16} - 4x^2$ ______
10. $49x^2 - 64y^2$ ______
11. $9m^4 - 121n^8$ ______
12. $x^{32} - 16$ ______
13. $36k^4 - 25p^2$ ______
14. $t^2 - 289$ ______

Directions Solve the problem.

15. Mr. Finney's bedroom has a closet in the corner that is square in shape, measuring 3 feet on a side. Including this closet space, Mr. Finney's bedroom makes a perfect square.

Write an expression to show the difference between the area of the two squares—total bedroom minus closet. Then factor the expression.

______

______

 Algebra

TRL

Activity 58

Writing About Mathematics

Can you use the model to factor $8y^3 - 8$? Explain why or why not.

EXAMPLE 2 Find the factors of $9y^4 - 1$.

Step 1 Find the square roots of a and b:
$\sqrt{9y^4} = 3y^2$ and $\sqrt{1} = 1$

Step 2 Place the values in the model.
$9y^4 - 1 = (3y^2 + 1)(3y^2 - 1)$

Find the factors of $25x^6 - 4y^2$.
$\sqrt{25x^6} = 5x^3$ and $\sqrt{4y^2} = 2y$
$25x^6 - 4y^2 = (5x^3 + 2y)(5x^3 - 2y)$

Exercise A Use the model to factor these differences. Check your answers using arithmetic.

1. $144 - 100$ 44 **3.** $36 - 25$ 11 **5.** $121 - 81$ 40
2. $81 - 49$ 32 **4.** $25 - 16$ 9 **6.** $100 - 49$ 51

Exercise B Use the model to factor these expressions. Check your answers using multiplication.

7. $y^2 - 49$ **9.** $p^2 - 121$ **11.** $z^2 - 225$
8. $m^2 - 81$ **10.** $q^2 - 169$ **12.** $t^6 - 36$

Exercise C Factor these expressions. Check your answers.

13. $49x^2 - 1$ **15.** $36t^4 - 121$ **17.** $25r^8 - 1$
14. $25m^2 - 25$ **16.** $64x^6 - 49$ **18.** $100x^{10} - 100$

Exercise D Write these expressions as a product.

19. $49x^4 - 25y^2$ **21.** $36a^2b^2 - 1$ **23.** $81m^2 - 64n^{10}$
20. $121y^4 - 144z^6$ **22.** $225k^8 - 169h^4$ **24.** $625h^6 - 324h^8$

PROBLEM SOLVING

Exercise E Solve the problem.

25. A square fountain is planned for a city plaza. The plan calls for the plaza to be paved in decorative tiles. What area will the tiles need to cover? 319 m^2

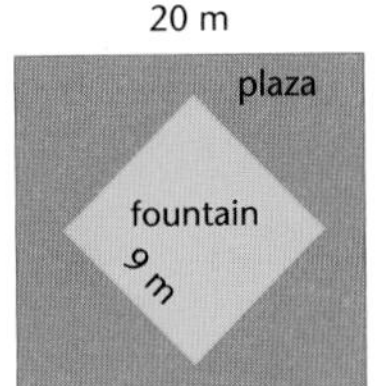

7. $(y + 7)(y - 7)$
8. $(m + 9)(m - 9)$
9. $(p + 11)(p - 11)$
10. $(q + 13)(q - 13)$
11. $(z + 15)(z - 15)$
12. $(t^3 + 6)(t^3 - 6)$
13. $(7x + 1)(7x - 1)$
14. $(5m - 5)(5m + 5)$
15. $(6t^2 + 11)(6t^2 - 11)$
16. $(8x^3 - 7)(8x^3 + 7)$
17. $(5r^4 + 1)(5r^4 - 1)$
18. $(10x^5 - 10)(10x^5 + 10)$
19. $(7x^2 - 5y)(7x^2 + 5y)$
20. $(11y^2 - 12z^3)(11y^2 + 12z^3)$
21. $(6ab + 1)(6ab - 1)$
22. $(15k^4 - 13h^2)(15k^4 + 13h^2)$
23. $(9m + 8n^5)(9m - 8n^5)$
24. $(25h^3 - 18h^4)(25h^3 + 18h^4)$

Show a sample using the FOIL method. Students should note that the O and I elements of the FOIL method cancel each other out. Substitute real numbers in the factors (square roots of perfect squares) to demonstrate.

3 Reinforce and Extend

LEARNING STYLES

Visual/Spatial

As students present their answers to Exercise C on the board, use a geometric model like that on page 166 to explain their solutions.

GROUP PROBLEM SOLVING

Have students work together in small groups to create models of rooms within rooms. They may find actual rooms (a closet within a bedroom is one example) to measure and create models to scale, or you may give them hypothetical situations. Have them draw their models on posterboard with A^2 set inside B^2. Ask them to color their models to show the area representing $a^2 - b^2$.

AT HOME

Have students work in groups of four or five to analyze the amount of area reserved for handicapped parking in several small parking lots. Have groups meet to decide

- what information they need to gather
- how they will gather the information
- how $a^2 - b^2$ can be used

Lesson at a Glance

Chapter 6 Lesson 6

Overview This lesson introduces perfect square trinomials and shows how they are factored.

Objectives

- To identify perfect square trinomials
- To model the binomial factors of a perfect square trinomial geometrically
- To factor perfect square trinomials

Student Pages 168–171

Teacher's Resource Library 

Workbook Activity 63

Activity 59

Alternative Activity 59

Mathematics Vocabulary

perfect square trinomial

Warm-Up Activity

Write $(a + b)(a + b)$ on the board. Ask, "What does this represent?" *(A binomial term multiplied by itself, or squared)* Have students complete the calculation independently and confirm the polynomial as $a^2 + 2ab + b^2$. Have students read page 168 for an introduction to another kind of polynomial, involving perfect squares in a new way.

Teaching the Lesson

Review the commutative property of multiplication as you go over the second line of each example. Ask, "Why does $ab + ba = 2ab$?" *(Because $ab = ba$)* Have students locate a^2, $2ab$, and b^2 in the geometric model of each example to be sure they grasp the concept visually.

Lesson 6 Factoring Expressions: $a^2 + 2ab + b^2$

Perfect square trinomial

The result of multiplying a binomial by itself or squaring a binomial

You can use what you know about multiplying binomials to find the factors of some trinomials.

EXAMPLE 1
$$(a + b)(a + b) = (a + b)^2 = a(a + b) + b(a + b)$$
$$= a^2 + ab + ba + b^2$$

Using the commutative property of multiplication:

$$= a^2 + 2ab + b^2$$

$a^2 + 2ab + b^2$ is a **perfect square trinomial.**

You can use geometry to visualize this process.

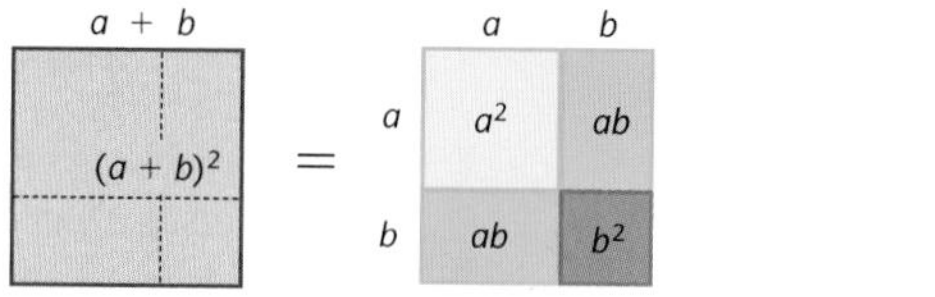

a + b; a + b; $(a + b)^2$ = a, b; a, b; a^2, ab, ab, b^2

$$\text{Area of } (a + b)^2 = (a + b)(a + b)$$
$$= (a \bullet a) + (a \bullet b) + (a \bullet b) + (b \bullet b)$$
$$(a + b)^2 = a^2 + 2ab + b^2$$

EXAMPLE 2
$$(a - b)(a - b) = (a - b)^2 = a(a - b) - b(a - b)$$
$$= a^2 - ab - ba + b^2$$

Using the commutative property of multiplication:

$$= a^2 - 2ab + b^2$$

$a^2 - 2ab + b^2$ is a **perfect square trinomial.**

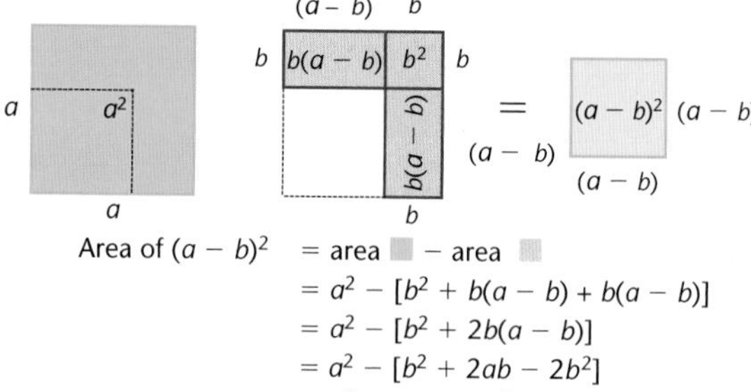

$$\text{Area of } (a - b)^2 = \text{area} \;\blacksquare\; - \text{area} \;\blacksquare$$
$$= a^2 - [b^2 + b(a - b) + b(a - b)]$$
$$= a^2 - [b^2 + 2b(a - b)]$$
$$= a^2 - [b^2 + 2ab - 2b^2]$$
$$= a^2 - [2ab - b^2]$$
$$(a - b)^2 = a^2 - 2ab + b^2$$

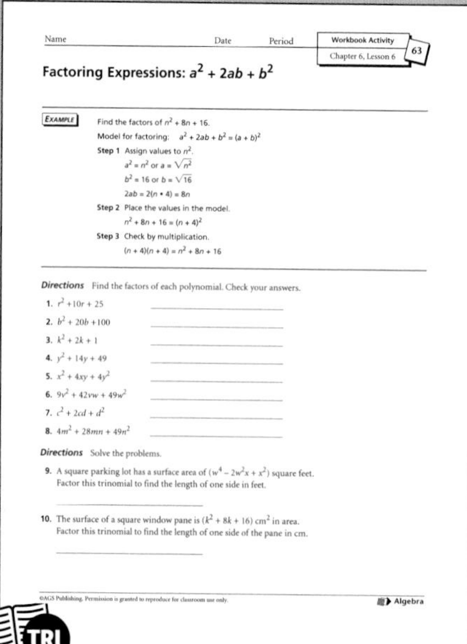

Name Date Period **Workbook Activity 63** Chapter 6, Lesson 6

Factoring Expressions: $a^2 + 2ab + b^2$

EXAMPLE Find the factors of $n^2 + 8n + 16$.

Model for factoring: $a^2 + 2ab + b^2 = (a + b)^2$

Step 1 Assign values to n^2.

$a^2 = n^2$ or $a = \sqrt{n^2}$

$b^2 = 16$ or $b = \sqrt{16}$

$2ab = 2(n \bullet 4) = 8n$

Step 2 Place the values in the model.

$n^2 + 8n + 16 = (n + 4)^2$

Step 3 Check by multiplication.

$(n + 4)(n + 4) = n^2 + 8n + 16$

Directions Find the factors of each polynomial. Check your answers.

1. $r^2 + 10r + 25$ ______
2. $b^2 + 20b + 100$ ______
3. $k^2 + 2k + 1$ ______
4. $y^2 + 14y + 49$ ______
5. $x^2 + 4xy + 4y^2$ ______
6. $9v^2 + 42vw + 49w^2$ ______
7. $c^2 + 2cd + d^2$ ______
8. $4m^2 + 28mn + 49n^2$ ______

Directions Solve the problems.

9. A square parking lot has a surface area of $(w^4 - 2w^2x + x^2)$ square feet. Factor this trinomial to find the length of one side in feet.

10. The surface of a square window pane is $(k^2 + 8k + 16)$ cm^2 in area. Factor this trinomial to find the length of one side of the pane in cm.

 Algebra

TRL

Workbook Activity 63

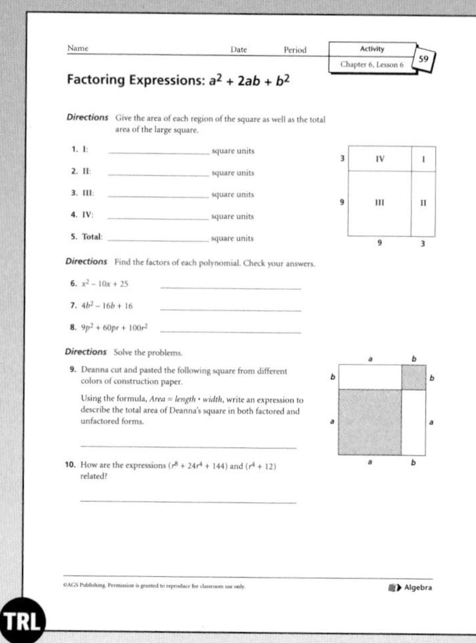

Name Date Period **Activity 59** Chapter 6, Lesson 6

Factoring Expressions: $a^2 + 2ab + b^2$

Directions Give the area of each region of the square as well as the total area of the large square.

1. I: ______ square units
2. II: ______ square units
3. III: ______ square units
4. IV: ______ square units
5. Total: ______ square units

Directions Find the factors of each polynomial. Check your answers.

6. $x^2 - 10x + 25$ ______
7. $4b^2 - 16b + 16$ ______
8. $9p^2 + 60pr + 100r^2$ ______

Directions Solve the problems.

9. Deanna cut and pasted the following square from different colors of construction paper.

   Using the formula, *Area = length • width*, write an expression to describe the total area of Deanna's square in both factored and unfactored forms.

10. How are the expressions $(r^8 + 24r^4 + 144)$ and $(r^4 + 12)$ related?

 Algebra

TRL

Activity 59

Rule The perfect square trinomial can be factored using the model: $a^2 + 2ab + b^2 = (a + b)^2$.

EXAMPLE 3 Use the model to find the factors of $x^2 + 4x + 4$.

Step 1 Assign values to $x^2 + 4x + 4$ from the model:

$a^2 = x^2$ or $a = x$

$b^2 = 4$ or $b = 2$, this means that

$2ab = 2(2x) = 4x$

Step 2 Place the values in the model.

$x^2 + 4x + 4 = (x + 2)(x + 2) = (x + 2)^2$

EXAMPLE 4 Find the factors of $x^2 + 6x + 9$.

Step 1 Assign values from the model:

$a^2 = x^2$ or $a = x$

$b^2 = 9$ or $b = 3$, this means that

$2ab = 2(3x) = 6x$

Step 2 Place the values in the model.

$x^2 + 6x + 9 = (x + 3)(x + 3) = (x + 3)^2$

Exercise A Give the area of each region of the square as well as the total area of the large square.

1. 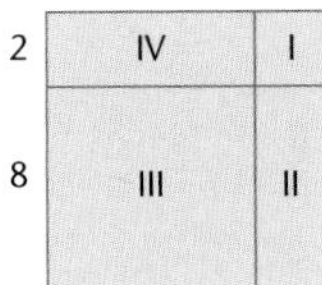

I = 4 sq. units, II = 16 sq. units, III = 64 sq. units, IV = 16 sq. units, total = 100 sq. units

COMMON ERROR

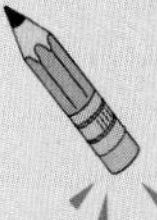

Some students make errors with + and − signs in multiplying factors. Have them work through the derivation of $a^2 - 2ab + b^2$ and $a^2 + 2ab + b^2$ on the board, circling − elements in one color and + elements in another.

3 Reinforce and Extend

LEARNING STYLES

Body/Kinesthetic

Students who have difficulty understanding the factoring examples on page 169 may benefit from working in small groups to create geometric models of each example, patterned after those on page 168.

LEARNING STYLES

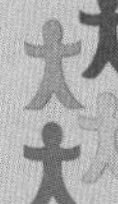

LEP/ESL

Students who struggle with factoring trinomials may benefit from the mnemonic device FOIL. It shows how elements of each binomial are distributed over one another:

FIRST OUTSIDE INSIDE LAST

$(a + b)(a + b)$

Have students work together to create poster-size models of the binomials for the perfect square trinomial: $(a - b)(a - b)$ and $(a + b)(a + b)$

Then have them show each product of the multiplications performed to derive the perfect square trinomial using the FOIL method. Suggest that they use arrows or color coding, etc., to show clearly how $-2ab$ and $+2ab$ are derived.

Learning Styles

Auditory/Verbal

Have students explain how they know b must be negative for the trinomial $a^2 - 2ab + b^2$. *(a is positive, yet the sum of the ab products is negative; therefore, b must be negative; b^2 is positive because a negative times a negative gives a positive.)*

Learning Styles

Visual/Spatial

Link the geometric models in Exercise A to the polynomial model. Reproduce each model on the board and have students identify each number and roman numeral as a, b, $(a - b)$, a^2, or b^2. *[E.g., in item 1, $a = 8$, $b = 2$, $IV = (a - b)$, $I = b^2$, etc.]*

2.

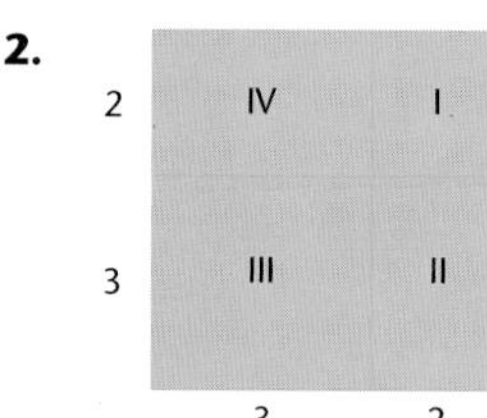

I = 4 sq. units, II = 6 sq. units, III = 9 sq. units, IV = 6 sq. units, total = 25 sq. units

3.

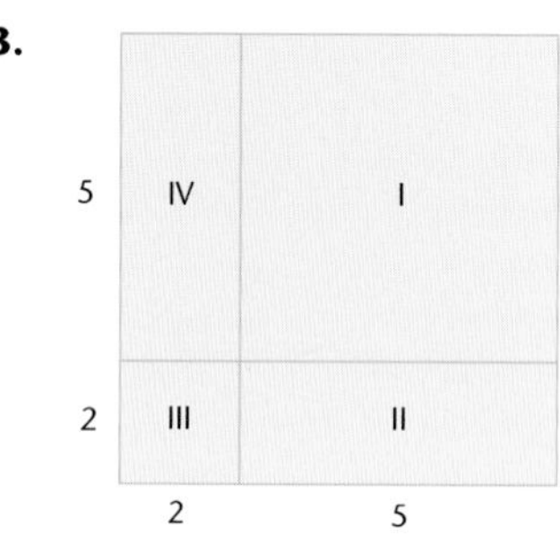

I = 25 sq. units, II = 10 sq. units, III = 4 sq. units, IV = 10 sq. units, total = 49 sq. units

Exercise B Use the model to find the factors of these perfect square trinomials.

4. $m^2 - 24m + 144$ $(m - 12)^2$

5. $x^2 + 24x + 144$ $(x + 12)^2$

6. $p^2 - 18p + 81$ $(p - 9)^2$

7. $t^2 + 18t + 81$ $(t + 9)^2$

8. $z^2 + 30z + 225$ $(z + 15)^2$

9. $x^2 + 26x + 169$ $(x + 13)^2$

Exercise C Find the factors of these trinomials.

10. $4m^2 + 48m + 144$ $(2m + 12)^2$

11. $4r^2 - 48r + 144$ $(2r - 12)^2$

Writing About Mathematics

Is $64m^5 + 128m^3 + 64m^2$ a perfect square trinomial? Tell why or why not. Find all the factors of the trinomial.

12. $16x^4 - 16x^2 + 4$ $(4x^2 - 2)^2$

13. $81p^6 + 90p^3 + 25$ $(9p^3 + 5)^2$

14. $4x^2 - 60x + 225$ $(2x - 15)^2$

15. $25x^4 + 50x^2 + 25$ $(5x^2 + 5)^2$

16. $36y^2 - 156y + 169$ $(6y - 13)^2$

17. $144b^4 - 24b^2 + 1$ $(12b^2 - 1)^2$

18. $49q^8 + 28q^4 + 4$ $(7q^4 + 2)^2$

PROBLEM SOLVING

Exercise D Solve each problem.

19. An architect drew this sketch to show how she would enlarge an existing room. The area of the existing room is 49 square units. The area of the new room will be 100 square units. What is the length and width of each region?

IV | I

III | II, existing room

$II = 7 \cdot 7, I = 7 \cdot 3,$
$III = 7 \cdot 3, IV = 3 \cdot 3$

20. Use the diagram below to show that the area of the large square is $16y^2 - 8y + 1$.

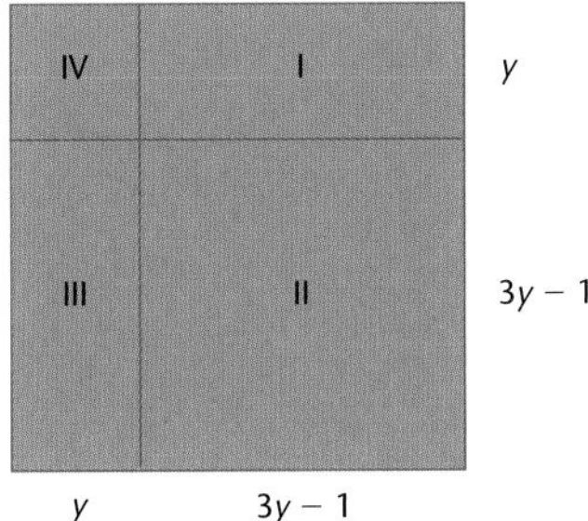

Area $= [y + (3y - 1)]^2$. Students may find the area by multiplication or by adding the areas of each region.

Area by addition $=$
$y^2 + 2(3y - 1)y + (3y - 1)^2 =$
$(6y - 2)y + y^2 + (3y - 1)^2 =$
$6y^2 - 2y + y^2 + (3y - 1)(3y - 1) =$
$6y^2 - 2y + y^2 + 9y^2 - 3y - 3y + 1 =$
$6y^2 + y^2 + 9y^2 - 2y - 6y + 1 =$
$16y^2 - 8y + 1$

Group Problem Solving

Have groups of three or four students serve as "editorial staff" for a newsletter. Provide each group with a square photograph or image (2 x 2, 1 x 1, 3 x 3, and so on) and a piece of paper (8 x 8) for one "page" of the newsletter. Have the group determine

- How much area should be allowed as a margin
- How much of the printed area the photograph will fill
- How much area will remain for text

Require students to show their calculations, mark up the page, place the photograph, and indicate where text will go. Finally, have a representative of each group explain the process to the class.

Online Connection

Students can read about the fascinating origin of zero at www.sciam.com/askexpert_question.cfm?articleID=000A41D6-B959-1C71-9EB7809EC588F2D7&catID=3&topicID=11. After students have read this article, have them work in groups to write a paragraph about (or list examples of) what mathematics, the world, and their lives might be like if zero did not exist.

Lesson at a Glance

Chapter 6 Lesson 7

Overview This lesson explains the zero product property.

Objectives

- To recognize that a product of 0 results when one or both factors is 0
- To solve equations whose factors = 0

Student Pages 172–173

Teacher's Resource Library 

Workbook Activity 64

Activity 60

Alternative Activity 60

1 Warm-Up Activity

Write the following on the board:

$9 \cdot a = 0$

$3^3 \cdot b = 0$

$a \cdot b = 0$

and have students solve for a and b. Ask, "If the product of two unknown numbers is zero, what can you tell about the numbers? How do you know this?"

2 Teaching the Lesson

Be sure students understand that the solutions to equations [of the type $(x + 1)(x - 2) = 0$] in this lesson create two answers (either $x = -1$ *or* $x = 2$).

Exercise B requires students to apply their understanding of this type of equation. Before assigning the exercise, work together through problem 15 and one or more additional problems like the following:

$(x - 3)(x - 2) = 0$

($x = 3$ or $x = 2$)

$(5x + 5)(x - 10) = 0$

($x = -1$ or $x = 10$)

Lesson 7 Zero as a Factor

You already know that 0 times any number equals zero. So if $3x = 0$, you know that x must equal 0.

Suppose you know that the product of two unknown numbers is 0. What are the numbers?

Let a, b be the two numbers, then

$ab = 0$

Either a or b or both must be zero because

if	$a = 0$,	then $(0)(b) = 0$	True
if	$b = 0$,	then $(a)(0) = 0$	True
if	$a = 0$ and $b = 0$,	then $(0)(0) = 0$	True

Conclusion: $ab = 0$ whenever $a = 0$ or $b = 0$, or $a = b = 0$

EXAMPLE 1 Find the value of the variable.

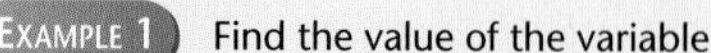

$5y = 0$ Since $5 \neq 0$, y must be 0.

$y = 0$ because $(5)(0) = 0$

EXAMPLE 2

$3x^2 = 0$ Since $3 \neq 0$, x^2 must be 0.

$x^2 = 0$ because $(3)(0) = 0$, $x = 0$

$x = 0$

EXAMPLE 3

$5(x + 1) = 0$ Since $5 \neq 0$, $x + 1$ must be 0.

$(x + 1) = 0$ because $(5)(0) = 0$

so $(x + 1) = 0$ and $x = -1$

Check. $5(x - 1) = 5(-1 + 1) = 5(0) = 0$

EXAMPLE 4

$(x + 1)(x - 2) = 0$ implies

$(x + 1) = 0$ because $(0)(x - 2) = 0$

or $(x - 2) = 0$ because $(x + 1)(0) = 0$

if $(x + 1) = 0$ then $x = -1$

Check. $(-1 + 1)(-1 - 2) = 0(-3) = 0$

if $(x - 2) = 0$ then $x = 2$

Check. $(2 + 1)(2 - 2) = 3(0) = 0$

so $x = -1$ or $x = 2$

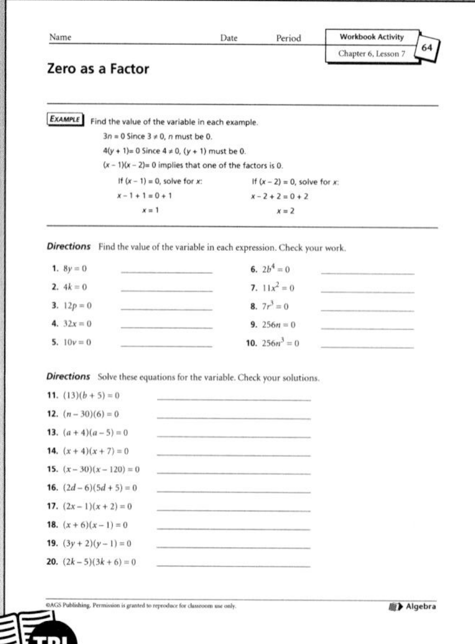

Name Date Period | Workbook Activity 64 | Chapter 6, Lesson 7

Zero as a Factor

EXAMPLE Find the value of the variable in each example.

$3n = 0$ Since $3 \neq 0$, n must be 0.

$4(y + 1) = 0$ Since $4 \neq 0$, $(y + 1)$ must be 0.

$(x - 1)(x - 2) = 0$ implies that one of the factors is 0.

If $(x - 1) = 0$, solve for x: $x - 1 + 1 = 0 + 1$, $x = 1$

If $(x - 2) = 0$, solve for x: $x - 2 + 2 = 0 + 2$, $x = 2$

Directions Find the value of the variable in each expression. Check your work.

1. $8y = 0$ ____
2. $4k = 0$ ____
3. $12p = 0$ ____
4. $32x = 0$ ____
5. $10v = 0$ ____
6. $2b^4 = 0$ ____
7. $11x^2 = 0$ ____
8. $7r^3 = 0$ ____
9. $256n = 0$ ____
10. $256n^3 = 0$ ____

Directions Solve these equations for the variable. Check your solutions.

11. $(13)(b + 5) = 0$ ____
12. $(n - 30)(6) = 0$ ____
13. $(a + 4)(a - 5) = 0$ ____
14. $(x + 4)(x + 7) = 0$ ____
15. $(x - 30)(x - 120) = 0$ ____
16. $(2d - 6)(5d + 5) = 0$ ____
17. $(2x - 1)(x + 2) = 0$ ____
18. $(x + 6)(x - 1) = 0$ ____
19. $(3y + 2)(y - 1) = 0$ ____
20. $(2k - 5)(3k + 6) = 0$ ____

 Algebra

TRL

Workbook Activity 64

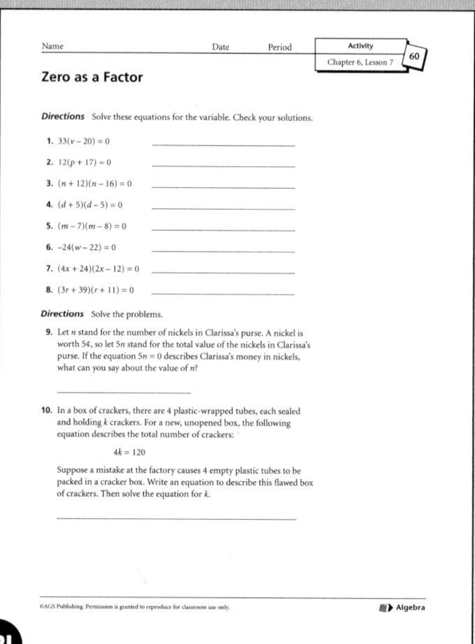

Name Date Period | Activity 60 | Chapter 6, Lesson 7

Zero as a Factor

Directions Solve these equations for the variable. Check your solutions.

1. $33(v - 20) = 0$ ____
2. $12(p + 17) = 0$ ____
3. $(n + 12)(n - 16) = 0$ ____
4. $(d + 5)(d - 5) = 0$ ____
5. $(m - 7)(m - 8) = 0$ ____
6. $-24(w - 22) = 0$ ____
7. $(4x + 24)(2x - 12) = 0$ ____
8. $(3r + 39)(r + 11) = 0$ ____

Directions Solve the problems.

9. Let n stand for the number of nickels in Clarissa's purse. A nickel is worth 5¢, so let $5n$ stand for the total value of the nickels in Clarissa's purse. If the equation $5n = 0$ describes Clarissa's money in nickels, what can you say about the value of n?

____

10. In a box of crackers, there are 4 plastic-wrapped tubes, each sealed and holding k crackers. For a new, unopened box, the following equation describes the total number of crackers:

$4k = 120$

Suppose a mistake at the factory causes 4 empty plastic tubes to be packed in a cracker box. Write an equation to describe this flawed box of crackers. Then solve the equation for k.

____

 Algebra

TRL

Activity 60

Exercise A Find the value of the variable in each expression. Check your work.

1. $4m = 0$ $m = 0$
2. $34k = 0$ $k = 0$
3. $16y = 0$ $y = 0$
4. $23x = 0$ $x = 0$
5. $12x^2 = 0$ $x^2 = 0, x = 0$
6. $14y^3 = 0$ $y^3 = 0, y = 0$
7. $21b^4 = 0$ $b^4 = 0, b = 0$
8. $44m^2 = 0$ $m^2 = 0, m = 0$
9. $9x^3 = 0$ $x^3 = 0, x = 0$
10. $33d^2 = 0$ $d^2 = 0, d = 0$

Exercise B Solve these equations for the variable. Check your solutions.

11. $17(x - 5) = 0$
12. $21(y + 1) = 0$
13. $12(m + 21) = 0$
14. $12(m + 4) = 0$
15. $(n - 12)(n + 4) = 0$
16. $(x - 6)(x + 5) = 0$
17. $14(m - 4) = 0$
18. $(3x - 9)(x + 1) = 0$
19. $(4x - 6)(x + 6) = 0$
20. $(x - 6)^2(x + 5) = 0$
21. $(9z - 18)(12z + 6) = 0$
22. $(4t - 12)(5t - 25) = 0$
23. $(3x + 6)(2x - 10) = 0$
24. $(5x - 5)(14x + 28) = 0$
25. $(4p - 4)(13p + 27) = 0$

11. $x = 5$
12. $y = -1$
13. $m = -21$
14. $m = -4$
15. $n = 12$ or $n = -4$
16. $x = 6$ or $x = -5$
17. $m = 4$
18. $x = 3$ or $x = -1$
19. $x = \frac{6}{4} = 1\frac{1}{2}$ or $x = -6$
20. $x = 6$ or $x = -5$
21. $z = -\frac{1}{2}$ or $z = 2$
22. $t = 3$ or $t = 5$
23. $x = -2$ or $x = 5$
24. $x = 1$ or $x = -2$
25. $p = 1$ or $p = -\frac{27}{13}$

TRY THIS $(2x^2 - 32)(x - 9) = 0$

$(2x^2 - 32) = 0$ or $(x - 9) = 0$; if $(2x^2 - 32) = 0$, then $2x^2 = 32$, $x^2 = 16$ and $x = 4$ or $x = -4$; if $x - 9 = 0$, $x = 9$

Try This

Solving the first binomial $(2x^2 - 32)$ requires students to add a step: finding the square root. Remind them that they practiced finding square roots in Lesson 5, pages 166–167.

MANIPULATIVES

Zero as a Factor

Materials: Algebra Tiles, Manipulatives Master 4 (Factor Frame)

Group Practice: Using the examples $5(x + 1)$ and $(x + 1)(x - 2)$, build a model of the factors that contain a variable. To find the value of the variable, use the Zero Rule and replace the unknown piece with the appropriate number of unit pieces to make the factor equal zero. The number of units used to replace the unknown piece represents the value of the variable that satisfies the equation.

Student Practice: Have students use models for Exercise B, Problems 11–18, 20, and 22–23. Have students sketch each model and write its symbolic equivalent.

3 Reinforce and Extend

LEARNING STYLES

Visual/Spatial

Students who are visual learners will benefit from seeing a graph of a factored quadratic equation since it clearly shows two solutions for x. Inform students that such graphs on the x, y axes are mathematical models. (Graphing equations will be studied in depth in Chapter 10.) For these problems, y is set at 0, so the solutions for x appear on the x number line.

MENTAL MATH

To accustom students to the new step of finding the value of x in binomial factors, give the following problems orally, and have students answer orally:

$x + 20 = 0$	*($x = -20$)*
$x - 9 = 0$	*($x = 9$)*
$x - 12 = 0$	*($x = 12$)*
$x + 3 = 0$	*($x = -3$)*
$x + 13 = 0$	*($x = -13$)*

Then have students think of a general mathematical rule to express the relationship between the sign of x and the sign of the factor of c. *(Here is one possibility: For $x + c_1 = 0$, $x = -c_1$ and for $x - c_1 = 0$, $x = +c_1$ where c_1 is a factor of c in a trinomial equation.)*

Lesson at a Glance

Chapter 6 Lesson 8

Overview This lesson introduces quadratic equations and shows how to solve them using zero as a factor.

Objectives

- To identify the form of a quadratic equation
- To find solutions for quadratic equations by substituting values equal to zero

Student Pages 174–177

Teacher's Resource Library 

Workbook Activity 65

Activity 61

Alternative Activity 61

Mathematics Vocabulary

quadratic equation
solution

Warm-Up Activity

Write the following equation on the board:

$3x^2 + 6x = 24$

Ask students to identify the form of polynomial equation this represents. (If students have difficulty, remind them that they may subtract an equal number from both sides of the equation: $3x^2 + 6x - 24 = 0$.) Explain that $ax^2 + bx + c = 0$ is a quadratic equation and that in this lesson, students will apply what they know about factoring to solving quadratic equations.

Teaching the Lesson

Write the following equation on the board and ask students how they could solve it using the quadratic equation model:

$3x^2 + 5x = 12$

Stress the importance of substituting the solutions into the original equation to check answers (step 4 of each example).

Lesson 8 Solving Quadratic Equations—Factoring

Quadratic equation
An equation in the form of $ax^2 + bx + c = 0$

Solution
The value of a variable that makes an open statement true

Recall that if

$$\begin{aligned} (x+1)(x-2) &= 0 \quad \text{then either} \\ (x+1) &= 0 \quad \text{and } x = -1 \text{ or} \\ (x-2) &= 0 \quad \text{and } x = +2 \end{aligned}$$

Also recall you can rewrite $(x + 1)(x - 2)$ as a trinomial:

$$\begin{aligned} (x+1)(x-2) &= x(x-2) + 1(x-2) \\ &= x^2 - 2x + x - 2 \\ &= x^2 - x - 2 \end{aligned}$$

So, $(x + 1)(x - 2) = 0$ is the same as $x^2 - x - 2 = 0$

$x^2 - x - 2 = 0$ is an example of a **quadratic equation.** *Quadratic* means square and in a quadratic equation the highest power of the variable is 2. The expression is an equation because it is equal to zero.

> **Rule** The general form of a quadratic equation is $ax^2 + bx + c = 0$.

$x = -1$ and $x = +2$ are called **solutions** to the quadratic equation $x^2 - x - 2 = 0$. When these values are substituted for x in the equation, the resulting statements are true.

Let $x = -1$, then $x^2 - x - 2 =$
$(-1)^2 - (-1) - 2 = 1 + 1 - 2 = 0$ True

Let $x = 2$, then $x^2 - x - 2 =$
$(2)^2 - 2 - 2 = 4 - 4 = 0$ True

Therefore, -1 and 2 represent the solutions for $x^2 - x - 2 = 0$. To solve a quadratic equation, you must find the solutions for the equation.

EXAMPLE 1 Solve $x^2 + 3x + 2 = 0$.

Step 1 Factor the equation. $x^2 + 3x + 2 = (x + 2)(x + 1) = 0$

Step 2 Set each factor equal to 0. $x + 2 = 0$ or $x + 1 = 0$

Step 3 Solve each factor for x. $x + 2 = 0, x = -2$ or $x + 1 = 0, x = -1$

Step 4 Check. Let $x = -2$, $x^2 + 3x + 2 = (-2)^2 + 3(-2) + 2 = 4 - 6 + 2 = 0$ True
Let $x = -1$, $x^2 + 3x + 2 = (-1)^2 + 3(-1) + 2 = 1 - 3 + 2 = 0$ True
The solutions are -2 and -1.

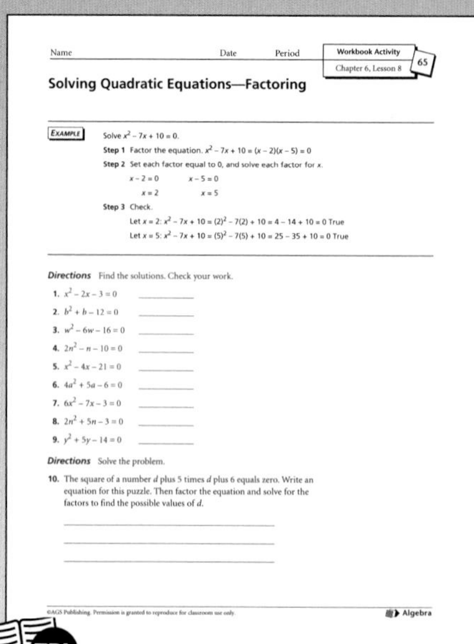

Name Date Period | Workbook Activity 65 | Chapter 6, Lesson 8

Solving Quadratic Equations—Factoring

EXAMPLE Solve $x^2 - 7x + 10 = 0$.

Step 1 Factor the equation. $x^2 - 7x + 10 = (x - 2)(x - 5) = 0$

Step 2 Set each factor equal to 0, and solve each factor for x.
$x - 2 = 0$ $x - 5 = 0$
$x = 2$ $x = 5$

Step 3 Check.
Let $x = 2$: $x^2 - 7x + 10 = (2)^2 - 7(2) + 10 = 4 - 14 + 10 = 0$ True
Let $x = 5$: $x^2 - 7x + 10 = (5)^2 - 7(5) + 10 = 25 - 35 + 10 = 0$ True

Directions Find the solutions. Check your work.

1. $x^2 - 2x - 3 = 0$ ______
2. $b^2 + b - 12 = 0$ ______
3. $w^2 - 6w - 16 = 0$ ______
4. $2n^2 - n - 10 = 0$ ______
5. $x^2 - 4x - 21 = 0$ ______
6. $4a^2 + 5a - 6 = 0$ ______
7. $6x^2 - 7x - 3 = 0$ ______
8. $2n^2 + 5n - 3 = 0$ ______
9. $y^2 + 5y - 14 = 0$ ______

Directions Solve the problem.

10. The square of a number d plus 5 times d plus 6 equals zero. Write an equation for this puzzle. Then factor the equation and solve for the factors to find the possible values of d.

Algebra

Workbook Activity 65

Name Date Period | Activity 61 | Chapter 6, Lesson 8

Solving Quadratic Equations—Factoring

Directions Find the solutions. Check your work.

1. $a^2 - 9a - 10 = 0$ ______
2. $2n^2 - 3n - 20 = 0$ ______
3. $3x^2 + x - 52 = 0$ ______

Directions Solve the problems.

4. Two times the square of a number y equals 13 times y minus 15. The following equation restates this information:
$2y^2 = 13y - 15$
Next, you can change the equation into a trinomial for factoring:
$2y^2 - 13y + 15 = 13y - 15 - 13y + 15$
$2y^2 - 13y + 15 = 0$
Factor the trinomial and solve for y. List the possible values for y.

5. A touching square and rectangle share a common side, n. (See the diagram.) The area of the square is described by n^2 and the area of the rectangle by $3n$. The sum of these two areas is 40 square units. The following equation restates this information:
$n^2 + 3n = 40$
Now you can change this equation into a trinomial for factoring:
$n^2 + 3n - 40 = 40 - 40$
$n^2 + 3n - 40 = 0$
Factor this trinomial and solve for n to find the length of side n in the diagram. Explain why only one of the possible solutions is reasonable.

n
A = n²
n
A = 3n
3

Algebra

Activity 61

Example 2 Solve $2m^2 - m - 3 = 0$.

Step 1 Factor the equation. The factors of 2 are 1 and 2, and the factors of 3 are 1 and 3. Arrange these factors as many ways as possible.

$(2m - 1)(m + 3)$

$(2m + 1)(m - 3)$

$(m - 1)(2m + 3)$

$(m + 1)(2m - 3)$

Step 2 Decide which arrangement is equal to $2m^2 - m - 3$, the given equation.

$(2m - 1)(m + 3) = 2m^2 + 5m - 3$

$(2m + 1)(m - 3) = 2m^2 - 5m - 3$

$(m - 1)(2m + 3) = 2m^2 + m - 3$

$(m + 1)(2m - 3) = 2m^2 - m - 3$

Step 3 Since $(m + 1)(2m - 3) = 2m^2 - m - 3$, the given equation, set $(m + 1)$ and $(2m - 3)$ equal to zero. Then solve.

$m + 1 = 0 \qquad 2m - 3 = 0$

$m = -1 \qquad 2m = 3$

$m = \frac{3}{2}$

Step 4 Check.

Let $m = -1$, then $2m^2 - m - 3 = 2(-1)^2 - (-1) - 3$
$= 2(1) + 1 - 3$
$= 2 + 1 - 3$
$= 3 - 3$
$= 0$ True

Let $m = \frac{3}{2}$, then $2m^2 - m - 3 = 2(\frac{3}{2})^2 - (\frac{3}{2}) - 3$
$= 2(\frac{9}{4}) - \frac{3}{2} - 3$
$= \frac{18}{4} - \frac{3}{2} - 3$
$= \frac{18}{4} - \frac{6}{4} - 3$
$= \frac{12}{4} - 3$
$= 3 - 3$
$= 0$ True

Manipulatives

Quadratic Equations

Materials: Algebra Tiles, Manipulatives Master 4 (Factor Frame)

Group Practice: Review the procedures for factoring trinomials. Using the examples in the text and the Algebra Tiles, factor the polynomial. To find the root of each factor, remove the unknown piece(s). Apply the Zero Rule and replace the unknown piece with as many unit pieces as are needed to make the factor equal 0. The root is the value represented by the pieces that replace the unknown piece.

Student Practice: Have students use models for Exercise A, Problems 1–8, 10–12, and Exercise B, Problems 17 and 18, to solve the equations or to check answers obtained by using the method used in the examples.

3 Reinforce and Extend

Learning Styles

LEP/ESL

Students who have not grasped the factoring of trinomials will be unable to solve quadratic equations by factoring. Use problems in Exercise B to reteach the concepts in Lesson 4. Have students work in pairs. Assign a problem to each pair. Ask them to determine

- the numbers that represent a, b, and c
- the factors of a and c

Then have students work out all possible ways factors could be distributed in the binomial multiplicands. To keep track of factors, have students use one color for factors of a and another color for factors of c.

Mental Math

Before students solve quadratic equations, revisit the concepts of squares and their factors. Ask, "Why are there no negative numbers with square roots?" *(No real number squared gives a negative result: negative • negative = positive.)* Give numbers and have students tell whether they are perfect squares. Give trinomials and have students tell whether the terms in the factors are positive or negative.

Learning Styles

Interpersonal/ Group Learning

Before students begin Exercise A, assess their understanding of factoring by asking, "Why are two solutions possible?" *(A factored trinomial creates two binomials with x. Either one can equal 0.)* Have students work in pairs to complete Exercise A. Half the pairs do the odd-numbered problems, half do the even-numbered problems. Combine odd and even pairs into groups of four and have each pair explain their work to the other. Bring the class together again and discuss problems and insights.

Exercise A Solve each of these quadratic equations. Be sure to check your work.

1. $x^2 + 5x + 6 = 0$ $-2, -3$
2. $m^2 - 4m - 12 = 0$ $+6, -2$
3. $a^2 - 6a + 8 = 0$ $+2, +4$
4. $x^2 + 5x - 24 = 0$ $+3, -8$
5. $y^2 + 3y - 18 = 0$ $-6, +3$
6. $m^2 - 8m - 20 = 0$ $+10, -2$
7. $t^2 - t - 20 = 0$ $+5, -4$
8. $y^2 - 4y - 5 = 0$ $+5, -1$
9. $x^2 + 16x - 17 = 0$ $+1, -17$
10. $q^2 - q - 30 = 0$ $+6, -5$
11. $x^2 + 7x + 12 = 0$ $-3, -4$
12. $y^2 - 9y + 14 = 0$ $+2, +7$
13. $2t^2 - 12t - 32 = 0$ $8, -2$
14. $2d^2 - 18d - 20 = 0$ $10, -1$
15. $2x^2 + 13x + 15 = 0$ $\frac{-3}{2}, -5$

Exercise B Find the solutions. Check your work.

16. $8n^2 - 40n - 48 = 0$ $6, -1$
17. $2x^2 + 4x - 30 = 0$ $3, -5$
18. $3x^2 - 6x - 9 = 0$ $3, -1$
19. $4x^2 + 18x - 36 = 0$ $1\frac{1}{2}, -6$
20. $6x^2 - 18x - 60 = 0$ $-2, 5$

Estimation Activity

Estimate: Find the product.

13×17 8×14

Solution:
Use the distributive property to help figure out products.

Think:	$(10 + 3)17$	$8(10 + 7)$
Do:	$10 \times 17 = 170$ $3 \times 17 = 51$	$8 \times 10 = 80$ $8 \times 4 = 32$
Total:	$170 + 51 = 221$	$80 + 32 = 112$

Exercise C Find the solutions. Be sure to factor completely.

21. $3b^2 + 15b + 12 = 0$ see below

22. $2p^2 - 16p + 30 = 0$

23. $12x^2 + 18x + 6 = 0$

24. $3y^2 + 12y - 36 = 0$

25. $12c^2 + 60c + 72 = 0$

PROBLEM SOLVING

Exercise D Solve the problems.

These possibilities exist for some quadratic equations.

A The equation has no solution.

B The equation has one solution.

C The equation has two solutions.

Study the following equations. For each equation, choose A, B, or C.

26. $x^2 = 9$ C

27. $x^2 + 9 = 25$ C

28. $x^2 + 1 = 0$ A

29. $2x^2 - 10 = -10$ B

30. $25x^2 = 49$ C

Technology Connection

Measuring Mattes

When you frame a picture, you can use the quadratic equation to find the dimensions of the matte that goes around the picture. The equation calculates the exact, or geometric, center of the matte. But there is a piece of technology that solves the same problem—a print positioner. It positions a print in the optical center of a matte. Optical center means exactly centered between left and right, but slightly above center between top and bottom. What will they think of next?

21. $3(b^2 + 5b + 4) = 3(b + 4)(b + 1)$, solutions are $-4, -1$

22. $2(p^2 - 8p + 15) = 2(p - 5)(p - 3)$, solutions are $+5, +3$

23. $6(2x^2 + 3x + 1) = 6(2x + 1)(x + 1)$, solutions are $-\frac{1}{2}, -1$

24. $3(y^2 + 4y - 12) = 3(y + 6)(y - 2)$, solutions are $-6, +2$

25. $12(c^2 + 5c + 6) = 12(c + 3)(c + 2)$, solutions are $-2, -3$

Group Problem Solving

Review the formula for finding the area of a rectangle: $A = lw$. Have students work in groups of four to solve the following problem by factoring a quadratic equation:

A rectangular sign has a length l and a width 4 feet less than twice the length ($2l$). By law, you may not put up a sign with an area greater than 48 square feet. Find the largest dimensions your sign may have. *($l = 6$, $w = 8$)*

Have groups write their solutions on the board or an overhead transparency and discuss how they decided which of the two solutions of the quadratic equation must be thrown out. *(Negative 4, because length cannot be a negative number)*

Learning Styles

Auditory/Verbal

Go over Exercise B orally, having students use the steps in the example at the top of page 167 to explain their solutions.

Lesson at a Glance

Chapter 6 Application

Overview This application explains how to apply the factoring of quadratic equations to computing areas of shapes whose dimensions are unknown.

Objective

- To apply the quadratic equation to compute the dimensions of a rectangle (dimensions unknown) within a second rectangle (dimensions given)

Student Page 178

Teacher's Resource Library 

Application Activity 6

Everyday Algebra 6

1 Warm-Up Activity

Exhibit several framed certificates, photographs, or pictures that have mattes. Ask students to identify the areas in each. *(Frame, matte, and picture)* Solicit student ideas about how the framer decided on the exact dimensions of the matte once he or she chose the frame for the picture. Inform students that they will now learn to apply what they know about factoring quadratic equations to solve problems such as this.

2 Teaching the Lesson

Work through the example with students, copying the model onto the board or an overhead transparency. Establish what is known. *(Area of inner rectangle; dimensions of outer rectangle)* Ask, "What part of the model do we have to find out about?" *(The portion outside the picture)* Have students explain what x, $20 - 2x$, and $14 - 2x$ represent on the model. *(x = width of the matte; $20 - 2x$ = width of picture; $14 - 2x$ = length of picture)*

Write the formula for the area of a rectangle on the board. Have volunteers fill in the elements for this problem, using the model on the board to explain their work.

Frame Factor Factoring equations is useful for computing the area of a shape without knowing the exact dimensions.

EXAMPLE 1 The overall dimensions of this picture frame are 20 in. by 14 in. The picture inside the frame has an area of 160 in^2. How wide should the matte surrounding the picture be?

20 in. | $20 - 2x$ | x | 14 in. | $14 - 2x$

Step 1 Area = length • width

$160 = (20 - 2x)(14 - 2x)$

$= 20 \bullet 14 - 20 \bullet 2x - 28x + 4x^2$

$280 - 68x + 4x^2 = 160$ or $4x^2 - 68x + 280 = 160$

Step 2 Set equation equal to zero.

$4x^2 - 68x + 280 - 160 = 160 - 160$

$4x^2 - 68x + 120 = 0$

Factor 4 from each term. $4(x^2 - 17x + 30) = 0(4)$

$x^2 - 17x + 30 = 0$ $(x - 15)(x - 2) = 0$ So either $x = 15$ or $x = 2$.

Check. $160 = (20 - 2x)(14 - 2x)$ for $x = 15$. Substituting 15 in the equation leads to a negative length, which is impossible, so 15 is not a solution.

Check. $160 = (20 - 2x)(14 - 2x)$ for $x = 2$ $160 = (20 - 2 \bullet 2)(14 - 2 \bullet 2)$

$160 = (16)(10)$ True. The matte should be 2 inches wide.

Exercise Factor to solve each problem.

1. The outside edges of a rectangular frame are 3 ft by 4 ft. The matte covers $\frac{1}{2}$ the area inside the frame. How wide is the matte? $\frac{1}{2}$ ft or 6 in.

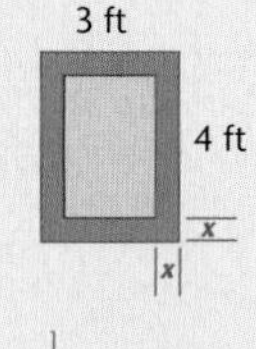

2. The area of a walkway around a rectangular garden is equal to the area of the garden alone. The garden measures 6 m by 9 m. What is the width of the walkway? $1\frac{1}{2}$ m

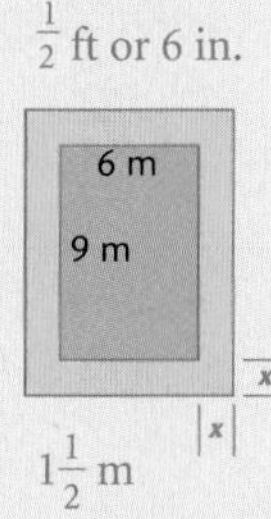

3. If the sides of a square are lengthened by 3 ft, the area of the square becomes 81 ft^2. What is the length of the side of the original square? 6 ft

$x + 3$ | x | x | $x +$

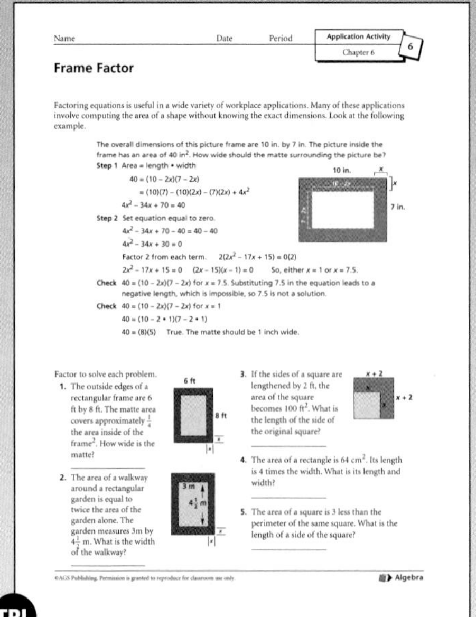

Name Date Period **Application Activity 6** Chapter 6

Frame Factor

Factoring equations is useful in a wide variety of workplace applications. Many of these applications involve computing the area of a shape without knowing the exact dimensions. Look at the following example.

The overall dimensions of this picture frame are 10 in. by 7 in. The picture inside the frame has an area of 40 in^2. How wide should the matte surrounding the picture be?

Step 1 Area = length • width

$40 = (10 - 2x)(7 - 2x)$

$= (10)(7) - (10)(2x) - (7)(2x) + 4x^2$

$4x^2 - 34x + 70 = 40$

Step 2 Set equation equal to zero.

$4x^2 - 34x + 70 - 40 = 40 - 40$

$4x^2 - 34x + 30 = 0$

Factor 2 from each term. $2(2x^2 - 17x + 15) = 0(2)$

$2x^2 - 17x + 15 = 0$ $(2x - 15)(x - 1) = 0$ So, either $x = 1$ or $x = 7.5$.

Check $40 = (10 - 2x)(7 - 2x)$ for $x = 7.5$. Substituting 7.5 in the equation leads to a negative length, which is impossible, so 7.5 is not a solution.

Check $40 = (10 - 2x)(7 - 2x)$ for $x = 1$

$40 = (10 - 2 \bullet 1)(7 - 2 \bullet 1)$

$40 = (8)(5)$ True. The matte should be 1 inch wide.

10 in. | x | 7 in.

Factor to solve each problem.

1. The outside edges of a rectangular frame are 6 ft by 8 ft. The matte area covers approximately $\frac{1}{4}$ the area inside of the frame^2. How wide is the matte? ______ (6 ft, 8 ft, x)
2. The area of a walkway around a rectangular garden is equal to twice the area of the garden alone. The garden measures 3m by $4\frac{1}{2}$ m. What is the width of the walkway? ______ (3 m, $4\frac{1}{2}$ m, x)
3. If the sides of a square are lengthened by 2 ft, the area of the square becomes 100 ft^2. What is the length of the side of the original square? ______ ($x + 2$, x)
4. The area of a rectangle is 64 cm^2. Its length is 4 times the width. What is its length and width? ______
5. The area of a square is 3 less than the perimeter of the same square. What is the length of a side of the square? ______

 Algebra

Application Activity 6

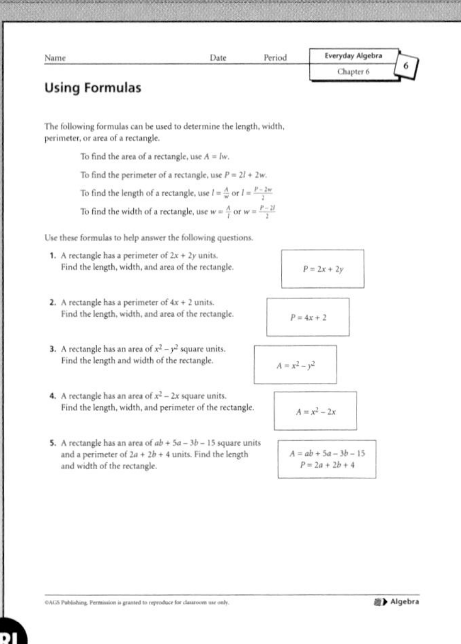

Name Date Period **Everyday Algebra 6** Chapter 6

Using Formulas

The following formulas can be used to determine the length, width, perimeter, or area of a rectangle.

To find the area of a rectangle, use $A = lw$.

To find the perimeter of a rectangle, use $P = 2l + 2w$.

To find the length of a rectangle, use $l = \frac{A}{w}$ or $l = \frac{P - 2w}{2}$

To find the width of a rectangle, use $w = \frac{A}{l}$ or $w = \frac{P - 2l}{2}$

Use these formulas to help answer the following questions.

1. A rectangle has a perimeter of $2x + 2y$ units. Find the length, width, and area of the rectangle. $P = 2x + 2y$
2. A rectangle has a perimeter of $4x + 2$ units. Find the length, width, and area of the rectangle. $P = 4x + 2$
3. A rectangle has an area of $x^2 - y^2$ square units. Find the length and width of the rectangle. $A = x^2 - y^2$
4. A rectangle has an area of $x^2 - 2x$ square units. Find the length, width, and perimeter of the rectangle. $A = x^2 - 2x$
5. A rectangle has an area of $ab + 5a - 3b - 15$ square units and a perimeter of $2a + 2b + 4$ units. Find the length and width of the rectangle. $A = ab + 5a - 3b - 15$ $P = 2a + 2b + 4$

 Algebra

Everyday Algebra 6

Chapter 6 REVIEW

Write the letter of the correct answer.

1. What is the greatest common factor of 24 and 36? A

A 12 **C** 4

B 8 **D** 16

2. What is the greatest common factor for $54pq$, $108p$, and $27p$? B

A 9 **C** $3p$

B $27p$ **D** 27

Factor the expression. Write the letter of the correct answer.

3. $24m^2 - 8$ B

A $m - 1$ **C** $3(8m^2 - 2)$

B $8(3m^2 - 1)$ **D** $24m^2 - (2 \cdot 4)$

4. $4x^4 - 32x^3 + 28x^2$ D

A $4x^2$ **C** $4x(x - 8)$

B $x^2 - 8x + 7$ **D** $4x^2(x - 7)(x - 1)$

5. $p^2 - 81$ C

A $p - 9$ **C** $(p + 9)(p - 9)$

B $p + 9$ **D** $(p - 9)^2$

6. $15x^2 - 35x + 10$ A

A $(5x - 10)(3x - 1)$ **C** $(3x + 1)(5x + 10)$

B $(3x + 5)(5x + 5)$ **D** $(3x - 5)(5x - 5)$

7. Solve for m. $13(m + 6) = 0$ C

A $m = 6$ **C** $m = -6$

B $m = -7$ **D** $m = 19$

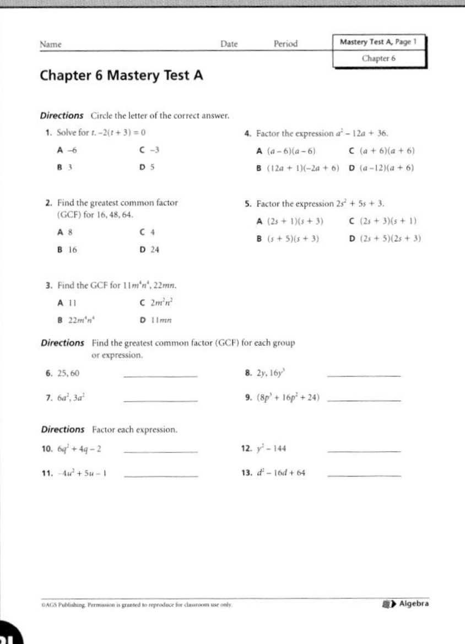

Name Date Period | Mastery Test A, Page 1 | Chapter 6

Chapter 6 Mastery Test A

Directions Circle the letter of the correct answer.

1. Solve for t. $-2(t + 3) = 0$

A -6 **C** -3

B 3 **D** 5

2. Find the greatest common factor (GCF) for 16, 48, 64.

A 8 **C** 4

B 16 **D** 24

3. Find the GCF for $11m^4n^4$, $22mn$.

A 11 **C** $2m^2n^2$

B $22m^4n^4$ **D** $11mn$

4. Factor the expression $a^2 - 12a + 36$.

A $(a - 6)(a - 6)$ **C** $(a + 6)(a + 6)$

B $(12a + 1)(-2a + 6)$ **D** $(a - 12)(a + 6)$

5. Factor the expression $2s^2 + 5s + 3$.

A $(2s + 1)(s + 3)$ **C** $(2s + 3)(s + 1)$

B $(s + 5)(s + 3)$ **D** $(2s + 5)(2s + 3)$

Directions Find the greatest common factor (GCF) for each group or expression.

6. 25, 60 ________

7. $6a^2, 3a^2$ ________

8. $2y, 16y^3$ ________

9. $(8p^3 + 16p^2 + 24)$ ________

Directions Factor each expression.

10. $6q^2 + 4q - 2$ ________

11. $-4u^2 + 5u - 1$ ________

12. $y^2 - 144$ ________

13. $d^2 - 16d + 64$ ________

 Algebra

TRL

Name Date Period | Mastery Test A, Page 2 | Chapter 6

Chapter 6 Mastery Test A, continued

Directions Solve each equation for the variable.

14. $-5r = 0$ ________

15. $(2a - 2)(a + 1) = 0$ ________

16. $(5m - 5)(-3m + 6) = 0$ ________

17. $(k^2 - k - 6) = 0$ ________

18. $(8y^2 + 6y - 9) = 0$ ________

Directions Solve.

19. What is the area of this rectangle? ________

y

$x + 6$

20. What is the length of one side of this square? ________

$A = 4x^2 - 4xy + y^2$ square units

 Algebra

TRL

Chapter 6 Mastery Test A

3 Reinforce and Extend

CAREER CONNECTION

Invite an artist, gallery manager, or experienced frame shop employee to come to class to explain (and, if possible, demonstrate) the algebra used in matting and framing photographs and artworks.

LEARNING STYLES

Body/Kinesthetic

Have students work in pairs and use measurement equipment with paper and pencil or floor space and chalk to create the shapes in problems 1, 3, and 4. As they solve the problems, have them write in the dimensions they find. Then have them check their answers against the model.

Chapter 6 Review

Each set of problems in the Chapter Review includes an example and solution to illustrate the concept. Use the given examples for reteaching the materials in Chapter 6. For additional practice, refer to the Supplementary Problems for Chapter 6 (pages 416–417).

Chapter 6 Mastery Test 

The Teacher's Resource Library includes parallel forms of the Chapter 6 Mastery Test. The difficulty level of the two forms is equivalent. You may wish to use one form as a pretest and the other form as a posttest.

MANIPULATIVES

M **Review**

Materials: Algebra Tiles, Manipulatives Master 4 (Factor Frame)

Group Practice: Review procedures for factoring polynomials and solving quadratic equations using the Algebra Tiles.

Student Practice: Encourage students to use Algebra Tiles to check their work in Chapter Review problems 13, 14, 28, and 40, and Supplementary Problems 32–34 and 36–38 on pages 416–417. Then have students sketch each model and write its symbolic equivalent.

ALTERNATIVE ASSESSMENT

Alternative Assessment items correlate with student Goals for Learning at the beginning of this chapter.

- **To completely factor integers**
Have students work in groups to make a table of prime factorization for integers from 51 through 100. Have students discuss their methods for factoring. Compare the table with the table in the textbook for prime factors of integers from 1 through 50. Ask if they notice any patterns. *(The prime numbers from 51 to 100 are 53, 61, 67, 71, 73, 79, 83, 89, and 97.)*

- **To find the greatest common factor of polynomials**
Have students explain the steps they use to find the greatest common factor. Then discuss them as a class.

- **To factor trinomials**
Write the following expressions on the board:

1. $2x^2 + 17x + 9$

2. $3x^2 + 9x + 6$

3. $x^2 + 4x + 4$

Have students explain the differences in the three problems. *(Examples 1 and 2 have a number besides 1 for the coefficient a. The coefficient of x^2 can be factored out in example 2.)* Next, have the students solve the problems using

Find the solutions for these equations.

Example: $x^2 + 5x + 6 = 0$ Solution: $x^2 + 5x + 6 = 0$
$(x + 3)(x + 2) = 0$
$(x + 3) = 0;\ x = -3$
$(x + 2) = 0;\ x = -2$

Answer	Problem	Problem	Answer
$a = -2$ or $a = +4$	**8.** $a^2 - 2a - 8 = 0$	**15.** $4z^2 = 9$	$z = -\frac{3}{2}$ or $z = \frac{3}{2}$
$x = -\frac{1}{2}$ or $x = -4$	**9.** $2x^2 + 9x + 4 = 0$	**16.** $x^2 + 45 = -18x$	$x = -15$ or $x =$
$x = 2$ or $x = -\frac{2}{3}$	**10.** $6x^2 - 8x = 8$	**17.** $y^2 - 121 = 0$	$y = +11$ or $y =$
$x = 0$ or $x = -2$	**11.** $9x^2 = -18x$	**18.** $b^3 - 16b = 0$	$b = 0$ or $b = +4,$ or $b = -4$
$x = -2$ or $x = -3$	**12.** $3x^2 + 15x = -18$	**19.** $5c^2 + 45c = 0$	$c = 0$ or $c = -9$
$y = 1$ or $y = \frac{3}{2}$	**13.** $4y^2 - 10y + 6 = 0$	**20.** $x^2 + 6x = -5$	$x = -1$ or $x =$
$b = \frac{1}{5}$ or $b = 3$	**14.** $5b^2 - 16b = -3$		

Find the solution to each problem.

Example: What is the area of the rectangle?
Solution: $A = (10)(x + 1)$
$A = 10x + 10$

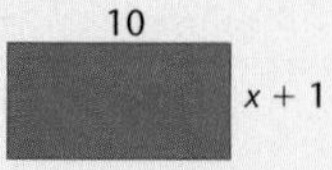

21. What is the area of the rectangle? $a^2 - b^2$

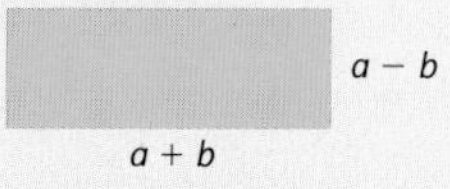

22. A pond and its square deck are part of a garden. What area of the garden is not occupied by the pond and its deck? If the diameter of the pond is 10 ft, what is the area of the garden not occupied by the pond and its deck? $9y^2 - y^2$; $900 - 100 = 800$ square feet

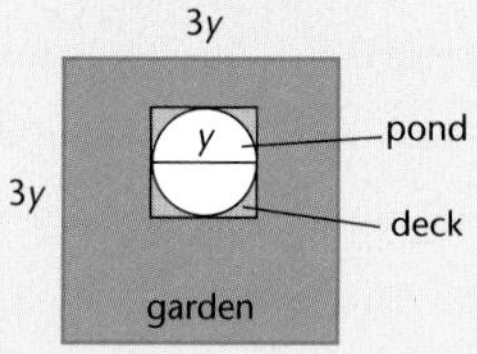

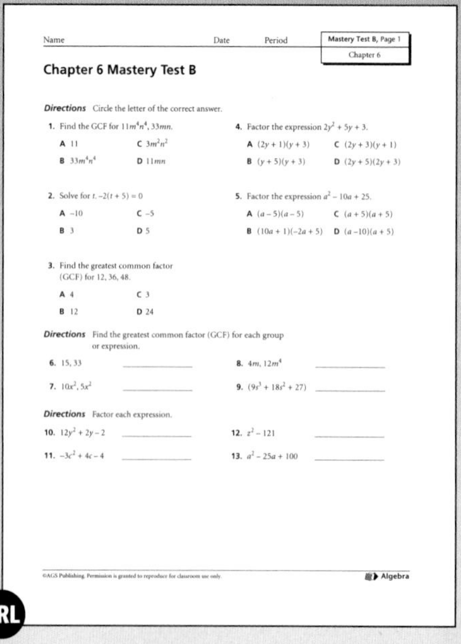

Name Date Period **Mastery Test B, Page 1** Chapter 6

Chapter 6 Mastery Test B

Directions Circle the letter of the correct answer.

1. Find the GCF for $11m^4n^4$, $33mn$.
A 11 C $3m^2n^2$
B $33m^4n^4$ D $11mn$

2. Solve for t. $-2(t + 5) = 0$
A −10 C −5
B 3 D 5

3. Find the greatest common factor (GCF) for 12, 36, 48.
A 4 C 3
B 12 D 24

4. Factor the expression $2y^2 + 5y + 3$.
A $(2y + 1)(y + 3)$ C $(2y + 3)(y + 1)$
B $(y + 5)(y + 3)$ D $(2y + 5)(2y + 3)$

5. Factor the expression $a^2 - 10a + 25$.
A $(a - 5)(a - 5)$ C $(a + 5)(a + 5)$
B $(10a + 1)(-2a + 5)$ D $(a - 10)(a + 5)$

Directions Find the greatest common factor (GCF) for each group or expression.

6. 15, 33 ______
7. $10x^2, 5x^2$ ______
8. $4m, 12m^4$ ______
9. $(9s^3 + 18s^2 + 27)$ ______

Directions Factor each expression.

10. $12y^2 + 2y - 2$ ______
11. $-3c^2 + 4c - 4$ ______
12. $z^2 - 121$ ______
13. $a^2 - 25a + 100$ ______

 Algebra

TRL

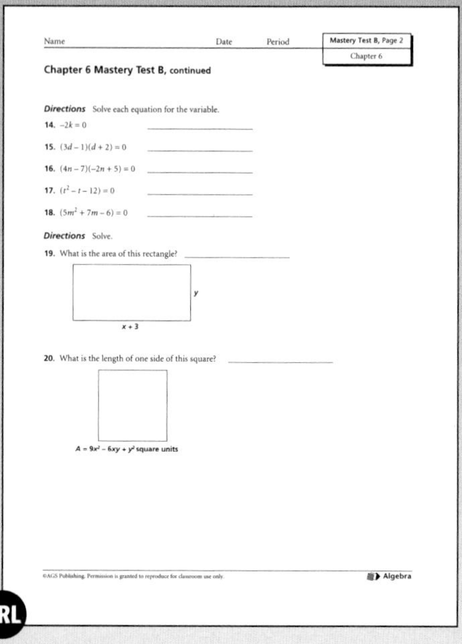

Name Date Period **Mastery Test B, Page 2** Chapter 6

Chapter 6 Mastery Test B, continued

Directions Solve each equation for the variable.

14. $-2k = 0$ ______
15. $(3d - 1)(d + 2) = 0$ ______
16. $(4n - 7)(-2n + 5) = 0$ ______
17. $(t^2 - t - 12) = 0$ ______
18. $(5m^2 + 7m - 6) = 0$ ______

Directions Solve.

19. What is the area of this rectangle? ______

y
x + 3

20. What is the length of one side of this square? ______

$A = 9x^2 - 6xy + y^2$ square units

 Algebra

TRL

Chapter 6 Mastery Test B

23. I = length and width = 8; II = length 4, width 8, III = length and width = 4, IV = length 8, width 4

24. either subtract the smaller area from the larger, 144 − 64 = 80 square units; or add the areas of each of the additional regions, 80 square units

25. $9a^2 + 6ab + b^2$

26. width = 4 cm, length = 7 cm

27. width = 5 units, length = 12 units

28. width = 9 m, length = 12 m

29. 7 cm

30. 2 ft

23. This sketch shows how a contractor plans to enlarge an existing family room. The area of the existing room is 64 square units. The area of the new room will be 144 square units. What is the length and width of each region?

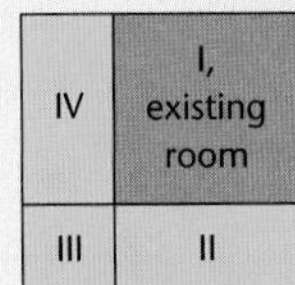

24. Describe two ways to find the area of the addition in problem 23.

25. What is the area of the large square?

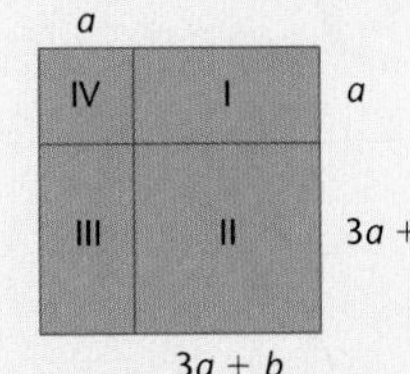

26. A rectangle has a length 3 cm greater than its width. The area of the rectangle is 28 cm². What is the length and width of the rectangle?

27. The length of a rectangle is two more than twice its width. The area of the rectangle is 60 units. What is the length and width of the rectangle?

28. A rectangle has an area of 108 m². Its width is 3 m less than its length. What are the dimensions of the rectangle?

29. The sides of a square are increased by 4 cm. The area of the newly created square is 121 cm². What was the original length of one side of the square?

30. Each side of a square is lengthened by 6 ft. This makes the area of the square 64 ft². What was the original length of a side of the square?

Test-Taking Tip

When studying for a test, review any tests or quizzes you took earlier that cover the same information.

Alternative Assessment, continued

trial and error. *[1. $(2x + 9)(x + 1)$; 2. $3(x + 2)(x + 1)$; 3. $(x + 2)(x + 2)$]* Have three students come to the board and check the solutions using the FOIL method.

■ **To factor algebraic expressions**
Have students work in pairs to use manipulatives such as paper clips to represent algebraic expressions. One partner creates an expression and the other represents it with the manipulatives. Then have them switch roles. Have them start with simple expressions where the manipulatives represent numbers and then use the manipulatives as variables. Tell students to create problems where they can use the GCF to factor the expression.

■ **To identify zero as a factor**
Have students work in groups to work through a series of increasingly complicated equations equal to zero, such as $5x^2 = 0$; $5x^2 - 125 = 0$; $x^3 = 0$; $(x - 7)(x + 12) = 0$. Have the first student solve for the variable and have the others check the answer. Then have the next student solve the next equation and so on. *($x = 0$; $x = 5$; $x = 0$; $x = 7$ or -12. Add more such examples.)*

■ **To use factoring as a means of solving equations**
Have students play an algebraic form of telephone, working in groups of three. Have them create several equations that can be solved by factoring. Note: Tell students it is easy to create equations if they write the factors first and then multiply them out using the FOIL method. Have the first student keep the factored equations and pass a copy of the whole equations to a partner to solve. Have a third student check the factored equations by the FOIL method. Pass the finished product back to the original student to see if the answers are the same. If the answers are not, ask the group to find the mistake.

Chapter

Planning Guide

Data, Statistics, and Probability

		Student Text Lesson: Student Pages	Vocabulary	Practice Exercises	Solutions Key
Lesson 1	Organizing Data	184–187	✔	✔	✔
Lesson 2	Range, Mean, Median, and Mode	188–191	✔	✔	✔
Lesson 3	Box-and-Whiskers Plots	192–195	✔	✔	✔
Lesson 4	The Probability Fraction	196–199	✔	✔	✔
Lesson 5	Probability and Complementary Events	200–203	✔	✔	✔
Lesson 6	Tree Diagrams and Sample Spaces	204–205	✔	✔	✔
Lesson 7	Dependent and Independent Events	206–209	✔	✔	✔
Lesson 8	The Fundamental Principle of Counting	210–213	✔	✔	✔
Application	Multistage Experiments	214		✔	✔

Chapter Activities

Teacher's Resource Library

Estimation Exercise 7: Estimating Probability with a Spinner

Application Activity 7: Multistage Experiments

Everyday Algebra 7: Studying Graph Impressions

Community Connection 7: License Possibilities

Teacher's Edition

Chapter 7 Project

Assessment Options

Student Text

Chapter 7 Review

Teacher's Resource Library

Chapter 7 Mastery Tests A and B

Chapters 1–7 Midterm Mastery Test

Student Text Features							Teaching Strategies							Learning Styles						Teacher's Resource Library			
Estimation Activity	Algebra in Your Life	Technology Connection	Writing About Mathematics	Try This	Problem Solving	Calculator Practice	Online Connection	Common Error	Applications Home, Career, Community	Mental Math	Manipulatives	Calculator	Group Problem Solving	Auditory/Verbal	Visual/Spatial	Logical/Mathematical	Body/Kinesthetic	Interpersonal/Group Learning	LEP/ESL	Activities	Alternate Activities	Workbook Activities	Self-Study Guide
	187								186						185					62	62	66	✔
						191		189	191	189		191		191				190	190	63	63	67	✔
194			194	194			194	193										193		64	64	68	✔
		199							198	199	197				198		197, 199			65	65	69	✔
					203						201		203	202		203			202	66	66	70	✔
				205							205						205		205	67	67	71	✔
			209	209				207	208	208	207		209	209			208			68	68	72	✔
					212–213			211	211			212	212				213			69	69	73–74	✔
									215														✔

Software Options

Skill Track Software

Use the Skill Track Software for *Algebra* for additional reinforcement of this chapter. The software provides multiple-choice assessment items for students to access by computer.

Solutions Key

Use the Solutions Key with this chapter to help students who may need additional assistance. The Solutions Key CD provides solutions for every exercise in the student edition.

Other Resources

Alternative Activities

The Teacher's Resource Library (TRL) contains a set of worksheets written at a second-grade reading level called Alternative Activities. They cover the same content as the regular Activities.

Manipulatives

See the Manipulative activities in this chapter for hands-on modeling of the content.

1–6 Number Cubes
Blank Game Spinners
Two-Color Counters
Unit Cubes

Chapter at a Glance

Chapter 7: Data, Statistics, and Probability

pages 182–217

(Answer Keys for the Teacher's Resource Library begin on page 530 of this Teacher's Edition.)

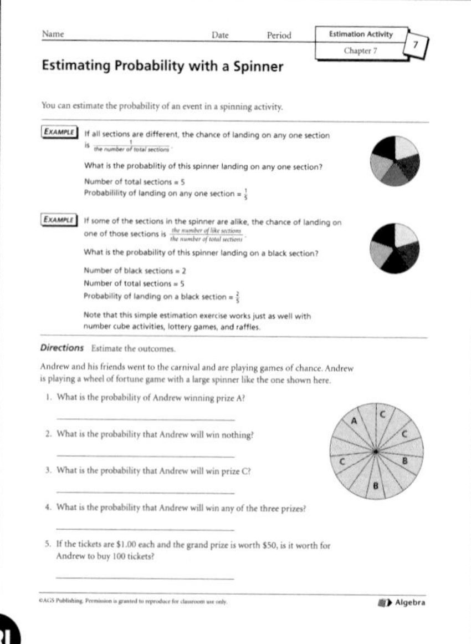

Name Date Period | Estimation Activity 7, Chapter 7

Estimating Probability with a Spinner

You can estimate the probability of an event in a spinning activity.

EXAMPLE If all sections are different, the chance of landing on any one section is $\frac{1}{\text{the number of total sections}}$.

What is the probablitiy of this spinner landing on any one section?

Number of total sections = 5
Probabilility of landing on any one section = $\frac{1}{5}$

EXAMPLE If some of the sections in the spinner are alike, the chance of landing on one of those sections is $\frac{\text{the number of like sections}}{\text{the number of total sections}}$.

What is the probability of this spinner landing on a black section?

Number of black sections = 2
Number of total sections = 5
Probability of landing on a black section = $\frac{2}{5}$

Note that this simple estimation exercise works just as well with number cube activities, lottery games, and raffles.

Directions Estimate the outcomes.

Andrew and his friends went to the carnival and are playing games of chance. Andrew is playing a wheel of fortune game with a large spinner like the one shown here.

1. What is the probability of Andrew winning prize A?
2. What is the probability that Andrew will win nothing?
3. What is the probability that Andrew will win prize C?
4. What is the probability that Andrew will win any of the three prizes?
5. If the tickets are $1.00 each and the grand prize is worth $50, is it worth for Andrew to buy 100 tickets?

Algebra

TRL

Estimation Exercise 7

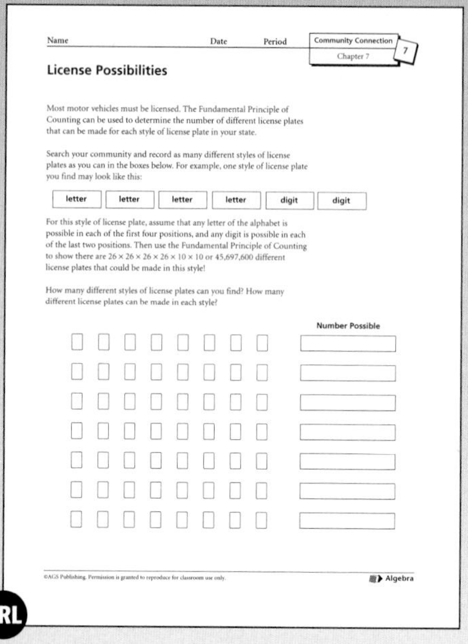

Name Date Period | Community Connection 7, Chapter 7

License Possibilities

Most motor vehicles must be licensed. The Fundamental Principle of Counting can be used to determine the number of different license plates that can be made for each style of license plate in your state.

Search your community and record as many different styles of license plates as you can in the boxes below. For example, one style of license plate you find may look like this:

letter	letter	letter	letter	digit	digit

For this style of license plate, assume that any letter of the alphabet is possible in each of the first four positions, and any digit is possible in each of the last two positions. Then use the Fundamental Principle of Counting to show there are $26 \times 26 \times 26 \times 26 \times 10 \times 10$ or 45,697,600 different license plates that could be made in this style!

How many different styles of license plates can you find? How many different license plates can be made in each style?

Number Possible

Algebra

TRL

Community Connection 7

Chapter 7: Data, Statistics, and Probability

Suppose the weather forecast calls for a 60 percent chance of rain. This prediction is based on similar past conditions and corresponding times of past years. In 60 percent of past cases, it rained. In 40 percent, it didn't rain. People who predict the weather collect, record, and study statistics on weather. They use this data to make predictions. You can use data and probability to predict many things besides weather. What are the chances you'll get heads in a coin toss or draw the winning card? Figure it out!

In Chapter 7, you will read and interpret data.

Goals for Learning

- To organize data into graphs
- To read and interpret graphic representations
- To determine range and measures of central tendency
- To compute probabilities and complementary events involving statistics

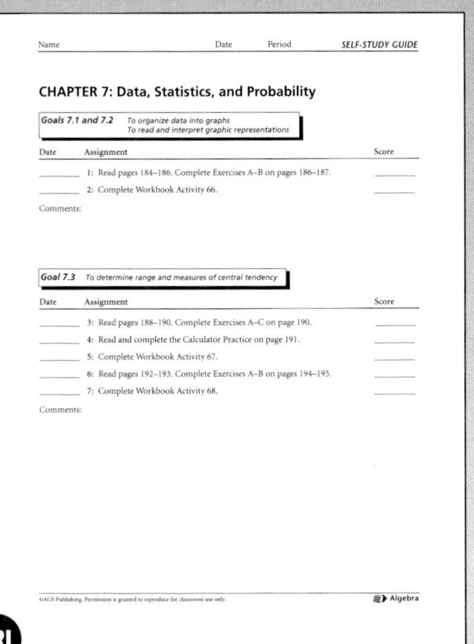

Name Date Period *SELF-STUDY GUIDE*

CHAPTER 7: Data, Statistics, and Probability

Goals 7.1 and 7.2 *To organize data into graphs*
To read and interpret graphic representations

Date	Assignment	Score
______	1: Read pages 184–186. Complete Exercises A–B on pages 186–187.	______
______	2: Complete Workbook Activity 66.	______

Comments:

Goal 7.3 *To determine range and measures of central tendency*

Date	Assignment	Score
______	3: Read pages 188–190. Complete Exercises A–C on page 190.	______
______	4: Read and complete the Calculator Practice on page 191.	______
______	5: Complete Workbook Activity 67.	______
______	6: Read pages 192–193. Complete Exercises A–B on pages 194–195.	______
______	7: Complete Workbook Activity 68.	______

Comments:

Name Date Period *SELF-STUDY GUIDE*

CHAPTER 7: Data, Statistics, and Probability, continued

Goal 7.4 *To compute probabilities and complementary events involving statistics*

Date	Assignment	Score
______	8: Read pages 196–198. Complete Exercises A–D on pages 198–199.	______
______	9: Complete Workbook Activity 69.	______
______	10: Read pages 200–201. Complete Exercises A–C on pages 202–203.	______
______	11: Complete Workbook Activity 70.	______
______	12: Read pages 204–205. Complete Exercises A–B on page 205.	______
______	13: Complete Workbook Activity 71.	______
______	14: Read pages 206–208. Complete Exercises A–C on pages 208–209.	______
______	15: Complete Workbook Activity 72.	______
______	16: Read pages 210–212. Complete Exercises A–B on pages 212–213.	______
______	17: Complete Workbook Activities 73–74.	______
______	18: Read and complete the Application Exercise on page 214.	______
______	19: Complete the Chapter 7 Review on pages 215–217.	______

Comments:

Student's Signature ______________________ Date ____________

Instructor's Signature ______________________ Date ____________

 Algebra

TRL

Chapter 7 Self-Study Guide

Introducing the Chapter

Use the information in the chapter opener to help students understand that data, or numerical facts, become helpful tools when organized and analyzed through graphs and measurements.

Have students list uses they have seen for statistics and graphs and bring to class examples they find in newspapers, and magazines, and on television such as weather forecasts. Invite students to explain what the measurement or comparison shows and who it helps. Keep a running list and have students add and categorize new examples as chapter lessons are completed.

Chapter Project

Have small groups of students gather data and generate statistics about the students in their class. For example, they might collect data about the hours of television watched per day. Then use the data to construct graphs; calculate mean, median, and mode; and calculate probabilities as they progress through the chapter.

Have the groups compile their results into a magazine using graphics, calculations, and explanatory paragraphs.

Teacher's Resource

The AGS Publishing Teaching Strategies in Math Transparencies may be used with this chapter. They add an interactive dimension to expand and enhance the program content.

Career Interest Inventory

The AGS Publishing Harrington-O'Shea Career Decision-Making System-Revised (CDM) may be used with this chapter. Students can use the CDM to explore their interests and identify careers. The CDM defines career areas that are indicated by students' responses on the inventory.

Lesson at a Glance

Chapter 7 Lesson 1

Overview This lesson explains how to organize data in frequency tables, stem-and-leaf plots, bar graphs, and histograms.

Objectives

- To manipulate data for ease of interpretation
- To create a stem-and-leaf plot, a frequency table, a histogram, and a bar graph to display data
- To compare the types of data displays and analyze their strengths

Student Pages 184–187

Teacher's Resource Library 

Workbook Activity 66

Activity 62

Alternative Activity 62

Mathematics Vocabulary

bar graph
data
frequency
frequency table
histogram
stem-and-leaf plot

Warm-Up Activity

Students will already be aware that our society runs on information. Many people gather data about teenagers' habits. Poll students to collect data about the type of music they buy most often: rap, rock and roll, alternative, mixed (house/free style music). Discuss how this information might be used and who might use it. Ask the class to suggest alternative ways the data could be organized for easy comparison. Allow pairs of students five minutes to come up with a format that will organize the data. They can compare each other's efforts.

Teaching the Lesson

After students have read the lesson, have the class compare the tables and graphs on pages 184–186 and explain how each was organized. Which do they find easiest to interpret? Why?

Lesson 1 Organizing Data

Frequency table
A way of showing the count of items or number of times in different groups or categories

Data
Information given in numbers

Stem-and-Leaf Plot
A way of showing place value by separating the data by powers of ten

Information can be organized and shown in many different ways. A **frequency table** is a method of summarizing data. The following data table shows how old some adults were when they bought their first home.

How old were you when you bought your first home? (in years)		
63	24	35
31	44	61
41	36	23
48	54	49
27	60	37
42	24	50
29	43	29
30	56	41

The frequency table was made using the **data** from the table. The frequency table is much easier to read and interpret than the data table.

Frequency Table		
Interval	**Tally**	**Frequency**
0–9		0
10–19		0
20–29	𝍸 I	6
30–39	𝍸	5
40–49	𝍸 II	7
50–59	III	3
60–69	III	3
70–79		0

A stem-and-leaf plot is another way to show how frequently data occur. **A stem-and-leaf plot** organizes and displays data using stems and leafs. In the following stem-and-leaf plot, the first data value is made up of a stem of 1 and a leaf of 0. The stem (1) represents the place value of the tens place (1 ten) and the leaf (0) represents the place value of the ones place (0 ones). So stem (1) and leaf (0) represents 1 ten—(10) + 0—ones (0), or 10 + 0 = 10.

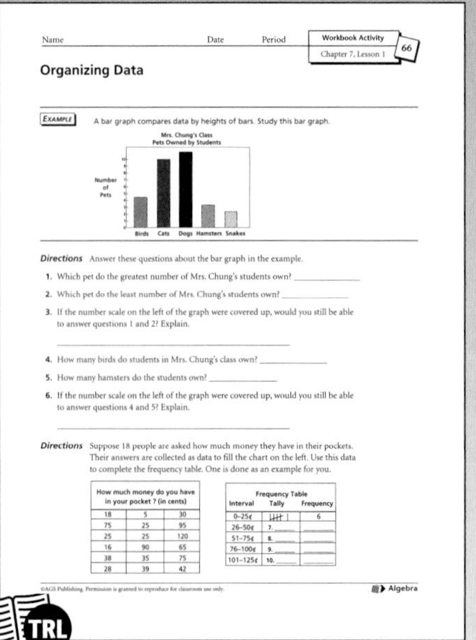

Name Date Period | Workbook Activity 66 | Chapter 7, Lesson 1

Organizing Data

EXAMPLE A bar graph compares data by heights of bars. Study this bar graph.

Directions Answer these questions about the bar graph in the example.

1. Which pet do the greatest number of Mrs. Chung's students own? ______
2. Which pet do the least number of Mrs. Chung's students own? ______
3. If the number scale on the left of the graph were covered up, would you still be able to answer questions 1 and 2? Explain. ______
4. How many birds do students in Mrs. Chung's class own? ______
5. How many hamsters do the students own? ______
6. If the number scale on the left of the graph were covered up, would you still be able to answer questions 4 and 5? Explain. ______

Directions Suppose 18 people are asked how much money they have in their pockets. Their answers are collected as data to fill the chart on the left. Use this data to complete the frequency table. One is done as an example for you.

How much money do you have in your pocket? (in cents)		
18	5	30
75	25	95
25	25	120
16	90	65
38	35	75
28	39	42

Frequency Table		
Interval	Tally	Frequency
0–25¢	𝍸 I	6
26–50¢	7. ____	____
51–75¢	8. ____	____
76–100¢	9. ____	____
101–125¢	10. ____	____

 Algebra

Workbook Activity 66

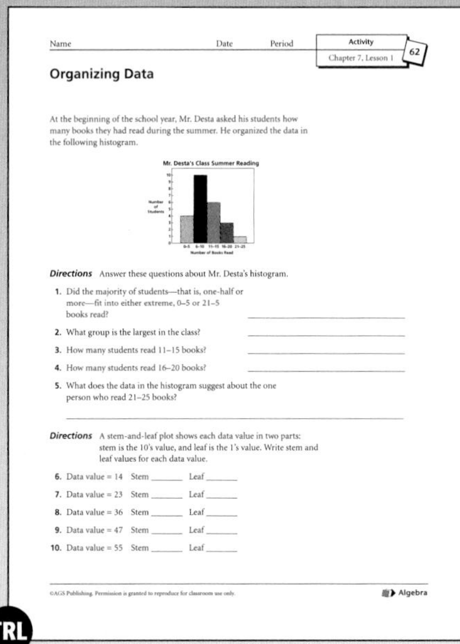

Name Date Period | Activity 62 | Chapter 7, Lesson 1

Organizing Data

At the beginning of the school year, Mr. Desta asked his students how many books they had read during the summer. He organized the data in the following histogram.

Directions Answer these questions about Mr. Desta's histogram.

1. Did the majority of students—that is, one-half or more—fit into either extreme, 0–5 or 21–5 books read? ______
2. What group is the largest in the class? ______
3. How many students read 11–15 books? ______
4. How many students read 16–20 books? ______
5. What does the data in the histogram suggest about the one person who read 21–25 books? ______

Directions A stem-and-leaf plot shows each data value in two parts: stem is the 10's value, and leaf is the 1's value. Write stem and leaf values for each data value.

6. Data value = 14 Stem ______ Leaf ______
7. Data value = 23 Stem ______ Leaf ______
8. Data value = 36 Stem ______ Leaf ______
9. Data value = 47 Stem ______ Leaf ______
10. Data value = 55 Stem ______ Leaf ______

 Algebra

Activity 62

Bar Graph

A way of showing how information can be compared using rectangular bars

Time Spent Studying (in minutes)	
1	0 0 5 5 5
2	0 5 5
3	0 0 0 5
4	5

1 | 0 = 10

This stem-and-leaf plot shows:

- there are 13 data values
- the data values 15 and 30 occur most often
- the greatest data value is 45
- the least data value is 10

A **bar graph** uses rectangular bars to show data. The bar graph below shows the number of minutes five students spent getting ready for school.

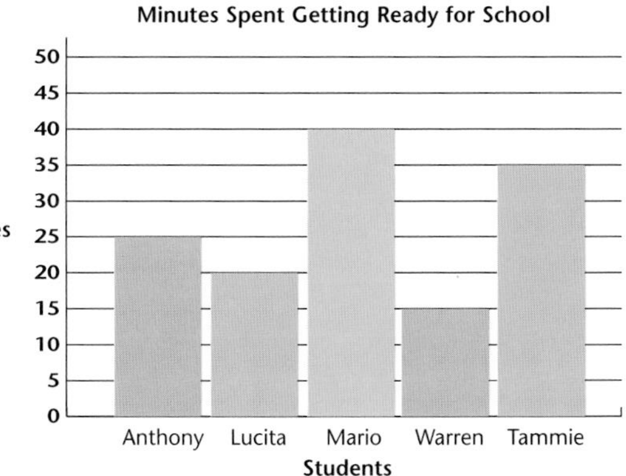

This bar graph contains

- a title
- horizontal and vertical axes with labels
- individual data values

To compare data shown by a bar graph, compare the heights of the bars. The tallest bars represent the greatest data values.

Be sure students understand that each leaf in a stem-and-leaf plot is the last (or ones) digit of one numerical piece of data. The stem shows the left-hand portion of the number. Each leaf goes to the right of its stem, so that 337 and 338 would be represented as

33 | 7 8

Check understanding by having students explain how many individuals spend 10 minutes studying *(two)*, 15 minutes *(three)*, etc.

3 Reinforce and Extend

Learning Styles

Visual/Spatial

Provide data like the following to small groups of students.

- Life expectancy in the United States: 1900, 47.3; 1930, 59.7; 1960, 69.7; 1990, 75.4
- Time spent exercising each day, in minutes: 30, 15, 60, 25, 20, 15, 10, 30, 35, 25, 0, 15, 20, 30

Invite groups to organize their data using one of the display formats described in this lesson. Have each group draw its graph or table on the board, an overhead transparency, or poster board and explain its meaning to the class.

At Home

Students can use data analysis to track their spending habits. Invite them to record their purchases for a week by category (snacks, personal items, music, etc.) Then have them create stem-and-leaf plots showing the amount of money spent on each purchase in a given category—e.g., snacks purchased in one week. Students can then analyze each category, asking questions such as

- How often do I make these purchases each week?
- What amount do I spend most frequently on this purchase?
- What percent of my income is spent on this category?

Histogram
A way of showing the frequency of data using rectangular bars and the area they contain

A **histogram** uses rectangular bars and area to represent the frequency of data. The histogram below shows how a class scored on a recent quiz.

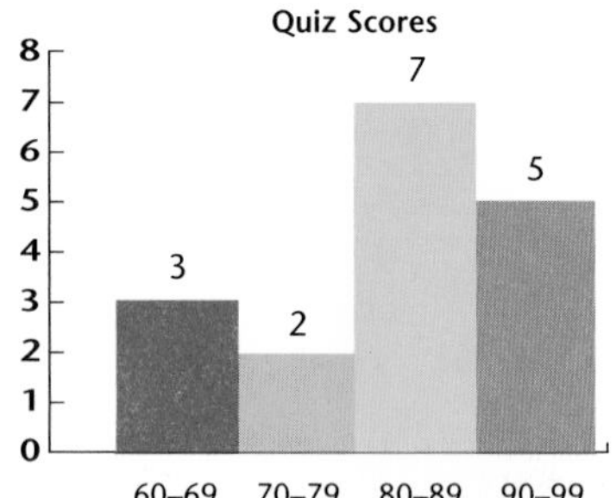

This histogram contains
- a title
- horizontal and vertical axes with regular intervals and labels
- data

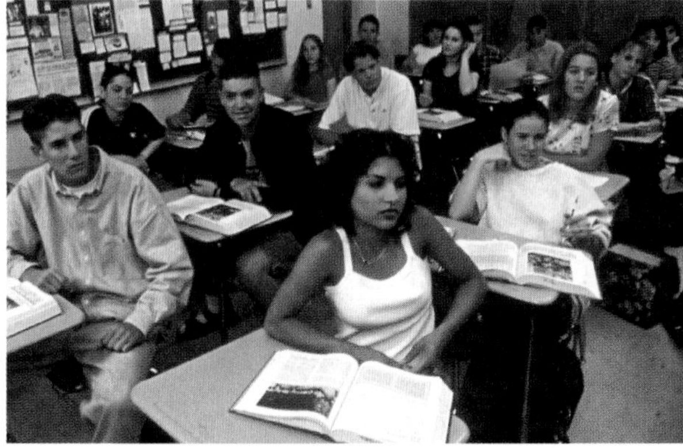

See Teacher's Edition page for answers.

Exercise A Consider the data in the chart.

1. Display the data in a stem-and-leaf plot.
2. Display the data in a frequency table.
3. Display the data in a bar graph.
4. Display the data in a histogram.

Age in Years		
21	2	13
10	11	7
20	19	26
27	14	6
3	30	25
4	20	11
16	22	4
12	5	24

Answers to Problems 1–10

1.

Stem	Leaves							
0	2	3	4	4	5	6	7	
1	0	1	1	2	3	4	6	9
2	0	0	1	2	4	5	6	7
3	0							

2.

Frequency Table		
Interval	Tally	Frequency
0–9	~~IIII~~ II	7
10–19	~~IIII~~ III	8
20–29	~~IIII~~ III	8
30–39	I	1

3.

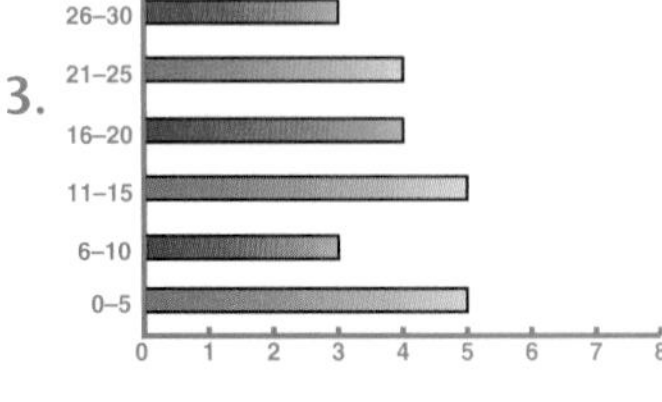

4.

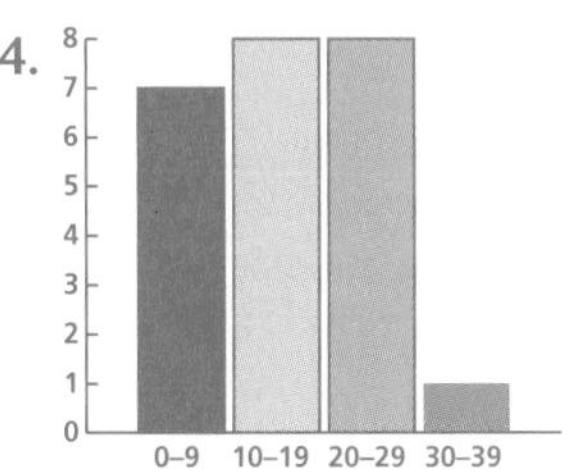

5. They all give a visual display of the data. **6.** A frequency table summarizes data, a stem and leaf plot organizes data, a bar graph uses rectangles to show data, and a histogram uses intervals and rectangular bars. **7.** 4, 11, and 20 occur most often. 2, 3, 5, 6, 7, 10, 12, 13, 14, 16, 19, 21, 22, 24, 25, 26, 27, and 30 occur the least. **8.** Stem-and-leaf plot **9.** Sample answer: frequency table **10.** Stem-and-leaf plot. It lists data from least to greatest.

See Teacher's Edition page for answers.

Exercise B Use the graphs you made in Exercise A to answer these questions.

5. How are the graphs alike?

6. How are the graphs different?

7. Which data value occurs most often? Which occurs least often?

8. In which graph can you most easily find the data value or values that occur most often?

9. In which graph can you most easily find the data value or values that occur least often?

10. In which graph is the greatest data value easiest to find? In which graph is the least data value easiest to find? Explain.

Algebra in Your Life

Making a Budget

How much money do you spend? Here's a way to find out. Get a small notebook. Divide each page into columns and title each column. You might use these titles: recreation, clothes, gifts, food, gasoline, and savings. Carry your notebook with you everywhere. For three months, record everything you spend. After three months, divide the total amount you've spent in each category by three. This will give you the average of what you spend each month. From that information, you can develop a budget you can work with.

Math History

One of the greatest sources of statistical data about the United States comes from the U.S. Census Bureau. However, taking a census is not new. The ancient Romans were among the first government or culture to take a census. Roman census-takers recorded information about people and their property. The information was used to figure the amount of taxes that a family or person would have to pay the Roman government. In fact, the word census comes from a Latin word meaning "to tax." The United States Constitution requires that a census be taken every ten years. The U.S. Census Bureau analyzes the census information gathered by census-takers, questionnaires, and other means. Federal and state governments, businesses, academic institutions, and other organizations use census data and statistics for making projections of population trends and for decision-making.

Lesson at a Glance

Chapter 7 Lesson 2

Overview This lesson defines range, mean, median, and mode and explains how to calculate each for a given set of data.

Objectives

- To define *mean*, *median*, and *mode* as measures of central tendency describing data with a set range
- To calculate the mean, median, and mode of given sets of data

Student Pages 188–191

Teacher's Resource Library 

Workbook Activity 67

Activity 63

Alternative Activity 63

Mathematics Vocabulary

mean
measures of central tendency
median
mode
range

Warm-Up Activity

Draw on the board a configuration like the following:

A •	B • • • • •
D • • • •	C • • • • • • • • •

Explain that the rectangles represent stores in a mall, and the dots represent shoppers. Have students determine the high and low numbers of shoppers. Ask pairs of students to discuss how they would determine the *average* number of shoppers per store. Discuss what this number represents.

Explain that people frequently look at related sets of numbers (standardized test scores, earnings, temperatures, etc.) to determine their central tendencies and assign them meanings. Use student responses here to introduce the concepts of *median, mean, mode,* and *range* as numerical descriptions of data.

Lesson 2 Range, Mean, Median, and Mode

Range
The difference between the greatest and least values in a set of data

Mean
The sum of the values in a set of data divided by the number of pieces of data in the set

The stem-and-leaf plot you learned about in Lesson 1 uses numerals to display data. Range, median, mean, and mode are numerical ways to describe data.

Study this set of data: {$6.50, $7.31, $10.00, $25.95, $10.00, $4.50, $2.13, $6.50, $10.00}

The **range** of the set of data is the difference between the greatest and least values. To compute the range, subtract the least value from the greatest value.

$25.95	greatest value
–$2.13	least value
$23.82	

The range is $23.82.

The arithmetic **mean** of a set of data is the sum of the values in the set divided by the number of values in the set.

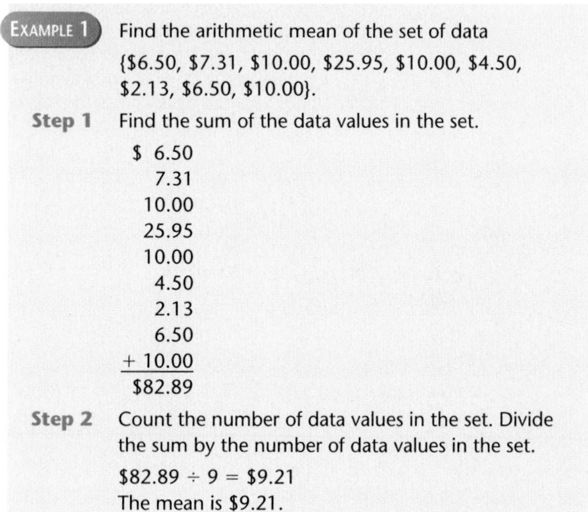

EXAMPLE 1 Find the arithmetic mean of the set of data {$6.50, $7.31, $10.00, $25.95, $10.00, $4.50, $2.13, $6.50, $10.00}.

Step 1 Find the sum of the data values in the set.

$ 6.50
7.31
10.00
25.95
10.00
4.50
2.13
6.50
+ 10.00
$82.89

Step 2 Count the number of data values in the set. Divide the sum by the number of data values in the set.

$82.89 ÷ 9 = $9.21

The mean is $9.21.

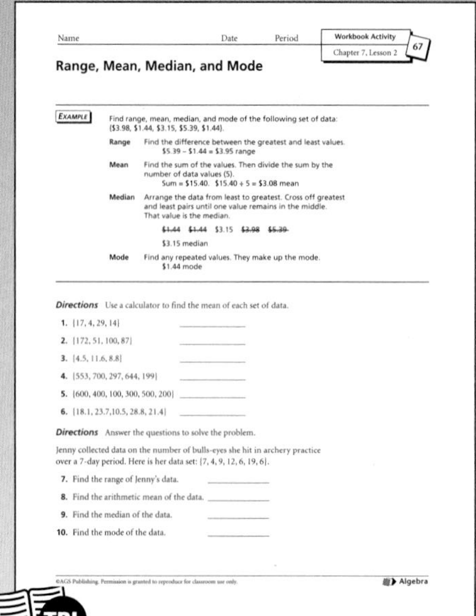

Name Date Period **Workbook Activity 67** Chapter 7, Lesson 2

Range, Mean, Median, and Mode

EXAMPLE Find range, mean, median, and mode of the following set of data: {$3.98, $1.44, $3.15, $5.39, $1.44}.

Range Find the difference between the greatest and least values.
$5.39 – $1.44 = $3.95 range

Mean Find the sum of the values. Then divide the sum by the number of data values (5).
Sum = $15.40. $15.40 ÷ 5 = $3.08 mean

Median Arrange the data from least to greatest. Cross off greatest and least pairs until one value remains in the middle. That value is the median.
~~$1.44~~ ~~$1.44~~ $3.15 ~~$3.98~~ ~~$5.39~~
$3.15 median

Mode Find any repeated values. They make up the mode.
$1.44 mode

Directions Use a calculator to find the mean of each set of data.

1. {17, 4, 29, 14} ______
2. {172, 51, 100, 87} ______
3. {4.5, 11.6, 8.8} ______
4. {553, 700, 297, 644, 199} ______
5. {600, 400, 100, 300, 500, 200} ______
6. {18.1, 23.7,10.5, 28.8, 21.4} ______

Directions Answer the questions to solve the problem.

Jenny collected data on the number of bulls-eyes she hit in archery practice over a 7-day period. Here is her data set: {7, 4, 9, 12, 6, 19, 6}.

7. Find the range of Jenny's data. ______
8. Find the arithmetic mean of the data. ______
9. Find the median of the data. ______
10. Find the mode of the data. ______

 Algebra

TRL

Workbook Activity 67

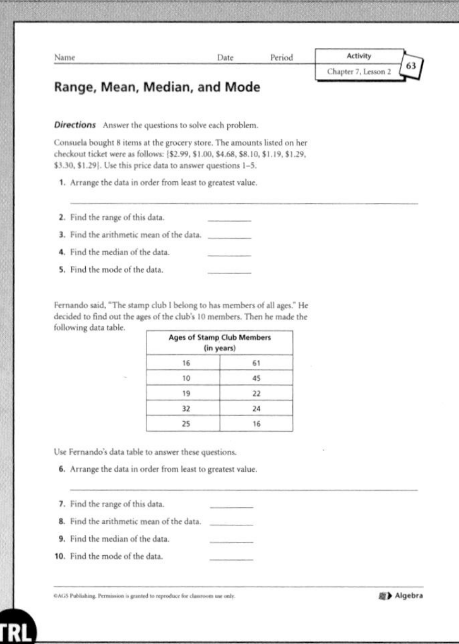

Name Date Period **Activity 63** Chapter 7, Lesson 2

Range, Mean, Median, and Mode

Directions Answer the questions to solve each problem.

Consuela bought 8 items at the grocery store. The amounts listed on her checkout ticket were as follows: {$2.99, $1.00, $4.68, $8.10, $1.19, $1.29, $3.30, $1.29}. Use this price data to answer questions 1–5.

1. Arrange the data in order from least to greatest value.
______
2. Find the range of this data. ______
3. Find the arithmetic mean of the data. ______
4. Find the median of the data. ______
5. Find the mode of the data. ______

Fernando said, "The stamp club I belong to has members of all ages." He decided to find out the ages of the club's 10 members. Then he made the following data table.

Ages of Stamp Club Members (in years)	
16	61
10	45
19	22
32	24
25	16

Use Fernando's data table to answer these questions.

6. Arrange the data in order from least to greatest value.
______
7. Find the range of this data. ______
8. Find the arithmetic mean of the data. ______
9. Find the median of the data. ______
10. Find the mode of the data. ______

 Algebra

TRL

Activity 63

Median
The middle value in an ordered set of data

The **median** of a set of data is the middle value when the set is ordered from greatest to least or least to greatest.

EXAMPLE 2 Find the median of the set of data {\$10.00, \$25.95, \$2.13, \$10.00, \$7.31, \$6.50, \$10.00, \$6.50, \$4.50}.

Step 1 Order the data values from greatest to least or from least to greatest.

\$25.95 \$10.00 \$10.00 \$10.00 \$7.31 \$6.50 \$6.50 \$4.50 \$2.13

Step 2 Cross off the greatest and least values in the set. Continue crossing off greatest and least pairs until one value remains in the middle of the set.

~~\$25.95~~ ~~\$10.00~~ ~~\$10.00~~ ~~\$10.00~~ \$7.31 ~~\$6.50~~ ~~\$6.50~~ ~~\$4.50~~ ~~\$2.13~~

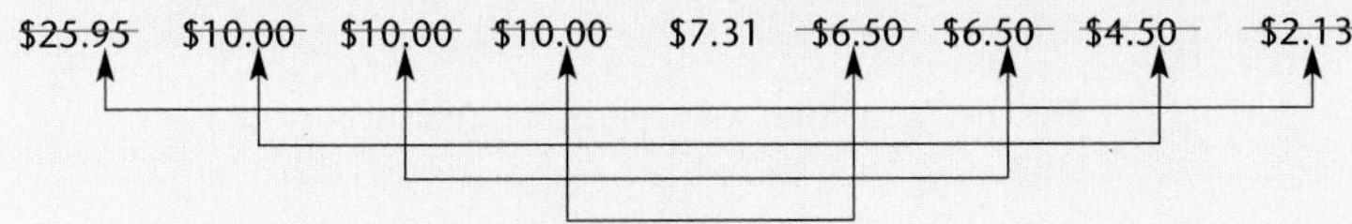

The data value remaining in the middle of the set is the median.
The median of the set of data is \$7.31.

The data set above has an odd number of values. Any set of data that has an odd number of values will always have a middle value. However, some sets of data have an even number of values. To find the median of such a set, arrange the values in order from greatest to least or least to greatest, and cross off greatest and least pairs until two values remain in the middle of the set. The median is the mean, or average, of these values.

EXAMPLE 3 Find the median of the set of data {9, 4, 2, 10}.

Step 1 Arrange the values from greatest to least or least to greatest.

2 4 9 10

Step 2 Cross off greatest and least pairs until two values remain in the middle of the set.

~~2~~ 4 9 ~~10~~

Step 3 Find the mean of the two values in the middle of the set. Add the values, then divide by 2 because there are 2 values in the set.

$$\begin{array}{r} 4 \\ +9 \\ \hline 13 \end{array} \qquad 13 \div 2 = 6.5 \text{ or } 6\tfrac{1}{2}$$

The median of the set of data is 6.5 or $6\frac{1}{2}$.

2 Teaching the Lesson

After students have read the lesson, assess understanding of median by having them explain why it is necessary to add middle values and divide by 2 in some data samples. *(When there is an even number of data items, the exact midpoint is halfway between the two center numbers. Adding them and dividing by 2 calculates this point halfway between them, the exact middle of the range.)*

Common Error

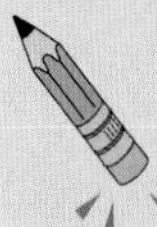

Many students confuse *mean* and *median*. The *mean* is the average and is calculated by addition and division. The *median* is the value located in the middle of the range, found by manipulating data and counting. You may wish to sponsor a poster contest among students to invent the best mnemonic device or visualization technique for keeping the terms (and the processes) straight. Post the best entries for student reference.

3 Reinforce and Extend

Mental Math

Provide simple example data sets orally and have students practice calculating the mean without using pencil and paper:

4, 5, 7, 8 *(24 ÷ 4 = 6)*

10, 20, 30, 40 *(100 ÷ 4 = 25)*

2, 4, 6 *(12 ÷ 3 = 4)*

25, 25, 30, 35, 35 *(150 ÷ 5 = 30)*

Learning Styles

LEP/ESL

ESL students may have difficulty with the concepts of median and mode. Have students work in groups of 7 to 10 with a set of data. Give some sets even and some odd numbers of items. Assign each student one value in the set of data. Have students line up in number order. Ask students representing the median (or the numbers on either side of it in the case of even-numbered sets) and the mode to identify themselves by stepping forward. One group member not in line explains how to calculate median using names and numbers of group members in line.

Learning Styles

Interpersonal/ Group Learning

Create sets of data such as the following on 3 x 5 cards:

- bake sale earnings: $33, $111, $59, $75, $59

  (67.4, 59, 59, 78)

- high temperatures in March: 66, 49, 52, 62, 45, 52, 70, 57, 55

  (56.4w, 55, 52, 25)

- concert ticket prices: $25, $30, $35, $35, $37, $40, $50, $55

  (38.38, 36, 35, 30)

Have students form small groups, draw a card, and work cooperatively to calculate the mean, median, mode, and range for each group of data.

Mode
The value or values that occur most often in a set of data

Measures of central tendency
The mean, median, and mode of a set of data

The **mode** of a set of data is the value or values that occur most often. To compute the mode of a set of data, count the number of times each value appears. The value or values that appear most often is the mode.

Example 4 Find the mode of the set of data
{1, 8, 6, 8, 2, 4, 9, 6}.
↑ ↑ ↑ ↑

The values 8 and 6 appear twice. All of the other values appear only once. Therefore, the modes are 8 and 6.

The mean, median, and mode are **measures of central tendency.** Each describes a set of data in a different way.

Exercise A Use this data set for the following exercise.
{8.2, 3.005, 2.03, 14, 7.75, 3, 1.01, 3.005}

1. Compute the range. 14 − 1.01 = 12.99

2. Compute the mean. 5.25

3. Compute the median. 3.005

4. Compute the mode. 3.005

Exercise B

Students' answers will vary.

5. Create a set of data that contains at least six values. Compute the range, mean, median, and mode of the set.

Exercise C

Students' answers for problems 6–9 will vary.

6. Create a data set that contains five values and has a range of 10.

7. Create a data set that contains four values and has a mean of 24.

8. Create a data set that contains seven values and has a median of 2.75.

9. Create a data set that contains three values and has a mode of $\frac{1}{3}$.

10. Which measure—range, mean, median, or mode—best describes the ages of your classmates? Explain. The mode, because almost everyone is the same age.

Calculator Practice

A calculator can be used to compute the arithmetic mean, or average, of a set of data.

EXAMPLE 5 Find the average of the set of data {4.1, 2.5, 13.8}.

Step 1 Use a calculator to find the sum of the data values in the set.

Enter 4.1 [+] 2.5 [+] 13.8 [=]

Step 2 The calculator will display 20.4.

Divide by 3—the number of data values in the set.

Press [÷] 3 [=] The display reads 6.8.

The average of {4.1, 2.5, 13.8} is 6.8.

If your calculator has a sum [Σ+] key and a mean [$\bar{x}$] key, enter 4.1 [Σ+] 2.5 [Σ+] 13.8 [Σ+]. Then press [$\bar{x}$].
(On most calculators, you will need to press [SHIFT] [$\bar{x}$] or [2nd] [$\bar{x}$].) The display reads 6.8.

Exercise D Use a calculator to find the average of each set of data.

11. $\{12, 21, 34, 7\}$ 18.5

12. $\{3.2, 16.5, 9.1\}$ 9.6

13. $\{110, 158, 86\}$ 118

14. $\{73.02, 11.145, 11.955\}$ 32.04

15. $\{10, 550, 212, 623, 1914.06\}$ 661.812

Career Connection

Invite as guest speaker an insurance adjuster, municipal employee, or other worker who deals with statistics. Request that he or she demonstrate for students how finding the mean, median, mode, and range is important in the job and explain uses to which the data are put.

Learning Styles

Auditory/Verbal

Be sure students understand that *mode* is an existing value or values within the set of data, not a calculation. Write on the board sets of data with one mode, two or more modes, and no modes. Have each student order and analyze one set of data and determine the mode(s), if any. As the student works, ask him or her to explain the steps in the process and how the answer was obtained.

Calculator

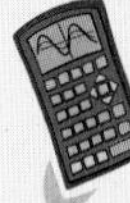

Have students count off by fives and form five groups with at least four members per group. Then invite students to use calculators to find the mean shoe size of their group. As students record their shoe sizes, alert them to write half sizes as decimals (8.5, not $8\frac{1}{2}$). Question groups to be sure they are adding all sizes before dividing by the number of members in the group.

Lesson at a Glance

Chapter 7 Lesson 3

Overview This lesson explains how to construct a box-and-whiskers plot to illustrate the concentration and spread of data in a set.

Objectives

- To explain the usefulness of box-and-whiskers plots for representing large sets of data
- To learn a five-step process for creating a box-and-whiskers plot

Student Pages 192–195

Teacher's Resource Library 

Workbook Activity 68

Activity 64

Alternative Activity 64

Mathematics Vocabulary

box-and-whiskers plot
lower quartile
upper quartile

Warm-Up Activity

Review the concepts *median, quartile,* and *number line.* Draw a number line on the board, numbered 1–9, and ask students to find the median of the numbers on the line. *(5)* Divide the number line at that point and ask what the median value does. *(Separates the data into an upper and lower half)* Challenge the class to invent a way to find the midpoints of the upper half and the lower half. Ask what this process does to the data. *(Divides it into four quarters)*

Teaching the Lesson

Work through the example with students, step by step. In step 3, have students explain how they would calculate the median if there were an even number of items. In step 4, check to be sure students understand they are finding the points to divide the data into four portions. Each portion will contain a fourth of the *quantity* of data.

Lesson 3 Box-and-Whiskers Plots

Box-and-whiskers plot
A way to describe the concentration and the spread of data in a set

Lower quartile
The median of the scores below the median

Upper quartile
The median of the scores above the median

The bar graph and histogram you learned about in Lesson 1 are visual ways to represent data. A **box-and-whiskers plot** is another visual way to describe the concentration and the spread of data in a set. A box-and-whiskers plot with its box and two whiskers looks like this:

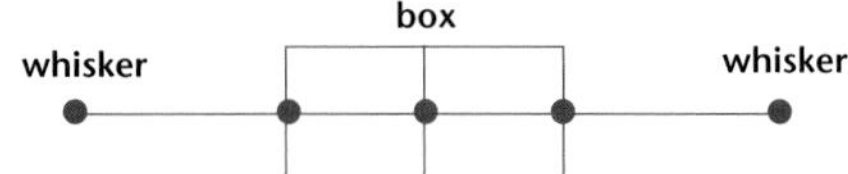

EXAMPLE 1 Construct a box-and-whiskers plot for the data set. The data represents the number of points seven players on a basketball team scored during a game.

{8, 3, 13, 10, 17, 12, 5}

Step 1 Arrange the data in order from greatest to least or least to greatest.

3 5 8 10 12 13 17

Step 2 Identify the greatest and least values of the data. These values are called the upper and lower extremes.

3 5 8 10 12 13 17
↑ lower extreme ↑ upper extreme

Step 3 Find the median of the data.

3 5 8 10 12 13 17
↑ median

Step 4 Find the median of all of the scores below the median. This median is called the **lower quartile.** Then find the median of all of the scores above the median. This median is called the **upper quartile.**

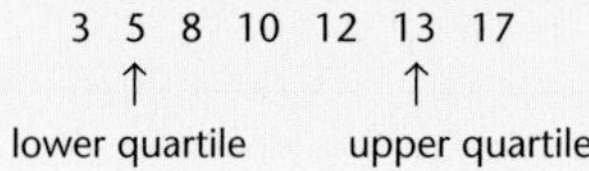

3 5 8 10 12 13 17
↑ lower quartile ↑ upper quartile

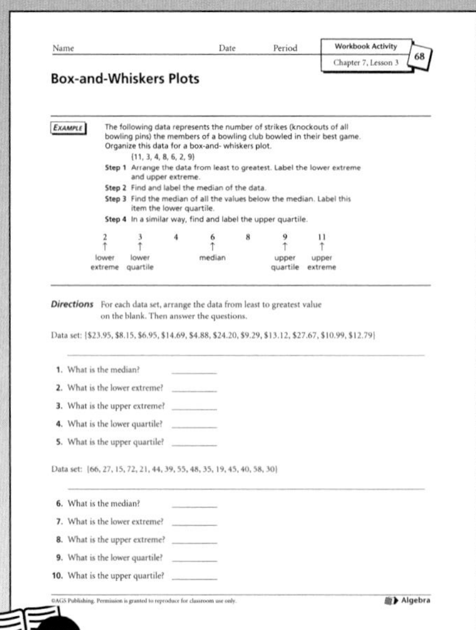

Name Date Period | Workbook Activity 68 | Chapter 7, Lesson 3

Box-and-Whiskers Plots

EXAMPLE The following data represents the number of strikes (knockouts of all bowling pins) the members of a bowling club bowled in their best game. Organize this data for a box-and- whiskers plot.

{11, 3, 4, 8, 6, 2, 9}

Step 1 Arrange the data from least to greatest. Label the lower extreme and upper extreme.
Step 2 Find and label the median of the data.
Step 3 Find the median of all the values below the median. Label this item the lower quartile.
Step 4 In a similar way, find and label the upper quartile.

2 (lower extreme) 3 (lower quartile) 4 6 (median) 8 9 (upper quartile) 11 (upper extreme)

Directions For each data set, arrange the data from least to greatest value on the blank. Then answer the questions.

Data set: {\$23.95, \$8.15, \$6.95, \$14.69, \$4.88, \$24.20, \$9.29, \$13.12, \$27.67, \$10.99, \$12.79}

1. What is the median? ________
2. What is the lower extreme? ________
3. What is the upper extreme? ________
4. What is the lower quartile? ________
5. What is the upper quartile? ________

Data set: {66, 27, 15, 72, 21, 44, 39, 55, 48, 35, 19, 45, 40, 58, 30}

6. What is the median? ________
7. What is the lower extreme? ________
8. What is the upper extreme? ________
9. What is the lower quartile? ________
10. What is the upper quartile? ________

 Algebra

Workbook Activity 68

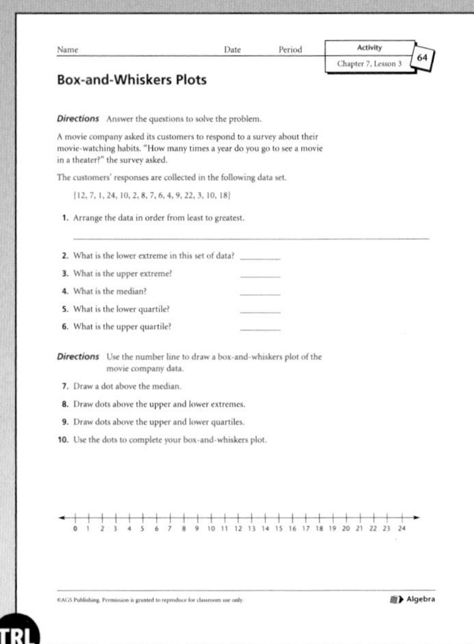

Name Date Period | Activity 64 | Chapter 7, Lesson 3

Box-and-Whiskers Plots

Directions Answer the questions to solve the problem.

A movie company asked its customers to respond to a survey about their movie-watching habits. "How many times a year do you go to see a movie in a theater?" the survey asked.

The customers' responses are collected in the following data set.

{12, 7, 1, 24, 10, 2, 8, 7, 6, 4, 9, 22, 3, 10, 18}

1. Arrange the data in order from least to greatest.
2. What is the lower extreme in this set of data? ________
3. What is the upper extreme? ________
4. What is the median? ________
5. What is the lower quartile? ________
6. What is the upper quartile? ________

Directions Use the number line to draw a box-and-whiskers plot of the movie company data.

7. Draw a dot above the median.
8. Draw dots above the upper and lower extremes.
9. Draw dots above the upper and lower quartiles.
10. Use the dots to complete your box-and-whiskers plot.

0 1 2 3 4 5 6 7 8 9 10 11 12 13 14 15 16 17 18 19 20 21 22 23 24

 Algebra

Activity 64

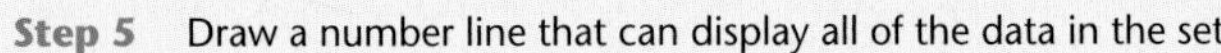

Step 5 Draw a number line that can display all of the data in the set.

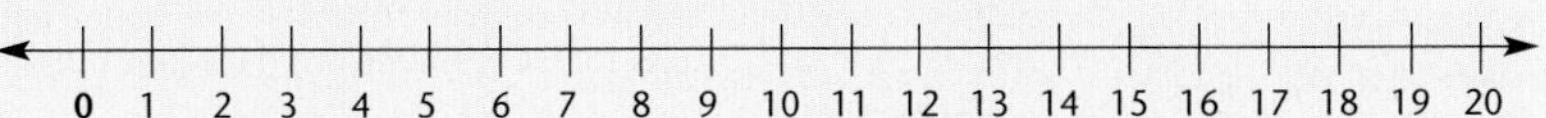

Step 6 Above the number line, draw five dots: one to represent the median, one to represent each extreme, and one to represent each quartile.

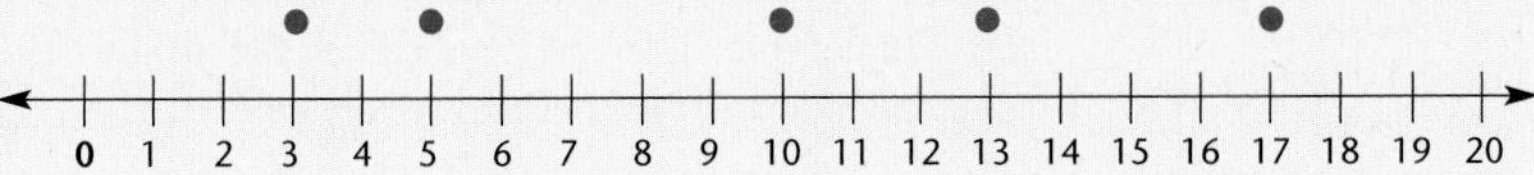

Step 7 Draw a box or rectangle from the lower to the upper quartile. Draw a vertical segment in the box to represent the median. Then draw horizontal segments or whiskers to connect the box to the extremes.

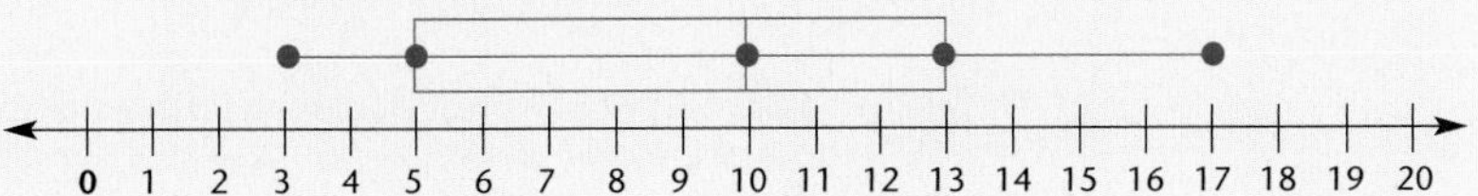

The box in a box-and-whiskers plot contains approximately 50% of the data. The box-and-whiskers plot above tells you that the middle 50% of the data range, or cluster, is from 5 to 13. Box-and-whiskers plots are especially useful when comparing large sets of data.

Common Error

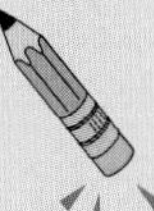

Students may confuse the number line with the set of data. Be sure they understand that the line and its numbers simply provide a visual marker above which quartiles of the actual set of data can be displayed. Duplicate the box-and-whiskers plot on the board. Have students point to the dots that show where

- the lower fourth of the data begins
- the upper fourth of the data begins
- the midpoint of the data is located

Try This

In many cases, the mean will be in the box. However, students should understand that extreme values can influence the average, so that it does not represent the middle range of values and falls on a whisker. Have students calculate the mean for the data in Exercise A. *(44.9 or 45, same as the median)* Then have them recalculate the mean with the upper extreme changed to 100. *(48.7 or 49, on the right whisker)*

3 Reinforce and Extend

Learning Styles

Interpersonal/ Group Learning

After students have completed Exercise A, have them work in groups of four to create box-and-whiskers plots for sets of data with extreme values (that is, with some values far from the median or mean):

- Gasoline mileage (miles per gallon)

  9 18 20 21 23 24 38

- Added tax per gallon of gas (in cents)

  5 6 7 8 10 20 35

Ask students to describe differences in the appearance of the plots with extreme values. *(One or more whiskers is proportionally longer than the box.)* Ask, "What signal does this send about the data and the measurement of its central tendencies (represented by the box)?" *(The imbalance in the plot shows that extreme values may distort the measures of central tendency. This may result in statistics that are misleading, as when "average" salaries for a company are computed. One or two very high salaries raise the average far above what most people are actually making.)*

ONLINE CONNECTION

Students can visit http://illuminations.nctm.org/imath/6-8/BoxModel/student/index.html.

From this website, they can use an interactive simulation called a "box model" to explore the relationship between actual probability and theoretical probability.

This website was created by NCTM and correlates with the NCTM Standard on probability.

Writing About Mathematics

Survey your classmates. Ask them to estimate the average number of minutes they study each week. Record the data you collect and construct a box-and-whiskers plot from it.

1. 39, 40, 41, 42, 44, 44, 45, 45, 47, 48, 49, 49, 51; upper extreme 51
2. lower extreme 39
3. median 45
4. upper quartile 48.5; lower quartile 41.5

Exercise A Use the following data set {42, 48, 44, 45, 41, 39, 45, 49, 47, 44, 40, 51, 49} to make a box-and-whiskers plot.

1. Arrange the data in order from greatest to least or least to greatest. Identify the greatest value of the data and label it upper extreme.
2. Identify the least value of the data and label it lower extreme.
3. Find the median of the data and label it median.
4. Find the median of all of the data above the median and label it upper quartile. Find the median of all of the data below the median and label it lower quartile.
5. Draw a number line that can display all of the data in the set. Draw dots for the median, both extremes, and both quartiles. Draw a box or rectangle from the lower to the upper quartile. Draw a vertical segment in the box to represent the median. Then draw horizontal segments or whiskers to connect the box to the extremes.

See Teach Edition p answer.

TRY THIS If a box-and-whiskers plot would also include the mean of the data, would the mean be in the box or on a whisker? Explain.

Estimation Activity

Estimate: Find the average (mean) of a set of numbers.

Find the average of 39, 42, 44, 45, 47, 48, 51

Solution: Take the highest and lowest numbers and add them.
51 + 39 = 90
Divide by 2 90 ÷ 2 = 45

The estimated average is 45.

194 Chapter 7 Data, Statistics, and Probability

Answer to Problem 5

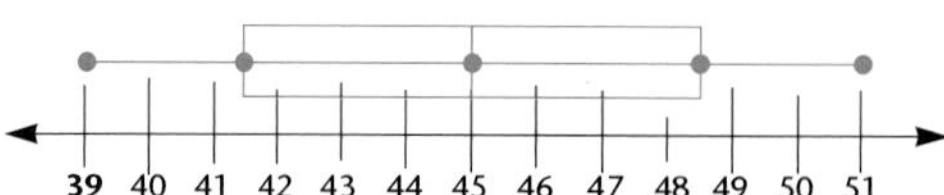

6. 12, 14, 15, 16, 16, 17, 18, 20, 21, 21, 22, ; upper extreme 22

7. lower extreme 12

8. median 17

9. upper quartile 21; lower quartile 15

Exercise B Use the following data set {18, 16, 12, 22, 21, 16, 20, 21, 14, 17, 15} to make a box-and-whiskers plot.

6. Arrange the data in order from greatest to least or least to greatest. Identify the greatest value of the data and label it upper extreme.

7. Identify the least value of the data and label it lower extreme.

8. Find the median of the data and label it median.

9. Find the median of all of the data above the median and label it upper quartile. Find the median of all of the data below the median and label it lower quartile.

10. Draw a number line that can display all of the data in the set. Draw dots for the median, both extremes, and both quartiles. Draw a box or rectangle from the lower to the upper quartile. Draw a vertical segment in the box to represent the median. Then draw horizontal segments or whiskers to connect the box to the extremes.
See Teacher's Edition page for answer.

Lesson at a Glance

Chapter 7 Lesson 4

Overview This lesson explains probability and how to calculate it.

Objectives

- To identify the number of favorable outcomes and possible outcomes in an event
- To calculate the probability that an outcome will occur

Student Pages 196–199

Teacher's Resource Library 

Workbook Activity 69
Activity 65
Alternative Activity 65

Mathematics Vocabulary

probability
statistics
theoretical probability

Warm-Up Activity

Draw a large circle on a piece of paper and divide it into three equal wedges: one white, one red, and one blue. Place a pencil in the circle's center and ask, "When I spin the pencil, how likely is it that the pencil point will land on red?" Encourage students to explain their answers. Then hold the pencil above the floor and ask, "If I drop the pencil, how likely is it that it will land on the floor? What is the probability that it will land on the ceiling?" Encourage students to explain their reasoning. Ask them to describe the number of possible results in each problem. How did this affect their answers?

Teaching the Lesson

Make sure students understand these essentials about the concept of probability *(P)*:

- *P* expresses the likelihood that the desired outcome will occur.
- Each possible outcome is equally likely to occur in any given trial.

Lesson 4 The Probability Fraction

Statistics
Numerical facts about people, places, or things

Probability
The chance or likelihood of an event occurring

In Lesson 2, you explored the mean, median, and mode of a set of data. Mean, median, and mode are examples of **statistics.** Statistics also include **probability**—the chance or likelihood that an outcome will occur.

Probability experiments always include an event and one or more outcomes. To find the probability (*P*) that an outcome will occur, use the fraction

$$P = \frac{\text{number of favorable outcomes}}{\text{number of possible outcomes}}$$

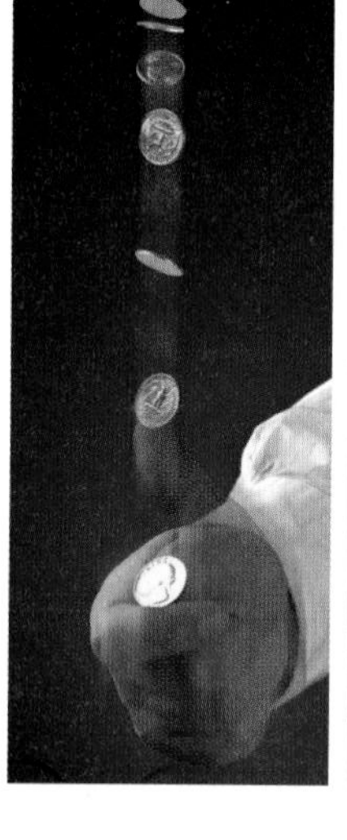

Example 1 Suppose a coin is tossed once. What is the probability *P* that the coin will land heads up?

Step 1 Use the probability fraction.

$$P = \frac{\text{number of favorable outcomes}}{\text{number of possible outcomes}}$$

Step 2 Find the denominator. Since there are two possible outcomes when the coin is tossed—the coin will land either heads up or tails up—the denominator is two.

$$P = \frac{\text{number of favorable outcomes}}{2}$$

Step 3 Find the numerator. Since one outcome is favorable—the coin landing heads up—the numerator is one.

$$P = \frac{1}{2}$$

The probability of tossing a coin and having it land heads up is $\frac{1}{2}$.

Since you know how to change a fraction to a percent, you can also say that the probability of flipping a coin and having it land heads up is 50%. This is because $\frac{1}{2} = 50\%$.

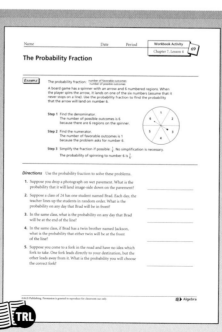

Name Date Period **Workbook Activity 69** Chapter 7, Lesson 4

The Probability Fraction

Example The probability fraction: $\frac{\text{number of favorable outcomes}}{\text{number of possible outcomes}}$

A board game has a spinner with an arrow and 6 numbered regions. When the player spins the arrow, it lands on one of the six numbers (assume that it never stops on a line). Use the probability fraction to find the probability that the arrow will land on number 6.

Step 1 Find the denominator.
The number of possible outcomes is 6 because there are 6 regions on the spinner.

Step 2 Find the numerator.
The number of favorable outcomes is 1 because the problem asks for number 6.

Step 3 Simplify the fraction if possible: $\frac{1}{6}$. No simplification is necessary.
The probability of spinning to number 6 is $\frac{1}{6}$.

Directions Use the probability fraction to solve these problems.

1. Suppose you drop a photograph on wet pavement. What is the probability that it will land image-side down on the pavement? ______
2. Suppose a class of 24 has one student named Brad. Each day, the teacher lines up the students in random order. What is the probability on any day that Brad will be in front? ______
3. In the same class, what is the probability on any day that Brad will be at the end of the line? ______
4. In the same class, if Brad has a twin brother named Jackson, what is the probability that either twin will be at the front of the line? ______
5. Suppose you come to a fork in the road and have no idea which fork to take. One fork leads directly to your destination, but the other leads away from it. What is the probability you will choose the correct fork? ______

 Algebra

TRL

Workbook Activity 69

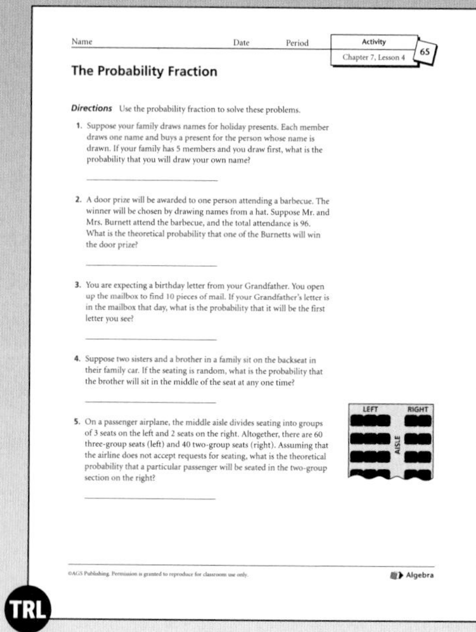

Name Date Period **Activity 65** Chapter 7, Lesson 4

The Probability Fraction

Directions Use the probability fraction to solve these problems.

1. Suppose your family draws names for holiday presents. Each member draws one name and buys a present for the person whose name is drawn. If your family has 5 members and you draw first, what is the probability that you will draw your own name? ______
2. A door prize will be awarded to one person attending a barbecue. The winner will be chosen by drawing names from a hat. Suppose Mr. and Mrs. Burnett attend the barbecue, and the total attendance is 96. What is the theoretical probability that one of the Burnetts will win the door prize? ______
3. You are expecting a birthday letter from your Grandfather. You open up the mailbox to find 10 pieces of mail. If your Grandfather's letter is in the mailbox that day, what is the probability that it will be the first letter you see? ______
4. Suppose two sisters and a brother in a family sit on the backseat in their family car. If the seating is random, what is the probability that the brother will sit in the middle of the seat at any one time? ______
5. On a passenger airplane, the middle aisle divides seating into groups of 3 seats on the left and 2 seats on the right. Altogether, there are 60 three-group seats (left) and 40 two-group seats (right). Assuming that the airline does not accept requests for seating, what is the theoretical probability that a particular passenger will be seated in the two-group section on the right? ______

 Algebra

TRL

Activity 65

Theoretical probability

The predicted likelihood of what should happen in an experiment

EXAMPLE 2 Suppose the 1–6 number cube at the right is rolled once. What is the probability of rolling an even number?

Step 1 Use the probability fraction.

$$P = \frac{\text{number of favorable outcomes}}{\text{number of possible outcomes}}$$

Step 2 Find the denominator. Since there are six possible outcomes when the cube is rolled—1, 2, 3, 4, 5, or 6—the denominator is six.

$$P = \frac{\text{number of favorable outcomes}}{6}$$

Step 3 Find the numerator. Since three outcomes are favorable—2, 4, or 6—the numerator is three.

$$P = \frac{3}{6}$$

Step 4 Simplify if possible.

$$P = \frac{3}{6} = \frac{1}{2}$$

The probability of rolling a 1–6 number cube and rolling an even number is $\frac{1}{2}$ or 50%.

In each of these examples, the probability you found is the **theoretical probability** of each event. Theoretical probability describes what will happen if the experiment is performed many times. In other words, if you toss a coin many times, the probability that the coin lands heads up (or tails up) approaches $\frac{1}{2}$ or 50%, and if you roll a 1–6 number cube many times, the probability of an even (or odd) outcome approaches $\frac{1}{2}$ or 50%.

The theoretical probability of any event will always be 0, 1, or a fraction between 0 and 1.

- *P* is a ratio of the desired outcome to the number of possible outcomes.

To assess understanding, have students explain why the probability of an event cannot be greater than 1. *(You cannot have more successes than tries.)*

Manipulatives

Probability Experiment

Materials: 1–6 Number Cubes

Group Practice: After discussing the theoretical probability in the second example, use a number cube to conduct a probability experiment. Roll the number cube 10 to 20 times, having students record the number that comes up with each roll. Show students how to use this data to describe the actual outcome of the event as a fraction in simplest form. Compare the actual outcome with its theoretical probability and discuss the results. Repeat again if necessary.

Student Practice: Instruct students to use the cubes in the same way to conduct their own probability experiments with the events in Exercise A, Problems 1–6, then report the actual outcome as a simplified fraction.

3 Reinforce and Extend

Learning Styles

Body/Kinesthetic

Students who learn best through touch and movement should work through the second example (page 197) using a number cube. Have them model each possible outcome with the number cube, sketch the outcomes on paper, and circle the favorable outcomes (2, 4, 6) to corroborate the text calculations.

Learning Styles

Visual/Spatial

Create a game show-type of spinner (or draw one on the board), adding dollar amounts or prizes in each segment. For example:

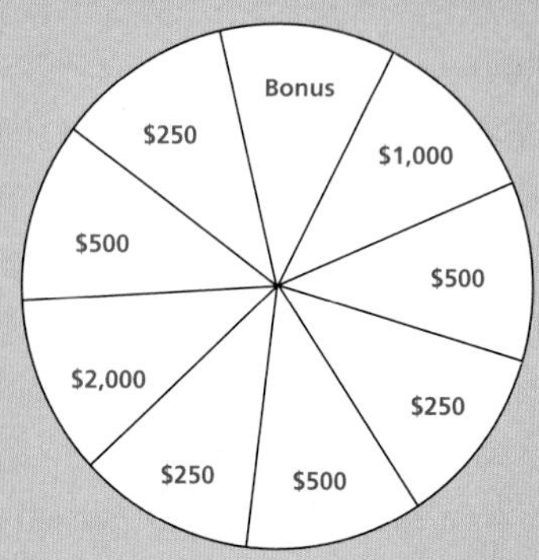

Have students work in pairs to answer questions like these:

- Find (P) of the spinner landing on $250. $(\frac{3}{9} = \frac{1}{3})$
- Find (P) of the spinner landing on $500. $(\frac{3}{9} = \frac{1}{3})$
- Find (P) of the spinner landing on $1,000. $(\frac{1}{9})$
- Find (P) of the spinner landing on Bonus. $(\frac{1}{9})$

At Home

Have students watch or listen to several weather broadcasts and note any references to probability. Invite students to explain how they think the probability was calculated.

Example 3 The probability of rolling a 1–6 number cube and rolling a 7 is zero because the outcome 7 is not possible. $P = \frac{0}{6} = 0$

Example 4 The probability of tossing a coin and having it land heads up or tails up is one because either outcome is favorable. $P = \frac{2}{2} = 1$

Exercise A In a probability experiment, a 1–6 number cube is rolled once. Find the theoretical probability (P) of each event. Express your answer as a fraction in simplest form.

1. $P(2)$ $\frac{1}{6}$
2. $P(3 \text{ or } 5)$ $\frac{2}{6} = \frac{1}{3}$
3. $P(\text{odd number})$ $\frac{3}{6} = \frac{1}{2}$
4. $P(2, 3, \text{or } 4)$ $\frac{3}{6} = \frac{1}{2}$
5. $P(\text{prime number})$ $\frac{3}{6} = \frac{1}{2}$
6. $P(\text{composite number})$ $\frac{2}{6} = \frac{1}{3}$

Exercise B In a probability experiment, a painted cube is rolled once. One side of the cube is painted red, two sides are painted yellow, and three sides are painted green. Find the theoretical probability (P) of each event.

7. $P(\text{yellow})$ $\frac{2}{6} = \frac{1}{3}$
8. $P(\text{green})$ $\frac{3}{6} = \frac{1}{2}$
9. $P(\text{red})$ $\frac{1}{6}$
10. $P(\text{yellow or green})$ $\frac{5}{6}$
11. $P(\text{blue})$ 0
12. $P(\text{red or yellow or green})$ $\frac{6}{6} = 1$

Exercise C Suppose you write each letter of your first name on a slip of paper. All the slips of paper are the same size. The slips are placed in a bag and you take out one slip, without looking. Students' answers will vary.

13. Find (P) of getting a vowel.

14. Find (P) of getting a consonant.

15. Find (P) of getting the first letter of your name.

16. Find (P) of getting the last letter of your name.

Exercise D

Students' answers for problems 17–19 will vary.

17. Describe an experiment that has a probability of 1.

18. Describe an experiment that has a probability of 0.

19. Describe an experiment that has a probability that is greater than 0 but less than 1.

20. Why can't the probability of any event ever exceed 1?

Technology Connection

Cell Phones + Pagers = More Phone Numbers

The number of ways we can "reach out and touch" one another continues to multiply. Less than a decade ago, there was usually one telephone number per household. Now a household may have a phone line for the computer, two or three cell phones, and a pager. All of these lines need a number different from the regular phone line. Phone companies began running out of numbers. The solution was to add more area codes. Adding just three digits has increased the combinations of phone numbers by the millions!

20. By definition, $P = \left(\frac{\text{number or favorable outcomes}}{\text{number of possible outcomes}}\right)$ can never exceed 1.

Mental Math

Review the process of converting simple fractions to percentages. Have students mentally calculate the percentage represented by each of the following fractions:

$\frac{1}{4}$ *(25%)*

$\frac{1}{8}$ *(12.5%)*

$\frac{1}{3}$ *($33.\overline{3}$%)*

$\frac{1}{5}$ *(20%)*

$\frac{3}{4}$ *(75%)*

$\frac{2}{3}$ *($66.\overline{6}$%)*

Learning Styles

Body/Kinesthetic

Have students create paper models of the painted cube in Exercise B and explain their answers to problems 7–12 to the class using the model as a visual aid.

Lesson at a Glance

Chapter 7 Lesson 5

Overview This lesson explains how to classify probabilities as not likely or very likely, more likely or less likely. It then shows how to determine the complement of a probability event.

Objectives

- To classify outcomes as certain, impossible, very likely, not likely, more likely, or less likely
- To calculate probability of events and their complements

Student Pages 200–203

Teacher's Resource Library 

Workbook Activity 70

Activity 66

Alternative Activity 66

Mathematics Vocabulary

complement of a probability event

Warm-Up Activity

Have students imagine they are going to conduct a poll to find out which radio stations classmates listen to. Have them design a form listing radio stations on the left and a range of responses on the right. List on the board the choices participants should be able to circle (e.g., always, never, almost always, almost never, sometimes). Have students order the responses. Place the responses on a line and ask students which end correlates to a probability of 0 and which to a probability of 1.

Teaching the Lesson

Define *complement* for students as "the amount or number needed to fill or complete." Using this definition, ask them to identify the complement in each of the following:

- a pint + ___ = 1 quart
- quarter + ___ = $1

Lesson 5 Probability and Complementary Events

Remember that the probability of any outcome occurring is 0, 1, or a fraction between 0 and 1. The word *impossible* is sometimes used to describe a probability of 0, and the word *certain* is sometimes used to describe a probability of 1.

0 — 1

impossible — certain

Phrases are sometimes used to describe a probability between 0 and 1. These phrases include *not likely* and *very likely*.

EXAMPLE 1 Suppose you roll a 1–6 number cube once and are looking for an outcome of 1, 2, 3, 4, or 5. You are *very likely* to be successful because there are five favorable outcomes (1, 2, 3, 4, 5) in the event and only one unfavorable outcome (6).

Suppose you roll a 1–6 number cube once and are looking for an outcome of 6. You are *not likely* to be successful because there is only one favorable outcome (6) in the event and five unfavorable outcomes (1, 2, 3, 4, 5).

Phrases such as *more likely* and *less likely* are sometimes used when probabilities are compared.

EXAMPLE 2 Suppose each letter of the alphabet is written on a slip of paper. All the slips of paper are the same size and are folded in the same way. If you choose one slip without looking, you will be *more likely* to choose a consonant than a vowel because there are 21 consonants and only 5 vowels in the alphabet. Also, you will be *less likely* to choose a vowel than a consonant for the same reason.

These words and phrases are used in a general way to describe probability. Probability can also be described in a specific or exact way. Recall that you explored how to find the probability of an outcome occurring. You can also find the probability of an outcome *not* occurring.

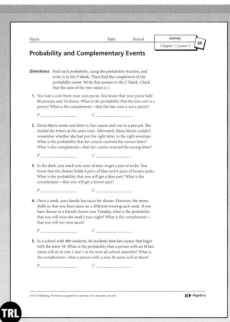

Name Date Period — Workbook Activity 70 — Chapter 7, Lesson 5

Probability and Complementary Events

EXAMPLE

- Suppose you toss a 1–6 number cube. It is *certain* that the outcome will be in the set {1, 2, 3, 4, 5, 6}.
- Suppose you toss a coin. It is *impossible* that the outcome will be both heads and tails.
- Suppose you close your eyes and point at random to a key on your computer keyboard. It is *likely* that you will point to a letter or number key.
- In the same situation, it is *not likely* that you will point to the letter *Q*.

Directions Write one of the following words on the blank to describe the probability of each event: *certain, impossible, likely, not likely.*

1. With eyes closed, you pick a crayon at random from your box of 48 crayons. The color you pick is green. ________
2. The sun will come up tomorrow morning. ________
3. The first card you draw from a deck of regular playing cards is an ace. ________
4. Opening a book randomly, you open it to page 132. ________
5. Your book has 286 pages. You open the book randomly to page 400. ________
6. A pollster sends a questionnaire to 40 households in your community of 800 total households. One of these questionnaires arrives in your mailbox. ________
7. If you roll a 1–6 number cube, the number that rolls up will be the square of another integer. ________
8. If you roll a 1–6 number cube, the number that rolls up will be the square root of an integer. ________
9. The next person you pass on the sidewalk has a birthday in January. ________
10. You take one egg out of a dozen eggs in the refrigerator. It is *not* the last egg in the carton. ________

 Algebra

Workbook Activity 70

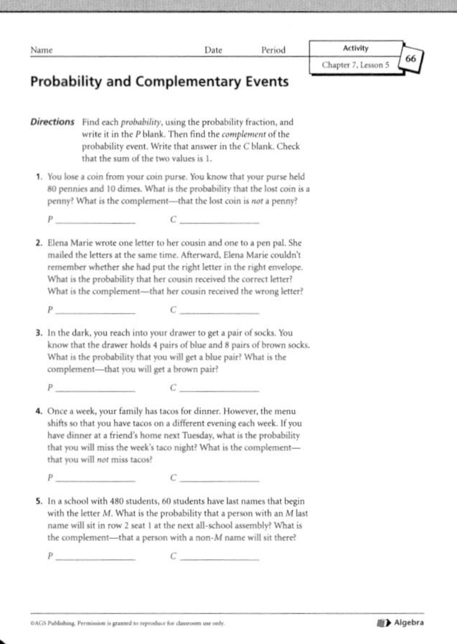
Name Date Period — Activity 66 — Chapter 7, Lesson 5

Probability and Complementary Events

Directions Find each *probability*, using the probability fraction, and write it in the *P* blank. Then find the *complement* of the probability event. Write that answer in the *C* blank. Check that the sum of the two values is 1.

1. You lose a coin from your coin purse. You know that your purse held 80 pennies and 10 dimes. What is the probability that the lost coin is a penny? What is the complement—that the lost coin is *not* a penny?

   P ________ *C* ________
2. Elena Marie wrote one letter to her cousin and one to a pen pal. She mailed the letters at the same time. Afterward, Elena Marie couldn't remember whether she had put the right letter in the right envelope. What is the probability that her cousin received the correct letter? What is the complement—that her cousin received the wrong letter?

   P ________ *C* ________
3. In the dark, you reach into your drawer to get a pair of socks. You know that the drawer holds 4 pairs of blue and 8 pairs of brown socks. What is the probability that you will get a blue pair? What is the complement—that you will get a brown pair?

   P ________ *C* ________
4. Once a week, your family has tacos for dinner. However, the menu shifts so that you have tacos on a different evening each week. If you have dinner at a friend's home next Tuesday, what is the probability that you will miss the week's taco night? What is the complement—that you will *not* miss tacos?

   P ________ *C* ________
5. In a school with 480 students, 60 students have last names that begin with the letter *M*. What is the probability that a person with an *M* last name will sit in row 2 seat 1 at the next all-school assembly? What is the complement—that a person with a non-*M* name will sit there?

   P ________ *C* ________

 Algebra

Activity 66

Complement of a probabilty event

The set of outcomes that are not in the event

EXAMPLE 3 What is the probability of tossing a coin and not getting an outcome that is heads?

Step 1 Use the probability fraction.

$P = \frac{\text{number of favorable outcomes}}{\text{number of possible outcomes}}$

Step 2 Find the denominator. Since there are two possible outcomes when the coin is tossed—the coin will land either heads up or tails up—the denominator is two.

$P = \frac{\text{number of favorable outcomes}}{2}$

Step 3 Find the numerator. Since you are looking for an outcome that is not heads, the outcome that is favorable is tails. There is one favorable outcome.

$P = \frac{1}{2}$

The probability of tossing a coin and not getting an outcome that is heads is $\frac{1}{2}$. It is also an example of the complement of a probability event. The **complement of a probability event** is the set of outcomes that are not in the event.

EXAMPLE 4 Find (*P*) not blue.

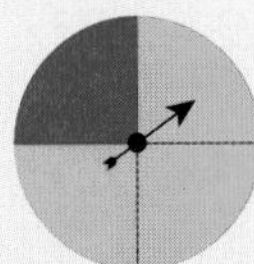

Since the probability of the spinner pointing to blue is $\frac{1}{4}$, the probability of the spinner not pointing to blue is $\frac{3}{4}$, because $\frac{1}{4} + \frac{3}{4} = \frac{4}{4} = 1$.

(*P*) not blue $= \frac{3}{4}$

- $\frac{1}{4} +$ ___ $= 1$
- $\frac{1}{2}$ chance of heads + ___ chance of tails $= \frac{2}{2}$ or 1 (total possible outcomes)

Invite students to create an equation that expresses the relationship between a probability and its complement. The following example is reasonable:

P_1 (desired outcome) + P_2 (all other outcomes) = 1 (total possibilities)

Where P_1 and P_2 are probabilities.

MANIPULATIVES

Probability Experiment

Materials: Blank Game Spinners

Group Practice: Show students how to color their spinners to match the spinner pictured with Exercise B on page 203 in the text. Review how to perform a probability experiment (see the Chapter 7, Lesson 4 Manipulatives Activity) and simplify the data. Conduct an experiment on *P* (orange and not yellow). Perform 10 to 20 trials, simplify the data, and compare the actual outcome to the theoretical probability.

Student Practice: Instruct students to use their spinners to conduct experiments on Problems 9–18 in Exercise B. Have them describe the outcome of their experiments as a fraction in simplest form and compare it to the theoretical probability of each event.

3 Reinforce and Extend

LEARNING STYLES

Auditory/Verbal

Complete Exercise A orally in class. Ask volunteers to read aloud each sentence with their chosen word or phrase. Then ask them to explain why they chose that word or phrase to complete that sentence.

LEARNING STYLES

LEP/ESL

Help ESL students learn the modifiers *more likely* and *less likely*, *not likely* and *very likely* by associating them with fractions on the number line. Reproduce the following on the board:

0			1
not likely	less likely	more likely	very likely

As students calculate probabilities for events, have them locate the fraction on the line and state the probability along with its likelihood—e.g., "there is a 1-in-8 probability that ________, so it is not likely."

You may wish to have LEP students review adding of fractions. Then have them work fraction problems like the following:

$\frac{1}{3} + \frac{2}{3} = (1)$

$\frac{3}{8} + \frac{5}{8} = (1)$

$\frac{4}{10} + \frac{6}{10} = (1)$

Finally, have students explain in their own words what two fractions must be added together to total 1 and create an algebraic equation showing the relationship.

Exercise A Write each sentence on a sheet of paper. Use one of these words or phrases to complete each sentence: *certain, impossible, very likely, not likely, more likely, less likely.*

1. The probability of tossing a coin and getting an outcome of heads or tails is ______. certain
2. An outcome of 2 or 4 on a 1–6 number cube is ______ than an outcome of any odd number. less likely
3. An outcome of tossing a coin and getting an outcome of tails is ______ than rolling a 1–6 number cube and getting an outcome of 3. more likely
4. The probability of tossing a coin and getting an outcome of heads and tails is ______. impossible
5. An outcome of an odd number on a 1–6 number cube is ______ than an outcome of 3 or 5. more likely
6. The probability of tossing a coin and getting an outcome of heads and tails is ______ than the probability of flipping a coin and getting an outcome of heads or tails. impossible or less likely
7. It is ______ that a person was born during the month of February. not likely
8. It is ______ that a person's age is a one-digit or a two-digit number. very likely

Exercise B Refer to the spinner at the right. Express the probability of each event below as a fraction in simplest form.

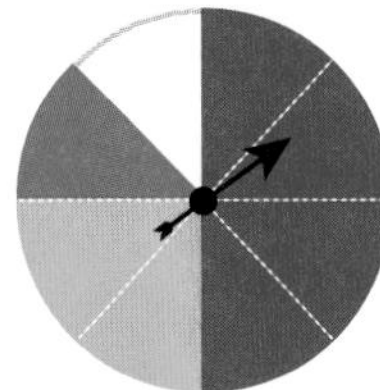

9. P (blue) $\frac{1}{2}$

10. P (orange) $\frac{1}{4}$

11. P (green) $\frac{1}{8}$

12. P (not white) $\frac{7}{8}$

13. P (not orange) $\frac{3}{4}$

14. P (not white and not blue) $\frac{3}{8}$

15. P (white or green) $\frac{1}{4}$

16. P (green or not blue) $\frac{1}{2}$

17. P (blue or white) $\frac{5}{8}$

18. P (not green and not white) $\frac{3}{4}$

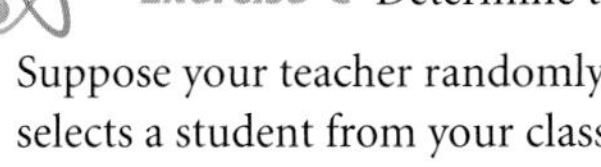

PROBLEM SOLVING

Exercise C Determine the probability in each of the following problems.

19. Suppose your teacher randomly selects a student from your class. What is the probability that the student selected is you?

$\frac{1}{\text{(number of students in the class)}}$

20. Suppose your teacher randomly selects a student from your class. What is the probability that the student selected is not male?

$\frac{\text{(number of females)}}{\text{(total number of students)}}$

LEARNING STYLES

Logical/Mathematical

Before assigning Exercise B, have students study the spinner and convert the geometric shapes into fractions of the whole. Ask,

"Into how many equal portions is the spinner divided?" *(8)*

"What portion of the spinner is gray? *($\frac{1}{8}$)*

"What portion is yellow?" *($\frac{4}{8}$ or $\frac{1}{2}$)*

GROUP PROBLEM SOLVING

Have students work together in groups of three or four to discuss and solve the following:

The Ski Club is having a raffle to raise money for a ski trip. Two hundred tickets have been sold at $10 a ticket. The holder of the winning ticket will receive free lodging at Alpine Ski Resort—worth $100.

1. Find the probability that you will *not* win if you buy one ticket.
2. Decide your chances of winning (certain, very likely, more likely, less likely, not likely, or impossible) if you
   a. buy 10 tickets *(not likely)*
   b. buy 2 tickets *(not likely)*
   c. buy no tickets *(impossible)*
   d. buy 180 tickets *(very likely)*
3. Write a paragraph explaining why it is foolish to buy 10 tickets.

Invite groups to post and compare their answers and to explain how they solved the problems.

Lesson at a Glance

Chapter 7 Lesson 6

Overview This lesson models the use of a tree diagram to show possible combinations in a sample space.

Objective

- To diagram all possible outcomes when two independent events occur simultaneously

Student Pages 204–205

Teacher's Resource Library 

Workbook Activity 71

Activity 67

Alternative Activity 67

Mathematics Vocabulary

sample space

Warm-Up Activity

Ask students to determine how many different combinations are possible when three toppings for a pizza may be ordered. Have students draw pizza shapes on paper and provide them with colored paper shapes representing, say, pepperoni, mushrooms, and green peppers. Working in pairs, students can model the possibilities. Use their outcomes to introduce the concept of sample space. Tell them that this lesson will show them an efficient and orderly way to find all the possible outcomes in a sample space.

Teaching the Lesson

Ask students why *tree diagram* is an appropriate name for this model. *(It has branches.)* Monitor understanding of the process by introducing a third birth into the problem. Have volunteers copy the first example tree diagram onto the board and add appropriate possibilities for the third child. Then elicit explanation from students as they trace the possible combinations to show eight possible outcomes. Ask, "Why is order of the three items so important? That is, why couldn't they simply say there are only four possibilities: 3 boys, 3 girls, 2 boys and 1 girl, or 2 girls and 1 boy?" *(The events occur in a specific sequence.)*

Lesson 6 Tree Diagrams and Sample Spaces

> ***Sample space***
> *The set of all possible outcomes of an experiment*

In probability, a **sample space** is the set of all possible outcomes of an experiment. A tree diagram can be used to generate a sample space.

EXAMPLE 1 There are two children in a family. What is the probability that the first child is a girl and the second child is a boy? Use a tree diagram to solve.

Step 1 Show the possible outcomes for the first child. The first child could be a girl or a boy.

first child → girl boy

Step 2 Show the possible outcomes for the second child. If the first child was a girl, the second child could be a girl or a boy. If the first child was a boy, the second child could be a girl or a boy.

first child → girl boy

second child → girl boy girl boy

Step 3 Draw branches for your tree diagram. Each complete branch represents one possible outcome.

first child → girl boy

second child → girl boy girl boy

The sample space shows there are four possible combinations of children: (girl, girl), (girl, boy), (boy, girl), and (boy, boy). The probability that the first child was a girl and the second child was a boy is one of those combinations, or $\frac{1}{4}$.

EXAMPLE 2 A coin is tossed and the spinner at the right is spun once. What is the probability that the coin will land tails up and the spinner will point to 3?

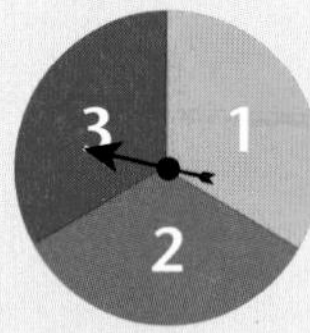

Step 1 Show the possible outcomes for the coin.

coin → heads tails

Name Date Period | Workbook Activity 71 | Chapter 7, Lesson 6

Tree Diagrams and Sample Spaces

EXAMPLE A child is asked to select one crayon and one picture for coloring. Crayon choices are blue or red. The picture choices are a balloon or a star. What is the probability that the child will select *red* and a *star*?

Color choices: blue red

Picture choices: balloon star balloon star

The 4 possible choices: • blue and balloon • blue and star • red and balloon • red and star

The probability is $\frac{1}{4}$. P (red, star) = $\frac{1}{4}$

Directions Suppose the child is still asked to choose between a blue or red crayon but is now offered 3 picture choices: balloon, star, or box. Use a tree diagram to determine the probability of each outcome.

1. Find P (red, box) ______
2. Find P (red, star) ______
3. Find P (blue, not star) ______
4. Find P (blue, balloon) ______
5. Find P (not blue, not balloon) ______
6. Find P (blue *or* red, box) ______
7. Find P (red, *any* picture) ______
8. Find P (*any* color, *any* picture) ______

Directions Solve the problems.

9. Suppose that runners may choose to run in the 5-km or 10-km race. What is the probability that the next runner to sign up will be female and will choose the 5-km race? ______
10. For the same event, what is the probability that the next runner to sign up will be of either sex and will choose the 10-km race? ______

 Algebra

TRL **Workbook Activity 71**

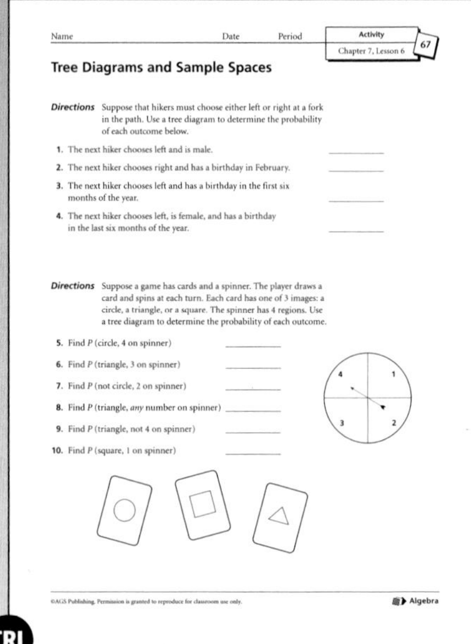
Name Date Period | Activity 67 | Chapter 7, Lesson 6

Tree Diagrams and Sample Spaces

Directions Suppose that hikers must choose either left or right at a fork in the path. Use a tree diagram to determine the probability of each outcome below.

1. The next hiker chooses left and is male. ______
2. The next hiker chooses right and has a birthday in February. ______
3. The next hiker chooses left and has a birthday in the first six months of the year. ______
4. The next hiker chooses left, is female, and has a birthday in the last six months of the year. ______

Directions Suppose a game has cards and a spinner. The player draws a card and spins at each turn. Each card has one of 3 images: a circle, a triangle, or a square. The spinner has 4 regions. Use a tree diagram to determine the probability of each outcome.

5. Find P (circle, 4 on spinner) ______
6. Find P (triangle, 3 on spinner) ______
7. Find P (not circle, 2 on spinner) ______
8. Find P (triangle, *any* number on spinner) ______
9. Find P (triangle, not 4 on spinner) ______
10. Find P (square, 1 on spinner) ______

 Algebra

TRL **Activity 67**

Step 2 Show the possible outcomes for the spinner.

coin → heads tails

spinner → 1 2 3 1 2 3

If the outcome of the coin is heads, the outcome of the spinner can be 1, 2, or 3.

If the outcome of the coin is tails, the outcome of the spinner can be 1, 2, or 3.

Step 3 Draw branches for your tree diagram.

coin → heads tails

spinner → 1 2 3 1 2 3

The sample space shows there are six possible combinations: (heads and 1), (heads and 2), (heads and 3), (tails and 1), (tails and 2), (tails and 3). The probability that the coin was tails and the spinner pointed to 3 is one of those combinations, or $\frac{1}{6}$.

Exercise A Suppose you spin the spinner at the right and toss a coin. Use a tree diagram to determine the probability of each outcome below.

1. Find P (heads and 1) $\frac{1}{8}$
2. Find P (tails and an odd number) $\frac{1}{4}$
3. Find P (tails and a multiple of 3) $\frac{1}{8}$
4. Find P (heads and a prime number) $\frac{1}{4}$
5. Find P (not heads and not 4) $\frac{3}{8}$
6. Find P (not tails and not a whole number) 0
7. Find P (heads or tails and a whole number) 1

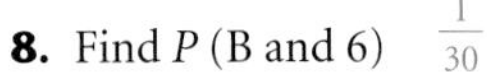

How many different outcomes are possible if two 1–6 number cubes are rolled? What is the probability of rolling a 6 with each cube?

ferent
mes; $\frac{1}{36}$

Exercise B Suppose you spin the spinner at the right and roll a 1–6 number cube.

8. Find P (B and 6) $\frac{1}{30}$
9. Find P (R and an even number) $\frac{1}{10}$
10. Find P (M or V and 4) $\frac{1}{15}$
11. Find P (a consonant and a composite number) $\frac{4}{15}$
12. Find P (a vowel and a multiple of 1) $\frac{1}{5}$
13. Find P (not M and not an odd number) $\frac{2}{5}$
14. Find P (not B or not E and not a multiple of 2) $\frac{3}{10}$
15. Find P (not B and 6) $\frac{2}{15}$

Try This

Ask students to comment about any difficulties they had with the assignment. With 36 possible outcomes, the tree diagram becomes unwieldy and time consuming to construct. Students should realize this method is not realistic when dealing with large quantities of data, with many possible outcomes.

Manipulatives

Probability Experiment

Materials: Blank Game Spinners, Two-Color Counters (or coins), 1–6 Number Cubes

Group Practice: Color a spinner to match the one in the example and conduct a probability experiment on the event in the example, P (tails and 3). Repeat 10 to 20 trials spinning the arrow, tossing the chip (or coin), and recording the outcomes of each trial. Determine the actual outcome of the event and compare to the theoretical probability.

Student Practice: Have students color their spinners to match the spinners in Exercises A and B. Have them conduct probability experiments with some or all of the events named in Exercises A and B. Use the actual outcome to compare to the theoretical probability to see if their answers are reasonable.

3 Reinforce and Extend

Learning Styles

Body/Kinesthetic

Use cardboard and a brad to construct a spinner; divide it into thirds. Have students manipulate the spinner and a coin to demonstrate the possible outcomes. Ask volunteers to create a second spinner, divided into fourths, and demonstrate the possible outcomes for the same events. Model the tree diagram for this sample space on the board, and have students explain its organization as they trace possible outcomes.

Learning Styles

LEP/ESL

For ESL students, emphasize the meaning of the concepts "all possible outcomes" and "possible combinations." After they explain the combinations, ask, "Are there any other results that could happen?"

Lesson at a Glance

Chapter 7 Lesson 7

Overview This lesson explains how to determine the probability of events that are dependent or independent of one another.

Objectives

- To recognize events in a probability experiment as dependent or independent
- To calculate the probability of successive events that are dependent or independent

Student Pages 206–209

Teacher's Resource Library 

Workbook Activity 72

Activity 68

Alternative Activity 68

Mathematics Vocabulary

dependent event
independent event

1 Warm-Up Activity

Have two students each hold a hand of five different cards including one ace apiece, so that the class can see them, but the students cannot see each other's cards. Ask students to discuss the probability that an ace will be drawn at random. Have each student draw a card from the other. Now ask, "Has the probability of drawing an ace changed? Why?" Explain that some events have an effect on the outcome of other events. In this lesson, students will learn to identify dependent and independent sequences of events and to show how probability is changed when the first event affects the second event.

2 Teaching the Lesson

Assess understanding of the probability calculation in the first example by asking students to explain what the multiplicands in the problem $P = \frac{2}{4} \cdot \frac{1}{3}$ each mean. Point out the simplification of $\frac{2}{12}$ to $\frac{1}{6}$ in Step 3 of the first example. Explain that a 2-in-12 chance of occurrence is the same as a 1-in-6 chance.

Lesson 7 Dependent and Independent Events

Probability consists of events, trials, and outcomes. A coin toss, for example, is an event, tossing the coin is a trial, and (heads) and (tails) are the outcomes that could occur. Events in a probability experiment can be dependent or independent

EXAMPLE 1 Suppose a bag contains four marbles, all the same size. Two marbles are red and two marbles are yellow. You reach into the bag, choose a marble, record its color, and put the marble in your pocket. Then you take another marble from the bag. What is the probability that you will take out two yellow marbles? The experiment contains two events. Find the probability of each event.

Step 1 Find the probability of the first event—taking a yellow marble from the bag.
Use the probability fraction.

$$P = \frac{\text{number of favorable outcomes}}{\text{number of possible outcomes}}$$

In this event, there are four possible outcomes because there are four marbles in the bag. The denominator of the fraction is four. Since choosing either yellow marble that is in the bag is a favorable outcome, the numerator of the fraction is 2. The probability of this event is $\frac{2}{4}$.

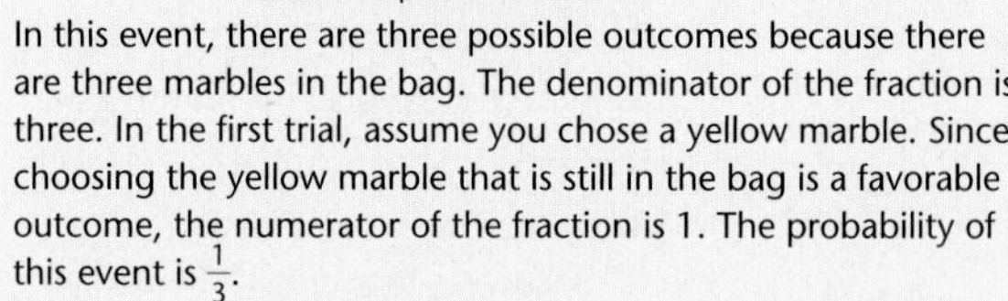

Step 2 Find the probability of the second event—taking a yellow marble from the bag. Remember, you put the first marble that was taken from the bag in your pocket.

$$P = \frac{\text{number of favorable outcomes}}{\text{number of possible outcomes}}$$

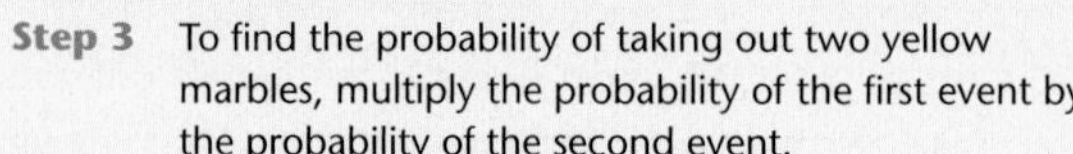

In this event, there are three possible outcomes because there are three marbles in the bag. The denominator of the fraction is three. In the first trial, assume you chose a yellow marble. Since choosing the yellow marble that is still in the bag is a favorable outcome, the numerator of the fraction is 1. The probability of this event is $\frac{1}{3}$.

Step 3 To find the probability of taking out two yellow marbles, multiply the probability of the first event by the probability of the second event.

$$P = \frac{2}{4} \bullet \frac{1}{3} = \frac{2}{12} = \frac{1}{6}$$

Name Date Period | Workbook Activity 72 | Chapter 7, Lesson 7

Dependent and Independent Events

EXAMPLE Suppose 2 children take one pencil each from the same box of 10 pencils. Half of the pencils have erasers, half do not. The first child chooses a pencil, then the second child chooses. What is the probability that both will choose a pencil with an eraser?

These events are dependent.

- The probability of an eraser for child A's choice is $\frac{5}{10}$, or $\frac{1}{2}$.
- The probability of an eraser for child B's choice is $\frac{5-1}{10-1}$, or $\frac{4}{9}$.

Suppose instead that each child chooses from an identical separate box of pencils. These events are independent, so each probability is identical.

Directions Write whether the events are *dependent* or *independent*.

1. Each of 5 children chooses and keeps a marble from a bag of 5 marbles. ____________
2. A player in a board game rolls a number cube. Then a different player rolls the cube. ____________
3. A clothing store has one of a particular shirt left. One man buys the shirt. Then another man comes in, asking to buy the same shirt. ____________
4. Three children always sit on the backseat of their family car. Today, the first child sits in the middle. Then the second child sits down. ____________
5. One person draws a card from the deck, looks at it, and puts it back into the deck. The next person then draws from the deck. ____________
6. At the start of a board game, one person selects her playing piece from a bag of 7 pieces. Then you select your piece. ____________
7. A grab bag holds 3 wrapped gifts: one red, one blue, and one green. You take the gift wrapped in red. Then the person on your right takes one. ____________
8. A friend shows you a card trick, having you select 1 card out of 5. Then your friend repeats the same trick with someone else. ____________
9. Two trains are on the same track line. Train number one slows down. Train number two then slows down. ____________
10. A vase in a flower shop holds 3 flowers. After you take one, the florist replaces it. Then another person takes one. ____________

 Algebra

TRL

Workbook Activity 72

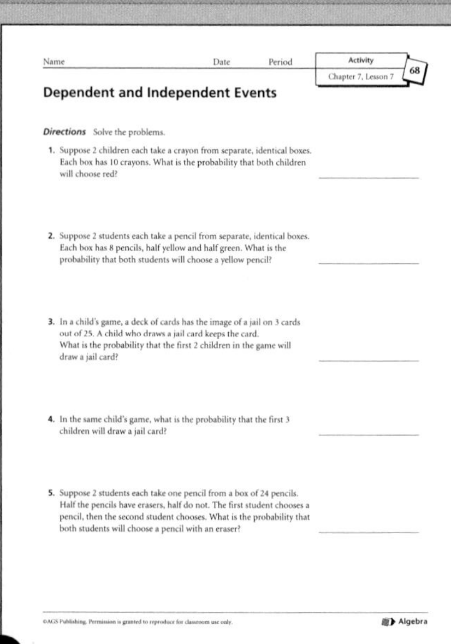

Name Date Period | Activity 68 | Chapter 7, Lesson 7

Dependent and Independent Events

Directions Solve the problems.

1. Suppose 2 children each take a crayon from separate, identical boxes. Each box has 10 crayons. What is the probability that both children will choose red? ____________
2. Suppose 2 students each take a pencil from separate, identical boxes. Each box has 8 pencils, half yellow and half green. What is the probability that both students will choose a yellow pencil? ____________
3. In a child's game, a deck of cards has the image of a jail on 3 cards out of 25. A child who draws a jail card keeps the card. What is the probability that the first 2 children in the game will draw a jail card? ____________
4. In the same child's game, what is the probability that the first 3 children will draw a jail card? ____________
5. Suppose 2 students each take one pencil from a box of 24 pencils. Half the pencils have erasers, half do not. The first student chooses a pencil, then the second student chooses. What is the probability that both students will choose a pencil with an eraser? ____________

 Algebra

TRL

Activity 68

Dependent event

In a probability experiment, the outcome of one event is affected by the outcome of any other event

The probability of the outcome is $\frac{1}{6}$. The events in this experiment were dependent. In **dependent events,** the outcome of the first event affects the outcome of all other events in the experiment.

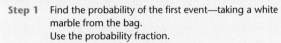

EXAMPLE 2 Suppose a bag contains four marbles, all the same size. Two marbles are black and two marbles are white. You reach into the bag, choose a marble, and record its color. Then you replace the marble in the bag and take out a marble again. What is the probability that you will take out two white marbles? The experiment contains two events. Find the probability of each event.

Step 1 Find the probability of the first event—taking a white marble from the bag.
Use the probability fraction.

$$P = \frac{\text{number of favorable outcomes}}{\text{number of possible outcomes}}$$

In this event, there are four possible outcomes because there are four marbles in the bag. The denominator of the fraction is four. Since choosing either white marble that is in the bag is a favorable outcome, the numerator of the fraction is 2. The probability of this event is $\frac{2}{4}$.

Step 2 Find the probability of the second event—taking a white marble from the bag. Remember, you put the first marble that was taken from the bag back into the bag.

$$P = \frac{\text{number of favorable outcomes}}{\text{number of possible outcomes}}$$

In this event, there again are four possible outcomes because there are four marbles in the bag. The denominator of the fraction is four. Since choosing either white marble that is in the bag is a favorable outcome, the numerator of the fraction is 2. The probability of this event is $\frac{2}{4}$.

Step 3 To find the probability of taking out two white marbles, multiply the probability of the first event by the probability of the second event.

$$P = \frac{2}{4} \bullet \frac{2}{4} = \frac{4}{16} = \frac{1}{4}$$

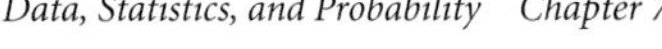

$P = \frac{2}{4} \bullet \frac{1}{3}$ each mean. Point out the simplification of $\frac{2}{12}$ to $\frac{1}{6}$ in Step 3 of the first example. Explain that a 2-in-12 chance of occurrence is the same as a 1-in-6 chance.

Common Error

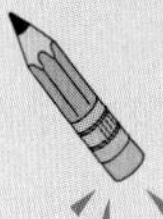

Careless thinking may cause some students to forget to adjust the number of possible outcomes when an item is removed. Have them diagram on scratch paper the number of items in the bag before and after each trial.

Manipulatives

Simulating Probability with Unit Cubes

Materials: Unit Cubes

Group Practice: Use the Unit Cubes to represent the group of marbles used in each example. Have students carry out the actions in the example. Go through the example together so students can see the outcomes of each trial and make the connection that the fractions represent the outcomes.

Student Practice: Have students use Unit Cubes to find the probabilities in Exercises B and C.

Reinforce and Extend

Learning Styles

Body/Kinesthetic

Exercise A assesses students' ability to identify events as independent or dependent. To apply what they have learned, students create and act out their own problems like those in Exercise A. (Example events include eating M&Ms and picking a number from 1 to 10.) Have students write their problems, exchange them with a partner, and teach their partner using their "props."

At Home

When students complete the Writing About Mathematics activity, discuss the difference between theoretical probability (a ratio of favorable outcomes to possible outcomes) and experimental probability (a ratio of successes to number of tries). As a family project, students might conduct an experiment in which all family members flip a coin 10 times, each recording the number of heads. Have students report to the class how the family's average compared to the theoretical probability of 50% and explain any difference.

Mental Math

Students will need to reduce fractions to simplest terms in Exercises B and C. Have them practice this skill mentally by giving the following orally:

$\frac{4}{12}$	$(\frac{1}{3})$	$\frac{6}{24}$	$(\frac{1}{4})$
$\frac{7}{14}$	$(\frac{1}{2})$	$\frac{7}{21}$	$(\frac{1}{3})$
$\frac{8}{48}$	$(\frac{1}{6})$	$\frac{8}{60}$	$(\frac{2}{15})$
$\frac{9}{12}$	$(\frac{3}{4})$	$\frac{10}{25}$	$(\frac{2}{5})$
$\frac{13}{39}$	$(\frac{1}{3})$	$\frac{40}{100}$	$(\frac{2}{5})$

The probability of the outcome is $\frac{1}{4}$. The events in this experiment were independent. In **independent events,** the outcome of an event does not affect the outcome of any other event in the experiment.

Independent event

In a probability experiment, the outcome of any event does not affect the outcome of any other event

Exercise A

1. To find the probability of tossing five tails in a row, you toss the same coin five times. Are the events in the experiment dependent or independent? Explain.
2. Suppose a consonant of the alphabet is chosen at random and removed. Then a different consonant is chosen. Are the events in the experiment dependent or independent? Explain.
3. Suppose a number cube is rolled and the outcome is 6. The cube is rolled a second time and again the outcome is 6. If the cube is rolled again, what will the outcome be? Explain.

1. Independent events; any toss does not affect the previous toss or the next toss of the coin.
2. Dependent events; once the consonant is chosen, it cannot be chosen again.
3. These are independent events. The next outcome will be 1, 2, 3, 4, 5, or 6.

Exercise B

Suppose a bag contains 6 marbles. All the marbles are the same size. One marble is green, two marbles are orange, and three marbles are purple. A marble will be taken from the bag two times. Each time a marble is taken out, it is replaced.

4. Find *P* (orange and green). $\frac{1}{18}$
5. Find *P* (green and purple). $\frac{1}{12}$
6. Find *P* (not purple and not orange). $\frac{1}{3}$

Exercise C

Suppose a bag contains 8 marbles. All the marbles are the same size. One marble is red, two marbles are white, and five marbles are blue. A marble will be taken from the bag two times. Each time a marble is taken, it is *not* replaced.

7. Find P (white and red). $\frac{1}{28}$

8. Find P (blue and white). $\frac{5}{28}$

9. Find P (red and not white). $\frac{5}{56}$

10. Find P (blue). $\frac{5}{14}$

TRY THIS Look again at Exercise C. Suppose you take out a marble three times. What is the probability of (red and white and blue)? Express your answer as a percent rounded to the nearest whole number. 3%

Writing About Mathematics

You might expect to get 5 heads and 5 tails in 10 coin tosses. Toss a coin 10 times. Tally the results. Compare your results to your prediction.

Try This

Remind students that the marbles are not replaced in this exercise. Students may wish to simulate the activity and then create other problems for classmates to try.

Group Problem Solving

Have students work in small groups to solve the following problem:

Eleven basketball teammates all want to start in the first game of the season. Only five will be selected. Set up a drawing that will decide the starting five at random. Decide whether the drawings are independent or dependent. Calculate the probability of being chosen on the first, second, third, fourth, and fifth drawings.

Ask groups to write a description of the probability problem and record the steps in their experiment, using the examples in the text as a model. Have groups present their findings and explain their methods to the class.

Learning Styles

Auditory/Verbal

Assess student understanding of independent and dependent events. Number 3 x 5 cards 1 through 10 and place them in a container. Have students explain the probability of drawing an even-numbered card. *(5 in 10, or 1 in 2)* Draw a card at random and record its number before returning it to the container. Ask, "Now what is the probability that the next card drawn will be an even number?" *(the same, 5 in 10, or 1 in 2)* Repeat the process, but do not return the card for the second trial. Have students explain in their own words why the events are *dependent* when the card is not replaced in the container.

Lesson at a Glance

Chapter 7 Lesson 8

Overview This lesson explains how to use the fundamental principle of counting to find the number of possible outcomes.

Objective

- To explain how the fundamental principle of counting can be used to find the number of possible outcomes or the permutations in a set

Student Pages 210–213

Teacher's Resource Library 

Workbook Activity 73–74

Activity 69

Alternative Activity 69

Mathematics Vocabulary

factorial notation
fundamental principle of counting
permutation

1 Warm-Up Activity

Ask students how they would find the number of possible combinations for an odd number of four digits (made up of integers between 1 and 5). Discuss why a tree diagram (or any pictorial method) would not work well for such large numbers of combinations. Introduce the lesson by asking students to read it to find a simpler method of finding all possible outcomes.

2 Teaching the Lesson

After students have read page 210, ask them to explain in their own words why the calculation 3 • 2 gives the number of possible routes from Detroit to Cheyenne, passing through Lincoln. *(The first leg of the journey has three possibilities and the second has two. Multiplying gives the total number of choices.)* Have them determine the possible choices if there are 4 different ways to drive from Lincoln to Cheyenne. *(12)*

Lesson 8 The Fundamental Principle of Counting

Fundamental principle of counting

A general rule that states that if one task can be completed p different ways, and a second task can be completed q different ways, the first task followed by the second task can be completed p • q, or pq, different ways

Recall that a tree diagram can be used to generate a sample space.

EXAMPLE 1 Suppose you plan to travel from Detroit, Michigan, to Cheyenne, Wyoming, and pass through Lincoln, Nebraska, on the way. If there are three different roads you can travel from Detroit to Lincoln and two different roads you can travel from Lincoln to Cheyenne, how many different ways can you travel from Detroit to Cheyenne? Make a tree diagram.

Step 1 Show the different roads you can travel from Detroit to Lincoln. There are three different roads you can travel from Detroit to Lincoln.

Detroit
Lincoln

Step 2 Show the different roads you can travel from Lincoln to Cheyenne. There are two different roads you can travel from Lincoln to Cheyenne.

Step 3 Since there are 3 different roads you can travel from Detroit to Lincoln, and 2 different roads you can travel from Lincoln to Cheyenne, there are 3 • 2 or 6 different ways you can travel from Detroit to Cheyenne and pass through Lincoln.

A tree diagram helps you find all of the different ways without forgetting any.

Another method you could use to find the answer is the fundamental principle of counting. The **fundamental principle of counting** is a general rule that states that you can multiply the number of choices for each task to find the total number of choices.

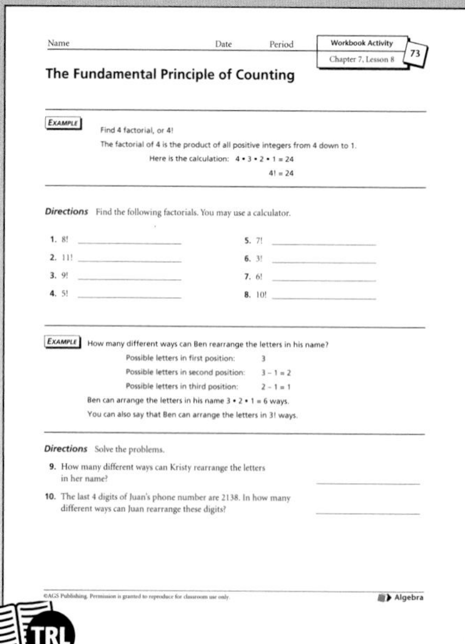

Name Date Period

Workbook Activity 73
Chapter 7, Lesson 8

The Fundamental Principle of Counting

EXAMPLE Find 4 factorial, or 4!
The factorial of 4 is the product of all positive integers from 4 down to 1.
Here is the calculation: 4 • 3 • 2 • 1 = 24
4! = 24

Directions Find the following factorials. You may use a calculator.

1. 8! ______
2. 11! ______
3. 9! ______
4. 5! ______
5. 7! ______
6. 3! ______
7. 6! ______
8. 10! ______

EXAMPLE How many different ways can Ben rearrange the letters in his name?
Possible letters in first position: 3
Possible letters in second position: 3 – 1 = 2
Possible letters in third position: 2 – 1 = 1
Ben can arrange the letters in his name 3 • 2 • 1 = 6 ways.
You can also say that Ben can arrange the letters in 3! ways.

Directions Solve the problems.

9. How many different ways can Kristy rearrange the letters in her name? ______
10. The last 4 digits of Juan's phone number are 2138. In how many different ways can Juan rearrange these digits? ______

 Algebra

Workbook Activity 73

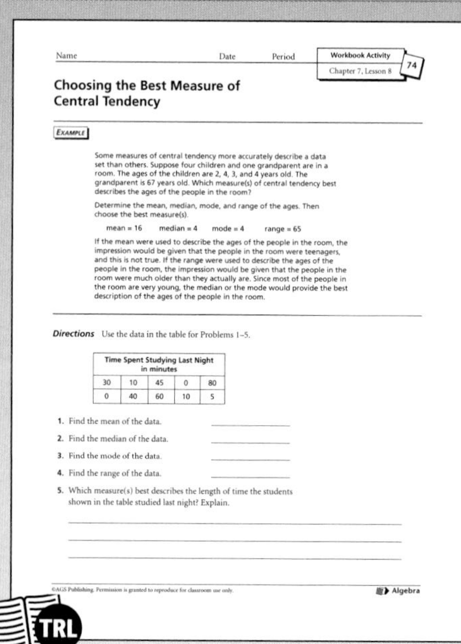

Name Date Period

Workbook Activity 74
Chapter 7, Lesson 8

Choosing the Best Measure of Central Tendency

EXAMPLE

Some measures of central tendency more accurately describe a data set than others. Suppose four children and one grandparent are in a room. The ages of the children are 2, 4, 3, and 4 years old. The grandparent is 67 years old. Which measure(s) of central tendency best describes the ages of the people in the room?

Determine the mean, median, mode, and range of the ages. Then choose the best measure(s).

mean = 16 median = 4 mode = 4 range = 65

If the mean were used to describe the ages of the people in the room, the impression would be given that the people in the room were teenagers, and this is not true. If the range were used to describe the ages of the people in the room, the impression would be given that the people in the room were much older than they actually are. Since most of the people in the room are very young, the median or the mode would provide the best description of the ages of the people in the room.

Directions Use the data in the table for Problems 1–5.

Time Spent Studying Last Night in minutes				
30	10	45	0	80
0	40	60	10	5

1. Find the mean of the data. ______
2. Find the median of the data. ______
3. Find the mode of the data. ______
4. Find the range of the data. ______
5. Which measure(s) best describes the length of time the students shown in the table studied last night? Explain.

 Algebra

Workbook Activity 74

Permutation

An arrangement of some or all of a set of numbers in a specific order

Factorial notation

The product of all positive integers from a given integer to 1 represented by the symbol (!)

EXAMPLE 2 How many different ways can Geri rearrange the letters of her name? Use the fundamental principle of counting to find out.

Step 1 Find the number of letters Geri could use for the first letter of her name.

4			

Any of four letters—G, E, R, or I—could be used for the first letter of her name.

Step 2 Find the number of letters Geri could use for the second letter of her name.

4 •	3 •		

A letter must have been used for the first letter of her name. So there are three letters remaining to choose from.

Step 3 Find the number of letters Geri could use for the third letter of her name.

4 •	3 •	2 •	

Two letters—one for the first letter in her name and one for the second—have been used. So there are two letters remaining to choose from.

Step 4 Find the number of letters Geri could use for the last letter of her name.

4 •	3 •	2 •	1

Three letters have been used, and only one letter remains.

Geri can arrange the letters of her name $4 \cdot 3 \cdot 2 \cdot 1$ or 24 different ways.

The ways in which the members of a set can be arranged in an ordered fashion are called **permutations.** You can use the fundamental principle of counting to determine the number of permutations in a set.

The computation $4 \cdot 3 \cdot 2 \cdot 1 = 24$ is an example of a factorial. The factorial is the product of all positive integers from a given integer to 1 and is represented by the symbol (!). In **factorial notation,** $4! = 4 \cdot 3 \cdot 2 \cdot 1 = 24$.

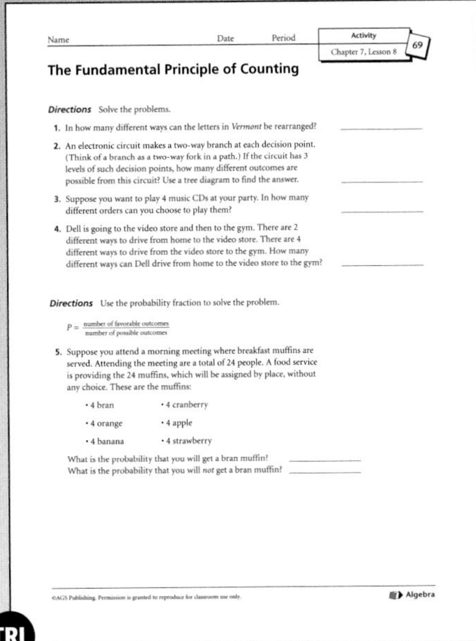

Name Date Period Activity 69 Chapter 7, Lesson 8

The Fundamental Principle of Counting

Directions Solve the problems.

1. In how many different ways can the letters in *Vermont* be rearranged? ________
2. An electronic circuit makes a two-way branch at each decision point. (Think of a branch as a two-way fork in a path.) If the circuit has 3 levels of such decision points, how many different outcomes are possible from this circuit? Use a tree diagram to find the answer. ________
3. Suppose you want to play 4 music CDs at your party. In how many different orders can you choose to play them? ________
4. Dell is going to the video store and then to the gym. There are 2 different ways to drive from home to the video store. There are 4 different ways to drive from the video store to the gym. How many different ways can Dell drive from home to the video store to the gym? ________

Directions Use the probability fraction to solve the problem.

$P = \frac{\text{number of favorable outcomes}}{\text{number of possible outcomes}}$

5. Suppose you attend a morning meeting where breakfast muffins are served. Attending the meeting are a total of 24 people. A food service is providing the 24 muffins, which will be assigned by place, without any choice. These are the muffins:

   - 4 bran
   - 4 cranberry
   - 4 orange
   - 4 apple
   - 4 banana
   - 4 strawberry

   What is the probability that you will get a bran muffin? ________
   What is the probability that you will *not* get a bran muffin? ________

Algebra

TRL

Activity 69

When students have completed page 211, check their understanding by having them complete the four steps using their first or last name (whichever has 5 letters or more).

COMMON ERROR

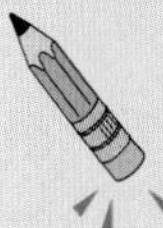

Some students may add rather than multiply the choices in a factorial notation. This confusion may arise from the fact that tree diagrams represent all choices pictorially and can be added. Explain that, unlike the tree diagram, the fundamental counting principle requires multiplying the number of choices for each stage.

3 Reinforce and Extend

IN THE COMMUNITY

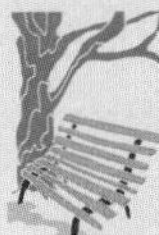

Direct students to find or make a map of their community. On it, have them locate their residence, school, and one other place they go regularly, such as a store, park, church, or friend's home. Give these directions:

1. Highlight the routes you could take to travel from home to school and then to your third familiar place.
2. Beneath your map, show how many routes are possible to travel to all three by
   a. drawing a tree diagram.
   b. using the fundamental principle of counting.

Calculator

Before students complete Exercise B, have them check their calculators for a factorial key and calculate several factorials:

$5! = 5 \cdot 4 \cdot 3 \cdot 2 \cdot 1 = 120$

$8! = 8 \cdot 7 \cdot 6 \cdot 5 \cdot 4 \cdot 3 \cdot 2 \cdot 1 = 40{,}320$

$10! = 10 \cdot 9 \cdot 8 \cdot 7 \cdot 6 \cdot 5 \cdot 4 \cdot 3 \cdot 2 \cdot 1 = 3{,}628{,}800$

Group Problem Solving

Have students form groups of five. Distribute to each group a catalog or sales brochure featuring products with choices of several features (for example, sweaters in assorted sizes and colors; bikes with alternative tires, sizes, and brakes). Direct groups to choose an article to order and list all the choices that must be made in the order. Then have students use the fundamental principle of counting to calculate the number of different possibilities for their order.

Example 3 Find 4!.

Find the product $4 \bullet 3 \bullet 2 \bullet 1$.

$4! = 24$

Find 6!.

Find the product $6 \bullet 5 \bullet 4 \bullet 3 \bullet 2 \bullet 1$.

$6! = 720$

When finding factorials, you may find it helpful to use a calculator. If you use a scientific calculator, look for the [!] key.

PROBLEM SOLVING

Exercise A Identify the number of arrangements possible for each of the following situations.

1. Choose any two letters of the alphabet. How many different ways can those letters be arranged? 2
2. Suppose that you want to read three books, and you can read them in any order. In how many different ways can you read the books? 6
3. Five students are waiting in a line. As they wait, how many different ways can they arrange themselves in that line? 120
4. How many different ways can Tamika, Miguel, Blevian, Trina, and Mark be seated in five chairs if Miguel must always sit in the first chair? 24
5. Jason has four winter hats, three scarves, and three pairs of mittens. How many different combinations of one hat, one scarf, and one pair of mittens can Jason wear? 36

PROBLEM SOLVING

Exercise B Use a calculator for these exercises.

6. A computer password is made up of four characters. Two characters must be letters of the alphabet and two characters must be digits (numbers). If no characters can be repeated, how many different passwords are possible? 58,500

7. A student is taking a true/false quiz. The quiz has ten questions. If the student guesses every answer, how many different arrangements of answers are possible? 1,024

8. Some of the license plates on automobiles display six characters—the first three characters are letters of the alphabet and the last three characters are digits (numbers). Characters may be repeated any number of times. How many different license plates of this style can be made? 17,576,000

9. Consider the phone number 924-xxxx. How many different phone numbers are possible with a 924 prefix? 10,000

10. How many different orders of finish can there be if there are eight people in a race and each person finishes the race? 40,320

LEARNING STYLES

Body/Kinesthetic

Have students model problem 5 in Exercise A to verify the answer provided by factorial notation. This not only reinforces the accuracy of the method but also illustrates how ill-suited the tree diagram is for handling large numbers of stages and outcomes.

Lesson at a Glance

Chapter 7 Application

Overview This lesson illustrates an application of calculating probability for experiments with multiple stages.

Objective

- To apply the fundamental principle of counting to probability problems with multiple stages

Student Page 214

Teacher's Resource Library 

Application Activity 7

Everyday Algebra 7

1 Warm-Up Activity

Here students will apply what they have learned about probability. Review earlier concepts by asking questions such as the following:

- What is probability? *(the likelihood that something will happen)*
- How can you calculate probability? *(Determine the number of possible outcomes and favorable outcomes. Make a fraction, putting favorable outcomes in the numerator and possible outcomes in the denominator.)*
- How can you calculate the probability of two events? *(Find each probability and multiply the two fractions.)*

2 Teaching the Lesson

Work through the example with students. Then have them work in pairs to complete this problem:

A bag contains 4 cookies that are the same size, shape, and weight. One is peanut butter, one is oatmeal, and two are sugar cookies.

- What is the probability that the cookies will be picked in this order: oatmeal, sugar, peanut butter, sugar? $(\frac{1}{4} \cdot \frac{2}{3} \cdot \frac{1}{2} \cdot \frac{1}{1}) = \frac{2}{24} = \frac{1}{12})$

Application $\pi^2 \Sigma + \Omega \sqrt{x^2} \% \neq y \geq n = \nabla 3_0 \circ \pi$

Multistage Experiments

To find the probability that any outcome in an experiment will occur, use the fraction

$$P = \frac{\text{number of favorable outcomes}}{\text{number of possible outcomes}}$$

Some probability experiments are multistage experiments. To find the probability of a multistage experiment, first determine the probability of each stage. Then find the product of the probabilities.

Example 1 The following box contains the letters that spell the word mathematics. | m a t h e m a t i c s |

Suppose you were to draw a letter from the box without looking and not replace it. Then you repeat the procedure three more times. What is the probability that you will first draw *c*, then *a*, then *t*, and then *s* to spell the word *cats*?

Step 1 Find the probability of each stage. Remember that you do not replace the letter after each draw.

Stage 1: Drawing the letter *c*. $P = \frac{1}{11}$

Stage 2: Drawing the letter *a*. $P = \frac{2}{10}$

Stage 3: Drawing the letter *t*. $P = \frac{2}{9}$

Stage 4: Drawing the letter *s*. $P = \frac{1}{8}$

Step 2 Find the product of the probability for each stage.

$\frac{1}{11} \bullet \frac{2}{10} \bullet \frac{2}{9} \bullet \frac{1}{8} = \frac{4}{7{,}920}$ or $\frac{1}{1{,}980}$

Exercise Suppose a launched rocket must burn three separate stages of fuel to reach orbit. The probability of failure for the first stage is $\frac{1}{10}$, for the second stage is $\frac{1}{10}$, and for the third stage is $\frac{1}{100}$.

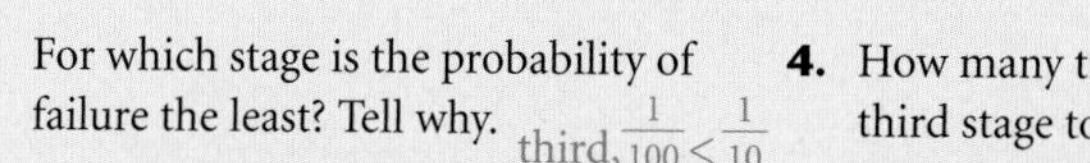

1. For which stage is the probability of failure the least? Tell why. *third, $\frac{1}{100} < \frac{1}{10}$*
2. For which stage is the probability of success the greatest? Tell why. *third, $\frac{99}{100} > \frac{9}{10}$*
3. Determine the probability of an overall failure. (Stages 1, 2, and 3 all fail.) *$\frac{1}{10{,}000}$*
4. How many times less likely is the third stage to fail than the first or second stage? Explain. *10 times, $\frac{1}{10} \div \frac{1}{100} = 1$*
5. In one million launches of this rocket, how many launches would you expect to fail? *100, sample explanation: $\frac{1 \text{ failure}}{10{,}000 \text{ launches}} = \frac{100 \text{ failures}}{1{,}000{,}000 \text{ launches}}$*

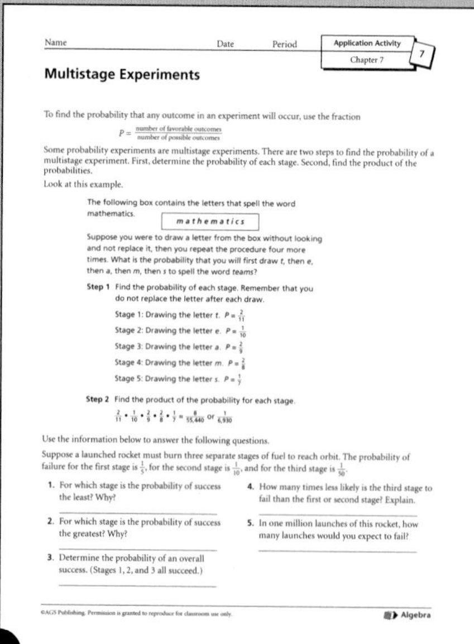

Name Date Period | Application Activity 7 | Chapter 7

Multistage Experiments

To find the probability that any outcome in an experiment will occur, use the fraction

$$P = \frac{\text{number of favorable outcomes}}{\text{number of possible outcomes}}$$

Some probability experiments are multistage experiments. There are two steps to find the probability of a multistage experiment. First, determine the probability of each stage. Second, find the product of the probabilities.

Look at this example.

The following box contains the letters that spell the word mathematics. | m a t h e m a t i c s |

Suppose you were to draw a letter from the box without looking and not replace it, then you repeat the procedure four more times. What is the probability that you will first draw *t*, then *e*, then *a*, then *m*, then *s* to spell the word *teams*?

Step 1 Find the probability of each stage. Remember that you do not replace the letter after each draw.

Stage 1: Drawing the letter *t*. $P = \frac{2}{11}$

Stage 2: Drawing the letter *e*. $P = \frac{1}{10}$

Stage 3: Drawing the letter *a*. $P = \frac{2}{9}$

Stage 4: Drawing the letter *m*. $P = \frac{2}{8}$

Stage 5: Drawing the letter *s*. $P = \frac{1}{7}$

Step 2 Find the product of the probability for each stage.

$\frac{2}{11} \bullet \frac{1}{10} \bullet \frac{2}{9} \bullet \frac{2}{8} \bullet \frac{1}{7} = \frac{8}{55{,}440}$ or $\frac{1}{6{,}930}$

Use the information below to answer the following questions.

Suppose a launched rocket must burn three separate stages of fuel to reach orbit. The probability of failure for the first stage is $\frac{1}{5}$, for the second stage is $\frac{1}{10}$, and for the third stage is $\frac{1}{50}$.

1. For which stage is the probability of success the least? Why?
2. For which stage is the probability of success the greatest? Why?
3. Determine the probability of an overall success. (Stages 1, 2, and 3 all succeed.)
4. How many times less likely is the third stage to fail than the first or second stage? Explain.
5. In one million launches of this rocket, how many launches would you expect to fail?

 Algebra

TRL

Application Activity 7

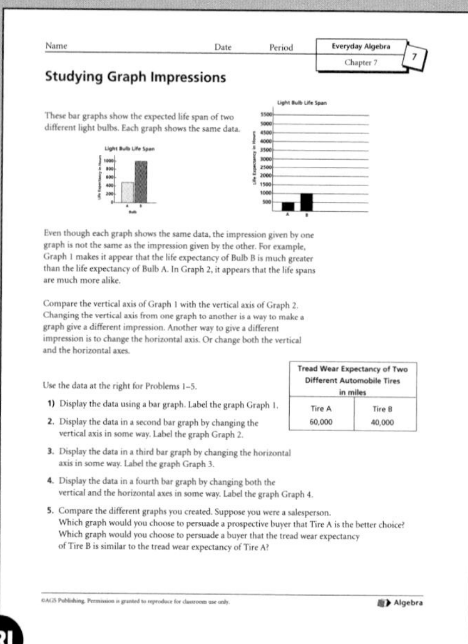

Name Date Period | Everyday Algebra 7 | Chapter 7

Studying Graph Impressions

These bar graphs show the expected life span of two different light bulbs. Each graph shows the same data.

Even though each graph shows the same data, the impression given by one graph is not the same as the impression given by the other. For example, Graph 1 makes it appear that the life expectancy of Bulb B is much greater than the life expectancy of Bulb A. In Graph 2, it appears that the life spans are much more alike.

Compare the vertical axis of Graph 1 with the vertical axis of Graph 2. Changing the vertical axis from one graph to another is a way to make a graph give a different impression. Another way to give a different impression is to change the horizontal axis. Or change both the vertical and the horizontal axes.

Tread Wear Expectancy of Two Different Automobile Tires in miles	
Tire A	Tire B
60,000	40,000

Use the data at the right for Problems 1–5.

1) Display the data using a bar graph. Label the graph Graph 1.
2. Display the data in a second bar graph by changing the vertical axis in some way. Label the graph Graph 2.
3. Display the data in a third bar graph by changing the horizontal axis in some way. Label the graph Graph 3.
4. Display the data in a fourth bar graph by changing both the vertical and the horizontal axes in some way. Label the graph Graph 4.
5. Compare the different graphs you created. Suppose you were a salesperson. Which graph would you choose to persuade a prospective buyer that Tire A is the better choice? Which graph would you choose to persuade a buyer that the tread wear expectancy of Tire B is similar to the tread wear expectancy of Tire A?

 Algebra

TRL

Everyday Algebra 7

Chapter 7 REVIEW

Use the data in the table to answer questions 1 through 4. Write the letter of the correct answer.

Age in Years		
37	30	84
42	4	49
14	11	13
21	28	51
54	61	26

1. What is the mean of the data in the table? C

A 30 C 35

B 51 D 37

2. What is the median of the data in the table? B

A 35 C 11

B 30 D 80

3. What is the range of the data in the table? A

A 80 C 35

B 30 D 88

4. What is the mode of the data in the table? B

A 11 C 30

B no mode D 35

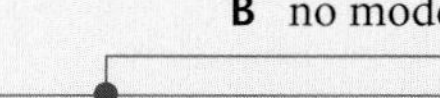

250 255 260 265 270 275 280

Use the box-and-whiskers plot above to answer questions 5 through 7. Write the letter of the correct answer.

5. Which values represent the quartiles? B

A 251 and 272 C 251 and 279

B 255 and 272 D 264 and 279

6. Which value represents the median? D

A 250 C 255

B 132 D 264

7. Which values represent the extremes? C

A 255 and 272 C 251 and 279

B 251 and 255 D 272 and 279

Name Date Period | Mastery Test A, Page 1 Chapter 7

Chapter 7 Mastery Test A

Directions Circle the letter of the correct answer.

1. Find the mean of the data in the table.
   A 95
   B 83.5
   C 90
   D 87.5

Quiz Scores			
88	92	93	81
73	98	97	99
90	81	72	89
84	86	90	87

2. Find the mode(s) of the data in the table.
   A 87.5
   B 81, 90
   C 83.5
   D 72, 99
3. Find the range of the data in the table.
   A 72 to 99
   B 87.5
   C 81 to 90
   D 72 to 87

Directions Use the box-and-whiskers plot for questions 4–5.

30 31 32 33 34 35 36 37 38 39 40 41 42 43 44 45 46 47 48 49 50

4. Which value represents the median?
   A 35
   B 40
   C 45
   D 47
5. Which values represent the quartiles?
   A 35 and 45
   B 35 and 47
   C 36 and 47
   D 36 and 45

 Algebra

TRL

Name Date Period | Mastery Test A, Page 2 Chapter 7

Chapter 7 Mastery Test A, continued

Directions In a probability experiment, a painted cube is rolled once. One side of the cube is painted blue, four sides are painted white, and one side is painted green. Express the theoretical probability (P) of each event as a fraction in simplest form.

6. P (green) ________ 8. P (black) ________

7. P (white) ________ 9. P (green or blue) ________

Directions Refer to the spinner at the right. Express the theoretical probability of each event below as a fraction in simplest form.

1 4 6 10

10. P (even number) ________

11. P (an odd number and an even number) ________

Directions Suppose a bag contains 10 marbles. All of the marbles are the same size. Six marbles are black, three marbles are gray, and one marble is white. A marble will be taken from the bag two times. Each time a marble is taken, it is not replaced.

12. Find P (gray and white). ________

13. Find P (black and not gray). ________

Directions Solve.

14. Suppose four coins are tossed at the same time. What fraction in simplest form describes the theoretical probability that all of the coins will land tails-up?

____

15. Eight desks have been placed in a classroom for eight students. How many different ways can the eight students arrange themselves in the eight chairs?

____

 Algebra

TRL

Chapter 7 Mastery Test A

3 Reinforce and Extend

Career Connection

Invite interested students to research the track record of launches by NASA and report on actual percentages of failures and successes. Encourage students to locate on-line information about career possibilities in space science and recommended math preparation for those careers.

Chapter 7 Review

Each set of problems in the Chapter Review includes an example and solution to illustrate the concept. Use the given examples for reteaching the materials in Chapter 7. For additional practice, refer to the Supplementary Problems for Chapter 7 (pages 418–419).

Chapter 7 Mastery Test 

The Teacher's Resource Library includes parallel forms of the Chapter 7 Mastery Test. The difficulty level of the two forms is equivalent. You may wish to use one form as a pretest and the other form as a posttest.

Chapters 1–7 Midterm Mastery Test

The Teacher's Resource Library includes the Midterm Mastery Test. This test is pictured on page 527 of this Teacher's Edition. The Midterm Mastery Test assesses the major learning objectives for Chapters 1–7.

Answers to Chapter Review Problem 5

5.

Stem	Leaf
0	4
1	1 3 4
2	1 6 8
3	0 7
4	2 9
5	1 4
6	1
7	
8	4

Answers to Chapter Review, continued

Problems 6–7

6.

Frequency Table		
Interval	Tally	Frequency
0–9	|	1
10–19	|||	3
20–29	|||	3
30–39	||	2
40–49	||	2
50–59	||	2
60–69	|	1
70–79		0
80–89	|	1

7.

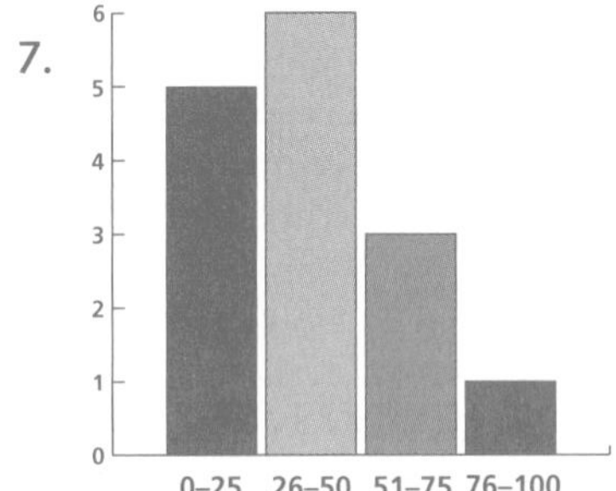

Alternative Assessment

Alternative Assessment items correlate with student Goals for Learning at the beginning of this chapter.

■ **To organize data into graphs**
Have students find representations of different kinds of graphs on the Internet, in newspapers, or in magazines and bring them to class. Discuss the data each kind of graph represents. Determine whether certain graphs represent certain kinds of data better than other kinds of graphs. *(Bar graphs show comparison, histograms show ranges and frequency and are similar to stem and leaf plots in that respect. Stem and leaf plots show mean, median, and mode.)*

■ **To read and interpret graphic representations**
Have students discuss the data represented in the graphs they bring to class (see above). Ask students to think about what information might not be included in the graphs. *(Students should see that graphs usually are accompanied by text that explains the data more fully.)*

Decide if the probability of each of the following events is 0, 1, close to 0, or close to 1.

Example: A day of the week is chosen at random. The name of the weekday begins with a B.
Solution: Since no day of the week has a name that begins with B, the outcome is impossible, and the event has a probability of zero.

8. A person is chosen at random. The second digit of the person's age is 7. close to 0

9. A month of the year has only 27 days. 0

10. A person is born in winter, spring, or summer. close to 1

11. A day of the week chosen at random ends with the letter *y*. 1

In a probability experiment, two 1–6 number cubes are rolled once. Find the theoretical probability (*P*) of each event. Express your answer as a fraction in simplest form.

Example: *P* (1, 2)
Solution: Find the probability of each outcome and then find the product of the probabilities. $\frac{1}{6} \bullet \frac{1}{6} = \frac{1}{36}$

12. *P* (1, 1) $\frac{1}{36}$

13. *P* (0, 4) 0

14. *P* (3, 3 or 6, 6) $\frac{1}{18}$

15. *P* (a multiple of 2 and a multiple of 3) $\frac{1}{6}$

16. *P* (1 and 1 or 2 and 2 or 5 and 5 or 6 and 6) $\frac{1}{9}$

17. *P* (a prime number and not a prime number) $\frac{1}{4}$

Solve the following probabilities involving marbles.

Example: A bag contains 3 marbles—one red, one blue, and one white. Each time a marble is taken out, it is not replaced. Find the probability (*P*) of choosing a blue marble and then a red one.
Solution: $P\text{ (blue)} = \frac{1}{3}$ $P\text{ (red)} = \frac{1}{2}$ $P\text{ (blue and red)}\ \frac{1}{3} \bullet \frac{1}{2} = \frac{1}{6}$

Suppose a bag contains 5 marbles. One is white, two are red, and two are yellow. Each time a marble is taken out, it is replaced.

18. $\frac{4}{25}$ 19. $\frac{2}{25}$

18. Find *P* (red and yellow). **19.** Find *P* (yellow and white).

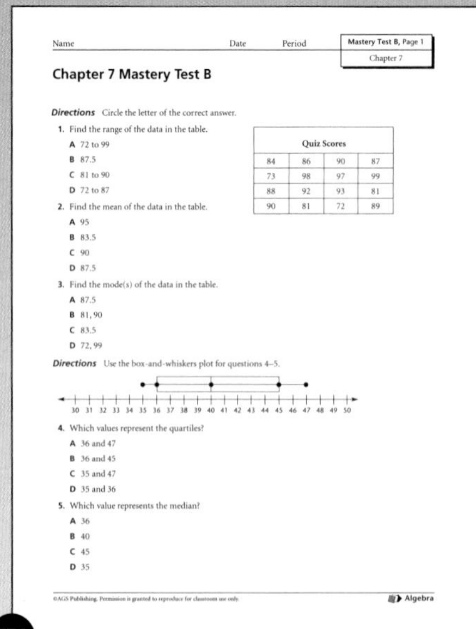

Name Date Period

Mastery Test B, Page 1
Chapter 7

Chapter 7 Mastery Test B

Directions Circle the letter of the correct answer.

1. Find the range of the data in the table.
   - A 72 to 99
   - B 87.5
   - C 81 to 90
   - D 72 to 87

Quiz Scores			
84	86	90	87
73	98	97	99
88	92	93	81
90	81	72	89

2. Find the mean of the data in the table.
   - A 95
   - B 83.5
   - C 90
   - D 87.5
3. Find the mode(s) of the data in the table.
   - A 87.5
   - B 81, 90
   - C 83.5
   - D 72, 99

Directions Use the box-and-whiskers plot for questions 4–5.

30 31 32 33 34 35 36 37 38 39 40 41 42 43 44 45 46 47 48 49 50

4. Which values represent the quartiles?
   - A 36 and 47
   - B 36 and 45
   - C 35 and 47
   - D 35 and 36
5. Which value represents the median?
   - A 36
   - B 40
   - C 45
   - D 35

©AGS Publishing. Permission is granted to reproduce for classroom use only. Algebra

TRL

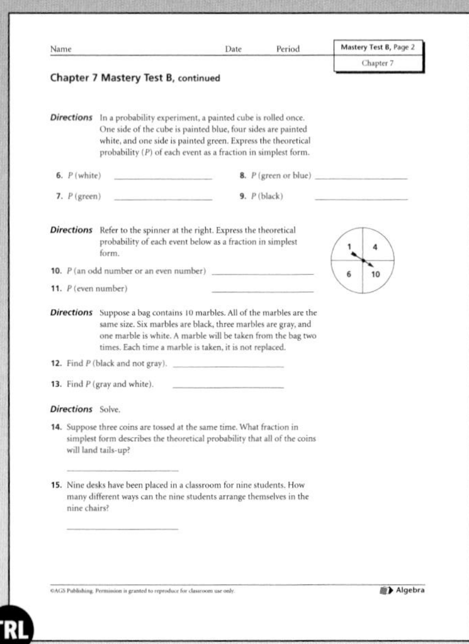

Name Date Period

Mastery Test B, Page 2
Chapter 7

Chapter 7 Mastery Test B, continued

Directions In a probability experiment, a painted cube is rolled once. One side of the cube is painted blue, four sides are painted white, and one side is painted green. Express the theoretical probability (*P*) of each event as a fraction in simplest form.

6. *P* (white) ________ 8. *P* (green or blue) ________

7. *P* (green) ________ 9. *P* (black) ________

Directions Refer to the spinner at the right. Express the theoretical probability of each event below as a fraction in simplest form.

10. *P* (an odd number or an even number) ________
11. *P* (even number) ________

Directions Suppose a bag contains 10 marbles. All of the marbles are the same size. Six marbles are black, three marbles are gray, and one marble is white. A marble will be taken from the bag two times. Each time a marble is taken, it is not replaced.

12. Find *P* (black and not gray). ________
13. Find *P* (gray and white). ________

Directions Solve.

14. Suppose three coins are tossed at the same time. What fraction in simplest form describes the theoretical probability that all of the coins will land tails-up?

    ____

15. Nine desks have been placed in a classroom for nine students. How many different ways can the nine students arrange themselves in the nine chairs?

    ____

©AGS Publishing. Permission is granted to reproduce for classroom use only. Algebra

TRL

Chapter 7 Mastery Test B, 2 pages

Use the spinner at the right.

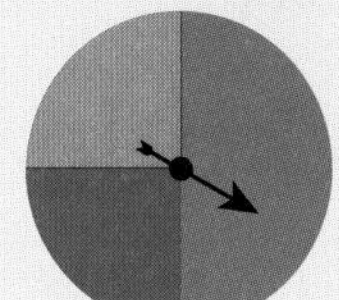

Example: Describe an event that could not happen.
Solution: The pointer cannot point to yellow because yellow is not on the spinner.

20. Describe an event that is certain.

21. Describe an event that is impossible.

Answer the following questions.

Example: Three chairs are arranged in a row. How many different ways can three students sit in those chairs?
Solution: Any of the three students can sit in the first chair. Once a person is in that chair, any of the two other students can sit in the middle chair. The remaining student sits in the last chair. The students can sit in $3 \bullet 2 \bullet 1 = 6$ different ways.

22. Four friends are waiting in a line. How many different ways can they arrange themselves in that line? 24 ways

23. If six horses start and finish a race, how many different orders of finish are possible? 720 ways

24. Jan has five books. How many different ways can she arrange the books on her shelf? 120 ways

25. Miguel and his three friends say their names aloud one at a time. In how many different ways can they recite their names? 24 ways

20. Answers will vary. Sample answer: Spinning the spinner once and getting an outcome of orange, blue, or green.

21. Answers will vary. Sample answer: Spinning the spinner once and getting an outcome of black.

Test-Taking Tip

It is a good idea to double-check the location of numbers or other data that you identify in a table or chart.

Alternative Assessment, continued

■ **To determine range and measures of central tendency**
Have students determine the range and measures of central tendency of the histograms they bring to class. Ask students how a histogram might be used to measure the quality of a company's products. *(Almost all manufacturing uses quality control, and histograms are one way to measure the quality of products. If possible, bring in a quality control expert to explain how range and measures of central tendency are used in manufacturing. If you can't find a quality control expert, ask a representative of an manufacturing industry in your area to speak about these concepts to your class.)*

■ **To compute probabilities and complementary events involving statistics**
Have students explain why the sum of a probability of an event and its complement always equals 1. Have them give examples using a number cube and by flipping a coin to determine heads or tails. *(The reason the probability of an event and its complement always equals 1 is because the probability and complement are two parts of a single whole. The number 1 equals the event. The probability and complement total the single event.)*

Chapter

Planning Guide

Fractions and Algebra

		Student Text Lesson: Student Pages	Vocabulary	Practice Exercises	Solutions Key
Lesson 1	**Fractions as Rational Numbers**	220–221	✔	✔	✔
Lesson 2	**Algebraic Fractions—Rational Numbers**	222–223	✔	✔	✔
Lesson 3	**Multiplying/Dividing Algebraic Fractions**	224–225		✔	✔
Lesson 4	**Complex Fractions and the LCM**	226–229	✔	✔	✔
Lesson 5	**Least Common Multiples and Prime Factors**	230–231		✔	✔
Lesson 6	**Sums and Differences**	232–233		✔	✔
Lesson 7	**Proportions and Fractions in Equations**	234–237		✔	✔
Lesson 8	**More Solutions to Equations with Fractions**	238–241		✔	✔
Lesson 9	**Denominators and Zero**	242–243	✔	✔	✔
Application	**Working Fractions**	244		✔	✔

Chapter Activities

Teacher's Resource Library

Estimation Exercise 8: Estimating Products and Quotients of Fractions

Application Activity 8: Working Fractions

Everyday Algebra 8: Solving Distance Problems

Community Connection 8: Weather Forecasts

Teacher's Edition

Chapter 8 Project

Assessment Options

Student Text

Chapter 8 Review

Teacher's Resource Library

Chapter 8 Mastery Tests A and B

Student Text Features							Teaching Strategies							Learning Styles						Teacher's Resource Library			
Estimation Activity	Algebra in Your Life	Technology Connection	Writing About Mathematics	Try This	Problem Solving	Calculator Practice	Online Connection	Common Error	Applications Home, Career, Community	Mental Math	Manipulatives	Calculator	Group Problem Solving	Auditory/Verbal	Visual/Spatial	Logical/Mathematical	Body/Kinesthetic	Interpersonal/Group Learning	LEP/ESL	Activities	Alternate Activities	Workbook Activities	Self-Study Guide
			221					221	221						221					70	70	75	✔
			223								223		223					223		71	71	76	✔
			225					224		225									225	72	72	77	✔
			229	229	229		227	227	229	228		228	229	227						73	73	78	✔
			231					231				231				231				74	74	79	✔
233									233	233							233			75	75	80	✔
				237	236			235				237	237				235	236	236	76	76	81	✔
		239	241		241	240			241			240	239	239						77	77	82–83	✔
	242		243					242	243		243		243		243					78	78	84	✔
													245					244					✔

Software Options

Skill Track Software

Use the Skill Track Software for *Algebra* for additional reinforcement of this chapter. The software provides multiple-choice assessment items for students to access by computer.

Solutions Key

Use the Solutions Key with this chapter to help students who may need additional assistance. The Solutions Key CD provides solutions for every exercise in the student edition.

Other Resources

Alternative Activities

The Teacher's Resource Library (TRL) contains a set of worksheets written at a second-grade reading level called Alternative Activities. They cover the same content as the regular Activities.

Manipulatives

See the Manipulative activities in this chapter for hands-on modeling of the content.

Pattern Blocks
Algebra Tiles

Chapter at a Glance

Chapter 8: Fractions and Algebra
pages 218–247

Lessons

Skill Track for Algebra 

Teacher's Resource Library TRL

Workbook Activities 75–84
Activities 70–78
Alternative Activities 70–78
Application Activity 8
Estimation Exercise 8
Everyday Algebra 8
Community Connection 8
Chapter 8 Self-Study Guide
Chapter 8 Mastery Tests A and B
(Answer Keys for the Teacher's Resource Library begin on page 530 of this Teacher's Edition.)

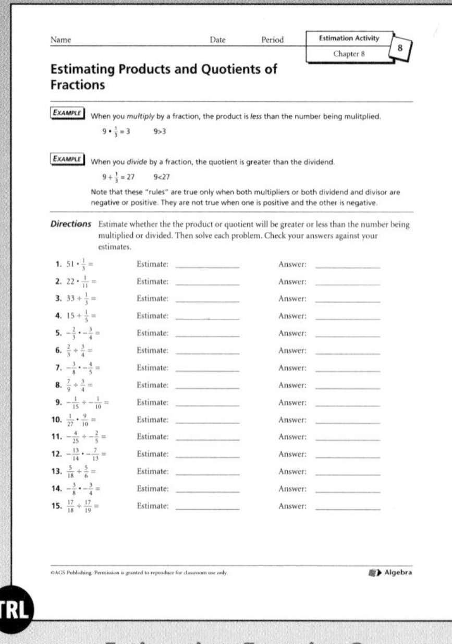

Name Date Period **Estimation Activity** Chapter 8 **8**

Estimating Products and Quotients of Fractions

EXAMPLE When you *multiply* by a fraction, the product is *less* than the number being mulitplied.

$9 \cdot \frac{1}{3} = 3 \qquad 9 > 3$

EXAMPLE When you *divide* by a fraction, the quotient is greater than the dividend.

$9 \div \frac{1}{3} = 27 \qquad 9 < 27$

Note that these "rules" are true only when both multipliers or both dividend and divisor are negative or positive. They are not true when one is positive and the other is negative.

Directions Estimate whether the the product or quotient will be greater or less than the number being multiplied or divided. Then solve each problem. Check your answers against your estimates.

1. $51 \cdot \frac{1}{3} =$ Estimate: ______ Answer: ______
2. $22 \cdot \frac{1}{11} =$ Estimate: ______ Answer: ______
3. $33 \div \frac{1}{3} =$ Estimate: ______ Answer: ______
4. $15 \div \frac{1}{5} =$ Estimate: ______ Answer: ______
5. $-\frac{2}{3} \cdot -\frac{3}{4} =$ Estimate: ______ Answer: ______
6. $\frac{2}{3} \div \frac{3}{4} =$ Estimate: ______ Answer: ______
7. $-\frac{3}{8} \cdot -\frac{4}{5} =$ Estimate: ______ Answer: ______
8. $\frac{7}{9} \div \frac{3}{4} =$ Estimate: ______ Answer: ______
9. $-\frac{1}{15} \div -\frac{1}{10} =$ Estimate: ______ Answer: ______
10. $\frac{1}{27} \cdot \frac{9}{10} =$ Estimate: ______ Answer: ______
11. $-\frac{4}{25} \div -\frac{2}{5} =$ Estimate: ______ Answer: ______
12. $-\frac{13}{14} \cdot -\frac{7}{13} =$ Estimate: ______ Answer: ______
13. $\frac{5}{18} \div \frac{5}{6} =$ Estimate: ______ Answer: ______
14. $-\frac{3}{8} \cdot -\frac{3}{4} =$ Estimate: ______ Answer: ______
15. $\frac{17}{18} \div \frac{17}{19} =$ Estimate: ______ Answer: ______

 Algebra

TRL

Estimation Exercise 8

Name Date Period **Community Connection** Chapter 8 **8**

Weather Forecasts

Weather forecasts use probability in the form of a percent or a fraction to describe the chance of precipitation. Have you ever wondered how often a precipitation forecast is correct?

Use the chart below to help determine how often a precipitation forecast for your community is correct. Each day for one month, record in a journal the forecast for the next day. On the following chart, record the accuracy of the previous days' forecast. For example, suppose a 30% chance of precipitation was forecast for Tuesday. On Wednesday, record a tally in the 30% column for *Y* (yes) if precipitation occurred or a tally for *N* (no) if precipitation did not occur. Also on Wednesday record in your journal the forecast for Thursday. And so on.

At the end of one month, work cooperatively to analyze the data and describe the accuracy of the forecasts.

0%		10%		20%		30%		40%		50%		60%		70%		80%		90%		100%	
Y	N	Y	N	Y	N	Y	N	Y	N	Y	N	Y	N	Y	N	Y	N	Y	N	Y	N

 Algebra

TRL

Community Connection 8

Chapter

8 Fractions and Algebra

We live in a three-dimensional world. Objects have height, width, and depth, or thickness. The amount of space any object takes up is its volume. Whether it is one of the great pyramids of Egypt or a grain of curry powder, every object has volume. You have been learning to apply your algebra skills to formulas. You can apply these skills to the formula for finding volume. To calculate the volume of a pyramid, for example, you will need to know how to multiply fractions. When you multiply one-third ($\frac{1}{3}$) of the pyramid's height by the area of its base, you find exactly how much space the entire pyramid occupies. With a little practice, working with fractions in algebra can be easy.

In Chapter 8, you will study and use fractions in algebraic equations.

Goals for Learning

- To write fractions in their simplest form
- To find the greatest common factor of two or more fractions
- To multiply and divide algebraic fractions
- To simplify complex fractions
- To find the least common multiple and prime factors of algebraic fractions
- To add and subtract algebraic fractions
- To solve problems involving proportions and fractions
- To solve equations with algebraic fractions

219

Name Date Period *SELF-STUDY GUIDE*

CHAPTER 8: Fractions and Algebra

Goals 8.1 and 8.2 *To write fractions in their simplest form*
To find the greatest common factor of two or more fractions

Date	Assignment	Score
______	1: Read pages 220–221. Complete Exercises A–B on page 221.	______
______	2: Complete Workbook Activity 75.	______
______	3: Read pages 222–223. Complete Exercises A–B on page 223.	______
______	4: Complete Workbook Activity 76.	______

Comments:

Goal 8.3 *To multiply and divide algebraic fractions*

Date	Assignment	Score
______	5: Read pages 224–225. Complete Exercises A–B on page 225.	______
______	6: Complete Workbook Activity 77.	______

Comments:

Goals 8.4 and 8.5 *To simplify complex fractions*
To find the least common multiple and prime factors of algebraic fractions

Date	Assignment	Score
______	7: Read pages 226–228. Complete Exercises A–C on pages 228–229.	______
______	8: Complete Workbook Activity 78.	______
______	9: Read pages 230–231. Complete Exercises A–B on page 231.	______
______	10: Complete Workbook Activity 79.	______

Comments:

 Algebra

TRL

Name Date Period *SELF-STUDY GUIDE*

CHAPTER 8: Fractions and Algebra, continued

Goal 8.6 *To add and subtract algebraic fractions*

Date	Assignment	Score
______	11: Read page 232. Complete Exercise A on page 233.	______
______	12: Complete Workbook Activity 80.	______

Comments:

Goal 8.7 *To solve problems involving proportions and fractions*

Date	Assignment	Score
______	13: Read pages 234–235. Complete Exercises A–B on pages 236–237.	______
______	14: Complete Workbook Activity 81.	______

Comments:

Goal 8.8 *To solve equations with algebraic fractions*

Date	Assignment	Score
______	15: Read pages 238–239. Complete Exercises A, B, D on pages 239–241.	______
______	16: Read and complete the Calculator Practice on pages 240–241.	______
______	17: Complete Workbook Activities 82–83.	______
______	18: Read pages 242–243. Complete Exercise A on page 243.	______
______	19: Complete Workbook Activity 84.	______
______	20: Read and complete the Application Exercise on page 244.	______
______	21: Complete the Chapter 8 Review on pages 245–247.	______

Comments:

Student's Signature ______________ Date ______

Instructor's Signature ______________ Date ______

 Algebra

TRL

Chapter 8 Self-Study Guide

Introducing the Chapter

Use the chapter opener as an opportunity to tell students we live in a three-dimensional world. All objects have height, width, or thickness. This includes a grain of curry or a great pyramid of Egypt. You can apply your algebraic skills to formulas with fractions to find out how much space a huge pyramid takes, or a tiny grain of curry.

Chapter Project

Have student groups create a teaching guide for the chapter. The guide will consist of nine sections, one for each lesson in the chapter. Have each group:

- Write a paragraph explaining how to solve one problem from each lesson in the chapter.
- Include five problems with appropriate solutions.
- Give an example for each concept taught in the lesson.

Make sure that the members of each group assign all tasks involved in the project.

Teacher's Resource

The AGS Publishing Teaching Strategies in Math Transparencies may be used with this chapter. They add an interactive dimension to expand and enhance the program content.

Career Interest Inventory

The AGS Publishing Harrington-O'Shea Career Decision-Making System-Revised (CDM) may be used with this chapter. Students can use the CDM to explore their interests and identify careers. The CDM defines career areas that are indicated by students' responses on the inventory.

Lesson at a Glance

Chapter 8 Lesson 1

Overview This lesson shows how to find the greatest common factor and how to use the greatest common factor to write fractions in simplest form.

Objectives

- To find the greatest common factor
- To write factions in simplest form using greatest common factors

Student Pages 220–221

Teacher's Resource Library TRL

Workbook Activity 75

Activity 70

Alternative Activity 70

Mathematics Vocabulary

rational number
simplest form

1 Warm-Up Activity

Ask students to look at the following fractions:

$\frac{68}{136}$ $\frac{18}{36}$ $\frac{52}{104}$ $\frac{31}{62}$ $\frac{55}{110}$

Ask, "What do all these fractions have in common?" *(All these fractions can be simplified to $\frac{1}{2}$.)* Discuss the meaning of equivalent fractions, which will lead to fractions as rational numbers.

2 Teaching the Lesson

Using the fractions from the Warm-Up Activity, show how the greatest common factor can be used to write each fraction in simplest form.

Fraction	GCF	Simplest Form
$\frac{68}{136}$	68	$\frac{1}{2}$
$\frac{18}{36}$	18	$\frac{1}{2}$
$\frac{52}{104}$	52	$\frac{1}{2}$
$\frac{31}{62}$	31	$\frac{1}{2}$
$\frac{55}{110}$	55	$\frac{1}{2}$

Lesson 1 Fractions as Rational Numbers

Rational number
Any number that is expressed as an integer or as a ratio between two integers when 0 does not serve as the denominator

Simplest form
A fraction in which the only common factor of the numerator and denominator is 1

A fraction is one or more parts of a whole. Examples of fractions include $\frac{1}{3}$, $\frac{-3}{4}$, and $\frac{0}{10}$. Fractions such as $\frac{1}{3}$ are positive. Fractions such as $\frac{3}{-4}$ or $\frac{-3}{4}$ or $-\frac{3}{4}$ are negative. When simplified, fractions such as $\frac{0}{10}$ are neither positive nor negative because $\frac{0}{10} = 0$.

Fractions are examples of **rational numbers.**

These numbers are rational numbers:

$\frac{1}{3}$, $\frac{-1}{3}$, $\frac{1}{-3}$, $\frac{5}{-7}$, $\frac{0}{5}$, and $\frac{-7}{5}$

These numbers are not rational numbers:

$\frac{0}{0}$, $\frac{1}{0}$, or $\frac{n}{0}$ where n = any number.

Each of these fractions is equivalent to $\frac{1}{2}$.

$$\frac{1}{2} = \frac{2}{4} = \frac{3}{6} = \frac{4}{8} = \frac{5}{10} = \frac{6}{12} = \frac{7}{14} = \ldots \frac{1(n)}{2(n)} \text{ for all } n \neq 0.$$

The fraction $\frac{1}{2}$ is in **simplest form** because the greatest common factor of the numerator (1) and the denominator (2) is 1.

Remember that a proportion is an equation made up of two equal ratios. For example, $\frac{6}{12} = \frac{1}{2}$ is a proportion. To check, use cross products $6 \bullet 2 = 12$ and $12 \bullet 1 = 12$. Since the cross products are equal, $\frac{6}{12} = \frac{1}{2}$ is a true proportion.

Rule To write a fraction in simplest form, divide the numerator and denominator by the greatest common factor (GCF).

EXAMPLE 1 Write $\frac{6}{12}$ in simplest form.

Step 1 Write the prime factorization of 6 and 12.

$\frac{6}{12} = \frac{2 \bullet 3}{2 \bullet 2 \bullet 3}$

Step 2 Identify the common prime factors. The product of the common prime factors is the GCF.

$\frac{2 \bullet 3}{2 \bullet 2 \bullet 3}$ $2 \bullet 3 = 6$

Step 3 Divide the numerator and denominator of the fraction you want to simplify by 6.

$\frac{6}{12} \div \frac{6}{6} = \frac{1}{2}$

Step 4 Check your work. Use the idea that if two rational numbers are equivalent, they form a true proportion. In a true proportion, the cross products are equal.

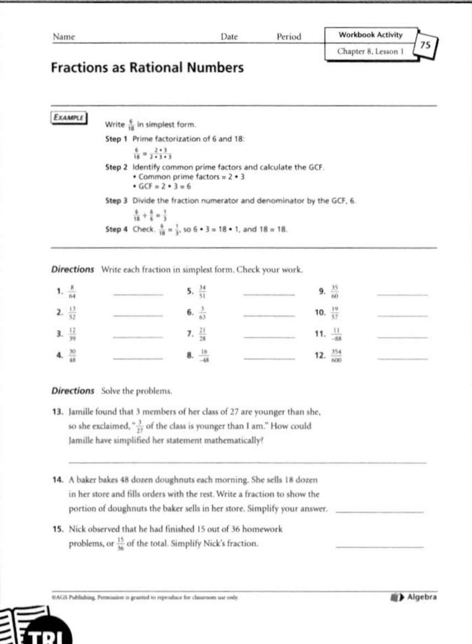

Name Date Period — Workbook Activity 75 — Chapter 8, Lesson 1

Fractions as Rational Numbers

EXAMPLE Write $\frac{6}{18}$ in simplest form.

Step 1 Prime factorization of 6 and 18:
$\frac{6}{18} = \frac{2 \bullet 3}{2 \bullet 3 \bullet 3}$

Step 2 Identify common prime factors and calculate the GCF.
• Common prime factors = $2 \bullet 3$
• GCF = $2 \bullet 3 = 6$

Step 3 Divide the fraction numerator and denominator by the GCF, 6.
$\frac{6}{18} \div \frac{6}{6} = \frac{1}{3}$

Step 4 Check. $\frac{6}{18} = \frac{1}{3}$, so $6 \bullet 3 = 18 \bullet 1$, and $18 = 18$.

Directions Write each fraction in simplest form. Check your work.

1. $\frac{8}{64}$ ____ 5. $\frac{34}{51}$ ____ 9. $\frac{35}{60}$ ____
2. $\frac{13}{52}$ ____ 6. $\frac{3}{63}$ ____ 10. $\frac{19}{57}$ ____
3. $\frac{12}{39}$ ____ 7. $\frac{21}{28}$ ____ 11. $\frac{11}{-88}$ ____
4. $\frac{30}{48}$ ____ 8. $\frac{16}{-48}$ ____ 12. $\frac{354}{600}$ ____

Directions Solve the problems.

13. Jamille found that 3 members of her class of 27 are younger than she, so she exclaimed, "$\frac{3}{27}$ of the class is younger than I am." How could Jamille have simplified her statement mathematically?
14. A baker bakes 48 dozen doughnuts each morning. She sells 18 dozen in her store and fills orders with the rest. Write a fraction to show the portion of doughnuts the baker sells in her store. Simplify your answer.
15. Nick observed that he had finished 15 out of 36 homework problems, or $\frac{15}{36}$ of the total. Simplify Nick's fraction.

 Algebra

TRL

Workbook Activity 75

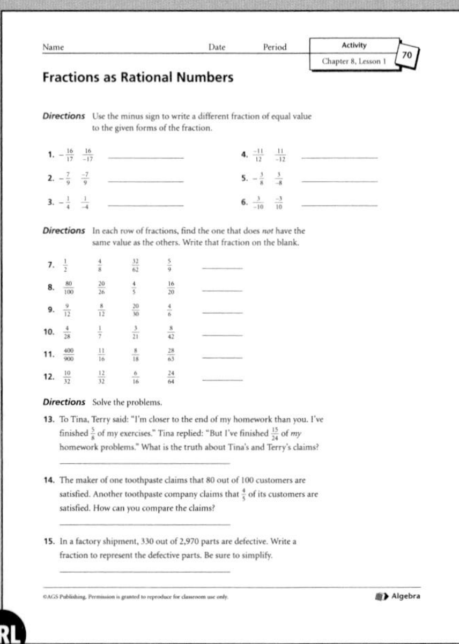

Name Date Period — Activity 70 — Chapter 8, Lesson 1

Fractions as Rational Numbers

Directions Use the minus sign to write a different fraction of equal value to the given forms of the fraction.

1. $-\frac{16}{17}$ $\frac{16}{-17}$ ____ 4. $\frac{-11}{12}$ $\frac{11}{-12}$ ____
2. $-\frac{7}{9}$ $\frac{-7}{9}$ ____ 5. $-\frac{3}{8}$ $\frac{3}{-8}$ ____
3. $-\frac{1}{4}$ $\frac{1}{-4}$ ____ 6. $\frac{3}{-10}$ $\frac{-3}{10}$ ____

Directions In each row of fractions, find the one that does *not* have the same value as the others. Write that fraction on the blank.

7. $\frac{1}{2}$ $\frac{4}{8}$ $\frac{32}{62}$ $\frac{5}{9}$ ____
8. $\frac{80}{100}$ $\frac{20}{26}$ $\frac{4}{5}$ $\frac{16}{20}$ ____
9. $\frac{9}{12}$ $\frac{8}{12}$ $\frac{20}{30}$ $\frac{4}{6}$ ____
10. $\frac{4}{28}$ $\frac{1}{7}$ $\frac{3}{21}$ $\frac{8}{42}$ ____
11. $\frac{400}{900}$ $\frac{11}{16}$ $\frac{8}{18}$ $\frac{28}{63}$ ____
12. $\frac{10}{32}$ $\frac{12}{32}$ $\frac{6}{16}$ $\frac{24}{64}$ ____

Directions Solve the problems.

13. To Tina, Terry said: "I'm closer to the end of my homework than you. I've finished $\frac{5}{8}$ of my exercises." Tina replied: "But I've finished $\frac{15}{24}$ of *my* homework problems." What is the truth about Tina's and Terry's claims?
14. The maker of one toothpaste claims that 80 out of 100 customers are satisfied. Another toothpaste company claims that $\frac{4}{5}$ of its customers are satisfied. How can you compare the claims?
15. In a factory shipment, 330 out of 2,970 parts are defective. Write a fraction to represent the defective parts. Be sure to simplify.

 Algebra

TRL

Activity 70

EXAMPLE 2 Write $-\frac{1}{2}$ in two other forms.

$$-\frac{1}{2} = (-1)\frac{1}{2} = \left[\frac{-1}{1}\right] \cdot \frac{1}{2} = \frac{-1 \cdot 1}{2} = \frac{-1}{2} \text{ or}$$

$$-\frac{1}{2} = (-1)\frac{1}{2} = \left[\frac{1}{-1}\right] \cdot \frac{1}{2} = \frac{1}{-1 \cdot 2} = \frac{1}{-2}$$

Exercise A Find the GCF, then use it to write each fraction in simplest form. Check your work.

1. $\frac{9}{63}$ $\frac{1}{7}$

2. $\frac{21}{63}$ $\frac{1}{3}$

3. $\frac{-16}{64}$ $\frac{-1}{4}$

4. $\frac{15}{75}$ $\frac{1}{5}$

5. $\frac{18}{72}$ $\frac{1}{4}$

6. $\frac{36}{-81}$ $\frac{4}{-9}$

7. $\frac{12}{144}$ $\frac{1}{12}$

8. $-(\frac{25}{225})$ $\frac{-1}{9}$

9. $\frac{18}{81}$ $\frac{2}{9}$

10. $\frac{-19}{38}$ $\frac{-1}{2}$

11. $\frac{42}{64}$ $\frac{21}{32}$

12. $\frac{24}{192}$ $\frac{1}{8}$

13. $\frac{27}{72}$ $\frac{3}{8}$

14. $\frac{14}{-28}$ $\frac{1}{-2}$

Exercise B Write each fraction in simplest form. Check your work.

15. $\frac{121}{891}$ $\frac{11}{81}$

16. $\frac{43}{172}$ $\frac{1}{4}$

17. $\frac{43}{-215}$ $\frac{1}{-5}$

18. $\frac{95}{-135}$ $\frac{19}{-27}$

19. $\frac{90}{135}$ $\frac{2}{3}$

20. $\frac{16}{128}$ $\frac{1}{8}$

21. $\frac{270}{720}$ $\frac{3}{8}$

22. $\frac{-42}{441}$ $\frac{-2}{21}$

23. $\frac{125}{-525}$ $\frac{5}{-21}$

24. $-(\frac{81}{405})$ $-\frac{1}{5}$

25. $\frac{81}{405}$ $\frac{1}{5}$

Writing About Mathematics

Explain why $\frac{-a}{b} = \frac{a}{-b} = -[\frac{a}{b}]$ are equivalent expressions in which a and b are integers and $b \neq 0$. You may use numbers to illustrate your answer.

Also, go over some other examples:

Fraction	GCF	Simplest Form
$\frac{21}{28}$	7	$\frac{3}{4}$
$\frac{-30}{36}$	6	$\frac{-5}{6}$
$\frac{24}{-27}$	3	$\frac{8}{-9}$
$\frac{50}{80}$	10	$\frac{5}{8}$
$\frac{70}{75}$	5	$\frac{14}{15}$

Common Error

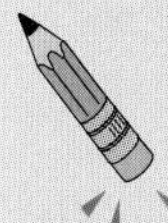

When writing fractions in simplest form, students may find a common factor but not the greatest common factor. Remind them that a fraction is in simplest form only when the greatest common factor in the resulting fraction is no greater than 1.

3 Reinforce and Extend

Learning Styles

Visual/Spatial

Have students draw and shade rectangles to represent simplified fractions. The simplified fraction is drawn using vertical lines in the rectangle, and horizontal lines are drawn to show the greatest common factors. For example, to show that $\frac{2}{4}$ equals $\frac{1}{2}$, start by drawing a rectangle, then draw a vertical line down the middle. Shade half and label it $\frac{1}{2}$. Next, to show the greatest common factor of 2, draw a horizontal line. (One line shows a factor of two, two lines show a factor of three, and so on.) Label the line GCF = 2.

Career Connection

Many stockbrokers watch some type of stock quotes, which are quoted in fractions. They must write the fractions in simplest form on many different documents. Have students watch a business channel that offers stock quotes, copy 25 fractional quotes, and write them in simplest form.

Lesson at a Glance

Chapter 8 Lesson 2

Overview This lesson shows how to write algebraic fractions in simplest form.

Objective

- To write algebraic fractions in simplest form

Student Pages 222–223

Teacher's Resource Library TRL

Workbook Activity 76

Activity 71

Alternative Activity 71

Mathematics Vocabulary

algebraic fraction
rational expression

1 Warm-Up Activity

Propose this problem to the class:

A scientist found that the decay rate of a certain substance was $\frac{2x^2}{x^3}$.

He made a table of his results using the decay rate.

Value of x	Rate of Decay ($\frac{2x^2}{x^3}$)
10	0.2
8	0.25
4	0.5
2	1.0
1	2.0
0	totally decayed

Study this table to discover an easier way for the scientist to make his calculations. *(Write $\frac{2x^2}{x^3}$ in simplest form as $\frac{2}{x}$.)*

2 Teaching the Lesson

Encourage students to write their problems out in expanded notation in both the numerator and denominator to find the greatest common factor.

Lesson 2 Algebraic Fractions—Rational Expressions

> ***Algebraic fraction***
> *A single algebraic term divided by a single algebraic term*
>
> ***Rational expression***
> *An algebraic expression divided by another algebraic expression*

The expressions $\frac{x^2}{x^3}$ and $\frac{15x^2}{45x^3}$ are examples of **algebraic fractions.** Like all fractions, algebraic fractions can be simplified, or written in simplest form.

EXAMPLE 1 Simplify $\frac{x^2}{x^3}$.

Step 1 Find the GCF of the numerator and the denominator.

$\frac{x^2}{x^3} = \frac{x \bullet x}{x \bullet x \bullet x}$ The GCF is $x \bullet x$ or x^2.

Step 2 Divide both the numerator and the denominator by the GCF.

$\frac{x^2}{x^3} \div \frac{x^2}{x^2} = \frac{1}{x}$

Step 3 Does $\frac{x^2}{x^3} = \frac{1}{x}$? Check by comparing the cross products.

$x^2 \bullet x = x^3 \bullet 1$

$x^3 = x^3$ True

EXAMPLE 2 Simplify $\frac{15x^2}{45x^3}$.

Step 1 Find the GCF of the numerator and the denominator.

$\frac{15x^2}{45x^3} = \frac{3 \bullet 5 \bullet x \bullet x}{3 \bullet 3 \bullet 5 \bullet x \bullet x \bullet x}$ The GCF is $15x^2$.

Step 2 Divide both the numerator and the denominator by the GCF.

$\frac{15x^2}{45x^3} = \frac{15x^2}{45x^3} \div \frac{15x^2}{15x^2} = \frac{1}{3x}$

Step 3 Check. Does $\frac{15x^2}{45x^3} = \frac{1}{3x}$?

$15x^2 \bullet 3x = 45x^3 \bullet 1$

$45x^3 = 45x^3$ True

A **rational expression** is a fraction that compares two algebraic expressions. Many rational expressions can be written in simplest form.

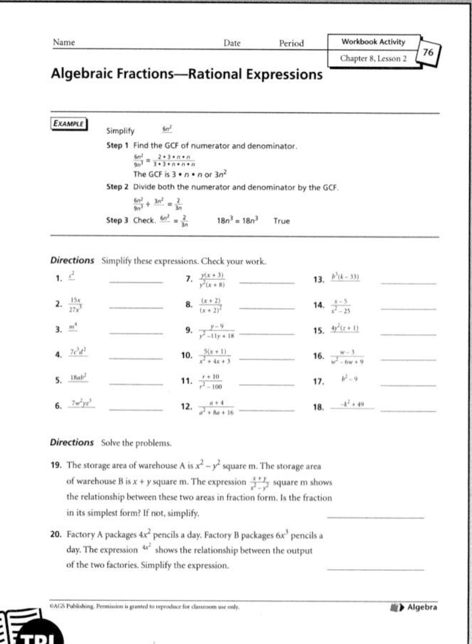

Name Date Period — Workbook Activity 76, Chapter 8, Lesson 2

Algebraic Fractions—Rational Expressions

EXAMPLE Simplify $\frac{6n^2}{}$

Step 1 Find the GCF of numerator and denominator.

$\frac{6n^2}{9n^3} = \frac{2 \bullet 3 \bullet n \bullet n}{3 \bullet 3 \bullet n \bullet n \bullet n}$

The GCF is $3 \bullet n \bullet n$ or $3n^2$

Step 2 Divide both the numerator and denominator by the GCF.

$\frac{6n^2}{9n^3} \div \frac{3n^2}{} = \frac{2}{3n}$

Step 3 Check. $\frac{6n^2}{} = \frac{2}{3n}$ $18n^3 = 18n^3$ True

Directions Simplify these expressions. Check your work.

1. $\frac{c^2}{}$ ____
2. $\frac{15x}{27x^3}$ ____
3. $\frac{m^4}{}$ ____
4. $\frac{7c^3d^2}{}$ ____
5. $\frac{18ab^2}{}$ ____
6. $\frac{7w^2yz^3}{}$ ____
7. $\frac{y(x+3)}{y^2(x+8)}$ ____
8. $\frac{(x+2)}{(x+2)^2}$ ____
9. $\frac{y-9}{y^2-11y+18}$ ____
10. $\frac{5(x+1)}{x^2+4x+3}$ ____
11. $\frac{r+10}{r^2-100}$ ____
12. $\frac{a+4}{a^2+8a+16}$ ____
13. $\frac{b^3(k-33)}{}$ ____
14. $\frac{x-5}{x^2-25}$ ____
15. $\frac{4y^2(z+1)}{}$ ____
16. $\frac{w-3}{w^2-6w+9}$ ____
17. b^2-9 ____
18. $\frac{-k^2+49}{}$ ____

Directions Solve the problems.

19. The storage area of warehouse A is $x^2 - y^2$ square m. The storage area of warehouse B is $x + y$ square m. The expression $\frac{x+y}{x^2-y^2}$ square m shows the relationship between these two areas in fraction form. Is the fraction in its simplest form? If not, simplify. ____
20. Factory A packages $4x^2$ pencils a day. Factory B packages $6x^3$ pencils a day. The expression $4x^2$ shows the relationship between the output of the two factories. Simplify the expression. ____

 Algebra

TRL

Workbook Activity 76

Name Date Period — Activity 71, Chapter 8, Lesson 2

Algebraic Fractions—Rational Expressions

Directions Decide whether each fraction is in its simplest form. If it is, write *yes*. If it is not, write *no* and simplify.

1. $\frac{2x}{6x^3}$ ____
2. $\frac{y}{14}$ ____
3. $\frac{16^3p^2}{48n^5p^3}$ ____
4. $\frac{11x^4y^4z^4}{66x^4y^4z^4}$ ____
5. $\frac{r^2}{22}$ ____
6. $\frac{1}{7n^2}$ ____
7. $\frac{b+9}{b^2-81}$ ____
8. $\frac{x+2}{x^3}$ ____
9. $\frac{a^5b^7c^4d^3}{a^5b^7c^4d^3}$ ____
10. $\frac{y-2}{y^5}$ ____
11. $\frac{5}{9b^2}$ ____
12. $\frac{n+11}{n^2-121}$ ____
13. $\frac{y+2}{y^2+5y+6}$ ____
14. $\frac{k-11}{k+14}$ ____
15. $\frac{1}{n+6}$ ____
16. $\frac{c^5d^3x^{15}y^{15}}{c^5d^3x^{15}y^{15}}$ ____
17. $\frac{k^2-144}{(k+12)(k-12)}$ ____
18. $\frac{x+2}{y(x-3)}$ ____
19. $\frac{x^2-1}{x^2+1}$ ____
20. $\frac{2x-1}{2x^2-7x+3}$ ____

Directions Simplify each expression. Check your work.

21. $\frac{x-64}{x^2+10x+16}$ ____
22. $\frac{-w^2+81}{w^2+8w-9}$ ____
23. $\frac{3x-5}{6x^2-x-15}$ ____

Directions Solve the problems.

24. A scientist calculates that one molecule is $\frac{x+5}{x^2+8x+15}$ the size of a different molecule. Can the scientist simplify his fraction? If so, simplify it. ____
25. Scientists compare temperature changes in 2 distant parts of the world over a period of time. If the net (overall) temperature change is upward, the scientists record a positive number. If the net change is downward, they record a negative number. After completing the experiment, they compare the data in fraction form: $\frac{-4}{12}$. Simplify the fraction, writing it in 2 different forms. ____

 Algebra

TRL

Activity 71

EXAMPLE 3 Simplify $\frac{(x + 2)}{(x + 2)^3}$.

Step 1 If possible, factor the numerator and denominator.

$$\frac{(x + 2)}{(x + 2)^3} = \frac{(x + 2)}{(x + 2)(x + 2)(x + 2)}$$

Step 2 Simplify. $\frac{\cancel{(x + 2)}}{\cancel{(x + 2)}(x + 2)(x + 2)} = \frac{1}{(x + 2)(x + 2)}$ or $\frac{1}{(x + 2)^2}$

Step 3 Check. Does $\frac{(x + 2)}{(x + 2)^3} = \frac{1}{(x + 2)^2}$?

$\frac{(x + 2)}{(x + 2)^3} = \frac{1}{(x + 2)^2} \rightarrow (x + 2)(x + 2)^2 = (x + 2)^3 \bullet 1$

$(x + 2)^3 = (x + 2)^3$ True

EXAMPLE 4 Simplify $\frac{(x - 4)}{(x^2 - 8x + 16)}$.

Step 1 If possible, factor the numerator and denominator.

$$\frac{(x - 4)}{(x^2 - 8x + 16)} = \frac{x - 4}{(x - 4)(x - 4)}$$

Step 2 Simplify. $\frac{\cancel{x - 4}}{\cancel{(x - 4)}(x - 4)} = \frac{1}{(x - 4)}$

Step 3 Check. Does $\frac{(x - 4)}{(x^2 - 8x + 16)} = \frac{1}{(x - 4)}$?

$\frac{(x - 4)}{(x^2 - 8x + 16)} = \frac{1}{(x - 4)}$ or $(x - 4)(x - 4) = x^2 - 8x + 16$

Exercise A Use the GCF to simplify these expressions. Check your work.

1. $\frac{m^5}{m^6}$ ($\frac{1}{m}$)
2. $\frac{r^5}{r^3}$ (r^2)
3. $\frac{5x^3}{25x^2}$ ($\frac{x}{5}$)
4. $\frac{-45x^2}{90x^3}$ ($-\frac{1}{2x}$)
5. $\frac{125x^7}{25x^5}$ ($5x^2$)
6. $\frac{13m^2n^2}{-39mn^2}$ ($\frac{(m)}{-3}$)
7. $\frac{42xy}{63x^2y^3}$ ($\frac{2}{3xy^2}$)
8. $\frac{56r^2s^2}{28r^3s^3}$ ($\frac{2}{(rs)}$)
9. $\frac{72x^3y^3z^3}{-144x^2y^2z}$ ($\frac{(xyz^2)}{-2}$)
10. $\frac{(x - 3)}{(x - 3)^3}$ ($\frac{1}{(x - 3)^2}$)
11. $\frac{(-a^2 - 4)}{(a^2 + 4)^2}$ ($\frac{-1}{(a^2 + 4)}$)
12. $\frac{(m - 6)}{m^2 - 36}$ ($\frac{1}{(m + 6)}$)
13. $\frac{(x^2 - 25)}{(x + 5)}$ ($(x - 5)$)
14. $\frac{(d - 7)}{(d^2 - 49)}$ ($\frac{1}{d + 7}$)

Exercise B Simplify. Check your work.

15. $\frac{(-x^2 + 25)}{(x + 5)}$ ($(-x + 5)$)
16. $\frac{-(r - 12)}{(r^2 - 24r + 144)}$ ($\frac{-1}{(r - 12)}$)
17. $\frac{(w^2 + 14w + 49)}{(w + 7)}$ ($(w + 7)$)
18. $\frac{(-n^2 + 36)}{(n - 6)(n^2 + 12n + 36)}$ ($\frac{-1}{(n + 6)}$)
19. $\frac{(a - 4)}{(a^2 - 6a + 8)}$ ($\frac{1}{(a - 2)}$)
20. $\frac{(-m - 8)}{(m^2 + 5m - 24)}$ ($\frac{-1}{(m - 3)}$)

Writing About Mathematics

What happens when you simplify $\frac{(16x^3y^2)}{(56x5y^3)}$ using $2xy$ instead of the GCF? Can you still factor completely? Explain.

MANIPULATIVES

Review of Simplifying Expressions

Materials: Pattern Blocks

Group Practice: Review the procedures for simplifying variables with exponents by stacking a shape for each factor of the variable. Review how to stack the stacks and add shapes to find the product. To divide, place the denominator model directly below the numerator model. Pair up shapes from the numerator and denominator and remove, explaining that each pair represents 1. The quotient is represented by the remaining unpaired shapes. Emphasize that different shapes, like different variables, cannot be combined.

Student Practice: Have students use the blocks to simplify the variables in Exercise A, Problems 1–9.

Reinforce and Extend

LEARNING STYLES

Interpersonal/ Group Learning

Divide the class into groups of two or three. Have each group write three algebraic fractions with the GCF of $2x$, $15d^3$ and $(y + 4)$. Have the groups write an explanation of how to solve each problem and then solve the problems.

GROUP PROBLEM SOLVING

Have students use 2, x, and 9 to write an algebraic fraction using only positive integers under the following conditions.

- Write an expression that will have the greatest value. ($\frac{9x}{2}$)
- Write an expression that will have the least value. ($\frac{2}{9x}$)
- Write an expression in which the denominator will be 18. [$\frac{x}{(2)(9)}$]

Lesson at a Glance

Chapter 8 Lesson 3

Overview This lesson demonstrates how to find the product and quotient of algebraic fractions.

Objective

- To find the product and quotient of algebraic fractions

Student Pages 224–225

Teacher's Resource Library 

Workbook Activity 77

Activity 72

Alternative Activity 72

1 Warm-Up Activity

Understanding reciprocals provides a foundation not only for solving equations but also for dividing algebraic fractions. Write these expressions on the board:

$\frac{20}{5}$ $\quad 20(\frac{1}{5})$

$\frac{20}{2}$ $\quad 20(\frac{1}{2})$

$\frac{20}{4}$ $\quad 20(\frac{1}{4})$

Have students simplify each expression. *(4, 4, 10, 10, 5, 5)* Ask, "What pattern do you see?" *(Multiplying by the reciprocal gives you the same answer as dividing by the denominator of a fraction whose numerator is 1.)*

2 Teaching the Lesson

Discuss the examples on pages 224 and 225 with the students. You may wish to reproduce the examples on the board and work through them while students follow along in their books.

Common Error

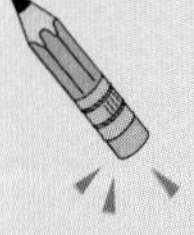

Some students may find the reciprocal of the dividend rather than the reciprocal of the divisor. Stress the rule that when dividing fractions you take only the reciprocal of the divisor. The dividend must remain the same.

Lesson 3 Multiplying and Dividing Algebraic Fractions

Recall that the reciprocal of any non-zero number x is $\frac{1}{x}$. Dividing by a number is the same as multiplying by its reciprocal. For example, $12 \div 3 = 4$ is the same as $(12)(\frac{1}{3})$. Both equal 4.

In algebra, you divide fractions by multiplying by the reciprocal of the divisor.

$\frac{a}{b} \div \frac{c}{d} = \frac{a}{b} \bullet \frac{d}{c}$ $\qquad \frac{c}{d}$ and $\frac{d}{c}$ are reciprocals.

> Follow the same method you learned to check basic division facts. To check $6 \div 3 = 2$, multiply the quotient (2) by the divisor (3). The product of the quotient and the divisor should equal the dividend: $(2)(3) = 6$.

Example 1 Find the quotient of $\frac{3}{4} \div \frac{2}{3}$.

Step 1 Write the equation.

Step 2 Divide by multiplying by the reciprocal.

$\frac{3}{2}$ is the reciprocal of $\frac{2}{3}$.

$\frac{3}{4} \div \frac{2}{3} = \frac{3}{4} \bullet \frac{3}{2}$

$\frac{3}{4} \div \frac{2}{3} = \frac{3}{4} \bullet \frac{3}{2} = \frac{9}{8}$

Step 3 Simplify if possible.

$\frac{9}{8} = 1\frac{1}{8}$.

Step 4 Check. Does $\frac{3}{4} \div \frac{2}{3} = 1\frac{1}{8}$?

$\frac{3}{4}$	$\div$	$\frac{2}{3}$	$=$	$1\frac{1}{8}$
dividend		divisor		quotient

Quotient • divisor = dividend

$\frac{9}{8} \bullet \frac{2}{3} = \frac{9 \bullet 2}{8 \bullet 3} = \frac{18}{24} = \frac{3}{4}$ True

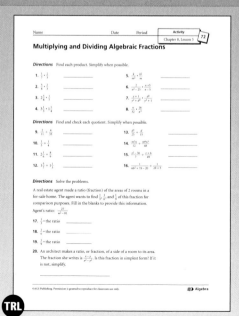

Workbook Activity 77 — Multiplying and Dividing Algebraic Fractions (Chapter 8, Lesson 3)

Activity 72 — Multiplying and Dividing Algebraic Fractions (Chapter 8, Lesson 3)

Workbook Activity 77

Activity 72

EXAMPLE 2 Find the quotient of $1\frac{1}{2}x \div \frac{3x^2}{4}$.

Step 1 Rewrite $1\frac{1}{2}$ as an improper fraction.

$1\frac{1}{2}x \div \frac{3x^2}{4} = \frac{3x}{2} \div \frac{3x^2}{4}$

Step 2 Divide by multiplying by the reciprocal.

In this example, $\frac{3x^2}{4}$ and $\frac{4}{3x^2}$ are reciprocals.

$\frac{3x}{2} \div \frac{3x^2}{4} = \frac{3x}{2} \bullet \frac{4}{3x^2} = \frac{12x}{6x^2}$

Step 3 Simplify if possible.

$\frac{12x}{6x^2} = \frac{2 \bullet \cancel{2} \bullet \cancel{3} \bullet \cancel{x}}{\cancel{2} \bullet \cancel{3} \bullet \cancel{x} \bullet x} = \frac{2}{x}$

Step 4 Check. Does $1\frac{1}{2}x \div \frac{3x^2}{4} = \frac{2}{x}$?

$1\frac{1}{2}x$	$\div$	$\frac{3x^2}{4}$	$=$	$\frac{2}{x}$
dividend		divisor		quotient

Quotient • divisor = dividend

$\frac{2}{x} \bullet \frac{3x^2}{4} = \frac{6x^2}{4x} = \frac{\cancel{2} \bullet 3 \bullet x \bullet \cancel{x}}{\cancel{2} \bullet 2 \bullet \cancel{x}} = \frac{3x}{2}$ or $1\frac{1}{2}x$ True

Writing About Mathematics

Show why a number times its reciprocal is equal to 1. Explain your work.

Exercise A Find each product. Simplify your answers whenever possible.

1. $\frac{3}{4} \bullet \frac{5}{6}$ $\quad \frac{5}{8}$
2. $\frac{7}{8} \bullet \frac{2}{3}$ $\quad \frac{7}{12}$
3. $(3\frac{1}{3}) \bullet \frac{4}{5}$ $\quad 2\frac{2}{3}$
4. $(2\frac{7}{8})(1\frac{5}{6})$ $\quad 5\frac{13}{48}$
5. $(\frac{x}{a^2})(\frac{a^3}{x^2})$ $\quad \frac{a}{x}$
6. $(\frac{d}{t^2}) \bullet \frac{d^2}{t}$
7. $\frac{1}{(a^2 - 25)} \bullet \frac{(a + 5)}{(a - 5)}$
8. $\frac{(x + 1)}{(b^2x^2 + b^2)} \bullet \frac{(b^2)}{(x + 1)}$
9. $\frac{(1 - x^2)}{(b^2x^2 - 1)} \bullet \frac{(bx + 1)}{(x + 1)}$
10. $\frac{(a^2 + 10a + 25)}{(b - 5)} \bullet \frac{(b^2 - 10b + 25)}{(a + 5)}$

6. $\frac{d^3}{t^3}$
7. $\frac{1}{(a - 5)^2}$
8. $\frac{1}{(x^2 + 1)}$
9. $\frac{(1 - x)}{(bx - 1)}$
10. $(a + 5)(b - 5)$

Exercise B Find and check each quotient. Simplify your answers whenever possible

11. $\frac{3}{4} \div \frac{5}{6}$ $\quad \frac{9}{10}$
12. $\frac{7}{8} \div \frac{2}{3}$ $\quad 1\frac{5}{16}$
13. $(3\frac{1}{3}) \div \frac{4}{5}$ $\quad 4\frac{1}{6}$
14. $(2\frac{7}{8}) \div (1\frac{5}{6})$ $\quad 1\frac{25}{44}$
15. $(\frac{x}{a^2}) \div (\frac{a^3}{x^2})$ $\quad \frac{x^3}{a^5}$
16. $(\frac{-d}{t^2}) \div \frac{d^2}{t}$
17. $\frac{1}{(a^2 - 25)} \div \frac{(a + 5)}{(a - 5)}$
18. $\frac{(x + 1)}{(b^2x^2 + b^2)} \div \frac{(b^2)}{(x + 1)}$
19. $\frac{(x^2 - 1)}{(b^2x^2 - 1)} \div \frac{(bx + 1)}{(x + 1)}$
20. $\frac{(a^2 + 10a + 25)}{(b - 5)} \div \frac{(b^2 - 10b + 25)}{(a + 5)}$

16. $\frac{-1}{td}$
17. $\frac{1}{(a + 5)^2}$
18. $\frac{(x + 1)^2}{b^4(x^2 + 1)}$
19. $\frac{(x - 1)(x + 1)^2}{(bx - 1)(bx + 1)^2}$
20. $\frac{(a + 5)^3}{(b - 5)^3}$

3 Reinforce and Extend

LEARNING STYLES

LEP/ESL

Multiplying and dividing algebraic fractions may be difficult for some students. Give them exercises using the same fractions in the same order but different operations. For example,

$\frac{5x^2}{3} \bullet \frac{6x}{5}$ $\qquad \frac{5x^2}{3} \div \frac{6x}{5}$

$\frac{3}{4} \bullet \frac{8}{9}$ $\qquad \frac{3}{4} \div \frac{8}{9}$

$2\frac{1}{2} \bullet \frac{5}{6}$ $\qquad 2\frac{1}{2} \div \frac{5}{6}$

$\frac{1}{(y - 16)} \bullet (y + 4)$

$\frac{1}{(y - 16)} \div (y + 4)$

$(b + 2) \bullet (b - 2)$

$(b + 2) \div (b - 2)$

Have students explain what they are doing and why.

MENTAL MATH

Have students calculate these problems mentally.

$\frac{3}{4x} \bullet \frac{4x}{3}$	(1)
$\frac{6y^2}{5} \div \frac{6y^2}{10}$	(2)
$(2c + 5) \div (2c + 5)$	(1)
$\frac{(x + 4)}{(x^2 + 16)} \bullet \frac{(x^2 + 16)}{(x + 4)}$	(1)
$\frac{15}{16} \div \frac{15}{32}$	(2)

MATH HISTORY

The symbols for mathematical and algebraic operations come from various sources. Many were used in practice long before they appeared in any printed or published form. One of the earliest documents showing a plus sign (+) is a German manuscript written in 1456. The Latin word *et*, which means "and" indicated addition as in "5 et 7." The person who wrote the manuscript used a shortened form that looked somewhat like +. Most scholars agree, however, that the first published use of the plus sign was in a Dutch book, *Een sonderlinghe boeck in dye edel conste Arithmetica*, written by Giel Vander Hoecke and printed in 1514. The book also used the minus sign (−) to indicate subtraction.

Lesson at a Glance

Chapter 8 Lesson 4

Overview This lesson demonstrates how to find the least common multiple for a pair of numbers and how to simplify complex fractions.

Objectives

- To find the least common multiple for a pair of numbers
- To simplify complex fractions

Student Pages 226–229

Teacher's Resource Library 

Workbook Activity 78

Activity 73

Alternative Activity 73

Mathematics Vocabulary

complex fraction
least common multiple (LCM)

Warm-Up Activity

Have students write fractions from these division problems.

$5 \div 8$	$(\frac{5}{8})$
$13 \div 16$	$(\frac{13}{16})$
$1 \div 2$	$(\frac{1}{2})$
$7 \div 8$	$(\frac{7}{8})$
$3 \div 4$	$(\frac{3}{4})$

This will lead into the discussion of complex fractions and the LCM.

Teaching the Lesson

Present the material in two different ways. First, go over the example on page 226. This example shows how a complex fraction can be rewritten as a division problem. Second, go over the examples on page 227. These examples show how the LCM can be used to simplify complex fractions. Third, go over the examples on page 227 as division problems. Some students may find this is much easier than finding the LCM.

Lesson 4 Complex Fractions and the LCM

Complex fraction
A fraction in which the numerator, the denominator, or both the numerator and the denominator are fractions

Least common multiple (LCM)
The smallest number that two or more numbers can divide into without leaving a remainder

Recall there are two ways to represent a whole number division computation.

$12 \div 4 = 3$ and $\frac{12}{4} = 3$

There are also two ways to represent division of fractions.

$\frac{3}{2} \div \frac{3}{4} = 2$ can also be written as $\frac{\frac{3}{2}}{\frac{3}{4}} = 2.$

$\frac{\frac{3}{2}}{\frac{3}{4}}$ is an example of a **complex fraction.**

Other examples of complex fractions include

$\frac{3}{\frac{5}{7}} \qquad \frac{\frac{1}{3}}{5} \qquad \frac{x}{\frac{a}{b}} \qquad \frac{\frac{a}{b}}{\frac{c}{d}}$

You can simplify a complex fraction by removing the denominator in each fractional part.

EXAMPLE 1 Simplify $\frac{\frac{1}{3}}{5}$.

Step 1 One way to simplify complex fractions is to think of the fraction bar as a division symbol.

$\frac{\frac{1}{3}}{5} = \frac{1}{3} \div 5$

Step 2 Find $\frac{1}{3} \div 5$.

Write the whole number 5 as the improper fraction $\frac{5}{1}$.

$\frac{1}{3} \div 5 = \frac{1}{3} \div \frac{5}{1} = \frac{1}{3} \bullet \frac{1}{5} = \frac{1}{15}$

To find a quotient of two fractions, multiply the dividend by the reciprocal of the divisor.

Another way to simplify complex fractions is to find and multiply the numerator and denominator by the **least common multiple,** or **LCM,** of the two denominators.

Workbook Activity 78 — Complex Fractions and the LCM

Activity 73 — Complex Fractions and the LCM

EXAMPLE 2

Simplify $\dfrac{\frac{2}{15}}{\frac{3}{10}}$.

Step 1 Find the LCM of each denominator.

Multiples of 15: 15, **30**, 45, 60, 75, ...

Multiples of 10: 10, 20, **30**, 40, 50, ...

The LCM is 30.

Step 2 Multiply the numerator and denominator of the complex fraction by 30.

$$\dfrac{\frac{2}{15}}{\frac{3}{10}} \bullet \frac{30}{30}$$

Multiplying by $\frac{30}{30}$ is the same as multiplying by $\frac{1}{1}$ or 1—multiplying by 1 does not change the value of the fraction.

Step 3 Simplify.

$$\dfrac{\frac{2}{15}}{\frac{3}{10}} \bullet \frac{30}{30} = \dfrac{\frac{2}{15}}{\frac{3}{10}} \bullet \dfrac{\frac{30}{1}}{\frac{30}{1}} = \dfrac{\frac{60}{15}}{\frac{90}{10}} = \frac{4}{9}$$

EXAMPLE 3

Simplify $\dfrac{\frac{5}{7x}}{\frac{2}{3x}}$.

Step 1 Find the LCM of each denominator.

Multiples of $7x$: $7x$, $14x$, $\mathbf{21x}$, $28x$, $35x$, $42x$, ...

Multiples of $3x$: $3x$, $6x$, $9x$, $12x$, $15x$, $18x$, $\mathbf{21x}$, $24x$, $27x$, ...

The LCM is $21x$.

Step 2 Multiply the numerator and denominator of the complex fraction by $21x$.

$$\dfrac{\frac{5}{7x}}{\frac{2}{3x}} \bullet \frac{21x}{21x}$$

Step 3 Simplify.

$$\dfrac{\frac{5}{7x}}{\frac{2}{3x}} \bullet \frac{21x}{21x} = \dfrac{\frac{5}{7x}}{\frac{2}{3x}} \bullet \dfrac{\frac{21x}{1}}{\frac{21x}{1}} = \dfrac{\frac{105x}{7x}}{\frac{42x}{3x}} = \frac{15}{14} = 1\frac{1}{14}$$

COMMON ERROR

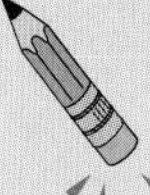

When dividing fractions, some students will take the reciprocal of both fractions. Stress to students that they should take the reciprocal of the second fraction only.

3 Reinforce and Extend

LEARNING STYLES

Auditory/Verbal

Have students write a paragraph on how to find the least common multiple and how to simplify complex fractions. Have each student read the paragraph to the class. To evaluate the oral paragraphs, have the audience listen for

____ clear explanation.

____ specific examples.

____ correct solutions.

ONLINE CONNECTION

Even 0.5% interest makes a big difference in the amount you pay for a car or home loan. Give students a hypothetical loan amount for a home or car and have them look through local newspapers to find loan rates from three loan institutions. Then have them visit www.bankrate.com/brm/popcalc2.asp?nav=calc_loan_payment&page=default to calculate loan payments using the interest rates they've found in the newspaper from the three loan institutions.

Calculator

Have students use their calculators to simplify these problems.

$\frac{1}{\frac{654}{981}}$ $(1\frac{1}{2})$

$\frac{7}{\frac{699}{833}}$ $(8\frac{239}{699})$

$\frac{10}{\frac{577}{55}}$ $(\frac{550}{577})$

$\frac{2}{\frac{332}{525}}$ $(3\frac{27}{166})$

$\frac{6}{\frac{125}{369}}$ $(17\frac{89}{125})$

Mental Math

Have students look at the following problems to find a pattern.

$\frac{4}{\frac{1}{2}} = 8$

$\frac{5}{\frac{1}{2}} = 10$

$\frac{7}{\frac{1}{2}} = 14$

$\frac{8}{\frac{1}{2}} = 16$

$\frac{10}{\frac{1}{2}} = 20$

Then have students solve these problems mentally.

$\frac{50}{\frac{1}{2}}$ *(100)* $\frac{75}{\frac{1}{2}}$ *(150)*

$\frac{200}{\frac{1}{2}}$ *(400)* $\frac{1000}{\frac{1}{2}}$ *(2,000)*

$\frac{2500}{\frac{1}{2}}$ *(5,000)*

Example 4 $\frac{a}{b} \div \frac{c}{d}$ can be written as $\frac{\frac{a}{b}}{\frac{c}{d}}$

and $\frac{\frac{a}{b}}{\frac{c}{d}} \bullet \frac{(\frac{d}{c})}{(\frac{d}{c})} = \frac{\frac{ad}{bc}}{\frac{\cancel{cd}}{\cancel{dc}}} = \frac{ad}{bc}$.

Therefore, the rule for division of fractions is

$\frac{a}{b} \div \frac{c}{d} = \frac{a}{b} \bullet \frac{d}{c}$.

Exercise A Find the least common multiple for each pair.

1. 3, 4 12
2. 5, 2 10
3. 7, 8 56
4. 6, 7 42
5. 4, 9 36
6. 8, 3 24
7. 7, 21 21
8. 10, 12 60
9. 18, 6 18
10. $4a, 7a$ $28a$
11. $8n, 2n$ $8n$
12. $9x, 7x$ $63x$
13. $4r, 5r$ $20r$
14. $4m, 25m$ $100m$
15. $9b, 11b$ $99b$

Exercise B Simplify.

16. $\frac{1}{\frac{3}{5}}$ $1\frac{2}{3}$
17. $\frac{4}{\frac{1}{2}}$ 8
18. $\frac{\frac{2}{3}}{7}$ $\frac{2}{21}$
19. $\frac{\frac{5}{6}}{3}$ $\frac{5}{18}$
20. $\frac{\frac{3}{4}}{2}$ $\frac{3}{8}$
21. $\frac{4}{\frac{11}{12}}$ $4\frac{4}{11}$
22. $\frac{6}{\frac{7}{8}}$ $6\frac{6}{7}$
23. $\frac{\frac{3}{8}}{5}$ $\frac{3}{40}$
24. $\frac{10}{\frac{1}{5}}$ 50
25. $\frac{\frac{3}{8}}{\frac{2}{3}}$ $\frac{9}{16}$

26.	$\dfrac{\frac{2}{5}}{\frac{5}{6}}$	$\frac{12}{25}$	31.	$\dfrac{\frac{6}{25n}}{\frac{3}{4n}}$	$\frac{8}{25}$
27.	$\dfrac{\frac{2}{3}}{\frac{3}{4}}$	$\frac{8}{9}$	32.	$\dfrac{\frac{2x}{3}}{5x}$	$\frac{2}{15}$
28.	$\dfrac{\frac{2}{9}}{\frac{3}{7}}$	$\frac{14}{27}$	33.	$\dfrac{\frac{1}{2a}}{\frac{5}{6a}}$	$\frac{3}{5}$
29.	$\dfrac{\frac{1}{2n}}{\frac{9}{10n}}$	$\frac{5}{9}$	34.	$\dfrac{\frac{3x}{16}}{\frac{1}{4}}$	$\frac{3x}{4}$
30.	$\dfrac{\frac{4}{7x}}{\frac{2}{9x}}$	$2\frac{4}{7}$	35.	$\dfrac{\frac{1}{8h}}{\frac{2}{9}}$	$\frac{9}{16h}$

Writing About Mathematics

Take any two prime numbers, such as 3 and 5. Can you figure out an easy way to find their LCM? Test your theory by trying it out on another pair of prime numbers.

PROBLEM SOLVING

Exercise C Use the formulas $d = rt$, $r = \frac{d}{t}$, and $t = \frac{d}{r}$ to solve these problems, in which d = distance in miles, r = speed in miles per hour, and t = time in hours.

These facts are related to driving each day of a five-day vacation.

Day 1: 45 miles per hour; 5.5 hours

Day 2: $264\frac{1}{2}$ miles; $5\frac{3}{4}$ hours

Day 3: $13\frac{1}{2}$ miles per hour; $10\frac{1}{8}$ miles

Day 4: $2\frac{3}{4}$ hours; 77 miles

Day 5: $97\frac{1}{2}$ miles; 39 miles per hour

36. Find the distance driven on Day 1. 247.5 miles

37. Find the average rate of speed on Day 2. 46 mph

38. Find the time spent driving on Day 3. 45 minutes

39. Find the average rate of speed on Day 4. 28 mph

40. Find the time spent driving on Day 5. $2\frac{1}{2}$ hours

TRY THIS Simplify this complex fraction:

$\dfrac{x}{\frac{a}{b}}$ $\quad \frac{xb}{a}$

Try This

Have students first simplify simpler problems such as the following:

$\dfrac{4}{\frac{5}{b}}$ $\quad (\frac{4b}{5})$

$\dfrac{4}{\frac{a}{b}}$ $\quad (\frac{4b}{a})$

Group Problem Solving

To extend students' thinking, have small groups of students write their own complex fractions under the following conditions. Five problems must be algebraic, and five must be numerical. The solutions to the problems must be 1, 2, 3, 4, 5, 6, 7, 8, 9, and 10. Call on one group to give you one of its complex fractions. Call on another group to simplify that fraction.

At Home

Have students use a map to find distances between places in their community or state. Then ask them to use these numbers to write word problems about distance, time, and rate similar to those in Exercise C. Have pairs of students exchange and solve each other's problems.

Lesson at a Glance

Chapter 8 Lesson 5

Overview This lesson explains how to use prime factorization to find the least common multiple and how to use factorization to simplify complex fractions.

Objectives

- To use prime factorization to find the least common multiple
- To use factorization to simplify complex fractions

Student Pages 230–231

Teacher's Resource Library 

Workbook Activity 79

Activity 74

Alternative Activity 74

 Warm-Up Activity

Have students use their calculators to find the least common multiple of each pair of numbers by listing their multiples.

16 and 36	*(144)*
12 and 30	*(60)*
18 and 42	*(126)*
24 and 14	*(168)*
12 and 9	*(36)*

Note to students that listing multiples is one way to find the least common multiple. This will lead into discussion on how to use prime factorization to find the least common multiple.

 Teaching the Lesson

Write the example on page 230 on the board to show how prime factorization can be used to find the least common multiple, which can be used to simplify a complex fraction. Using the same process, show students how the algebraic example on page 230 can be solved.

Lesson 5 Least Common Multiples and Prime Factors

Recall that you can find the least common multiple (LCM) of two numbers by listing the multiples of each number. You can also find the LCM using prime factors.

EXAMPLE 1 Simplify $\dfrac{\frac{5}{12}}{\frac{3}{10}}$ using prime factors.

Step 1 List the prime factors of 12 and 10.

$12 = 2 \cdot 2 \cdot 3$

$10 = 2 \cdot 5$

Step 2 Count the greatest number of times each prime factor occurs in either factorization.

The greatest number of times the factor 2 appears is twice.

$12 = 2 \cdot 2 \cdot 3$

$10 = 2 \cdot 5$

The greatest number of times the factor 3 appears is once.

$12 = 2 \cdot 2 \cdot 3$

$10 = 2 \cdot 5$

The greatest number of times the factor 5 appears is once.

$12 = 2 \cdot 2 \cdot 3$

$10 = 2 \cdot 5$

Step 3 Find the product of the greatest number of times each factor appears.

$2 \cdot 2 \cdot 3 \cdot 5 = 60$

The LCM of 12 and 10 is 60.

Step 4 Multiply both the numerator and the denominator by 60.

$$\dfrac{\frac{5}{12}}{\frac{3}{10}} \cdot \frac{60}{60} = \dfrac{\frac{300}{12}}{\frac{180}{10}} = \frac{25}{18} = 1\frac{7}{18}$$

Name Date Period | Workbook Activity 79 | Chapter 8, Lesson 5

Least Common Multiples and Prime Factors

EXAMPLE Find the LCM of 12 and 10.

Step 1 List prime factors of the denominators, 12 and 10.

$12 = 2 \cdot 2 \cdot 3$ $10 = 2 \cdot 5$

Step 2 Count prime factors:

- greatest number of times 2 appears: twice $(2 \cdot 2)$
- greatest number of times 3 appears: once (3)
- greatest number of times 5 appears: once (5)

Step 3 Find the product of the above:

$2 \cdot 2 \cdot 3 \cdot 5 = 60 =$ LCM of 12 and 10

Directions Using prime factorization, find the least common multiple for each pair.

1. 3, 8 ______
2. 15, 25 ______
3. 14, 38 ______
4. 6, 14 ______
5. 16, 10 ______
6. 5, 7 ______
7. x^4y, xy^2 ______
8. cd^4, c^2d^3 ______

Directions Solve the problems.

9. A store display has 2 blinking lights. One blinks every 15 seconds and the other blanks every 12 seconds. After how many seconds will the lights blink at the same instant? (Hint: find the LCM of the numbers.) ______

10. Geri has play blocks that are 4 inches tall. Bette has blocks that are 6 inches tall. Suppose the two tots each stack their own blocks into towers, side by side. What is the *least* height at which both towers can be the same height? ______

 Algebra

TRL

Workbook Activity 79

Name Date Period | Activity 74 | Chapter 8, Lesson 5

Least Common Multiples and Prime Factors

Directions Use factorization to simplify these complex fractions. Write the answers in simplest form.

1. $\dfrac{\frac{1}{3}}{\frac{3}{4}}$ ______
2. $\dfrac{\frac{2}{5}}{\frac{7}{9}}$ ______
3. $\dfrac{\frac{7}{11}}{\frac{1}{2}}$ ______
4. $\dfrac{\frac{2}{5}}{\frac{8}{15}}$ ______
5. $\dfrac{\frac{11}{20}}{\frac{5}{6}}$ ______
6. $\dfrac{\frac{9}{10}}{\frac{1}{10}}$ ______
7. $\dfrac{ak}{\frac{k}{a}}$ ______
8. $\dfrac{\frac{15}{18}}{\frac{22}{27}}$ ______
9. $\dfrac{\frac{2b^2}{9x^2}}{\frac{3b}{2x^2}}$ ______
10. $\dfrac{\frac{7}{n-1}}{4}$ ______
11. $\dfrac{\frac{5}{7n}}{\frac{2}{3n}}$ ______
12. $\dfrac{\frac{5a^2}{9b^2}}{\frac{3a}{ab^2}}$ ______

Directions Solve the problems.

13. In a toy store, 2 toy trains are set up to run continuously. One train completes its circle every 24 seconds. The other completes its circle every 36 seconds. After how many seconds will the two trains be at their starting points at the same instant? (Hint: find the LCM.) ______

14. Two thicknesses of paper are produced in a paper factory. The better paper stacks 42 pages per cm height. The cheaper paper stacks 56 pages per cm height. To what height, in cm, must the two papers be stacked, side by side, for the heights of the stacks to become equal? ______

15. An electric company operates two power plants. At Power Station 1, the older plant, engineers perform full maintenance every 6 months. At Station 2, a new plant, they perform full maintenance every 9 months. Occasionally, full maintenance for both plants falls on the same month. How often does this happen? ______

 Algebra

TRL

Activity 74

Writing About Mathematics

Which method for dividing fractions do you prefer? Why?

$\frac{3}{4} \div \frac{1}{2} = \frac{3}{4} \bullet \frac{2}{1} =$

$\frac{3 \bullet 2}{4 \bullet 1} = \frac{6}{4} = \frac{3}{2} = 1\frac{1}{2}$

or $\frac{3}{4} \div \frac{1}{2} = \frac{\frac{3}{4}}{\frac{1}{2}} =$

$\frac{\frac{3}{4}}{\frac{1}{2}} \bullet \frac{4}{4} = \frac{\frac{3}{4} \bullet \frac{4}{1}}{\frac{1}{2} \bullet \frac{4}{1}} = \frac{3}{2}$

$= 1\frac{1}{2}$

EXAMPLE 2 Simplify $\dfrac{\frac{a}{b^2}}{\frac{c}{bd}}$.

Step 1 Find the LCM of b^2 and bd.

$b^2 = b \bullet b \quad bd = b \bullet d$

The LCM of b^2 and bd is $b \bullet b \bullet d$ or b^2d.

Step 2 Multiply both the numerator and the denominator by b^2d.

$$\frac{\frac{a}{b^2}}{\frac{c}{bd}} \bullet \frac{b^2d}{b^2d} = \frac{\frac{ab^2d}{b^2}}{\frac{cb^2d}{bd}} = \frac{ad}{bc}$$

Exercise A Using prime factorization, find the least common multiple for each pair.

1. 3, 5 15
2. 2, 8 8
3. 6, 10 30
4. 12, 3 12
5. 7, 28 28
6. 18, 24 72
7. 21, 14 42
8. a^2b^2, a^3bc a^3b^2c
9. x^3y^2, x^2y x^3y^2
10. r^3s^2t, r^2t r^3s^2t

Exercise B Use factorization to simplify these complex fractions. Write your answer in simplest form.

11. $\dfrac{\frac{2}{3}}{\frac{1}{2}}$ $1\frac{1}{3}$
12. $\dfrac{\frac{4}{5}}{\frac{7}{15}}$ $1\frac{5}{7}$
13. $\dfrac{\frac{7}{18}}{\frac{5}{27}}$ $2\frac{1}{10}$
14. $\dfrac{\frac{9}{20}}{\frac{3}{4}}$ $\frac{3}{5}$
15. $\dfrac{\frac{ax}{x}}{b}$ ab
16. $\dfrac{\frac{yx}{b}}{\frac{x}{bx}}$ xy
17. $\dfrac{\frac{8a^3}{6y^3}}{\frac{2a}{24y^2}}$ $\frac{16a^2}{y}$
18. $\dfrac{\frac{a}{x^2}}{\frac{a^2}{x^3}}$ $\frac{x}{a}$
19. $\dfrac{\frac{mn^2}{mn}}{\frac{x^2}{mn}}$ $\frac{mn^2}{x^2}$
20. $\dfrac{\frac{4xy^2}{8x^2}}{\frac{xy}{12x^3}}$ $6xy$

Common Error

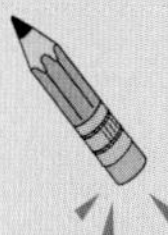

Stress that in prime factorization you can only use prime numbers. Some students will try to use composite numbers, such as 4, 6, 9, and so on. To help prevent students from using composite numbers, write the first ten prime numbers on the board:

The First Ten Prime Numbers

2 3 5 7 11 13 17 19 23 29

Then ask students to explain why the following are not examples of prime factorization.

$12 = 6 \cdot 2$

(6 is a composite number.)

$25 = 1 \cdot 5 \cdot 5$

(1 is not prime.)

$36 = 4 \cdot 9$

(4 and 9 are composite numbers.)

$100 = 25 \cdot 2 \cdot 2$

(25 is a composite number.)

$51 = 51$

(51 is a composite number.)

3 Reinforce and Extend

Calculator

Have students use their calculators to find the original numbers from these prime factorizations.

$2 \cdot 3 \cdot 5 \cdot 7 \cdot 11 \cdot 13$

(30,030)

$3 \cdot 7 \cdot 11 \cdot 17 \cdot 23 \cdot 37$

(3,341,877)

$x \cdot x \cdot 5 \cdot 19 \cdot 53 \cdot 97$

($488{,}395x^2$)

$y \cdot y \cdot y \cdot 2 \cdot 7 \cdot 67 \cdot 71$

($66{,}598y^3$)

$m \cdot m \cdot m \cdot m \cdot 19 \cdot 43 \cdot 47$

($38{,}399m^4$)

Learning Styles

Logical/Mathematical

Have each student pick four composite numbers between 100 and 1,000 and find the prime factorizations. For example,

$121 = 11 \cdot 11$

$200 = 2 \cdot 2 \cdot 2 \cdot 5 \cdot 5$

$925 = 5 \cdot 5 \cdot 37$

$620 = 2 \cdot 2 \cdot 5 \cdot 31$

Have students write the factored form on a piece of paper. Ask pairs of students to exchange papers and find the original numbers.

Lesson at a Glance

Chapter 8 Lesson 6

Overview This lesson demonstrates how to use the LCM to add or subtract fractions and write them in simplest form.

Objectives

- To use the LCM to add or subtract fractions
- To write fractions in simplest form

Student Pages 232–233

Teacher's Resource Library 

Workbook Activity 80

Activity 75

Alternative Activity 75

1 Warm-Up Activity

Draw these number lines on the board and ask students to write a number sentence to describe each.

Student response: $\frac{5}{8} + \frac{7}{8} = 1\frac{4}{8} = 1\frac{1}{2}$

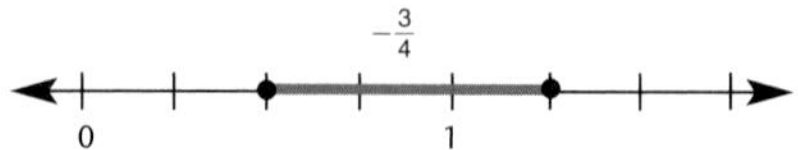

Student response: $1\frac{1}{4} - \frac{3}{4} = \frac{2}{4} = \frac{1}{2}$

Teaching the Lesson

Explain the examples on page 232 by doing them on the board. Note to students the connection between numerical fractions and algebraic fractions. Both can be added or subtracted, both require finding the LCM, and both can be written in simplest form.

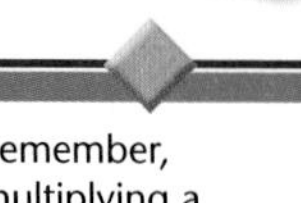

Lesson 6 Sums and Differences

Algebra and arithmetic have a great deal in common. For example, to add or subtract arithmetic or algebraic fractions with unlike denominators, you must first find a common denominator.

> Remember, multiplying a number by 1 does not change the value of the number.

EXAMPLE 1 Subtract $\frac{1}{10}$ from $\frac{3}{4}$.

Step 1 The denominators are unlike. Find the LCM of 4 and 10.

$4 = 2 \bullet 2$

$10 = 2 \bullet 5$

The LCM of 4 and 10 is $2 \bullet 2 \bullet 5 = 20$.

Step 2 Multiply each fraction by 1 in a form that will make the denominator 20.

$\frac{3}{4} - \frac{1}{10} = \frac{3}{4} \bullet \left[\frac{5}{5}\right] - \frac{1}{10}\left[\frac{2}{2}\right] = \frac{15}{20} - \frac{2}{20} = \frac{15-2}{20} = \frac{13}{20}$

Follow the same method when adding or subtracting algebraic fractions.

EXAMPLE 2 Find the sum of $\frac{3}{y} + \frac{2}{y}$.

Because the fractions have like denominators, you can add without rewriting.

$\frac{3}{y} + \frac{2}{y} = \frac{3+2}{y} = \frac{5}{y}$

Find the sum of $\frac{3}{x^2y^5} + \frac{2}{xy^3}$.

Step 1 The denominators are unlike. Find the LCM of x^2y^5 and xy^3.

$x^2y^5 = x \bullet x \bullet y \bullet y \bullet y \bullet y \bullet y$

$xy^3 = x \bullet y \bullet y \bullet y$

The LCM of x^2y^5 and xy^3 is $x \bullet x \bullet y \bullet y \bullet y \bullet y \bullet y = x^2y^5$.

Step 2 Multiply each fraction by a form of 1 so that each fraction denominator is x^2y^5.

$\frac{3}{x^2y^5}\left[\frac{1}{1}\right] + \frac{2}{xy^3}\left[\frac{xy^2}{xy^2}\right] = \frac{3}{x^2y^5} + \frac{2xy^2}{x^2y^5}$

Step 3 Simplify by adding the fractions.

$\frac{3}{x^2y^5} + \frac{2xy^2}{x^2y^5} = \frac{3 + 2xy^2}{x^2y^5}$

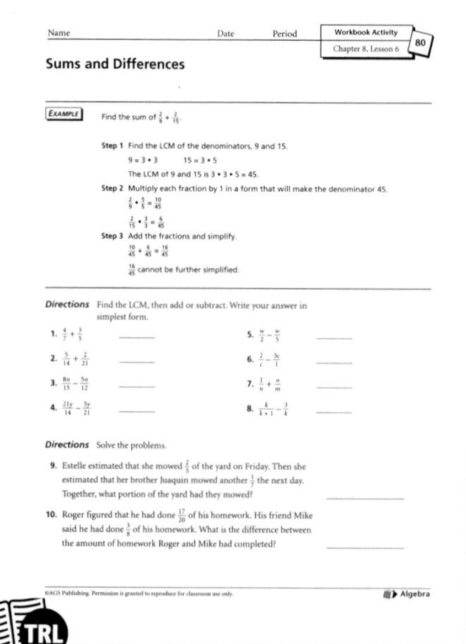

Name Date Period **Workbook Activity 80** Chapter 8, Lesson 6

Sums and Differences

EXAMPLE Find the sum of $\frac{2}{9} + \frac{2}{15}$.

Step 1 Find the LCM of the denominators, 9 and 15.

$9 = 3 \bullet 3$ $15 = 3 \bullet 5$

The LCM of 9 and 15 is $3 \bullet 3 \bullet 5 = 45$.

Step 2 Multiply each fraction by 1 in a form that will make the denominator 45.

$\frac{2}{9} \bullet \frac{5}{5} = \frac{10}{45}$

$\frac{2}{15} \bullet \frac{3}{3} = \frac{6}{45}$

Step 3 Add the fractions and simplify.

$\frac{10}{45} + \frac{6}{45} = \frac{16}{45}$

$\frac{16}{45}$ cannot be further simplified.

Directions Find the LCM, then add or subtract. Write your answer in simplest form.

1. $\frac{4}{7} + \frac{3}{5}$ ____
2. $\frac{5}{14} + \frac{2}{21}$ ____
3. $\frac{8n}{15} - \frac{5n}{12}$ ____
4. $\frac{21y}{14} - \frac{5y}{21}$ ____
5. $\frac{w}{2} - \frac{w}{5}$ ____
6. $\frac{2}{c} - \frac{3c}{1}$ ____
7. $\frac{1}{n} + \frac{n}{m}$ ____
8. $\frac{k}{k+1} - \frac{3}{k}$ ____

Directions Solve the problems.

9. Estelle estimated that she mowed $\frac{2}{5}$ of the yard on Friday. Then she estimated that her brother Juaquin mowed another $\frac{1}{7}$ the next day. Together, what portion of the yard had they mowed? ____
10. Roger figured that he had done $\frac{17}{20}$ of his homework. His friend Mike said he had done $\frac{3}{8}$ of his homework. What is the difference between the amount of homework Roger and Mike had completed? ____

 Algebra

TRL

Workbook Activity 80

Name Date Period **Activity 75** Chapter 8, Lesson 6

Sums and Differences

Directions Find the LCM of each pair.

1. 5, 12 ____
2. 2, 9 ____
3. 3, 7 ____
4. 11, 2 ____
5. 36, 24 ____
6. 27, 18 ____
7. 49, 21 ____
8. $6x$, $9x$ ____
9. $10w$, $15w$ ____
10. $9a^3$, $21a^2$ ____
11. d^5, $2d$ ____
12. mn^4, m^2n^3 ____

Directions Add or subtract. Write the answer in simplest form.

13. $\frac{1}{3} + \frac{7}{8}$ ____
14. $\frac{7}{9} + \frac{1}{5}$ ____
15. $\frac{4}{9} - \frac{2}{3}$ ____
16. $\frac{5}{12} + \frac{7}{18}$ ____
17. $\frac{2}{9} - \frac{-1}{10}$ ____
18. $\frac{3}{xy} + \frac{2}{3}$ ____
19. $\frac{11}{w} + \frac{7}{r}$ ____
20. $\frac{d+2}{5d} + \frac{d+4}{15d}$ ____
21. $\frac{1}{r} + \frac{1}{2r}$ ____
22. $\frac{4}{15} - \frac{6}{35}$ ____
23. $\frac{5}{a} - \frac{4}{3a}$ ____
24. $\frac{21k}{14} - \frac{5k}{21}$ ____
25. $\frac{-y}{9} + \frac{m}{10}$ ____
26. $\frac{x+1}{2} - \frac{3}{5}$ ____
27. $\frac{p}{2} - \frac{p}{5}$ ____
28. $\frac{a+5}{ab} - \frac{a-1}{a^2b}$ ____

Directions Solve the problems.

29. Keri has $\frac{2}{9}$ of a pizza, and Lisa has $\frac{1}{5}$ of a pizza. Together, what part of a whole pizza do they have? ____
30. In sewing class, cutting out a pattern takes $\frac{1}{5}$ of an hour, while sewing in a zipper takes $\frac{11}{12}$ of an hour. What is the time difference between these tasks, expressed as a fraction of an hour? ____

 Algebra

TRL

Activity 75

Exercise A Find the LCM, then add or subtract. Write your answer in simplest form.

1. $\frac{3}{4} + \frac{7}{8}$ $1\frac{5}{8}$
2. $\frac{3}{4} - \frac{7}{8}$ $\frac{-1}{8}$
3. $\frac{7}{8} + \frac{5}{24}$ $1\frac{1}{12}$
4. $\frac{7}{8} - \frac{5}{25}$ $\frac{27}{40}$
5. $\frac{3}{10} + \frac{3}{5}$ $\frac{9}{10}$
6. $\frac{4}{9} + \frac{4}{7}$ $1\frac{1}{63}$
7. $1\frac{1}{2} - \frac{5}{7}$ $\frac{11}{14}$
8. $-3\frac{2}{3} - \frac{5}{7}$ $-4\frac{8}{21}$
9. $4\frac{1}{8} + \frac{3}{5}$ $4\frac{29}{40}$
10. $\frac{2}{a} + \frac{3}{b}$ $\frac{3a + 2b}{ab}$
11. $\frac{10}{x} - \frac{7}{y}$ $\frac{10y - 7x}{xy}$
12. $\frac{5}{2} + \frac{2}{h}$ $\frac{5h + 4}{2h}$
13. $\frac{-2}{x^2} + \frac{3}{y}$ $\frac{3x^2 - 2y}{x^2y}$
14. $\frac{13}{p} - \frac{1}{2r}$ $\frac{26r - p}{2pr}$
15. $\frac{1}{a} + \frac{3}{a^2}$ $\frac{a + 3}{a^2}$
16. $\frac{9}{mn} - \frac{2}{np}$ $\frac{9p - 2m}{mnp}$
17. $\frac{25}{ab} - \frac{4}{acd}$ $\frac{25cd - 4b}{abcd}$
18. $\frac{2a}{p^2} + \frac{1}{pq}$ $\frac{2aq + p}{p^2q}$
19. $\frac{5x}{c^2d} - \frac{3x}{d^2c}$ $\frac{5dx - 3cx}{c^2d^2}$
20. $\frac{7a}{ab} + \frac{c}{b^2c}$ $\frac{7abc + ac}{ab^2c}$
21. $\frac{3}{a^2b} + \frac{4}{ab^2}$ $\frac{3b + 4a}{a^2b^2}$
22. $\frac{5}{x^2y^3} - \frac{7}{xy^2}$ $\frac{5 - 7xy}{x^2y^3}$
23. $\frac{5y}{ax^2} + \frac{7x}{ay^2}$ $\frac{5y^3 + 7x^3}{ax^2y^2}$
24. $\frac{3y}{m^2n} + \frac{3m}{ym}$ $\frac{3y^2 + 3m^2n}{m^2ny}$
25. $\frac{3xy}{4a^2b} + \frac{2a^2b}{7xy}$ $\frac{21x^2y^2 + 8a^4b^2}{28a^2bxy}$

Estimation Activity

Estimate: Find the sum of a set of mixed numbers.

$1\frac{1}{8} + 2\frac{3}{4} + 5\frac{1}{3} + 6\frac{2}{3} = ?$

Solution: Round to the nearest whole number. For fractions less than $\frac{1}{2}$, round down. For fractions $\frac{1}{2}$ and higher, round up.

$1 + 3 + 5 + 7 = 16$

The estimated sum is 16.

3 Reinforce and Extend

Learning Styles

Body/Kinesthetic

Have students model the addition and subtraction of fractions with fraction bars. Students can also construct fraction bars by drawing equal-size rectangles, cutting them out, and coloring halves red, thirds blue, eighths yellow, etc. After students model several problems, have them explain how to find the LCM with fraction bars and how to model equivalent fractions using the LCM.

At Home

Have students look in the business section of a newspaper to find ten local stocks and calculate the previous day's closing prices for the stocks. Ask each student to make four columns with the headings *Stock Name, Closing Price, Change,* and *Yesterday's Close* and write the appropriate information in each column for each stock. For example,

Stock Name	*Closing Price*
ABC Comp.	$55\frac{7}{8}$
Melock Inc.	$13\frac{15}{16}$
Zerro LP.	5

Change	*Yesterday's Close*
$+\frac{1}{8}$	$55\frac{7}{8} - \frac{1}{8} = 55\frac{3}{4}$
$-1\frac{7}{8}$	$13\frac{15}{16} + 1\frac{7}{8} = 15\frac{13}{16}$
$+3\frac{1}{2}$	$5 - 3\frac{1}{2} = 1\frac{1}{2}$

Mental Math

Have students estimate each sum or difference by rounding each fraction to the nearest half.

$\frac{6}{5} + \frac{7}{8}$ *(estimate 2)*

$4\frac{3}{8} - 2\frac{1}{5}$ *(estimate $2\frac{1}{2}$)*

$\frac{2}{9} - \frac{5}{8}$ *(estimate $-\frac{1}{2}$)*

$\frac{6x}{3} - \frac{2x}{5}$ *(estimate $\frac{3x}{2}$)*

$\frac{4y}{7} + \frac{6y}{13}$ *(estimate y)*

Lesson at a Glance

Chapter 8 Lesson 7

Overview This lesson demonstrates how proportions can be solved using fractions.

Objective

- To solve proportions using fractions

Student Pages 234–237

Teacher's Resource Library TRL

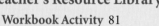

Workbook Activity 81

Activity 76

Alternative Activity 76

Warm-Up Activity

Ask students several questions to stimulate what they already know about proportions. For example, "If it takes a farmer 3 days to plant 7 acres of corn, how long will it take the farmer to plant 21 acres?" *(9 days)* "If a lawyer needs 6 days to prepare 2 cases, how many cases can be prepared in 36 days?" *(12 cases)* "If it takes Martha 15 minutes to complete one page of science homework, how much can she finish in 1 hour?" *(4 pages)*

Teaching the Lesson

Discuss the questions in the Warm-Up Activity and show how they can be set up as proportions. Then solve the problems by using cross products. Finally, go over the examples on pages 234 and 235.

Lesson 7 Proportions and Fractions in Equations

Recall that two equivalent rational numbers (such as $\frac{1}{2} = \frac{3}{6}$) form a proportion and in that proportion the cross products are equal.

$$(2 \cdot 3) = (1 \cdot 6)$$
$$6 = 6 \qquad \text{True}$$

You can check if $\frac{3}{4} = \frac{75}{100}$.

Using cross products, if (3)(100) is equal to the product (4)(75), the fractions are equivalent. Check if the products are equal.

$$(3)(100) = (4)(75)$$
$$300 = 300 \qquad \text{True}$$

You can use this idea to solve for an unknown in a proportion.

EXAMPLE 1 Solve $\frac{3}{n} = \frac{75}{100}$ for n.

Step 1 Set up the cross products.

$$(75)(n) = (3)(100)$$
$$75n = 300$$

Step 2 Solve for n.

$$\frac{75n}{75} = \frac{300}{75}$$
$$n = 4$$

Step 3 Check. (3)(100) = (4)(75)

$$300 = 300 \qquad \text{True}$$

You can also use this idea to solve for this unknown. Rectangle *A* has a base of 45 m and a height of 30 m. Rectangle *B*, a similar rectangle, has a height of 15 m.

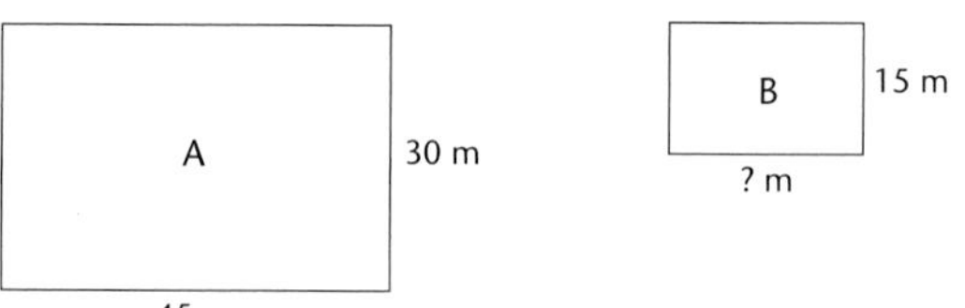

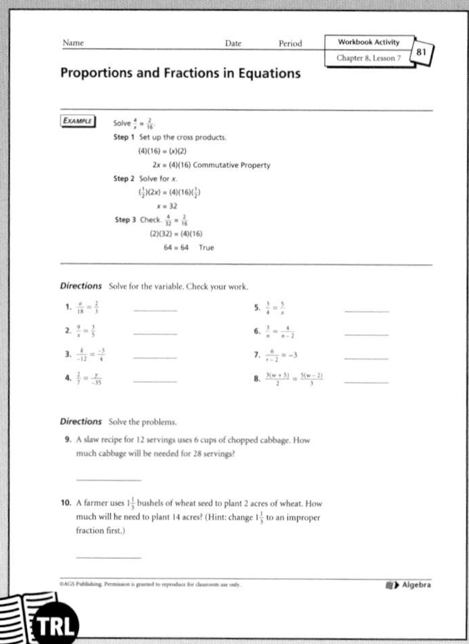

Name Date Period

Workbook Activity 81
Chapter 8, Lesson 7

Proportions and Fractions in Equations

EXAMPLE Solve $\frac{4}{x} = \frac{2}{16}$.

Step 1 Set up the cross products.

$(4)(16) = (x)(2)$

$2x = (4)(16)$ Commutative Property

Step 2 Solve for x.

$(\frac{1}{2})(2x) = (4)(16)(\frac{1}{2})$

$x = 32$

Step 3 Check. $\frac{4}{32} = \frac{2}{16}$

$(2)(32) = (4)(16)$

$64 = 64$ True

Directions Solve for the variable. Check your work.

1. $\frac{a}{18} = \frac{2}{3}$ ______
2. $\frac{9}{x} = \frac{3}{5}$ ______
3. $\frac{k}{-12} = \frac{-3}{4}$ ______
4. $\frac{2}{7} = \frac{y}{-35}$ ______
5. $\frac{3}{4} = \frac{5}{x}$ ______
6. $\frac{3}{n} = \frac{4}{n-2}$ ______
7. $\frac{6}{r-2} = -3$ ______
8. $\frac{3(w+5)}{2} = \frac{5(w-2)}{3}$ ______

Directions Solve the problems.

9. A slaw recipe for 12 servings uses 6 cups of chopped cabbage. How much cabbage will be needed for 28 servings?

______

10. A farmer uses $1\frac{1}{3}$ bushels of wheat seed to plant 2 acres of wheat. How much will he need to plant 14 acres? (Hint: change $1\frac{1}{3}$ to an improper fraction first.)

______

 Algebra

TRL

Workbook Activity 81

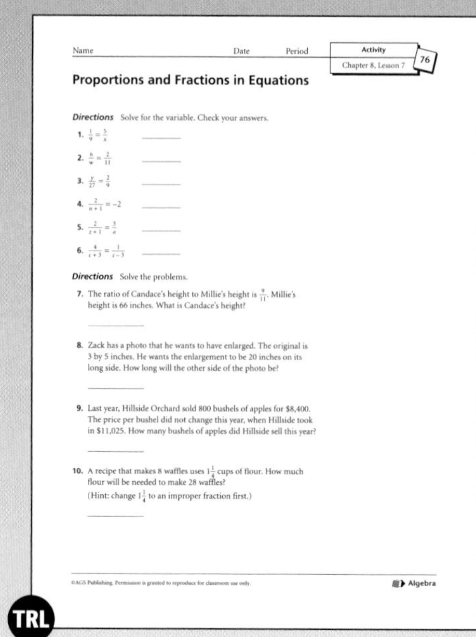

Name Date Period

Activity 76
Chapter 8, Lesson 7

Proportions and Fractions in Equations

Directions Solve for the variable. Check your answers.

1. $\frac{1}{9} = \frac{5}{x}$ ______
2. $\frac{6}{w} = \frac{2}{11}$ ______
3. $\frac{y}{27} = \frac{2}{9}$ ______
4. $\frac{2}{n+1} = -2$ ______
5. $\frac{2}{z+1} = \frac{3}{z}$ ______
6. $\frac{4}{c+3} = \frac{1}{c-3}$ ______

Directions Solve the problems.

7. The ratio of Candace's height to Millie's height is $\frac{9}{11}$. Millie's height is 66 inches. What is Candace's height?

______

8. Zack has a photo that he wants to have enlarged. The original is 3 by 5 inches. He wants the enlargement to be 20 inches on its long side. How long will the other side of the photo be?

______

9. Last year, Hillside Orchard sold 800 bushels of apples for $8,400. The price per bushel did not change this year, when Hillside took in $11,025. How many bushels of apples did Hillside sell this year?

______

10. A recipe that makes 8 waffles uses $1\frac{1}{4}$ cups of flour. How much flour will be needed to make 28 waffles? (Hint: change $1\frac{1}{4}$ to an improper fraction first.)

______

 Algebra

TRL

Activity 76

EXAMPLE 2 How long is the base of rectangle *B*?

Step 1 Set up a proportion.

$$\frac{\text{height of rectangle } A}{\text{height of rectangle } B} = \frac{\text{base of rectangle } A}{\text{base of rectangle } B}$$

$$\frac{30 \text{ m}}{15 \text{ m}} = \frac{45 \text{ m}}{\text{base of rectangle } B}$$

Step 2 Set up the cross products. Then solve for the unknown.

$$(30 \text{ m})(\text{base of rectangle } B) = (15 \text{ m})(45 \text{ m})$$

$$(\text{base of rectangle } B) = \frac{(15 \text{ m})(45 \text{ m})}{(30 \text{ m})}$$

$$\text{base of rectangle } B = 22.5 \text{ m}$$

Step 3 Check. $(15 \text{ m})(45 \text{ m}) = (30 \text{ m})(22.5 \text{ m})$

$675 \text{ m} = 675 \text{ m}$ True

Use cross products to solve this equation.

EXAMPLE 3 Solve $\frac{8}{4x - 1} = \frac{3}{x + 3}$ for x.

Step 1 Set up the cross products.

$(8)(x + 3) = (4x - 1)(3)$

Step 2 Solve for x.

$8(x + 3) = (4x - 1)(3)$

$8x + 24 = 12x - 3$

$27 = 4x$

$x = \frac{27}{4} = 6\frac{3}{4}$

Step 3 Check. $(8)(x + 3) = (4x - 1)(3)$

$(8)(6\frac{3}{4} + 3) = (27 - 1)(3)$

$78 = 78$ True

Common Error

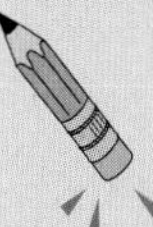

Some students may be confused about how to set up an equation using cross products. Stress that in using cross products, the numerator of one proportion is multiplied by the denominator of the other proportion. Thus, we *cross* the equal sign to multiply the numerator by the denominator.

3 Reinforce and Extend

Learning Styles

Body/Kinesthetic

Have students find and use their pulse rate as a proportion. Have one student be the timer to announce to the class when to start counting their heartbeats and when to stop counting. Have the timer time for one minute. Repeat this process three times to get three measurements. Have each student record his or her pulse rate as a proportion to every thirty seconds.

For example, $\frac{35 \text{ beats}}{30 \text{ seconds}}$.

Using the proportion in the middle, have students calculate how many times their hearts beat in a minute, hour, day, week, month, year, and decade.

Learning Styles

LEP/ESL

Have students classify each number or variable for problems 1 through 15 on page 236 as numerator, denominator, ratio, and proportion. This will help them better understand instructions written in English involving fractions.

Learning Styles

Interpersonal/ Group Learning

Have students work in groups of two or three on the problems on pages 236 and 237. All group members work out the problems on separate sheets of paper and check each other's answers. If they find their answers differ, they go over the problem together to find where the error was made and to correct it.

Exercise A Solve for the variable. Check your work.

1. $\frac{x}{4} = \frac{75}{100}$ 3
2. $\frac{3}{4} = \frac{x}{100}$ 75
3. $\frac{3}{4} = \frac{75}{x}$ 100
4. $\frac{2y}{3} = 8$ 12
5. $\frac{-4y}{5} = 12$ −15
6. $\frac{5x}{12} = 10$ 24
7. $\frac{5m}{7} = 35$ 49
8. $\frac{h}{6} = \frac{3}{9}$ 2
9. $\frac{d}{7} = \frac{-4}{28}$ −1
10. $\frac{(x+1)}{8} = \frac{-3(x+2)}{4}$ $-1\frac{6}{7}$
11. $\frac{(x-4)}{25} = \frac{x+2}{9}$ $-5\frac{3}{8}$
12. $\frac{(x-5)}{6} = \frac{(x+5)}{11}$ 17
13. $\frac{(x+4)}{3} = \frac{(x+4)}{3(x-4)}$ 5, −4
14. $\frac{3}{(y+2)} = \frac{6}{(y+4)}$ 0
15. $\frac{4x}{(x+1)} = \frac{4}{7}$ $\frac{1}{6}$

PROBLEM SOLVING

Exercise B Use what you know about proportions and fractions to solve these problems.

16. The plans for a doghouse are drawn to a scale of 1 in. equals $\frac{3}{4}$ ft. What is the distance from the ground to the top of the roof?
$2\frac{5}{8}$ feet

17. There are 10 girls in Mitchell's algebra class of 18 students. Only 5 girls are in his history class, but the ratio of girls to boys is the same as in his algebra class. How many students are in Mitchell's history class?
9 students

18. A model railroad is built to $\frac{1}{87}$th the size of a real train. The gauge (track width) for a train is about $\frac{5}{8}$ of an inch. What is the (approximate) actual track width of the railroad? $54\frac{3}{8}$ inches

19. On a map of the United States, Anchorage, Alaska, is 8.1 cm from Olympia, Washington. Denver, Colorado, is the same distance from Charleston, West Virginia. The map scale indicates that 2 cm = 500 km. About how far apart are the cities of Anchorage and Olympia? 2,025 km

20. In order to win a "Guess the Number of Jelly Beans" contest, Jamie bought a jar exactly like the one in the contest. His jar is 12 inches high. He placed 55 jelly beans in the jar. The jelly beans filled $\frac{7}{8}$ in. of the jar. About how many jelly beans will the filled jar hold? about 754 jelly beans

Anchorage, Alaska, is located at the base of the Chugach Mountains.

TRY THIS Consider $3x = 15y$ and $3x = 5 \cdot 6$. Which proportion can you solve and why? Use this information to think about this question. In order to solve a proportion such as $\frac{a}{b} = \frac{c}{d}$, how many constants and how many variables do you need to know? Explain.

$3x = 5 \cdot 6$; If a proportion has three constants and one unknown, it can be solved. The expression $3x = 15y$ has two unknowns.

Try This

A common problem-solving strategy is to solve a simpler problem first.

Solve $2m = 4$ *($m = 2$)*

Solve $a = 2b$ *(infinite solutions $a = 1$ $b = \frac{1}{2}$, $a = 2$ $b = 1, \ldots$)*

Therefore, $a = 2b$ doesn't have exactly one solution.

Group Problem Solving

Have the class work out the solutions for problems 1 through 8 on page 236 using cross products. Have them study the problems and solutions. Ask, "How can you solve these problems without using cross products?" Notice that in each problem a factor can be added or removed to produce the equivalent proportion. For example, in $\frac{x}{4} = \frac{75}{100}$, the factor of 25 can be removed from 100. $100 \div 25 = 4$. Therefore, $75 \div 25 = 3$, and the value of $x = 3$.

Calculator

Have students use their calculators to solve for the variable.

$\frac{45}{60} = \frac{96}{x}$ *(128)*

$\frac{69}{161} = \frac{y}{147}$ *(63)*

$\frac{m}{288} = \frac{504}{672}$ *(216)*

$\frac{728}{n} = \frac{736}{828}$ *(819)*

$\frac{469}{536} = \frac{p}{408}$ *(357)*

Lesson at a Glance

Chapter 8 Lesson 8

Overview The lesson shows how to solve equations using multiplication and division.

Objective

- To solve equations using multiplication and division

Student Pages 238–241

Teacher's Resource Library 

Workbook Activities 82–83

Activity 77

Alternative Activity 77

1 Warm-Up Activity

Have students find the value of n.

$\frac{2}{3} \cdot n = 1 \qquad (n = \frac{3}{2})$

$\frac{8}{15} \cdot n = 1 \qquad (n = \frac{15}{8})$

$\frac{6}{11} \cdot n = 1 \qquad (n = \frac{11}{6})$

$n \cdot \frac{5}{8} = 1 \qquad (n = \frac{8}{5})$

$n \cdot \frac{8}{15} = 1 \qquad (n = \frac{15}{8})$

2 Teaching the Lesson

Go over the examples on pages 238 and 239 on how to solve equations using multiplication and division. Encourage students to discuss each step in the process and to ask questions about steps they do not understand.

Lesson 8 More Solutions to Equations with Fractions

The equation $(\frac{3}{4})x = 15$ can be solved using two different methods.

You can solve the equation using multiplication:

$$(\frac{3}{4})x = 15$$

Multiply both sides of the equation by 4.

$$4 \cdot (\frac{3}{4})x = 4 \cdot 15$$

$$3x = 60$$

$$x = 20$$

Check: $(\frac{3}{4})(20) = \frac{60}{4} = 15$ True

Or, you can solve the equation using division.

$$\frac{3}{4}x = 15$$

Divide both sides of the equation by $\frac{3}{4}$.

$$\frac{\frac{3}{4}}{\frac{3}{4}}\ x = \frac{15}{\frac{3}{4}}$$

$$x = \frac{15}{\frac{3}{4}} = \frac{60}{3} = 20$$

EXAMPLE 1 Solve $(\frac{2}{3})x = -5$ using multiplication and using division.

Solutions:

$(\frac{2}{3})x = -5$	$(\frac{2}{3})x = -5$
$(3) \cdot (\frac{2}{3})x = (3) \cdot (-5)$	$\frac{\frac{2}{3}}{\frac{2}{3}}\ x = \frac{-5}{\frac{2}{3}}$
$2x = -15$	
$x = -7\frac{1}{2}x$	$= -5[\frac{3}{2}] = \frac{-15}{2} = -7\frac{1}{2}$

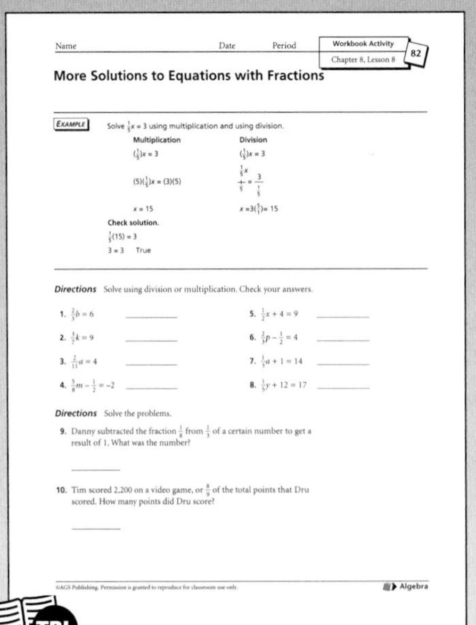

Name Date Period — Workbook Activity 82, Chapter 8, Lesson 8

More Solutions to Equations with Fractions

EXAMPLE Solve $\frac{1}{5}x = 3$ using multiplication and using division.

Multiplication	Division
$(\frac{1}{5})x = 3$	$(\frac{1}{5})x = 3$
$(5)(\frac{1}{5})x = (3)(5)$	$\frac{\frac{1}{5}x}{\frac{1}{5}} = \frac{3}{\frac{1}{5}}$
$x = 15$	$x = 3(\frac{5}{1}) = 15$

Check solution.

$\frac{1}{5}(15) = 3$

$3 = 3$ True

Directions Solve using division or multiplication. Check your answers.

1. $\frac{2}{3}b = 6$ ______
2. $\frac{3}{7}k = 9$ ______
3. $\frac{2}{11}a = 4$ ______
4. $\frac{5}{8}m - \frac{1}{2} = -2$ ______
5. $\frac{1}{2}x + 4 = 9$ ______
6. $\frac{2}{3}p - \frac{1}{2} = 4$ ______
7. $\frac{1}{3}a + 1 = 14$ ______
8. $\frac{1}{5}y + 12 = 17$ ______

Directions Solve the problems.

9. Danny subtracted the fraction $\frac{1}{8}$ from $\frac{1}{3}$ of a certain number to get a result of 1. What was the number? ______

10. Tim scored 2,200 on a video game, or $\frac{8}{9}$ of the total points that Dru scored. How many points did Dru score? ______

Algebra

Workbook Activity 82

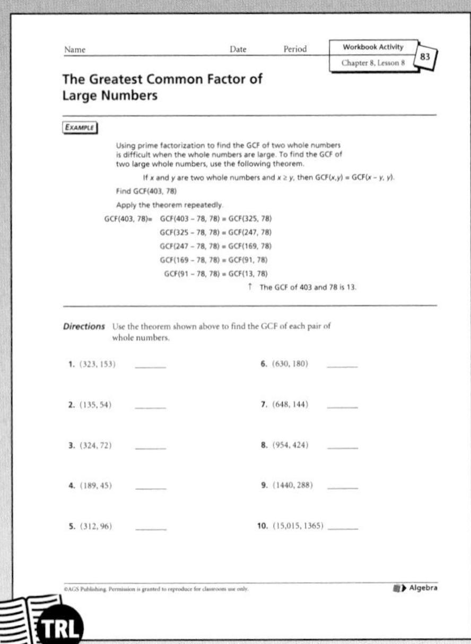

Name Date Period — Workbook Activity 83, Chapter 8, Lesson 8

The Greatest Common Factor of Large Numbers

EXAMPLE

Using prime factorization to find the GCF of two whole numbers is difficult when the whole numbers are large. To find the GCF of two large whole numbers, use the following theorem.

If x and y are two whole numbers and $x \geq y$, then GCF(x,y) = GCF$(x - y, y)$.

Find GCF(403, 78)

Apply the theorem repeatedly.

GCF(403, 78) = GCF(403 − 78, 78) = GCF(325, 78)
GCF(325 − 78, 78) = GCF(247, 78)
GCF(247 − 78, 78) = GCF(169, 78)
GCF(169 − 78, 78) = GCF(91, 78)
GCF(91 − 78, 78) = GCF(13, 78)
↑ The GCF of 403 and 78 is 13.

Directions Use the theorem shown above to find the GCF of each pair of whole numbers.

1. (323, 153) ______
2. (135, 54) ______
3. (324, 72) ______
4. (189, 45) ______
5. (312, 96) ______
6. (630, 180) ______
7. (648, 144) ______
8. (954, 424) ______
9. (1440, 288) ______
10. (15,015, 1365) ______

Algebra

Workbook Activity 83

EXAMPLE 2 If you subtract $\frac{1}{2}$ from $\frac{2}{3}$ of a number, the result is 2. What is the number?

Step 1 Let n = the number. Write an equation describing the number.

$(\frac{2}{3})n - \frac{1}{2} = 2$

Step 2 Solve the equation using multiplication or division.

$(\frac{2}{3})n - \frac{1}{2} = 2$

$6 \bullet [(\frac{2}{3})n - \frac{1}{2}] = 6 \bullet 2$

$4n - 3 = 12$

$4n = 15 \quad n = \frac{15}{4}$ or $3\frac{3}{4}$

Step 3 Check.

$(\frac{2}{3})(\frac{15}{4}) - \frac{1}{2} = 2$

$\frac{30}{12} - \frac{6}{12} = 2$

$\frac{24}{12} = 2$ True

Exercise A Solve each equation using multiplication and using division. Check each method you use.

1. $(\frac{3}{4})y = 18$ 24

2. $(\frac{3}{4})x = 33$ 44

3. $(\frac{7}{8})m = 49$ 56

4. $(\frac{9}{15})t = 81$ 135

5. $(\frac{5}{7})h = -35$ −49

6. $(\frac{2}{3})m = 7$ $10\frac{1}{2}$

7. $(\frac{5}{9})d = 15$ 27

8. $(\frac{3}{7})p - \frac{1}{3} = 1$ $3\frac{1}{9}$

9. $(\frac{4}{9})x = 5 + \frac{1}{9}$ $11\frac{1}{2}$

Technology Connection

Computerized Taps

Quarter notes, eighth notes, or half notes? Now buglers don't have to know the difference when they play Taps at a veteran's funeral. Currently, there aren't enough buglers around, and families of veterans do not think playing a recording of Taps on a CD player is dignified. So, the U.S. Pentagon has developed a bugle with a computerized chip insert that plays Taps. Now, buglers only have to press a button, wait five seconds, hold the bugle to their lips, and pretend to blow as Taps plays.

3 Reinforce and Extend

LEARNING STYLES

Auditory/Verbal

The first time you read the following problem aloud, have students simply listen. The second time you read the problem, ask students to write down the important information they will need to solve the problem.

Mike and Lisa read in the Sunday newspaper that a local resident is running for the state legislature. The article states that $\frac{3}{8}$ or 5,022 people in Louisville voted for the candidate. How many voters are there in Louisville? *(13,392 voters)*

GROUP PROBLEM SOLVING

Have students form groups of two or three. Each group is to write three word problems with the solutions on a separate piece of paper. The word problems must be solved by using a fraction to multiply or divide an equation. Have each group exchange problems with another group and work out that group's problems. Have them check with the original group to see whether their solutions are correct. Select several problems to review with the class.

Name Date Period Activity 77 Chapter 8, Lesson 8

More Solutions to Equations with Fractions

Directions Check the computations. You can use a calculator. Write *correct* or *not correct* for the given answer.

1. $\frac{2}{5}n = 6; n = 15$ ______
2. $\frac{3}{4}a = 63; a = 84$ ______
3. $\frac{4}{7}y = 28; y = 35$ ______
4. $\frac{7}{10}k = 49; k = 70$ ______
5. $\frac{3}{10}n = 21; n = 60$ ______
6. $\frac{4}{7}y = 28; y = 49$ ______
7. $\frac{2}{3}w + \frac{1}{3}w = 27; w = 24$ ______
8. $\frac{4}{5}r + \frac{3}{20}r = 38; r = 40$ ______

Directions Solve using division or multiplication. Check your answers.

9. $\frac{2}{15}x = 4$ ______
10. $\frac{7}{9}y = 7$ ______
11. $\frac{1}{3}b + 2 = 13$ ______
12. $\frac{1}{3}w + 1 = \frac{1}{2}w$ ______
13. $\frac{1}{5}x - \frac{1}{3}x = -8$ ______

Directions Solve the problems.

14. Merle added the fraction $\frac{1}{6}$ to $\frac{1}{4}$ of a number, getting 4 as a result. What was the number? ______
15. To her cousin Crystal, Jeanne observed: "My zip code is 3 times four-fifths of your zip code." If Jeanne's zip code is 60660, what is Crystal's? ______

 Algebra

TRL

Activity 77

Calculator

Ask students to use their calculators to solve these problems.

$(82.766)c = 36{,}582.572$
($c = 442$)

$(375.65)x = 46{,}396.5315$
($x = 123.51$)

$(72.50)a = 69{,}672.5$
($a = 961$)

$(66.125)g = 5577.64375$
($g = 84.35$)

$(3.1456)y = 56.6208$
($y = 18$)

Exercise B Solve using division *or* multiplication. Check your answers.

10. $(\frac{4}{9})m + \frac{1}{9} = 5$ 11

11. $(\frac{6}{7})x - \frac{2}{3} = 4$ $5\frac{4}{9}$

12. $4 - (\frac{2}{3})z = \frac{1}{2}$ $5\frac{1}{4}$

13. $12 - (\frac{6}{7})y = 5$ $8\frac{1}{6}$

14. $(\frac{2}{3})x - \frac{4}{7} = 6$ $9\frac{6}{7}$

15. $(\frac{5}{6})m - (\frac{2}{3})m = 14$ 84

16. $(\frac{7}{8})y + (1\frac{1}{2})y = 8$ $3\frac{7}{19}$

17. $(\frac{3}{7})x - (\frac{2}{3})x = -6$ $25\frac{1}{5}$

Suppose you use pencil and paper to determine that $n = 6$ in the equation $\frac{3}{4}n + \frac{1}{2} = 5$. To check your answer using a calculator, follow these steps.

Example 3 Substitute $n = 6$ into the equation $\frac{3}{4}n + \frac{1}{2} = 5$.

$\frac{3}{4}(6) + \frac{1}{2} = 5$

Then press (3 ÷ 4) (6) + (1 ÷ 2) =

The calculator display will read 5.

If you have a calculator with a fraction key $a^{b}/_{c}$, follow these steps:

Press 3 $a^{b}/_{c}$ 4 × 6 + 1 $a^{b}/_{c}$ 2 =

The calculator display will read 5.

Writing About Mathematics

Write a word problem that can be solved using an equation with fractions. Solve it, then challenge a classmate to solve it. (Hint: You can use problems 23, 24, and 25 to help.)

Exercise C Use a calculator to check these computations. If the answer is correct, write *correct*. If the answer is not correct, write *not correct*.

18. $\frac{3}{8}a = 64; a = 24$ not correct

19. $\frac{4}{5}b = 105; b = 94$ not correct

20. $\frac{1}{10}c + \frac{1}{2} = 1; c = 5$ correct

21. $\frac{2}{3}d + \frac{1}{3} = 18; d = 28$ not correct

22. Tell how you might use a calculator to check a computation that has a fraction for an answer.
Sample answer: Use division to find the decimal equivalent for the fraction.

PROBLEM SOLVING

Exercise D Write and solve equations using division or multplication.

23. Keisha and Jamaal take the same standard math test. The ratio of their scores is 4 to 5. The difference in their scores is 15. What are their scores?

24. Everitt is twice as old as Danny. The difference in their ages is 6 years. How old is Everitt? How old is Danny?

25. Ella scores 54 points in a basketball game. This is $\frac{2}{3}$ of her team's points. How many points does the team score?

23. Their scores are 75 and 60.

24. Everitt is 12 years old and Danny is 6 years old.

25. 81 points

CAREER CONNECTION

Technical writers write instructional manuals for VCRs, compact disc players, radios, lawn mowers, computer programs, and so on. They must write instructions as clearly as possible, since many readers have never used the particular product they are writing about. Ask students to imagine that they are technical writers writing instructions for someone who knows very little about solving equations with fractions. Have them conclude their instructions with a generalization about solving equations with fractions and give four examples of how the generalization can be used.

Lesson at a Glance

Chapter 8 Lesson 9

Overview This lesson explains how to determine for which values an expression is undefined.

Objective

- To determine the values for which an expression is undefined

Student Pages 242–243

Teacher's Resource Library 

Workbook Activity 84

Activity 78

Alternative Activity 78

Mathematics Vocabulary

undefined

1 Warm-Up Activity

Have students use their calculators to evaluate the following expression using the values 2, 3, 4, 5, and 6. Have them record their answers.

$\frac{6}{x-3}$ *(−6, error, 6, 3, 2)*

2 Teaching the Lesson

Discuss the solutions to the Warm-Up Activity. Elicit from students that division by zero results in an undefined term.

Common Error

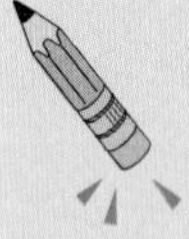

Encourage students to analyze each problem carefully, because there may be more than one value that will make the term undefined. Initially, some students will only find one value and move on to the next problem without considering the possibility that another value exists.

Lesson 9 Denominators and Zero

Undefined

A term used without a specific mathematical definition

Recall that for any rational number $\frac{a}{b}$, $b \neq 0$. You know that $\frac{12}{3} = 4$ because $12 = 3 \cdot 4$. Likewise, $\frac{a}{b} = c$ means $a = bc$. Now, look at $\frac{a}{0} = c$. This means that $a = 0 \cdot c$. But $a = 0$ is false, so division by zero is **undefined** because no quotient works.

Rule The expressions $\frac{1}{0}$ and $\frac{a}{0}$ are undefined because division by zero is not defined.

Therefore, the denominators in algebraic expressions must never be zero.

If $x = 2$ in the expression $\frac{1}{(x-2)}$, then $\frac{1}{(x-2)} = \frac{1}{(2-2)} = \frac{1}{0}$.

Since division by zero is not defined, $\frac{1}{(x-2)}$ can have any value except 2. This is usually written $\frac{1}{(x-2)}$ for $x \neq 2$.

Sometimes a solution is a value that is both positive and negative, such as $x = +2$ and $x = -2$. The solution $x = +2$ and $x = -2$ can be written in a simpler way by just writing $x = \pm 2$.

Example 1 For what value of x is $\frac{1}{(x+\frac{1}{2})}$ undefined?

If $x + \frac{1}{2} = 0$, then $x = -\frac{1}{2}$ makes the fraction undefined.

For what values of x is $\frac{1}{(x^2-4)}$ undefined?

If $x^2 - 4 = 0$, then the fraction is undefined.

$x^2 = 4$, $x = \pm 2$ makes the fraction undefined.

$x = \pm 2$ makes the fraction undefined.

Algebra in Your Life

When $\frac{1}{4}$ Inch Equals One Foot

When constructing anything from a house to a skyscraper, builders follow an architect's drawings. Architects can't make drawings that are the same size as the buildings, so they make scale drawings. A measurement of one foot of the building might only equal a quarter inch on the plan. Architects have to do the math to "scale down" a building for the drawing. Builders have to "scale up" the plans to know how long to cut a timber or how large a window should be.

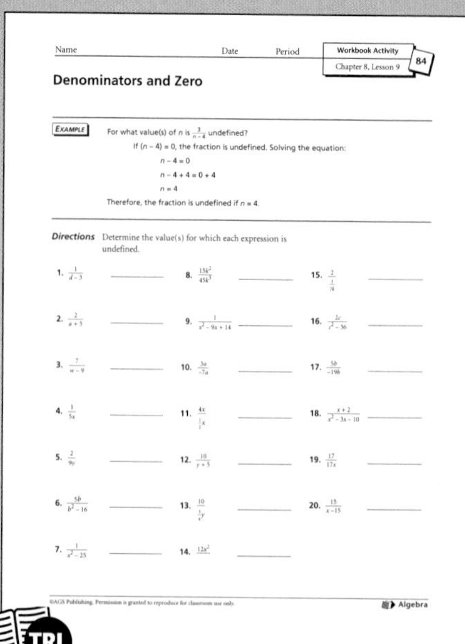

Name ____ Date ____ Period ____ Workbook Activity 84 Chapter 8, Lesson 9

Denominators and Zero

Example For what value(s) of n is $\frac{3}{n-4}$ undefined?

If $(n-4) = 0$, the fraction is undefined. Solving the equation:

$n - 4 = 0$

$n - 4 + 4 = 0 + 4$

$n = 4$

Therefore, the fraction is undefined if $n = 4$.

Directions Determine the value(s) for which each expression is undefined.

1. $\frac{1}{d-3}$ ____
2. $\frac{2}{a+5}$ ____
3. $\frac{7}{w-9}$ ____
4. $\frac{1}{5x}$ ____
5. $\frac{2}{9y}$ ____
6. $\frac{5b}{b^2-16}$ ____
7. $\frac{1}{x^2-25}$ ____
8. $\frac{15k^2}{45k^3}$ ____
9. $\frac{1}{x^2-9x+14}$ ____
10. $\frac{3a}{-7a}$ ____
11. $\frac{4x}{\frac{1}{2}x}$ ____
12. $\frac{10}{y+5}$ ____
13. $\frac{10}{\frac{3}{4}y}$ ____
14. $12x^2$ ____
15. $\frac{2}{\frac{1}{7k}}$ ____
16. $\frac{2c}{c^2-36}$ ____
17. $\frac{5b}{-19b}$ ____
18. $\frac{x+2}{x^2-3x-10}$ ____
19. $\frac{17}{17x}$ ____
20. $\frac{15}{x-15}$ ____

 Algebra

Workbook Activity 84

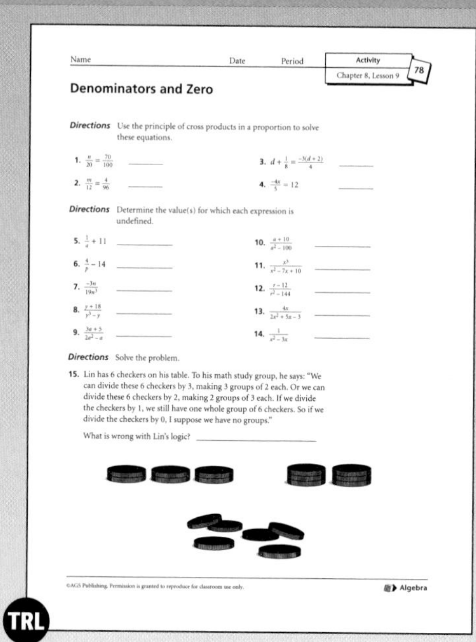

Name ____ Date ____ Period ____ Activity 78 Chapter 8, Lesson 9

Denominators and Zero

Directions Use the principle of cross products in a proportion to solve these equations.

1. $\frac{n}{20} = \frac{70}{100}$ ____
2. $\frac{m}{12} = \frac{4}{96}$ ____
3. $d + \frac{1}{8} = \frac{-3(d+2)}{4}$ ____
4. $\frac{-4x}{5} = 12$ ____

Directions Determine the value(s) for which each expression is undefined.

5. $\frac{1}{a} + 11$ ____
6. $\frac{4}{p} - 14$ ____
7. $\frac{-3n}{19n^3}$ ____
8. $\frac{y+18}{y^3-y}$ ____
9. $\frac{3a+5}{2a^2-a}$ ____
10. $\frac{a+10}{a^2-100}$ ____
11. $\frac{x^3}{x^2-7x+10}$ ____
12. $\frac{r-12}{r^2-144}$ ____
13. $\frac{4x}{2x^2+5x-3}$ ____
14. $\frac{1}{x^2-3x}$ ____

Directions Solve the problem.

15. Lin has 6 checkers on his table. To his math study group, he says: "We can divide these 6 checkers by 3, making 3 groups of 2 each. Or we can divide these 6 checkers by 2, making 2 groups of 3 each. If we divide the checkers by 1, we still have one whole group of 6 checkers. So if we divide the checkers by 0, I suppose we have no groups."

What is wrong with Lin's logic? ____

 Algebra

Activity 78

Writing About Mathematics

Describe why you cannot divide any number by zero. What would the quotient be?

EXAMPLE 2 For what values of y is $\frac{y}{y(y + 1)}$ undefined?

If $y(y + 1) = 0$, then the fraction is undefined.

Either $y = 0$ or $y + 1 = 0$ makes the fraction undefined.

Therefore, both $y = 0$ and $y = -1$ make the fraction undefined.

Exercise A Determine the value(s) for which each expression is undefined.

1. $\frac{1}{x - 4}$ $x = 4$
2. $\frac{3}{v - 3}$ $v = 3$
3. $\frac{10}{c + 5}$ $c = -5$
4. $\frac{-2m}{25m^4}$ $m = 0$
5. $\frac{4a}{-7b}$ $b = 0$
6. $\frac{-45x^2}{90x^3}$ $x = 0$
7. $\frac{13m^2n^3}{-39mn^2}$ $m = 0$ and/or $n = 0$
8. $\frac{(x - 3)}{(x - 3)^3}$ $x = 3$
9. $\frac{(a^2 + 4)^2}{(-a^2 + 4)}$ $a = +2$ or $a = -2$
10. $\frac{(m - 6)}{(m^2 - 36)}$ $m = +6$ or $m = -6$
11. $\frac{-(r - 12)}{(r^2 - 24r + 144)}$ $r = 12$
12. $\frac{(w^2 + 14w + 49)}{(w + 7)}$ $w = -7$
13. $\frac{(-n^2 + 36)}{(n - 6)(n^2 + 12n + 36)}$ $n = +6$ or $n = -6$
14. $\frac{(a - 4)}{(a^2 - 6a + 8)}$ $a = +4$ or $a = +2$
15. $\frac{(-m - 8)}{(m^2 + 5m - 24)}$ $m = -8$ or $m = +3$
16. $\frac{(x^2 + 2x)}{(x^2 + 5x + 6)}$ $x = -2$ or $x = -3$
17. $\frac{(x^2 + 7x + 12)}{(9 - x^2)(x + 4)}$ $x = -3, x = -4$, or $x = +3$
18. $\frac{(x + 1)}{(x^2 + 5x + 4)}$ $x = -4$ or $x = -1$
19. $\frac{(b - 3)}{(b^2 - 9b + 20)}$ $b = +5$ or $b = +4$
20. $\frac{(2a + 1)}{(2a^2 - a - 1)}$ $a = +1$ or $a = \frac{-1}{2}$

MANIPULATIVES

Finding Undefined Values

Materials: Algebra Tiles

Group Practice: Review procedures for factoring polynomials and finding roots of factors. Establish the connection between finding values that make an expression undefined and finding roots of equations or factors. Use the Algebra Tiles to find the undefined values of the variables in the examples, modeling the denominator and replacing the unknown pieces with unit pieces to make the expression equal zero.

Student Practice: Have students use Algebra Tiles to find the undefined values of the expressions in Exercise A, Problems 1–3, 12, 14–16, 18–20. Have students sketch each model and write its symbolic equivalent.

3 Reinforce and Extend

LEARNING STYLES

Visual/Spatial

Give each student an index card on which to write an expression in which at least one value will make the expression undefined. Have each student write the value or values on the back of the card. Collect all the cards. Use the set of cards as flashcards. Hold up a card for students to see and have them find the value or values as quickly as they can.

GROUP PROBLEM SOLVING

Challenge the class to write ten expressions in which the values that will make the expression undefined are between 2 and 8. Call on one student for the numerator, and call on another student for the denominator. After the class completes ten expressions, add another condition: The next ten expressions must have exponents in the denominators.

Lesson at a Glance

Chapter 8 Application

Overview This lesson demonstrates the application of rational numbers and fractional equivalents to solve work problems.

Objective

- To use rational numbers and fractional equivalents to solve work problems

Student Page 244

Teacher's Resource Library 

Application Activity 8

Everyday Algebra 8

1 Warm-Up Activity

Ask the class to estimate the answer to this problem.

Juanita can paint the kitchen in $5\frac{1}{2}$ hours. Mike can paint the same room in 7 hours. How long will it take them to paint the room together?

The students will know that each person can paint half of the kitchen in half of the time. Therefore, they will estimate about 6 hours for the entire job or about 3 hours per person.

2 Teaching the Lesson

Discuss with the class how they know it will take about 6 hours to paint the kitchen. This discussion will serve as an introduction to the concept of work problems. Go over the example on page 244.

3 Reinforce and Extend

Learning Styles

Interpersonal/ Group Learning

Have a student read aloud a problem on page 244. Ask the class to discuss the problem and offer an appropriate estimate of the amount of time needed to complete the work. Do this for all five problems. Next, have students work in pairs to solve the problems.

Application $\pi^2 \Sigma + \Omega \sqrt{x^2}\ \% \neq y \geq n = \nabla 30^\circ \pi$

Working Fractions

One of the most useful applications of rational numbers and fractional equivalents is the work problem. Work problems rely on the fact that work done by one person + work done by a second person = total amount of work completed.

Example 1 It takes Steve 3 hours to clear a mile of riverbank. Seela can clear the riverbank in 4 hours. If Steve and Seela work together, how quickly can the riverbank be cleared?

Let x = the time, in hours, for both workers to clear the riverbank.

Because Steve can clear the riverbank in 3 hours, you know that in one hour he can clear $\frac{1}{3}$ of the riverbank, and in x hours $\frac{x}{3}$ of the bank. Because Seela can clear the riverbank in 4 hours, you know that in one hour she can clear $\frac{1}{4}$ of the riverbank, and in x hours $\frac{x}{4}$ of the bank.

Set up an equation that describes the work problem:

part of the bank cleared by Steve in x hours + part of the bank cleared by Seela = 1 (entire riverbank cleared)

$$\frac{x}{3} + \frac{x}{4} = 1$$

Use what you know about fractional equations to solve the equation.

$$\frac{x}{3} + \frac{x}{4} = 1$$

$$12 \bullet [\frac{x}{3} + \frac{x}{4}] = 12 \bullet 1$$

$$4x + 3x = 12$$

$$7x = 12$$

$$x = \frac{12}{7} \text{ or } 1\frac{5}{7} \text{ hours}$$

Exercise Find the solutions to the following problems.

1. Marc can mow Bobolink Meadow in 7 hours. Earlene can mow it in 6 hours. How long will it take Earlene and Marc, working together, to mow Bobolink Meadow? $3\frac{3}{13}$ hours
2. In 3 hours, Mai can complete a series of water-quality tests. Harry needs $3\frac{1}{2}$ hours to complete the same tests. If they work together, how long will it take them to complete the tests? $1\frac{8}{13}$ hours
3. Emile can survey the East River in 4 hours. Daniel can survey the same area in 5 hours. If they work together, how quickly can they survey the river? $2\frac{2}{9}$ hours

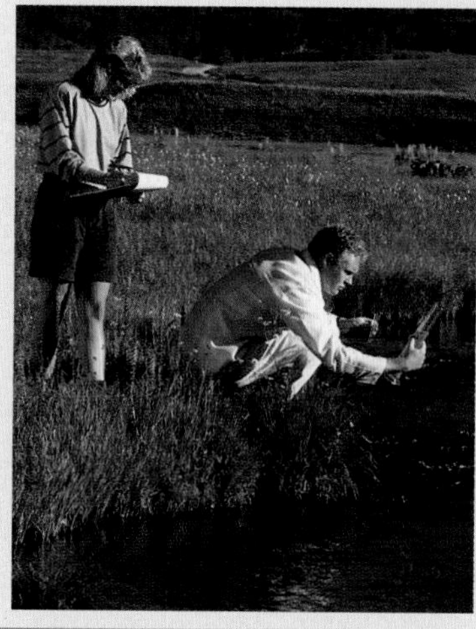

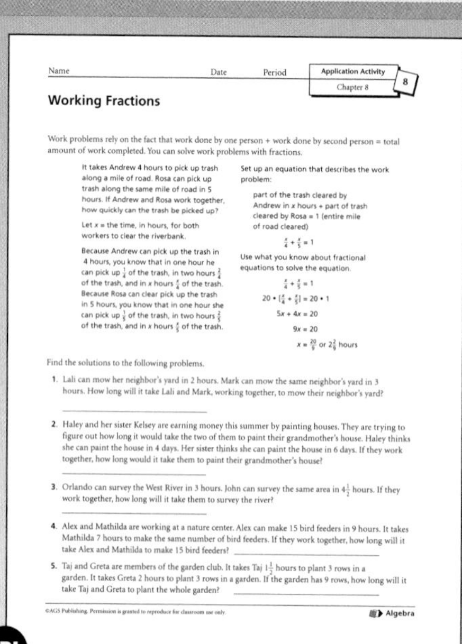

Name Date Period — Application Activity, Chapter 8 — 8

Working Fractions

Work problems rely on the fact that work done by one person + work done by second person = total amount of work completed. You can solve work problems with fractions.

It takes Andrew 4 hours to pick up trash along a mile of road. Rosa can pick up trash along the same mile of road in 5 hours. If Andrew and Rosa work together, how quickly can the trash be picked up?

Let x = the time, in hours, for both workers to clear the riverbank.

Because Andrew can pick up the trash in 4 hours, you know that in one hour he can pick up $\frac{1}{4}$ of the trash, in two hours $\frac{2}{4}$ of the trash, and in x hours $\frac{x}{4}$ of the trash. Because Rosa can clear pick up the trash in 5 hours, you know that in one hour she can pick up $\frac{1}{5}$ of the trash, in two hours $\frac{2}{5}$ of the trash, and in x hours $\frac{x}{5}$ of the trash.

Set up an equation that describes the work problem:

part of the trash cleared by Andrew in x hours + part of trash cleared by Rosa = 1 (entire mile of road cleared)

$$\frac{x}{4} + \frac{x}{5} = 1$$

Use what you know about fractional equations to solve the equation.

$$\frac{x}{4} + \frac{x}{5} = 1$$

$$20 \bullet [\frac{x}{4} + \frac{x}{5}] = 20 \bullet 1$$

$$5x + 4x = 20$$

$$9x = 20$$

$$x = \frac{20}{9} \text{ or } 2\frac{2}{9} \text{ hours}$$

Find the solutions to the following problems.

1. Lali can mow her neighbor's yard in 2 hours. Mark can mow the same neighbor's yard in 3 hours. How long will it take Lali and Mark, working together, to mow their neighbor's yard? ____
2. Haley and her sister Kelsey are earning money this summer by painting houses. They are trying to figure out how long it would take the two of them to paint their grandmother's house. Haley thinks she can paint the house in 4 days. Her sister thinks she can paint the house in 6 days. If they work together, how long would it take them to paint their grandmother's house? ____
3. Orlando can survey the West River in 3 hours. John can survey the same area in $4\frac{1}{2}$ hours. If they work together, how long will it take them to survey the river? ____
4. Alex and Mathilda are working at a nature center. Alex can make 15 bird feeders in 9 hours. It takes Mathilda 7 hours to make the same number of bird feeders. If they work together, how long will it take Alex and Mathilda to make 15 bird feeders? ____
5. Taj and Greta are members of the garden club. It takes Taj $1\frac{1}{2}$ hours to plant 3 rows in a garden. It takes Greta 2 hours to plant 3 rows in a garden. If the garden has 9 rows, how long will it take Taj and Greta to plant the whole garden? ____

 Algebra

TRL

Application Activity 8

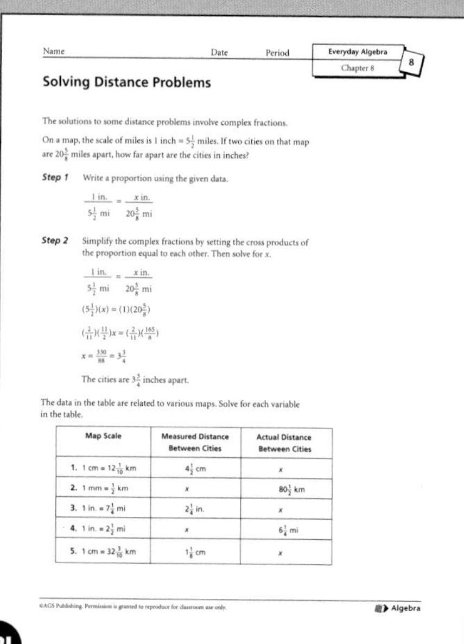

Name Date Period — Everyday Algebra, Chapter 8 — 8

Solving Distance Problems

The solutions to some distance problems involve complex fractions.

On a map, the scale of miles is 1 inch = $5\frac{1}{2}$ miles. If two cities on that map are $20\frac{5}{8}$ miles apart, how far apart are the cities in inches?

Step 1 Write a proportion using the given data.

$$\frac{1 \text{ in.}}{5\frac{1}{2} \text{ mi}} = \frac{x \text{ in.}}{20\frac{5}{8} \text{ mi}}$$

Step 2 Simplify the complex fractions by setting the cross products of the proportion equal to each other. Then solve for x.

$$\frac{1 \text{ in.}}{5\frac{1}{2} \text{ mi}} = \frac{x \text{ in.}}{20\frac{5}{8} \text{ mi}}$$

$$(5\tfrac{1}{2})(x) = (1)(20\tfrac{5}{8})$$

$$(\tfrac{2}{11})(\tfrac{11}{2})x = (\tfrac{2}{11})(\tfrac{165}{8})$$

$$x = \tfrac{330}{88} = 3\tfrac{3}{4}$$

The cities are $3\frac{3}{4}$ inches apart.

The data in the table are related to various maps. Solve for each variable in the table.

Map Scale	Measured Distance Between Cities	Actual Distance Between Cities
1. 1 cm = $12\frac{1}{10}$ km	$4\frac{1}{2}$ cm	x
2. 1 mm = $\frac{1}{2}$ km	x	$80\frac{1}{2}$ km
3. 1 in. = $7\frac{1}{4}$ mi	$2\frac{1}{4}$ in.	x
4. 1 in. = $2\frac{1}{2}$ mi	x	$6\frac{1}{4}$ mi
5. 1 cm = $32\frac{3}{10}$ km	$1\frac{1}{8}$ cm	x

 Algebra

TRL

Everyday Algebra 8

Chapter 8 REVIEW

Write the letter of the correct answer.

1. What is $\frac{48}{72}$ in simplest form? C

   A $\frac{24}{36}$ C $\frac{2}{3}$
   B 0.667   D 24

2. Multiply $2\frac{1}{2} \cdot 4\frac{2}{3}$. A

   A $11\frac{2}{3}$ C $23\frac{1}{3}$
   B 45   D 3

3. Divide $ab^3 \div a^2b$. B

   A $\frac{ab}{a^2b}$ C $\frac{(ab)^3}{a^2b}$
   B $\frac{b^2}{a}$ D $\frac{a}{b^2}$

4. Simplify $\frac{6}{\frac{7}{8}}$. A

   A $6\frac{6}{7}$ C $\frac{8}{7}$
   B 48   D $8\frac{6}{7}$

5. Find the sum of $\frac{3}{x} + \frac{5}{x^2}$. D

   A $\frac{3x}{x^2}$ C $\frac{3x}{5x^2}$
   B $\frac{3x^2}{5x}$ D $\frac{(3x + 5)}{x^2}$

6. Find the difference of $\frac{15}{xy} - \frac{4}{xz}$. C

   A $\frac{15z}{xyz}$ C $\frac{(15z - 4y)}{xyz}$
   B $\frac{11}{(y - z)}$ D $\frac{15}{(xyz - 4)}$

7. Solve for x. $\frac{x}{5} = \frac{80}{100}$ A

   A 4   C 160
   B $6\frac{1}{4}$ D 40

Group Problem Solving

Assign each of the problems on page 244 to five small groups. Ask the groups to consider what would happen if there were a third person involved in the work. Have them rewrite their problem, adding a third person and his or her work rate, and then solve the new problem. Allow time for the groups to report on their reconstructed problems and what they discovered when they added new data.

Chapter 8 Review

Each set of problems in the Chapter Review includes an example and solution to illustrate the concept. Use the given examples for reteaching the materials in Chapter 8. For additional practice, refer to the Supplementary Problems for Chapter 8 (pages 420–421).

Chapter 8 Mastery Test 

The Teacher's Resource Library includes parallel forms of the Chapter 8 Mastery Test. The difficulty level of the two forms is equivalent. You may wish to use one form as a pretest and the other form as a posttest.

Alternative Assessment

Alternative Assessment items correlate with student Goals for Learning at the beginning of this chapter.

- **To write fractions in their simplest form**

Have students think of themselves in terms of the groups they belong to—their families, their friends, their class—and write them as fractions. Example: I'm one of five people in my family so I'm $\frac{1}{5}$ of the family unit. Then have them think of the larger groups in which they are members. Example: my family belongs to a hiking club of 40 members. Direct students to write these as fractions—the family is $\frac{5}{40}$ or $\frac{1}{8}$ of the hiking group. Remind students to write the fractions in simplest terms.

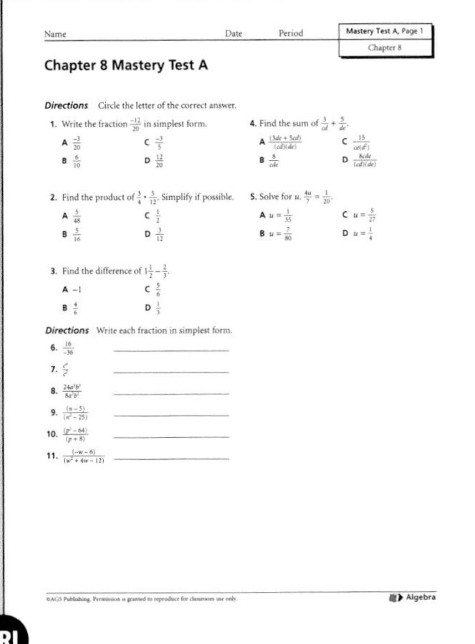

Name Date Period | Mastery Test A, Page 1 | Chapter 8

Chapter 8 Mastery Test A

Directions Circle the letter of the correct answer.

1. Write the fraction $\frac{-12}{20}$ in simplest form.
   A $\frac{-3}{20}$ C $\frac{-3}{5}$ B $\frac{6}{10}$ D $\frac{12}{20}$
2. Find the product of $\frac{3}{4} \cdot \frac{5}{12}$. Simplify if possible.
   A $\frac{5}{48}$ C $\frac{1}{2}$ B $\frac{5}{16}$ D $\frac{3}{12}$
3. Find the difference of $1\frac{1}{2} - \frac{2}{3}$.
   A −1   C $\frac{5}{6}$ B $\frac{4}{6}$ D $\frac{1}{3}$
4. Find the sum of $\frac{3}{cd} + \frac{5}{de}$.
   A $\frac{(3de + 5cd)}{(cd)(de)}$ C $\frac{15}{ce(d^2)}$ B $\frac{8}{cde}$ D $\frac{8cde}{(cd)(de)}$
5. Solve for u. $\frac{4u}{7} = \frac{1}{20}$.
   A $u = \frac{1}{35}$ C $u = \frac{5}{27}$ B $u = \frac{7}{80}$ D $u = \frac{1}{4}$

Directions Write each fraction in simplest form.

6. $\frac{16}{-36}$ ______
7. $\frac{c^4}{c^2}$ ______
8. $\frac{24a^5b^3}{8a^3b^2}$ ______
9. $\frac{(n-5)}{(n^2-25)}$ ______
10. $\frac{(p^2-64)}{(p+8)}$ ______
11. $\frac{(-w-6)}{(w^2+4w-12)}$ ______

 Algebra

TRL

Name Date Period | Mastery Test A, Page 2 | Chapter 8

Chapter 8 Mastery Test A, continued

Directions Find each product or quotient. Simplify your answers whenever possible.

12. $\frac{a}{b^3} \cdot \frac{b^3}{a}$ ______
13. $\frac{1}{(c^2-4)} \cdot \frac{(c-2)}{(c+2)}$ ______
14. $\frac{(p^2+6p+9)}{(q-4)} \cdot \frac{(q^2-8q+16)}{(p+3)}$ ______
15. $\frac{7}{8} \div \frac{1}{4}$ ______
16. $\frac{g}{h^2} \div \frac{h^2}{g}$ ______
17. $\frac{(y^2+3y-10)}{(x-3)} \div \frac{(y+5)}{(x-3)}$ ______

Directions Simplify each complex fraction.

18. $\frac{4}{\frac{1}{3}}$ ______
19. $\frac{\frac{1}{5}}{10}$ ______
20. $\frac{\frac{1}{3x}}{\frac{4}{6x}}$ ______
21. $\frac{\frac{ab}{c}}{\frac{a}{bc}}$ ______

Directions For which value or values is each expression undefined?

22. $\frac{1}{c+2}$ ______
23. $\frac{-3k}{16k^2}$ ______
24. $\frac{n-7}{n^2-49}$ ______

Directions Solve.

25. Jon stores his extra golf balls in a box that is $14\frac{1}{2}$ inches tall. One layer of balls that has a height of $1\frac{13}{16}$ inches completely fills the bottom of the box. If that layer is made up of 40 balls, how many balls can fit in the remainder of the box? ______

 Algebra

TRL

Chapter 8 Mastery Test A

Alternative Assessment, continued

■ **To find the greatest common factor of two or more fractions**
Have students use manipulatives such as paper clips to make pairs of fractions that have a greatest common factor. Then have students find the greatest common factors of another student's problems.

■ **To multiply and divide algebraic fractions**
Separate students into groups of five. Have the first person in the group think of an algebraic expression with one term for the numerator and one for the denominator, such as $\frac{3a}{4b}$. Have the second person add (or subtract) an algebraic expression to the first one—$\frac{3a + 6b}{2b - 2a}$. The third student decides whether the fraction should be divided or multiplied. For this example, the problem will be multiplied. The fourth student figures out two expressions, one for the numerator and denominator of the second term—$\frac{b - a}{6a + 3b}$. The fifth student performs the operation. If possible, allow enough time for each student to perform each of the roles. *(The solution for the example above is* $\frac{3a + 6b}{2b - 2a} \cdot \frac{b - a}{6a + 3b} = \frac{a + 2b}{(b - a)(2a + b)}$.*)*

■ **To simplify complex fractions**
Have students think of two examples of how complex fractions are used in real life. Have them create and then solve two problems based on the examples. Example: if someone runs $5\frac{3}{4}$ miles in $54\frac{5}{8}$ minutes, how many minutes does it take to run one mile? *Answer: 9.5 minutes.*

■ **To find the least common multiple and prime factors of algebraic fractions**
Have students create algebraic fractions using their names and or a friend's or relative's name (long names can be cut in two and placed in the numerator and denominator positions). Then have the students simplify the expression and, using prime factorization, find the least common multiple. You can go a step

Chapter 8 REVIEW - continued

Write each fraction in simplest form.

Example: $\frac{8}{10}$ Solution: $\frac{8}{10} = \frac{2 \cdot 2 \cdot 2}{2 \cdot 5}$ GCF = 2 $\frac{8}{10} \div \frac{2}{2} = \frac{4}{5}$

8. $\frac{12}{36}$ $\frac{1}{3}$
9. $\frac{47}{235}$ $\frac{1}{5}$
10. $\frac{13}{-169}$ $\frac{1}{-13}$
11. $\frac{x^4}{x^5}$ $\frac{1}{x}$
12. $\frac{225y^9}{25y^5}$ $9y^4$
13. $\frac{49mn}{63m^2n^2}$ $\frac{7}{9mn}$
14. $\frac{36xz^2}{72x^2z}$ $\frac{z}{2x}$
15. $\frac{(y^2 - 9)}{y + 3}$ $(y - 3)$
16. $\frac{(x^4 + 7x^3 + 12x^2)}{(x^3 + 8x^2 + 15x)}$ $\frac{x(x + 4)}{(x + 5)}$

Multiply or divide. Simplify your answers.

Example: $\frac{3}{4} \div \frac{4}{5}$ Solution: $\frac{3}{4} \div \frac{4}{5} = \frac{3}{4} \cdot \frac{5}{4} = \frac{15}{16}$

17. $\frac{1}{(x^2 - 9)} \cdot \frac{(x - 3)}{(x + 3)}$ $\frac{1}{(x + 3)^2}$
18. $\frac{1}{(y^2 - 9)} \cdot \frac{(y + 3)}{(y - 3)}$ $\frac{1}{(y - 3)^2}$
19. $\frac{5}{7} \div \frac{2}{3}$ $1\frac{1}{14}$
20. $\frac{(z + 3)}{(z - 3)} \div \frac{1}{(z^2 - 9)}$ $(z + 3)^2$

Simplify these complex fractions. Simplify your answers.

Example: $\frac{\frac{3}{5}}{2}$ Solution: $\frac{\frac{3}{5}}{2} = \frac{3}{5} \div 2 = \frac{3}{5} \div \frac{2}{1} = \frac{3}{5} \cdot \frac{1}{2} = \frac{3}{10}$

21. $\frac{\frac{a}{x}}{\frac{x}{b}}$ $\frac{ab}{x^2}$
22. $\frac{\frac{b}{y^2}}{\frac{b^2}{y^3}}$ $\frac{y}{b}$

Solve for the variable. Check your work.

Example: $\frac{6}{a} = \frac{2}{3}$ Solution: $\frac{6}{a} = \frac{2}{3}$ $2a = 6(3)$ $2a = 18$ $a = 9$
Check. $2(9) = 6(3)$ $18 = 18$

23. $\frac{20}{5} = \frac{80}{y}$ 20
24. $\frac{h}{7} = \frac{3}{35}$ $\frac{3}{5}$
25. $\frac{5}{9}h = -45$ -81
26. $\frac{5}{9}m = 4\frac{1}{9}$ $7\frac{2}{5}$
27. $\frac{1}{6}x - \frac{2}{3}x = 14$ -28
28. $\frac{3x}{2} = -45$ -30
29. $\frac{(3x - 5)}{2} = -45$ $-28\frac{1}{3}$
30. $\frac{3(x - 5)}{2} = -45$ -25
31. $\frac{2}{3} + \frac{5}{6} = 9x$ $\frac{1}{6}$

246 *Chapter 8 Fractions and Algebra*

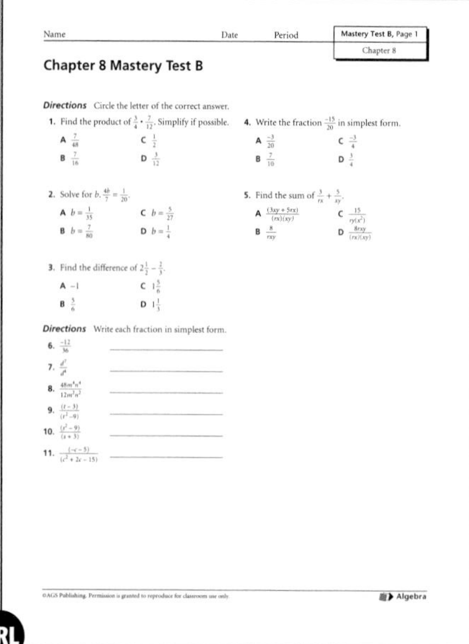

Chapter 8 Mastery Test B

32. $\dfrac{3x}{(x-1)^2}$

33. $\dfrac{(x+3)^2+(x-5)^2}{(x-5)(x+3)}$

34. $\dfrac{9ac^2-ac}{abc^2}$

35. $\dfrac{3mp+5n}{n^2p^2}$

36. 276 votes

37. about 833 deer

38. $1\frac{13}{15}$ hours

39. 10 feet

40. 12

Find the sum or difference.

Example: $\frac{3}{4}-\frac{1}{8}$ Solution: $\frac{3}{4}-\frac{1}{8}=\frac{3}{4}\left[\frac{2}{2}\right]-\frac{1}{8}\left[\frac{1}{1}\right]=\frac{6}{8}-\frac{1}{8}=\frac{5}{8}$

32. $\dfrac{3}{(x-1)}+\dfrac{3}{(x-1)^2}$

33. $\dfrac{(x+3)}{(x-5)}+\dfrac{(x-5)}{(x+3)}$

34. $\dfrac{9a}{ab}-\dfrac{c}{bc^2}$

35. $\dfrac{3m}{n^2p}+\dfrac{5}{p^2n}$

Solve these problems. Write your answer in simplest form.

Example: The scale on a map is 1 cm = 20 miles. How many cm represent 180 miles?
Solution: $\frac{1}{20}=\frac{x}{180}$ (1)(180) = (20)(x) 180 = 20x x = 9

36. John won the class election by a margin of 3 to 2. He received 414 votes. How many votes did the other candidate get?

37. Conservationists capture, tag, and release 250 deer in a preserve. Later, 150 deer are caught for observation; 45 of them are already tagged. About how many deer are in the preserve?

38. In four hours, Edgar can collect 100 spittle bugs. Gene collects the same number in $3\frac{1}{2}$ hours. If they work together, how quickly can they catch 100 bugs?

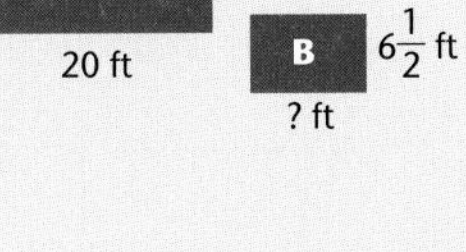

39. Rectangle A has a base of 20 ft and a height of 13 ft. Rectangle B, a similar rectangle, has a height of $6\frac{1}{2}$ ft. How long is the base of rectangle B?

40. One third a number equals 5 less than $\frac{3}{4}$ of the number. What is the number?

Test-Taking Tip

If you have time, compute problems a second time. Then check your original answer.

further and have the students simplify the expression using factorization. Example: The names Aaron, Ronald, and Brian can become $\frac{\text{aaron/ron}}{\text{ald/brian}}$. Simplified it would be $\frac{\text{ba}^2\text{rin}}{\text{ld}}$.

■ To add and subtract algebraic fractions

Have students create an algebraic fraction by using the first letter of their birthday month as a variable in either the numerator or denominator position and the number of their birthday day in the other position. Example: A student with the birthday April 27 can write the fraction as $\frac{a}{27}$ or $\frac{27}{a}$. Then have the students pair up and add and subtract their personalized expressions. Remind the students that they must have like denominators before they can find the solution.

■ To solve problems involving proportions and fractions

Have students bring in a favorite recipe—or provide a variety of recipes that students can choose from. Direct students to write down the ingredients needed for some multiple of the recipe, for example five or six times as much. Then have students divide the proportionally larger recipe by $\frac{2}{3}$, $\frac{3}{4}$ or $\frac{3}{8}$.

■ To solve equations with algebraic fractions

Have students think about measurements that affect them personally—such as time, distance, prices, etc. Then have students develop questions about some of these real-life issues and explain how they can be solved using algebraic fractions. Example: If it takes me 2 hours to clean the house and it takes my brother 1 hour and 15 minutes, how fast can we clean the house together? If x equals the total time it takes to clean the house, then in x hours I can clean a fraction $\frac{x}{2}$ of the house, and my brother can clean a fraction of $\frac{x}{(\frac{5}{4})}$. The total of these fractions would equal "1" which is the entire house being cleaned. Solution: $x = 46\frac{2}{13}$ minutes. Then have students exchange questions and solve them.

Chapter

Planning Guide

Linear Equations and Inequalities in the Coordinate Plane

		Student Text Lesson: Student Pages	Vocabulary	Practice Exercises	Solutions Key
Lesson 1	The Coordinate System	250–253	✔	✔	✔
Lesson 2	Graphing Equations	254–255		✔	✔
Lesson 3	Intercepts of Lines	256–257	✔	✔	✔
Lesson 4	Slopes of Lines	258–262	✔	✔	✔
Lesson 5	Writing Linear Equations	263–264	✔	✔	✔
Lesson 6	Lines as Functions	265–267	✔	✔	✔
Lesson 7	Domain and Range of a Function	268–271		✔	✔
Lesson 8	Graphing Inequalities: $y < mx + b$, $y > mx + b$	272–275		✔	✔
Lesson 9	Graphing Inequalities: $y \leq mx + b$, $y \geq mx + b$	276–279		✔	✔
Lesson 10	Graphs Without Numbers	280–281		✔	✔
Application	Graphing	282		✔	✔

Chapter Activities

Teacher's Resource Library

Estimation Exercise 9: Estimating Slope
Application Activity 9: Graphing
Everyday Algebra 9: Comparing Slopes
Community Connection 9: Slope in Construction

Teacher's Edition

Chapter 9 Project

Assessment Options

Student Text

Chapter 9 Review

Teacher's Resource Library

Chapter 9 Mastery Tests A and B

Student Text Features							Teaching Strategies							Learning Styles						Teacher's Resource Library			
Estimation Activity	Algebra in Your Life	Technology Connection	Writing About Mathematics	Try This	Problem Solving	Calculator Practice	Online Connection	Common Error	Applications Home, Career, Community	Mental Math	Manipulatives	Calculator	Group Problem Solving	Auditory/Verbal	Visual/Spatial	Logical/Mathematical	Body/Kinesthetic	Interpersonal/Group Learning	LEP/ESL	Activities	Alternate Activities	Workbook Activities	Self-Study Guide
			252		253			251	252	253			253				251		252	79	79	85	✔
				255														255		80	80	86	✔
			257					256						259	257					81	81	87	✔
	262		261		262	261	262	259	259			260	261	260						82	82	88	✔
			264										264							83	83	89	✔
			267											266	266					84	84	90	✔
		270						270								271			269	85	85	91	✔
275													272							86	86	92	✔
								276										278	277	87	87	93	✔
									281						281					88	88	94	✔
																		282					✔

Software Options

Skill Track Software

Use the Skill Track Software for *Algebra* for additional reinforcement of this chapter. The software provides multiple-choice assessment items for students to access by computer.

Solutions Key

Use the Solutions Key with this chapter to help students who may need additional assistance. The Solutions Key CD provides solutions for every exercise in the student edition.

Other Resources

Alternative Activities

The Teacher's Resource Library (TRL) contains a set of worksheets written at a second-grade reading level called Alternative Activities. They cover the same content as the regular Activities.

Chapter at a Glance

Chapter 9: Linear Equations and Inequalities in the Coordinate Plane

pages 248–285

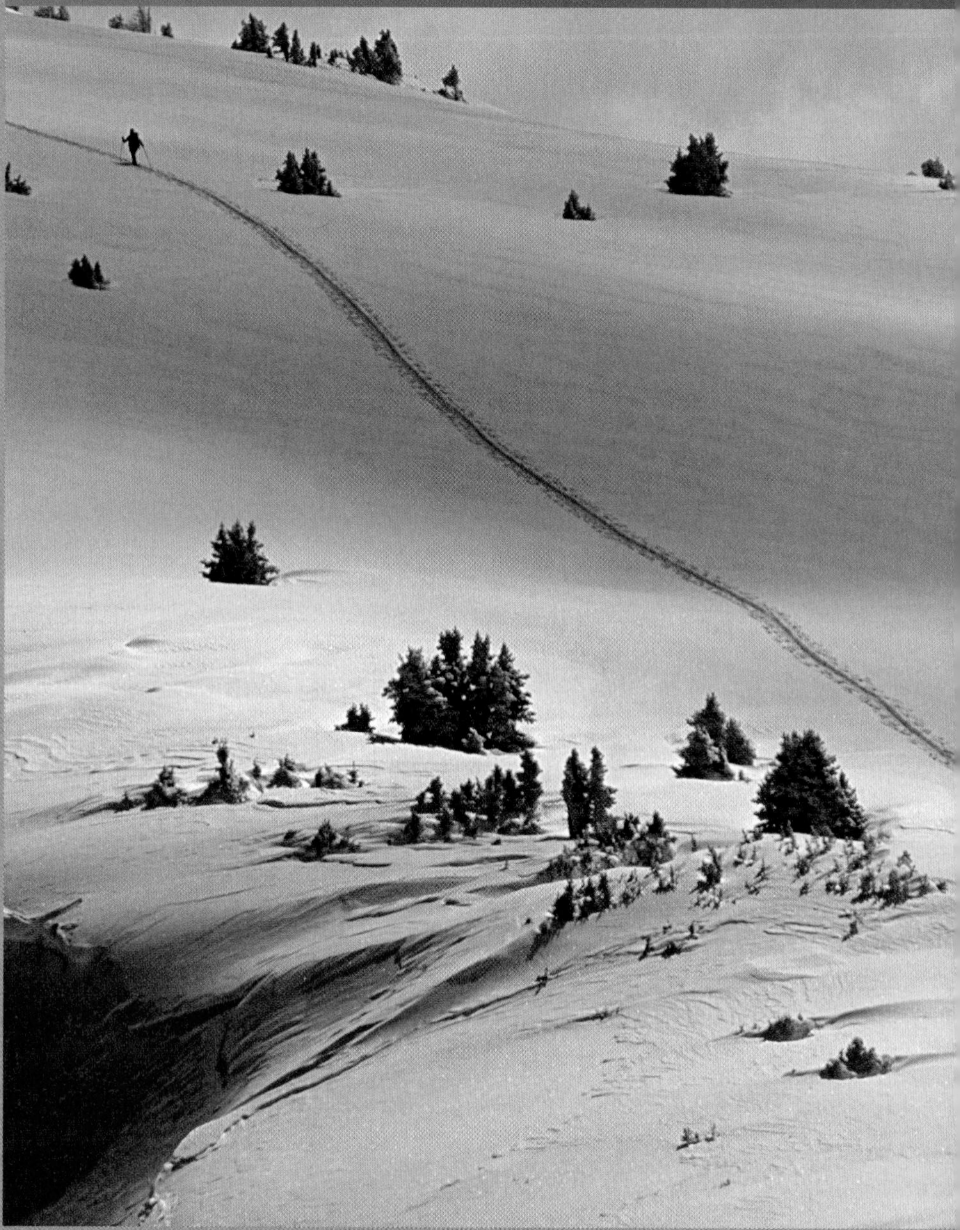

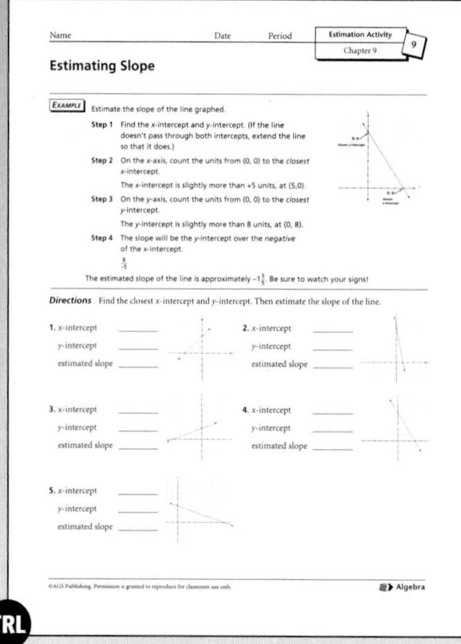

Name Date Period | Estimation Activity 9 | Chapter 9

Estimating Slope

EXAMPLE Estimate the slope of the line graphed.

Step 1 Find the *x*-intercept and *y*-intercept. (If the line doesn't pass through both intercepts, extend the line so that it does.)

Step 2 On the *x*-axis, count the units from (0, 0) to the *closest* *x*-intercept.

The *x*-intercept is slightly more than +5 units, at (5,0).

Step 3 On the *y*-axis, count the units from (0, 0) to the *closest* *y*-intercept.

The *y*-intercept is slightly more than 8 units, at (0, 8).

Step 4 The slope will be the *y*-intercept over the *negative* of the *x*-intercept.

$\frac{8}{-5}$

The estimated slope of the line is approximately $-1\frac{3}{5}$. Be sure to watch your signs!

Directions Find the closest *x*-intercept and *y*-intercept. Then estimate the slope of the line.

1. *x*-intercept ______
   y-intercept ______
   estimated slope ______
2. *x*-intercept ______
   y-intercept ______
   estimated slope ______
3. *x*-intercept ______
   y-intercept ______
   estimated slope ______
4. *x*-intercept ______
   y-intercept ______
   estimated slope ______
5. *x*-intercept ______
   y-intercept ______
   estimated slope ______

 Algebra

TRL

Estimation Exercise 9

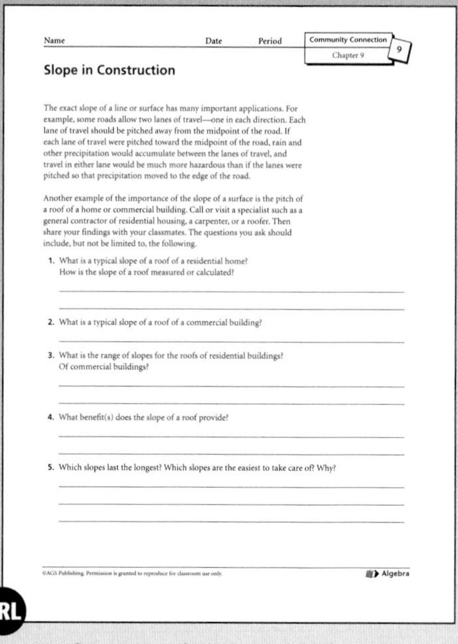

Name Date Period | Community Connection 9 | Chapter 9

Slope in Construction

The exact slope of a line or surface has many important applications. For example, some roads allow two lanes of travel—one in each direction. Each lane of travel should be pitched away from the midpoint of the road. If each lane of travel were pitched toward the midpoint of the road, rain and other precipitation would accumulate between the lanes of travel, and travel in either lane would be much more hazardous than if the lanes were pitched so that precipitation moved to the edge of the road.

Another example of the importance of the slope of a surface is the pitch of a roof of a home or commercial building. Call or visit a specialist such as a general contractor of residential housing, a carpenter, or a roofer. Then share your findings with your classmates. The questions you ask should include, but not be limited to, the following.

1. What is a typical slope of a roof of a residential home? How is the slope of a roof measured or calculated?
2. What is a typical slope of a roof of a commercial building?
3. What is the range of slopes for the roofs of residential buildings? Of commercial buildings?
4. What benefit(s) does the slope of a roof provide?
5. Which slopes last the longest? Which slopes are the easiest to take care of? Why?

 Algebra

TRL

Community Connection 9

Chapter

Linear Equations and Inequalities in the Coordinate Plane

Nordic, or cross-country, skiing takes practice and strength. Advanced skiers can ski up steep slopes. To compare the steepness of two hills, you could graph the slope of a ski trail on a coordinate plane. The points in the horizontal line on the *x*-axis represent the flat plane of the earth. Next, you'd plot points in a line on the *y*-axis. This line would be tilted like the slant of the ski trail. Using the formula for slope, you could find the angle between the *x*- and *y*- lines. The wider the angle, the steeper the hill. And the steeper the hill, the more work it takes to reach the top.

In Chapter 9, you will study, create and interpret graphs.

Goals for Learning

- ◆ To identify the parts of a graph
- ◆ To locate and plot points in the coordinate system
- ◆ To solve equations for ordered pairs and graph a line
- ◆ To find the *x*-intercept and *y*-intercept of a graph
- ◆ To determine the slope of a line
- ◆ To write and solve an equation of a straight line
- ◆ To identify and evaluate functions
- ◆ To determine the range of a function with a given domain
- ◆ To graph inequalities
- ◆ To interpret and create graphs without numbers

249

Introducing the Chapter

Use the chapter opener as an opportunity to alert students that linear equations and inequalities form the foundation for using various graphs. For example, using graphs, skiers can determine the slope of ski trails. The steeper the slope, the more work it is to climb to the top.

Chapter Project

Encourage students to work in groups of four to produce a 10-minute video that presents information about coordinate graphs or uses coordinate graphs to describe a physical phenomenon. Allow students to choose one of these projects or their own project.

- *Where in the World*, a show that uses the worldwide coordinate system to locate specific places on earth.
- *Scream With Me*, a show that compares and contrasts the slopes of several famous roller coasters.
- *Treasure Hunt*, a game show where contestants use coordinate pairs as clues to be the first to reach buried treasure.

Teacher's Resource

The AGS Publishing Teaching Strategies in Math Transparencies may be used with this chapter. They add an interactive dimension to expand and enhance the program content.

Career Interest Inventory

The AGS Publishing Harrington-O'Shea Career Decision-Making System-Revised (CDM) may be used with this chapter. Students can use the CDM to explore their interests and identify careers. The CDM defines career areas that are indicated by students' responses on the inventory.

Name ______ Date ______ Period ______ *SELF-STUDY GUIDE*

CHAPTER 9: Linear Equations and Inequalities in the Coordinate Plane

Goals 9.1 and 9.2 *To identify the parts of a graph*
To locate and plot points in the coordinate system

Date	Assignment	Score
______	1: Read pages 250–251. Complete Exercises A–D on pages 252–253.	______
______	2: Complete Workbook Activity 85.	______

Comments:

Goal 9.3 and 9.4 *To solve equations for ordered pairs and graph a line*
To find the x-intercept and y-intercept of a graph

Date	Assignment	Score
______	3: Read page 254. Complete Exercises A–B on page 255.	______
______	4: Complete Workbook Activity 86.	______
______	5: Read pages 256–257. Complete Exercises A–C on page 257.	______
______	6: CompleteWorkbook Activity 87.	______

Comments:

Goal 9.5 *To determine the slope of a line*

Date	Assignment	Score
______	7: Read pages 258–259. Complete Exercises A, B, D, and E on pages 260–262.	______
______	8: Read and complete the Calculator Practice on page 261.	______
______	9: Complete Workbook Activity 88.	______

Comments:

Goals 9.6 and 9.7 *To write and solve an equation of a straight line*
To identify and evaluate functions

Date	Assignment	Score
______	10: Read pages 263–264. Complete Exercises A–C on page 264.	______
______	11: Complete Workbook Activity 89.	______
______	12: Read pages 265–266. Complete Exercises A–B on pages 266–267.	______
______	13: Complete Workbook Activity 90.	______

Comments:

 Algebra

TRL

Name ______ Date ______ Period ______ *SELF-STUDY GUIDE*

CHAPTER 9: Linear Equations and Inequalities, continued

Goal 9.8 *To determine range of a function with a given domain*

Date	Assignment	Score
______	14: Read pages 268–269. Complete Exercises A–C on pages 269–271.	______
______	15: Complete Workbook Activity 91.	______

Comments:

Goal 9.9 *To graph inequalities*

Date	Assignment	Score
______	16: Read pages 272–274. Complete Exercise A on page 274.	______
______	17: Complete Workbook Activity 92.	______
______	18: Read pages 276–277. Complete Exercises A–B on pages 278–279.	______
______	19: Complete Workbook Activity 93.	______

Comments:

Goal 9.10 *To interpret and create graphs without numbers*

Date	Assignment	Score
______	20: Read page 280. Complete Exercises A–B on page 281.	______
______	21: Complete Workbook Activity 94.	______
______	22: Read and complete the Application Exercise on page 282.	______
______	23: Complete the Chapter 9 Review on pages 283–285.	______

Comments:

Student's Signature ______ Date ______

Instructor's Signature ______ Date ______

©AGS Publishing. Permission is granted to reproduce for classroom use only. Algebra

TRL

Chapter 9 Self-Study Guide

Lesson at a Glance

Chapter 9 Lesson 1

Overview This lesson introduces the coordinate system and indicates how to represent points using ordered pairs of numbers.

Objectives

- To identify the parts of a graph
- To locate and plot points in the coordinate system

Student Pages 250–253

Teacher's Resource Library 

Workbook Activity 85

Activity 79

Alternative Activity 79

Mathematics Vocabulary

ordered pair
origin
quadrant
***x*-axis**
***y*-axis**

Warm-Up Activity

Initiate a discussion with students about the instructions needed to find a buried treasure or to get to a specific city. Draw out from students that the instructions generally include two components: an indication of direction (for example, north, south, left, right) and an indication of distance (such as 5 paces, 4 blocks, 30 miles). Encourage students to keep these factors in mind as they begin their study of coordinate systems.

Teaching the Lesson

Demonstrate the example, Point P located at (4, 3), on the board or on an overhead projector. Indicate to students that the x-value of P is 4 units to the right of the origin and the y-value of P is 3 units up from the origin. Ask volunteers to locate points $Q\,(-4, 3)$, $R\,(4, -3)$ and $S\,(-4, -3)$ on the same coordinate system.

Lesson 1 The Coordinate System

***X*-axis**
The horizontal axis in a coordinate system

***Y*-axis**
The vertical axis in a coordinate system

Origin
The point at which the axes in a coordinate system intersect

Quadrant
Region of a coordinate plane bounded by the x- and y-axes

Ordered pair
Two real numbers that locate a point in the plane

The coordinate system is made up of two number lines that are perpendicular to each other. Using these axes, you can name every point in the plane.

The horizontal number line is known as the ***x*-axis,** and the vertical number line is known as the ***y*-axis.**

The point at which the axes meet, or intersect, is known as the **origin.**

The x-axis and the y-axis divide the coordinate system into four regions called **quadrants.**

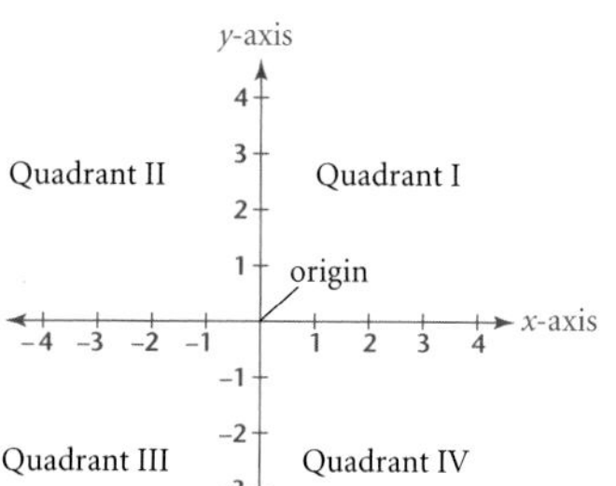

Rule In the coordinate system, any point P can be represented by an **ordered pair** of real numbers written in the form (x, y).

In an ordered pair of real numbers written in the form (x, y), the x-value is always first and the y-value is always second.

EXAMPLE 1 To locate a point in the coordinate system:

First, determine the x-value of the point by drawing or imagining a perpendicular line from the point to the x-axis.

Second, determine the y-value of the point by drawing or imagining a perpendicular line from the point to the y-axis.

Then write the ordered pair in the form (x, y).

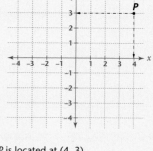

Locate Point P. Point P is located at (4, 3).

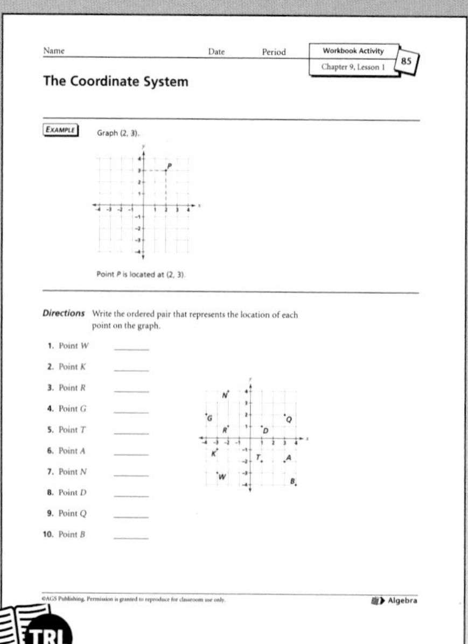

Name Date Period — Workbook Activity 85, Chapter 9, Lesson 1

The Coordinate System

EXAMPLE Graph (2, 3).

Point P is located at (2, 3).

Directions Write the ordered pair that represents the location of each point on the graph.

1. Point W ______
2. Point K ______
3. Point R ______
4. Point G ______
5. Point T ______
6. Point A ______
7. Point N ______
8. Point D ______
9. Point Q ______
10. Point B ______

 Algebra

Workbook Activity 85

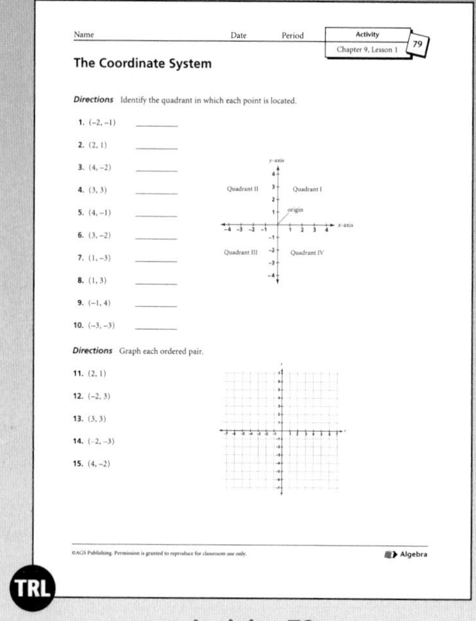

Name Date Period — Activity 79, Chapter 9, Lesson 1

The Coordinate System

Directions Identify the quadrant in which each point is located.

1. (−2, −1) ______
2. (2, 1) ______
3. (4, −2) ______
4. (3, 3) ______
5. (4, −1) ______
6. (3, −2) ______
7. (1, −3) ______
8. (1, 3) ______
9. (−1, 4) ______
10. (−3, −3) ______

Directions Graph each ordered pair.

11. (2, 1)
12. (−2, 3)
13. (3, 3)
14. (−2, −3)
15. (4, −2)

 Algebra

Activity 79

To *graph* a point on the coordinate system means to draw a *dot* where the point is located.

Example 2 Graph $(-3, 2)$.

Recall that in the ordered pair $(-3, 2)$, -3 represents the x-value and 2 represents the y-value.

To graph $(-3, 2)$, begin at the origin and move 3 units to the left. Then move 2 units up.

Draw a dot and label the point $(-3, 2)$.

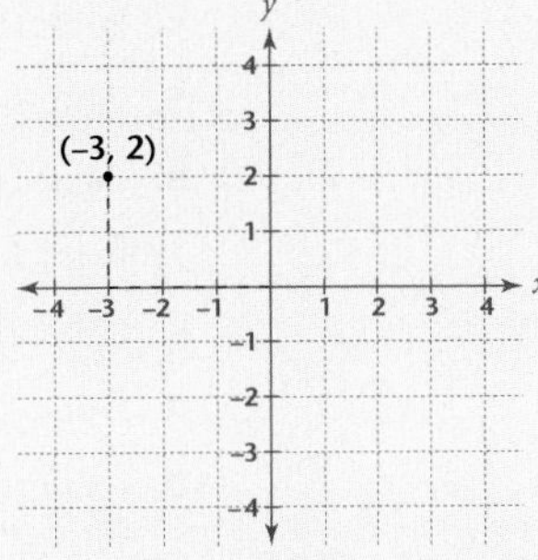

Example 3 Graph Point H at $(2, 0)$.

Begin at the origin and move 2 units to the right. Because the y-value is 0, no further movement is required.

Draw a dot and label the point H.

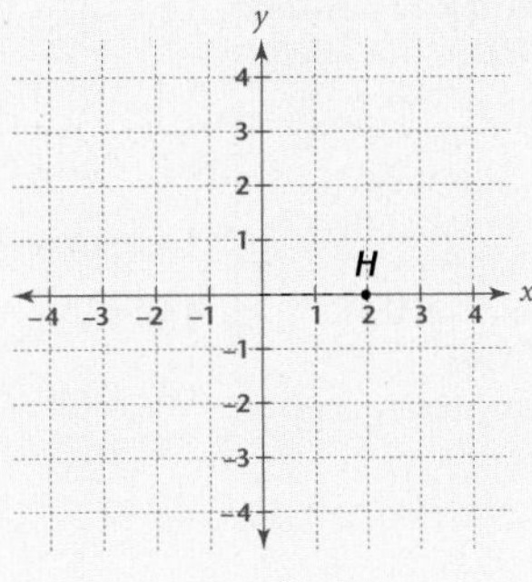

Common Error

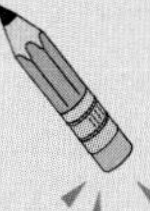

As they gain familiarity with coordinate systems, students may lose track of the order in ordered pairs. Stress to students that in an ordered pair the x-value is always first, and the y-value is always second. Help students establish consistent graphing skills by always plotting the x-value of an ordered pair first.

3 Reinforce and Extend

Learning Styles

Body/Kinesthetic

Prepare a set of 42 cards, 2 cards for each number from 0 to 20. Also prepare two "negative" cards and two "positive" cards. Mark a coordinate grid on the classroom floor. If the floor is covered in square tiles, use the corners of the tiles as grid intersections. Have students draw two number cards and two cards to indicate positive or negative. Direct students to use the cards to form an ordered pair. Then have them move to the location on the coordinate grid that matches the ordered pair they drew. Direct students to hold up their cards to indicate their location.

In the Community

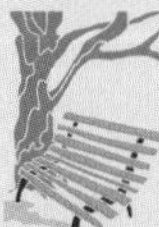

Point out to students that sometimes it is important that a description of a point applies to one and only one location. Offer as an example the need to make certain that the legal description of a parcel of land describes one and only one land parcel. Ask students to form three study teams. The first team can determine the legal description of the land occupied by their school. The information is kept by the county and is usually accessible through the county clerk's office. The second team can investigate how legal descriptions were composed for parcels of land in most of the United States. (These descriptions originally included meridians, ranges, townships, sections, and subdivisions.) The third team might investigate how this older type of land description is being converted to a geographic coordinate system in some western states. Information about this conversion may be obtained through the Bureau of Land Management.

Learning Styles

LEP/ESL

Have students work in pairs to write complete sentences describing the points in Exercise B. Using problem 11, provide a model sentence for students: "Point *Y* is 1 unit to the right of the *y*-axis and 2 units above the *x*-axis." For each problem, one student should write the sentence, and the partner should plot the point described. Encourage students to exchange roles after each problem.

Exercise A Write the ordered pair that represents the location of each point.

1. Point *B* (2, 1)
2. Point *W* (−1, 3)
3. Point *K* (3, −2)
4. Point *R* (−4, 0)
5. Point *N* (−2, −2)
6. Point *Q* (1, −4)
7. Point *L* (0, 1)
8. Point *T* (−1, −1)
9. Point *G* (−3, 1)
10. Point *A* (0, 0)

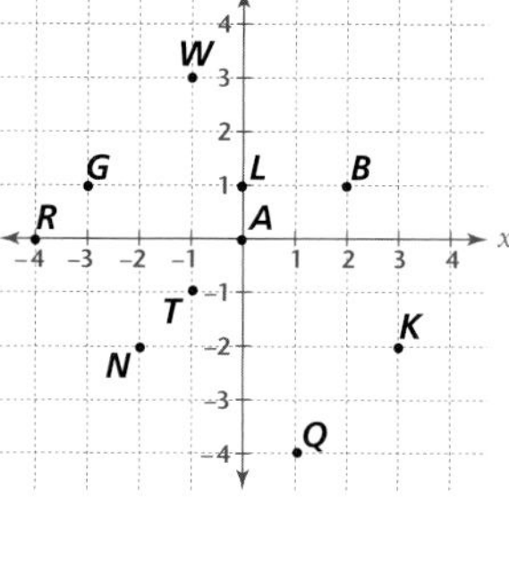

Writing About Mathematics

What is true about the *y*-value of any point on the *x*-axis? What is true about the *x*-value of any point on the *y*-axis?

Exercise B Draw a coordinate system like the one shown and graph the following points.

11. Point *Y* at (1, 2)
12. Point *V* at (0, −4)
13. Point *C* at (−3, −1)
14. Point *D* at (4, 0)
15. Point *F* at (−2, −4)
16. Point *Z* at (0, 3)

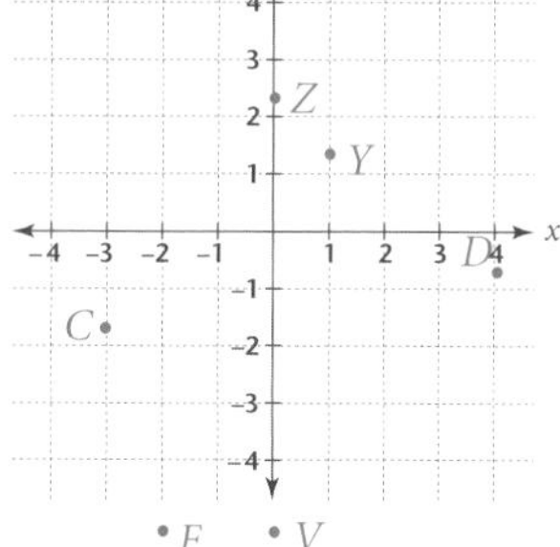

Exercise C Identify the quadrant in which each point is located.

17. (3, 3) Quadrant I

18. (−1, −3) Quadrant III

19. (−2, 1) Quadrant II

20. (2, −1) Quadrant IV

21. (−3, 2) Quadrant II

22. (−2, −3) Quadrant III

PROBLEM SOLVING

Exercise D Answer each question.

23. For exercise, Amy walks eight blocks east. After walking four blocks north, twelve blocks west, and four blocks south, she stops to rest. At that time, Amy is how many blocks away from her starting point? 4 blocks

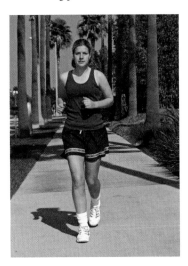

24. Mario is lost and asks two people for directions. The first person says that Mario should drive four blocks west and then five blocks north. The second person says that Mario should drive five blocks west and then four blocks north. Are the directions given by each person the same? Explain.

25. Suppose a north-south line and an east-west line pass through the exact middle of the contiguous United States. If the north-south line represents the y-axis and the east-west line represents the x-axis, in which quadrant of the United States do you live?

24. No, sample explanation: The point (−4, +5) is in a different location than the point (−5, +4).

25. Answers will vary.

MENTAL MATH

Gather a set of 42 cards, 2 cards for each number from 0 to 20, and two "negative" cards and two "positive" cards. Draw two number and two sign cards, then post them as an ordered pair on the board or overhead projector. Ask students to identify in which quadrant of the coordinate system the ordered pair lies.

GROUP PROBLEM SOLVING

Have students work in groups of four. Encourage them to use a coordinate system to describe the bus routes for their school. Suggest that they place the school at (0, 0), the origin. Then have them plot the routes of the buses that bring students to the school. Indicate that they may find it easiest to plot the last pickup first and then work their way back to the first pickup point. Have each group plot a different bus route. Display all the routes. Encourage students to suggest ways in which the routes can be made shorter or more efficient.

Lesson at a Glance

Chapter 9 Lesson 2

Overview This lesson demonstrates how to produce an ordered pair solution to an equation and use the ordered pair to graph the line of the equation.

Objectives

- To produce ordered pairs that represent solutions to equations
- To graph the line of an equation using ordered pairs

Student Pages 254–255

Teacher's Resource Library 

Workbook Activity 86

Activity 80

Alternative Activity 80

Warm-Up Activity

Remind students that in equations involving x and y, they can choose a value for x, substitute it in the equation, and find the value for y for which the equation is true.

Teaching the Lesson

Use the example $y = 2x$ to demonstrate how to choose a value for x and then solve for the appropriate value of y. Then using a coordinate system on the board or overhead projector, work with students to plot points to determine the graph of the equation $y = 2x$.

Try This

Ask students to offer ways in which they can prove they have the correct equation. *(Graph the equation, choose any point P along the line of the equation, and show that the x and y coordinates for P are equal.)*

Lesson 2 Graphing Equations

Since ordered pairs are represented by (x, y), an equation can be used to represent x and y. You can then substitute numbers for x, solve for y, plot the points (x, y), and graph the line of the equation.

EXAMPLE 1 Graph $y = 2x$.

Step 1 Assign values for x. For example, let $x = -1$, 0, 1, and 2.

Step 2 Solve $y = 2x$ for y. Display the results in a table.

$y = 2x$	
x	y
−1	−2
0	0
1	2
2	4

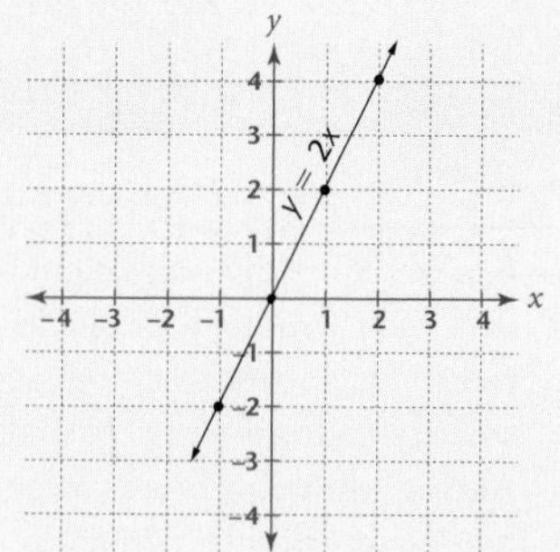

Step 3 Plot the points shown in the table, then graph the line.

The graph of the equation $y = 2x$ forms a straight line.

EXAMPLE 2 Graph $y = 2x - 3$.

Step 1 Assign two values for x. Let $x = -1$ and $x = 1$.

Step 2 Solve for y.

$y = 2x - 3$	$y = 2x - 3$
$y = 2(-1) - 3$	$y = 2(1) - 3$
$y = -2 - 3$	$y = 2 - 3$
$y = -5$	$y = -1$
When $x = -1$, $y = -5$.	When $x = 1$, $y = -1$.
$(-1, -5)$	$(1, -1)$

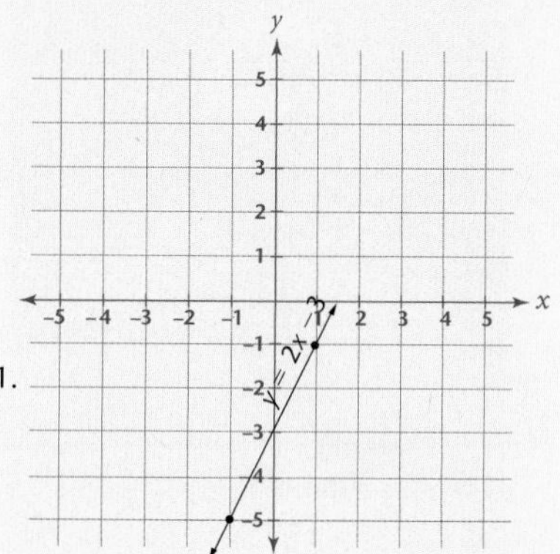

Step 3 Plot the points $(-1, -5)$ and $(1, -1)$. Then graph and label the line.

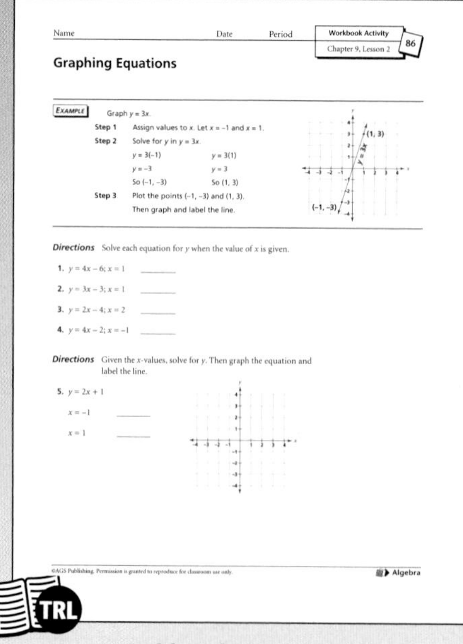

Name Date Period

Workbook Activity 86 — Chapter 9, Lesson 2

Graphing Equations

EXAMPLE Graph $y = 3x$.

Step 1 Assign values to x. Let $x = -1$ and $x = 1$.

Step 2 Solve for y in $y = 3x$.

$y = 3(-1)$	$y = 3(1)$
$y = -3$	$y = 3$
So $(-1, -3)$	So $(1, 3)$

Step 3 Plot the points $(-1, -3)$ and $(1, 3)$. Then graph and label the line.

Directions Solve each equation for y when the value of x is given.

1. $y = 4x - 6$; $x = 1$ ______
2. $y = 3x - 3$; $x = 1$ ______
3. $y = 2x - 4$; $x = 2$ ______
4. $y = 4x - 2$; $x = -1$ ______

Directions Given the x-values, solve for y. Then graph the equation and label the line.

5. $y = 2x + 1$

   $x = -1$ ______

   $x = 1$ ______

 Algebra

Workbook Activity 86

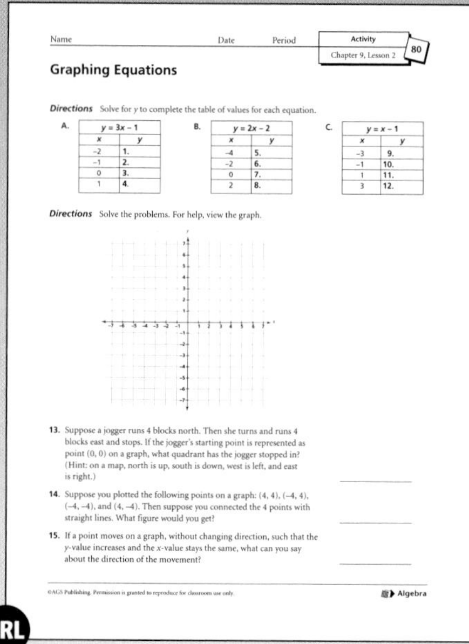

Name Date Period

Activity 80 — Chapter 9, Lesson 2

Graphing Equations

Directions Solve for y to complete the table of values for each equation.

A.

$y = 3x - 1$	
x	y
−2	1.
−1	2.
0	3.
1	4.

B.

$y = 2x - 2$	
x	y
−4	5.
−2	6.
0	7.
2	8.

C.

$y = x - 1$	
x	y
−3	9.
−1	10.
1	11.
3	12.

Directions Solve the problems. For help, view the graph.

13. Suppose a jogger runs 4 blocks north. Then she turns and runs 4 blocks east and stops. If the jogger's starting point is represented as point (0, 0) on a graph, what quadrant has the jogger stopped in? (Hint: on a map, north is up, south is down, west is left, and east is right.) ______
14. Suppose you plotted the following points on a graph: (4, 4), (−4, 4), (−4, −4), and (4, −4). Then suppose you connected the 4 points with straight lines. What figure would you get? ______
15. If a point moves on a graph, without changing direction, such that the y-value increases and the x-value stays the same, what can you say about the direction of the movement? ______

 Algebra

Activity 80

Whenever you graph a line, it is a good idea to graph three points instead of two. The third point will act as a check to be sure the points you chose are correct.

Exercise A Copy and complete the table of values for each equation.

1.

$y = x$	
x	y
–2	–2
–1	–1
0	0
1	1
2	2

2.

$y = 3x$	
x	y
–5	–15
–3	–9
–1	–3
1	3
3	9

3.

$y = 2x + 1$	
x	y
–4	–7
–2	–3
0	1
2	5
4	9

See Teacher's Edition page for answers to problems 4–10.

Exercise B Copy and complete a table of values for each equation. Then graph and label the line of each equation.

4.

$y = x$	
x	y
–1	–1
0	0
1	1

5.

$y = 3x$	
x	y
–1	–3
0	0
1	3

6.

$y = 2x + 1$	
x	y
–1	–1
0	1
1	3

7.

$y = 2x - 1$	
x	y
–1	–3
0	–1
1	1

8.

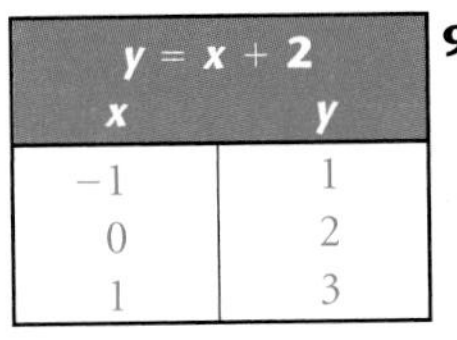

$y = x + 2$	
x	y
–1	1
0	2
1	3

9.

$y = x - 3$	
x	y
–1	–4
0	–3
1	–2

10.

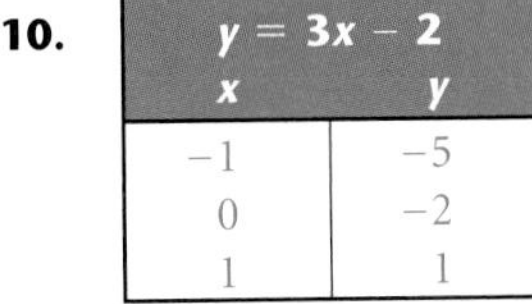

$y = 3x - 2$	
x	y
–1	–5
0	–2
1	1

TRY THIS A straight line passes through (100, 100) and the origin. What is the equation of the line? $y = x$

3 Reinforce and Extend

Learning Styles

Interpersonal Group Learning

Have students work in small groups to write, solve, and graph the inverse of the equations in problems 5–10 in Exercise B. For example, $y = 3x$ becomes $x = 3y$; $y = 2x + 1$ becomes $x = 2y + 1$. Ask the groups to describe the similarities and differences between their graphs and the graphs of the equations for Exercise B.

Answers to Problems 4–10

4.

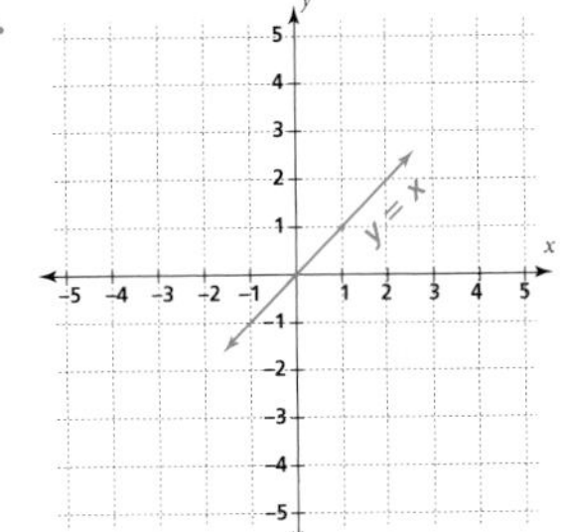

5.

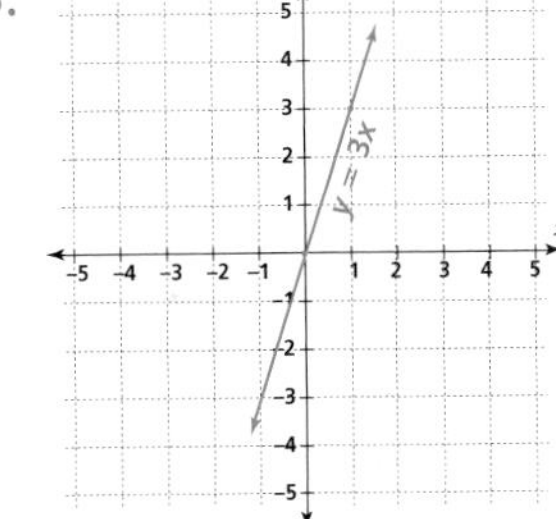

6.

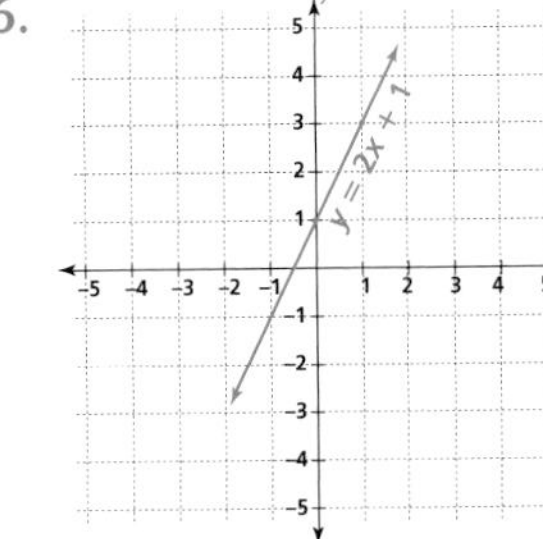

7.

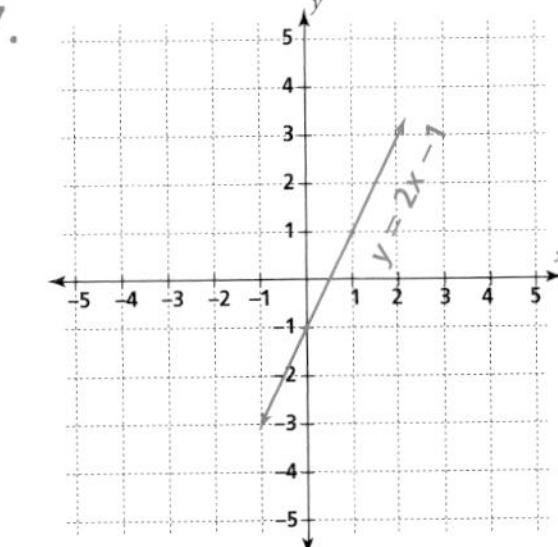

8.

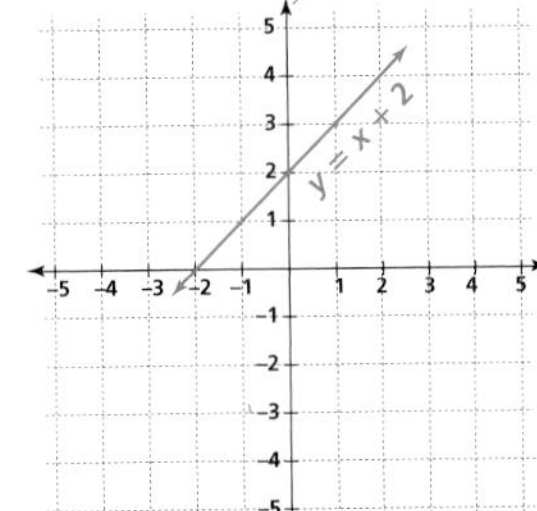

9.

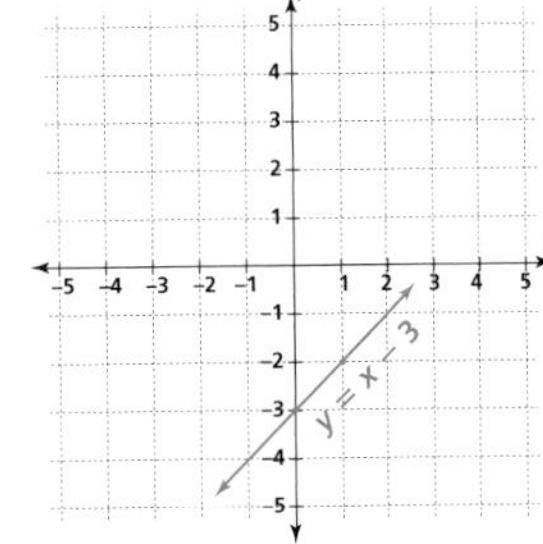

10.

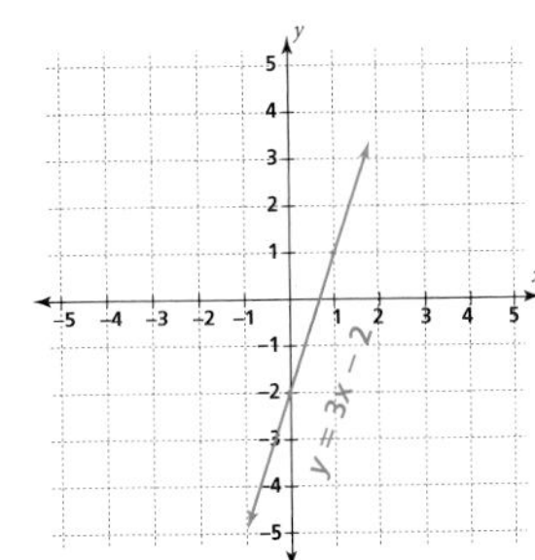

Lesson at a Glance

Chapter 9 Lesson 3

Overview This lesson explores the usefulness of the x- and y-intercepts of graphs.

Objective

- To find the x- and y-intercepts of a graph

Student Pages 256–257

Teacher's Resource Library 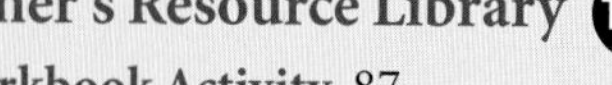

Workbook Activity 87

Activity 81

Alternative Activity 81

Mathematics Vocabulary

***x*-intercept**
***y*-intercept**

Warm-Up Activity

Discuss with students the values associated with the x- and y-axes of the coordinate system. Lead students to the generalization that the points along the y-axis are those for which $x = 0$ and the points along the x-axis are those for which $y = 0$.

Teaching the Lesson

Make certain students recognize the x- and y-intercepts of the graph of $y = 2x + 1$. You may want to duplicate the graph on the board or an overhead projector. Label both the x- and y-axes and the x- and y-intercepts.

Common Error

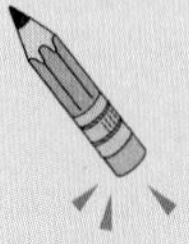

Students may become confused as they work with x- and y-intercepts. Help them recognize that the y-intercept for an equation, the point where the equation crosses the y-axis, represents the location at which $x = 0$. In a similar manner, the x-intercept for an equation, the point where the equation crosses the x-axis, represents the location at which $y = 0$.

Lesson 3 Intercepts of Lines

***y*-intercept**
The point at which a graph intersects the y-axis

In the previous lesson, you explored the graph of $y = 2x + 1$.

The graph passes through the point (0, 1). Since (0, 1) is a point on the y-axis, (0, 1) is called the ***y*-intercept** of the graph.

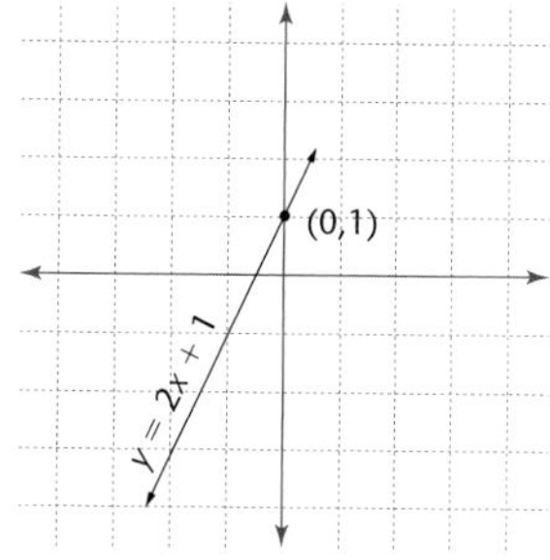

The y-intercept of a graph is the point at which a graph intersects the y-axis.

To find the y-intercept of a graph, substitute $x = 0$ into the equation of the graph and solve for y.

EXAMPLE 1 Find the y-intercept of $y = 3x + 1$.

Step 1 Let $x = 0$.

Step 2 Substitute $x = 0$ into the equation $y = 3x + 1$ and solve for y.

$y = 3x + 1$
$y = 3(0) + 1$
$y = 0 + 1$
$y = 1$

Step 3 Write an ordered pair to represent the y-intercept.

The y-intercept of $y = 3x + 1$ is (0, 1).

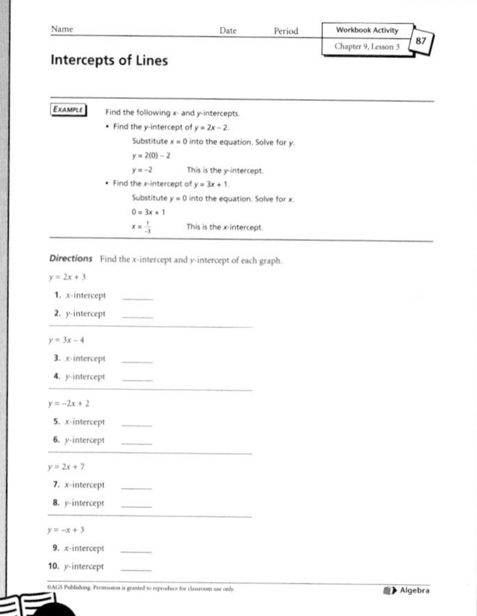

Name Date Period — Workbook Activity 87, Chapter 9, Lesson 3

Intercepts of Lines

EXAMPLE Find the following x- and y-intercepts.

- Find the y-intercept of $y = 2x - 2$.
  Substitute $x = 0$ into the equation. Solve for y.
  $y = 2(0) - 2$
  $y = -2$ This is the y-intercept.
- Find the x-intercept of $y = 3x + 1$.
  Substitute $y = 0$ into the equation. Solve for x.
  $0 = 3x + 1$
  $x = \frac{1}{-3}$ This is the x-intercept.

Directions Find the x-intercept and y-intercept of each graph.

$y = 2x + 3$
1. x-intercept ______
2. y-intercept ______

$y = 3x - 4$
3. x-intercept ______
4. y-intercept ______

$y = -2x + 2$
5. x-intercept ______
6. y-intercept ______

$y = 2x + 7$
7. x-intercept ______
8. y-intercept ______

$y = -x + 3$
9. x-intercept ______
10. y-intercept ______

 Algebra

Workbook Activity 87

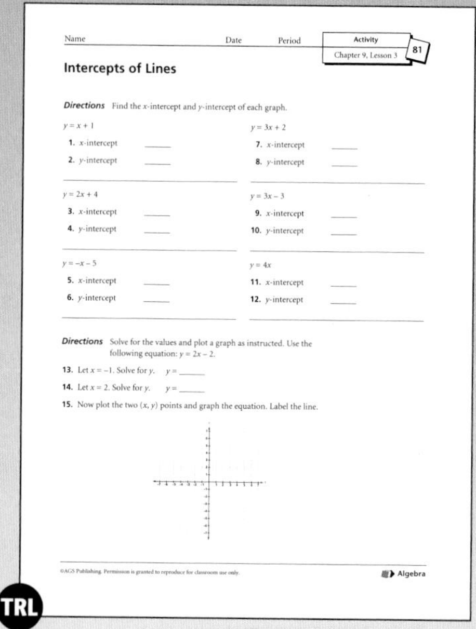

Name Date Period — Activity 81, Chapter 9, Lesson 3

Intercepts of Lines

Directions Find the x-intercept and y-intercept of each graph.

$y = x + 1$
1. x-intercept ______
2. y-intercept ______

$y = 2x + 4$
3. x-intercept ______
4. y-intercept ______

$y = -x - 5$
5. x-intercept ______
6. y-intercept ______

$y = 3x + 2$
7. x-intercept ______
8. y-intercept ______

$y = 3x - 3$
9. x-intercept ______
10. y-intercept ______

$y = 4x$
11. x-intercept ______
12. y-intercept ______

Directions Solve for the values and plot a graph as instructed. Use the following equation: $y = 2x - 2$.

13. Let $x = -1$. Solve for y. $y =$ ______
14. Let $x = 2$. Solve for y. $y =$ ______
15. Now plot the two (x, y) points and graph the equation. Label the line.

 Algebra

Activity 81

x-intercept

The point at which a graph intersects the x-axis

Writing About Mathematics

Will every graph have an x-intercept and a y-intercept? Explain.

Look again at the graph of $y = 2x + 1$.

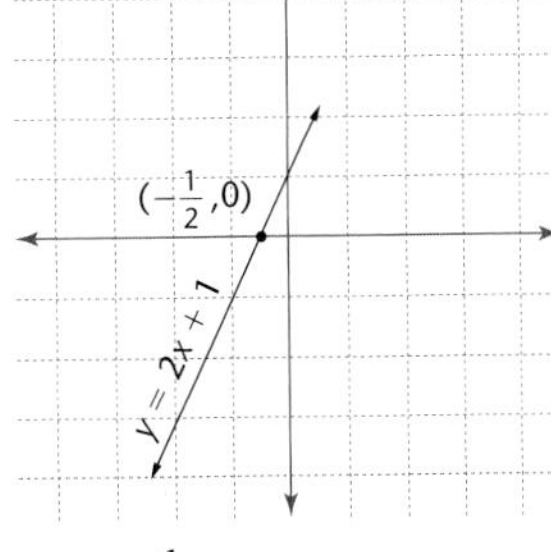

The graph also passes through the point $(-\frac{1}{2}, 0)$. Since $(-\frac{1}{2}, 0)$ is a point on the x-axis, $(-\frac{1}{2}, 0)$ is called the **x-intercept** of the graph.

The x-intercept of a graph is the point at which a graph intersects the x-axis. The x-intercept is also known as the root of the equation. To find the x-intercept of a graph, substitute $y = 0$ into the equation of the graph and solve for x.

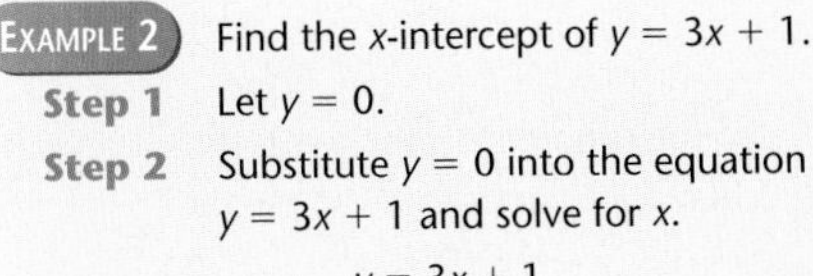

EXAMPLE 2 Find the x-intercept of $y = 3x + 1$.

Step 1 Let $y = 0$.

Step 2 Substitute $y = 0$ into the equation $y = 3x + 1$ and solve for x.

$$y = 3x + 1$$
$$0 = 3x + 1$$
$$-1 = 3x$$
$$-\frac{1}{3} = x$$

Step 3 Write an ordered pair to represent the x-intercept.

The x-intercept of $y = 3x + 1$ is $(-\frac{1}{3}, 0)$.

Exercise A Answer these questions.

1. Explain how to find the y-intercept of a graph.
2. Explain how to find the x-intercept of a graph.

1. Substitute $x = 0$ into the equation of the graph and solve for y. Write an ordered pair in the form (x, y).

2. Substitute $y = 0$ into the equation of the graph and solve for x. Write an ordered pair in the form (x, y).

Exercise B Find the x-intercept and y-intercept of each graph.

3. $y = x + 1$ — x-int. = −1; y-int. = 1
4. $y = x - 1$ — x-int. = 1; y-int. = −1
5. $y = x - 3$ — x-int. = 3; y-int. = −3
6. $y = x + 2$ — x-int. = −2; y-int. = 2
7. $y = 2x$ — x-int. = 0; y-int. = 0
8. $y = 3x$ — x-int. = 0; y-int. = 0
9. $y = 2x - 1$ — x-int. = $\frac{1}{2}$; y-int. = −1
10. $y = 4x - 4$ — x-int. = 1; y-int. = −4
11. $y = -x + 1$ — x-int. = 1; y-int. = 1
12. $y = -2x + 8$ — x-int. = 4; y-int. = 8
13. $y = -3x - 9$ — x-int. = −3; y-int. = −9
14. $y = -2x - 5$ — x-int. = $-\frac{5}{2}$; y-int. = −5

Exercise C Answer this question. Sample answer: when the graph passes through the origin

15. When are the x-intercept and the y-intercept of a graph identical?

3 Reinforce and Extend

Learning Styles

Auditory/Verbal

Ask pairs of students to explain the x- and y-intercepts of a graph to one another in their own words. Encourage them to include the following in their explanation: the location of the intercept in the coordinate plane, the value of x for the y-intercept, and the value of y for the x-intercept.

Learning Styles

Visual/Spatial

Suggest that students use the x- and y-intercepts to graph each of the problems in Exercise B. Students can work in pairs. One student can use the intercepts to graph the equation; the other can confirm the graph by finding another ordered pair for which the equation is true. Have students describe how the intercepts can be used in graphing equations.

Lesson at a Glance

Chapter 9 Lesson 4

Overview This lesson introduces the concept of the slope of a line.

Objective

- To determine the slope of a line

Student Pages 258–262

Teacher's Resource Library 

Workbook Activity 88

Activity 82

Alternative Activity 82

Mathematics Vocabulary

acute
obtuse
slope

Warm-Up Activity

Engage students in a discussion about slope. Ask them to supply examples such as ski slopes, toboggan hills, or playground slides. Have them identify characteristics of slope such as length, height, steepness, shallowness, and so on.

Teaching the Lesson

Work with students to develop an intuitive notion of slope. Point out that slope is a measure of how steeply a line rises or falls. Slope tells how many units a line goes up or down for every unit the line goes to the left or right. On a coordinate grid, draw several lines of increasing slope. Ask students to identify which lines are the steepest. Have them predict which lines would have the greatest slope. *(the same lines)*

To convince students who may not believe that they can assign either ordered pair the value (x_1, y_1), work through the second and third examples. Make sure students realize that in the first instance, (x_1, y_1) is assigned to $(1, 0)$, and in the second instance, the same ordered pair is assigned (x_2, y_2). Have students explain in their own words why the slope of the line would be the same no matter which ordered pair was chosen as (x_1, y_1).

Lesson  4 Slopes of Lines

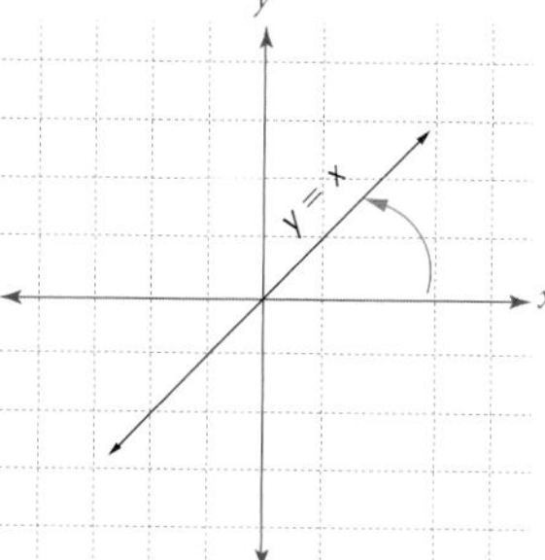

Slope
A measure of the steepness of a line

Acute
An angle smaller than a 90° angle

Obtuse
An angle larger than a 90° angle and smaller than a 180° angle

The coefficient of x controls the **slope,** or steepness, of a graph.

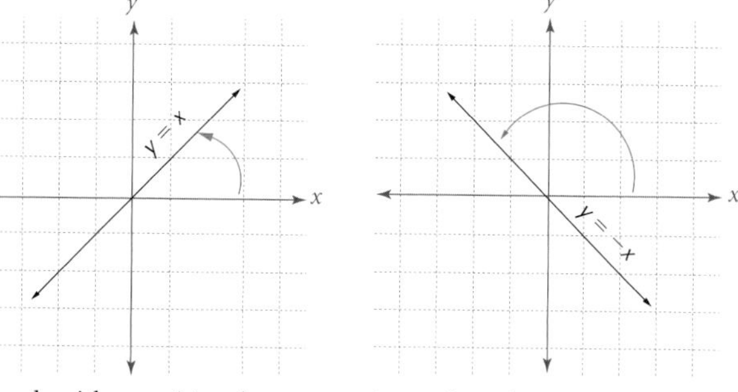

A graph with a *positive* slope creates an **acute** angle with the positive direction of the x-axis.

A graph with a *negative* slope creates an **obtuse** angle with the positive direction of the x-axis.

Remember, ordered pairs are written in the form (x, y).

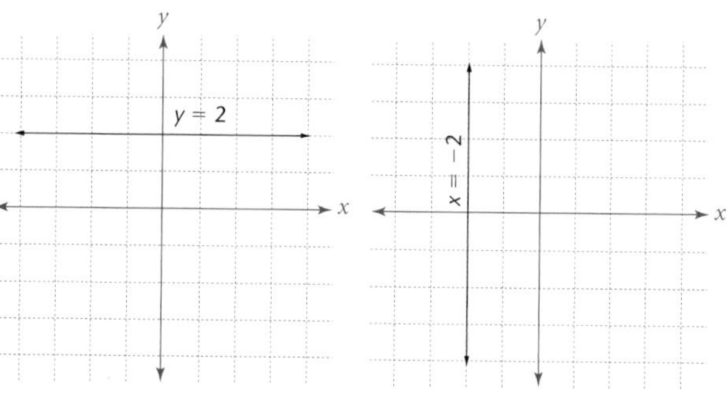

A graph with a *slope of zero* is parallel to the x-axis.

A graph with a slope that is *undefined* is parallel to the y-axis.

Roofs have slope. Is the slope of each roof the same or different?

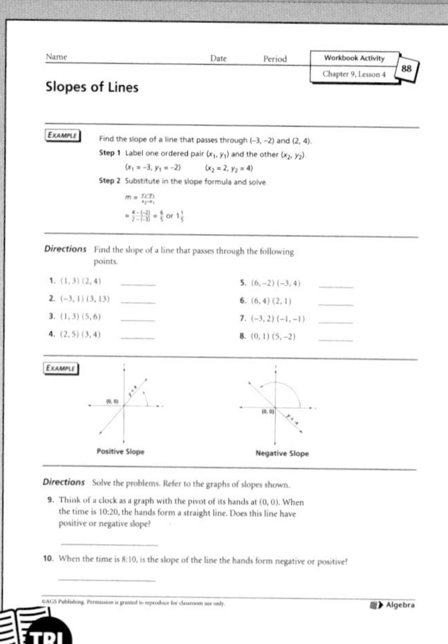

Name Date Period **Workbook Activity 88** Chapter 9, Lesson 4

Slopes of Lines

EXAMPLE Find the slope of a line that passes through (–3, –2) and (2, 4).

Step 1 Label one ordered pair (x_1, y_1) and the other (x_2, y_2).

$(x_1 = -3, y_1 = -2)$ $(x_2 = 2, y_2 = 4)$

Step 2 Substitute in the slope formula and solve.

$m = \frac{y_2 - y_1}{x_2 - x_1}$

$= \frac{4-(-2)}{2-(-3)} = \frac{6}{5}$ or $1\frac{1}{5}$

Directions Find the slope of a line that passes through the following points.

1. (1, 3) (2, 4) ______
2. (–3, 1) (3, 13) ______
3. (1, 3) (5, 6) ______
4. (2, 5) (3, 4) ______
5. (6, –2) (–3, 4) ______
6. (6, 4) (2, 1) ______
7. (–3, 2) (–1, –1) ______
8. (0, 1) (5, –2) ______

EXAMPLE

(0, 0) Positive Slope

(0, 0) Negative Slope

Directions Solve the problems. Refer to the graphs of slopes shown.

9. Think of a clock as a graph with the pivot of its hands at (0, 0). When the time is 10:20, the hands form a straight line. Does this line have positive or negative slope?

10. When the time is 8:10, is the slope of the line the hands form negative or positive?

 Algebra

Workbook Activity 88

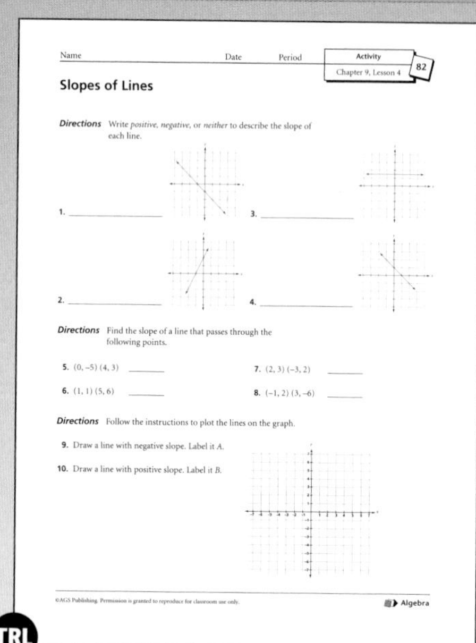

Name Date Period **Activity 82** Chapter 9, Lesson 4

Slopes of Lines

Directions Write *positive, negative,* or *neither* to describe the slope of each line.

1. ______
2. ______
3. ______
4. ______

Directions Find the slope of a line that passes through the following points.

5. (0, –5) (4, 3) ______
6. (1, 1) (5, 6) ______
7. (2, 3) (–3, 2) ______
8. (–1, 2) (3, –6) ______

Directions Follow the instructions to plot the lines on the graph.

9. Draw a line with negative slope. Label it *A*.
10. Draw a line with positive slope. Label it *B*.

 Algebra

Activity 82

Formula for Slope

If you know two points on a straight line, use the formula $m = \frac{y_2 - y_1}{x_2 - x_1}$ to find the slope of that line. In the formula, m = slope.

EXAMPLE 1 Find the slope of a line that passes through (−2, 5) and (2, −3).

Step 1 Label one ordered pair (x_1, y_1) and label the other (x_2, y_2).

$$\underset{(x_1,\ y_1)}{(-2,\ 5)} \qquad \underset{(x_2,\ y_2)}{(2,\ -3)}$$

Step 2 Substitute the x_1, y_1, x_2, and y_2 values into the formula $m = \frac{y_2 - y_1}{x_2 - x_1}$.

$m = \frac{-3 - 5}{2 - (-2)} = -\frac{8}{4} = -2$ The slope of the line is −2.

EXAMPLE 2 Find the slope of a line that passes through (1, 0) and (5, 2).

Step 1 Label one ordered pair (x_1, y_1) and label the other (x_2, y_2).

$$\underset{(x_1,\ y_1)}{(1,\ 0)} \qquad \underset{(x_2,\ y_2)}{(5,\ 2)}$$

Step 2 Substitute the x_1, y_1, x_2, and y_2 values into the formula $m = \frac{y_2 - y_1}{x_2 - x_1}$.

$m = \frac{2 - 0}{5 - 1} = \frac{2}{4} = \frac{1}{2}$ The slope of the line is $\frac{1}{2}$.

You can label either ordered pair (x_1, y_1) or (x_2, y_2).

EXAMPLE 3 Find the slope of a line that passes through (1, 0) and (5, 2).

Step 1 This time label the second ordered pair (x_1, y_1) and label the first ordered pair (x_2, y_2).

$$\underset{(x_1,\ y_1)}{(5,\ 2)} \qquad \underset{(x_2,\ y_2)}{(1,\ 0)}$$

Step 2 Substitute the x_1, y_1, x_2, and y_2 values into the formula $m = \frac{y_2 - y_1}{x_2 - x_1}$.

$m = \frac{0 - 2}{1 - 5} = \frac{-2}{-4} = \frac{2}{4} = \frac{1}{2}$ The slope of the line is $\frac{1}{2}$.

As you can see, the way that ordered pairs are labeled does not affect the slope of the line.

COMMON ERROR

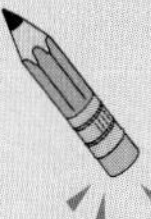

Be sure students understand that to find the slope of a line they need to subtract one x coordinate from the other x coordinate and one y coordinate from the other y coordinate. In error, some students may try to determine slope by subtracting x and y components, essentially computing $(x_1 - y_1) \div (x_2 - y_2)$.

3 Reinforce and Extend

AT HOME

Point out to students that carpenters often speak of slope in terms of $\frac{\text{rise}}{\text{run}}$. Have students find the slope or $\frac{\text{rise}}{\text{run}}$ of any stairs they might have at their home. Suggest that they draw a picture of the stairs, showing how high (the rise) and how wide (the run) each stair is. They can find the slope of one stair or, by counting the number of stairs and multiplying, they can find the slope of the entire stairway. Post students' findings as part of a class bulletin board.

CALCULATOR

Provide calculator practice in computing slope and using parentheses. Have students find the slopes of lines that pass through the following pairs of points. For each pair of points, have one student recite aloud the sequence of calculator keys used to find the slope. Have students exchange roles after each calculation.

(2, 3) (1, 6)	$(-\frac{1}{3})$
(−3, 4) (−4, 3)	(1)
(2, 2) (4, 8)	$(\frac{1}{3})$
(3, 1) (4, 6)	$(\frac{1}{5})$
(−3, −1) (4, −6)	$(-\frac{7}{5})$
(−2, −2) (−3, −6)	$(\frac{1}{4})$

LEARNING STYLES

Auditory/Verbal

Suggest that students work in pairs. The partners should take turns explaining slope in their own words. They might use the problems in Exercise C or D and make statements such as "The slope of the line is two. That means the line moves two units upward for every unit it moves to the right."

There are two ways to label ordered pairs when using the formula for slope. $(x_1, y_1) = (1, 0)$ and $(x_2, y_2) = (5, 2)$ or $(x_1, y_1) = (5, 2)$ and $(x_2, y_2) = (1, 0)$ Either way gives the same answer when using the formula for slope.

1. The graph should create an acute angle with the positive direction of the *x*-axis.
2. The graph should create an obtuse angle with the positive direction of the *x*-axis.

Exercise A Draw a coordinate system. Use it for this exercise.

1. Draw a line that has a positive slope. Label the line *A*.

2. Draw a line that has a negative slope. Label the line *B*.

3. Draw a line whose slope is neither positive nor negative. Label the line *C*. The graph must be parallel to either the *x*- or *y*-axis.

Exercise B Describe the slope of each line. Write positive, negative, or neither.

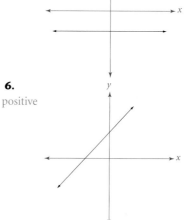

4. negative

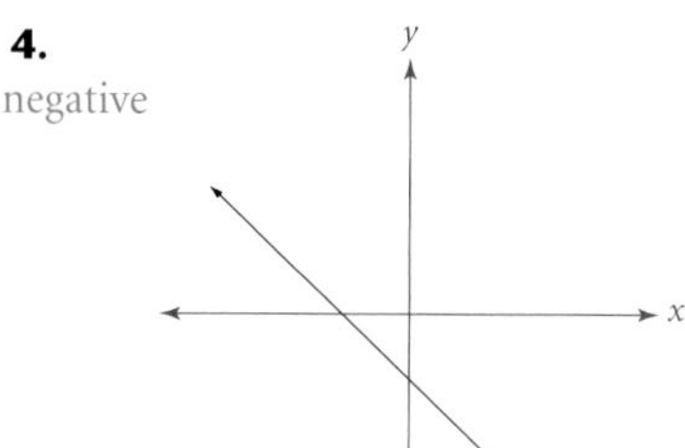

5. neither

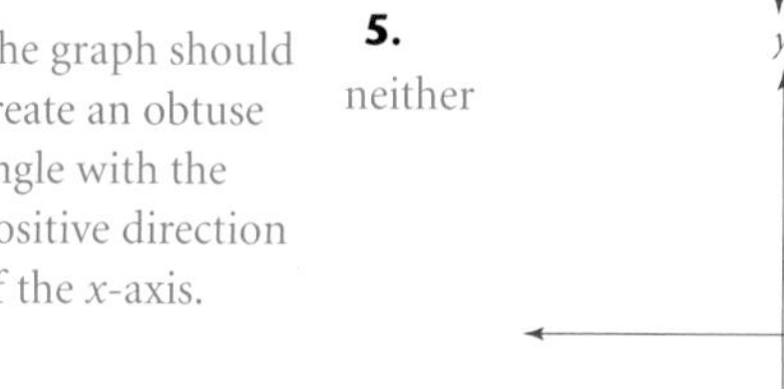

6. positive

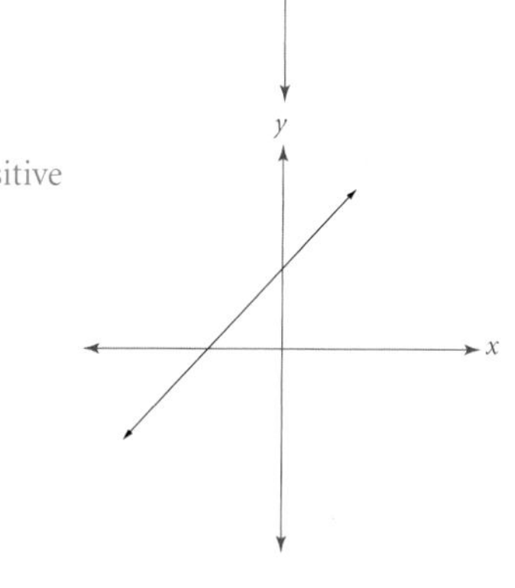

You can use a calculator to check your answer whenever you find the slope of a line.

EXAMPLE 4 Suppose the slope formula looks like this after substituting x- and y-values:

$$\frac{-6-(-2)}{1-5} = 1$$

To check, input the entire numerator in a set of parentheses and input the entire denominator in a set of parentheses:

Press: (− 6 − (− 2)) ÷ (1 − 5) =

The calculator will display 1.

Writing About Mathematics

Imagine coasting down a short but steep hill on a bicycle. If the slope of the hill could be measured, would it be closer to $\frac{1}{2}$ or $\frac{2}{1}$? Explain.

Exercise C Use a calculator to compute each slope.

7. $\frac{-1-(-1)}{2-3}$ $m = 0$

8. $\frac{-9-5}{-3-4}$ $m = 2$

9. $\frac{5-(-3)}{-2-2}$ $m = -2$

10. $\frac{-1-(-7)}{-6-(-3)}$ $m = -2$

11. How can you use a calculator to check a slope computation that has a fraction or mixed number for an answer?

11. Change the fraction or mixed number to a decimal. Use a calculator to check the slope calculation. Then compare decimal answers.

Exercise D Find the slope of the line that passes through the following points.

12. $(-3, -3)$ $(3, 3)$ $m = 1$

13. $(1, -6)$ $(4, -6)$ $m = 0$

14. $(-3, -2)$ $(5, 1)$ $m = \frac{3}{8}$

15. $(2, 6)$ $(5, 0)$ $m = -2$

16. $(4, 3)$ $(2, 2)$ $m = \frac{1}{2}$

17. $(-1, 5)$ $(5, 5)$ $m = 0$

Group Problem Solving

Suggest that small groups of students work to find the slope of the bleachers in the gym or the slope of the auditorium seating in their school. Indicate that the groups will have to present their methods, including an explanation of how they measured, estimated, or computed the y and x values they used. Invite the groups to present their findings as a "How To" segment for a local cable TV program.

Online Connection

Have students read about map making at math.rice.edu/~lanius/pres/map/mapcoo.html. Here they will learn what coordinate systems have to do with geography. This site provides a wealth of information on map making and has links to related math problems. Recommended sites include www.usgs.gov/, a site of the U.S. Geological Survey which provides several suggested activities for teachers and students, and www.indo.com/cgi-bin/dist, which provides an online distance calculator to nearly anywhere on Earth.

PROBLEM SOLVING

Exercise E Use the data given to answer each question.

Bicycle Trail 1: Slope $= \frac{1}{100}$

Bicycle Trail 2: Slope $= \frac{2}{15}$

Bicycle Trail 3: Slope $= -\frac{1}{25}$

18. Elena is making a scale drawing of the trails. Which trail or trails are downhill? Which are uphill? Trail 3; Trails 1 and 2

19. Aaron wants to avoid riding on the steepest trail. Which trail should he avoid? Trail 2

20. Robby rides the least steep trail almost every day. Which trail does he ride? Trail 1

Algebra in Your Life

It's All Downhill from Here

Have you ever seen a sign along a roadway that says "Trucks Check Brakes Grade 6%." What does that mean? It means there's a hill ahead. The steepness or slope of the road is called its grade. The grade is measured in percents. It is calculated the same way you find the slope of a line in algebra. If the slope is too steep, the trucker could lose control and wreck. Amazing as it may seem, people use algebra to help prevent traffic accidents!

Lesson 5 Writing Linear Equations

Linear equation
An equation whose graph is a straight line

If the graph of an equation is a straight line, the equation is a **linear equation**. The general form for all linear equations is

$y = mx + b$ where m is the slope of the line and b is the y-intercept
(↑ slope, ↑ y-intercept)

The equation $y = 2x + 1$ is an example of a linear equation.
(↑ slope, ↑ y-intercept)
It has a slope of 2 and a y-intercept of 1.

If you know the values of m and b, you can use the general form $y = mx + b$ to write the equation of a line.

EXAMPLE 1 Write the equation of a line whose slope is 3 and y-intercept is $\frac{1}{2}$.

Solution Given $m = 3$ and $b = \frac{1}{2}$, $y = mx + b$ becomes $y = 3x + \frac{1}{2}$.

If you are given two points through which a line passes, you can write the equation of the line.

EXAMPLE 2 Write the equation of a line that passes through (7, 1) and (−2, 3).

Step 1 Compute the slope. $m = \frac{y_2 - y_1}{x_2 - x_1} = \frac{3 - 1}{-2 - 7} = -\frac{2}{9}$

Step 2 Substitute $-\frac{2}{9}$ for m in $y = mx + b$. $y = -\frac{2}{9}x + b$

Step 3 Compute the y-intercept. Since both points (7, 1) and (−2, 3) are on the line, substitute either point into $y = -\frac{2}{9}x + b$, then solve for b.
Use the point (−2, 3); $x = -2$ and $y = 3$:
$y = -\frac{2}{9}x + b$
$3 = -\frac{2}{9}(-2) + b \quad 3 = \frac{4}{9} + b \quad 2\frac{5}{9} = b$

Step 4 Write the equation of the line by substituting the values you computed for m and b in $y = mx + b$. Since $m = -\frac{2}{9}$ and $b = 2\frac{5}{9}$, $y = mx + b$ becomes $y = -\frac{2}{9}x + 2\frac{5}{9}$.

Lesson at a Glance

Chapter 9 Lesson 5

Overview This lesson introduces students to the general form for all linear equations: $y = mx + b$.

Objectives

- To recognize $y = mx + b$ as the general form for a linear equation
- To write an equation that describes a line with a given slope and passing through given points

Student Pages 263–264

Teacher's Resource Library 

Workbook Activity 89

Activity 83

Alternative Activity 83

Mathematics Vocabulary

linear equation

Warm-Up Activity

Point out to students that they are already familiar with linear equations. The equations in the previous four lessons were all linear equations—equations of lines.

Teaching the Lesson

Use the second example as a demonstration tool. Stress step 3, computing the y-intercept by using points on the line of the equation.

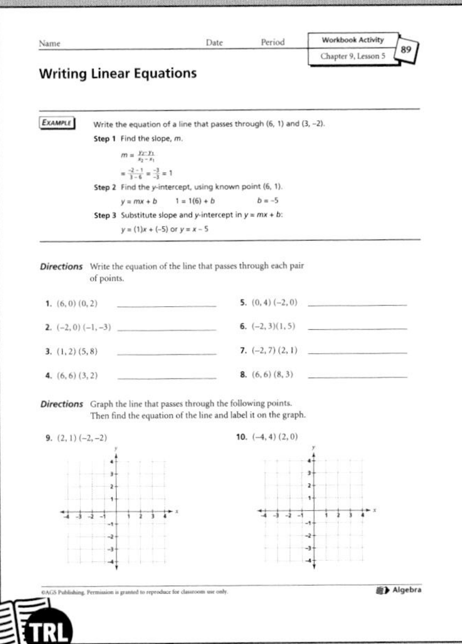

Name Date Period — Workbook Activity 89, Chapter 9, Lesson 5

Writing Linear Equations

EXAMPLE Write the equation of a line that passes through (6, 1) and (3, −2).
Step 1 Find the slope, m.
$m = \frac{y_2 - y_1}{x_2 - x_1}$
$= \frac{-2 - 1}{3 - 6} = \frac{-3}{-3} = 1$
Step 2 Find the y-intercept, using known point (6, 1).
$y = mx + b \quad 1 = 1(6) + b \quad b = -5$
Step 3 Substitute slope and y-intercept in $y = mx + b$:
$y = (1)x + (-5)$ or $y = x - 5$

Directions Write the equation of the line that passes through each pair of points.

1. (6, 0) (0, 2) ______
2. (−2, 0) (−1, −3) ______
3. (1, 2) (5, 8) ______
4. (6, 6) (3, 2) ______
5. (0, 4) (−2, 0) ______
6. (−2, 3)(1, 5) ______
7. (−2, 7) (2, 1) ______
8. (6, 6) (8, 3) ______

Directions Graph the line that passes through the following points. Then find the equation of the line and label it on the graph.

9. (2, 1) (−2, −2)
10. (−4, 4) (2, 0)

 Algebra

TRL **Workbook Activity 89**

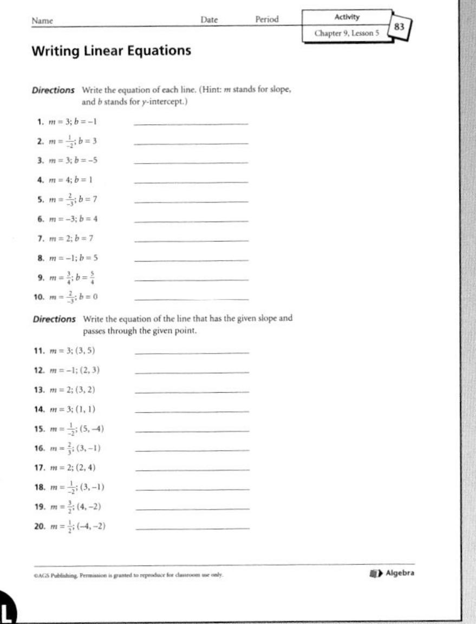

Name Date Period — Activity 83, Chapter 9, Lesson 5

Writing Linear Equations

Directions Write the equation of each line. (Hint: m stands for slope, and b stands for y-intercept.)

1. $m = 3; b = -1$ ______
2. $m = \frac{1}{-2}; b = 3$ ______
3. $m = 3; b = -5$ ______
4. $m = 4; b = 1$ ______
5. $m = \frac{2}{-3}; b = 7$ ______
6. $m = -3; b = 4$ ______
7. $m = 2; b = 7$ ______
8. $m = -1; b = 5$ ______
9. $m = \frac{3}{4}; b = \frac{5}{4}$ ______
10. $m = \frac{2}{-3}; b = 0$ ______

Directions Write the equation of the line that has the given slope and passes through the given point.

11. $m = 3$; (3, 5) ______
12. $m = -1$; (2, 3) ______
13. $m = 2$; (3, 2) ______
14. $m = 3$; (1, 1) ______
15. $m = \frac{1}{-2}$; (5, −4) ______
16. $m = \frac{2}{3}$; (3, −1) ______
17. $m = 2$; (2, 4) ______
18. $m = \frac{1}{-2}$; (3, −1) ______
19. $m = \frac{3}{2}$; (4, −2) ______
20. $m = \frac{1}{2}$; (−4, −2) ______

 Algebra

TRL **Activity 83**

3 Reinforce and Extend

Group Problem Solving

Invite small groups of students to develop a five-question True-or-False quiz. Questions should focus on the role that slope and y-intercepts play in linear equations. Students might prepare questions such as "In $y = mx + b$, b gives the value of y when $x = 0$." *(true)* Have groups answer one another's quiz questions. Students might vote on the best questions and post them for use as study aids.

Answers to Problems 4–10

4.

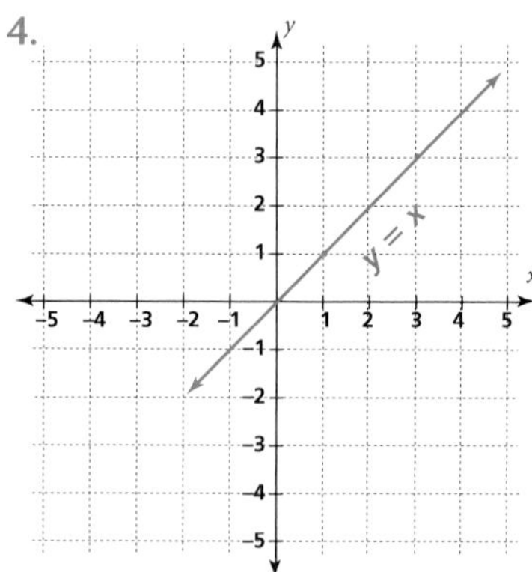

The remaining graphs should display the following information:

5. The graph should pass through $(0, 0)$ and $(2, 4)$; $y = 2x$
6. The graph should pass through $(-1, 2)$ and $(3, -6)$; $y = -2x$
7. The graph should pass through $(5, 0)$ and $(0, 10)$; $y = -2x + 10$
8. The graph should pass through $(-4, -1)$ and $(4, 7)$; $y = x + 3$
9. The graph should pass through $(-2, 0)$ and $(-6, -1)$; $y = \frac{1}{4}x + \frac{1}{2}$
10. The graph should pass through $(1, 8)$ and $(2, -16)$; $y = -24x + 32$

Example 3 Write the equation of a line that has a slope of $\frac{1}{2}$ and passes through $(-1, 2)$.

Step 1 Since the slope is given, substitute $\frac{1}{2}$ for m in $y = mx + b$. $\quad y = \frac{1}{2}x + b$

Step 2 Compute the y-intercept. Substitute the point $(-1, 2)$ into $y = \frac{1}{2}x + b$, then solve for b.
Given the point $(-1, 2)$, $x = -1$ and $y = 2$:
$y = \frac{1}{2}x + b$
$2 = \frac{1}{2}(-1) + b \qquad 2 = -\frac{1}{2} + b \qquad 2\frac{1}{2} = b$

Step 3 Write the equation of the line by substituting the values you computed for m and b in $y = mx + b$.
Since $m = \frac{1}{2}$ and $b = 2\frac{1}{2}$, $y = mx + b$ becomes
$y = \frac{1}{2}x + 2\frac{1}{2}$.

Writing About Mathematics

Can $y = mx + b$ be used to write an equation of a line that passes through (1, 0) and (1, 10)? Explain.

Exercise A Write the equation of each line.

1. $m = 2; b = 1$ $\quad y = 2x + 1$
2. $m = 3; b = -3$ $\quad y = 3x - 3$
3. $m = -2; b = 5$ $\quad y = -2x + 5$

Exercise B Graph the line that passes through the following points. Then write the equation of each line.

4. $(1, 1)\ (3, 3)$
5. $(0, 0)\ (2, 4)$
6. $(-1, 2)\ (3, -6)$
7. $(5, 0)\ (0, 10)$
8. $(-4, -1)\ (4, 7)$
9. $(-2, 0)\ (-6, -1)$
10. $(1, 8)\ (2, -16)$

See Teacher's Edition page for answers.

Exercise C Write the equation of the line that has the given slope and passes through the given point.

11. $m = 5; (5, 5)$
12. $m = 10; (-1, -4)$
13. $m = \frac{1}{2}; (1, 6)$
14. $m = \frac{3}{4}; (8, 4)$
15. $m = 2; (4, 8)$

11. $y = 5x - 20$ 12. $y = 10x + 6$ 13. $y = \frac{x + 11}{2}$ or $y = \frac{1}{2}x + \frac{11}{2}$
14. $y = \frac{3}{4}x - 2$ 15. $y = 2x$

Lesson 6 Lines as Functions

Dependent variable
The value of the y variable that depends on the value of x

Independent variable
The value of x that determines the value of y

Function
A rule that associates every x-value with one and only one y-value

Vertical line test
A way of determining whether a graph is a function; if a vertical line intersects a graph in more than 1 point, the graph is not a function

If you make a table of values for the equation $y = \frac{3}{2}x + 7$, you will find that for each value you choose for x, the value of y changes. Because the value of y depends on the value you choose for x, y is known as the **dependent variable** and x is known as the **independent variable**. Another way to describe the same idea is to say that y is a **function** of x.

To use the language of functions, use the symbol $f(x)$ in place of y.

$y = mx + b$ is the same as $f(x) = mx + b$.

(The symbol $f(x)$ is read "the function of x.")

Rewrite $y = \frac{3}{2}x + 7$ as $f(x) = \frac{3}{2}x + 7$

Rule A function is a rule that associates every x-value with one and only one y-value.

All equations of the form $f(x) = mx + b$ are functions. To decide whether the graph of an equation is a function, perform a **vertical line test**—if a vertical line crosses the graph more than once, the graph is not a function because the x-value of the vertical line is associated with more than one y-value.

EXAMPLE 1 Is the graph at the right a function?

Solution No; a vertical line crosses the graph more than once—for every x-value, there is more than one y-value.

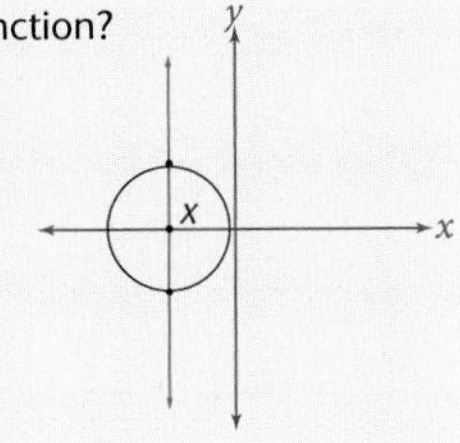

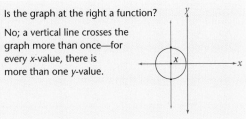

Lesson at a Glance

Chapter 9 Lesson 6

Overview This lesson introduces students to functions.

Objectives

- To identify graphs that represent functions
- To evaluate functions

Student Pages 265–267

Teacher's Resource Library TRL

Workbook Activity 90

Activity 84

Alternative Activity 84

Mathematics Vocabulary

dependent variable
function
independent variable
vertical line test

1 Warm-Up Activity

Help students relate the term *function* to their everyday lives. Pose situations in which one event is a function of another: whether a car moves is a function of (depends on) how much gas is in the tank; whether a team wins is a function of (depends on) how well the team plays, and so on. Indicate to students that in mathematical circles, *functions* have specific characteristics.

2 Teaching the Lesson

Indicate to students that $y = mx + b$ and $f(x) = mx + b$ are two ways of stating the same information. Point out that the significant characteristic of a function is that for every value of x, there is one and only one related value of y.

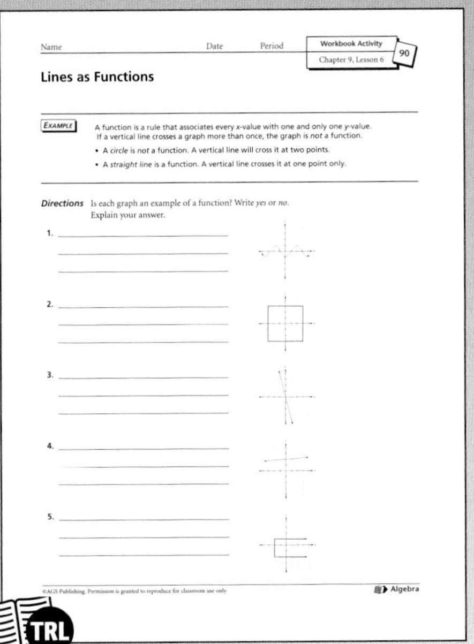

Name Date Period Workbook Activity 90 Chapter 9, Lesson 6

Lines as Functions

EXAMPLE A function is a rule that associates every x-value with one and only one y-value. If a vertical line crosses a graph more than once, the graph is *not* a function.

- A *circle* is *not* a function. A vertical line will cross it at two points.
- A *straight line* is a function. A vertical line crosses it at one point only.

Directions Is each graph an example of a function? Write *yes* or *no*. Explain your answer.

1. ______
2. ______
3. ______
4. ______
5. ______

 Algebra

TRL

Workbook Activity 90

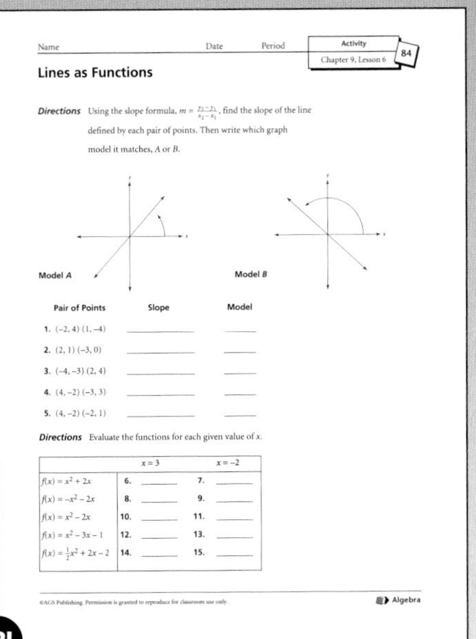

Name Date Period Activity 84 Chapter 9, Lesson 6

Lines as Functions

Directions Using the slope formula, $m = \frac{y_2 - y_1}{x_2 - x_1}$, find the slope of the line defined by each pair of points. Then write which graph model it matches, *A* or *B*.

Model *A* Model *B*

Pair of Points	Slope	Model
1. (–2, 4) (1, –4)	______	______
2. (2, 1) (–3, 0)	______	______
3. (–4, –3) (2, 4)	______	______
4. (4, –2) (–3, 3)	______	______
5. (4, –2) (–2, 1)	______	______

Directions Evaluate the functions for each given value of x.

	$x = 3$	$x = -2$
$f(x) = x^2 + 2x$	6. ______	7. ______
$f(x) = -x^2 - 2x$	8. ______	9. ______
$f(x) = x^2 - 2x$	10. ______	11. ______
$f(x) = x^2 - 3x - 1$	12. ______	13. ______
$f(x) = \frac{1}{2}x^2 + 2x - 2$	14. ______	15. ______

 Algebra

TRL

Activity 84

Reinforce and Extend

Learning Styles

Visual/Spatial

Have students copy the graphs shown in Exercise A. For each graph, ask students to apply the vertical line test. Have them attempt to draw a line that intersects the graph at more than one point. Have students post their efforts, indicating whether each graph passed or failed the vertical line test.

Learning Styles

Auditory/Verbal

Encourage pairs of students to write the functions in problems 7–10 in Exercise B as equations. Then have them determine whether or not the equations are linear. *(The equations are not linear; they are not of the form $y = mx + b$.)* Have volunteers share their reasoning with the class.

Example 2 Is the graph at the right a function?

Solution Yes; a vertical line crosses the graph only once—for every x-value, there is one and only one y-value.

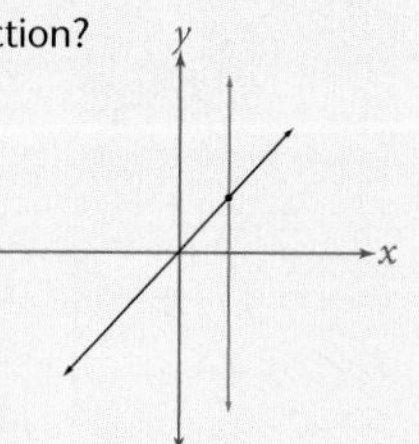

To evaluate a function means to substitute a value for x and solve for $f(x)$.

Example 3 Evaluate $f(x) = x^2 + x - 1$ given $x = 3$.

Solution
$f(x) = x^2 + x - 1$
$f(3) = 3^2 + 3 - 1$
$f(3) = 11$

Exercise A Is each graph an example of a function? Write yes or no.

1. yes

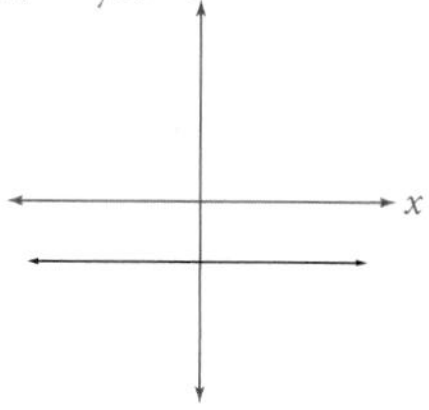

2. no

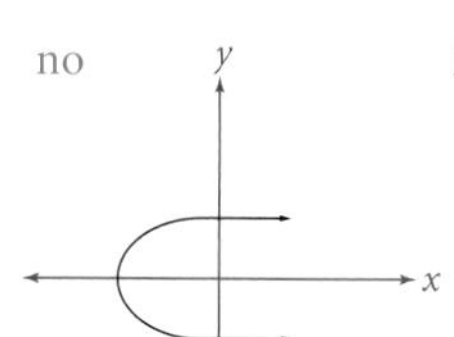

3. yes

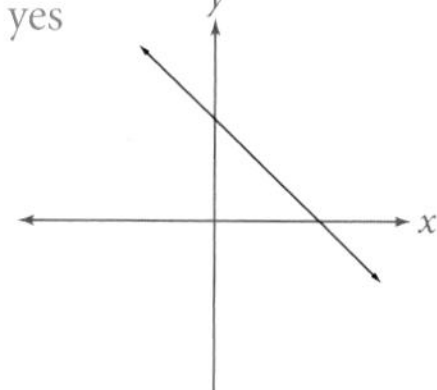

4. yes

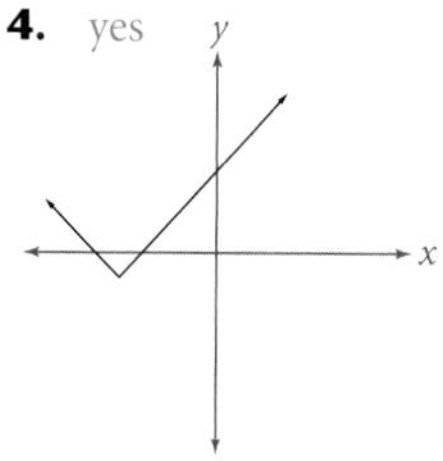

5. yes

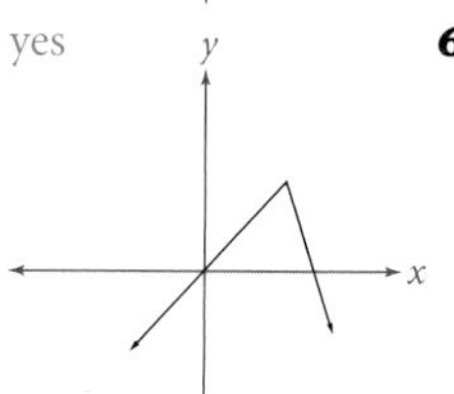

6. no

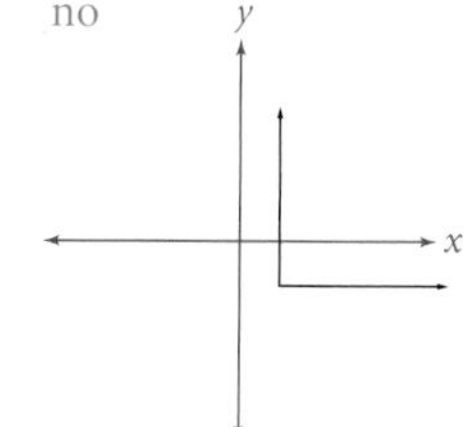

Writing About Mathematics

In your local newspaper, find a line graph. Is this graph an example of a function? Explain why or why not.

Exercise B Evaluate each function two times. Use $x = 2$ and $x = -4$.

7. $f(x) = x^2 + x$ $f(2) = 6; f(-4) = 12$

8. $f(x) = x^2 - x$ $f(2) = 2; f(-4) = 20$

9. $f(x) = 4x^2 - x$ $f(2) = 14; f(-4) = 68$

10. $f(x) = -2x^2 + x$ $f(2) = -6; f(-4) = -36$

11. $f(x) = -x^2 + 3x$ $f(2) = 2; f(-4) = -28$

12. $f(x) = x^2 - 6x$ $f(2) = -8; f(-4) = 40$

13. $f(x) = -3x^2 + x - 1$ $f(2) = -11; f(-4) = -53$

14. $f(x) = 4x^2 - x - 4$ $f(2) = 10; f(-4) = 64$

15. $f(x) = 1.5x^2 + 3x$ $f(2) = 12; f(-4) = 12$

Linear Equations and Inequalities in the Coordinate Plane **267**

Lesson at a Glance

Chapter 9 Lesson 7

Overview This lesson demonstrates several different ways to determine the domain and range of a graphed function.

Objective

- To find the domain and range using two sets of ordered pairs on a line
- To calculate the range of a function given the domain
- To determine the domain and range of a function using a graph

Student Pages 268–271

Teacher's Resource Library 

Workbook Activity 91

Activity 85

Alternative Activity 85

Warm-Up Activity

Reinforce the concept of an algebraic function by asking students if any of them has an auto-dial or speed dial feature on their telephone or cell phone. Explain that programming a speed dial is similar to an algebraic function—a single key or "function" button is programmed to produce a series of numbers (a phone number). For a phone, $f(x)$ is a phone number. On the keypad of the phone, $f(1)$ might be the fire department phone number, $f(3)$ might be a parent's telephone number at work, $f(5)$ might be a friend's phone number in another state, etc. Remind students that in algebra, a function is a rule that sets up a relationship between an x-value and a y-value.

Teaching the Lesson

Begin by drawing a coordinate plane on the board and drawing a line between point $(-3, -3)$ and $(4,4)$.Using the diagram in the example box as a guide, discuss the meanings of range and domain using the plane you drew. Explain that the domain is $-3, -1, 2, 4$. Because $y = f(x) = x$, the range is the same as the domain in this example. It is important that students understand that the domain contains x-values and the range contains

Lesson 7 Domain and Range of a Function

Domain
The independent variables, or set of x–values, of a function

Range
The dependent variables, or set of y–values, of a function

The set of x-values, the independent variables that are used in a function, is called the **domain** of the function. The corresponding set of y-values, the dependent variables, is called the **range** of the function.

Example 1 $y = f(x) = 2x - 1$

Let the domain be $-1, 0, 2, 5$.

Determine the range.

Substitute the domain values in $f(x)$ to determine the range.

$x = -1 \quad y = f(-1) = 2(-1) - 1 = -3$ so $y = -3$

$x = 0 \quad y = f(0) = 2(0) - 1 = -1$ so $y = -1$

$x = 2 \quad y = f(2) = 2(2) - 1 = 3$ so $y = 3$

$x = 5 \quad y = f(5) = 2(5) - 1 = 9$ so $y = 9$

The range is $-3, -1, 3, 9$.

Example 2 Look at the graph for $f(x) = x - 1$ for $1 \le x \le 4$

What is the range?

Find the endpoints of the range by evaluating $f(1)$ and $f(4)$.

$f(1) = 1 - 1 = 0$

$f(4) = 4 - 1 = 3$

So the range is $0 \le y \le 3$.

range
domain
5
–5
1 2 3 4

Note: domain: $1 \le x \le 4$

range: $f(1) \le y \le f(4)$

The range of the dependent variable depends on the domain.

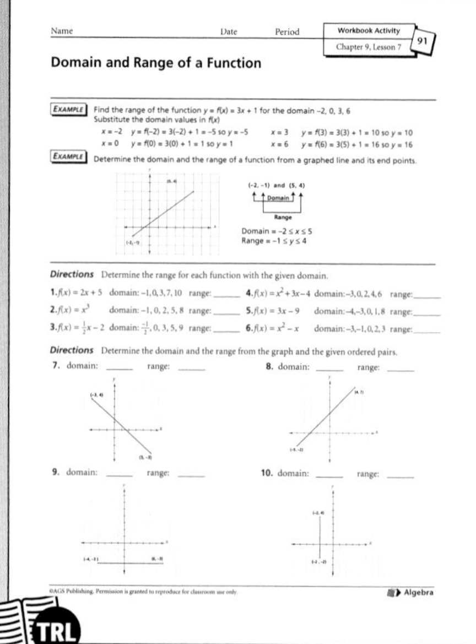

Name Date Period | Workbook Activity 91 | Chapter 9, Lesson 7

Domain and Range of a Function

Example Find the range of the function $y = f(x) = 3x + 1$ for the domain $-2, 0, 3, 6$
Substitute the domain values in $f(x)$

$x = -2 \quad y = f(-2) = 3(-2) + 1 = -5$ so $y = -5$ $\qquad x = 3 \quad y = f(3) = 3(3) + 1 = 10$ so $y = 10$

$x = 0 \quad y = f(0) = 3(0) + 1 = 1$ so $y = 1$ $\qquad x = 6 \quad y = f(6) = 3(5) + 1 = 16$ so $y = 16$

Example Determine the domain and the range of a function from a graphed line and its end points.

$(-2, -1)$ and $(5, 4)$
Domain
Range
Domain $= -2 \le x \le 5$
Range $= -1 \le y \le 4$

Directions Determine the range for each function with the given domain.

1. $f(x) = 2x + 5$ domain: $-1, 0, 3, 7, 10$ range: ______
2. $f(x) = x^3$ domain: $-1, 0, 2, 5, 8$ range: ______
3. $f(x) = \frac{1}{2}x - 2$ domain: $\frac{-1}{2}, 0, 3, 5, 9$ range: ______
4. $f(x) = x^2 + 3x - 4$ domain: $-3, 0, 2, 4, 6$ range: ______
5. $f(x) = 3x - 9$ domain: $-4, -3, 0, 1, 8$ range: ______
6. $f(x) = x^2 - x$ domain: $-3, -1, 0, 2, 3$ range: ______

Directions Determine the domain and the range from the graph and the given ordered pairs.

7. domain: ______ range: ______
8. domain: ______ range: ______
9. domain: ______ range: ______
10. domain: ______ range: ______

Algebra

Workbook Activity 91

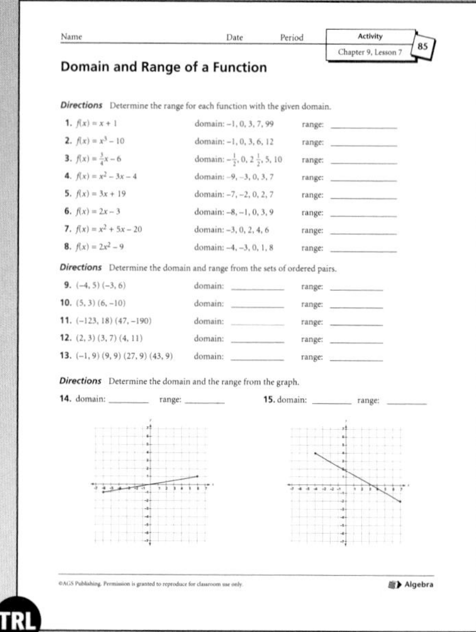

Name Date Period | Activity 85 | Chapter 9, Lesson 7

Domain and Range of a Function

Directions Determine the range for each function with the given domain.

1. $f(x) = x + 1$ domain: $-1, 0, 3, 7, 99$ range: ______
2. $f(x) = x^3 - 10$ domain: $-1, 0, 3, 6, 12$ range: ______
3. $f(x) = \frac{3}{4}x - 6$ domain: $-\frac{1}{2}, 0, 2\frac{1}{2}, 5, 10$ range: ______
4. $f(x) = x^2 - 3x - 4$ domain: $-9, -3, 0, 3, 7$ range: ______
5. $f(x) = 3x + 19$ domain: $-7, -2, 0, 2, 7$ range: ______
6. $f(x) = 2x - 3$ domain: $-8, -1, 0, 3, 9$ range: ______
7. $f(x) = x^2 + 5x - 20$ domain: $-3, 0, 2, 4, 6$ range: ______
8. $f(x) = 2x^2 - 9$ domain: $-4, -3, 0, 1, 8$ range: ______

Directions Determine the domain and range from the sets of ordered pairs.

9. $(-4, 5)\ (-3, 6)$ domain: ______ range: ______
10. $(5, 3)\ (6, -10)$ domain: ______ range: ______
11. $(-123, 18)\ (47, -190)$ domain: ______ range: ______
12. $(2, 3)\ (3, 7)\ (4, 11)$ domain: ______ range: ______
13. $(-1, 9)\ (9, 9)\ (27, 9)\ (43, 9)$ domain: ______ range: ______

Directions Determine the domain and the range from the graph.

14. domain: ______ range: ______
15. domain: ______ range: ______

Algebra

Activity 85

EXAMPLE 3 Use the graph at the right to determine the domain and range of the graphed function.

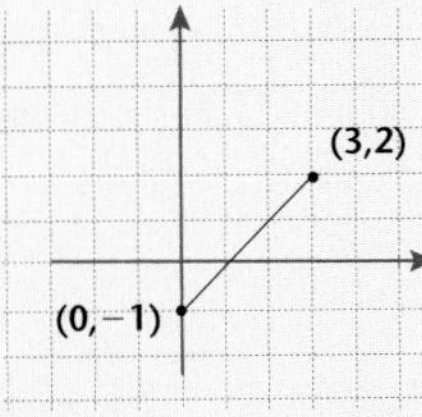

The ordered pairs $(0, -1)$ and $(3, 2)$ give the endpoints of the intervals of domain and range.

$(0, -1)$ and $(3, 2)$

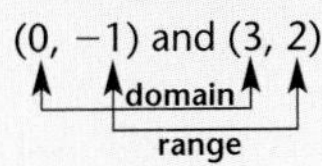

domain: $0 \le x \le 3$

range: $-1 \le y \le 2$

> **Remember:**
> 1. The domain includes all the x-values needed to define the function. The domain is found on the x-axis. You can choose the domain. It is independent.
> 2. The range includes all the y-values, which depend directly on the domain-values substituted in the function. The range is found on the y-axis. It is dependent on the domain.

Exercise A Determine the range for each function with the given domain.

1. Range: $-7, -5, 1, 9, 15$	**1.** $f(x) = 2x - 5$	domain: $-1, 0, 3, 7, 10$
2. Range: $-1, 0, -25, -81, -10{,}000$	**2.** $f(x) = -x^2$	domain: $-1, 0, 5, 9, 100$
3. Range: $\frac{7}{4}, 2, 3, \frac{7}{2}, 4$	**3.** $f(x) = \frac{1}{2}x + 2$	domain: $-\frac{1}{2}, 0, 2, 3, 4$
4. Range: $3, 3, 6, 11, 18$	**4.** $f(x) = x^2 + 2x + 3$	domain: $-2, 0, 1, 2, 3$
5. Range: $-2, 0, 5, 8, 22$	**5.** $f(x) = 2x + 6$	domain: $-4, -3, -\frac{1}{2}, 1, 8$

y-values. Discuss the examples shown in the lesson, emphasizing that there are different ways of determining the domain and range: you can calculate range using the function and a given domain; you can find the range and domain based on the ordered pairs of the two end points of a graphed line; and you can determine the range and domain from a line on a coordinate plane.

3 Reinforce and Extend

LEARNING STYLES

LEP/ESL

Both the words *range* and *domain* have several meanings, which might be confusing to some students. For example, "range" can mean the distance a vehicle can travel on a full tank of fuel, a cooking stove, a prairie (as in Home on the Range), or a series of things in a row (the algebraic meaning). "Domain" can mean an area of land owned by someone, a country or territory that is controlled by a government, the sphere of knowledge someone has, or a set of numbers or variables in a function. Reinforce the definitions that are used in this lesson.

Common Error

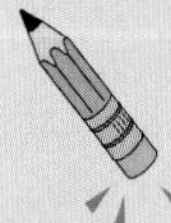

Students may not understand that the domain is variable and the range is non-variable. The range is always based on the x-value. The range is always based on y as a function of x, not the other way around.

Exercise B Determine the range for each function, given the domain and the graph.

6. $f(x) = -x + 2$ for $-2 \leq x \leq 4$

Range: $-2 \leq y \leq 4$

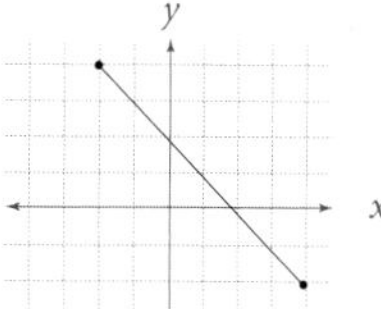

7. $f(x) = 3$ for $-3 \leq x \leq 4$

Range: $y = 3$

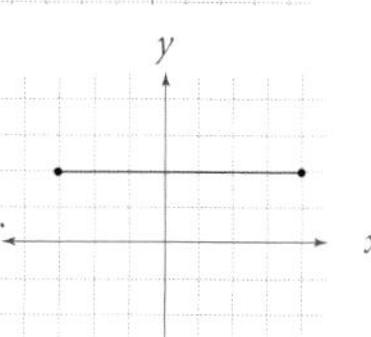

8. $f(x) = \frac{1}{3}x + 2$ for $-7 \leq x \leq 10$

Range: $-\frac{1}{3} \leq y \leq 5\frac{1}{3}$

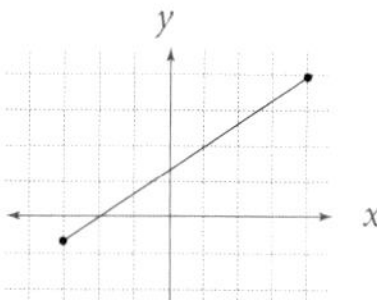

9. $f(x) = x^2$ for $-2 \leq x \leq 2$

Range: $y = 4$

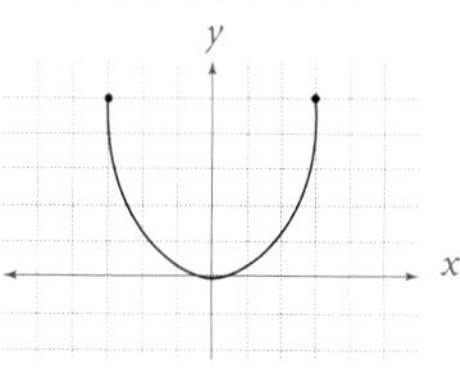

10. $f(x) = |x|$ for $-5 \leq x \leq 5$

Range: $y = 5$

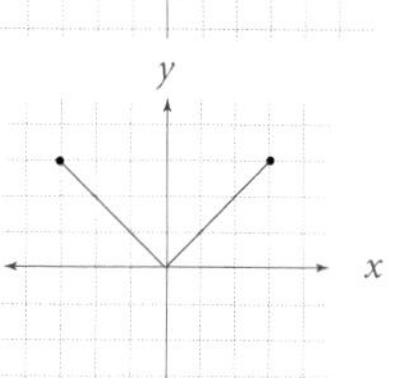

Exercise C Determine the domain and the range from the graph and the given ordered pairs.

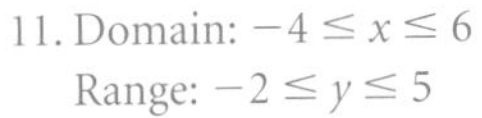
11. Domain: $-4 \le x \le 6$
Range: $-2 \le y \le 5$

12. Domain: $-5 \le x \le 3$
Range: $-\frac{1}{2} \le y \le 2$

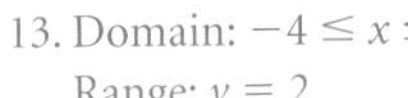
13. Domain: $-4 \le x \le 5$
Range: $y = 2$

14. Domain: $-2 \le x \le 3$
Range: $-2 \le y \le 3$

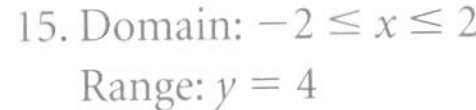
15. Domain: $-2 \le x \le 2$
Range: $y = 4$

11.

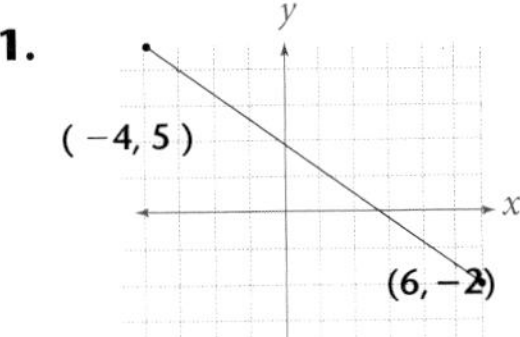

12.

y
x
(3, 2)
$(-5, -\frac{1}{2})$

13.

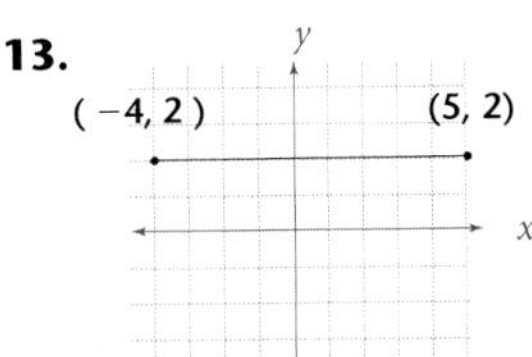

14.

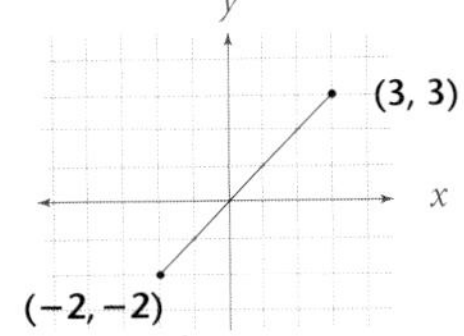

15.

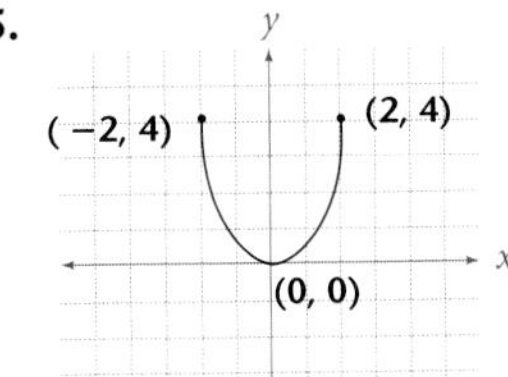

Technology Connection

Graphing Tools

If you have access to the Internet, there are lots of graphing tools available. Go to a search engine, type in the words "online graphing tools," and you'll find several you can download for free. (There are many you can buy them, as well.) Computer spreadsheet and even word-processing programs are capable of making graphs, too. All these graphing tools function the same way. You plug in a formula or data, and the tool will display the resulting graph.

LEARNING STYLES

Logical Mathematical

Have students explain how the range of a function depends on the value of x. (The range of a function contains y-values based on a function. The function might be $y = 3x - 7$ or $y = x + 29$. The value of x determines the value of y. y is a dependent variable, so the range is dependent.)

Lesson at a Glance

Chapter 9 Lesson 8

Overview This lesson presents methods for graphing inequalities.

Objective

- To graph inequalities in which y is greater than or less than $mx + b$.

Student Pages 272–275

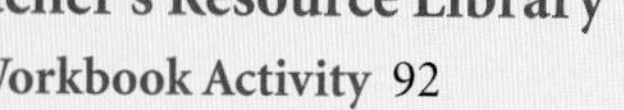

Teacher's Resource Library TRL

Workbook Activity 92

Activity 86

Alternative Activity 86

1 Warm-Up Activity

Provide the following puzzle to students: "I am thinking of two numbers. What are the possible relationships between the numbers?"

Help students conclude there are three possibilities: the numbers are equal, the first number is greater than the second, or the first number is less than the second.

2 Teaching the Lesson

Work through the three possibilities for point (x, y) and the equation for $y = x + 1$ with students. The points are on the line, the points are above the line, or the points are below the line.

3 Reinforce and Extend

Group Problem Solving

Suggest that pairs of students discuss the example graphs, making statements that describe how points in the shaded areas of the graphs relate to the inequality. For example, "Substituting any ordered pair in the shaded region of $y < 3x + 1$ will give a true statement." Students should test the accuracy of their statements by substituting values and solving the inequalities.

Lesson 8 Graphing Inequalities: $y < mx + b$, $y > mx + b$

A line in a plane divides a plane into three parts: the points on the line, the points above the line, and the points below the line.

For any point (x, y), three possibilities exist:

1. (x, y) is on $y = x + 1$
   Example $(0, 1) \rightarrow y = x + 1 \rightarrow 1 = 0 + 1 \rightarrow 1 = 1$
   True, (0,1) is on the line.
2. (x, y) is above $y = x + 1$
   Example $(-2, 5) \rightarrow y = x + 1 \rightarrow 5 = -2 + 1 \rightarrow 5 = -1$
   False, $(-2, 5)$ is *not* on the line.
   However $(-2, 5) \rightarrow y > x + 1 \rightarrow 5 > -2 + 1 \rightarrow 5 > -1$ True
   Conclusion $y > x + 1$ represents the region above $y = x + 1$.
3. (x, y) is below $y = x + 1$
   Example $(5, -2) \rightarrow y = x + 1 \rightarrow -2 = 5 + 1 \rightarrow -2 = 6$
   False, $(5, -2)$ is *not* on the line.
   However $(5, -2) \rightarrow y < x + 1 \rightarrow -2 < 5 + 1 \rightarrow -2 < 6$ True
   Conclusion $y < x + 1$ represents the region below $y = x + 1$.

This graph shows all three possibilities.

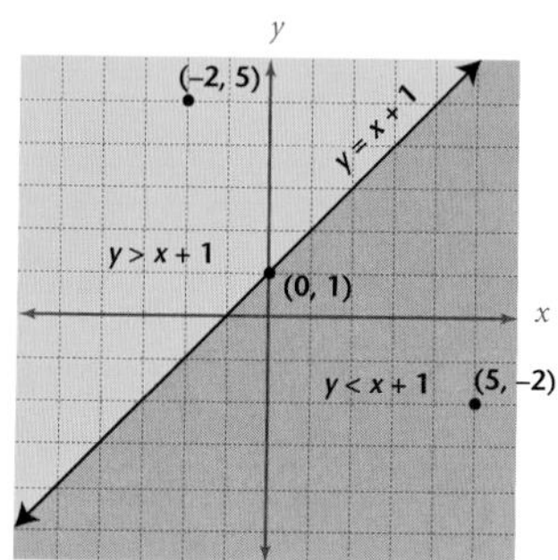

Whenever you graph inequalities, begin by sketching the equality, then decide whether you need to shade the region above or below the line.

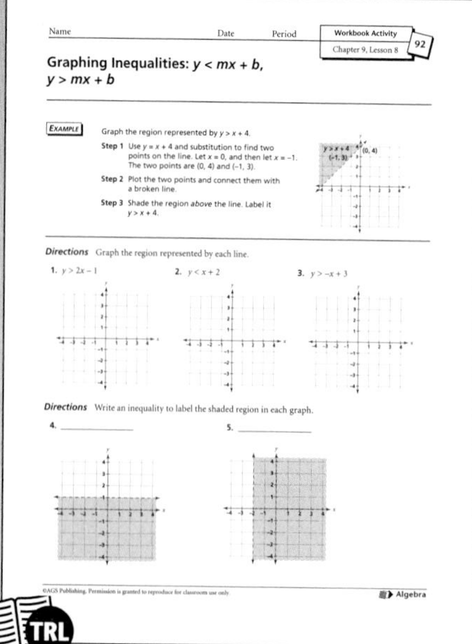

Name Date Period | Workbook Activity 92 | Chapter 9, Lesson 8

Graphing Inequalities: $y < mx + b$, $y > mx + b$

EXAMPLE Graph the region represented by $y > x + 4$.

Step 1 Use $y = x + 4$ and substitution to find two points on the line. Let $x = 0$, and then let $x = -1$. The two points are (0, 4) and (−1, 3).

Step 2 Plot the two points and connect them with a broken line.

Step 3 Shade the region *above* the line. Label it $y > x + 4$.

Directions Graph the region represented by each line.

1. $y > 2x - 1$
2. $y < x + 2$
3. $y > -x + 3$

Directions Write an inequality to label the shaded region in each graph.

4. ________
5. ________

 Algebra

Workbook Activity 92

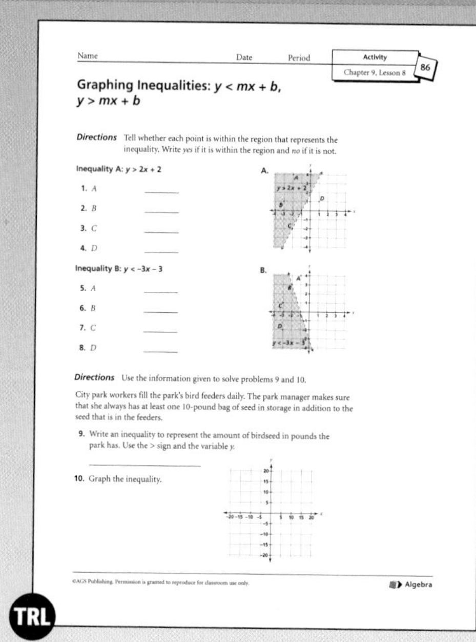

Name Date Period | Activity 86 | Chapter 9, Lesson 8

Graphing Inequalities: $y < mx + b$, $y > mx + b$

Directions Tell whether each point is within the region that represents the inequality. Write *yes* if it is within the region and *no* if it is not.

Inequality A: $y > 2x + 2$

1. *A* ________
2. *B* ________
3. *C* ________
4. *D* ________

Inequality B: $y < -3x - 3$

5. *A* ________
6. *B* ________
7. *C* ________
8. *D* ________

Directions Use the information given to solve problems 9 and 10.

City park workers fill the park's bird feeders daily. The park manager makes sure that she always has at least one 10-pound bag of seed in storage in addition to the seed that is in the feeders.

9. Write an inequality to represent the amount of birdseed in pounds the park has. Use the > sign and the variable y.
   ____
10. Graph the inequality.

 Algebra

Activity 86

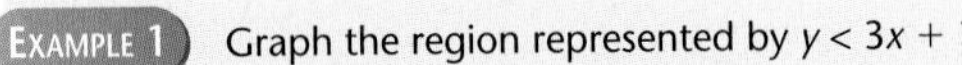

Example 1 Graph the region represented by $y < 3x + 1$.

Step 1 Use $y = 3x + 1$ and substitution to find two points on the line. Plot the points and then draw a broken line and label the line $y < 3x + 1$.

Step 2 $y < 3x + 1$ represents the region below the broken line. Check by choosing a point such as (5, 1) that is located below the broken line.

$y < 3x + 1$

$1 < 3(5) + 1$

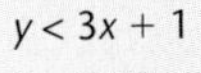

$1 < 16$ True

Step 3 Shade the region below the broken line without touching the broken line.

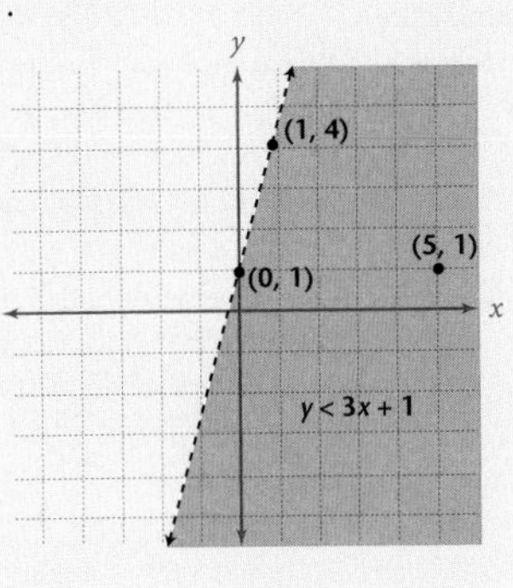

Example 2 Graph the region represented by $y > 3$.

Step 1 All ordered pairs having a y-value of 3 are on a horizontal line that passes through $y = 3$. So $y > 3$ is parallel to the x-axis. Draw a broken line and label the line $y > 3$.

Step 2 $y > 3$ represents the region above the broken line. Check by choosing a point such as (4, 5) that is located above the broken line.

$y > 3$

$5 > 3$ True

Step 3 Shade the region above the broken line without touching the broken line.

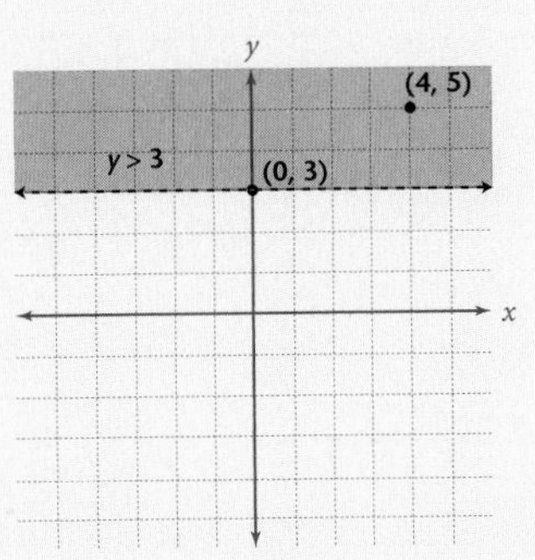

Answers to Problems 1–15

1.
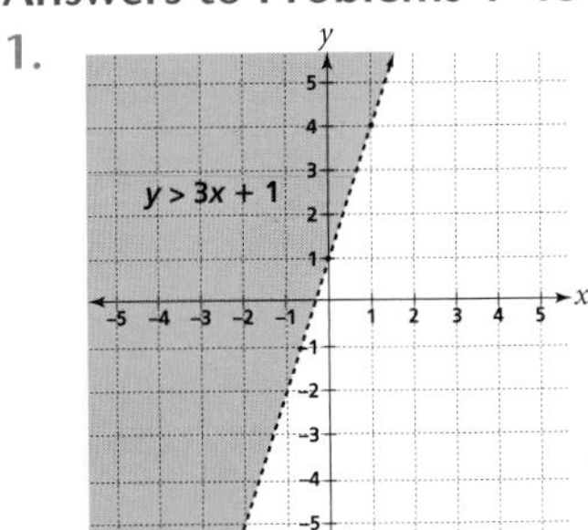

2.
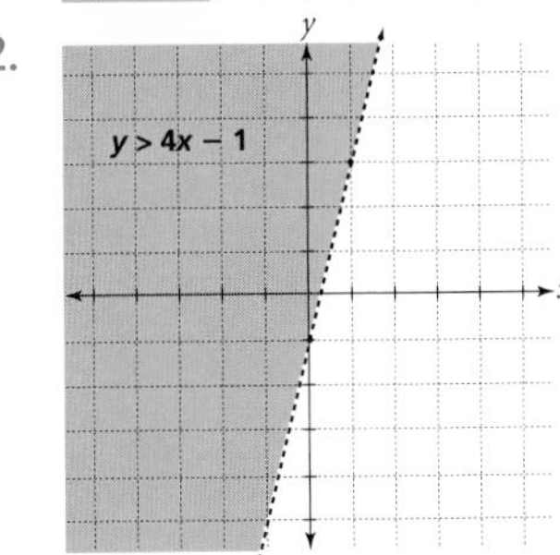

3.
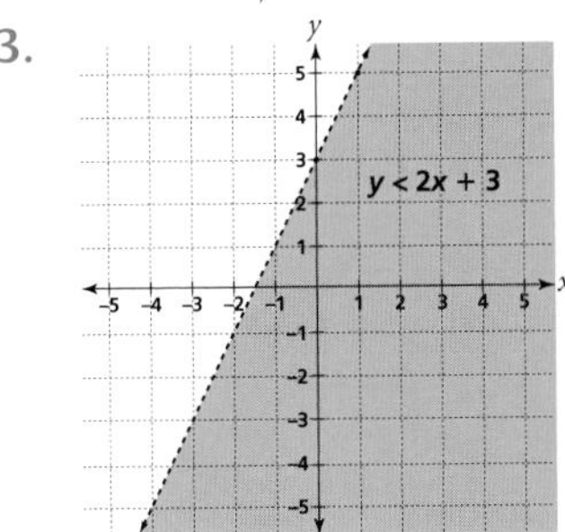

4.
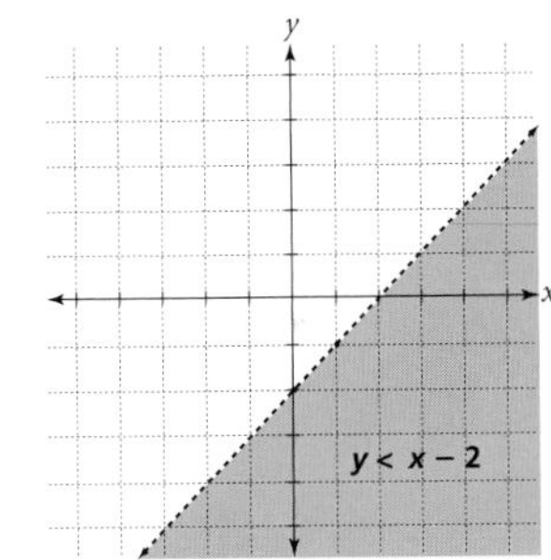

5.
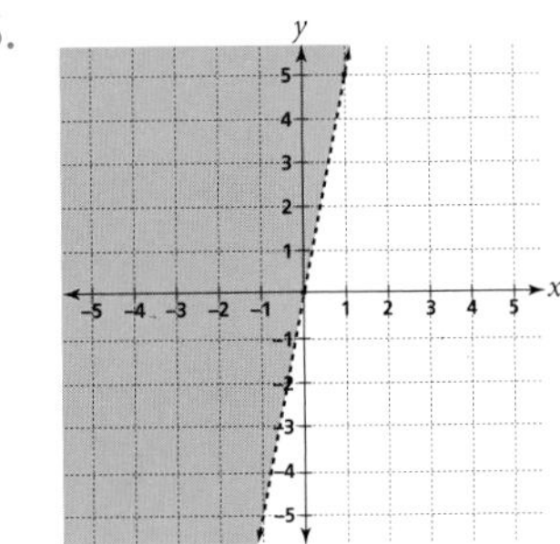

6. The graph should be a broken line passing through (−2, 2) and (2, 2). The region below the broken line should be shaded.
7. The graph should be a broken line passing through (6, 2) and (6, −2). The region to the right of the broken line should be shaded.
8. The graph should be a broken line passing through (−3, 2) and (−3, −2). The region to the left of the broken line should be shaded.
9. The graph should be a broken line passing through (−1, 1) and (1, 1). The region above the broken line should be shaded.
10. The graph should be a broken line passing through (−1, −1) and (1, −1). The region below the broken line should be shaded.
11. The graph should be a broken line passing through (0, 4) and (1, 5). The region above the broken line should be shaded.
12. The graph should be a broken line passing through (0, 0) and (1, 4). The region to the right of the broken line should be shaded.
13. The graph should be a broken line passing through (−1, −2) and (1, −2). The region above the broken line should be shaded.
14. The graph should be a broken line passing through (4, 1) and (4, −1). The region to the left of the broken line should be shaded.
15. The graph should be a broken line passing through (−1, 2) and (−1, −2). The region to the right of the broken line should be shaded.

Math History

Carl Friedrich Gauss was the first mathematician to prove definitively the fundamental theorem of algebra, which states: An equation to the first power has one root. An equation to the second power has two roots. An equation to the third power has three roots. An equation to the *n*th power has *n* roots. Born in 1777, Gauss achieved great success in both mathematics and science and was considered a mathematical prodigy. He applied mathematics to many disciplines including astronomy, electricity, and magnetism. He published over a hundred articles, essays, and books. Many scholars consider his manuscript *Disquisitiones Arithmeticae*, published in 1801, as one of the most important books on number theory in the history of mathematics.

Example 3 Graph the region represented by $x < -1$.

Step 1 All ordered pairs having an x-value of -1 are on a vertical line that passes through $x = -1$. So $x < -1$ is perpendicular to the y-axis. Draw a broken line and label the line $x < -1$.

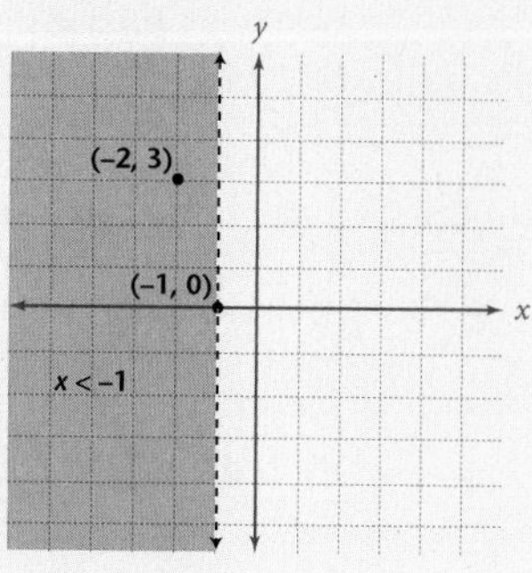

Step 2 $x < -1$ represents the region to the left of the broken line. Check by choosing a point such as $(-2, 3)$ that is located to the left of the broken line.

$x < -1$

$-2 < -1$ True

Step 3 Shade the region to the left of the broken line without touching the broken line.

Exercise A Graph the region represented by each line.

See Teacher's Edition page for answers to problems 1–15.

1. $y > 3x + 1$

2. $y > 4x - 1$

3. $y < 2x + 3$

4. $y < x - 2$

5. $y > 5x$

6. $y < 2$

7. $x > 6$

8. $x < -3$

9. $y > 1$

10. $y < -1$

11. $y > x + 4$

12. $y < 4x$

13. $y > -2$

14. $x < 4$

15. $x > -1$

Estimation Activity

Estimate: The graph shows the population growth in Johnsonville. If the population grows the same amount as it did between 1970 and 1980, what will the population of Johnsonville be in 2010?

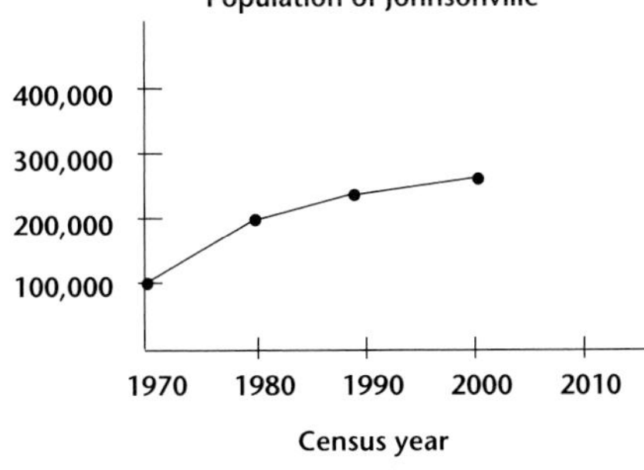

Solution: Look at the information on the graph and use it to solve the problem.

Between 1970 and 1980, the population grew from 100,000 to 200,000, an increase of 100,000. The last population data on the graph shows the population at 250,000. So, you can estimate that the population in 2100 will be 350,000.

Linear Equations and Inequalities in the Coordinate Plane **275**

Lesson at a Glance

Chapter 9 Lesson 9

Overview This lesson expands information on how to graph inequalities that include equalities.

Objectives

- To graph inequalities in which y is greater than or equal to or less than or equal to $mx + b$
- To write an inequality that describes a given graph

Student Pages 276–279

Teacher's Resource Library TRL

Workbook Activity 93

Activity 87

Alternative Activity 87

Warm-Up Activity

Remind students that given a point $P = (x, y)$ and the inequality $y \geq mx + b$, P is on the line of the inequality, above the line, or below the line. Have them infer that the same conditions apply for the inequality $y \leq mx + b$.

Teaching the Lesson

Help students make the generalization that regions below the line $y = mx + b$ represent values that yield the inequality $y < mx + b$ and that regions above the line represent values that yield the inequality $y > mx + b$.

Common Error

Students sometimes confuse the symbols <, > and ≤, ≥. Point out to students that they can use the symbol itself to keep the meaning accurate. Indicate that the smaller part of the symbol always points to the lesser quantity, while the open or wider part of the symbol always points to the greater quantity.

Lesson 9 Graphing Inequalities: $y \leq mx + b$, $y \geq mx + b$

Graphs of inequalities also include inequalities such as $y \leq x + 1$ and $y \geq x + 1$. In these cases, you must *include* equality in the graphs of these regions.

Example 1 Graph the region represented by $y \leq x + 1$.

Step 1 Use $y = x + 1$ and substitution to find two points on the line. Plot the points and then draw a solid line and label the line $y \leq x + 1$.

Step 2 $y \leq x + 1$ represents the region below the solid line. Check by choosing a point such as (0, 0) that is located below the solid line.

$y \leq x + 1$
$0 \leq 0 + 1$
$0 \leq 1$ True

Step 3 Shade the region *below* the solid line. Include the line in your shading.

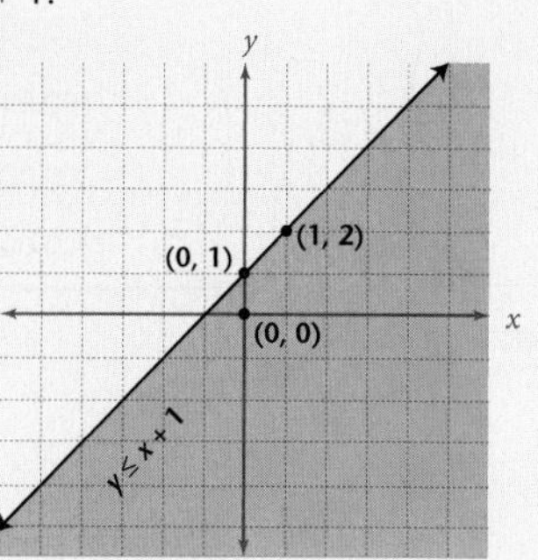

Example 2 Graph the region represented by $y \geq x + 1$.

Step 1 Use $y = x + 1$ and substitution to find two points on the line. Plot the points and then draw a solid line and label the line $y \geq x + 1$.

Step 2 $y \geq x + 1$ represents the region above the solid line. Check by choosing a point such as $(-5, 5)$ that is located above the solid line.

$y \geq x + 1$
$5 \geq -5 + 1$
$5 \geq -4$ True

Step 3 Shade the region above the solid line. Include the line in your shading.

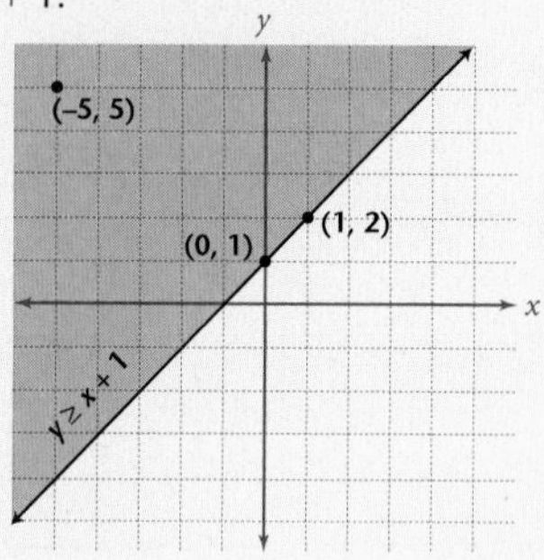

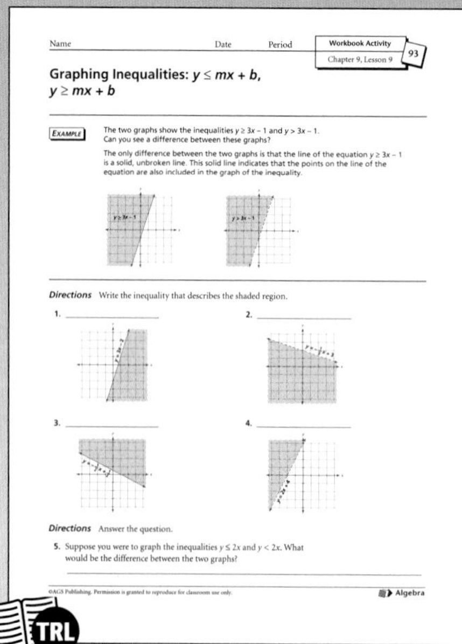

Name Date Period | Workbook Activity 93 | Chapter 9, Lesson 9

Graphing Inequalities: $y \leq mx + b$, $y \geq mx + b$

Example The two graphs show the inequalities $y \geq 3x - 1$ and $y > 3x - 1$. Can you see a difference between these graphs?

The only difference between the two graphs is that the line of the equation $y \geq 3x - 1$ is a solid, unbroken line. This solid line indicates that the points on the line of the equation are also included in the graph of the inequality.

Directions Write the inequality that describes the shaded region.

1. ______
2. ______
3. ______
4. ______

Directions Answer the question.

5. Suppose you were to graph the inequalities $y \leq 2x$ and $y < 2x$. What would be the difference between the two graphs?

 Algebra

Workbook Activity 93

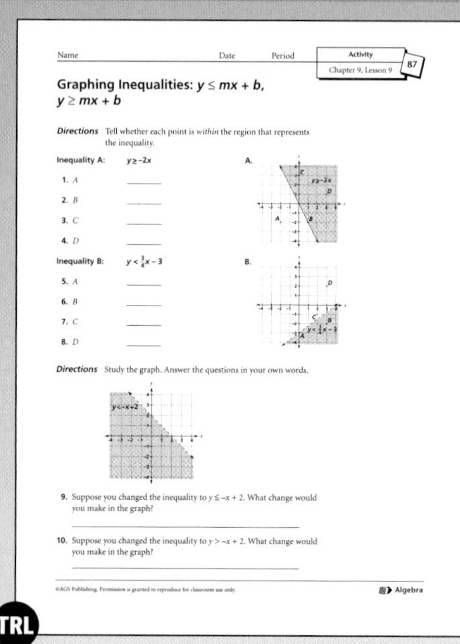

Name Date Period | Activity 87 | Chapter 9, Lesson 9

Graphing Inequalities: $y \leq mx + b$, $y \geq mx + b$

Directions Tell whether each point is *within* the region that represents the inequality.

Inequality A: $y \geq -2x$

1. *A* ______
2. *B* ______
3. *C* ______
4. *D* ______

Inequality B: $y < \frac{3}{4}x - 3$

5. *A* ______
6. *B* ______
7. *C* ______
8. *D* ______

Directions Study the graph. Answer the questions in your own words.

9. Suppose you changed the inequality to $y \leq -x + 2$. What change would you make in the graph?

10. Suppose you changed the inequality to $y > -x + 2$. What change would you make in the graph?

 Algebra

Activity 87

You can write the algebraic inequality represented by a graph if you are given a graph and the equation of the line of the graph.

Example 3 Write the inequality that describes the shaded region.

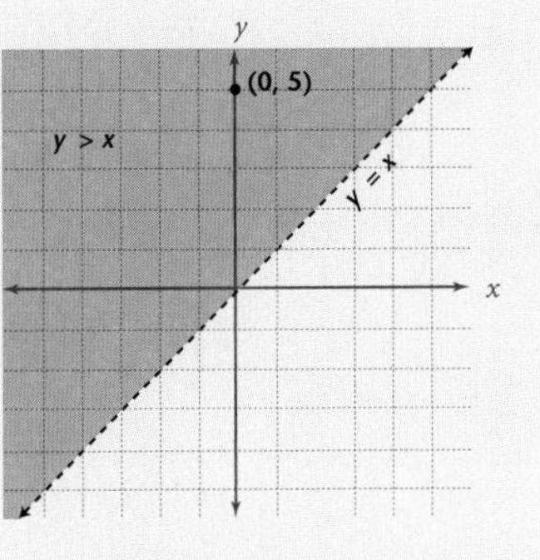

Step 1 Since the shaded region is defined by a broken line, the inequality does not include =. Since the shaded region is above $y = x$, the inequality is >, and $y > x$ is the inequality that describes the shaded region.

Step 2 Check by choosing a point such as (0, 5) that is located in the shaded region.

$y > x$

$5 > 0$ True

Example 4 Write the inequality that describes the shaded region.

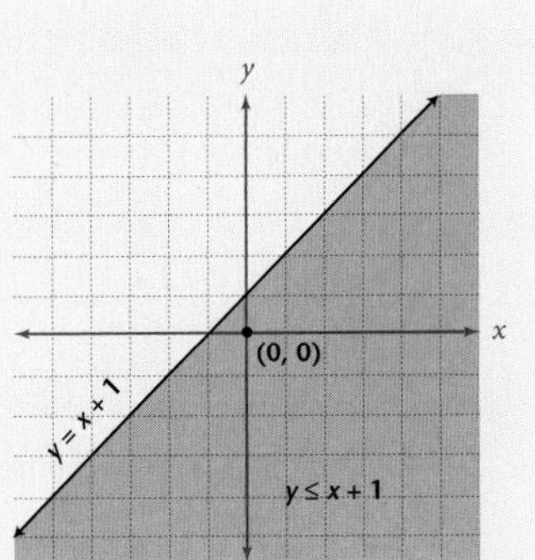

Step 1 Since the shaded region is defined by a solid line, the inequality includes =. Since the shaded region is *below* $y = x + 1$, the inequality is <, and $y \leq x + 1$ is the inequality that describes the shaded region.

Step 2 Check by choosing a point such as (0, 0) that is located in the shaded region.

$y \leq x + 1$

$0 \leq 0 + 1$

$0 \leq 1$ True

3 Reinforce and Extend

Learning Styles

LEP/ESL

Have pairs of students discuss the example graphs. Suggest one student choose a point on the graph either on the line or in the shaded or unshaded regions and give the coordinates to his or her partner. The partner should then describe which region includes the chosen coordinates—the line, the region above the line, or the region below the line.

Learning Styles

Interpersonal/ Group Learning

Ask students to consider the information in problems 11–14. Have them discuss the following questions: Could they complete the problems without knowing the equation for the line? *(no)* Could they complete the problems without knowing two of the points along the line? *(yes)* Suppose they were given only two points on the line and the slope of the line. Would they have enough information to complete the problem? *(Yes, they can use the slope and two points to write the equation of the line.)*

See Teacher's Edition page for answers to problems 1–10.

Exercise A Graph the region represented by each line.

1. $y \geq x + 2$

2. $y \leq x + 2$

3. $y \leq 2x - 1$

4. $y < 3x + 3$

5. $y \geq -2x$

6. $y \leq 5x$

7. $y > -1$

8. $y \leq 4$

9. $x > 2$

10. $x \geq -3$

Exercise B Write the inequality that describes each shaded region.

11.

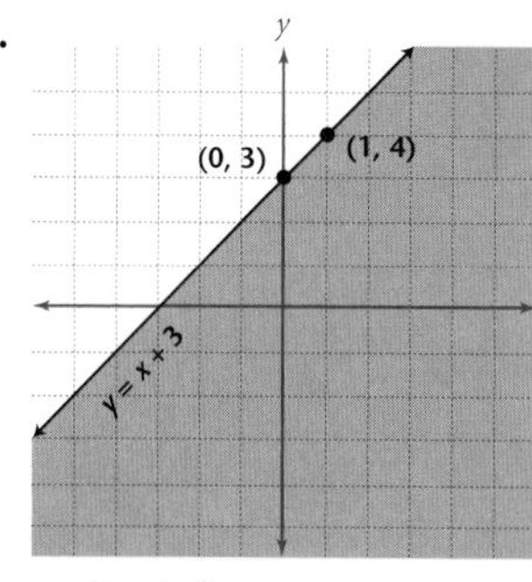

$y \leq x + 3$

12.

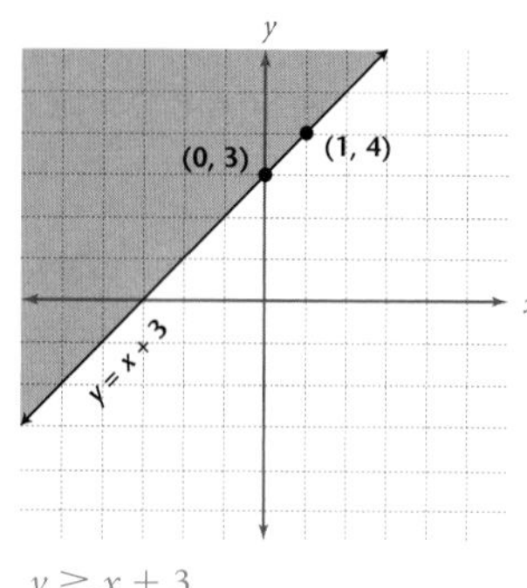

$y \geq x + 3$

13.

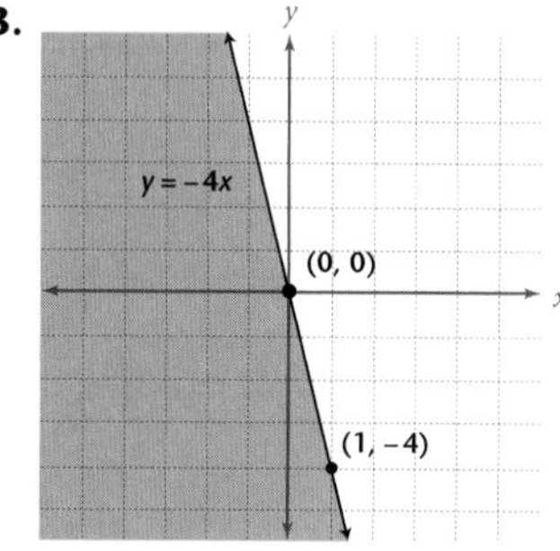

$y \leq -4x$

14.

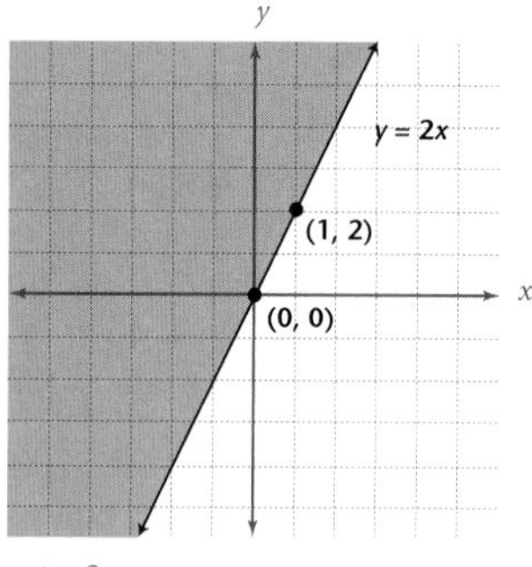

$y \geq 2x$

15.

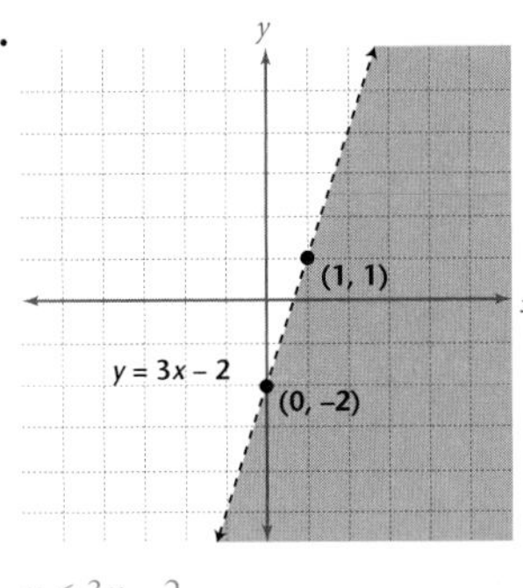

$y < 3x - 2$

16.

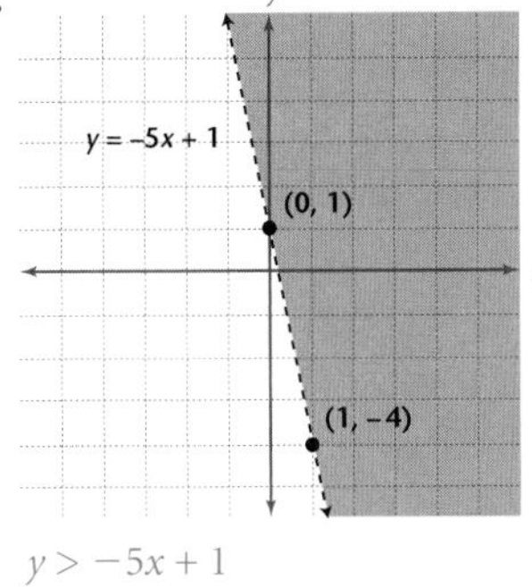

$y > -5x + 1$

17.

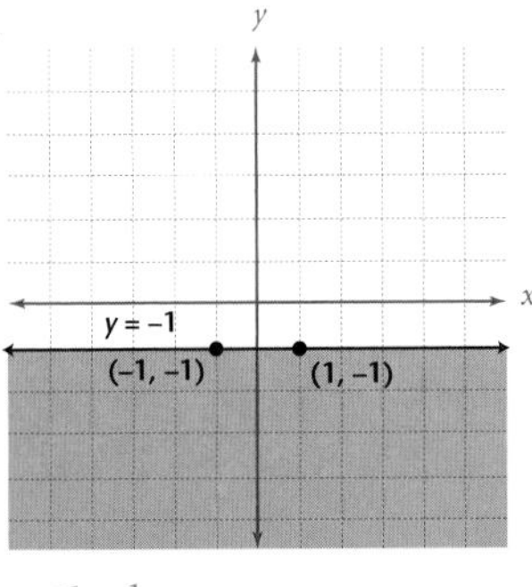

$y \leq -1$

18.

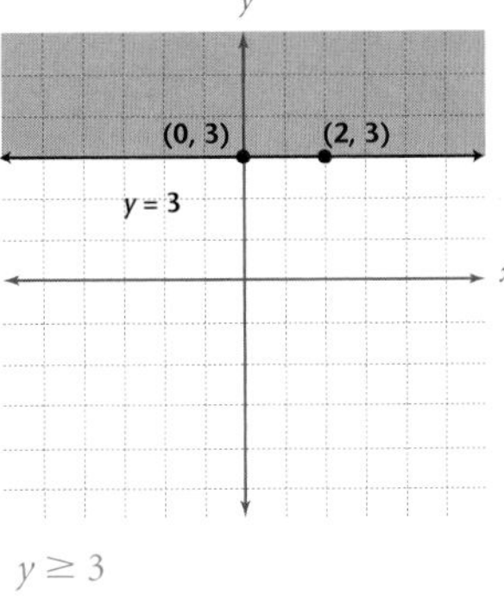

$y \geq 3$

19.

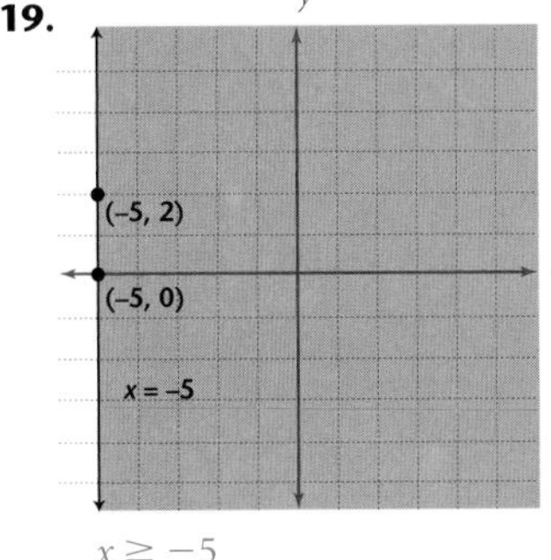

$x \geq -5$

20.

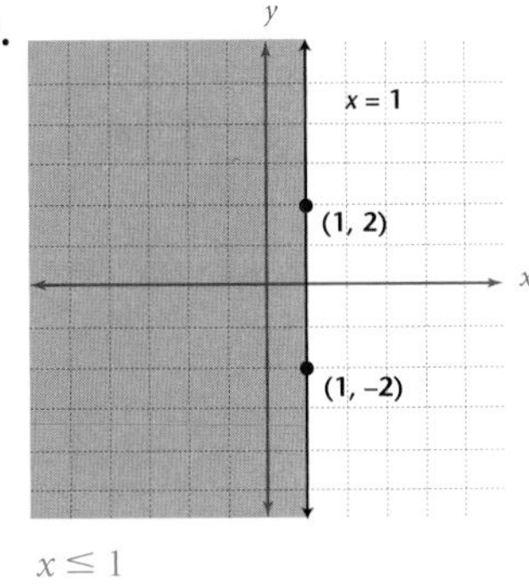

$x \leq 1$

Answers to Problems 1–10

1.

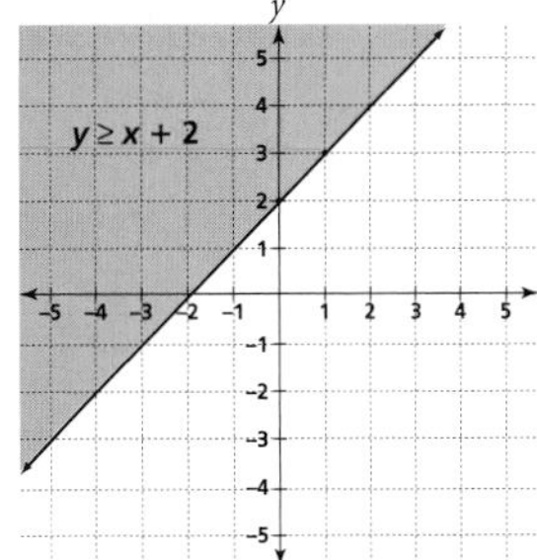

2.

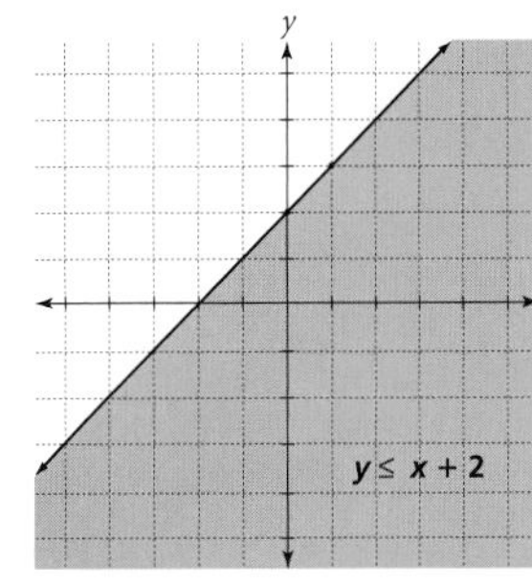

3.

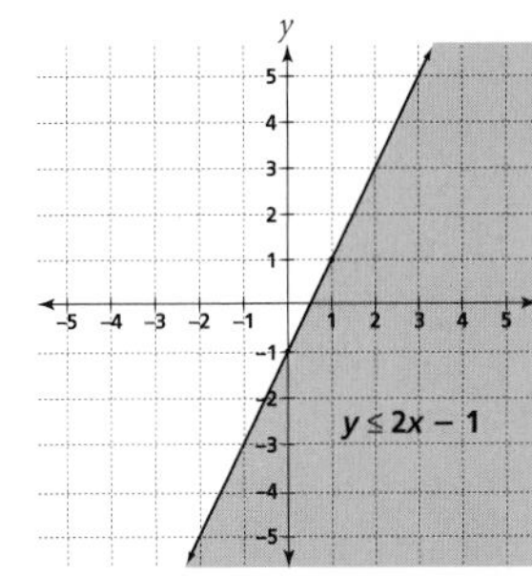

4.

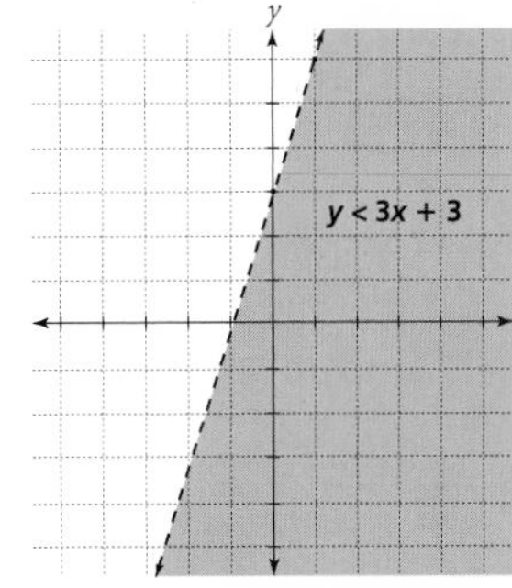

5.

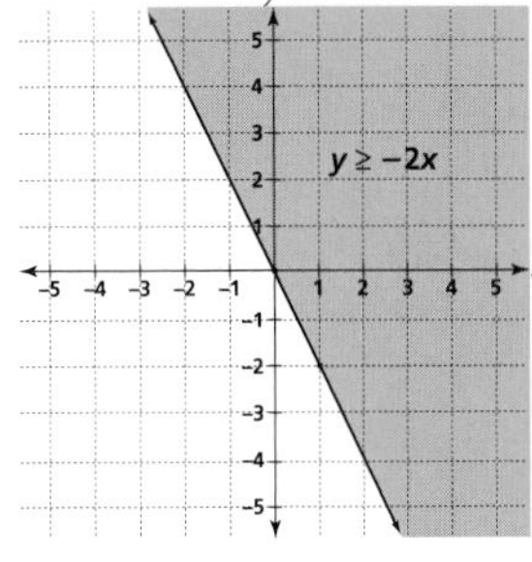

6. The graph should be a solid line passing through (0, 0) and (1, 5). The region below the solid line should be shaded.

7. The graph should be a broken line passing through (0, −1) and (1, −1). The region above the broken line should be shaded.

8. The graph should be a solid line passing through (0, 4) and (2, 4). The region below the solid line should be shaded.

9. The graph should be a broken line passing through (2, 0) and (2, 2). The region to the right of the broken line should be shaded.

10. The graph should be a solid line passing through (−3, 0) and (−3, 3). The region to the left of the solid line should be shaded.

Lesson at a Glance

Chapter 9 Lesson 10

Overview This lesson introduces graphs without numbers.

Objective

- To interpret and create graphs without numbers

Student Pages 280–281

Teacher's Resource Library 

Workbook Activity 94

Activity 88

Alternative Activity 88

Warm-Up Activity

Point out to students that graphs can provide a picture of an event and make the event clearer or easier to understand. Engage students in a discussion of the kinds of graphs they may have seen during television shows about hospitals or medical procedures. Point out that the electronic picture of a heartbeat helps doctors "see" how a person's heart is working. Indicate to students there are other instances in which a graph of an event can help describe or clarify the event.

Teaching the Lesson

If feasible, demonstrate the first graph using a helium-filled balloon. As an alternative, you might ask a volunteer to mime the action of a rising, then bursting balloon using a basketball or soccer ball as a model.

Lesson 10 Graphs Without Numbers

Every graph is a picture of something that has happened sometime in the past or is happening now.

Look at the graph at the right. It tells a story. Use your imagination—what story might it be telling?

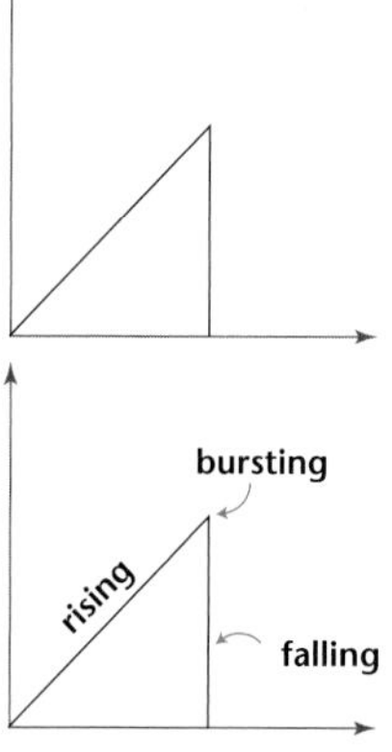

Possible solution:
Suppose the horizontal axis, or x-axis, represents time, and the vertical axis, or y-axis, represents height above ground. The graph shows how a balloon filled with helium rises until it bursts and falls to the ground.

Note that the graph shows only the first quadrant. This makes both axes positive and you can assume the origin of the graph is (0, 0).

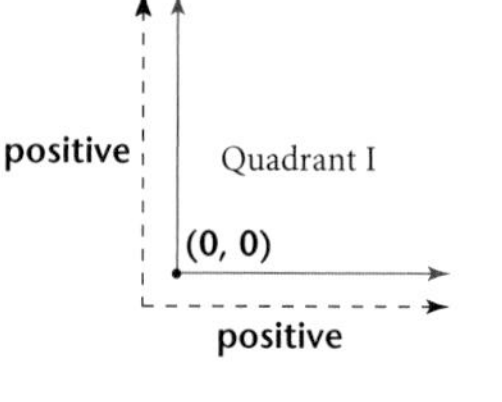

Look at the graph at the right. It too tells a story. Again use your imagination—what story might it be telling?

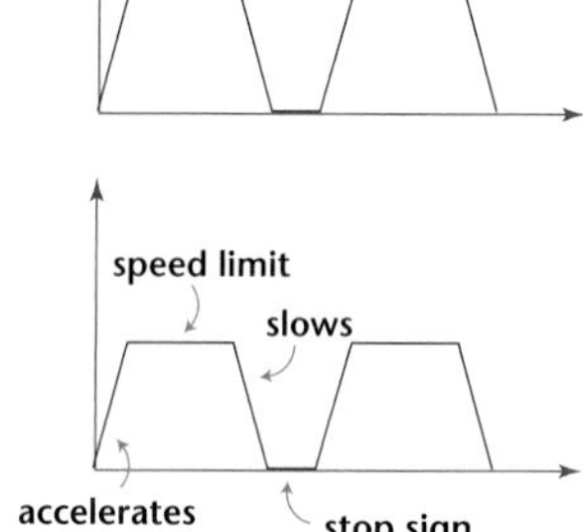

Possible solution:
Suppose the x-axis represents time and the y-axis represents speed. The graph shows how an automobile driver accelerates from 0 miles per hour to the speed limit. The driver maintains a steady speed for a while and then slows and stops for a stop sign. The process then repeats itself.

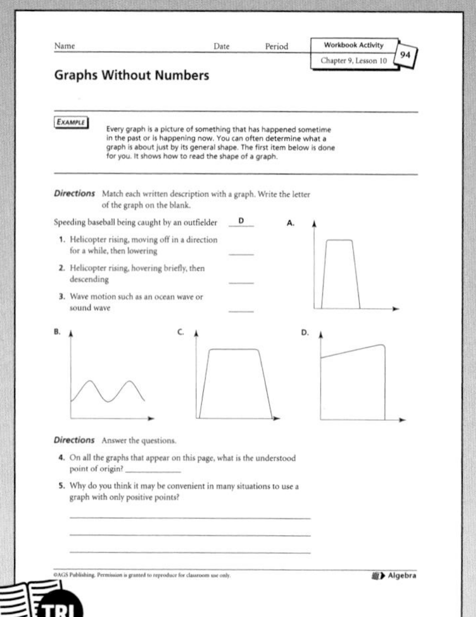

Name Date Period — Workbook Activity 94, Chapter 9, Lesson 10

Graphs Without Numbers

EXAMPLE Every graph is a picture of something that has happened sometime in the past or is happening now. You can often determine what a graph is about just by its general shape. The first item below is done for you. It shows how to read the shape of a graph.

Directions Match each written description with a graph. Write the letter of the graph on the blank.

Speeding baseball being caught by an outfielder D

1. Helicopter rising, moving off in a direction for a while, then lowering ____
2. Helicopter rising, hovering briefly, then descending ____
3. Wave motion such as an ocean wave or sound wave ____

A. B. C. D.

Directions Answer the questions.

4. On all the graphs that appear on this page, what is the understood point of origin? ____
5. Why do you think it may be convenient in many situations to use a graph with only positive points?

 Algebra

Workbook Activity 94

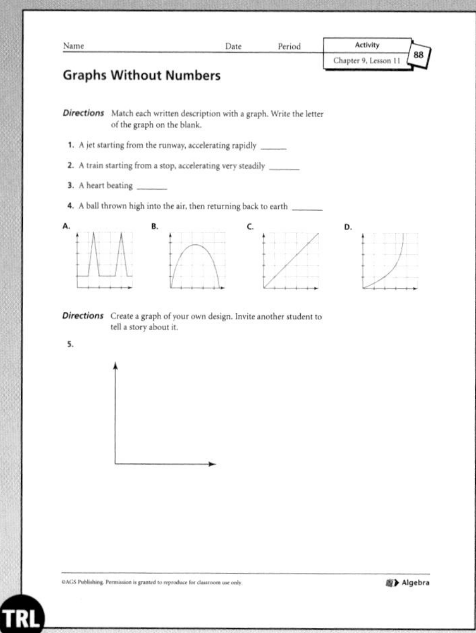

Name Date Period — Activity 88, Chapter 9, Lesson 11

Graphs Without Numbers

Directions Match each written description with a graph. Write the letter of the graph on the blank.

1. A jet starting from the runway, accelerating rapidly ____
2. A train starting from a stop, accelerating very steadily ____
3. A heart beating ____
4. A ball thrown high into the air, then returning back to earth ____

A. B. C. D.

Directions Create a graph of your own design. Invite another student to tell a story about it.

5.

 Algebra

Activity 88

Exercise A What story might each of these graphs be telling?

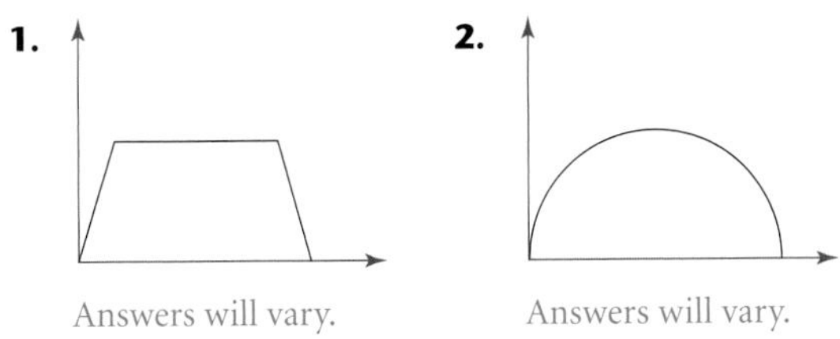

1. Answers will vary.
2. Answers will vary.

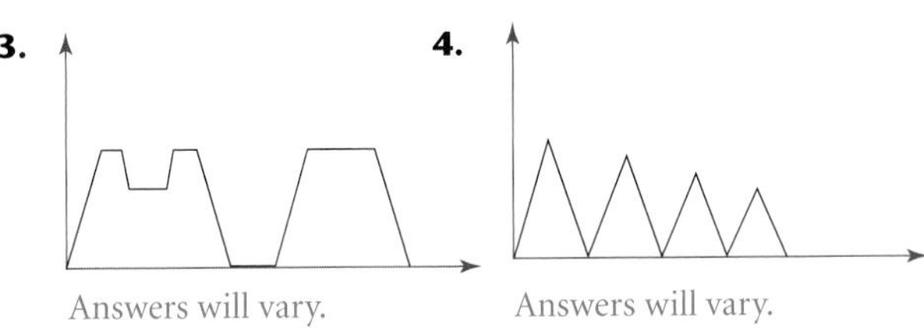

3. Answers will vary.
4. Answers will vary.

Exercise B

5. Create a graph of your own design. Invite another student to tell a story about it. Check students' graphs.

Reinforce and Extend

Learning Styles

Visual/Spatial

Encourage students to create a storyboard that illustrates an event such as stop-and-go driving, the action of a pendulum, or the path down a ski hill or up a skateboard ramp. Direct students to prepare a graph to illustrate the event. A section of the graph should be completed for each frame of the storyboard. Invite students to post their graphs and storyboards on a class bulletin board.

Career Connection

Ask students to investigate the area of medical technology and find out how different kinds of visual displays and graphs are used in medicine. Mention electroencephalograms and electrocardiograms as two possibilities. How are they used? Who uses them? Encourage students to use the answer to the second question to begin a list of medical-related careers.

Lesson at a Glance

Chapter 9 Application

Overview This lesson applies the process of plotting points on a coordinate plane to graph polygons.

Objective

- To plot points and draw lines to create polygons on a coordinate plane

Student Page 282

Teacher's Resource Library 

Application Activity 9

Everyday Algebra 9

1 Warm-Up Activity

Ask students to discuss their familiarity with connect-the-dot pictures. If feasible, bring in several simple connect-the-dot pictures as reminders.

2 Teaching the Lesson

Point out to students that connecting three points in the coordinate plane gives a triangle. The order in which the points are connected does not affect the final shape. Have students predict whether the same is true when they connect four or more points in the coordinate plane.

3 Reinforce and Extend

LEARNING STYLES

Interpersonal/ Group Learning

Invite students to work in groups of four to devise a drawing game based on coordinate geometry. Each team should work together to design a simple, recognizable shape such as an outline of a house, airplane, or automobile. Then the team should translate the drawing into a series of coordinates and directions for connecting the coordinates. Teams can exchange coordinates and directions, using them to produce the original shape.

Application $\pi^2 \Sigma + \Omega \sqrt{x^2} \% \neq y \geq n = \nabla 30^\circ \pi$ 

Graphing

In the coordinate system, you can connect points with line segments to form polygons and other figures. For example, the points (2, 1), (6, 1), and (3, 3) form a triangle when connected with line segments.

EXAMPLE 1 To graph any point in the coordinate system:

Step 1 Locate the *x*-value of the pair by starting at the origin and moving left or right the appropriate number of units on the *x*-axis.

Step 2 Locate the *y*-value of the point by moving up or down the appropriate number of units from the *x*-value.

Step 3 Mark the point.

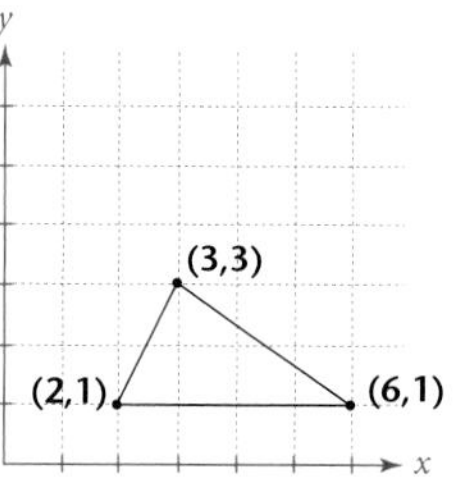

Exercise Make each graph to find the answer.

1. Graph these points: (0, 0), (5, 0), (0, −3). Then draw a line from (0, 0) to (5, 0), from (5, 0) to (0, −3), and from (0, −3) to (0, 0). What shape is the figure? triangle
2. Graph these points: (2, 6), (4, 6), (0, 4), (6, 4), (4, 2), (2, 2). Connect the points using line segments. What figure is formed? hexagon
3. Name four points in the coordinate system that form a rectangle when connected. (1, 1), (3, 1), (1, 4), (3, 4)
4. Name five points in the coordinate system that form a pentagon, or five-sided figure, when connected. (1, 1), (−1, 1), (2, 2), (−2, 2), (0, 3)
5. Name four points in the coordinate system that form a square when connected. (0, 0), (2, 0), (2, 2), (0, 2)

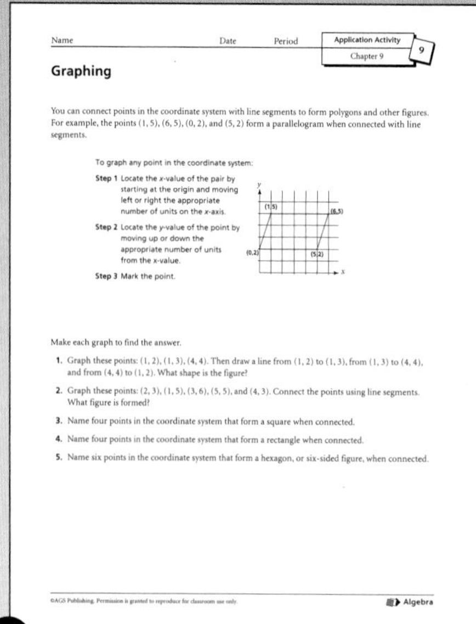

Name Date Period **Application Activity 9** Chapter 9

Graphing

You can connect points in the coordinate system with line segments to form polygons and other figures. For example, the points (1, 5), (6, 5), (0, 2), and (5, 2) form a parallelogram when connected with line segments.

To graph any point in the coordinate system:

Step 1 Locate the *x*-value of the pair by starting at the origin and moving left or right the appropriate number of units on the *x*-axis.

Step 2 Locate the *y*-value of the point by moving up or down the appropriate number of units from the x-value.

Step 3 Mark the point.

Make each graph to find the answer.

1. Graph these points: (1, 2), (1, 3), (4, 4). Then draw a line from (1, 2) to (1, 3), from (1, 3) to (4, 4), and from (4, 4) to (1, 2). What shape is the figure?
2. Graph these points: (2, 3), (1, 5), (3, 6), (5, 5), and (4, 3). Connect the points using line segments. What figure is formed?
3. Name four points in the coordinate system that form a square when connected.
4. Name four points in the coordinate system that form a rectangle when connected.
5. Name six points in the coordinate system that form a hexagon, or six-sided figure, when connected.

 Algebra

Application Activity 9

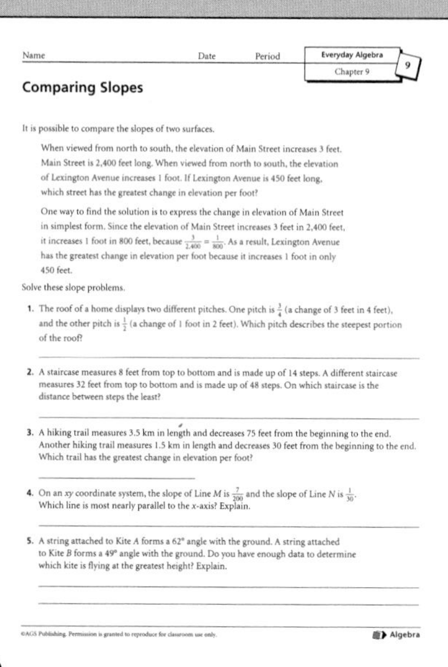

Name Date Period **Everyday Algebra 9** Chapter 9

Comparing Slopes

It is possible to compare the slopes of two surfaces.

When viewed from north to south, the elevation of Main Street increases 3 feet. Main Street is 2,400 feet long. When viewed from north to south, the elevation of Lexington Avenue increases 1 foot. If Lexington Avenue is 450 feet long, which street has the greatest change in elevation per foot?

One way to find the solution is to express the change in elevation of Main Street in simplest form. Since the elevation of Main Street increases 3 feet in 2,400 feet, it increases 1 foot in 800 feet, because $\frac{3}{2,400} = \frac{1}{800}$. As a result, Lexington Avenue has the greatest change in elevation per foot because it increases 1 foot in only 450 feet.

Solve these slope problems.

1. The roof of a home displays two different pitches. One pitch is $\frac{3}{4}$ (a change of 3 feet in 4 feet), and the other pitch is $\frac{1}{2}$ (a change of 1 foot in 2 feet). Which pitch describes the steepest portion of the roof?
2. A staircase measures 8 feet from top to bottom and is made up of 14 steps. A different staircase measures 32 feet from top to bottom and is made up of 48 steps. On which staircase is the distance between steps the least?
3. A hiking trail measures 3.5 km in length and decreases 75 feet from the beginning to the end. Another hiking trail measures 1.5 km in length and decreases 30 feet from the beginning to the end. Which trail has the greatest change in elevation per foot?
4. On an *xy* coordinate system, the slope of Line *M* is $\frac{7}{200}$ and the slope of Line *N* is $\frac{1}{30}$. Which line is most nearly parallel to the *x*-axis? Explain.
5. A string attached to Kite *A* forms a 62° angle with the ground. A string attached to Kite *B* forms a 49° angle with the ground. Do you have enough data to determine which kite is flying at the greatest height? Explain.

 Algebra

Everyday Algebra 9

Chapter 9 REVIEW

Use the graph at the left for questions 1 and 2.
Write the letter of the correct answer.

1. Find the ordered pair that represents the location of point R. C

A $(0, -3)$ **C** $(-3, 0)$

B $(3, 0)$ **D** $(-1, -3)$

2. Find the ordered pair that represents the location of point Z. A

A $(2, -1)$ **C** $(-1, 2)$

B $(-1, 0)$ **D** $(2, 1)$

Write the letter of the correct answer.

3. What is the x-intercept and the y-intercept of the graph $y = x + 3$? C

A x-intercept $= (0, 0)$, y-intercept $= (0, 3)$

B x-intercept $= (-3, 0)$, y-intercept $= (0, 0)$

C x-intercept $= (-3, 0)$, y-intercept $= (0, 3)$

D x-intercept $= (3, 0)$, y-intercept $= (0, 3)$

4. What is the x-intercept and the y-intercept of the graph $y = 4x - 1$? B

A x-intercept $= (-4, 0)$, y-intercept $= (0, 1)$

B x-intercept $= (\frac{1}{4}, 0)$, y-intercept $= (0, -1)$

C x-intercept $= (4, 0)$, y-intercept $= (0, -1)$

D x-intercept $= (-\frac{1}{4}, 0)$, y-intercept $= (0, 1)$

5. Find the slope (m) of the line that passes through the points $(-1, -1)$ $(2, 2)$. C

A $m = -1$ **C** $m = 1$

B $m = -3$ **D** $m = 2$

6. What is the equation of the line with $m = 4$ that passes through the point $(2, 8)$? B

A $y = 8x + 4$ **C** $y = x + 2$

B $y = 4x$ **D** $y = 2x + 8$

Chapter 9 Review

Each set of problems in the Chapter Review includes an example and solution to illustrate the concept. Use the given examples for reteaching the materials in Chapter 9. For additional practice, refer to the Supplementary Problems for Chapter 9 (pages 422–423).

Chapter 9 Mastery Test 

The Teacher's Resource Library includes parallel forms of the Chapter 9 Mastery Test. The difficulty level of the two forms is equivalent. You may wish to use one form as a pretest and the other form as a posttest.

Alternative Assessment

Alternative Assessment items correlate with student Goals for Learning at the beginning of this chapter.

■ **To identify the parts of a graph**
Have students work in groups to invent ways to remember the parts of a graph and what they mean. They should include the terms x-axis, y-axis, ordered pair, origin, point, and quadrant. Have groups share their ideas and memory-joggers with the class. *(Example: To remember which number is x and which number is y in an ordered pair, remember that x comes before y in the alphabet.)*

■ **To locate and plot points in the coordinate system**
Draw a large coordinate system on the board or on an overhead. Plot and label the following points on the coordinate system: A = $(-2, -3)$; B = $(-4, 5)$; C = $(3, 4)$; D = $(6, -1)$. Ask which quadrant each point is in. Ask the coordinates for each point. Have students plot points for $(4, 7)$; $(-3, -4)$; $(5, -5)$; and $(-5, 5)$. *(A = Quadrant III; B = Quadrant II; C = Quadrant I; D = Quadrant IV.)*

■ **To solve equations for ordered pairs and graph a line**
Have students demonstrate what happens when ordered pairs do not fall on the graph of a line. Example: What happens to the equation $y = x + 2$ when the ordered pair $(5, 5)$ is substituted for the values x and y?

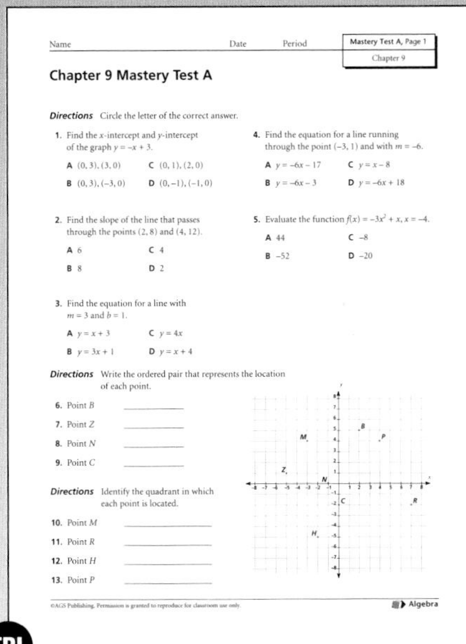

Name Date Period | Mastery Test A, Page 1 | Chapter 9

Chapter 9 Mastery Test A

Directions Circle the letter of the correct answer.

1. Find the x-intercept and y-intercept of the graph $y = -x + 3$.
   A (0, 3), (3, 0) **C** (0, 1), (2, 0)
   B (0, 3), (–3, 0) **D** (0, –1), (–1, 0)

2. Find the slope of the line that passes through the points (2, 8) and (4, 12).
   A 6 **C** 4
   B 8 **D** 2

3. Find the equation for a line with $m = 3$ and $b = 1$.
   A $y = x + 3$ **C** $y = 4x$
   B $y = 3x + 1$ **D** $y = x + 4$

4. Find the equation for a line running through the point (–3, 1) and with $m = -6$.
   A $y = -6x - 17$ **C** $y = x - 8$
   B $y = -6x - 3$ **D** $y = -6x + 18$

5. Evaluate the function $f(x) = -3x^2 + x$, $x = -4$.
   A 44 **C** –8
   B –52 **D** –20

Directions Write the ordered pair that represents the location of each point.

6. Point B ________
7. Point Z ________
8. Point N ________
9. Point C ________

Directions Identify the quadrant in which each point is located.

10. Point M ________
11. Point R ________
12. Point H ________
13. Point P ________

©AGS Publishing. Permission is granted to reproduce for classroom use only. Algebra

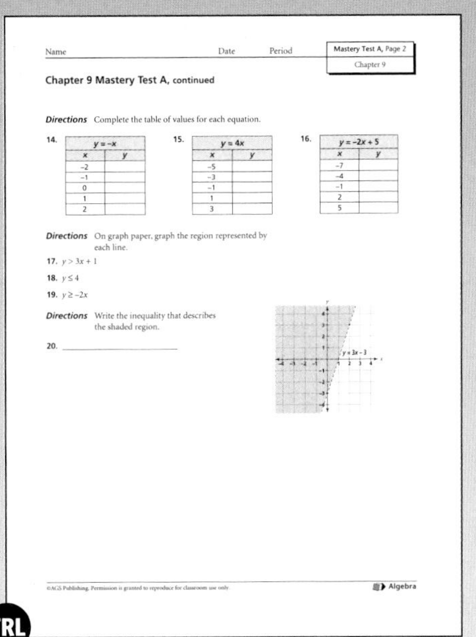

Name Date Period | Mastery Test A, Page 2 | Chapter 9

Chapter 9 Mastery Test A, continued

Directions Complete the table of values for each equation.

14.

$y = -x$	
x	y
–2	
–1	
0	
1	
2	

15.

$y = 4x$	
x	y
–5	
–3	
–1	
1	
3	

16.

$y = -2x + 5$	
x	y
–7	
–4	
–1	
2	
5	

Directions On graph paper, graph the region represented by each line.

17. $y > 3x + 1$
18. $y \leq 4$
19. $y \geq -2x$

Directions Write the inequality that describes the shaded region.

20. ________________

$y = 3x - 3$

©AGS Publishing. Permission is granted to reproduce for classroom use only. Algebra

Chapter 9 Mastery Test A

Answers to Problems 20–23 in the Chapter Review

20.

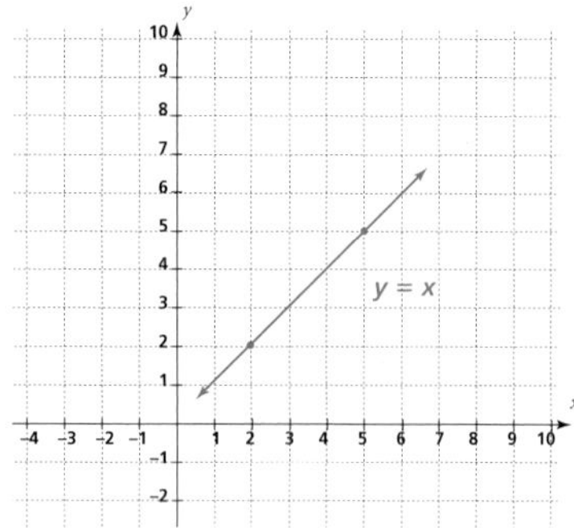

21.

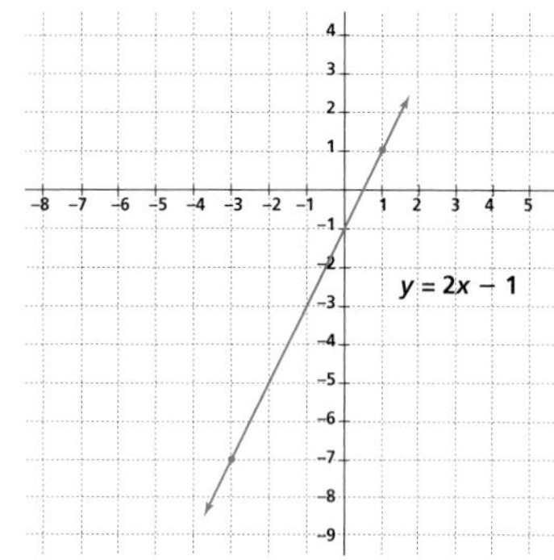

22.

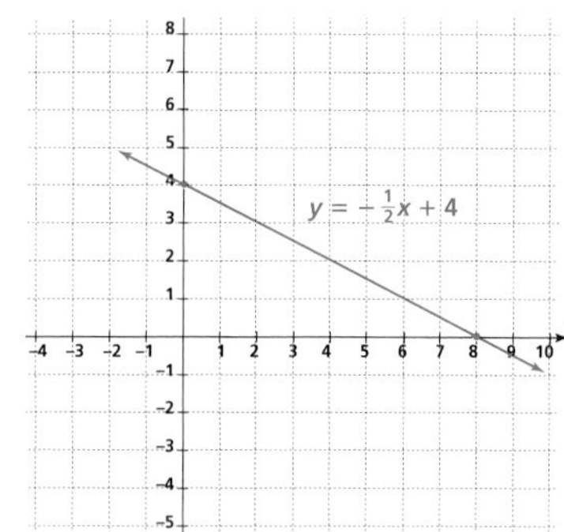

23.

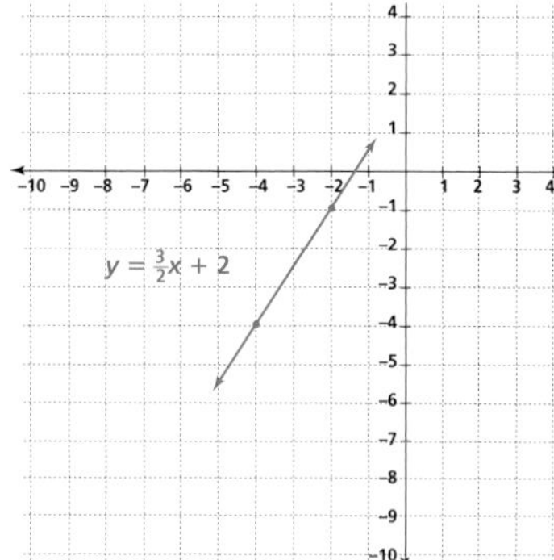

Draw a coordinate system and graph the following points.

Example: Point A at (1, 3)
Solution: Move 1 unit to the right.
Then move up 3 units. Draw the point.

7. Point M at (1, 2)

8. Point S at (0, –4)

9. Point H at (–3, –1)

10. Point Q at (4, 0)

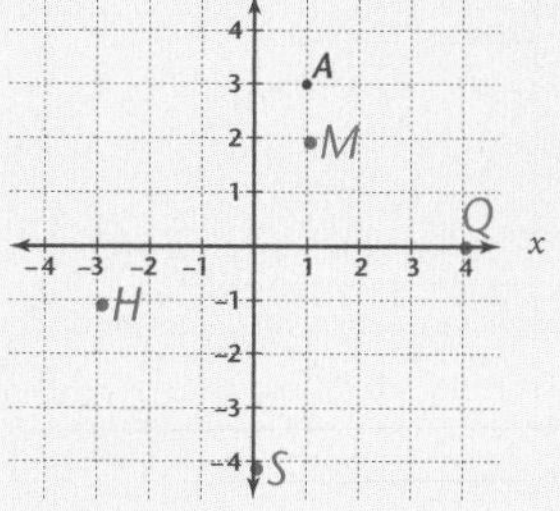

Find the slope of the line that passes through the following points.

Example: (1, 0) (−1, 2) Solution: $m = \frac{y_2 - y_1}{x_2 - x_1} = \frac{2 - 0}{-1 - 1} = \frac{2}{-2} = -1$

11. (3, −6) (−1, −2) $m = -1$

12. (−8, 1) (4, −1) $m = -\frac{1}{6}$

13. (0, 4) (8, 0) $m = -\frac{1}{2}$

See Teacher's Edition page for answers to problems 14–17.

Graph the line that passes through the following points. Then write the equation of each line.

Example: (1, 1) (3, 2) Solution: $m = \frac{y_2 - y_1}{x_2 - x_1}$

$m = \frac{2 - 1}{3 - 1}$ $m = \frac{1}{2}$

$y = mx + b$ $y = \frac{1}{2}(3) + b$

$2 = \frac{3}{2} + b$ $\frac{1}{2} = b$

$y = \frac{1}{2}x + \frac{1}{2}$

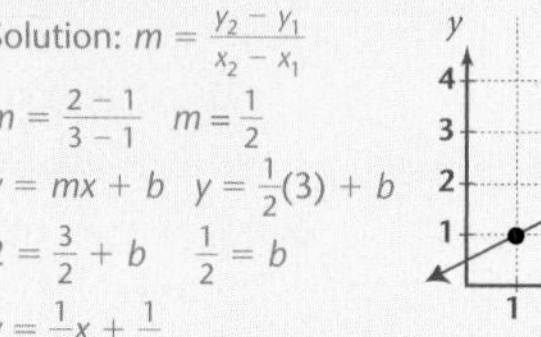

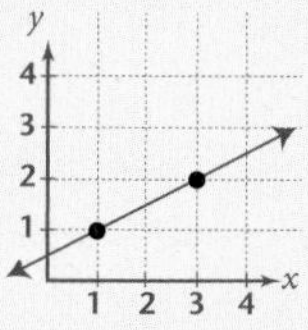

14. (2, 2) (5, 5)

15. (−3, −7) (1, 1)

16. (0, 4) (8, 0)

17. (−2, −1) (−4, −4)

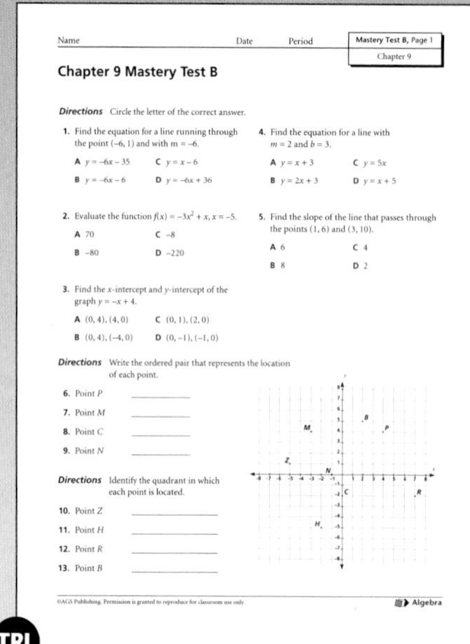

Name Date Period | Mastery Test B, Page 1 | Chapter 9

Chapter 9 Mastery Test B

Directions Circle the letter of the correct answer.

1. Find the equation for a line running through the point (–6, 1) and with m = –6.
   A $y = -6x - 35$ C $y = x - 6$
   B $y = -6x - 6$ D $y = -6x + 36$

2. Evaluate the function $f(x) = -3x^2 + x, x = -5$.
   A 70 C –8
   B –80 D –220

3. Find the x-intercept and y-intercept of the graph $y = -x + 4$.
   A (0, 4), (4, 0) C (0, 1), (2, 0)
   B (0, 4), (–4, 0) D (0, –1), (–1, 0)

4. Find the equation for a line with $m = 2$ and $b = 3$.
   A $y = x + 3$ C $y = 5x$
   B $y = 2x + 3$ D $y = x + 5$

5. Find the slope of the line that passes through the points (1, 6) and (3, 10).
   A 6 C 4
   B 8 D 2

Directions Write the ordered pair that represents the location of each point.

6. Point P ________
7. Point M ________
8. Point C ________
9. Point N ________

Directions Identify the quadrant in which each point is located.

10. Point Z ________
11. Point H ________
12. Point R ________
13. Point B ________

Algebra

TRL

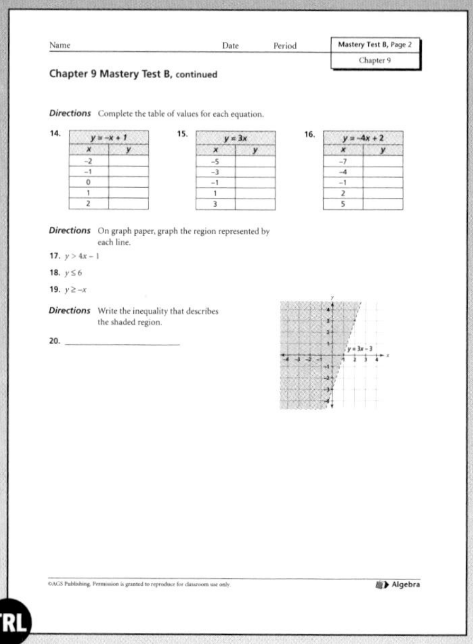

Name Date Period | Mastery Test B, Page 2 | Chapter 9

Chapter 9 Mastery Test B, continued

Directions Complete the table of values for each equation.

14.

$y = -x + 1$	
x	y
–2	
–1	
0	
1	
2	

15.

$y = 3x$	
x	y
–5	
–3	
–1	
1	
3	

16.

$y = -4x + 2$	
x	y
–7	
–4	
–1	
2	
5	

Directions On graph paper, graph the region represented by each line.

17. $y > 4x - 1$
18. $y \le 6$
19. $y \ge -x$

Directions Write the inequality that describes the shaded region.

20. ________________

$y = 3x - 3$

Algebra

TRL

Chapter 9 Mastery Test B

Is each graph an example of a function? Write *yes* or *no*.

Example: Solution: no

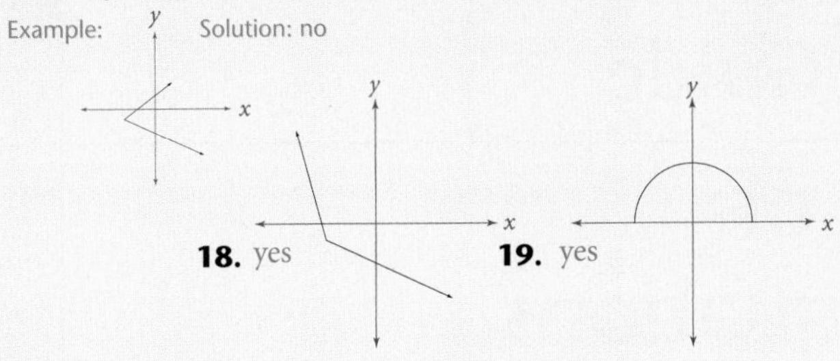

18. yes **19.** yes

Evaluate each function two times. Use $x = -1$ and $x = 2$.

Example: $f(x) = x + 1$ Solution: $f(-1) = -1 + 1$ $f(-1) = 0$ $f(2) = 2 + 1$ $f(2) = 3$

20. $f(x) = x^2 + x$ $f(-1) = 0; f(2) = 6$

21. $f(x) = x^2 - x$ $f(-1) = 2; f(2) = 2$

22. $f(x) = -x^2 - x$ $f(-1) = 0; f(2) = -6$

Graph the region represented by each line.

Example: $y > x + 1$ Solution: Find two points: (1, 2) (2, 3)
Check using (0, 5). $y > x + 1$
$5 > 0 + 1$ True

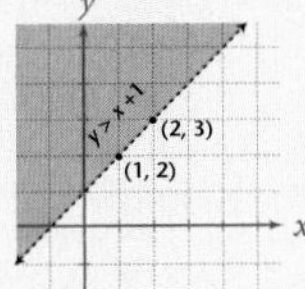

23. $y < 2x + 1$

24. $y > 4$

23\. The graph should be a broken line passing through (0, 1) and (1, 3). The region to the right of the broken line should be shaded.

24\. The graph should be a broken line passing through (0, 4) and (1, 4). The region above the broken line should be shaded.

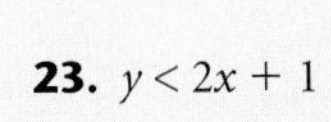

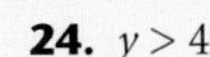

Write the inequality that describes the shaded region.

Example:

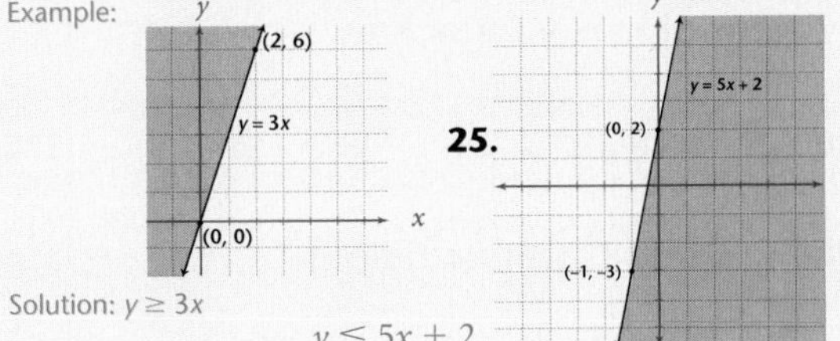

Solution: $y \geq 3x$

25. $y \leq 5x + 2$

Test-Taking Tip When you create a graph from a chart of data, check the number of facts you are supposed to record from the chart.

Alternative Assessment, continued

(The equation becomes false; that is, values that make an equation false can never fall on the graph of a line.)

■ **To find the *x*-intercept and *y*-intercept of a graph**
Have students describe the kinds of lines that have no *x*-intercept and the kinds that have no *y*-intercept. *(Lines parallel to the x-axis have no x-intercept, all the y values in the ordered pairs are the same, and the equation takes the form y = some number; lines parallel to the y-axis have no y-intercept, all the x values in the ordered pairs are the same, and the equation takes the form x = some number.)*

■ **To determine the slope of a line**
Have students calculate the slope of a line that passes through (−2, 5) and (2, −3). Then, have students discuss why only two sets of ordered pairs are needed to determine the slope of a line. *(m = −2. Only one straight line can pass through two points; so, the slope of a straight line can be calculated using only two sets of ordered pairs.)*

■ **To write and solve an equation of a straight line**
Have students describe three ways to find the equation of a straight line and give one example of each. *(If they know the slope and y-intercept, if they know the slope and a given point, or if they know two points, then they can write and solve an equation of a straight line. Students should use the general form of all linear equations—y = mx + b—to write their equations.)*

■ **To identify and evaluate functions**
Have each student draw an "input-output" machine, which is essentially a two-column table with the labels input and output. Have them determine values for the input column and corresponding values for two or three of the corresponding output. Then ask the students to pass their "machines" to another student who will determine the functional relationship. (In the following example, 3 is added to each input to produce the output. So, the answers for the last three items are 16, 22, and 25.)

input	output
4	7
8	11
10	13
13	?
19	?
22	?

■ **To graph inequalities**
Have students draw three number lines and three coordinate planes. Ask them to graph different inequalities on each of them. Ask them to list similarities and differences. (Similarities: shaded area on the coordinate plane, the shaded area on a number line, and the dotted line and the open circle represent similar ideas. Differences: a number line is one-dimensional and a coordinate system is two-dimensional.)

■ **To interpret and create graphs without numbers**
Have each student draw a graph without numbers and then write an explanation of the graph on a separate piece of paper. Post all graphs and their explanations separately. Ask students to match the explanations to the graphs. Discuss the results of accurate and inaccurate matches. *(Since some students may try to make their graphs too difficult to discern, discuss that all graphs should be easily identifiable because graphs are supposed to convey information more quickly than words.)*

Chapter

Planning Guide

Systems of Linear Equations

		Student Text Lesson			
		Student Pages	Vocabulary	Practice Exercises	Solutions Key
Lesson 1	Parallel Lines	288–291	✔	✔	✔
Lesson 2	Describing Parallel Lines	292–293		✔	✔
Lesson 3	Intersecting Lines—Common Solutions	294–297	✔	✔	✔
Lesson 4	Solving Linear Equations—Substitution	298–301		✔	✔
Lesson 5	Solving Linear Equations—Elimination	302–303		✔	✔
Lesson 6	Graphing Systems of Linear Equations	304–305		✔	✔
Lesson 7	*And* Statements—Conjunctions	306–309	✔	✔	✔
Lesson 8	Problem Solving Using Linear Equations	310–313		✔	✔
Lesson 9	Introduction to Matrices: Addition and Subtraction	314–317		✔	✔
Lesson 10	Multiplication of Matrices	318–321		✔	✔
Application	Using Venn Diagrams	322		✔	✔

Chapter Activities

Teacher's Resource Library

Estimation Exercise 10: Estimating Intersection

Application Activity 10: Using Venn Diagrams

Everyday Algebra 10: Graphing Linear Equations

Community Connection 10: Line Graphs

Teacher's Edition

Chapter 10 Project

Assessment Options

Student Text

Chapter 10 Review

Teacher's Resource Library

Chapter 10 Mastery Tests A and B

Student Text Features							Teaching Strategies							Learning Styles						Teacher's Resource Library			
Estimation Activity	Algebra in Your Life	Technology Connection	Writing About Mathematics	Try This	Problem Solving	Calculator Practice	Online Connection	Common Error	Applications Home, Career, Community	Mental Math	Manipulatives	Calculator	Group Problem Solving	Auditory/Verbal	Visual/Spatial	Logical/Mathematical	Body/Kinesthetic	Interpersonal/Group Learning	LEP/ESL	Activities	Alternate Activities	Workbook Activities	Self-Study Guide
			291	291	291			289					291				290			89	89	95	✔
			293	293					293	293					293					90	90	96	✔
	296						296		295					295				295	296	91	91	97	✔
301						301		299			299	300	300							92	92	98	✔
			303					303			303					303				93	93	99	✔
								305			305		305							94	94	100	✔
		309	308, 309										308					307		95	95	101	✔
			312		313			312	312				313							96	96	102	✔
								315									316	317	315	97	97	103	✔
					321			319	320								319			98	98	104	✔
								322	323		323												✔

Software Options

Skill Track Software

Use the Skill Track Software for *Algebra* for additional reinforcement of this chapter. The software provides multiple-choice assessment items for students to access by computer.

Solutions Key

Use the Solutions Key with this chapter to help students who may need additional assistance. The Solutions Key CD provides solutions for every exercise in the student edition.

Other Resources

Alternative Activities

The Teacher's Resource Library (TRL) contains a set of worksheets written at a second-grade reading level called Alternative Activities. They cover the same content as the regular Activities.

Manipulatives

See the Manipulative activities in this chapter for hands-on modeling of the content. The following TRL pages can also be used:

Manipulatives Master 5 (Basic Sentence Mat)
Pattern Blocks
Unit Cubes

Chapter at a Glance

Chapter 10: Systems of Linear Equations
pages 286–325

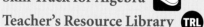

Lessons

Skill Track for Algebra 

Teacher's Resource Library TRL

- Workbook Activities 95–104
- Activities 89–98
- Alternative Activities 89–98
- Application Activity 10
- Estimation Exercise 10
- Everyday Algebra 10
- Community Connection 10
- Chapter 10 Self-Study Guide
- Chapter 10 Mastery Tests A and B

(Answer Keys for the Teacher's Resource Library begin on page 530 of this Teacher's Edition.)

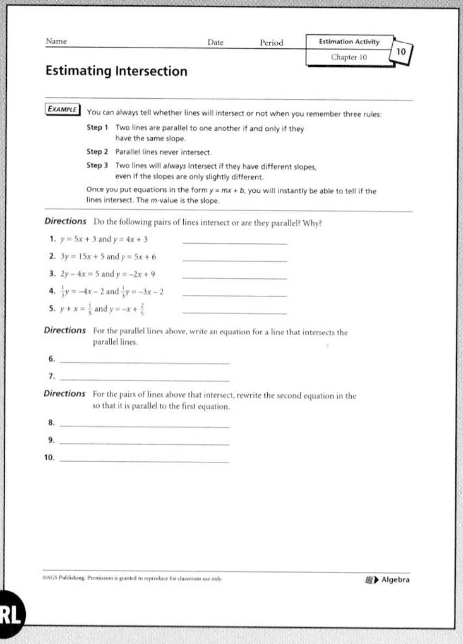

Name Date Period | Estimation Activity 10 | Chapter 10

Estimating Intersection

EXAMPLE You can always tell whether lines will intersect or not when you remember three rules:

Step 1 Two lines are parallel to one another if and only if they have the same slope.

Step 2 Parallel lines never intersect.

Step 3 Two lines will *always* intersect if they have different slopes, even if the slopes are only slightly different.

Once you put equations in the form $y = mx + b$, you will instantly be able to tell if the lines intersect. The m-value is the slope.

Directions Do the following pairs of lines intersect or are they parallel? Why?

1. $y = 5x + 3$ and $y = 4x + 3$ ______
2. $3y = 15x + 5$ and $y = 5x + 6$ ______
3. $2y - 4x = 5$ and $y = -2x + 9$ ______
4. $\frac{1}{3}y = -4x - 2$ and $\frac{1}{3}y = -3x - 2$ ______
5. $y + x = \frac{1}{5}$ and $y = -x + \frac{2}{5}$ ______

Directions For the parallel lines above, write an equation for a line that intersects the parallel lines.

6. ______
7. ______

Directions For the pairs of lines above that intersect, rewrite the second equation in the so that it is parallel to the first equation.

8. ______
9. ______
10. ______

 Algebra

TRL

Estimation Exercise 10

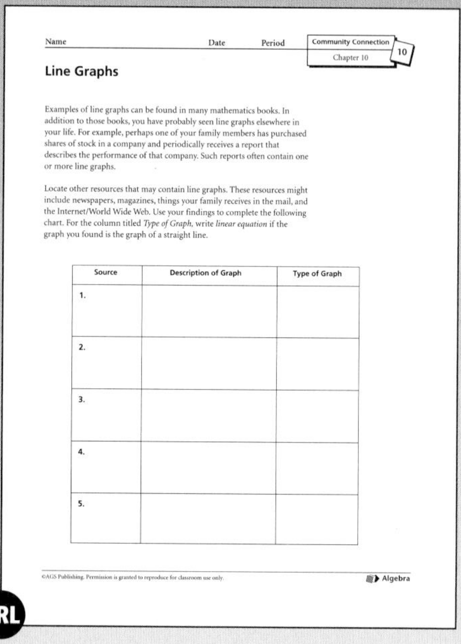

Name Date Period | Community Connection 10 | Chapter 10

Line Graphs

Examples of line graphs can be found in many mathematics books. In addition to those books, you have probably seen line graphs elsewhere in your life. For example, perhaps one of your family members has purchased shares of stock in a company and periodically receives a report that describes the performance of that company. Such reports often contain one or more line graphs.

Locate other resources that may contain line graphs. These resources might include newspapers, magazines, things your family receives in the mail, and the Internet/World Wide Web. Use your findings to complete the following chart. For the column titled *Type of Graph,* write *linear equation* if the graph you found is the graph of a straight line.

Source	Description of Graph	Type of Graph
1.		
2.		
3.		
4.		
5.		

 Algebra

TRL

Community Connection 10

Chapter

Systems of Linear Equations

As the city of Chicago grew larger, city planners developed a flat graph to create a street system. The easiest design called for straight roads that were parallel and perpendicular to each other. We graph straight lines by solving a series of equations, called linear equations. To be parallel, lines (as well as streets) must have the same slope. Each linear equation determines a point on the graph. With a list of four or five points, we can draw a straight line. Systems of equations are used for graphing two or more lines, including parallel and intersecting lines. City planners use equation systems when designing new communities or neighborhoods.

In Chapter 10, you will learn about systems of linear equations.

Goals for Learning

- ◆ To write and solve equations for parallel lines
- ◆ To determine whether a system of equations has a common solution
- ◆ To use substitution or elimination to find the common solution for a system of equations
- ◆ To graph equations to find the common solution
- ◆ To evaluate conjunctions
- ◆ To solve problems using systems of linear equations
- ◆ To add, subtract, and multipy matrices

Name Date Period ***SELF-STUDY GUIDE***

CHAPTER 10: Systems of Linear Equations

Goal 10.1 *To write and solve equations for parallel lines*

Date	Assignment	Score
______	1: Read pages 288–290. Complete Exercises A–D on pages 290–291.	______
______	2: Complete Workbook Activity 95.	______
______	3: Read pages 292–293. Complete Exercises A–B on page 293.	______
______	4: Complete Workbook Activity 96.	______

Comments:

Goal 10.2 *To determine whether a system of equations has a common solution*

Date	Assignment	Score
______	5: Read pages 294–295. Complete Exercises A–B on pages 296–297.	______
______	6: Complete Workbook Activity 97.	______

Comments:

Goal 10.3 *To use substitution or elimination to find the common solution for a system of equations*

Date	Assignment	Score
______	7: Read pages 298–299. Complete Exercise A on page 300.	______
______	8: Read and complete the Calculator Practice on page 301.	______
______	9: Complete Workbook Activity 98.	______
______	10: Read pages 302–303. Complete Exercise A on page 303.	______
______	11: Complete Workbook Activity 99.	______

Comments:

 Algebra

TRL

Name Date Period ***SELF-STUDY GUIDE***

CHAPTER 10: Systems of Linear Equations, continued

Goal 10.4 *To graph equations to find the common solution*

Date	Assignment	Score
______	12: Read pages 304–305. Complete Exercise A on page 305.	______
______	13: Complete Workbook Activity 100.	______

Comments:

Goal 10.5 *To evaluate conjunctions*

Date	Assignment	Score
______	14: Read pages 306–307. Complete Exercises A–B on pages 308–309.	______
______	15: Complete Workbook Activity 101.	______

Comments:

Goal 10.6 *To solve problems using systems of linear equations*

Date	Assignment	Score
______	16: Read pages 310–312. Complete Exercises A–B on page 313.	______
______	17: Complete Workbook Activity 102.	______

Comments:

Goal 10.7 *To add, subtract, and multiply matrices*

Date	Assignment	Score
______	18: Read pages 314–315. Complete Exercise A–D on pages 315–317.	______
______	19: Complete Workbook Activity 103.	______
______	20: Read pages 318–320. Complete Exercises A–C on pages 320–321.	______
______	21: Complete Workbook Activity 104.	______
______	22: Read and complete the Application Exercise on page 322.	______
______	23: Complete the Chapter 10 Review on pages 323–325.	______

Comments:

Student's Signature ______________ Date ______

Instructor's Signature ______________ Date ______

 Algebra

TRL

Chapter 10 Self-Study Guide

Introducing the Chapter

Use the information in the chapter opener to help students understand that city planners use equation systems of straight lines to design communities or neighborhoods. Many cities, such as Chicago, were developed along a flat graph of straight lines. That is why Chicago's streets are parallel and perpendicular to each other.

Chapter Project

Many examples of linear equations exist in any classroom. Have pairs of students examine their classroom tiled floor or ceiling and choose a pair of parallel, perpendicular, or intersecting lines. After completing the first three lessons of the chapter, ask each pair to begin designing a coordinate system to create an equation for each line. After completing the chapter, invite each pair to identify their lines, identify an equation for each line, and explain how a coordinate system was developed and used to generate the equation of each line.

Teacher's Resource

The AGS Publishing Teaching Strategies in Math Transparencies may be used with this chapter. They add an interactive dimension to expand and enhance the program content.

Career Interest Inventory

The AGS Publishing Harrington-O'Shea Career Decision-Making System-Revised (CDM) may be used with this chapter. Students can use the CDM to explore their interests and identify careers. The CDM defines career areas that are indicated by students' responses on the inventory.

Lesson at a Glance

Chapter 10 Lesson 1

Overview This lesson introduces linear equations in the form of parallel lines and the standard form of linear equations.

Objective

- To write the equation of a line parallel to a given line and passing through the y-intercept

Student Pages 288–291

Teacher's Resource Library 

Workbook Activity 95

Activity 89

Alternative Activity 89

Mathematics Vocabulary

parallel lines

Warm-Up Activity

Invite students to work in small groups and, without using pencil or paper, determine how many different pairs of parallel lines exist in a cube. *(18)* Then point out that parallel lines are both straight lines and examples of linear equations.

Teaching the Lesson

In the first example on page 288, have students note that the equation of each line is written in the form $y = mx + b$. Explain that a linear equation in the form $y = mx + b$ is said to be in *standard form.* When a linear equation is written in standard form, the value of m represents the slope of the line and the value of b represents the y-intercept, or the location at which the line intersects the y-axis.

After students complete the example at the bottom of page 289, point out that a coordinate system contains an infinite number of parallel lines. The lines may or may not be parallel to an axis. Although the lines in a pair of parallel lines share the same slope, they do not share the same y-intercept. Then ask, "Suppose one line on a coordinate system intersects the y-axis. Another line does not intersect the

Lesson 1 Parallel Lines

> ***Parallel lines***
> *Lines that have the same slope*

In Chapter 9, you saw that an equation such as $y = mx + b$ or $f(x) = mx + b$ describes a straight line. You also saw that the coefficient of the x-term, m, tells you the slope of the line.

Example 1

$y = 3x$	slope $m = 3$
$y = 3x + 2$	slope $m = 3$
$y = 3x + 4$	slope $m = 3$
$y = 3x - 2$	slope $m = 3$

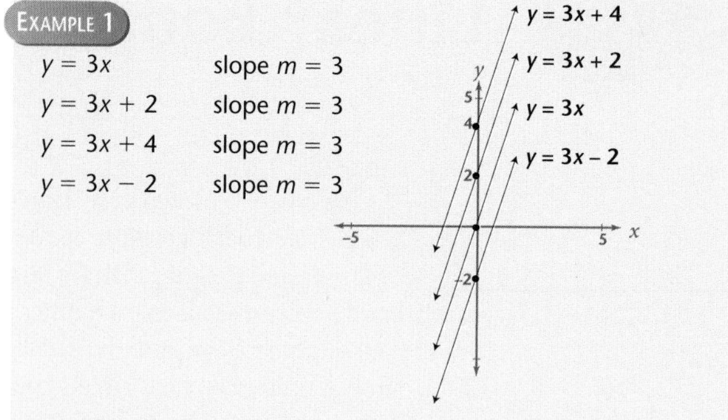

All these lines have the same slope, and all these lines are **parallel lines.**

> **Rule** Two lines are parallel to one another if and only if they have the same slope.

There are some special cases of parallel lines that are useful to remember.

All lines defined by the equation y = constant are horizontal lines. They are all parallel to the x-axis and parallel to each other.

All horizontal lines

- are parallel to each other,
- are parallel to the x-axis,
- have slope $m = 0$,
- have an equation of the form $y = 0(x)$ + constant.

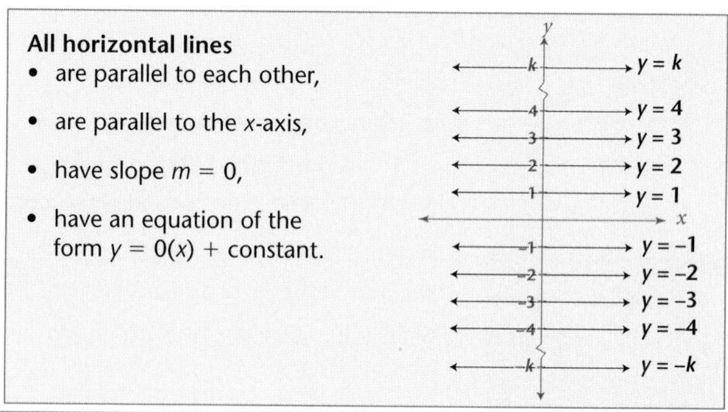

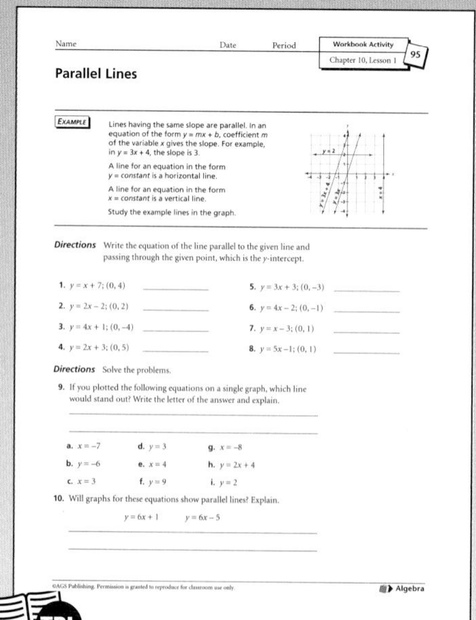

Name Date Period **Workbook Activity 95** Chapter 10, Lesson 1

Parallel Lines

Example Lines having the same slope are parallel. In an equation of the form $y = mx + b$, coefficient m of the variable x gives the slope. For example, in $y = 3x + 4$, the slope is 3.

A line for an equation in the form y = *constant* is a horizontal line.

A line for an equation in the form x = *constant* is a vertical line.

Study the example lines in the graph.

Directions Write the equation of the line parallel to the given line and passing through the given point, which is the y-intercept.

1. $y = x + 7$; (0, 4) ______
2. $y = 2x - 2$; (0, 2) ______
3. $y = 4x + 1$; (0, –4) ______
4. $y = 2x + 3$; (0, 5) ______
5. $y = 3x + 3$; (0, –3) ______
6. $y = 4x - 2$; (0, –1) ______
7. $y = x - 3$; (0, 1) ______
8. $y = 5x - 1$; (0, 1) ______

Directions Solve the problems.

9. If you plotted the following equations on a single graph, which line would stand out? Write the letter of the answer and explain.

a. $x = -7$ d. $y = 3$ g. $x = -8$
b. $y = -6$ e. $x = 4$ h. $y = 2x + 4$
c. $x = 3$ f. $y = 9$ i. $y = 2$

10. Will graphs for these equations show parallel lines? Explain.

$y = 6x + 1$ $y = 6x - 5$

 Algebra

TRL

Workbook Activity 95

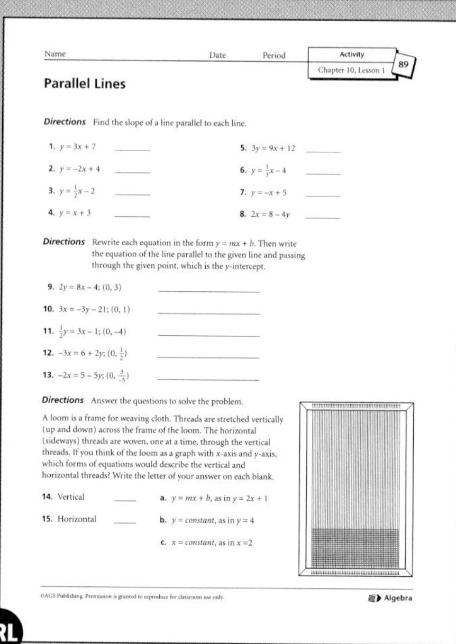

Name Date Period **Activity 89** Chapter 10, Lesson 1

Parallel Lines

Directions Find the slope of a line parallel to each line.

1. $y = 3x + 7$ ______
2. $y = -2x + 4$ ______
3. $y = \frac{1}{2}x - 2$ ______
4. $y = x + 3$ ______
5. $3y = 9x + 12$ ______
6. $y = \frac{1}{3}x - 4$ ______
7. $y = -x + 5$ ______
8. $2x = 8 - 4y$ ______

Directions Rewrite each equation in the form $y = mx + b$. Then write the equation of the line parallel to the given line and passing through the given point, which is the y-intercept.

9. $2y = 8x - 4$; (0, 3) ______
10. $3x = -3y - 21$; (0, 1) ______
11. $\frac{1}{2}y = 3x - 1$; (0, –4) ______
12. $-3x = 6 + 2y$; $(0, \frac{1}{2})$ ______
13. $-2x = 5 - 5y$; $(0, \frac{3}{-5})$ ______

Directions Answer the questions to solve the problem.

A loom is a frame for weaving cloth. Threads are stretched vertically (up and down) across the frame of the loom. The horizontal (sideways) threads are woven, one at a time, through the vertical threads. If you think of the loom as a graph with x-axis and y-axis, which forms of equations would describe the vertical and horizontal threads? Write the letter of your answer on each blank.

14. Vertical ______
15. Horizontal ______

a. $y = mx + b$, as in $y = 2x + 1$
b. y = *constant*, as in $y = 4$
c. x = *constant*, as in $x = 2$

 Algebra

TRL

Activity 89

Recall the point (0, y) is a point on the y-axis. This is called the y-intercept for the line $y = mx + b$.

All lines defined by the equation $x =$ constant are parallel to the y-axis and parallel to each other.

All vertical lines

- are parallel to each other,
- are parallel to the y-axis,
- have undefined slope,
- have an equation of the form x = constant.

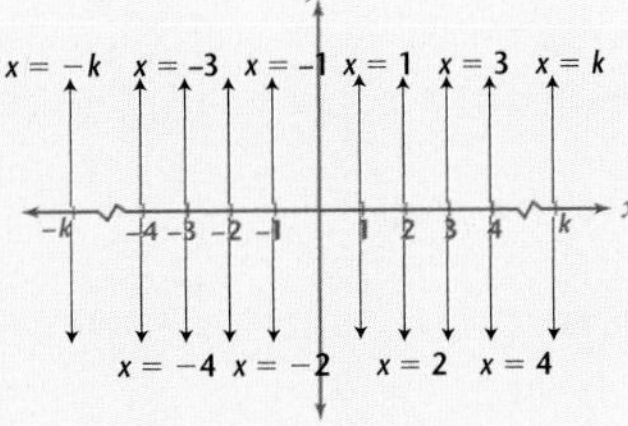

EXAMPLE 2 Find the equation of a line parallel to the line $y = -\frac{3}{4}x + 2$ and passing through the y-intercept (0, −2).

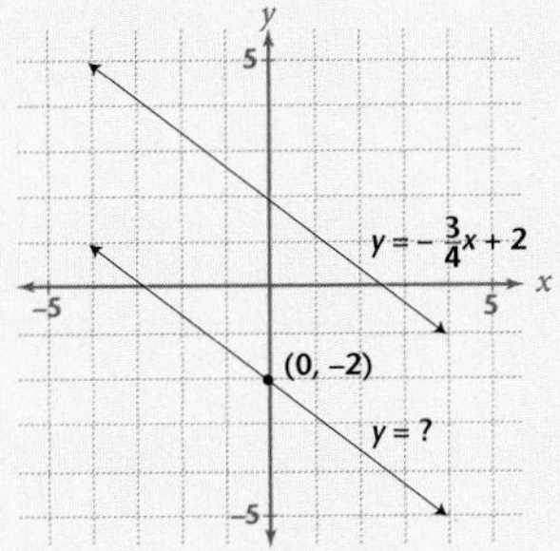

Step 1 Write the equation of the parallel line in the form $y = mx + b$. You will find values for m (slope) and b (y-intercept).

Step 2 Determine the slope of the parallel line. Because the slope of parallel lines is the same, the slope of the second line must be $-\frac{3}{4}$, so $m = -\frac{3}{4}$.

$y = -\frac{3}{4}x + b$

Step 3 Because the line passes through the y-intercept (0, −2), $y = -2$ when $x = 0$, so $b = -2$. Substitute −2 for b.

$y = -\frac{3}{4}x - 2$

The parallel lines are $y = -\frac{3}{4}x + 2$ and $y = -\frac{3}{4}x - 2$.

y-axis. Can the lines be parallel lines? Why or why not?" *(No; Sample explanation: Any line that does not intersect the y-axis is parallel to the y-axis, and any line that does intersect the y-axis cannot be parallel to the y-axis.)*

After students complete the example on page 290, write the equations $y = -3x + 2$ and $6x = -2y + 4$ on the board. Ask "How can the slope of two or more lines easily be compared?" *(The slope of two or more lines can easily be compared if the equation of each line is written in standard form.)* "What is the equation of each line in standard form?" *($y = -3x + 2$ and $y = -3x + 2$)* "How do the slopes of the lines compare?" *(The slopes are identical; the lines are parallel.)*

Common Error

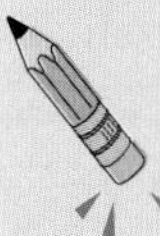

As the equations in problems 10–12 are rewritten in standard form, remind students that whatever operation they choose to perform on one side of an equation, they must remember to also perform the same operation on the opposite side of the equation.

3 Reinforce and Extend

Learning Styles

Body/Kinesthetic

Have students sketch a coordinate system, plot the points (−4, 7) and (4, 3), and draw a line that passes through the points. Remind students that another way to describe the slope of a line is to use the ratio $\frac{\text{rise}}{\text{run}}$. Then challenge students to use the ratio to locate and draw a line parallel to the given line.

Try This

When the formula $m = \frac{y_2 - y_1}{x_2 - x_1}$ is used to determine the slope of a line that is parallel to the y-axis, the value $x_2 - x_1$ is always zero. Because division by zero is undefined, the slope of any line parallel to the y-axis is said to be undefined.

Answer to Try This

A line of the form $x =$ constant or $x =$ any number means the line is vertical and parallel to the y-axis. The slope of any two points on the line gives a zero for the $x_2 - x_1$ portion of the slope formula. Division by zero is undefined.

EXAMPLE 3 Find the equation of a line parallel to the line $3x = 4y + 4$ and passing through the y-intercept (0, 3).

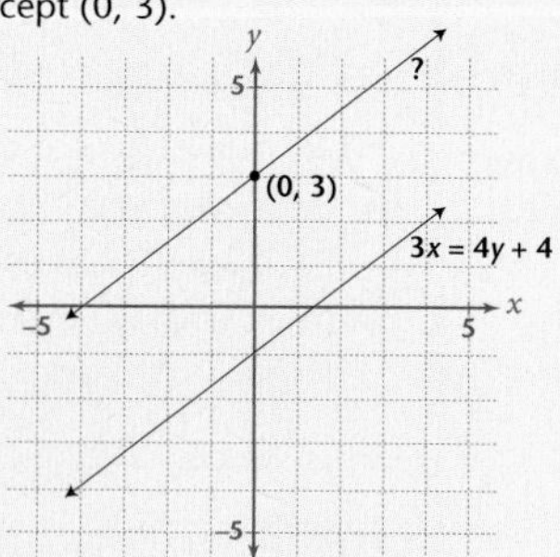

Step 1 Rewrite $3x = 4y + 4$ so that it is in the form $y = mx + b$.

$3x = 4y + 4$

$4y = 3x - 4$

$y = \frac{3}{4}x - 1$

Step 2 Determine the slope of the parallel line. Because the slope of parallel lines is the same, the slope of the second line must be $\frac{3}{4}$, so $m = \frac{3}{4}$.

$y = \frac{3}{4}x + b$

Step 3 Because the line passes through the y-intercept (0, 3), $y = 3$ when $x = 0$, so $b = 3$. Substitute 3 for b.

$y = \frac{3}{4}x + 3$

The equations for the parallel lines are $y = \frac{3}{4}x - 1$ and $y = \frac{3}{4}x + 3$ or $3x = 4y + 4$ and $3x = 4y - 12$.

Exercise A Find the slope of a line parallel to each line.

1. $y = 2x - 3$ $\quad m = 2$
2. $y = \frac{1}{3}x - 4$ $\quad m = \frac{1}{3}$
3. $y = -\frac{4}{9}x + 1$ $\quad m = -\frac{4}{9}$
4. $8y = -7x + 16$ $\quad m = -\frac{7}{8}$
5. $-5x = 10 - 2y$ $\quad m = \frac{5}{2}$ or $m = 2\frac{1}{2}$

Writing About Mathematics

Write a general statement about the direction of parallel lines that have a negative slope.

Exercise B Write the equation of the line parallel to the given line and passing through the given point, which is the y-intercept. Check your answer by graphing the lines.

6. $y = 2x - 4$; $(0, 4)$ $y = 2x + 4$

7. $y = 3x - 5$; $(0, -2)$ $y = 3x - 2$

8. $y = -\frac{3}{5}x + 2$; $(0, 6)$ $y = -\frac{3}{5}x + 6$

9. $y = -\frac{1}{2}x$; $(0, -3)$ $y = -\frac{1}{2}x - 3$

Exercise C Rewrite each equation in the form $y = mx + b$. Then write the equation of the line parallel to the given line and passing through the given point, which is the y-intercept.

10. $2y = x + 2$; $(0, 3)$ rewrite as $y = \frac{x}{2} + 1$; $y = \frac{x}{2} + 3$

11. $3y = 3x + 3$; $(0, 3)$ rewrite as $y = x + 1$; $y = x + 3$

12. $9x - 3y = 12$; $(0, 2)$ rewrite as $y = 3x - 4$; $y = 3x + 2$

PROBLEM SOLVING

Exercise D Answer the following questions.

13. Antonio says that the greatest and least slope of a line that lies only in Quadrants I and II is the same as the greatest and least slope of a line that lies only in Quadrant III and Quadrant IV. Is he correct? yes

14. Antonio decides to use a number line to show the possible slope of a line that lies in Quadrant I and Quadrant III of a graph. What does his number line look like? an open circle at zero and a shaded line to the right; the slope of any line in Quadrants I and III is $m > 0$

15. Carrie uses a number line to show the possible slope of a line that lies in Quadrant II and Quadrant IV of a graph. Does her number line look like Antonio's? no

TRY THIS Show why lines of the form x = constant have an undefined slope. HINT: Plot two points along the line and then look at the value for $m = \frac{y_2 - y_1}{x_2 - x_1}$. See Teacher's Edition for answer.

Group Problem Solving

Have students work in groups of three or four to discuss and solve the following problem:

Suppose a fence is to be erected around a rectangular area. The fence will be supported by vertical posts that are spaced 8 feet apart. Describe a way to ensure that the posts on each side of the rectangular area are parallel to each other.

Invite groups to share their strategies with one another.

Math History

Leonhard Euler was a Swiss mathematician who advanced the concepts of pure mathematics in geometry, algebra, and number theory. Euler, sometimes referred to as "the most productive mathematician in history," was born in 1707 in Basel, Switzerland. After graduating from the University of Basel, Euler taught at the St. Petersburg Academy of Science in St. Petersburg, Russia. Euler introduced many familiar algebraic and geometric notations in use today, including Σ for sum, the letters a, b, and c for the sides of a triangle, the symbol π for the ratio of a circle's circumference to its diameter, and the notation $f(x)$ for a function.

Lesson at a Glance

Chapter 10 Lesson 2

Overview This lesson introduces equations for parallel lines that pass through a given point.

Objective

- To write the equation of a line parallel to a given line and passing through a given point

Student Pages 292–293

Teacher's Resource Library 

Workbook Activity 96

Activity 90

Alternative Activity 90

1 Warm-Up Activity

Have students recall the standard form of any linear equation and identify the different elements of a linear equation that is written in standard form. *(The standard form of a linear equation is $y = mx + b$ where m = the slope of the line and b = the y-intercept of the line.)*

Teaching the Lesson

As students work through the examples and problems on pages 292 and 293, remind them to perform the same operation to *both* sides of an equation whenever they rewrite an equation in standard form.

Try This

Remind students that when an ordered pair is used to describe the location of a point on the coordinate system, the ordered pair is always given in the form (x, y). In the point (c, d), c represents the x-value or distance from the y-axis and d represents the y-value or distance from the x-axis.

Lesson 2 Describing Parallel Lines

In Lesson 1, you wrote equations for parallel lines with different y-intercepts. Now you'll explore how to write equations for parallel lines passing through any point (x, y) using the same linear equation: $y = mx + b$.

EXAMPLE 1 Write the equation of a line that is parallel to the line $y = -2x + 5$ and passes through the point $(-3, 4)$.

Step 1 For the lines to be parallel, the slope of the second line must be the same as the slope of the first:
$y = -2x + 5$, so $m = -2$
$y = -2x + b$

Step 2 Because the line passes through $(-3, 4)$, you know that $y = -2x + b$ must be true when $x = -3$ and $y = 4$.
$(-3, 4)$ is on line $y = -2x + b$

Step 3 Substitute the values for y and x in the equation and solve for b.
$(-3, 4)$ is on line $y = -2x + b$, so
$4 = -2(-3) + b$
$-2 = b$

Step 4 Place the value for b in the equation of the parallel line.
$y = -2x = b, b = -2,$
$y = -2x + (-2)$
Therefore, $y = -2x + (-2)$ is parallel to $y = -2x + 5$ and passes through $(-3, 4)$.

EXAMPLE 2 Write the equation of a line that is parallel to the line $2y - 3x = 6$ and passes through the point $(2, 4)$.

Step 1 Rewrite $2y - 3x = 6$ in the form $y = mx + b$.
$2y - 3x = 6$ becomes $y = \frac{3}{2}x + 3$

Step 2 Because they are parallel, the slope of the second line must be the same as the slope of the first:
$y = \frac{3}{2}x + 3$, so $m = \frac{3}{2}$
$y = \frac{3}{2}x + b$

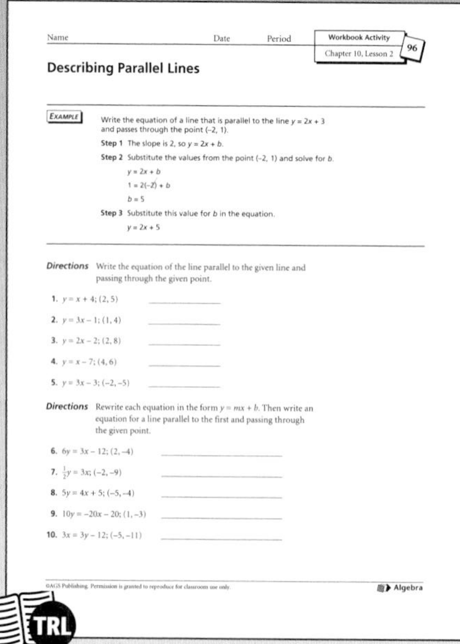

Name Date Period — Workbook Activity 96 — Chapter 10, Lesson 2

Describing Parallel Lines

EXAMPLE Write the equation of a line that is parallel to the line $y = 2x + 3$ and passes through the point $(-2, 1)$.

Step 1 The slope is 2, so $y = 2x + b$.

Step 2 Substitute the values from the point $(-2, 1)$ and solve for b.
$y = 2x + b$
$1 = 2(-2) + b$
$b = 5$

Step 3 Substitute this value for b in the equation.
$y = 2x + 5$

Directions Write the equation of the line parallel to the given line and passing through the given point.

1. $y = x + 4$; $(2, 5)$ ______
2. $y = 3x - 1$; $(1, 4)$ ______
3. $y = 2x - 2$; $(2, 8)$ ______
4. $y = x - 7$; $(4, 6)$ ______
5. $y = 3x - 3$; $(-2, -5)$ ______

Directions Rewrite each equation in the form $y = mx + b$. Then write an equation for a line parallel to the first and passing through the given point.

6. $6y = 3x - 12$; $(2, -4)$ ______
7. $\frac{1}{2}y = 3x$; $(-2, -9)$ ______
8. $5y = 4x + 5$; $(-5, -4)$ ______
9. $10y = -20x - 20$; $(1, -3)$ ______
10. $3x = 3y - 12$; $(-5, -11)$ ______

 Algebra

Workbook Activity 96

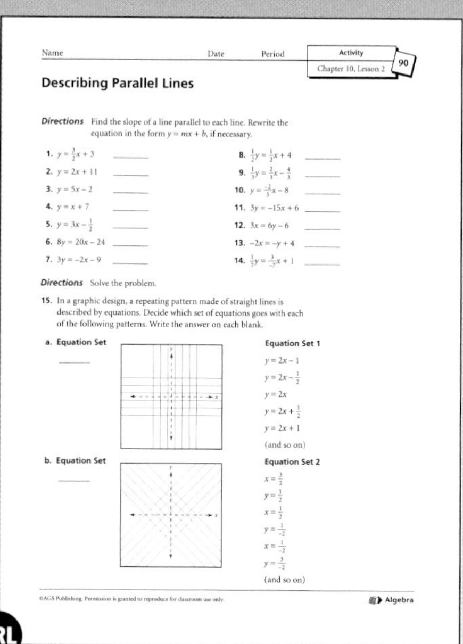

Name Date Period — Activity 90 — Chapter 10, Lesson 2

Describing Parallel Lines

Directions Find the slope of a line parallel to each line. Rewrite the equation in the form $y = mx + b$, if necessary.

1. $y = \frac{3}{2}x + 3$ ______
2. $y = 2x + 11$ ______
3. $y = 5x - 2$ ______
4. $y = x + 7$ ______
5. $y = 3x - \frac{1}{2}$ ______
6. $8y = 20x - 24$ ______
7. $3y = -2x - 9$ ______
8. $\frac{1}{2}y = \frac{1}{2}x + 4$ ______
9. $\frac{1}{3}y = \frac{2}{3}x - \frac{4}{3}$ ______
10. $y = \frac{-2}{3}x - 8$ ______
11. $3y = -15x + 6$ ______
12. $3x = 6y - 6$ ______
13. $-2x = -y + 4$ ______
14. $\frac{1}{7}y = \frac{3}{-7}x + 1$ ______

Directions Solve the problem.

15. In a graphic design, a repeating pattern made of straight lines is described by equations. Decide which set of equations goes with each of the following patterns. Write the answer on each blank.

a. Equation Set ______

Equation Set 1
$y = 2x - 1$
$y = 2x - \frac{1}{2}$
$y = 2x$
$y = 2x + \frac{1}{2}$
$y = 2x + 1$
(and so on)

b. Equation Set ______

Equation Set 2
$x = \frac{3}{2}$
$y = \frac{1}{2}$
$x = \frac{1}{2}$
$y = \frac{1}{-2}$
$x = \frac{1}{-2}$
$y = \frac{3}{-2}$
(and so on)

 Algebra

Activity 90

Writing About Mathematics

How many lines are parallel to the line $y = 3x + 1$? How would you write an equation for all the lines?

Example 2 *(continued)*

Step 3 Because the line passes through (2, 4), you know that $y = \frac{3}{2}x + b$ must be true when $x = 2$ and $y = 4$.

(2, 4) is on line $y = \frac{3}{2}x + b$, so

$4 = \frac{3}{2}(2) + b$

$4 = 3 + b$

$1 = b$

Step 4 Place the value for b in the equation of the parallel line.

$y = \frac{3}{2}x + 1$

Therefore, $y = \frac{3}{2}x + 1$ is parallel to $2y - 3x = 6$ and passes through (2, 4).

1. $y = 2x - 10$
2. $y = 3x - 15$
3. $y = -\frac{3}{5}x + 2$
4. $y = -\frac{3}{5}x + \frac{1}{10}$
5. $y = -\frac{1}{2}x - \frac{1}{2}$
6. $y = 2x + 9$
7. $y = -2x + 8$
8. $y = -\frac{2}{5}x + \frac{3}{2}$
9. $y = 2x - 1$

Exercise A Write the equation of the line parallel to the given line and passing through the given point.

1. $y = 2x - 4$; $(6, 2)$	**6.** $y = 2x$; $(-2, 5)$
2. $y = 3x - 5$; $(4, -3)$	**7.** $y = -2x$; $(5, -2)$
3. $y = -\frac{3}{5}x + 2$; $(0, 2)$	**8.** $y = -(\frac{2}{5})x + 3$; $(\frac{5}{4}, 1)$
4. $y = -\frac{3}{5}x + 2$; $(-\frac{3}{2}, 1)$	**9.** $y = 2x - 4$; $(1, 1)$
5. $y = -\frac{1}{2}x$; $(3, -2)$	

Exercise B Rewrite each equation in the form $y = mx + b$. Then write an equation for a line parallel to the first and passing through the given point.

10. $2y = x + 2$; $(1, 2)$	**13.** $4y - 2x = 5$; $(0, 0)$
11. $3y = 3x + 3$; $(3, 5)$	**14.** $10 = y - 2x$; $(-1, -3)$
12. $\frac{y}{2} = -2x - 3$; $(4, 2)$	**15.** $9x = 3y - 12$; $(4, 1)$

sample answers: $y = mx + (d - mc)$ or $y = mx + (c - md)$

TRY THIS Given a line $y = mx + b$, write the equation for a line parallel to the line and passing through point (c, d).

10. rewrite as $y = \frac{x}{2} + 1$; $y = \frac{x}{2} + \frac{3}{2}$
11. rewrite as $y = x + 1$; $y = x + 2$
12. rewrite as $y = -4x - 6$; $y = -4x + 18$
13. rewrite as $y = \frac{x}{2} + \frac{5}{4}$; $y = \frac{x}{2}$
14. rewrite as $y = 2x + 10$; $y = 2x - 1$
15. rewrite as $y = 3x + 4$; $y = 3x - 11$

3 Reinforce and Extend

At Home

Explain that whenever a home is constructed, it is important that various lines and plane surfaces in that home are parallel to each other. For example, for a window to open and close properly, it is important that the frame in which a window rests, and the frame of the window itself, be parallel. Invite students to find or think of other examples of parallel lines and surfaces in their homes and share their findings with their classmates.

Learning Styles

Visual/Spatial

Draw a vertical line on the board. Invite students to identify other lines, line segments, or plane surfaces in the classroom that are likely to be parallel to the given line. Then repeat the activity after drawing a horizontal line on the board.

Mental Math

Write the following linear equations on the board:

$2y = 2x + 2$	($y = x + 1$)
$-3y = -3x + 24$	($y = x - 8$)
$5y = 5x + 10$	($y = x + 2$)
$-2y = -2x + 10$	($y = x - 5$)
$3y = 3x - 3$	($y = x - 1$)
$-y = -x - 4$	($y = x + 4$)
$4y = 4x - 8$	($y = x - 2$)

Ask volunteers to change each equation to standard form mentally.

Lesson at a Glance

Chapter 10 Lesson 3

Overview This lesson introduces intersecting lines and their common solutions.

Objective

- To determine if a system of equations has a common solution

Student Pages 294–297

Teacher's Resource Library 

Workbook Activity 97

Activity 91

Alternative Activity 91

Mathematics Vocabulary

common solution
intersecting lines
system of equations

Warm-Up Activity

Invite students to use the word *intersect* and the phrase *parallel lines* in a sentence that states a mathematical truth. *(Sample answer: Parallel lines never intersect.)*

Teaching the Lesson

Have students recall from their study of geometry that the common solution of a system of equations can only be one point because two intersecting lines in the same plane (coplanar) intersect at exactly one point.

Also have students recall skew lines from their study of geometry. If possible, display a cube or rectangular prism and identify different skew lines. Explain that skew lines exist in different planes and do not have a common solution. Because a coordinate system exists in only one plane, skew lines are not considered to be a part of a system of equations. However, along with parallel lines, skew lines are examples of lines that do not share a common solution.

Point out that a system of equations must contain two equations, but can contain more. Although the systems of equations in this lesson each contain only two equations, systems can contain three, four, or more equations.

Lesson 3 Intersecting Lines—Common Solutions

System of equations
Equations describing two or more lines

Intersecting lines
Lines with one point in common

Common solution
The ordered pair of real numbers that two intersecting lines share

The equations describing two or more lines are called a **system of equations**. In Lessons 1 and 2, you examined parallel lines in a graph. In this lesson, you will examine **intersecting lines** in a graph. Intersecting lines are lines that share one point in the graph.

Two Parallel Lines

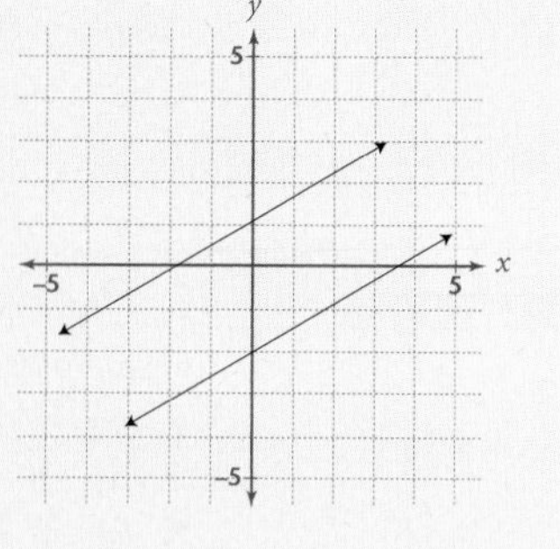

NO COMMON POINTS

Therefore, there is no common solution.

Two Intersecting Lines

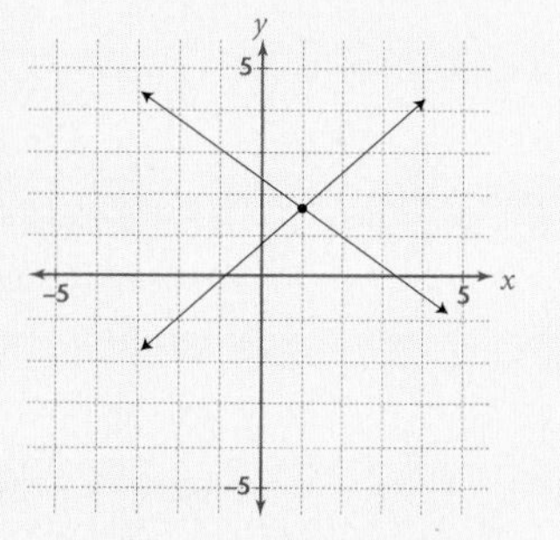

ONE COMMON POINT

Therefore, there must be exactly one ordered pair that makes both equations true. This is called the **common solution.**

Intersecting lines have a common solution. Parallel lines do not have a common solution.

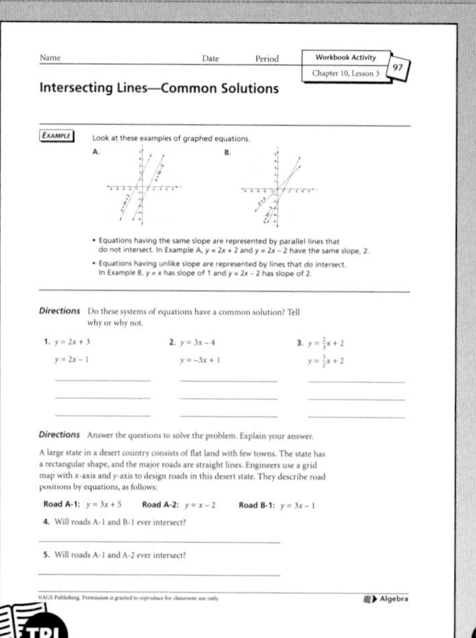

Name Date Period — Workbook Activity 97, Chapter 10, Lesson 3

Intersecting Lines—Common Solutions

EXAMPLE Look at these examples of graphed equations.

A. B.

- Equations having the same slope are represented by parallel lines that do not intersect. In Example A, $y = 2x + 2$ and $y = 2x - 2$ have the same slope, 2.
- Equations having unlike slope are represented by lines that *do* intersect. In Example B, $y = x$ has slope of 1 and $y = 2x - 2$ has slope of 2.

Directions Do these systems of equations have a common solution? Tell why or why not.

1. $y = 2x + 3$, $y = 2x - 1$
2. $y = 3x - 4$, $y = -3x + 1$
3. $y = \frac{2}{3}x + 2$, $y = \frac{3}{2}x + 2$

Directions Answer the questions to solve the problem. Explain your answer.

A large state in a desert country consists of flat land with few towns. The state has a rectangular shape, and the major roads are straight lines. Engineers use a grid map with x-axis and y-axis to design roads in this desert state. They describe road positions by equations, as follows:

Road A-1: $y = 3x + 5$ **Road A-2:** $y = x - 2$ **Road B-1:** $y = 3x - 1$

4. Will roads A-1 and B-1 ever intersect?
5. Will roads A-1 and A-2 ever intersect?

 Algebra

Workbook Activity 97

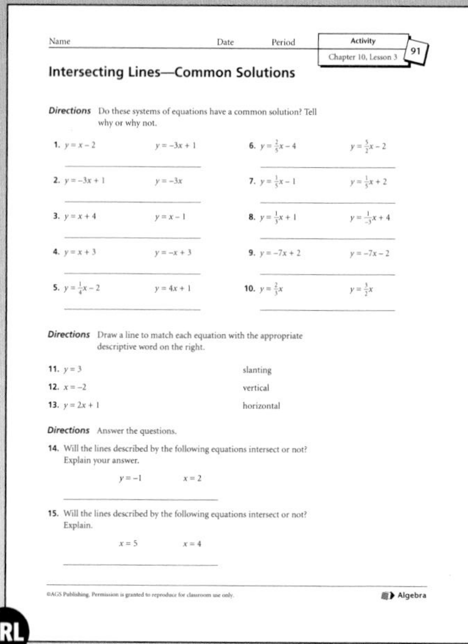

Name Date Period — Activity 91, Chapter 10, Lesson 3

Intersecting Lines—Common Solutions

Directions Do these systems of equations have a common solution? Tell why or why not.

1. $y = x - 2$ $y = -3x + 1$
2. $y = -3x + 1$ $y = -3x$
3. $y = x + 4$ $y = x - 1$
4. $y = x + 3$ $y = -x + 3$
5. $y = \frac{1}{4}x - 2$ $y = 4x + 1$
6. $y = \frac{2}{5}x - 4$ $y = \frac{5}{2}x - 2$
7. $y = \frac{1}{5}x - 1$ $y = \frac{1}{5}x + 2$
8. $y = \frac{1}{3}x + 1$ $y = \frac{1}{-3}x + 4$
9. $y = -7x + 2$ $y = -7x - 2$
10. $y = \frac{2}{3}x$ $y = \frac{3}{2}x$

Directions Draw a line to match each equation with the appropriate descriptive word on the right.

11. $y = 3$ slanting
12. $x = -2$ vertical
13. $y = 2x + 1$ horizontal

Directions Answer the questions.

14. Will the lines described by the following equations intersect or not? Explain your answer.
$y = -1$ $x = 2$
15. Will the lines described by the following equations intersect or not? Explain.
$x = 5$ $x = 4$

 Algebra

Activity 91

Example 1 Does the system of equations have a common solution?

system: $y = 2x + 2$
$y = 2x - 1$

The slopes are equal; $m = 2$ for both equations. Therefore, the lines are parallel and there is no common solution.

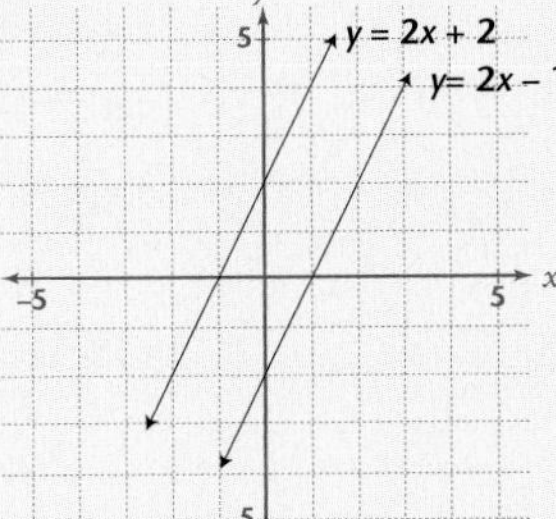

system: $y = x$
$y = -x + 2$

The slopes are not equal. The lines intersect and have a common solution.

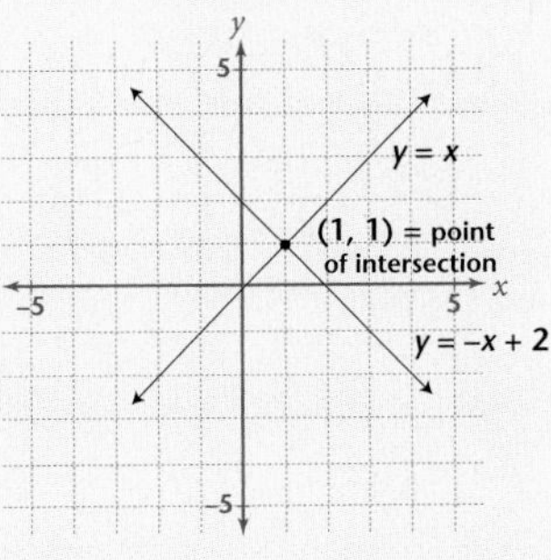

You can determine whether a system has a common solution by looking at the algebraic expressions. You do not need to make or look at a graph of the line.

Example 2 Does the system of equations have a common solution?

system: $y = 5x + 1$
$y = 5x - \frac{1}{2}$

Since the slopes are equal, $m = 5$ for both equations. The lines are parallel and they do not intersect. Therefore, they have no common solution.

system: $y = -3x + 1$
$y = x + 2$

Since the slopes $m = -3$ and $m = 1$ are not equal, the lines intersect and there is a common solution.

3 Reinforce and Extend

Learning Styles

Interpersonal/ Group Learning

Suggest students work in groups of four. Challenge each group to write the equations of three different lines that intersect at exactly one point.

Learning Styles

Auditory/Verbal

Encourage students to work in groups of four or five to discuss and solve the following problem:

On a coordinate system, prove that the *x*- and *y*-axes are perpendicular to each other.

Invite groups to record the steps they used to solve the problem. Then have them share their problem-solving approach and proof with one another.

Career Connection

Invite students to research CAD, or Computer-Aided Design, as a career. Encourage them to find the answers to questions such as these:

What does a person with CAD skills do?

What kind of education and/or training does the person need?

In what fields can a person with CAD skills work?

Ask students to consider whether or not they would be interested in CAD as a career.

LEARNING STYLES

LEP/ESL

Ask students to name words from their native language that have the same meaning as *common, intersecting,* and *system.* Then ask them to write the terms *common solution, intersecting lines,* and *system of equations* on a sheet of paper and give several examples of each. The sheet can then be kept for reference as the remainder of the chapter is completed.

ONLINE CONNECTION

Have students visit www.math.csusb.edu/notes/logic/lognot/node1.html to learn the symbols used in truth table constructions. Then have students do some truth table problems at www.math.csusb.edu/notes/quizzes/tablequiz/tablepractice.html. After students feel comfortable solving these problems, have them generate some truth tables of their own. They can pass them to a partner to solve. Discuss disagreements as a class.

Exercise A Do these systems of equations have a common solution? Give a reason for your answer.

1. $y = 2x - 4$

$y = 2x - 5$

no,

$m = 2$ for each, parallel

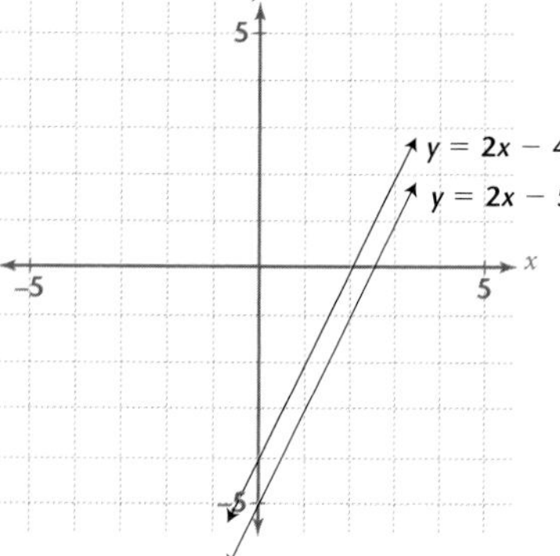

2. $y = \frac{1}{2}x - 4$

$y = -\frac{1}{2}x - 5$

yes,

$m = \frac{1}{2}$ and $m = -\frac{1}{2}$, lines intersect

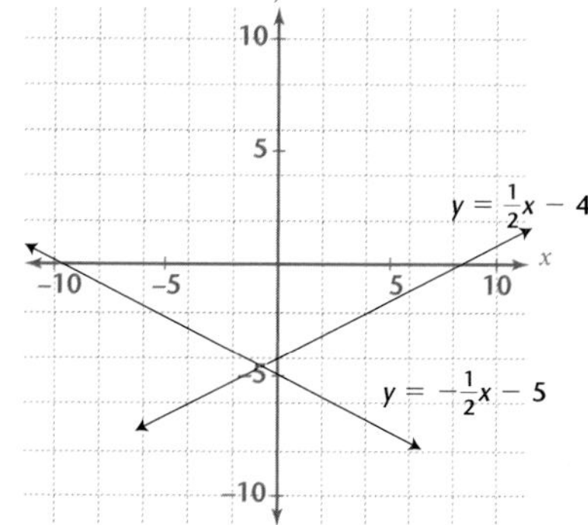

Algebra in Your Life

Life in a Parallel Universe

Parallel lines are found everywhere. Think about things you see that are shaped like rectangles. Homes, windows, and doors all have parallel lines. So do skyscrapers or roads. Look around you—what else can you find that is an example of parallel lines?

Exercise B Do these systems of equations have a common solution? Tell why or why not.

3. $y = -\frac{4}{9}x + 1$
$y = -\frac{9}{4}x + 1$

yes, slopes not equal, lines intersect

4. $y = -\frac{3}{5}x + 2$
$y = -\frac{3}{5}x$

no, slopes equal, lines parallel

5. $y = -\frac{3}{5}x + 2$
$y = -\frac{5}{3}x + 2$

yes, slopes not equal, lines intersect

The boards on this fence are parallel to each other. Parallel lines have no common solutions.

Lesson at a Glance

Chapter 10 Lesson 4

Overview This lesson introduces the substitution method of solving a system of linear equations.

Objective

- To use the substitution method to find the common solution of a system of linear equations

Student Pages 298–301

Teacher's Resource Library TRL

Workbook Activity 98

Activity 92

Alternative Activity 92

1 Warm-Up Activity

Write the equation $y = 2(x + 1)$ on the board. Have students solve the equation for y given the following x-values.

$x = 1$ $(y = 4)$

$x = -3$ $(y = -4)$

$x = 0$ $(y = 2)$

$x = -1$ $(y = 0)$

$x = \frac{1}{2}$ $(y = 3)$

Upon completion of the activity, point out that in order to find the value of y, a substitution was made—a value for x was substituted into the equation.

2 Teaching the Lesson

After discussing the examples, you might choose to explain that there is more than one way to find the common solution of a system of linear equations. On the board, write the equations $y = x + 1$ and $x + y = 5$. Point out that in the first equation, y is expressed in terms of x, and have students find the common solution by substituting $x + 1$ for y. *(2, 3)* Then ask students to express x in terms of y in the second equation. *($x = -y + 5$)* and again find the common solution. *(2, 3)* Compare the solutions and point out that a common solution of a system of linear equations can be found by expressing y in terms of x or expressing x in terms of y.

Lesson 4 Solving Linear Equations—Substitution

You can find the common solution for a system of linear equations algebraically. Remember, a common solution is an ordered pair of real numbers that, when substituted in each equation, makes each equation a true statement.

EXAMPLE 1 Find the common solution for the system:

$y = 3x + 1$

$y = x + 5$

Step 1 Notice that in the second equation, y is expressed in terms of x. That is, $y = x + 5$. Substitute this value of y into the first equation.

$y = 3x + 1$ $x + 5 = 3x + 1$

Step 2 Solve the equation for x.

$x + 5 = 3x + 1$

$5 = 3x - 1x + 1$

$4 = 2x$

$2 = x$

Step 3 Substitute this value of x in either equation to find the value of y.

$y = x + 5$

$y = 2 + 5 = 7$ The common solution is the ordered pair (2, 7).

Step 4 Check your work. Substitute (2, 7) for x and y in each equation. Determine whether the statements are true.

$y = 3x + 1$ $y = x + 5$

$7 = 3(2) + 1$ $7 = 2 + 5$

$7 = 7$ True $7 = 7$ True

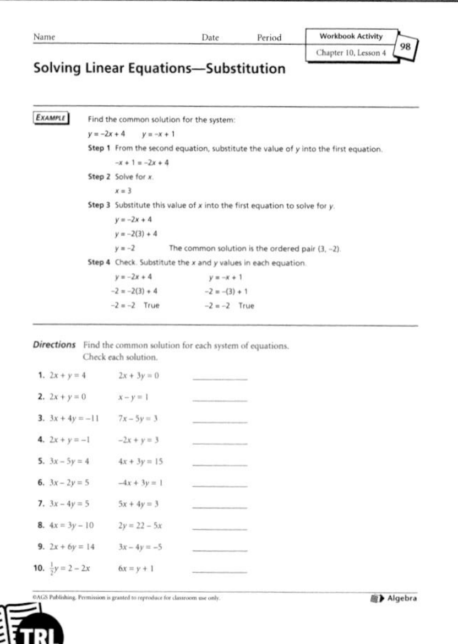

Name Date Period | Workbook Activity 98 | Chapter 10, Lesson 4

Solving Linear Equations—Substitution

EXAMPLE Find the common solution for the system:

$y = -2x + 4$ $y = -x + 1$

Step 1 From the second equation, substitute the value of y into the first equation.

$-x + 1 = -2x + 4$

Step 2 Solve for x.

$x = 3$

Step 3 Substitute this value of x into the first equation to solve for y.

$y = -2x + 4$

$y = -2(3) + 4$

$y = -2$ The common solution is the ordered pair (3, –2).

Step 4 Check. Substitute the x and y values in each equation.

$y = -2x + 4$ $y = -x + 1$

$-2 = -2(3) + 4$ $-2 = -(3) + 1$

$-2 = -2$ True $-2 = -2$ True

Directions Find the common solution for each system of equations. Check each solution.

1. $2x + y = 4$ $2x + 3y = 0$ ________
2. $2x + y = 0$ $x - y = 1$ ________
3. $3x + 4y = -11$ $7x - 5y = 3$ ________
4. $2x + y = -1$ $-2x + y = 3$ ________
5. $3x - 5y = 4$ $4x + 3y = 15$ ________
6. $3x - 2y = 5$ $-4x + 3y = 1$ ________
7. $3x - 4y = 5$ $5x + 4y = 3$ ________
8. $4x = 3y - 10$ $2y = 22 - 5x$ ________
9. $2x + 6y = 14$ $3x - 4y = -5$ ________
10. $\frac{1}{2}y = 2 - 2x$ $6x = y + 1$ ________

 Algebra

TRL

Workbook Activity 98

Name Date Period | Activity 92 | Chapter 10, Lesson 4

Solving Linear Equations—Substitution

Directions Study each system of equations. Find the system that does not have a common solution. Write that letter on the blank.

1. ______ a. $y = -4x + 4$, $y = 6x - 1$ c. $y = 2x + 3$, $y = 2x - 1$

   b. $y = -2x + 4$, $y = \frac{2}{-3}x$ d. $y = x + 2$, $y = -x + 2$

Directions Find the common solution for each system of equations. Check each solution.

2. $x + y = 3$ $3x - y = 1$ ________
3. $3x + 2y = 12$ $y = 2x - 1$ ________
4. $2x + 3y = 2$ $3x = 2y + 16$ ________
5. $x - y = 4$ $3x + 2y = 7$ ________
6. $x + y = 7$ $5x - 3y = 11$ ________
7. $5x + 2y = 7$ $3x - 2y = 9$ ________
8. $\frac{2}{3}x - \frac{1}{2}y = 1$ $\frac{1}{2}x + \frac{1}{3}y = 5$ ________
9. $4x - y - 1 = 0$ $2x = 17 - y$ ________

Directions Use a calculator to check each common solution. Write either *correct* or *not correct*.

10. $3x - y = -7$ $5y + 5 = -5x$ $(-2, 1)$ ________
11. $y = 3x - 2$ $2x + y = 8$ $(4, 2)$ ________
12. $4x + 3y = 5$ $5x + 3y = 2$ $(-3, \frac{17}{3})$ ________
13. $2x + y = -5$ $3x + 5y = -4$ $(-3, 2)$ ________
14. $x + 2y = 1$ $5x + 3y = 26$ $(7, 3)$ ________
15. $y = 2x + 5$ $x + 2y = -5$ $(-3, -1)$ ________

 Algebra

TRL

Activity 92

Example 2 Find the common solution for the system:

$2x - 3y = 15$

$x + y = 6$

Step 1 You can use either equation to solve for either x or y. Solve $x + y = 6$ for x. Substitute this value of x in the first equation.

$x + y = 6$, solving for x gives $x = -y + 6$

$2x - 3y = 15$

$2(-y + 6) - 3y = 15$

Step 2 Solve the equation for y.

$2(-y + 6) - 3y = 15$

$-2y + 12 - 3y = 15$

$-5y = 3$

$y = -\frac{3}{5}$

Step 3 Substitute this value of y into either equation to find the value of x.

$x + y = 6$

$x - \frac{3}{5} = 6$

$x = 6 + \frac{3}{5} = 6\frac{3}{5}$ or $\frac{33}{5}$

The common solution is the ordered pair $(\frac{33}{5}, -\frac{3}{5})$.

Step 4 Check. Substitute $(\frac{33}{5}, -\frac{3}{5})$ for x and y in each equation. Determine whether the statements are true.

$2x - 3y = 15$	$x + y = 6$
$2(\frac{33}{5}) - 3(-\frac{3}{5}) = 15$	$-\frac{3}{5} + \frac{33}{5} = 6$
$\frac{66}{5} + \frac{9}{5} = 15$	$\frac{30}{5} = 6$ True
$\frac{75}{5} = 15$ True	

Common Error

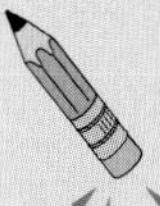

After a substitution has been made in any system of equations, students may discover that two or more computations can be performed at any time. Remind them of the need to follow the order of operations.

Manipulatives

M Modeling Equations

Materials: Pattern Blocks, Unit Cubes, two copies of Manipulatives Master 5 (Basic Sentence Mat) for each student

Group Practice: Build models of the equations in the example and place one model on each Basic Sentence Mat. Write the symbolic equivalent above each model. Model each step in the example, substituting one of the unknown pieces with pieces representing the equivalent term. To solve for the variable, add inverses of terms to be removed to both sides of the Basic Sentence Mat. Apply the Zero Rule to remove pairs of opposites and simplify. Divide Unit Cubes evenly among each unknown piece to find the value of $1x$ or $1y$. To solve for the remaining unknown variable, replace the known variable piece with Unit Cubes and solve. Check work by rebuilding both original equations, using Unit Cubes in place of the unknown pieces. In the second example, replace each unknown piece with the pieces that represent the equivalent term.

Student Practice: Have students use models for Exercise A, Problems 1–2 and 5–7, and Supplementary Problems 11–20 on page 424.

Reinforce and Extend

Group Problem Solving

Encourage students to work in groups of four to discuss and solve the following problem:

Generate a system of equations that does not have a common solution.

Calculator

Explain that another way to check if a common solution is correct is to graph the system of equations. Invite students to rewrite the equations in each system in standard form and then graph the equations using a graphing calculator. The common solution that was computed can then be compared to the common solution displayed by the calculator.

Exercise A Find the common solution for each system of equations. Check your solution.

1. $y + x = 5$ $(1, 4)$
$2x + y = 6$

2. $6 + 2x = y$ $(-4, -2)$
$y = x + 2$

3. $2x = 3y + 2$ $(-\frac{20}{7}, -\frac{18}{7})$
$5y + 10 = x$

4. $\frac{x + y}{2} = \frac{7}{4}$ $(\frac{5}{2}, 1)$
$4x + 2y = 12$

5. $x = 2y$ $(-4, -2)$
$3x = y - 10$

6. $6 + x = y + 4$ $(0, 2)$
$2x + 3y = 6$

7. $3x + 2y = 7$ $(3, -1)$
$4x + 3y = 9$

8. $x + 2y = 7$ $(-83, 45)$
$3y + 2x = -31$

Intersecting lines have common solutions. These roads are an example of intersecting lines.

Calculator Practice

Suppose that you determine the common solution for the equations $4x + 6y = 12$ and $x - y = -2$ is $x = 0$ and $y = 2$. Use a calculator to check.

EXAMPLE 3

Step 1 Choose one equation and substitute for x and y.
$4x + 6y = 12 = 4(0) + 6(2) = 12$

Step 2 Input the $4(0) + 6(2) =$ portion of the equation.
Press 4 [×] 0 [+] 6 [×] 2 [=]
If the calculator gives an answer of 12, your x and y solutions for that equation are correct.

Step 3 Repeat the procedure for the other equation.

Exercise B Use a calculator to check each common solution. If the solution is correct, write *correct.* If the solution is not correct, write *not correct.*

9. $x = 4y$ $\quad 6x = 2y - 20$ $\quad (56, 14)$ not correct

10. $x + y = 10$ $\quad 4x + 2y = 12$ $\quad (-4, 14)$ correct

Estimation Activity

Estimate: Which has a greater slope: a rise of 3 meters per kilometer or 3 inches per foot?

Solution: Use the slope formula and compare the fractions. The larger fraction will have the greater slope.

$$\text{slope} = \frac{\text{rise}}{\text{run}}$$

$$\frac{3\text{ m}}{1\text{ km}} = \frac{3\text{ m}}{1000\text{ m}} = \frac{3}{1000}$$

$$\frac{3''}{1'} = \frac{3''}{12''} = \frac{1}{4}$$

$$\frac{1}{4} > \frac{3}{1000}$$

The slope of 3 inches per foot has the greater slope.

Systems of Linear Equations **301**

Lesson at a Glance

Chapter 10 Lesson 5

Overview This lesson introduces the elimination method of solving a system of linear equations.

Objective

- To use the elimination method to find the common solution of a system of linear equations

Student Pages 302–303

Teacher's Resource Library 

Workbook Activity 99

Activity 93

Alternative Activity 93

1 Warm-Up Activity

Prerequisite skills for the completion of this lesson include adding and subtracting variables. Invite students to practice their addition and subtraction skills by writing the following computations on the board. Encourage volunteers to demonstrate how to find the solutions to the computations.

$(3x + 7y + 1) + (8x + y + 4)$
$(11x + 8y + 5)$

$(10x - 5y + 2) + (2x - 6y + 6)$
$(12x - 11y + 8)$

$(x - 6y - 1) - (3x + 12y - 1)$
$(-4x - 18y)$

$(-15x + 9y - 11) - (-5x - 5y + 2)$
$(-10x + 14y - 13)$

2 Teaching the Lesson

Systems of linear equations sometimes include one or more fractions. Remind students that to clear an equation of a fraction, they should multiply by the reciprocal of the fraction. For example, to clear the equation $2x + \frac{1}{2}y = -8$ of $\frac{1}{2}$, multiply both sides of the equation by $\frac{2}{1}$.

$$2x + \frac{1}{2}y = -8$$
$$\frac{2}{1}(2x + \frac{1}{2}y) = (-8)\frac{2}{1}$$
$$\frac{4}{1}x + \frac{2}{2}y = -\frac{16}{1}$$
$$4x + y = -16$$

Lesson 5 Solving Linear Equations—Elimination

There is another way to find the common solution for a system of equations. You can use your knowledge of linear equations to eliminate one of the variables.

EXAMPLE 1 Find the common solution for the system: $x + 2y = 5$
$-x + y = 13$

Step 1 Add the two equations to eliminate the x term.

$$\begin{aligned} x + 2y &= 5 \\ -x + y &= 13 \\ \hline 0 + 3y &= 18 \text{ or } y = 6 \end{aligned}$$

Step 2 Substitute the value of y into either equation.

$$\begin{aligned} x + 2y &= 5 \\ x + 2(6) &= 5 \\ x &= 5 - 12 \text{ or } x = -7 \end{aligned}$$

The common solution, or the point of intersection, is $(-7, 6)$.

Step 3 Check your work. Substitute $(-7, 6)$ for x and y in each equation. Determine whether the statements are true.

$x + 2y = 5$	$-x + y = 13$
$(-7) + 2(6) = 5$	$-(-7) + 6 = 13$
$-7 + 12 = 5$	$7 + 6 = 13$
$5 = 5$ True	$13 = 13$ True

EXAMPLE 2 Find the common solution for the system: $2y + 5x = 10$
$-y + x = 2$

Step 1 Multiply the second equation by 2. Then add to eliminate the y-term.

$$\begin{aligned} 2y + 5x &= 10 \\ -2y + 2x &= 4 \\ \hline 0 + 7x &= 14 \text{ or } x = 2 \end{aligned}$$

Step 2 Substitute the value of x into either equation.

$$\begin{aligned} 2y + 5x &= 10 \\ 2y + 5(2) &= 10 \\ 2y &= 10 - 10 \\ 2y &= 0 \text{ or } y = 0 \end{aligned}$$

The common solution, or the point of intersection, is $(2, 0)$.

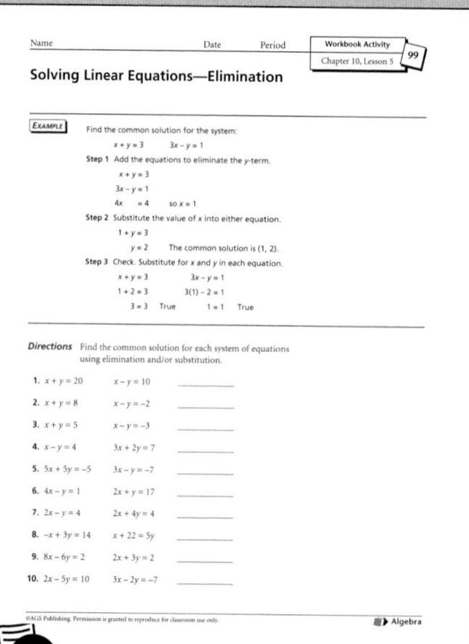

Name Date Period — Workbook Activity 99, Chapter 10, Lesson 5

Solving Linear Equations—Elimination

EXAMPLE Find the common solution for the system:
$x + y = 3$ $3x - y = 1$

Step 1 Add the equations to eliminate the y-term.
$x + y = 3$
$3x - y = 1$
$4x = 4$ so $x = 1$

Step 2 Substitute the value of x into either equation.
$1 + y = 3$
$y = 2$ The common solution is (1, 2).

Step 3 Check. Substitute for x and y in each equation.
$x + y = 3$ $3x - y = 1$
$1 + 2 = 3$ $3(1) - 2 = 1$
$3 = 3$ True $1 = 1$ True

Directions Find the common solution for each system of equations using elimination and/or substitution.

1. $x + y = 20$ $x - y = 10$ ______
2. $x + y = 8$ $x - y = -2$ ______
3. $x + y = 5$ $x - y = -3$ ______
4. $x - y = 4$ $3x + 2y = 7$ ______
5. $5x + 5y = -5$ $3x - y = -7$ ______
6. $4x - y = 1$ $2x + y = 17$ ______
7. $2x - y = 4$ $2x + 4y = 4$ ______
8. $-x + 3y = 14$ $x + 22 = 5y$ ______
9. $8x - 6y = 2$ $2x + 3y = 2$ ______
10. $2x - 5y = 10$ $3x - 2y = -7$ ______

 Algebra

Workbook Activity 99

Name Date Period — Activity 93, Chapter 10, Lesson 5

Solving Linear Equations—Elimination

Directions Write whether each of these systems of equations has a common solution or not. Explain your answer. (Hint: If the equation is not already in the form $y = mx + b$, you will need to rewrite it first.)

1. $y = -x + 2$ $y = 2x + 1$ ______
2. $y = 2x + 2$ $y = 2x - 1$ ______
3. $2y = 4 - \frac{3}{2}x$ $3x + 4y = 2$ ______
4. $y = -3x + 1$ $y = x + 2$ ______
5. $2x + y = -6$ $4x = 8 - 2y$ ______

Directions Find the common solution for each system of equations using elimination and/or substitution.

6. $x + y = 2$ $2x - y = 1$ ______
7. $x - y = -5$ $x + y = 1$ ______
8. $2x + y = 5$ $3x - y = 0$ ______
9. $2x - 3y = -11$ $3x + 3y = 21$ ______
10. $y = 2x - 8$ $3x + 2y = 12$ ______
11. $2y = 6x + 2$ $3x + 4y = -26$ ______
12. $2x + y = -2$ $-2x - 3y = -6$ ______
13. $\frac{x}{3} + y = 3$ $4x + 2y = 0$ ______
14. $4x + 3y = 24$ $4x - 3y = -24$ ______
15. $2x + 3y = 9$ $5x + 2y = 17$ ______

 Algebra

TRL

Activity 93

EXAMPLE 2 *(continued)*

Step 3 Check your work. Substitute (2, 0) for x and y in each equation. Determine whether the statements are true.

$$\begin{aligned} 2y + 5x &= 10 \\ 2(0) + 5(2) &= 10 \\ 0 + 10 &= 10 \\ 10 &= 10 \quad \text{True} \end{aligned} \qquad \begin{aligned} -y + x &= 2 \\ -(0) + 2 &= 2 \\ 2 &= 2 \quad \text{True} \end{aligned}$$

EXAMPLE 3 Find the common solution for the system: $2y + x = 4$
$3y + x = 6$

Step 1 Multiply the second equation by -1. Then add to eliminate the x-term.

$$\begin{aligned} 2y + x &= 4 \\ -3y - x &= -6 \\ \hline -y + 0 &= -2 \text{ or } y = 2 \end{aligned}$$

Step 2 Substitute the value of y in either equation.

$$\begin{aligned} 2y + x &= 4 \\ 2(2) + x &= 4 \\ x &= 4 - 4 \text{ or } x = 0 \end{aligned}$$

The common solution, or the point of intersection, is (0, 2).

Step 3 Check your work. Substitute (0, 2) for x and y in each equation. Determine whether the statements are true.

$$\begin{aligned} 2y + x &= 4 \\ 2(2) + 0 &= 4 \\ 4 + 0 &= 4 \\ 4 &= 4 \quad \text{True} \end{aligned} \qquad \begin{aligned} 3y + x &= 6 \\ 3(2) + 0 &= 6 \\ 6 + 0 &= 6 \\ 6 &= 6 \quad \text{True} \end{aligned}$$

Writing About Mathematics

Which method do you prefer to use—substitution or elimination? Why?

Exercise A Find the common solution for each system of equations using elimination. Check your solution.

1. $2y + x = 4$, $3y - x = 6$ (0, 2)
2. $y + x = 5$, $2x + y = 6$ (1, 4)
3. $6 + 2x = y$, $y = x + 2$ $(-4, -2)$
4. $x + \frac{y}{2} = 3$, $2x + 2y = 7$ $(\frac{5}{2}, 1)$
5. $x = 2y$, $3x = y - 10$ $(-4, -2)$
6. $3x + 2y = 6$, $6x + 2y = 10$ $(\frac{4}{3}, 1)$
7. $\frac{3}{4}x + y = 14$, $3x + 2y = 52$ (16, 2)
8. $3x - y = 10$, $4x + y = 15$ $(\frac{25}{7}, \frac{5}{7})$
9. $4x + 2y = 8$, $4y - 4x = 10$ $(\frac{1}{2}, 3)$
10. $4x - 3y = 1$, $2x + 3y = 2$ $(\frac{1}{2}, \frac{1}{3})$

Reinforce and Extend

Learning Styles

Logical/Mathematical

To help visual learners better understand that a common solution of a system of linear equations is the intersection of the graphs of those equations, invite students to choose one exercise from page 303, rewrite each equation in standard form, and input and view the equations using a graphing calculator. The point representing the intersection of the graphs should be the same as the point that was found using the elimination method.

Common Error

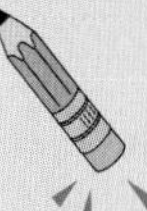

When solving a linear equation by elimination, it will sometimes be necessary to multiply both sides of an equation by a constant. Remind students that

$(+) \cdot (+) = (+)$

$(+) \cdot (-) = (-)$

$(-) \cdot (+) = (-)$

$(-) \cdot (-) = (+)$

Manipulatives

Modeling Equations

Materials: Pattern Blocks, Unit Cubes, two copies of Manipulatives Master 5 (Basic Sentence Mat) for each student

Group Practice: Build models of both equations used in the example, placing one model on each Basic Sentence Mat. To combine the equations, move the pieces from one Basic Sentence Mat to the other. Use the Zero Rule to remove pairs of opposites and eliminate one of the variables. If one equation needs to be multiplied by some factor before being combined with the other, increase the number of pieces in each term proportionally. For example, if the equation needs to be multiplied by -2, double the number of pieces in each term and move them to the opposite area on the Basic Sentence Mat. Continue modeling the subsequent steps, following the procedures in the Chapter 10, Lesson 4 Manipulatives activity.

Student Practice: Have students use models for Exercise A, Problems 1–3, 5, and 9–10, and Supplementary Problems 11–20 on page 424.

Lesson at a Glance

Chapter 10 Lesson 6

Overview This lesson introduces the graphing method of solving a system of linear equations.

Objective

- To find the common solution of a system of linear equations by graphing

Student Pages 304–305

Teacher's Resource Library 

Workbook Activity 100

Activity 94

Alternative Activity 94

1 Warm-Up Activity

Invite students to consider this scenario:

For exercise one evening, Jerod left home and walked four blocks north, nine blocks west, one block south, five blocks east, three blocks south, and then paused to rest. At that time, Jerod was how far from home? In what direction should he walk to go directly home? *(4 blocks; east)*

Encourage a volunteer to use the board to demonstrate how a coordinate system can be used to find the solution.

2 Teaching the Lesson

Have students recall that to create a table of values, they should substitute values for x and solve for y, *or* substitute values for y and solve for x. Also point out the benefit of generating a table of values that contains three points for the graph of any equation. Although only two points are necessary to graph a linear equation, three points helps ensure that the graph is correct. If only two points are generated and graphed, there is no way of knowing if one or both points are incorrect.

Lesson 6 Graphing Systems of Linear Equations

Another way you can find the common solution for two intersecting lines is to graph the lines. Occasionally, the graph's solution may not be as precise as an algebraic solution. Even so, the graph will give you a picture of the lines and an approximation of the point of intersection.

EXAMPLE 1 Use a graph to find the common solution for

$x + y = 6$

$x - y = 4$

Step 1 Find the x- and y-intercepts of each line.

$x + y = 6$

$y = 6 - x$

x	y
0	6
6	0

$x - y = 4$

$-y = 4 - x$

$y = x - 4$

x	y
0	−4
4	0

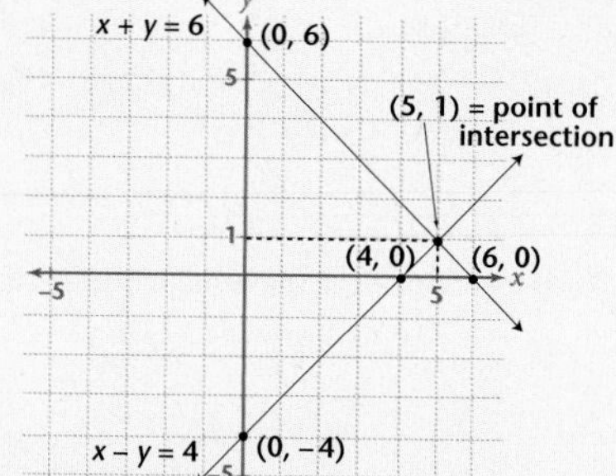

Step 2 Read the point of intersection from the graph. In this case, the common solution is (5, 1).

Step 3 Check your work. Substitute (5, 1) for x and y in each equation. Determine whether the statements are true.

$x + y = 6$ $\quad$ $x - y = 4$

$5 + 1 = 6$ $\quad$ $5 - 1 = 4$

$6 = 6$ True $\quad$ $4 = 4$ True

EXAMPLE 2 Use a graph to find the common solution for $y = 5$ $\quad 2x + y = 6$

Step 1 Find the x- and y-intercepts of each line.

$y = 5$ A horizontal line through $y = 5$

$2x + y = 6$

$y = 6 - 2x$

x	y
0	6
3	0

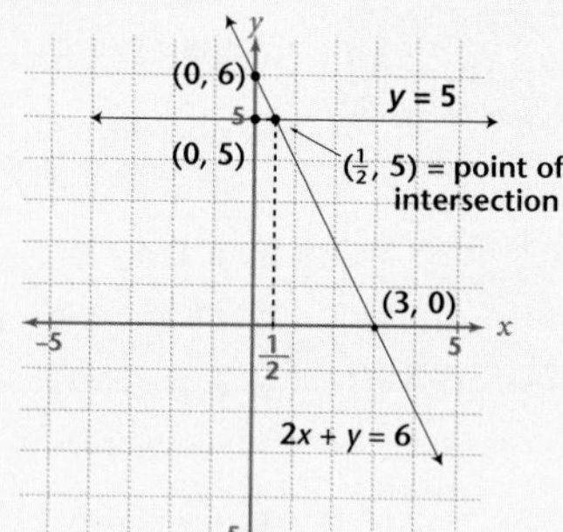

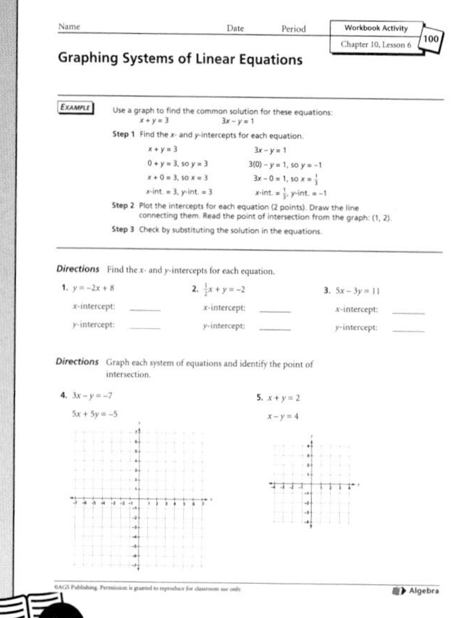

Name Date Period — Workbook Activity 100 — Chapter 10, Lesson 6

Graphing Systems of Linear Equations

EXAMPLE Use a graph to find the common solution for these equations: $x + y = 3$ $\quad 3x - y = 1$

Step 1 Find the x- and y-intercepts for each equation.

$x + y = 3$: $0 + y = 3$, so $y = 3$; $x + 0 = 3$, so $x = 3$; x-int. = 3, y-int. = 3

$3x - y = 1$: $3(0) - y = 1$, so $y = -1$; $3x - 0 = 1$, so $x = \frac{1}{3}$; x-int. = $\frac{1}{3}$, y-int. = −1

Step 2 Plot the intercepts for each equation (2 points). Draw the line connecting them. Read the point of intersection from the graph: (1, 2).

Step 3 Check by substituting the solution in the equations.

Directions Find the x- and y-intercepts for each equation.

1. $y = -2x + 8$ x-intercept: ____ y-intercept: ____
2. $\frac{1}{2}x + y = -2$ x-intercept: ____ y-intercept: ____
3. $5x - 3y = 11$ x-intercept: ____ y-intercept: ____

Directions Graph each system of equations and identify the point of intersection.

4. $3x - y = -7$, $5x + 5y = -5$
5. $x + y = 2$, $x - y = 4$

©AGS Publishing. Permission is granted to reproduce for classroom use only. Algebra

Workbook Activity 100

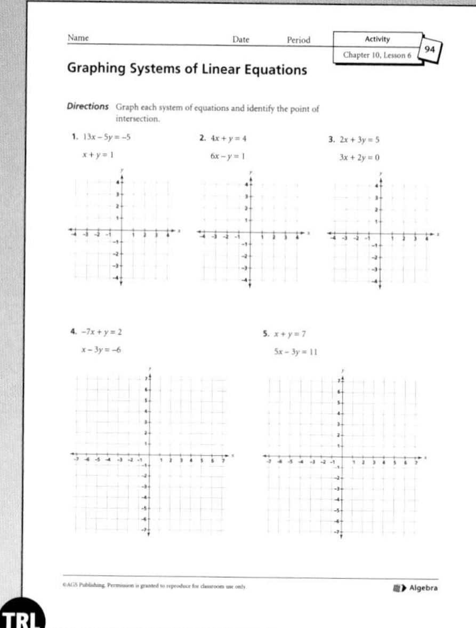

Name Date Period — Activity 94 — Chapter 10, Lesson 6

Graphing Systems of Linear Equations

Directions Graph each system of equations and identify the point of intersection.

1. $13x - 5y = -5$, $x + y = 1$
2. $4x + y = 4$, $6x - y = 1$
3. $2x + 3y = 5$, $3x + 2y = 0$
4. $-7x + y = 2$, $x - 3y = -6$
5. $x + y = 7$, $5x - 3y = 11$

©AGS Publishing. Permission is granted to reproduce for classroom use only. Algebra

Activity 94

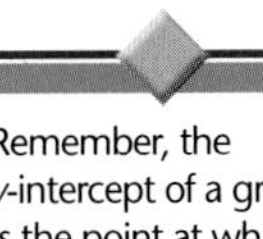

Remember, the y-intercept of a graph is the point at which a graph intersects the y-axis. The x-intercept of a graph is the point at which a graph intersects the x-axis. The x-intercept is also known as the root of the equation.

EXAMPLE 2 *(continued)*

Step 2 Read the point of intersection from the graph. In this case, the common solution is $(\frac{1}{2}, 5)$.

Step 3 Check your work. Substitute $(\frac{1}{2}, 5)$ for x and y in each equation. Determine whether the statements are true.

$y = 5$ | $x + y = 6$
$5 = 5$ True | $2(\frac{1}{2}) + 5 = 6$
 | $1 + 5 = 6$ True

A special case of intersection includes those lines that are parallel to the x-axis and y-axis.

EXAMPLE 3 Find the points of intersection for these systems of equations.

$x = 1$, $y = 5$ | $x = -1$, $y = 0$ | $x = 3$, $y = -2$

Graph each line using the given values of x and y.
Then read the common solution from the point of intersection.

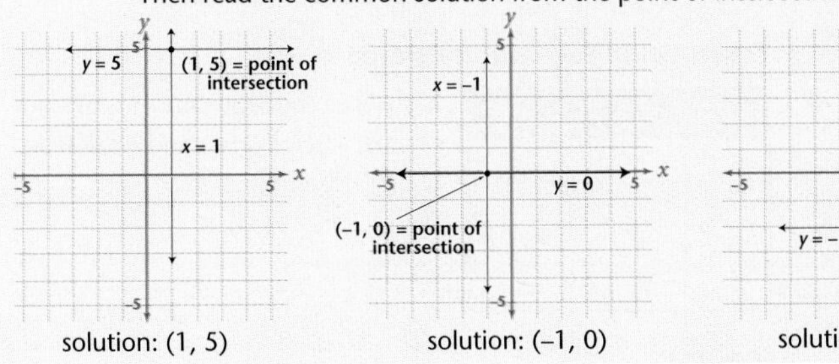

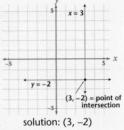

solution: (1, 5) | solution: (−1, 0) | solution: (3, −2)

Exercise A Graph each system of equations. Find the point of intersection.

1. $x = 2$, $y = -3$ $(2, -3)$

2. $x = 4$, $y = 4$ $(4, 4)$

3. $x = 3$, $y = -3$ $(3, -3)$

4. $x = 1$, $y = 3$ $(1, 3)$

5. $x = 2$, $2x + y = 4$ $(2, 0)$

6. $y = -3$, $3y = 4 - x$ $(13, -3)$

7. $y = 2$, $4x + 2y = 7$ $(\frac{3}{4}, 2)$

8. $x = -3$, $3y + 2x = 4$ $(-3, \frac{10}{3})$

9. $-x + 2y = 4$, $x + 5y = 10$ $(0, 2)$

10. $-3x + 2y = 10$, $4y + 3x = 20$ $(0, 5)$

11. $4x + 2y = 12$, $3x - 2y = 9$ $(3, 0)$

12. $4x + y = 10$, $3y - 23 = 2x$ $(\frac{1}{2}, 8)$

13. $x + 5y = 6$, $x + 2y = 9$ $(11, -1)$

14. $2x - y = 6$, $4x + y = 18$ $(4, 2)$

15. $3x + 6 = y$, $2x - 3y = 10$ $(-4, -6)$

COMMON ERROR

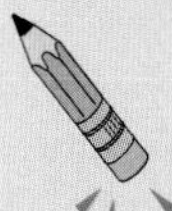

When plotting points that have been generated by a table of values, remind students that the x-value represents horizontal distance or distance from the y-axis, and the y-value represents vertical distance or distance from the x-axis.

MANIPULATIVES

Modeling Equations

Materials: Pattern Blocks, Unit Cubes, two copies of Manipulatives Master 5 (Basic Sentence Mat) for each student

Group Practice: Review procedures for solving systems of equations from the Chapter 10, Lessons 4 and 5 Manipulatives activities. Show students how to evaluate a system to determine which method would be better to use.

Student Practice: Have students use manipulatives to check their work in Exercise A, Problems 5–6, 9–11, 13 and 15.

3 Reinforce and Extend

GROUP PROBLEM SOLVING

Encourage small groups of students to work cooperatively and generate a system of equations that has the origin of a coordinate system as a common solution and, along with the x- and y-axes, divides the coordinate system into eight equal areas. *(Possible answer: $y = x$ and $y = -x$)*

After the activity has been completed, invite volunteers from each group to share their problem-solving approach and their answers with one another.

Lesson at a Glance

Chapter 10 Lesson 7

Overview This lesson introduces conjunctions in the form of *and* statements.

Objective

- To determine the truth-value of a conjunction

Student Pages 306–309

Teacher's Resource Library 

Workbook Activity 101

Activity 95

Alternative Activity 95

Mathematics Vocabulary

conjunction

Warm-Up Activity

Copy the following table on the board.

x	y	$x + y$
1	7	8
	− 3	
2		

Point out that in this table, the value of the $x + y$ column depends on the value of x *and* depends on the value of y. If the value of x is not known, and/or the value of y is not known, the value of $x + y$ cannot be determined. In other words, both the value of x and the value of y combine to influence the value of $x + y$.

Teaching the Lesson

In mathematics, compound statements represent a form of logic. In the study of logic, variables are used to represent simple statements, which, in and of themselves, are either true or false. When two simple statements are combined or joined to create a compound statement, a conjunction is formed. When evaluating the truth-value of a conjunction, the truth-value of each simple statement that forms the conjunction must be considered.

To help students better understand how the simple statements of a conjunction

Lesson 7 *And* Statements—Conjunctions

Conjunction

Two or more simple statements connected by "and"

In Lesson 6, you learned that the common solution for a system of linear equations is the point of intersection—the single point that is on each of the lines. In other words, the point must belong to the first line *and* the second line. The statement "the point must belong to the first line *and* the second line" is an example of a **conjunction**. Two simple statements connected by *and* are called a conjunction.

A truth table is a table of true (T) and false (F) values.

Rule for Conjunctions

A conjunction is TRUE whenever both simple statements are true. All other conjunctions are FALSE.

You can let p and q stand for simple sentences that can be either true or false. You can use the symbol ^ to stand for *and*. Then you can use this information to make a truth table to show when the conjunction is true and when it is false.

Truth Table for Conjunctions

p	q	$p \wedge q$
T	T	T
T	F	F
F	T	F
F	F	F

Note that the only true conjunction occurs when both p and q are true. If one statement is false, the conjunction is false.

EXAMPLE 1 Graph the lines $y = 2$ and $x = 4$. Refer to the graph to check the truth-value of each statement and the truth-value of each conjunction. Use the truth table at the top of page 307.

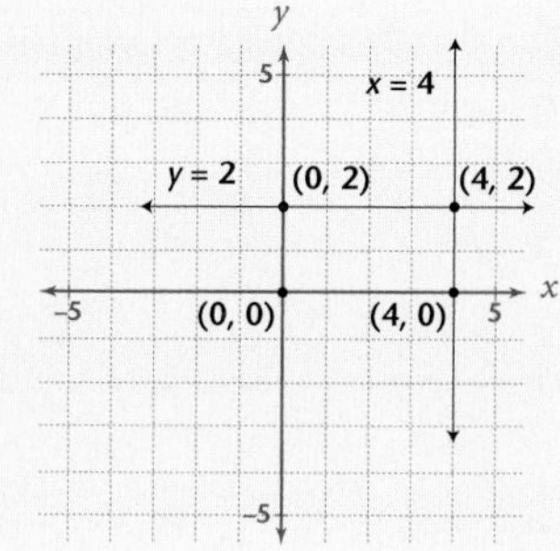

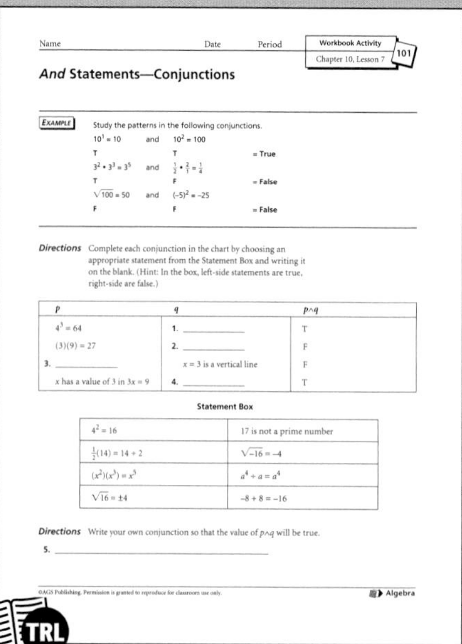

Name Date Period

Workbook Activity 101
Chapter 10, Lesson 7

***And* Statements—Conjunctions**

EXAMPLE Study the patterns in the following conjunctions.

$10^1 = 10$	and	$10^2 = 100$	
T		T	= True
$3^2 \cdot 3^3 = 3^5$	and	$\frac{1}{2} \cdot \frac{2}{1} = \frac{1}{4}$	
T		F	= False
$\sqrt{100} = 50$	and	$(-5)^2 = -25$	
F		F	= False

Directions Complete each conjunction in the chart by choosing an appropriate statement from the Statement Box and writing it on the blank. (Hint: In the box, left-side statements are true, right-side are false.)

p	q	$p \wedge q$
$4^3 = 64$	1. ________	T
$(3)(9) = 27$	2. ________	F
3. ________	$x = 3$ is a vertical line	F
x has a value of 3 in $3x = 9$	4. ________	T

Statement Box

$4^2 = 16$	17 is not a prime number
$\frac{1}{2}(14) = 14 \div 2$	$\sqrt{-16} = -4$
$(x^2)(x^3) = x^5$	$a^4 + a = a^4$
$\sqrt{16} = \pm 4$	$-8 + 8 = -16$

Directions Write your own conjunction so that the value of $p \wedge q$ will be true.

5. ______________________

Algebra

Workbook Activity 101

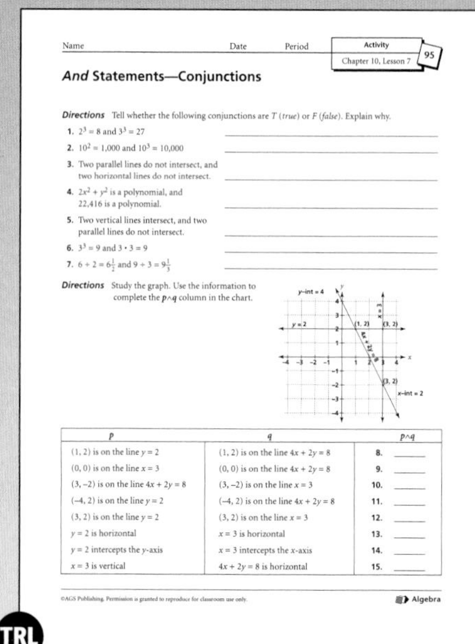

Name Date Period

Activity 95
Chapter 10, Lesson 7

***And* Statements—Conjunctions**

Directions Tell whether the following conjunctions are *T* (*true*) or *F* (*false*). Explain why.

1. $2^3 = 8$ and $3^3 = 27$ ______
2. $10^2 = 1{,}000$ and $10^3 = 10{,}000$ ______
3. Two parallel lines do not intersect, and two horizontal lines do not intersect. ______
4. $2x^2 + y^2$ is a polynomial, and 22,416 is a polynomial. ______
5. Two vertical lines intersect, and two parallel lines do not intersect. ______
6. $3^3 = 9$ and $3 \cdot 3 = 9$ ______
7. $6 \div 2 = 6\frac{1}{2}$ and $9 \div 3 = 9\frac{1}{3}$ ______

Directions Study the graph. Use the information to complete the $p \wedge q$ column in the chart.

p	q	$p \wedge q$
(1, 2) is on the line $y = 2$	(1, 2) is on the line $4x + 2y = 8$	8. ______
(0, 0) is on the line $x = 3$	(0, 0) is on the line $4x + 2y = 8$	9. ______
(3, –2) is on the line $4x + 2y = 8$	(3, –2) is on the line $x = 3$	10. ______
(–4, 2) is on the line $y = 2$	(–4, 2) is on the line $4x + 2y = 8$	11. ______
(3, 2) is on the line $y = 2$	(3, 2) is on the line $x = 3$	12. ______
$y = 2$ is horizontal	$x = 3$ is horizontal	13. ______
$y = 2$ intercepts the y-axis	$x = 3$ intercepts the x-axis	14. ______
$x = 3$ is vertical	$4x + 2y = 8$ is horizontal	15. ______

Algebra

Activity 95

p	^	q	p ^ q
(4, 2) is on the line $y = 2$ T	and	(4, 2) is on the line $x = 4$ T	T
(0, 2) is on the line $y = 2$ T	and	(0, 2) is on the line $x = 4$ F	F
(4, 0) is on the line $y = 2$ F	and	(4, 0) is on the line $x = 4$ T	F
(0, 0) is on the line $y = 2$ F	and	(0, 0) is on the line $x = 4$ F	F

EXAMPLE 2 Tell whether the following conjunctions are true or false. Give a reason.

$2 + 2 = 4$ and $3^2 = 9$ True

T T

Both statements are true. The conjunction is true.

$2 \cdot 2 = 4$ and squares are circles False

T F

Only one statement is true. The conjunction is false.

$\sqrt{9} = 3$ and $3 \neq 5$ True

T T

Both statements are true. The conjunction is true.

Is p ^ q true or false when $p = 2 + 3 = 5$ and $q = 15 \div 3 \neq 5$?

Evaluate each statement:

$2 + 3 = 5$ is true, so p is true.

$15 \div 3 \neq 5$ is false, so q is false.

Therefore, by the rule of conjunctions, p ^ q is false.

influence its truth-value, you might choose to invite a volunteer to stand and ask the volunteer to say "My first name is _____ and my last name is _____." Point out to the remainder of the class that the conjunction is true because the student used his or her real first and last names in the conjunction. If the student had used a first name and/or a last name that was not real, the conjunction would not be true.

In the conjunction truth tables on pages 306 and 307, have students note that if any element of a conjunction is false, the truth-value of the entire conjunction is false.

3 Reinforce and Extend

LEARNING STYLES

Interpersonal/ Group Learning

Suggest students work in groups of three to practice determining the truth-value of simple statements. Ask each group to create a ten-question true/false quiz. The quiz should consist of ten simple statements that are known by the group to be true or false. The content of any statement does not necessarily have to be limited to the domain of mathematics. Two examples of such statements are

The record high temperature in degrees Fahrenheit in the state of Alaska is 100°. *(true)*

Neptune is the seventh planet from the sun in our solar system. *(false)*

Ask groups to exchange quizzes. You might choose to elicit a "friendly" competition—which group can generate the greatest number of correct answers to the quizzes?

Group Problem Solving

Encourage students to work in groups of four to consider the following scenario and decide if it is true or false.

All *c*'s are *d*'s.

Some *e*'s are *c*'s.

Some *e*'s are not *d*'s.

Therefore, some *e*'s are *d*'s. *(true)*

Invite groups to share their method of determining the truth-value of the scenario with each other.

Writing About Mathematics

If you know that p is true, what must be the truth-value of q in order for $p \wedge q$ to be true? Give an example.

6. False, angles in a triangle add up to 360° is false
7. False, all vertical lines have a slope of 1 is false
8. False, dividing by $\frac{3}{4}$ is the same as multiplying by $-\frac{4}{3}$ is false
9. False, $2^2 + 2^3 = 2^5$ is false
10. True, both are true
11. False, $6 + 7 = 15$ is false
12. False, $4\frac{2}{7} = 30$ is false

Exercise A Tell whether the following conjunctions are true or false. Explain why.

1. $2 + 2 = 4$ and $2^2 = 4$ True, both are true
2. $2^3 = 8$ and $8 = 2 \cdot 2 \cdot 2$ True, both are true
3. $4 \div 0 = 0$ and $4 \cdot 0 = 0$ False, $4 \div 0 = 0$ is false
4. $4 \div 4 = 1$ and $4 \cdot 1 \neq 5$ True, both are true
5. $6 \cdot 0 = 0$ and $6 + 0 = 6$ True, both are true
6. Angles in a triangle add up to 360°, and there are four right angles in a square.
7. All parallel lines have the same slope, and all vertical lines have a slope of 1.
8. Dividing by $\frac{3}{4}$ is the same as multiplying by $-\frac{4}{3}$, and $3\frac{1}{2}$ has the same value as $\frac{14}{4}$.
9. $2^2 + 2^3 = 2^5$ and $a^2 + a^2 = 2a^2$
10. $-x = 12$ is the same as $x = -12$ and $3^3 = 27$
11. $\frac{42}{7} = 6$ and $6 + 7 = 15$
12. $4\frac{2}{7} = 30$ and $\frac{3}{2}x = (1\frac{1}{2})x$

Truth Table for Conjunctions

p	q	$p \wedge q$
T	T	T
T	F	F
F	T	F
F	F	F

> **Writing About Mathematics**
>
> If p is false, is it possible to make $p \wedge q$ true? Explain.

Exercise B What is the truth-value of $p \wedge q$ in the following exercises?

13. $p = 4^3 = 64, q = 23 - 15 = 8$ — True, both are true

14. $p = 2 + 6 = 8, q = 4 + 4 = 8$ — True, both are true

15. p = Parallel lines have the same slope.
$q = 0 \div 0$ is undefined. — True, both are true

16. p = All triangles have one right angle. — False, p is false
q = All circles have $4 \cdot 90°$.

17. p = All squares have four sides. — True, both are true
q = All rectangles have a perimeter.

18. p = All numbers greater than 100 are prime. — False,
q = Some numbers greater than 100 are prime. — p is false

19. $p = x^2 \cdot x^3 = x^5$
q = for all lines, slope $(m) > 0$ — False, q is false

20. $p = x^6 \div x^2 = x^3$
$q = a^2 + b^2 = (ab)^2$ — False, both are false

> **Technology Connection**
>
> **Search Engines**
>
> Many Internet search engines use *and statements* to help limit and focus a search. Try this: type a word into a search engine. Notice the number of Web sites that show up. Add a second word to your search phrase (separated from the first by a comma), and you get fewer sites. Type a third word, and you get even fewer sites. That's because you get only the Web sites with all three words—word 1 AND word 2 AND word 3.

Lesson at a Glance

Chapter 10 Lesson 8

Overview This lesson introduces problem solving using linear equations.

Objective

- To use linear equations to solve problems

Student Pages 310–313

Teacher's Resource Library TRL

Workbook Activity 102

Activity 96

Alternative Activity 96

1 Warm-Up Activity

Although students are aware that variables are used to represent unknown quantities, remind them that any letter of the alphabet can be used to represent a variable. Ask students to identify the unknown quantity in each of the following statements and represent the unknown quantity in terms of the variable *x*.

Ten added to a number creates a sum of 14. *(a number; $x = 14 - 10$ or 4)*

A mother's age is 25 years greater than her son's age. The son is 9 years old. *(the mother's age; $x = 9 + 25$ or 34)*

The product of a negative integer and 6 is –27. *(a negative integer; $x = -27 \div 6$ or $-4\frac{1}{2}$)*

2 Teaching the Lesson

This lesson completes the study of various methods that can be used to solve a system of linear equations. After discussing the example on page 310, remind students that the solution to the problem could have been obtained, for example, by substitution. Demonstrate on the board how substitution could have been used.

Since $x + y = 10$, $x = 10 - y$; substitute $10 - y$ for x in either equation.

$$x - y = 4$$
$$(10 - y) - y = 4$$
$$10 - 2y = 4$$
$$-2y = -6$$
$$y = 3$$

Lesson 8 Problem Solving Using Linear Equations

You can solve certain word problems by setting up and then solving systems of equations.

EXAMPLE 1 The sum of two numbers is 10 and the difference of the same two numbers is 4. What are the numbers?

Step 1 Let x = one number, let y = the other number. Write an equation for each condition.

$x + y = 10$ The sum is 10.

$x - y = 4$ The difference is 4.

Step 2 Solve the system of equations. In this case, elimination works well.

$$\begin{array}{r} x + y = 10 \\ + \ x - y = 4 \\ \hline 2x + 0y = 14 \\ 2x = 14 \\ x = 7 \end{array}$$

Substitute 7 for x in either equation.

$$x + y = 10$$
$$7 + y = 10$$
$$y = 3$$

You found that $x = 7$ and $y = 3$. The two numbers are 7 and 3.

Step 3 Check.

$x + y = 10$	$x - y = 4$
$7 + 3 = 10$	$7 - 3 = 4$
$10 = 10$ True	$4 = 4$ True

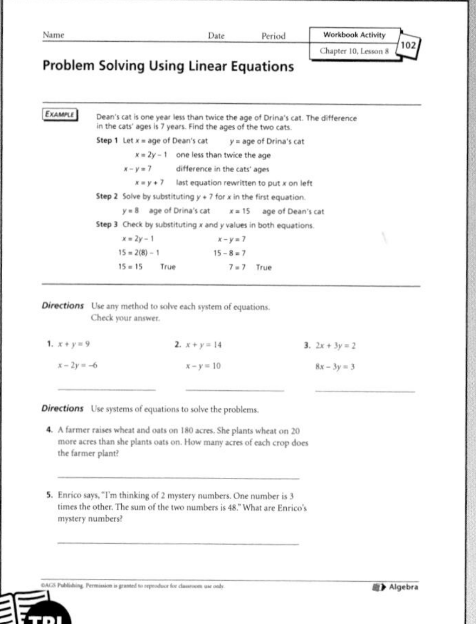

Name Date Period **Workbook Activity 102** Chapter 10, Lesson 8

Problem Solving Using Linear Equations

EXAMPLE Dean's cat is one year less than twice the age of Drina's cat. The difference in the cats' ages is 7 years. Find the ages of the two cats.

Step 1 Let x = age of Dean's cat y = age of Drina's cat

$x = 2y - 1$ one less than twice the age

$x - y = 7$ difference in the cats' ages

$x = y + 7$ last equation rewritten to put x on left

Step 2 Solve by substituting $y + 7$ for x in the first equation.

$y = 8$ age of Drina's cat $x = 15$ age of Dean's cat

Step 3 Check by substituting x and y values in both equations.

$x = 2y - 1$	$x - y = 7$
$15 = 2(8) - 1$	$15 - 8 = 7$
$15 = 15$ True	$7 = 7$ True

Directions Use any method to solve each system of equations. Check your answer.

1. $x + y = 9$, $x - 2y = -6$
2. $x + y = 14$, $x - y = 10$
3. $2x + 3y = 2$, $8x - 3y = 3$

Directions Use systems of equations to solve the problems.

4. A farmer raises wheat and oats on 180 acres. She plants wheat on 20 more acres than she plants oats on. How many acres of each crop does the farmer plant?

5. Enrico says, "I'm thinking of 2 mystery numbers. One number is 3 times the other. The sum of the two numbers is 48." What are Enrico's mystery numbers?

 Algebra

TRL

Workbook Activity 102

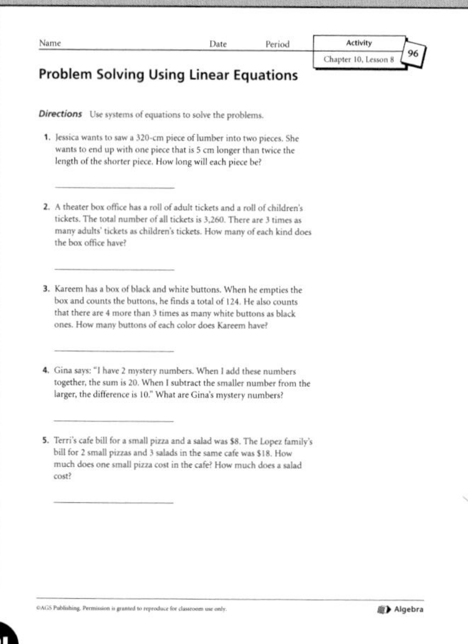

Name Date Period **Activity 96** Chapter 10, Lesson 8

Problem Solving Using Linear Equations

Directions Use systems of equations to solve the problems.

1. Jessica wants to saw a 320-cm piece of lumber into two pieces. She wants to end up with one piece that is 5 cm longer than twice the length of the shorter piece. How long will each piece be?

2. A theater box office has a roll of adult tickets and a roll of children's tickets. The total number of all tickets is 3,260. There are 3 times as many adults' tickets as children's tickets. How many of each kind does the box office have?

3. Kareem has a box of black and white buttons. When he empties the box and counts the buttons, he finds a total of 124. He also counts that there are 4 more than 3 times as many white buttons as black ones. How many buttons of each color does Kareem have?

4. Gina says: "I have 2 mystery numbers. When I add these numbers together, the sum is 20. When I subtract the smaller number from the larger, the difference is 10." What are Gina's mystery numbers?

5. Terri's cafe bill for a small pizza and a salad was $8. The Lopez family's bill for 2 small pizzas and 3 salads in the same cafe was $18. How much does one small pizza cost in the cafe? How much does a salad cost?

 Algebra

TRL

Activity 96

Remember to answer the question in the problem after you find the values for x and y.

Notice there are three steps to solve these problems. First, decide which variable in the problem will be x and which variable will be y. Write an equation for each condition using the variables x and y. Second, solve the system of equations. Third, check your answer. Substitute the value for x and y in your equations. Also, reread the problem and decide if your answer makes sense.

EXAMPLE 2 A father's age is three less than two times the son's age. The difference in their ages is 30 years. Find the ages of father and son.

Step 1 Let x = father's age and let y = son's age. Write an equation for each condition.

$x = 2y - 3$ Three less than twice son's age.

$x - y = 30$ The difference is 30.

Step 2 Solve the system of equations. In this case, substitution works well.

$x = 2y - 3$

$x - y = 30$ becomes

$(2y - 3) - y = 30$

$y - 3 = 30$

$y = 30 + 3$ or $y = 33$

Substitute 33 for y in either equation.

$x = 2y - 3$ becomes

$x = 2(33) - 3$

$x = 66 - 3$ or $x = 63$

The father's age is 63, the son's age is 33.

Step 3 Check.

$x - y = 30$	$x = 2y - 3$
$63 - 33 = 30$	$63 = 2(33) - 3$
$30 = 30$ True	$63 = 66 - 3$
	$63 = 63$ True

Since $y = 3$, substitute 3 for y in either equation.

$$x - y = 4$$
$$x - (3) = 4$$
$$x = 7$$

After discussing the example on page 311, remind students that the solution to the problem could have been obtained, for example, by graphing. In order to graph the equations, a table of values would need to be generated for each equation. You might choose to copy the following table of values on the board:

$x = 2y - 3$	
x	y
−7	−2
−3	0
1	2

$x - y = 30$	
x	y
35	5
30	0
25	5

Explain that the solution to the system may be somewhat difficult to find because the x-values in the second table are so great. These values will necessitate either the use of a greater axis interval, or a graph that is physically large. As a result, graphing appears (in this example) to not be a particularly attractive way of finding the solution.

Also point out that the solution to some systems of linear equations may be a value that cannot be easily graphed (for example, $\frac{1}{5}, \frac{1}{12}$). For this reason, graphing may sometimes not be a preferred method of generating the solution to a system of linear equations.

Common Error

When solving a system of linear equations by elimination, remind students that either the x- or the y-value will "disappear" if the elimination is performed properly. If both values are still present after the elimination has been performed, the elimination was not performed properly.

3 Reinforce and Extend

In the Community

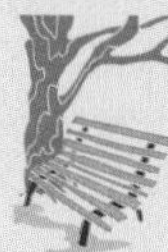

Encourage students to name a variety of vocations that are part of the economy of their community and conjecture which of those vocations may require the skill of modeling a problem using a system of linear equations and finding the common solution to that system.

Writing About Mathematics

Write a word problem of your own. Exchange problems with a partner and solve one another's problems. (Be sure you solve and check your own problem first.)

Example 3 Rosa's best time in a race is 2 seconds faster than her second-best time. Her second-best time is $1\frac{1}{4}$ times her best time. What is her best time? What is her second-best time?

Step 1 Let x = second-best time, let y = best time. Write an equation for each condition.

best time: $x - y = 2$ (two seconds faster than second-best time)

second-best time: $x = 1\frac{1}{4}y$ ($1\frac{1}{4}$ times the best time)

Step 2 Solve the system of equations. In this case, substitution works well.

$x = \frac{5}{4}y$

$x - y = 2$ becomes

$\frac{5}{4}y - y = 2$

$\frac{1}{4}y = 2$ or $y = 8$

Substitute 8 for y in either equation.

$x - y = 2$ becomes

$x - 8 = 2$

$x = 2 + 8$ or $x = 10$

Rosa's second-best time is 10 seconds, and her best time is 8 seconds.

Step 3 Check.

$x - y = 2$	$x = \frac{5}{4}y$
$10 - 8 = 2$	$10 = \frac{5}{4}(8)$
$2 = 2$ True	$10 = \frac{5 \cdot 8}{4}$
	$10 = 10$ True

and 16
3 and 12
ais week
54, last
eek $18
miles
2
econds;
6 seconds
ighest 47,
west 17
mityville
4,
ohnstown
0
lark $56,
liguel
69.50
aWayne
2,
havonne
8
his
nonth
$20,
nighest
$60

PROBLEM SOLVING

Exercise A Set up and solve a system of equations to find the answers. Check your answers.

1. The sum of two numbers is 24 and the difference of the same two numbers is 8. What are the numbers?

2. A mother's age is three less than three times her daughter's age. The sum of their ages is 45. Find the ages of the mother and daughter.

3. This week Leah earned three times as much as she earned last week. During both weeks, Leah earned $72. How much did she earn each week?

4. While walking for exercise, Mia is able to walk only $\frac{3}{4}$ as far on Saturday as she walked on Friday. On Saturday she walks $1\frac{1}{2}$ miles. How many miles did she walk on Friday?

5. Christopher's best time in a race is 4 seconds faster than his second-best time. His second-best time is $1\frac{1}{3}$ times slower than his best time. What is his best time? What is his second-best time?

Exercise B Set up and solve a system of equations to answer the questions. Check your answers.

6. In a 50-question test, the highest score in class is three times the lowest score minus four. The difference between the highest and the lowest scores is 30. What are the highest and lowest scores?

7. In one game, the Amityville football team scores $\frac{3}{5}$ as many points as the Johnstown team. Johnstown wins the game by 16 points. What is each team's score?

8. Mark and Miguel compare paychecks. Miguel makes $13.50 more than Mark. Their combined wages for the week are $125.50. How much does each earn?

9. DaWayne is $1\frac{1}{2}$ times as old as his younger sister Shavonne. DaWayne is also 14 years older than Shavonne. What are their ages?

10. At Makita's Market, this month's electric bill is $\frac{1}{3}$ as much as the market's highest bill. This bill is also $40 less than the highest bill. How much is this month's bill? How much is the highest bill?

GROUP PROBLEM SOLVING

Encourage students to work in pairs to generate a system of linear equations that can be used to model the following problem and find the common solution of the system using elimination, substitution, or graphing.

An adult ticket to a football game costs $6. A student ticket costs $2.50. If ticket sales totaled $1,394, how many tickets of each kind were sold? *(124 adult tickets and 260 student tickets)*

Invite one or more volunteers from different groups to demonstrate on the board the different methods that were used to find the common solution.

Lesson at a Glance

Chapter 10 Lesson 9

Overview This lesson introduces the concept of a matrix and demonstrates how to add or subtract matrices.

Objectives

- To define the dimension of a matrix
- To identify the row and column of a matrix entry
- To find the sum of two matrices (addition)
- To find the difference between two matrices (subtraction)

Student Pages 314–317

Teacher's Resource Library 

Workbook Activity 103

Activity 97

Alternative Activity 97

1 Warm-Up Activity

Ask the class if they've ever heard the word "matrix." Some students may mention the film with the title *The Matrix*. Tell them that the film was well-named because it was about a fictional, computer-controlled world controlled by a very complex arrangement of numbers—the computer program. Tell them that the matrices they will be working with will be very simple, nothing like the one in the film. Point out that there are many kinds of matrices. In fact, the seating arrangement in most classrooms—rows of desks—is a form of matrix.

2 Teaching the Lesson

Begin by discussing the definition of a matrix. Point out that there can be small matrices of two entries/members or much larger matrices that contain hundreds of entries/members. Work through the examples presented. Emphasize how entries/members are identified by the subscript showing row and column. Remind students that to add or subtract two matrices, the matrices must have the same dimensions. You cannot add a 2 x 4 matrix with a 3 x 7 matrix, for example. As a class, work

Lesson 9 Introduction to Matrices: Addition and Subtraction

Matrix
Any rectangular arrangement of numbers or symbols

A **matrix** is any rectangular arrangement of numbers or symbols. The plural of matrix is **matrices.** A matrix of m rows and n columns is a matrix with dimensions $m \times n$, which is read "m by n."

EXAMPLE 1 This is a 2×3 matrix.

$$\begin{array}{l} \text{Row 1} \rightarrow \\ \text{Row 2} \rightarrow \end{array} \begin{bmatrix} -2 & 5 & 7 \\ \pi & \frac{1}{2} & 0 \end{bmatrix}$$

$$\begin{array}{ccc} \uparrow & \uparrow & \uparrow \\ \text{Column 1} & \text{Column 2} & \text{Column 3} \end{array}$$

EXAMPLE 2 This is a 3×3 matrix.

This is a square matrix. In a square matrix, the number of rows equals the number of columns, $m = n$.

$$\text{Rows} \begin{array}{l} \rightarrow \\ \rightarrow \\ \rightarrow \end{array} \begin{bmatrix} 5 & -1 & \frac{1}{2} \\ \pi & \sqrt{2} & 1 \\ 1 & 0 & 7 \end{bmatrix}$$

$$\begin{array}{ccc} \uparrow & \uparrow & \uparrow \\ 1 & 2 & 3 \end{array}$$

Columns

EXAMPLE 3 This is a 2×1 matrix.

$$\begin{array}{l} \text{Row 1} \rightarrow \\ \text{Row 2} \rightarrow \end{array} \begin{bmatrix} x \\ -10 \end{bmatrix}$$

$$\begin{array}{c} \uparrow \\ 1 \\ \text{Column} \end{array}$$

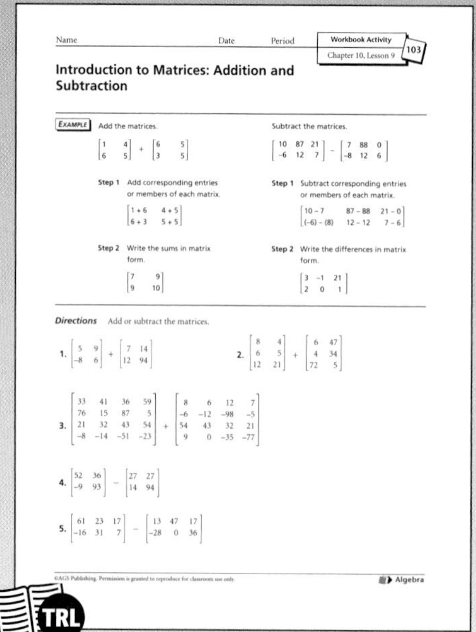

Name Date Period

Workbook Activity 103 — Chapter 10, Lesson 9

Introduction to Matrices: Addition and Subtraction

EXAMPLE Add the matrices.

$$\begin{bmatrix} 1 & 4 \\ 6 & 5 \end{bmatrix} + \begin{bmatrix} 6 & 5 \\ 3 & 5 \end{bmatrix}$$

Step 1 Add corresponding entries or members of each matrix.

$$\begin{bmatrix} 1+6 & 4+5 \\ 6+3 & 5+5 \end{bmatrix}$$

Step 2 Write the sums in matrix form.

$$\begin{bmatrix} 7 & 9 \\ 9 & 10 \end{bmatrix}$$

Subtract the matrices.

$$\begin{bmatrix} 10 & 87 & 21 \\ -6 & 12 & 7 \end{bmatrix} - \begin{bmatrix} 7 & 88 & 0 \\ -8 & 12 & 6 \end{bmatrix}$$

Step 1 Subtract corresponding entries or members of each matrix.

$$\begin{bmatrix} 10-7 & 87-88 & 21-0 \\ (-6)-(8) & 12-12 & 7-6 \end{bmatrix}$$

Step 2 Write the differences in matrix form.

$$\begin{bmatrix} 3 & -1 & 21 \\ 2 & 0 & 1 \end{bmatrix}$$

Directions Add or subtract the matrices.

1. $\begin{bmatrix} 5 & 9 \\ -8 & 6 \end{bmatrix} + \begin{bmatrix} 7 & 14 \\ 12 & 94 \end{bmatrix}$

2. $\begin{bmatrix} 8 & 4 \\ 6 & 5 \\ 12 & 21 \end{bmatrix} + \begin{bmatrix} 6 & 47 \\ 4 & 34 \\ 72 & 5 \end{bmatrix}$

3. $\begin{bmatrix} 33 & 41 & 36 & 59 \\ 76 & 15 & 87 & 5 \\ 21 & 32 & 43 & 54 \\ -8 & -14 & -51 & -23 \end{bmatrix} + \begin{bmatrix} 8 & 6 & 12 & 7 \\ -6 & -12 & -98 & -5 \\ 54 & 43 & 32 & 21 \\ 9 & 0 & -35 & -77 \end{bmatrix}$

4. $\begin{bmatrix} 52 & 36 \\ -9 & 93 \end{bmatrix} - \begin{bmatrix} 27 & 27 \\ 14 & 94 \end{bmatrix}$

5. $\begin{bmatrix} 61 & 23 & 17 \\ -16 & 31 & 7 \end{bmatrix} - \begin{bmatrix} 13 & 47 & 17 \\ -28 & 0 & 36 \end{bmatrix}$

Algebra

TRL

Workbook Activity 103

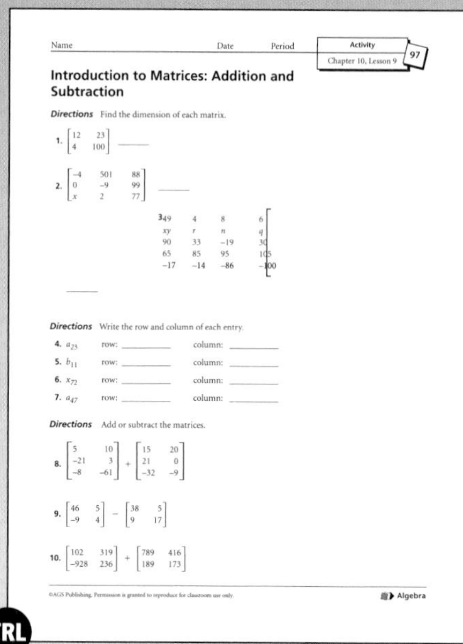

Name Date Period

Activity 97 — Chapter 10, Lesson 9

Introduction to Matrices: Addition and Subtraction

Directions Find the dimension of each matrix.

1. $\begin{bmatrix} 12 & 23 \\ 4 & 100 \end{bmatrix}$ ______

2. $\begin{bmatrix} -4 & 501 & 88 \\ 0 & -9 & 99 \\ x & 2 & 77 \end{bmatrix}$ ______

3. $\begin{bmatrix} 49 & 4 & 8 & 6 \\ xy & r & n & q \\ 90 & 33 & -19 & 30 \\ 65 & 85 & 95 & 105 \\ -17 & -14 & -86 & -100 \end{bmatrix}$ ______

Directions Write the row and column of each entry.

4. a_{23} row: ______ column: ______
5. b_{11} row: ______ column: ______
6. x_{72} row: ______ column: ______
7. a_{47} row: ______ column: ______

Directions Add or subtract the matrices.

8. $\begin{bmatrix} 5 & 10 \\ -21 & 3 \\ -8 & -61 \end{bmatrix} + \begin{bmatrix} 15 & 20 \\ 21 & 0 \\ -32 & -9 \end{bmatrix}$

9. $\begin{bmatrix} 46 & 5 \\ -9 & 4 \end{bmatrix} - \begin{bmatrix} 38 & 5 \\ 9 & 17 \end{bmatrix}$

10. $\begin{bmatrix} 102 & 319 \\ -928 & 236 \end{bmatrix} + \begin{bmatrix} 789 & 416 \\ 189 & 173 \end{bmatrix}$

Algebra

TRL

Activity 97

EXAMPLE 4 This is a 3 × 3 matrix.

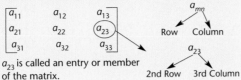

$$\begin{bmatrix} a_{11} & a_{12} & a_{13} \\ a_{21} & a_{22} & a_{23} \\ a_{31} & a_{32} & a_{33} \end{bmatrix}$$

a_{mn} → Row, Column

a_{23} → 2nd Row, 3rd Column

a_{23} is called an entry or member of the matrix.

Rule To add or subtract matrices, you add or subtract corresponding entries or members. The two matrices must have the same dimensions.

EXAMPLE 5 Add.

$$\begin{bmatrix} 2 & 3 & 1 \\ 5 & 3 & -6 \end{bmatrix} + \begin{bmatrix} 10 & 5 & -1 \\ 6 & 3 & -2 \end{bmatrix}$$

$$\begin{bmatrix} 2+10 & 3+5 & 1+(-1) \\ 5+6 & 3+3 & -6+(-2) \end{bmatrix} = \begin{bmatrix} 12 & 8 & 0 \\ 11 & 6 & -8 \end{bmatrix}$$

EXAMPLE 6 Subtract.

$$\begin{bmatrix} 2 & 3 & 1 \\ 5 & 3 & -6 \end{bmatrix} - \begin{bmatrix} 10 & 5 & -1 \\ 6 & 3 & -2 \end{bmatrix}$$

$$\begin{bmatrix} 2-10 & 3-5 & 1-(-1) \\ 5-6 & 3-3 & -6-(-2) \end{bmatrix} = \begin{bmatrix} -8 & -2 & 2 \\ -1 & 0 & -4 \end{bmatrix}$$

Exercise A Write the dimension of each matrix.

1. $\begin{bmatrix} a & b \\ c & d \end{bmatrix}$ 2 × 2

2. $\begin{bmatrix} x & 1 & 2 \\ 7 & 3 & -\frac{1}{2} \end{bmatrix}$ 2 × 3

3. $[\,1 \quad 9 \quad \sqrt{2} \quad \pi\,]$ 1 × 4

4. $\begin{bmatrix} x & y \\ 3 & 5 \\ -1 & 2 \end{bmatrix}$ 3 × 2

5. $\begin{bmatrix} a_{11} & a_{12} & a_{13} & a_{14} \\ a_{21} & a_{22} & a_{23} & a_{24} \end{bmatrix}$ 2 × 4

through the first problem in each of the four exercise sets before assigning students to solve them independently.

3 Reinforce and Extend

LEARNING STYLES

LEP/ESL

There is a significant amount of new vocabulary associated with this lesson. Review the terms *matrix, matrices, row, column, entry, member,* and *dimension* with students who may have problems with learning new terms or associating the terms with a mathematical concept. Draw a matrix on the board and have students demonstrate their understanding of new vocabulary by identifying a row, a column, an entry, and the dimensions of the matrix.

COMMON ERROR

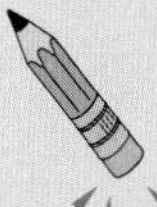

Students may confuse what number stands for the row and what number stands for the column in a matrix entry such as a_{37}. Tell students that they should always think of the location of an entry by its row and column (as opposed to column and row). That way they can remember first number is the row and the second number is the column.

Learning Styles

Body/Kinesthetic

Draw two matrices with the same dimensions on the board. Give a location, such as "row 4, column 5" and have students use their finger to move down to the row and across to the column and identify the entries in the location. Repeat this exercise with various locations. You can extend the activity by then having students add or subtract the corresponding entries in the two matrices.

6. row 2, column 2
7. row 5, column 1
8. row 6, column 4
9. row 9, column 9
10. row 6, column 3
11. row 1, column 7
12. row 1, column 1
13. row 2, column 8
14. row 4, column 4
15. row 7, column 2

Exercise B Give the row and column of each entry.

6. a_{22}
7. a_{51}
8. a_{64}
9. a_{99}
10. a_{63}
11. a_{17}
12. a_{11}
13. a_{28}
14. a_{44}
15. a_{72}

Exercise C Add.

16. $\begin{bmatrix} 1 & 2 \\ 3 & 4 \end{bmatrix} + \begin{bmatrix} -1 & 0 \\ 5 & -3 \end{bmatrix}$

17. $\begin{bmatrix} 5 & 1 & 6 \\ 2 & -1 & 0 \end{bmatrix} + \begin{bmatrix} 5 & 1 & 7 \\ 2 & -3 & -5 \end{bmatrix}$

18. $\begin{bmatrix} 3x & 3x & y \\ 7 & 6 & -3 \end{bmatrix} + \begin{bmatrix} x & -x & 2y \\ 6 & -7 & -5 \end{bmatrix}$

19. $\begin{bmatrix} 2 & \frac{1}{2} & 7 \\ 6 & 3 & 5 \\ 1 & 2 & 1 \end{bmatrix} + \begin{bmatrix} a & x & y \\ -7 & 4 & -5 \\ 2 & 3 & 7 \end{bmatrix}$

20. $\begin{bmatrix} 5 & 1 & 6 \\ \sqrt{2} & 7 & 3 \\ 9 & 1 & 6 \end{bmatrix} + \begin{bmatrix} 0 & 0 & 0 \\ 0 & 0 & 0 \\ 0 & 0 & 0 \end{bmatrix}$

16. $\begin{bmatrix} 0 & 2 \\ 8 & 1 \end{bmatrix}$

17. $\begin{bmatrix} 10 & 2 & 13 \\ 4 & -4 & -5 \end{bmatrix}$

18. $\begin{bmatrix} 4x & 2x & 3y \\ 13 & -1 & -8 \end{bmatrix}$

19. $\begin{bmatrix} 2+a & \frac{1}{2}+x & 7+y \\ -1 & 7 & 0 \\ 3 & 5 & 8 \end{bmatrix}$

20. $\begin{bmatrix} 5 & 1 & 6 \\ \sqrt{2} & 7 & 3 \\ 9 & 1 & 6 \end{bmatrix}$

Exercise D Subtract.

21. $\begin{bmatrix} 2 & 4 \\ 6 & 8 \end{bmatrix} - \begin{bmatrix} 3 & -1 \\ -2 & 0 \end{bmatrix}$

22. $\begin{bmatrix} -1 & 0 & 1 \\ -2 & 1 & -3 \end{bmatrix} - \begin{bmatrix} 4 & -1 & 1 \\ 0 & -1 & 3 \end{bmatrix}$

23. $\begin{bmatrix} x & 2x & y \\ 4 & 8 & 1 \end{bmatrix} - \begin{bmatrix} 2x & x & -y \\ 2 & -1 & 3 \end{bmatrix}$

24. $\begin{bmatrix} 3 & 1 & 6 \\ 0 & -5 & 2 \\ -3 & 2 & 4 \end{bmatrix} - \begin{bmatrix} a & b & c \\ 1 & 4 & -2 \\ 0 & 1 & 0 \end{bmatrix}$

25. $\begin{bmatrix} 8 & 9 & 20 & -6 \\ 0 & 23 & -15 & 4 \end{bmatrix} - \begin{bmatrix} 8 & -9 & 4 & 7 \\ 31 & 75 & 18 & 20 \end{bmatrix}$

21. $\begin{bmatrix} -1 & 5 \\ 8 & 8 \end{bmatrix}$

22. $\begin{bmatrix} -5 & 1 & 0 \\ -2 & 2 & -6 \end{bmatrix}$

23. $\begin{bmatrix} -x & x & 2y \\ 2 & 9 & -2 \end{bmatrix}$

24. $\begin{bmatrix} 3-a & 1-b & 6-c \\ -1 & -9 & 4 \\ -3 & 1 & 4 \end{bmatrix}$

25. $\begin{bmatrix} 0 & 18 & 16 & -13 \\ -31 & -52 & -33 & -16 \end{bmatrix}$

Learning Styles

Interpersonal/ Group Learning

If your class is set up with desks in rows, have small groups of students put together a matrix seating chart. Each student in the class is an "entry" or "member." Groups should create a matrix with students' names and locations. For example, Keesha $_{34}$ would mean that Keesha sits in the fourth desk in the third row.

Lesson at a Glance

Chapter 10 Lesson 10

Overview This lesson shows students how to multiply and find the product of two matrices.

Objectives

- To identify two matrices that can be multiplied together
- To find the product of two matrices

Student Pages 318–321

Teacher's Resource Library 

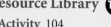

Workbook Activity 104

Activity 98

Alternative Activity 98

1 Warm-Up Activity

From the sports page, read a list of several final scores (some with the winning score first, some with the winning score second) and have students write the scores as you read them. After you've read five or six scores, ask students to describe how they wrote the scores down. (Most will write them down in the order they were given.) Ask students if it matters what order the scores were displayed to know which team won. (It doesn't matter.) Explain that in some situations the way numbers are displayed or ordered can make a big difference. For example, if the entries in two matrices are not displayed in a certain way, you cannot multiply them.

2 Teaching the Lesson

Explain that it is very simple to multiply a matrix by a single number. You just multiply each entry by the number. Multiplying a matrix by another matrix is much trickier, but if you follow the rules, it isn't difficult. Go through the section and examples about row x column multiplication with the class. Make sure students understand the concept of multiplying a row by a column. Their success at this skill depends on their fully understanding this concept. Move on to the section of the lesson about multiplying corresponding entries and adding the products. Go through the

Lesson 10 Multiplication of Matrices

To multiply a matrix by a number, simply multiply each entry by that number.

EXAMPLE 1 Let $A = \begin{bmatrix} 2 & 1 \\ 10 & -1 \end{bmatrix}$ Find $3A$.

$$③\begin{bmatrix} 2 & 1 \\ 10 & -1 \end{bmatrix} = ③A = \begin{bmatrix} ③ \cdot 2 & ③ \cdot 1 \\ ③ \cdot 10 & ③ (-1) \end{bmatrix} = \begin{bmatrix} 6 & 3 \\ 30 & -3 \end{bmatrix}$$

EXAMPLE 2

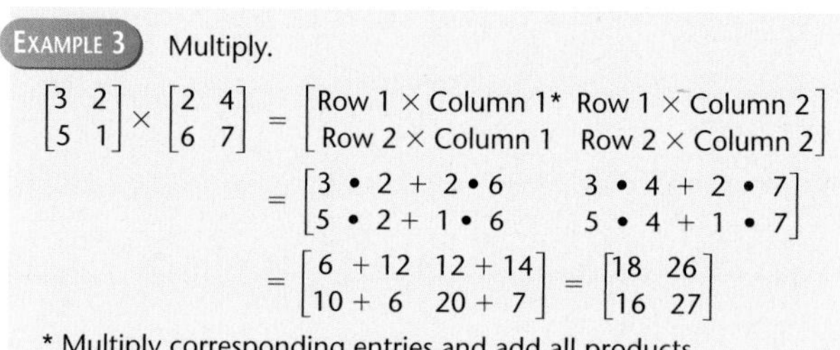

$$t\begin{bmatrix} a_{11} & a_{12} & a_{13} \dots a_{1n} \\ a_{21} & a_{22} & a_{23} \dots a_{2n} \\ a_{31} & a_{32} & a_{33} \dots a_{3n} \\ \cdot & \cdot & \cdot \quad \cdot \\ \cdot & \cdot & \cdot \quad \cdot \\ \cdot & \cdot & \cdot \quad \cdot \\ \cdot & \cdot & \cdot \quad \cdot \\ a_{m1} & a_{m2} & a_{m3} \dots a_{mn} \end{bmatrix} = \begin{bmatrix} ta_{11} & ta_{12} & ta_{13} \dots ta_{1n} \\ ta_{21} & ta_{22} & ta_{23} \dots ta_{2n} \\ ta_{31} & ta_{32} & ta_{33} \dots ta_{3n} \\ \cdot & \cdot & \cdot \quad \cdot \\ \cdot & \cdot & \cdot \quad \cdot \\ \cdot & \cdot & \cdot \quad \cdot \\ \cdot & \cdot & \cdot \quad \cdot \\ ta_{m1} & ta_{m2} & ta_{m3} \dots ta_{mn} \end{bmatrix}$$

To multiply a matrix by another matrix, you use row × column multiplication. Two matrices, A and B can be multiplied if the number of columns in A is the same as the number of rows in B. All square matrices of the same dimension can be multiplied.

EXAMPLE 3 Multiply.

$$\begin{bmatrix} 3 & 2 \\ 5 & 1 \end{bmatrix} \times \begin{bmatrix} 2 & 4 \\ 6 & 7 \end{bmatrix} = \begin{bmatrix} \text{Row 1} \times \text{Column 1*} & \text{Row 1} \times \text{Column 2} \\ \text{Row 2} \times \text{Column 1} & \text{Row 2} \times \text{Column 2} \end{bmatrix}$$

$$= \begin{bmatrix} 3 \cdot 2 + 2 \cdot 6 & 3 \cdot 4 + 2 \cdot 7 \\ 5 \cdot 2 + 1 \cdot 6 & 5 \cdot 4 + 1 \cdot 7 \end{bmatrix}$$

$$= \begin{bmatrix} 6 + 12 & 12 + 14 \\ 10 + 6 & 20 + 7 \end{bmatrix} = \begin{bmatrix} 18 & 26 \\ 16 & 27 \end{bmatrix}$$

* Multiply corresponding entries and add all products.

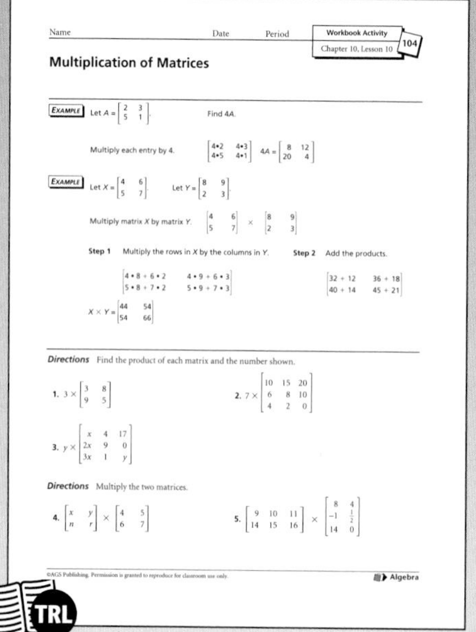

Name Date Period | Workbook Activity 104 | Chapter 10, Lesson 10

Multiplication of Matrices

EXAMPLE Let $A = \begin{bmatrix} 2 & 3 \\ 5 & 1 \end{bmatrix}$. Find $4A$.

Multiply each entry by 4. $\begin{bmatrix} 4 \cdot 2 & 4 \cdot 3 \\ 4 \cdot 5 & 4 \cdot 1 \end{bmatrix}$ $4A = \begin{bmatrix} 8 & 12 \\ 20 & 4 \end{bmatrix}$

EXAMPLE Let $X = \begin{bmatrix} 4 & 6 \\ 5 & 7 \end{bmatrix}$. Let $Y = \begin{bmatrix} 8 & 9 \\ 2 & 3 \end{bmatrix}$.

Multiply matrix X by matrix Y. $\begin{bmatrix} 4 & 6 \\ 5 & 7 \end{bmatrix} \times \begin{bmatrix} 8 & 9 \\ 2 & 3 \end{bmatrix}$

Step 1 Multiply the rows in X by the columns in Y. **Step 2** Add the products.

$\begin{bmatrix} 4 \cdot 8 + 6 \cdot 2 & 4 \cdot 9 + 6 \cdot 3 \\ 5 \cdot 8 + 7 \cdot 2 & 5 \cdot 9 + 7 \cdot 3 \end{bmatrix}$ $\begin{bmatrix} 32 + 12 & 36 + 18 \\ 40 + 14 & 45 + 21 \end{bmatrix}$

$X \times Y = \begin{bmatrix} 44 & 54 \\ 54 & 66 \end{bmatrix}$

Directions Find the product of each matrix and the number shown.

1. $3 \times \begin{bmatrix} 3 & 8 \\ 9 & 5 \end{bmatrix}$ **2.** $7 \times \begin{bmatrix} 10 & 15 & 20 \\ 6 & 8 & 10 \\ 4 & 2 & 0 \end{bmatrix}$

3. $y \times \begin{bmatrix} x & 4 & 17 \\ 2x & 9 & 0 \\ 3x & 1 & y \end{bmatrix}$

Directions Multiply the two matrices.

4. $\begin{bmatrix} x & y \\ n & r \end{bmatrix} \times \begin{bmatrix} 4 & 5 \\ 6 & 7 \end{bmatrix}$ **5.** $\begin{bmatrix} 9 & 10 & 11 \\ 14 & 15 & 16 \end{bmatrix} \times \begin{bmatrix} 8 & 4 \\ -1 & \frac{1}{2} \\ 14 & 0 \end{bmatrix}$

 Algebra

Workbook Activity 104

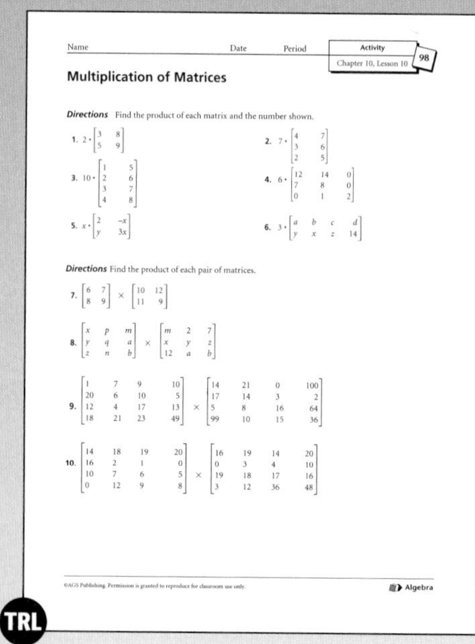

Name Date Period | Activity 98 | Chapter 10, Lesson 10

Multiplication of Matrices

Directions Find the product of each matrix and the number shown.

1. $2 \cdot \begin{bmatrix} 3 & 8 \\ 5 & 9 \end{bmatrix}$ **2.** $7 \cdot \begin{bmatrix} 4 & 7 \\ 3 & 6 \\ 2 & 5 \end{bmatrix}$

3. $10 \cdot \begin{bmatrix} 1 & 5 \\ 2 & 6 \\ 3 & 7 \\ 4 & 8 \end{bmatrix}$ **4.** $6 \cdot \begin{bmatrix} 12 & 14 & 0 \\ 7 & 8 & 0 \\ 0 & 1 & 2 \end{bmatrix}$

5. $x \cdot \begin{bmatrix} 2 & -x \\ y & 3x \end{bmatrix}$ **6.** $3 \cdot \begin{bmatrix} a & b & c & d \\ y & x & z & 14 \end{bmatrix}$

Directions Find the product of each pair of matrices.

7. $\begin{bmatrix} 6 & 7 \\ 8 & 9 \end{bmatrix} \times \begin{bmatrix} 10 & 12 \\ 11 & 9 \end{bmatrix}$

8. $\begin{bmatrix} x & p & m \\ y & q & a \\ z & n & b \end{bmatrix} \times \begin{bmatrix} m & 2 & 7 \\ x & y & z \\ 12 & a & b \end{bmatrix}$

9. $\begin{bmatrix} 1 & 7 & 9 & 10 \\ 20 & 6 & 10 & 5 \\ 12 & 4 & 17 & 13 \\ 18 & 21 & 23 & 49 \end{bmatrix} \times \begin{bmatrix} 14 & 21 & 0 & 100 \\ 17 & 14 & 3 & 2 \\ 5 & 8 & 16 & 64 \\ 99 & 10 & 15 & 36 \end{bmatrix}$

10. $\begin{bmatrix} 14 & 18 & 19 & 20 \\ 16 & 2 & 1 & 0 \\ 10 & 7 & 6 & 5 \\ 0 & 12 & 9 & 8 \end{bmatrix} \times \begin{bmatrix} 16 & 19 & 14 & 20 \\ 0 & 3 & 4 & 10 \\ 19 & 18 & 17 & 16 \\ 3 & 12 & 36 & 48 \end{bmatrix}$

 Algebra

Activity 98

EXAMPLE 4 Multipy.

$$A_{23} \times B_{32} = \begin{bmatrix} 2 & x & y \\ -1 & 0 & 5 \end{bmatrix} \times \begin{bmatrix} 1 & x \\ 2 & y \\ 3 & z \end{bmatrix}$$

$$= \begin{bmatrix} \text{Row 1} \times \text{Column 1*} & \text{Row 1} \times \text{Column 2} \\ \text{Row 2} \times \text{Column 1} & \text{Row 2} \times \text{Column 2} \end{bmatrix}$$

$$= \begin{bmatrix} 2 \bullet 1 + x \bullet 2 + y \bullet 3 & 2 \bullet x + x \bullet y + y \bullet z \\ -1 \bullet 1 + 0 \bullet 2 + 5 \bullet 3 & -1 \bullet x + 0 \bullet y + 5 \bullet z \end{bmatrix}$$

$$= \begin{bmatrix} 2 + 2x + 3y & 2x + xy + yz \\ -1 + 0 + 15 & -x + 0 + 5z \end{bmatrix}$$

$$= \begin{bmatrix} 2 + 2x + 3y & 2x + xy + yz \\ 14 & -x + 5z \end{bmatrix}$$

* Multiply corresponding entries and add all products.

Note: A_{23} times $B_{32} = C_{22}$ $\qquad A_{23} \times B_{32} = C_{22}$

Product Matrix

In general: A_{mn} times $B_{np} = C_{mp}$ $\qquad A_{mn} \times B_{np} = C_{mp}$

Product Matrix

Each entry in a matrix contains two pieces of information:

- First, a number or a symbol.
- Second, a location within the matrix.

A business can use this information to evaluate its inventory.

EXAMPLE 5 The price of canned goods per one can is given in matrix *A*. The number of cans of each product on the shelf is shown in matrix *B*. $A \times B$ = Total dollar value of the items on the shelf.

A_{13} = [\$1.29/can of peas \$2.19/can of carrots \$0.98/can of lentils]

= [1.29 2.19 0.98]

$$B_{31} = \begin{bmatrix} \text{10 cans of peas} \\ \text{15 cans of carrots} \\ \text{25 cans of lentils} \end{bmatrix} = \begin{bmatrix} 10 \\ 15 \\ 25 \end{bmatrix}$$

Note: the position denotes the correct price.

examples thoroughly, because the process can be confusing, although the actual computations are relatively simple.

3 Reinforce and Extend

COMMON ERROR

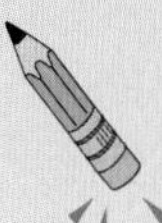

Remind students that they must add all the products of the corresponding entries. This step is often overlooked by students learning to multiply matrices.

LEARNING STYLES

Body/Kinesthetic

Use the example about pricing cans on the shelf (or a similar example) and set up an actual physical matrix with various items on shelves. Create another matrix with prices. Have students physically take an entry from price the matrix and match it to the entry in on the shelf. You can reinforce the concept of adding products by having more than one item in a location.

In the Community

Invite a computer programmer from a local company to come to the class and talk about the ways companies set up various matrices for pricing products, tracking sales, calculating sales commissions, and so on. Have the programmer explain how they set up databases that are matrices. If possible, have the programmer bring printouts of reports or other examples of how matrices are used.

Example 5 *Continued*

$A_{13} \times B_{31}$ = Product Matrix$_{11}$ which will give the total dollar value of the three types of canned vegetables on the shelf.

$$[1.29 \;\; 2.19 \;\; 0.98] \times \begin{bmatrix} 10 \\ 15 \\ 25 \end{bmatrix} = [(1.29)(10) + (2.19)(15) + (0.98)(25)]$$

$$= 12.90 + 32.85 + 24.50$$

$$= 70.25$$

The total value of the canned goods is $70.25.

Exercise A Multiply.

1. $3\begin{bmatrix} 16 & 0 \\ 5 & 1 \end{bmatrix}$

2. $x\begin{bmatrix} 3 & 5 & x \\ 1 & 2 & y \end{bmatrix}$

3. $7\begin{bmatrix} x & y \\ 3 & 15 \end{bmatrix}$

4. $(ab)\begin{bmatrix} 1 & x & a \\ -3 & y & 0 \\ b & z & -a \end{bmatrix}$

5. $y^2\begin{bmatrix} 3x & -x & a \\ 4 & 14 & 0 \\ -6 & 10 & -y^2 \\ y & 1 & xy \end{bmatrix}$

1. $\begin{bmatrix} 48 & 0 \\ 15 & 3 \end{bmatrix}$

2. $\begin{bmatrix} 3x & 5x & x^2 \\ x & 2x & xy \end{bmatrix}$

3. $\begin{bmatrix} 7x & 7y \\ 21 & 105 \end{bmatrix}$

4. $\begin{bmatrix} ab & abx & a^2b \\ -3ab & aby & 0 \\ ab^2 & abz & -a^2b \end{bmatrix}$

5. $\begin{bmatrix} 3xy^2 & -xy^2 & ay^2 \\ 4y^2 & 14y^2 & 0 \\ -6y^2 & 10y^2 & -y^4 \\ y^3 & y^2 & xy^3 \end{bmatrix}$

Exercise B Multiply.

6. $\begin{bmatrix} a & b \\ c & d \end{bmatrix} \times \begin{bmatrix} 2 & 3 \\ 4 & 5 \end{bmatrix}$ $\begin{bmatrix} 2a + 4b & 3a + 5b \\ 2c + 4d & 3c + 5d \end{bmatrix}$

7. $\begin{bmatrix} 1 & 0 & 2 \\ 1 & 1 & 6 \\ 3 & 2 & 1 \end{bmatrix} \times \begin{bmatrix} 1 & 0 & 0 \\ 0 & 1 & 0 \\ 0 & 0 & 1 \end{bmatrix}$ $\begin{bmatrix} 1 & 0 & 2 \\ 1 & 1 & 6 \\ 3 & 2 & 1 \end{bmatrix}$

8. $\begin{bmatrix} 3 & -2 & x \\ \frac{1}{2} & 5 & 6 \\ 7 & 10 & y \end{bmatrix} \times \begin{bmatrix} x & 4 & -1 \\ 11 & 5 & 3 \\ 20 & y & \frac{1}{4} \end{bmatrix}$ $\begin{bmatrix} 23x - 22 & 2 + xy & \frac{1}{4}x - 9 \\ \frac{1}{2}x + 175 & 27 + 6y & 16 \\ 7x + 110 + 2y & 78 + y^2 & 23 + \frac{1}{4}y \end{bmatrix}$

PROBLEM SOLVING

Exercise C

9. Show that $A \times B \neq B \times A$.

Let $A = \begin{bmatrix} 1 & 2 \\ 3 & 4 \end{bmatrix}$ $B = \begin{bmatrix} 1 & 0 \\ -1 & 1 \end{bmatrix}$ $AB = \begin{bmatrix} -1 & 2 \\ -1 & 4 \end{bmatrix}$ $BA = \begin{bmatrix} 1 & 2 \\ 2 & 2 \end{bmatrix}$

10. Al sells three different brands of sparkplugs. Quick Start sparkplugs cost $11.60 per box. Power Up sparkplugs cost $18.50 per box. Ultimate sparkplugs cost $42.00 per box. There are 17 boxes of Quick Start sparkplugs on the top shelf, 20 boxes of Power Up sparkplugs on the middle shelf, and 8 boxes of Ultimate spark plugs on the bottom shelf. Set up a matrix for the price of the sparkplugs and another matrix for the number of boxes and location of the sparkplugs. Multiply the two matrices to find the value of Al's sparkplug inventory. $903.20

Lesson at a Glance

Chapter 10 Application

Overview This lesson introduces Venn diagrams

Objective

- To use Venn diagrams to model and solve problems

Student Page 322

Teacher's Resource Library 

Application Activity 10

Everyday Algebra 10

1 Warm-Up Activity

Explain that in mathematics, it is important that every set be well-defined and not vague or ambiguous in any way. Write the following phrases on the board:

The set of interesting books.
The set of pennies in circulation.
The set of cities in a state.
The set of months in a year.
The set of people in a city.

Invite students to provide reasons why each set is or is not well-defined.

2 Teaching the Lesson

Explain that a set is a collection or group of objects. The objects in any set are known as elements, or members of the set. The universal set (***U***), or universe, is the set of all of the elements that are being considered. A Venn diagram consists of one or more subsets of the universal set.

Common Error

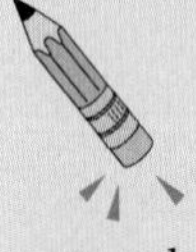

Students sometimes fail to check an answer that was generated using a Venn diagram. Explain that one way to check an answer is to count the number of unique members of each subset. This sum should be equal to the number of members in the universe.

Answer to Problem 2

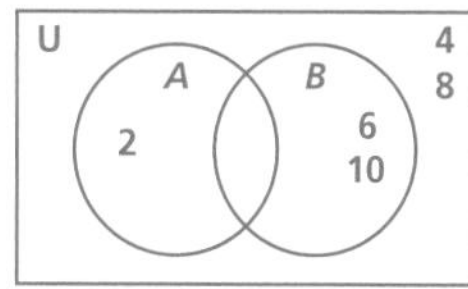

Application

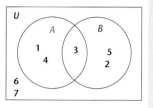

Using Venn Diagrams

Venn diagrams represent one of the most common applications of conjunction and disjunction. A Venn diagram is a way to illustrate ideas in logic.

Example 1 A Venn diagram consists of a universal set and various subsets. In this Venn diagram, the universal set U contains the integers 1–7. Subset A contains the integers 1, 3, and 4. Subset B contains the integers 2, 3, and 5.

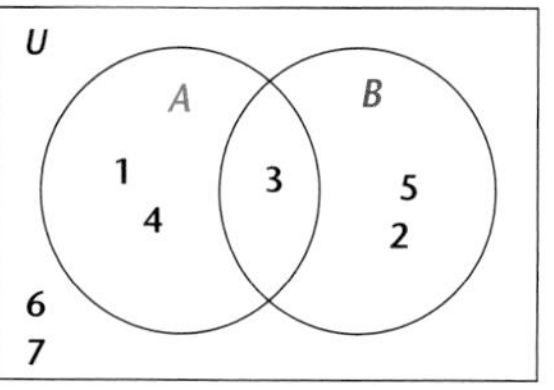

The union of sets A and B is written $A \cup B$ and represents the set of all elements in A or in B or in both A and B. In this Venn diagram, $A \cup B = \{1, 2, 3, 4, 5\}$.

The intersection of sets A and B is written $A \cap B$ and represents the set of all elements common to both A and B. In this Venn diagram, $A \cap B = \{3\}$.

A set that contains no elements is called an *empty set*, or *null set*. The symbol $\varnothing$ or { } is used to designate the empty set.

Exercise Find the answer to each problem.

1. Use the Venn diagram to find U, $A \cup B$, and $A \cap B$.

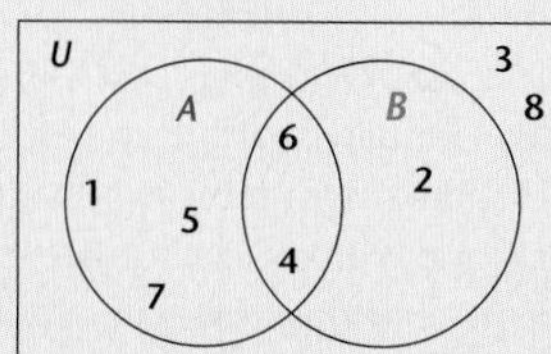

$U = \{1, 2, 3, 4, 5, 6, 7, 8\}$; $A \cup B = \{1, 2, 4, 5, 6, 7\}$; $A \cap B = \{4, 6\}$

2. Draw a Venn diagram that displays these elements: $U = \{2, 4, 6, 8, 10\}$, $A \cup B = \{2, 6, 10\}$, and $A \cap B = \varnothing$.
3. How many different Venn diagrams can be drawn to show $U = \{1, 2, 3\}$, $A \cup B = \{1, 2, 3\}$, and $A \cap B = \varnothing$? 8
4. A survey of 24 high school freshmen found that 13 of the students surveyed were taking mathematics and science courses, 0 students were taking science and no mathematics, and 9 students were taking mathematics and no science. How many students were not taking a science or a mathematics course? two students
5. Given A = the set of all the letters in your first name, and B = all the letters in your last name, what is U? $A \cup B$? $A \cap B$? Answers will vary.

See Teacher's Edition page for the answer to problem 2.

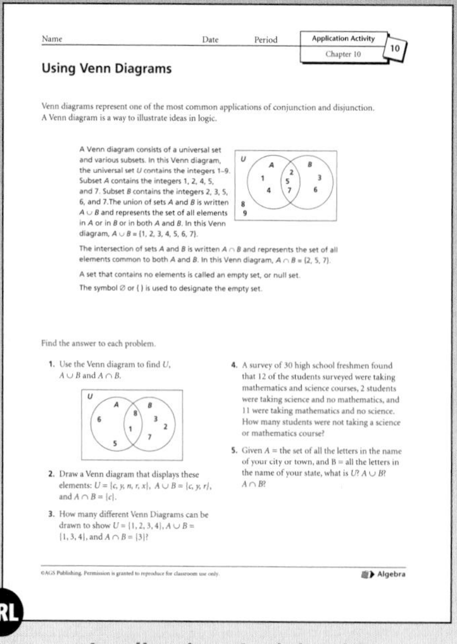

Name Date Period **Application Activity 10** Chapter 10

Using Venn Diagrams

Venn diagrams represent one of the most common applications of conjunction and disjunction. A Venn diagram is a way to illustrate ideas in logic.

A Venn diagram consists of a universal set and various subsets. In this Venn diagram, the universal set U contains the integers 1–9. Subset A contains the integers 1, 2, 4, 5, and 7. Subset B contains the integers 2, 3, 5, 6, and 7. The union of sets A and B is written $A \cup B$ and represents the set of all elements in A or in B or in both A and B. In this Venn diagram, $A \cup B = \{1, 2, 3, 4, 5, 6, 7\}$.

The intersection of sets A and B is written $A \cap B$ and represents the set of all elements common to both A and B. In this Venn diagram, $A \cap B = \{2, 5, 7\}$.

A set that contains no elements is called an empty set, or null set.

The symbol $\varnothing$ or { } is used to designate the empty set.

Find the answer to each problem.

1. Use the Venn diagram to find U, $A \cup B$ and $A \cap B$.
2. Draw a Venn diagram that displays these elements: $U = \{c, y, n, r, x\}$, $A \cup B = \{c, y, r\}$, and $A \cap B = \{c\}$.
3. How many different Venn Diagrams can be drawn to show $U = \{1, 2, 3, 4\}$, $A \cup B = \{1, 3, 4\}$, and $A \cap B = \{3\}$?
4. A survey of 30 high school freshmen found that 12 of the students surveyed were taking mathematics and science courses, 2 students were taking science and no mathematics, and 11 were taking mathematics and no science. How many students were not taking a science or mathematics course?
5. Given A = the set of all the letters in the name of your city or town, and B = all the letters in the name of your state, what is U? $A \cup B$? $A \cap B$?

 Algebra

TRL **Application Activity 10**

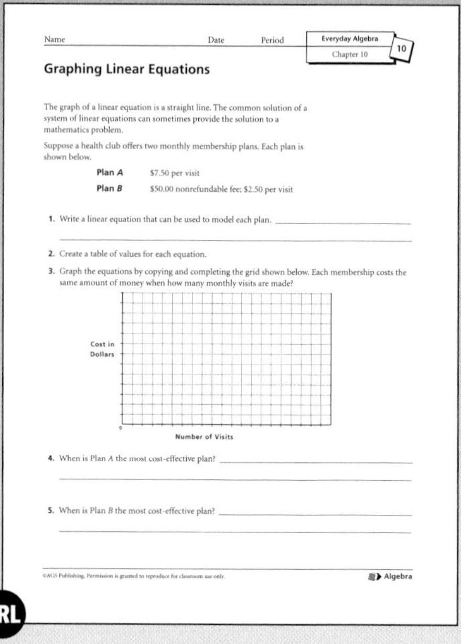

Name Date Period **Everyday Algebra 10** Chapter 10

Graphing Linear Equations

The graph of a linear equation is a straight line. The common solution of a system of linear equations can sometimes provide the solution to a mathematics problem.

Suppose a health club offers two monthly membership plans. Each plan is shown below.

Plan *A* $7.50 per visit

Plan *B* $50.00 nonrefundable fee; $2.50 per visit

1. Write a linear equation that can be used to model each plan.
2. Create a table of values for each equation.
3. Graph the equations by copying and completing the grid shown below. Each membership costs the same amount of money when how many monthly visits are made?

Cost in Dollars — 0 — Number of Visits

4. When is Plan A the most cost-effective plan?
5. When is Plan B the most cost-effective plan?

 Algebra

TRL **Everyday Algebra 10**

Chapter 10 REVIEW

Find the point of intersection for each pair of equations. Write the letter of the correct answer.

1. $y = 2x - 2 \quad y = x + 1$ C

A $(4, 3)$ C $(3, 4)$

B $(1, 2)$ D $(0, 0)$

2. $y = x + 4 \quad y = 3x$ B

A $(-2, 3)$ C $(0, -2)$

B $(2, 6)$ D $(3, 2)$

3. $y = 2x + 1 \quad y = x + 1$ C

A $(\frac{-1}{2}, 0)$ C $(0, 1)$

B $(0, 2)$ D $(-2, 2)$

Set up and solve a system of equations to answer the questions. Write the letter of the correct answer.

4. One number is six more than another number. Four times the smaller number is the same as three times the larger number. What are the unknown numbers? A

A 18 and 24 C 3 and 4

B 9 and15 D 18 and 10

5. Two angles are supplementary. (Their sum = 180°.) The larger angle is 90° more than the smaller angle. What are the measurements of the angles? D

A 45° and 45° C 90° and 45°

B 65° and 115° D 135° and 45°

6. Andy is three years younger than Bobby. When their ages are added together, the sum is 23. How old is Bobby? C

A 10 years old C 13 years old

B 12 years old D 23 years old

Name Date Period | Mastery Test A, Page 1 | Chapter 10

Chapter 10 Mastery Test A

Directions Circle the letter of the correct answer.

1. Find the slope of a line parallel to the line $-3x = 4y - 2$.

A $m = \frac{1}{2}$ C $m = \frac{-3}{4}$

B $m = -3$ D $m = -2$

2. Choose the equation of the line parallel to the line that passes $x - 2$ that passes through the point $(0, 4)$.

A $y = x + 4$ C $y = x + 2$

B $y = 4x - 2$ D $y = 2x + 4$

3. Choose the equation of the line parallel to the line $5 = -10x - 5y$ that passes through the point $(-2, 5)$.

A $y = -2x + 1$ C $y = x - 5$

B $y = -12x + 5$ D $y = 5x + 11$

4. Find a common solution for the system of equations $y = 3x + 5$ and $y = -5x - 3$.

A $(3, -2)$ C $(1, 5)$

B $(-1, 2)$ D $(-1, -5)$

5. Find a common solution for the system of equations $-3y + x = 9$ and $6x + y = -3$.

A $(1, -4)$ C $(0, -3)$

B $(-3, 0)$ D $(2, -6)$

Directions Find a common solution for each system of equations.

6. $y = x - 1$
$y = 2x - 5$ ______

7. $x = -5y$
$x + y = 8$ ______

 Algebra

TRL

Name Date Period | Mastery Test A, Page 2 | Chapter 10

Chapter 10 Mastery Test A, continued

Directions On a coordinate system on graph paper, graph each system of equations on the same set of axes. Name the point of intersection.

8. $y = 2x - 1$
$y = x + 1$ ______

9. $-2x = -2y - 4$
$-6 = 3y - 6x$ ______

Directions Tell whether the following conjunctions are *true* or *false*.

10. A line with a slope of zero is parallel to the x-axis, and a line with an undefined slope is parallel to the y-axis.

______

11. Multiplying a number n by the reciprocal of 3 is the same as $\frac{x}{3}$, and all integers divided by zero equal zero.

______

12. All parallel lines have the same slope, and not all systems of equations have a common solution.

______

Directions Solve.

13. The perimeter of a rectangle is 120 feet. The width of the rectangle is equal to one-half the length. Find the length and width of the rectangle.

______

14. The area of a rectangle is 576 m^2. The length of the rectangle is 4 times greater than the width. What are the length and width of the rectangle?

______

15. One integer is 8 less than another integer. The product of the lesser integer and −5 is 28 more than the greater integer. What are the integers?

______

 Algebra

TRL

Chapter 10 Mastery Test A

Reinforce and Extend

CAREER CONNECTION

Ask students to think of jobs or careers in which a knowledge of sets and subsets might help people perform their work more efficiently. An example would be catering. Suggest that students look at help-wanted ads, search the Internet, and ask family members and friends for jobs or careers to consider.

Chapter 10 Review

Each set of problems in the Chapter Review includes an example and solution to illustrate the concept. Use the given examples for reteaching the materials in Chapter 10. For additional practice, refer to the Supplementary Problems for Chapter 10 (pages 424–425).

MANIPULATIVES

Modeling Equations

Materials: Pattern Blocks, Unit Cubes, two copies of Manipulatives Master 5 (Basic Sentence Mat) for each student

Group Practice: Review procedures for solving systems of equations from the Chapter 10, Lessons 4 and 5 Manipulatives activities. Show students how to evaluate a system to determine which method would be better to use.

Student Practice: Have students use models to solve systems of equations or to check their work in Chapter Review Problems 11–13, 16–18, and 20 using either method.

Chapter 10 Mastery Test 

The Teacher's Resource Library includes parallel forms of the Chapter 10 Mastery Test. The difficulty level of the two forms is equivalent. You may wish to use one form as a pretest and the other form as a posttest.

Alternative Assessment

Alternative Assessment items correlate with student Goals for Learning at the beginning of this chapter.

■ **To write and solve equations for parallel lines**
Have students choose a word or acronym of at least three letters, such as NBA or FBI. Have students draw this word on a graph using a ruler and have them use block lettering so that only straight lines are on the graph. Ask students to determine how many parallel lines there are. For NBA, you will have 4 vertical and 4 horizontal lines, and possibly 2 diagonal parallel lines—depending on how you draw the N and the A.

■ **To determine whether a system of equations has a common solution**
Have students explain how to determine if a system of equations has a common solution without graphing. *(If the slope of the equations is the same, there is no common solution because the lines are parallel. If the slope is different, there is a common solution because at some point the lines will intersect.)*

■ **To use substitution or elimination to find the common solution for a system of equations**
Have students explain how they determine when to use substitution and when to use elimination to solve equations. *(Substitution is usually the method to choose when there is a simple substitution for one of the variables, such as in the system $a + b = 200$ and $2a + 4b = 500$. It is easy to solve the first equation for a or b and substitute that value in the second equation.)*

■ **To graph equations to find the common solution**
Have students graph systems of equations and, using the graph, determine the solution to the system. Additional systems of equations in the Supplementary Problems are in the back of the textbook. Substitute the solution into the equation and check algebraically.

Write the equation of the line parallel to the given line and passing through the given point. Check your answer by graphing the lines.

Example: $y = 3x + 2$; $(0, 5)$ Solution: $y = mx + b$, $5 = 3(0) + b$, $b = 5$, so parallel line is $y = 3x + 5$

7. $y = 2x - 5$; $(0, 10)$ $y = 2x + 10$

8. $y = -\frac{1}{3}x$; $(0, -3)$ $y = -\frac{1}{3}x - 3$

9. $2y = x + 2$; $(0, 4)$ $y = \frac{1}{2}x + 4$ or $2y = x + 8$

10. $y = 2x - 3$; $(6, 2)$ $y = 2x - 10$

11. $y = 3x$; $(3, 6)$ $y = 3x - 3$

12. $y = 2x - 6$; $(1, 1)$ $y = 2x - 1$

Find a common solution for each system.

Example: $y = 2x + 4$, $y = x - 2$ Solution: $x - 2 = 2x + 4$, $-2 = x + 4$, $-6 = x$; $y = 2x + 4$, $y = 2(-6) + 4$, $y = -12 + 4$, $y = -8$; $(-6, -8)$

13. $y = x - 2$, $y = \frac{1}{2}x$ $(4, 2)$

14. $8 + 2x = y$, $y = x + 2$ $(-6, -4)$

15. $x = 3y$, $3x = y + 8$ $(3, 1)$

16. $3y = x - 1$, $6y = x$ $(2, \frac{1}{3})$

17. $x = 5y + 5$, $x + 2y = 10$ $(8\frac{4}{7}, \frac{5}{7})$

18. $2y = 5x - 1$, $3x = y + 3$ $(5, 12)$

Name Date Period | Mastery Test B, Page 1 | Chapter 10

Chapter 10 Mastery Test B

Directions Circle the letter of the correct answer.

1. Choose the equation of the line parallel to the line $y = 4x - 2$ that passes through the point $(0, 4)$.
A $y = x + 4$ **B** $y = 4x + 4$ **C** $y = x + 2$ **D** $y = 2x + 4$

2. Find a common solution for the system of equations $-3y + 12x = 9$ and $x - y = 0$.
A $(-1, 1)$ **B** $(2, 3)$ **C** $(1, 1)$ **D** $(-2, 3)$

3. Find the slope of a line parallel to the line $-x = 2y + 5$.
A $m = \frac{-1}{2}$ **B** $m = -1$ **C** $m = 2$ **D** $m = -2$

4. Choose the equation of the line parallel to the line $5 = -10x - 10y$ that passes through the point $(-2, 1)$.
A $y = -2x + 1$ **B** $y = -10x + 5$ **C** $y = -x - 1$ **D** $y = 5x + 10$

5. Find a common solution for the system of equations $y = 3$ and $y = 3x - 3$.
A $(3, 2)$ **B** $(2, 3)$ **C** $(-3, 1)$ **D** $(-2, -3)$

Directions Find a common solution for each system of equations.

6. $y = x + 1$, $y = 3x - 2$ ______

7. $y = -3y$, $x + y = 6$ ______

 Algebra

TRL

Name Date Period | Mastery Test B, Page 2 | Chapter 10

Chapter 10 Mastery Test B, continued

Directions On a coordinate system on graph paper, graph each system of equations on the same set of axes. Name the point of intersection.

8. $y = 3x + 1$, $y = x - 1$ ______

9. $-x = -3y - 6$, $-4 = 2y - 8x$ ______

Directions Tell whether the following conjunctions are *true* or *false*.

10. A line with a slope of zero is parallel to the x-axis, and a line with an undefined slope is parallel to the y-axis. ______

11. Multiplying a number n by the reciprocal of 3 is the same as $\frac{x}{3}$, and all integers divided by zero equal zero. ______

12. All parallel lines have the same slope, and not all systems of equations have a common solution. ______

Directions Solve.

18. The perimeter of a rectangle is 180 feet. The width of the rectangle is equal to one-half the length. Find the length and width of the rectangle. ______

19. The area of a rectangle is 256 m^2. The length of the rectangle is 4 times greater than the width. What are the length and width of the rectangle? ______

20. One integer is 6 less than another integer. The product of the lesser integer and -7 is 42 more than the greater integer. What are the integers? ______

 Algebra

TRL

Chapter 10 Mastery Test B

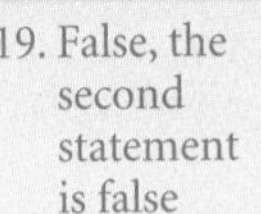

19. False, the second statement is false
20. True, both statements are true
21. False, both statements are false
22. False, the second statement is false

Tell whether the following conjunctions are true or false. Explain.

Example: Two dimes = 30¢, and two pennies = 2¢.
Solution: False, the first statement is false. Two dimes = 20¢.

19. All parallel lines have the same slope, and all vertical lines have a slope of 1.

20. Dividing by $\frac{6}{7}$ is the same as multiplying by $\frac{7}{6}$, and $3\frac{1}{2}$ has the same value as $\frac{14}{4}$.

21. $x^a \cdot x^b = x^{a \cdot b}$, and $4\frac{1}{3}$ has the same value as $\frac{5}{3}$.

22. All weeks have seven days, and all months have 30 days.

Set up and solve a system of equations to answer questions 23–25. Check your answers.

Example: Tom is 2 times plus 1 year older than his sister. The difference in their ages is 5 years. How old is Tom? How old is his sister?
Solution: Let x = the sister's age and y = Tom's age.

$y = 2x + 1$
$y - x = 5$ or $y = 5 + x$
$5 + x = 2x + 1$
$4 = x$

The sister is 4 years old so Tom is 2(4) + 1 = 9 years old.
Check: 9 − 4 = 5. True 9 = 2 • 4 + 1 True

23. The difference between two complementary angles is 34°. What are the angles? (Complementary angles are angles whose sum = 90°.) 62° and 28°

24. The perimeter of a rectangle is 200 ft. The width of the rectangle is 20 ft less than the length. What is the length and width of the rectangle? length = 60 ft, width = 40 ft

25. Markette is 4 years older than Earlene. Earlene's age is $\frac{4}{5}$ Markette's age. What are their ages?
Markette is 20; Earlene is 16.

Test-Taking Tip

When you read word problems, watch for numbers that are written in word form.

Answers to Problems 21–23

21.

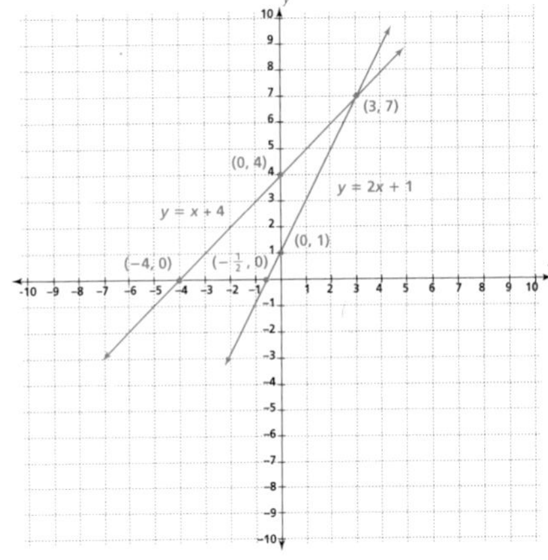

22.

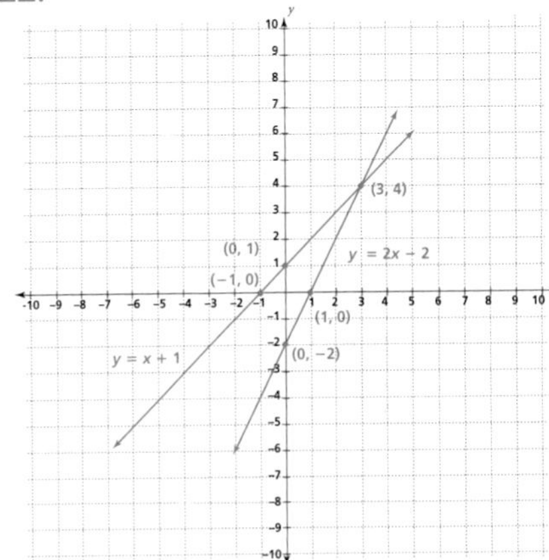

23.

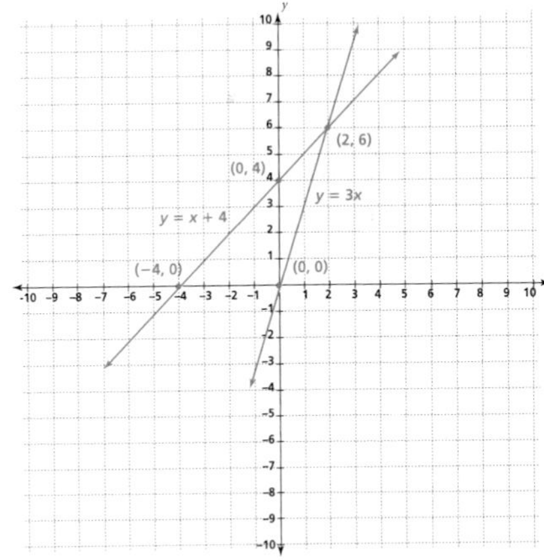

■ To evaluate conjunctions

Separate students into groups of three. Direct each student to draw a graph of two linear equations. (Example: eI: $x = 3$ and eII: $y = x + 2$) Then have students pass their graphs to the group member on their right. This person must create a conjunction table with three rows of *and* statements. Last, have students pass the graph with the table to the third person in the group who determines if the conjunctions are true or false. Example:

p	∧	q	p∧q
Example of *p* statement: (0, 3) lies on eI *(false)*	and	Example of *q* statement: When $x = 0$, $y = 2$ in eII *(true)*	*(false)*

■ To solve problems using systems of linear equations

Have student volunteers come to the board to translate portions of word problems into algebraic expressions. Do this until the entire word problem is completed. Then have the whole class find the solution individually. Example: Teacher says, "Together, Josh and Aaron are 26 years old." Student translates: $a + j = 26$. Teacher says, "Aaron is 2 years older than Josh." Student translates: $a - 2 = j$. Teacher asks, "How old is Josh?" Students solve on paper for the solution, which in this example is 12. Note: Several similar problems are in the Supplementary Problems section in the back of the textbook, or you can create your own.

Chapter

Planning Guide

Irrational Numbers and Radical Expressions

		Student Pages	Vocabulary	Practice Exercises	Solutions Key
		Student Text Lesson			
Lesson 1	Rational Numbers as Decimals	328–331	✔	✔	✔
Lesson 2	Rational Number Equivalents	332–333		✔	✔
Lesson 3	Irrational Numbers as Decimals	334–335	✔	✔	✔
Lesson 4	Products of Quotients and Radicals	336–337		✔	✔
Lesson 5	Sums and Differences of Radicals	338–339		✔	✔
Lesson 6	Radicals and Fractions	340–341	✔	✔	✔
Lesson 7	Radicals in Equations	342–345		✔	✔
Lesson 8	Radicals and Exponents	346–347	✔	✔	✔
Lesson 9	Drawing and Using a Square Root Graph	348–349		✔	✔
Application	Falling Objects and Soaring Rockets	350		✔	✔

Chapter Activities

Teacher's Resource Library

Estimation Exercise 11: Estimating the Dimensions of a Square Given Its Area

Application Activity 11: Falling Objects and Soaring Rockets

Everyday Algebra 11: Converting Measurements

Community Connection 11: Measurement Conversion

Teacher's Edition

Chapter 11 Project

Assessment Options

Student Text

Chapter 11 Review

Teacher's Resource Library

Chapter 11 Mastery Tests A and B

Student Text Features							Teaching Strategies							Learning Styles						Teacher's Resource Library			
Estimation Activity	Algebra in Your Life	Technology Connection	Writing About Mathematics	Try This	Problem Solving	Calculator Practice	Online Connection	Common Error	Applications Home, Career, Community	Mental Math	Manipulatives	Calculator	Group Problem Solving	Auditory/Verbal	Visual/Spatial	Logical/Mathematical	Body/Kinesthetic	Interpersonal/Group Learning	LEP/ESL	Activities	Alternate Activities	Workbook Activities	Self-Study Guide
	331			331	331	330		329	330			331	331						330	99	99	105	✔
		333						333							333				333	100	100	106	✔
					335		335			335			335							101	101	107	✔
				337				337		337										102	102	108	✔
			339	339				339						339					339	103	103	109	✔
								341					341							104	104	110	✔
345					344				342, 343				343				343			105	105	111–112	✔
						347						347				347				106	106	113	✔
										349		349								107	107	114	✔
									351									350					✔

Software Options

Skill Track Software

Use the Skill Track Software for *Algebra* for additional reinforcement of this chapter. The software provides multiple-choice assessment items for students to access by computer.

Solutions Key

Use the Solutions Key with this chapter to help students who may need additional assistance. The Solutions Key CD provides solutions for every exercise in the student edition.

Other Resources

Alternative Activities

The Teacher's Resource Library (TRL) contains a set of worksheets written at a second-grade reading level called Alternative Activities. They cover the same content as the regular Activities.

Chapter at a Glance

Chapter 11: Irrational Numbers and Radical Expressions

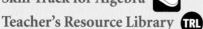

pages 326–353

(Answer Keys for the Teacher's Resource Library begin on page 530 of this Teacher's Edition.)

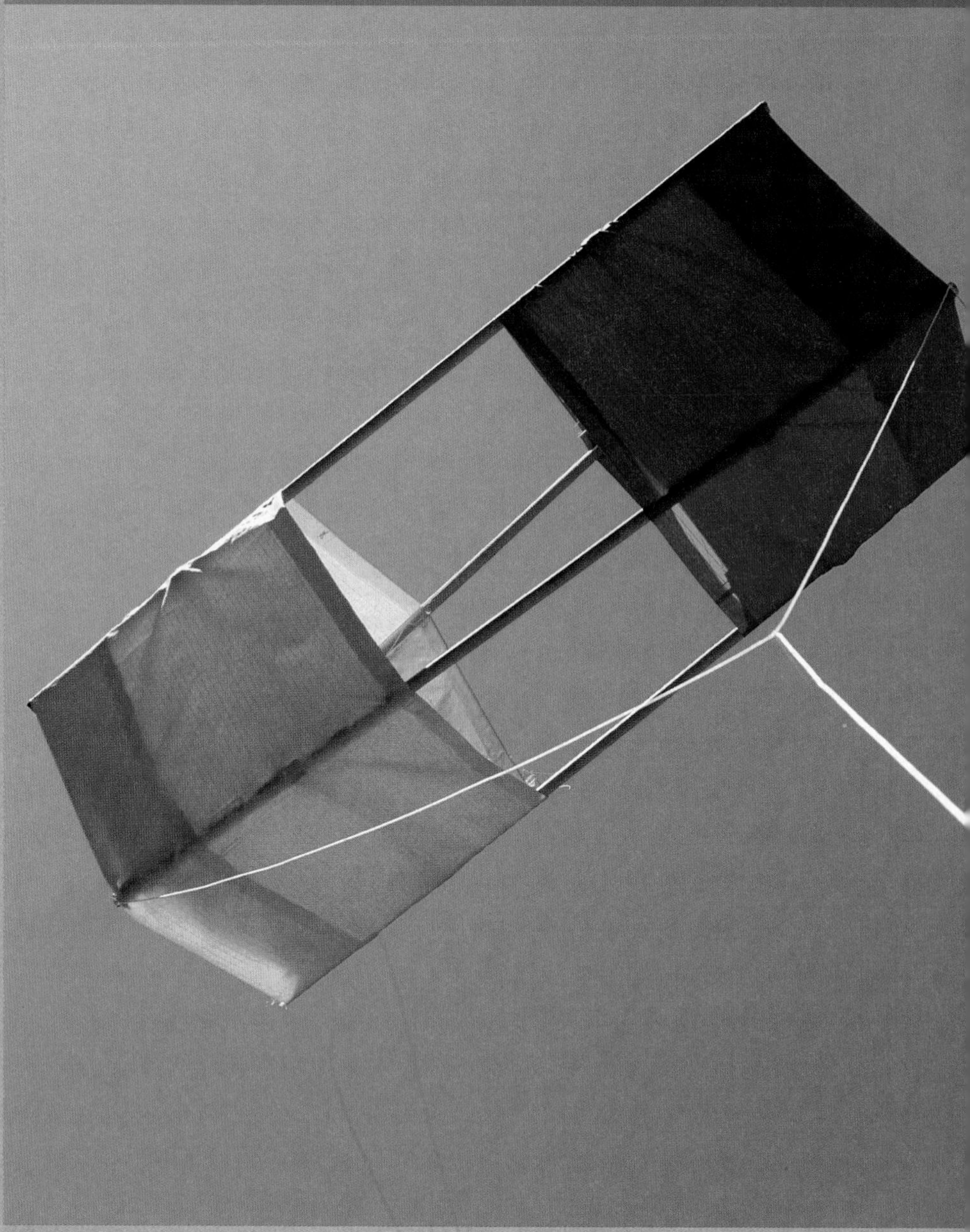

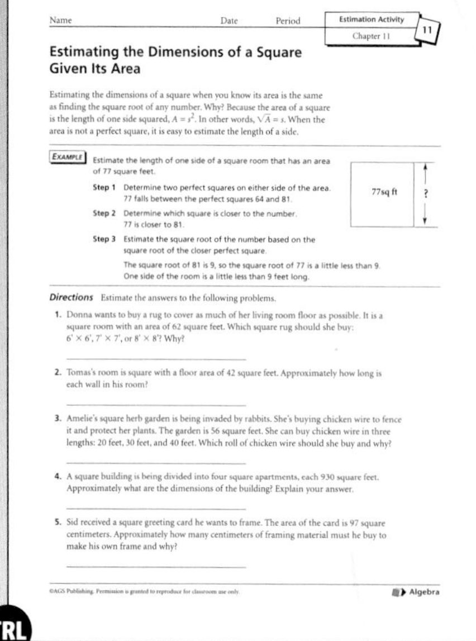

Name Date Period | Estimation Activity 11 | Chapter 11

Estimating the Dimensions of a Square Given Its Area

Estimating the dimensions of a square when you know its area is the same as finding the square root of any number. Why? Because the area of a square is the length of one side squared, $A = s^2$. In other words, $\sqrt{A} = s$. When the area is not a perfect square, it is easy to estimate the length of a side.

EXAMPLE Estimate the length of one side of a square room that has an area of 77 square feet.

Step 1 Determine two perfect squares on either side of the area. 77 falls between the perfect squares 64 and 81.

Step 2 Determine which square is closer to the number. 77 is closer to 81.

Step 3 Estimate the square root of the number based on the square root of the closer perfect square.

The square root of 81 is 9, so the square root of 77 is a little less than 9. One side of the room is a little less than 9 feet long.

Directions Estimate the answers to the following problems.

1. Donna wants to buy a rug to cover as much of her living room floor as possible. It is a square room with an area of 62 square feet. Which square rug should she buy: 6' × 6', 7' × 7', or 8' × 8'? Why?
2. Tomas's room is square with a floor area of 42 square feet. Approximately how long is each wall in his room?
3. Amelie's square herb garden is being invaded by rabbits. She's buying chicken wire to fence it and protect her plants. The garden is 56 square feet. She can buy chicken wire in three lengths: 20 feet, 30 feet, and 40 feet. Which roll of chicken wire should she buy and why?
4. A square building is being divided into four square apartments, each 930 square feet. Approximately what are the dimensions of the building? Explain your answer.
5. Sid received a square greeting card he wants to frame. The area of the card is 97 square centimeters. Approximately how many centimeters of framing material must he buy to make his own frame and why?

 Algebra

TRL

Estimation Exercise 11

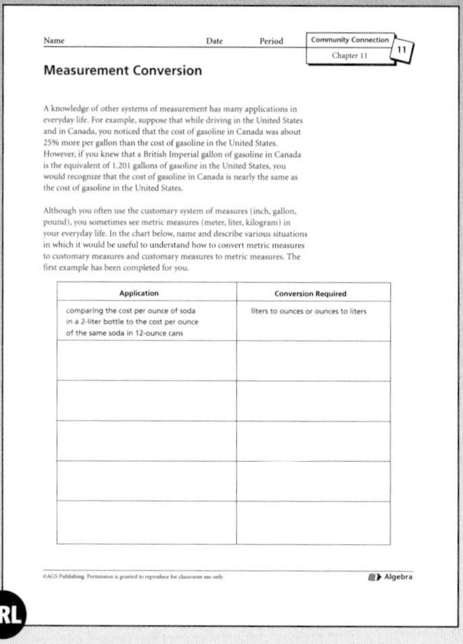

Name Date Period | Community Connection 11 | Chapter 11

Measurement Conversion

A knowledge of other systems of measurement has many applications in everyday life. For example, suppose that while driving in the United States and in Canada, you noticed that the cost of gasoline in Canada was about 25% more per gallon than the cost of gasoline in the United States. However, if you knew that a British Imperial gallon of gasoline in Canada is the equivalent of 1.201 gallons of gasoline in the United States, you would recognize that the cost of gasoline in Canada is nearly the same as the cost of gasoline in the United States.

Although you often use the customary system of measures (inch, gallon, pound), you sometimes see metric measures (meter, liter, kilogram) in your everyday life. In the chart below, name and describe various situations in which it would be useful to understand how to convert metric measures to customary measures and customary measures to metric measures. The first example has been completed for you.

Application	Conversion Required
comparing the cost per ounce of soda in a 2-liter bottle to the cost per ounce of the same soda in 12-ounce cans	liters to ounces or ounces to liters

 Algebra

TRL

Community Connection 11

Chapter

Irrational Numbers and Radical Expressions

Suppose you needed eight paper squares for a huge box kite. You want each square to have an area of 16 square feet. What length should the sides of the squares be? You need a number that multiplied by itself equals 16. For 16, that number is its square root, 4. Four is a rational number that can be written as the fraction $\frac{4}{1}$. Not all square roots come out so neatly. Some numbers are irrational. They cannot be written as fractions. For instance, the square root of 2 is 1.414213… The number goes on and on. Let's just say it's somewhere between 1 and 2 on the number line.

In Chapter 11, you will investigate irrational numbers and radicals.

Goals for Learning

- To distinguish rational and irrational numbers
- To find the rational number equivalents of decimal expansions
- To find the roots of radicals
- To simplify radical expressions
- To add, subtract, multiply, and divide radicals
- To rationalize the denominator of a fraction
- To solve equations with radicals and exponents
- To use a graph to find square root

Introducing the Chapter

Use the information in the chapter opener to help students understand that they can use algebra to help them build a box kite or a bird house or tree house. Not all square roots for a box can be written as a fraction. For example, the square root of 5 is 2.23606797. The number continues on and on with no repeating pattern. Students will learn about these irrational numbers in this chapter.

Chapter Project

After each lesson, have students compile or add to a list of persons or vocations that may require a proficiency of the skills that were presented in the lesson. For example, a skill presented in Lesson 1 is converting from degrees Fahrenheit to degrees Celsius and vice versa. Have students repeat the procedure after every lesson. After completing the chapter, ask them to share their lists and explain why each skill is important to the persons or vocations on their lists.

Teacher's Resource

The AGS Publishing Teaching Strategies in Math Transparencies may be used with this chapter. They add an interactive dimension to expand and enhance the program content.

Career Interest Inventory

The AGS Publishing Harrington-O'Shea Career Decision-Making System-Revised (CDM) may be used with this chapter. Students can use the CDM to explore their interests and identify careers. The CDM defines career areas that are indicated by students' responses on the inventory.

Name Date Period **SELF-STUDY GUIDE**

CHAPTER 11: Irrational Numbers and Radical Expressions

Goal 11.1 *To distinguish between rational and irrational numbers*

Date	Assignment	Score
______	1: Read pages 328–329. Complete Exercises A and C on pages 330–331.	______
______	2: Read and complete the Calculator Practice on page 330.	______
______	3: Complete Workbook Activity 105.	______

Comments:

Goal 11.2 *To find the rational number equivalents of decimal expansions*

Date	Assignment	Score
______	4: Read pages 332–333. Complete Exercises A–B on page 333.	______
______	5: Complete Workbook Activity 106.	______

Comments:

Goal 11.3 *To find the roots of radicals*

Date	Assignment	Score
______	6: Read pages 334–335. Complete Exercises A–B on page 335.	______
______	7: Complete Workbook Activity 107.	______

Comments:

Goals 11.4 and 11.5 *To simplify radical expressions; to add, subtract, multiply, and divide radicals*

Date	Assignment	Score
______	8: Read pages 336–337. Complete Exercises A–B on page 337.	______
______	9: Complete Workbook Activity 108.	______
______	10: Read pages 338–339. Complete Exercises A–B on page 339.	______
______	11: Complete Workbook Activity 109.	______

Comments:

 Algebra

TRL

Name Date Period **SELF-STUDY GUIDE**

CHAPTER 11: Irrational Numbers and Radical Expressions, continued

Goal 11.6 *To rationalize the denominator of a fraction*

Date	Assignment	Score
______	12: Read pages 340–341. Complete Exercises A–B on page 341.	______
______	13: Complete Workbook Activity 110.	______

Comments:

Goal 11.7 *To solve equations with radicals and exponents*

Date	Assignment	Score
______	14: Read pages 342–343. Complete Exercises A–C on pages 344–345.	______
______	15: Complete Workbook Activities 111–112.	______
______	16: Read pages 346–347. Complete Exercises A–C on page 347.	______
______	17: Read and complete the Calculator Practice on page 347.	______
______	18: Complete Workbook Activity 113.	______

Comments:

Goal 11.8 *To use a graph to find square root*

Date	Assignment	Score
______	19: Read pages 348–349. Complete Exercise A on page 349.	______
______	20: Complete Workbook Activity 114.	______
______	21: Read and complete the Application Exercise on page 350.	______
______	22: Complete the Chapter 11 Review on pages 351–353.	______

Comments:

Student's Signature ______________________ Date __________

Instructor's Signature ______________________ Date __________

 Algebra

TRL

Chapter 11 Self-Study Guide

Lesson at a Glance

Chapter 11 Lesson 1

Overview This lesson introduces the set of real numbers.

Objective

- To write the decimal expansion of rational numbers

Student Pages 328–331

Teacher's Resource Library 

Workbook Activity 105

Activity 99

Alternative Activity 99

Mathematics Vocabulary

decimal expansion
irrational number
repeating decimal expansion
terminating decimal expansion

1 Warm-Up Activity

Have students recall that a rational number can be represented by $\frac{a}{b}$ where $b \neq 0$. Then ask, "When a rational number appears in the form $\frac{a}{b}$, why can't $b = 0$? *(Division by zero is undefined.)* "What are some examples of rational numbers?" *(Examples include proper fractions such as $\frac{1}{3}$, improper fractions such as $\frac{5}{2}$, decimals such as 0.14, and integers such as -6.)* "How is the rational number $\frac{1}{2}$ different from the rational number $\frac{1}{3}$?" *(The division $1 \div 2$ terminates, or ends; the division $1 \div 3$ does not.)*

2 Teaching the Lesson

The set of real numbers is made up of two distinct subsets—the set of rational numbers and the set of irrational numbers. Explain that a set is a group or collection (in this case, the group of real numbers), and a subset contains at least one element or member of the set. As an example, you might choose to identify by name one student in your class. Point out that the student is a subset, or member of, the entire set of students in class.

Lesson 1 Rational Numbers as Decimals

> ***Irrational number***
> *A real number, such as $\sqrt{2}$, that cannot be written in the form $\frac{a}{b}$ in which a and b are whole numbers and $b \neq 0$*

The set of real numbers contains those numbers you can find on the number line.

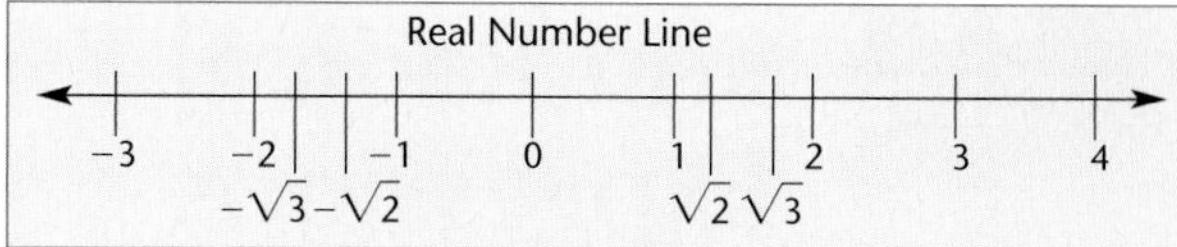

For every point on the real number line, there is one and only one real number. For every real number, there is one and only one point on the number line.

The set of real numbers can be grouped into two distinct subsets:

rational numbers such as $1, \frac{2}{3}, -\frac{7}{8}$, and so on,

and **irrational numbers** such as $\sqrt{2}, \sqrt{3}, \sqrt[3]{2}$, and so on.

Rational numbers have the form $\frac{a}{b}$, in which a and b are integers (positive or negative whole numbers and 0) and $b \neq 0$.

> Recall that a rational number is any number that is expressed as an integer or as a ratio between two integers when 0 does not serve as the denominator.

All integers are rational numbers because they can be written in the form $\frac{a}{b}$ where $b = 1$. For instance,

$5 = \frac{5}{1}, -7 = -\frac{7}{1}, 0 = \frac{0}{1}$, and so on.

One way to identify a rational number that is not an integer is to look at the number written as a decimal. To write a rational number as a decimal, divide the numerator by the denominator.

Name Date Period | Workbook Activity 105 | Chapter 11, Lesson 1

Rational Numbers as Decimals

EXAMPLE Is the decimal form of these fractions *terminating* or *repeating*? $\frac{1}{5}$ $\frac{2}{3}$

Step 1 Divide numerator by denominator. Divide numerator by denominator.

$5\overline{)1.000}$ = .2000; 10; 0 $3\overline{)2.000000}$ = .666 ...; 18; 20; 18; 20 ...

Step 2 $\frac{1}{5} = 0.2\overline{0}$ Terminating $\frac{2}{3} = 0.\overline{6}$ Repeating

Directions Write the decimal expansion for these rational numbers. Tell whether each is *terminating* or *repeating*.

1. $\frac{1}{4}$ ______ 6. $\frac{1}{9}$ ______
2. $\frac{4}{5}$ ______ 7. $\frac{7}{8}$ ______
3. $\frac{19}{20}$ ______ 8. $\frac{11}{25}$ ______
4. $\frac{5}{6}$ ______ 9. $\frac{1}{5}$ ______
5. $\frac{2}{15}$ ______ 10. $\frac{2}{7}$ ______

Directions Using a calculator, perform the division to change each fraction into an expanded decimal. Tell whether each is *terminating* or *repeating*.

11. $\frac{1}{11}$ ______ 16. $\frac{1}{13}$ ______
12. $\frac{8}{9}$ ______ 17. $\frac{7}{10}$ ______
13. $\frac{3}{8}$ ______ 18. $\frac{13}{15}$ ______
14. $\frac{1}{16}$ ______ 19. $\frac{6}{7}$ ______
15. $\frac{3}{4}$ ______ 20. $\frac{69}{80}$ ______

 Algebra

TRL Workbook Activity 105

Name Date Period | Activity 99 | Chapter 11, Lesson 1

Rational Numbers as Decimals

Directions Find the expanded decimal for each fraction and fill in the chart. You may use a calculator.

Rational Number	Decimal Expansion
1. $\frac{4}{11}$	______
2. $\frac{3}{7}$	______
3. $\frac{3}{13}$	______
4. $\frac{3}{5}$	______
5. $\frac{19}{21}$	______
6. $\frac{5}{7}$	______
7. $\frac{3}{3}$	______

Directions Use the formula for converting between Fahrenheit and Celsius degrees to solve the problems.

To find Celsius equivalent, $°C = \frac{5}{9}(°F - 32)$ To find the Fahrenheit equivalent, $°F = \frac{9}{5}(°C) + 32$

8. When she had a strep throat, Meg ran a high fever of 104°F. What would her temperature be in Celsius? ______
9. While traveling in Japan, the Scheffers heard that the temperature in the city they were visiting was 29°C. What was the temperature in degrees Fahrenheit? ______
10. Drake's cooking thermometer has a Celsius scale. His recipe states, "Remove the mixture from the burner when the temperature reaches 254°F." What temperature should Drake look for on his Celsius cooking thermometer? ______

 Algebra

TRL Activity 99

Decimal expansion

Writing a number, such as a fraction, as a decimal

Terminating decimal expansion

A decimal sequence that ends in all 0s

Repeating decimal expansion

A decimal sequence in which the numbers repeat in exactly the same order

EXAMPLE 1 Write $\frac{2}{5}$ as a decimal.

$\frac{2}{5}$ is the same as $2 \div 5$ or $5\overline{)2.0}$ = 0.4

$\frac{2}{5} = 0.4$ The decimal places after 4 are all occupied by 0s.

So, $\frac{2}{5} = 0.4000....$ This can be written as $0.4\overline{0}$.

$0.4\overline{0}$ is called the **decimal expansion** of $\frac{2}{5}$.

A decimal expansion ending in all zeroes is called a **terminating decimal expansion.**

EXAMPLE 2 Write $\frac{1}{3}$ as a decimal.

$\frac{1}{3}$ is the same as $1 \div 3$ or $3\overline{)1.0}$ = 0.33

$\frac{1}{3} = 0.333...$ or $0.\overline{3}$.

The 3 repeats an infinite number of times in the decimal.

EXAMPLE 3 Write $\frac{1}{7}$ as a decimal.

$\frac{1}{7}$ is the same as $1 \div 7$ or $7\overline{)1.0}$ = 0.142

Use a calculator to find this decimal expansion.

Press 1 [÷] 7 [=] 0.142857

↑ ↑

repeating pattern

$\frac{1}{7} = 0.142857142857... = 0.\overline{142857}$

↑ ↑

repeating pattern

A decimal expansion in which one or more digits repeat in exactly the same order is called a **repeating decimal expansion.** Rational numbers have either terminating or repeating decimal expansions.

After discussing the example at the top of page 329, have students note that an answer of 0.4 would not be the correct decimal expansion of $\frac{2}{5}$. The function of a decimal expansion is to show the digit or digits in a rational number that repeat, without regard to the place or value of the digit(s). Finding the decimal expansion of a rational number will sometimes produce a decimal that does not appear to be in simplest form.

After discussing the remaining examples on page 329, caution students to be careful when using a calculator to find the decimal expansion of a number. Explain that some calculators show a greater number of digits in their displays than others. For this reason, depending on the decimal expansion and depending on the calculator, it may sometimes be difficult to be sure which digits repeat simply by looking at a display. Encourage students to take the time to perform a long division any time a question exists with respect to which digits in a decimal expansion repeat and which digits do not.

COMMON ERROR

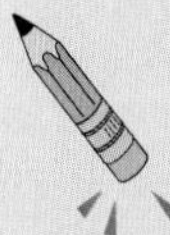

Prior to having students perform the problems on page 330, remind them that a decimal expansion of a rational number should include only the digit or digits that repeat. It should not include a repeating digit or digits more than once. For example, an answer of $0.2\overline{0}$ for the decimal expansion of $\frac{1}{5}$ is different from an answer of $0.\overline{200}$. The answer $0.2\overline{0}$ is correct; $0.\overline{200}$ is not.

On page 331, have students note that the formula for changing degrees Celsius to degrees Fahrenheit contains two operations—multiplication and addition, and note that the formula for changing degrees Fahrenheit to degrees Celsius contains the operations of multiplication and subtraction. Prior to completing problems 18–25, remind students to follow the order of operations when using each formula.

MATH HISTORY

Sofya Kovalevsky was born in Russia in 1850. Married at age 18, she and her husband moved to Germany. Because she was a woman, she was not allowed to enroll at a university. However, she took private classes with Karl Weierstass at the University of Berlin and eventually received her Ph.D. from the University of Göttigen. Her paper on the theory of partial differential equations was published in a prestigious journal. In 1888, she won the Prix Bordin from the French Academy of Science for her paper, "On the Rotation of a Solid Body about a Fixed Point." Her work in trigonometry helped further clarify the sine function. Along with her mathematical accomplishments, Kovalevsky was a novelist who wrote about her native Russia.

Reinforce and Extend

In the Community

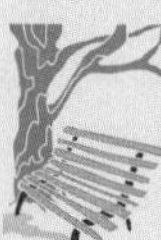

Invite students to name or find places in their community where the temperature is recorded and/or displayed both in degrees Fahrenheit and degrees Celsius.

Career Connection

Point out that travel agents, tour guides, and people who travel outside the United States find it useful to be able to convert degrees Fahrenheit to degrees Celsius. Have pairs of students create and present skits based on situations that demonstrate how this skill proves to be useful to a travel agent, tour guide, or traveler.

Learning Styles

LEP/ESL

Ask students to name words from their native language that are used to describe terms such as rational and irrational numbers and repeating and terminating decimal expansions. Then ask them to write the terms on a sheet of paper and give several examples of each. The sheet can then be kept for reference as the remainder of the chapter is completed.

1. $0.6\overline{0}$, terminating
2. $0.\overline{2}$, repeating
3. $0.\overline{5}$, repeating
4. $0.\overline{7}$, repeating
5. $0.\overline{18}$, repeating
6. $0.\overline{27}$, repeating
7. $0.\overline{63}$, repeating
8. $0.\overline{714285}$, repeating
9. $0.\overline{15}$, repeating
10. $0.\overline{84}$, repeating
11. $0.12\overline{0}$, terminating
12. $0.28\overline{0}$, terminating
13. $0.41\overline{6}$, repeating
14. $0.08\overline{3}$, repeating
15. $0.7\overline{3}$; repeating

Exercise A Write the decimal expansions for these rational numbers. Tell whether the expansions are terminating or repeating.

1. $\frac{3}{5}$	**6.** $\frac{3}{11}$	**11.** $\frac{3}{25}$
2. $\frac{2}{9}$	**7.** $\frac{7}{11}$	**12.** $\frac{7}{25}$
3. $\frac{5}{9}$	**8.** $\frac{5}{7}$	**13.** $\frac{5}{12}$
4. $\frac{7}{9}$	**9.** $\frac{5}{33}$	**14.** $\frac{1}{12}$
5. $\frac{2}{11}$	**10.** $\frac{28}{33}$	**15.** $\frac{11}{15}$

Use your calculator to change fractions to expanded decimals.

Example 4 Change $\frac{5}{9}$ to a decimal.

Press 5 ÷ 9 =

The display reads 0.555555555 or 0.555555556 because of rounding.

You can write the repeating decimal expansion as $0.\overline{5}$.

Exercise B Use your calculator to find the expanded decimal for each fraction in the chart. Copy the chart onto a sheet of paper. Use long division to check any repeating expansions.

16.

Rational Number	$\frac{1}{1}$	$\frac{1}{2}$	$\frac{1}{3}$	$\frac{1}{4}$	$\frac{1}{5}$	$\frac{1}{6}$	$\frac{1}{7}$	$\frac{1}{8}$	$\frac{1}{9}$	$\frac{1}{10}$
Decimal Expansion	1	0.5	$0.\overline{3}$	0.25	0.2	$0.1\overline{6}$		0.125	$0.\overline{1}$	0.1

17.

Rational Number	$\frac{1}{1}$	$\frac{1}{2}$	$\frac{2}{3}$	$\frac{3}{4}$	$\frac{4}{5}$	$\frac{5}{6}$	$\frac{6}{7}$	$\frac{7}{8}$	$\frac{8}{9}$	$\frac{9}{10}$
Decimal Expansion	1	0.5	$0.\overline{6}$	0.75	0.8	$0.8\overline{3}$		0.875	$0.\overline{8}$	0.9

$0.\overline{142857}$ $0.\overline{857142}$

PROBLEM SOLVING

Rational and irrational numbers can be used to describe much of the world in which you live. For example, to change degrees Celsius to degrees Fahrenheit or to change degrees Fahrenheit to degrees Celsius, use one of these formulas:

$$°F = (\frac{9}{5})(°C) + 32 \qquad °C = (\frac{5}{9})(°F - 32)$$

In these formulas, $\frac{9}{5}$ is a rational number and $\frac{5}{9}$ is an irrational number.

TRY THIS

What is the normal temperature of the human body in degrees Celsius?

37°C

Exercise C Suppose you visit distant countries and experience the following temperatures in degrees Celsius. Change the temperatures to degrees Fahrenheit.

18. 34°C 93.2°F

19. -18°C -0.4°F

20. 25°C 77°F

21. -4°C 24.8°F

Suppose a tourist visiting the United States experiences the following temperatures in degrees Fahrenheit. Change the temperatures to degrees Celsius.

22. 104°F 40°C

23. 46°F $7.\overline{7}$°C

24. -10°F $-23.\overline{3}$°C

25. 70°F $21.\overline{1}$°C

Algebra in Your Life

The Square of the Hypotenuse

Roofing contractors use the Pythagorean theorem to figure out the length of the rafters in a building. Rafters run parallel to one another. They are the diagonal boards on which the roof of a building is laid. A rafter represents the unknown hypotenuse of a right triangle. To find the length of a rafter you need to find the square root of the triangle's hypotenuse. If roofing contractors couldn't calculate square roots, they wouldn't be able to measure rafters correctly.

Try This

The prerequisite knowledge required to successfully answer the question is the fact that the body temperature of a typical human being is about 98.6°F.

Calculator

Remind students that to change a fraction to a decimal, they simply need to divide the numerator of the fraction by the denominator. It is not necessary to use any fraction-related functions a calculator may possess.

Group Problem Solving

Encourage students to work in pairs or groups of three to discuss and answer the following questions:

What is the boiling point of water, in degrees Celsius? *(100°C)*

What is the freezing point of water, in degrees Celsius? *(0°C)*

A temperature of 0° Fahrenheit is equivalent to what Celsius temperature? *($-17.\overline{7}$°C)*

What Celsius air temperature is comfortable for swimming in a lake or ocean? *(Sample answer: 35°C)*

Upon completion of the activity, invite groups to compare answers.

Lesson at a Glance

Chapter 11 Lesson 2

Overview This lesson introduces equivalent fractions for decimal numbers.

Objective

- To determine the rational number that represents a repeating or terminating decimal expansion

Student Pages 332–333

Teacher's Resource Library 

Workbook Activity 106

Activity 100

Alternative Activity 100

1 Warm-Up Activity

Have students identify the fraction in simplest form that represents each of the following decimal numbers.

0.5	$(\frac{1}{2})$
0.25	$(\frac{1}{4})$
0.7	$(\frac{7}{10})$
$0.\overline{3}$	$(\frac{1}{3})$
0.75	$(\frac{3}{4})$
$0.\overline{6}$	$(\frac{2}{3})$
0.09	$(\frac{9}{100})$
0.3	$(\frac{3}{10})$
0.61	$(\frac{61}{100})$
1.0	$(\frac{1}{1}$ *or 1*$)$

Point out that because a decimal number is a rational number, all decimal numbers can be expressed as fractions.

2 Teaching the Lesson

As students discuss and work through the examples on pages 332 and 333, help them understand that writing a rational number equivalent for a decimal expansion involves multiplying both sides of an equation by a value that will enable subtraction to eliminate the repeating portion of the decimal expansion.

Lesson 2 Rational Number Equivalents

You can use what you know about solving equations to find the rational number that represents a repeating or terminating decimal expansion.

EXAMPLE 1 What rational number is equal to $0.45\overline{0}$?

Because $0.45\overline{0}$ is a terminating decimal expansion, you can write it as $0.45 = \frac{45}{100}$.

Simplify.

$\frac{45}{100} = \frac{9}{20}$, so $\frac{45}{100} = \frac{9}{20} = 0.450$

EXAMPLE 2 What rational number is equal to $0.\overline{3}$?

Step 1 For a repeating decimal expansion, let $x =$ the expansion written as a repeating decimal.
In this case, $x = 0.333...$

Step 2 Multiply both sides of the equation to place the repeating digit(s) to the left of the decimal.
In this case, multiply by 10.

$10(x) = (10)0.3333...$
$10x = 3.333...$

Step 3 Subtract the repeating decimal.

$$\begin{aligned} 10x &= 3.333... \\ -\ x &= 0.333... \\ \hline 9x &= 3.000... \\ 9x &= 3 \end{aligned}$$

(The repeating part of the decimal subtracts to 0.)

Step 4 Simplify.

$x = \frac{3}{9} = \frac{1}{3}$, so $\frac{1}{3} = 0.\overline{3}$

EXAMPLE 3 What rational number is equal to $1.0\overline{51}$?

Step 1 Let $x = 1.0515151...$

Step 2 Multiply both sides of the equation to place the repeating digit(s) to the left of the decimal.
In this case, multiply by 1,000.

$1{,}000(x) = (1{,}000)1.0515151...$
$1{,}000x = 1{,}051.51...$

Name Date Period **Workbook Activity 106** Chapter 11, Lesson 2

Rational Number Equivalents

EXAMPLE What rational number is equal to $0.58\overline{3}$?

Step 1 Let $x = 0.58333...$

Step 2 Multiply to place the first repeating digit(s) to the *left* of the decimal.

$(1000)x = (1000)0.583333...$ Simplify: $1000x = 583.333...$

Step 3 Multiply to place the repeating digit(s) to the *right* of the decimal.

$(100)x = (100)0.583333...$ Simplify: $100x = 58.333...$

Step 4 Subtract the smaller from the larger result.

$1000x = 583.333...$
$-100x = 58.333...$
$900x = 525.000$

$x = \frac{525}{900}$ Simplify: $\frac{525}{900} \div \frac{75}{75} = \frac{7}{12}$

Directions Find the rational number equivalents for these decimal expansions. Show your work.

1. $0.1\overline{3}$ ______
2. $0.8\overline{3}$ ______
3. $0.\overline{1}$ ______
4. $0.\overline{6}$ ______
5. $0.8\overline{6}$ ______
6. $0.\overline{8}$ ______
7. $0.1\overline{6}$ ______
8. $0.\overline{36}$ ______
9. $0.\overline{18}$ ______
10. $0.\overline{4}$ ______

 Algebra

TRL

Workbook Activity 106

Name Date Period **Activity 100** Chapter 11, Lesson 2

Rational Number Equivalents

Directions For each decimal expansion on the *left*, find a rational equivalent (fraction) on the *right*. Circle that fraction.

1. $0.5\overline{0}$	$\frac{2}{7}$	$\frac{2}{4}$	$\frac{2}{3}$
2. $0.9\overline{0}$	$\frac{6}{7}$	$\frac{4}{5}$	$\frac{18}{20}$
3. $0.0\overline{83}$	$\frac{83}{100}$	$\frac{1}{12}$	$\frac{1}{5}$
4. $0.2\overline{6}$	$\frac{1}{4}$	$\frac{3}{14}$	$\frac{4}{15}$
5. $0.875\overline{0}$	$\frac{7}{8}$	$\frac{8}{9}$	$\frac{13}{14}$
6. $0.\overline{3}$	$\frac{6}{18}$	$\frac{7}{18}$	$\frac{5}{18}$
7. $0.75\overline{0}$	$\frac{2}{3}$	$\frac{9}{12}$	$\frac{9}{13}$
8. $0.458\overline{3}$	$\frac{4}{7}$	$\frac{3}{5}$	$\frac{11}{24}$
9. $0.\overline{6}$	$\frac{8}{12}$	$\frac{8}{13}$	$\frac{7}{12}$
10. $0.0625\overline{0}$	$\frac{1}{14}$	$\frac{1}{16}$	$\frac{1}{15}$

Directions Find the rational number equivalents for these decimal expansions.

11. $0.35\overline{0}$ ______
12. $0.7\overline{3}$ ______
13. $0.85\overline{0}$ ______
14. $0.6\overline{1}$ ______
15. $0.62\overline{0}$ ______
16. $0.9\overline{4}$ ______
17. $0.\overline{81}$ ______
18. $0.945\overline{0}$ ______

Directions Solve the problems.

19. Suppose you divide an apple pie into 6 equal wedges. Each slice will be $\frac{1}{6}$ of the total pie. In decimal expansion, how much of the pie is one slice? ______
20. Consider the same apple pie. If only one person takes a slice for dessert, $\frac{5}{6}$ of the pie will remain in the pie pan. In decimal expansion, what portion of the whole pie remains in the pan? ______

 Algebra

TRL

Activity 100

EXAMPLE 3 *(continued)*

Step 3 Multiply both sides of $x = 1.0515151...$ so the repeating part of the expansion immediately follows the decimal. In this case, multiply by 10.

$(10)x = (10)1.05151...$
$10x = 10.5151...$

Step 4 Subtract the products from one another.

$$\begin{array}{rl} 1{,}000x = & 1{,}051.5151... \\ -\quad 10x = & 10.5151... \\ \hline 990x = & 1{,}041.0000... \\ 990x = & 1{,}041 \end{array}$$

(The repeating part of the decimal subtracts to 0.)

Step 5 Simplify.

$x = \frac{1041}{900} = \frac{347}{330}$

so $\frac{347}{330} = 1.0\overline{51}$

Exercise A Find the rational number equivalents for these decimal expansions. Write your answers in lowest terms.

1. $0.4\overline{0}$ $\frac{2}{5}$
2. $0.75\overline{0}$ $\frac{3}{4}$
3. $0.36\overline{0}$ $\frac{9}{25}$
4. $0.52\overline{0}$ $\frac{13}{25}$
5. $0.\overline{81}$ $\frac{9}{11}$
6. $0.\overline{09}$ $\frac{1}{11}$
7. $0.0\overline{75}$ $\frac{5}{66}$
8. $0.5\overline{3}$ $\frac{8}{15}$

Exercise B Find the rational number equivalents for these decimal expansions.

9. $0.7\overline{3}$ $\frac{11}{15}$
10. $0.\overline{07}$ $\frac{7}{99}$
11. $0.\overline{13}$ $\frac{13}{99}$
12. $0.15\overline{90}$ $\frac{7}{44}$
13. $0.\overline{153846}$ $\frac{2}{13}$
14. $1.\overline{153846}$ $\frac{15}{13}$
15. $0.0\overline{0495}$ $\frac{1}{202}$

Technology Connection

Software Programs Use Formulas

Balancing your checkbook is easy when you use a software program. Just enter the amounts of your checks and deposits in the right place. The software calculates your balance for you. In the same way, other software programs help businesses to do payroll. They also help insurance companies to figure out premiums, and scientists to calculate the growth of bacteria and viruses. These software programs all use formulas with variables!

COMMON ERROR

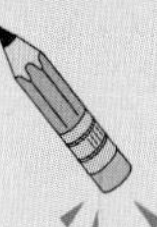

Remind students that if they choose, for example, to multiply one side of an equation by 10, they must also multiply the other side of the equation by 10. The same operation must be performed to *both* sides of an equation.

3 Reinforce and Extend

LEARNING STYLES

Visual/Spatial

Write the following pattern on the board.

$\frac{1}{9} = 0.\overline{1}$

$\frac{2}{9} = 0.\overline{2}$

$\frac{3}{9} = 0.\overline{3}$

Invite students to continue the pattern and then work cooperatively to discover other patterns and share those patterns with their classmates.

LEARNING STYLES

LEP/ESL

Explain that the word *Equivalents* in the title of the lesson means *naming the same number.* Invite volunteers to name in their native language synonyms, or words or phrases that mean the same as, *equivalent* or *equivalents.*

Lesson at a Glance

Chapter 11 Lesson 3

Overview This lesson introduces rational and irrational roots of integers.

Objective

- To use a calculator to find the roots of radicals and identify the roots as rational or irrational

Student Pages 334–335

Teacher's Resource Library TRL

Workbook Activity 107

Activity 101

Alternative Activity 101

Mathematics Vocabulary

radical
radical sign

Warm-Up Activity

Remind students that the integer 5, when multiplied by itself, creates a product of 25. Working in groups of four, challenge students to use a calculator and find a decimal value in tenths, which when multiplied by itself, as closely approximates 12 as possible without being greater than 12. Repeat the activity several times using other whole numbers. Each time, challenge each group to find the number using fewer guesses or trials than the other groups in the classroom.

Teaching the Lesson

Not all calculators require a user to perform the same steps when finding the root of a number. For example, to find the root of 36, some calculators will require the user to input 36, then press the radical key. Other calculators will require a user to first press the radical key, then enter 36 and press the equals key. Prior to assigning homework exercises, make sure each student understands the sequence that is required by his or her calculator for generating roots.

Lesson 3 Irrational Numbers as Decimals

> ***Radical***
> *A number that is written with the radical sign*
>
> ***Radical sign***
> *The mathematical symbol ($\sqrt{\ }$) placed before a number or algebraic expression to indicate that the root should be found*

Recall that the set of real numbers can be grouped into two distinct subsets—rational numbers and irrational numbers.

Irrational numbers include the square root, cube root, and *n*th root of many numbers. These numbers are sometimes called roots, or **radicals**, because they are written with the **radical sign** ($\sqrt{\ }$). For example, $\sqrt{2}$, $\sqrt{3}$, $\sqrt[3]{2}$, and so on.

It is important to note that not all radicals or roots are irrational. For instance, $\sqrt{4} = 2$, $\sqrt[3]{-8} = -2$, and $\sqrt[5]{32} = 2$. In each case, the root is an integer. You know that integers are also rational numbers, so these roots are *not* irrational.

Use your calculator to find the decimal expansion of irrational numbers.

> Remember, a root is an equal factor of a number or expression. Roots, or radicals, that cannot be written in the form $\frac{a}{b}$ in which a and b are whole numbers and $b \neq 0$ are called irrational numbers.

EXAMPLE 1 Write the decimal expansion for $\sqrt{2}$.

Use a calculator to find the decimal expansion of $\sqrt{2}$.

Press 2 [$\sqrt{\ }$]. (On many calculators, the answer will be displayed after the [$\sqrt{\ }$] is pressed. On some calculators, you will have to press [=] for the answer to be displayed.)

The display reads 1.4142136.

This expansion does *not* end in zeroes and it does *not* have a repeating pattern. Therefore, $\sqrt{2}$ is *not* a rational number. Because the display of some calculators is limited to 8 digits, $\sqrt{2} = 1.4142136\ldots$ is an approximation of the complete decimal expansion. This is often written using "$\approx$," a symbol standing for *approximately equal.*

So $\sqrt{2} \approx 1.4142136$, which is an irrational number.

The decimal expansion of an irrational number is nonterminating and nonrepeating.

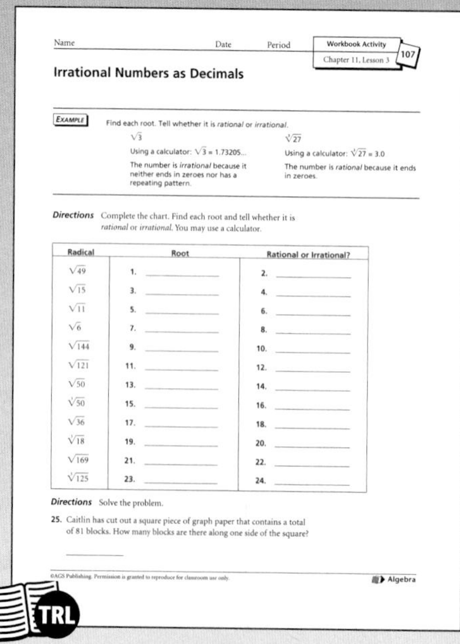

Name Date Period | Workbook Activity 107 | Chapter 11, Lesson 3

Irrational Numbers as Decimals

EXAMPLE Find each root. Tell whether it is *rational* or *irrational*.

$\sqrt{3}$ — Using a calculator: $\sqrt{3} = 1.73205...$ The number is *irrational* because it neither ends in zeroes nor has a repeating pattern.

$\sqrt[3]{27}$ — Using a calculator: $\sqrt[3]{27} = 3.0$ The number is *rational* because it ends in zeroes.

Directions Complete the chart. Find each root and tell whether it is *rational* or *irrational*. You may use a calculator.

Radical	Root	Rational or Irrational?
$\sqrt{49}$	1. ______	2. ______
$\sqrt{15}$	3. ______	4. ______
$\sqrt{11}$	5. ______	6. ______
$\sqrt{6}$	7. ______	8. ______
$\sqrt{144}$	9. ______	10. ______
$\sqrt{121}$	11. ______	12. ______
$\sqrt{50}$	13. ______	14. ______
$\sqrt[3]{50}$	15. ______	16. ______
$\sqrt{36}$	17. ______	18. ______
$\sqrt[3]{18}$	19. ______	20. ______
$\sqrt{169}$	21. ______	22. ______
$\sqrt[3]{125}$	23. ______	24. ______

Directions Solve the problem.

25. Caitlin has cut out a square piece of graph paper that contains a total of 81 blocks. How many blocks are there along one side of the square? ______

 Algebra

TRL

Workbook Activity 107

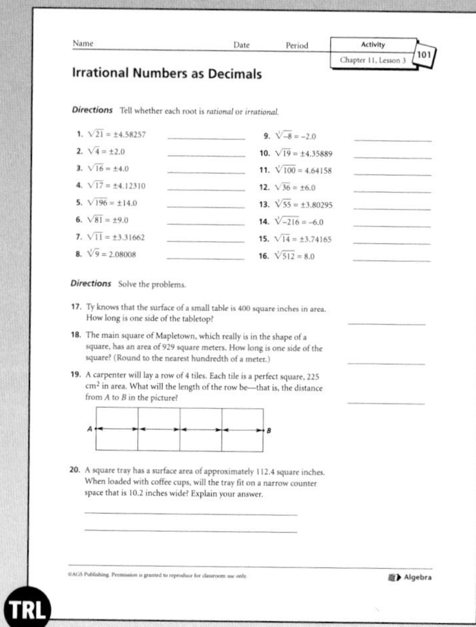

Name Date Period | Activity 101 | Chapter 11, Lesson 3

Irrational Numbers as Decimals

Directions Tell whether each root is *rational* or *irrational*.

1. $\sqrt{21} = \pm 4.58257$ ______
2. $\sqrt{4} = \pm 2.0$ ______
3. $\sqrt{16} = \pm 4.0$ ______
4. $\sqrt{17} = \pm 4.12310$ ______
5. $\sqrt{196} = \pm 14.0$ ______
6. $\sqrt{81} = \pm 9.0$ ______
7. $\sqrt{11} = \pm 3.31662$ ______
8. $\sqrt[3]{9} = 2.08008$ ______
9. $\sqrt[3]{-8} = -2.0$ ______
10. $\sqrt{19} = \pm 4.35889$ ______
11. $\sqrt[3]{100} = 4.64158$ ______
12. $\sqrt{36} = \pm 6.0$ ______
13. $\sqrt[3]{55} = \pm 3.80295$ ______
14. $\sqrt[3]{-216} = -6.0$ ______
15. $\sqrt{14} = \pm 3.74165$ ______
16. $\sqrt[3]{512} = 8.0$ ______

Directions Solve the problems.

17. Ty knows that the surface of a small table is 400 square inches in area. How long is one side of the tabletop? ______
18. The main square of Mapletown, which really is in the shape of a square, has an area of 929 square meters. How long is one side of the square? (Round to the nearest hundredth of a meter.) ______
19. A carpenter will lay a row of 4 tiles. Each tile is a perfect square, 225 cm^2 in area. What will the length of the row be—that is, the distance from A to B in the picture? ______

20. A square tray has a surface area of approximately 112.4 square inches. When loaded with coffee cups, will the tray fit on a narrow counter space that is 10.2 inches wide? Explain your answer.

______

______

 Algebra

TRL

Activity 101

EXAMPLE 2 Write a decimal expansion for $\sqrt[3]{2}$. Tell whether it is rational or irrational.

Use a calculator to find the cube root. Note that the cube root key may look like $\sqrt[3]{x}$, $\sqrt[3]{\ }$, or $\sqrt[x]{y}$ depending on the calculator.

Press 2 $\sqrt[3]{x}$. The display shows 1.259921.

The decimal is not terminating and not repeating, so $\sqrt[3]{2}$ is irrational.

The area of a square is 30 cm². What is the length of one side (s) of the square?

Area $= s^2$, so $\sqrt{\text{area}} = s$

30 cm²

s

s

You can estimate the length of one side by comparing the area to known squares:

$\sqrt{25} < \sqrt{30} < \sqrt{36}$ so $5 < s < 6$

Use a calculator to make a closer approximation.

Press 30 $\sqrt{\ }$. The display shows 5.477225.

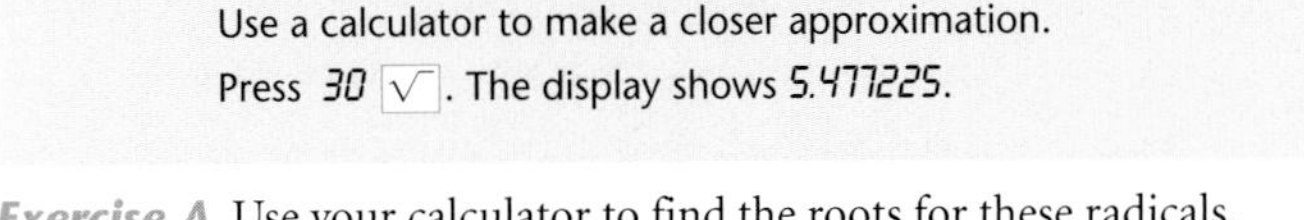

Exercise A Use your calculator to find the roots for these radicals. Tell whether they are rational or irrational.

1. $\sqrt[3]{400}$ 7.368, irrational
2. $\sqrt[4]{400}$ 4.472, irrational
3. $\sqrt[5]{400}$ 3.314, irrational
4. $\sqrt[3]{512}$ 8, rational
5. $\sqrt[3]{45}$ 3.557, irrational
6. $\sqrt[9]{512}$ 2, rational
7. $\sqrt[10]{1024}$ 2, rational
8. $\sqrt[2]{30}$ 5.477, irrational
9. $\sqrt[8]{256}$ 2, rational
10. $\sqrt{55}$ 7.416, irrational

PROBLEM SOLVING

Exercise B Answer the following questions.

11. Hisako is building a square birdhouse with a 36 in.² floor. How long will each side of the birdhouse be? 6 in.
12. Sharon wants to make a square poster with an area of about 500 cm². What will be the length of each side of the square, rounded to the nearest hundredth? 22.36 cm
13. Jesse's room has an area of 160 ft². What is the length of one side of the square room? Round to the nearest hundredth. 12.65 ft
14. A store has a square floor space with an area of 1,600 ft². Can you find the exact length of a side of this square? Explain.
15. A building is divided into four square offices with each having 49 square units. What is the area of the building (larger square)? What is the length of a side of the larger square?

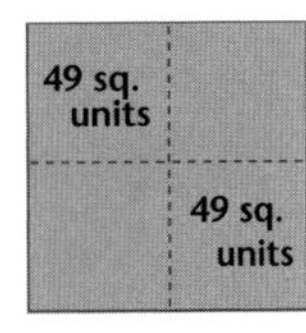

Yes. 0 = 40². ause 600 is tional nber, it xact.

196 are units; units

3 Reinforce and Extend

MENTAL MATH

Invite volunteers to name the following roots.

$\sqrt{100}$	*(10)*
$\sqrt[3]{8}$	*(2)*
$\sqrt{64}$	*(8)*
$\sqrt[3]{64}$	*(4)*
$\sqrt[3]{27}$	*(9)*
$\sqrt{144}$	*(12)*
$\sqrt{400}$	*(20)*
$\sqrt[4]{16}$	*(2)*
$\sqrt{900}$	*(30)*
$\sqrt[3]{8000}$	*(20)*

GROUP PROBLEM SOLVING

Have students recall that the Pythagorean theorem ($a^2 + b^2 = c^2$ where c represents the hypotenuse or longest side of a right triangle and a and b represent the legs opposite the hypotenuse) can be used to determine the measure of one side of a right triangle if the measures of the other two sides are known. Encourage students to work in pairs and use a calculator to find the diagonal measure of each square described in problems 11–15 on page 297. Ask students to round their answers to the nearest tenth. *[11) 8.5 in. 12) 31.6 cm 13) 17.9 ft 14) 56.6 ft 15) 9.9 units and/or 19.8 units]*

ONLINE CONNECTION

At www.lerc.nasa.gov/WWW/K-12/BGA/Sheri/Newton%27s_Second_Law_int.htm, students can practice their algebra problem-solving skills and learn something about aerodynamics. The site directs them to read about Newton's First and Second Laws of Motion and then solve a problem set around the Wright Brothers' first sustained, controlled flight. Have students click on "Activity" to read the activity. You can print out the worksheet for students by clicking on "Worksheet." An answer key is also linked to the site.

Lesson at a Glance

Chapter 11 Lesson 4

Overview This lesson introduces radicals that are not in simplest form.

Objective

- To simplify radicals using multiplication or division

Student Pages 336–337

Teacher's Resource Library 

Workbook Activity 108

Activity 102

Alternative Activity 102

Warm-Up Activity

Invite a volunteer to explain the concept of greatest common factor (GCF). Then have students determine the GCF of these number pairs.

3, 6	*(3)*	10, 45	*(5)*
12, 18	*(6)*	14, 35	*(7)*
5, 13	*(1)*	36, 54	*(18)*

Teaching the Lesson

Remind students that the procedure to follow to simplify a radical that includes a fraction is much the same as the procedure that is followed to write a fraction in simplest form. Write the fraction $\frac{4}{8}$ on the board and point out that the equivalent fraction $\frac{1}{2}$ is found by dividing both the numerator and the denominator by the common factor 2 (two times) or the greatest common factor 4 (one time). Explain that to simplify a radical that includes a fraction is similar in the sense that the same root of *both* the numerator and the denominator is taken.

Try This

Have students consider the integer and variable value of the numerator and denominator of each expression individually. For example, in the first expression, have students determine the three identical integer values that when multiplied together create a product of 27 *(3)*, then determine the three identical variable values that when multiplied together create a product of y^6 *(y^2)*. This

Lesson 4 Products and Quotients of Radicals

The rules for multiplying or dividing radicals can be illustrated by the following examples.

Example 1 Find the product of $\sqrt{4} \bullet \sqrt{25}$.

$$\sqrt{4} \bullet \sqrt{25} = (2) \bullet (5) = 10$$
$$\sqrt{100} = 10$$
$$\text{so } \sqrt{4} \bullet \sqrt{25} = \sqrt{4 \bullet 25} = \sqrt{100} = 10$$

Find the product of $\sqrt{4} \bullet \sqrt{9}$.

$$\sqrt{4} \bullet \sqrt{9} = (2) \bullet (3) = 6$$
$$\sqrt{36} = 6$$
$$\text{so } \sqrt{4} \bullet \sqrt{9} = \sqrt{4 \bullet 9} = \sqrt{36} = 6$$

These examples form the first rule of radicals.

Rule $\sqrt{a} \bullet \sqrt{b} = \sqrt{a \bullet b}$, for $a > 0$ and $b > 0$

A similar rule exists for working with expressions that contain radicals in both the numerator and the denominator. Consider these examples.

Example 2 Find the quotient of $\frac{\sqrt{16}}{\sqrt{4}}$.

$$\frac{\sqrt{16}}{\sqrt{4}} = \frac{(4)}{(2)} = 2$$
$$\sqrt{\frac{16}{4}} = \sqrt{4} = 2$$
$$\text{so } \frac{\sqrt{16}}{\sqrt{4}} = \sqrt{\frac{16}{4}} = \sqrt{4} = 2$$

Find the quotient of $\frac{\sqrt{36}}{\sqrt{4}}$.

$$\frac{\sqrt{36}}{\sqrt{4}} = \frac{(6)}{(2)} = 3$$
$$\sqrt{\frac{36}{4}} = \sqrt{9} = 3$$
$$\text{so } \frac{\sqrt{36}}{\sqrt{4}} = \sqrt{\frac{36}{4}} = \sqrt{9} = 3$$

These examples demonstrate the rule of radicals for fractions.

Rule $\frac{\sqrt{a}}{\sqrt{b}} = \sqrt{\frac{a}{b}}$, where $a \geq 0$ and $b > 0$

Name Date Period — Workbook Activity 108, Chapter 11, Lesson 4

Products and Quotients of Radicals

Example Simplify $\sqrt{48}$.

$\sqrt{48} = \sqrt{16 \bullet 3} = \sqrt{16} \bullet \sqrt{3} = 4\sqrt{3}$

Simplify $\sqrt{27x^3}$.

$\sqrt{27x^3} = \sqrt{27} \bullet \sqrt{x^3} = (\sqrt{9} \bullet \sqrt{3})(\sqrt{x^2} \bullet \sqrt{x}) = (3\sqrt{3})(x\sqrt{x}) = 3x\sqrt{3x}$

Check. $(3x\sqrt{3x})^2 = 9x^2 \bullet 3x = 27x^3$ True

Directions Simplify the following radicals. Check your answers.

1. $\sqrt{12}$ ______	13. $\sqrt{3a^2}$ ______
2. $\sqrt{20}$ ______	14. $\sqrt{45x^2y^3}$ ______
3. $\sqrt{48}$ ______	15. $\sqrt{8x^3y^3}$ ______
4. $\sqrt{18}$ ______	16. $\sqrt{25x^2y^3}$ ______
5. $\sqrt{32}$ ______	17. $\sqrt{1{,}000}$ ______
6. $\sqrt{50}$ ______	18. $\sqrt{396x^2}$ ______
7. $\sqrt{84}$ ______	19. $\sqrt{9x^2y}$ ______
8. $\sqrt{180a^2b^3}$ ______	20. $\sqrt{32k^3}$ ______
9. $\sqrt{98}$ ______	21. $\sqrt{12a^7y^7}$ ______
10. $\sqrt{45}$ ______	22. $\sqrt{18x^3y^5}$ ______
11. $\sqrt{16xy^2}$ ______	23. $\sqrt{50a^3b^5}$ ______
12. $\sqrt{96}$ ______	24. $\sqrt{192}$ ______

Directions Solve the problem.

25. To repair a wall, Van and Mai have cut out a square piece of wallboard whose area is 396 square inches. The length of one side of this piece is $\sqrt{396}$ inches. Use the first rule of radicals to simplify this expression. ______

 Algebra

TRL **Workbook Activity 108**

Name Date Period — Activity 102, Chapter 11, Lesson 4

Products and Quotients of Radicals

Directions Simplify the following expressions. Check your work.

1. $\sqrt{\frac{36}{49}}$ ______	9. $\sqrt{52}$ ______
2. $\sqrt{a^5b^4}$ ______	10. $\sqrt{\frac{4a^6}{49b^8}}$ ______
3. $\sqrt{\frac{9}{25}}$ ______	11. $\sqrt{\frac{9x^2}{25y^4}}$ ______
4. $\sqrt{\frac{16}{21}}$ ______	12. $\sqrt{\frac{169}{w^2}}$ ______
5. $\sqrt{\frac{x^2}{64}}$ ______	13. $\sqrt{\frac{49}{144}}$ ______
6. $\sqrt{\frac{4}{81}}$ ______	14. $\sqrt{\frac{26}{25}}$ ______
7. $\sqrt{\frac{c^2}{36}}$ ______	15. $\sqrt{\frac{15a}{36a^4}}$ ______
8. $\sqrt{(a+b)^4}$ ______	16. $\sqrt{\frac{18xy^2}{25x}}$ ______

Directions Solve the problems.

17. A square assembly platform in a factory has an area of 120 square meters. One side of the platform is $\sqrt{120}$ meters long. Simplify this radical as much as possible, using the first rule of radicals. ______

18. Montoya has carefully cut out a perfectly square section of graph paper. She counts all the blocks in the square, then takes a square root of this number. Will Montoya's square root equal the number of blocks in one side of the graph-paper square? Explain. ______

19. The formula for the area of a circle is $A = \pi r^2$. If a particular circle has an area of $(\pi \cdot 147)$ square units, what is the length of the radius, r? Use the first rule of radicals to write the answer in simplest form. ______

radius

20. Cynthia is a real estate agent. In one of her properties, a large square room has an area of 405 square feet. To find the length of one side of the room, Cynthia writes $\sqrt{405}$ feet. Simplify this expression, using the first rule of radicals. ______

 Algebra

TRL **Activity 102**

You can use these rules to simplify some types of radicals.

See Teacher's Edition page for answers to problems 1–25.

Answers for Try This. . .

$\frac{3y^2}{4z}$ $\frac{4y}{2x^2} = \frac{2y}{x^2}$

EXAMPLE 3 Simplify $\sqrt{200}$.

Factor 200 using the largest possible perfect squares:

$\sqrt{200} = \sqrt{100 \cdot 2} = \sqrt{100} \cdot \sqrt{2} = 10\sqrt{2}$.

Check: $(10\sqrt{2})^2 = 200$ $100 \cdot 2 = 200$ True

You cannot factor 2 any further—you are finished simplifying.

Suppose you had factored 200 as $8 \cdot 25$? You would then have $\sqrt{200} = \sqrt{25 \cdot 8} = \sqrt{25} \cdot \sqrt{8} = 5\sqrt{8}$.

But 8 can be factored further, leading to

$5\sqrt{8} = 5\sqrt{4 \cdot 2} = 5 \cdot \sqrt{4} \cdot \sqrt{2} = 5 \cdot 2 \cdot \sqrt{2} = 10\sqrt{2}$.

Simplify $\sqrt{(16x^3)}$.

$\sqrt{(16x^3)} = \sqrt{16} \cdot \sqrt{x^3} = \sqrt{16} \cdot \sqrt{x^2} \cdot \sqrt{x} = 4 \cdot x \cdot \sqrt{x}$

Check. $(4x\sqrt{x})^2 = 16x^3$ $16x^2 \cdot x = 16x^3$ True

Simplify $\sqrt{\frac{25y^6}{x^3}}$, $\sqrt{\frac{25y^6}{x^3}} = \frac{(\sqrt{25} \cdot \sqrt{y^6})}{\sqrt{x^3}} = \frac{\sqrt{25} \cdot \sqrt{y^3} \cdot y^3}{\sqrt{x^2} \cdot x} = \frac{5y^3}{x\sqrt{x}}$

Check. $(\frac{5y^3}{x\sqrt{x}})^2 = \frac{25y^6}{x^3}$ $\frac{25y^6}{x^2x} = \frac{25y^6}{x^3}$ True

TRY THIS

Simplify these expressions.

$\sqrt[3]{\frac{27y^6}{64z^3}}$ and $\sqrt[4]{\frac{256y^4}{16x^8}}$

Exercise A Simplify the following radicals. Be sure to check your answers.

1. $\sqrt{2500}$
2. $\sqrt{500}$
3. $\sqrt{196}$
4. $\sqrt{441}$
5. $\sqrt{25a^2}$
6. $\sqrt{27y^3}$
7. $\sqrt{25x^4y^5}$
8. $\sqrt{225z^7}$
9. $\sqrt{90x^5}$
10. $\sqrt{72t^2}$
11. $\sqrt{1{,}089m^2n^4}$
12. $\sqrt{288y^3z^5}$

Exercise B Simplify the following expressions. Check your work.

13. $\sqrt{\frac{16}{81}}$
14. $\sqrt{\frac{81}{225}}$
15. $\sqrt{\frac{75}{36}}$
16. $\sqrt{\frac{36x^6}{y^4}}$
17. $\sqrt{\frac{27}{y^3}}$
18. $\sqrt{\frac{x^2}{25y^3}}$
19. $\sqrt{\frac{16y^2}{25x^4}}$
20. $\sqrt{\frac{49x^3}{100y^4}}$
21. $\sqrt{\frac{81h^6}{27y^2}}$
22. $\sqrt{\frac{441j^2}{9h^4}}$
23. $\sqrt{\frac{243x^6}{90y^2}}$
24. $\sqrt{\frac{48m^3}{56n^5}}$
25. $\sqrt{\frac{36d^2}{24t^4}}$

procedure should then be repeated for the denominator of the expression. In other words, the simplification of each of these expressions will involve four individual steps. One or more additional steps may be involved if the various roots combine to create an answer that can be simplified.

COMMON ERROR

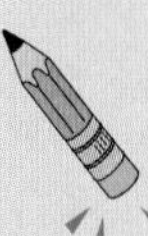

Students may sometimes decide that a value such as $\sqrt{27}$ cannot be simplified because they failed to consider all of the ways that 27 can be rewritten as the product of two factors. To help students find all of the possible factors of a number, explain that they should consider all of the factors of a number up to the root of that number. For example, to find all of the possible factors of 27, first approximate the square root of 27 (< 6) and consider all of the factors to that root: $1 \times ?$, $2 \times ?$, $3 \times ?$, $4 \times ?$, $5 \times ?$, and $6 \times ?$. Applying this procedure whenever the square root of a number needs to be found will help ensure that no factors are overlooked.

3 Reinforce and Extend

MENTAL MATH

Ask volunteers to perform these computations.

12^2	*(144)*
0.3^2	*(0.09)*
100^2	*(10,000)*
0.2^3	*(0.008)*
$1{,}000^2$	*(1,000,000)*
20^3	*(8,000)*

Answers to Problems 1–25

1. $\sqrt{25} \cdot \sqrt{100} = 5 \cdot 10 = 50$
2. $\sqrt{100} \cdot \sqrt{5} = 10\sqrt{5}$
3. $\sqrt{49} \cdot \sqrt{4} = 7 \cdot 2 = 14$
4. $\sqrt{49} \cdot \sqrt{9} = 7 \cdot 3 = 21$
5. $\sqrt{5a \cdot 5a} = 5a$
6. $\sqrt{9} \cdot \sqrt{3} \cdot \sqrt{y^2} \cdot \sqrt{y} = \sqrt{9} \cdot \sqrt{y^2} \cdot \sqrt{3} \cdot \sqrt{y} = 3y \cdot \sqrt{3y}$
7. $\sqrt{25} \cdot \sqrt{x^4} \cdot \sqrt{y^4}\sqrt{y} = 5x^2y^2 \cdot \sqrt{y}$
8. $\sqrt{25} \cdot \sqrt{9} \cdot \sqrt{z^6} \cdot \sqrt{z} = 5 \cdot 3 \cdot z^3 \cdot \sqrt{z} = 15z^3\sqrt{z}$
9. $\sqrt{9} \cdot \sqrt{10} \cdot \sqrt{x^4} \cdot \sqrt{x} = 3 \cdot \sqrt{10} \cdot x^2\sqrt{x} = 3x^2\sqrt{10x}$
10. $\sqrt{36} \cdot \sqrt{2} \cdot \sqrt{t^2} = 6 \cdot t \cdot \sqrt{2} = 6t\sqrt{2}$
11. $\sqrt{121} \cdot \sqrt{9} \cdot \sqrt{m^2} \cdot \sqrt{n^4} = 11 \cdot 3 \cdot mn^2 = 33mn^2$
12. $\sqrt{144} \cdot \sqrt{2} \cdot \sqrt{y^2} \cdot \sqrt{y} \cdot \sqrt{z^4} \cdot \sqrt{z} = 12 \cdot \sqrt{2} \cdot y \cdot \sqrt{y} \cdot z^2 \cdot \sqrt{z} = 12yz^2 \cdot \sqrt{2yz}$
13. $\frac{\sqrt{16}}{\sqrt{81}} = \frac{4}{9}$
14. $\frac{\sqrt{81}}{\sqrt{225}} = \frac{9}{15}$
15. $\frac{(\sqrt{25} \cdot \sqrt{3})}{\sqrt{36}} = \frac{5\sqrt{3}}{6}$
16. $\frac{\sqrt{(36 \cdot x^6)}}{\sqrt{y^4}} = \frac{6x^3}{y^2}$
17. $\frac{\sqrt{27}}{\sqrt{y^3}} = \frac{(\sqrt{9} \cdot \sqrt{3})}{\sqrt{y^2} \cdot \sqrt{y}} = \frac{3\sqrt{3}}{y\sqrt{y}}$
18. $\frac{\sqrt{x^2}}{\sqrt{25y^3}} = \frac{x}{5y\sqrt{y}}$
19. $\frac{\sqrt{16y^2}}{\sqrt{25x^4}} = \frac{4y}{5x^2}$
20. $\frac{\sqrt{49x^3}}{\sqrt{100y^4}} = \frac{\sqrt{49} \cdot \sqrt{x^2} \cdot \sqrt{x}}{\sqrt{100} \cdot \sqrt{y^4}} = \frac{7x\sqrt{x}}{10y^2}$
21. $\frac{\sqrt{81h^6}}{\sqrt{27y^2}} = \frac{9h^3}{\sqrt{9} \cdot \sqrt{3} \cdot \sqrt{y^2}} = \frac{9h^3}{3y \cdot \sqrt{3}} = \frac{3h^3}{y\sqrt{3}}$
22. $\frac{(\sqrt{49} \cdot \sqrt{9} \cdot \sqrt{j^2})}{(\sqrt{9} \cdot \sqrt{h^4})} = \frac{(7 \cdot 3 \cdot j)}{3 \cdot h^2} = \frac{7j}{h^2}$
23. $\frac{(\sqrt{81} \cdot \sqrt{3} \cdot \sqrt{x^6})}{(\sqrt{9} \cdot \sqrt{10} \cdot \sqrt{y^2})} = \frac{9 \cdot \sqrt{3} \cdot x^3}{3 \cdot \sqrt{10} \cdot y} = \frac{3x^3\sqrt{3}}{y\sqrt{10}}$
24. $\frac{\sqrt{16} \cdot \sqrt{3} \cdot \sqrt{m^2} \cdot \sqrt{m}}{\sqrt{4} \cdot \sqrt{14} \cdot \sqrt{n^4} \cdot \sqrt{n}} = \frac{4m\sqrt{3m}}{2n^2\sqrt{14n}} = \frac{2m\sqrt{3m}}{n^2\sqrt{14n}}$
25. $\frac{\sqrt{4} \cdot \sqrt{9} \cdot \sqrt{d^2}}{\sqrt{4} \cdot \sqrt{6} \cdot \sqrt{t^4}} = \frac{3d}{t^2\sqrt{6}}$

Lesson at a Glance

Chapter 11 Lesson 5

Overview This lesson introduces addition and subtraction of radicals.

Objective

- To find the sum or difference of two radicals

Student Pages 338–339

Teacher's Resource Library 

Workbook Activity 109

Activity 103

Alternative Activity 103

Warm-Up Activity

Remind students that the addition or subtraction of fractions or variables is only possible when the variables in an expression or the denominators of the fractions are *alike*. Have students determine if it is possible to compute the following sums or differences. If it is possible, invite volunteers to name the sum or difference in simplest form. If it is not possible, invite volunteers to tell why.

$\frac{3}{10} + \frac{7}{10}$ *(1)*

$\frac{4}{a} - \frac{2}{b}$

(not possible; denominators are unlike)

$\frac{5}{y} + \frac{11}{y}$ $(\frac{16}{y})$

$24m + 6n - m$

$(23m + 6n \text{ or } 6n + 23m)$

$10w - 18w$ $(-8w)$

Encourage students to keep the concept of *like* and *unlike* terms in mind as they complete the lesson.

Teaching the Lesson

To prove that it is not possible to add or subtract radicals of the same value, write the following on the board.

$\sqrt{9} + \sqrt{9} = 3 + 3$ or 6 because $\sqrt{9} = 3$.

$\sqrt{9} + \sqrt{9} \neq \sqrt{18}$ because $\sqrt{18} = 4.2426$.

Lesson 5 Sums and Differences of Radicals

You already know that the sum of $a + 2a$ is $3a$. In much the same way, the sum of $\sqrt{3} + 2\sqrt{3}$ is $3\sqrt{3}$. You can show why this is true if you factor the expressions.

$$\sqrt{3} + 2\sqrt{3} = 1\sqrt{3} + 2\sqrt{3} = (1 + 2)\sqrt{3} = 3\sqrt{3}.$$

However, you cannot add expressions in which the radicals are different. For example, the terms $2\sqrt{5}$ and $5\sqrt{2}$ have different radicals and cannot be added or subtracted.

In some cases, you can simplify radicals so that the resulting terms can be added or subtracted.

Numbers under the $\sqrt{\ }$ are equal	Numbers under the $\sqrt{\ }$ are *not* equal
$2\sqrt{5} + \sqrt{5} = 3\sqrt{5}$	$\sqrt{5} + \sqrt{2}$
$3\sqrt{7} - \sqrt{7} = 2\sqrt{7}$	$2\sqrt{7} - \sqrt{5}$
$5\sqrt{3} - 2\sqrt{3} = 3\sqrt{3}$	$5\sqrt{2} - 5\sqrt{3}$
These radicals can be added or subtracted.	These radicals *cannot* be added or subtracted.

Rule Like radicals can be added or subtracted; unlike radicals cannot.

EXAMPLE 1 Find the sum of $\sqrt{2} + \sqrt{8}$.

First, simplify the terms of the expression.

$\sqrt{2} + \sqrt{8} = \sqrt{2} + \sqrt{(4 \bullet 2)}$

$= \sqrt{2} + (\sqrt{4} \bullet \sqrt{2})$. Then factor and add:

$= (1)\sqrt{2} + (2)\sqrt{2}$

$= 3\sqrt{2}$

Subtract $\sqrt{27} - \sqrt{3}$

Simplify. $\sqrt{27} - \sqrt{3} = \sqrt{(9 \bullet 3)} - \sqrt{3}$

$= (\sqrt{9} \bullet \sqrt{3}) - \sqrt{3}$. Factor and subtract:

$= (3)\sqrt{3} - (1)\sqrt{3}$

$= 2\sqrt{3}$

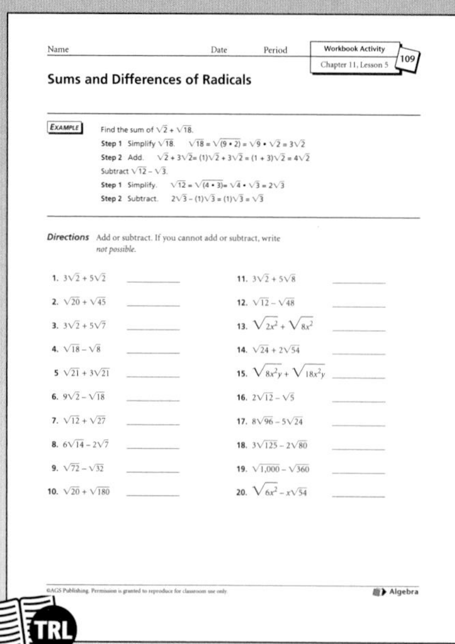

Name Date Period — Workbook Activity 109, Chapter 11, Lesson 5

Sums and Differences of Radicals

EXAMPLE Find the sum of $\sqrt{2} + \sqrt{18}$.

Step 1 Simplify $\sqrt{18}$. $\sqrt{18} = \sqrt{(9 \bullet 2)} = \sqrt{9} \bullet \sqrt{2} = 3\sqrt{2}$

Step 2 Add. $\sqrt{2} + 3\sqrt{2} = (1)\sqrt{2} + 3\sqrt{2} = (1 + 3)\sqrt{2} = 4\sqrt{2}$

Subtract $\sqrt{12} - \sqrt{3}$.

Step 1 Simplify. $\sqrt{12} = \sqrt{(4 \bullet 3)} = \sqrt{4} \bullet \sqrt{3} = 2\sqrt{3}$

Step 2 Subtract. $2\sqrt{3} - (1)\sqrt{3} = (1)\sqrt{3} = \sqrt{3}$

Directions Add or subtract. If you cannot add or subtract, write *not possible.*

1. $3\sqrt{2} + 5\sqrt{2}$ _____
2. $\sqrt{20} + \sqrt{45}$ _____
3. $3\sqrt{2} + 5\sqrt{7}$ _____
4. $\sqrt{18} - \sqrt{8}$ _____
5. $\sqrt{21} + 3\sqrt{21}$ _____
6. $9\sqrt{2} - \sqrt{18}$ _____
7. $\sqrt{12} + \sqrt{27}$ _____
8. $6\sqrt{14} - 2\sqrt{7}$ _____
9. $\sqrt{72} - \sqrt{32}$ _____
10. $\sqrt{20} + \sqrt{180}$ _____
11. $3\sqrt{2} + 5\sqrt{8}$ _____
12. $\sqrt{12} - \sqrt{48}$ _____
13. $\sqrt{2x^2} + \sqrt{8x^2}$ _____
14. $\sqrt{24} + 2\sqrt{54}$ _____
15. $\sqrt{8x^2y} + \sqrt{18x^2y}$ _____
16. $2\sqrt{12} - \sqrt{5}$ _____
17. $8\sqrt{96} - 5\sqrt{24}$ _____
18. $3\sqrt{125} - 2\sqrt{80}$ _____
19. $\sqrt{1{,}000} - \sqrt{360}$ _____
20. $\sqrt{6x^2} - x\sqrt{54}$ _____

 Algebra

TRL

Workbook Activity 109

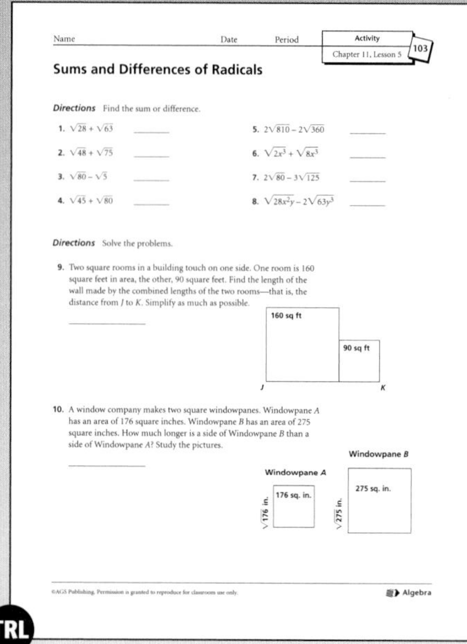

Name Date Period — Activity 103, Chapter 11, Lesson 5

Sums and Differences of Radicals

Directions Find the sum or difference.

1. $\sqrt{28} + \sqrt{63}$ _____
2. $\sqrt{48} + \sqrt{75}$ _____
3. $\sqrt{80} - \sqrt{5}$ _____
4. $\sqrt{45} + \sqrt{80}$ _____
5. $2\sqrt{810} - 2\sqrt{360}$ _____
6. $\sqrt{2x^3} + \sqrt{8x^3}$ _____
7. $2\sqrt{80} - 3\sqrt{125}$ _____
8. $\sqrt{28x^2y} - 2\sqrt{63y^3}$ _____

Directions Solve the problems.

9. Two square rooms in a building touch on one side. One room is 160 square feet in area, the other, 90 square feet. Find the length of the wall made by the combined lengths of the two rooms—that is, the distance from J to K. Simplify as much as possible. _____

10. A window company makes two square windowpanes. Windowpane A has an area of 176 square inches. Windowpane B has an area of 275 square inches. How much longer is a side of Windowpane B than a side of Windowpane A? Study the pictures. _____

 Algebra

TRL

Activity 103

Writing About Mathematics

Is the square root of a number always less than the number itself? In symbol form, is $\sqrt{x} < x$ true for all positive, real numbers? Try some examples. Explain your answer.

EXAMPLE 2 Subtract $2\sqrt{8} - \sqrt{32}$

Simplify. Then factor and subtract:

$$2\sqrt{8} - \sqrt{32} = 2(\sqrt{4} \bullet \sqrt{2}) - (\sqrt{16} \bullet \sqrt{2})$$
$$= 2(2 \bullet \sqrt{2}) - 4(\sqrt{2})$$
$$= 4\sqrt{2} - 4\sqrt{2} = 0$$

Exercise A If possible, find the sum or difference.

1. $\sqrt{2} + 5\sqrt{2}$ $6\sqrt{2}$
2. $\sqrt{2} - 5\sqrt{2}$ $-4\sqrt{2}$
3. $3\sqrt{7} - 2\sqrt{7}$ $\sqrt{7}$
4. $2\sqrt{7} + 7\sqrt{2}$
5. $\sqrt{64} + \sqrt{16}$ 12
6. $\sqrt{13} - \sqrt{11}$
7. $3\sqrt{75} - 4\sqrt{27}$ $3\sqrt{3}$
8. $2\sqrt{28} + 4\sqrt{112}$ $20\sqrt{7}$
9. $5\sqrt{8} - \sqrt{2}$ $9\sqrt{2}$
10. $\sqrt{27} + \sqrt{3}$ $4\sqrt{3}$
11. $\sqrt{52} - 2\sqrt{13}$ 0
12. $\sqrt{21} - 2\sqrt{23}$

Exercise B Simplify, then add or subtract.

13. $\sqrt{24} + \sqrt{36}$
14. $2\sqrt{108} + 3\sqrt{36}$
15. $\sqrt{24} + 3\sqrt{48}$
16. $2\sqrt{7} + 3\sqrt{28}$
17. $4\sqrt{40} + 6\sqrt{60}$
18. $4\sqrt{125} - 3\sqrt{25}$
19. $6\sqrt{36x^4} - \sqrt{25x^4}$
20. $4\sqrt{64x^2} - 3\sqrt{16x^2}$

13. $2\sqrt{6} + 6$
14. $12\sqrt{3} + 18$
15. $2\sqrt{6} + 12\sqrt{3}$
16. $8\sqrt{7}$
17. $8\sqrt{10} + 12\sqrt{15}$
18. $20\sqrt{5} - 15$
19. $31x^2$
20. $20x$

TRY THIS Simplify, then factor and subtract this expression: $2\sqrt{64x^2} - 3\sqrt{49x^2}$ $-5x$

4. cannot be simplified or added
6. cannot be simplified or subtracted
12. cannot be simplified or subtracted

$\sqrt{49} - \sqrt{16} = 7 - 4$ or 3
because $\sqrt{49} = 7$ and $\sqrt{16} = 4$.

$\sqrt{49} - \sqrt{16} \neq \sqrt{49-16}$ or $\sqrt{33}$
because $\sqrt{33} = 5.7446$.

Try This

If some students have difficulty finding a correct solution, encourage them to find the square root of each element of the radicals:

$\sqrt{64} = 8$

$\sqrt{x^2} = x$

$\sqrt{49} = 7$

$\sqrt{x^2} = x$

Common Error

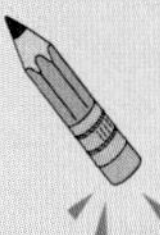

Remind students that the sum of radicals such as $\sqrt{2} + \sqrt{2}$ is $2\sqrt{2}$, not $\sqrt{4}$.

3 Reinforce and Extend

Learning Styles

Auditory/Verbal

Invite several volunteers to each choose a homework exercise and demonstrate and explain the solution on the board. Encourage class members in the audience to ask questions.

Learning Styles

Interpersonal/ Group Learning

Suggest students work in groups of three to develop a method for using a calculator to check the answers to problems 1–20 on page 339.

Lesson at a Glance

Chapter 11 Lesson 6

Overview This lesson introduces fractional radicals.

Objective

- To simplify fractional radicals by rationalizing their denominators

Student Pages 340–341

Teacher's Resource Library 

Workbook Activity 110

Activity 104

Alternative Activity 104

Mathematics Vocabulary

conjugate
rationalizing the denominator

Warm-Up Activity

Write the following computations on the board.

$\frac{1}{2} + \frac{3}{4}$

$\frac{4}{g} - \frac{2}{gh}$

Have students recall that it is possible to simplify each expression by finding its sum or difference. Invite a volunteer to demonstrate how to find the sum and invite another to demonstrate how to find the difference. After the demonstrations, point out that each expression was simplified by multiplying one or both terms of each expression by a form of the whole number 1.

Teaching the Lesson

Prior to discussing the lesson, have students recall that the products of binomial expressions such as $(a + b)(a - b)$ and $(x - y)(x + y)$ generate binomial products. *[$(a + b)(a - b) = a^2 - ab + ab - b^2$ or $a^2 - b^2$ and $(x - y)(x + y) = x^2 + xy - xy - y^2$ or $x^2 - y^2$]*

Lesson 6 Radicals and Fractions

> ***Rationalizing the denominator***
> *Changing a fraction with an irrational number to an equivalent fraction with a rational number*
>
> ***Conjugate***
> *A factor that when multiplied rationalizes (or simplifies) an expression*

Remember that $\sqrt{\frac{1}{4}} = \frac{\sqrt{1}}{\sqrt{4}} = \frac{1}{2}$ and that, in general, $\sqrt{\frac{a}{b}} = \frac{\sqrt{a}}{\sqrt{b}}$ when $b \neq 0$. And, you can evaluate $\frac{\sqrt{2}}{2}$ by rewriting it as $\sqrt{2} \div 2$. How would you evaluate $\frac{2}{\sqrt{2}}$? You know that $\frac{2}{\sqrt{2}}$ is the same as $2 \div \sqrt{2}$. But what value can you assign to the denominator? A value of 1.4? 1.41? 1.414?

You can avoid choosing a value by multiplying the fraction by 1 in the form of $\frac{\sqrt{2}}{\sqrt{2}}$. Remember, multiplying by 1 does not change the value of a number or expression.

$$\frac{2}{\sqrt{2}} = \frac{2}{\sqrt{2}} \cdot \left[\frac{\sqrt{2}}{\sqrt{2}}\right] = \frac{2\sqrt{2}}{2} = \sqrt{2}$$

↑ irrational number ↑ [1] ↑ rational number

You have now changed the denominator from an irrational number to a rational number.

The process of changing a fraction with an irrational denominator to an equivalent fraction with a rational denominator is called **rationalizing the denominator.**

EXAMPLE 1 Rationalize the denominators of $\frac{1}{\sqrt{3}}$, $\frac{2\sqrt{2}}{\sqrt{3}}$, and $\frac{\sqrt{2}}{2\sqrt{5}}$.

$\frac{1}{\sqrt{3}}$	$\frac{2\sqrt{2}}{\sqrt{3}}$	$\frac{\sqrt{2}}{2\sqrt{5}}$
$= \frac{1}{\sqrt{3}} \cdot \left[\frac{\sqrt{3}}{\sqrt{3}}\right]$	$= \frac{2\sqrt{2}}{\sqrt{3}} \cdot \left[\frac{\sqrt{3}}{\sqrt{3}}\right]$	$= \frac{\sqrt{2}}{2\sqrt{5}} \cdot \left[\frac{\sqrt{5}}{\sqrt{5}}\right]$
$= \frac{\sqrt{3}}{(\sqrt{3} \cdot \sqrt{3})}$	$= \frac{(2\sqrt{2} \cdot \sqrt{3})}{(\sqrt{3} \cdot \sqrt{3})}$	$= \frac{(\sqrt{2} \cdot \sqrt{5})}{(2 \cdot \sqrt{5} \cdot \sqrt{5})}$
$= \frac{\sqrt{3}}{3}$	$= \frac{2\sqrt{6}}{3}$	$= \frac{\sqrt{10}}{10}$

You can use the same process to rationalize a denominator such as $3 + \sqrt{2}$. Notice in the following example that you will multiply $(3 + \sqrt{2})$ by $(3 - \sqrt{2})$ to rationalize the denominator. The terms $(3 + \sqrt{2})$ and $(3 - \sqrt{2})$ are called **conjugates** of one another.

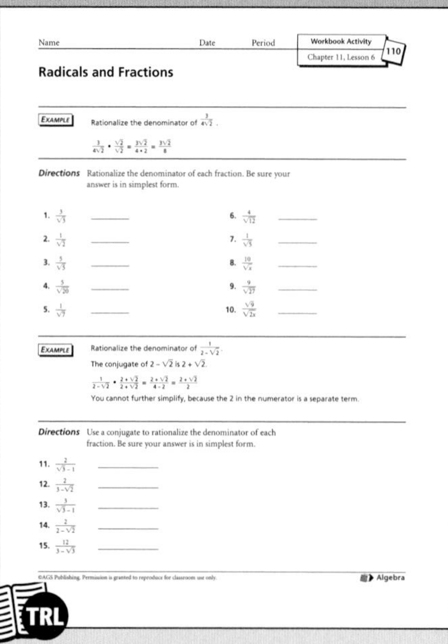

Name Date Period | Workbook Activity 110 | Chapter 11, Lesson 6

Radicals and Fractions

EXAMPLE Rationalize the denominator of $\frac{3}{4\sqrt{2}}$.

$\frac{3}{4\sqrt{2}} \cdot \frac{\sqrt{2}}{\sqrt{2}} = \frac{3\sqrt{2}}{4 \cdot 2} = \frac{3\sqrt{2}}{8}$

Directions Rationalize the denominator of each fraction. Be sure your answer is in simplest form.

1. $\frac{3}{\sqrt{3}}$ ______ 6. $\frac{4}{\sqrt{12}}$ ______
2. $\frac{1}{\sqrt{2}}$ ______ 7. $\frac{1}{\sqrt{5}}$ ______
3. $\frac{5}{\sqrt{5}}$ ______ 8. $\frac{10}{\sqrt{x}}$ ______
4. $\frac{5}{\sqrt{20}}$ ______ 9. $\frac{9}{\sqrt{27}}$ ______
5. $\frac{1}{\sqrt{7}}$ ______ 10. $\frac{\sqrt{9}}{\sqrt{2x}}$ ______

EXAMPLE Rationalize the denominator of $\frac{1}{2 - \sqrt{2}}$.
The conjugate of $2 - \sqrt{2}$ is $2 + \sqrt{2}$.
$\frac{1}{2 - \sqrt{2}} \cdot \frac{2 + \sqrt{2}}{2 + \sqrt{2}} = \frac{2 + \sqrt{2}}{4 - 2} = \frac{2 + \sqrt{2}}{2}$
You cannot further simplify, because the 2 in the numerator is a separate term.

Directions Use a conjugate to rationalize the denominator of each fraction. Be sure your answer is in simplest form.

11. $\frac{2}{\sqrt{3} - 1}$ ______
12. $\frac{2}{3 - \sqrt{2}}$ ______
13. $\frac{3}{\sqrt{3} - 1}$ ______
14. $\frac{2}{2 - \sqrt{2}}$ ______
15. $\frac{12}{3 - \sqrt{3}}$ ______

 Algebra

Workbook Activity 110

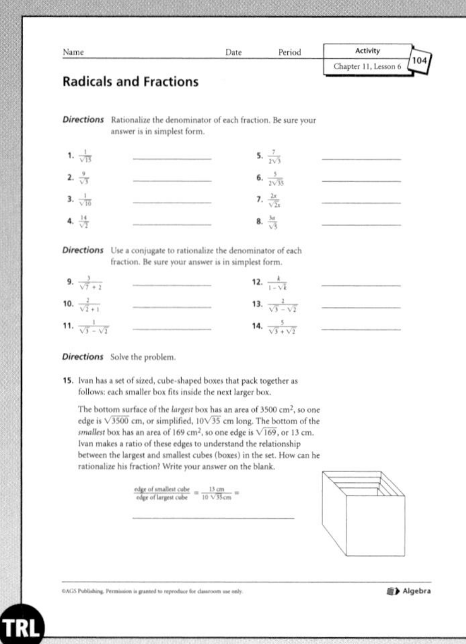

Name Date Period | Activity 104 | Chapter 11, Lesson 6

Radicals and Fractions

Directions Rationalize the denominator of each fraction. Be sure your answer is in simplest form.

1. $\frac{1}{\sqrt{15}}$ ______ 5. $\frac{7}{2\sqrt{3}}$ ______
2. $\frac{9}{\sqrt{3}}$ ______ 6. $\frac{5}{2\sqrt{35}}$ ______
3. $\frac{1}{\sqrt{10}}$ ______ 7. $\frac{2x}{\sqrt{2x}}$ ______
4. $\frac{14}{\sqrt{2}}$ ______ 8. $\frac{3a}{\sqrt{3}}$ ______

Directions Use a conjugate to rationalize the denominator of each fraction. Be sure your answer is in simplest form.

9. $\frac{3}{\sqrt{7} + 2}$ ______ 12. $\frac{k}{1 - \sqrt{k}}$ ______
10. $\frac{2}{\sqrt{2} + 1}$ ______ 13. $\frac{2}{\sqrt{3} - \sqrt{2}}$ ______
11. $\frac{1}{\sqrt{3} - \sqrt{2}}$ ______ 14. $\frac{5}{\sqrt{3} + \sqrt{2}}$ ______

Directions Solve the problem.

15. Ivan has a set of sized, cube-shaped boxes that pack together as follows: each smaller box fits inside the next larger box.

The bottom surface of the *largest* box has an area of 3500 cm^2, so one edge is $\sqrt{3500}$ cm, or simplified, $10\sqrt{35}$ cm long. The bottom of the *smallest* box has an area of 169 cm^2, so one edge is $\sqrt{169}$, or 13 cm. Ivan makes a ratio of these edges to understand the relationship between the largest and smallest cubes (boxes) in the set. How can he rationalize his fraction? Write your answer on the blank.

$\frac{\text{edge of smallest cube}}{\text{edge of largest cube}} = \frac{13 \text{ cm}}{10\sqrt{35} \text{cm}} =$

______

 Algebra

Activity 104

Remember, if you multiply the numerator and denominator by the same number, the value of the fraction does not change.

EXAMPLE 2 Rationalize the denominator of $\frac{2}{(3 + \sqrt{2})}$.

In this case, you will need to multiply by 1 in the form of $[\frac{3 - \sqrt{2}}{(3 - \sqrt{2})}]$.

$$\frac{2}{(3 + \sqrt{2})} \bullet [\frac{3 - \sqrt{2}}{(3 - \sqrt{2})}] = \frac{(2)(3 - \sqrt{2})}{(3 + \sqrt{2})(3 - \sqrt{2})}$$

$$= \frac{(2)(3 - \sqrt{2})}{3(3 - \sqrt{2}) + \sqrt{2}(3 - \sqrt{2})} = \frac{(2)(3 - \sqrt{2})}{9 - 3\sqrt{2} + 3\sqrt{2} - 2}$$

$$= \frac{6 - 2\sqrt{2}}{9 - 0 - 2} = \frac{6 - 2\sqrt{2}}{7}$$

In general, this multiplication follows the pattern of the difference between two perfect squares.

$$(a + \sqrt{b})(a - \sqrt{b}) = a^2 - (\sqrt{b})^2 = a^2 - b$$

11. $5\sqrt{5} - 10$ or $-5(2 - \sqrt{5})$

12. $\sqrt{6} - \sqrt{3}$

13. $\frac{(9\sqrt{5} - 15)}{4}$

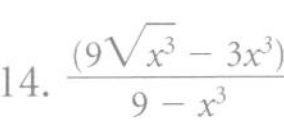

14. $\frac{(9\sqrt{x^3} - 3x^3)}{9 - x^3}$ or $\frac{[3(3\sqrt{x^3} - x^3)]}{9 - x^3}$

15. $\frac{[3y(3 + \sqrt{y^3})]}{9 - y^3}$

Rule To rationalize a denominator of the form $a + \sqrt{b}$ or $a - \sqrt{b}$, multiply both the numerator and the denominator by the conjugate of the denominator.

EXAMPLE 3 Rationalize the denominator of $\frac{2}{(3 - \sqrt{5})}$.

Multiply $(3 - \sqrt{5})$ by its conjugate, $(3 + \sqrt{5})$.

$$\frac{2}{(3 - \sqrt{5})} = \frac{2}{(3 - \sqrt{5})} \bullet \frac{(3 + \sqrt{5})}{(3 + \sqrt{5})}$$

$$= \frac{(6 + 2\sqrt{5})}{(9 - 5)} = \frac{(6 + 2\sqrt{5})}{4} = \frac{(3 + \sqrt{5})}{2}$$

Exercise A Rationalize the denominator of each fraction. Be sure your answer is in simplest form.

1. $\frac{(4)\sqrt{3}}{\sqrt{2}}$ $2\sqrt{6}$
2. $\frac{(6)\sqrt{8}}{\sqrt{3}}$ $4\sqrt{6}$
3. $\frac{(3\sqrt{7})}{\sqrt{5}}$ $\frac{(3\sqrt{35})}{5}$
4. $\frac{(3\sqrt{5})}{(3\sqrt{15})}$ $\frac{\sqrt{3}}{3}$
5. $\frac{(2\sqrt{12})}{(3\sqrt{6})}$ $\frac{2\sqrt{2}}{3}$
6. $\frac{(3\sqrt{21})}{(2\sqrt{7})}$ $\frac{(3\sqrt{3})}{2}$
7. $\frac{(5\sqrt{35})}{(3\sqrt{7})}$ $\frac{(5\sqrt{5})}{3}$
8. $\frac{(4\sqrt{14})}{(2\sqrt{28})}$ $\sqrt{2}$

Exercise B Use a conjugate to rationalize the denominator of each fraction. Be sure your answer is in simplest form.

9. $\frac{2}{(2 + \sqrt{2})}$ 9. $2 - \sqrt{2}$
10. $\frac{6}{(3 + \sqrt{3})}$ 10. $3 - \sqrt{3}$
11. $\frac{5}{(2 + \sqrt{5})}$
12. $\frac{\sqrt{3}}{(1 + \sqrt{2})}$
13. $\frac{3\sqrt{5}}{(3 + \sqrt{5})}$
14. $\frac{3\sqrt{x^3}}{(3 + \sqrt{x^3})}$
15. $\frac{3y}{(3 - \sqrt{y^3})}$

See above for answers to problems 11–15

COMMON ERROR

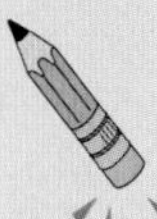

Remind students that if they choose, for example, to multiply the denominator of a fraction by $(4 + \sqrt{5})$, they must also multiply the numerator of that fraction by $(4 + \sqrt{5})$. The same operation must be performed to *both* the numerator and denominator of a fraction.

3 Reinforce and Extend

GROUP PROBLEM SOLVING

Encourage students to work in groups of three to discuss and solve the following problem:

Use the Pythagorean theorem to find the value of *a*. *(32)*

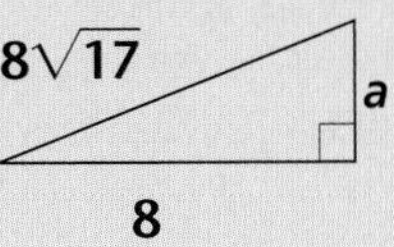

Lesson at a Glance

Chapter 11 Lesson 7

Overview This lesson introduces equations that contain a radical and a variable or unknown.

Objective

- To determine the value of a variable in an equation that contains a radical

Student Pages 342–345

Teacher's Resource Library TRL

Workbook Activities 111–112

Activity 105

Alternative Activity 105

Warm-Up Activity

Invite students to consider and solve the following riddles.

"I am thinking of a fraction. When you subtract $\frac{3}{4}$ and add $\frac{1}{2}$ to the fraction, the result is $\frac{1}{4}$. What is the fraction?" *($\frac{1}{2}$)*

"I am thinking of a positive integer. When you subtract −3 and add −7 to the number, the result is 6. What is the integer?" *(10)*

"I am thinking of a negative integer. When you add 11 to the integer, then find the square root of the sum, the result is 3. What is the integer?" *(−2)*

"I am thinking of a positive whole number. When you cube the number, then take its square root, the result is 8. What is the number?" *(4)*

"I am thinking of a fraction. When you square the fraction, then take its fourth root, the answer is $\frac{1}{3}$. What is the fraction?" *($\frac{1}{9}$)*

Teaching the Lesson

Prior to discussing the examples beginning on page 342, write the equation $x + 2 = 9$ on the board and remind students that the answer $x = 7$ is found by subtracting 2 from both sides of the equation. Explain that adding, subtracting, multiplying, or dividing both sides of an equation by the same number helps to *isolate* the variable. When an

Lesson 7 Radicals in Equations

Suppose you were asked to solve this puzzle: "The square root of a number is 10. What is the number?" You could solve the puzzle by letting n equal the number and writing the puzzle in terms of an equation:

$$\sqrt{n} = 10$$

You already know that you can multiply each side of an equation by an equivalent of 1 without changing the value of the equation. In this case, you can "square" both sides of the equation:

$$(\sqrt{n})^2 = (10)^2$$

And then solve for n: $n = 100$

EXAMPLE 1 Find x when $(\sqrt{3x}) = 4$.

First, square both sides of the equation.

$(\sqrt{3x})^2 = 4^2$ Then solve for x.

$3x = 16$

$x = \frac{16}{3}$

Check: $\sqrt{[3(\frac{16}{3})]} = 4$

$\sqrt{16} = 4$ True

EXAMPLE 2 Find x when $[\sqrt{x - 1}] = 5$.

Square both sides of the equation, then solve for x.

$[\sqrt{(x - 1)}]^2 = 5^2$

$x - 1 = 25$

$x = 26$

Check: $\sqrt{(26 - 1)} = 5$

$\sqrt{25} = 5$ True

EXAMPLE 3 Find x when $12 - \sqrt{3x} = 4$.

Step 1 In this case, you must first isolate the variable. Place the term with the variable on one side of the equation and place all other terms on the opposite side of the equation.

$12 - \sqrt{3x} = 4$ is the same as $-\sqrt{3x} = -8$.

Name Date Period

Workbook Activity 111 — Chapter 11, Lesson 7

Radicals in Equations

EXAMPLE Solve for x: $\sqrt{x} + 2 = 13$

Step 1 Isolate the variable, x. $\sqrt{x} + 2 - 2 = 13 - 2$

$\sqrt{x} = 11$

Step 2 Square both sides. $(\sqrt{x})^2 = 11^2$

$x = 121$

Step 3 Check. $\sqrt{121} + 2 = 13$

$11 + 2 = 13$ $13 = 13$

True

Directions Solve each equation for the variable. Check your answers.

1. $\sqrt{x} = 5$ ________
2. $\sqrt{n} = 8$ ________
3. $\sqrt{k + 3} = 2$ ________
4. $\sqrt{a} = 13$ ________
5. $\sqrt{r + 8} = 12$ ________
6. $\sqrt{y - 5} = 5$ ________
7. $\sqrt{m} = 16$ ________
8. $\sqrt{4n - 3} = 3$ ________

Directions Solve the problems. Show the equation as well as your answer.

9. Kristen challenges you with this puzzle: "Add the square root of a mystery number to the square root of 100. The result is 19. What is the mystery number?"

____

10. Jaime buys a square tablecloth. The package label declares, "The area of this tablecloth is 800 square inches." What is the length of a side of the cloth? (Express your answer as a simplified radical.)

____

 Algebra

TRL

Workbook Activity 111

Name Date Period

Workbook Activity 112 — Chapter 11, Lesson 7

Simplifying Equations with Radicals

EXAMPLE One way to simplify an equation containing a radical sign is to raise each side of the equation to the second power.

Suppose an object is dropped from a tall building. At the moment the object reaches a velocity of 24 feet per second, how far has the object fallen? Use the formula $V = \sqrt{64d}$ where V = velocity in feet per second and d = distance in feet.

Solution: $V = \sqrt{64d}$

$24 = \sqrt{64d}$

$(24)^2 = (\sqrt{64d})^2$

$576 = 64d$

$9 = d$ The object has fallen 9 feet.

Directions Use a calculator to solve these problems.

1. Suppose the formula $V = \sqrt{32d}$ is used to find the distance in feet (d) an object falls at a velocity (V) measured in feet per second. An object is dropped from the edge of a roof. At the moment the object reaches a velocity of 36 feet per second, it hits the ground. How far did the object fall? ________
2. Suppose the formula $S = 5.5\sqrt{d}$ is used to determine the distance in feet (d) it takes an automobile to stop if it were traveling a certain speed in miles per hour (S). Find the distance it would take an automobile traveling 70 miles per hour to stop. Round your answer to the nearest whole number. ________
3. Suppose the formula $d = 0.25\sqrt{h}$ is used to determine the height in inches (h) that a submarine periscope must be for an observer looking through that periscope to see an object that is a distance of (d) miles away. How far does a submarine periscope have to extend above the water to see a surface ship that is 1 mile away? ________
4. A rectangle measures 4 inches by 6 inches. What is the length in inches, to the nearest tenth, of a diagonal of that rectangle? Use the formula $a^2 + b^2 = c^2$, where a and b represent the legs of a right triangle and c represents the hypotenuse. ________
5. A 16-foot ladder is leaning against the side of a building. If the bottom of the ladder is 8 feet from the side of the building, how far above the ground does the ladder touch the building? Use the formula $a^2 + b^2 = c^2$, where a and b represent the legs of a right triangle and c represents the hypotenuse, and round your answer to the nearest tenth. ________

 Algebra

TRL

Workbook Activity 112

EXAMPLE 3 *(continued)*

Step 2 Square both sides of the equation and solve for x.

$$-\sqrt{3x} = -8$$
$$(-\sqrt{3x})^2 = (-8)^2$$
$$3x = 64$$
$$x = \frac{64}{3}$$

Check: $12 - \sqrt{3x} = 4$

$$12 - \sqrt{3(\tfrac{64}{3})} = 4$$
$$12 - \sqrt{64} = 4$$
$$12 - 8 = 4 \quad \text{True}$$

You may also need to use radicals when presented with some formulas.

EXAMPLE 4 What is the length of the side of a square whose area is A?

Write the question in equation form: $A = s^2$. Then solve for s. Your answer is in simplified radical form.

$$A = s^2, \sqrt{A} = s \text{ or } s = \sqrt{A}$$

What is the length of the side of a square whose area is 25 cm^2?

$$s = \sqrt{A}$$
$$s = \sqrt{25} \text{ or } 5 \text{ cm}$$

What is the radius of a circle whose area is A?

Write the question in equation form: $A = \pi r^2$.

Isolate r^2 on one side of the equation.

$$A = \pi r^2 \text{ is the same as } \frac{A}{\pi} = r^2.$$

A
r

Solve for r.

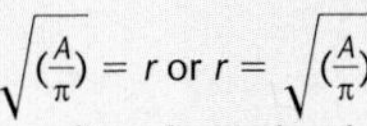

$$\sqrt{\left(\frac{A}{\pi}\right)} = r \text{ or } r = \sqrt{\left(\frac{A}{\pi}\right)}$$

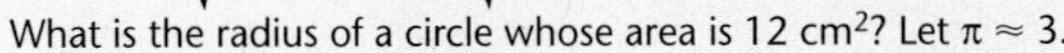

What is the radius of a circle whose area is 12 cm^2? Let $\pi \approx 3$.

$$r = \sqrt{\left(\frac{A}{\pi}\right)}$$
$$r = \sqrt{\frac{12}{3}}$$
$$r = \sqrt{4} \text{ or } 2 \text{ cm}$$

unknown in the form of a variable is isolated in any equation, the value of the variable becomes known.

After discussing the example at the bottom of page 343, explain that the formula $\frac{A}{\pi} = r^2$ is derived from the formula $A = \pi r^2$ by isolating r^2. This isolation is accomplished by dividing both sides of the equation by π:

$$A = \pi r^2$$
$$\frac{A}{\pi} = \frac{\pi r^2}{\pi}$$
$$\frac{A}{\pi} = r^2$$

3 Reinforce and Extend

LEARNING STYLES

Body/Kinesthetic

Invite students to use graph paper or other classroom materials to model problems 14–20 on pages 344 and 345.

GROUP PROBLEM SOLVING

Encourage students to work in groups of three to discuss and solve the following problem:

Does $\sqrt{x} - \sqrt{y} = \sqrt{(x - y)}$? Explain.

(The statement is true if $y = 0$ or if $x = 0$ and $y = 0$. The statement is false for all other values of x and y.)

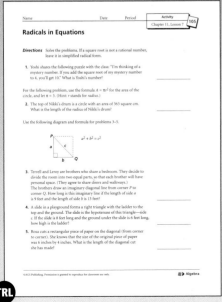

Name Date Period | Activity 105 | Chapter 11, Lesson 7

Radicals in Equations

Directions Solve the problems. If a square root is not a rational number, leave it in simplified radical form.

1. Yoshi shares the following puzzle with the class: "I'm thinking of a mystery number. If you add the square root of my mystery number to 4, you'll get 10." What is Yoshi's number? ________

For the following problem, use the formula $A = \pi r^2$ for the area of the circle, and let $\pi = 3$. (Hint: r stands for *radius*.)

2. The top of Nikki's drum is a circle with an area of 363 square cm. What is the length of the radius of Nikki's drum? ________

Use the following diagram and formula for problems 3–5.

P
a
c
b
Q

$$a^2 + b^2 = c^2$$

3. Terrell and Leroy are brothers who share a bedroom. They decide to divide the room into two equal parts, so that each brother will have personal space. (They agree to share doors and walkways.) The brothers draw an imaginary diagonal line from corner P to corner Q. How long is this imaginary line if the length of side a is 9 feet and the length of side b is 13 feet? ________
4. A slide in a playground forms a right triangle with the ladder to the top and the ground. The slide is the hypotenuse of this triangle—side c. If the slide is 8 feet long and the ground under the slide is 6 feet long, how high is the ladder? ________
5. Rosa cuts a rectangular piece of paper on the diagonal (from corner to corner). She knows that the size of the original piece of paper was 6 inches by 4 inches. What is the length of the diagonal cut she has made? ________

 Algebra

TRL

Activity 105

In the Community

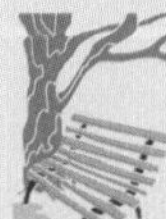

Have students note the scenario presented in problem 14 on page 344. Point out that many businesses (such as those in a shopping mall) pay rent that is based on the number of square feet the business occupies. Invite students to name various businesses and other organizations in their community that may pay rent in terms of square footage. You might choose to challenge a group of students to create and implement a way to find the typical rent (per square foot) that is charged in your community and share their findings with their classmates.

Exercise A Solve each equation for the unknown.

1. $\sqrt{n} = 7$ $n = 49$
2. $\sqrt{x} = 4$ $x = 16$
3. $\sqrt{2y} = 6$ $y = 18$
4. $\sqrt{4m} = 8$ $m = 16$
5. $\sqrt{5y} = 35$ $y = 245$
6. $\sqrt{z} = \frac{3}{2}$ $z = \frac{9}{4}$
7. $\sqrt{3x} = 7$ $x = 16\frac{1}{3}$
8. $\sqrt{4x} = 6$ $x = 9$

Exercise B Solve each equation for x. Check your answers.

9. $13 - \sqrt{x} = 5$ $x = 64$
10. $29 - \sqrt{x} = 13$ $x = 256$
11. $43 - \sqrt{x} = 18$ $x = 625$
12. $\sqrt{x} - 9 = 16$ $x = 625$
13. $\sqrt{(2x - 1)} = 16$ $x = 128\frac{1}{2}$

PROBLEM SOLVING

Exercise C Solve each problem.

14. In the new mall, each store has a square floor space of 36 square units. What is the length of one side of the store? 6 units

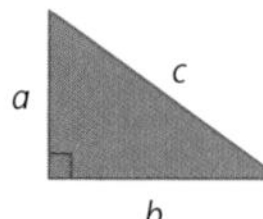

15. Gina rides her bike around a square park that has 49 square units. What is the length of one side of the park? 7 units
16. Carrie has drawn a right triangle. She asks you to determine the lengths of the sides of the triangle by using the formula $a^2 + b^2 = c^2$. Solve for a, b, and c.

a
c
b
$a^2 + b^2 = c^2$

$a = \sqrt{c^2 - b^2}$

$b = \sqrt{c^2 - a^2}$

$c = \sqrt{a^2 + b^2}$

The formula for the area of a circle with radius r is $A = \pi r^2$. Use this formula for Problems 17 and 18.

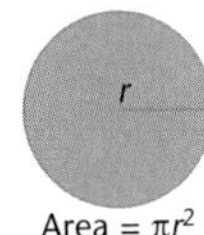

17. The small, circular area rug in Jackson's room has an area of 1,200 square inches. What is the length of the rug's radius? (Use $\pi \approx 3$.) You may use radicals in your answer. 20 in.

18. Juanita draws a chalk circle on the sidewalk after tying the chalk to a length of string and taping the string to the ground. The length of the string is equal to the radius of the circle. How long is her string if the circle has an area of 81 square units? (Use $\pi \approx 3$.) $\sqrt{27}$ units or 5.196 units

The formula for the volume of a cylinder with radius r is $V = \pi r^2 h$. Use this formula for Problems 19 and 20.

19. Cal is making a lid for a can shaped like a cylinder. What is the radius of the circle Cal must make for the lid? The volume (V) of the cylinder is 600 cubic units and its height is 200 units. What is its radius? (Use $\pi \approx 3$.) 1 unit

20. An auto mechanic pours used oil into a cylindrical drum. What is the radius of the lid of the drum if the drum's volume is 1,200 cubic units and its height is 16 units? (Use $\pi \approx 3$.) 5 units

Estimation Activity

Estimate: Predict the nature of the roots from the graphed solution.

1\.

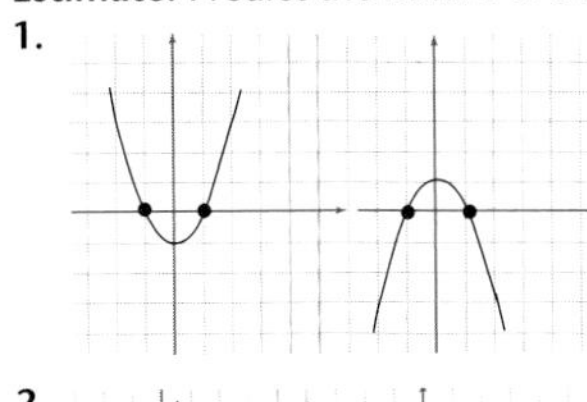

2\.

3\.

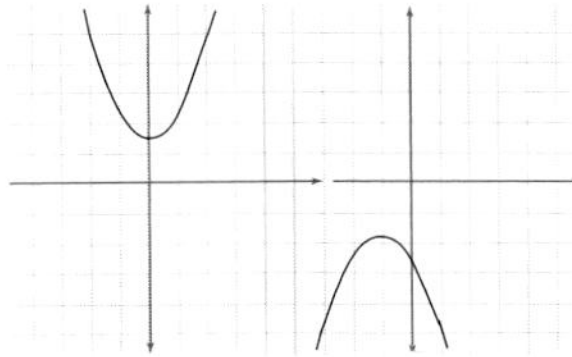

Solution: Each type of root results in a similar graph. By knowing the shape of the line, you can predict the nature of the root.

Answers: **1.** two real roots
2. two equal real roots
3. no real roots (complex roots)

AT HOME

Have students note the scenario presented in problem 16 on page 344 and invite them to name other carpeting-related or other home-improvement formulas that are sometimes used by a homeowner consumer.

[Sample answers: Use $A = lw$ (where l = the measure of the length and w = the measure of the width) to find the area of a rectangular floor to carpet or to find the area of a rectangular wall or other rectangular surface to paint; use $n = \frac{A}{9}$ (where A = area of a surface in square feet) to find the number of square yards in a given number of square feet; use $x = 144y$ where y = a measure in square feet to find the number of square inches in a given number of square feet.]

Lesson at a Glance

Chapter 11 Lesson 8

Overview This lesson introduces expressions that, when rewritten or simplified, contain fractional exponents.

Objective

- To rewrite and simplify expressions that contain radicals

Student Pages 346–347

Teacher's Resource Library TRL

Workbook Activity 113

Activity 106

Alternative Activity 106

Mathematics Vocabulary

radicand

1 Warm-Up Activity

Ask students to solve each of these equations for the unknown.

$x + 2 = 17$	$(x = 15)$
$b - 5 = -8$	$(b = -3)$
$-3r = 12$	$(r = -4)$
$\frac{n}{4} = -20$	$(n = -80)$
$q = 81$	$(q = 9)$
$c = -9$	$(c = -3)$

Upon completion of the activity, remind students that any letter of the alphabet can be used to represent an unknown, and that to solve an equation for an unknown, the same operation must be performed on *both* sides of the equation.

2 Teaching the Lesson

After discussing the examples on pages 346 and 347, prove that $\sqrt[2]{x} = x^{\frac{1}{2}}$ by writing the expression $\sqrt[2]{16} = 16^{\frac{1}{2}}$ on the board and inviting students to use a calculator to find the values of $\sqrt[2]{16}$ and $16^{\frac{1}{2}}$.

(Students will find that $\sqrt[2]{16} = 4$ and $16^{\frac{1}{2}} = 4$.)

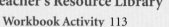

Lesson 8 Radicals and Exponents

Radicand

A number under the radical sign ($\sqrt{\ }$)

Recall that $x \cdot x^2 = x^3$, $y^2 \cdot y^3 = y^5$, and, in general, $n^a \cdot n^b = n^{(a+b)}$.

In algebra, you will sometimes need to find products of terms containing radicals, such as $x \cdot \sqrt{x}$ and $(y^2)\sqrt[3]{y}$. To find these products, you will need to rewrite the radicals using exponents.

> The nth root of x is written $x^{\frac{1}{n}}$.
>
> Using symbols, $\sqrt[n]{x} = x^{\frac{1}{n}}$.

To write the radical using exponents, you need to write the **radicand** as the base raised to a power.

$\sqrt[2]{x} = x^{\frac{1}{2}}$	$\sqrt[3]{x} = x^{\frac{1}{3}}$	$\sqrt[6]{x} = x^{\frac{1}{6}}$
↑ radicand	↑ base	↑ power

The $\sqrt{x}$ represents the square or second root of x. The 2 is understood and not usually written. $\sqrt{x} = \sqrt[2]{x}$.

Recall that

$$\sqrt{(a \cdot b)} = \sqrt{a} \cdot \sqrt{b}$$

$$(a \cdot b)^{\frac{1}{2}} = a^{\frac{1}{2}} \cdot b^{\frac{1}{2}}$$

> In general,
>
> $\sqrt[n]{(a \bullet b)} = \sqrt[n]{a} \bullet \sqrt[n]{b}$, and $(a \bullet b)^{\frac{1}{n}} = a^{\frac{1}{n}} \bullet b^{\frac{1}{n}}$.

EXAMPLE 1 Write $\sqrt[5]{xy}$ using exponents.

$$\sqrt[5]{xy} = x^{\frac{1}{5}} \bullet y^{\frac{1}{5}}$$

Write $\sqrt[3]{4x}$ using exponents.

$$\sqrt[3]{4x} = 4^{\frac{1}{3}} \bullet x^{\frac{1}{3}}$$

Write $x \bullet \sqrt{x}$ with exponents and simplify.

$$x \bullet \sqrt{x} = x \bullet x^{\frac{1}{2}} = x^{(1+\frac{1}{2})} = x^{\frac{3}{2}}$$

Write $y^2 \bullet \sqrt[3]{y}$ with exponents and simplify.

$$y^2 \bullet \sqrt[3]{y} = y^2 \bullet y^{\frac{1}{3}} = y^{(2+\frac{1}{3})} = y^{(2\frac{1}{3})}$$

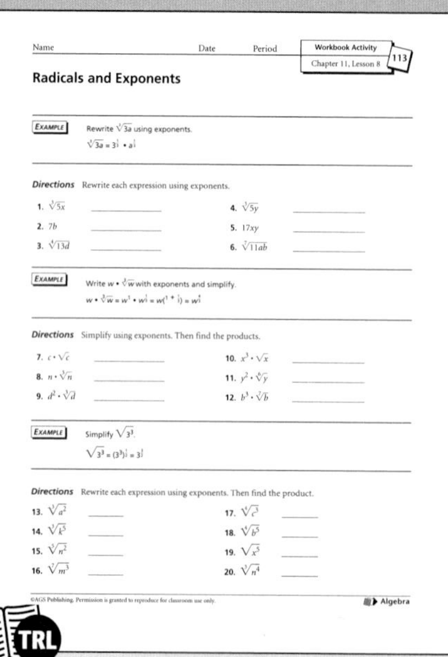

Name Date Period — Workbook Activity 113, Chapter 11, Lesson 8

Radicals and Exponents

EXAMPLE Rewrite $\sqrt[4]{3a}$ using exponents.
$\sqrt[4]{3a} = 3^{\frac{1}{4}} \cdot a^{\frac{1}{4}}$

Directions Rewrite each expression using exponents.

1. $\sqrt[3]{5x}$ ______
2. $7b$ ______
3. $\sqrt[4]{13d}$ ______
4. $\sqrt[3]{5y}$ ______
5. $17xy$ ______
6. $\sqrt[7]{11ab}$ ______

EXAMPLE Write $w \cdot \sqrt[3]{w}$ with exponents and simplify.
$w \cdot \sqrt[3]{w} = w^1 \cdot w^{\frac{1}{3}} = w^{(1+\frac{1}{3})} = w^{\frac{4}{3}}$

Directions Simplify using exponents. Then find the products.

7. $c \cdot \sqrt{c}$ ______
8. $n \cdot \sqrt[3]{n}$ ______
9. $d^2 \cdot \sqrt[3]{d}$ ______
10. $x^3 \cdot \sqrt{x}$ ______
11. $y^2 \cdot \sqrt[6]{y}$ ______
12. $b^3 \cdot \sqrt[7]{b}$ ______

EXAMPLE Simplify $\sqrt{3^3}$.
$\sqrt{3^3} = (3^3)^{\frac{1}{2}} = 3^{\frac{3}{2}}$

Directions Rewrite each expression using exponents. Then find the product.

13. $\sqrt[3]{a^2}$ ______
14. $\sqrt[3]{k^5}$ ______
15. $\sqrt[5]{n^2}$ ______
16. $\sqrt[7]{m^3}$ ______
17. $\sqrt[4]{c^3}$ ______
18. $\sqrt[4]{b^5}$ ______
19. $\sqrt{x^5}$ ______
20. $\sqrt[3]{n^4}$ ______

 Algebra

TRL

Workbook Activity 113

Name Date Period — Activity 106, Chapter 11, Lesson 8

Radicals and Exponents

Directions Rewrite each expression using exponents.

1. $\sqrt[3]{n}$ ______
2. $\sqrt{y}$ ______
3. $\sqrt{3d}$ ______
4. $\sqrt[5]{x}$ ______
5. $\sqrt[4]{k}$ ______
6. $\sqrt[3]{9x}$ ______
7. $\sqrt[6]{3a}$ ______
8. $\sqrt[5]{7k}$ ______

Directions Simplify using exponents. Then find the products.

9. $a^3 \cdot \sqrt{a}$ ______
10. $x^2 \cdot \sqrt[3]{x}$ ______
11. $\sqrt{d} \cdot \sqrt[3]{d}$ ______
12. $n^3 \cdot \sqrt[4]{n}$ ______
13. $y \cdot \sqrt[3]{y}$ ______

Directions Use a calculator to find the square root or cube root of a number.

14. $\sqrt{4^4}$ ______
15. $\sqrt[3]{27^2}$ ______
16. $\sqrt{9^4}$ ______
17. $\sqrt[3]{3^6}$ ______
18. $\sqrt{16^3}$ ______
19. $\sqrt{25^3}$ ______
20. $\sqrt[3]{64^2}$ ______
21. $\sqrt{10^6}$ ______
22. $\sqrt[3]{125^2}$ ______
23. $\sqrt{10^8}$ ______

Directions Solve the problems.

24. Filipe has a puzzle to share. "I'm thinking of a number that has a square root equal to two times the square root of 16." What is the number in Filipe's puzzle? ______
25. The top of a large square urn (pot) for planting flowers has a surface area of 304 square inches. What is the length of one side of the square top? (Express the answer as a simplified radical.) ______

 Algebra

TRL

Activity 106

You can find square roots, cube roots, and even *n*th roots by rewriting and simplifying radical expressions.

EXAMPLE 2 $\sqrt[3]{x^3} = \sqrt[3]{(x \bullet x \bullet x)} = x^{\frac{1}{3}} \bullet x^{\frac{1}{3}} \bullet x^{\frac{1}{3}} = x^{(\frac{1}{3} + \frac{1}{3} + \frac{1}{3})} = x^1 = x$

And, $\sqrt[3]{x^3}$ can be written as $(x^3)^{\frac{1}{3}}$, which equals $x^{(3 \bullet \frac{1}{3})} = x^1 = x$.

$$\sqrt[n]{x^m} = (x^m)^{\frac{1}{n}}$$

Simplify $\sqrt[3]{8^2}$.

$\sqrt[3]{8^2} = (8^2)^{\frac{1}{3}} = 8^{\frac{2}{3}}$

In words, $8^{\frac{2}{3}}$ means the cube root of 8, squared, or 2^2, which is 4.

$\sqrt[3]{8^2} = 2^2 = 4$ or cube root of 8 squared, or $\sqrt[3]{8^2} = \sqrt[3]{64} = 4$

Rewrite $\sqrt[4]{x^5}$ using exponents.

$\sqrt[4]{x^5} = (x^5)^{\frac{1}{4}} = x^{(5 \bullet \frac{1}{4})} = x^{\frac{5}{4}}$

Exercise A Rewrite the following using exponents.

1. $\sqrt[3]{y}$ $y^{\frac{1}{3}}$ **2.** $\sqrt[5]{m}$ $m^{\frac{1}{5}}$ **3.** $\sqrt[3]{4y}$ $4^{\frac{1}{3}} \cdot y^{\frac{1}{3}}$ **4.** $\sqrt[6]{2x}$ $2^{\frac{1}{6}} \cdot x^{\frac{1}{6}}$

Exercise B Simplify using exponents. Then find the products.

5. $x \cdot \sqrt[3]{x}$ $x^{\frac{4}{3}}$ **6.** $y^2 \cdot \sqrt[3]{y}$ $y^{\frac{7}{3}}$ **7.** $z \cdot \sqrt[3]{z}$ $z^{\frac{4}{3}}$ **8.** $m^2 \cdot \sqrt[5]{m}$ $m^{\frac{11}{5}}$

Exercise C Rewrite these expressions using exponents.

9. $\sqrt[3]{x^2}$ $x^{\frac{2}{3}}$ **10.** $\sqrt[5]{y^3}$ $y^{\frac{3}{5}}$ **11.** $\sqrt[4]{x^4}$ x **12.** $\sqrt[3]{k^4}$ $k^{\frac{4}{3}}$

Calculator Practice

You can use a calculator to find the square root or cube root of a number. The cube root key may look like $\sqrt[3]{\ }$, $\sqrt[3]{x}$, or $\sqrt[x]{y}$, depending on your calculator.

EXAMPLE 3 $\sqrt[3]{8^2} = 8^{\frac{2}{3}}$

Press 8 x^2. Display reads 64. Then press $\sqrt[3]{\ }$. Display reads 4. $\sqrt[3]{8^2} = 4$.

You could also press 8 × 8. Display reads 64. Then press $\sqrt[3]{\ }$. Display reads 4.

Exercise D Use a calculator to find the square root or cube root of a number.

13. $\sqrt{2^4}$ 4 **14.** $\sqrt[3]{3^3}$ 3 **15.** $\sqrt{10^4}$ 100

3 Reinforce and Extend

CALCULATOR

Some calculators may not have a key whose function is to find the cube (or lesser) root of a number. For such calculators, you might try the following method.

Simplify $\sqrt[3]{4913}$.

Locate the $\sqrt[x]{y}$ key. (Suppose it is a second-level function.)

Press 4913 2nd $\sqrt[x]{y}$ 3 =.

The display shows 17.

LEARNING STYLES

Logical/Mathematical

Suggest students consider the following pattern.

$\sqrt[2]{2^2} = 2$

$\sqrt[2]{3^2} = 3$

$\sqrt[2]{4^2} = 4$

$\sqrt[2]{5^2} = 5$

Invite students to create other patterns and share those patterns with their classmates.

Lesson at a Glance

Chapter 11 Lesson 9

Overview This lesson introduces the square root graph.

Objective

- To draw and use a square root graph

Student Pages 348–349

Teacher's Resource Library 

Workbook Activity 114

Activity 107

Alternative Activity 107

Warm-Up Activity

Ask students to name the following:

Name four points on the *xy* coordinate system that, when connected with four line segments, form a square. *[Sample answer: (1, 2), (1, 5), (4, 5), (4, 2)]*

Name four points on the *xy* coordinate system that, when connected with four line segments, form a square whose center is the origin of the graph. *[Sample answer: (–1, 1), (–1, –1), (1, –1), (1, 1)]*

Name four points on the *xy* coordinate system that, when connected with four line segments, form a square that exists in the first, third, and fourth quadrants of the graph. *[Sample answer: (2, 1), (5, –2), (2, –5), (–1, –2)]*

Before discussing the lesson, remind students that ordered pairs are always given in the form (x, y), and the x-value of an ordered pair describes horizontal distance from the vertical y-axis while the y-value of an ordered pair describes vertical distance from the horizontal x-axis.

Teaching the Lesson

In Step 3 of the example on page 348, the missing values for the chart are $\frac{9}{4}$ or $2\frac{1}{4}$, 4, $\frac{25}{4}$ or $6\frac{1}{4}$, 9, $\frac{49}{4}$ or $12\frac{1}{4}$, 16, $\frac{81}{4}$ or $20\frac{1}{4}$, and 25. After students complete Step 4, remind them that exact roots are represented by the various points that have been plotted on the graph. All

Lesson 9 Drawing and Using a Square Root Graph

You have used a calculator to approximate square roots that are irrational numbers. You can also find these square roots using a graph. Use the following steps to draw your own square root graph.

Example 1

Step 1 On graph paper, draw the first quadrant of the *xy* coordinate system. Mark the location of $x = 0, 1, 2, 3, 4$, and 5 along the x-axis.

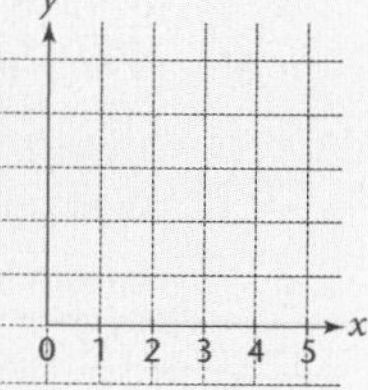

Step 2 On the y-axis, mark the values $y = 0, 5, 10, 15, 20$, and 25. These values will represent the squares of the numbers along the x-axis.

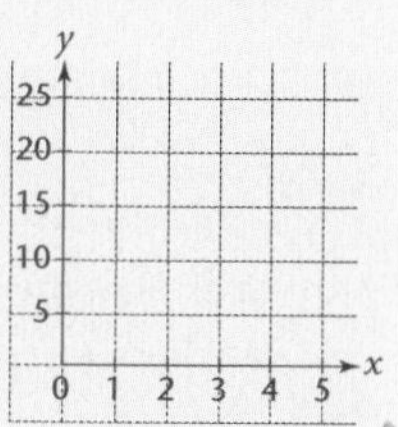

Step 3 On a separate sheet of paper, complete the following chart. Then find and label the ordered pairs (x, x^2).

x	0	$\frac{1}{2}$	1	$1\frac{1}{2}$	2	$2\frac{1}{2}$	3	$3\frac{1}{2}$	4	$4\frac{1}{2}$	5
x^2	0	$\frac{1}{4}$	1	$2\frac{1}{4}$	4	$6\frac{1}{4}$	9	$12\frac{1}{4}$	16	$20\frac{1}{4}$	25

Step 4 Connect the points you have plotted. This will produce a graph of $y = x^2$. Any point along the line has the coordinates (x, x^2).

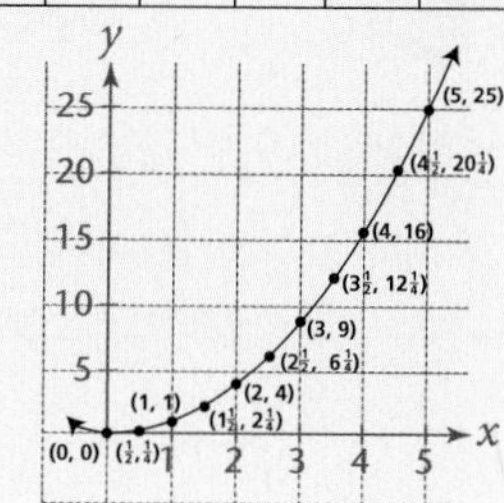

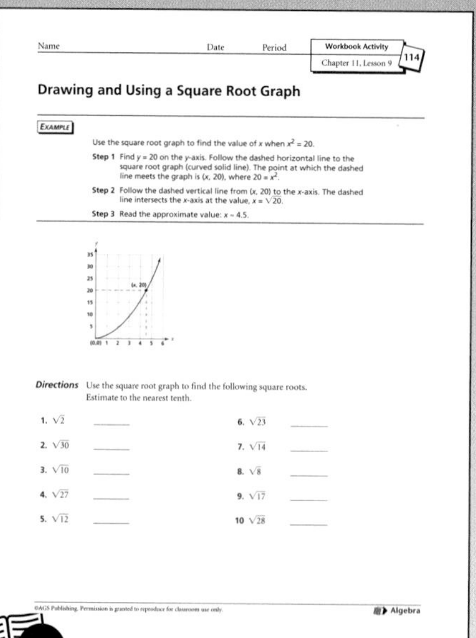

Name Date Period **Workbook Activity** Chapter 11, Lesson 9 114

Drawing and Using a Square Root Graph

Example

Use the square root graph to find the value of x when $x^2 = 20$.

Step 1 Find $y = 20$ on the y-axis. Follow the dashed horizontal line to the square root graph (curved solid line). The point at which the dashed line meets the graph is $(x, 20)$, where $20 = x^2$.

Step 2 Follow the dashed vertical line from $(x, 20)$ to the x-axis. The dashed line intersects the x-axis at the value, $x = \sqrt{20}$.

Step 3 Read the approximate value: $x \approx 4.5$.

Directions Use the square root graph to find the following square roots. Estimate to the nearest tenth.

1. $\sqrt{2}$ ______
2. $\sqrt{30}$ ______
3. $\sqrt{10}$ ______
4. $\sqrt{27}$ ______
5. $\sqrt{12}$ ______
6. $\sqrt{23}$ ______
7. $\sqrt{14}$ ______
8. $\sqrt{8}$ ______
9. $\sqrt{17}$ ______
10. $\sqrt{28}$ ______

 Algebra

Workbook Activity 114

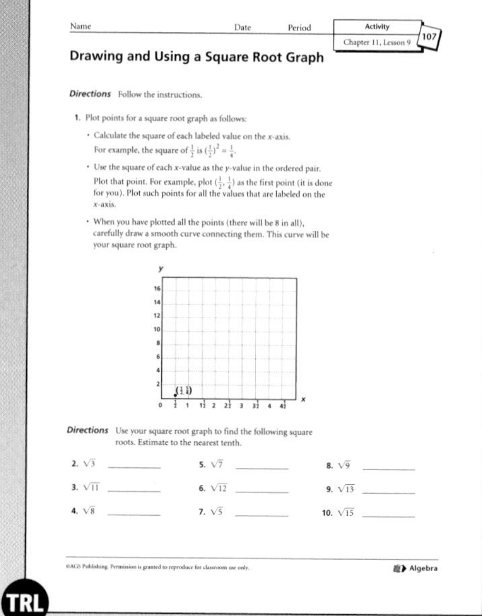

Name Date Period **Activity** Chapter 11, Lesson 9 107

Drawing and Using a Square Root Graph

Directions Follow the instructions.

1. Plot points for a square root graph as follows:
   - Calculate the square of each labeled value on the x-axis. For example, the square of $\frac{1}{2}$ is $(\frac{1}{2})^2 = \frac{1}{4}$.
   - Use the square of each x-value as the y-value in the ordered pair. Plot that point. For example, plot $(\frac{1}{2}, \frac{1}{4})$ as the first point (it is done for you). Plot such points for all the values that are labeled on the x-axis.
   - When you have plotted all the points (there will be 8 in all), carefully draw a smooth curve connecting them. This curve will be your square root graph.

Directions Use your square root graph to find the following square roots. Estimate to the nearest tenth.

2. $\sqrt{3}$ ______
3. $\sqrt{11}$ ______
4. $\sqrt{8}$ ______
5. $\sqrt{7}$ ______
6. $\sqrt{12}$ ______
7. $\sqrt{5}$ ______
8. $\sqrt{9}$ ______
9. $\sqrt{13}$ ______
10. $\sqrt{15}$ ______

 Algebra

Activity 107

To use the graph on page 348, complete the steps shown in the following example.

EXAMPLE 2 Find the value of x when $x^2 = 15$.

Recall that if $x^2 = 15$, then $x = \sqrt{15}$. You can approximate the value of $x = \sqrt{15}$ using a square root graph.

Step 1 Find $y = 15$ on the y-axis. Draw a horizontal line to the graph. The point at which the line meets the square root graph will be $(x, 15)$ where $15 = x^2$.

Step 2 Draw a perpendicular line from $(x, 15)$ to the x-axis. The perpendicular line will intersect the x-axis at the value $x = \sqrt{15}$. You can read the value of x from the graph. In this case, the value is approximately 3.9, so $x = \sqrt{15} \approx 3.9$.

Step 3 Compare this value to the calculator value. Press 15 [√]. Display reads 3.8729833.

So 3.9 from the graph approximates the calculator value of 3.8729833 rounded to nearest tenth.

Exercise A Follow these steps to make a square root graph.

Step 1 Use the long side of a sheet of graph paper as the x-axis. Label these values of x: $0, \frac{1}{2}, 1, 1\frac{1}{2}, 2, 2\frac{1}{2}, \ldots$ to $x = 10$.

Step 2 Label the y-axis, making the values by 10s, so that $y = 0$, 10, 20, 30, … and so on to $y = 100$.

Step 3 Find and label the ordered pairs $(0,0), (\frac{1}{2}, \frac{1}{4}), (1,1), \ldots$ and so on to $(10, 100)$.

Step 4 Connect the ordered pairs to graph the line $y = x^2$. Use your graph to approximate the following square roots. Confirm your graph value with a calculator value.

Approximate answers shown for problems 1–10.

1. $\sqrt{10}$ 3.2
2. $\sqrt{30}$ 5.5
3. $\sqrt{50}$ 7.1
4. $\sqrt{60}$ 7.7
5. $\sqrt{70}$ 8.4
6. $\sqrt{80}$ 8.9
7. $\sqrt{90}$ 9.5
8. $\sqrt{75}$ 8.7
9. $\sqrt{85}$ 9.2
10. $\sqrt{55}$ 7.4

other roots derived from the graph will be approximations.

Have students practice using the graph several times by asking them to use it to approximate the following roots (in addition to the root shown in the example on page 349).

$\sqrt{8}$ *(~2.8)*
$\sqrt{17}$ *(~4.1)*
$\sqrt{22}$ *(~4.7)*

3 Reinforce and Extend

CALCULATOR

The method that is used to find a square root using a calculator may vary, depending on the calculator. Some calculators will require a user to press the radical key first.

Simplify $\sqrt{84}$.

Press [√] 84 [=].

Other calculators will require a user to input the value first.

Press 84 [√] [=].

In both cases, the display shows 9.16515139.

MENTAL MATH

Invite volunteers to recall these common square roots.

$\sqrt{1}$ *(1)*
$\sqrt{4}$ *(2)*
$\sqrt{36}$ *(6)*
$\sqrt{100}$ *(10)*
$\sqrt{64}$ *(8)*
$\sqrt{16}$ *(4)*
$\sqrt{49}$ *(7)*
$\sqrt{81}$ *(9)*
$\sqrt{9}$ *(3)*
$\sqrt{144}$ *(12)*
$\sqrt{25}$ *(5)*
$\sqrt{121}$ *(11)*

Lesson at a Glance

Chapter 11 Application

Overview This lesson introduces the application of formulas related to moving objects.

Objectives

- To use a formula to find the velocity of a moving object

Student Page 350

Teacher's Resource Library TRL

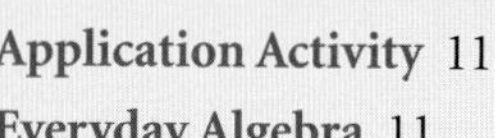

Application Activity 11

Everyday Algebra 11

Warm-Up Activity

Have students work in groups of four or five to consider the following scenario and answer the question it poses.

Suppose that in calm air, the air speed of a small plane is 125 miles per hour. Flying against the wind, the plane can fly 225 miles in the same amount of time it can fly 525 miles with the wind. What is the speed of the wind? *(50 mph)*

Teaching the Lesson

While discussing the example and prior to completing problems 1–5, remind students that the computations contained in a radical must be performed before a root can be extracted.

Reinforce and Extend

Learning Styles

Interpersonal Group Learning

Suggest students work in groups of three to discuss the following problem and use a calculator to solve it.

Suppose the formula to describe the distance it takes a moving automobile to achieve a complete stop is given by the formula $d = \sqrt{394s}$ where d = distance in feet and s = speed in miles per hour. At what speed is an automobile traveling if it takes 164 feet to stop? Round your answer to the nearest whole number. *(68 mph)*

Application $\pi^2 \Sigma + \Omega \sqrt{x^2} \% \neq y \geq n = \nabla 30° \pi$

Falling Objects

You might be surprised to know that "radical" is just the right description for falling objects. In the sixteenth and seventeenth centuries, Galileo Galilei did several experiments with falling objects. He found that the farther an object falls, the faster its velocity when it reaches the ground.

The velocity, v, of a falling object can be computed using the following expression: $v = \sqrt{2gh}$ in which h is the distance the object has fallen, and g is the acceleration due to gravity. On Earth, the acceleration due to gravity is about 32 feet per second squared, 32 ft/s^2.

Example 1 Find the velocity of an object after it has fallen 10 feet.

Use the expression $v = \sqrt{2gh}$.

In this example, $h = 10$ feet. (Use $g = 32$ ft/s^2.)

$$v = \sqrt{2gh}$$
$$= \sqrt{2(32)(10)}$$
$$= \sqrt{640}$$
$$= 25.3 \text{ feet per second}$$

You can find the velocity of falling le[aves] by using a formula.

Exercise Find the solutions.

1. Find the velocity of a falling object after it has fallen 50 feet. 56.6 feet per second
2. What is a falling object's velocity after it has fallen 100 meters? (Use $g = 9.8$ m/s^2.) 44.3 meters per second
3. Find the velocity of a falling object after it has fallen 1,000 meters. (Use $g = 9.8$ m/s^2.) 140 meters per second
4. Find the velocity of a falling object after it has fallen 300 feet. 138.6 feet per second
5. Find the velocity of a falling object after it has fallen 2,500 feet. 400 feet per second

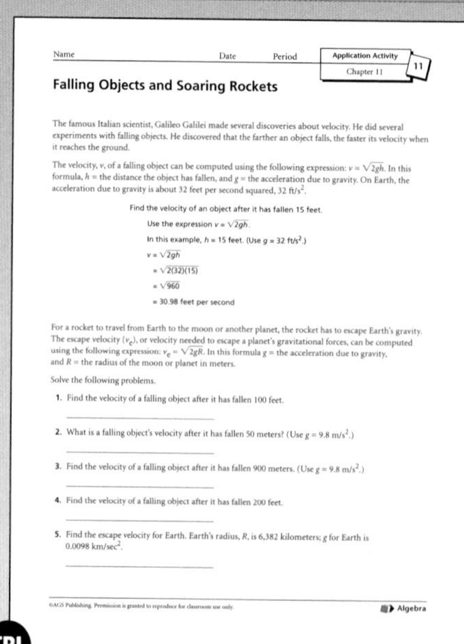

Name Date Period | Application Activity 11, Chapter 11

Falling Objects and Soaring Rockets

The famous Italian scientist, Galileo Galilei made several discoveries about velocity. He did several experiments with falling objects. He discovered that the farther an object falls, the faster its velocity when it reaches the ground.

The velocity, v, of a falling object can be computed using the following expression: $v = \sqrt{2gh}$. In this formula, h = the distance the object has fallen, and g = the acceleration due to gravity. On Earth, the acceleration due to gravity is about 32 feet per second squared, 32 ft/s^2.

Find the velocity of an object after it has fallen 15 feet.

Use the expression $v = \sqrt{2gh}$.

In this example, $h = 15$ feet. (Use $g = 32$ ft/s^2.)

$$v = \sqrt{2gh}$$
$$= \sqrt{2(32)(15)}$$
$$= \sqrt{960}$$
$$= 30.98 \text{ feet per second}$$

For a rocket to travel from Earth to the moon or another planet, the rocket has to escape Earth's gravity. The escape velocity (v_e), or velocity needed to escape a planet's gravitational forces, can be computed using the following expression: $v_e = \sqrt{2gR}$. In this formula g = the acceleration due to gravity, and R = the radius of the moon or planet in meters.

Solve the following problems.

1. Find the velocity of a falling object after it has fallen 100 feet.
2. What is a falling object's velocity after it has fallen 50 meters? (Use $g = 9.8$ m/s^2.)
3. Find the velocity of a falling object after it has fallen 900 meters. (Use $g = 9.8$ m/s^2.)
4. Find the velocity of a falling object after it has fallen 200 feet.
5. Find the escape velocity for Earth. Earth's radius, R, is 6,382 kilometers; g for Earth is 0.0098 km/sec^2.

 Algebra

TRL **Application Activity 11**

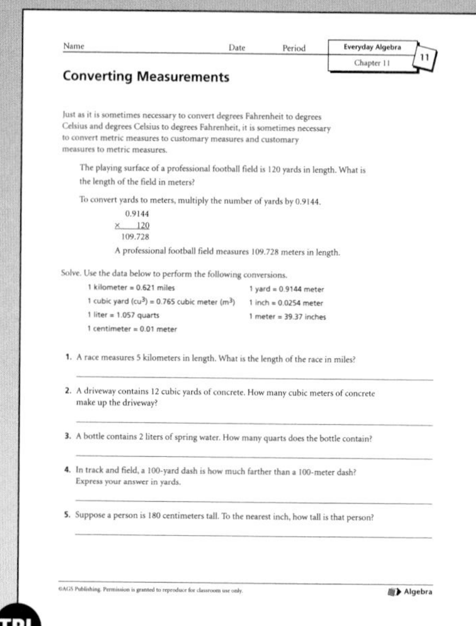

Name Date Period | Everyday Algebra 11, Chapter 11

Converting Measurements

Just as it is sometimes necessary to convert degrees Fahrenheit to degrees Celsius and degrees Celsius to degrees Fahrenheit, it is sometimes necessary to convert metric measures to customary measures and customary measures to metric measures.

The playing surface of a professional football field is 120 yards in length. What is the length of the field in meters?

To convert yards to meters, multiply the number of yards by 0.9144.

$$\begin{array}{r} 0.9144 \\ \times \quad 120 \\ \hline 109.728 \end{array}$$

A professional football field measures 109.728 meters in length.

Solve. Use the data below to perform the following conversions.

1 kilometer = 0.621 miles
1 yard = 0.9144 meter
1 cubic yard (cu^3) = 0.765 cubic meter (m^3)
1 inch = 0.0254 meter
1 liter = 1.057 quarts
1 meter = 39.37 inches
1 centimeter = 0.01 meter

1. A race measures 5 kilometers in length. What is the length of the race in miles?
2. A driveway contains 12 cubic yards of concrete. How many cubic meters of concrete make up the driveway?
3. A bottle contains 2 liters of spring water. How many quarts does the bottle contain?
4. In track and field, a 100-yard dash is how much farther than a 100-meter dash? Express your answer in yards.
5. Suppose a person is 180 centimeters tall. To the nearest inch, how tall is that person?

 Algebra

TRL **Everyday Algebra 11**

Chapter 11 REVIEW

Write the letter of the correct answer.

1. Find the decimal expansion of the number $\frac{5}{17}$, and identify it as a rational or irrational number. A

A 0.2941177 is irrational **C** 0.32941177 is irrational

B 0.20 is rational **D** 2.94128 is rational

2. Find the decimal expansion of the number $\sqrt{73}$, and identify it as a rational or irrational number. C

A 4.85 and rational **C** 8.54 and irrational

B 8.54 and rational **D** 6.08 and irrational

3. Find the rational number equivalent in lowest terms for the number 0.5625. C

A $\frac{16}{9}$ **C** $\frac{9}{16}$

B $\frac{15}{9}$ **D** $\frac{18}{32}$

4. Find the rational number equivalent in lowest terms for the number $0.4\overline{6}$. B

A $\frac{15}{7}$ **C** $\frac{21}{45}$

B $\frac{7}{15}$ **D** $\frac{14}{30}$

5. Simplify the expression $\sqrt{600}$. A

A $10\sqrt{6}$ **C** 60

B $5\sqrt{6}$ **D** 20

6. Simplify the expression $\sqrt{25x^4}$. D

A $2x^5$ **C** $5x$

B $5x^5$ **D** $5x^2$

7. A square has an area of 16,900 ft^2. What is the length of one side of the square? D

A 103.5 ft **C** 310 ft

B 105.3 ft **D** 130 ft

Career Connection

An aeronautical engineer is one example of a person who must have an understanding of moving objects both in the Earth's atmosphere and in free space. Invite students with Internet access to explore NASA's on-line educational resources at **www.gsfc.nasa.gov/forstudents/** and share their findings with their classmates.

Chapter 11 Review

Each set of problems in the Chapter Review includes an example and solution to illustrate the concept. Use the given examples for reteaching the materials in Chapter 11. For additional practice, refer to the Supplementary Problems for Chapter 11 (pages 426–427).

Chapter 11 Mastery Test 

The Teacher's Resource Library includes parallel forms of the Chapter 11 Mastery Test. The difficulty level of the two forms is equivalent. You may wish to use one form as a pretest and the other form as a posttest.

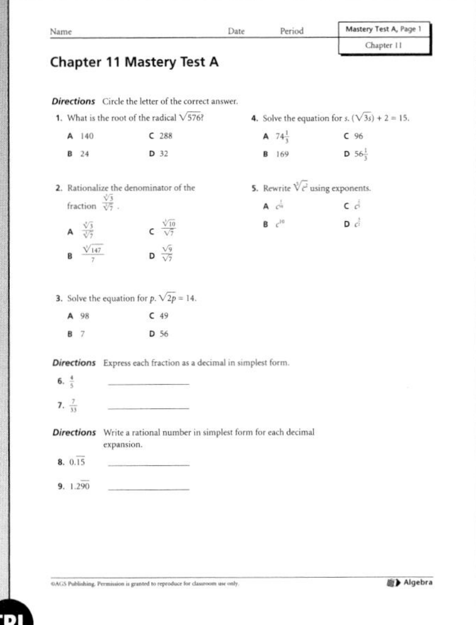

Name Date Period | Mastery Test A, Page 1 | Chapter 11

Chapter 11 Mastery Test A

Directions Circle the letter of the correct answer.

1. What is the root of the radical $\sqrt{576}$?

   A 140 **C** 288

   B 24 **D** 32

2. Rationalize the denominator of the fraction $\frac{\sqrt[3]{3}}{\sqrt[3]{7}}$.

   A $\frac{\sqrt[3]{3}}{\sqrt[3]{7}}$ **C** $\frac{\sqrt[3]{10}}{\sqrt{7}}$

   B $\frac{\sqrt[3]{147}}{7}$ **D** $\frac{\sqrt{9}}{\sqrt{7}}$

3. Solve the equation for p. $\sqrt{2p} = 14$.

   A 98 **C** 49

   B 7 **D** 56

4. Solve the equation for s. $(\sqrt{3s}) + 2 = 15$.

   A $74\frac{1}{3}$ **C** 96

   B 169 **D** $56\frac{1}{3}$

5. Rewrite $\sqrt[5]{c^2}$ using exponents.

   A $c^{\frac{1}{10}}$ **C** $c^{\frac{2}{5}}$

   B c^{10} **D** $c^{\frac{5}{2}}$

Directions Express each fraction as a decimal in simplest form.

6. $\frac{4}{5}$ ________

7. $\frac{7}{33}$ ________

Directions Write a rational number in simplest form for each decimal expansion.

8. $0.\overline{15}$ ________

9. $1.2\overline{90}$ ________

 Algebra

TRL

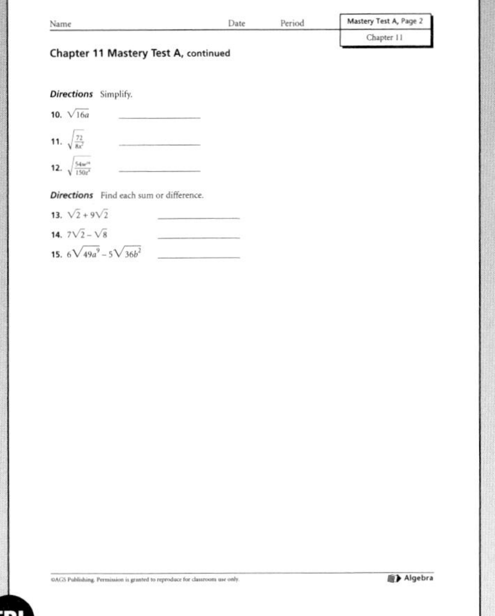

Name Date Period | Mastery Test A, Page 2 | Chapter 11

Chapter 11 Mastery Test A, continued

Directions Simplify.

10. $\sqrt{16a}$ ________

11. $\sqrt{\frac{72}{8x^2}}$ ________

12. $\sqrt{\frac{54w^{14}}{150z^2}}$ ________

Directions Find each sum or difference.

13. $\sqrt{2} + 9\sqrt{2}$ ________

14. $7\sqrt{2} - \sqrt{8}$ ________

15. $6\sqrt{49a^9} - 5\sqrt{36b^2}$ ________

 Algebra

TRL

Chapter 11 Mastery Test A

Alternative Assessment

Alternative Assessment items correlate with student Goals for Learning at the beginning of this chapter.

■ **To distinguish rational and irrational numbers**
Have students describe the differences between rational and irrational numbers. *(Rational numbers are numbers that can be expressed as an integer or as a ratio between two integers when 0 does not serve as the denominator. Irrational numbers are real numbers, such as $\sqrt{2}$, that cannot be written in the form $\frac{a}{b}$ in which a and b are whole numbers and $b \neq 0$.)*

■ **To find the rational number equivalents of decimal expansions**
Have students show how to find the rational number equivalent of the following decimal expansions. $0.\overline{4}$, $0.\overline{63}$, 0.8750, 0.20. Then have students describe the differences between the first two decimals and the last two. *($\frac{4}{9}$, $\frac{7}{11}$, $\frac{5}{8}$, $\frac{1}{5}$. The first two are repeating and the last two are terminal decimal expansions.)*

■ **To find the roots of radicals**
Have students describe one good way to find the roots of radicals without a calculator. *(An example would be to estimate the root. So, if the square root of 36 is 6 and the square root of 49 is 7, then the square root of 45 must be between 6 and 7.)*

■ **To simplify radical expressions**
Have students explain why knowing how to factor is essential to simplify radical expressions. *(Students' answers should reflect an understanding that all numbers can be factored unless they are prime. Mathematical, algebraic, and radical expressions should be simplified to make them easier to work with.)*

■ **To add, subtract, multiply, and divide radicals**
Have students explain how adding and subtracting radicals is different from multiplying and dividing them. *(Students' answers should include that it is impossible to add and subtract unlike radicals, but that unlike radicals can be multiplied and divided.)*

8. $0.2\overline{0}$; rational, terminating

9. $0.\overline{621}$; rational, repeating

10. 17; rational, terminating

11. 25; rational, terminating

Find the decimal expansions of these numbers. Identify each number as rational or irrational and tell why it is rational or irrational.

Example: $\frac{1}{4}$ Solution: $1.00 \div 4 = 0.25\overline{0}$ rational, terminating

8. $\frac{1}{5}$

9. $\frac{23}{37}$

10. $\sqrt{289}$

11. $\sqrt{625}$

Add or subtract these radicals.

Example: $\sqrt{9} + \sqrt{16}$ Solution: $3 + 4 = 7$

12. $\sqrt{3} + 6\sqrt{3}$ $7\sqrt{3}$

13. $3\sqrt{5} + 5\sqrt{3}$ (cannot be added)

14. $4\sqrt{8} - \sqrt{2}$ $7\sqrt{2}$

15. $2\sqrt{48} - 3\sqrt{72}$ $8\sqrt{3} - 18\sqrt{2}$

Rationalize the denominators of these fractions.

Example: $\frac{1}{\sqrt{5}}$ Solution: $\frac{1}{\sqrt{5}} = \frac{1}{\sqrt{5}} \bullet \frac{\sqrt{5}}{\sqrt{5}} = \frac{\sqrt{5}}{(\sqrt{5})(\sqrt{5})} = \frac{\sqrt{5}}{5}$

16. $\frac{(5\sqrt{35})}{(3\sqrt{7})}$ $\frac{5\sqrt{5}}{3}$

17. $\frac{(4\sqrt{7})}{(4 + \sqrt{7})}$ $\frac{(16\sqrt{7} - 28)}{9}$

18. $\frac{8\sqrt{x}}{\sqrt{2x}}$ $4\sqrt{2}$

19. $3x \div \frac{\sqrt{3x}}{4}$ $4\sqrt{3x}$

Rewrite using exponents.

Example: $\sqrt[3]{x^4}$ Solution: $\sqrt[3]{x^4} = (x^4)^{\frac{1}{3}} = x^{(4 \bullet \frac{1}{3})} = x^{\frac{4}{3}}$

20. $\sqrt[6]{x^5}$ $x^{\frac{5}{6}}$

21. $\sqrt{2}$ $2^{\frac{1}{2}}$

22. $\sqrt{11^3}$ $11^{\frac{3}{2}}$

23. $\sqrt[4]{13^3}$ $13^{\frac{3}{4}}$

Name Date Period | Mastery Test B, Page 1 | Chapter 11

Chapter 11 Mastery Test B

Directions Circle the letter of the correct answer.

1. Solve the equation for s. $(\sqrt{9s}) + 2 = 15$.
   A $27\frac{7}{9}$ C 96
   B 169 D $18\frac{7}{9}$

2. Solve the equation for p. $\sqrt{2p} = 16$.
   A 128 C 64
   B 8 D 32

3. What is $\sqrt[6]{c^2}$ using exponents?
   A $c^{\frac{1}{12}}$ C $c^{\frac{1}{3}}$
   B c^{12} D [illegible]

4. Find the root of the radical $\sqrt{676}$.
   A 140 C 388
   B 26 D 52

5. Rationalize the denominator of the fraction $\frac{3\sqrt{4}}{\sqrt{7}}$.
   A $\frac{9\sqrt{4}}{3\sqrt{7}}$ C $3\sqrt{8}$
   B $\frac{3\sqrt{28}}{7}$ D $\frac{\sqrt{9}}{\sqrt{7}}$

Directions Express each fraction as a decimal in simplest form.

6. $\frac{2}{5}$ ______

7. $\frac{8}{23}$ ______

Directions Write a rational number in simplest form for each decimal expansion.

8. $0.\overline{11}$ ______

9. $1.\overline{18}$ ______

 Algebra

TRL

Name Date Period | Mastery Test B, Page 2 | Chapter 11

Chapter 11 Mastery Test B, continued

Directions Simplify.

10. $\sqrt{9m^2}$ ______

11. $\sqrt{\frac{42}{6c^2}}$ ______

12. $\sqrt{\frac{48b^{12}}{100a^3}}$ ______

Directions Find each sum or difference.

13. $\sqrt{3} + 6\sqrt{3}$ ______

14. $5\sqrt{3} - \sqrt{27}$ ______

15. $4\sqrt{36p^{16}} - 3\sqrt{16p^2}$ ______

 Algebra

TRL

Chapter 11 Mastery Test B

Answer each of the following questions.

Example: The square root of a number is 5. What is the number?
Solution: $\sqrt{x} = 5 \quad x = 5^2 = 25$

24. 225

25. $r \approx 4$ units

26. $256y^4$

27. $r \approx 9$ units

28. $s \approx 28.46$; no, $\sqrt{810}$ does not repeat or terminate

See Teacher's Edition page for graphs for problems 29 and 30.

24. The square root of a number is 15. What is the number?

25. The volume of a cylinder is 240 cubic units. The height of the cylinder is 5 units. What is the radius? (Use $V = \pi r^2 h, \pi \approx 3$.)

26. The square root of a number is $16y^2$. What is the number?

27. The area of a circle is 243 square units. What is the approximate radius of the circle? (Use $A = \pi r^2, \pi \approx 3$.)

28. The area of a square is 810 units. What is the length of a side of the square? Can you find the exact length of the side? Explain.

Make and use a square root graph to approximate the following square roots. Label the x-axis with these values of x: $0, \frac{1}{2}, 1, 1\frac{1}{2}$, and so on to 10. Label the y-axis with the squares of the x values: $0, \frac{1}{4}, 1, 2.25, 4, 6.25$, and so on to 100. Find and label the ordered pairs $(0, 0), (\frac{1}{2}, \frac{1}{4})$ $(1, 1)$, and so on to $(10, 100)$.

29. $\sqrt{40}$

30. $\sqrt{85}$

When you read decimal numbers, get in the habit of reading them as mathematical language. For example, read 0.61 as "sixty-one hundredths" instead of "point 61."

■ **To rationalize the denominator of a fraction**

Have students write why they think it is important to rationalize the denominators of fractions. *(Students' answers should show that they cannot calculate with irrational numbers, so irrational numbers must be rationalized to work with them.)*

■ **To solve equations with radicals and exponents**

Have students write two expressions with radicals and two with expressions with exponents and radicals. Then have students exchange expressions with a partner and rewrite their partner's expressions with exponents. Example: The radical expression $\sqrt[3]{6}$ would be rewritten as $6^{\frac{1}{3}}$. The expression $a^2 \cdot \sqrt{a}$ would equal $a^{2\frac{1}{2}}$.

■ **To use a graph to find a square root**

Have students draw a square root graph to represent $x^2 = 16$. Ask them to think about what is true of all square root graphs. *(Students should have an upper right quadrant graph that shows several ordered pairs; the graph should include these three and with some in between: (0, 0), (1, 1), (2, 4), (3, 9), and (4, 16). All square root graphs show points (0, 0) and (1, 1).)*

Answers to Problems 39–40

39. Approximate answer: 6.3

40. Approximate answer: 9.2

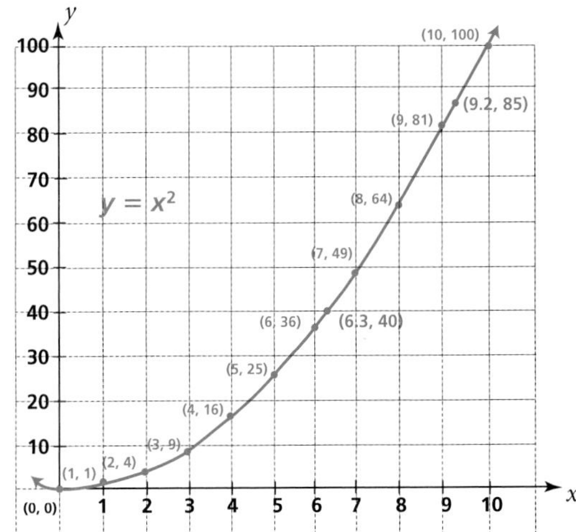

Chapter

Planning Guide

Geometry

		Student Text Lesson: Student Pages	Vocabulary	Practice Exercises	Solutions Key
Lesson 1	Angles and Angle Measure	356–359	✔	✔	✔
Lesson 2	Pairs of Lines in a Plane and in Space	360–363	✔	✔	✔
Lesson 3	Angle Measures in a Triangle	364–367		✔	✔
Lesson 4	Naming Triangles	368–369	✔	✔	✔
Lesson 5	Quadrilaterals	370–371	✔	✔	✔
Lesson 6	Congruent and Similar Triangles	372–375	✔	✔	✔
Lesson 7	Trigonometric Ratios	376–379	✔	✔	✔
Application	Using Geometric Shapes	380		✔	✔

Chapter Activities

Teacher's Resource Library

Estimation Exercise 12: Estimating the Measure of Angles

Application Activity 12: Using Geometric Shapes

Everyday Algebra 12: Finding the Sum of Angle Measures in a Figure

Community Connection 12: Geometric Shapes

Teacher's Edition

Chapter 12 Project

Assessment Options

Student Text

Chapter 12 Review

Teacher's Resource Library

Chapter 12 Mastery Tests A and B

Student Text Features							Teaching Strategies							Learning Styles						Teacher's Resource Library			
Estimation Activity	Algebra in Your Life	Technology Connection	Writing About Mathematics	Try This	Problem Solving	Calculator Practice	Online Connection	Common Error	Applications Home, Career, Community	Mental Math	Manipulatives	Calculator	Group Problem Solving	Auditory/Verbal	Visual/Spatial	Logical/Mathematical	Body/Kinesthetic	Interpersonal/Group Learning	LEP/ESL	Activities	Alternate Activities	Workbook Activities	Self-Study Guide
		359	359					358		359		359			357		358		357	108	108	115	✔
								361	361					363		361		362		109	109	116	✔
367													366	366			365		365	110	110	117	✔
				369	369				369	369			369							111	111	118	✔
									371										371	112	112	119	✔
	375			375					374						375		373	373		113	113	120	✔
					379	378	378		377			379	379			377	378			114	114	121	✔
								380					381					381					✔

Software Options

Skill Track Software

Use the Skill Track Software for *Algebra* for additional reinforcement of this chapter. The software provides multiple-choice assessment items for students to access by computer.

Solutions Key

Use the Solutions Key with this chapter to help students who may need additional assistance. The Solutions Key CD provides solutions for every exercise in the student edition.

Other Resources

Alternative Activities

The Teacher's Resource Library (TRL) contains a set of worksheets written at a second-grade reading level called Alternative Activities. They cover the same content as the regular Activities.

Chapter at a Glance

Chapter 12: Geometry
pages 354–383

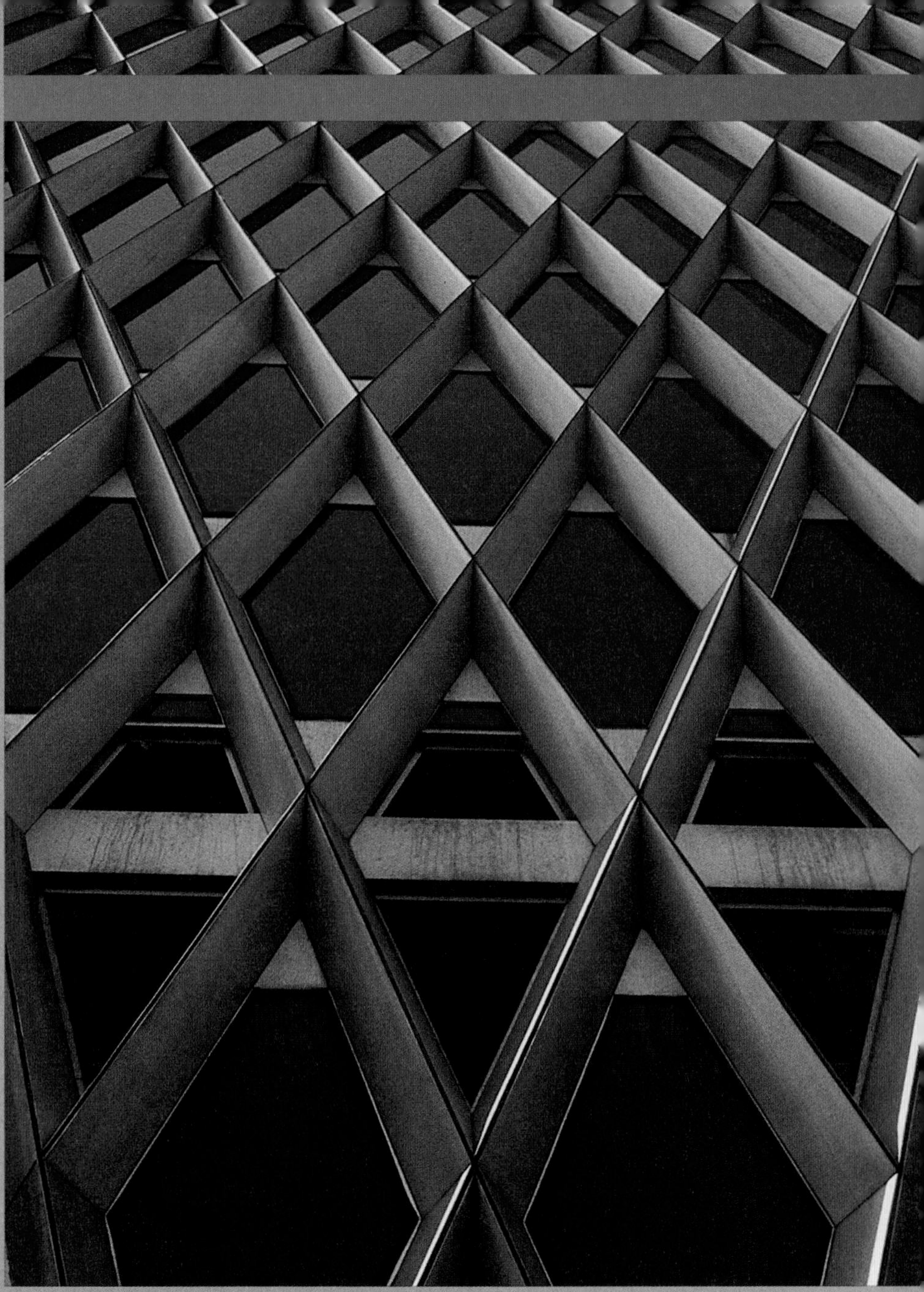

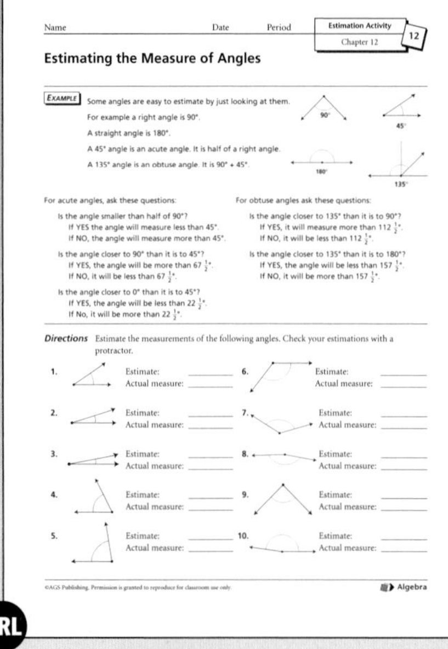

Name Date Period

Estimation Activity 12
Chapter 12

Estimating the Measure of Angles

EXAMPLE Some angles are easy to estimate by just looking at them.
For example a right angle is 90°.
A straight angle is 180°.
A 45° angle is an acute angle. It is half of a right angle.
A 135° angle is an obtuse angle. It is 90° + 45°.

For acute angles, ask these questions:

Is the angle smaller than half of 90°?
If YES the angle will measure less than 45°.
If NO, the angle will measure more than 45°.

Is the angle closer to 90° than it is to 45°?
If YES, the angle will be more than $67\frac{1}{2}°$.
If NO, it will be less than $67\frac{1}{2}°$.

Is the angle closer to 0° than it is to 45°?
If YES, the angle will be less than $22\frac{1}{2}°$.
If No, it will be more than $22\frac{1}{2}°$.

For obtuse angles ask these questions:

Is the angle closer to 135° than it is to 90°?
If YES, it will measure more than $112\frac{1}{2}°$.
If NO, it will be less than $112\frac{1}{2}°$.

Is the angle closer to 135° than it is to 180°?
If YES, the angle will be less than $157\frac{1}{2}°$.
If NO, it will be more than $157\frac{1}{2}°$.

Directions Estimate the measurements of the following angles. Check your estimations with a protractor.

1. Estimate: ______ Actual measure: ______
2. Estimate: ______ Actual measure: ______
3. Estimate: ______ Actual measure: ______
4. Estimate: ______ Actual measure: ______
5. Estimate: ______ Actual measure: ______
6. Estimate: ______ Actual measure: ______
7. Estimate: ______ Actual measure: ______
8. Estimate: ______ Actual measure: ______
9. Estimate: ______ Actual measure: ______
10. Estimate: ______ Actual measure: ______

Algebra

TRL

Estimation Exercise 12

Name Date Period

Community Connection 12
Chapter 12

Geometric Shapes

The world around you is filled with an infinite variety of geometric shapes. As you spend time outside the classroom, take the opportunity to observe various shapes in your world. Use your observations to complete the chart shown below.

Type of Shape	Location
1. acute angle	
2. right angle	
3. obtuse angle	
4. straight angle	
5. two supplementary angles	
6. two complementary angles	
7. two parallel lines	
8. two parallel lines and a transversal	
9. two intersecting lines	
10. two skew lines	
11. a pair of complementary angles	
12. a pair of supplementary angles	
13. a pair of alternate interior angles	
14. a pair of corresponding angles	
15. a right triangle	
16. an acute triangle	
17. an obtuse triangle	
18. a scalene triangle	
19. a right scalene triangle	
20. an isosceles triangle	
21. a right isosceles triangle	
22. an equilateral and equiangular triangle	
23. a quadrilateral	
24. a rectangle	
25. a parallelogram	
26. a square	
27. a rhombus	
28. a trapezoid	
29. two congruent triangles	
30. two similar triangles	

Algebra

TRL

Community Connection 12

Chapter

Geometry

Skyscrapers can provide geometry lessons about shapes, angles, and intersecting lines. The ancient Greeks believed everything in the universe was made from five basic shapes, called the "Platonic solids." They built a special rectangle called the Golden Section. The sides of this "golden" rectangle had a ratio of 1:1.6. The Greeks used this special rectangle in the Parthenon and other buildings. People thought it was pleasing to look at. Architects still use this 1:1.6 ratio for modern buildings. Architects use angles and lines to make pleasing geometric shapes a part of their buildings.

In Chapter 12, you will relate algebra to geometry.

Goals for Learning

- To name and determine the measure of angles
- To identify how lines are related in planes and space
- To use theorems to help solve problems involving triangles
- To name triangles by their characteristics
- To determine the measures of angles in quadrilaterals
- To use theorems to determine whether triangles are congruent or similar
- To use trigonometric ratios to solve problems

355

Name Date Period **SELF-STUDY GUIDE**

CHAPTER 12: Geometry

Goal 12.1 *To name and determine the measure of angles*

Date	Assignment	Score
________	1: Read pages 356–358. Complete Exercises A–D on page 359.	________
________	2: Complete Workbook Activity 115.	________

Comments:

Goal 12.2 *To identify how lines are related in planes and space*

Date	Assignment	Score
________	3: Read pages 360–362. Complete Exercises A–D on page 363.	________
________	4: Complete Workbook Activity 116.	________

Comments:

Goal 12.3 *To use theorems to help solve problems involving triangles*

Date	Assignment	Score
________	5: Read pages 364–366. Complete Exercises A–C on page 367.	________
________	6: Complete Workbook Activity 117.	________

Comments:

Goal 12.4 *To name triangles by their characteristics*

Date	Assignment	Score
________	7: Read pages 368–369. Complete Exercises A–B on page 369.	________
________	8: Complete Workbook Activity 118.	________

Comments:

 Algebra

TRL

Name Date Period **SELF-STUDY GUIDE**

CHAPTER 12: Geometry, continued

Goal 12.5 *To determine the measures of angles in quadrilaterals*

Date	Assignment	Score
________	9: Read pages 370–371. Complete Exercises A–B on page 371.	________
________	10: Complete Workbook Activity 119.	________

Comments:

Goal 12.6 *To use theorems to determine whether triangles are congruent or similar*

Date	Assignment	Score
________	11: Read pages 372–374. Complete Exercises A–C on page 375.	________
________	12: Complete Workbook Activity 120.	________

Comments:

Goal 12.7 *To use trigonometric ratios to solve problems*

Date	Assignment	Score
________	13: Read pages 376–378. Complete Exercises B–D on page 379.	________
________	14: Read and complete the Calculator Practice on page 378.	________
________	15: Complete Workbook Activity 121.	________
________	16: Read and complete the Application Exercise on page 380.	________
________	17: Complete the Chapter 12 Review on pages 381–383.	________

Comments:

Student's Signature ________________ Date ________

Instructor's Signature ________________ Date ________

 Algebra

TRL

Chapter 12 Self-Study Guide

Introducing the Chapter

Use the information in the chapter opener to expand students' awareness of the geometry all around them. For example, architects use geometric angles and lines to make interesting shapes as part of their buildings, including skyscrapers.

Chapter Project

Have students work in pairs to create a design for a building or park or a logo for an imaginary company that

- involves construction of lines, angles, triangles, and polygons.
- illustrates symmetry and congruence.

Begin by having pairs brainstorm and sketch several possible projects. As students complete each lesson, have them revisit their plan to incorporate what they have learned.

At the end of the chapter, have the pairs present their projects to the class. They should show all their versions and explain why they made changes. One copy of the final version should show specifics of angle measurement, construction of geometric figures, and explanations.

Teacher's Resource

The AGS Publishing Teaching Strategies in Math Transparencies may be used with this chapter. They add an interactive dimension to expand and enhance the program content.

Career Interest Inventory

The AGS Publishing Harrington-O'Shea Career Decision-Making System-Revised (CDM) may be used with this chapter. Students can use the CDM to explore their interests and identify careers. The CDM defines career areas that are indicated by students' responses on the inventory.

Lesson at a Glance

Chapter 12 Lesson 1

Overview This lesson defines types of angles and line segments and demonstrates computation of angle measures.

Objectives

- To classify angles as acute, right, obtuse, or straight
- To identify complementary and supplementary angles
- To calculate angle measure

Student Pages 356–359

Teacher's Resource Library 

Workbook Activity 115

Activity 108

Alternative Activity 108

Mathematics Vocabulary

adjacent angle
angle
complementary angles
ray
supplementary angles
vertex
vertical angles

Warm-Up Activity

Have students point out angles in the classroom and attempt to recreate them on the board. Ask them to categorize the angles in some logical way. Point out that angles are composed of lines and invite students to identify the parts of an angle and create a definition. Then have them read the lesson to learn the mathematical terms they need to refer to angles and lines.

Teaching the Lesson

Provide examples for each term in the lesson and have students work with them to become familiar with the vocabulary. Provide examples circumscribed by a circle to emphasize that the lines lie within a 360∞ plane and help show why a straight line describes 180∞. Be sure all angles are labeled with three letters. Ask, "Why is it wise to name angles with three letters?" *(to be able to identify a specific*

Lesson 1 Angles and Angle Measure

Ray
A set of points that is part of a line. It has one endpoint and extends infinitely in one direction.

Angle
A geometric figure made up of two rays with a common endpoint called a vertex

Vertex
A point common to both sides of an angle

Adjacent angle
An angle that shares a vertex and a common side with another angle

Geometric figures exist in many shapes and sizes. Two such figures are rays and angles. A **ray** is a set of points that is a part of a line. It has one endpoint and extends infinitely in one direction. An **angle** is a geometric figure formed by two rays that share a common endpoint called the **vertex.**

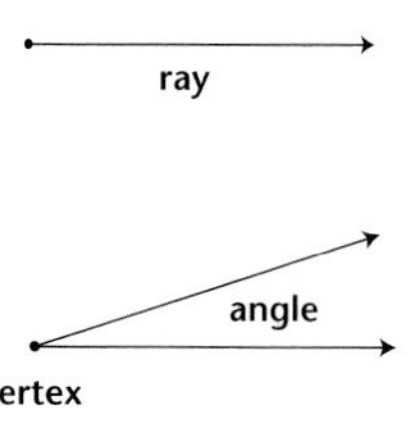

The symbol ∠ is used to designate an angle. Any angle can be read or named two ways. The angle at the right can be named ∠*ABC* or ∠*CBA*. Note that the vertex, *B*, is always the middle letter.

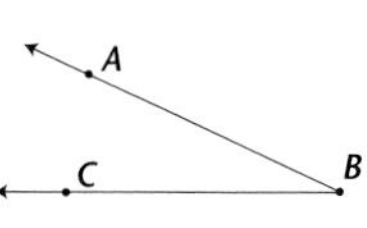

Angles are sometimes named by one letter or number.

∠1 and ∠2 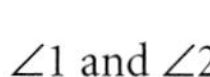

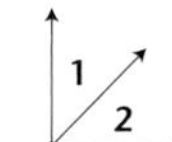

∠*a* and ∠*b* 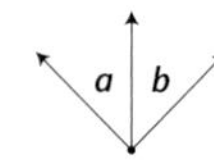

The basic unit of angle measure is the degree (°).
The measure of an angle is used to classify angles.

Measure (m) in degrees	Picture	Name of Angle
0° < m < 90°		acute
m = 90°		right
90° < m < 180°		obtuse
m = 180°		straight

Angles that share a common vertex and a common side are called **adjacent angles.**

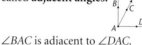

∠*BAC* is adjacent to ∠*DAC*.

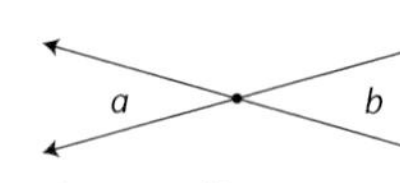

∠*a* is *not* adjacent to ∠*b*.

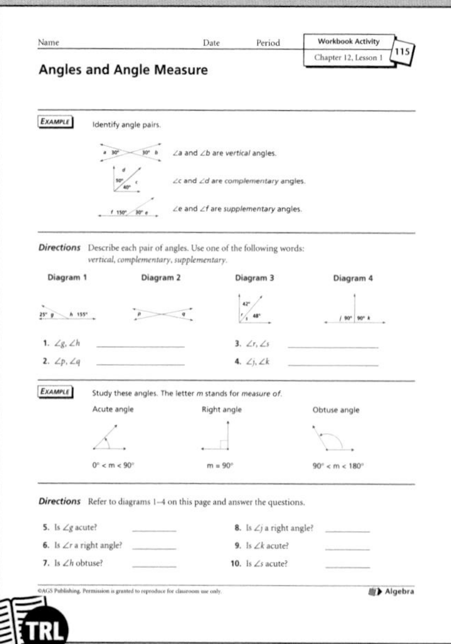

Name Date Period | Workbook Activity 115 | Chapter 12, Lesson 1

Angles and Angle Measure

EXAMPLE Identify angle pairs.

∠a and ∠b are *vertical* angles.
∠c and ∠d are *complementary* angles.
∠e and ∠f are *supplementary* angles.

Directions Describe each pair of angles. Use one of the following words: *vertical, complementary, supplementary.*

Diagram 1 Diagram 2 Diagram 3 Diagram 4

1. ∠g, ∠h ____
2. ∠p, ∠q ____
3. ∠r, ∠s ____
4. ∠j, ∠k ____

EXAMPLE Study these angles. The letter *m* stands for *measure of.*

Acute angle: 0° < m < 90°
Right angle: m = 90°
Obtuse angle: 90° < m < 180°

Directions Refer to diagrams 1–4 on this page and answer the questions.

5. Is ∠g acute? ____
6. Is ∠r a right angle? ____
7. Is ∠h obtuse? ____
8. Is ∠j a right angle? ____
9. Is ∠k acute? ____
10. Is ∠s acute? ____

©AGS Publishing. Permission is granted to reproduce for classroom use only. Algebra

Workbook Activity 115

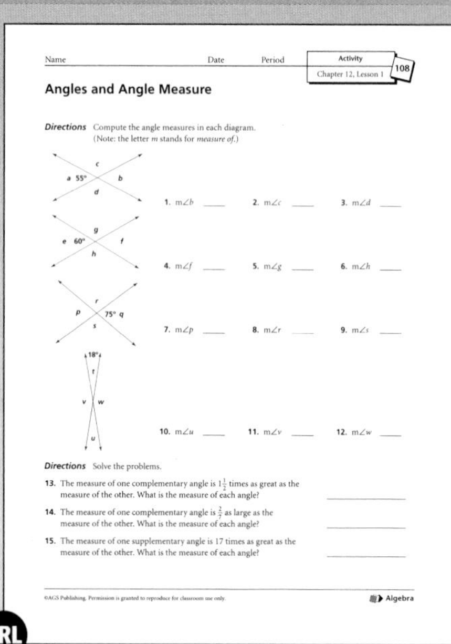

Name Date Period | Activity 108 | Chapter 12, Lesson 1

Angles and Angle Measure

Directions Compute the angle measures in each diagram. (Note: the letter *m* stands for *measure of.*)

1. m∠b ____ 2. m∠c ____ 3. m∠d ____
4. m∠f ____ 5. m∠g ____ 6. m∠h ____
7. m∠p ____ 8. m∠r ____ 9. m∠s ____
10. m∠u ____ 11. m∠v ____ 12. m∠w ____

Directions Solve the problems.

13. The measure of one complementary angle is $1\frac{1}{2}$ times as great as the measure of the other. What is the measure of each angle? ____
14. The measure of one complementary angle is $\frac{2}{7}$ as large as the measure of the other. What is the measure of each angle? ____
15. The measure of one supplementary angle is 17 times as great as the measure of the other. What is the measure of each angle? ____

©AGS Publishing. Permission is granted to reproduce for classroom use only. Algebra

Activity 108

Vertical angles

Pairs of opposite angles formed by intersecting lines. Vertical angles have the same measure.

Complementary angles

Two angles whose sum of their measures is 90°

Vertical angles are opposite pairs of angles formed when two lines intersect.

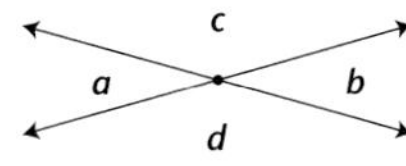

$\angle a$ and $\angle b$ are vertical angles. $\angle c$ and $\angle d$ are vertical angles.

It is possible to compute angle measures.

> The measure of a circle is 360°.
> The measure of a straight line is 180°.

EXAMPLE 1 Given $m\angle a = 20°$, find the measure (m) of $\angle b$, $\angle c$, and $\angle d$.

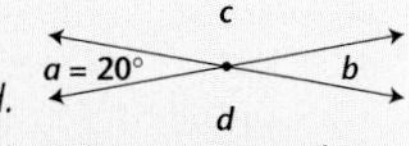

Step 1 Find the measure of $\angle c$. Recall that the measure of a straight angle is 180°. Since $\angle a$ and $\angle c$ are adjacent and form a straight angle, $m\angle a + m\angle c = 180°$.

$20° + m\angle c = 180°$
$m\angle c = 180° - 20°$
$m\angle c = 160°$

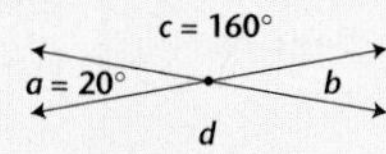

Step 2 Find the measure of $\angle d$. Since $\angle a$ and $\angle d$ are adjacent and form a straight angle, $m\angle a + m\angle d = 180°$.

$20° + m\angle d = 180°$
$m\angle d = 180° - 20°$
$m\angle d = 160°$

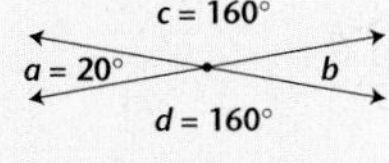

Step 3 Find the measure of $\angle b$. Since $\angle d$ and $\angle b$ are adjacent and form a straight angle, $m\angle d + m\angle b = 180°$.

$160° + m\angle b = 180°$
$m\angle b = 180° - 160°$
$m\angle b = 20°$

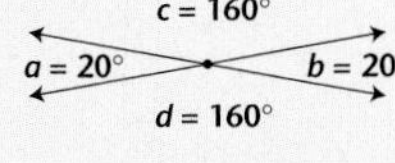

Recall that $\angle a$ and $\angle b$ are vertical angles. So are $\angle c$ and $\angle d$. Vertical angles have the same measure.

If the sum of the measures of two angles is 90°, the angles are **complementary angles.** Angles do not have to be adjacent to be complementary.

Examples of Complementary Angles

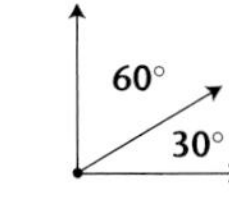

$60° + 30° = 90°$

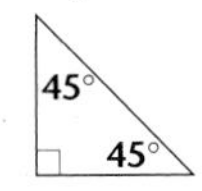

$45° + 45° = 90°$

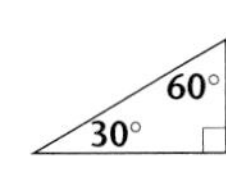

$30° + 60° = 90°$

angle where several are formed, and because angles have two sides and a vertex)

You may wish to show students how to measure angles using a protractor and let them create their own problems with complementary and supplementary angles.

Reinforce and Extend

LEARNING STYLES

Visual/Spatial

Cut out magazine pictures of objects that contain angles. Have students use a straightedge and pen to outline and identify angles within the objects, as well as parts of lines. Have them use the straightedge and a t-square to identify and differentiate right angles, straight angles, obtuse angles, and acute angles.

LEARNING STYLES

LEP/ESL

Write each vocabulary word on one side of a 3 x 5 card. On the other side, draw a clear example. Pair students and have them take turns identifying the examples by name. Be sure they can describe the qualities that make the illustration identifiable. After practice, draw additional examples on the board and have students see who can be first to identify the examples and match them with the cards.

Learning Styles

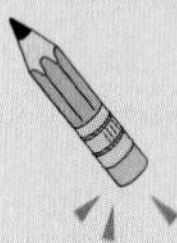

Body/Kinesthetic

Have students use a protractor to create several examples of acute, right, obtuse, and straight angles. Then have them point to and identify the parts of each angle and explain what defines it.

Common Error

Be sure students understand that angles may be oriented in any direction and have the same measure. Some students may assume incorrectly that angles "read" from a zero point on the *x*-axis. To avoid such mistakes, teach students to identify the angle in question by drawing an arc from one arm to the other, enclosing the vertex, and to estimate the size of the "opening" as "less than 90 degrees," "greater than 90 degrees," etc.

Math History

Benjamin Banneker is most often remembered for the work he did surveying the boundaries of Washington, D.C. However, Banneker's accomplishments extended far beyond surveying. Benjamin Banneker was born in 1731, the son of former slaves. Although he had little formal schooling, he became an accomplished inventor, writer, mathematician, astronomer, and surveyor. As a young man, Banneker constructed a clock with carved wooden gears. The clock kept perfect time for over 50 years. Banneker was also an astronomer and could accurately predict the occurrence of solar and lunar eclipses and when the sun and moon would rise and set. Thomas Jefferson wrote to him that Banneker's accomplishments clearly showed that African Americans were intellectually equal to Caucasians.

Example 2 Suppose that the measure of one complementary angle is five times greater than the measure of the other. What is the measure of each angle?

Step 1 Let $x =$ the measure of the lesser angle.

Let $5x =$ the measure of the greater angle.

Step 2 Since the sum of the measures of complementary angles is 90°, use the equation $x + 5x = 90°$ and solve for x.

$x + 5x = 90°$

$6x = 90°$

$x = 15°$

Since $x = 15°$, $5x = 5(15°)$ or 75°. The angles measure 15° and 75°.

Step 3 Check. $15° + 75° = 90°$

> ***Supplementary angles***
> *Two angles whose sum of their measures is 180°*

If the sum of the measures of two angles is 180°, the angles are **supplementary angles.** Angles do not have to be adjacent to be supplementary.

Examples of Supplementary Angles

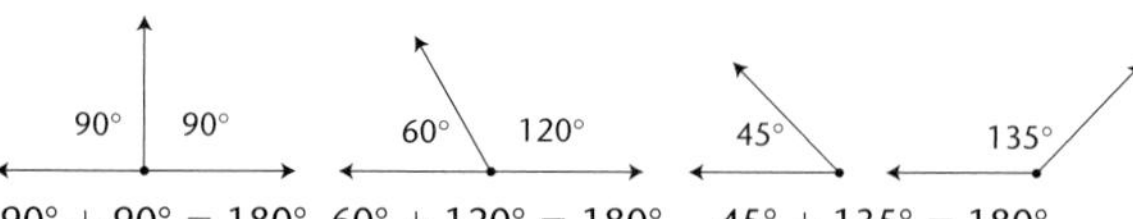

$90° + 90° = 180°$ $60° + 120° = 180°$ $45° + 135° = 180°$

Example 3 Suppose that the measure of one supplementary angle is $3\frac{1}{2}$ times greater than the measure of the other. What is the measure of each angle?

Step 1 Let $x =$ the measure of the lesser angle.

Let $3\frac{1}{2}x =$ the measure of the greater angle.

Step 2 Since the sum of the measures of supplementary angles is 180°, use the equation $x + 3\frac{1}{2}x = 180°$ and solve for x.

$x + 3\frac{1}{2}x = 180°$

$4\frac{1}{2}x = 180°$

$\frac{9}{2}x = 180°$

$x = 180°(\frac{2}{9})$

$x = (\frac{360°}{9})$

$x = 40°$

Since $x = 40°$, $3\frac{1}{2}(40°) = 140°$. The angles measure 40° and 140°.

Step 3 Check. $40° + 140° = 180°$

Writing About Mathematics

A square contains four right angles. Make a list of the different pairs of supplementary angles that can be formed. Explain how you know you have listed all such pairs.

Exercise A Classify each angle. Write *acute, right, obtuse,* or *straight.*

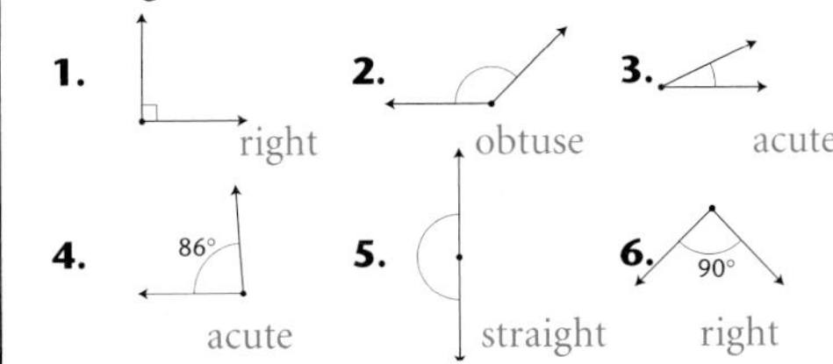

1. right
2. obtuse
3. acute
4. acute (86°)
5. straight
6. right (90°)

Exercise B Classify each pair of angles using the figure at the right. Write *vertical* or *adjacent.*

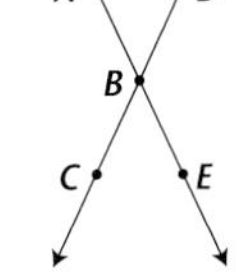

7. $\angle ABC$ and $\angle CBE$ — adjacent
8. $\angle DBA$ and $\angle EBC$ — vertical
9. $\angle CBA$ and $\angle DBE$ — vertical
10. $\angle EBD$ and $\angle ABD$ — adjacent

Exercise C Use the figure at the right.

11. Which angles are complementary? — 11. $\angle PQR$ and $\angle SQR$
12. Which angles are supplementary? — 12. $\angle PQS$ and $\angle TQS$ *or* $\angle PQR$ and $\angle RQT$

Exercise D Answer each question.

13. The measure of one supplementary angle is 2 times greater than the measure of the other. What is the measure of each angle? — 13. 60°; 120°
14. The measure of one complementary angle is 3 times greater than the measure of the other. What is the measure of each angle? — 14. 22.5°; 67.5°
15. The measure of one complementary angle is $\frac{1}{4}$ as large as the measure of the other. What is the measure of each angle? — 15. 18°; 72°

Technology Connection

Computer-Generated Tessellations

Have you seen the art of M. C. Escher? He is famous for his tessellations. Tessellations are repeating geometric forms in interesting patterns. Computer drawing programs let you make your own tessellations. Select a pattern. Then copy and paste your pattern, fitting it next to your original like pieces of a jigsaw puzzle. For some examples, type "computer-generated tessellations" into an Internet search engine. While you're at it, see if you can find some examples of M. C. Escher's art.

Mental Math

Call out the measure of an angle and have students identify it as acute, right, obtuse, or straight. Continue until students are confident in their ability to categorize angles. Then provide measures of pairs of angles and have students add them mentally and identify them as supplementary, complementary, or neither.

Calculator

Have students use a calculator to determine the measure of complementary or supplementary angles given the measure of the first angle in the pair. For example, for complementary angles, given one angle of 37°:

Press 90 [−] 37 [=].

The display shows 53.

The other angle is 53°.

For supplementary angles, given one angle of 76°:

Press 180 [−] 76 [=].

The display shows 104.

The other angle is 104°.

Lesson at a Glance

Chapter 12 Lesson 2

Overview This lesson contrasts relationships of pairs of lines in a plane and in space and explains the relationships among angles formed in a plane.

Objectives

- To identify lines as intersecting, parallel, or skew
- To identify angles created by a transversal as interior or exterior, supplementary, alternate interior, or corresponding
- To calculate the measures of angles within a set of parallel lines cut by a transversal

Student Pages 360–363

Teacher's Resource Library 

Workbook Activity 116

Activity 109

Alternative Activity 109

Mathematics Vocabulary

corresponding angles	plane
exterior angles	theorem
interior angles	transversal

Warm-Up Activity

Review the concepts of *parallel lines*, *perpendicular lines*, and *three-dimensional space*. Use a box for reference and have volunteers point out illustrations of a perfectly flat surface (plane), lines that meet and cross each other (intersecting lines), lines in a plane that never meet (parallel lines), and nonintersecting lines in two different planes (skew lines).

Teaching the Lesson

Be sure students can distinguish exterior and interior angles. Draw a set of lines with transversals on the board. As you point to each angle, have students identify it. If students have difficulty, refer them to the diagrams at the top of page 361, in which the shaded areas highlight first exterior, then interior, angles.

Lesson 2 Pairs of Lines in a Plane and in Space

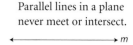

Plane
A two-dimensional flat surface

Transversal
A line that intersects two or more lines

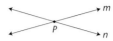

A **plane** can be thought of as a two-dimensional flat surface. Pairs of lines in a plane can exist in two different ways.

Lines in a Plane

Intersecting lines in a plane meet at exactly one point *P*.

Parallel lines in a plane never meet or intersect.

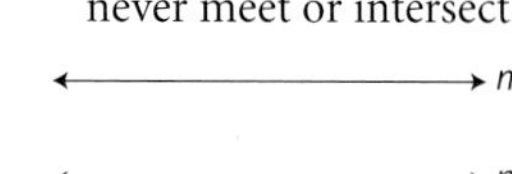

The symbol for parallel is $||$; $m || n$ is read "m is parallel to n."

Space is three-dimensional. Pairs of lines in space can exist in three different ways.

Lines in Space

Intersecting lines form a plane and meet in that plane.

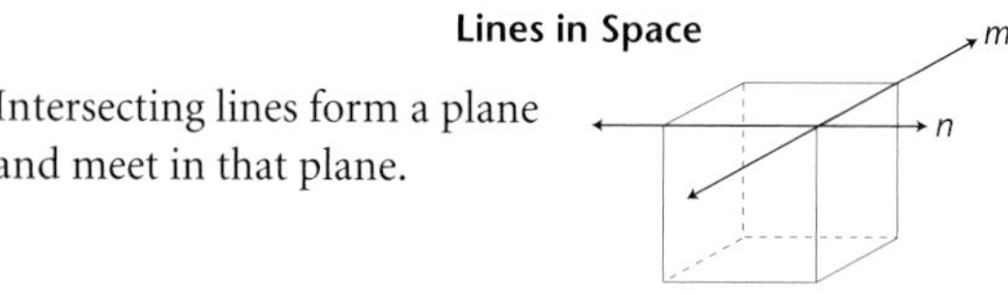

Parallel lines form a plane and do not meet.

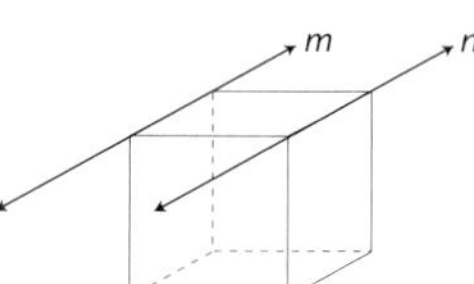

Skew lines are not parallel and do not intersect. Skew lines do not determine a plane.

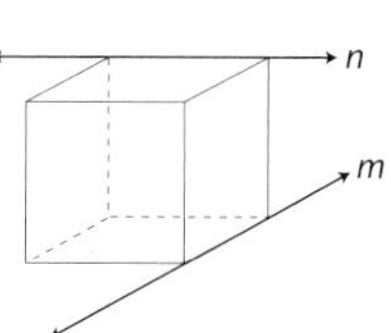

A **transversal** is a line that intersects two or more lines.

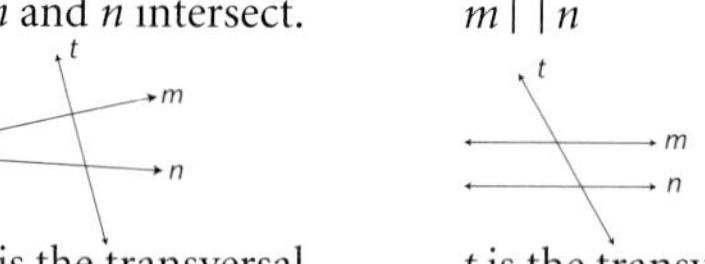

t is the transversal. *t* is the transversal.

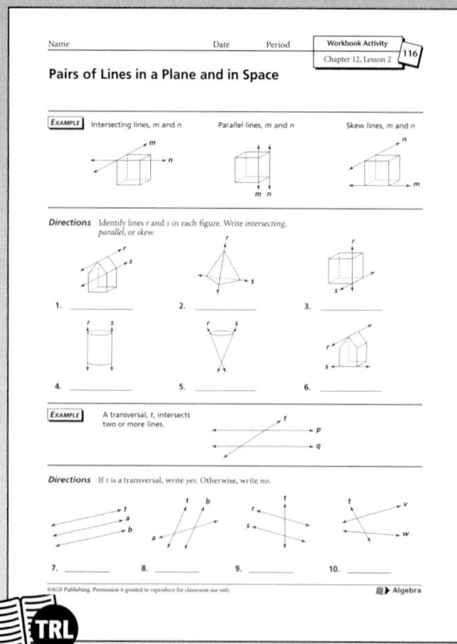

Name Date Period | Workbook Activity 116 | Chapter 12, Lesson 2

Pairs of Lines in a Plane and in Space

EXAMPLE Intersecting lines, *m* and *n* — Parallel lines, *m* and *n* — Skew lines, *m* and *n*

Directions Identify lines *r* and *s* in each figure. Write *intersecting*, *parallel*, or *skew*.

1. ______ 2. ______ 3. ______

4. ______ 5. ______ 6. ______

EXAMPLE A transversal, *t*, intersects two or more lines.

Directions If *t* is a transversal, write *yes*. Otherwise, write *no*.

7. ______ 8. ______ 9. ______ 10. ______

 Algebra

Workbook Activity 116

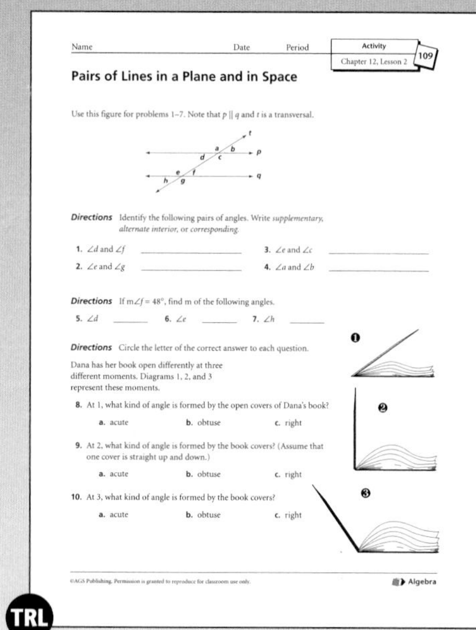

Name Date Period | Activity 109 | Chapter 12, Lesson 2

Pairs of Lines in a Plane and in Space

Use this figure for problems 1–7. Note that $p || q$ and *t* is a transversal.

Directions Identify the following pairs of angles. Write *supplementary*, *alternate interior*, or *corresponding*.

1. $\angle d$ and $\angle f$ ______ 3. $\angle e$ and $\angle c$ ______
2. $\angle e$ and $\angle g$ ______ 4. $\angle a$ and $\angle b$ ______

Directions If $m\angle f = 48°$, find m of the following angles.

5. $\angle d$ ______ 6. $\angle e$ ______ 7. $\angle h$ ______

Directions Circle the letter of the correct answer to each question.

Dana has her book open differently at three different moments. Diagrams 1, 2, and 3 represent these moments.

8. At 1, what kind of angle is formed by the open covers of Dana's book?
   a. acute b. obtuse c. right
9. At 2, what kind of angle is formed by the book covers? (Assume that one cover is straight up and down.)
   a. acute b. obtuse c. right
10. At 3, what kind of angle is formed by the book covers?
   a. acute b. obtuse c. right

 Algebra

Activity 109

Angles formed by transversals have special names.

Exterior angles are those angles outside lines cut by a transversal.

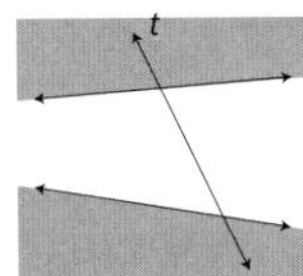

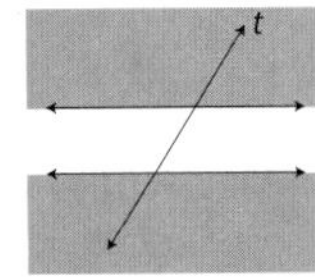

Interior angles are those angles inside, or between, lines cut by a transversal.

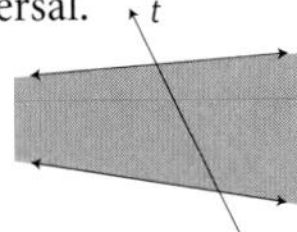

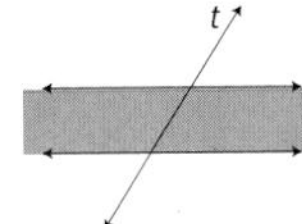

When parallel lines are cut by a transversal, certain angles will always be equal and others supplementary. Here is an example of $l \,||\, m$, t is the transversal.

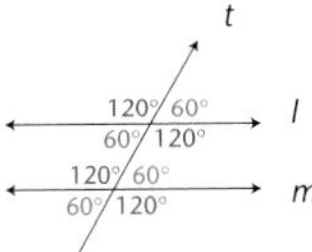

Alternate interior angles are equal:

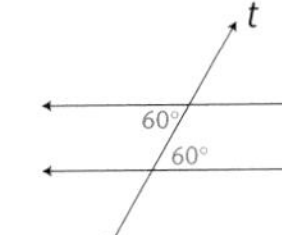

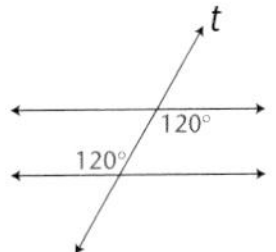

Interior angles on the same side of the transversal are supplementary:

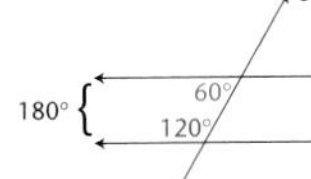

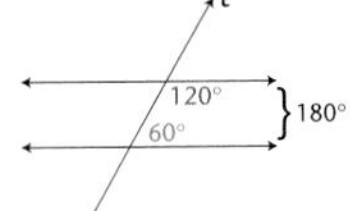

Corresponding angles are equal:

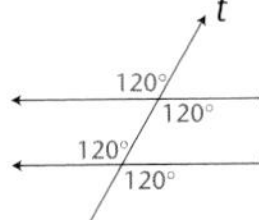

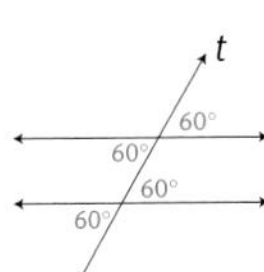

Each fact illustrated here is a **theorem** from geometry. This means these angles are always equal or supplementary as long as they are in the positions as shown in the diagrams.

Exterior angles
Angles that are formed outside two lines cut by a transversal

Interior angles
Angles that are formed inside, or between, two lines cut by a transversal

Corresponding angles
Interior and exterior angles on the same side of a transversal cutting through parallel lines

Theorem
A statement that can be proven

3 Reinforce and Extend

Career Connection

Have students investigate how geometry is used in carpentry or architecture. Ask them to note in particular ways in which parallel and perpendicular lines and corresponding angles are used. For example, a carpenter might use a miter box, which allows lumber to be sawed at an exact angle. A carpenter also might use knowledge of transversals and parallel lines to enable him or her to figure the measures of other angles. Encourage students to use sources such as encyclopedias, how-to manuals, the Internet, or interviews with carpenters or architects.

Common Error

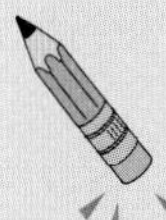

Because plane geometry problems are often set within the bounds of a geometric figure, students may not comprehend that the plane in which a line exists extends infinitely. It may be necessary for them to extend a line mentally in order to recognize that it intersects another line in the plane.

Learning Styles

Logical/Mathematical

Provide sets of lines with transversals. Make some lines parallel and some nonparallel. Have students study each set and guess whether the lines are parallel. Then have them check their guesses by measuring angles with a protractor and finding out whether alternate interior angles are equal.

Learning Styles

Interpersonal/ Group Learning

Have students work in groups of three or four to construct parallel lines cut by a transversal, using "found" materials such as straws or spaghetti. Suggest that they first solve the problem of how to ensure that the lines will be parallel. Then have them take measurements and make comparisons to verify the truth of the statement "Whenever a transversal cuts two parallel lines, the alternate interior angles that are formed are equal." Finally, have students reform the set of lines so that no parallel lines exist and determine how the statement above must be changed to remain true.

In this figure, $p \parallel q$ and t is a transversal.

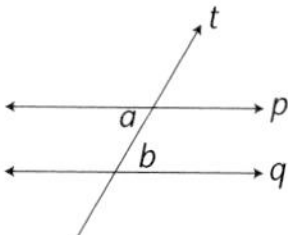

If you would measure $\angle a$ and $\angle b$, you would find that $m\angle a = m\angle b$. $\angle a$ and $\angle b$ are alternate interior angles. Whenever a transversal cuts two parallel lines, the alternate interior angles that are formed are equal.

Example 1 In the following figure, $p \parallel q$ and $m\angle a = 30°$. Find $m\angle b$, $m\angle c$, and $m\angle d$.

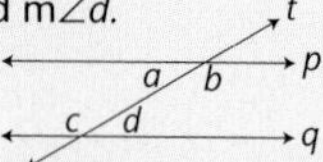

Step 1 If $p \parallel q$ and t is a transversal, then $m\angle a = m\angle d$ and $m\angle b = m\angle c$. This statement is true because it is a theorem from geometry.

Step 2 Since $m\angle a = 30°$, $m\angle d = 30°$ because alternate interior angles have the same measure.

Step 3 Recognize that $\angle a$ and $\angle b$ are supplementary angles because they form a straight line. Find $m\angle b$.

$m\angle a + m\angle b = 180°$
$30° + m\angle b = 180°$
$m\angle b = 180° - 30°$
$m\angle b = 150°$

Step 4 Since $m\angle b = 150°$, $m\angle c = 150°$ because alternate interior angles have the same measure.

In this figure, $p \parallel q$ and t is a transversal.

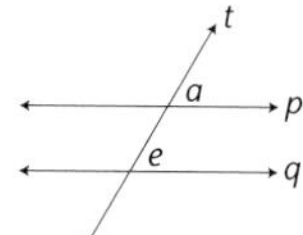

If you would measure $\angle a$ and $\angle e$, you would find that $m\angle a = m\angle e$. $\angle a$ and $\angle e$ are corresponding angles. Whenever a transversal cuts two parallel lines, the corresponding angles that are formed on the same side of the transversal are equal.

1. parallel
2. intersecting
3. parallel
4. skew
5. intersecting
6. parallel
7. exterior
8. exterior
9. interior
10. interior
11. exterior
12. interior
13. exterior
14. interior
15. supplementary
16. corresponding
17. supplementary
18. alternate interior
19. supplementary
20. corresponding
21. supplementary
22. alternate interior
23. corresponding
24. 108°
25. 72°
26. 108°
27. 72°
28. 72°
29. 108°
30. 108°

Exercise A Identify the lines shown in each figure. Write *intersecting*, *parallel*, or *skew*.

1. 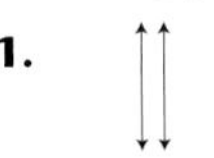

2. 

3.  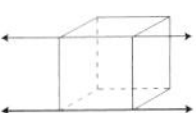

4. 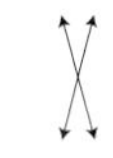

5. 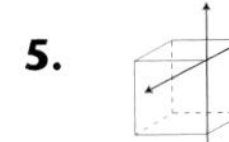

6. 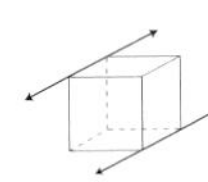

Exercise B Identify the angles shown in this figure. Write *interior* or *exterior*.

7. ∠1 **11.** ∠8

8. ∠7 **12.** ∠5

9. ∠4 **13.** ∠2

10. ∠3 **14.** ∠6

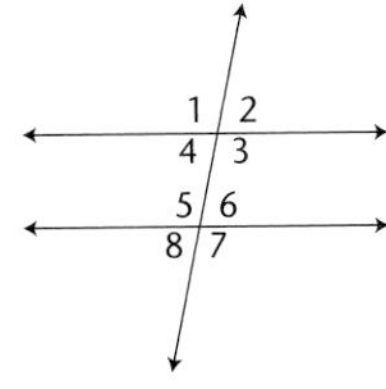

Exercise C In this figure, $p \mid\mid q$ and t is a transversal. Identify the following pairs of angles. Write *supplementary*, *alternate interior*, or *corresponding*.

15. ∠*e* and ∠*f* **20.** ∠*b* and ∠*f*

16. ∠*d* and ∠*h* **21.** ∠*b* and ∠*c*

17. ∠*b* and ∠*g* **22.** ∠*e* and ∠*c*

18. ∠*d* and ∠*f* **23.** ∠*a* and ∠*e*

19. ∠*d* and ∠*e*

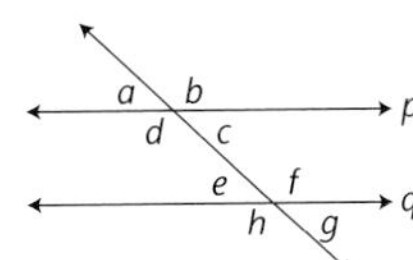

Exercise D In this figure, $p \mid\mid q$, t is a transversal, and $m\angle h = 72°$. Find the measure (m) of each of the following angles.

24. ∠*m* **28.** ∠*s*

25. ∠*l* **29.** ∠*j*

26. ∠*g* **30.** ∠*r*

27. ∠*k*

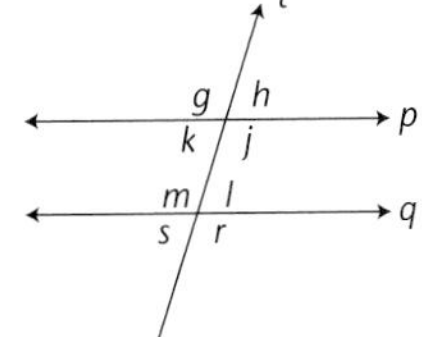

LEARNING STYLES

Auditory/Verbal

Use the figure for Exercise C to create mathematical statements such as these:

$a = b$ (*false*)

$a = c$ (*true*)

$g = c$ (*true*)

$e + h = 180°$ (*true*)

$d + g = 180°$ (*true*)

$d + b = 180°$ (*false*)

Have students refer to the figure to tell whether each statement is true or false.

Lesson at a Glance

Chapter 12 Lesson 3

Overview This lesson demonstrates the proofs of the theorems that the sum of the measures of the angles of any triangle is 180° and the measure of an exterior angle of a triangle is equal to the sum of the measures of the two nonadjacent interior angles.

Objectives

- To prove that the sum of the measures of the angles in any triangle is 180°
- To prove that the measure of any exterior angle of a triangle is equal to the sum of the measures of the two nonadjacent interior angles
- To find the measure of an angle within a triangle

Student Pages 364–367

Teacher's Resource Library 

Workbook Activity 117

Activity 110

Alternative Activity 110

Warm-Up Activity

Draw adjacent supplementary angles on the board and ask students to describe what they see. *(a straight line intersected by another, creating two angles)*

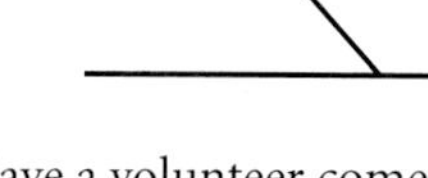

Have a volunteer come to the board and show how to create two triangles by adding two more lines. Then ask students to identify all angles and label them. Encourage them to think of a way they could find the measure of each angle within the triangles. What would they need to know?

Teaching the Lesson

Define *theorem* for students. (a rule that can be established or proved by using previously established or proved premises) Explain that a theorem uses known facts and a step-by-step logical process to prove a mathematical truth.

Lesson 3 Angle Measures in a Triangle

Any triangle is made up of three sides and three angles. The sides and angles of triangles share relationships that can be proven. For example, one way to discover the sum of the measures of the angles in any triangle is to do this experiment.

1. Draw any triangle.

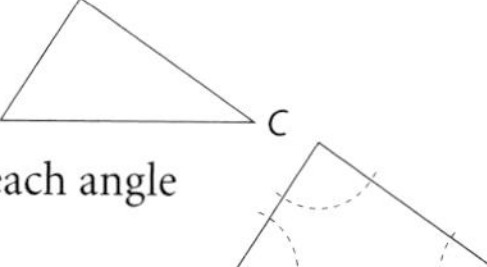

2. Using scissors, cut off each angle of the triangle.

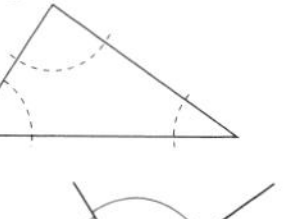

3. Place the angles adjacent to each other along a straight line.

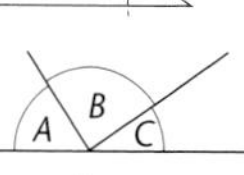

Since the exterior sides of the angles form a supplementary angle and the measure of a supplementary angle is 180°,

$m\angle A + m\angle B + m\angle C = 180°$.

You can also prove this as a theorem. This is an example of a proof.

EXAMPLE 1 **Theorem:** The sum of the measures of the angles in any triangle is 180°.

Prove $m\angle A + m\angle B + m\angle C$ in $\triangle ABC = 180°$.

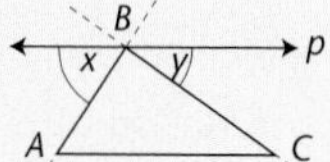

Step 1 $\triangle ABC$ is a triangle. Given.

Step 2 Draw Line $p \parallel AC$ through Point *B*. By construction.

Step 3 *AB* is a transversal of *p* and *AC*, so $m\angle x = m\angle A$ because alternate interior angles are equal.

Step 4 *BC* is a transversal of *p* and *AC*, so $m\angle y = m\angle C$ because alternate interior angles are equal.

Step 5 $\angle x + \angle B + \angle y$ are adjacent and form a straight angle. Since the measure of a straight angle is 180°, $m\angle x + m\angle B + m\angle y = 180°$ and by substitution $m\angle A + m\angle B + m\angle C = 180°$.

You can use this angle-sum theorem to solve problems like the following example.

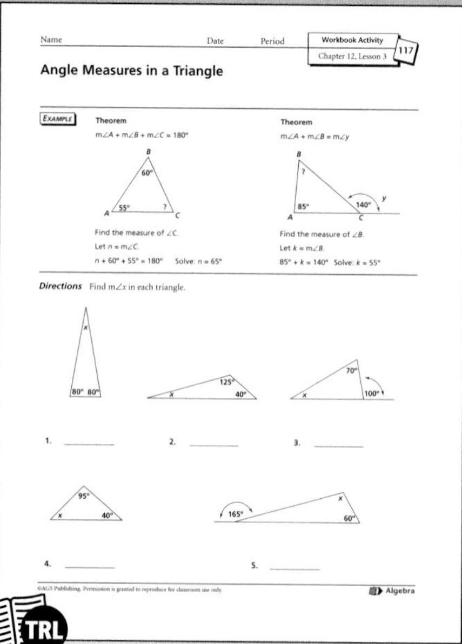

Name Date Period

Workbook Activity 117
Chapter 12, Lesson 3

Angle Measures in a Triangle

EXAMPLE

Theorem
$m\angle A + m\angle B + m\angle C = 180°$

Find the measure of $\angle C$.
Let $n = m\angle C$.
$n + 60° + 55° = 180°$ Solve: $n = 65°$

Theorem
$m\angle A + m\angle B = m\angle y$

Find the measure of $\angle B$.
Let $k = m\angle B$.
$85° + k = 140°$ Solve: $k = 55°$

Directions Find $m\angle x$ in each triangle.

1. _____ 2. _____ 3. _____

4. _____ 5. _____

Algebra

Workbook Activity 117

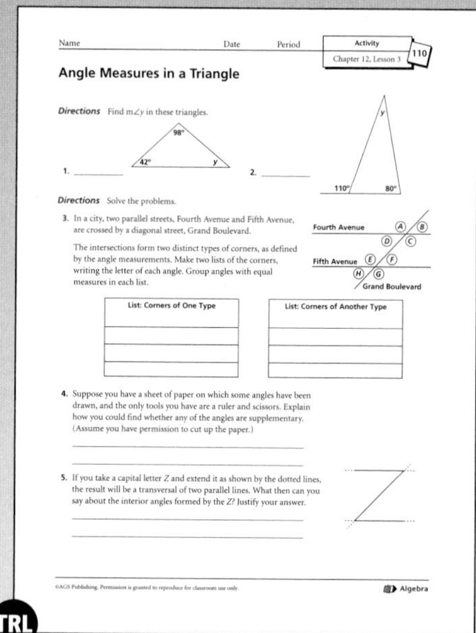

Name Date Period

Activity 110
Chapter 12, Lesson 3

Angle Measures in a Triangle

Directions Find $m\angle y$ in these triangles.

1. _____ 2. _____

Directions Solve the problems.

3. In a city, two parallel streets, Fourth Avenue and Fifth Avenue, are crossed by a diagonal street, Grand Boulevard.

   The intersections form two distinct types of corners, as defined by the angle measurements. Make two lists of the corners, writing the letter of each angle. Group angles with equal measures in each list.

List: Corners of One Type	List: Corners of Another Type

4. Suppose you have a sheet of paper on which some angles have been drawn, and the only tools you have are a ruler and scissors. Explain how you could find whether any of the angles are supplementary. (Assume you have permission to cut up the paper.)

5. If you take a capital letter *Z* and extend it as shown by the dotted lines, the result will be a transversal of two parallel lines. What then can you say about the interior angles formed by the *Z*? Justify your answer.

Algebra

Activity 110

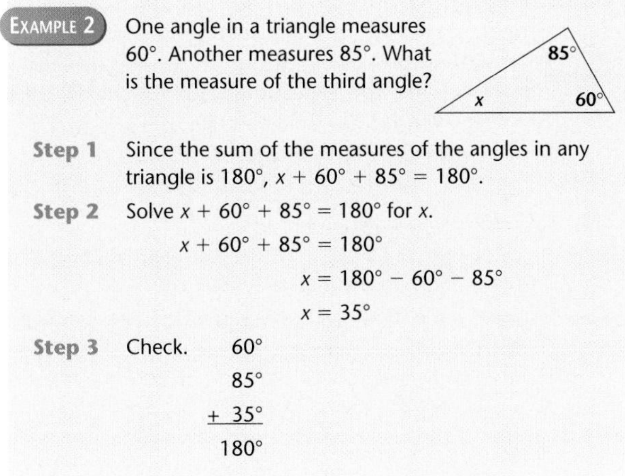

EXAMPLE 2 One angle in a triangle measures 60°. Another measures 85°. What is the measure of the third angle?

Step 1 Since the sum of the measures of the angles in any triangle is 180°, $x + 60° + 85° = 180°$.

Step 2 Solve $x + 60° + 85° = 180°$ for x.

$$x + 60° + 85° = 180°$$
$$x = 180° - 60° - 85°$$
$$x = 35°$$

Step 3 Check.

$$\begin{array}{r} 60° \\ 85° \\ \underline{+\ 35°} \\ 180° \end{array}$$

Other relationships exist in any triangle. For example, an exterior angle of a triangle is formed by extending one side of a triangle at any vertex.

B
exterior angle BCD
A C D

$\angle BCD$ is an exterior angle.

Any exterior angle of a triangle is supplementary to the adjacent interior angle.

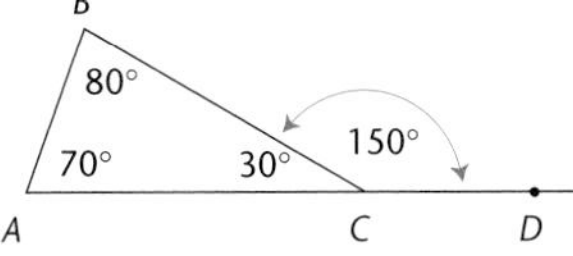

$\angle BCA$ is supplementary to $\angle BCD$, so

$$m\angle BCA + m\angle BCD = 180°$$
$$30° + m\angle BCD = 180°$$
$$m\angle BCD = 180° - 30°$$
$$m\angle BCD = 150°$$

In this example, note that the sum $m\angle A + m\angle B$ is equal to $m\angle BCD$. In other words, the sum of the measures of the two non-adjacent interior angles in any triangle is equal to the measure of the exterior angle.

Reproduce examples and problems on the board or an overhead and extend the sides of each triangle using dotted lines. This should enable students to see the system of angles, transversals, and exterior and interior angles used to prove the theorems.

Explain that a proof for a theorem does not have a set number of steps. It flows from logical proof and uses whatever number of steps are needed to establish truth. Next, have students work in small groups to analyze the proof for the second theorem. Assess students' understanding by having volunteers explain how they know the theorem is true.

3 Reinforce and Extend

Learning Styles

Body/Kinesthetic

As you introduce the lesson, have students draw triangles, cut out their angles, and place them adjacent along a straight line to verify for themselves that the sum of the measures of the angles equals 180°, or a straight angle.

Learning Styles

LEP/ESL

Success in completing this lesson depends upon how well students learned the definitions and concepts in Lesson 2. Copy the art from the theorem on page 364 on the board or an overhead. Extend segment AC. Have students label corresponding angles, exterior angles, interior angles, and transversal and define the terms. Then have them explain each step in proving the theorem in their own words.

Group Problem Solving

Draw the following figure on the board and present the problem. Have students work in groups of four to discuss possible solutions and try them out.

How many degrees are the sum total of the measures of the four angles? How can you prove it?

(360 degrees. Proofs will vary. Students may draw a diagonal line dividing the figure into two triangles and add the sum of the measures of the angles of both triangles.)

Learning Styles

Auditory/Verbal

Help students apply the algebraic component and show their understanding of the lesson's theorems by having them explain aloud how they derived their answers for Exercise B. For example, for problem 9, $m\angle y = 180° - m\angle p$ or $m\angle y = 180° - (m\angle Q + m\angle T)$.

Here is another example of a proof.

Example 3 **Theorem:** The measure of any exterior angle of a triangle is equal to the sum of the measures of the two non-adjacent interior angles.

In $\triangle ABC$, prove $m\angle A + m\angle B = m\angle BCD$.

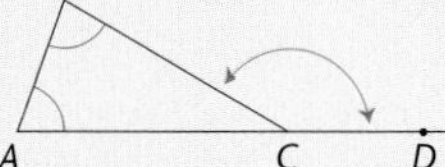

Step 1 $\triangle ABC$ is a triangle. Given.

Step 2 $m\angle A + m\angle B + m\angle C = 180°$. By theorem, the sum of the measures of the angles in any triangle is 180°.

Step 3 $m\angle C + m\angle BCD = 180°$. The sum of the measures of supplementary angles is 180°.

$m\angle A + m\angle B + m\angle C = 180°$ $\qquad$ $m\angle C + m\angle BCD = 180°$

$m\angle A + m\angle B = 180° - m\angle C$ $\qquad$ $m\angle BCD = 180° - m\angle C$

$m\angle A + m\angle B = m\angle BCD$

Quantities equal to the same quantity are equal to each other.

You can use this theorem to solve problems like the following examples.

Example 4 Given $\triangle ABC$, find $m\angle x$.

Step 1 By previous theorem, $60° + m\angle x = 130°$.

Step 2 Solve $60° + m\angle x = 130°$ for x.

$60° + m\angle x = 130°$

$m\angle x = 130° - 60°$

$m\angle x = 70°$

Example 5 In this triangle, $m\angle x = m\angle y$. The exterior angle measures 120°. Find $m\angle x$ and $m\angle y$.

Step 1 Find $m\angle y$. Since $\angle y$ and the exterior angle are supplementary, the sum of their measures is 180°.

$120° + y = 180°$

$y = 180° - 120°$

$y = 60°$

Step 2 Find $m\angle x$.

$y + x + x = 180°$

$60° + x + x = 180°$

$x + x = 180° - 60°$

$2x = 120°$

$x = 60°$

Step 3 Check. $\quad 60° + 60° + 60° = 180°$

Exercise A Find m∠*x*.

1. 70°

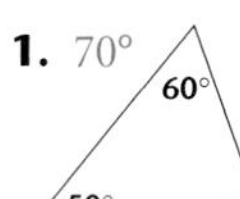

2. 50°

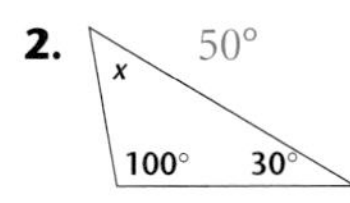

3. 45°

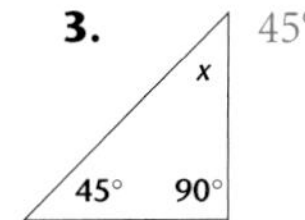

4. 110°

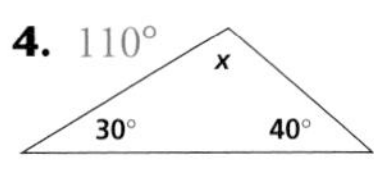

5. 105°

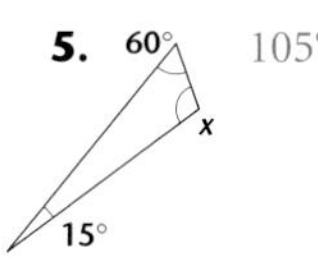

Exercise B Find m∠*y*.

6. 50°

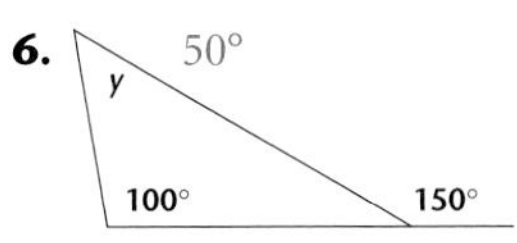

7. 40°

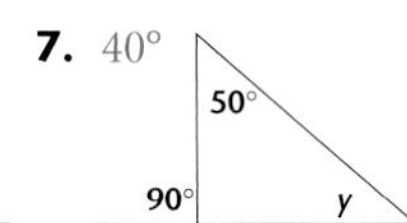

8. 94.5°

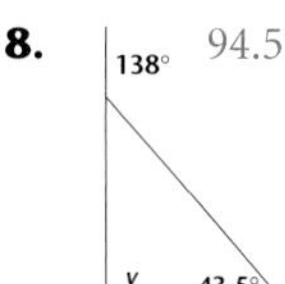

9. m∠*y* = 180° – m∠*P* *or*
m∠*y* = 180° – (m∠*Q* + m∠*T*)

Exercise C Answer this question. 360°; explanations will vary

10. If the sum of the measures of the angles in any triangle is 180°, what is the sum of the measures of the angles in any four-sided figure? Give a reason for your answer.

Estimation Activity

Estimate: What are the angle sums of a convex polygon?
Solution: Find the sum of all the angle measures.
Divide the convex polygon into non-overlapping triangles.
Multiply the number of triangles by 180°.

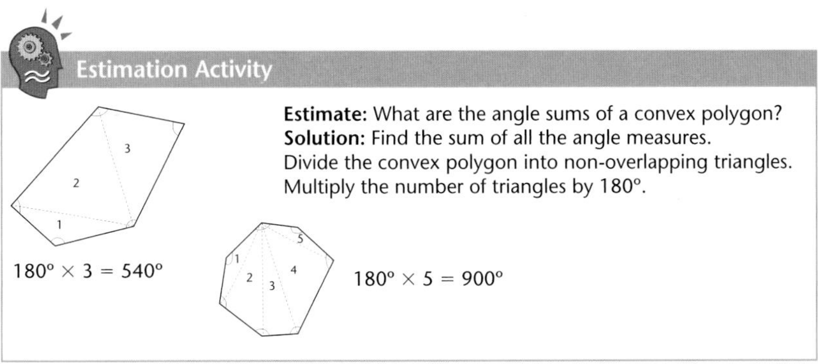

180° × 3 = 540°

180° × 5 = 900°

Lesson at a Glance

Chapter 12 Lesson 4

Overview This lesson classifies triangles by their angles and by their sides.

Objectives

- To identify triangles as acute, equiangular, obtuse, or right
- To identify triangles as scalene, isosceles, or equilateral

Student Pages 368–369

Teacher's Resource Library 

Workbook Activity 118

Activity 111

Alternative Activity 111

Mathematics Vocabulary

acute triangle
equiangular triangle
isosceles triangle
obtuse triangle
scalene triangle

Warm-Up Activity

Provide students with straws, wood craft sticks, straight plastic strips, or pieces of wood doweling in various lengths. Have them create triangles with three equal-length sides, two equal-length sides, and no equal-length sides and comment on what happens to the angles within the triangle with these variations.

Teaching the Lesson

Provide a variety of triangle shapes and practice time to be sure students become familiar with the vocabulary and types of triangles. Show students how to use arcs and tick marks to designate angles and sides that are equal or different in measure. Have them create triangles and mark their angles and sides with arcs and lines. Students can then exchange their triangles and use the shorthand designations to name them.

Lesson 4 Naming Triangles

Acute triangle
A triangle with three acute angles

Equiangular triangle
A triangle with three angles, each measuring 60°

Obtuse triangle
A triangle with one obtuse angle

Scalene triangle
A triangle with no equal sides

Isosceles triangle
A triangle with two sides of equal length

Triangles are named by their angles and by their sides.

Triangles Named by Their Angles

Acute

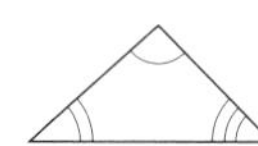

Each angle of an **acute triangle** measures less than 90°.

Equiangular

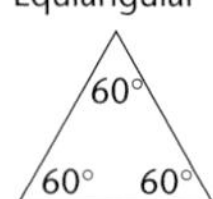

All of the angles of an **equiangular triangle** measure 60°.

Obtuse

One angle of an **obtuse triangle** measures more than 90°.

Right

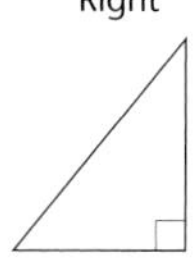

One angle of a right triangle measures 90°.

Triangles Named by Their Sides

Scalene

Each side of a **scalene triangle** is a different length.

Isosceles

Two sides of an **isosceles triangle** have the same length.

Equilateral

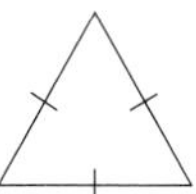

All of the sides of an equilateral triangle have the same length.

Lines may be used to mark the sides of a figure. A single line represents one side length, double lines another, and triple lines a third. For example, a triangle that has a single line marking each side has three sides of equal length.

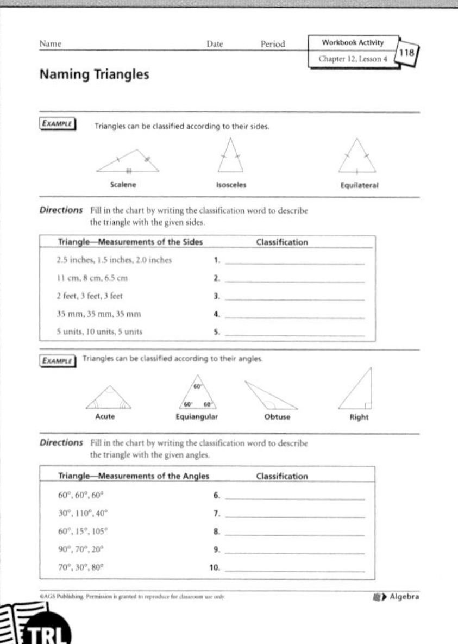

Name Date Period | Workbook Activity 118 | Chapter 12, Lesson 4

Naming Triangles

EXAMPLE Triangles can be classified according to their sides.

Scalene Isosceles Equilateral

Directions Fill in the chart by writing the classification word to describe the triangle with the given sides.

Triangle—Measurements of the Sides	Classification
2.5 inches, 1.5 inches, 2.0 inches	1. ______
11 cm, 8 cm, 6.5 cm	2. ______
2 feet, 3 feet, 3 feet	3. ______
35 mm, 35 mm, 35 mm	4. ______
5 units, 10 units, 5 units	5. ______

EXAMPLE Triangles can be classified according to their angles.

Acute Equiangular Obtuse Right

Directions Fill in the chart by writing the classification word to describe the triangle with the given angles.

Triangle—Measurements of the Angles	Classification
60°, 60°, 60°	6. ______
30°, 110°, 40°	7. ______
60°, 15°, 105°	8. ______
90°, 70°, 20°	9. ______
70°, 30°, 80°	10. ______

 Algebra

Workbook Activity 118

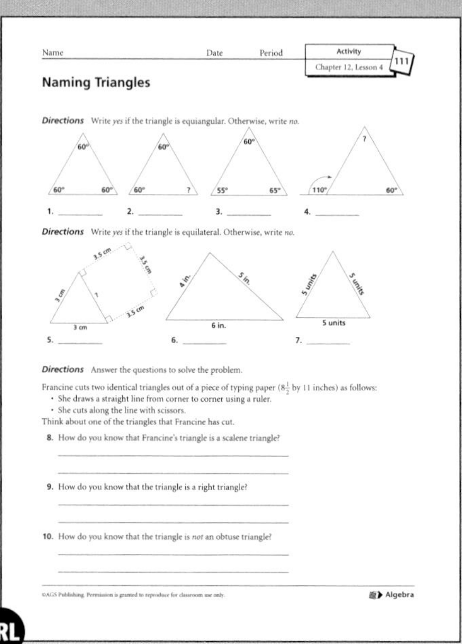

Name Date Period | Activity 111 | Chapter 12, Lesson 4

Naming Triangles

Directions Write *yes* if the triangle is equiangular. Otherwise, write *no*.

60° 60° 60° | 60° 60° ? | 60° 55° 65° | ? 110° 60°

1. ______ 2. ______ 3. ______ 4. ______

Directions Write *yes* if the triangle is equilateral. Otherwise, write *no*.

3.5 cm 3.5 cm 3.5 cm 3 cm ? 3 cm | 4 in. 5 in. 6 in. | 5 units 5 units 5 units

5. ______ 6. ______ 7. ______

Directions Answer the questions to solve the problem.

Francine cuts two identical triangles out of a piece of typing paper ($8\frac{1}{2}$ by 11 inches) as follows:
- She draws a straight line from corner to corner using a ruler.
- She cuts along the line with scissors.

Think about one of the triangles that Francine has cut.

8. How do you know that Francine's triangle is a scalene triangle?
9. How do you know that the triangle is a right triangle?
10. How do you know that the triangle is *not* an obtuse triangle?

 Algebra

Activity 111

You can use these characteristics of triangles to name triangles.

Arcs are used like lines to show angles. On a triangle that has two angles marked with a single arc, those two angles are of equal measure.

EXAMPLE 1 What name or names best describe this triangle?

Step 1 Consider the angles of the triangle. Because one angle measures more than 90°, it is an obtuse triangle.

Step 2 Consider the sides of the triangle. Because two sides have the same length, it is an isosceles triangle.

Step 3 Name the triangle: The triangle is *obtuse isosceles.*

TRY THIS

Find triangles used as graphs, illustrations, or decorations in newspapers and magazines. Measure the lengths of the sides and use lines to compare the sides of each triangle. Name the triangles by the lengths of their sides.

Exercise A Name each triangle.

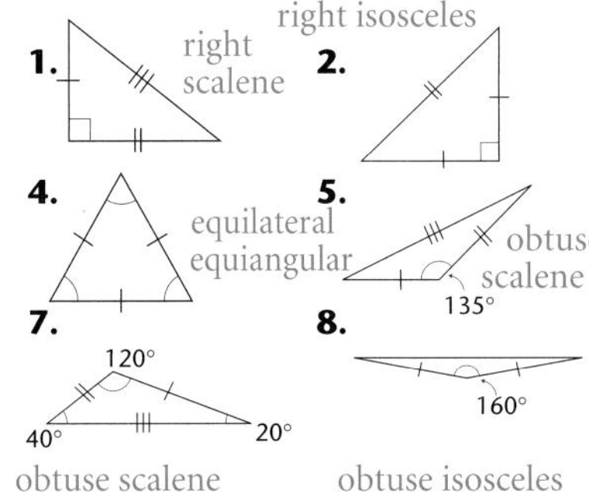

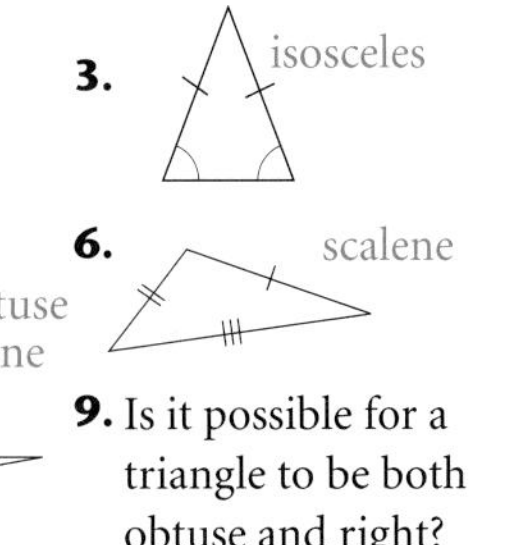

1. right scalene
2. right isosceles
3. isosceles
4. equilateral equiangular
5. obtuse scalene (135°)
6. scalene
7. (120°, 40°, 20°) obtuse scalene
8. (160°) obtuse isosceles

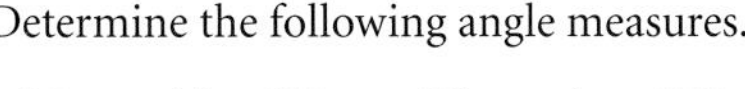

9. Is it possible for a triangle to be both obtuse and right? No. Sample explanation provided in Teacher's Edition.

PROBLEM SOLVING

Exercise B In this figure, a televison antenna is attached to the top of a rigid mast. The mast is attached to the roof of a home. Guy wires help prevent the mast and antenna from flowing over.

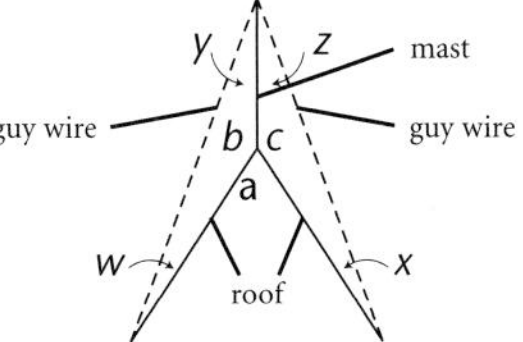

Determine the following angle measures.

10. $m\angle b$	150°	**13.** $m\angle c$	150°
11. $m\angle w$	10°	**14.** $m\angle x$	10°
12. $m\angle y$	20°	**15.** $m\angle z$	20°

In the figure, $m\angle a = 60°$, $m\angle b = m\angle c$, $m\angle y = m\angle z$, and $\frac{1}{2}m\angle y = m\angle w$

Answer to Problem 9

9. No. Sample explanation: The sum of the angles in any triangle is 180°. If one angle in that triangle is right, the sum of the measures of the other angles in the triangle is 180° − 90° or 90°. Since the measure of an obtuse angle is greater than 90°, either of the remaining angles in the triangle cannot be obtuse.

MENTAL MATH

Ask students which arithmetic operations(s) will make each of the following open statements true.

3 ■ 2 = 5	(+)
3 ■ 2 = 6	(•)
3 ■ 1 = 2	(−)
3 ■ 1 = 3	(÷)
2 ■ 1 = 2	(• or ÷)
2 ■ 2 = 4	(+ or •)

Try This

As students measure the sides of triangles, have them note which type(s) are prevalent. Ask that they analyze why each type of triangle was preferred in a given ad or graph. For example, does the context call for the symmetry of an equilateral or an isosceles triangle? Does a scalene triangle draw the eye more because of its irregularity?

3 Reinforce and Extend

IN THE COMMUNITY

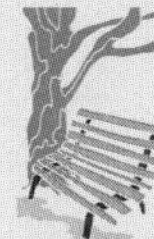

Have small groups of students visit a variety of community sites (malls, office buildings, stores, bridges, courtyards, parks, government offices, etc.) to observe how and where triangles are used in their architecture. For three sites, require students to measure the sides of the triangle, sketch it within its context (wall, floor, etc.), and show its angles. Encourage them to analyze the structure and offer an explanation why the triangles were used in the design.

GROUP PROBLEM SOLVING

Have students work in groups of four to create "impossible triangles." First, they must experiment with sides of different lengths. Can they construct a triangle with sides of 2, 3, and 5 inches? *(no)* 3, 4, and 8 inches? *(no)* 3, 4, and 6 inches *(yes)* Have them write combinations that will work and shuffle them in with those that will not. Read combinations aloud and have the class guess which sides can form triangles. Ask groups to use what they have observed to make a rule about triangles. *(In any triangle, the sum of the lengths of any two sides is greater than the length of the third side.)*

Lesson at a Glance

Chapter 12 Lesson 5

Overview This lesson presents five types of quadrilaterals and the measurement of their angles.

Objectives

- To identify and construct parallelogram, rectangle, rhombus, square, and trapezoid forms
- To compute the measures of the four angles of a quadrilateral

Student Pages 370–371

Teacher's Resource Library 

Workbook Activity 119

Activity 112

Alternative Activity 112

Mathematics Vocabulary

parallelogram **rectangle** **rhombus** **square** **trapezoid**

1 Warm-Up Activity

Have students experiment with triangle shapes they constructed in the previous lesson or construct new ones (some should be of equal size). Ask them to combine the shapes and see what new geometric shapes they can form. What type of shape is formed by the combination of two triangles? *(a quadrilateral, or a four-sided figure)* Have students read the lesson to discover the names and definitions for some of the shapes they have created.

2 Teaching the Lesson

Help students see the relationships among the types of quadrilaterals by creating true-false statements and explaining whether each is always true, always false, or sometimes true:

1) A square is a type of rectangle. *(always true)*

2) A rectangle is a square. *(sometimes true)*

3) A rhombus is a square. *(sometimes true)*

Lesson 5 Quadrilaterals

Parallelogram
A four-sided polygon with two pairs of equal and parallel sides

Trapezoid
A four-sided polygon with one pair of parallel sides and one pair of sides that are not parallel

Rectangle
A four-sided polygon with four right angles and the opposite sides equal

Square
A polygon with four equal sides and four right angles

Rhombus
A four-sided polygon with four parallel sides the same length

Quadrilaterals are polygons. In general, a quadrilateral has four sides, four angles, and two diagonals. The sum of the angle measures in any quadrilateral is 360°. This is shown by the fact that a triangle has 180° and two triangles make up every quadrilateral.

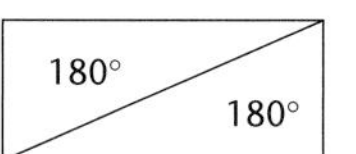

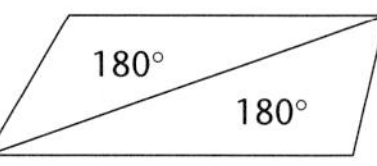

Quadrilaterals have special names.

Parallelogram
A quadrilateral with both pairs of opposite sides the same length and parallel

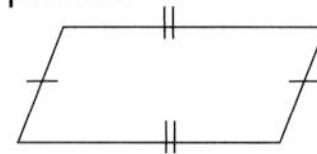

Rectangle
A parallelogram with four right angles

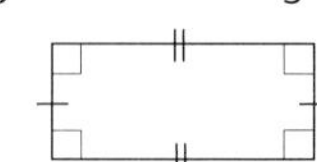

Square
A rectangle with all sides the same length

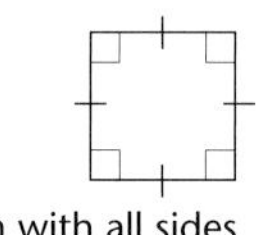

Rhombus
A parallelogram with all sides the same length

Trapezoid
A quadrilateral with only one pair of parallel sides

Right trapezoid
A quadrilateral with one pair of parallel sides and two right angles

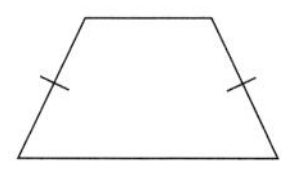

Isosceles trapezoid
A quadrilateral with one pair of parallel sides and two sides the same length

The angle measures of a quadrilateral can be computed.

EXAMPLE 1 In parallelogram *ABCD*, $m\angle A = 70°$.

Find $m\angle B$, $m\angle C$, and $m\angle D$.

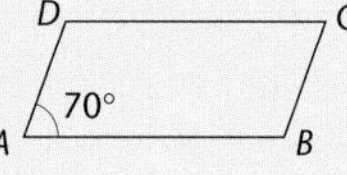

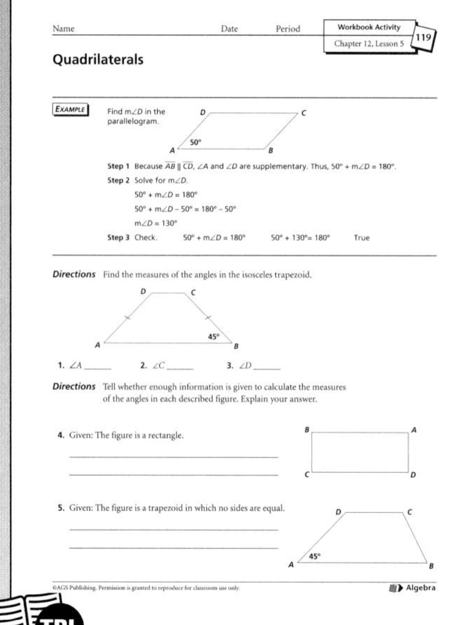

Name Date Period — Workbook Activity 119, Chapter 12, Lesson 5

Quadrilaterals

EXAMPLE Find $m\angle D$ in the parallelogram.

Step 1 Because $\overline{AB} \parallel \overline{CD}$, $\angle A$ and $\angle D$ are supplementary. Thus, $50° + m\angle D = 180°$.

Step 2 Solve for $m\angle D$.

$50° + m\angle D = 180°$

$50° + m\angle D - 50° = 180° - 50°$

$m\angle D = 130°$

Step 3 Check. $50° + m\angle D = 180°$ $50° + 130° = 180°$ True

Directions Find the measures of the angles in the isosceles trapezoid.

1. $\angle A$ ____ 2. $\angle C$ ____ 3. $\angle D$ ____

Directions Tell whether enough information is given to calculate the measures of the angles in each described figure. Explain your answer.

4. Given: The figure is a rectangle.

5. Given: The figure is a trapezoid in which no sides are equal.

 Algebra

Workbook Activity 119

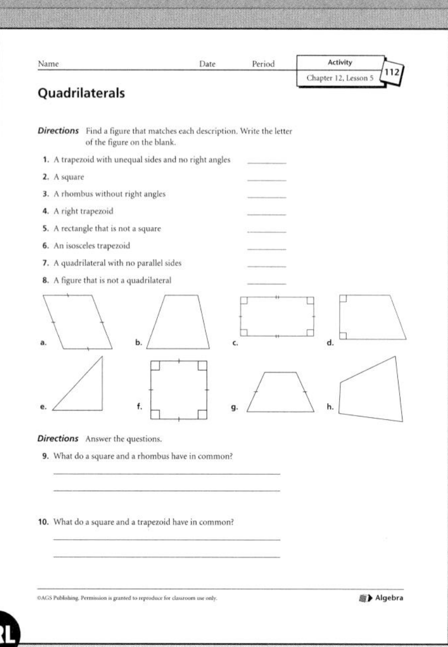

Name Date Period — Activity 112, Chapter 12, Lesson 5

Quadrilaterals

Directions Find a figure that matches each description. Write the letter of the figure on the blank.

1. A trapezoid with unequal sides and no right angles ____
2. A square ____
3. A rhombus without right angles ____
4. A right trapezoid ____
5. A rectangle that is not a square ____
6. An isosceles trapezoid ____
7. A quadrilateral with no parallel sides ____
8. A figure that is not a quadrilateral ____

a. b. c. d. e. f. g. h.

Directions Answer the questions.

9. What do a square and a rhombus have in common?

10. What do a square and a trapezoid have in common?

 Algebra

Activity 112

Example 1 *(continued)*

Step 1 Because $\overline{AB} \,||\, \overline{CD}$, $\angle A$ and $\angle D$ are supplementary. Find m$\angle D$.

$$m\angle A + m\angle D = 180°$$
$$70° + m\angle D = 180°$$
$$m\angle D = 180° - 70°$$
$$m\angle D = 110°$$

Step 2 Because $\overline{AD} \,||\, \overline{BC}$, $\angle C$ and $\angle D$ are supplementary. Find m$\angle C$.

$$m\angle C + m\angle D = 180°$$
$$m\angle C + 110° = 180°$$
$$m\angle C = 180° - 110°$$
$$m\angle C = 70°$$

Step 3 Because $\overline{AB} \,||\, \overline{CD}$, $\angle B$ and $\angle C$ are supplementary. Find m$\angle B$.

$$m\angle B + m\angle C = 180°$$
$$m\angle B + 70° = 180°$$
$$m\angle B = 180° - 70°$$
$$m\angle B = 110°$$

Exercise A Find the measures of the angles.

1. In right trapezoid $ABCD$, $\overline{AB} \,||\, \overline{DC}$. Find m$\angle D$ and m$\angle C$.

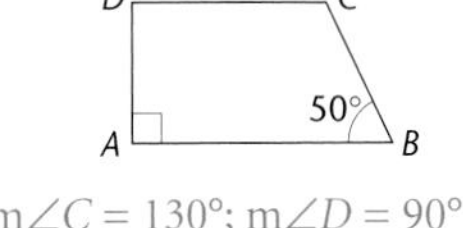

m$\angle C$ = 130°; m$\angle D$ = 90°

2. In rhombus $ABCD$, $\overline{AB} \,||\, \overline{CD}$, $\overline{BC} \,||\, \overline{AD}$, and m$\angle B$ = 142°. Find m$\angle A$, m$\angle C$, and m$\angle D$.

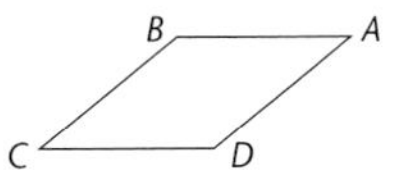

m$\angle A$ = 38°; m$\angle C$ = 38°; m$\angle D$ = 142°

Exercise B Draw each figure on graph paper. Then compute the measure of each unknown angle.

3. Draw rectangle $ABCD$. Draw each diagonal of the rectangle. What is the sum of the measures of the angles that are formed at the intersection of the diagonals? 360°
4. Draw square $ABCD$. Draw each diagonal of the square. What is the measure of each angle that is formed at the intersection of the diagonals? 90°
5. Draw a quadrilateral that has one pair of parallel sides and no sides the same length. Check students' drawings

4) A parallelogram is an isosceles trapezoid. *(always false)*
5) A right trapezoid is a trapezoid. *(always true)*
6) A rhombus is a trapezoid. *(always false)*
7) A trapezoid is an isosceles trapezoid. *(sometimes true)*

When students complete Exercise B, problem 5, have them label the quadrilateral they created. Ask them to explain why it cannot be an isosceles trapezoid, a rhombus, a square, a rectangle, or a parallelogram.

3 Reinforce and Extend

Learning Styles

LEP/ESL

Make examples of each type of quadrilateral cut from 4 x 6 cards. Write the name on the back of each. Have students work in pairs, with one partner describing the characteristics of the quadrilateral and naming it while the other holds the cards and verifies. Then have partners switch roles and repeat.

At Home

Have students locate a cardboard box at home and determine the following about it:

How many quadrilaterals make up its faces?

Measure each quadrilateral and name it (square, etc.).

Is the box formed from one continuous piece of cardboard?

Carefully disassemble the box to determine the size and shape of the piece(s) of cardboard from which it was formed.

Create your own design for a gift box using different quadrilateral shapes and triangles. Label each shape with its geometric name.

Lesson at a Glance

Chapter 12 Lesson 6

Overview This lesson introduces congruent and similar triangles and the theorems that prove congruence.

Objectives

- To identify triangles that are congruent
- To identify triangles that are similar
- To comprehend that triangles are congruent if they have two sides and an included angle that are equal or three equal corresponding sides or two angles and an included side that are equal

Student Pages 372–375

Teacher's Resource Library 

Workbook Activity 120

Activity 113

Alternative Activity 113

Mathematics Vocabulary

congruent
similar

Warm-Up Activity

Show several quadrilaterals and ask students to fold each one once to form two triangles. Ask, "What do you notice about the two triangles?" *(A rectangle, parallelogram, square, and rhombus form two identical triangles. A trapezoid forms two triangles that are not the same in size or angles.)* Have students read the lesson to find out about triangles that are alike.

Teaching the Lesson

To reinforce the concept of congruence, refer students to the models from the Warm-Up Activity (or have them create models of their own) and have them verify that the triangles within a square or rectangle fit over one another exactly. To model similarity, create a smaller square in a contrasting color, fold it into triangles, and place it on top of the larger model. Have students compare angle

Lesson 6 Congruent and Similar Triangles

Congruent
Figures that have the same size and shape

Figures that have exactly the same size and shape are **congruent.** The symbol for *congruent* is ≅. $\triangle ABC \cong \triangle DEF$ is read "Triangle *ABC* is congruent to triangle *DEF*."

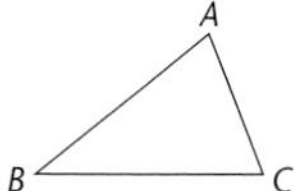

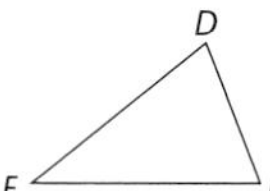

A diagonal divides each of these quadrilaterals into two triangles. Two triangles are congruent if their corresponding sides and angles are equal.

square

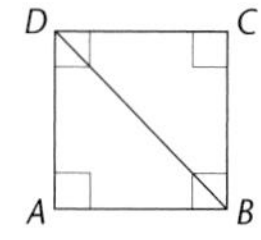

$\triangle ABD \cong \triangle CBD$.
If you fold the square along the diagonal, the triangles would match exactly.

rectangle

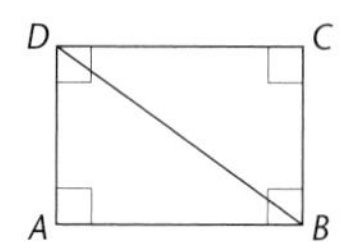

$\triangle ABD \cong \triangle CDB$.
If you cut along the diagonal and make two triangles, one triangle could be moved and placed exactly on top of the other.

right trapezoid

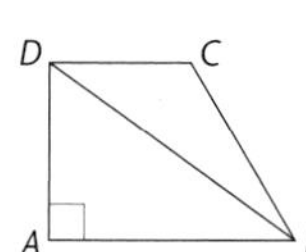

$\triangle ABD$ and $\triangle CBD$ are not congruent.
$\triangle ABD \ncong \triangle CBD$.
$\triangle ABD$ is a right triangle.
$\triangle CBD$ is not a right triangle.

Three theorems can help you determine whether two triangles are congruent.

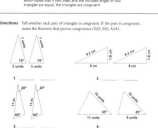

Name Date Period — Workbook Activity 120, Chapter 12, Lesson 6

Congruent and Similar Triangles

EXAMPLE Are these triangles congruent? Give a reason for the answer.

(4 in., 3 in.; 4 in., 3 in.)

Yes. They are congruent by the Side-Angle-Side (SAS) theorem, which states that if two sides and the included angle of two triangles are equal, the triangles are congruent.

Directions Tell whether each pair of triangles is congruent. If the pair is congruent, name the theorem that proves congruence (SAS, SSS, ASA).

1. (7 units, 74°, 5 units; 7 units, 74°, 5 units) ______ ______
2. (4.2 cm, 1.8 cm, 4 cm; 4.2 cm, 1.8 cm, 4 cm) ______ ______
3. (20°, 11 in., 60°; 20°, 11 in., 60°) ______ ______
4. (10 units, 45°, 11 units; 10 units, 45°, 9 units) ______ ______

Directions Answer the question.

5. Are all right triangles similar? Tell why or why not.

 Algebra

Workbook Activity 120

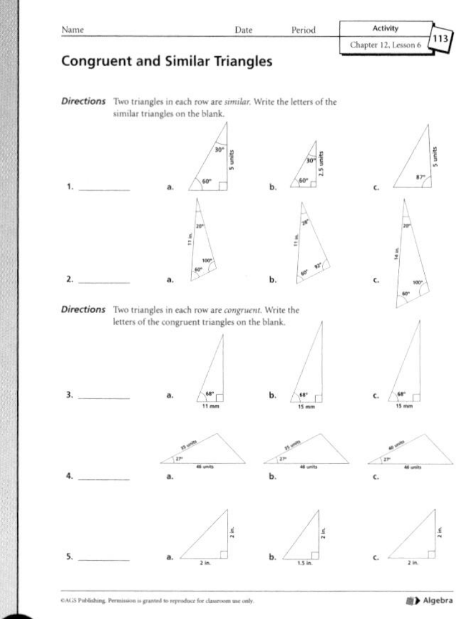
Name Date Period — Activity 113, Chapter 12, Lesson 6

Congruent and Similar Triangles

Directions Two triangles in each row are *similar.* Write the letters of the similar triangles on the blank.

1. ______ a. (30°, 5 units, 60°) b. (30°, 2.5 units, 60°) c. (5 units, 87°)
2. ______ a. (20°, 11 in., 100°, 60°) b. (28°, 11 in., 60°, 92°) c. (20°, 14 in., 100°, 60°)

Directions Two triangles in each row are *congruent.* Write the letters of the congruent triangles on the blank.

3. ______ a. (68°, 11 mm) b. (68°, 15 mm) c. (68°, 15 mm)
4. ______ a. (35 units, 27°, 46 units) b. (35 units, 27°, 46 units) c. (40 units, 27°, 46 units)
5. ______ a. (2 in., 2 in.) b. (2 in., 1.5 in.) c. (2 in., 2 in.)

 Algebra

Activity 113

The Side-Angle-Side Theorem (SAS)

If two sides and the included angle of two triangles are equal, then the triangles are congruent.

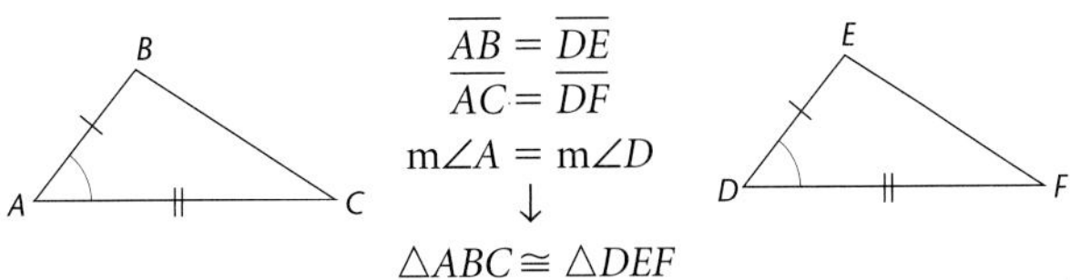

The Side-Side-Side Theorem (SSS)

If the corresponding sides of two triangles are equal, then the triangles are congruent.

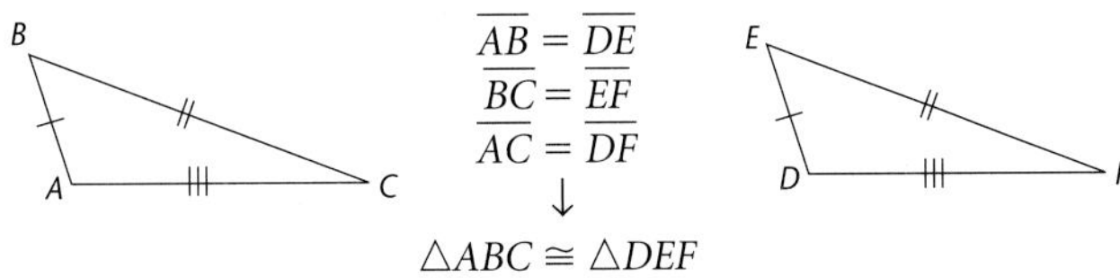

The Angle-Side-Angle Theorem (ASA)

If two angles and the included side of two triangles are equal, then the triangles are congruent.

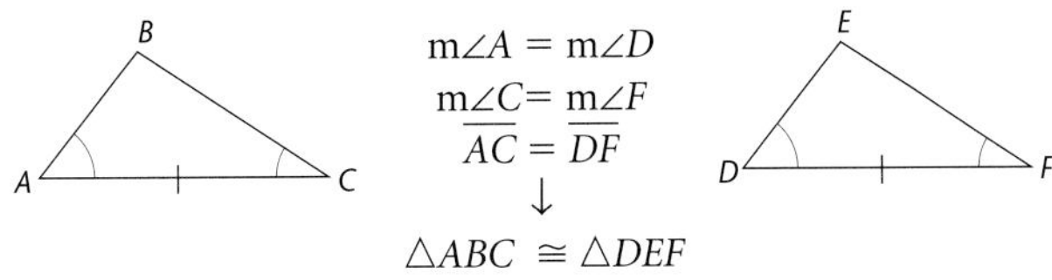

EXAMPLE 1 Given $\triangle ABC$ and $\triangle DEF$ with $m\angle A = m\angle D$, $AB = DE$, and $AC = DF$, determine whether the triangles are congruent. If the triangles are congruent, name the theorem that proves congruence.

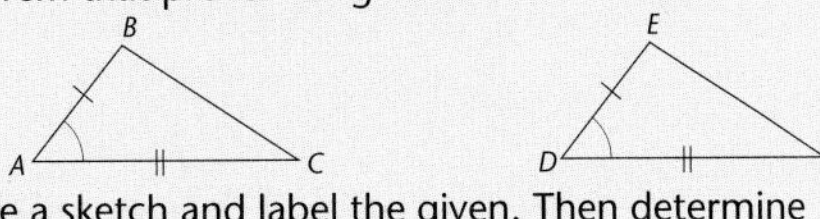

Solution Make a sketch and label the given. Then determine which theorem—SAS, SSS, or ASA—proves congruence. Answer: $\triangle ABC \cong \triangle DEF$ by SAS.

measures and side lengths of the two. Ask them to summarize the difference between similar and congruent triangles. *(Congruent triangles are identical. Similar triangles have the same proportions but are different sizes, like nesting shapes.)*

3 Reinforce and Extend

LEARNING STYLES

Interpersonal/ Group Learning

Set up stations at which you place pairs of triangles, some congruent, some similar, and some neither. At each station, provide just enough information for students to apply the SAS, SSS, or ASA theorems. (Note: For similar triangles, provide measures for two angles and a side.) Have small groups of students move from station to station, identifying the relationship between each pair of triangles.

LEARNING STYLES

Body/Kinesthetic

Use the concept of symmetry to further develop students' ability to recognize congruence. Inform students that symmetry exists within a figure when it may be folded so that one half fits exactly over the other. Provide models of the following types of triangles and have students experiment to see whether they are able to fold the triangles to create two congruent triangles. Then have students list the measures of the angles in the triangles they created.

isosceles triangle with angles of 70°, 70°, and 40° *(yes; 70°, 90°, and 20° degrees)*

right triangle with 45° angles *(yes; 45°, 45°, and 90°)*

scalene triangle *(no)*

equilateral triangle *(yes; 30°, 90°, and 60°)*

At Home

Geometric patterns that repeat are pleasing and useful in many aspects of our lives. Have students look at home for products or designs with shapes that demonstrate congruence or similarity. After students list their finds, ask them to design their own product that includes a pattern with congruent or similar triangles.

Example 2 Given $\triangle ABC$ and $\triangle DEF$ with $m\angle B = m\angle E$, $m\angle C = m\angle F$, and $\overline{BC} = \overline{EF}$, determine whether the triangles are congruent. If the triangles are congruent, name the theorem that proves congruence.

Solution Make a sketch and label the given. Then determine which theorem—SAS, SSS, or ASA—proves congruence. Answer: $\triangle ABC \cong \triangle DEF$ by ASA.

Example 3 Given $\triangle ABC$ and $\triangle DEF$ with $m\angle A = m\angle D$, $\overline{BC} = \overline{EF}$, and $\overline{AB} = \overline{DE}$, determine whether the triangles are congruent. If the triangles are congruent, name the theorem that proves congruence.

Solution Make a sketch and label the given. Then determine which theorem—SAS, SSS, or ASA—proves congruence. Answer: Because the given does not satisfy SAS, SSS, or ASA, $\triangle ABC$ is not congruent to $\triangle DEF$.

Similar

Figures that have the same shape but not the same size

Figures that have the same shape but not the same size are **similar.** The symbol for *similar* is ~. $\triangle ABC \sim \triangle DEF$ is read "Triangle *ABC* is similar to triangle *DEF*."

Similar triangles have equal corresponding angles but not equal corresponding sides. These triangles are similar because their corresponding angles are equal.

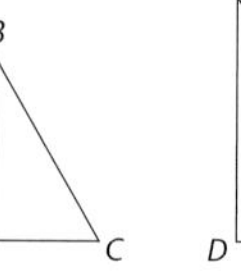

Example 4

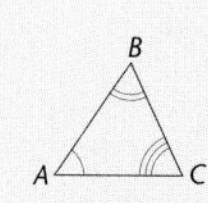

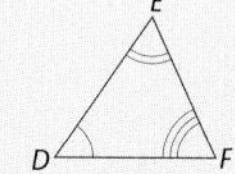

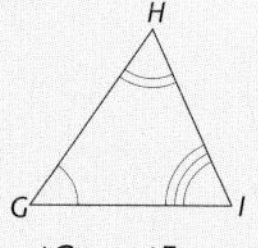

$\angle A = \angle D = \angle G$ $\quad$ $\angle B = \angle E = \angle H$ $\quad$ $\angle C = \angle F = \angle I$

Given $\triangle ABC \sim \triangle DEF$, $m\angle A = 55°$, and $m\angle B = 60°$, find $m\angle F$.

Step 1 Find $m\angle C$.

$m\angle A + m\angle B + m\angle C = 180°$

$55° + 60° + m\angle C = 180°$

$m\angle C = 180° - 55° - 60°$

$m\angle C = 65°$

Step 2 Find $m\angle F$.

Since the triangles are similar, their corresponding angles are equal, and $m\angle C = m\angle F$. So $m\angle F = 65°$.

TRY THIS

Draw three rectangles. Make two of the rectangles similar and make one that is not similar. Tell why the rectangles are similar or not similar.

Students' answers will vary.

Exercise A Name the theorem that proves congruence.

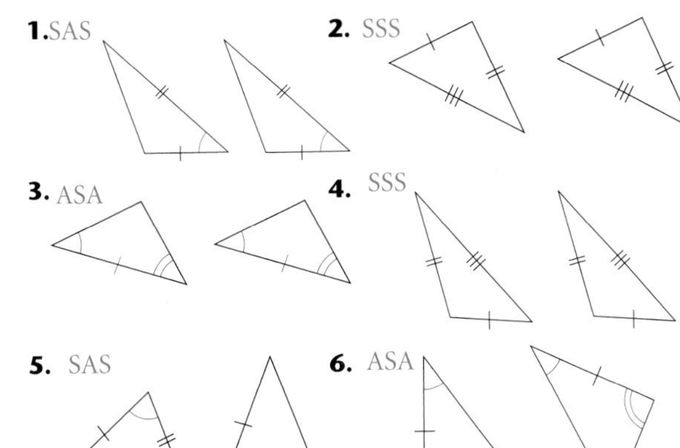

5. SAS **6.** ASA

Exercise B Find the measures of the angles.

7. Given $\triangle ABC \sim \triangle DEF$, $m\angle A = 88°$, and $m\angle B = 29°$, find $m\angle F$. 63°

8. Given $\triangle ABC \sim \triangle DEF$, $m\angle B = 30°$, and $m\angle C = 107°$, find $m\angle D$. 43°

Exercise C Answer these questions.

9. Are all isosceles triangles similar? Tell why or why not.

10. Which triangles are always similar?

9. No; isosceles triangles can have different sizes and different shapes

10. equilateral and equiangular triangles

Algebra in Your Life

The Golden Rectangle

The "golden rectangle" is considered the most pleasing of all geometric shapes. It uses a height-to-width ratio of 1:1.6. A 3 × 5 index card has ratio that is close to a golden rectangle. Architects and artists have used the golden rectangle for centuries. The ancient Greek temple, the Parthenon, fits almost perfectly inside a golden rectangle. Leonardo da Vinci's (1452–1519) painting, *Mona Lisa*, contains many golden rectangles. Today, package designers and advertisers often use the golden rectangle because of its appeal to consumers.

Try This

Have students create a definition for similar rectangles after they complete the activity. Suggest that their definitions have two parts:

1) how the sides are different *(different lengths)*

2) how the sides are similar *(They must be proportional.)*

Learning Styles

Visual/Spatial

Students may require some extra time and practice to become familiar with the symbols for "congruent to" and "similar to" and the abbreviations ASA, SSS, and SAS. Have students write each abbreviation and symbol on a separate piece of paper in marker, so that they are easily visible. On the overhead or board, present pairs of triangles. Introduce information about the triangles one item at a time. When students can decide whether triangles are similar or congruent, they hold up the appropriate card (≠ or ≈). Then ask them to hold up the card for the theorem they used.

Lesson at a Glance

Chapter 12 Lesson 7

Overview This lesson explains trigonometric ratios and the formulas for calculating sine, cosine, and tangent.

Objectives

- To identify the hypotenuse of a right triangle
- To comprehend the proportionality of right triangles
- To calculate sine, cosine, and tangent of angle A in a right triangle, with or without a calculator

Student Pages 376–379

Teacher's Resource Library 

Workbook Activity 121

Activity 114

Alternative Activity 114

Mathematics Vocabulary

trigonometric ratios

Warm-Up Activity

Give examples of ratios. Show that right triangles have sides with special ratios: $a^2 + b^2 = c^2$ where c is the length of the hypotenuse and a and b are the other two sides of a right triangle. Explain that in this lesson, students will learn the special, predictable ratios that exist within a right triangle.

Teaching the Lesson

Be sure students know the vocabulary needed to complete the section: hypotenuse, side adjacent, side opposite. Draw and label several right triangles and have students locate these sides for specific angles. Then provide measurements for each side and, when students have read the lesson, have them calculate sine, cosine, and tangent for several angles. When students are confident they can identify the sides that make up each ratio, work through the examples.

Lesson 7 Trigonometric Ratios

Trigonometric ratios

Angles measured by ratios of the sides of a right triangle

In right triangle ABC, the hypotenuse is AC, the side adjacent to $\angle A$ is AB, and the side opposite $\angle A$ is BC.

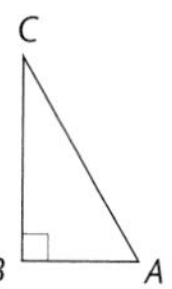

From the measures of the lengths of these sides, **trigonometric ratios** can be established.

Trigonometric ratios include

sine ratio of $\angle A = \dfrac{\text{the length of the side opposite } \angle A}{\text{the length of the hypotenuse}}$

The sine of $\angle A$ is written sin A.

cosine ratio of $\angle A = \dfrac{\text{the length of the side adjacent to } \angle A}{\text{the length of the hypotenuse}}$

The cosine of $\angle A$ is written cos A.

tangent ratio of $\angle A = \dfrac{\text{the length of the side opposite } \angle A}{\text{the length of the side adjacent to } \angle A}$

The tangent of $\angle A$ is written tan A.

Trigonometric ratios can be used in different ways to solve problems.

EXAMPLE 1 In right triangle ABC, find sin A, cos A, and tan A.

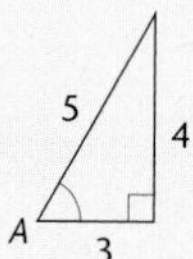

Step 1 $\sin A = \dfrac{\text{the length of the side opposite } \angle A}{\text{the length of the hypotenuse}} = \dfrac{4}{5} = 0.8$

Step 2 $\cos A = \dfrac{\text{the length of the side adjacent to } \angle A}{\text{the length of the hypotenuse}} = \dfrac{3}{5} = 0.6$

Step 3 $\tan A = \dfrac{\text{the length of the side opposite } \angle A}{\text{the length of the side adjacent to } \angle A} = \dfrac{4}{3} = 1.\overline{3}$

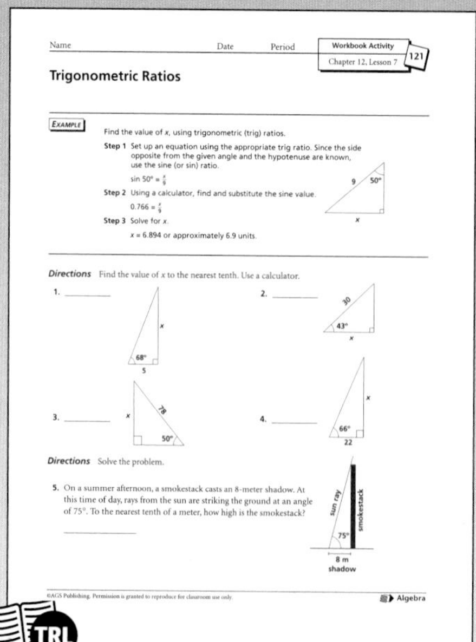

Name Date Period

Workbook Activity 121 — Chapter 12, Lesson 7

Trigonometric Ratios

EXAMPLE Find the value of x, using trigonometric (trig) ratios.

Step 1 Set up an equation using the appropriate trig ratio. Since the side opposite from the given angle and the hypotenuse are known, use the sine (or sin) ratio.

$\sin 50° = \frac{x}{9}$

Step 2 Using a calculator, find and substitute the sine value.

$0.766 = \frac{x}{9}$

Step 3 Solve for x.

$x = 6.894$ or approximately 6.9 units.

Directions Find the value of x to the nearest tenth. Use a calculator.

1. ______
2. ______
3. ______
4. ______

Directions Solve the problem.

5. On a summer afternoon, a smokestack casts an 8-meter shadow. At this time of day, rays from the sun are striking the ground at an angle of 75°. To the nearest tenth of a meter, how high is the smokestack?

______

Algebra

Workbook Activity 121

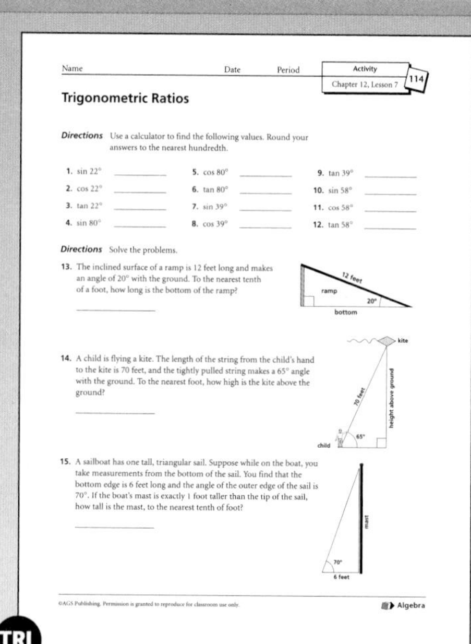

Name Date Period

Activity 114 — Chapter 12, Lesson 7

Trigonometric Ratios

Directions Use a calculator to find the following values. Round your answers to the nearest hundredth.

1. sin 22° ______	5. cos 80° ______	9. tan 39° ______
2. cos 22° ______	6. tan 80° ______	10. sin 58° ______
3. tan 22° ______	7. sin 39° ______	11. cos 58° ______
4. sin 80° ______	8. cos 39° ______	12. tan 58° ______

Directions Solve the problems.

13. The inclined surface of a ramp is 12 feet long and makes an angle of 20° with the ground. To the nearest tenth of a foot, how long is the bottom of the ramp?

______

14. A child is flying a kite. The length of the string from the child's hand to the kite is 70 feet, and the tightly pulled string makes a 65° angle with the ground. To the nearest foot, how high is the kite above the ground?

______

15. A sailboat has one tall, triangular sail. Suppose while on the boat, you take measurements from the bottom of the sail. You find that the bottom edge is 6 feet long and the angle of the outer edge of the sail is 70°. If the boat's mast is exactly 1 foot taller than the tip of the sail, how tall is the mast, to the nearest tenth of foot?

______

Algebra

Activity 114

EXAMPLE 2 In the right triangle shown here, find x. Round your answer to the nearest hundredth.

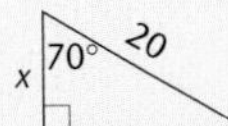

Step 1 Decide which trigonometric ratio to use. Since the measure of the hypotenuse is given and you need to find the length of the side adjacent to the 70° angle, use the cosine ratio and a calculator.

Step 2 $\cos A = \frac{\text{the length of the adjacent side}}{\text{the length of the hypotenuse}}$

$$\cos 70° = \frac{x}{20}$$
$$(20)\cos 70° = x$$
$$(20)(0.3420201) = x$$
$$6.840402 = x$$
$$6.84 = x \text{ (rounded to the nearest hundredth)}$$

EXAMPLE 3 Suppose you are standing 100 feet from the foot of a flagpole. The angle of elevation from the ground on which you are standing to the top of the flagpole is 20°. Find the height of the flagpole to the nearest foot.

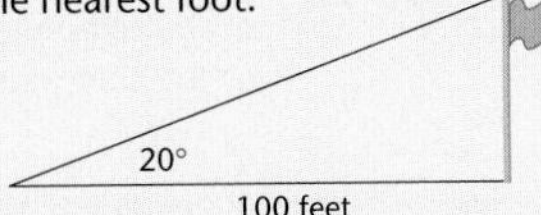

Step 1 You know that the length of the side adjacent to the 20° angle is 100 feet, and you are trying to find x, the side opposite. Use the tangent ratio:

$$\tan A = \frac{\text{opposite side}}{\text{adjacent side}}$$

Step 2 Find x.

$$\tan A = \frac{\text{the length of the opposite side}}{\text{the length of the adjacent side}}$$
$$\tan 20° = \frac{x}{100}$$
$$(100)(\tan 20°) = x$$
$$(100)(0.3639702) = x$$
$$36.39702 = x$$
$$36 \text{ feet} = x \text{ (rounded to the nearest foot)}$$

Reinforce and Extend

CAREER CONNECTION

Have students gather information on surveying, a career that requires the measurement of lengths and angles using trigonometry. Ask students to share their findings with their classmates.

LEARNING STYLES

Logical/Mathematical

Assess students' understanding of the sine ratio by asking them to explain why sin A can never be a whole number. Their explanations should make clear the understanding that the hypotenuse is always the longest side of a right triangle. Since it is the denominator of a fraction, the fraction will always be less than 1.

Learning Styles

Body/Kinesthetic

Have students use a geoboard to construct a right triangle and find the sine, cosine, and tangent of angles *A* and *B*. Then have them change the sizes of angles *A* and *B*, recalculate, and note any changes in the values of the trigonometric ratios. Ask that they formulate a true statement to express what they learned. For example, "As angle *A* in a right triangle approaches 90°, the value of sine ________." *(gets larger, approaches 1, or other reasonable answers)*

Online Connection

This is a two-part activity, both from the same Internet site. Have students go to www.maa.org/mathland/mathland_11_4.html to read the Problem at the Art Gallery. Part 1: Have them read about the map problem again. Then use a world atlas to see how cartographers today differentiate territories. Part 2: Copy the diagram for the 11-sided art gallery and Ivars Peterson's example solution. Ask students to work in groups to find other possible triangulations.

Example 4 A 30-foot-long ladder leaning against a house forms a 70° angle with the ground. To the nearest foot, how far above the ground does the ladder touch the house?

Step 1 You know the length of the hypotenuse and want to find the side opposite of the 70° angle.

Use the sine ratio: $\sin A = \frac{\text{opposite side}}{\text{hypotenuse}}$

Step 2 Find x.

$$\sin A = \frac{\text{opposite side}}{\text{hypotenuse}}$$
$$\sin 70° = \frac{x}{30}$$
$$(30)(\sin 70°) = x$$
$$(30)(0.9396926) = x$$
$$28.190779 = x$$
$$28 \text{ feet} = x \text{ (rounded to the nearest foot)}$$

Calculator Practice Using a calculator can help you find trigonometric ratios easily.

Example 5 Angle A of a right triangle is 50°. The measure of the hypotenuse is 5. You want to know the length of the side opposite to the 50° angle.

$\sin 50° = \frac{x}{5}$

$5(\sin 50°) = x$

Use your calculator to find the answer.

Press 50 [SIN]. The display reads 0.766044. Press [×] 5 [=]. The display reads 3.83022.

Round to the nearest hundredth. 3.83 is the length of the side opposite the 50° angle.

Exercise A Use a calculator to find the following values. Round your answers to the nearest hundredth.

1. sin 15° 0.26 **2.** cos 15° 0.97 **3.** tan 15° 0.27

Exercise B Use a calculator to find the following values.

4. sin C 0.6

5. cos C 0.8

6. tan C 0.75

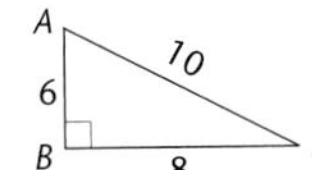

Exercise C Use a calculator to find the value for x. Round your answers to the nearest hundredth.

7.

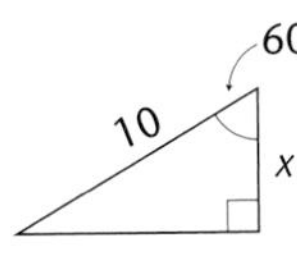

$x = 5$

8.

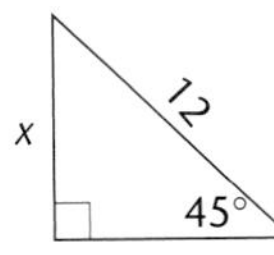

$x = 8.49$

PROBLEM SOLVING

Exercise D Answer these questions.

9. On the shore of a pond, $\overline{AC}$ measures 100 feet, $\angle A = 90°$, and $\angle C = 60°$.

To the nearest foot, find the distance from A to B. 173 feet

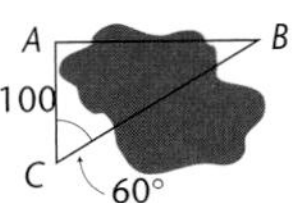

10. Suppose you are standing 2 miles away from a tall building and you see the lights on the top of the building. The angle of elevation from you to the lights is 25°.

To the nearest 100 feet, how far above ground are the lights?

4,900 feet

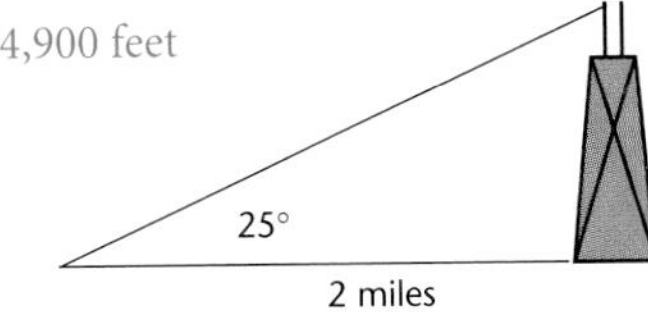

Surveyors use line and angle measures to determine distances and areas.

CALCULATOR

To apply trigonometry, it is necessary to understand the use of a scientific calculator or a table of trigonometric ratios. Have students locate the sin, cos, and tan keys on their calculators and work through the example as you discuss it in class. As they complete Exercises A, B, and C, check students' procedures to be sure they are using their calculators correctly.

You may wish to have students explore relationships among the sine, cosine, and tangent functions using their calculators. Provide a list of trigonometric ratios students are to find involving right triangles. Ask that they prove or disprove this identity with their calculations:

$\sin(90° - x) = \cos(x)$

GROUP PROBLEM SOLVING

Divide students into groups of three or four to discuss and solve the following problem:

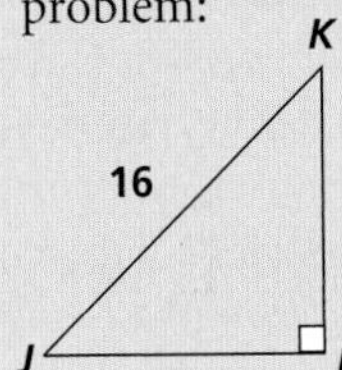

Suppose $JK = 16$ feet and $\tan K = 1$.

Find the lengths of JL and KL.

Find the measure of each angle in the triangle.

Have students write a paragraph explaining how they solved the problem. *(Explanations should show understanding that tan K can only be 1 if JL and KL are the same length. Because of the Pythagorean theorem, if JL and KL both = x, then x ≈ 11.3.*

Angle L = 90°. Angles K and J must total 90° and they must be equal; therefore, they are each 45°.)

Lesson at a Glance

Chapter 12 Application

Overview This application explores the number of diagonals that can exist in a geometric shape, as a predictable pattern, related to the number of sides.

Objectives

- To determine the number of diagonals that can be drawn in a figure
- To detect the pattern that predicts the number of diagonals in a shape with n sides

Student Page 380

Teacher's Resource Library 

Application Activity 12
Everyday Algebra 12

1 Warm-Up Activity

Present a variety of polygons on the board or overhead. Remind the class that polygons take their names from the number of sides. Have students count the sides and name each: *triangle, quadrilateral, pentagon, hexagon, heptagon, octagon, nonagon, decagon,* etc. Ask students to define *diagonal (line segment that joins two nonconsecutive vertices, or points where sides meet)* and have volunteers attempt to draw a diagonal in each example polygon.

2 Teaching the Lesson

Ask students to explain the effect of drawing diagonals within a polygon. *(They divide the polygon into triangles.)* Through examples drawn on the board, demonstrate to students that the diagonals drawn from any vertex divide the polygon with n sides into $(n - 2)$ triangles.

Common Error

Sometimes students have difficulty counting the number of diagonals in polygons with many sides. Suggest that they mark each diagonal with a tick mark as they count it to avoid counting the same one twice.

Application $\pi^2 \Sigma + \Omega \sqrt{x^2} \% \neq y \geq n = \nabla 30° \pi$

Using Geometric Shapes

Geometric figures exist in an infinite variety of shapes and sizes.

In some geometric figures, diagonals can be drawn.

Example 1 Two different diagonals can be drawn in a square.

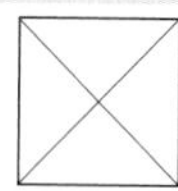

No diagonals can be drawn in a triangle.

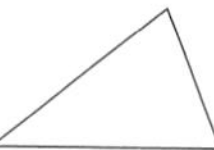

In a pentagon, five diagonals can be drawn.

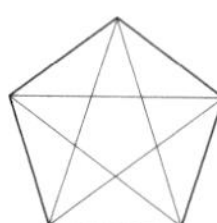

Exercise Determine the number of diagonals that can be drawn in each figure.

1. a hexagon **2.** an octagon

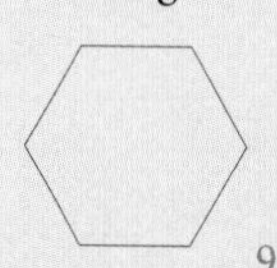

9

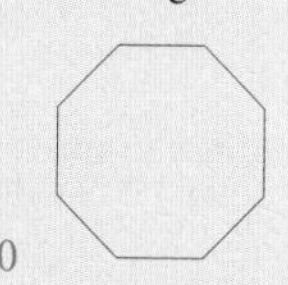

20

The number of diagonals that can be drawn in these geometric figures is predictable. Think again about the number of diagonals that can be drawn in a triangle (three sides), square (four sides), pentagon (five sides), hexagon (six sides), and octagon (eight sides). Find a pattern. Then use the pattern to predict the number of diagonals that can be drawn in the following shapes.

3. a heptagon (seven sides) 14
4. a decagon (ten sides) 35
5. a dodecagon (12 sides) 54

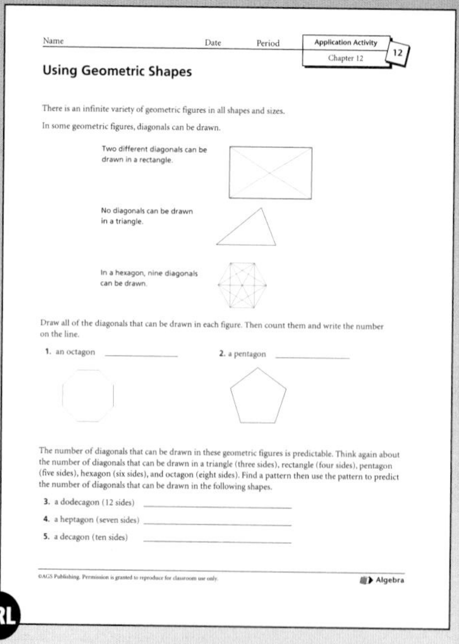

Name Date Period — Application Activity, Chapter 12, 12

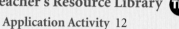

Using Geometric Shapes

There is an infinite variety of geometric figures in all shapes and sizes.

In some geometric figures, diagonals can be drawn.

Two different diagonals can be drawn in a rectangle.

No diagonals can be drawn in a triangle.

In a hexagon, nine diagonals can be drawn.

Draw all of the diagonals that can be drawn in each figure. Then count them and write the number on the line.

1. an octagon ________ **2.** a pentagon ________

The number of diagonals that can be drawn in these geometric figures is predictable. Think again about the number of diagonals that can be drawn in a triangle (three sides), rectangle (four sides), pentagon (five sides), hexagon (six sides), and octagon (eight sides). Find a pattern then use the pattern to predict the number of diagonals that can be drawn in the following shapes.

3. a dodecagon (12 sides) ________
4. a heptagon (seven sides) ________
5. a decagon (ten sides) ________

 Algebra

TRL **Application Activity 12**

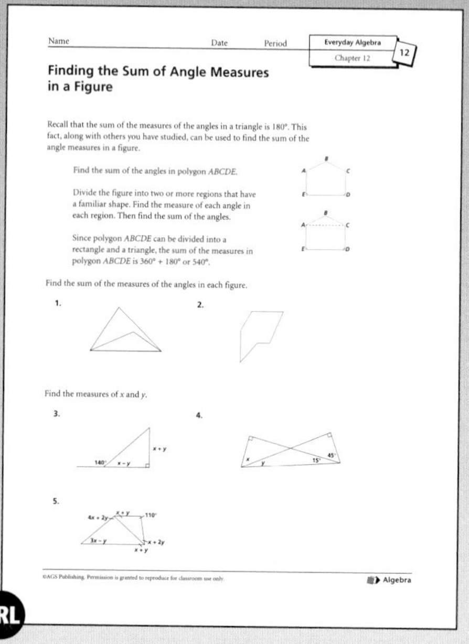

Name Date Period — Everyday Algebra, Chapter 12, 12

Finding the Sum of Angle Measures in a Figure

Recall that the sum of the measures of the angles in a triangle is 180°. This fact, along with others you have studied, can be used to find the sum of the angle measures in a figure.

Find the sum of the angles in polygon *ABCDE*.

Divide the figure into two or more regions that have a familiar shape. Find the measure of each angle in each region. Then find the sum of the angles.

Since polygon *ABCDE* can be divided into a rectangle and a triangle, the sum of the measures in polygon *ABCDE* is 360° + 180° or 540°.

Find the sum of the measures of the angles in each figure.

1. **2.**

Find the measures of x and y.

3. (140°, $x - y$, $x + y$) **4.** (x, y, 15°, 45°)

5. ($4x + 2y$, $x + y$, 110°, $3x - y$, $x + 2y$, $x + y$)

 Algebra

TRL **Everyday Algebra 12**

Chapter 12 REVIEW

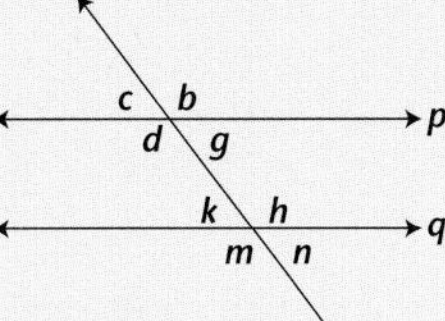

Use this figure and the information that $p \parallel q$, t is a transversal, and $m\angle c = 52.4°$ for questions 1 through 4. Write the letter of the correct answer.

1. Find the measure of $\angle d$. D
   - A $\angle d = 128.6°$
   - B $\angle d = 52.4°$
   - C $\angle d = 128.4°$
   - D $\angle d = 127.6°$
2. Find the measure of $\angle h$. A
   - A $\angle h = 127.6°$
   - B $\angle h = 90°$
   - C $\angle h = 52.4°$
   - D $\angle h = 180°$
3. Find the measure of $\angle k$. B
   - A $\angle k = 45°$
   - B $\angle k = 52.4°$
   - C $\angle k = 227.4°$
   - D $\angle k = 108.4°$
4. Find the measure of $\angle n$. C
   - A $\angle n = 127.6°$
   - B $\angle n = 90°$
   - C $\angle n = 52.4°$
   - D $\angle n = 45°$

Write the letter of the correct answer.

5. Find $m\angle x$. B

   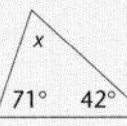

   - A $m\angle x = 129°$
   - B $m\angle x = 67°$
   - C $m\angle x = 88°$
   - D $m\angle x = 113°$
6. Find $m\angle x$. B

   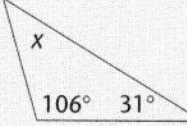

   - A $m\angle x = 53°$
   - B $m\angle x = 43°$
   - C $m\angle x = 137°$
   - D $m\angle x = 40°$
7. Find $m\angle x$. A

   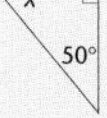

   - A $m\angle x = 40°$
   - B $m\angle x = 30°$
   - C $m\angle x = 50°$
   - D $m\angle x = 130°$

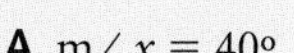

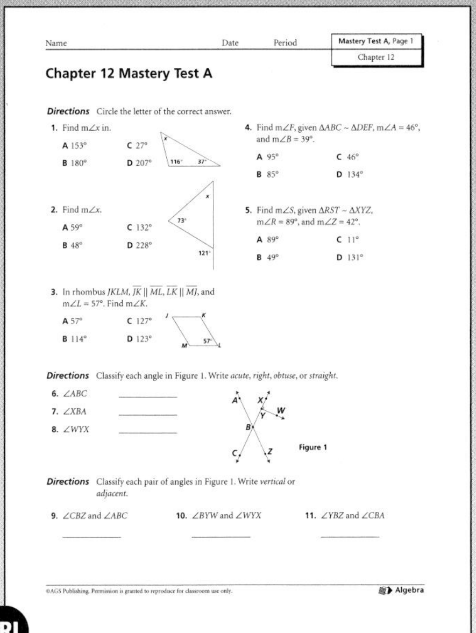

Name Date Period | Mastery Test A, Page 1 | Chapter 12

Chapter 12 Mastery Test A

Directions Circle the letter of the correct answer.

1. Find $m\angle x$ in.
   A 153° C 27° B 180° D 207°
2. Find $m\angle x$.
   A 59° C 132° B 48° D 228°
3. In rhombus $JKLM$, $\overline{JK} \parallel \overline{ML}$, $\overline{LK} \parallel \overline{MJ}$, and $m\angle L = 57°$. Find $m\angle K$.
   A 57° C 127° B 114° D 123°
4. Find $m\angle F$, given $\Delta ABC \sim \Delta DEF$, $m\angle A = 46°$, and $m\angle B = 39°$.
   A 95° C 46° B 85° D 134°
5. Find $m\angle S$, given $\Delta RST \sim \Delta XYZ$, $m\angle R = 89°$, and $m\angle Z = 42°$.
   A 89° C 11° B 49° D 131°

Directions Classify each angle in Figure 1. Write *acute*, *right*, *obtuse*, or *straight*.

6. $\angle ABC$ ______
7. $\angle XBA$ ______
8. $\angle WYX$ ______

Figure 1

Directions Classify each pair of angles in Figure 1. Write *vertical* or *adjacent*.

9. $\angle CBZ$ and $\angle ABC$ ______ 10. $\angle BYW$ and $\angle WYX$ ______ 11. $\angle YBZ$ and $\angle CBA$ ______

©AGS Publishing. Permission is granted to reproduce for classroom use only. Algebra

TRL

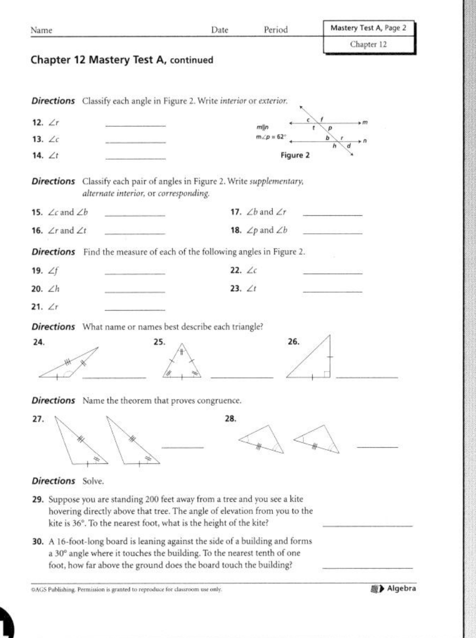

Name Date Period | Mastery Test A, Page 2 | Chapter 12

Chapter 12 Mastery Test A, continued

Directions Classify each angle in Figure 2. Write *interior* or *exterior*.

12. $\angle r$ ______
13. $\angle c$ ______
14. $\angle t$ ______

$m \parallel n$, $m\angle p = 62°$ Figure 2

Directions Classify each pair of angles in Figure 2. Write *supplementary*, *alternate interior*, or *corresponding*.

15. $\angle c$ and $\angle b$ ______
16. $\angle r$ and $\angle t$ ______
17. $\angle b$ and $\angle r$ ______
18. $\angle p$ and $\angle b$ ______

Directions Find the measure of each of the following angles in Figure 2.

19. $\angle f$ ______
20. $\angle h$ ______
21. $\angle r$ ______
22. $\angle c$ ______
23. $\angle t$ ______

Directions What name or names best describe each triangle?

24. ______ 25. ______ 26. ______

Directions Name the theorem that proves congruence.

27. ______ 28. ______

Directions Solve.

29. Suppose you are standing 200 feet away from a tree and you see a kite hovering directly above that tree. The angle of elevation from you to the kite is 36°. To the nearest foot, what is the height of the kite? ______
30. A 16-foot-long board is leaning against the side of a building and forms a 30° angle where it touches the building. To the nearest tenth of one foot, how far above the ground does the board touch the building? ______

©AGS Publishing. Permission is granted to reproduce for classroom use only. Algebra

TRL

Chapter 12 Mastery Test A

Reinforce and Extend

Learning Styles

Interpersonal/ Group Learning

To better perceive the pattern, have students construct a table.

	No. of sides				
	3	4	5	6	7
No. of diagonals	0	2	5		

Ask them to analyze the information in the table and try to find a pattern among the numbers. *(The pattern is add 2, add 3, add 4, and so on, with each additional side of the polygon.)*

Group Problem Solving

Divide the class into groups of four. First have them enlarge the table they created for the Group Learning activity to include polygons of 6, 7, 8, 9, 10, 11, and 12 sides. Then have the groups experiment with the numbers of sides and diagonals within the pattern to try to derive a formula for finding the number of diagonals of any polygon, given the number of sides (n). *(number of diagonals of a polygon with n sides* $= n\frac{(n-3)}{2}$*)*

Chapter 12 Review

Each set of problems in the Chapter Review includes an example and solution to illustrate the concept. Use the given examples for reteaching the materials in Chapter 12. For additional practice, refer to the Supplementary Problems for Chapter 12 (pages 428–429).

Chapter 12 Mastery Test 

The Teacher's Resource Library includes parallel forms of the Chapter 12 Mastery Test. The difficulty level of the two forms is equivalent. You may wish to use one form as a pretest and the other form as a posttest.

ALTERNATIVE ASSESSMENT

Alternative Assessment items correlate with student Goals for Learning at the beginning of this chapter.

■ **To name and determine the measure of angles**
On a sheet of paper, have students use a protractor and a ruler to draw two straight angles, two right angles, two obtuse angles, and two right angles. Tell students to mix them up so that no two of the same kind of angle are next to one another. Have students exchange papers with a partner. Students should then classify each angle and use a protractor to measure each angle. *(To extend this assessment, have students draw two lines crossing, then having partners show vertical, complementary, and supplementary angles.)*

■ **To identify how lines are related in planes and space**
Have students use manipulatives, such as a 5 x 5 geoboard and a set of rubber bands, to demonstrate parallel, intersecting, and skew lines. Have students label their lines parallel, intersecting, or skew. If geoboards are not available, have students draw their examples on graph or dot paper. *(To extend this assessment, have students use manipulatives to demonstrate their understanding of exterior, interior, and corresponding angles.)*

■ **To use theorems to help solve problems involving triangles**
Have students draw triangles and figures similar to—but not the same angle measurements as—the ones shown in the examples in Lesson 3, and then use a protractor to measure the angles and to demonstrate that each of the theorems is true. Students should label the size of each angle in the triangle or figure. *(Students' work should reflect the accuracy of each theorem.)*

■ **To name triangles by their characteristics**
Have students explain why triangles can be both isosceles and right, or scalene and right, but not obtuse and right. *(Isosceles and scalene triangles are named by the relative length of their sides, so the size of the angles is*

Classify each angle or pair of angles. Line $m \parallel n$. Write *acute, right, obtuse, straight, adjacent, complementary, supplementary, interior, exterior, alternate interior,* or *corresponding.* For any angle or pair of angles, more than one name may apply.

Example: $\angle p$ Solution: $\angle p$, interior, right angle

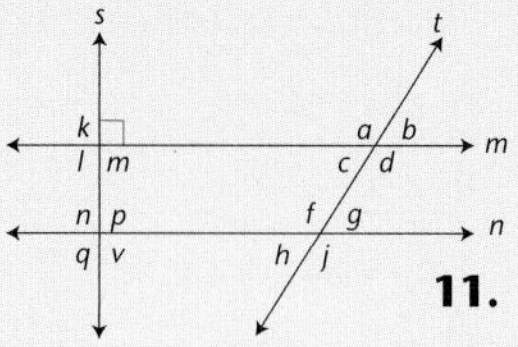

8. $\angle a$ — 8. obtuse; exterior

9. $\angle g$ — 9. acute; interior

10. $\angle j$ and $\angle h$ — 10. straight; adjacent; supplementary; exterior

11. $\angle d$ and $\angle f$ — 11. obtuse; interior; alternate interior

12. $\angle m$ and $\angle p$ — 12. right; straight; supplementary; interior

Find each angle.

Example: In parallelogram $ABCD$, $\overline{AB} \parallel \overline{CD}$, $\overline{AD} \parallel \overline{BC}$, and $m\angle A = 75°$. Find $m\angle B$, $m\angle C$, and $m\angle D$.
Solution: $\angle A$ and $\angle D$ are supplementary.
$m\angle D + 75° = 180°$, $m\angle D = 180° - 75°$,
$m\angle D = 105°$; $\angle D$ and $\angle C$ are supplementary.
$m\angle C + 105° = 180°$, $m\angle C = 180° - 105°$,
$m\angle C = 75°$; $\angle C$ and $\angle B$ are supplementary.
$m\angle B + 75° = 180°$, $m\angle B = 180° - 75°$, $m\angle B = 105°$

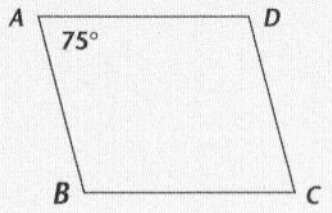

13. In right trapezoid $ABCD$, $\overline{AB} \parallel \overline{DC}$. Find $m\angle D$ and $m\angle C$.

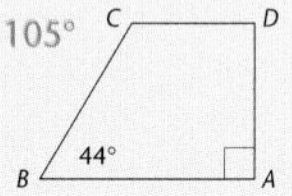

$m\angle C = 136°$; $m\angle D = 90°$

14. In rhombus $ABCD$, $\overline{AB} \parallel \overline{CD}$, $\overline{BC} \parallel \overline{AD}$, and $m\angle B = 146°$. Find $m\angle A$, $m\angle C$, and $m\angle D$.

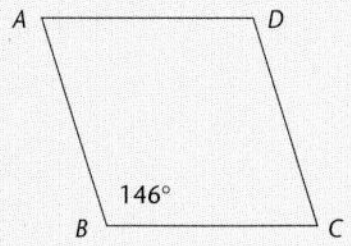

$m\angle A = 34°$; $m\angle C = 34°$; $m\angle D = 146°$

Name the theorem that proves congruence.

Example:
Solution: The Side-Side-Side Theorem

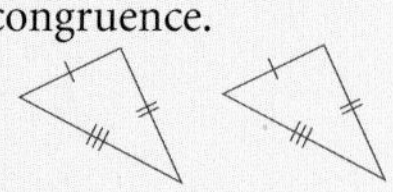

15. 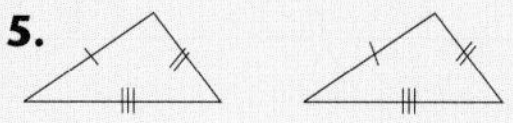 SSS

16. 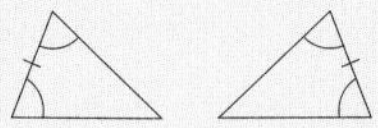 ASA

Name Date Period | Mastery Test B, Page 1 | Chapter 12

Chapter 12 Mastery Test B

Directions Circle the letter of the correct answer.

1. Find m∠S, given ΔRST ~ ΔXYZ, m∠R = 89°, and m∠Z = 42°.
   A 89° C 11°
   B 49° D 131°

2. In rhombus JKLM, $\overline{JK} \parallel \overline{ML}$, $\overline{LK} \parallel \overline{MJ}$, and m∠L = 57°. Find m∠K.
   A 57° C 127°
   B 114° D 123°

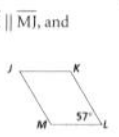

3. Find m∠F, given ΔABC ~ ΔDEF, m∠A = 46°, and m∠B = 39°.
   A 95° C 46°
   B 85° D 134°

4. Find m∠x.
   A 153° C 27°
   B 180° D 207°

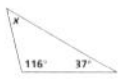

5. Find m∠x.
   A 59° C 132°
   B 48° D 228°

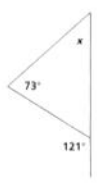

Directions Classify each angle in Figure 1. Write *acute, right, obtuse,* or *straight.*

6. ∠XBA ________
7. ∠WYX ________
8. ∠ABC ________

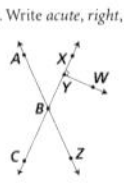

Figure 1

Directions Classify each pair of angles in Figure 1. Write *vertical* or *adjacent.*

9. *∠BYW and ∠WYX* ________
10. ∠YBZ *and* XBA ________
11. *∠CBZ and ∠ABC* ________

 Algebra

Name Date Period | Mastery Test B, Page 2 | Chapter 12

Chapter 12 Mastery Test B, continued

Directions Classify each angle in Figure 2. Write *interior* or *exterior.*

12. ∠c ________
13. ∠t ________
14. ∠r ________

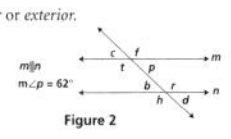

Figure 2

Directions Classify each pair of angles in Figure 2. Write *supplementary, alternate interior,* or *corresponding.*

15. ∠p and ∠b ________
16. ∠b and ∠r ________
17. ∠c and ∠b ________
18. ∠r and ∠t ________

Directions Find the measure of each of the following angles in Figure 2.

19. ∠r ________
20. ∠t ________
21. ∠c ________
22. ∠f ________
23. ∠h ________

Directions What name or names best describe each triangle?

24. 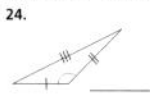 ________
25.  ________
26. 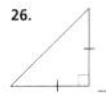 ________

Directions Name the theorem that proves congruence.

27. 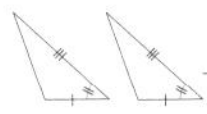 ________
28.  ________

Directions Solve.

29. Suppose you are standing 200 feet away from a tree and you see a kite hovering directly above that tree. The angle of elevation from you to the kite is 36°. To the nearest foot, what is the height of the kite? ________

30. A 16-foot-long board is leaning against the side of a building and forms a 30° angle where it touches the building. To the nearest tenth of one foot, how far above the ground does the board touch the building? ________

 Algebra

TRL TRL

Chapter 12 Mastery Test B

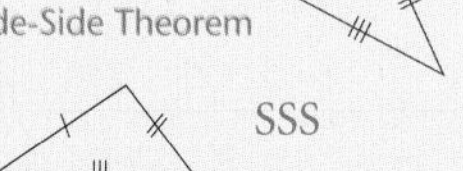

Find each angle.

Example: Given $\triangle ABC \sim \triangle DEF$, $m\angle A = 90°$, and $m\angle B = 45°$, find $m\angle F$. Solution: Find $m\angle C$. $m\angle A + m\angle B + m\angle C = 180°$, $m\angle C + 90° + 45° = 180°$, $m\angle C = 180° - 135°$, $m\angle C = 45°$, $m\angle C = m\angle F = 45°$

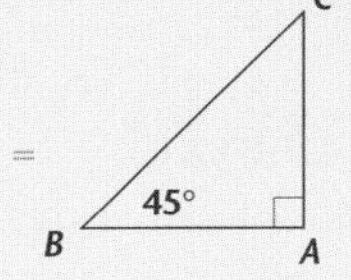

17. Given $\triangle ABC \sim \triangle DEF$, $m\angle A = 73°$, and $m\angle B = 31°$, find $m\angle F$. $m\angle F = 76°$

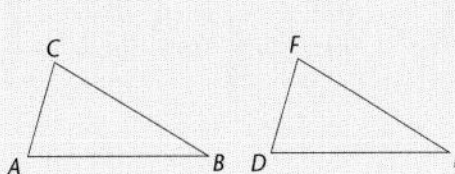

18. Given $\triangle ABC \sim \triangle DEF$, $m\angle B = 28°$, and $m\angle F = 38°$, find $m\angle A$. $m\angle A = 114°$

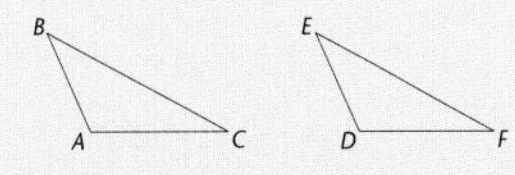

Answer these questions. You may use a calculator.

Example: Suppose that you are planting flowers along one side of a flower bed that is in the shape of a right triangle. You know that the hypotenuse of the triangle is 30 feet and that the angle opposite to the side you want to plant is 50°. What is the length of the side you are going to plant? Round to the nearest foot.

Solution: $\sin 50° = \frac{x}{30}$, $30(\sin 50°) = (30)0.766 = 22.9813 = 23$ feet

19. Suppose you are standing 150 feet away from a tree and you see a hawk hovering directly above that tree. The angle of elevation from you to the hawk is 21°. To the nearest foot, how far above ground is the hawk? 58 feet

20. Suppose that a painter has leaned a 3-meter ladder against a wall so that the ladder forms a 70° angle with the floor. To the nearest tenth of a meter, how far above the floor does the ladder touch the wall? 2.8 meters

Test-Taking Tip

Drawing pictures and diagrams is one way to help you understand and solve problems.

irrelevant in terms of naming them. Right and obtuse triangles are named by their angles, so a triangle must be one or the other.)

■ **To determine the measures of angles in quadrilaterals**

Have students draw several quadrilaterals without right angles. Have them measure the angles and add them to show that the sum of angles in all quadrilaterals is 360°. *(Drawings will vary. To extend this assessment, challenge students to draw a quadrilateral with as large and as small an angle as they can. Discuss how close they can get to an angle of 180 degrees for one of the angles.)*

■ **To use theorems to determine whether triangles are congruent or similar**

Have students draw pairs of triangles to demonstrate each of the three theorems in Lesson 6: side-angle-side, side-side-side, and angle-side-angle. Then have students explain why each of the theorems requires three measures. *(If only one or two measures are used, those measures could be equal, but the triangles could still not be congruent.)*

■ **To use trigonometric ratios to solve problems**

Have students work in groups to write a jingle, rap, or some other memory device to remember the trigonometric ratios of sine, cosine, and tangent. *(Many mathematical mnemonic devices are on the Internet.)*

Chapter

Planning Guide

Quadratic Equations

		Student Text Lesson			
		Student Pages	Vocabulary	Practice Exercises	Solutions Key
Lesson 1	Solutions by Factoring	386–389	✔	✔	✔
Lesson 2	Writing the Equations from Their Roots	390–391		✔	✔
Lesson 3	Solving by Completing the Square	392–395	✔	✔	✔
Lesson 4	Solving Using the Quadratic Formula	396–397	✔	✔	✔
Lesson 5	Graphing Quadratic Equations	398–401	✔	✔	✔
Application	Using Quadratic Equations	402		✔	✔

Chapter Activities

Teacher's Resource Library

Estimation Exercise 13: Estimating Whether a Quadratic Equation Has a Solution

Application Activity 13: Using Quadratic Equations

Everyday Algebra 13: Graphic Quadratic Equations

Community Connection 13: CAD—Computer-Aided Design

Teacher's Edition

Chapter 13 Project

Assessment Options

Student Text

Chapter 13 Review

Teacher's Resource Library

Chapter 13 Mastery Tests A and B

Chapters 1–13 Final Mastery Test

Student Text Features							Teaching Strategies							Learning Styles						Teacher's Resource Library			
Estimation Activity	Algebra in Your Life	Technology Connection	Writing About Mathematics	Try This	Problem Solving	Calculator Practice	Online Connection	Common Error	Applications Home, Career, Community	Mental Math	Manipulatives	Calculator	Group Problem Solving	Auditory/Verbal	Visual/Spatial	Logical/Mathematical	Body/Kinesthetic	Interpersonal/Group Learning	LEP/ESL	Activities	Alternate Activities	Workbook Activities	Self-Study Guide
387			389		389			388	389		388		389		389					115	115	122	✔
				391	391						391		391	391						116	116	123	✔
	394	395					394	393	393		393	393	393							117	117	124	✔
								397		397	397						397			118	118	125	✔
						401		399	399			401	401			399			400	119	119	126	✔
											403		402										✔

Software Options

Skill Track Software

Use the Skill Track Software for *Algebra* for additional reinforcement of this chapter. The software provides multiple-choice assessment items for students to access by computer.

Solutions Key

Use the Solutions Key with this chapter to help students who may need additional assistance. The Solutions Key CD provides solutions for every exercise in the student edition.

Other Resources

Alternative Activities

The Teacher's Resource Library (TRL) contains a set of worksheets written at a second-grade reading level called Alternative Activities. They cover the same content as the regular Activities.

Manipulatives

See the Manipulative activities in this chapter for hands-on modeling of the content. The following TRL pages can also be used:

Manipulatives Master 3 (Sentence Mat)
Manipulatives Master 4 (Factor Frame)
Algebra Tiles

Chapter at a Glance

Chapter 13: Quadratic Equations

pages 384–405

(Answer Keys for the Teacher's Resource Library begin on page 530 of this Teacher's Edition.)

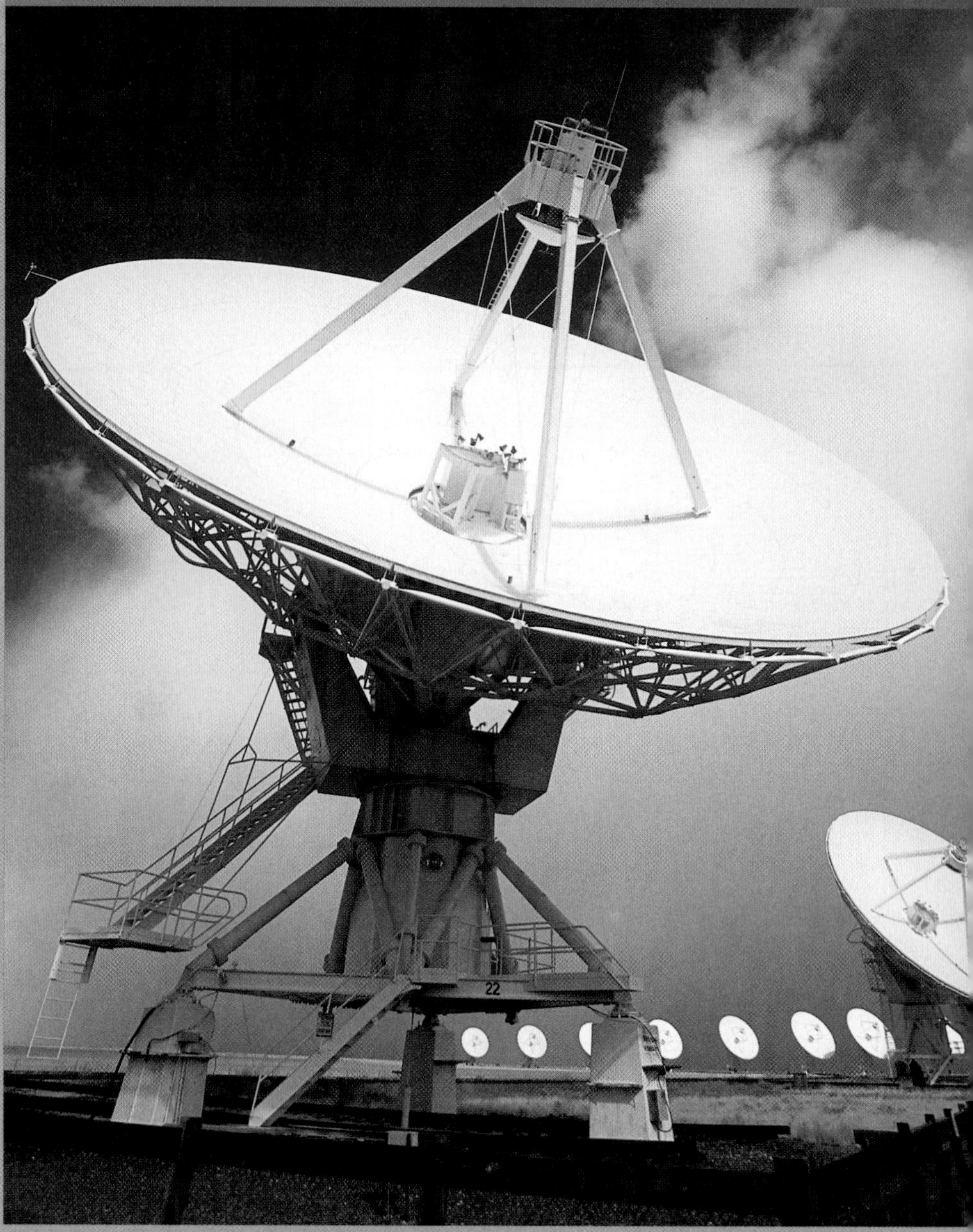

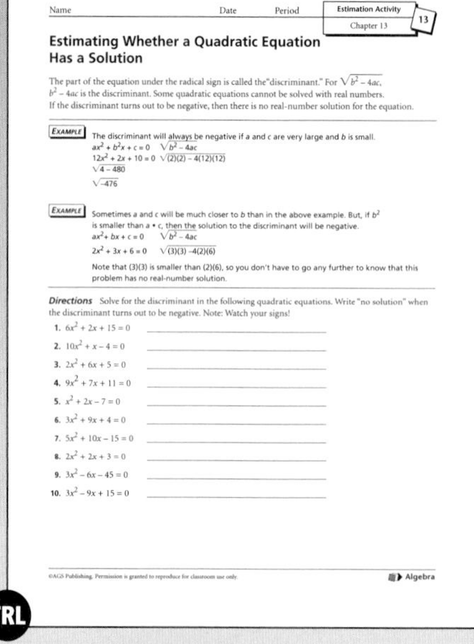

Name Date Period | Estimation Activity 13 | Chapter 13

Estimating Whether a Quadratic Equation Has a Solution

The part of the equation under the radical sign is called the "discriminant." For $\sqrt{b^2 - 4ac}$, $b^2 - 4ac$ is the discriminant. Some quadratic equations cannot be solved with real numbers. If the discriminant turns out to be negative, then there is no real-number solution for the equation.

EXAMPLE The discriminant will always be negative if a and c are very large and b is small.

$ax^2 + b^2x + c = 0$ $\quad \sqrt{b^2 - 4ac}$

$12x^2 + 2x + 10 = 0$ $\quad \sqrt{(2)(2) - 4(12)(12)}$

$\sqrt{4 - 480}$

$\sqrt{-476}$

EXAMPLE Sometimes a and c will be much closer to b than in the above example. But, if b^2 is smaller than $a \cdot c$, then the solution to the discriminant will be negative.

$ax^2 + bx + c = 0$ $\quad \sqrt{b^2 - 4ac}$

$2x^2 + 3x + 6 = 0$ $\quad \sqrt{(3)(3) - 4(2)(6)}$

Note that (3)(3) is smaller than (2)(6), so you don't have to go any further to know that this problem has no real-number solution.

Directions Solve for the discriminant in the following quadratic equations. Write "no solution" when the discriminant turns out to be negative. Note: Watch your signs!

1. $6x^2 + 2x + 15 = 0$ ________
2. $10x^2 + x - 4 = 0$ ________
3. $2x^2 + 6x + 5 = 0$ ________
4. $9x^2 + 7x + 11 = 0$ ________
5. $x^2 + 2x - 7 = 0$ ________
6. $3x^2 + 9x + 4 = 0$ ________
7. $5x^2 + 10x - 15 = 0$ ________
8. $2x^2 + 2x + 3 = 0$ ________
9. $3x^2 - 6x - 45 = 0$ ________
10. $3x^2 - 9x + 15 = 0$ ________

 Algebra

TRL

Estimation Exercise 13

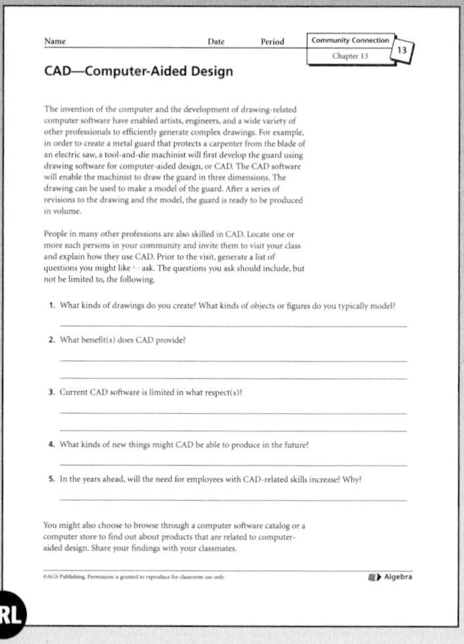

Name Date Period | Community Connection 13 | Chapter 13

CAD—Computer-Aided Design

The invention of the computer and the development of drawing-related computer software have enabled artists, engineers, and a wide variety of other professionals to efficiently generate complex drawings. For example, in order to create a metal guard that protects a carpenter from the blade of an electric saw, a tool-and-die machinist will first develop the guard using drawing software for computer-aided design, or CAD. The CAD software will enable the machinist to draw the guard in three dimensions. The drawing can be used to make a model of the guard. After a series of revisions to the drawing and the model, the guard is ready to be produced in volume.

People in many other professions are also skilled in CAD. Locate one or more such persons in your community and invite them to visit your class and explain how they use CAD. Prior to the visit, generate a list of questions you might like to ask. The questions you ask should include, but not be limited to, the following.

1. What kinds of drawings do you create? What kinds of objects or figures do you typically model?
2. What benefit(s) does CAD provide?
3. Current CAD software is limited in what respect(s)?
4. What kinds of new things might CAD be able to produce in the future?
5. In the years ahead, will the need for employees with CAD-related skills increase? Why?

You might also choose to browse through a computer software catalog or a computer store to find out about products that are related to computer-aided design. Share your findings with your classmates.

 Algebra

TRL

Community Connection 13

Chapter

13 Quadratic Equations

Satellite dishes are everywhere, including backyards! These dishes are antennas designed to send and receive signals. The signals are bounced off of satellites orbiting the earth. The dish shape is an arc, or parabola. You create parabolas when you pitch a baseball or turn on a drinking fountain. To plot parabolas on a graph, we use quadratic equations. You've plotted straight lines using linear equations to the power of one. Soon you'll be able to graph a curved line by using an equation with a second power or exponent. The direction your parabola opens depends upon the type of quadratic equation you use.

In Chapter 13, you will solve and graph quadratic equations.

Goals for Learning

- ◆ To solve quadratic equations by factoring
- ◆ To write quadratic equations from their roots
- ◆ To solve quadratic equations by completing the square
- ◆ To use the quadratic formula to solve quadratic equations
- ◆ To graph quadratic equations

385

Introducing the Chapter

Have students note that satellite dishes are everywhere—in backyards, on roof tops, and in space. The shape of the dish is an arc, or parabola.To determine the dimensions of a parabola, you will need to use quadratic equations. By using quadratic equations, students can plot parabolas on a graph.

Chapter Project

Ask each student to pair with a partner. After each lesson in the chapter has been completed, ask students to maintain a log or other record of the kinds of problems that can be modeled using quadratic equations. Upon completion of the chapter, have students create a problem that can be modeled and solved using a quadratic equation. Then have the class work cooperatively to model and solve the problems generated by each pair of students

Teacher's Resource

The AGS Publishing Teaching Strategies in Math Transparencies may be used with this chapter. They add an interactive dimension to expand and enhance the program content.

Career Interest Inventory

The AGS Publishing Harrington-O'Shea Career Decision-Making System-Revised (CDM) may be used with this chapter. Students can use the CDM to explore their interests and identify careers. The CDM defines career areas that are indicated by students' responses on the inventory.

Name ______ Date ______ Period ______ *SELF-STUDY GUIDE*

CHAPTER 13: Quadratic Equations

Goal 13.1 *To solve quadratic equations by factoring*

Date	Assignment	Score
______	1: Read pages 386–388. Complete Exercises A–C on pages 388–389.	______
______	2: Complete Workbook Activity 122.	______

Comments:

Goal 13.2 *To write quadratic equations from their roots*

Date	Assignment	Score
______	3: Read pages 390–391. Complete Exercises A–B on page 391.	______
______	4: Complete Workbook Activity 123.	______

Comments:

Goal 13.3 *To solve quadratic equations by completing the square*

Date	Assignment	Score
______	5: Read pages 392–393. Complete Exercises A–B on pages 394–395.	______
______	6: Complete Workbook Activity 124.	______

Comments:

 Algebra

TRL

Name ______ Date ______ Period ______ *SELF-STUDY GUIDE*

CHAPTER 13: Quadratic Equations, continued

Goal 13.4 *To use the quadratic formula to solve quadratic equations*

Date	Assignment	Score
______	7: Read pages 396–397. Complete Exercises A–B on page 397.	______
______	8: Complete Workbook Activity 125.	______

Comments:

Goal 13.5 *To graph quadratic equations*

Date	Assignment	Score
______	9: Read pages 398–400. Complete Exercises A–C on pages 400–401.	______
______	10: Read and complete the Calculator Practice on page 401.	______
______	11: Complete Workbook Activity 126.	______
______	12: Read and complete the Application Exercise on page 402.	______
______	13: Complete the Chapter 13 Review on pages 403–405.	______

Comments:

Student's Signature ______ Date ______

Instructor's Signature ______ Date ______

 Algebra

TRL

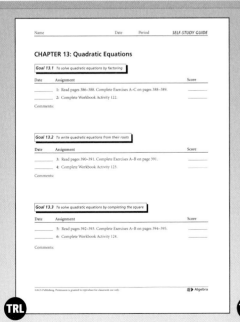

Chapter 13 Self-Study Guide

Lesson at a Glance

Chapter 13 Lesson 1

Overview This lesson introduces quadratic equations that can be solved by factoring.

Objective

- To find the root(s) of a quadratic equation by factoring

Student Pages 386–389

Teacher's Resource Library 

Workbook Activity 122

Activity 115

Alternative Activity 115

Mathematics Vocabulary

set of roots

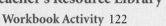

Warm-Up Activity

Have students recall that the solution of an equation is any value that makes the equation true.

Write the following equations on the board and invite volunteers to describe the solutions.

$x + 7 = 0$	(-7)
$x - 3 = 0$	(3)
$x - (-8) = 0$	(-8)
$x + 2 = 0$	(-2)
$x - 5 = 0$	(5)
$x + 4 = 0$	(-4)
$x + (-9) = 0$	(9)
$x - (+1) = 0$	(1)
$x + 14 = 0$	(-14)
$x - (-11) = 0$	(-11)

Choose several of the equations and encourage a volunteer to use the board and demonstrate how each equation can be checked.

Teaching the Lesson

Before discussing the lesson, have students recall their study of factoring in Chapter 6 by asking them to name the common factors, and the greatest common factor, of each of these groups of expressions.

Lesson 1 Solutions by Factoring

> ***Set of roots***
> *The set of numbers that make an equation true*

Recall that a quadratic equation is of the form $ax^2 + bx + c = 0$, where a, b, and c are real numbers, and $a \neq 0$.

The root of an equation is the value of the variable that makes the equation true. The **set of roots** for an equation forms the solution set for the equation.

Some quadratic equations can be solved by factoring.

EXAMPLE 1 Find the roots, or the solution set, of $x^2 + 3x + 2 = 0$.

Step 1 Factor the equation.

$$x^2 + 3x + 2 = 0$$
$$(x + 2)(x + 1) = 0$$

Step 2 Remember, $ab = 0$ if and only if $a = 0$ or $b = 0$.

Therefore, for $(x + 2)(x + 1) = 0$ to be true, either $x + 2 = 0$ or $x + 1 = 0$.

Set each factor equal to zero, and solve for x.

$x + 2 = 0$ or $x + 1 = 0$

$x = -2$ or $x = -1$

Step 3 Check.

Let $x = -2$		Let $x = -1$	
$x^2 + 3x + 2 \stackrel{?}{=} 0$		$x^2 + 3x + 2 \stackrel{?}{=} 0$	
$(-2)^2 + 3(-2) + 2 \stackrel{?}{=} 0$		$(-1)^2 + 3(-1) + 2 \stackrel{?}{=} 0$	
$4 - 6 + 2 \stackrel{?}{=} 0$		$1 - 3 + 2 \stackrel{?}{=} 0$	
$0 = 0$	True	$0 = 0$	True

The solution set is -2 and -1.

> When you check an open statement, use $\stackrel{?}{=}$ until you reach the answer. If the equality holds, write *True.* If the equality does not hold, write *False*.

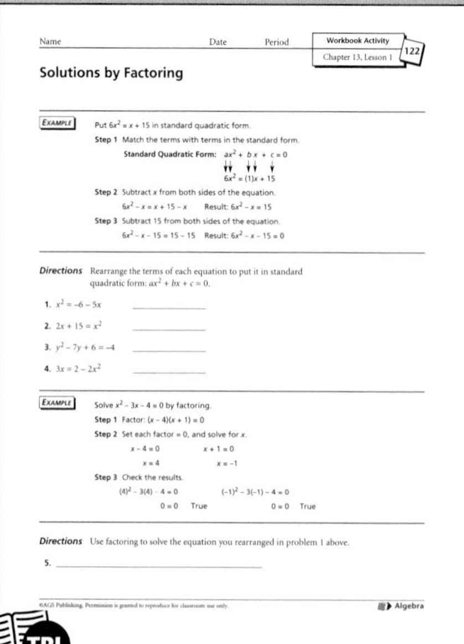

Name Date Period | Workbook Activity 122 | Chapter 13, Lesson 1

Solutions by Factoring

EXAMPLE Put $6x^2 = x + 15$ in standard quadratic form.

Step 1 Match the terms with terms in the standard form.

Standard Quadratic Form: $ax^2 + bx + c = 0$

$6x^2 = (1)x + 15$

Step 2 Subtract x from both sides of the equation.

$6x^2 - x = x + 15 - x$ Result: $6x^2 - x = 15$

Step 3 Subtract 15 from both sides of the equation.

$6x^2 - x - 15 = 15 - 15$ Result: $6x^2 - x - 15 = 0$

Directions Rearrange the terms of each equation to put it in standard quadratic form: $ax^2 + bx + c = 0$.

1. $x^2 = -6 - 5x$ ______
2. $2x + 15 = x^2$ ______
3. $y^2 - 7y + 6 = -4$ ______
4. $3x = 2 - 2x^2$ ______

EXAMPLE Solve $x^2 - 3x - 4 = 0$ by factoring.

Step 1 Factor: $(x - 4)(x + 1) = 0$

Step 2 Set each factor = 0, and solve for x.

$x - 4 = 0$ $x + 1 = 0$

$x = 4$ $x = -1$

Step 3 Check the results.

$(4)^2 - 3(4) - 4 = 0$ $(-1)^2 - 3(-1) - 4 = 0$

$0 = 0$ True $0 = 0$ True

Directions Use factoring to solve the equation you rearranged in problem 1 above.

5. ______

 Algebra

Workbook Activity 122

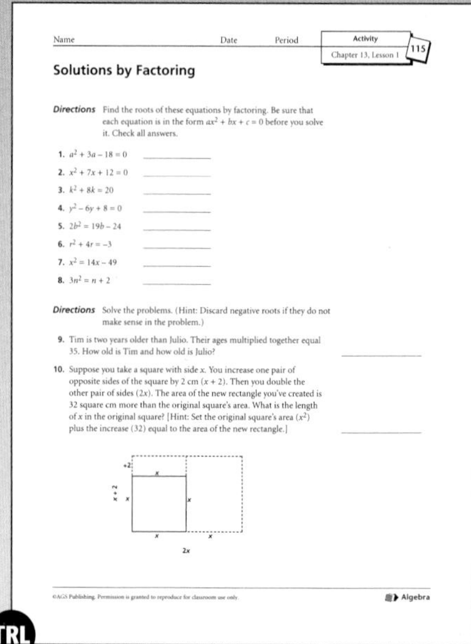

Name Date Period | Activity 115 | Chapter 13, Lesson 1

Solutions by Factoring

Directions Find the roots of these equations by factoring. Be sure that each equation is in the form $ax^2 + bx + c = 0$ before you solve it. Check all answers.

1. $a^2 + 3a - 18 = 0$ ______
2. $x^2 + 7x + 12 = 0$ ______
3. $k^2 + 8k = 20$ ______
4. $y^2 - 6y + 8 = 0$ ______
5. $2b^2 = 19b - 24$ ______
6. $r^2 + 4r = -3$ ______
7. $x^2 = 14x - 49$ ______
8. $3n^2 = n + 2$ ______

Directions Solve the problems. (Hint: Discard negative roots if they do not make sense in the problem.)

9. Tim is two years older than Julio. Their ages multiplied together equal 35. How old is Tim and how old is Julio? ______
10. Suppose you take a square with side x. You increase one pair of opposite sides of the square by 2 cm $(x + 2)$. Then you double the other pair of sides $(2x)$. The area of the new rectangle you've created is 32 square cm more than the original square's area. What is the length of x in the original square? [Hint: Set the original square's area (x^2) plus the increase (32) equal to the area of the new rectangle.] ______

 Algebra

Activity 115

EXAMPLE 2 Find the roots, or the solution set, of $2x^2 + 7x = 15$.

Step 1 Write the equation so that the sum of the terms equals zero.

$2x^2 + 7x - 15 = 0$

Step 2 Factor the equation.

$$2x^2 + 7x - 15 = 0$$
$$(2x - 3)(x + 5) = 0$$

Step 3 Because $ab = 0$ if and only if $a = 0$ or $b = 0$,

either $2x - 3 = 0$ or $x + 5 = 0$.

$x = \frac{3}{2}$ or $x = -5$

Step 4 Check.

Let $x = \frac{3}{2}$	Let $x = -5$
$2x^2 + 7x - 15 \stackrel{?}{=} 0$	$2x^2 + 7x - 15 \stackrel{?}{=} 0$
$2(\frac{3}{2})^2 + 7(\frac{3}{2}) - 15 \stackrel{?}{=} 0$	$2(-5)^2 + 7(-5) - 15 \stackrel{?}{=} 0$
$\frac{18}{4} + \frac{21}{2} - 15 \stackrel{?}{=} 0$	$50 - 35 - 15 \stackrel{?}{=} 0$
$\frac{9}{2} + \frac{21}{2} - 15 \stackrel{?}{=} 0$	$0 = 0$
$\frac{30}{2} - 15 \stackrel{?}{=} 0$	True
$0 = 0$	
True	

The roots are $\frac{3}{2}$ and -5.

Estimation Activity

Estimate: The pond on Li's farm is an odd shape. He has a scale drawing of the farm that shows the pond. How can Li estimate the area of the pond?

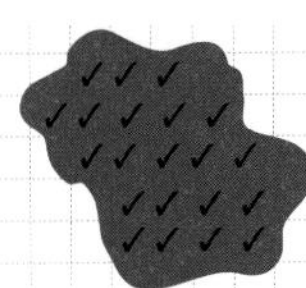

Solution: Draw a grid to a known scale over the scale drawing. Count the number of squares and estimate the area of the partial squares. Checked squares on the grid are totally within the area of the pond. Other units must be estimated.

MATH HISTORY

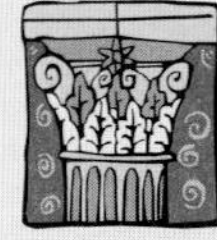

"Magic" squares have been around a long time. According to Chinese legend, the first magic square, or *lo-shu*, was given to Emperor Yu around 2200 B.C. As he stood by the side of the Huang River, Emperor Yu was visited by a giant tortoise. The lo-shu was on the tortoise's shell. The shell was divided into nine equal sections forming a 3 × 3 square. Numbers were arranged in each square so that their sum equaled 15 no matter which way the Emperor added—across, down or diagonally. Since then, many people have created lo-shu puzzles in squares. One of America's founding fathers, Benjamin Franklin, was fascinated by magic squares and created them in his spare time.

$12b^2, 8$	$(1, 4; GCF = 4)$
$3y, y$	$(y; GCF = y)$
$5gh^2, 10g^2h$	$(1, 5, g, h; GCF = 5gh)$
$2x, 2x^2$	$(1, 2, x; GCF = 2x)$
$6a^3, 3a^2$	$(1, 3, a, a^2; GCF = 3a^2)$

After completing Step 3, encourage students, whenever possible, to perform the computation required to check the roots of an equation mentally.

Have students note that the example is different from the example on page 386 in the sense that the coefficient of the x^2 term is not 1. Explain that the value of the coefficient of the x^2 is not relevant; both equations can still be solved by factoring.

Point out that all of the examples that have been discussed in this lesson have had a solution set that contains two roots. To show that a quadratic equation may have only one root, copy the following example on the board.

$$x^2 - 4x + 4 = 0$$
$$(x - 2)(x - 2) = 0$$
$$(x - 2) = 0 \qquad (x - 2) = 0$$
$$x = 2 \qquad x = 2$$

Explain that finding the set of roots for a quadratic equation by factoring is one of several ways by which the set of roots for a quadratic equation can be found. As their study of the chapter progresses, students will learn other methods of finding the set of roots for a quadratic equation. Because they will be asked to find the set of roots for many different equations, remind students that their practice with each method will enable them to choose an efficient method each time they need to find the set of roots for a quadratic equation.

Manipulatives

Modeling Quadratic Equations

Materials: Algebra Tiles, Manipulatives Master 3 (Sentence Mat), Manipulatives Master 4 (Factor Frame)

Group Practice: Build a model of the polynomial used in the first example in the text. Arrange the pieces inside the Factor Frame so that they meet the two conditions, applying the Zero Rule when necessary. (See page T9, "Using the Factor Frame," for more detailed instructions). To find the factors, fill in the left and top portions of the Factor Frame with the appropriate Algebra Tiles pieces. To find the root of each factor, place the model of each factor on the Sentence Mat. Solve for the unknown by adding the inverse of the constant to both sides of the Sentence Mat. Apply the Zero Rule to remove pairs of opposites and isolate the variable.

Student Practice: Have students use models for Exercise A, Problems 1–2, 4–5, and 10, and Exercise B, Problems 11 and 17–18.

Common Error

Incorrect answers are sometimes caused by incorrect factoring. Encourage students to check if their factoring of an equation is correct *before* they set each of the factors equal to zero and solve.

You can use what you know about quadratic equations to solve some problems.

Example 3 The product of two consecutive integers is 72. What are the integers?

Step 1 Write the problem as an equation. Let x represent the first integer, and let $x + 1$ represent the next integer.

$(x)(x + 1) = 72$

Step 2 Multiply and rearrange terms so the equation is in the form $ax^2 + bx + c = 0$.

$x^2 + x - 72 = 0$

Step 3 Factor, then solve for x.

$(x - 8)(x + 9) = 0$

either $x - 8 = 0$ or $x + 9 = 0$

If $x = 8$, the integers are 8 and 9.

If $x = -9$, the integers are -9 and -8.

Step 4 Check.

Let $x = 8$			Let $x = -9$		
$x(x + 1)$	$\stackrel{?}{=}$	72	$x(x + 1)$	$\stackrel{?}{=}$	72
$8 \bullet 9$	$\stackrel{?}{=}$	72	$-9(-8)$	$\stackrel{?}{=}$	72
72	=	72	72	=	72
	True			True	

Exercise A Find the roots of these equations by factoring. Check your answers.

1. $x^2 + 5x + 6 = 0$
2. $x^2 + 5x = 0$
3. $y^2 + 11y + 30 = 0$
4. $x^2 - 8x + 16 = 0$
5. $x^2 + 6x + 5 = 0$
6. $3x^2 + x - 2 = 0$
7. $6x^2 - 4x - 10 = 0$
8. $2y^2 + 12y + 10 = 0$
9. $12x^2 + 5x - 2 = 0$
10. $-x^2 + 12x = 0$ (Hint: Multiply both sides by -1.)

1. $-2, -3$
2. $0, -5$
3. $-5, -6$
4. 4
5. $-1, -5$
6. $\frac{2}{3}, -1$
7. $\frac{5}{3}, -1$
8. $-1, -5$
9. $-\frac{2}{3}, \frac{1}{4}$
10. $0, 12$

Writing About Mathematics

Choose one of the problems from Exercise B. Explain the steps you used to factor the equation.

Exercise B Rewrite these equations in the form $ax^2 + bx + c = 0$. Then find the roots.

11. $t^2 + 6t = -9$ — -3
12. $3x^2 - 12 = 5x$ — $-\frac{4}{3}, 3$
13. $3x^2 = 9x + 30$ — $-2, 5$
14. $4x^2 + 4x = 48$ — $-4, 3$
15. $5y^2 = 7y$ — $0, \frac{7}{5}$
16. $3x^2 - 7x = 20$ — $-\frac{5}{3}, 4$
17. $14 = x^2 - 5x$ — $7, -2$
18. $m^2 - 5m = 18 + 2m$ — $9, -2$
19. $3z^2 - 2 = -z$ — $\frac{2}{3}, -1$
20. $x^2 + 5x = 36$ — $4, -9$

PROBLEM SOLVING

Exercise C Answer each problem.

21. The area of a rectangular floor is 36 square units. The length is 4 times greater than its width. What are the length and width of the floor? length 12, width 3
22. The product of Miguel's and Maria's ages is 108. Miguel is 3 years older than Maria. What are their ages? Maria, 9; Miguel, 12
23. Mai can install one more computer chip every hour than Tom can. The product of the number of computer chips Mai installs in an hour and the number of computer chips Tom installs in an hour is 420. How many computer chips does Mai install in an hour? How many chips does Tom install? Mai, 21 chips; Tom, 20 chips
24. Janet is one year older than her best friend. Their ages multiplied together equal 56. How old is Janet? How old is her friend? Janet's friend, 7; Janet, 8
25. Jesse is 2 years older than Kristen. The product of their ages is 48. How old is Jesse? How old is Kristen? (Hint: Let one integer be x and the other be $x + 2$.) Kristen, 6; Jesse, 8

3 Reinforce and Extend

LEARNING STYLES

Visual/Spatial

Have students recall that the graph of a linear equation such as $y = x - 2$ is a straight line. To help students better understand what a quadratic equation represents, ask them to choose an equation with a known solution from the lesson and view the graph of the equation using a graphing calculator. Point out that the graph of a quadratic equation is a parabola. Then invite students to compare the set of roots for their equation to the graph of the equation and describe any relationship they may share.

GROUP PROBLEM SOLVING

Encourage students to work in groups to discuss and solve these problems:

The floor of a rectangular room used for storage has an area of 136 square feet. The length of the room is 1 foot longer than twice its width. What are the dimensions of the room? *(17 feet by 8 feet)*

The sum of the squares of two numbers is 89. The sum of the numbers is ±13. What are the numbers? *(5 and 8; −5 and −8)*

The perimeter of a photograph is 19 inches. The area of the photograph is 21 square inches. What is the measure of the length and the width of the photograph? *(length: 6 inches; width: $3\frac{1}{2}$ inches)*

Invite groups to share different ways of finding the solutions with one another.

AT HOME

Invite students to measure the length and width of a rectangular room in their home and then use those dimensions to write a word problem that can be solved by factoring. When students return to class, ask them to exchange and solve the problems. If some students have difficulty writing a problem, encourage them to use the format from problem 21 on page 389 as a model.

Lesson at a Glance

Chapter 13 Lesson 2

Overview This lesson introduces the concept of using the roots of a quadratic equation to generate the equation.

Objective

- To write a quadratic equation given the roots of the equation

Student Pages 390–391

Teacher's Resource Library TRL

Workbook Activity 123

Activity 116

Alternative Activity 116

Warm-Up Activity

The factors shown below represent the roots of various quadratic equations. Write the factors on the board and invite students to mentally compute the root(s) of each equation.

$(x - 2)(x - 9) = 0$
($x = 2; x = 9$)

$(x + \frac{1}{3})(x - 3) = 0$
($x = -\frac{1}{3}; x = 3$)

$(x - 1)(x + \frac{4}{9}) = 0$
($x = 1; x = -\frac{4}{9}$)

$(x + 15)(x + 5) = 0$
($x = -15; x = -5$)

$(x - 18)(x + \frac{1}{2}) = 0$
($x = 18; x = -\frac{1}{2}$)

$(x + 12)(x + 12) = 0$
($x = -12$)

Teaching the Lesson

Have students recall from their study of Chapter 9 that the general (or standard) form of a line is given as $y = mx + b$. Explain that a general or standard form of an equation is a reference point that lends some consistency to the study of those equations. Make sure students are familiar with the fact that the general or standard form of a quadratic equation is $ax^2 + bx + c = 0$.

Prior to discussing the examples, remind students of the concept of factoring they

Lesson 2 Writing the Equations from Their Roots

> Remember, if $a = 0$ and $b = 0$, then $ab = 0$. Multiply. Then write in general form.

You can factor to find the roots of a quadratic equation. You can also reverse the process of factoring—if you know the roots of a quadratic equation, you can find the equation itself. For example, suppose the roots of an equation are

$x = 1$ or $x = -2$.

You can find the factors of the equation by setting each root equation equal to zero.

$x = 1$ or $x = -2$
$x - 1 = 0$ or $x + 2 = 0$
$(x - 1)(x + 2) = 0$
$x^2 + x - 2 = 0$

> r_1 and r_2 are the roots of the quadratic equation $(x - r_1)(x - r_2) = 0$.

EXAMPLE 1 The roots of a quadratic equation are 1 and 2. What is the general form of the equation?

Step 1 The roots are values of x that satisfy the equation, so $x = 1$ or $x = 2$.

Step 2 Set each factor equal to zero.
$(x - 1) = 0$ or $(x - 2) = 0$

Step 3 Multiply the factors.
$(x - 1)(x - 2) = 0$

Step 4 Use the distributive property to place the equation in general form. $x^2 - 3x + 2 = 0$

EXAMPLE 2 The roots of a quadratic equation are $\frac{2}{3}$ and -2. What is the general form of the equation?

Step 1 If the roots are $\frac{2}{3}$ and -2, then $x = \frac{2}{3}$ or $x = -2$.

Step 2 Set each factor equal to zero.
$(x - \frac{2}{3}) = 0$ or $(x + 2) = 0$

Step 3 Multiply each side of the first equation by 3 to remove the fraction.
$3(x - \frac{2}{3}) = 3 \bullet 0$ or $3x - 2 = 0$

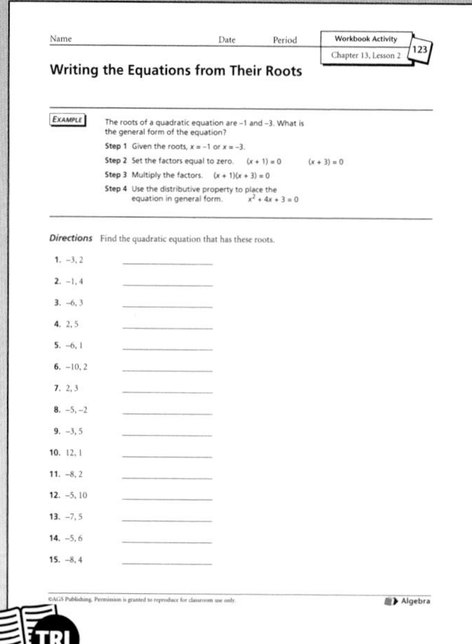

Name Date Period | Workbook Activity 123 | Chapter 13, Lesson 2

Writing the Equations from Their Roots

EXAMPLE The roots of a quadratic equation are –1 and –3. What is the general form of the equation?

Step 1 Given the roots, $x = -1$ or $x = -3$.

Step 2 Set the factors equal to zero. $(x + 1) = 0$ $(x + 3) = 0$

Step 3 Multiply the factors. $(x + 1)(x + 3) = 0$

Step 4 Use the distributive property to place the equation in general form. $x^2 + 4x + 3 = 0$

Directions Find the quadratic equation that has these roots.

1. –3, 2 ________
2. –1, 4 ________
3. –6, 3 ________
4. 2, 5 ________
5. –6, 1 ________
6. –10, 2 ________
7. 2, 3 ________
8. –5, –2 ________
9. –3, 5 ________
10. 12, 1 ________
11. –8, 2 ________
12. –5, 10 ________
13. –7, 5 ________
14. –5, 6 ________
15. –8, 4 ________

 Algebra

TRL

Workbook Activity 123

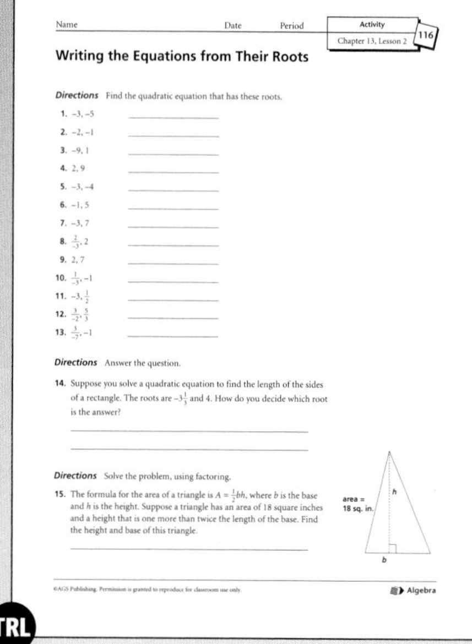

Name Date Period | Activity 116 | Chapter 13, Lesson 2

Writing the Equations from Their Roots

Directions Find the quadratic equation that has these roots.

1. –3, –5 ________
2. –2, –1 ________
3. –9, 1 ________
4. 2, 9 ________
5. –3, –4 ________
6. –1, 5 ________
7. –3, 7 ________
8. $\frac{2}{-3}$, 2 ________
9. 2, 7 ________
10. $\frac{1}{-3}$, –1 ________
11. –3, $\frac{1}{2}$ ________
12. $\frac{3}{-2}$, $\frac{5}{3}$ ________
13. $\frac{3}{-7}$, –1 ________

Directions Answer the question.

14. Suppose you solve a quadratic equation to find the length of the sides of a rectangle. The roots are $-3\frac{1}{3}$ and 4. How do you decide which root is the answer?
____

Directions Solve the problem, using factoring.

15. The formula for the area of a triangle is $A = \frac{1}{2}bh$, where b is the base and h is the height. Suppose a triangle has an area of 18 square inches and a height that is one more than twice the length of the base. Find the height and base of this triangle.
____

 Algebra

TRL

Activity 116

Example 2 *(continued)*

Step 4 Multiply the factors.

$(3x - 2)(x + 2) = 0$

Step 5 Use the distributive property to place the equation in general form.

$3x^2 + 4x - 4 = 0$

Exercise A Find the quadratic equation that has these roots.

1. $-2, -3$ — $x^2 + 5x + 6 = 0$
2. $2, 4$ — $x^2 - 6x + 8 = 0$
3. $6, 4$ — $x^2 - 10x + 24 = 0$
4. $-6, 4$ — $x^2 + 2x - 24 = 0$
5. $6, -4$ — $x^2 - 2x - 24 = 0$
6. $-6, -4$ — $x^2 + 10x + 24 = 0$
7. $-7, 4$ — $x^2 + 3x - 28 = 0$
8. $6, -7$ — $x^2 + x - 42 = 0$
9. $8, 11$ — $x^2 - 19x + 88 = 0$
10. $-3, -7$ — $x^2 + 10x + 21 = 0$
11. $2, -5$ — $x^2 + 3x - 10 = 0$
12. $-2, 5$ — $x^2 - 3x - 10 = 0$
13. $3, 5$ — $x^2 - 8x + 15 = 0$
14. $\frac{2}{3}, 3$ — $3x^2 - 11x + 6 = 0$
15. $\frac{4}{5}, 5$ — $5x^2 - 29x + 20 = 0$
16. $\frac{3}{4}, 1$ — $4x^2 - 7x + 3 = 0$
17. $-\frac{3}{2}, -1$ — $2x^2 + 5x + 3 = 0$
18. $-\frac{4}{3}, 1$ — $3x^2 + x - 4 = 0$
19. $-\frac{4}{3}, 2$ — $3x^2 - 2x - 8 = 0$
20. $-\frac{3}{5}, 3$ — $5x^2 - 12x - 9 = 0$
21. $\frac{1}{2}, 3$ — $2x^2 - 7x + 3 = 0$
22. $0, \frac{2}{3}$ — $3x^2 - 2x = 0$
23. $\frac{4}{7}, 7$ — $7x^2 - 53x + 28 = 0$

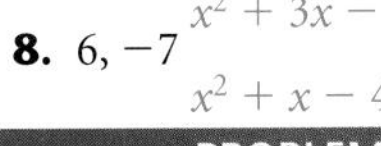

PROBLEM SOLVING

Exercise B Solve each problem.

24. Denise says that it is impossible for one of the roots of a quadratic equation to be zero. Is she correct? If not, give an example. If yes, tell why.
    No; $x^2 - 8x = 0$, the roots are 0 and 8

25. Nate wants to prove that both roots of a quadratic equation could be zero. Write the quadratic equation to determine whether Nate is correct. Explain your answer.
    No, you could only have one root, and it would equal zero: $x^2 = 0$

TRY THIS Write two roots of an equation. Ask a classmate to write the quadratic equation for those roots. Solve the equation to check that it was done correctly.

Answers will vary.

studied in the previous lesson by encouraging a volunteer to factor the quadratic equation $x^2 - x - 6$ on the board. $(x - 3)(x + 2)$ Then as students discuss the examples in the lesson, occasionally remind them that writing a quadratic equation given the roots of the equation is the reverse of factoring.

Before assigning students to complete some or all of Exercise A, remind them to always check their work by making sure each answer they write is in the general form $ax^2 + bx + c = 0$.

Try This

You might choose to have students perform this activity in pairs or small groups before requiring them to complete other exercises on the page.

Manipulatives

Modeling Quadratic Equations

Materials: Algebra Tiles, Manipulatives Master 3 (Sentence Mat), Manipulatives Master 4 (Factor Frame)

Group Practice: Using the first example in the text, build models of the factors and place them on the left and top portion of the Factor Frame. Multiply the factors using the distributive property. To find the polynomial for the quadratic equation, fill in the rectangle with the pieces that represent the products of the factors.

Student Practice: Have students use models for Exercise A, Problems 1–7 and 10–13.

Group Problem Solving

Encourage students to work in groups of four to discuss and solve the following problem:

Which quadratic equation has -3 and 4 as its solution set? *(c)*

a. $x^2 + x - 12 = 0$
b. $x^2 + x + 12 = 0$
c. $x^2 - x - 12 = 0$
d. $x^2 - x + 12 = 0$

3 Reinforce and Extend

Learning Styles

Auditory/Verbal

Encourage a volunteer to choose a problem from page 391 and use the board to demonstrate how to find *and check* the solution. Invite classmates to ask questions they may have.

Lesson at a Glance

Chapter 13 Lesson 3

Overview This lesson introduces the completing the square method of solving quadratic equations.

Objectives

- To find the roots of quadratic equations by completing the square

Student Pages 392–395

Teacher's Resource Library TRL

Workbook Activity 124

Activity 117

Alternative Activity 117

Mathematics Vocabulary

completing the square

1 Warm-Up Activity

Factoring perfect square trinomials is a prerequisite skill for solving quadratic equations by completing the square. Write the following quadratic equations on the board. Then encourage volunteers to use the board to factor the equations.

$x^2 + 6x + 9$ $(x + 3)^2$

$x^2 - 14x + 49$ $(x - 7)^2$

$x^2 + 8x + 16$ $(x + 4)^2$

$x^2 + x + 1$ $(x + 1)^2$

$x^2 - 18x + 81$ $(x - 9)^2$

$x^2 - 4x + 4$ $(x - 2)^2$

$x^2 + 12x + 36$ $(x + 6)^2$

$x^2 - 16x + 64$ $(x - 8)^2$

$x^2 + 10x + 25$ $(x + 5)^2$

2 Teaching the Lesson

Explain that the factoring performed in Lesson 1 of this chapter represents one way to find the roots or the solution set of a quadratic equation. However, not all quadratic equations can be easily solved by factoring.

For example, write the quadratic equation $x^2 + 10x - 10$ on the board and invite several volunteers to factor it. After students discover that factoring the

Lesson 3 Solving by Completing the Square

Completing the square

Finding the roots of a perfect square trinomial

One method you can use to solve a quadratic equation is called **completing the square.**

Completing the square works because $(x + b)^2 = x^2 + 2bx + b^2$, and $x^2 + 2bx + b^2$ is a perfect square trinomial. You can find the roots of a perfect square trinomial by finding the square root of each side of the equation.

EXAMPLE 1 Find the roots of $x^2 + 4x + 1 = 0$.

Step 1 Rewrite the equation so that the variable is on one side of the equation, and the constant is on the other.

$x^2 + 4x + 1 = 0$ becomes $x^2 + 4x = -1$.

Step 2 Add a constant to each side of the equation so that the expression on the left is a perfect square trinomial. $x^2 + 4x + \blacksquare^2 = -1 + \blacksquare^2$

Step 3 Find the value of the constant, $\blacksquare$. Remember, the model perfect square trinomial is

$x^2 + 2bx + b^2 = (x + b)^2$ In this case, $2bx = 4x$.

$x^2 + 4x + \blacksquare^2 = -1 + \blacksquare^2$ so $2 \cdot \blacksquare = 4$, and $\blacksquare = 2$.

Step 4 Rewrite the equation with the value $\blacksquare = 2$, $\blacksquare^2 = 4$.

$x^2 + 4x + \blacksquare^2 = -1 + \blacksquare^2$ becomes

$x^2 + 4x + 4 = -1 + 4$.

Step 5 Factor the perfect square trinomial, then find the square root of each side of the equation.

$x^2 + 4x + 4 = -1 + 4$

$(x + 2)^2 = 3$

$\sqrt{(x + 2)^2} = \sqrt{3}$

$x + 2 = \pm\sqrt{3}$

$x = -2 \pm \sqrt{3}$

The roots of the equation are $-2 + \sqrt{3}$ and $-2 - \sqrt{3}$.

Step 6 Check.

Let $x = -2 + \sqrt{3}$

$x^2 + 4x + 1 \stackrel{?}{=} 0$

$(-2 + \sqrt{3})^2 + 4(-2 + \sqrt{3}) + 1 \stackrel{?}{=} 0$

$(4 - 4\sqrt{3} + 3) - 8 + 4\sqrt{3} + 1 \stackrel{?}{=} 0$

$0 = 0$

True

Let $x = -2 - \sqrt{3}$

$x^2 + 4x + 1 \stackrel{?}{=} 0$

$(-2 - \sqrt{3})^2 + 4(-2 - \sqrt{3}) + 1 \stackrel{?}{=} 0$

$(4 + 4\sqrt{3} + 3) - 8 - 4\sqrt{3} + 1 \stackrel{?}{=} 0$

$0 = 0$

True

Name Date Period

Workbook Activity 124
Chapter 13, Lesson 3

Solving by Completing the Square

EXAMPLE Find the roots of $x^2 + 4x - 3 = 0$ by completing the square.

Step 1 Rewrite the equation so that the constant is isolated.

$x^2 + 4x = 3$

Step 2 Find the constant that must be added to complete the square. Take $\frac{1}{2}$ of the x coefficient and square it.

$\frac{1}{2}(4) = 2$ $2^2 = 4$

Step 3 Add the constant to both sides of the equation.

$x^2 + 4x + 4 = 3 + 4$ Result: $x^2 + 4x + 4 = 7$

Step 4 Factor the trinomial on the left side, and solve for x.

$(x + 2)^2 = 7$ Therefore, $x + 2 = \pm\sqrt{7}$

$x = -2 + \sqrt{7}$ or $x = -2 - \sqrt{7}$

Step 5 Check by substituting the roots in the equation.

Directions Find the roots of each equation by completing the square.

1. $x^2 + 4x + 3 = 0$ ________
2. $x^2 - 2x = 0$ ________
3. $m^2 - 6m - 7 = 0$ ________
4. $k^2 + 12k = 0$ ________
5. $y^2 + 8y - 9 = 0$ ________
6. $x^2 - 10x = 0$ ________
7. $x^2 - 6x + 2 = 0$ ________
8. $a^2 - 4a - 12 = 0$ ________
9. $x^2 - 2x - 15 = 0$ ________
10. $d^2 - 2d - 24 = 0$ ________

Algebra

TRL

Workbook Activity 124

Name Date Period

Activity 117
Chapter 13, Lesson 3

Solving by Completing the Square

Directions Find the roots of each equation by completing the square.

1. $y^2 + 5y - 6 = 0$ ________
2. $r^2 = 8r - 15$ ________
3. $a^2 + 8a + 8 = 0$ ________
4. $2x^2 = 12x - 16$ ________
5. $3y^2 + 9 = -12y$ ________
6. $2n^2 + 4n - 2 = 0$ ________
7. $4y^2 + 4y - 3 = 0$ ________

Directions Write an equation to represent the facts in each problem. Then solve by completing the square.

8. A rectangle is 3 inches longer on one pair of sides than the other. Its area is approximately 12 square inches. To the nearest tenth of an inch, what are the measurements of the length and width of the rectangle? (Hint: Use a decimal fraction to complete the square.)

____

9. Leah can run 2 more laps in an hour than can Terri. The product of the number of laps each can run in an hour is 24. How many laps can each of these runners run?

____

10. A part made in a factory is a rectangular grid (a crisscross pattern such as on graph paper). The grid is made up of regularly spaced holes. There are 8 more holes in each long row (grid length) than in a short row (grid width). In all, the grid has 153 holes. How many holes are in each long row and in each short row?

____

Algebra

TRL

Activity 117

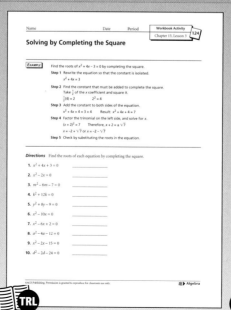

Recall that a quadratic equation is of the form $ax^2 + bx + c = 0$, where a, b, and c are real numbers and $a \neq 0$.

EXAMPLE 2 Find the roots of $x^2 + 6x + 1 = 0$ by completing the square.

Step 1 Rewrite the equation so that the variable is on one side of the equation, the constant on the other.

$x^2 + 6x + 1 = 0$ becomes $x^2 + 6x = -1$.

Step 2 Add a constant to each side of the equation so that the expression on the left is a perfect square trinomial.

$x^2 + 6x + ■^2 = -1 + ■^2$

Step 3 Find the value of the constant, ■. Remember, the model perfect square trinomial is

$x^2 + 2bx + b^2 = (x + b)^2$ In this case, $2bx = 6x$

$x^2 + 6x + ■^2 = -1 + ■^2$ so $2 \bullet ■ = 6$, and $■ = 3$.

Step 4 Rewrite the equation using the value $■ = 3$, $■^2 = 9$.

$x^2 + 6x + ■^2 = -1 + ■^2$ becomes

$x^2 + 6x + 9 = -1 + 9$.

Step 5 Factor the perfect square trinomial, then find the square root of each side of the equation.

$$\begin{aligned} x^2 + 6x + 9 &= -1 + 9 \\ (x + 3)^2 &= 8 \\ \sqrt{(x + 3)^2} &= \sqrt{8} \\ x + 3 &= \pm 2\sqrt{2} \\ x &= -3 \pm 2\sqrt{2} \end{aligned}$$

The roots of the equation are $-3 + 2\sqrt{2}$ and $-3 - 2\sqrt{2}$.

Step 6 Check.

Let $x = -3 + 2\sqrt{2}$

$$\begin{aligned} x^2 + 6x + 1 &\stackrel{?}{=} 0 \\ (-3 + 2\sqrt{2})^2 + 6(-3 + 2\sqrt{2}) + 1 &\stackrel{?}{=} 0 \\ (9 - 12\sqrt{2} + 8) + (-18 + 12\sqrt{2}) + 1 &\stackrel{?}{=} 0 \\ 0 &= 0 \end{aligned}$$

True

Let $x = -3 - 2\sqrt{2}$

$$\begin{aligned} x^2 + 6x + 1 &\stackrel{?}{=} 0 \\ (-3 - 2\sqrt{2})^2 + 6(-3 - 2\sqrt{2}) + 1 &\stackrel{?}{=} 0 \\ (9 + 12\sqrt{2} + 8) - (18 - 12\sqrt{2}) + 1 &\stackrel{?}{=} 0 \\ 0 &= 0 \end{aligned}$$

True

equation is difficult or does not seem to be possible, point out that the equation does have roots, but the roots are very difficult to find by factoring. As a result, another method called completing the square can be used to find the roots.

Common Error

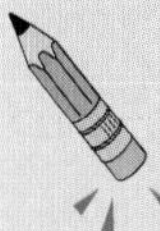

Completing the square of a quadratic equation involves identifying and adding a constant to the equation. Remind students that after a constant is identified, that constant must be added to *both* sides of the equation.

Manipulatives

Modeling Quadratic Equations

Materials: Algebra Tiles, Manipulatives Master 3 (Sentence Mat), Manipulatives Master 4 (Factor Frame)

Group Practice: Review how to use Algebra Tiles to factor polynomials and find roots of equations. (See the Chapter 13, Lesson 1 Manipulatives activity.)

Student Practice: Have students use models to check their answers obtained by completing the square in Exercise A, Problems 1–2, 4–9, 11, 13, and 15–16. Students should factor the polynomials and find the roots of the factors.

In the Community

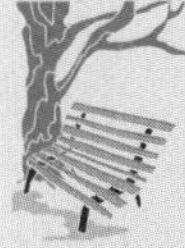

Many businesses rely on an understanding of quadratic equations in order to operate in an efficient way. For example, a form that can be folded into a cardboard box having no lid is cut from a large sheet of cardboard. A quadratic equation can be used to determine how many forms can be obtained and how much waste will be generated. Invite students to describe how other businesses in their community may benefit from or use quadratic equations.

Calculator

Invite students to work in small groups and develop and implement a method for using a calculator to check their answers.

Reinforce and Extend

Group Problem Solving

Suggest students work in pairs and solve problem 9 on page 394 two different times—once by completing the square and once by factoring. Then have each partner name the method he or she prefers and tell why.

ONLINE CONNECTION

Have students read the radio transcript reprinted at www.uh.edu/engines/epi847.htm about why they should continue to study mathematics. This episode of the National Public Radio show *Engines of Our Ingenuity* addresses the relationship of nonlinear equations to the real world. *Engines of Our Ingenuity* is a syndicated radio show written and produced by John Lienhard, professor of mechanical engineering and history at the University of Houston, Houston, Texas.

Exercise A Find the roots of these equations by completing the square.

1. $x^2 + 6x + 5 = 0$ — $-1, -5$
2. $y^2 - 3y = 18$ — $6, -3$
3. $2x^2 + 6x = 0$ — $0, -3$
4. $m^2 + 4m - 12 = 0$ — $2, -6$
5. $x^2 - 4x = 5$ — $5, -1$
6. $z^2 - 8z + 15 = 0$ — $5, 3$
7. $x^2 + 2x = 15$ — $3, -5$
8. $t^2 + 9t = -18$ — $-6, -3$
9. $x^2 - 6x + 8 = 0$ — $2, 4$
10. $x^2 - 2x - 4 = 0$ — $1 \pm \sqrt{5}$

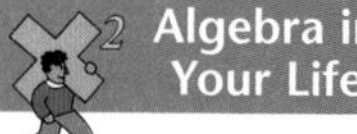

Algebra in Your Life

The First American Indian Astronaut John Bennett Herrington became interested in mathematics when he worked as a surveyor's assistant. The surveyor showed him how to use mathematics to convert instrument sightings into useful information for road construction. After high school, Herrington earned a degree in applied mathematics, joined the Navy, and became a test pilot. In the Navy, he earned a master's degree in aeronautical engineering and joined NASA. On his first flight into space, Herrington carried with him several objects honoring his heritage.

Exercise B Find the roots of these equations by completing the square.

11. $x^2 - 12 = 4x$ $\quad 6, -2$

12. $y^2 + 2y - 6 = 0$ $\quad -1 \pm \sqrt{7}$

13. $x^2 = -6x - 5$ $\quad -1, -5$

14. $d^2 - 3d = 6$ $\quad \frac{(3 \pm \sqrt{33})}{2}$

15. $2m^2 + 4m = 6$ $\quad 1, -3$

16. $3x^2 - 6x - 24 = 0$ $\quad 4, -2$

17. $2y^2 - 3y = 3$ $\quad \frac{(3 \pm \sqrt{33})}{4}$

18. $3x^2 + 33x + 72 = 0$ $\quad -3, -8$

19. $x^2 - 6x - 17 = 0$ $\quad 3 \pm \sqrt{26}$

20. $4x^2 + 28x = 32$ $\quad -8, 1$

Technology Connection

Without a Calculator

Graphing a quadratic equation on a calculator takes seconds. Graphing it on paper can take a minute or so. Imagine having to do thousands of calculations and graphs with almost no technological help. Buckminster Fuller, developer of the geodesic dome, didn't even have a calculator. In the 1940s, Fuller had a mechanical adding machine that could only add and subtract. So it took him *two years* to complete the calculations he needed to build his first dome in 1948.

Lesson at a Glance

Chapter 13 Lesson 4

Overview This lesson introduces the quadratic formula method of solving quadratic equations.

Objective

- To find the roots of quadratic equations by using the quadratic formula

Student Pages 396–397

Teacher's Resource Library 

Workbook Activity 125

Activity 118

Alternative Activity 118

Mathematics Vocabulary

quadratic formula

Warm-Up Activity

Write the formula $A = 2l + 2w$ on the board. After reminding students that the formula can be used to determine the perimeter of a rectangle, ask them to use the formula to determine the perimeter of a rectangle that has a length of 15 inches and a width of 12 inches. *(54 inches)*

Then moderate a discussion in which students relate general ideas and principles to follow when working with formulas.

Teaching the Lesson

If students require an additional example of using the quadratic formula to find the roots of an equation, you might choose to copy the example below on the board.

If $2x^2 + 4x - 6 = 0$, then $a = 2$, $b = 4$, $c = -6$.

$$x = \frac{-4 \pm \sqrt{4^2 - 4(2)(-6)}}{2(2)}$$

$$x = \frac{-4 \pm \sqrt{16 + 48}}{4}$$

$$x = \frac{-4 \pm \sqrt{64}}{4}$$

$$x = \frac{-4 \pm 8}{4}$$

$$x = \frac{4}{4} \text{ or } 1 \text{ and } x = \frac{-12}{4} \text{ or } -3$$

Lesson 4 Solving Using the Quadratic Formula

In addition to factoring and completing the square, there is another tool you can use to find the roots of a quadratic equation. The steps below show how this tool is derived.

Step 1: Start with the general form of the quadratic equation. Divide by a so that the coefficient of x^2 is 1.

$ax^2 + bx + c = 0$ becomes

$$x^2 + \frac{b}{a}x + \frac{c}{a} = 0$$

Step 2: Rewrite so that the variables are on one side of the equation, constants on the other.

$$x^2 + \frac{b}{a}x = -\frac{c}{a}$$

Step 3: Add a constant to each side of the equation to complete the square.

$$x^2 + \frac{b}{a}x + ■ = -\frac{c}{a} + ■$$

To find the value of the constant, ■, look again at the model perfect square trinomial.

$$x^2 + 2cx + c^2 = (x + c)^2$$

In this case, $2cx = \frac{b}{a}x$, so $2c = \frac{b}{a}$, and $c = \frac{b}{2a}$, $c^2 = \frac{b^2}{4a^2}$.

Step 4: Rewrite the equation using the value $c = \frac{b}{2a}$, $c^2 = \frac{b^2}{4a^2}$.

$x^2 + \frac{b}{a}x + ■ = -\frac{c}{a} + ■$ becomes

$$x^2 + \frac{b}{a}x + [\frac{b^2}{4a^2}] = -\frac{c}{a} + [\frac{b^2}{4a^2}].$$

Factor the left side. Place the right side over the common denominator $4a^2$.

$(x + \frac{b}{2a})^2 = \frac{b^2 - 4ac}{4a^2}$ Take the square root of each side.

$(x + \frac{b}{2a}) = \pm\sqrt{\frac{b^2 - 4ac}{4a^2}}$ Simplify. Take the square root of $4a^2$.

$x + \frac{b}{2a} = \pm\frac{\sqrt{b^2 - 4ac}}{2a}$ Rearrange terms.

$x = -\frac{b}{2a} \pm \frac{\sqrt{b^2 - 4ac}}{2a}$ Place over common denominator.

$x = \frac{-b \pm \sqrt{b^2 - 4ac}}{2a}$	This is the quadratic formula.

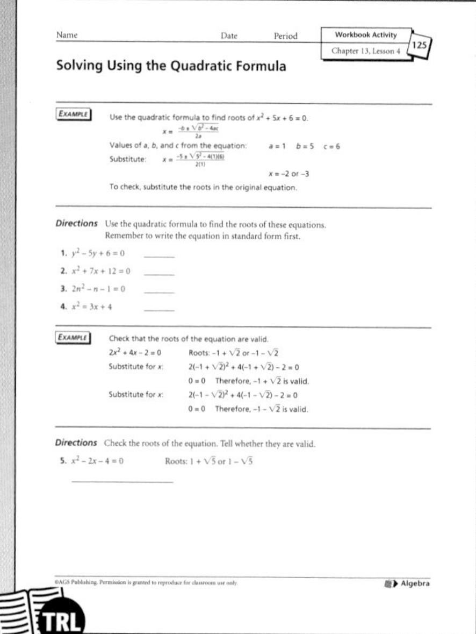

Name Date Period

Workbook Activity 125
Chapter 13, Lesson 4

Solving Using the Quadratic Formula

EXAMPLE Use the quadratic formula to find roots of $x^2 + 5x + 6 = 0$.

$x = \frac{-b \pm \sqrt{b^2 - 4ac}}{2a}$

Values of a, b, and c from the equation: $a = 1$ $b = 5$ $c = 6$

Substitute: $x = \frac{-5 \pm \sqrt{5^2 - 4(1)(6)}}{2(1)}$

$x = -2$ or -3

To check, substitute the roots in the original equation.

Directions Use the quadratic formula to find the roots of these equations. Remember to write the equation in standard form first.

1. $y^2 - 5y + 6 = 0$ ______
2. $x^2 + 7x + 12 = 0$ ______
3. $2n^2 - n - 1 = 0$ ______
4. $x^2 = 3x + 4$ ______

EXAMPLE Check that the roots of the equation are valid.

$2x^2 + 4x - 2 = 0$ Roots: $-1 + \sqrt{2}$ or $-1 - \sqrt{2}$

Substitute for x: $2(-1 + \sqrt{2})^2 + 4(-1 + \sqrt{2}) - 2 = 0$

$0 = 0$ Therefore, $-1 + \sqrt{2}$ is valid.

Substitute for x: $2(-1 - \sqrt{2})^2 + 4(-1 - \sqrt{2}) - 2 = 0$

$0 = 0$ Therefore, $-1 - \sqrt{2}$ is valid.

Directions Check the roots of the equation. Tell whether they are valid.

5. $x^2 - 2x - 4 = 0$ Roots: $1 + \sqrt{5}$ or $1 - \sqrt{5}$

______

Algebra

Workbook Activity 125

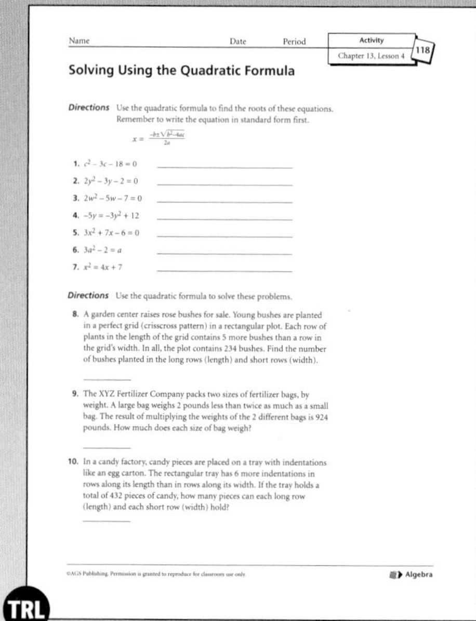

Name Date Period

Activity 118
Chapter 13, Lesson 4

Solving Using the Quadratic Formula

Directions Use the quadratic formula to find the roots of these equations. Remember to write the equation in standard form first.

$x = \frac{-b \pm \sqrt{b^2 - 4ac}}{2a}$

1. $c^2 - 3c - 18 = 0$ ______
2. $2y^2 - 3y - 2 = 0$ ______
3. $2w^2 - 5w - 7 = 0$ ______
4. $-5y = -3y^2 + 12$ ______
5. $3x^2 + 7x - 6 = 0$ ______
6. $3a^2 - 2 = a$ ______
7. $x^2 = 4x + 7$ ______

Directions Use the quadratic formula to solve these problems.

8. A garden center raises rose bushes for sale. Young bushes are planted in a perfect grid (crisscross pattern) in a rectangular plot. Each row of plants in the length of the grid contains 5 more bushes than a row in the grid's width. In all, the plot contains 234 bushes. Find the number of bushes planted in the long rows (length) and short rows (width).

______

9. The XYZ Fertilizer Company packs two sizes of fertilizer bags, by weight. A large bag weighs 2 pounds less than twice as much as a small bag. The result of multiplying the weights of the 2 different bags is 924 pounds. How much does each size of bag weigh?

______

10. In a candy factory, candy pieces are placed on a tray with indentations like an egg carton. The rectangular tray has 6 more indentations in rows along its length than in rows along its width. If the tray holds a total of 432 pieces of candy, how many pieces can each long row (length) and each short row (width) hold?

______

Algebra

Activity 118

Quadratic formula

The formula that can be used to find the roots of any quadratic equation

$x = \frac{-b \pm \sqrt{b^2 - 4ac}}{2a}$

This value of x is true for any quadratic equation and is called the **quadratic formula.** You can use the formula to find the roots of any quadratic equation by substituting the coefficients a and b and the constant c.

EXAMPLE 1 Use the quadratic formula to find the roots of $x^2 - 8x = -15$.

Step 1 Compare the equation with the model $ax^2 + bx + c = 0$. Determine the values of a, b, and c.

In $x^2 - 8x + 15 = 0$, $a = 1$, $b = -8$, and $c = 15$.

Step 2 Substitute the values for a, b, and c in the general quadratic formula.

$$x = \frac{-b \pm \sqrt{b^2 - 4ac}}{2a} = \frac{-(-8) \pm \sqrt{(8)^2 - 4(1)(15)}}{2(1)} =$$

$$\frac{8 \pm \sqrt{64 - 60}}{2} = \frac{8 \pm \sqrt{4}}{2} = \frac{8 + 2}{2} \text{ and } \frac{8 - 2}{2}$$

The roots are 5 and 3.

Remember to begin by writing the equation in standard form. $x^2 - 8x + 15 = 0$

Step 3 Check.

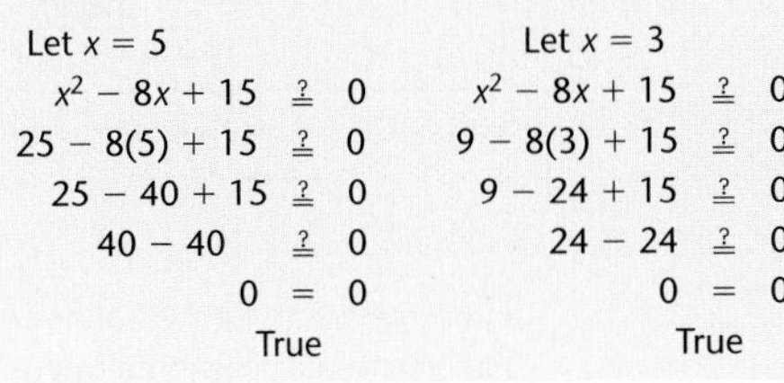

Let $x = 5$	Let $x = 3$
$x^2 - 8x + 15 \stackrel{?}{=} 0$	$x^2 - 8x + 15 \stackrel{?}{=} 0$
$25 - 8(5) + 15 \stackrel{?}{=} 0$	$9 - 8(3) + 15 \stackrel{?}{=} 0$
$25 - 40 + 15 \stackrel{?}{=} 0$	$9 - 24 + 15 \stackrel{?}{=} 0$
$40 - 40 \stackrel{?}{=} 0$	$24 - 24 \stackrel{?}{=} 0$
$0 = 0$	$0 = 0$
True	True

Exercise A Find the roots of these equations. Remember to write the equation in standard form first.

2, −4 **1.** $x^2 + 2x - 8 = 0$

4 **2.** $x^2 - 8x + 16 = 0$

2, 1 **3.** $m^2 + 2 = 3m$

4, 9 **4.** $x^2 - 13x = -36$

3, −3 **5.** $y^2 - 9 = 0$

5, −5 **6.** $x^2 - 25 = 0$

2, −4 **7.** $-x^2 - 2x = -8$

8. $6r^2 + r - 1 = 0$ $\frac{1}{3}, -\frac{1}{2}$

9. $-2x^2 + 11x = 15$ $\frac{5}{2}, 3$

10. $5y^2 - 8y + 3 = 0$ $\frac{3}{5}, 1$

11. $3x^2 + 2x - 7 = 0$ $\frac{(-1 \pm \sqrt{22})}{3}$

12. $2z^2 + 4z = 5$ $\frac{(-2 \pm \sqrt{14})}{2}$

13. $2x^2 + 7x + 3 = 0$ $-3, -\frac{1}{2}$

14. $x^2 - 10x = -22$ $5 \pm \sqrt{3}$

Exercise B

See Teacher's Edition page for answer.

15. Check that $\frac{(1 + \sqrt{7})}{3}$ and $\frac{(1 - \sqrt{7})}{3}$ are the roots of $3x^2 = 2x + 2$.

Answer to Problem 15

15. Substitute $x = \frac{(1 + \sqrt{7})}{3}$ in $3x^2 - 2x - 2 = 0$

$$3\left(\frac{1 + \sqrt{7}}{3}\right)^2 - 2\left(\frac{1 + \sqrt{7}}{3}\right) - 2 = 0$$

$$3\left(\frac{1 + 2\sqrt{7} + 7}{9}\right) - 2\left(\frac{1 + \sqrt{7}}{3}\right) - 2 = 0$$

$$\frac{8 + 2\sqrt{7}}{3} - 2\left(\frac{1 + \sqrt{7}}{3}\right) - 2 = 0$$

$$\frac{(8 + 2\sqrt{7} - 2 - 2\sqrt{7})}{3} - 2 = 0$$

$$\frac{6}{3} - 2 = 0$$

$$0 = 0$$

Check for $x = \frac{(1 - \sqrt{7})}{3}$ is similar.

COMMON ERROR

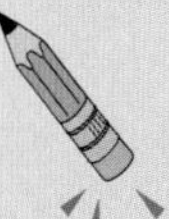

Incorrect substitutions sometimes occur when using the quadratic formula. Encourage students to check their substitutions before performing the computations in the formula.

MANIPULATIVES

M **Modeling Quadratic Equations**

Materials: Algebra Tiles, Manipulatives Master 3 (Sentence Mat), Manipulatives Master 4 (Factor Frame)

Group Practice: Review how to use Algebra Tiles to factor polynomials and find roots of equations. (See the Chapter 13, Lesson 1 Manipulatives activity.)

Student Practice: Have students use models to check their answers obtained by using the quadratic formula in Exercise A, Problems 1–7. Students should factor the polynomials and find the roots of the equation.

3 Reinforce and Extend

LEARNING STYLES

Body/Kinesthetic

On one or more sheets of paper, have students write an example for each different method they have learned for finding the roots of quadratic equations. Each example should consist of an equation and a complete solution and may include explanatory notes.

MENTAL MATH

Prior to completing the problems on page 397, ask students to identify the value of a, b, and c in each problem.

Lesson at a Glance

Chapter 13 Lesson 5

Overview This lesson introduces the graphs of quadratic equations.

Objectives

- To graph quadratic equations and identify the axis of symmetry of each graph

Student Pages 398–401

Teacher's Resource Library 

Workbook Activity 126

Activity 119

Alternative Activity 119

Mathematics Vocabulary

axis of symmetry
parabola
symmetry

Warm-Up Activity

Have students recall again that the graph of a linear equation such as $y = 2x - 1$ is a straight line. Write the following linear equations on the board. Then ask students to name three points on the line represented by each equation.

Sample answers shown.

$y = 2x - 1$ $(-2, -5), (0, -1), (2, 3)$

$y = -x + 4$ $(-1, 5), (0, 4), (1, 3)$

$y = 3x - 6$ $(-2, -12), (0, -6), (2, 0)$

$y = -4x$ $(-1, 4), (0, 0), (1, -4)$

$y = \frac{1}{2}x + \frac{1}{2}$ $(-4, -\frac{3}{2}), (0, \frac{1}{2}), (4, \frac{5}{2})$

Encourage a volunteer to summarize how to find points on a graph given the equation of the graph.

Teaching the Lesson

In both examples, a table of values has been generated for the given equation by substituting for x and solving for y. You might choose to point out that it is also possible to create a table of values by substituting for y and solving for x. However, since the general or standard form of a quadratic equation expresses y in terms of x, it typically takes less time to create a table of values by substituting

Lesson 5 Graphing Quadratic Equations

Parabola
A plane curve generated by a point that moves so that its distance from a fixed point is always the same as its distance from a fixed line

Recall that the graph of a linear equation (such as $y = x + 1$) is a straight line. Because a quadratic equation contains a second power, the graph of a quadratic equation is not a straight line. This means you will need to plot more than two points in order to determine the shape of the graph.

EXAMPLE 1 Graph $y = x^2 - 1$.

Step 1 Make a table of values. Substitute values for x to find the values of y.

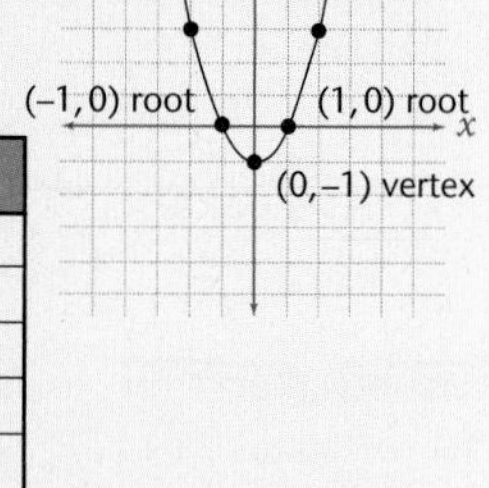

x	$y = x^2 - 1$	(x, y)
0	$0 - 1 = -1$	$(0, -1)$
1	$1 - 1 = 0$	$(1, 0)$ ROOT
-1	$(-1)^2 - 1 = 0$	$(-1, 0)$ ROOT
2	$4 - 1 = 3$	$(2, 3)$
-2	$(-2)^2 - 1 = 3$	$(-2, 3)$

Step 2 Plot points along the graph using the coordinates from the table. Connect the points starting with the least value of x and continuing to the greatest value.

The shape of the graph of $x^2 - 1 = y$ is known as a **parabola.** This particular parabola opens upward or "holds water." The turning point of a parabola, in this case, the point $(0, -1)$, is called the vertex.

EXAMPLE 2 Graph $y = -x^2 + 1$.

Step 1 Make a table of values for x and y.

x	$y = -x^2 + 1$	(x, y)
0	$0 + 1 = 1$	$(0, 1)$
1	$-(1^2) + 1 = 0$	$(1, 0)$ ROOT
-1	$-(-1)^2 + 1 = 0$	$(-1, 0)$ ROOT
2	$-(2^2) + 1 = -3$	$(2, -3)$
-2	$-(-2)^2 - 1 = -3$	$(-2, -3)$

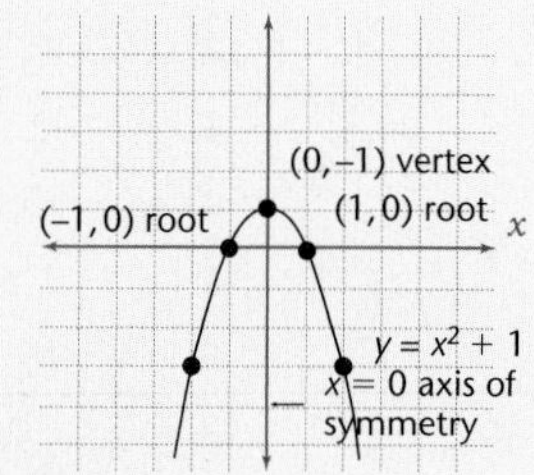

Step 2 Plot points along the graph using the coordinates from the table. Connect the points starting with the least value of x and continuing to the greatest value.

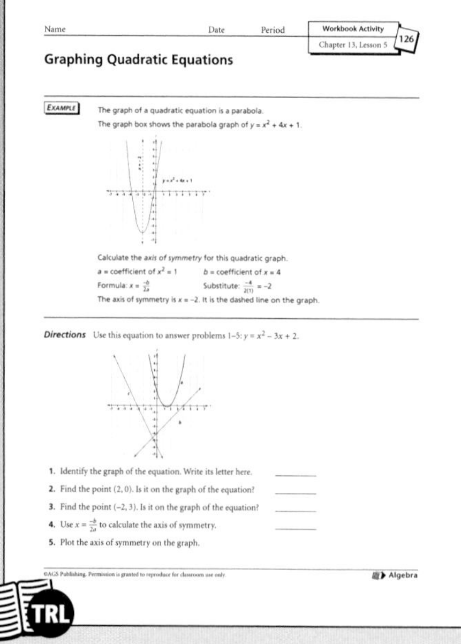

Name Date Period — Workbook Activity 126, Chapter 13, Lesson 5

Graphing Quadratic Equations

EXAMPLE The graph of a quadratic equation is a parabola.
The graph box shows the parabola graph of $y = x^2 + 4x + 1$.

Calculate the *axis of symmetry* for this quadratic graph.
a = coefficient of $x^2 = 1$ b = coefficient of $x = 4$
Formula: $x = \frac{-b}{2a}$ Substitute: $\frac{-4}{2(1)} = -2$
The axis of symmetry is $x = -2$. It is the dashed line on the graph.

Directions Use this equation to answer problems 1–5: $y = x^2 - 3x + 2$.

1. Identify the graph of the equation. Write its letter here. ______
2. Find the point (2, 0). Is it on the graph of the equation? ______
3. Find the point (–2, 3). Is it on the graph of the equation? ______
4. Use $x = \frac{-b}{2a}$ to calculate the axis of symmetry. ______
5. Plot the axis of symmetry on the graph.

 Algebra

TRL

Workbook Activity 126

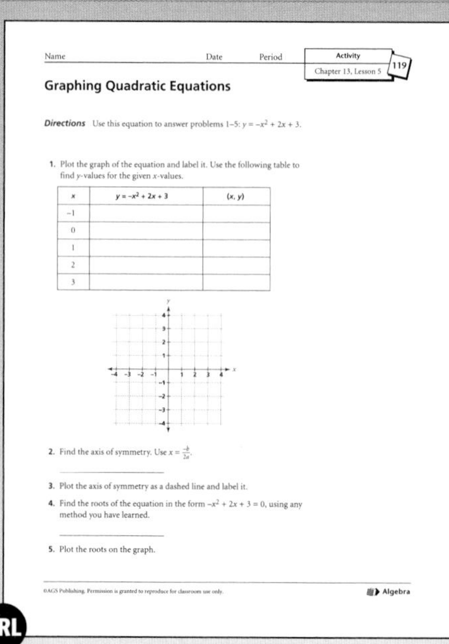

Name Date Period — Activity 119, Chapter 13, Lesson 5

Graphing Quadratic Equations

Directions Use this equation to answer problems 1–5: $y = -x^2 + 2x + 3$.

1. Plot the graph of the equation and label it. Use the following table to find y-values for the given x-values.

x	$y = -x^2 + 2x + 3$	(x, y)
–1		
0		
1		
2		
3		

2. Find the axis of symmetry. Use $x = \frac{-b}{2a}$.
3. Plot the axis of symmetry as a dashed line and label it.
4. Find the roots of the equation in the form $-x^2 + 2x + 3 = 0$, using any method you have learned.
5. Plot the roots on the graph.

 Algebra

TRL

Activity 119

Symmetry
The exact agreement of parts on opposite sides of a line

Axis of symmetry
A perpendicular line that passes through the midpoint between the roots

As in the first example, the shape of the graph of $-x^2 + 1 = y$ is also a parabola. However, the vertex of this parabola is (0, 1) and the parabola opens downward or "spills water."

If you look closely at each parabola, you will notice that it has **symmetry** about a line through the vertex. In other words, if you fold the graph along an imaginary line halfway between the two roots, the two halves of the graph will match exactly. This imaginary line is called the **axis of symmetry**. In these two examples, the line of symmetry is the y-axis.

> **Axis of Symmetry**
> The axis of symmetry is a perpendicular line that passes through the midpoint between the roots.

You can compute the x-value of the axis of symmetry using the quadratic formula.

$$x = \frac{-b \pm \sqrt{b^2 - 4ac}}{2a} = \frac{-b}{2a} \pm \frac{\sqrt{b^2 - 4ac}}{2a}$$

We can place these values along a number line:

axis of symmetry

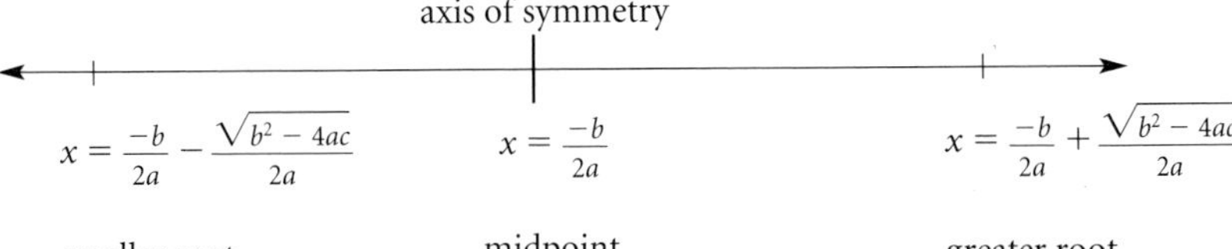

$x = \frac{-b}{2a} - \frac{\sqrt{b^2 - 4ac}}{2a}$ smaller root

$x = \frac{-b}{2a}$ midpoint

$x = \frac{-b}{2a} + \frac{\sqrt{b^2 - 4ac}}{2a}$ greater root

The number line shows that the x-value of the axis of symmetry is $x = \frac{-b}{2a}$.

Nature provides an example of symmetry. Both sides of the leaf match exactly.

for x and solving for y than it does to substitute for y and solve for x.

Have students note that the line of symmetry of a parabola is an imaginary line. Although it appears that there is a physical line of symmetry in the graphs of the equations on page 398, it is coincidental because the axis of symmetry and the y-axis of each graph represent the same line. It is important to note that the line of symmetry for the graph of a quadratic equation will be imaginary whenever the graph is not symmetric to an axis.

Prior to completing Exercise A at the bottom of the page 400, help students recognize that the axis of symmetry in problems 1–3 ($x = 0$) is the y-axis.

Before assigning problems for students to complete, note that graph paper exists in a variety of sizes with respect to the number of squares per inch. Quadratic equations can be difficult to graph if graph paper displays many squares per inch. Graph paper having 4 squares per inch typically works well for graphing the quadratic equations found in this chapter.

Common Error

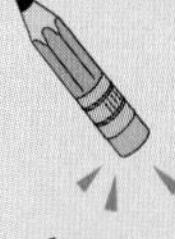

Remind students to follow the order of operations after they substitute values into an equation to create a table of values, and after they substitute values into the expression $x = \frac{-b}{2a}$ to find a parabola's axis of symmetry.

3 Reinforce and Extend

Learning Styles

Logical/Mathematical

Explain that the *vertex* of a parabola is the point at which the parabola changes direction. Have students study the parabolas shown on each page of this lesson and identify the vertex of each parabola.

Career Connection

Have students note that although the rocket pictured on the page is a model rocket, real rockets such as those that power a space shuttle into orbit have become part of our everyday life. Ask students to speculate what qualifications might be necessary to pilot or become a crew member on a space shuttle. Then invite them to use reference materials such as the Internet or those found in a library to discover the qualifications that are necessary to be a candidate to ride into space and share their findings with their classmates.

Learning Styles

LEP/ESL

Invite students to use English to name objects that display one or more lines of symmetry. (Examples of such objects include many geometric shapes such as regular polygons.) Then encourage students to identify a native language word or phrase that means the same as the word *symmetry* and share native-language words that mean the same as the objects that were described using English.

Example 3 Graph $y = x^2 + 2x - 3$ and identify its line of symmetry.

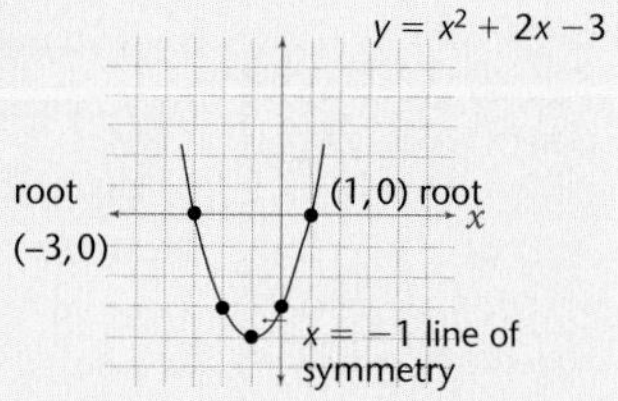

$y = x^2 + 2x - 3$

root (−3, 0)

(1, 0) root

$x = -1$ line of symmetry

Step 1 To graph the line of symmetry, compare the equation $y = x^2 + 2x - 3$ with the model, $ax^2 + bx + c = 0$. In this case, $a = 1$ and $b = 2$. Substitute these values in the expression for the line of symmetry.

$x = \frac{-b}{2a}$ becomes $x = \frac{-2}{2(1)} = -1$.

The line of symmetry is the line $x = -1$.

Step 2 To graph the equation, make a table of values for x and y.

x	$y = x^2 + 2x - 3$	(x, y)
0	$0 + 0 - 3 = -3$	(0, −3)
1	$1^2 + 2(1) - 3 = 0$	(1, 0) ROOT
−1	$(-1)^2 + 2(-1) - 3 = -4$	(−1, −4)
−2	$(-2)^2 + 2(-2) - 3 = -3$	(−2, −3)
−3	$(-3)^2 + 2(-3) - 3 = 0$	(−3, 0) ROOT

Step 3 Plot points along the graph using the coordinates from the table. Connect the points using the axis of symmetry as a guide.

Exercise A Graph the following equations. The axis of symmetry and the roots for each are given.

1. $y = x^2, x = 0; (0, 0)$

2. $y = -(x^2), x = 0; (0, 0)$

3. $y = x^2 - 1, x = 0; (1, 0), (-1, 0)$

Exercise B Find the axis of symmetry using the expression $x = \frac{-b}{2a}$. Find the roots of the equation, then graph the equation.

4. $y = 2x^2 - 2$

5. $y = x^2 - 8x + 16$

6. $y = x^2 - 7x + 12$

See Teacher's Edition page for answers to problems 1–6.

Answers to Problems 1–6

1.

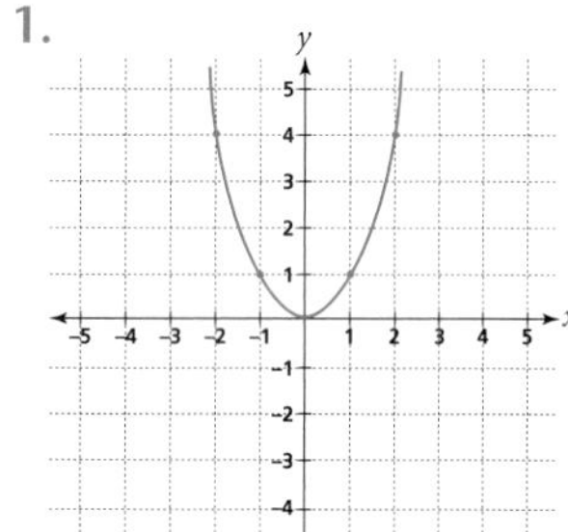

2.

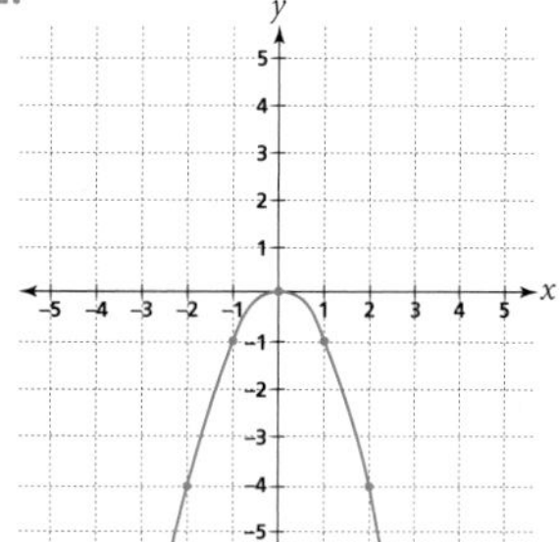

3.

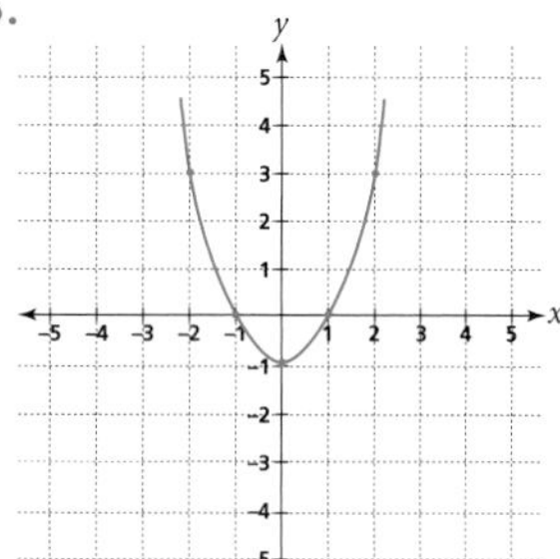

4.

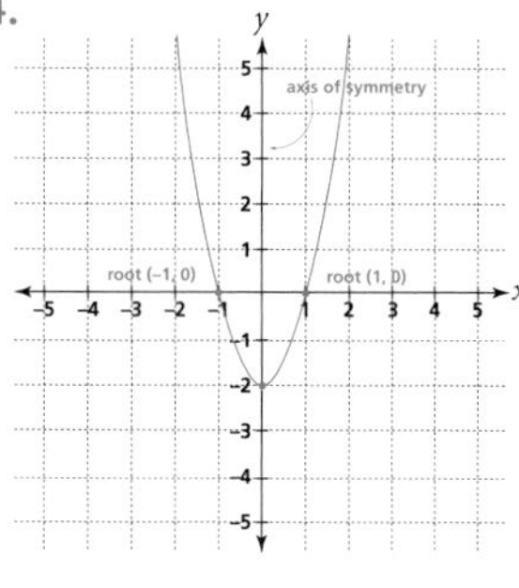

5.

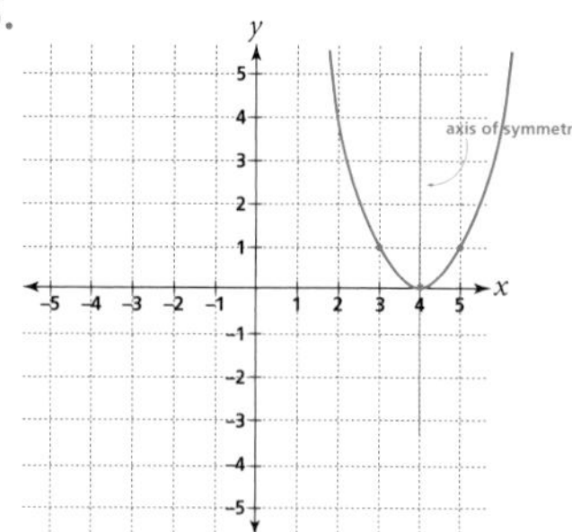

$x = 4; (4, 0)$

6.

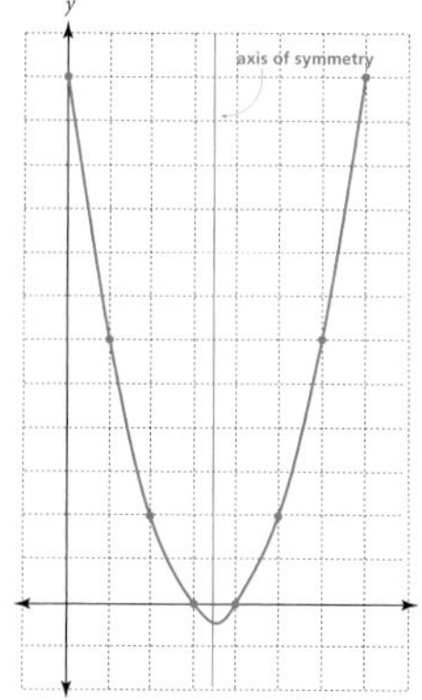

$x = 3.5; (3, 0); (4, 0)$

Calculator Practice If you have a graphing calculator, you can use it to graph linear or quadratic equations.

EXAMPLE 4 Graph $y = x^2 - 5$.

Step 1 Press GRAPH.

Step 2 Press $y(x)$ to go to the equation screen. Press CLEAR to remove any equations that may have been left in the calculator's memory. You will see this screen.

Y1 =
Y2 =
Y3 =
Y4 =
Y5 =

Step 3 Move the cursor to Y1 =, then press X ^ 2 − 5.

Step 4 Press GRAPH. The screen will display this graph.

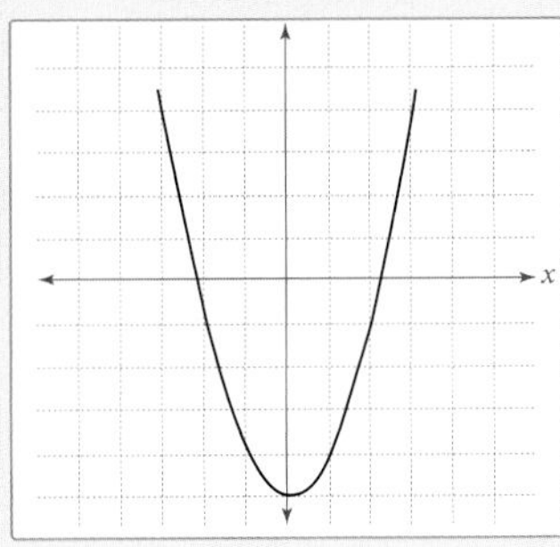

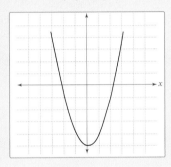

Exercise C Graph these equations. Use a graphing calculator if you have one.

7. $y = x^2 + 3$

8. $y = x^2 - 3$

9. $y = x^2 + 2x + 1$

10. $y = x^2 - 3x - 1$

See Teacher's Edition page for answers to problems 7–10.

9.

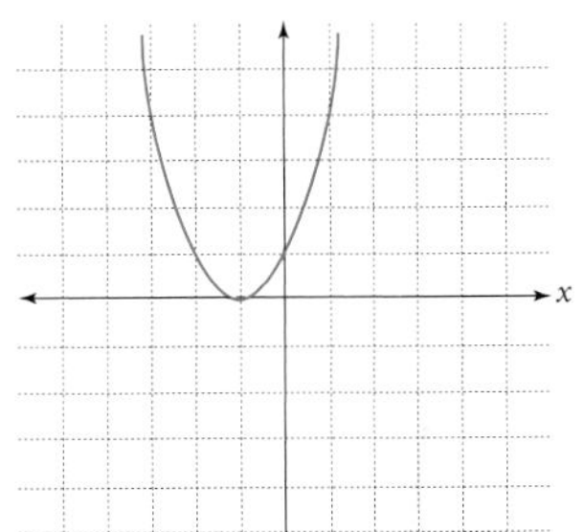

10.

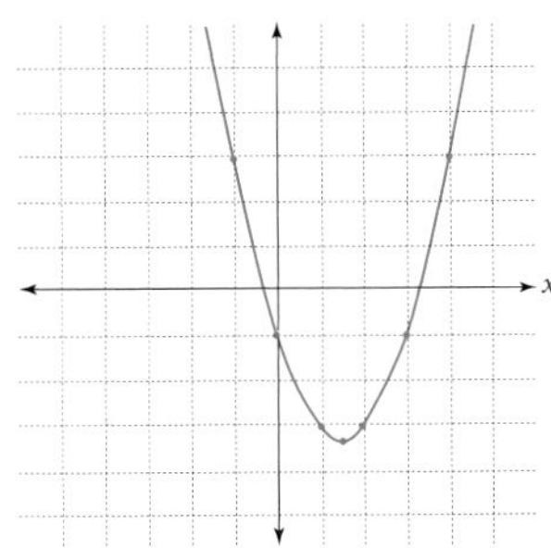

Calculator

The exact procedure that is required to graph equations may vary from calculator to calculator. Make sure students are familiar with the procedure that is required by their calculator to graph quadratic equations. You might choose to have students familiarize themselves with various graphing calculators if a variety of graphing calculators is readily available.

Group Problem Solving

Encourage students to work in groups of four to discuss and solve the following problem:

The graph of the equation $y = x^2 + 1$ is a parabola opening upward. The axis of symmetry of the graph is the y-axis and the *vertex,* or point at which the curve changes direction, is (0, 1). What is the equation of the graph if it were reflected through the x-axis? *($y = -x^2 - 1$)*

Invite groups to record the steps they used to solve the problem. Then have them share their problem-solving approach with one another.

Answers to Problems 7–10

7.

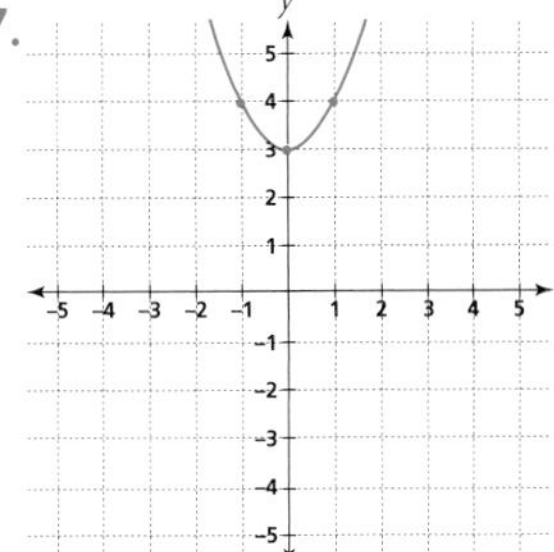

8.

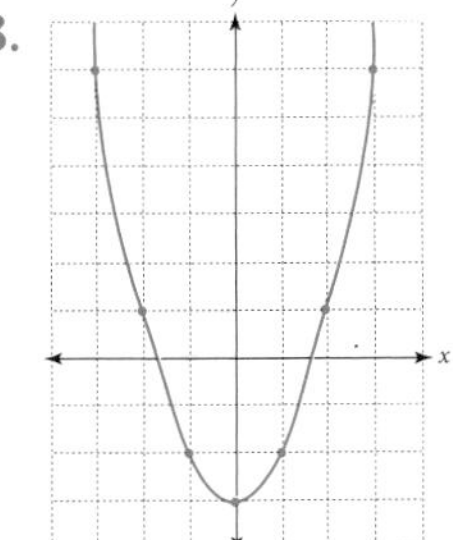

Lesson at a Glance

Chapter 13 Application

Overview This lesson introduces the application of a quadratic equation from the discipline of physical science.

Objective

- To use a quadratic equation to model the path of a rocket in flight

Student Page 402

Teacher's Resource Library 

Application Activity 13

Everyday Algebra 13

Warm-Up Activity

Invite volunteers to speculate what it might be like to ride in a space shuttle.

Teaching the Lesson

Remind students to follow the order of operations after substitutions for a, b, and c have been made in the quadratic formula.

Reinforce and Extend

Group Problem Solving

Encourage students to work in groups of three to discuss and solve the following problem:

The vertex of a parabola is $(0, -4)$ and the parabola passes through the point $(2, 0)$. Name another point the parabola passes through. *[The parabola passes through an infinite number of points, including $(-3, 5)$, $(-2, 0)$, $(-1, -3)$, $(1, -3)$, and $(3, 5)$.]*

Chapter 13 Review

Each set of problems in the Chapter Review includes an example and solution to illustrate the concept. Use the given examples for reteaching the materials in Chapter 13. For additional practice, refer to the Supplementary Problems for Chapter 13 (pages 430–431).

Application

Using Quadratic Equations

The quadratic equation can be used to model the path of a rocket in flight.

Example 1 A model rocket is launched vertically with a starting velocity of 100 feet per second. After how many seconds will the rocket be 50 feet above the ground?

Step 1 Use the vertical motion formula $h = -16t^2 + vt + s$.

h = height above ground in feet
t = time in seconds
v = starting velocity in feet per second
s = starting height in feet

$h = -16t^2 + vt + s$

$(50) = -16t^2 + 100(t) + 0$

$0 = -16t^2 + 100t - 50$

Step 2 Use the quadratic formula to find t.

$x = \frac{-b \pm \sqrt{b^2 - 4ac}}{2a}$

$t = \frac{-100 \pm \sqrt{(100)^2 - (4)(-16)(-50)}}{2(-16)}$

$t = \frac{-100 \pm \sqrt{6800}}{-32}$

$t = 0.55$ seconds and 5.70 seconds, rounded to the nearest hundredth.

The rocket will be 50 feet above the ground after 0.55 seconds and 5.70 seconds.

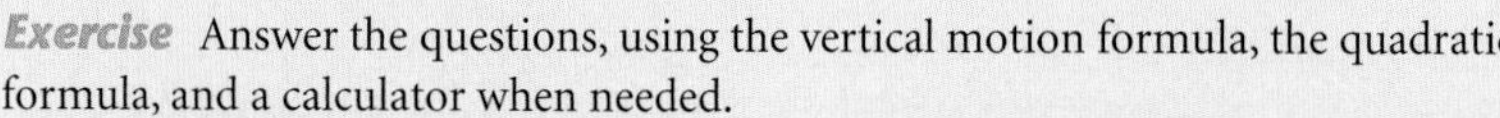

Exercise Answer the questions, using the vertical motion formula, the quadratic formula, and a calculator when needed.

1. After how many seconds will the rocket in the example be 100 feet above the ground?
   1.25 seconds and 5 seconds
2. After how many seconds will the rocket be 150 feet above the ground?
   2.5 seconds and 3.75 seconds
3. Look again at the example. Why is the model rocket 50 feet above the ground at two different times?
   The model rocket is at any height above ground twice—once on its way up and once on its way down.
4. Explain how you could estimate the total flight time of the rocket.
   See answer below.
5. Estimate the total flight time of the rocket.
   A good estimate is 6.25 seconds.

4. Find the time it takes the rocket to reach one foot above ground on its way down.

Name Date Period **Application Activity 13** Chapter 13

Using Quadratic Equations

You can model the path of a rocket in flight using the quadratic equation.

A model rocket is launched vertically with a starting velocity of 75 feet per second. After how many seconds will the rocket be 40 feet above the ground?

Step 1 Use the vertical motion formula $h = -16t^2 + vt + s$.

h = height above ground in feet
t = time in seconds
v = starting velocity in feet per second
s = starting height in feet

$h = -16t^2 + vt + s$

$40 = -16t^2 + 75t + 0$

$0 = -16t^2 + 75t - 40$

Step 2 Use the quadratic formula to find t.

$x = \frac{-b \pm \sqrt{b^2 - 4ac}}{2a}$

$t = \frac{-75 \pm \sqrt{(75)^2 - (4)(-16)(-40)}}{2(-16)}$

$t = \frac{-75 \pm \sqrt{3065}}{-32}$

$t = 0.61$ seconds and 4.07 seconds, rounded to the nearest hundredth.

The rocket will be 40 feet above the ground after 0.61 seconds and 4.07 seconds.

Answer the questions using the vertical motion formula, the quadratic formula, and a calculator when needed.

1. After how many seconds will the rocket in the example be 60 feet above the ground?
2. After how many seconds will the rocket be 75 feet above ground?
3. Look again at the example. Why is the model rocket 40 feet above the ground at two different times?
4. Explain how you could estimate the total flight time of the rocket.
5. Estimate the total flight time of the rocket.

 Algebra

Application Activity 13

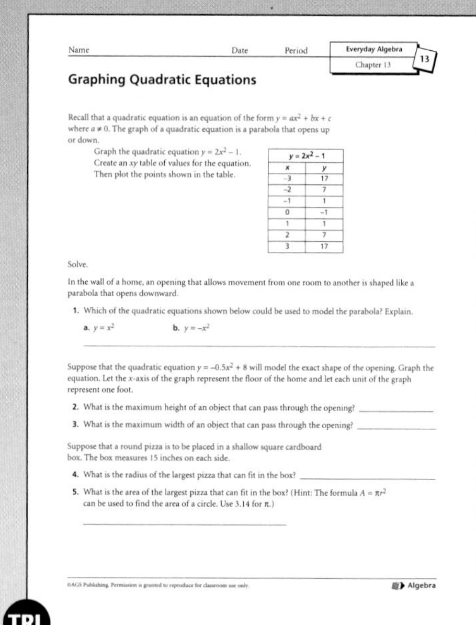

Name Date Period **Everyday Algebra 13** Chapter 13

Graphing Quadratic Equations

Recall that a quadratic equation is an equation of the form $y = ax^2 + bx + c$ where $a \neq 0$. The graph of a quadratic equation is a parabola that opens up or down.

Graph the quadratic equation $y = 2x^2 - 1$. Create an xy table of values for the equation. Then plot the points shown in the table.

$y = 2x^2 - 1$	
x	y
–3	17
–2	7
–1	1
0	–1
1	1
2	7
3	17

Solve.

In the wall of a home, an opening that allows movement from one room to another is shaped like a parabola that opens downward.

1. Which of the quadratic equations shown below could be used to model the parabola? Explain.
   a. $y = x^2$ b. $y = -x^2$

Suppose that the quadratic equation $y = -0.5x^2 + 8$ will model the exact shape of the opening. Graph the equation. Let the x-axis of the graph represent the floor of the home and let each unit of the graph represent one foot.

2. What is the maximum height of an object that can pass through the opening? ____
3. What is the maximum width of an object that can pass through the opening? ____

Suppose that a round pizza is to be placed in a shallow square cardboard box. The box measures 15 inches on each side.

4. What is the radius of the largest pizza that can fit in the box? ____
5. What is the area of the largest pizza that can fit in the box? (Hint: The formula $A = \pi r^2$ can be used to find the area of a circle. Use 3.14 for π.)

 Algebra

Everyday Algebra 13

Chapter 13 REVIEW

Write the letter of the correct answer.

1. Find the roots of this quadratic equation by factoring.
   $3x^2 - 2x - 21 = 0$ D
   - A $3, 7$
   - B $7, -3$
   - C $\frac{7}{3}, -3$
   - D $-\frac{7}{3}, 3$
2. Find the roots of this quadratic equation by factoring.
   $x^2 + 2x - 15 = 0$ B
   - A $-5, -3$
   - B $3, -5$
   - C $15, 1$
   - D $-1, 15$
3. What is the equation for the roots $\frac{3}{8}, -1$? C
   - A $8x^2 + 3x - 5 = 0$
   - B $8x^2 + 5x - 5 = 0$
   - C $8x^2 + 5x - 3 = 0$
   - D $8x^2 - 5x + 3 = 0$
4. What is the equation for the roots $1, -2$? A
   - A $x^2 + x - 2 = 0$
   - B $2x^2 + x - 2 = 0$
   - C $x^2 + 2x - 1 = 0$
   - D $x^2 + x - 1 = 0$
5. Solve the equation $x^2 - 4x - 21 = 0$ by completing the square. B
   - A $-3, -7$
   - B $7, -3$
   - C $3, -7$
   - D $3, 7$
6. Solve the equation $x^2 + 6x = -5$ by completing the square. B
   - A $1, 5$
   - B $-1, -5$
   - C $1, -5$
   - D $-1, 5$
7. Use the quadratic formula to find the roots of the equation: $3x^2 - 8x + 4 = 0$. D
   - A $\frac{2}{3}, -2$
   - B $2, -\frac{2}{3}$
   - C $-\frac{2}{3}, -2$
   - D $\frac{2}{3}, 2$

MANIPULATIVES

M Modeling Quadratic Equations

Materials: Algebra Tiles, Manipulatives Master 3 (Sentence Mat), Manipulatives Master 4 (Factor Frame)

Group Practice: Review how to use Algebra Tiles to factor polynomials and find roots of equations. (See the Chapter 13, Lesson 1 Manipulatives activity.)

Student Practice: Have students use manipulatives to solve Chapter Review Problems 1–4, 6–7, 9, and 12, and to check answers in Problems 14–15, 17–18, and 21–23.

Chapter 13 Mastery Test 

The Teacher's Resource Library includes parallel forms of the Chapter 13 Mastery Test. The difficulty level of the two forms is equivalent. You can use one form as a pretest and the other as a posttest.

Chapters 1–13 Final Mastery Test TRL

The Teacher's Resource Library includes the Final Mastery Test. This test is pictured on pages 528–529 of this Teacher's Edition. The Final Mastery Test assesses the major learning objectives of this text, with emphasis on Chapters 8–13.

ALTERNATIVE ASSESSMENT

Alternative Assessment items correlate with student Goals for Learning at the beginning of this chapter.

- **To solve quadratic equations by factoring**

Separate students into small groups. On the board, write and assign one equation for each group. Make the problems similar in difficulty. (Additional equations are in Supplementary Problems in the back of the textbook.) Have each group choose one student to write the final solution on the board. Have the groups evaluate the solutions of the other groups.

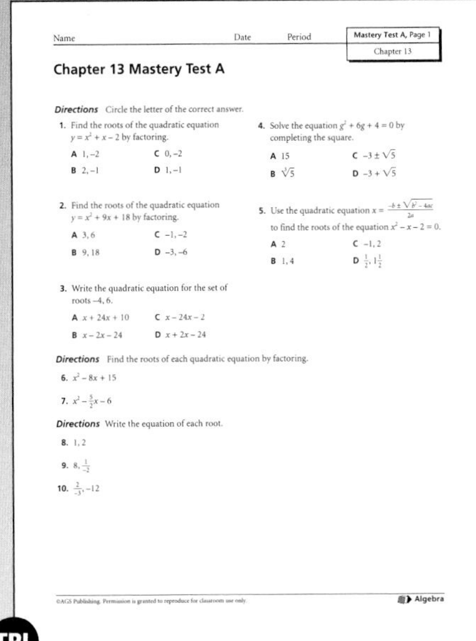

Name Date Period | Mastery Test A, Page 1 | Chapter 13

Chapter 13 Mastery Test A

Directions Circle the letter of the correct answer.

1. Find the roots of the quadratic equation $y = x^2 + x - 2$ by factoring.
   - A 1, –2
   - B 2, –1
   - C 0, –2
   - D 1, –1
2. Find the roots of the quadratic equation $y = x^2 + 9x + 18$ by factoring.
   - A 3, 6
   - B 9, 18
   - C –1, –2
   - D –3, –6
3. Write the quadratic equation for the set of roots –4, 6.
   - A $x + 24x + 10$
   - B $x - 2x - 24$
   - C $x - 24x - 2$
   - D $x + 2x - 24$
4. Solve the equation $g^2 + 6g + 4 = 0$ by completing the square.
   - A 15
   - B $\sqrt[3]{5}$
   - C $-3 \pm \sqrt{5}$
   - D $-3 + \sqrt{5}$
5. Use the quadratic equation $x = \frac{-b \pm \sqrt{b^2 - 4ac}}{2a}$ to find the roots of the equation $x^2 - x - 2 = 0$.
   - A 2
   - B 1, 4
   - C –1, 2
   - D $\frac{1}{2}, 1\frac{1}{2}$

Directions Find the roots of each quadratic equation by factoring.

6. $x^2 - 8x + 15$
7. $x^2 - \frac{5}{2}x - 6$

Directions Write the equation of each root.

8. 1, 2
9. $8, \frac{1}{-2}$
10. $\frac{2}{-3}, -12$

©AGS Publishing. Permission is granted to reproduce for classroom use only. Algebra

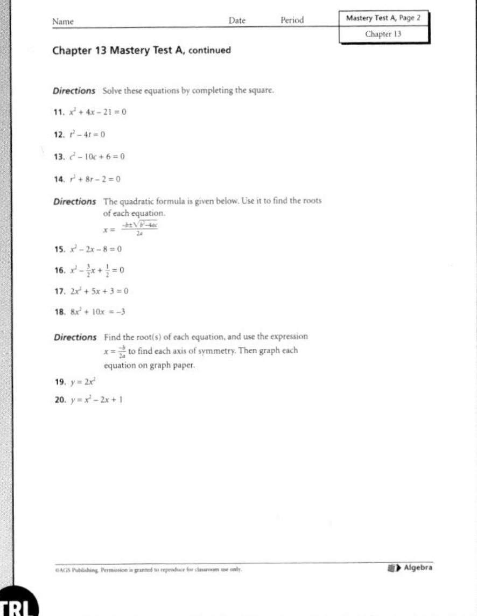

Name Date Period | Mastery Test A, Page 2 | Chapter 13

Chapter 13 Mastery Test A, continued

Directions Solve these equations by completing the square.

11. $x^2 + 4x - 21 = 0$
12. $t^2 - 4t = 0$
13. $c^2 - 10c + 6 = 0$
14. $r^2 + 8r - 2 = 0$

Directions The quadratic formula is given below. Use it to find the roots of each equation.
$x = \frac{-b \pm \sqrt{b^2 - 4ac}}{2a}$

15. $x^2 - 2x - 8 = 0$
16. $x^2 - \frac{3}{2}x + \frac{1}{2} = 0$
17. $2x^2 + 5x + 3 = 0$
18. $8x^2 + 10x = -3$

Directions Find the root(s) of each equation, and use the expression $x = \frac{-b}{2a}$ to find each axis of symmetry. Then graph each equation on graph paper.

19. $y = 2x^2$
20. $y = x^2 - 2x + 1$

©AGS Publishing. Permission is granted to reproduce for classroom use only. Algebra

Chapter 13 Mastery Test A

Answers to Problems 25–30

25.

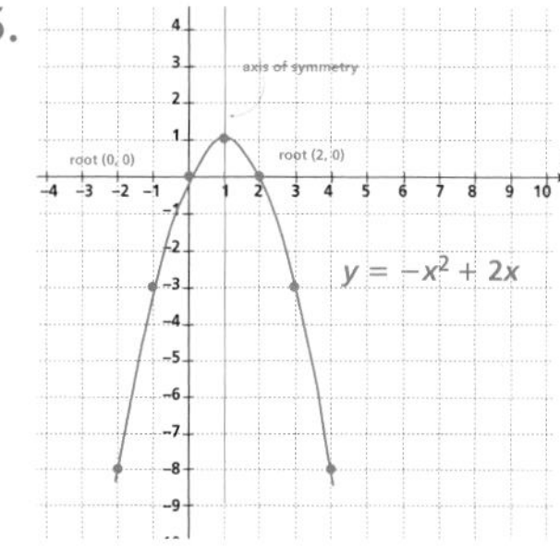

26.

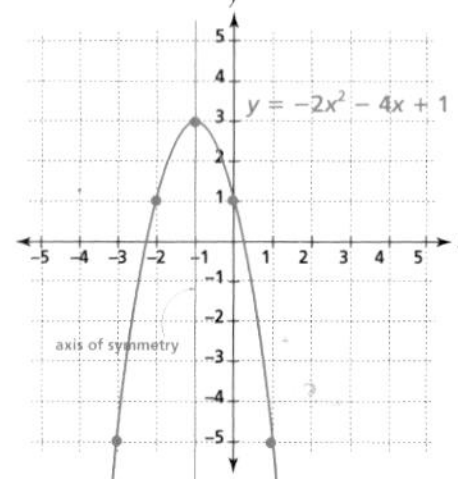

27.

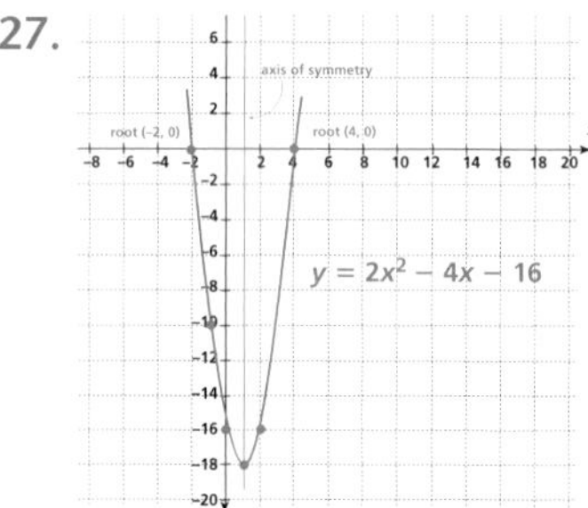

28.

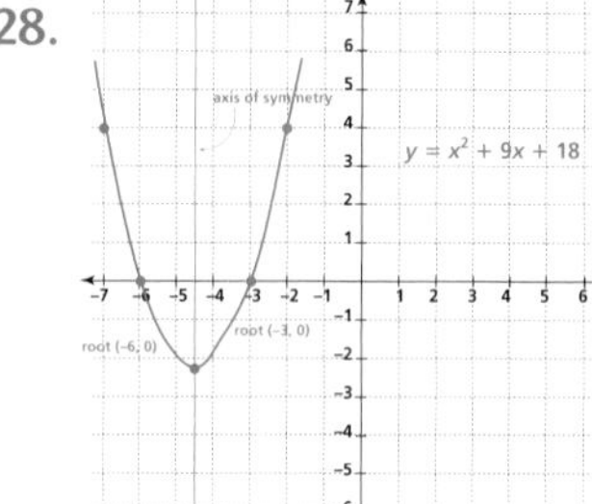

29.

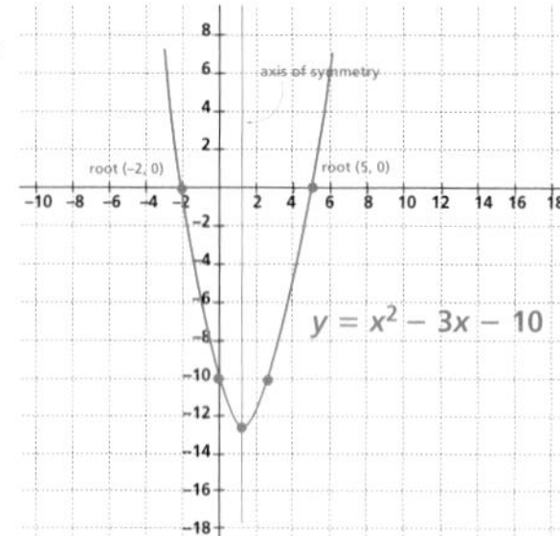

30.

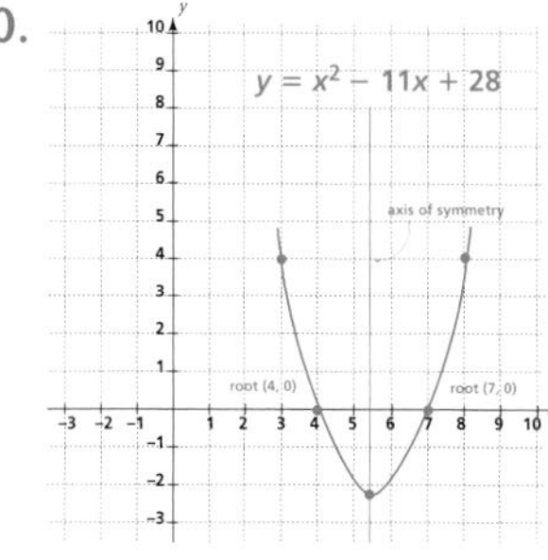

Chapter 13 REVIEW - continued

Find the roots of these quadratic equations by factoring.

Example: $x^2 - x - 12 = 0$ Solution: $x^2 - x - 12 = 0$, $(x + 3)(x - 4) = 0$
$x + 3 = 0$, $x - 4 = 0$, $x = -3$, $x = 4$

8. $x^2 - 5x + 6 = 0$ — 8. 2, 3

9. $-x^2 + 8x = 0$ — 9. 0, 8

10. $x^2 - 2x - 24 = 0$ — 10. −4, 6

11. $x^2 + 4x = 21$ — 11. −7, 3

Find the equations for these roots.

Example: −2, 5 Solution: $(x + 2)(x - 5) = x^2 - 5x + 2x - 10$
$= x^2 - 3x - 10$

12. −3, −8 — 12. $x^2 + 11x + 24 = 0$

13. 3, −6 — 13. $x^2 + 3x - 18 = 0$

14. −3, 6 — 14. $x^2 - 3x - 18 = 0$

15. $\frac{3}{4}$, 3 — 15. $4x^2 - 15x + 9 = 0$

Solve these equations by completing the square. Check your answers.

Example: $y^2 + 8y + 2 = 0$ Solution:

$$y^2 + 8y + 2 = 0$$
$$y^2 + 8y = -2$$
$$y^2 + 8y + 16 = -2 + 16$$
$$y^2 + 8y + 16 = 14$$
$$(y + 4)^2 = 14$$
$$\sqrt{(y + 4)} = \pm\sqrt{14}$$
$$y + 4 = \pm\sqrt{14}$$
$$y = -4 + \sqrt{14} \quad \text{or} \quad y = -4 - \sqrt{14}$$

16. $y^2 + 4y - 6 = 0$ — 16. $-2 \pm \sqrt{10}$

17. $x^2 + 6x - 16 = 0$ — 17. −8, 2

18. $d^2 - 8d = 0$ — 18. 0, 8

19. $2x^2 + 24x = 8$ — 19. $-6 \pm 2\sqrt{10}$

Use the quadratic formula to find the roots to these equations. Check your answers.

Example: $6x^2 + 7x - 5$ Solution:

$$x = \frac{-b \pm \sqrt{b^2 - 4ac}}{2a}$$
$$x = \frac{-7 \pm \sqrt{(7)^2 - 4(6)(-5)}}{2(6)}$$
$$x = \frac{-7 \pm \sqrt{169}}{12}$$
$$x = \frac{-7 + 13}{12} \quad \text{or} \quad x = \frac{-7 - 13}{12}$$
$$x = \frac{6}{12} \text{ or } \frac{1}{2} \quad \text{or} \quad x = \frac{-20}{12} \text{ or } -1.66$$

20. $4x^2 - 7 = 0$ — $\frac{\sqrt{7}}{2}, -\frac{\sqrt{7}}{2}$

21. $2x^2 - 7x - 9 = 0$ — $\frac{9}{2}, -1$

22. $y^2 + 4y - 5 = 0$ — −5, 1

23. $x^2 - 9x = -20$ — 4, 5

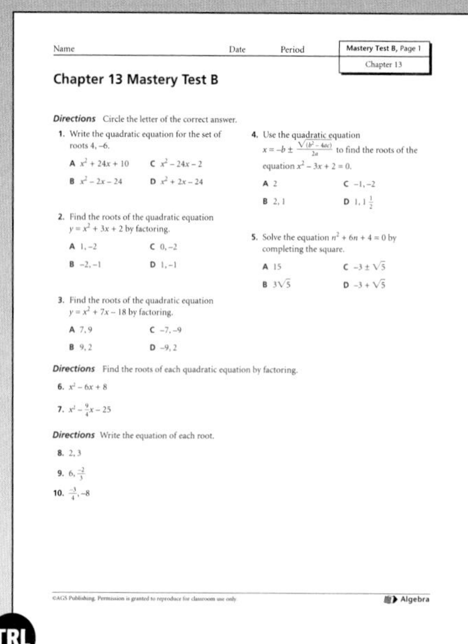
Name Date Period | Mastery Test B, Page 1 | Chapter 13

Chapter 13 Mastery Test B

Directions Circle the letter of the correct answer.

1. Write the quadratic equation for the set of roots 4, −6.
   - **A** $x^2 + 24x + 10$ **C** $x^2 - 24x - 2$
   - **B** $x^2 - 2x - 24$ **D** $x^2 + 2x - 24$
2. Find the roots of the quadratic equation $y = x^2 + 3x + 2$ by factoring.
   - **A** 1, −2 **C** 0, −2
   - **B** −2, −1 **D** 1, −1
3. Find the roots of the quadratic equation $y = x^2 + 7x - 18$ by factoring.
   - **A** 7, 9 **C** −7, −9
   - **B** 9, 2 **D** −9, 2
4. Use the quadratic equation $x = -b \pm \frac{\sqrt{(b^2 - 4ac)}}{2a}$ to find the roots of the equation $x^2 - 3x + 2 = 0$.
   - **A** 2 **C** −1, −2
   - **B** 2, 1 **D** 1, $1\frac{1}{2}$
5. Solve the equation $n^2 + 6n + 4 = 0$ by completing the square.
   - **A** 15 **C** $-3 \pm \sqrt{5}$
   - **B** $3\sqrt{5}$ **D** $-3 + \sqrt{5}$

Directions Find the roots of each quadratic equation by factoring.

6. $x^2 - 6x + 8$
7. $x^2 - \frac{9}{4}x - 25$

Directions Write the equation of each root.

8. 2, 3
9. 6, $\frac{-2}{3}$
10. $\frac{-3}{4}$, −8

 Algebra

TRL

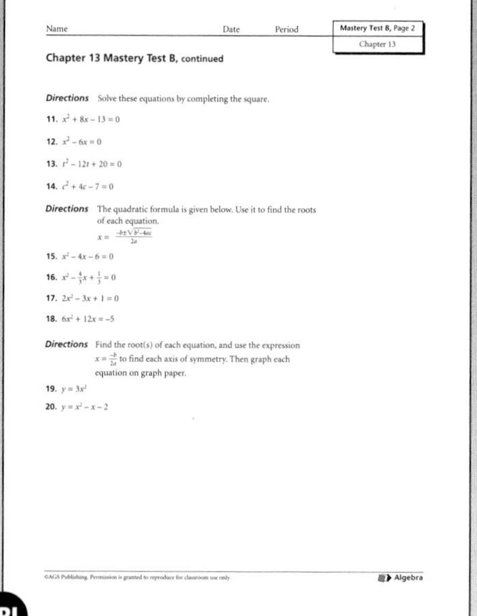
Name Date Period | Mastery Test B, Page 2 | Chapter 13

Chapter 13 Mastery Test B, continued

Directions Solve these equations by completing the square.

11. $x^2 + 8x - 13 = 0$
12. $x^2 - 6x = 0$
13. $t^2 - 12t + 20 = 0$
14. $c^2 + 4c - 7 = 0$

Directions The quadratic formula is given below. Use it to find the roots of each equation.
$x = \frac{-b \pm \sqrt{b^2 - 4ac}}{2a}$

15. $x^2 - 4x - 6 = 0$
16. $x^2 - \frac{4}{3}x + \frac{1}{3} = 0$
17. $2x^2 - 3x + 1 = 0$
18. $6x^2 + 12x = -5$

Directions Find the root(s) of each equation, and use the expression $x = \frac{-b}{2a}$ to find each axis of symmetry. Then graph each equation on graph paper.

19. $y = 3x^2$
20. $y = x^2 - x - 2$

 Algebra

TRL

Chapter 13 Mastery Test B

Find the axis of symmetry and the roots for these equations. Then graph the equation.

Example: $y = x^2 + x$ Solution: $x = -\frac{1}{2}$, (0, 0), (−1, 0)

24. $x = 1$, (0, 0), (2 ,0)

25. $x = -1$, $(\frac{2+\sqrt{6}}{-2}, 0)$, $(\frac{2-\sqrt{6}}{-2}, 0)$

26. $x = 1$, (−2, 0), (4, 0)

27. $x = -\frac{9}{2}$, (−3, 0), (−6, 0)

24. $y = -x^2 + 2x$

25. $y = -2x^2 - 4x + 1$

26. $y = 2x^2 - 4x - 16$

27. $y = x^2 + 9x + 18$

Answer these questions.

Example: The product of two consecutive integers is 72. What are the integers?
Solution: $x(x + 1) = 72$
$x^2 + x - 72 = 0$
$(x - 8)(x + 9) = 0$
$x - 8 = 0$ or $x + 9 = 0$
If $x = 8$, the integers are 8 and 9.
If $x = -9$, the integers are −8 and −9.

28. 7 and 8

29. 12 and 13

30. One is 5; the other is 7

28. The product of two consecutive positive integers is 56. What are the integers?

29. The product of two consecutive positive integers is 156. What are the integers?

30. The product of two brothers' ages is 35. They are two years apart. How old are they?

Test-Taking Tip

Whenever you solve an open sentence and find the value of a variable, always check your answer. Substitute the value you found for the variable in the equation. Then evaluate each side of the equation and check that the two sides are equal.

ALTERNATIVE ASSESSMENT, CONTINUED

■ **To write quadratic equations from their roots**
Have students choose a set of roots. Have students choose roots such as the number of students in class, ages, favorite numbers, etc. Have students give the roots to a partner, who will write the quadratic equations for the roots. Have partners check each other's results.

■ **To solve quadratic equations by completing the square**
Have students decide if the following problems are perfect squares. If yes, write Perfect Square after the equation. Then have them solve the problems.

$x + 50x = 0$ $(x^2 + 50x + 625 = 625;$ $x = 50$ or $x = 0)$

$x^2 + 2x = -1$ *(Perfect square)*

$x^2 - 2x = 10$ $(x^2 - 2x + 1 = 10 + 1;$ $(x - 1)^2 = 11x = 1 \pm \sqrt{11})$

$x^2 = -6x - 9$ *(Perfect square)*

$x^2 + 25 = 10x$ *(Perfect square)*

$-x - 4x + 4 = 0$ $(x^2 + 4x + 4 = 4$ $+ 4$ $(x + 2)^2 = 8; x = 2 \pm \sqrt{2})$

■ **To use the quadratic formula to solve quadratic equations**
Have students find the roots for the following equations.

$x^2 - 10x + 25 = 0$ *(5)*

$r^2 - 13x = -40$ *(5, 8)*

$m^2 - 49 = 0$ *(7, −7)*

$-b^2 - 2x = -12$ *(2, −6)*

■ **To graph quadratic equations**
Have students graph these quadratic equations on the same coordinate plane between the points given: $\frac{1}{4}x^2 + x + 3$ for points (−4, 3) through (0,3); $\frac{1}{4}x^2 - x + 3$ for points (0, 3) through (3, 4); and $\frac{1}{16}x^2 - 4$ for points (−4, −3) through (4, −3).

Chapter 1 Supplementary Problems

Write *true* or *false* for each statement.

1. $6 + 3 = 18$ false, $6 + 3 = 9$

2. $2 \cdot 6 = 12$ true

3. $\frac{40}{8} = 32$ false, $\frac{40}{8} = 5$

4. $25 - 13 = 38$ false, $25 - 13 = 12$

5. $21 \div 3 = 7$ true

Classify each expression, name the operation, and identify any variables.

6. $20 + 4$ numerical; addition

7. $8y$ algebraic; multiplication; y

8. $2d - 14$ algebraic; multiplication, subtraction; d

9. $n \div 3$ algebraic; division; n

10. $4 \cdot 6$ numerical; multiplication

Find the absolute value.

11. $|5|$ 5

12. $|-22|$ 22

13. $|+18|$ 18

14. $|-16|$ 16

15. $|25|$ 25

Find each sum.

16. $-8 + 15$ 7

17. $9 + 12$ 21

18. $-5 + (-11)$ -16

19. $3 + (-10)$ -7

20. $-4 + 7$ 3

Find each difference.

21. $5 - (-6)$ 11

22. $7 - 9$ -2

23. $-3 - 4$ -7

24. $-2 - (-8)$ 6

25. $+10 - 1$ 9

Find each product.

26. $(7)(4)$ 28

27. $(6)(-5)$ -30

28. $(-3)(-9)$ 27

29. $(11)(-3)$ -33

30. $(-12)(2)$ -24

406 *Supplementary Problems Algebra*

Find each quotient.

31. $36 \div (-6)$ -6

32. $-72 \div (-9)$ 8

33. $27 \div 3$ 9

34. $-80 \div 10$ -8

35. $-49 \div (-7)$ 7

Simplify each expression.

36. $3n + n$ $4n$

37. $4v - 14 + 12v$ $16v - 14$

38. $-5x + 3 + 10x$ $5x + 3$

39. $b + 4b - 8$ $5b - 8$

40. $6g + (-8g) - 18$ $-2g - 18$

Combine like terms to simplify each expression.

41. $2y + 3y + 4 + 6c$ $5y + 4 + 6c$

42. $7r - 4f + 8 + 6r - 3f$ $13r - 7f + 8$

43. $t + 4t - 9 + 2b - 4b$ $5t - 9 + (-2b)$

44. $3x + (-5b) + (-2x) + 15 + 5b$ $x + 15$

45. $6 + d - 8s - 4d + 5$ $11 + (-3d) - 8s$

Simplify each expression.

46. $a^5 \cdot a^4$ a^9

47. $c^7 \cdot c \cdot c^3$ c^{11}

48. $m^{10} \div m^5$ m^5

49. $z^9 \cdot z \cdot z^5 \cdot z^3$ z^{18}

50. $\frac{y^{15}}{y^2}$ y^{13}

Solve each problem using a formula.

51. Perimeter formula for a square: $P = 4s$. Find the perimeter, when $s = 12$ cm. 48 cm

52. Perimeter formula for a regular nonagon: $P = 9s$. Find the perimeter, when $s = 13$ m. 117 m

53. Perimeter formula for a regular decagon: $P = 10s$. What is the length of each side, when the perimeter is 120 km? 12 km

54. Perimeter formula for an equilateral triangle: $P = 3s$. What is the length of each side, when the perimeter is 72 dm? 24 dm

55. Perimeter formula for a triangle: $P = a + b + c$. What is the length of side b, when the perimeter is 132 mm, $a = 38$ mm, and $c = 59$ mm? 35 mm

Algebra Supplementary Problems **407**

Chapter 2 Supplementary Problems

Find each sum using expanded notation.

1. $6y + 9y$ $15y$ **3.** $x + 4x$ $5x$ **5.** $7j + 7j$ $14j$

2. $15a - 2a$ $13a$ **4.** $13n + 21n$ $34n$

Rewrite each expression showing the commutative property of multiplication.

6. mq qm **8.** $3(6t)$ $(6t)3$ **10.** $(12v)(i)$ $(i)(12v)$

7. $(2s)(5c)$ $(5c)(2s)$ **9.** $(7k)(10e)$ $(10e)(7k)$

Rewrite each expression showing the associative property of addition.

11. $(5 + 4z) + 3$ $5 + (4z + 3)$ **14.** $(8 + r) + k$ $8 + (r + k)$

12. $(3d + f) + 7$ $3d + (f + 7)$ **15.** $6b + (9c + 11e)$ $(6b + 9c) + 11e$

13. $25g + (2w + 14)$ $(25g + 2w) + 14$

Copy the problems. Find the products by multiplying the factors in parentheses first.

16. $(4 \cdot 25)3 = 4(25 \cdot 3)$ $300 = 300$ **19.** $6(2 \cdot 10) = (6 \cdot 2)10$ $120 = 120$

17. $40(2 \cdot 5) = (40 \cdot 2)5$ $400 = 400$ **20.** $5(5 \cdot 4) = (5 \cdot 5)4$ $100 = 100$

18. $(9 \cdot 2)50 = 9(2 \cdot 50)$ $900 = 900$

Use the distributive property to simplify each expression.

21. $3(x - j)$ $3x - 3j$ **24.** $8(-f + -g)$ $-8f + (-8g)$

22. $4(7w + -5)$ $28w + (-20)$ **25.** $-2(-k + 4)$ $2k + (-8)$

23. $-6(2 + z)$ $-12 + (-6z)$

Use the distributive property to factor each expression.

26. $15m + 5y$ $5(3m + y)$ **28.** $mc - mh$ $m(c - h)$ **30.** $-wr - wh^3$ $-w(r + h^3)$

27. $-9n - 7n$ $-n(9 + 7)$ **29.** $qy^4 + qs^2$ $q(y^4 + s^2)$

408 *Supplementary Problems Algebra*

Copy and fill in the missing number or letter.

31. $6 + ■ = 0$ -6

32. $9 - ■ = 0$ 9

33. $-c^3 + ■ = 0$ c^3

34. $u + ■ = 0$ $-u$

35. $-2 + ■ = 0$ 2

What is the reciprocal of each term? Check by multiplying.

36. 4 $\frac{1}{4}$; $(4)\left(\frac{1}{4}\right) = 1$

37. $\frac{1}{p}$ p; $\left(\frac{1}{p}\right)(p) = 1$

38. m^5 $\frac{1}{m^5}$; $\left(\frac{1}{m^5}\right)(m^5) = 1$

39. $\frac{1}{h}$ h; $\left(\frac{1}{h}\right)(h) = 1$

40. 15 $\frac{1}{15}$; $(15)\left(\frac{1}{15}\right) = 1$

Use your calculator to find the square root of each term.

41. $\sqrt{5.0625}$ 2.25

42. $\sqrt{985.96}$ 31.4

43. $\sqrt{335.9889}$ 18.33

44. $\sqrt{320.41}$ 17.9

45. $\sqrt{27.3529}$ 5.23

Use your calculator to simplify each term.

46. $(3u)^4$ $81u^4$

47. $(-5y)^3$ $-125y^3$

48. $(2a)^6$ $64a^6$

49. $(-16d)^2$ $256d^2$

50. $(-11n)^3$ $-1331n^3$

Use the order of operations to simplify.

51. $4x + 3x(4)$ $16x$

52. $3h(4 + 7) - 6h$ $27h$

53. $10s - s(4) + 7s$ $13s$

54. $g^3 + 6(g^3 + 2g^3)$ $19g^3$

55. $5m^2 + (3m)(2m)$ $11m^2$

Algebra Supplementary Problems **409**

Chapter 3 Supplementary Problems

Find the root of each equation by writing T (true) or F (false) for each value.

1.	$5p = 25$	$p = 4, 5, 8, 20$	F, T, F, F
2.	$7n = 42$	$n = 6, 10, 25, 42$	T, F, F, F
3.	$3x = 12$	$x = 1, 3, 4, 9$	F, F, T, F
4.	$8k = 40$	$k = 2, 3, 4, 5$	F, F, F, T
5.	$6y = 18$	$y = 2, 3, 12, 18$	F, T, F, F

Find the solution for each equation.

6. $a - 3 = 15$ 16

7. $p - 20 = 39$ 59

8. $w - (-6) = 5$ -1

9. $f - 13 = 20$ 33

10. $n - (-8) = 6$ -2

11. $g + 15 = 23$ 8

12. $y + 2.4 = 8$ 5.6

13. $u + (-6) = 17$ 23

14. $c + 16.9 = 29.7$ 12.8

15. $t + (-13) = 42$ 55

16. $5h = 35$ 7

17. $2q = 48$ 24

18. $-8.6v = 77.4$ -9

19. $-19.3i = -115.8$ 6

20. $7.6d = 60.8$ 8

21. $\frac{3}{4}j = 6$ 8

22. $\frac{8}{9}j = 16$ 18

23. $-\frac{2}{5}c = -10$ 25

24. $\frac{7}{16}m = -21$ -48

25. $\frac{1}{8}b = 2$ 16

26. $3f - 2 = 13$ 5

27. $2y - 10 = 14$ 12

28. $\frac{5}{7}r + (-6) = 29$ 49

29. $8t + 0 = 0$ 0

30. $\frac{2}{3}m - (-4) = 8$ 6

31. $P = 5s$ for s $s = \frac{P}{5}$

32. $V = lwh$ for l $l = \frac{V}{(wh)}$

33. $C = 2\pi r$ for r $r = \frac{C}{2\pi}$

34. $s = \frac{P}{10}$ for P $P = 10s$

35. $A = \frac{1}{2}(bh)$ for h $h = \frac{2A}{b}$

410 *Supplementary Problems Algebra*

Use the Pythagorean theorem to solve each problem.

36. $a = 6, b = ■, c = 10$ 8

37. $a = 15, b = 20, c = ■$ 25

38. $a = ■, b = 40, c = 50$ 30

39. $a = 18, b = ■, c = 30$ 24

40. $a = ■, b = 28, c = 35$ 21

Graph each of the equalities or inequalities on a number line.

41. $x > 0$

42. $x \leq 2$

43. $-2 \leq x \leq 2$

44. $x \geq -4$

45. $x \neq 1$

See page 416 for answers to problems 41-45

Solve each inequality.

46. $b + 3 < 6$ $b < 3$

47. $\frac{3}{5}e \geq 9$ $e \geq 15$

48. $t + (-9) > -3$ $t > 6$

49. $-4m < 16$ $m > -4$

50. $-\frac{1}{5}g \leq 3$ $g \geq -15$

Algebra Supplementary Problems **411**

Chapter 4 Supplementary Problems

Write an equation and solve each question.

1. Five times a number decreased by 4 is 26. What is the number?
$5 \bullet x - 4 = 26; 6$

2. The sum of two consecutive integers is –21. What are the integers?
$x + (x + 1) = -21; -10, -11$

3. The sum of three consecutive odd integers is 51. What are the integers?
$x + (x + 2) + (x + 4) = 51; 15, 17, 19$

4. Sixty subtracted from eight times some number is 4. What is the number?
$8x - 60 = 4; 8$

Use the 1% solution to solve each problem.

5. Aaron earns $3,000 a month. He invests $45 a month in a mutual fund. What percent of his income is invested in a mutual fund? 1.5%

6. Sarah wants to buy a CD player that costs $300. She has already saved $231. What percent of the total has she saved? 77%

7. Juan has an annual income of $42,000. He saves 4% of his income. How much does he save? $1,680

8. Linda has 24 classical music CDs in her collection. 12% of her CDs are classical music. How many CDs does she have in her collection? 200 CDs

Find the percent of each number.

9. 26% of 88 22.88

10. 37% of 950 351.5

11. 64% of 25 16

12. 81% of 515 417.15

Solve each problem using kilometers or miles.

13. Michelle rides her bike for $3\frac{1}{3}$ hours at a speed of $15\frac{1}{2}$ kilometers per hour. How far does she travel? $51\frac{2}{3}$ km

14. DeNorris drives $162\frac{1}{2}$ miles in $2\frac{1}{2}$ hours. What is his average speed? 65 mph

15. Maria and Patty jog for $1\frac{3}{4}$ hours at a rate of 18 kilometers per hour. How many kilometers do they jog? $31\frac{1}{2}$ km

16. Eliza and Mike walk at a rate of 4 miles per hour for $1\frac{1}{2}$ hours and 6 miles per hour for $\frac{1}{2}$ hour. What is their average speed? $4\frac{1}{2}$ miles per hour

412 *Supplementary Problems Algebra*

Use your calculator to tell how many nickels and dimes are in each problem.

17. $1.75, three times more dimes than nickels 5 nickels and 15 dimes

18. $3.00, three times more nickels than dimes 36 nickels and 12 dimes

19. $11.25, four times more dimes than nickels 25 nickels and 100 dimes

20. $1.20, six times more nickels than dimes 18 nickels and 3 dimes

Find the interest, principal, or rate of interest. ($I = prt$)

21. Principal: $2,500 Rate: 6% Time: 2 years Interest: ■ $300

22. Principal: ■ $625 Rate: 8% Time: 4 years Interest: $200

23. Principal: $900 Rate: ■ 5% Time: 3 years Interest: $135

24. Principal: $800 Rate: 13% Time: 5 years Interest: ■ $520

Solve each problem.

25. Cashews cost $3 per pound and peanuts cost $2.50 a pound. Three pounds of cashews and three pounds of peanuts are mixed. What is the cost for one pound of the mixture? $2.75

26. Walnuts cost $6 per pound and peanuts cost $3.50 a pound. Four pounds of walnuts and three pounds of peanuts are mixed. What is the cost for one pound of the mixture? $4.93

27. A mixture of peanuts and walnuts sells for $3.00 per pound. How many pounds of peanuts at $1.50 per pound should be mixed with 12 pounds of walnuts at $4.00 per pound? 8 pounds

28. The price for one pound of a mixture of cashews and walnuts is $5.75. The total cost of the mixture is $34.50. What is the total number of pounds in the mixture? 6 pounds

Find the missing term in each proportion

29. $\frac{3}{x} = \frac{18}{24}$ 4

30. $\frac{6}{9} = \frac{14}{y}$ 21

31. $\frac{m}{8} = \frac{20}{32}$ 5

32. $\frac{4}{7} = \frac{32}{w}$ 56

33. $\frac{z}{20} = \frac{6}{12}$ 10

34. $\frac{12}{c} = \frac{24}{64}$ 32

35. $\frac{6}{18} = \frac{b}{36}$ 12

Algebra Supplementary Problems **413**

Chapter 5 Supplementary Problems

Show why these statements are true.

1. $(y^3)^3 = y^9$ **2.** $(a^2)^4 = a^8$ **3.** $[(x + y)^3]^2 = (x + y)^6$

See below.

Find the quotient.

4. $(9^9) \div (9^6)$ 9^3

5. $\frac{7^8}{7^4}$ 7^4

6. $\frac{n^5}{n^3}, n \neq 0$ n^2

7. $(5g + 3y)^{10} \div (5g + 3y)^4, 5g + 3y \neq 0$ $(5g + 3y)^6$

8. $\frac{(h - i)^8}{(h - i)^3}, h - i \neq 0$ $(h - i)^5$

1. $(y \cdot y \cdot y)(y \cdot y \cdot y)(y \cdot y \cdot y) = y^9$
2. $(a \cdot a)(a \cdot a)(a \cdot a)(a \cdot a) = a^8$
3. $(x + y)(x + y)(x + y)(x + y)$
   $(x + y)(x + y) = (x + y)^6$

Write the following numbers in scientific notation.

9. 0.00000000554 $5.54 \bullet 10^{-9}$

10. 9,000,000 $9 \bullet 10^6$

11. 0.00000078 $7.85 \bullet 10^{-7}$

Write the following numbers in standard notation.

12. $2.6(10^5)$ 260,000

13. $3.14(10^{-3})$ 0.00314

14. $5.21(10^6)$ 5,210,000

Find the sum, difference, product, or quotient. Be sure your answers are in scientific notation.

15. $2.7(10^{-3}) + 3.4(10^{-3})$ $6.1\ (10^{-3})$

16. $8.3(10^8) - 4.9(10^8)$ $3.4(10^8)$

17. $1.3(10^{-2}) \cdot 2.1(10^{-6}) \cdot 2(10^{10})$ $5.46 \bullet 10^2$

18. $1.6(10^3) \div 3.2(10^{-8})$ $5 \bullet 10^{10}$

19. $2.2(10^{-7}) \cdot 2.1(10^{-3}) \cdot 4.0(10^8)$ $1.848 \bullet 10^{-1}$

414 *Supplementary Problems Algebra*

Find the sum and difference for each pair of polynomials.

20. $2x^2 + 5x + 1$ See below.

$-2x^2 + 6x + 3$

21. $c^4 + c^2 + 3c + 1$

$2c^4 + 3c^2 + c + 5$

22. $-3w^5 - 6w^4 - 2w^3 - w^2 - w - 5$

$w^5 + 6w^4 + 2w^3 + w^2 - w + 5$

23. $k^5 + k^3 + 3$

$k^4 + w^2 + 5$

24. $n^5 + n^3 + n - 3$

$n^7 + n^2$

25. $8d^7 + 3d^6 + 9d^3$

$d^2 + d - 8$

Find the product.

26. $(y + 4)(y + 3)$ $y^2 + 7y + 12$

27. $(b - 4)(b + 4)$ $b^2 - 16$

28. $3n^3(n^2 + 2n - 8)$ $3n^5+6n^4-24n^3$

29. $(-4x^2 - 5)(x^2 - 5)$ $-4x^4+15x^2+25$

30. $(c^3 + c^2)^2$ $c^6 + 2c^5 + c^4$

31. $(3z + 1)(z - 2)$ $3z^2 - 5z - 2$

32. $(u^3 + 3)(2u^2 + 5u + 4)$ $2u^5 + 5u^4 + 4u^3 + 6u^2 + 15u + 12$

33. $(3y^3 - 6)(4y^5 - y)$ $12y^8 - 24y^5 - 3y^4 + 6y$

Find the quotients. Identify any remainder. Use multiplication to check your answer.

34. $\frac{(24x^2 + 32x - 24)}{8}$ $3x^2 + 4x - 3$

35. $\frac{(30y^3 - 36y^2 + 42y + 48)}{-6}$ $-5y^3 + 6y^2 - 7y - 8$

36. $\frac{(h^2 - 2h)^2}{(h^2 - 2h)}$ $(h^2 + 2h)$

37. $\frac{(4s^2 - 12s)}{2s(s - 3)}$ 2

38. $(42t^3 + 70t^2 - 21t) \div 7t$ $6t^2 + 10t - 3$

39. $(2y^2 + 2y) \div (y + 1)$ $2y$

40. $(25x^3 - 5x^2 + x - 2)(7x^3 - 4x^2) \div (7x^3 - 4x^2)$ $(25x^3 - 5x^2 + x - 2)$

20. $11x + 4$; $4x^2 - x - 2$

21. $3c^4 + 4c^2 + 4c + 6$; $-c^4 - 2c^2 + 2c - 4$

22. $-2w^5 - 2w$; $-4w^5 - 12w^4 - 4w^3 - 2w^2 - 10$

23. $k^5 + k^4 + k^3 + w^2 + 8$; $k^5 - k^4 + k^3 - w^2 - 2$

24. $n^7 + n^5 + n^3 + n^2 + n - 3$; $-n^7 + n^5 + n^3 - n^2 + n - 3$

25. $8d^7 + 3d^6 + 9d^3 + d^2 + d - 8$; $8d^7 + 3d^6 + 9d^3 - d^2 - d + 8$

Algebra Supplementary Problems **415**

Chapter 6 Supplementary Problems

Find the GCF for these groups.

1. 25, 75 — 25

2. 22, 121 — 11

3. 36, 27 — 9

4. $16x, 20x^2, 12x^3$ — $4x$

5. $15a^3d, 25ad^3$ — $5ad$

Find the GCF for these expressions.

6. $20j^4 + 10$ — 10

7. $18x^3 + 24x^2 + 42x$ — $6x$

8. $25c^4 - 35c^3 - 45c^2 - 55$ — 5

9. $-21x^5y^5 - 63x^4y^2 - 56x^2y^2 + 14xy^2$ — $7xy^2$

10. $13w^3t^2 - 26wt$ — $13wt$

Factor the following expressions. Check by multiplying.

11. $x^2 - x - 56$ — $(x+7)(x-8)$

12. $c^2 + 6c + 9$ — $(c+3)(c+3)$

13. $y^2 - y - 12$ — $(y-4)(y+3)$

14. $3m^2 + 24m + 36$ — $3(m+2)(m+6)$

15. $5x^4 + 5x^3 - 60x^2$ — $5x^2(x-3)(x+4)$

16. $6e^2 + 33e + 42$ — $(2e+7)(3e+6)$

17. $12n^2 - 26n + 10$ — $(3n-5)(4n-2)$

18. $3z^2 + 35z - 52$ — $(z+13)(3z-4)$

19. $10s^2 + 17s + 6$ — $(2s+1)(5s+6)$

20. $3v^4 + 15v^3 + 18v^2$ — $3v^2(v-2)(v+3)$

21. $b^2 - 81$ — $(b - 9)(b + 9)$

22. $q^2 - 400$ — $(q - 20)(q + 20)$

23. $36g^2 - 49$ — $(6g - 7)(6g + 7)$

24. $81r^2 - 16$ — $(9r - 4)(9r + 4)$

25. $25w^4 - 9x^2$ — $(5w^2-3x)(5w^2+3x)$

416 *Supplementary Problems Algebra*

Find the factors of these perfect square trinomials.

26. $i^2 - 26i + 169$ $(i - 13)(i - 13)$

27. $y^2 + 16y + 64$ $(y + 8)(y + 8)$

28. $k^2 - 20k + 100$ $(k - 10)(k - 10)$

29. $p^2 + 22p + 121$ $(p + 11)(p + 11)$

30. $m^2 - 44m + 484$ $(m - 22)(m - 22)$

Find the value of the variable in each expression.

31. $3d = 0$ 0

32. $6(x + 4) = 0$ -4

33. $(h - 4)(h + 6) = 0$ 4 and -6

34. $(2y - 4)(3y + 6) = 0$ 2 and -2

35. $6(3b - 12)(b + 9) = 0$ 4 and -9

Solve each of these quadratic equations. Be sure to check your work.

36. $x^2 + 10x + 24 = 0$ -4 and -6

37. $y^2 - 9y + 18 = 0$ 3 and 6

38. $b^2 + 11b + 28 = 0$ -4 and -7

39. $6s^2 - 12s + 6 = 0$ 1

40. $10x^2 + 60x + 80 = 0$ -2 and -4

Algebra Supplementary Problems **417**

Chapter 7 Supplementary Problems

Use the following words to fill in the ■: *box-and-whiskers plot, dependent, frequency, fundamental principle of counting, histogram, impossible, independent, mean, mode, probability, range, sample space,* and *stem-and-leaf plot.*

1. A ■ table is a method used to summarize data. frequency

2. When data is organized and displayed using stems and leaves, it is called a ■. stem-and-leaf plot

3. A bar graph that uses intervals is called a ■. histogram

4. The difference between the highest and lowest values is the ■ of data. range

5. The sum of the values in a set of data divided by the total number of values is called the ■. mean

6. The value that occurs the most is called the ■. mode

7. To show the concentration and spread of data in a set, one uses a ■. box-and-whiskers plot

8. The chance that an outcome will occur is called ■. probability

9. An event that has a probability of zero is called an ■ event. impossible

10. The set of all possible outcomes of an experiment is called a ■. sample space

11. The outcome of one event affects the outcome of another event in ■ events. dependent

12. The outcome of one event has no effect on the outcome of another event in ■ events. independent

13. A general rule that states you can multiply the numbers of choices to find the total number of choices is called the ■. fundamental principle of counting

Use the chart on English test scores for problems 14–21.

English Test Scores							
59	73	87	59	90	80	58	69
60	63	78	96	59	68	81	85
90	73	64	98	97	75	77	91

14. Display the data in a stem-and-leaf plot. See page 458 for answer.

15. How many students had scores lower than 60? 4

16. How many students scored 75 or higher? 13

17. What score occurred the most? 59

18. What was the lowest score? 58

19. What was the highest score? 98

20. How many students received scores between 62 and 76? 7

21. Display the data in a histogram using intervals of 10. See page 458 for answer.

418 *Supplementary Problems Algebra*

Use this data set {$3.39, $4.77, $9.07, $1.40, $6.23, $7.25, $2.23, $4.77, $5.01} for problems 22–25.

22. Find the range. $7.67

23. Find the mean. $4.90

24. Find the median. $4.77

25. Find the mode. $4.77

Use the box-and-whiskers plot for problems 26–30.

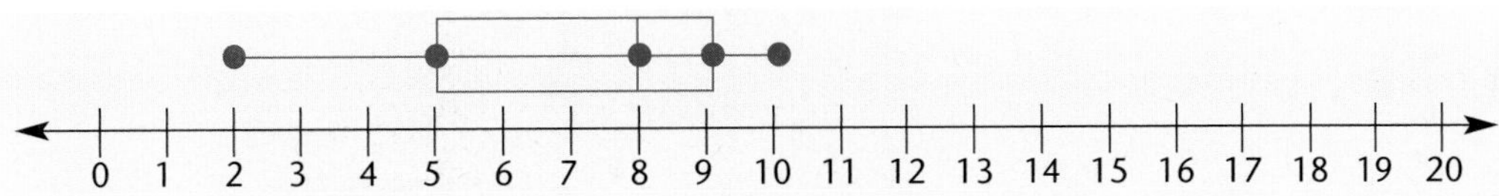

26. What is the upper extreme? 10

27. What is the lower extreme? 2

28. What is the median? 8

29. Where is the middle cluster of data? between 5 and 9

30. What is the range? 8

A 1–6 number cube is rolled once. Find the theoretical probability (*P*) of each event. Express your answer as a fraction in simplest form.

31. *P* (3) $\frac{1}{6}$

32. *P* (even number) $\frac{1}{2}$

33. *P* (0) 0

34. *P* (a factor of 6) $\frac{2}{3}$

Suppose you roll a 1–6 number cube and toss a coin. Use a tree diagram to determine the probability of each event.

35. *P* (heads and 2) $\frac{1}{12}$

36. *P* (tails and a number less than 4) $\frac{1}{4}$

37. *P* (not heads and not 3) $\frac{5}{12}$

A bag contains 10 marbles of equal size. One marble is blue, one is white, three are yellow, and five are red. A marble is taken from the bag two times. Each time a marble is taken, it is not replaced.

38. Find *P* (red and red) $\frac{2}{9}$

39. Find *P* (blue and white) $\frac{1}{90}$

40. Find *P* (yellow and blue) $\frac{1}{30}$

Algebra Supplementary Problems **419**

Chapter 8 Supplementary Problems

Reduce each fraction to its lowest terms.

1. $\frac{35}{45}$ $\quad \frac{7}{9}$

2. $\frac{200}{250}$ $\quad \frac{4}{5}$

3. $\frac{16}{24}$ $\quad \frac{2}{3}$

4. $-\frac{12}{144}$ $\quad -\frac{1}{12}$

5. $\frac{21}{42}$ $\quad \frac{1}{2}$

6. $\frac{c^8}{c^3}$ $\quad c^5$

7. $\frac{24s^7}{6s^2}$ $\quad 4s^5$

8. $\frac{45hg^3}{63h^4g^5}$ $\quad \frac{5}{7h^3g^2}$

9. $\frac{18x^5y^3}{81x^5y}$ $\quad \frac{2y^2}{9}$

10. $\frac{(p^2 - 16)}{(p + 4)}$ $\quad (p - 4)$

11. $\frac{(y^2 + 7y + 12)}{(y + 4)}$ $\quad (y + 3)$

12. $\frac{(m + 6)}{(m^2 + 2m - 24)}$ $\quad \frac{1}{(m - 4)}$

13. $\frac{(x^4 + 15x^3 + 56x^2)}{(2x^3 + 30x^2 + 112x)}$ $\quad \frac{x}{2}$

Multiply or divide. Reduce your answers to lowest terms.

14. $5\frac{1}{3} \cdot 6\frac{2}{9}$ $\quad 33\frac{5}{27}$

15. $\frac{7}{8} \div \frac{2}{5}$ $\quad 2\frac{3}{16}$

16. $\frac{1}{(y^2 - 16)} \cdot \frac{(y + 4)}{(y - 4)}$ $\quad \frac{1}{(y - 4)^2}$

17. $\frac{(d + 6)}{(d - 6)} \div \frac{(d + 6)}{(d^2 - 36)}$ $\quad (d + 6)$

18. $e^2f^3 \div ef^2$ $\quad ef$

19. $3\frac{3}{4} \cdot \frac{7}{8}$ $\quad 3\frac{9}{32}$

Simplify these complex fractions. Write your answers in lowest terms.

20. $\frac{9}{\frac{3}{4}}$ $\quad 12$

21. $\frac{\frac{3}{16}}{\frac{15}{16}}$ $\quad \frac{1}{5}$

22. $\frac{\frac{c}{u}}{\frac{u}{d}}$ $\quad \frac{cd}{u^2}$

23. $\frac{\frac{x^2}{w^3}}{\frac{x^3}{w^2}}$ $\quad \frac{1}{xw}$

Find each sum or difference.

24. $(\frac{5}{8}) - (\frac{5}{16})$ $\quad \frac{5}{16}$

25. $(\frac{2}{y}) + (\frac{y}{3^2})$ $\quad \frac{(18 + y^2)}{9y}$

26. $\frac{5}{(b - 1)} + \frac{4}{(b - 1)^2}$ $\quad \frac{5b - 1}{(b - 1)^2}$

27. $\frac{2}{(k + 2)} - \frac{1}{(k - 3)}$ $\quad \frac{k - 8}{(k - 3)(k + 2)}$

28. $\frac{3x}{(x - 8)} - \frac{6x}{(x + 8)}$ $\quad \frac{-3x\,(x - 24)}{x + 8)(x - 8)}$

29. $\frac{9}{(v^2 - 9)} - \frac{3}{(v + 3)}$ $\quad \frac{-3\,(v - 6)}{(v + 3)(v - 3)}$

420 *Supplementary Problems Algebra*

Solve for each variable.

30. $\frac{n}{16} = \frac{75}{80}$ 15

31. $\frac{g}{8} = \frac{72}{64}$ 9

32. $\frac{13}{11} = \frac{p}{65}$ 76.8

33. $\frac{5}{7}a = -35$ −49

34. $3\frac{1}{2}t = 5\frac{1}{4}$ $1\frac{1}{2}$

35. $\frac{7}{8}x - \frac{3}{4}x = 15$ 120

36. $\frac{3}{2}d = -9$ −6

37. $\frac{(2c - 6)}{3} = 7$ 13.5

38. $\frac{2(r - 4)}{5} = -3$ $-3\frac{1}{2}$

39. $\frac{1}{2} + \frac{9}{16} = \frac{n}{4}$ $4\frac{1}{4}$

40. $\frac{3}{8} - \frac{5}{8} = \frac{q}{3}$ $-\frac{3}{4}$

Solve these problems. Make sure your answers are in lowest terms.

41. Gloria received four-fifths of the election votes. 385 students voted. How many votes did Gloria receive?

42. The Washington High School football team's winning ratio is 4 to 3. They won 12 games. How many games did they lose?

43. George has $\frac{3}{4}$ pounds of raspberries. Each jelly recipe needs $\frac{3}{16}$ pounds of raspberries. How many recipes can he make?

44. The scale drawing of Jefferson Park reads 2 cm : 7 km. The width of the park is $3\frac{9}{10}$ cm. How many kilometers wide is the park?

45. Jenny's survey reveals that $\frac{5}{8}$ of the students at Washington High School watch $2\frac{1}{2}$ hours of television on Friday night. There are 648 students at the high school. How many hours of television do they watch altogether on Friday night?

41. 308 votes

42. 9 games

43. 4 jelly recipes

44. $13\frac{13}{20}$ km

45. $1{,}012\frac{1}{2}$ hours of television

Algebra Supplementary Problems **421**

Chapter 9 Supplementary Problems

Write the ordered pair that represents the location of each point.

1. Point B $(4, 0)$

2. Point D $(-3, -1)$

3. Point A $(-2, 4)$

4. Point E $(0, -3)$

5. Point C $(1, -1)$

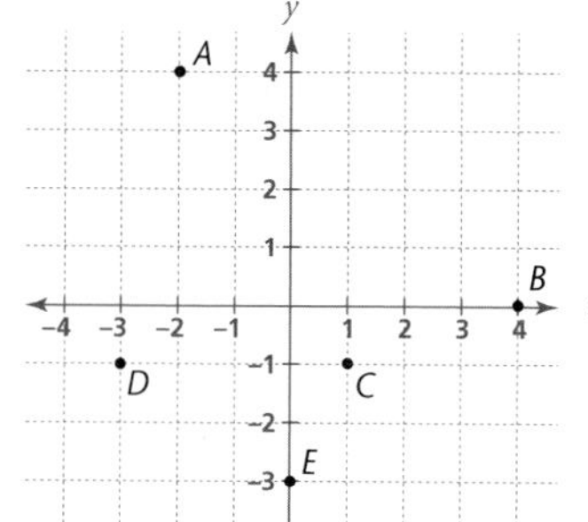

Draw a coordinate system and graph the following points.

6. Point X at $(2, -1)$

7. Point V at $(-4, 1)$

8. Point S at $(0, 4)$

9. Point M at $(-3, -5)$

See page 458 for answers to problems 6–9.

Copy and complete the table of values for each equation.

10.

$y = x - 2$	
x	**y**
−1	−3
0	−2
1	−1

11.

$y = 3x + 1$	
x	**y**
−1	−2
0	1
1	4

Find the x-intercept and the y-intercept of each graph.

12. $y = x + 1$ x-intercept $= (-1, 0)$; y-intercept $= (0, 1)$

13. $y = x - 4$ x-intercept $= (4, 0)$; y-intercept $= (0, -4)$

14. $y = -2x + 3$ x-intercept $= (\frac{3}{2}, 0)$; y-intercept $= (0, 3)$

15. $y = 5x - 2$ x-intercept $= (\frac{2}{5}, 0)$; y-intercept $= (0, -2)$

Find the slope of the line that passes through the following points.

16. $(3, 6)(-2, -4)$ $m = 2$

17. $(2, 5)(-1, -4)$ $m = 3$

18. $(0, 2)(-6, 8)$ $m = -1$

19. $(2, -2)(1, -3)$ $m = 1$

422 *Supplementary Problems Algebra*

Graph the line that passes through the following points. Then write the equation of each line.

20. $(0, -3)(2, -1)$

21. $(5, -3)(-1, 3)$

See page 459 for answers to problems 20–23.

22. $(4, 3)(-2, 0)$

23. $(0, 0)(-2, 4)$

Write the equation of the line that has the given slope and passes through the given point.

24. $m = 3; (2, 7)$ $y = 3x + 1$

25. $m = -1; (4, -5)$ $y = -x - 1$

26. $m = 4; (3, 8)$ $y = 4x - 4$

27. $m = \frac{1}{2}; (-4, -1)$ $y = \frac{1}{2}x + 1$

Is each graph an example of a function? Write *yes* or *no.*

28.

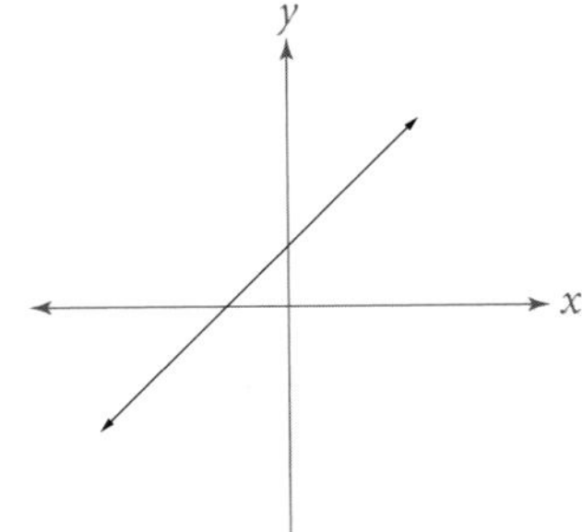

yes

29.

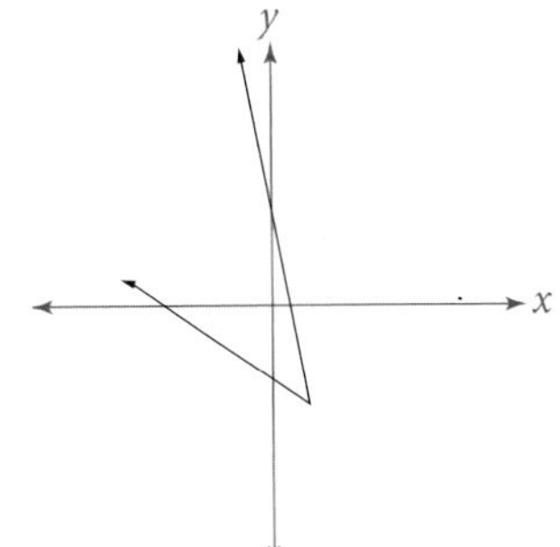

no

Evaluate each function two times. Use $x = 3$ and $x = -2$.

30. $f(x) = -x^2 + x$
$-6; -6$

31. $f(x) = 2x^2 + x$
$21; 6$

32. $f(x) = x^2 + 2x$
$15; 0$

Graph the region represented by each line.

33. $y > -3x$

34. $y \leq x - 3$

35. $y < x - 1$

See pages 459–460 for answers to problems 33–35.

Algebra Supplementary Problems **423**

Chapter 10 Supplementary Problems

Write the equation of the line parallel to the given line and passing through the given point. Check your answer by graphing the lines.

1. $y = 3x - 2; (3, 9)$ $y = 3x$
2. $y = x + 4; (2, 2)$ $y = x - 4$
3. $2y = 8x - 8; (1, 6)$ $y = 4x + 2$
4. $y - 5 = -2x; (0, 0)$ $y = -2x$
5. $2y = x - 4; (6, 5)$ $y = \frac{x}{2} + 2$
6. $8x - 2y = -10; (2, 5)$ $y = 4x + 5$
7. $3y - 3x = 18; (3, -5)$ $y = x - 8$
8. $6x = -2y + 16; (0, 1)$ $y = -3x + 1$
9. $2y + 16 = 6x; (1, 7)$ $y = 3x + 4$
10. $4y - 8x = -12; (2, 5)$ $y = 2x + 1$

See pages 460–461 for graphs of problems 1–10.

Find a common solution for the systems that have one.
Write *none* if the system does not have a common solution.

11. $y = 3x - 2$; $y = x + 4$ (3, 7)
12. $y = 5x - 3$; $9x + 3 = 3y$ (2, 7)
13. $2y = x + 2$; $3y = x + 6$ (6, 4)
14. $-4x = -y - 3$; $-2x = -y - 5$ (−1, −7)
15. $y = 4x + 6$; $y - 3x = 4$ (−2, −2)
16. $y + 2x = -1$; $y + x = 3$ (−4, 7)
17. $y - x = -7$; $y = 3x - 11$ (2, −5)
18. $2x = y - 5$; $2y = 4x - 14$ none
19. $5y - 5x = -5$; $y = 2x - 5$ (4, 3)
20. $2y + x = 4$; $y + 12 = 3x$ (4, 0)

Graph each system of equations on the same set of axes. Name the point of intersection.

See pages 461–462 for answers to problems 21–23.

21. $y = x + 1$; $y = 2x - 1$
22. $y = 3x + 1$; $y = x + 3$
23. $y = 3x$; $y = x + 4$

424 *Supplementary Problems Algebra*

Tell whether the following conjunctions are true or false. Explain.

24. All intersecting lines have the same slope, and all vertical lines have slopes that are equal to zero.
False, all parallel lines have the same slope

25. Subtracting four is the same as adding negative four, and 2 is the same as $\frac{22}{11}$. True

26. $3(6b + 2) = 18b + 2$, and the reciprocal of $\frac{3}{8}$ is $\frac{8}{3}$.
False, $3(6b + 2) = 18b + 3$

27. There are 12 eggs in a dozen, and there are 169 eggs in 12 dozen.
False, there are 144 eggs in 12 dozen

Graph each four-sided figure. Write the equations of the lines that form the figure.

28. A square with the vertices at (2, 3), (4, 1), (2, 1), (4, 3)

29. A square with the vertices at (1, 4), (2, 5), (1, 5), (2, 4)

30. A rectangle with the vertices at (3, –2), (–5, 4), (3, 4), (–5, –2)

See page 462 for answers to problems 28–30.

Set up and solve a system of equations to answer the questions.

31. One number is 36 more than the second number. Seven times the smaller number is the larger number. What are the numbers? The numbers are 6 and 42.

32. The difference between two supplementary angles is 130 degrees. What are the angles? (Supplementary angles are two angles whose sum equals 180 degrees.) 25 degrees and 155 degrees

33. The difference between two supplementary angles is 20 degrees. What are the angles?
80 degrees and 100 degrees

34. Two angles are complementary. The larger angle is eight times the smaller angle. What are the angles? (Complementary angles are two angles whose sum equals 90 degrees.)
10 degrees and 80 degrees

35. The perimeter of a rectangle is 300 feet. The width of the rectangle is 10 feet more than the length. What are the length and width of the rectangle?

length = 70 feet; width = 80 feet

Algebra Supplementary Problems **425**

Chapter 11 Supplementary Problems

Write the decimal expansions for these rational numbers. Tell whether the expansions are terminating or repeating.

1. $\frac{7}{8}$ $0.875\overline{0}$, terminating

2. $\frac{2}{3}$ $0.\overline{6}$, repeating

3. $\frac{1}{16}$ $0.625\overline{0}$, terminating

4. $\frac{4}{11}$ $0.\overline{36}$, repeating

5. $\frac{5}{8}$ $0.625\overline{0}$. terminating

Find the rational number equivalents for these decimal expansions. Be sure your answer is in lowest terms.

6. $0.6\overline{0}$ $\frac{3}{5}$

7. $0.8\overline{3}$ $\frac{5}{6}$

8. $0.9375\overline{0}$ $\frac{15}{16}$

9. $0.15625\overline{0}$ $\frac{5}{32}$

10. $0.\overline{2}$ $\frac{2}{9}$

Use your calculator to find the roots for these radicals. Tell whether they are rational or irrational.

11. $\sqrt[8]{6{,}561}$ 3; rational

12. $\sqrt[7]{1{,}024}$ 2.6918004; irrational

13. $\sqrt[5]{243}$ 3; rational

14. $\sqrt[3]{900}$ 9.6548938; irrational

15. $\sqrt[4]{2{,}100}$ 6.7694724; irrational

Simplify the following radicals. Be sure to check your answers.

16. $\sqrt{1{,}296}$ 36

17. $\sqrt{2{,}704x^6y^2}$ $52x^3y$

18. $\sqrt{\frac{64}{81}}$ $\frac{8}{9}$

19. $\sqrt{\frac{25g^4}{36a^2}}$ $\frac{5g^2}{6a}$

20. $\sqrt{\frac{49t^6}{121b^8}}$ $\frac{7t^3}{11b^4}$

Simplify, then add or subtract.

21. $\sqrt{100} + \sqrt{25}$ 15

22. $3\sqrt{18} - 3\sqrt{2}$ $6\sqrt{2}$

23. $2\sqrt{75} + 8\sqrt{3}$ $18\sqrt{3}$

24. $4\sqrt{48} - 4\sqrt{27}$ $4\sqrt{3}$

25. $2\sqrt{12x^2} + \sqrt{48x^2}$ $8x\sqrt{3}$

426 *Supplementary Problems Algebra*

Rationalize or conjugate the denominator of each fraction. Be sure your answer is in simplest form.

26. $3\frac{\sqrt{2}}{\sqrt{5}}$ $3\sqrt{\frac{10}{5}}$

27. $\frac{6\sqrt{28}}{2\sqrt{7}}$ 6

28. $\frac{5\sqrt{35}}{2\sqrt{7}}$ $\frac{5\sqrt{5}}{2}$

29. $\frac{2}{(2+\sqrt{3})}$ $(4-2\sqrt{3})$

30. $\frac{2\sqrt{5}}{(4+\sqrt{5})}$ $\frac{8\sqrt{5}-10}{11}$

Solve each equation for the unknown.

31. $\sqrt{n} = 64$ 8

32. $\sqrt{2x} = 4$ 8

33. $\sqrt{c} = \frac{5}{6}$ $\frac{25}{36}$

34. $\sqrt{x} + 4 = 10$ 36

35. $25 - \sqrt{y} = 8$ 289

Simplify using exponents, then find the products.

36. $y^3 \cdot \sqrt[5]{y}$ $y^{3\frac{1}{5}}$

37. $m \cdot \sqrt{m}$ $m^{1\frac{1}{2}}$

38. $\sqrt[3]{w} \cdot w^3$ w

39. $q^5 \cdot \sqrt[4]{q}$ $q^{5\frac{1}{4}}$

40. $d^3 \cdot \sqrt[7]{d}$ $d^{3\frac{1}{7}}$

Algebra Supplementary Problems **427**

Chapter 12 Supplementary Problems

Classify each angle or pairs of angles. Write *acute, right, obtuse, straight, adjacent, complementary, supplementary, interior, exterior, alternate interior, vertical,* or *corresponding*. For any angle or pair of angles, more than one name may apply. Line $x \parallel y$.

1. $\angle i$ obtuse and interior

2. $\angle n$ right and exterior

3. $\angle b$ and $\angle i$ alternate interior and obtuse

4. $\angle c$ and $\angle e$ right and corresponding

5. $\angle k$ and $\angle f$ supplementary and exterior

6. $\angle h$ and $\angle j$ acute and vertical

7. $\angle p$ and $\angle o$ supplementary and interior

8. $\angle a$ and $\angle b$ obtuse and corresponding

9. $\angle d$ and $\angle n$ right and corresponding

10. $\angle h$ and $\angle k$ acute and exterior

In this figure, line $a \parallel$ line b, c is the transversal, and measure of angle $x = 65.7°$. Find the measure (m) of each of the following angles.

11. $m\angle w$ 65.7°

12. $m\angle t$ 65.7°

13. $m\angle y$ 114.3°

14. $m\angle s$ 114.3°

15. $m\angle u$ 114.3°

16. $m\angle v$ 65.7°

17. $m\angle z$ 114.3°

In each triangle, find m$\angle x$.

18. 62°

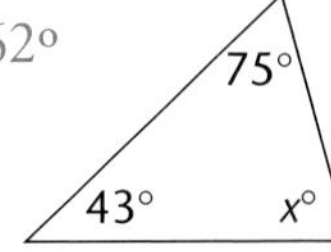

20. 45°

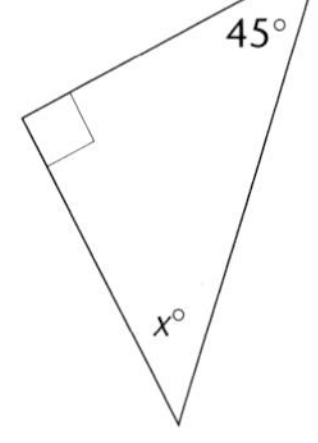

22. 60°

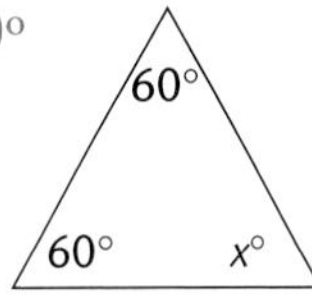

19. 76°

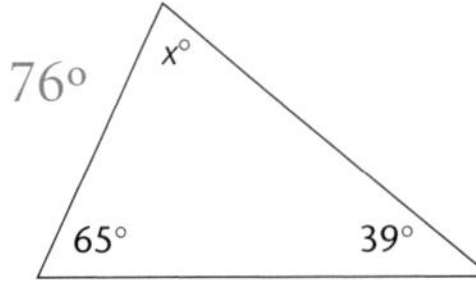

21. 72°

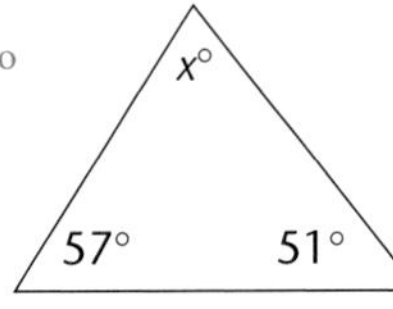

Name the theorem that proves congruence.

23. SSS

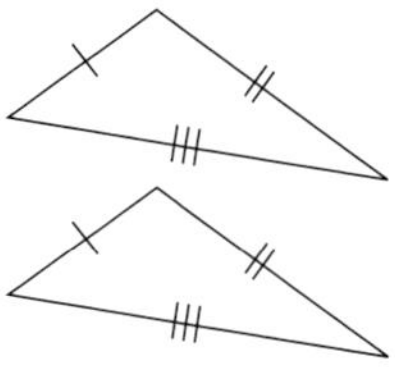

24. SAS

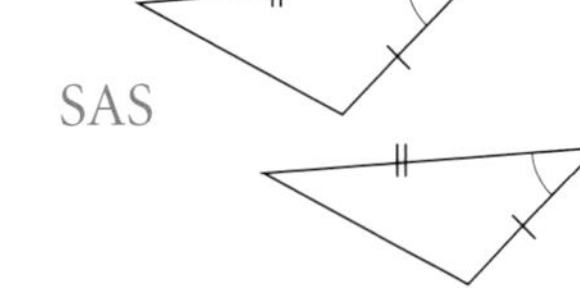

25. ASA

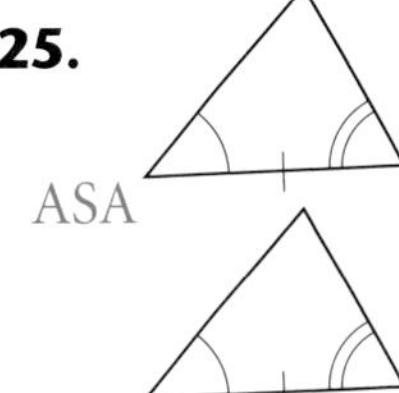

Use your calculator to find the following values.

26. tan 45° 1

27. sin 90° 1

28. cos 60° 0.5

29. cos 90° 0

30. sin 30° 0.5

31. Mildred stands 45 feet from a tree to measure the angle to the top of the tree. The angle measures 65°. How tall is the tree to the nearest foot? 97 feet

32. A 25-foot guy wire is attached to the top of a telephone pole. The guy wire forms a 45° angle with the ground. How tall is the telephone pole to the nearest foot? 18 feet

33. On a particular day, when the sun was setting, it caused the Bryan Library to cast a shadow at an angle of 32° The shadow was 100 feet long. How tall is the Bryan Library to the nearest foot? 62 feet

34. Angle A of a right triangle is 38°. The hypotenuse is 6 feet. What is the length of the opposite side to the nearest tenth? 3.7 feet

35. Angle A of a right triangle is 52°. The hypotenuse is 41 meters. What is the length of the adjacent side to the nearest tenth? 25.2 meters

Algebra Supplementary Problems **429**

Chapter 13 Supplementary Problems

Find the roots of these quadratic equations by factoring.

1. $x^2 - 10x = -21$ $\quad x = 7, x = 3$

2. $x^2 - x - 30 = 0$ $\quad x = 6, x = -5$

3. $2x^2 + 4x = 0$ $\quad x = 0, x = -2$

4. $x^2 + 11x + 24 = 0$ $\quad x = -3, x = -8$

5. $5x^2 - 9x = 2$ $\quad x = -\frac{1}{5}, x = 2$

6. $x^2 - 16x + 55 = 0$ $\quad x = 5, x = 11$

Find the equations for these roots.

7. $-4, 3$ $\quad x^2 + x - 12$

8. $6, 7$ $\quad x^2 - 13x + 42$

9. $8, -2$ $\quad x^2 - 6x - 16$

10. $\frac{1}{2}, 3$ $\quad 2x^2 - 7x + 3$

11. $4, -\frac{2}{3}$ $\quad 3x^2 - 10x - 8$

12. $1, -6$ $\quad x^2 + 5x - 6$

Solve these equations by completing the square.

13. $m^2 + 6m + 2 = 0$ $\quad m = -3 + \sqrt{7}$ or $-3 - \sqrt{7}$

14. $c^2 + 8c - 10 = 0$ $\quad c = -4 + \sqrt{26}$ or $-4 - \sqrt{26}$

15. $v^2 + 4v - 11 = 0$ $\quad v = -2 + \sqrt{15}$ or $-2 - \sqrt{15}$

16. $x^2 - 14x = -10$ $\quad x = 7 + \sqrt{39}$ or $7 - \sqrt{39}$

17. $4d^2 + 8d = 2$ $\quad d = -1 + \sqrt{\frac{3}{2}}$ or $-1 - \sqrt{\frac{3}{2}}$

18. $y^2 - 10y = -20$ $\quad y = 5 + \sqrt{5}$ or $5 - \sqrt{5}$

430 *Supplementary Problems Algebra*

Use the quadratic formula to find the roots to these equations. Check your answers.

19. $2x^2 + 7x - 4 = 0$ $x = -4$ or $x = \frac{1}{2}$

20. $y^2 + 14y + 33 = 0$ $y = -3$ or $y = -11$

21. $2x^2 + 3x - 2 = 0$ $x = -2$ or $x = \frac{1}{2}$

22. $y^2 + 6y - 16 = 0$ $y = -8$ or $y = 2$

23. $y^2 - 2y - 15 = 0$ $y = -3$ or $y = 5$

24. $2x^2 - 11x + 14 = 0$ $x = \frac{7}{2}$ or $x = 2$

Find the axis of symmetry and the roots for these equations. Then graph the equation.

25. $y = x^2 + 6x + 8$ $x = -3, (-4, 0), (-2, 0)$

26. $y = 2x^2 - 5x - 3$ $x = \frac{5}{4}, (-\frac{1}{2}, 0), (3, 0)$

27. $y = -x^2 + 10x - 24$ $x = 5, (4, 0), (6, 0)$

28. $y = x^2 - 12x + 27$ $x = 6, (3, 0), (9, 0)$

29. $y = x^2 + x - 2$ $x = -\frac{1}{2}, (-2, 0), (1, 0)$

30. $y = 2x^2 + 5x + 3$ $x = -\frac{5}{4}, (-\frac{3}{2}, 0), (-1, 0)$

Answer these questions.

31. The product of two consecutive positive integers is 182. What are the integers? 13,14

32. The product of two consecutive odd integers is 255. What are the integers? 15, 17 or −15, −17

33. The product of two consecutive even integers is 288. What are the integers? 16, 18 or −16, −18

34. The product of two sisters' ages is 72. They are one year apart. How old are they? 8 and 9 years old

35. Trixie is 8 years older than her brother. The product of their ages is 33. How old is Trixie? How old is her brother? Trixie is 11 years old. Her brother is 3 years old.

Algebra Supplementary Problems **431**

Selected Answers and Solutions

CHAPTER 1

Lesson 1, page 3

1. 12 = 12 true **3.** 12 = 12 true **5.** 7 = 8 false **7.** 24 = 22 false **9.** 36 = 36 true **11.** true **13.** false **15.** true **17.** open **19.** true **21.** 7 = 10 false **23.** 10 = 10 true **25.** 45 = 40 false **27.** 2 = 4 false **29.** 4 = 4 true

Lesson 2, pages 4–5

1. algebraic because it includes a variable and an operation, division **3.** algebraic, addition **5.** numerical, subtraction **7.** algebraic, addition and multiplication **9.** algebraic, multiplication and multiplication **11.** d, the value of d is unknown **13.** e **15.** k **17.** y **19.** n **21.** multiplication, $2x$ means 2 times some unknown number x **23.** multiplication and subtraction **25.** multiplication and division **27.** multiplication **29.** multiplication **31.** numerical because it contains only numbers, addition **33.** algebraic, multiplication, x **35.** algebraic, multiplication and addition, y **37.** numerical, multiplication **39.** algebraic, multiplication and addition, m **41.** 3 • 7, there are seven days in one week **43.** 3 + 18 **45.** 3 • n

Lesson 3, page 7

1. −4; on a number line, −4 and 4 are the same distance from zero **3.** −6 **5.** −11 **7.** 24 **9.** −9 **11.** 2, the distance of −2 from 0 is 2 **13.** 4 **15.** 6 **17.** 3 **19.** 8 **21.** +15 yards, −8 yards; a gain is + and a loss is − ; the team is 7 yards from where it started. **23.** 4° warmer **25.** Use a number line to indicate the time.

Try This

Answers will vary. Sample answer: −2 because a countdown usually begins with a negative real number and ends at zero.

Lesson 4, page 9

1. 5 + 8 = 13 **3.** 4 **5.** −8 **7.** −2 **9.** −4 **11.** −6 **13.** −4 **15.** 0 **16.** −5°F + 4°F = −1°F **17.** −2°F **19.** 0°F **21.** 8°F **23.** 10°F **25.** −5°C + (−5°C) = −5°C − 5°C = −10°C **27.** 6°C **29.** −11°C **31.** −170 **33.** 231 **35.** −493

Lesson 5, page 11

1. 5 + −4; 1 **3.** −5 + 6; 1 **5.** −7 + −5; −12 **7.** −3 + 10; 7 **9.** 8 + 1; 9 **11.** −6 + −2; −8 **13.** 9 + −6 = 3 **15.** 8 + 8 = 16 **17.** 12 + 3 = 15 **19.** 7 + −9 = −2 **21.** 3 + −6 = −3 **23.** 5 + −8 = −3 **25.** 6 + 9 = 15 **27.** 8 + −2 = 6 **28.** 153°F, add the absolute value of each number **29.** 18°F

Lesson 6, page 13

1. 56, (positive) • (positive) = (positive) **3.** −30 **5.** 81 **7.** 60 **9.** −60 **11.** 63 **13.** 24 **15.** 30 **17.** −50 **19.** −20 **21.** positive, (negative) • (negative) = (positive) **23.** positive **25.** zero **27.** positive **29.** 12 feet, (4)(3) = 12

432 *Selected Answers and Solutions Algebra*

Lesson 7, page 15
1. 7, (positive) ÷ (positive) = (positive) **3.** −4 **5.** 9 **7.** 6 **9.** –8 **11.** 0 **13.** 10 **15.** 7 **17.** 8 **19.** 3 **21.** negative, (positive) ÷ (negative) = (negative) **23.** negative **25.** positive **27.** negative **29.** +, (positive) ÷ (positive) = (positive)

Lesson 8, pages 16–17
1. $2m$, $1m + 1m = 2m$ **3.** $3v$ **5.** $4c$ **6.** $3m$, $2m + 1m = 3m$ **7.** $10h$ **9.** $8k$ **11.** $5p + 8p + 6 = 13p + 6$ **13.** $10y - 4$ **15.** $9 + 4c$ **17.** $6q - 2q - 3 = 4q - 3$ **19.** $20v + 9v + 9 = 29v + 9$ **21.** $-5g$ **23.** $-12m$ **25.** $28x$ **27.** $2r - 18r + 18 = -16r + 18$ **29.** $15u - 17u - 18 = -2u - 18$ **31.** $9c$, $1c + 9c = 10c$ **33.** $-6e$ **35.** $-10z$ **36.** $4x + 20$, a sum is the result of addition **37.** $2n - 30$ or $30 - 2n$ **39.** $4p - 3$

Lesson 9, pages 18–19
1. $8x + 4 + 7b$, the like terms are $5x$ and $3x$ **3.** $16 + 2a + 9u$ **5.** $7y + 17y + 10p + 10p + 18 = 24y + 20p + 18$ **7.** $m + 2m + 10 + 7t = 3m + 10 + 7t$ **9.** $8w - 4w - 13 + y = 4w - 13 + y$ **11.** $8u - 4u + 7b + 2b + 17 = 4u + 9b + 17$ **13.** $9g - 7g + 2 + 15 + 16r - 13r = 2g + 17 + 3r$ **15.** $3m - m + 7y - 6y + 5 = 2m + y + 5$ **16.** $-9t - 14 + (-5c)$ or $-9t - 14 - 5c$, the like terms are $7t$ and $-16t$, and $9c$ and $-14c$ **17.** $8 + (-16c) + (-16b)$ or $8 - 16c - 16b$ **19.** $3x + 3x + (-17) + 21f - (-21f) = 6x + (-17) + 42f$ **21.** $y - 2y - 14 + 30c + 16c = -y - 14 + 46c$ **23.** $40j + (-32m) + 16$ or $40j - 32m + 16$ **25.** $9m - 6m + 14 + 4r + 12r = 3m - 14 + 16r$ **26.** false, the expression simplifies to $-2m + 15c - 4$ **27.** false, $44x + 9 + 6m$ **29.** false, $7 + 6y + 8m$

Lesson 10, page 21
1. true, $23 = 2 \cdot 2 \cdot 2 = 8$ **3.** false, m^7 **5.** true **7.** true **9.** false, a^{20} **11.** $w^{8+7} = w^{15}$ **13.** $b^2 + 1 = b^3$ **15.** $v^7 + 7 = v^{14}$ **17.** $d^{4+3+1} = d^8$ **19.** $t^{1+8+10} = t^{19}$ **21.** $x^{3+1+5+4} = x^{13}$ **23.** $g^{14-3} = g^{11}$ **25.** $v^{2+2+8+7} = v^{19}$ **26.** 4 **27.** $4 + 3 = 7$ **29.** $1 + 2 = 3$ **31.** $12 - 6 = 6$ **33.** 3 **35.** 15 **36.** 390,625 **37.** 16.81 **39.** 0.0001

Lesson 11, pages 22–25
1. $P = s + s + s + s$, $P = 4s$ **3.** 40 m **5.** $P = a + b + c$ **7.** 90 cm **9.** $P = l + w + l + w$ or $P = 2l + 2w$ **11.** 38 cm **13.** $P = s + s + s + s + s$, $P = 5s$ **15.** 40 cm **17.** $P = s + s + s + s = 4s$ **19.** 32 km **21.** square **22.** $P = s + s + s + s + s + s$, $P = 6s$ **23.** 60 mm **25.** 12 m

Chapter 1 Application, page 26
1. 175 mph − 53 mph = 122 mph **3.** 155 mph + 15 mph = 170 mph **5.** 305 mph − 41 mph = 264 mph

Chapter 1 Review, pages 27–29
1. 2 **3.** 5 **5.** a^9b^6 **7.** algebraic expression **9.** algebraic expression **11.** numerical expression **13.** 3 **15.** 14 **17.** −4; +4 and −4 are the same distance from zero **19.** 1.5 **21.** $-\frac{3}{4}$ **23.** 28 **25.** 8 **27.** −1 **29.** −5 **31.** −60 **33.** 0 **35.** −10 **37.** 0 **39.** $-5y + 15$ **41.** $-2.2k$ **43.** $-22v + 8r$ **45.** n^8 **47.** e^5g^5 **49.** n^6 **51.** j^6 **53.** 45 km **55.** 16 m

Algebra *Selected Answers and Solutions* **433**

CHAPTER 2

Lesson 1, page 33

1. 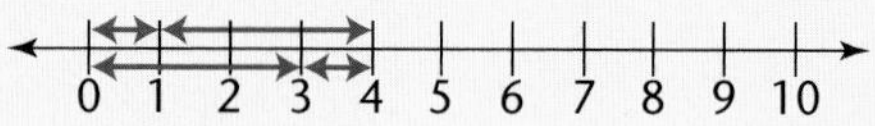 0 1 2 3 4 5 6 7 8 9 10

3. 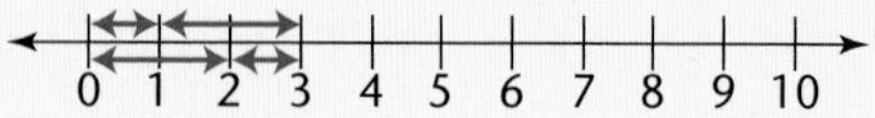 0 1 2 3 4 5 6 7 8 9 10

5. 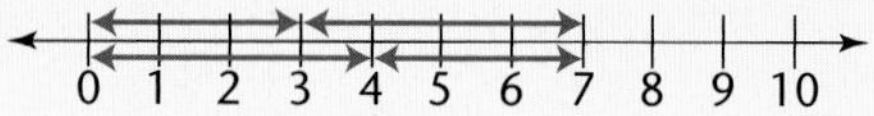 0 1 2 3 4 5 6 7 8 9 10

7. 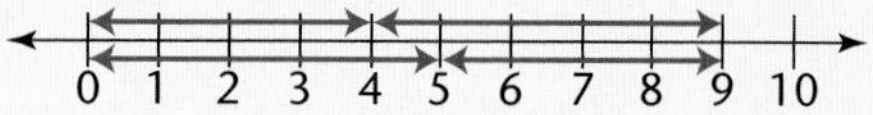 0 1 2 3 4 5 6 7 8 9 10

9. 0 1 2 3 4 5 6 7 8 9 10

11. $x + x + x + x + x + x = 6x$ **13.** $t + t + t + t + t + t = 6t$ **15.** $m + m + m + m + m + m + m = 7m$ **17.** $y + y + y = 3y$ **19.** $3 + a$ **21.** $y + x$ **23.** $8g + 5g$ **25.** $7r + 4r$ **27.** $y + 2x$ **29.** $7p + 6p$ **31.** $2q + 16q$ **33.** $10 + x$ **35.** $y + 5y$

Lesson 2, page 35

1. 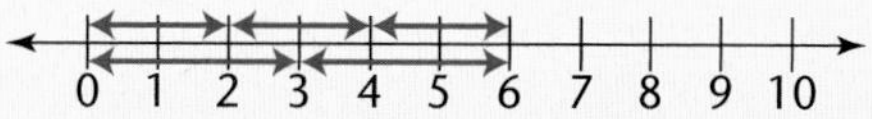 0 1 2 3 4 5 6 7 8 9 10

3.  0 1 2 3 4 5 6 7 8 9 10 11 12 13 14 15

5. 0 1 2 3 4 5 6 7 8 9 10

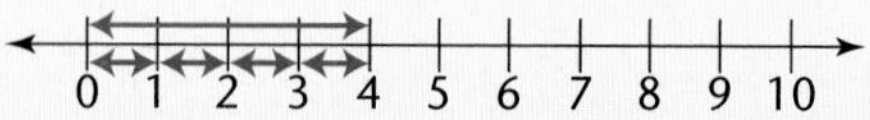

7. Factors: 5 and 3. Product: $5 \cdot 3 = 15$. **9.** Factors: 3 and 2. Product: $3 \cdot 2 = 6$. **11.** ba **13.** wz **15.** $(2)(3z)$ **17.** $(9w)h$ **19.** yes; because the pizza contains all three ingredients, the order of the ingredients is not important **21.** yes **23.** no **25.** no

Lesson 3, page 37

1. $25 = 25$; $(4 + 6) + 15 = (10) + 15 = 25$; $4 + (6 + 15) = 4 + (21) = 25$ **3.** $27 = 27$ **5.** $37 = 37$ **7.** $63 = 63$ **9.** $72 = 72$ **11.** $(x + y) + z = x + (y + z)$; the associative property of addition is used to group sums in different ways **13.** $(g + h) + j = g + (h + j)$ **15.** $(w + 4c) + p = w + (4c + p)$ **17.** $(4f + 9y) + 2x = 4f + (9y + 2x)$ **19.** $(21k + 13u) + 16s = 21k + (13u + 16s)$ **21.** $(3 + 6) + z$; the associative property of addition is used to group sums in different ways **23.** $(2b + 3c) + 8$ **25.** $5s + (3d + 28)$

Try This

No. The order of the numbers cannot be changed in subtraction without changing the result.

Lesson 4, pages 39–41

1. $300 = 300$; $(3 \cdot 5)20 = (15)20 = 300$; $3(5 \cdot 20) = 3(100) = 300$ **3.** $260 = 260$ **5.** $135 = 135$ **7.** $170 = 170$ **9.** $400 = 400$ For problems 11 and 13, other answers are possible. **11.** $(3 \cdot 5)4 = 60$ cubic units and $3(5 \cdot 4) = 60$ cubic units **13.** $(7 \cdot 4)3 = 84$ cubic units and $7(4 \cdot 3) = 84$ cubic units **15.** $(1w)h = 1(wh)$; the associative property of multiplication is used to group factors in different ways **17.** $(fp)n = f(pn)$ **19.** $(mk)s = m(ks)$

Lesson 5, page 43

1. 10; 5; the 4 outside the parentheses is distributed using multiplication to each number inside the parentheses **3.** b; 14 **5.** 6; 7 **7.** 29; n **9.** $4a + 4b$; the 4 outside the parentheses is distributed using multiplication to each variable inside the

434 *Selected Answers and Solutions Algebra*

parentheses **11.** $-2d + -2k$ **13.** $-4a + -4b$ **15.** $9v + -81$ **17.** $8z + 32$ **19.** $-3x + -12$ **20.** 77; $7(6 + 5) = 7(6) + 7(5) = 42 + 35 = 77$ square units **21.** $10(5) + 10(4) = 90$ square units **23.** $n(8) + n(4) = 12n$ square units **25.** $x(y) + x(z) = xy + xz$ square units

Lesson 6, page 45

1. a is the common factor; it is common to both $2a$ and $3a$ **3.** x **5.** $2b$ **7.** $-z$ **9.** a **11.** $4(x + y)$; 4 is the common factor **13.** $3(j - p)$ **15.** $6(y + z)$ **17.** $-4(m + y)$ **19.** $a(x - y)$ **21.** $a(-s + j)$ **23.** $-u(v + m)$ **25.** $b(x^2 + y^2)$ **27.** $w(x^4 + m^2)$ **29.** $9(b + c)$; 9 is the common factor of $9b$ and $9c$

Lesson 7, page 47

1. 3 **3.** x^2 **5.** 5 **7.** $-a$ **9.** 0; the product of any number and zero is zero **11.** 0 **13.** 0 **14.** Possible answer: They are opposites. **15.** $5°F - (-5°F) = 10°F$

Lesson 8, page 49

1. $\frac{5}{5}, \frac{1}{2} \cdot \frac{5}{5} = \frac{5}{10}$ **3.** $\frac{2}{2}$ **5.** $\frac{4}{4}$ **7.** $\frac{k}{k}$ **9.** $\frac{3}{3}$ **11.** 3; $(\frac{1}{3})(\frac{3}{1}) = 1$; the product of any nonzero number and its reciprocal is 1 **13.** $\frac{1}{c}$; $(c)(\frac{1}{c}) = 1$ **15.** $\frac{1}{n^2}$; $(n^2)(\frac{1}{n^2}) = 1$ **17.** d; $(\frac{1}{d})(d) = 1$ **19.** 4 ; $4(\frac{1}{4}) = 1$

Lesson 9, pages 52–53

1. $\sqrt{36} = 6$; $62 = 36$ **3.** $3 < \sqrt{15} < 4$; $\sqrt{15}$ is between $\sqrt{9}$, which is 3, and $\sqrt{16}$, which is 4 **5.** $2 < \sqrt{7} < 3$ **7.** $9 < \sqrt{83} < 10$ **9.** 25.6 **11.** 1.75

Lesson 10, page 55

1. 7 and -7; $(7)^2 = 49$ and $(-7)^2 = 49$ **3.** b^3 or $-b^3$ **5.** -2 **7.** $-x^2$ **9.** 8 and -8; $\sqrt{64} = +8$ and -8 **11.** 2 and -2 **13.** 4 and -4 **15.** $-125x^3$ **17.** $256m^4$ **19.** $256w^2$ **21.** $-243n^5$ **23.** $729v^6$ **25.** $1{,}296a^4$

Lesson 11, page 57

1. -7; multiply first, then subtract **3.** $5 + 4 = 9$ **5.** $2 \cdot 2 = 4$ **7.** $-39 + -3 = -42$ **9.** $10 - 30 = -20$ **11.** $8 + 3 = 11$ **13.** $4c$; multiply first, then subtract **15.** $8k + 6k + 12k = 26k$ **17.** $25y + (-18y) = 7y$ **19.** $4b^2 + 3b^2 = 7b^2$ **21.** $5z^2 - z^2 = 4z^2$ **23.** 2($10) + $5 − $5 = $20 profit; profit = money earned − cost **25.** $5.00 + 3($8.00) = $29.00

Chapter 2 Application, page 58

1. 10 blocks; $\sqrt{100} = 10$ **3.** 18 blocks **5.** 32 blocks

Chapter 2 Review, pages 59–61

1. $(3y)(5n)$ **3.** 140 **5.** 49 **7.** $37n$ **9.** $b + 3x$ **11.** $8a + 14g$ For problems 13–17, other answers are possible: **13.** $h + (t + s)$ **15.** $2m + (6n + s)$ **17.** $4b + (x + 2)$ **19.** $100 = 100$ **21.** $6m + 6n$ **23.** $-2x + 2z$ **25.** $-7h + -7p$ **27.** $5(n + s)$ **29.** $b(2 + 3)$ **31.** -8 **33.** $-w$ **35.** 5 **37.** 8 **39.** c **41.** 8 and -8 **43.** 216 **45.** $-27y^3$ **47.** $16m^4$ **49.** $49j^2$

Algebra Selected Answers and Solutions 435

CHAPTER 3

Lesson 1, pages 64–65

1. $9x = 36$; represent an unknown such as "some number" with a variable such as x **3.** $9x - 18 = 0$ **5.** $5x + 3 = 28$ **7.** $3x = 27$ **9.** $10x - 13 = 47$ **11.** $x - 6 = 25$ **13.** $x - 4 = 10$ **15.** $2(5) = 14$ F, $2(6) = 14$ F, $2(7) = 14$ T, $2(8) =$ F **17.** F, F, F, T **19.** F, F, T, F **21.** T, F, F, F **23.** T, F, F, F **25.** F, F, T, F

Try This

Methods will vary; $y = 39$

Lesson 2, page 67

1. $x = 16$; add 7 to both sides of the equation; $x + 7 = 9 + 7$ **3.** 11 **5.** 23 **7.** 37 **9.** 47 **11.** 55 **13.** 92 **15.** $m = 7$; rewrite the equation as $m + (+2) = 9$, then subtract 2 from both sides **17.** 0 **19.** −6 **21.** $x = \$9.50$; solve the equation $x - \$4.50 = \$5.00$ **23.** \$21.33 **25.** \$6.24

Lesson 3, page 69

1. $x = 6$; subtract 4 from both sides of the equation **3.** 3 **5.** 5 **7.** 13 **9.** 14 **11.** 9 **13.** 0 **15.** 7 **17.** 2.4 **19.** 4.4 **21.** $c = 12$; add +3 to each side of the equation **23.** 14 **25.** 45 **27.** \$8.77; \$13.99 − \$5.22 = \$8.77 **29.** \$72.00

Lesson 4, page 71

1. $x = 5$; divide both sides of the equation by 5 **3.** 4 **5.** 10 **7.** 9 **9.** 2 **11.** 2 **13.** 4 **15.** 6 **17.** −50 **19.** 6 **21.** −2 **23.** 9 **25.** −11 **27.** $x = 4$; write the equation $13x = 52$, then divide each side by 13 **29.** $-6g = 66$; $g = -11$

Lesson 5, page 73

1. $x = 6$; multiply each side by $\frac{2}{1}$, the reciprocal of $\frac{1}{2}$ **3.** 35 **5.** 20 **7.** 15 **9.** 7 **11.** 32 **13.** 16 **15.** 40 **17.** −40 **19.** 50 **21.** −20 **23.** 60 **25.** 36 **27.** $x = 24$ students; solve the equation $\frac{2}{3}x = 16$ by multiplying each side by $\frac{3}{2}$, the reciprocal of $\frac{2}{3}$ **29.** 18 questions

Lesson 6, page 75

1. $x = 4$; add 6 to each side of the equation, then divide each side of the equation by 3 **3.** 5 **5.** 6 **7.** 1 **9.** 8 **11.** 5 **13.** 10 **15.** 0 **17.** $b = 6$; subtract 20 from each side of the equation, then divide each side of the equation by −6 **19.** 0 **21.** −8 **23.** 6 **25.** −7 **26.** $s =$ 442 square miles; follow the order of operations—multiply first, then add **27.** 573 square miles **29.** 71 square miles

Lesson 7, page 77

1. $x = \frac{b}{-a}$; isolate the variable x by dividing each side of the equation by $-a$ **3.** $x = \frac{a}{b}$ **5.** $x = \frac{-a}{b}$ **7.** $x = \frac{-c}{(b + a)}$ **9.** $x = \frac{-b}{c}$ **11.** $x = \frac{c}{(b - a)}$ **13.** $x = \frac{a}{(c - b)}$ **15.** $x = \frac{-a}{(c + b)}$ **17.** $x = \frac{c}{(b + a)}$ **19.** $x = \frac{-b}{(c + a)}$

Lesson 8, page 79

1. $h = \frac{A}{b}$; isolate the variable h by dividing each side of the equation by b **3.** $s = \frac{P}{3}$ **5.** $d = \frac{W}{f}$ **7.** $b = \frac{A}{h}$ **9.** $s = \frac{P}{5}$ **11.** $r = \frac{d}{t}$ **13.** $F = \frac{W}{d}$ **15.** $h = \frac{(b_1 + b_2)}{2A}$ **17.** $a = P - c$ **19.** $d = An$ **21.** $s = \frac{1}{2A}$ **23.** $a = sP$ **25.** $A = (\frac{c}{d}) - b$

436 *Selected Answers and Solutions Algebra*

Lesson 9, pages 81–83

1. $a^2 = 50$; solve $a^2 + 50 = 100$ for a^2 by subtracting 50 from each side of the equation **3.** 26 **5.** 51 **6.** $c = 41$; solve $a^2 + b^2 = c^2$ when $a = 9$ and $b = 40$ **7.** 8 **9.** 53.1 **11.** 26.6 **12.** $c = 5$ blocks; sketch a diagram; in the diagram, the path Martin walked represents the legs of a right triangle. Use $a^2 + b^2 = c^2$ to find the hypotenuse. **13.** 8 feet **15.** 26 feet

Lesson 10, pages 86–87

1. $x = 6$; the closed dot means 6 is a solution; no other solutions are shown **3.** $x \neq 9$ **5.** $x \neq -5$ **7.** $x > 1$ **8.** open dot on 2, arrow left; the open dot means do not include the number 2, and the left arrow means include all of the numbers less than 2 **9.** closed dot on 2 **11.** closed dot on -3, arrow left **13.** open dot on -4, arrow right **15.** open dots on 1 and 4, line connecting 1 and 4 **17.** closed dots on -8 and 8, line connecting -8 and 8 **19.** open dot on 3, arrow right, arrow left **20.** T; on a number line, 1 is to the left of 10, so 1 is less than 10 **21.** T **23.** T **25.** F

Lesson 11, page 89

1. $x > 6$; solve for x by subtracting 4 from each side of the inequality **3.** $w > 7$ **5.** $g \leq 20$ **7.** $m < -14$ **9.** $c > -4$; solve for c by dividing each side of the inequality by -5 **11.** $t \leq 10$ **13.** $x < -4$ **15.** $m \geq -3$ **17.** $p < 95$; use the symbol $<$ to represent "less than" **19.** $i < 2{,}500$

Chapter 3 Application, page 90

1. 548 feet **3.** 948 feet **5.** 448 feet

Chapter 3 Review, pages 91–93

1. $m = 7$ **3.** $x = 32$ **5.** $h = -2$ **7.** $x = \frac{b}{(c + a)}$ **9.** $14x + 5 = 33$ **11.** $8x = 24$ **13.** $A = wh$ **15.** $A = \frac{bh}{2}$ **17.** $c = 10$ **19.** $c = 20$ **21.** closed dot at -2 **23.** open dot at 6, arrow left, arrow right **25.** closed dots at -9 and 2, connected by darkened line segment **27.** $b \geq 18$ **29.** $v < 9$

CHAPTER 4

Lesson 1, page 97

1. $n + 1$; on a number line, the next consecutive integer is 1 greater than any previous integer **3.** $n - 2$ **4.** 3; write and solve the equation $7n - 2 = 19$ **5.** -8 **7.** 10, 12, 14 **9.** Responses will vary. Possible answer: $2n + 2m = 2(n + m)$; use variables such as n and m to represent two unknown integers

Lesson 2, page 99

1. 34%; write and solve the equation for "\$850 is what percent of \$2,500?" **3.** 32,800 seats are filled. **5.** 6 people **7.** 500 books **9.** 24 stations

Lesson 3, pages 101–103

1. 10; to find a percent of a number, change the percent to a decimal, then multiply **3.** 41 **5.** $331\frac{1}{2}$ **7.** 135 **9.** $13\frac{1}{2}$ **11.** 100%; a whole is represented by 100% **13.** $37\frac{1}{2}\%$ **15.** 100 freshmen

Algebra *Selected Answers and Solutions* **437**

16. to find a percent of a number, change the percent to a decimal, then multiply

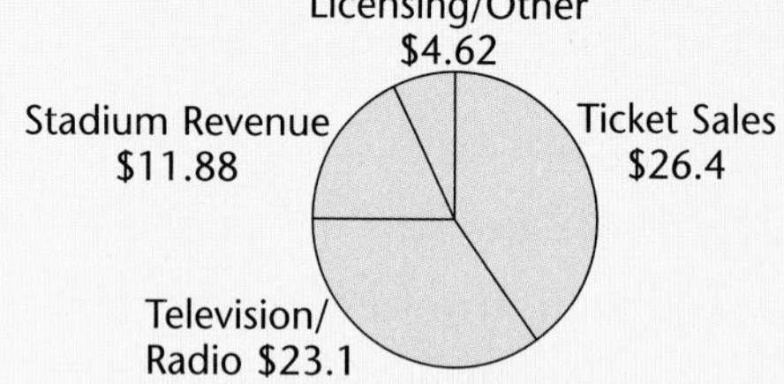

17.

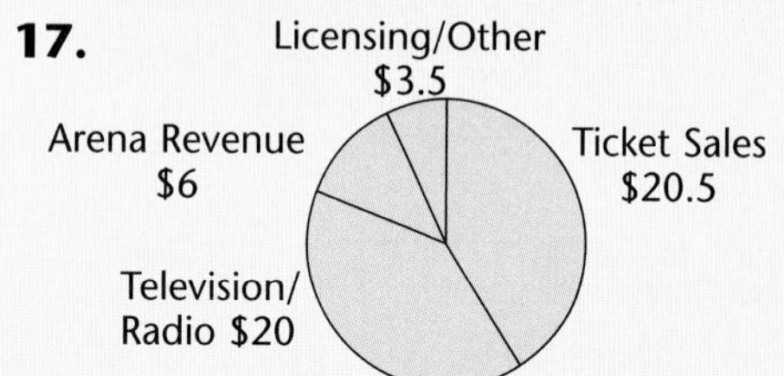

19.

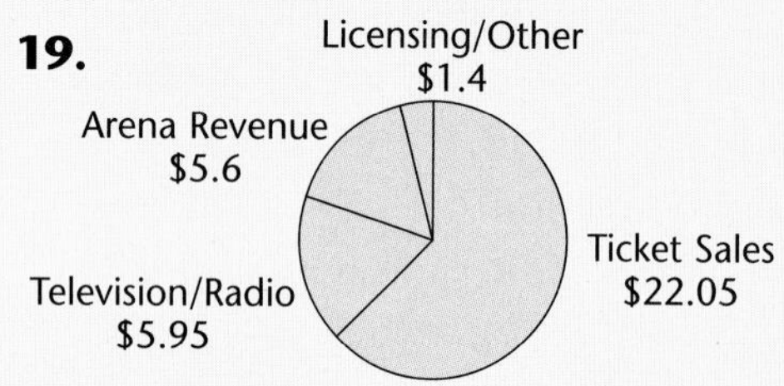

Lesson 4, pages 105–107

1. 3 hours; use the formula $t = \frac{d}{r}$ when $d = 165$ and $r = 55$ **3.** $d = 39\frac{7}{8}$ *km*; use the formula $d = rt$ when $r = 2\frac{3}{4}$ and $t = 14\frac{1}{2}$ **5.** $8\frac{1}{2}$ *km* per hour

Lesson 5, pages 109–110

1. a) 24 of each coin; let $5x$ represent the number of nickels and $10x$ represent the number of dimes, then solve $5x + 10x =$ \$3.60 for x b) $2x = 48$; 48 coins **3.** a) 12 dimes and 24 half-dollars b) 36 coins **5.** 12 dimes and 24 nickels; let $2x(5¢)$ represent the number of nickels and $1x(10¢)$ represent the number of dimes, then solve $2x(5¢) + 1x(10¢) =$ \$2.40 for x **7.** 20 nickels and 80 dimes **9.** 2 nickels and 16 dimes

Lesson 6, pages 112–113

1. \$165; use the formula $I = prt$ when $p =$ \$3,000, $r = 5.5\%$, and $t = 1$ year, change the percent to a decimal and solve for I **3.** \$2,300 **4.** $\frac{640}{(.04 \cdot 1)} = \$16{,}000$ **5.** \$5,600 **7.** \$1,312.50; use the formula $I = prt$ when $p =$ \$4,200, $r = 6.25\%$, and $t = 5$ years, change the percent to a decimal and solve for I **9.** \$48

Lesson 7, page 115

1. \$3.25; add the cost of the cashews (\$4 • 4) to the cost of the peanuts (\$2.50 • 4), then divide by 8, the number of pounds in the mixture **3.** 24 pounds of peanuts, 16 pounds of walnuts **5.** \$1.00

Try This

Possible response: $V = \frac{C}{A}$

Lesson 8, page 117

1. a) $\frac{64}{40} = \frac{8}{5}$; express a ratio as a fraction, then write the fraction in simplest form b) $\frac{40}{64} = \frac{5}{8}$ c) $\frac{40}{104} = \frac{5}{13}$ d) $\frac{64}{104} = \frac{8}{13}$ **3.** a) $\frac{3}{2}$ b) $\frac{2}{3}$ c) $\frac{1}{8}$ d) $\frac{1}{12}$ **4.** $n = 6$; solve a proportion by setting the cross products equal to each other, then solve for the unknown; $(2)(9) = (3)(n)$ **5.** $y = 3$ **7.** $n = 9$ **9.** $x = 5$ **11.** $y = 3$ **13.** $n = 40$ **15.** $x = 40$

438 *Selected Answers and Solutions Algebra*

Chapter 4 Application, page 118

1. 90 laps **3.** \$11.88 **5.** $9\frac{1}{3}$ inches

Chapter 4 Review, pages 119–121

1. 45 **3.** 450 **5.** \$3.75 **7.** 37, 38, 39 **9.** 400 **11.** 1,200 **13.** 19 nickels, 38 dimes **15.** 8 nickels, 2 dimes, and 6 quarters **17.** $x = 3$ **19.** $26\frac{2}{3}$ mph

CHAPTER 5

Lesson 1, page 125

1. $(3 \cdot 3)(3 \cdot 3)(3 \cdot 3) = 9 \cdot 9 \cdot 9 = 729$ or $3^6 = 729$ **3.** $x^{3 \cdot 4} = x^{12}$ **5.** $m^{4 \cdot 4} = m^{16}$ **7.** $(2x + 3y)^{4 \cdot 2} = (2x + 3y)^8$ **8.** $(3^5) \div (3^3) = 3^{5-3} = 3^2 = 9$ **9.** 4 **11.** y^2 **13.** $(x + y)^3$ **15.** $\frac{3 \cdot 3 \cdot 3 \cdot 3 \cdot 3}{3 \cdot 3 \cdot 3 \cdot 3 \cdot 3} = 1, 3^{5-5} = 3^0 = 1$ **17.** $x^{7-7} = x^0 = 1, \frac{1}{1} = 1$ **19.** $(p + q)^{3-3} = 1, \frac{1}{1} = 1$

Lesson 2, pages 127–128

1. $\frac{4 \cdot 4 \cdot 4 \cdot 4 \cdot 4}{4 \cdot 4 \cdot 4 \cdot 4 \cdot 4 \cdot 4 \cdot 4 \cdot 4 \cdot 4} = \frac{1}{4^4} = 4^{-4}$ **3.** 10^{-5} **5.** 10^{-10} **7.** 15^{-2} **9.** 203^{-4} **11.** $x^{5-7} = x^{-2}$ **13.** $(x + 2y)^{-4}$ **15.** $(x + y)^{-3}$ **17.** $(-3m - 9)^{-3}$ **19.** $3^{-2} = \frac{1}{3^2}$ **21.** $\frac{1}{10^{23}}$ **23.** $\frac{2}{y^6}$ **25.** $\frac{1}{4^2}$

Lesson 3, page 130

1. $1.86 \cdot 105$ **3.** $2.76 \cdot 10^{11}$ **5.** $1.34254 \cdot 10^3$ **7.** $1 \cdot 10^{-10}$ **9.** $9.3542 \cdot 10^8$ **11.** 0.00328 **13.** 186 **15.** 5,280 **17.** 0.0000000000000000000000000016 **19.** 11,122

Lesson 4, pages 132–133

1. $(1.4 \cdot 6.3)(10^{3-4}) = 8.82 \cdot 10^{-1}$ **3.** $6.4481201 \cdot 10^7$ **5.** $3.6712 \cdot 10^{13}$ **7.** $5.12 \cdot 10^4$ **9.** $9.711765 \cdot 10^{-15}$ **11.** $(6.8 \div 3.4)(10^{2-6}) = 2.0 \cdot 10^{-4}$ **13.** $4 \cdot 10^7$ **15.** $5.45 \cdot 10^3$ **17.** $1.25 \cdot 10^{-13}$ **19.** $1.29 \cdot 10^{-2}$

Lesson 5, page 135

1. binomial in y **3.** trinomial in x **5.** polynomial in p **7.** trinomial in y **9.** polynomial in b **11.** 2 **13.** 4 **15.** 3 **17.** 7 **19.** 3 **21.** $x^3 + x + 1$ **23.** $b^5 + 1$ **25.** $4r^n$ **26.** Responses will vary. Possible answer: negative exponent **27.** is not a sum or difference **29.** is not a sum or difference

Lesson 6, page 137

1. $4y^6 + 2y^5 + 2y^3 - 4y^2 + 28$ **3.** $-2b^4 - 4b^2 + 5b - 5$ **5.** $4x^4 + 11x^3 + 17x^2 + 17x + 4$ **7.** $-5x^7 + 6x^6 - 6x^5 - 7x^3 + 2x^2 - 9x + 6$ **9.** $2x^7 - 6x^6 + x^5 - 3x^3 - 2x^2 + 16x - 16$ **11.** $-4y^6 + 2y^5 + 4y^2 + 14y + 38$ **13.** $4b^4 + 2b^3 + 9b - 5$ **15.** $6x^6 + x^5 + 12$ **17.** $4x^4 + 3x^3 + 13x^2 - 17x + 4$ **19.** $(x + 5) + (x + 5) + (x^2) + (x^2) = 2x^2 + 2x + 10$

Lesson 7, page 139

1. $(x + 2)(8x - 2) = (8x^2 - 2x) + (16x - 4) = 8x^2 + 14x - 4$ **3.** $b^8 + 2b^7 + b^6$ **5.** $60x^5 - 239x^3 - 68x$ **7.** $2x^6 + 4x^5 + 2x^4 - x^3 - 2x^2 - x$ **9.** $10m^5 + 50m^4 + 4m^3 + 10m^2 - 50m$ **11.** $(a + 2b) \cdot (a + 2b) = a^2 + 2ab + 2ba + 4b^2 = a^2 + 4ab + 4b^2$ **13.** $x^2 + 4x + 3$ **15.** $3x^2 + 12x + 9$

Try This

$(ax + ay + az) + (bx + by + bz) + (cx + cy + cz)$

Lesson 8, page 141

1. $(x + y)^2 = x^2 + 2xy + y^2$ **3.** $m^2 - n^2$ **5.** $x^2 + 4x + 4$ **7.** $z^2 - 9$ **9.** $x^2 - 25$ **11.** $x^2 + 6x + 9$ **12.** $(z + 4)(z + 4)(z + 4) = z^3 + 12z^2 + 48z + 64$

Algebra Selected Answers and Solutions 439

13. $x^3 + 6x^2 = 11x + 6$ **15.** $m^3 - m^2n - mn^2 + n^3$

Try This

$a^4 + 4a^3b + 6a^2b^2 + 4ab^3 + b^4$

Lesson 9, page 143

1. $(16x^2 \div 4) + (4 \div 4) = 4x^2 + 1$ **3.** $-4x^3 + 3x^2 - 2x + 1$ **5.** $m^2 - m + 1$ **7.** $26x^2 + 4x$ **9.** $23x^4 - 41x^2 + 31$ **11.** $25x^5 - 14x - 9$ **13.** $15y^4 + y^3 + 5y^2 - 17y + 1$ **15.** $-a^4 + 12a^3 + 18a^2 + 20$

Lesson 10, pages 146–147

1. $x - 4$ **3.** $x - 2$ **5.** $x + 10$ **7.** $x + 4$ **9.** $x - 2$ **11.** $x - 5$ r1 **13.** $x + 2$ r-5 **15.** $x - 6$ r2 **16.** $5m^2 - 2$ **17.** $-4m + 3$ r-31 **19.** $3y^2 - 5$ **21.** $x^2 + 5x - 2$ **23.** $y^2 - 4y + 6$ r21 **25.** $5z$ r1

Lesson 11, page 149

1. $P(0, -1) = 1$ **3.** $P(\frac{1}{2}, -4) = 14\frac{1}{4}$ **5.** $P(\frac{1}{3}, 9) = 84\frac{1}{9}$ **7.** $P(-1, -1) = -1$ **9.** $P(9, 1) = 819$ **11.** $P(1, 1, 1) = 4$ **13.** $P(2, -1, 2) = 34$ **15.** $P(1, -2, -3) = 25$

Chapter 5 Application, page 150

1. \$1,050.63 **3.** \$1,104.49 **5.** \$1,268.24

Chapter 5 Review, pages 151–153

1. $(x \cdot x \cdot x \cdot x \cdot x \cdot x) \cdot (x \cdot x \cdot x \cdot x \cdot x \cdot x) \cdot (x \cdot x \cdot x \cdot x \cdot x \cdot x)$ **3.** 4 **5.** $4.0(10^9)$ **7.** $7.3(10^{-4})$ **9.** $1.0374(10^{-7})$ **11.** $2.5(10^{-9})$ **13.** $5x^4 + x^3 - 6x^2 + 8x + 17$; $-x^4 - 9x^3 - 6x^2 + 8x + 3$ **15.** $m^5 + m^4 + m^3 + m^2$; $m^5 - m^4 + m^3 - m^2 - 10$ **17.** $18x^4 + 2x^3 - 14x^2$ **19.** $-12y^3 - 12y^2 - 12y - 12$ **21.** $4x^2 - 5x - 6$ **23.** $2m^7 - 3m^6 + 2m^4 + 10m^3 + 15m^2 + 10$ **25.** $6x^3 - 5x^2 + 4x - 2$ **27.** 3 **29.** $(x^2 - 7x)$ or $x(x - 7)$

CHAPTER 6

Lesson 1, pages 158–159

1. $2^2 \cdot 3^2$, $36 = 2 \cdot 2 \cdot 3 \cdot 3$ and $72 = 2 \cdot 2 \cdot 2 \cdot 3 \cdot 3$ **3.** 3 **5.** $2^2 \cdot 3$ **7.** $3 \cdot 11$ **9.** 5^2 **11.** $3x$; $3x^2 = 3 \cdot x \cdot x$ and $3x = 3 \cdot x$ **13.** m^2 **15.** $4x$ **17.** $7xy$ **19.** $4xy$ **21.** 47; 48, 49 composite numbers **23.** 33 **25.** since $180 = 20 \cdot 9$, $180 = (22 \cdot 5)(32)$ or $22 \cdot 32 \cdot 5$ **26.** 72 **27.** 1,125 **29.** 3,705,625

Lesson 2, page 161

1. $3(x^2 + 1)$; 3 is common to $3x^2$ and to 3 **3.** $m^2(n^2 + 3)$ **5.** $6(x^3 + 3x^2 + 4)$ **7.** $8(2m^3 + 3m^2 + 2)$ **9.** $16x(2x^4 + 4x^3 + 1)$ **11.** $a^4(-3a^2 - 4a - 1)$ or $-a^4(3a^2 + 4a + 1)$ **13.** $6y(-4x^2 + x^2y + 5y)$ **15.** $3xy^2(-5x^2 - 15x - 11)$ or $-3xy^2(5x^2 + 15x + 11)$ **17.** $17xy(x - 2)$ **19.** $5t(-8t + ts + 4s^2)$

Lesson 3, page 163

1. $(x + 2)(x + 3)$; the expression $x^2 + 5x + 6$ has no common factors **3.** $(a - 2)(a - 4)$ **5.** $(y + 6)(y - 3)$ **7.** $(t - 5)(t + 4)$ **9.** $(x - 1)(x + 17)$ **10.** $x^2(x^2 + 7x + 12) = x^2(x + 4)(x + 3)$ **11.** $2b(b^2 + 5b + 4) = 2b(b + 4)(b + 1)$ **13.** $(a^2 + 3)(a^2 + 4)$ **14.** $(2x + 1)(3x - 2)$; $6x^2 - x - 2 = (2x + 1)(3x - 2)$ **15.** $2(x + 1) + 2(x + 3) = 4x + 8$

Lesson 4, page 165

1. $(3y + 2)(y + 4)$; the expression $3x^2 + 14y + 8$ has no common factors **3.** $(2c + 3)(3c + 5)$ **5.** $(2m + 4)(10m + 5)$ **7.** $(20y + 1)(y + 20)$ **9.** $(7x - 3)(x + 1)$; the expression $7x^2 + 4x - 3$ has no common factors **11.** $(7x - 2)(7x + 3)$ **13.** $(3y + 4)(2y - 6)$ **15.** $(3x - 7)(2x - 4)$

440 *Selected Answers and Solutions Algebra*

17. $(3x - 8)(x + 2)$ **18.** $4x(x + 4)(x + 1)$; $4x^3 + 20x^2 + 16x = 4x(x^2 + 5x + 4) = 4x(x + 4)(x + 1)$ **19.** $2x^2(3x + 8)(2x - 1)$

Lesson 5, page 167

1. 44 **3.** 11 **5.** 40 **7.** $(y + 7)(y - 7)$; the expression $y^2 - 49$ has no common factors **9.** $(p + 11)(p - 11)$ **11.** $(z + 15)(z - 15)$ **13.** $(7x + 1)(7x - 1)$; the expression $49x^2 - 1$ has no common factors **15.** $(6t^2 + 11)(6t^2 - 11)$ **17.** $(5r^4 + 1)(5r^4 - 1)$ **19.** $(7x^2 - 5y)(7x^2 + 5y)$; the expression $49x^4 - 25y^2$ has no common factors **21.** $(6ab + 1)(6ab - 1)$ **23.** $(9m + 8n^5)(9m - 8n^5)$ **25.** 319 m^2; subtract the area of the fountain from the area of the plaza $(20 \cdot 20) - (9 \cdot 9) = 400 - 81 = 319$ m^2

Lesson 6, pages 169–171

1. I = $2 \cdot 2$ or 4 sq. units, II = $2 \cdot 8$ or 16 sq. units, III = $8 \cdot 8$ or 64 sq. units, IV = $8 \cdot 2$ or 16 sq. units, total = 100 sq. units **3.** I = 25 sq. units, II = 10 sq. units, III = 4 sq. units, IV = 10 sq. units, total = 49 sq. units **4.** $(m - 12)^2$; $m^2 - 24m + 144 = (m - 12)(m - 12)$ **5.** $(x + 12)^2$ **7.** $(t + 9)^2$ **9.** $(x + 13)^2$ **10.** $(2m + 12)^2$; $4m^2 + 48m + 144 = (12m + 12)(2m + 12)$ **11.** $(2r - 12)^2$ **13.** $(9p^3 + 5)^2$ **15.** $(5x^2 + 5)^2$ **17.** $(12b^2 - 1)^2$ **19.** I = $7 \cdot 7$, II = $7 \cdot 3$, III = $7 \cdot 3$, IV = $3 \cdot 3$; to have an area of 100 square units, the new room must measure $10 \cdot 10$

Lesson 7, page 173

1. $m = 0$; any number times zero is zero **3.** $y = 0$ **5.** $x^2 = 0, x = 0$ **7.** $b^4 = 0, b = 0$ **9.** $x^3 = 0, x = 0$ **11.** $x = 5$; $17(5 - 5) = 17(0) = 0$ **13.** $m = -21$ **15.** $n = 12$ or $n = -4$ **17.** $m = 4$ **19.** $x = \frac{6}{4} = 1\frac{1}{2}$ or $x = -6$ **21.** $z = -\frac{1}{2}$ or $z = 2$ **23.** $x = -2$ or $x = 5$ **25.** $p = 1$ or $p = -\frac{27}{13}$

Try This

$(2x^2 - 32) = 0$ or $(x - 9) = 0$ if $(2x^2 - 32) = 0$, then $2x^2 = 32$, $x^2 = 16$ and $x = 4$ or $x = -4$; if $x - 9 = 0$, $x = 9$

Lesson 8, pages 176–177

1. $-2, -3$; $x^2 + 5x + 6 = (x + 2)(x + 3)$ **3.** $+2, +4$ **5.** $-6, +3$ **7.** $+5, -4$ **9.** $+1, -17$ **11.** $-3, -4$ **13.** $8, -2$ **15.** $\frac{-3}{2}, -5$ **16.** $(2n - 12)(4n + 4) = 0$, solutions are $6, -1$ **17.** $3, -5$ **19.** $1\frac{1}{2}, -6$ **21.** $3(b^2 + 5b + 4) = 3(b + 4)(b + 1)$, solutions are $-4, -1$ **23.** $6(2x^2 + 3x + 1) = 6(2x + 1)(x + 1)$, solutions are $-\frac{1}{2}, -1$ **25.** $12(c^2 + 5c + 6) = 12(c + 3)(c + 2)$, solutions are $-2, -3$ **26.** C **27.** C **29.** B

Chapter 6 Application, page 178

1. $\frac{1}{2}$ ft or 6 in. **3.** 6 ft

Chapter 6 Review, pages 179–181

1. $3 \cdot 22$ **3.** $8(3m^2 - 1)$ **5.** $(p - 9)(p + 9)$ **7.** $m = -6$ **9.** $x = -\frac{1}{2}$ or $x = -4$ **11.** $x = 0$ or $x = -2$ **13.** $y = 1$ or $y = \frac{3}{2}$ **15.** $z = -\frac{3}{2}$ or $z = \frac{3}{2}$ **17.** $y = +11$ or $y = -11$ **19.** $c = 0$ or $c = -9$ **21.** $a^2 - b^2$ **23.** I = length and width = 8; II = length 4, width 8, III = length and width = 4, IV = length 8, width 4 **25.** $9a^2 + 6ab + b^2$ **27.** width = 5 units, length = 12 units **29.** 7 cm

Algebra Selected Answers and Solutions **441**

CHAPTER 7

Lesson 1, pages 186–187

1. In each data value, use the digit in the tens place for the stem and the digit in the ones place for the leaf. Write each tens digit only once.

Stem	Leaves							
0	2	3	4	4	5	6	7	
1	0	1	1	2	3	4	6	9
2	0	0	1	2	4	5	6	7
3	0							

3.

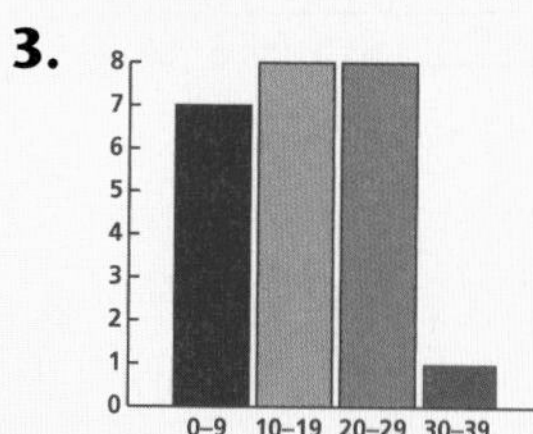

For problems 5 and 9, other answers are possible and, in some cases, likely.
5. Sample answer: They all give a visual display of the data. **7.** 4, 11, and 20 occur most often. 2, 3, 5, 6, 7, 10, 12, 13, 14, 16, 19, 21, 22, 24, 25, 26, 27, and 30 occur least often. **9.** Sample answer: frequency table

Lesson 2, pages 190–191

1. 14 – 1.01 = 12.99; to compute the range, subtract the least value in the set from the greatest 3. 3.005 5. Answers will vary. 6. Answers will vary.
7, 9. Answers will vary. 11. 18.5; find the sum of the values in the set, then divide by 4; 74 ÷ 4 = 18.5 13. 118 15. 661.812

Lesson 3, pages 194–195

1. 39, 40, 41, 42, 44, 44, 45, 45, 47, 48, 49, 49, 51; upper extreme 51 **3.** median 45

5.

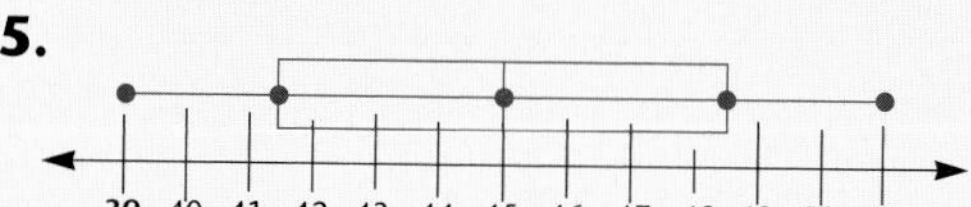

7. lower extreme 12 **9.** upper quartile 21; lower quartile 15

Lesson 4, pages 198–199

1. $\frac{1}{6}$; the number cube has 6 possible outcomes; there is 1 favorable outcome of rolling a 2 **3.** $\frac{3}{6} = \frac{1}{2}$ **5.** $\frac{3}{6} = \frac{1}{2}$ **7.** $\frac{2}{6} = \frac{1}{3}$; two of the six sides of the cube are yellow **9.** $\frac{1}{6}$ **11.** $\frac{0}{6}$ or 0 **13, 15, 17, 19.** Answers will vary.

Lesson 5, pages 202–203

1. certain; a coin has 2 possible outcomes; a toss of heads or tails represents 2 favorable outcomes; $P = \frac{2}{2}$ or $P = 1$ **3.** more likely **5.** more likely **7.** not likely **9.** $\frac{1}{2}$; divide the spinner into 8 equal parts; 4 of those parts are yellow; $\frac{4}{8} = \frac{1}{2}$ **11.** $\frac{1}{8}$ **13.** $\frac{3}{4}$ **15.** $\frac{1}{4}$ **17.** $\frac{5}{8}$ **19.** $\frac{1}{\text{(number of students in the class.)}}$; there is only 1 favorable outcome in this experiment—your name being chosen

Lesson 6, page 205

1. $(\frac{1}{2})(\frac{1}{4}) = \frac{1}{8}$; find the product of the probability of each event **3.** $\frac{1}{8}$ **5.** $\frac{3}{8}$ **7.** 1 **8.** $(\frac{1}{5})(\frac{1}{6}) = \frac{1}{30}$; find the product of the probability of each event **9.** $\frac{1}{10}$ **11.** $\frac{4}{15}$ **13.** $\frac{2}{5}$ **15.** $\frac{2}{15}$

Try This

36 different outcomes; $\frac{1}{36}$

442 *Selected Answers and Solutions Algebra*

Lesson 7, pages 208–209

1. Independent events, any toss does not affect the previous toss or the next toss of the coin **3.** These are independent events; the next outcome will be 1, 2, 3, 4, 5, or 6 **4.** $(\frac{2}{6})(\frac{1}{6}) = \frac{1}{18}$; find the product of the probability of each event **5.** $\frac{1}{12}$ **7.** $(\frac{2}{8})(\frac{1}{7}) = \frac{1}{28}$; find the product of the probability of each event; in the second event; there will only be 7 marbles left in the bag because the marble taken during the first event was not replaced **9.** $\frac{5}{56}$

Try This

3%

Lesson 8, pages 212–213

1. 2; if, for example, you choose the letters *A* and *B*, the letters can be arranged two ways—*A*, *B* or *B*, *A* **3.** 120 **5.** 36 **6.** 58,500; the first letter in the password has 26 possibilities, the second letter has 25 possibilities; the first digit has 10 possibilities (0 – 9) and the second digit has 9 possibilities; 26 • 25 • 10 • 9 = 58,500 **7.** 1,024 **9.** 10,000

Chapter 7 Application, page 214

1. third, $\frac{1}{100} < \frac{1}{10}$ **3.** $\frac{1}{10{,}000}$ **5.** 100, sample explanation:

$$\frac{1 \text{ failure}}{10{,}000 \text{ launches}} = \frac{100 \text{ failures}}{1{,}000{,}000 \text{ launches}}$$

Chapter 7 Review, pages 215–217

1. 35 **3.** 80 **5.** 255 and 272 **7.** 251 and 279 **9.** $P = 0$ **11.** $P = 1$ **13.** $P = 0$ **15.** $P = \frac{1}{6}$ **17.** $P = \frac{1}{4}$ **19.** $P = \frac{2}{25}$ **21.** Answers will vary. Sample answer: The spinner will land on black. **23.** 720 ways **25.** 24 ways

CHAPTER 8

Lesson 1, page 221

1. $\frac{1}{7}$; the GCF of 9 and 63 is 9; $\frac{9}{63} \div \frac{9}{9} = \frac{1}{7}$ **3.** $\frac{-1}{4}$ **5.** $\frac{1}{4}$ **7.** $\frac{1}{12}$ **9.** $\frac{2}{9}$ **11.** $\frac{21}{32}$ **13.** $\frac{3}{8}$ **15.** $\frac{11}{81}$; the GCF of 121 and 891 is 11; $\frac{121}{89} \div \frac{11}{11} = \frac{11}{81}$ **17.** $\frac{1}{-5}$ **19.** $\frac{2}{3}$ **21.** $\frac{3}{8}$ **23.** $\frac{5}{-21}$ **25.** $\frac{1}{5}$

Lesson 2, page 223

1. $\frac{1}{m}$; the GCF of m^5 and m^6 is m^5; $\frac{m^5}{m^6} \div \frac{m^5}{m^5} = \frac{1}{m^1}$ or $\frac{1}{m}$ **3.** $5x$ **5.** $5x^2$ **7.** $\frac{2}{3xy^2}$ **9.** $(\frac{xyz^2}{-2})$ **11.** $\frac{-1}{(a^2 + 4)}$ **13.** $(x - 5)$ **15.** $(-x + 5)$; $\frac{(-x^2 + 25)}{(x + 5)} = \frac{-(x^2 - 25)}{(x + 5)} = \frac{-(x^2 - 5)(x + 5)}{(x + 5)} = \frac{-(x - 5)}{1}$ or $-x + 5$ **17.** $(w + 7)$ **19.** $\frac{1}{(a - 2)}$

Lesson 3, page 225

1. $\frac{5}{8}$; $\frac{3}{4} \cdot \frac{5}{6} = \frac{15}{24} \div \frac{3}{3} = \frac{5}{8}$ **3.** $2\frac{2}{3}$ **5.** $\frac{a}{x}$ **7.** $\frac{1}{(a - 5)^2}$ **9.** $\frac{(1 - x)}{(bx - 1)}$ **11.** $\frac{9}{10}$; $\frac{3}{4} \div \frac{5}{6} = \frac{3}{4} \cdot \frac{6}{5} = \frac{18}{20} = \frac{9}{10}$ **13.** $4\frac{1}{6}$ **15.** $\frac{x^3}{a^5}$ **17.** $\frac{1}{(a + 5)^2}$ **19.** $\frac{(x - 1)(x + 1)^2}{(bx - 1)(bx + 1)^2}$

Algebra Selected Answers and Solutions **443**

Lesson 4, pages 228–229

1. 12; 12 is the first common multiple of 3 and 4 **3.** 56 **5.** 36 **7.** 21 **9.** 18 **11.** $8n$ **13.** $20r$ **15.** $99b$ **16.** $1\frac{2}{3}$; $1 \div \frac{3}{5}1 = 1 \cdot \frac{5}{3} = \frac{5}{3} = 1\frac{2}{3}$ **17.** 8 **19.** $\frac{5}{18}$ **21.** $4\frac{4}{11}$ **23.** $\frac{3}{40}$ **25.** $\frac{9}{16}$ **27.** $\frac{8}{9}$ **29.** $\frac{5}{9}$ **31.** $\frac{8}{25}$ **33.** $\frac{3}{5}$ **35.** $\frac{9}{16h}$ **36.** 247.5 mi.; $d = rt$, $d = 45 \cdot 5.5$, $d = 247.5$ **37.** 46 mph **39.** 28 mph

Try This

$\frac{xb}{a}$

Lesson 5, page 231

1. 15; 15 is the first common multiple of 3 and 5 **3.** 30 **5.** 28 **7.** 42 **9.** x^3y^2 **11.** $1\frac{1}{3}$; $\frac{2}{3} \div \frac{1}{2} = \frac{2}{3} \cdot \frac{2}{1} = \frac{4}{3} = 1\frac{1}{3}$ **13.** $2\frac{1}{10}$ **15.** ab **17.** $\frac{16a^2}{y}$ **19.** $\frac{mn^2}{x^2}$

Lesson 6, page 233

1. $1\frac{5}{8}$; $\frac{3}{4} + \frac{7}{8} = \frac{6}{8} + \frac{7}{8} = \frac{13}{8} = 1\frac{5}{8}$ **3.** $1\frac{1}{12}$ **5.** $\frac{9}{10}$ **7.** $\frac{11}{14}$ **9.** $4\frac{29}{40}$ **11.** $\frac{10y - 7x}{xy}$ **13.** $\frac{3x^2 - 2y}{x^2y}$ **15.** $\frac{a + 3}{a^2}$ **17.** $\frac{25cd - 4b}{abcd}$ **19.** $\frac{5dx - 3cx}{c^2d^2}$ **21.** $\frac{3b + 4a}{a^2b^2}$ **23.** $\frac{5y^3 + 7x^3}{ax^2y^2}$ **25.** $\frac{21x^2y^2 + 8a^4b^2}{28a^2bxy}$

Lesson 7, pages 236–237

1. 3; set the cross products equal to each other, then solve for x; $100x = 300$, so $x = 3$ **3.** 100 **5.** -15 **7.** 49 **9.** -1 **11.** $-5\frac{3}{8}$ **13.** 5, -4 **15.** $\frac{1}{6}$ **16.** $2\frac{5}{8}$ feet; solve $\frac{1 \text{ in.}}{\frac{3}{4} \text{ ft}} = \frac{3\frac{1}{2} \text{ in.}}{x}$ for x **17.** 9 students **19.** 2,025 km

Try This

$3x = 5 \cdot 6$; if a proportion has three constants and one unknown, it can be solved; the expression $3x = 15y$ has two unknowns

Lesson 8, pages 239–241

1. 24; multiply both sides of the equation by $\frac{4}{3}$, the reciprocal of $\frac{3}{4}$ **3.** 56 **5.** -49 **7.** 27 **9.** $11\frac{1}{2}$ **10.** 11; subtract $\frac{1}{9}$ from both sides, then multiply both sides by $\frac{9}{4}$, the reciprocal of $\frac{4}{9}$ **11.** $5\frac{4}{9}$ **13.** $8\frac{1}{6}$ **15.** 84 **17.** $25\frac{1}{5}$ **18.** not correct **19.** not correct **21.** not correct **23.** Their scores are 75 and 60. **25.** 81 points

Lesson 9, page 243

1. $x = 4$; if $x = 4$, the denominator is undefined because $4 - 4 = 0$ **3.** $c = -5$ **5.** $b = 0$ **7.** $m = 0$ and/or $n = 0$ **9.** $a = +2$ or $a = -2$ **11.** $r = 12$ **13.** $n = +6$ or $n = -6$ **15.** $m = -8$ or $m = +3$ **17.** $x = -3$ or $x = -4$ or $x = +3$ **19.** $b = +5$ or $b = +4$

Chapter 8 Application, page 244

1. $3\frac{1}{13}$ hours **3.** $2\frac{2}{9}$ hours

Chapter 8 Review, pages 245–247

1. $\frac{2}{3}$ **3.** $\frac{b^2}{a}$ **5.** $\frac{(3x + 5)}{x^2}$ **7.** $x = 4$ **9.** $\frac{1}{5}$ **11.** $\frac{1}{x}$ **13.** $\frac{7}{9mn}$ **15.** $(y - 3)$ **21.** $\frac{ab}{x^2}$ **23.** 20 **25.** -81 **27.** -28 **29.** $-28\frac{1}{3}$ **31.** $13\frac{1}{2}$ **33.** $\frac{(x + 3)^2 + (x - 5)^2}{(x + 3)(x - 5)}$ **35.** $\frac{3mp + 5n}{n^2p^2}$ **37.** about 833 deer **39.** 10 feet

444 Selected Answers and Solutions Algebra

CHAPTER 9

Lesson 1, pages 252–253

1. (2, 1); point B is located 2 units right and 1 unit up **3.** (3, –2) **5.** (–2, –2) **7.** (0, 1) **9.** (–3, 1) **11.** To plot any point, move left or right first, then move up or down. **13, 15.**

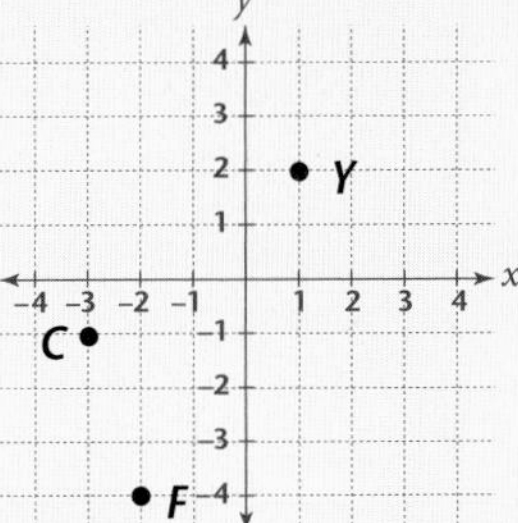

17. Quadrant I; point (3, 3. is three units to the right of the origin and 3 units up. **19.** Quadrant II **21.** Quadrant II **23.** 4 blocks; make a diagram on grid paper. Write north at the top of the page, south at the bottom, east at the right, and west at the left. **25.** Answers will vary.

Lesson 2, page 255

1. $y = x$ x $-2, -1, 0, 1, 2$ y $-2, -1, 0, 1, 2$; choose a value for x, then substitute that value into the equation and solve for y **3.** $y = 2x + 1$ x $-4, -2, 0, 2, 4$ y $-7, -3, 1, 5, 9$ For problems 4–9, choose a value for x, then substitute that value into the equation and solve for y **4.** $y = x$ x $-1, 0, 1$ y $-1, 0, 1$ The graph should pass through the points (0, 0) and (1, 1) **5.** $y = 3x$, x $-1, 0, 1$ y $-3, 0, 3$ The graph should pass through the points (0, 0) and (1, 3) **7.** $y = 2x - 1$ x $-1, 0, 1$ y $-3, -1, 1$ The graph should pass through the points (0, −1) and (1, 1) 9. $y = x - 3$ x $-1, 0, 1$ y $-4, -3, -2$ The graph should pass through the points (0, −3) and (1, −2)

Try This

$y = x$

Lesson 3, page 257

1. Substitute $x = 0$ into the equation of the graph and solve for y. Write an ordered pair in the form (x, y). **3.** x-intercept $= -1$; y-intercept $= 1$. To find the y-intercept, substitute $x = 0$ into the equation and solve for y. To find the x-intercept, substitute $y = 0$ into the equation and solve for x. **5.** x-intercept $= 3$; y-intercept $= -3$ **7.** x-intercept $= 0$; y-intercept $= 0$ **9.** x-intercept $= \frac{1}{2}$; y-intercept $= -1$ **11.** x-intercept $= 1$; y-intercept $= 1$ **13.** x-intercept $= -3$; y-intercept $= -9$ **15.** Sample answer: when the graph passes through the origin

Lesson 4, pages 260–262

1. The graph should create an acute angle with the positive direction of the x-axis; a line with a positive slope moves upward when read from left to right. **3.** The graph must be parallel to either the x- or y-axis. **4.** negative; a line with a negative slope moves downward when read from left to right. **5.** neither **7.** $m = 0; \frac{-1-(-1)}{2-3} = \frac{-1+1}{2-3} = \frac{0}{-1}$ or 0 **9.** $m = -2$ **11.** Change the fraction or mixed number to a decimal. Use a calculator to check the slope calculation. Then compare decimal answers. **12.** $m = 1$; to find the slope of a line, use the formula $\frac{y_2 - y_1}{x_2 - x_1}$ **13.** $m = 0$ **15.** $m = -2$

Algebra Selected Answers and Solutions **445**

17. $m = 0$ **18.** Trail 3; Trails 1 and 2; a negative slope is downhill. A positive slope is uphill. **19.** Trail 2

Lesson 5, page 264

1. $y = 2x + 1$; substitute $m = 2$ and $b = 1$ into $y = mx + b$, the general form for any linear equation **3.** $y = -2x + 5$
4. The graph should pass through (1, 1) and (3, 3); $y = x$; first use $\frac{y_2 - y_1}{x_2 - x_1}$ to find the slope of the line. Then substitute the slope and either point into $y = mx + b$ and solve for b. Substitute m and b into $y = mx + b$ to find the equation of the line. **5.** The graph should pass through (0, 0) and (2, 4); $y = 2x$ **7.** The graph should pass through (5, 0) and (0, 10); $y = -2x + 10$ **9.** The graph should pass through $(-2, 0)$ and $(-6, -1)$; $y = \frac{1}{4}x + \frac{1}{2}$ **11.** $y = 5x - 20$; substitute the slope and the point into $y = mx + b$ to find b. Then substitute m and b into $y = mx + b$ to find the equation of the line.
13. $y = \frac{x+11}{2}$ or $y = \frac{1}{2}x + \frac{11}{2}$ **15.** $y = 2x$

Lesson 6, pages 266–267

1. yes; a vertical line intersects the graph only once **3.** yes **5.** yes **7.** $f(2) = 6$; $f(-4) = 12$; to evaluate a function, substitute the given values into the function one at a time, and solve for $f(x)$
9. $f(2) = 14$; $f(-4) = 68$ **11.** $f(2) = 2$; $f(-4) = -28$ **13.** $f(2) = -11$; $f(-4) = -53$ **15.** $f(2) = 12$; $f(-4) = 12$

Lesson 7, pages 269–271

1. Range: $-7 \leq y \leq 15$ **3.** Range: $1 \leq y \leq 4$ **5.** Range: $-2 \leq y \leq 24$
6. Range: $-2 \leq y \leq 4$ **7.** Range: $y = 3$ **9.** Range: $y = 4$ **11.** Domain: $-4 \leq x \leq -2$ Range: $-2 \leq y \leq 5$ **13.** Domain: $-4 \leq x \leq 5$ Range: $y = 2$

Lesson 8, page 274

1.

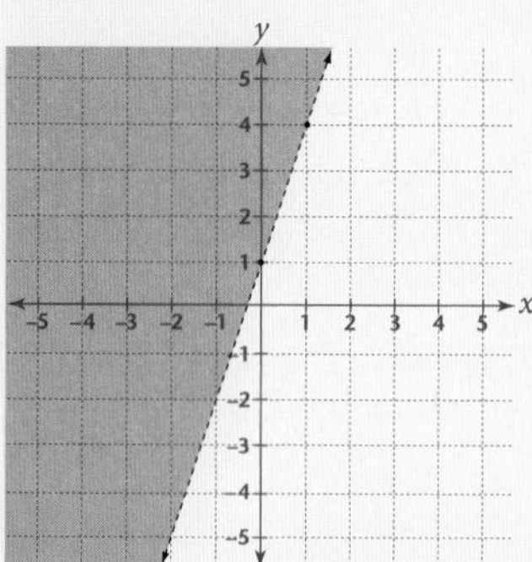

3.

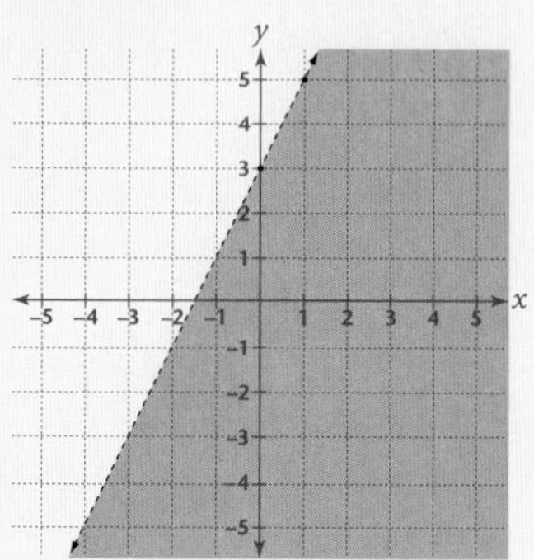

5.

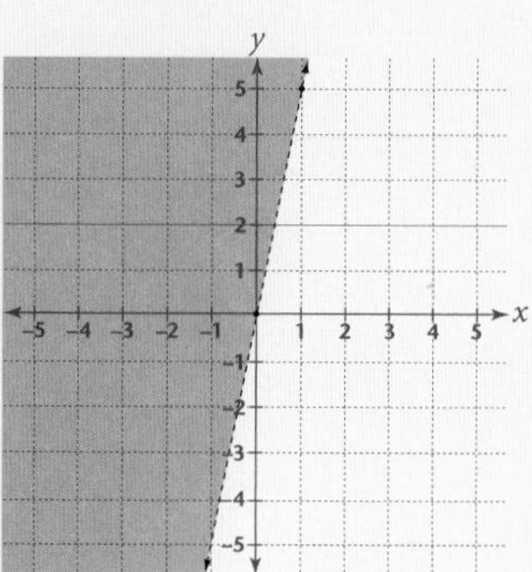

446 *Selected Answers and Solutions* *Algebra*

7.

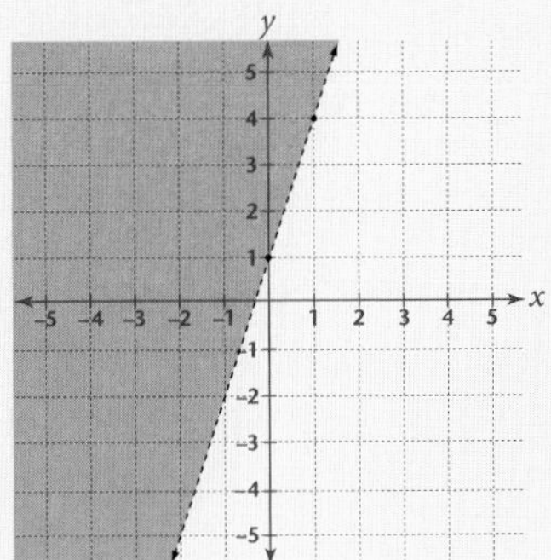

9.

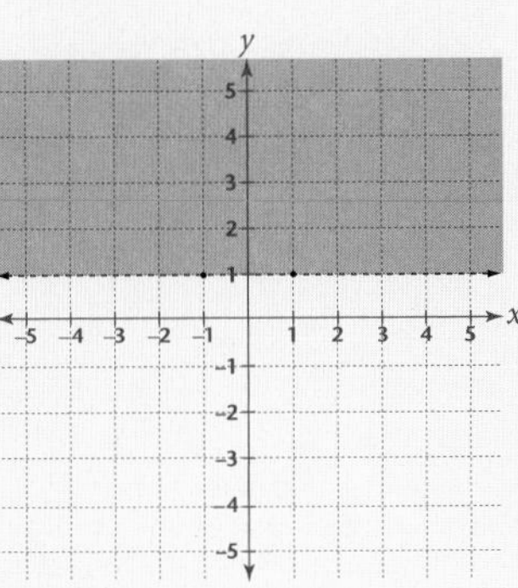

11.

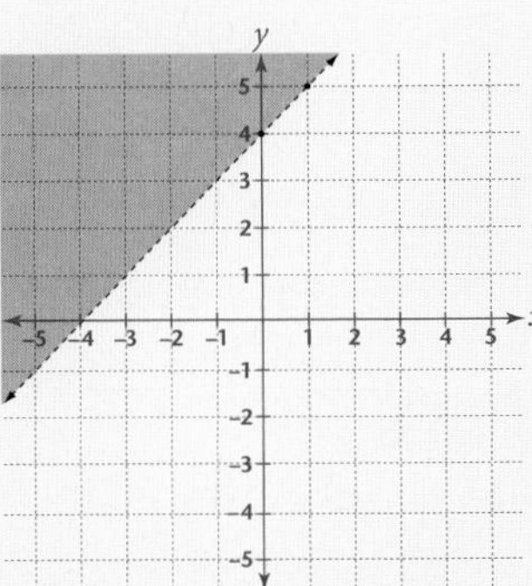

13.

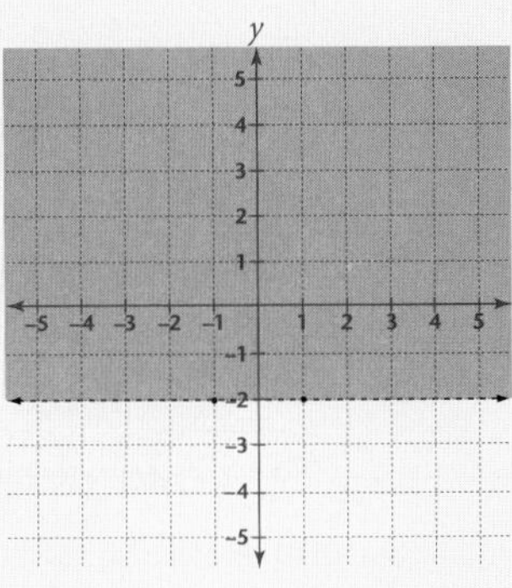

15.

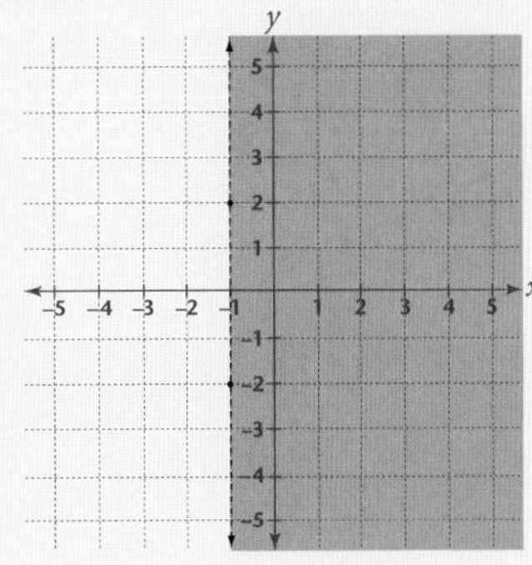

Lesson 9, pages 278–279

1. Choose a value for x, solve the equation for y, and write an ordered pair. Repeat. Graph the line connecting the points with a solid line because the inequality is $\geq$ or $\leq$. Choose a point to help decide which area to shade.

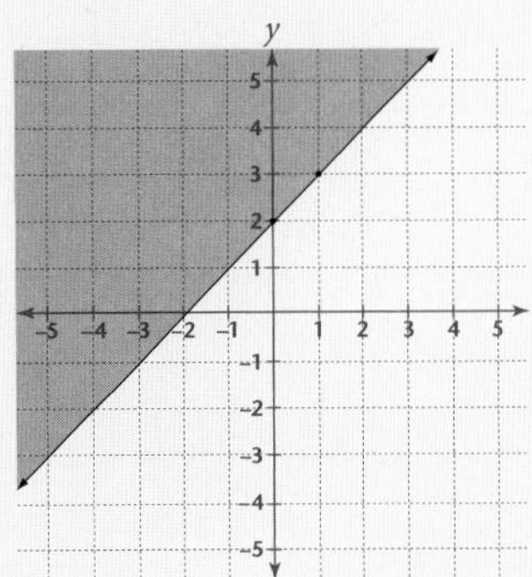

3.

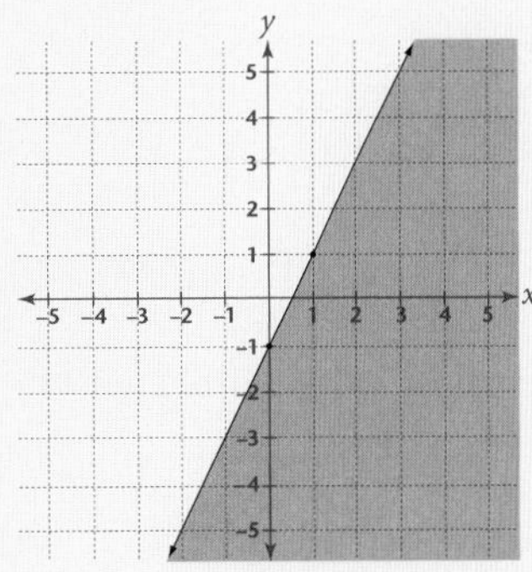

Algebra *Selected Answers and Solutions* **447**

5.

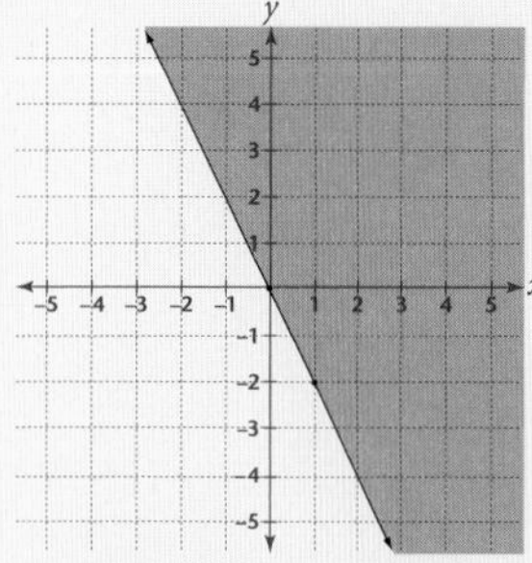

7.

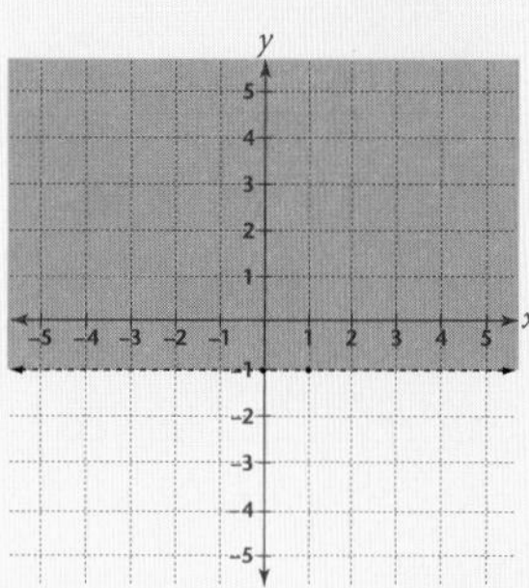

9.

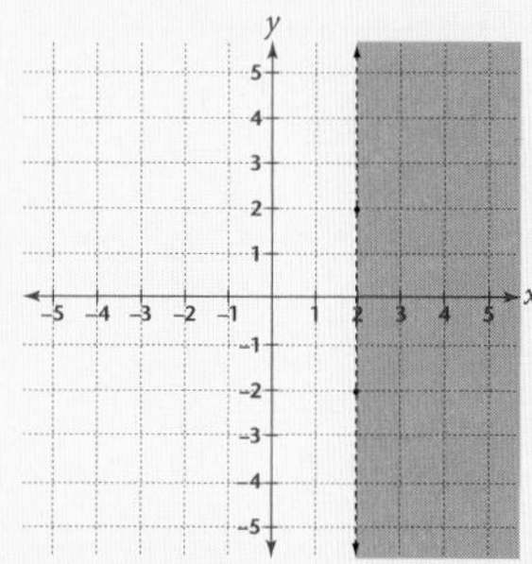

11. $y \leq x + 3$; Choose a point in the shaded region. Substitute that point into the equation of the line. Choose $\geq$ or $\leq$ if the graph is a solid line, or $<$ or $>$ if the graph is a broken line. **13.** $y \leq -4x$ **15.** $y < 3x - 2$ **17.** $y \leq -1$ **19.** $x \geq -5$

Lesson 10, page 281

1. Answers will vary. The graph increases, remains flat for some period of time, then decreases at the same rate it increased. **3.** Answers will vary. **5.** Graphs and stories will vary.

Chapter 9 Application, page 282

1. triangle **3.** Sample answer: (1, 1), (3, 1), (1, 4), (3, 4) **5.** Sample answer: (0, 0), (2, 0), (2, 2), (0, 2)

Chapter 9 Review, pages 283–285

1. (–3, 0) **3.** x-intercept = (−3, 0); y-intercept = (0, 3) **5.** $m = 1$ **7., 9.**

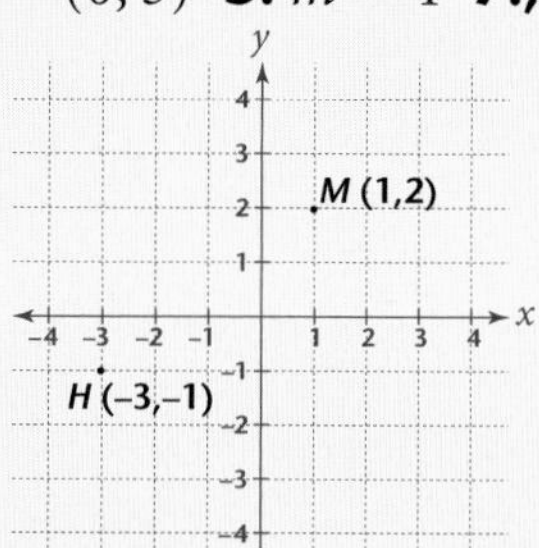

11. $m = -1$ **13.** $m = -\frac{1}{2}$ **15.** The graph should pass through (1, 1) and (−3, −7); $y = 2x - 1$ **17.** The graph should pass through (−2, −1) and (−4, −4); $y = \frac{3}{2}x + 2$ **19.** yes **21.** $f(-1) = 2$; $f(2) = 2$ **23.** The graph should be a broken line passing through (0, 1) and (1, 3). The region to the right of the broken line should be shaded. **25.** $y \leq 5x + 2$

CHAPTER 10

Lesson 1, pages 290–291

1. $m = 2$; the slope of a line is written in the form $y = mx + b$ **3.** $m = \frac{4}{9}$ **5.** $m = \frac{5}{2}$ or $m = 2\frac{1}{2}$; the slope of a line parallel to a given line is the same as the given line. The y-intercept of the parallel line is 4 because a point on that line is (0, 4) and because when $x = 0$, $y = b$. **6.** $y = 2x + 4$ **7.** $y = 3x - 2$ **9.** $y = -\frac{1}{2}x - 3$ **10.** rewrite as $y = 2x + 1$; $y = 2x + 3$; divide each side of the given equation by 2 to rewrite

448 *Selected Answers and Solutions Algebra*

the equation in the form $y = mx + b$ **11.** rewrite as $y = x + 1; y = x + 3$ **13.** yes; the only lines on a graph that can lie only in Quadrants I and II, and only in Quadrants III and IV, are lines that are parallel to the x-axis. Since the slope of the x-axis of any graph is zero, the slope of any line parallel to the x-axis is also zero. **15.** no

Try This

Lines of the form $x =$ constant or $x =$ any number means the line is vertical and parallel to the y-axis. The slope of any two points on the line gives a zero for the $x_2 - x_1$ portion of the slope formula. Division by zero is undefined.

Lesson 2, page 293

1. $y = 2x - 10$; substitute $(6, 2)$ into $y = mx + b$ to find the y-intercept of the line. The line must also have the same slope (2) of the given line. **3.** $y = -\frac{3}{5}x + 2$ **5.** $y = -\frac{1}{2}x - \frac{1}{2}$ **7.** $y = -2x + 8$ **9.** $y = 2x - 1$ **10.** $y = \frac{x}{2} + 1; y = \frac{x}{2} + \frac{3}{2}$; divide each side of the given equation by 2 to find $y = \frac{x}{2} + 1$. Then substitute $(1, 2)$ into $y = mx + b$ to find the y-intercept of a line that has the same slope as the given line. **11.** rewrite as $y = x + 1; y = x + 2$ **13.** rewrite as $y = \frac{x}{2} + \frac{5}{4}; y = \frac{x}{2}$ **15.** rewrite as $y = 3x + 4; y = 3x - 11$

Try This

Sample answers: $y = mx + (d - mc)$ or $y = mx + (c - md)$

Lesson 3, pages 296–297

1. no; $m = 2$ for each, parallel; in order for a system of equations to have a solution, two or more lines in that system must intersect **3.** yes, slopes not equal, lines intersect; a common solution for a system of equations is the point or points of intersection of the lines in that system **5.** yes, slopes not equal, lines intersect

Lesson 4, pages 300–301

1. $(1, 4)$; solve $y + x = 5$ for x: $x = 5 - y$. Substitute $x = 5 - y$ into $2x + y = 6$ to find that $y = 4$. Substitute $y = 4$ into either equation to find that $x = 1$. Check. **3.** $(-\frac{20}{7}, -\frac{18}{7})$ **5.** $(-4, -2)$ **7.** $(3, -1)$ **9.** not correct

Lesson 5, page 303

1. $(0, 2)$; add the equations to eliminate the x term. Substitute the value of y into either equation. Check your work by substituting the point into both equations. If both equations are true, then the common solution is correct. **3.** $(-4, -2)$ **5.** $(-4, -2)$ **7.** $(16, 2)$ **9.** $(\frac{1}{2}, 3)$

Lesson 6, page 305

1. $(2, -3)$ Create a table of values to find the x- and y-intercepts of each line. Use the points in the table to graph the lines. Identify the point of intersection, then check by substituting the x- and y-value for the point into each equation. **3.** $(3, -3)$ **5.** $(2, 0)$ **7.** $(\frac{3}{4}, 2)$ **9.** $(0, 2,)$ **11.** $(3, 0)$ **13.** $(11, -1)$ **15.** $(-4, -6)$

Algebra Selected Answers and Solutions **449**

Lesson 7, pages 308–309

1. True, both are true **3.** False, $4 \div 0 = 0$ is false **5.** True, both are true **7.** False, all vertical lines have a slope of 1 is false **9.** False, $2^2 + 23 = 25$ is false **11.** False, $6 + 7 = 15$ is false **13.** True, both are true **15.** True, both are true **17.** True, both are true **19.** False, q is false

Lesson 8, page 313

1. 8 and 16; solve $x + y = 24$ or $x - y = 8$ for x or y. Then substitute to find the other value. **3.** this week \$54, last week \$18 **5.** 12 seconds, 16 seconds **7.** Amityville 24 points, Johnstown 40 points; let a = Amityville's score and j = Johnstown's score. Solve $\frac{3}{5}j = a$ and $a + 16 = j$ for a and j. **9.** Shavonne is 28 and DaWayne is 42.

Lesson 9, pages 315–317

1. 2×2 **3.** 1×4 **5.** 2×4 **6.** row 2, column 2 **7.** row 5, column 1 **9.** row 9, column 9 **11.** $\begin{bmatrix} 0 & 2 \\ 8 & 1 \end{bmatrix}$ **13.** $\begin{bmatrix} 10x & 2x & 3y \\ 13 & -1 & -8 \end{bmatrix}$

15. $\begin{bmatrix} 5 & 1 & 6 \\ \sqrt{2} & 7 & 3 \\ 9 & 1 & 6 \end{bmatrix}$ **16.** $\begin{bmatrix} -1 & 5 \\ 8 & 8 \end{bmatrix}$

17. $\begin{bmatrix} -5 & 1 & 0 \\ -2 & 2 & -6 \end{bmatrix}$ **19.** $\begin{bmatrix} 3-a & 1-b & 6-c \\ -1 & -9 & -4 \\ -3 & 1 & 4 \end{bmatrix}$

Lesson 10, pages 320–321

1. $\begin{bmatrix} 48 & 0 \\ 15 & 3 \end{bmatrix}$ **3.** $\begin{bmatrix} 7x & 7y \\ 21 & 105 \end{bmatrix}$

5. $\begin{bmatrix} 3xy^2 & -xy^2 & ay^2 \\ 4y^2 & 14y^2 & 0 \\ -6y^2 & 10y^2 & -y^4 \\ y^3 & y^2 & xy^3 \end{bmatrix}$

7. $\begin{bmatrix} 1 & 0 & 2 \\ 1 & 1 & 6 \\ 3 & 2 & 1 \end{bmatrix}$

Chapter 10 Application, page 322

1. $U = \{1, 2, 3, 4, 5, 6, 7, 8\}$; $A \cup B = \{1, 2, 4, 5, 6, 7\}$; $A \cap B = \{4, 6\}$ **3.** 8 **5.** Answers will vary.

Chapter 10 Review, pages 323–325

1. (3, 4) **3.** (0, 1) **5.** 135° and 45° **7.** $y = 2x + 10$ **9.** $y = \frac{x}{2} + 4$ or $2y = x + 8$ **11.** $y = 3x - 3$ **13.** (4, 2) **15.** (3, 1) **17.** $(8\frac{4}{7}, \frac{5}{7})$ **19.** False, the second statement is not true **21.** False, both statements are false **23.** 62° and 28° **25.** Markette is 20 and Earlene is 16.

CHAPTER 11

Lesson 1, pages 330–331

1. $0.\overline{60}$, terminating; $\frac{3}{5} = 3 \div 5 = 0.6 = 0.\overline{60}$ **3.** $0.\overline{5}$, repeating **5.** $0.\overline{18}$, repeating **7.** $0.\overline{63}$, repeating **9.** $0.\overline{15}$, repeating **11.** $0.12\overline{0}$, terminating **13.** $0.41\overline{6}$, repeating **15.** $0.7\overline{3}$; repeating

16. Decimal Expansion 1 0.5 $0.\overline{3}$ 0.25 0.2 $0.1\overline{6}$ $0.\overline{142857}$ 0.125 $0.\overline{1}$ 0.1

17. Decimal Expansion 1 0.5 $0.\overline{6}$ 0.75 0.8 $0.8\overline{3}$ $0.\overline{857142}$ 0.875 $0.\overline{8}$ 0.9

18. 93.2°F; $°F = (\frac{9}{5})(34) + 32$; $°F = \frac{306}{5} + 32$; $°F = 61.2 + 32$; $°F = 93.2$

19. −0.4°F **21.** 24.8°F **22.** 40°C; $°C = (\frac{5}{9})(104 - 32)$; $°C = (\frac{5}{9})(72)$; $°C = \frac{360}{9}$; $°C = 40$ **23.** $7.\overline{7}$°C **25.** $21.\overline{1}$°C

450 *Selected Answers and Solutions* *Algebra*

Try This
37°C

Lesson 2, page 333

1. $\frac{2}{5}$; $0.4\overline{0} = \frac{4}{10} \div \frac{2}{2} = \frac{2}{5}$ **3.** $\frac{9}{25}$ **5.** $\frac{9}{11}$ **7.** $\frac{5}{66}$ **9.** $\frac{11}{15}$; let $x = 0.7\overline{3}$; $10x = 7.\overline{3}$ and $100x = 73.\overline{3}$; $(100x = 73.\overline{3}) - (10x = 7.\overline{3}) = 90x = 66$; $x = \frac{66}{90}$ or $\frac{11}{15}$ **11.** $\frac{13}{99}$ **13.** $\frac{2}{13}$ **15.** $\frac{1}{202}$

Lesson 3, page 335

1. 7.368 irrational **3.** 3.314 irrational **5.** 3.557 irrational **7.** 2 rational **9.** 2 rational **11.** 6 in.; since the area of a square is (side)2, finding the square root of the area will give you the length of a side of the square **13.** 12.65 ft **15.** 196 square units; 14 units

Lesson 4, page 337

1. $\sqrt{25} \cdot \sqrt{100} = 5 \cdot 10 = 50$ **3.** $\sqrt{49} \cdot \sqrt{4} = 7 \cdot 2 = 14$ **5.** $\sqrt{5a \cdot 5a} = 5a$ **7.** $\sqrt{25} \cdot \sqrt{x^4} \cdot \sqrt{y^4} \cdot \sqrt{y} = 5x^2y^2 \cdot \sqrt{y}$ **9.** $\sqrt{9} \cdot \sqrt{10} \cdot \sqrt{x^4} \cdot \sqrt{x} = 3 \cdot \sqrt{10} \cdot x^2\sqrt{x} = 3x^2\sqrt{(10x)}$ **11.** $\sqrt{121} \cdot \sqrt{9} \cdot \sqrt{m^2} \cdot \sqrt{n^4} = 11 \cdot 3 \cdot mn^2 = 33mn^2$ **13.** $\frac{\sqrt{16}}{\sqrt{18}} = \frac{4}{9}$ **15.** $\frac{\sqrt{25} \cdot \sqrt{3}}{\sqrt{36}} = \frac{5\sqrt{3}}{6}$

17. $\frac{\sqrt{27}}{\sqrt{y^3}} = \frac{\sqrt{9} \cdot \sqrt{3}}{\sqrt{y^2} \cdot \sqrt{y}} = \frac{3\sqrt{3}}{y\sqrt{y}}$

19. $\frac{\sqrt{(16y^2)}}{\sqrt{(25x^4)}} = \frac{4y}{5x^2}$ **21.** $\frac{\sqrt{81h^6}}{\sqrt{27y^2}} = \frac{9h^3}{\sqrt{9} \cdot \sqrt{3} \cdot \sqrt{y^2}} = \frac{9h^3}{3y \cdot \sqrt{3}} = \frac{3h^3}{y\sqrt{3}}$

23. $\frac{(\sqrt{81} \cdot \sqrt{3} \cdot \sqrt{x^6})}{(\sqrt{9} \cdot \sqrt{10} \cdot \sqrt{y^2})} = \frac{9 \cdot \sqrt{3} \cdot x^3}{3 \cdot \sqrt{10} \cdot y} = \frac{3x^3\sqrt{3}}{y\sqrt{10}}$ **25.** $\frac{\sqrt{4} \cdot \sqrt{9} \cdot \sqrt{d^2}}{\sqrt{4} \cdot \sqrt{6} \cdot \sqrt{t^4}} = \frac{3d}{t^2\sqrt{6}}$

Try This

$\frac{\sqrt[3]{(27y^6)}}{\sqrt[3]{(64z^3)}} = \frac{3y^2}{4z} = \frac{\sqrt[4]{(256y^4)}}{\sqrt[4]{(16x^8)}} = \frac{4y}{2x^2} = \frac{2y}{x^2}$

Lesson 5, page 339

1. $6\sqrt{2}$; $\sqrt{2} + 5\sqrt{2} = 1\sqrt{2} + 5\sqrt{2} = 6\sqrt{2}$ **3.** $\sqrt{7}$ **5.** 12 **6.** cannot be simplified or subtracted **7.** $3\sqrt{3}$ **9.** $9\sqrt{2}$ **11.** 0 **13.** $2\sqrt{6} + 6$; $\sqrt{24} + \sqrt{36} = \sqrt{6 \cdot 4} + \sqrt{36} = 2\sqrt{6} + 6$ **15.** $2\sqrt{6} + 12\sqrt{3}$ **17.** $8\sqrt{10} + 12\sqrt{15}$ **19.** $31x^2$

Try This

$-5x$

Lesson 6, page 341

1. $2\sqrt{6}$; $\frac{(4\sqrt{3} \cdot \sqrt{2})}{(\sqrt{2} \cdot \sqrt{2})} = \frac{4\sqrt{6}}{2} = 2\sqrt{6}$

3. $\frac{(3\sqrt{35})}{5}$ **5.** $\frac{(2\sqrt{2})}{3}$ **7.** $\frac{(5\sqrt{5})}{3}$

9. $2 - \sqrt{2}$; $\frac{2}{(2 + \sqrt{2})} \cdot \frac{(2 - \sqrt{2})}{(2 - \sqrt{2})} = \frac{4 - 2\sqrt{2}}{4 - 2} = \frac{4 - 2\sqrt{2}}{2} = 2 - 2\sqrt{2}$

11. $5\sqrt{5} - 10$ or $-5(2 - \sqrt{5})$

13. $\frac{(9\sqrt{5} - 15)}{4}$ **15.** $\frac{[3y(3 + y^3)]}{9 - y^3}$

Lesson 7, pages 344–345

1. $n = 49$ **3.** $y = 18$ **5.** $y = 245$ **7.** $x = 16\frac{1}{3}$ **9.** $x = 64$ **11.** $x = 625$ **13.** $x = 128\frac{1}{2}$ **14.** 6 units; since the area of a square is $(\text{side})^2$, finding the square root of the area will give you the length of a side of the square **15.** 7 units **17.** 20 inches **19.** 1 unit

Algebra Selected Answers and Solutions **451**

Lesson 8, page 347

1. $y^{\frac{1}{3}}$ **3.** $4^{\frac{1}{3}} \cdot y^{\frac{1}{3}}$ **5.** $x^{\frac{4}{3}}; x \cdot \sqrt[3]{x} = x \cdot x^{\frac{1}{3}} = x^{(1+\frac{1}{3})} = x^{\frac{4}{3}}$ **7.** $z^{\frac{4}{3}}$ **9.** $x^{\frac{2}{3}}; \sqrt[3]{x^2} = (x^2)^{\frac{1}{3}} = (x)^{2 \cdot \frac{1}{3}} = x^{\frac{2}{3}}$ **11.** x **13.** 4 **15.** 100

Lesson 9, page 349

Approximate answers shown for **1–10.**
1. 3.2 **3.** 7.1 **5.** 8.4 **7.** 9.5 **9.** 9.2

Chapter 11 Application, page 350

1. 56.6 feet per second **3.** 140 meters per second **5.** 400 feet per second

Chapter 11 Review, pages 351–353

1. 0.2941177; irrational, nonrepeating nonterminating **3.** $\frac{9}{16}$ **5.** $10\sqrt{6}$
7. 130 ft **9.** $0.\overline{621}$; rational, repeating
11. 25; rational, terminating **13.** cannot be added **15.** $8\sqrt{3} - 18\sqrt{2}$
17. $\frac{(16\sqrt{7} - 28)}{9}$ **19.** $4\sqrt{3x}$ **21.** $2^{\frac{1}{2}}$
23. $13^{\frac{3}{4}}$ **25.** $r \approx 4$ units **27.** $r \approx 9$ units

29.

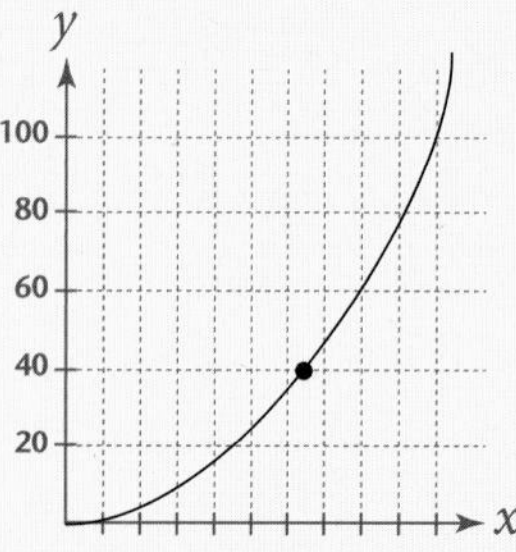

CHAPTER 12

Lesson 1, page 359

1. right; an angle that measures exactly 90° is a right angle **3.** acute **5.** straight **7.** adjacent; angles that share a common side are adjacent **9.** vertical **11.** $\angle PQR$ and $\angle SQR$; the sum of the measures of complementary angles is 90° **13.** 60°; 120°; the sum of the measures of supplementary angles is 180° **15.** 18°; 72°

Lesson 2, page 363

1. parallel; parallel lines never intersect **3.** parallel **5.** intersecting **7.** exterior; an exterior angle opens away, or toward the outside, of a figure **9.** interior
11. exterior **13.** exterior
15. supplementary; the sum of the measures of supplementary angles is 180°
17. supplementary **19.** supplementary
21. supplementary **23.** corresponding
24. 108°; 180° − 72° = 108° **25.** 72°
27. 72° **29.** 108°

Lesson 3, page 367

1. 70°; $x = 180° - 50° - 60°$ or $x = 70°$ **3.** 45° **5.** 105° **7.** 40°; find the measure of the angle adjacent to the 90° angle; 180° − 90° or 90°. Then find y: $y = 180° - 90° - 50° = 40°$. **9.** $m\angle Y = 180° - m\angle P$ or $180° - m\angle Q + m\angle T$ **10.** 360°; since there are four 90° angles in a square, the sum of the measures of the angles in a four-sided figure is (4)(90°) or 360°

452 *Selected Answers and Solutions Algebra*

Lesson 4, page 369

1. right scalene; in the triangle, one angle measures 90°, and none of the sides of the triangle have the same measure **3.** isosceles **5.** obtuse scalene **7.** obtuse scalene **9.** No. Sample explanation: The sum of the angles in any triangle is 180°. If one angle in that triangle is right, the sum of the measures of the other angles in the triangle is 180° − 90° or 90°. Since the measure of an obtuse angle is greater than 90°, neither of the remaining angles in the triangle can be obtuse. **10.** 150°; the sum of the measures of $\angle a$, $\angle b$, and $\angle c$ is 360°; since the measure of $\angle a$ is 60°, the sum of the measures of $\angle b$ and $\angle c$ is 360° − 60° or 300° **11.** 10° **13.** 150° **15.** 20°

Lesson 5, page 371

1. $m\angle C = 130°$; $m\angle D = 90°$; since the measure of $\angle D$ is 90°, the measure of $\angle C$ = 360° − 90° − 90° − 50° or 130° **3.** 360°; the sum of the measures of the angles forms a circle **5.** Check your drawing.

Lesson 6, page 375

1. SAS; in the triangles, the corresponding sides are adjacent to the same angle **3.** ASA **5.** SAS **7.** 63°; in any triangle, the sum of the angle measures is 180° **9.** No; isosceles triangles can have different sizes and different shapes

Try This

Answers will vary.

Lesson 7, pages 378–379

1. 0.26 **3.** 0.27 **4.** 0.6 **5.** 0.8 **7.** $x = 5$; use the cosine ratio because the length of the hypotenuse is known and you are trying to find the length of the adjacent side **9.** 173 feet; use the tangent ratio because the length of the adjacent side is known and you are trying to find the length of the opposite side

Chapter 12 Application, page 380

1. 9 **3.** 14 **5.** 54

Chapter 12 Review, pages 381–383

1. m $\angle d = 127.6°$ **3.** m $\angle k = 52.4°$ **5.** m $\angle x = 67°$ **7.** m $\angle x = 40°$ **9.** acute; interior **11.** obtuse; interior; alternate interior **13.** m $\angle D = 90°$ **15.** SSS **17.** m $\angle f = 76°$ **19.** 58 feet

CHAPTER 13

Lesson 1, pages 388–389

1. −2, −3; $(x + 3)(x + 2) = 0$; $x + 3 = 0$, $x = -3$; $x + 2 = 0$; $x = -2$ **3.** −5, −6 **5.** −1, −5 **7.** $\frac{5}{3}$, −1 **9.** $-\frac{2}{3}$, $\frac{1}{4}$ **11.** −3; $t^2 + 6t + 9 = 0$; $(t + 3)(t + 3) = 0$; $t + 3 = 0$, $t = -3$ **13.** −2, 5 **15.** 0, $\frac{7}{5}$ **17.** 7, −2 **19.** $\frac{2}{3}$, −1 **21.** length 12, width 3; since the area of a rectangle is found using the formula $A = lw$, use the equation $(x)(4x) = 36$. Solve for x, then solve for $4x$. **23.** Mai puts in 21 chips; Tom puts in 20 **25.** Kristen is 6; Jesse is 8

Lesson 2, page 391

1. $x^2 + 5x + 6 = 0$; since $x = -2$ and $x = -3$, $x + 2 = 0$ and $x + 3 = 0$; $(x + 2)(x + 3) = x^2 + 5x + 6$ **3.** $x^2 - 10x + 24 = 0$ **5.** $x^2 - 2x - 24 = 0$ **7.** $x^2 + 3x - 28 = 0$ **9.** $x^2 - 19x + 88 = 0$ **11.** $x^2 + 3x - 10 = 0$ **13.** $x^2 - 8x + 15 = 0$ **15.** $5x^2 - 29x + 20 = 0$ **17.** $2x^2 + 5x + 3 = 0$ **19.** $3x^2 - 2x - 8 = 0$

Algebra Selected Answers and Solutions **453**

21. $2x^2 - 7x + 3 = 0$ **23.** $7x^2 - 53x + 28 = 0$ **24.** No; for example, in the equation $x^2 - 8x = 0$, the roots are 0 and 8 **25.** No; you could only have one root, and it would equal zero: $x^2 = 0$

Lesson 3, pages 394–395

1. $-1, -5$; rewrite $x^2 + 6x + 5 = 0$ as $x^2 + 6x = -5$. Add the constant $+9$ to each side of the equation: $x^2 + 6x + 9 = 9 - 5$. Factor: $(x + 3)2 = 4$. Find the square root of each side: $\sqrt{(x+3)^2} = \sqrt{4}$; $x + 3 = {}^{\pm}2$. Find the roots: $x = -3 \, {}^{\pm}2$, or $x = -3 + 2$ and $x = -3 - 2$. **3.** $0, -3$ **5.** $5, -1$ **7.** $3, -5$ **9.** $2, 4$ **11.** $6, -2$ **13.** $-1, -5$ **15.** $1, -3$ **17.** $\frac{(3 \pm \sqrt{33})}{4}$ **19.** $3 \pm \sqrt{26}$

Lesson 4, page 397

1. $2, -4$; use the quadratic formula and substitute 1 for a, 2 for b, and -8 for c. **3.** $2, 1$ **5.** $3, -3$ **7.** $2, -4$ **9.** $\frac{5}{2}, 3$ **11.** $\frac{(-1 \pm \sqrt{22})}{3}$ **13.** $-3, -\frac{1}{2}$

15. Substitute $x = \frac{1 + \sqrt{7}}{3}$ in $3x^2 - 2x - 2 = 0$; $3(\frac{1 + \sqrt{7}}{3})^2 - 2(\frac{1 + \sqrt{7}}{3}) - 2 = 0$; $3(\frac{1 + 2\sqrt{7} + 7}{9}) - 2(\frac{1 + \sqrt{7}}{3}) - 2 = 0$; $\frac{8 + 2\sqrt{7}}{3} - 2(\frac{1 + \sqrt{7}}{3}) - 2 = 0$; $\frac{(8 + 2\sqrt{7} - 2 - 2\sqrt{7})}{3} - 2 = 0$; $\frac{6}{3} - 2 = 0$; $0 = 0$. Check for $x = \frac{1 - \sqrt{7}}{3}$ is similar.

Lesson 5, pages 400–401

1.

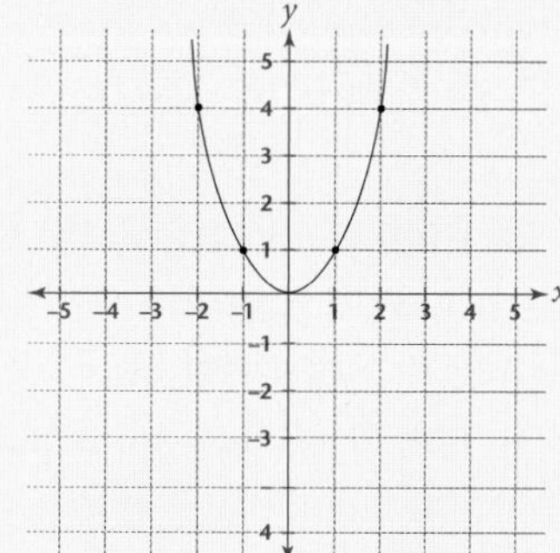

Make a table of values for the equation $y = x^2$. Points on the graph include $(0, 0)$, $(1, 1)$, $(-1, 1)$, $(2, 4)$, $(-2, 4)$, $(3, 9)$, $(-3, 9)$, $(4, 16)$, and $(-4, 16)$

3.

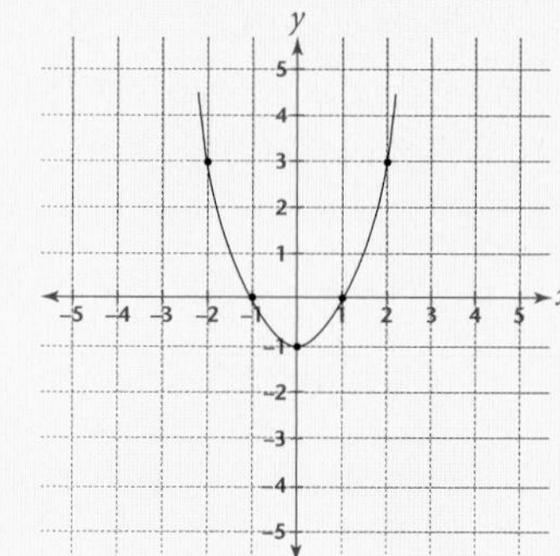

4.

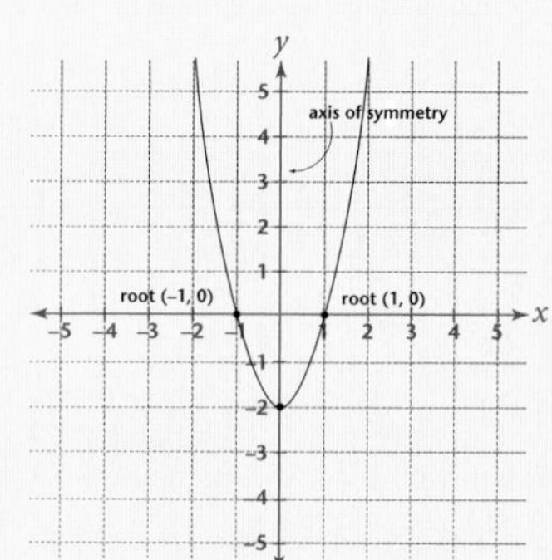

$x = 0$; $(-1, 0)$, $(1, 0)$; In the equation $x = \frac{-b}{2a}$, substitute 2 for a and 0 for b; the axis of symmetry is $\frac{-0}{2(2)} = \frac{0}{4} = 0$, or $x = 0$. To find the roots of the equation, set the equation equal to zero and solve.

454 *Selected Answers and Solutions Algebra*

5.

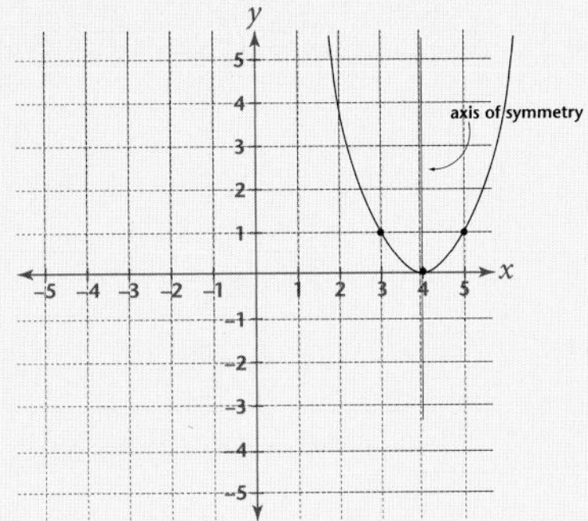

$x = 4; (4, 0)$

7.

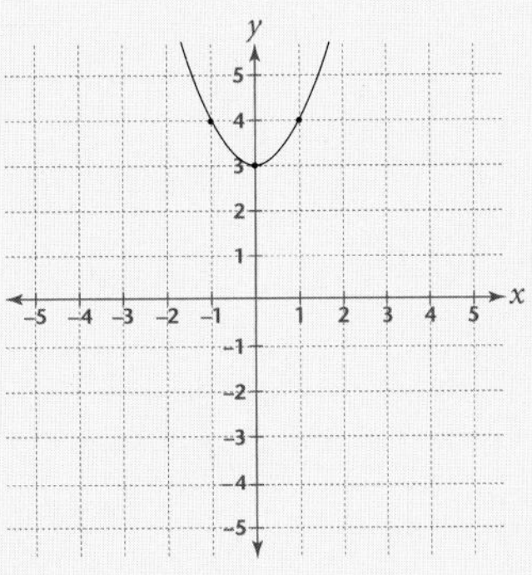

9.

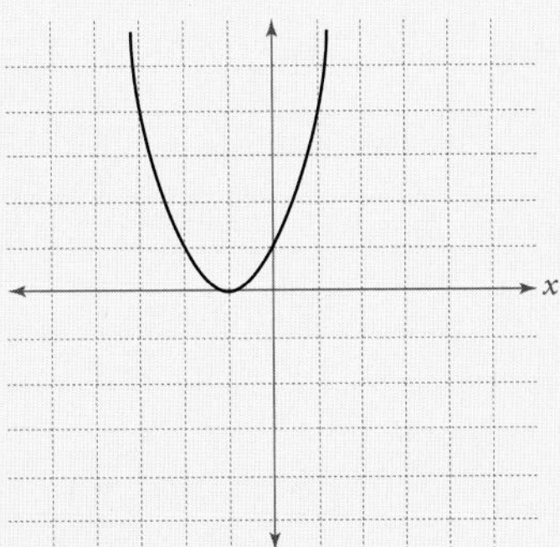

Chapter 13 Application, page 402

1. 1.25 seconds and 5 seconds
3. The model rocket is at any height above ground twice—once on its way up and once on its way down. **5.** A good estimate is 6.25 seconds.

Chapter 13 Review, pages 403–405

1. $-\frac{7}{3}, 3$ **3.** $8x^2 + 5x - 3 = 0$ **5.** $7, -3$ **7.** $x = 2$ or $x = \frac{2}{3}$ **9.** $x = 0$ or $x = 8$ **11.** $x = -7$ or $x = 3$ **13.** $x^2 + 3x - 18 = 0$ **15.** $4x^2 - 15x + 9 = 0$ **17.** $x = -8$ or $x = 2$ **19.** $x = -6 \pm 2\sqrt{10}$ **21.** $x = \frac{9}{2}$ or $x = -1$ **23.** $x = 5$ or $x = 4$ **25.** $x = -1, (\frac{2 + \sqrt{6}}{-2}, 0)$, and $(\frac{2 - \sqrt{6}}{-2}, 0)$

27. $x = \frac{-9}{2}, (-6, 0)$ and $(-3, 0)$

29. 12 and 13

Algebra Selected Answers and Solutions **455**

Supplementary Problems

CHAPTER 1

Pages 406–407

1. false, $6 + 3 = 9$ **2.** true **3.** false, $\frac{40}{8} = 5$ **4.** false, $25 - 13 = 12$ **5.** true **6.** numerical, addition **7.** algebraic, multiplication, y **8.** algebraic, multiplication and subtraction, d **9.** algebraic, division, n **10.** numerical, multiplication **11.** 5 **12.** 22 **13.** 18 **14.** 16 **15.** 25 **16.** 7 **17.** 21 **18.** -16 **19.** -7 **20.** 3 **21.** 11 **22.** -2 **23.** -7 **24.** 6 **25.** 9 **26.** 28 **27.** -30 **28.** 27 **29.** -33 **30.** -24 **31.** -6 **32.** 8 **33.** 9 **34.** -8 **35.** 7 **36.** $4n$ **37.** $16v - 14$ **38.** $5x + 3$ **39.** $5b - 8$ **40.** $-2g - 18$ **41.** $5y + 4 + 6c$ **42.** $13r - 7f + 8$ **43.** $5t - 9 + (-2b)$ **44.** $x + 15$ **45.** $11 + (-3d) - 8s$ **46.** a^9 **47.** c^{11} **48.** m^5 **49.** z^{18} **50.** y^{13} **51.** 48 cm **52.** 117 m **53.** 12 km **54.** 24 dm **55.** 35 mm

CHAPTER 2

Pages 408–409

1. $15y$ **2.** $13a$ **3.** $5x$ **4.** $34n$ **5.** $14j$ **6.** qm **7.** $(5c)(2s)$ **8.** $(6t)^3$ **9.** $(10e)(7k)$ **10.** $(i)(12v)$ **11.** $5 + (4z + 3)$ **12.** $3d + (f + 7)$ **13.** $(25g + 2w) + 14$ **14.** $8 + (r + k)$ **15.** $(6b + 9c) + 11e$ **16.** $300 = 300$ **17.** $400 = 400$ **18.** $900 = 900$ **19.** $120 = 120$ **20.** $100 = 100$ **21.** $3x - 3j$ **22.** $28w + (-20)$ **23.** $-12 + (-6z)$ **24.** $-8f + (-8g)$ **25.** $2k + (-8)$ **26.** $5(3m + y)$ **27.** $-n(9 + 7)$ **28.** $m(c - h)$ **29.** $q(y^4 + s^2)$ **30.** $-w(r + h^3)$ **31.** -6 **32.** 9 **33.** c^3 **34.** $-u$ **35.** 2 **36.** $\frac{1}{4}$; $(4)(\frac{1}{4}) = 1$ **37.** p; $(\frac{1}{p})(p) = 1$ **38.** $\frac{1}{m^5}$; $(\frac{1}{m^5})(m^5) = 1$ **39.** h; $(\frac{1}{h})(h) = 1$ **40.** $\frac{1}{15}$; $(15)(\frac{1}{15}) = 1$ **41.** 2.25 **42.** 31.4 **43.** 18.33 **44.** 17.9 **45.** 5.23 **46.** $81u^4$ **47.** $-125y^3$ **48.** $64a^6$ **49.** $256d^2$ **50.** $-1{,}331n^3$ **51.** $16x$ **52.** $27h$ **53.** $13s$ **54.** $19g^3$ **55.** $11m^2$

CHAPTER 3

Pages 410–411

1. F, T, F, F **2.** T, F, F, F **3.** F, F, T, F **4.** F, F, F, T **5.** F, T, F, F **6.** 18 **7.** 59 **8.** -1 **9.** 33 **10.** -2 **11.** 8 **12.** 5.6 **13.** 23 **14.** 12.8 **15.** 55 **16.** 7 **17.** 24 **18.** -9 **19.** 6 **20.** 8 **21.** 8 **22.** 18 **23.** 25 **24.** -48 **25.** 16 **26.** 5 **27.** 12 **28.** 49 **29.** 0 **30.** 6 **31.** $s = \frac{P}{5}$ **32.** $l = (\frac{V}{wh})$ **33.** $r - \frac{C}{2\pi}$ **34.** $P = 10s$ **35.** $h = \frac{2A}{b}$ **36.** 8 **37.** 25 **38.** 30 **39.** 24 **40.** 21

41.

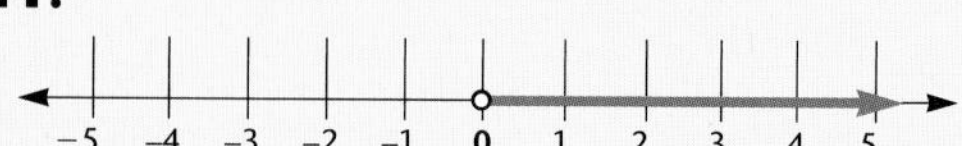

42.

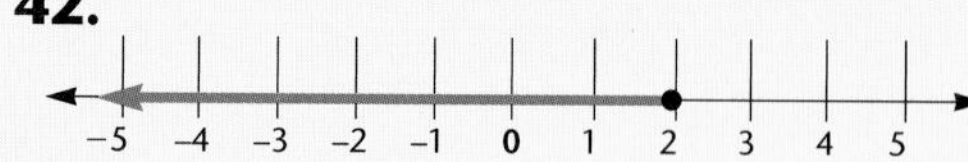

43.

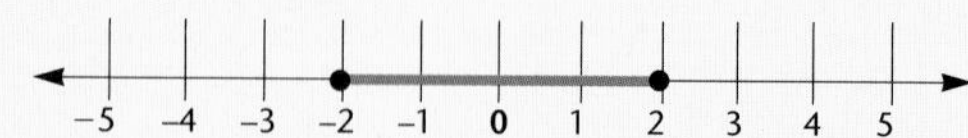

456 *Selected Answers and Solutions* *Algebra*

44.

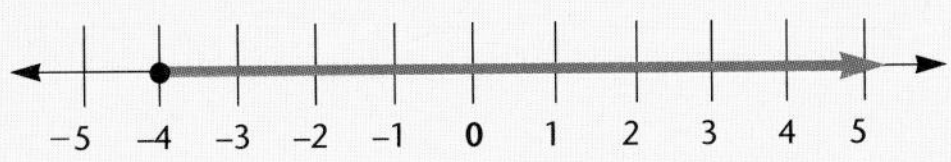

45.

–5 –4 –3 –2 –1 0 1 2 3 4 5

46. $b < 3$ **47.** $e \geq 15$ **48.** $t > 6$ **49.** m > -4 **50.** $g \geq -15$

CHAPTER 4

Pages 412–413

1. $5 \cdot x - 4 = 26$; 6 **2.** $x + (x + 1) = -21$; $-10, -11$ **3.** $x + (x + 2) + (x + 4) = 51$; 15, 17, 19 **4.** $8x - 60 = 4$; 8 **5.** 1.5% **6.** 77% **7.** $1,680 **8.** 200 CDs **9.** 22.88 **10.** 351.5 **11.** 16 **12.** 417.15 **13.** $51\frac{2}{3}$ km **14.** 65 mph **15.** $31\frac{1}{2}$ km **16.** $4\frac{1}{2}$ miles per hour **17.** 5 nickels and 15 dimes **18.** 36 nickels and 12 dimes **19.** 25 nickels and 100 dimes **20.** 18 nickels and 3 dimes **21.** $300 **22.** $625 **23.** 5% **24.** $520 **25.** $2.75 **26.** $4.93 **27.** 8 pounds **28.** 6 pounds **29.** 4 **30.** 21 **31.** 5 **32.** 56 **33.** 10 **34.** 32 **35.** 12

CHAPTER 5

Pages 414–415

1. $(y \cdot y \cdot y)(y \cdot y \cdot y)(y \cdot y \cdot y) = y^9$ **2.** $(a \cdot a)(a \cdot a)(a \cdot a)(a \cdot a) = a^8$ **3.** $(x + y)(x + y)(x + y)(x + y)(x + y)(x + y) = (x + y)^6$ **4.** 93 **5.** 74 **6.** n^2 **7.** $(5g + 3y)^6$ **8.** $(h - i)^5$ **9.** $5.54 \cdot 10^{-9}$ **10.** $9 \cdot 106$ **11.** $7.85 \cdot 10^{-7}$ **12.** 260,000 **13.** 0.00314 **14.** 5,210,000 **15.** $6.1(10^{-3})$ **16.** $3.4(10^8)$ **17.** $5.46 \cdot 102$ **18.** $5 \cdot 10^{-5}$ **19.** $1.848 \cdot 10^{-1}$ **20.** $11x + 4$; $4x^2 - x - 2$ **21.** $3c^4 + 4c^2 + 4c + 6$; $-c^4 - 2c^2 + 2c - 4$ **22.** $-2w^5 - 2w$; $-4w^5 - 12w^4 - 4w^3 - 2w^2 - 10$ **23.** $k^5 + k^4 + k^3 + w^2 + 8$; $k^5 - k^4 + k^3 - w^2 - 2$ **24.** $n^7 + n^5 + n^3 + n^2 + n - 3$; $-n^7 + n^5 + n^3 - n^2 + n - 3$ **25.** $8d^7 + 3d^6 + 9d^3 + d^2 + d - 8$; $8d^7 + 3d^6 + 9d^3 - d^2 - d + 8$ **26.** $y^2 + 7y + 12$ **27.** $b^2 - 16$ **28.** $3n^5 + 6n^4 - 24n^3$ **29.** $-4x^4 + 15x^2 + 25$ **30.** $c^6 + 2c^5 + c^4$ **31.** $3z^2 - 5z - 2$ **32.** $2u^5 + 5u^4 + 4u^3 + 6u^2 + 15u + 12$ **33.** $12y^8 - 24y^5 - 3y^4 + 6y$ **34.** $3x^2 + 4x - 3$ **35.** $-5y^3 + 6y^2 - 7y - 8$ **36.** $(h^2 + 2h)$ **37.** 2 **38.** $6t^2 + 10t - 3$ **39.** $2y$ **40.** $(25x^3 - 5x^2 + x - 2)$

CHAPTER 6

Pages 416–417

1. 25 **2.** 11 **3.** 9 **4.** $4x$ **5.** $5ad$ **6.** 10 **7.** $6x$ **8.** 5 **9.** $7xy^2$ **10.** $13wt$ **11.** $(x + 7)(x - 8)$ **12.** $(c + 3)(c + 3)$ **13.** $(y - 4)(y + 3)$ **14.** $3(m + 2)(m + 6)$ **15.** $5x^2(x - 3)(x + 4)$ **16.** $3(2e + 7)(e + 2)$ **17.** $2(2n - 1)(3n - 5)$ **18.** $(z + 13)(3z - 4)$ **19.** $(2s + 1)(5s + 6)$ **20.** $3v^2(v + 2)(v + 3)$ **21.** $(b - 9)(b + 9)$ **22.** $(q - 20)(q + 20)$ **23.** $(6g - 7)(6g + 7)$ **24.** $(9r - 4)(9r + 4)$ **25.** $(5w^2 - 3x)(5w^2 + 3x)$ **26.** $(i - 13)(i - 13)$ **27.** $(y + 8)(y + 8)$ **28.** $(k - 10)(k - 10)$ **29.** $(p + 11)(p + 11)$ **30.** $(m - 22)(m - 22)$ **31.** 0 **32.** -4 **33.** 4 and -6 **34.** 2 and -2 **35.** 4 and -9 **36.** -4 and -6 **37.** 3 and 6 **38.** -4 and -7 **39.** 1 **40.** -2 and -4

Algebra Selected Answers and Solutions **457**

CHAPTER 7

Pages 418–419

1. frequency **2.** stem-and-leaf plot **3.** histogram **4.** range **5.** mean **6.** mode **7.** box-and-whiskers plot **8.** probability **9.** impossible **10.** sample space **11.** dependent **12.** independent **13.** fundamental principle of counting

14.

5	8	9	9	9		
6	0	3	4	8	9	
7	3	3	5	7	8	
8	0	1	5	7		
9	0	0	1	6	7	8

15. 4 **16.** 13 **17.** 59 **18.** 58 **19.** 98 **20.** 7

21.

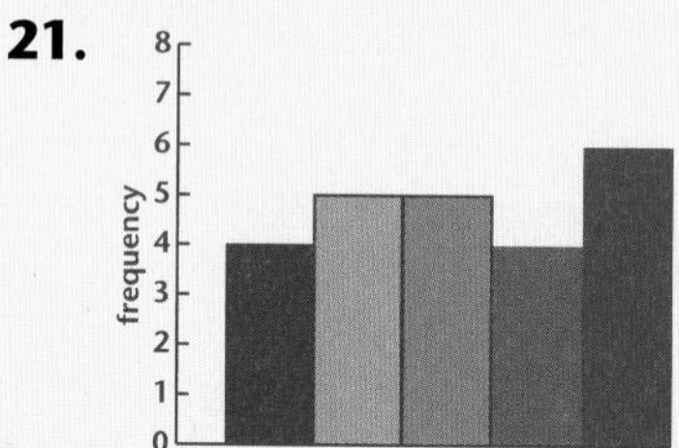

22. \$7.67 **23.** \$4.90 **24.** \$4.77 **25.** \$4.77 **26.** 10 **27.** 2 **28.** 8 **29.** between 5 and 9 **30.** 8 **31.** $\frac{1}{6}$ **32.** $\frac{1}{2}$ **33.** 0 **34.** $\frac{2}{3}$ **35.** $\frac{1}{12}$ **36.** $\frac{1}{4}$ **37.** $\frac{5}{12}$ **38.** $\frac{2}{9}$ **39.** $\frac{1}{90}$ **40.** $\frac{1}{30}$

CHAPTER 8

Pages 420–421

1. $\frac{7}{9}$ **2.** $\frac{4}{5}$ **3.** $\frac{2}{3}$ **4.** $-\frac{1}{12}$ **5.** $\frac{1}{2}$ **6.** c^5 **7.** $4s^5$ **8.** $\frac{5}{7h^3g^2}$ **9.** $\frac{2y^2}{9}$ **10.** $(p-4)$ **11.** $(y+3)$ **12.** $\frac{1}{(m-4)}$ **13.** $\frac{x}{2}$ **14.** $33\frac{5}{27}$ **15.** $2\frac{3}{16}$ **16.** $\frac{1}{(y-4)^2}$ **17.** $(d+6)$ **18.** ef **19.** $3\frac{9}{32}$ **20.** 12 **21.** $\frac{1}{5}$ **22.** $\frac{cd}{u^2}$ **23.** $\frac{1}{xw}$ **24.** $\frac{5}{16}$ **25.** $\frac{18+y^2}{9y}$ **26.** $\frac{5b-1}{(b-1)^2}$ **27.** $\frac{(k-8)}{(k-3)(k+2)}$ **28.** $\frac{-3x(x-24)}{(x+8)(x-8)}$ **29.** $\frac{-3}{(v+3)(v-3)}$ **30.** 15 **31.** 9 **32.** 76.8 **33.** −49 **34.** $1\frac{1}{2}$ **35.** 120 **36.** −6 **37.** 13.5 **38.** $-3\frac{1}{2}$ **39.** $4\frac{1}{4}$ **40.** $-\frac{3}{4}$ **41.** 308 votes **42.** 9 games **43.** 4 jelly recipes **44.** $13\frac{13}{20}$ km **45.** $1{,}012\frac{1}{2}$ hours of television

CHAPTER 9

Pages 422–423

1. (4, 0) **2.** (−3, −1) **3.** (−2, 4) **4.** (0, −3) **5.** (1, −1)

6.–9.

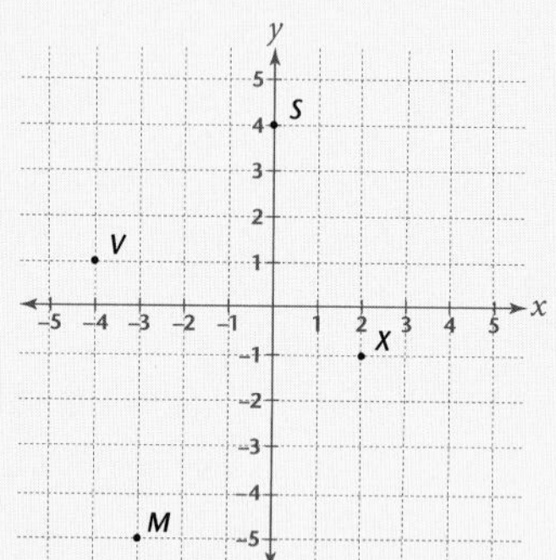

10.

$y = x - 2$	
x	**y**
−1	−3
0	−2
1	−1

11.

$y = 3x + 1$	
x	**y**
−1	−2
0	1
1	4

458 *Selected Answers and Solutions Algebra*

12. x-intercept $= (-1, 0)$; y-intercept $= (0, 1)$ **13.** x-intercept $= (4, 0)$; y-intercept $= (0, -4)$ **14.** x-intercept $= (3, 0)$; y-intercept $= (0, 3)$
15. x-intercept $= (\frac{2}{5}, 0)$; y-intercept $= (0, -2)$ **16.** $m = 2$ **17.** $m = 3$ **18.** $m = -1$ **19.** $m = 1$

20.

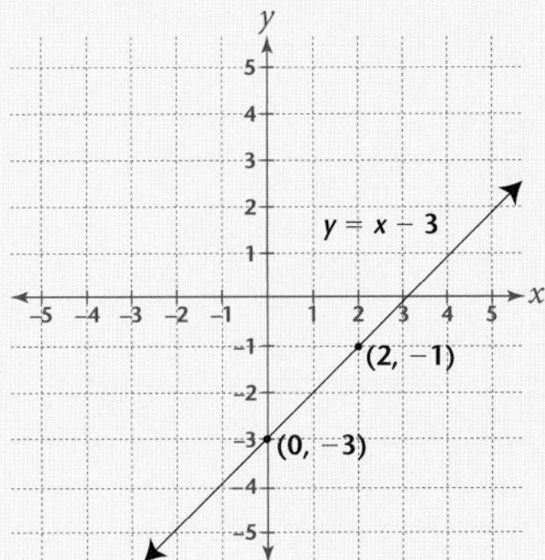

21.

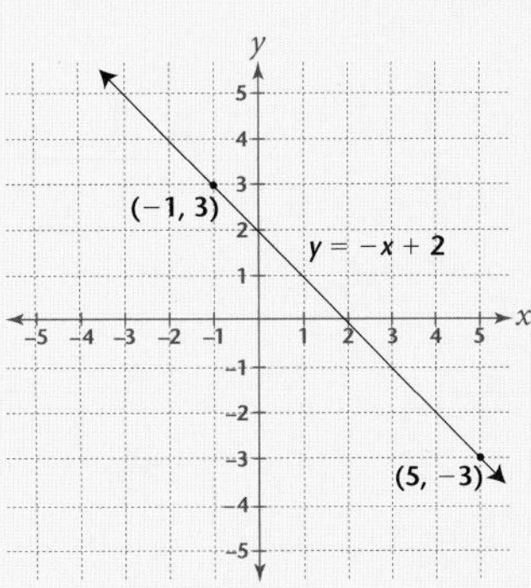

22.

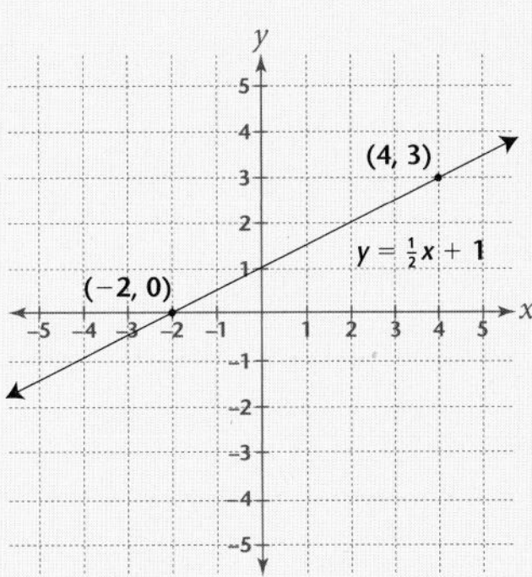

23.

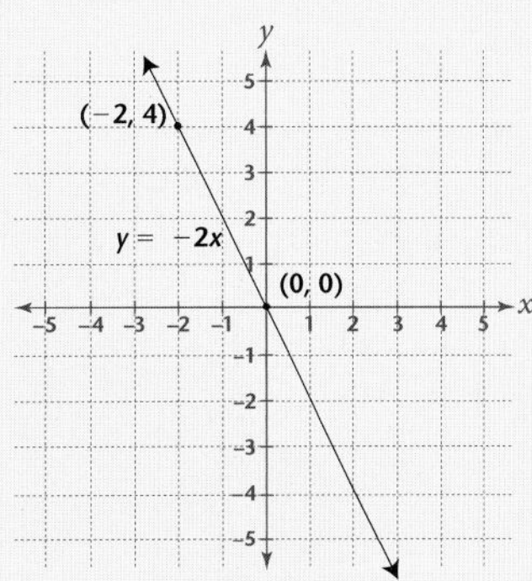

24. $y = 3x + 1$ **25.** $y = -x - 1$ **26.** $y = 4x - 4$ **27.** $y = \frac{1}{2}x + 1$ **28.** yes **29.** no
30. -6; -6 **31.** 21; 6 **32.** 15; 0

33.

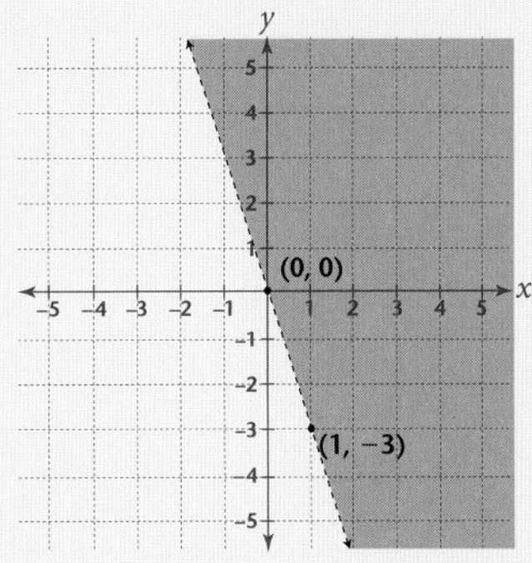

34.

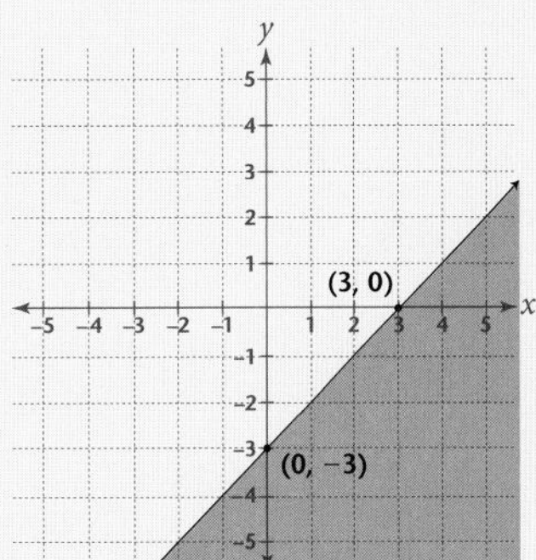

Algebra Selected Answers and Solutions **459**

35.

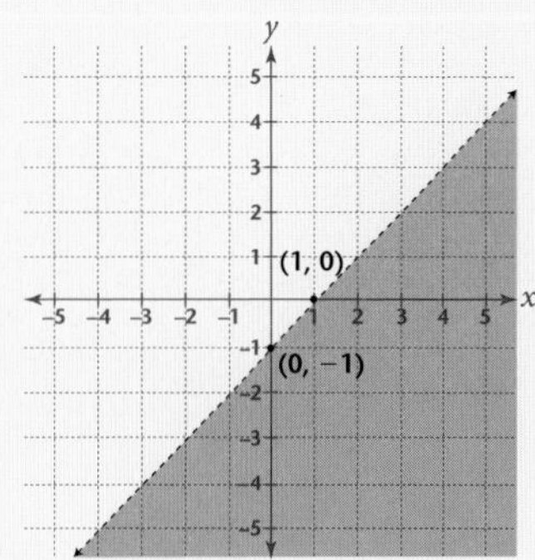

CHAPTER 10

Pages 424–425

1.

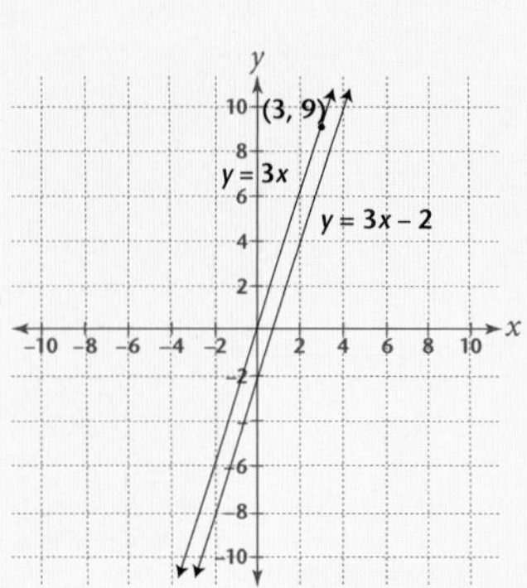

2.

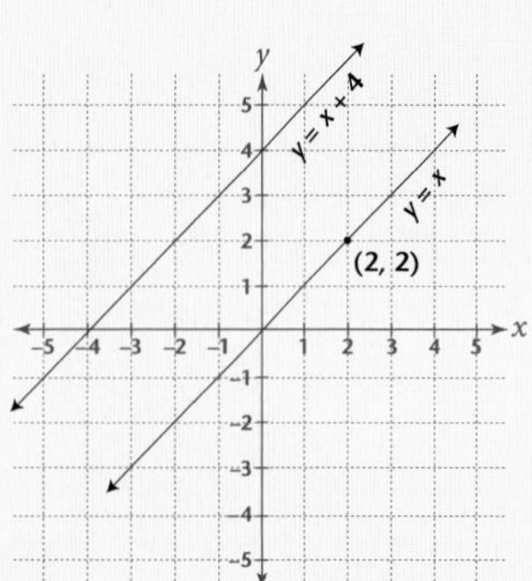

3.

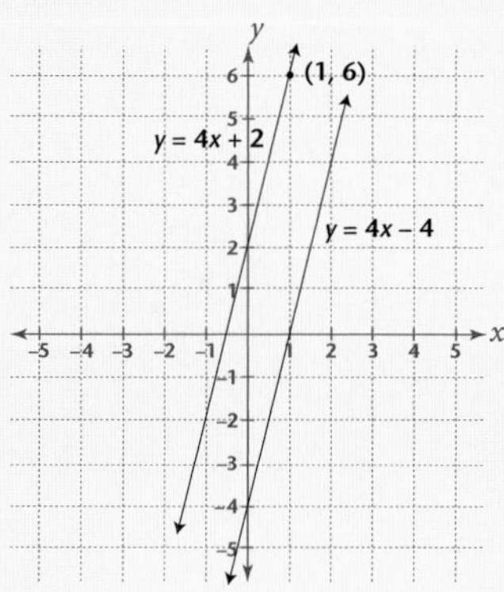

4.

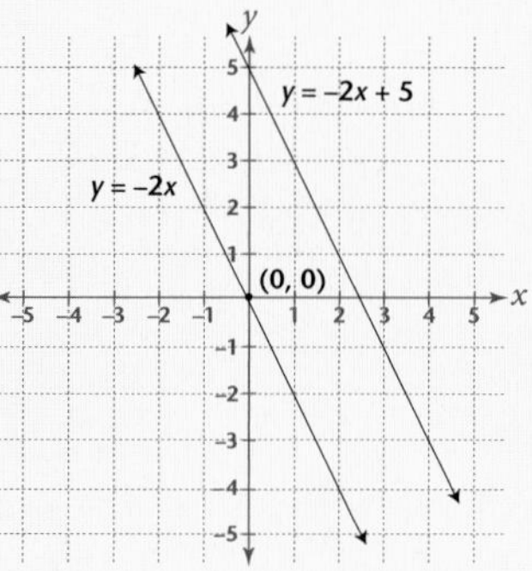

5.

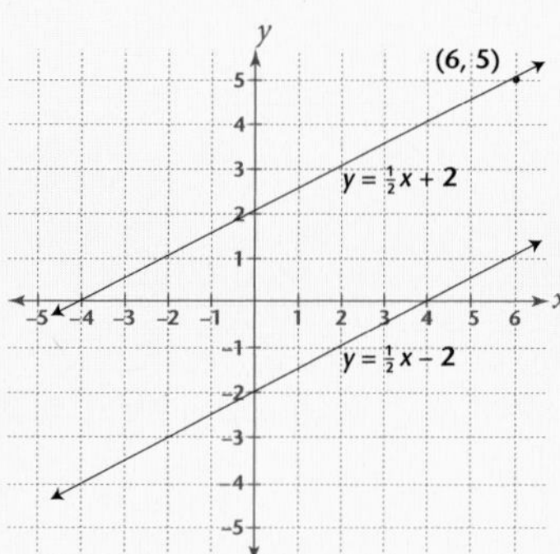

460 *Selected Answers and Solutions Algebra*

6.

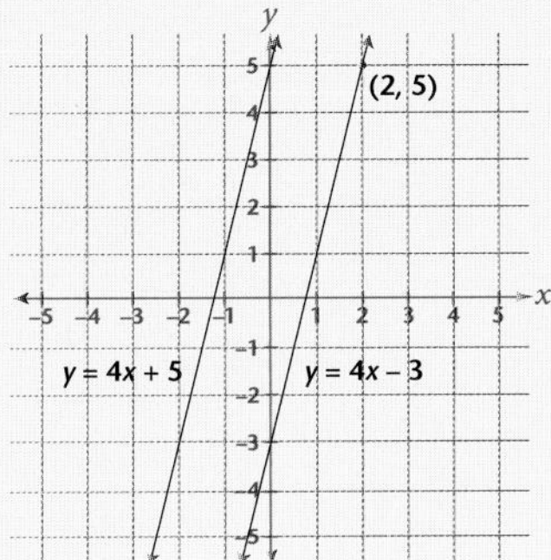

7.

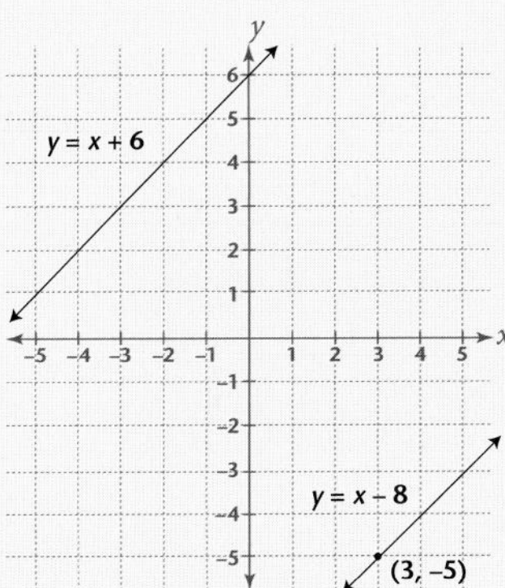

8.

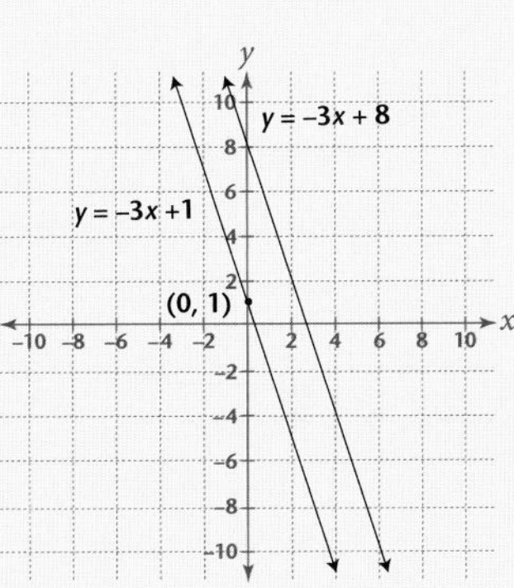

9.

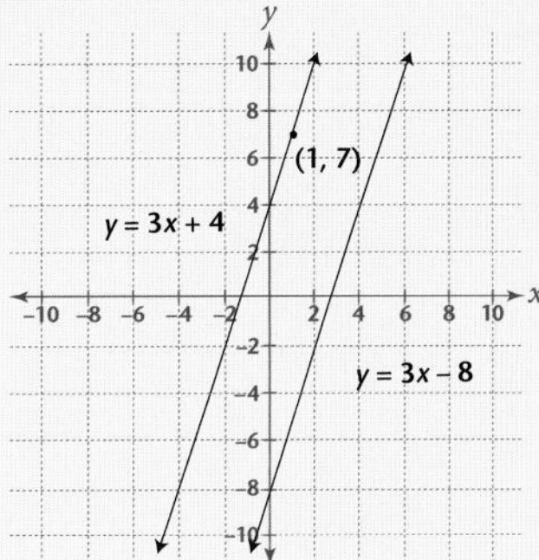

10.

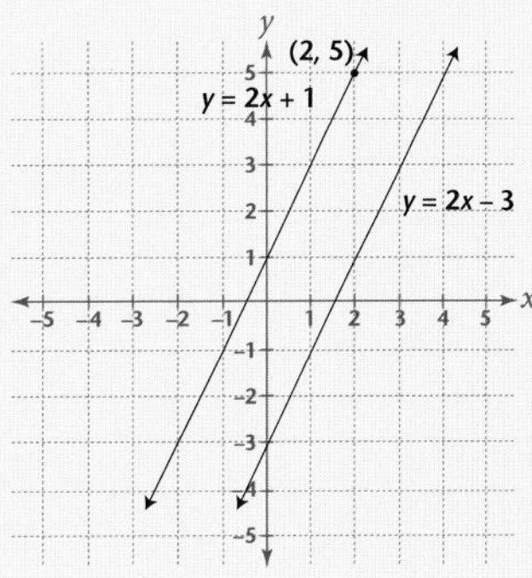

11. (3, 7) **12.** (2, 7) **13.** (6, 4)
14. (−1, −7) **15.** (−2, −2)
16. (−4, 7) **17.** (2, −5) **18.** none
19. (4, 3) **20.** (4, 0)
21. (2, 3)

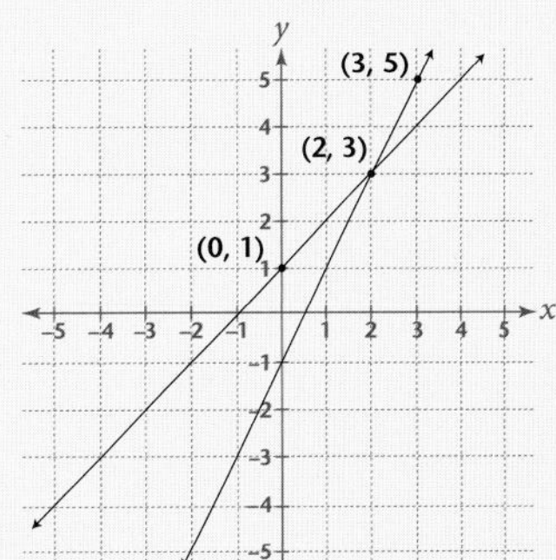

Algebra Selected Answers and Solutions **461**

22. (1, 4)

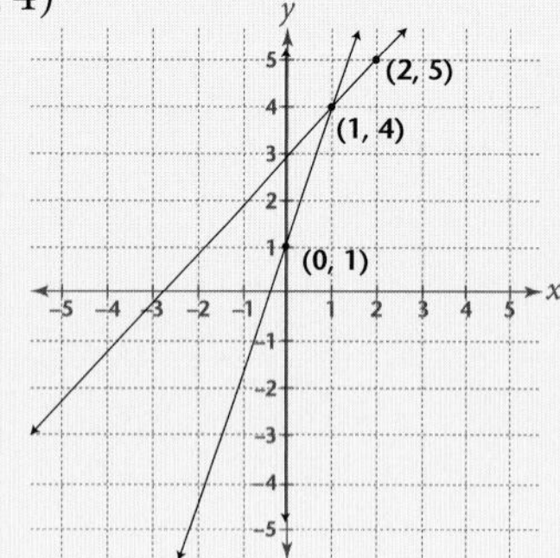

23. (2, 6)

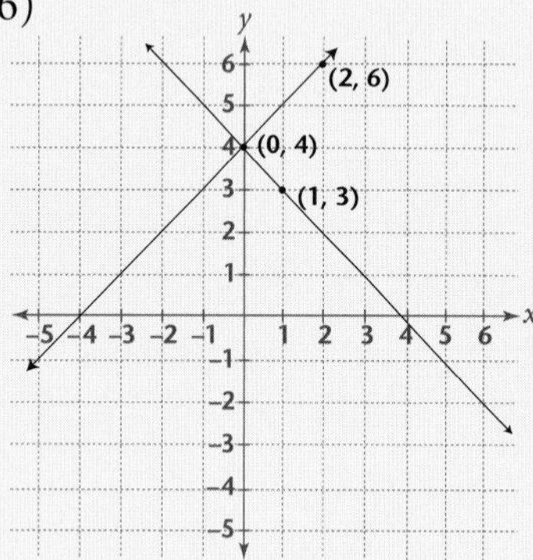

24. False, all parallel lines have the same slope **25.** True **26.** False, $3(6b + 2) = 18b + 3$ **27.** False, there are 144 eggs in 12 dozen

28. $x = 2, x = 4, y = 1, y = 3$

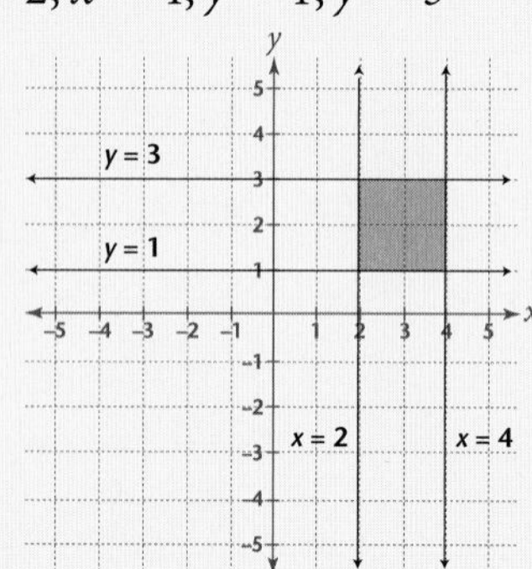

29. $x = 2, x = 1, y = 5, y = 4$

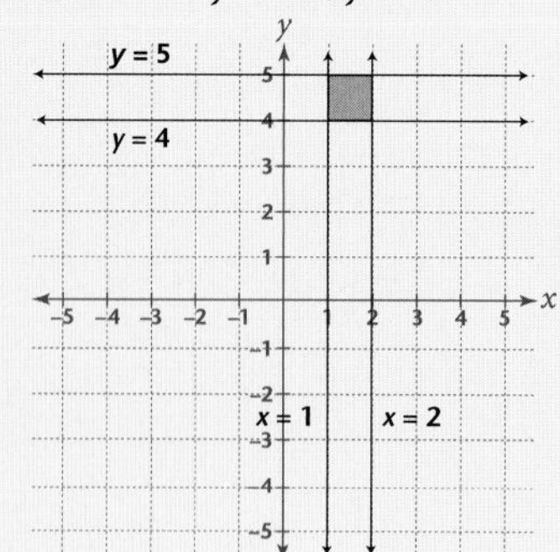

30. $x = 3, x = -5, y = -2, y = 4$

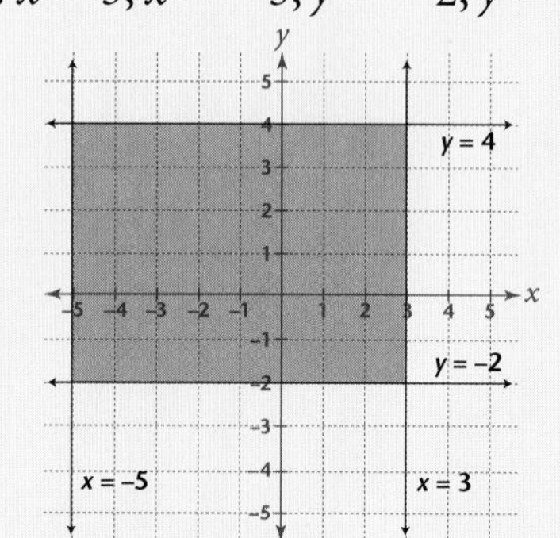

31. 6 and 42
32. 25 degrees and 155 degrees
33. 80 degrees and 100 degrees
34. 10 degrees and 80 degrees
35. length = 70 feet; width = 80 feet

CHAPTER 11

Pages 426–427

1. $0.875\overline{0}$, terminating **2.** $0.\overline{6}$, repeating **3.** $0.0625\overline{0}$, terminating **4.** $0.\overline{36}$, repeating **5.** $0.625\overline{0}$, terminating **6.** $\frac{3}{5}$ **7.** $\frac{5}{6}$ **8.** $\frac{15}{16}$ **9.** $\frac{5}{32}$ **10.** $\frac{2}{9}$ **11.** 3; rational **12.** 2.6918004; irrational **13.** 3; rational **14.** 9.6548938; irrational **15.** 6.7694724; irrational **16.** 36 **17.** $52x^3y$ **18.** $\frac{8}{9}$ **19.** $\frac{5g^2}{6a}$ **20.** $\frac{7t^3}{11b^4}$ **21.** 15 **22.** $6\sqrt{2}$ **23.** $18\sqrt{3}$ **24.** $4\sqrt{3}$

462 *Selected Answers and Solutions Algebra*

25. $8x\sqrt{3}$ **26.** $3\sqrt{\frac{10}{5}}$ **27.** 6 **28.** $\frac{5\sqrt{5}}{2}$
29. $(4 - 2\sqrt{3})$ **30.** $\frac{8\sqrt{5}-10}{11}$ **31.** 8
32. 8 **33.** $\frac{25}{36}$ **34.** 36 **35.** 289
36. $y^{3\frac{1}{5}}$ **37.** $m^{1\frac{1}{2}}$ **38.** w **39.** $q^{5\frac{1}{4}}$
40. $d^{3\frac{1}{7}}$

CHAPTER 12

Pages 428–429

1. obtuse and interior **2.** right and exterior **3.** alternate interior and obtuse **4.** right and corresponding **5.** supplementary and exterior **6.** acute and vertical **7.** supplementary and interior **8.** obtuse and corresponding **9.** right and corresponding **10.** acute and exterior **11.** 65.7° **12.** 65.7° **13.** 114.3° **14.** 114.3° **15.** 114.3° **16.** 65.7° **17.** 114.3° **18.** 62° **19.** 76° **20.** 45° **21.** 72° **22.** 60° **23.** SSS **24.** SAS **25.** ASA **26.** 1 **27.** 1 **28.** 0.5 **29.** 0 **30.** 0.5 **31.** 97 feet **32.** 18 feet **33.** 62 feet **34.** 3.7 feet **35.** 25.2 meters

CHAPTER 13

Pages 430–431

1. $x = 7, x = 3$ **2.** $x = 6, x = -5$ **3.** $x = 0, x = -2$ **4.** $x = -3, x = -8$ **5.** $x = -\frac{1}{5}, x = 2$ **6.** $x = 5, x = 11$ **7.** $x^2 + x - 12$ **8.** $x^2 - 13x + 42$ **9.** $x^2 - 6x - 16$ **10.** $2x^2 - 7x + 3$ **11.** $3x^2 - 10x - 8$ **12.** $x2 + 5x - 6$ **13.** $m = -3 + \sqrt{7}$ or $-3 - \sqrt{7}$ **14.** $c = -4 + \sqrt{26}$ or $-4 - \sqrt{26}$ **15.** $v = -2 + \sqrt{15}$ or $-2 - \sqrt{15}$ **16.** $x = 7 + \sqrt{39}$ or $7 - \sqrt{39}$ **17.** $d = -1 + \sqrt{\frac{3}{2}} - 1 - \sqrt{\frac{3}{2}} = \frac{-1 + \sqrt{3}}{2}$ or $\frac{-1 - \sqrt{3}}{2}$ **18.** $y = 5 + \sqrt{5}$ or $5 - \sqrt{5}$ **19.** $x = -4$ or $x = \frac{1}{2}$ **20.** $y = -3$ or $y = -11$ **21.** $x = -2$ or $x = \frac{1}{2}$ **22.** $y = -8$ or $y = 2$ **23.** $y = -3$ or $y = 5$ **24.** $x = \frac{7}{2}$ or $x = 2$
25. $x = -3, (-4, 0), (-2, 0)$

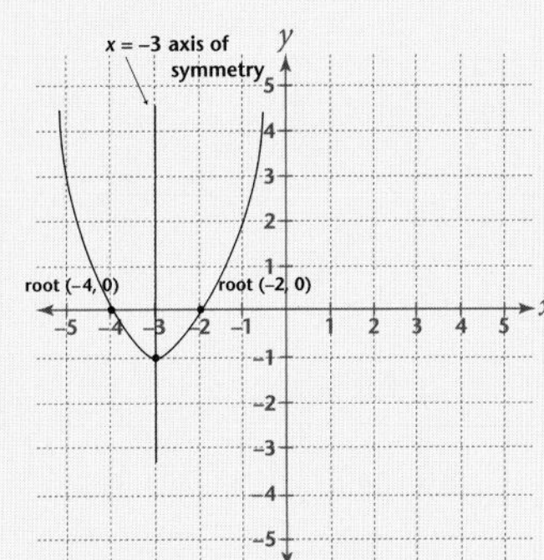

26. $x = \frac{5}{4}. (-\frac{1}{2}, 0), (3, 0)$

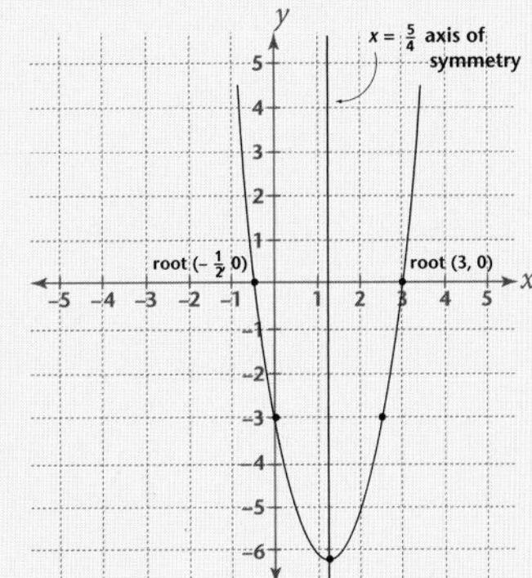

Algebra *Selected Answers and Solutions* **463**

27. $x = 5, (4, 0), (6, 0)$

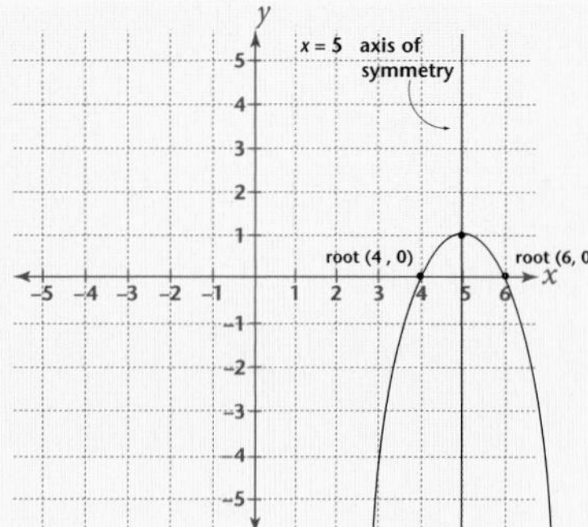

28. $x = 6, (3, 0), (9, 0)$

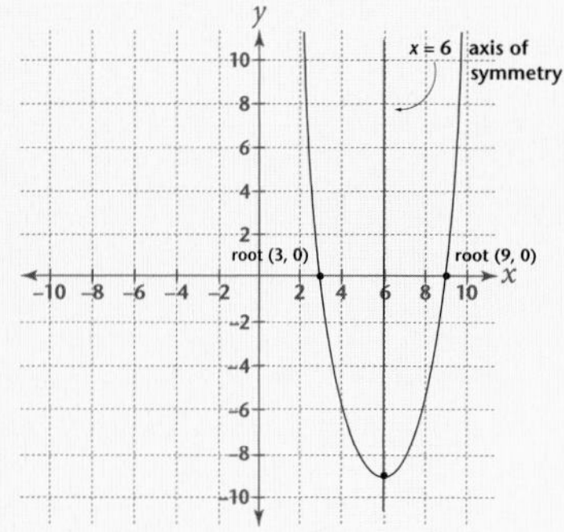

29. $x = -\frac{1}{2}, (-2, 0), (1, 0)$

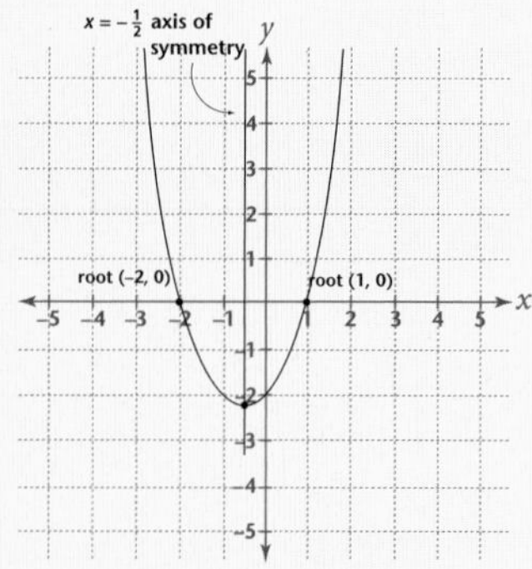

30. $x = -\frac{5}{4}, (-\frac{3}{2}, 0), (-1, 0)$

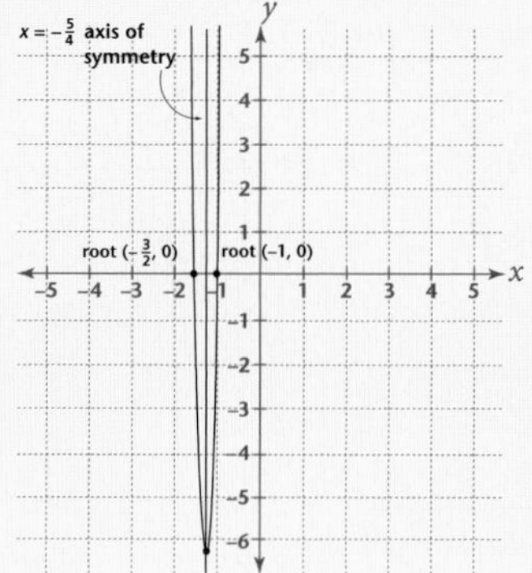

1. 13, 14 **32.** 15, 17 or $-15, -17$ **33.** 16, 18 or $-16, -18$ **34.** 8 and 9 years old **35.** Trixie is 11 years old. Her brother is 3 years old.

464 *Selected Answers and Solutions Algebra*

Review of Basic Skills

Review of Basic Skills 1, page 470

1. ones **2.** tens **3.** hundreds **4.** hundreds **5.** tens **6.** ones **7.** thousands **8.** hundreds **9.** tens **10.** ones **11.** hundreds **12.** thousands **13.** ones **14.** ten-thousands **15.** ten-thousands **16.** hundred-thousands **17.** thousands **18.** millions **19.** hundred-thousands **20.** hundred-millions

Review of Basic Skills 2, page 471

1. 10 **2.** 20 **3.** 190 **4.** 360 **5.** 1,890 **6.** 2,390 **7.** 4,020 **8.** 55,490 **9.** 63,560 **10.** 250,960 **11.** 100 **12.** 100 **13.** 300 **14.** 600 **15.** 800 **16.** 8,700 **17.** 13,400 **18.** 64,800 **19.** 267,500 **20.** 416,300 **21.** 1,000 **22.** 1,000 **23.** 5,000 **24.** 9,000 **25.** 10,000 **26.** 21,000 **27.** 46,000 **28.** 148,000 **29.** 250,000 **30.** 864,000

Review of Basic Skills 3, page 472

1. 6 **2.** 9 **3.** 8 **4.** 15 **5.** 19 **6.** 27 **7.** 113 **8.** 510 **9.** 1,017 **10.** 36 **11.** 118 **12.** 112 **13.** 377 **14.** 43,888 **15.** 110,682 **16.** 104,248 **17.** 256,818 **18.** 1,050 **19.** 2,107 **20.** 6,628

Review of Basic Skills 4, page 473

1. 4 **2.** 5 **3.** 10 **4.** 11 **5.** 32 **6.** 37 **7.** 141 **8.** 160 **9.** 404 **10.** 506 **11.** 309 **12.** 411 **13.** 736 **14.** 950 **15.** 40,736 **16.** 49,654 **17.** 1,692 **18.** 4,052 **19.** 873 **20.** 80,033 **21.** 59,960 **22.** 17,785 **23.** 493,000 **24.** 490,000 **25.** 400,000

Review of Basic Skills 5, page 474

1. 2, 4, 6, 8, 10, 12, 14, 16, 18, 20
2. 3, 6, 9, 12, 15, 18, 21, 24, 27, 30
3. 4, 8, 12, 16, 20, 24, 28, 32, 36, 40
4. 5, 10, 15, 20, 25, 30, 35, 40, 45, 50
5. 6, 12, 18, 24, 30, 36, 42, 48, 54, 60
6. 7, 14, 21, 28, 35, 42, 49, 56, 63, 70
7. 8, 16, 24, 32, 40, 48, 56, 64, 72, 80
8. 9, 18, 27, 36, 45, 54, 63, 72, 81, 90
9. 10, 20, 30, 40, 50, 60, 70, 80, 90, 100
10. 138 **11.** 182 **12.** 315 **13.** 252 **14.** 576 **15.** 162 **16.** 1,610 **17.** 987 **18.** 1,443 **19.** 3,312 **20.** 2,997 **21.** 3,087 **22.** 2,163 **23.** 6,768 **24.** 21,298 **25.** 48,020

Review of Basic Skills 6, page 475

1. 30 **2.** 500 **3.** 7,000 **4.** 60 **5.** 1,000 **6.** 1,400 **7.** 12,000 **8.** 270 **9.** 2,700 **10.** 27,000 **11.** 430 **12.** 4,300 **13.** 43,000 **14.** 2,670 **15.** 26,700 **16.** 267,000 **17.** 3,490 **18.** 34,900 **19.** 349,000 **20.** 3,490,000 **21.** 830 **22.** 8,300 **23.** 83,000 **24.** 5,860 **25.** 58,600 **26.** 586,000 **27.** 41,840 **28.** 418,400 **29.** 4,184,000 **30.** 41,840,000

Review of Basic Skills 7, page 476

1. 8 **2.** 7 **3.** 2 **4.** 4 **5.** 10 **6.** 6 **7.** 7 **8.** 7 **9.** 6 **10.** 9 **11.** 9 **12.** 9 **13.** 9 **14.** 7 **15.** 6 **16.** 23 **17.** 53 **18.** 123 **19.** 121 **20.** 207 **21.** 47 **22.** 17 **23.** 15 **24.** 50 **25.** 57

Algebra Selected Answers and Solutions **465**

Review of Basic Skills 8, page 477

1. $27\frac{3}{14}$ **2.** $15\frac{1}{39}$ **3.** $45\frac{6}{7}$ **4.** $9\frac{7}{71}$ **5.** $24\frac{7}{20}$ **6.** 591.52 **7.** 423.10 **8.** 2,838.33 **9.** 7,467.47 **10.** 17,082.15

Review of Basic Skills 9, page 478

1. 170 **2.** 304 **3.** 120 **4.** 460 **5.** 360 **6.** 502 **7.** 610 **8.** 6,011 **9.** 21,100 **10.** 4,300

Review of Basic Skills 10, page 479

1. 9 **2.** 16 **3.** 25 **4.** 36 **5.** 49 **6.** 64 **7.** 81 **8.** 100 **9.** 32 **10.** 625 **11.** 16 **12.** 27 **13.** 125 **14.** 1,000 **15.** 64 **16.** 900 **17.** 8,000 **18.** 121 **19.** 1,000,000 **20.** 1,000,000 **21.** 23 **22.** 24 **23.** 33 **24.** 92 **25.** 75 **26.** 105 **27.** 43 **28.** 923 **29.** 464 **30.** 106 **31.** 43 **32.** 44 **33.** 63 **34.** 65 **35.** 905 **36.** 433 **37.** 58 **38.** 364 **39.** 944 **40.** 1005

Review of Basic Skills 11, page 480

1. 7 **2.** 6 **3.** 12 **4.** 8 **5.** 23 **6.** 1 **7.** 8 **8.** 8 **9.** 5 **10.** 35 **11.** 43 **12.** 15 **13.** 25 **14.** 159 **15.** 22 **16.** 23 **17.** 45 **18.** 0 **19.** 10 **20.** 3

Review of Basic Skills 12, page 481

1. 47.4 **2.** 64.2 **3.** 53.2 **4.** 70.7 **5.** 62.7 **6.** 50.7 **7.** 61.7 **8.** 53.7 **9.** 68.6 **10.** 51.6 **11.** 103.5 **12.** 54.7 **13.** 95.3 **14.** 42.7 **15.** 41.2

Review of Basic Skills 13, page 482

1. $<$ **2.** $>$ **3.** $<$ **4.** $<$ **5.** $<$ **6.** $>$ **7.** $<$ **8.** $<$ **9.** $<$ **10.** $>$ **11.** $<$ **12.** $<$ **13.** $>$ **14.** $<$ **15.** $<$ **16.** $>$ **17.** $<$ **18.** $<$ **19.** $>$ **20.** $<$

Review of Basic Skills 14, page 483

1. $\frac{15}{30}$ **2.** $\frac{10}{24}$ **3.** $\frac{9}{21}$ **4.** $\frac{12}{18}$ **5.** $\frac{21}{36}$ **6.** $\frac{27}{39}$ **7.** $\frac{20}{35}$ **8.** $\frac{15}{40}$ **9.** $\frac{30}{35}$ **10.** $\frac{90}{100}$ **11.** $\frac{9}{33}$ **12.** $\frac{18}{39}$ **13.** $\frac{25}{60}$ **14.** $\frac{18}{45}$ **15.** $\frac{36}{64}$ **16.** $\frac{15}{65}$ **17.** $\frac{15}{51}$ **18.** $\frac{12}{38}$ **19.** $\frac{30}{550}$ **20.** $\frac{14}{630}$

Review of Basic Skills 15, page 484

1. $\frac{1}{2}$ **2.** $\frac{1}{23}$ **3.** $\frac{5}{11}$ **4.** $\frac{1}{5}$ **5.** $\frac{1}{3}$ **6.** $\frac{28}{29}$ **7.** $\frac{7}{9}$ **8.** $\frac{1}{9}$ **9.** $\frac{1}{7}$ **10.** $\frac{3}{4}$ **11.** $\frac{1}{5}$ **12.** $\frac{1}{4}$ **13.** $\frac{1}{2}$ **14.** $\frac{2}{11}$ **15.** $\frac{1}{2}$ **16.** $\frac{1}{4}$ **17.** $\frac{1}{3}$ **18.** $\frac{5}{22}$ **19.** $\frac{5}{26}$ **20.** $\frac{1}{2}$

Review of Basic Skills 16, page 485

1. $3\frac{3}{5}$ **2.** 6 **3.** $3\frac{1}{6}$ **4.** $4\frac{2}{3}$ **5.** $5\frac{3}{4}$ **6.** 6 **7.** $7\frac{3}{5}$ **8.** 6 **9.** $5\frac{1}{11}$ **10.** $3\frac{4}{5}$ **11.** $1\frac{5}{8}$ **12.** $6\frac{7}{8}$ **13.** $4\frac{2}{3}$ **14.** 8 **15.** 30 **16.** $7\frac{3}{4}$ **17.** $8\frac{1}{3}$ **18.** $8\frac{2}{7}$ **19.** $10\frac{1}{5}$ **20.** $12\frac{1}{3}$

Review of Basic Skills 17, page 486

1. $\frac{17}{5}$ **2.** $\frac{32}{5}$ **3.** $\frac{31}{6}$ **4.** $\frac{86}{12}$ **5.** $\frac{13}{6}$ **6.** $\frac{19}{2}$ **7.** $\frac{37}{9}$ **8.** $\frac{90}{11}$ **9.** $\frac{17}{3}$ **10.** $\frac{25}{3}$ **11.** $\frac{88}{13}$ **12.** $\frac{50}{3}$ **13.** $\frac{59}{8}$ **14.** $\frac{47}{3}$ **15.** $\frac{191}{14}$ **16.** $\frac{29}{3}$ **17.** $\frac{61}{10}$ **18.** $\frac{62}{3}$ **19.** $\frac{341}{21}$ **20.** $\frac{89}{8}$

Review of Basic Skills 18, page 487

1. $\frac{1}{3}$ **2.** $\frac{1}{2}$ **3.** $\frac{21}{51}$ **4.** $\frac{2}{15}$ **5.** $\frac{3}{7}$ **6.** $\frac{6}{55}$ **7.** $\frac{4}{63}$ **8.** $\frac{5}{44}$ **9.** $\frac{1}{27}$ **10.** $\frac{5}{24}$ **11.** $\frac{1}{22}$ **12.** $\frac{8}{45}$ **13.** $\frac{1}{14}$ **14.** $\frac{13}{112}$ **15.** $\frac{1}{6}$ **16.** $\frac{5}{104}$ **17.** $\frac{1}{8}$ **18.** $\frac{5}{9}$ **19.** $\frac{1}{2}$ **20.** $\frac{1}{8}$

466 *Selected Answers and Solutions Algebra*

Review of Basic Skills 19, page 488

1. $\frac{5}{6}$ **2.** $\frac{3}{5}$ **3.** $\frac{8}{21}$ **4.** $\frac{8}{35}$ **5.** $2\frac{2}{5}$ **6.** $1\frac{2}{15}$
7. $1\frac{39}{56}$ **8.** $1\frac{1}{4}$ **9.** 3 **10.** $3\frac{3}{25}$ **11.** $6\frac{1}{14}$
12. $11\frac{11}{35}$ **13.** $6\frac{1}{5}$ **14.** $2\frac{4}{9}$ **15.** $2\frac{41}{56}$
16. $17\frac{7}{8}$ **17.** $4\frac{1}{5}$ **18.** $5\frac{5}{8}$ **19.** 8 **20.** $5\frac{7}{8}$

Review of Basic Skills 20, page 489

1. $1\frac{2}{5}$ **2.** $2\frac{1}{2}$ **3.** $2\frac{2}{7}$ **4.** $4\frac{4}{5}$ **5.** $\frac{12}{35}$ **6.** $\frac{3}{4}$
7. $\frac{24}{25}$ **8.** $1\frac{1}{9}$ **9.** $2\frac{1}{12}$ **10.** 5 **11.** $1\frac{3}{5}$ **12.** $\frac{1}{2}$
13. $\frac{9}{10}$ **14.** $1\frac{1}{3}$ **15.** $\frac{2}{3}$ **16.** $1\frac{2}{3}$ **17.** $1\frac{7}{48}$
18. $\frac{35}{48}$ **19.** $\frac{7}{10}$ **20.** 2 **21.** $1\frac{7}{9}$ **22.** $\frac{7}{8}$
23. $2\frac{1}{6}$ **24.** $1\frac{1}{3}$ **25.** 1

Review of Basic Skills 21, page 490

1. 3 **2.** $7\frac{1}{3}$ **3.** $2\frac{2}{5}$ **4.** $3\frac{1}{4}$ **5.** $\frac{1}{10}$ **6.** $\frac{26}{45}$
7. $2\frac{1}{10}$ **8.** 10 **9.** 7 **10.** $4\frac{1}{2}$ **11.** 2 **12.** $3\frac{1}{2}$
13. 8 **14.** 6 **15.** 7 **16.** $8\frac{1}{3}$ **17.** $4\frac{1}{7}$
18. $7\frac{1}{9}$ **19.** $13\frac{1}{2}$ **20.** $15\frac{4}{5}$ **21.** $\frac{2}{3}$ **22.** $2\frac{1}{6}$
23. $1\frac{4}{5}$ **24.** $5\frac{2}{3}$ **25.** $2\frac{8}{11}$ **26.** $5\frac{2}{3}$ **27.** $1\frac{16}{19}$
28. $2\frac{16}{21}$ **29.** $1\frac{1}{4}$ **30.** $2\frac{22}{27}$

Review of Basic Skills 22, page 491

1. 3 **2.** $5\frac{1}{2}$ **3.** 8 **4.** 13 **5.** $7\frac{2}{3}$ **6.** $8\frac{1}{4}$ **7.** 10
8. $8\frac{1}{2}$ **9.** $8\frac{5}{16}$ **10.** $3\frac{1}{2}$ **11.** $11\frac{1}{2}$ **12.** $4\frac{13}{16}$
13. $6\frac{3}{16}$ **14.** $9\frac{4}{5}$ **15.** $7\frac{15}{16}$ **16.** 9 **17.** 4
18. 17 **19.** 7 **20.** 12

Review of Basic Skills 23, page 492

1. $\frac{3}{4}$ **2.** $\frac{8}{15}$ **3.** $1\frac{1}{4}$ **4.** $\frac{7}{10}$ **5.** $\frac{11}{12}$ **6.** $\frac{17}{30}$
7. $\frac{19}{30}$ **8.** $\frac{3}{4}$ **9.** $\frac{13}{14}$ **10.** $\frac{2}{3}$ **11.** $3\frac{5}{6}$ **12.** $7\frac{5}{6}$
13. $5\frac{1}{4}$ **14.** $5\frac{11}{12}$ **15.** $6\frac{7}{10}$ **16.** $5\frac{5}{12}$ **17.** $4\frac{5}{6}$
18. $10\frac{4}{5}$ **19.** $12\frac{11}{24}$ **20.** $12\frac{1}{32}$

Review of Basic Skills 24, page 493

1. $\frac{1}{4}$ **2.** $\frac{3}{7}$ **3.** $3\frac{1}{4}$ **4.** $4\frac{1}{4}$ **5.** $1\frac{2}{5}$ **6.** $2\frac{1}{2}$
7. $1\frac{1}{6}$ **8.** $2\frac{1}{4}$ **9.** $3\frac{1}{5}$ **10.** $3\frac{1}{2}$ **11.** $2\frac{1}{8}$ **12.** $\frac{1}{4}$
13. $1\frac{1}{8}$ **14.** $2\frac{1}{4}$ **15.** $3\frac{2}{5}$ **16.** 1 **17.** $2\frac{1}{17}$
18. $5\frac{11}{39}$ **19.** $2\frac{1}{5}$ **20.** $2\frac{1}{2}$

Review of Basic Skills 25, page 494

1. $\frac{1}{8}$ **2.** $\frac{1}{4}$ **3.** $1\frac{1}{8}$ **4.** $2\frac{1}{4}$ **5.** $4\frac{7}{20}$ **6.** $1\frac{1}{6}$
7. $3\frac{1}{8}$ **8.** $4\frac{1}{8}$ **9.** $3\frac{27}{100}$ **10.** $1\frac{31}{100}$ **11.** $7\frac{5}{8}$
12. $2\frac{1}{2}$ **13.** $4\frac{4}{9}$ **14.** $3\frac{1}{10}$ **15.** 7

Review of Basic Skills 26, page 495

1. $3\frac{3}{4}$ **2.** $3\frac{1}{4}$ **3.** $7\frac{1}{2}$ **4.** $2\frac{2}{3}$ **5.** $1\frac{1}{3}$ **6.** $2\frac{2}{5}$
7. $2\frac{3}{4}$ **8.** $2\frac{4}{7}$ **9.** $4\frac{7}{10}$ **10.** $4\frac{7}{9}$ **11.** $3\frac{1}{2}$
12. $3\frac{2}{3}$ **13.** $4\frac{3}{5}$ **14.** $1\frac{5}{6}$ **15.** $1\frac{7}{8}$ **16.** $4\frac{3}{4}$
17. $2\frac{5}{6}$ **18.** $6\frac{5}{6}$ **19.** $4\frac{1}{2}$ **20.** $4\frac{3}{5}$

Review of Basic Skills 27, page 496

1. tenths **2.** thousandths
3. ten-thousandths **4.** thousandths
5. hundred-thousandths **6.** millionths
7. thousandths **8.** hundreds
9. hundredths **10.** hundred-thousandths
11. $>$ **12.** $<$ **13.** $<$ **14.** $<$ **15.** $>$ **16.** $<$
17. $>$ **18.** $<$ **19.** $>$ **20.** $<$

Review of Basic Skills 28, page 497

1. 2.1, 2.06, 2.063 **2.** 0.1, 0.09, 0.089
3. 1.0, 1.04, 1.035 **4.** 0.2, 0.15, 0.155
5. 32.7, 32.70, 32.704 **6.** 7.6, 7.63, 7.630
7. 19.8, 19.81, 19.809 **8.** 34.0, 34.00, 34.004 **9.** 2.1, 2.06, 2.061 **10.** 139.4, 139.42, 139.418

Algebra Selected Answers and Solutions **467**

Review of Basic Skills 29, page 498
1. \$18.03 **2.** \$13.73 **3.** \$18.20 **4.** \$13.42 **5.** \$18.64 **6.** \$15.78 **7.** \$33.09 **8.** \$26.26 **9.** \$26.25 **10.** \$29.93 **11.** 15.32 **12.** 20.13 **13.** 12.11 **14.** 31.383 **15.** 64.403 **16.** 18.099 **17.** 11.617 **18.** 24.098 **19.** 86.0991 **20.** 28.8514

Review of Basic Skills 30, page 499
1. \$16.33 **2.** \$3.11 **3.** \$11.35 **4.** \$10 **5.** \$2.11 **6.** \$27.18 **7.** \$8.26 **8.** \$8.28 **9.** \$13.37 **10.** \$5.19 **11.** 5.09 **12.** 0.66 **13.** 1.09 **14.** 5.29 **15.** 5.79 **16.** 74.51 **17.** 21.81 **18.** 35.13 **19.** 36.73 **20.** 80.63

Review of Basic Skills 31, page 500
1. 2.8 **2.** 12 **3.** 18.9 **4.** 14.7 **5.** 33.5 **6.** 3.12 **7.** 15.86 **8.** 15.99 **9.** 8.04 **10.** 58.48 **11.** 3.159 **12.** 17.748 **13.** 7.408 **14.** 26.568 **15.** 14.094 **16.** 11.993 **17.** 36.036 **18.** 8.838 **19.** 27.434 **20.** 55.188

Review of Basic Skills 32, page 501
1. $2.9 \cdot 10^3$ **2.** $3.6 \cdot 10^3$ **3.** $8.75 \cdot 10^3$ **4.** $6.32 \cdot 10^3$ **5.** $33.5 \cdot 10^4$ **6.** $4.6 \cdot 10^4$ **7.** $7.11 \cdot 10^4$ **8.** $4 \cdot 10^5$ **9.** $4 \cdot 10^6$ **10.** $1.7 \cdot 10^9$ **11.** $3.8 \cdot 10^{-4}$ **12.** $39 \cdot 10^{-2}$ **13.** $41 \cdot 10^{-2}$ **14.** $72 \cdot 10^{-3}$ **15.** $7.2 \cdot 10^{-3}$ **16.** 8.1 • 10–3 **17.** 7.4 • 10–4 **18.** $1.2 \cdot 10^{-5}$ **19.** $1.23 \cdot 10^{-3}$ **20.** $2.46 \cdot 10^{-4}$

468 *Selected Answers and Solutions Algebra*

Review of Basic Skills 33, page 502

1. 2.35 **2.** 0.26 **3.** 0.25 **4.** 3.17 **5.** 6.5 **6.** 3.1 **7.** 7.1 **8.** 0.21 **9.** 7.1 **10.** 2.1 **11.** 3.1 **12.** 3.3 **13.** 20.5 **14.** 9.09 **15.** 6.1 **16.** 1.202 **17.** 6.1 **18.** 0.51 **19.** 1.02 **20.** 0.5

Review of Basic Skills 34, page 503

1. 7.2 **2.** 12.3 **3.** 11 **4.** 14.9 **5.** 55.7 **6.** 37.4 **7.** 96.7 **8.** 427 **9.** 0.002 **10.** 210.5 **11.** 210.5 **12.** 6,460 **13.** 810 **14.** 81 **15.** 8.1 **16.** 707 **17.** 33 **18.** 6,620 **19.** 532 **20.** 0.98

Review of Basic Skills 35, page 504

1. $\frac{14}{100}, \frac{7}{50}$ **2.** $\frac{15}{100}, \frac{3}{20}$ **3.** $\frac{75}{100}, \frac{3}{4}$ **4.** $\frac{36}{100}, \frac{9}{25}$ **5.** $\frac{79}{100}$ **6.** $\frac{15}{100}, \frac{3}{20}$ **7.** $\frac{159}{1000}$ **8.** $\frac{375}{1000}, \frac{3}{8}$ **9.** $\frac{875}{1000}, \frac{7}{8}$ **10.** $\frac{999}{1000}$ **11.** $\frac{42}{100}, \frac{21}{50}$ **12.** $\frac{65}{100}, \frac{13}{20}$ **13.** $\frac{60}{100}, \frac{3}{5}$ **14.** $\frac{45}{100}, \frac{9}{20}$ **15.** $\frac{50}{100}, \frac{1}{2}$ **16.** $\frac{168}{1000}, \frac{21}{125}$ **17.** $\frac{22}{100}, \frac{11}{50}$ **18.** $\frac{98}{100}, \frac{49}{50}$ **19.** $\frac{568}{1000}, \frac{71}{125}$ **20.** $\frac{72}{100}, \frac{18}{25}$

Review of Basic Skills 36, page 505

1. 0.1 **2.** 0.2 **3.** 0.5 **4.** 0.12 **5.** 0.18 **6.** 0.35 **7.** 0.36 **8.** 0.006 **9.** 0.024 **10.** 0.118 **11.** 0.4285714 **12.** 0.7142857 **13.** 0.6666666 **14.** 0.2222222 **15.** 0.3846153 **16.** 0.117647 **17.** 0.1578947 **18.** 0.2173913 **19.** 0.2068965 **20.** 0.1612903

Algebra Selected Answers and Solutions **469**

Manipulatives

Manipulative activities are included throughout the Review of Basic Skills. Use of the following manipulatives is suggested:

- Base Ten Blocks
- Base Ten Mat
- Cuisenaire Rods
- Manipulatives Master 4 (Factor Frame)

Manipulatives Masters are included with the AGS Algebra Teacher's Resource Library (TRL). Manipulatives can be ordered from AGS Publishing by calling 1-800-328-2560.

Review of Basic Skills 1

Place Value of Whole Numbers

Recall that 1,234 means 1 thousand + 2 hundreds + 3 tens + 4 ones.
So the place value of 1 is thousands, 2 is hundreds, 3 is tens, and 4 is ones.

Example 1 Write the place value of the underlined digit.

4,301 thousands
4,301 hundreds
4,301 tens
4,301 ones

Exercise Write the place value of the underlined digit.

1. 356 ones
2. 356 tens
3. 356 hundreds
4. 981 hundreds
5. 981 tens
6. 981 ones
7. 3,401 thousands
8. 3,401 hundreds
9. 3,401 tens
10. 3,401 ones

You may use this place value chart for larger numbers.

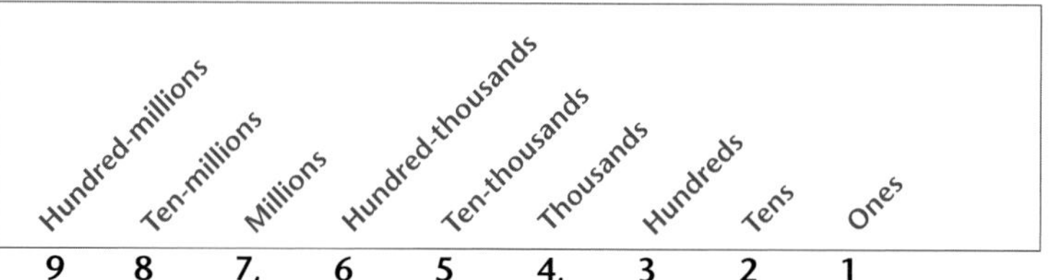

9 8 7, 6 5 4, 3 2 1

11. 3,485 hundreds
12. 6,379 thousands
13. 21,397 ones
14. 86,477 ten-thousands
15. 191,945 ten-thousands
16. 999,999 hundred-thousands
17. 4,676,000 thousands
18. 9,462,391 millions
19. 56,926,400 hundred-thousands
20. 879,940,604 hundred-millions

Review of Basic Skills 2

Rounding Whole Numbers

EXAMPLE 1	Round to the nearest:	Ten	Hundred	Thousand
Step 1	Find the place to be rounded.	1,582	1,582	1,582
Step 2	If the digit to the right is 5 or larger, add 1 to the place to be rounded.	1,582 ↑	1,582 ↑	1,582 ↑
Step 3	Change all digits to the right of the rounded place to 0s.	1,580	1,600	2,000

Exercise Round to the nearest ten.

1. 9 10 **4.** 356 360 **7.** 4,017 4,020 **10.** 250,960 250,960

2. 16 20 **5.** 1,888 1,890 **8.** 55,487 55,490

3. 191 190 **6.** 2,394 2,390 **9.** 63,561 63,560

Round to the nearest hundred.

11. 89 100 **14.** 561 600 **17.** 13,401 13,400 **20.** 416,313 416,300

12. 51 100 **15.** 840 800 **18.** 64,789 64,800

13. 284 300 **16.** 8,696 8,700 **19.** 267,476 267,500

Round to the nearest thousand.

21. 787 1,000 **24.** 8,634 9,000 **27.** 46,187 46,000 **30.** 864,217 864,000

22. 806 1,000 **25.** 9,500 10,000 **28.** 147,831 148,000

23. 5,350 5,000 **26.** 21,435 21,000 **29.** 250,011 250,000

MANIPULATIVES

Rounding Whole Numbers

Materials: Base Ten Blocks, Base Ten Mat

Group Practice: Place a model of the number to be rounded on the mat. Identify the place (column) to be rounded. If there are five or more units in the column to the right, trade them for one unit of the next higher place value. Place the new unit in the appropriate column. If there are less than five units in the column to the right, remove them from the column. Then remove all pieces to the right of the column to be rounded. Write the symbolic equivalent of the new model.

Student Practice: Have students use the blocks to round numbers in problems 1–4, 11–15, 21–22.

Manipulatives

Adding Whole Numbers

Materials: Base Ten Blocks, Base Ten Mat

Group Practice: Place models of the addends on the mat. Starting with the ones column, line up the unit cubes end to end, replacing ten cubes with a 10-rod in the tens column. Explain that there can be only nine units in any one column so each group of ten units is replaced with one unit in the next higher column. Write the symbolic equivalent for this step. Continue with the tens and hundreds columns, as necessary. Write the symbolic equivalent for the model of the sum.

Student Practice: Have students use the blocks to solve or check problems 1–8, 10–13, 18–19.

Review of Basic Skills 3

Adding Whole Numbers

Example 1 Try these in your head.

7 + 3 = ■ **Answer** 10

3 + 5 + 19 = ■ **Answer** 27

7 + 13 + 0 = ■ **Answer** 20

Example 2 2 + 451 + 26 = ■

Solution

```
   26 \
  451 -> Addends
+   2 /
  479   Sum
```

Example 3 Find the perimeter.

Solution

```
   30
   40
+  50
  120
```

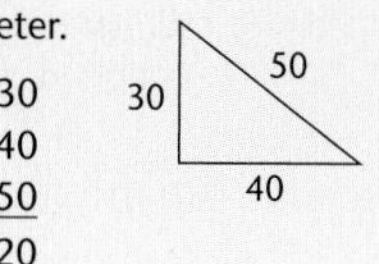

Exercise Do these in your head. Just write your answers.

1. 2 + 4 6
2. 2 + 4 + 3 9
3. 2 + 5 + 1 + 0 8
4. 2 + 0 + 3 + 10 15
5. 3 + 7 + 5 + 4 19
6. 6 + 7 + 4 + 10 27
7. 2 + 5 + 6 + 100 113
8. 500 + 2 + 7 + 1 510
9. 3 + 5 + 9 + 1,000 1,017

Write in vertical form, then add.

10. 9 + 27 36
11. 3 + 29 + 86 118
12. 7 + 14 + 91 112
13. 2 + 69 + 5 + 301 377
14. 26,487 + 17,401 43,888
15. 37,091 + 73,591 110,682
16. 100,847 + 3,401 104,248
17. 217,401 + 39,417 256,818

Find the perimeters.

18.

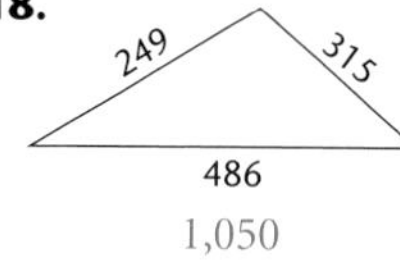

1,050

19.

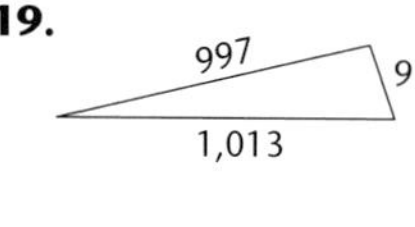

2,107

20.

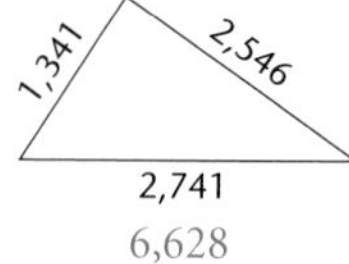

6,628

472 *Review of Basic Skills Algebra*

Review of Basic Skills 4

Subtracting Whole Numbers

Example 1 Try these in your head.

$7 - 3 = \blacksquare$ **Answer** 4

$28 - 10 = \blacksquare$ **Answer** 18

$13 - 3 + 0 = \blacksquare$ **Answer** 10

Example 2 Subtract 26 from 235.

Solution

```
  235  Minuend
-  26  Subtrahend
  209  Difference
```

Check.

```
   26
+ 209
  235
```

Example 3 208 − 35

Solution

```
  208
-  35
  173
```

Check.

```
  173
+  35
  208
```

Exercise Do these in your head. Just write the answers.

1. 9 − 5 4 **3.** 14 − 4 10 **5.** 42 − 10 32 **7.** 143 − 2 141 **9.** 409 − 5 404

2. 8 − 3 5 **4.** 19 − 8 11 **6.** 57 − 20 37 **8.** 167 − 7 160 **10.** 536 − 30 506

Write in vertical form, then subtract.

11. subtract 26 from 335 309

12. subtract 39 from 450 411

13. subtract 48 from 784 736

14. subtract 341 from 1,291 950

15. subtract 481 from 41,217 40,736

16. subtract 346 from 50,000 49,654

Write in vertical form, then subtract.

17. 2,113 − 421 1,692

18. 8,101 − 4,049 4,052

19. 6,714 − 5,841 873

20. 81,573 − 1,540 80,033

21. 72,451 − 12,491 59,960

22. 63,456 − 45,671 17,785

23. 493,146 − 146 493,000

24. 493,146 − 3,146 490,000

25. 493,146 − 93,146 400,000

Manipulatives

Subtracting Whole Numbers

Materials: Base Ten Blocks, Base Ten Mat

Group Practice: Using the example 235 – 26, place a model of 235 on the mat. It is necessary to regroup in order to subtract 6 from 5 in the ones column. Remove a 10-rod from the tens column and replace it with ten unit cubes in the ones column. Write the symbolic equivalent for this step. Subtract 6 cubes from 15 in the ones column, leaving 9 cubes. Subtract in the tens and hundreds columns, leaving the difference (209). Write the symbolic equivalent for the difference.

Student Practice: Have students use the blocks to solve or check problems 1–14.

Review of Basic Skills 5

Multipilying Whole Numbers

Multiplication is repeated addition.

6 • 3 means 6 threes. $\underbrace{3 + 3 + 3 + 3 + 3 + 3}_{18}$

6 • 3 = 18

You may want to practice your times tables before doing these problems.

Example 1 23 • 6 = ■

Solution

```
   23 ⟩ Factors
 ×  6
  138   Product
```

Example 2 46 • 35 = ■

Solution

```
    46 ⟩ Factors
  × 35
   230
+ 1 38
 1,610   Product
```

Exercise Do these in your head. Just write your answers.

1. 1 • 2, 2 • 2, 3 • 2, 4 • 2, 5 • 2, 6 • 2, 7 • 2, 8 • 2, 9 • 2, 10 • 2 — 2, 4, 6, 8, 10, 12, 14, 16, 18, 20
2. 1 • 3, 2 • 3, 3 • 3, 4 • 3, 5 • 3, 6 • 3, 7 • 3, 8 • 3, 9 • 3, 10 • 3 — 3, 6, 9, 12, 15, 18, 21, 24, 27, 30
3. 1 • 4, 2 • 4, 3 • 4, 4 • 4, 5 • 4, 6 • 4, 7 • 4, 8 • 4, 9 • 4, 10 • 4 — 4, 8, 12, 16, 20, 24, 28, 32, 36, 40
4. 1 • 5, 2 • 5, 3 • 5, 4 • 5, 5 • 5, 6 • 5, 7 • 5, 8 • 5, 9 • 5, 10 • 5 — 5, 10, 15, 20, 25, 30, 35, 40, 45, 50
5. 1 • 6, 2 • 6, 3 • 6, 4 • 6, 5 • 6, 6 • 6, 7 • 6, 8 • 6, 9 • 6, 10 • 6 — 6, 12, 18, 24, 30, 36, 42, 48, 54, 60
6. 1 • 7, 2 • 7, 3 • 7, 4 • 7, 5 • 7, 6 • 7, 7 • 7, 8 • 7, 9 • 7, 10 • 7 — 7, 14, 21, 28, 35, 42, 49, 56, 63, 70
7. 1 • 8, 2 • 8, 3 • 8, 4 • 8, 5 • 8, 6 • 8, 7 • 8, 8 • 8, 9 • 8, 10 • 8 — 8, 16, 24, 32, 40, 48, 56, 64, 72, 80
8. 1 • 9, 2 • 9, 3 • 9, 4 • 9, 5 • 9, 6 • 9, 7 • 9, 8 • 9, 9 • 9, 10 • 9 — 9, 18, 27, 36, 45, 54, 63, 72, 81, 90
9. 1 • 10, 2 • 10, 3 • 10, 4 • 10, 5 • 10, 6 • 10, 7 • 10, 8 • 10, 9 • 10, 10 • 10 — 10, 20, 30, 40, 50, 60, 70, 80, 90, 100

Multiply.

10. 23 • 6 138	**14.** 72 • 8 576	**18.** 37 • 39 1,443	**22.** 309 • 7 2,163
11. 26 • 7 182	**15.** 54 • 3 162	**19.** 46 • 72 3,312	**23.** 423 • 16 6,768
12. 35 • 9 315	**16.** 46 • 35 1,610	**20.** 81 • 37 2,997	**24.** 926 • 23 21,298
13. 63 • 4 252	**17.** 47 • 21 987	**21.** 49 • 63 3,087	**25.** 196 • 245 48,020

474 *Review of Basic Skills Algebra*

Review of Basic Skills 6

Multiplying Whole Numbers by Powers of 10

EXAMPLE 1 267 • 10 = ■

Solution

```
  267
×  10  ← One zero
2,670  ← One zero
```

EXAMPLE 2 342 • 100 = ■

Solution

```
   342
×  100  ← Two zeros
34,200  ← Two zeros
```

Exercise Do these in your head. Just write the answers.

1. 3 • 10 30
2. 5 • 100 500
3. 7 • 1,000 7,000
4. 3 • 20 60
5. 5 • 200 1,000
6. 7 • 200 1,400
7. 6 • 2,000 12,000
8. 9 • 30 270
9. 9 • 300 2,700
10. 9 • 3,000 27,000

Multiply.

11. 43 • 10 430
12. 43 • 100 4,300
13. 43 • 1,000 43,000
14. 267 • 10 2,670
15. 267 • 100 26,700
16. 267 • 1,000 267,000
17. 349 • 10 3,490
18. 349 • 100 34,900
19. 349 • 1,000 349,000
20. 349 • 10,000 3,490,000
21. 83 • 10 830
22. 83 • 100 8,300
23. 83 • 1,000 83,000
24. 586 • 10 5,860
25. 586 • 100 58,600
26. 586 • 1,000 586,000
27. 4,184 • 10 41,840
28. 4,184 • 100 418,400
29. 4,184 • 1,000 4,184,000
30. 4,184 • 10,000 41,840,000

Algebra Review of Basic Skills **475**

MANIPULATIVES

Division of Whole Numbers

Materials: Cuisenaire Rods, Manipulatives Master 4 (Factor Frame)

Group Practice: Using the example 21 ÷ 3, build a rectangular model of 21 using 3-rods and place it on the inside of the Factor Frame. Place a 3-rod on the left side of the frame to represent the divisor. Find the rod that represents the missing dimension of the rectangle (7-rod) and place it on the top of the frame. This rod represents the quotient (7).

Student Practice: Have students use the rods to solve or check problems 1–15.

Review of Basic Skills 7

Division of Whole Numbers

Division is repeated subtraction:

21 ÷ 3 = 7 because 21 – 3 = 18, 18 – 3 = 15, 15 – 3 = 12, 12 – 3 = 9,

9 – 3 = 6, 6 – 3 = 3, 3 – 3 = 0 There are 7 threes in 21.

You may want to practice basic division facts through ÷ 9 before doing these problems.

Division of Whole Numbers with Zero Remainders

EXAMPLE 1 576 ÷ 12 = *n*

Solution

```
     48
 12)576
   -48
     96
   - 96
      0 = Remainder
```

Check.

```
   48
 × 12
   96
 + 48
  576
```

Exercise Do these in your head. Just write the answers.

1. 24 ÷ 3	8	**6.** 24 ÷ 4	6	**11.** 45 ÷ 5	9
2. 14 ÷ 2	7	**7.** 35 ÷ 5	7	**12.** 63 ÷ 7	9
3. 14 ÷ 7	2	**8.** 49 ÷ 7	7	**13.** 81 ÷ 9	9
4. 12 ÷ 3	4	**9.** 48 ÷ 8	6	**14.** 56 ÷ 8	7
5. 30 ÷ 3	10	**10.** 18 ÷ 2	9	**15.** 54 ÷ 9	6

Divide.

16. 138 ÷ 6	23	**20.** 621 ÷ 3	207	**24.** 4,100 ÷ 82	50
17. 371 ÷ 7	53	**21.** 564 ÷ 12	47	**25.** 1,539 ÷ 27	57
18. 369 ÷ 3	123	**22.** 323 ÷ 19	17		
19. 484 ÷ 4	121	**23.** 540 ÷ 36	15		

Review of Basic Skills 8

Division of Whole Numbers with Fractional Remainders

Example 1 3,191 ÷ 25 = ■

Solution

$$\begin{array}{r} 127\frac{16}{25} \\ 25\overline{)3{,}191} \\ -25 \\ \hline 69 \\ -50 \\ \hline 191 \\ -175 \\ \hline 16 \end{array}$$

Write the remainder over the divisor.

Check.

$$\begin{array}{r} 127 \\ \times\ 25 \\ \hline 635 \\ +\ 254 \\ \hline 3{,}175 \\ +\ 16 \\ \hline 3{,}191 \end{array}$$

(+ 16: Remainder)

Exercise Divide. Write remainders as fractions. (These cannot be done with a calculator.)

1. 381 ÷ 14 $27\frac{3}{14}$
2. 586 ÷ 39 $15\frac{1}{39}$
3. 963 ÷ 21 $45\frac{18}{21} = 45\frac{6}{7}$
4. 646 ÷ 71 $9\frac{7}{71}$
5. 487 ÷ 20 $24\frac{7}{20}$

Estimate the quotients to the nearest thousand first, then use a calculator. Copy the calculator answer to the nearest hundredth.

6. 19,520 ÷ 33 591.52
7. 30,040 ÷ 71 423.10
8. 51,090 ÷ 18 2,838.33
9. 126,947 ÷ 17 7,467.47
10. 341,643 ÷ 20 17,082.15

Algebra Review of Basic Skills **477**

Review of Basic Skills 9

Division of Whole Numbers with Zeros in the Quotient

EXAMPLE 1 2,380 ÷ 14 = ■

Solution

```
     170
14 )2,380
   − 1 4
      98
    − 98
      00
```

Check.

```
   170
 ×  14
   680
+ 1 70
 2,380
```

EXAMPLE 1 4,864 ÷ 16 = ■

Solution

```
     304
16 )4,864
   − 4 8
     064
    − 64
       0
```

Check.

```
   304
 ×  16
 1,824
+ 3 04
 4,864
```

Exercise Divide. Do not use a calculator.

1. 2,380 ÷ 14 170
2. 4,864 ÷ 16 304
3. 2,040 ÷ 17 120
4. 5,980 ÷ 13 460
5. 16,200 ÷ 45 360
6. 31,626 ÷ 63 502
7. 19,520 ÷ 32 610
8. 138,253 ÷ 23 6,011
9. 738,500 ÷ 35 21,100
10. 103,200 ÷ 24 4,300

478 *Review of Basic Skills Algebra*

Review of Basic Skills 10

Numbers with Exponents

2^4 means $2 \cdot 2 \cdot 2 \cdot 2$.
So $2^4 = 2 \cdot 2 \cdot 2 \cdot 2 = 16$.

2^4 — Base, Exponent

2 is the base, 4 is the exponent.

Example 1 Find the value of 3^4.
Solution $3^4 = 3 \bullet 3 \bullet 3 \bullet 3$
$3^4 = 81$

Example 2 Write with an exponent $2 \bullet 2 \bullet 2$.
Solution $2 \bullet 2 \bullet 2 = 2^3$

Exercise Find the value of each.

1. 3^2	9	**8.** 10^2	100	**15.** 4^3	64
2. 4^2	16	**9.** 2^5	32	**16.** 30^2	900
3. 5^2	25	**10.** 25^2	625	**17.** 20^3	8,000
4. 6^2	36	**11.** 2^4	16	**18.** 11^2	121
5. 7^2	49	**12.** 3^3	27	**19.** $1{,}000^2$	1,000,000
6. 8^2	64	**13.** 5^3	125	**20.** 10^6	1,000,000
7. 9^2	81	**14.** 10^3	1,000		

Write with an exponent.

21. $2 \cdot 2 \cdot 2$	2^3	**28.** $92 \cdot 92 \cdot 92$	92^3	**35.** $90 \cdot 90 \cdot 90 \cdot 90 \cdot 90$	90^5
22. $2 \cdot 2 \cdot 2 \cdot 2$	2^4	**29.** $46 \cdot 46 \cdot 46 \cdot 46$	46^4	**36.** $43 \cdot 43 \cdot 43$	43^3
23. $3 \cdot 3 \cdot 3$	3^3	**30.** $10 \cdot 10 \cdot 10 \cdot 10 \cdot 10 \cdot 10$	10^6	**37.** $5 \cdot 5 \cdot 5 \cdot 5 \cdot 5 \cdot 5 \cdot 5 \cdot 5$	5^8
24. $9 \cdot 9$	9^2	**31.** $4 \cdot 4 \cdot 4$	4^3	**38.** $36 \cdot 36 \cdot 36 \cdot 36$	36^4
25. $7 \cdot 7 \cdot 7 \cdot 7 \cdot 7$	7^5	**32.** $4 \cdot 4 \cdot 4 \cdot 4$	4^4	**39.** $94 \cdot 94 \cdot 94 \cdot 94$	94^4
26. $10 \cdot 10 \cdot 10 \cdot 10 \cdot 10$	10^5	**33.** $6 \cdot 6 \cdot 6$	6^3	**40.** $100 \cdot 100 \cdot 100 \cdot 100 \cdot 100$	100^5
27. $81 \cdot 81$	81^2	**34.** $6 \cdot 6 \cdot 6 \cdot 6 \cdot 6$	6^5		

Manipulatives

Numbers with Exponents

Materials: Cuisenaire Rods

Group Practice: To model the square of a number, build a square with rods representing the value of the number to be squared. For example, to model 3^2, use 3-rods. Use multiplication to find the area of the square and write the symbolic equivalent. To find the cube of a number, build a cube using rods representing the value of the number to be cubed. For example, use 2-rods to model 2^3. To find the value of the cube, unstack the rods and rearrange them to form a rectangle. Multiply the dimensions to find the value and write the symbolic equivalent.

Student Practice: Have students use the rods to solve or check problems 1–8, 12–15.

Review of Basic Skills 11

Using the Order of Operations

Rule

1. Evaluate exponents first.
2. Multiply and divide from left to right in order.
3. Add and subtract from left to right in order.

EXAMPLE 1

	2	$+$	$3 \cdot 4$	$-$	$8 \div 4$	$=$	■
Solution	2	$+$	$3 \cdot 4$	$-$	$8 \div 4$	$=$	
			↓		↓		
	2	$+$	12	$-$	2	$=$	12

EXAMPLE 2

	2^3	$+$	$3 \cdot 4 \div 2$	$-$	$48 \div 4^2$	$=$	■
Solution	8	$+$	$3 \cdot 4 \div 2$	$-$	$48 \div 16$	$=$	
			↓		↓		
			$12 \div 2$		3	$=$	
			↓		↓		
	8	$+$	6	$-$	3	$=$	11

Exercise Use the rules for the order of operations. Find the answers.

1. $3 + 8 \cdot 2 \div 4$ 7
2. $5 + 9 \cdot 4 \div 12 - 2$ 6
3. $8 - 8 \div 4 + 3 \cdot 2$ 12
4. $13 - 16 \cdot 3 \div 12 - 1$ 8
5. $9 + 6 \cdot 3 - 8 \cdot 2 \div 4$ 23
6. $1 + 16 \cdot 3 \div 12 - 4$ 1
7. $14 + 32 \div 16 - 4 \cdot 2$ 8
8. $32 \div 16 + 9 \div 3 \cdot 2$ 8
9. $5 - 16 \div 4 + 1 + 3$ 5
10. $35 - 25 \cdot 4 \div 20 + 5$ 35
11. $2^3 + 8 \cdot 2^2 + 3$ 43
12. $8 - 6^2 \div 12 + 2 \cdot 5$ 15
13. $15 + 8^2 \div 4 - 6$ 25
14. $25 + 11^2 + 8 \cdot 2 - 3$ 159
15. $39 \div 13 + 12^2 \div 6 - 5$ 22
16. $52 + 12 \div 2^2 - 82 \div 2 + 3^2$ 23
17. $35 + 2^5 \div 2^4 \cdot 3^2 - 2^3$ 45
18. $18 \div 3^2 + 6 \cdot 8 \div 4^2 - 5$ 0
19. $4 \cdot 3 \cdot 5 \div 10 + 8 \cdot 2^3 \div 2^4$ 10
20. $9 - 16 \cdot 3 \div 12 + 8 \div 2^2 - 2^2$ 3

480 *Review of Basic Skills Algebra*

Review of Basic Skills 12

Finding an Average (Mean)

The word *mean* is sometimes used for *average.*

Rule

1. Add the numbers whose average or mean you want.
2. Divide the sum by the number of addends. The quotient is the average or mean.

Example 2 Find the average of 98, 88, 80, and 60.

Solution Add the numbers.

```
   98 )
   88 |
   80 } 4 addends
 + 60 )
  326
```

Then divide.

```
     81.5
 4 ) 326.0
   - 32
      06
    -  4
      20
    - 20
       0
```

Answer The average is 81.5.

Exercise Find the average for each set of numbers. Round to the nearest tenth.

1. 25, 63, 48, 52, 49 47.4
2. 98, 53, 42, 56, 72 64.2
3. 39, 40, 39, 62, 53, 86 53.2
4. 95, 83, 39, 42, 88, 77 70.7
5. 88, 62, 42, 53, 96, 35 62.7
6. 53, 60, 72, 43, 35, 39, 53 50.7
7. 91, 62, 39, 50, 42, 88, 60 61.7
8. 36, 19, 41, 63, 72, 64, 81 53.7
9. 39, 41, 62, 73, 96, 81, 92, 65 68.6
10. 40, 49, 51, 73, 29, 86, 29, 56 51.6
11. 100, 103, 96, 105, 105, 97, 102, 120 103.5
12. 36, 42, 85, 92, 30, 33, 88, 29, 62, 50 54.7
13. 109, 156, 95, 108, 90, 83, 45, 80, 90, 98, 93, 96 95.3
14. 40, 42, 43, 40, 41, 42, 43, 48, 44, 42, 45, 42 42.7
15. 40, 38, 37, 35, 42, 43, 36, 49, 48, 53, 42, 39, 34 41.2

Algebra Review of Basic Skills **481**

Review of Basic Skills 13

Comparing Fractions

Comparing fractions with *like* denominators—

Rule

Compare numerators: the larger the numerator, the larger the fraction.

EXAMPLE 1 Compare $\frac{5}{8}$ and $\frac{7}{8}$.

Solution The denominators are alike.

$5 < 7$, therefore $\frac{5}{8} < \frac{7}{8}$.

Comparing fractions with *unlike* denominators—

Rule

Change each fraction to a decimal. You may use a calculator. Compare decimals.

EXAMPLE 2 Compare $\frac{5}{8}$ and $\frac{3}{4}$.

Solution $\frac{5}{8}$ is

```
     0.625
  8 ) 5.0
    - 4 8
        20
      - 16
        40
      - 40
         0
```

$\frac{3}{4}$ is

```
     0.75
  4 ) 3.0
    - 2 8
       20
     - 20
        0
```

$0.625 < 0.75$, therefore $\frac{5}{8} < \frac{3}{4}$.

Exercise Compare the fractions. Write $<$ or $>$.

1. $\frac{1}{8}$ $\frac{3}{8}$	$<$	**6.** $\frac{5}{3}$ $\frac{2}{3}$	$>$	**11.** $\frac{3}{4}$ $\frac{7}{8}$	$<$	**16.** $\frac{3}{10}$ $\frac{3}{11}$	$>$
2. $\frac{6}{7}$ $\frac{5}{7}$	$>$	**7.** $\frac{8}{5}$ $\frac{9}{5}$	$<$	**12.** $\frac{3}{5}$ $\frac{3}{4}$	$<$	**17.** $\frac{9}{13}$ $\frac{11}{12}$	$<$
3. $\frac{3}{8}$ $\frac{5}{8}$	$<$	**8.** $\frac{1}{3}$ $\frac{2}{3}$	$<$	**13.** $\frac{6}{7}$ $\frac{5}{8}$	$>$	**18.** $\frac{6}{11}$ $\frac{7}{9}$	$<$
4. $\frac{7}{3}$ $\frac{11}{3}$	$<$	**9.** $\frac{4}{7}$ $\frac{5}{7}$	$<$	**14.** $\frac{3}{8}$ $\frac{5}{9}$	$<$	**19.** $\frac{7}{13}$ $\frac{8}{15}$	$>$
5. $\frac{5}{4}$ $\frac{7}{4}$	$<$	**10.** $\frac{11}{13}$ $\frac{9}{13}$	$>$	**15.** $\frac{6}{10}$ $\frac{7}{11}$	$<$	**20.** $\frac{9}{13}$ $\frac{6}{7}$	$<$

482 *Review of Basic Skills Algebra*

Review of Basic Skills 14

Changing Fractions to Higher Terms

EXAMPLE 1 Write $\frac{5}{6}$ as a fraction with 30 as the new denominator.

Step 1 $\frac{5}{6} = \frac{\blacksquare}{30}$

Step 2 Divide 30 by 6. $\quad 6\overline{)30}$ = 5

Step 3 Multiply $\frac{5}{6}$ by $\frac{5}{5}$. $\quad \frac{5 \cdot 5}{6 \cdot 5} = \frac{25}{30}$

Exercise Write each fraction with a new denominator.

Problem	Answer	Problem	Answer
1. $\frac{3}{6} = \frac{\blacksquare}{30}$	$\frac{15}{30}$	**11.** $\frac{3}{11} = \frac{\blacksquare}{33}$	$\frac{9}{33}$
2. $\frac{5}{12} = \frac{\blacksquare}{24}$	$\frac{10}{24}$	**12.** $\frac{6}{13} = \frac{\blacksquare}{39}$	$\frac{18}{39}$
3. $\frac{3}{7} = \frac{\blacksquare}{21}$	$\frac{9}{21}$	**13.** $\frac{5}{12} = \frac{\blacksquare}{60}$	$\frac{25}{60}$
4. $\frac{6}{9} = \frac{\blacksquare}{18}$	$\frac{12}{18}$	**14.** $\frac{6}{15} = \frac{\blacksquare}{45}$	$\frac{18}{45}$
5. $\frac{7}{12} = \frac{\blacksquare}{36}$	$\frac{21}{36}$	**15.** $\frac{9}{16} = \frac{\blacksquare}{64}$	$\frac{36}{64}$
6. $\frac{9}{13} = \frac{\blacksquare}{39}$	$\frac{27}{39}$	**16.** $\frac{3}{13} = \frac{\blacksquare}{65}$	$\frac{15}{65}$
7. $\frac{4}{7} = \frac{\blacksquare}{35}$	$\frac{20}{35}$	**17.** $\frac{5}{17} = \frac{\blacksquare}{51}$	$\frac{15}{51}$
8. $\frac{3}{8} = \frac{\blacksquare}{40}$	$\frac{15}{40}$	**18.** $\frac{6}{19} = \frac{\blacksquare}{38}$	$\frac{12}{38}$
9. $\frac{6}{7} = \frac{\blacksquare}{35}$	$\frac{30}{35}$	**19.** $\frac{6}{110} = \frac{\blacksquare}{550}$	$\frac{30}{550}$
10. $\frac{9}{10} = \frac{\blacksquare}{100}$	$\frac{90}{100}$	**20.** $\frac{7}{315} = \frac{\blacksquare}{630}$	$\frac{14}{630}$

MANIPULATIVES

Changing Fractions to Higher Terms

Materials: Cuisenaire Rods

Group Practice: Using the example, model $\frac{5}{6}$ by placing a 5-rod over a 6-rod. Model a denominator of 30 by building 30 using 6-rods. Point out that 6 is added five times, or multiplied by 5, to become 30. To complete the equivalent fraction, the numerator must also be added five times. Place five 5-rods over 30 to find the missing numerator (25). Write the symbolic equivalent of the model.

Student Practice: Have students use the rods to solve or check problems 1–18.

MANIPULATIVES

Renaming Fractions in Simplest Terms

Materials: Cuisenaire Rods, two copies of Manipulatives Master 4 (Factor Frame) for each student

Group Practice: Using the second example, rename $\frac{24}{30}$ in simplest terms. Factor 24 and 30 by building rectangles of areas 24 and 30 inside the Factor Frames, making sure one dimension is common to both rectangles. Place rods representing the dimensions, or factors, of each rectangle in the left and top portions of the frame. The GCD will be the largest rod common to both rectangles. The remaining rods represent the *simplest form* of the numerator and denominator after being divided by the GCD. Write the symbolic equivalent. Emphasize that to find the *greatest* common divisor, the rectangles must use the *largest* dimension common to both rectangles.

Student Practice: Have students use the rods to solve or check problems 1, 4–8, 10–13, 16–17, 19.

Review of Basic Skills 15

Renaming Fractions in Simplest Terms

Simplest terms means using the *smallest* numbers in both the numerator and the denominator of a fraction.

EXAMPLE 1 Rename $\frac{75}{100}$ in simplest terms.

Solution $\frac{75 \div 25}{100 \div 25} = \frac{3}{4}$

Choose a number that divides both the numerator and the denominator. If you do not use the largest common divisor, you may have to divide more than once.

EXAMPLE 2 Rename $\frac{24}{30}$ in simplest terms.

Solution $\frac{24 \div 3}{30 \div 3} = \frac{8}{10}$

The division process may occur more than once if the divisor is not large enough in the first step.

$\frac{8 \div 2}{10 \div 2} = \frac{4}{5}$

Answer $\frac{24}{30} = \frac{4}{5}$

Exercise Rename these fractions in simplest terms.

No.	Fraction	Answer	No.	Fraction	Answer	No.	Fraction	Answer
1.	$\frac{24}{48}$	$\frac{1}{2}$	**8.**	$\frac{6}{54}$	$\frac{1}{9}$	**15.**	$\frac{53}{106}$	$\frac{1}{2}$
2.	$\frac{10}{230}$	$\frac{1}{23}$	**9.**	$\frac{16}{112}$	$\frac{1}{7}$	**16.**	$\frac{18}{72}$	$\frac{1}{4}$
3.	$\frac{45}{99}$	$\frac{5}{11}$	**10.**	$\frac{39}{52}$	$\frac{3}{4}$	**17.**	$\frac{5}{15}$	$\frac{1}{3}$
4.	$\frac{5}{25}$	$\frac{1}{5}$	**11.**	$\frac{12}{60}$	$\frac{1}{5}$	**18.**	$\frac{55}{242}$	$\frac{5}{22}$
5.	$\frac{13}{39}$	$\frac{1}{3}$	**12.**	$\frac{16}{64}$	$\frac{1}{4}$	**19.**	$\frac{10}{52}$	$\frac{5}{26}$
6.	$\frac{56}{58}$	$\frac{28}{29}$	**13.**	$\frac{18}{36}$	$\frac{1}{2}$	**20.**	$\frac{48}{96}$	$\frac{1}{2}$
7.	$\frac{63}{81}$	$\frac{7}{9}$	**14.**	$\frac{22}{121}$	$\frac{2}{11}$			

484 *Review of Basic Skills Algebra*

Review of Basic Skills 16

Renaming Improper Fractions as Mixed Numbers

EXAMPLE 1 Rename $\frac{13}{5}$ as a mixed number.

Solution Divide numerator by denominator.

Write the remainder as a fraction.

$$\begin{array}{r} 2 \\ 5\overline{)13} \\ -10 \\ \hline 3 \end{array}\quad \text{Remainder}$$

Answer $2\frac{3}{5}$ Write the remainder over the divisor.

Mixed Numbers in Lowest Terms

Write mixed numbers in lowest terms.
This means to write the fraction part of a mixed number in lowest terms.

EXAMPLE 2 Write $3\frac{5}{15}$ in lowest terms.

Solution Rename $\frac{5}{15}$ in lowest terms.

$\frac{5 \div 5}{15 \div 5} = \frac{1}{3}$, so $3\frac{5}{15} = 3\frac{1}{3}$

Exercise Rename as mixed numbers in lowest terms or whole numbers.

1.	$\frac{18}{5}$	$3\frac{3}{5}$	**6.**	$\frac{12}{2}$	6	**11.**	$\frac{52}{32}$	$1\frac{5}{8}$	**16.**	$\frac{62}{8}$	$7\frac{3}{4}$
2.	$\frac{18}{3}$	6	**7.**	$\frac{38}{5}$	$7\frac{3}{5}$	**12.**	$\frac{55}{8}$	$6\frac{7}{8}$	**17.**	$\frac{50}{6}$	$8\frac{1}{3}$
3.	$\frac{19}{6}$	$3\frac{1}{6}$	**8.**	$\frac{66}{11}$	6	**13.**	$\frac{28}{6}$	$4\frac{2}{3}$	**18.**	$\frac{58}{7}$	$8\frac{2}{7}$
4.	$\frac{14}{3}$	$4\frac{2}{3}$	**9.**	$\frac{56}{11}$	$5\frac{1}{11}$	**14.**	$\frac{32}{4}$	8	**19.**	$\frac{52}{10}$	$5\frac{1}{5}$
5.	$\frac{23}{4}$	$5\frac{3}{4}$	**10.**	$\frac{19}{5}$	$3\frac{4}{5}$	**15.**	$\frac{90}{3}$	30	**20.**	$\frac{37}{3}$	$12\frac{1}{3}$

MANIPULATIVES

Renaming Improper Fractions as Mixed Numbers

Materials: Cuisenaire Rods

Group Practice: Using the example, label a number line in $\frac{1}{5}$ units with improper fractions through $\frac{20}{5}$. Explain that the expression $\frac{13}{5}$ means thirteen $\frac{1}{5}$ units and that on this number line, a cube (1-rod) represents a $\frac{1}{5}$ unit and a 5-rod represents a whole unit. Place thirteen cubes on the number line and write the symbolic equivalent. Next, replace each group of five cubes with a 5-rod. Explain that five $\frac{1}{5}$ units are the same as one whole unit. Write the symbolic equivalent of the mixed number model. Review the procedure in Basic Skill 15 to write the fraction in simplest terms.

Student Practice: Have students use the rods to solve or check problems 1–6 and 10.

Algebra Review of Basic Skills **485**

MANIPULATIVES

Renaming Mixed Numbers as Improper Fractions

Materials: Cuisenaire Rods

Group Practice: Using the example, label a number line in $\frac{1}{4}$ units through $\frac{12}{4}$. Represent $2\frac{3}{4}$ by placing two whole unit rods (4-rods) and three $\frac{1}{4}$ unit rods (cubes) on the number line. Replace each 4-rod with four cubes and count the cubes to find the improper fraction. Write the symbolic equivalent for each step, reminding students that the values of the rods change according to how the number line is labeled.

Student Practice: Have students use the rods for problems 1, 5, 6, 9.

Review of Basic Skills 17

Renaming Mixed Numbers as Improper Fractions

EXAMPLE 1 Write $2\frac{3}{4}$ as an improper fraction.

Step 1 Multiply the whole number by the denominator.

$2 \bullet 4 = 8$

Step 2 Add the numerator to the product from Step 1.

$3 + 8 = 11$

Step 3 Write the sum over the old denominator.

$\frac{11}{4}$

Answer $2\frac{3}{4} = \frac{11}{4}$

Exercise Rename these mixed numbers as improper fractions.

1. $3\frac{2}{5}$ $\frac{17}{5}$

2. $6\frac{2}{5}$ $\frac{32}{5}$

3. $5\frac{1}{6}$ $\frac{31}{6}$

4. $7\frac{2}{12}$ $\frac{86}{12}$

5. $2\frac{1}{6}$ $\frac{13}{6}$

6. $9\frac{1}{2}$ $\frac{19}{2}$

7. $4\frac{1}{9}$ $\frac{37}{9}$

8. $8\frac{2}{11}$ $\frac{90}{11}$

9. $5\frac{2}{3}$ $\frac{17}{3}$

10. $8\frac{1}{3}$ $\frac{25}{3}$

11. $6\frac{10}{13}$ $\frac{88}{13}$

12. $16\frac{2}{3}$ $\frac{50}{3}$

13. $7\frac{3}{8}$ $\frac{59}{8}$

14. $15\frac{2}{3}$ $\frac{47}{3}$

15. $13\frac{9}{14}$ $\frac{191}{14}$

16. $9\frac{2}{3}$ $\frac{29}{3}$

17. $5\frac{11}{10}$ $\frac{61}{10}$

18. $20\frac{2}{3}$ $\frac{62}{3}$

19. $16\frac{5}{21}$ $\frac{341}{21}$

20. $11\frac{1}{8}$ $\frac{89}{8}$

Review of Basic Skills 18

Multiplying Fractions

To multiply fractions, follow this simple rule.

> **Rule**
> To multiply two fractions, multiply numerator times numerator and denominator times denominator.

EXAMPLE 1 $\frac{5}{6} \bullet \frac{3}{4} = \blacksquare$

Solution $\frac{5 \bullet 3}{6 \bullet 4} = \frac{15}{24}$

$\frac{15}{24} = \frac{5}{8}$

Answer $\frac{5}{8}$

EXAMPLE 2 $7 \bullet \frac{4}{5} = \blacksquare$

Solution $\frac{7 \bullet 4}{1 \bullet 5} = \frac{28}{5}$

$\frac{28}{5} = 5\frac{3}{5}$

Answer $5\frac{3}{5}$

Exercise Multiply. Write your answers in lowest terms.

1. $\frac{1}{2} \bullet \frac{2}{3}$ $\frac{1}{3}$
2. $\frac{3}{5} \bullet \frac{5}{6}$ $\frac{1}{2}$
3. $\frac{7}{8} \bullet \frac{6}{13}$ $\frac{21}{52}$
4. $\frac{2}{9} \bullet \frac{3}{5}$ $\frac{2}{15}$
5. $\frac{6}{7} \bullet \frac{1}{2}$ $\frac{3}{7}$
6. $\frac{3}{11} \bullet \frac{2}{5}$ $\frac{6}{55}$
7. $\frac{2}{7} \bullet \frac{2}{9}$ $\frac{4}{63}$
8. $\frac{5}{11} \bullet \frac{1}{4}$ $\frac{5}{44}$
9. $\frac{1}{6} \bullet \frac{2}{9}$ $\frac{1}{27}$
10. $\frac{5}{6} \bullet \frac{1}{4}$ $\frac{5}{24}$
11. $\frac{3}{11} \bullet \frac{2}{12}$ $\frac{1}{22}$
12. $\frac{4}{5} \bullet \frac{2}{9}$ $\frac{8}{45}$
13. $\frac{4}{7} \bullet \frac{1}{8}$ $\frac{1}{14}$
14. $\frac{3}{16} \bullet \frac{13}{21}$ $\frac{13}{112}$
15. $\frac{5}{21} \bullet \frac{7}{10}$ $\frac{1}{6}$
16. $\frac{5}{24} \bullet \frac{3}{13}$ $\frac{5}{104}$
17. $\frac{6}{28} \bullet \frac{7}{12}$ $\frac{1}{8}$
18. $\frac{2}{3} \bullet \frac{5}{6}$ $\frac{5}{9}$
19. $\frac{12}{21} \bullet \frac{7}{8}$ $\frac{1}{2}$
20. $\frac{13}{32} \bullet \frac{8}{26}$ $\frac{1}{8}$

Algebra *Review of Basic Skills* **487**

MANIPULATIVES

Multiplying Mixed Numbers

Materials: Cuisenaire Rods

Group Practice: Using the example, label one number line in $\frac{1}{3}$ units and another in $\frac{1}{2}$ units. Model $3\frac{2}{3}$ by placing three 3-rods and two cubes on the first number line. Replace each 3-rod with 3 cubes and write the symbolic equivalent of the improper fraction ($\frac{11}{3}$). Repeat for $1\frac{1}{2}$. Multiply as shown in the example. To change products from improper fractions to mixed numbers, label a number line in $\frac{1}{2}$ units. Model $\frac{11}{2}$ by placing eleven cubes on the number line. To find the mixed number equivalent, replace each pair of cubes with a 2-rod, explaining that one whole unit is the same as two $\frac{1}{2}$ units. Write the symbolic equivalent of the mixed number ($5\frac{1}{2}$).

Student Practice: Have students use the rods to solve or check problems 1–8, 10–11, 14–18.

Multiplying Mixed Numbers

To multiply mixed numbers

1. Change them to improper fractions.
2. Multiply the fractions.
3. Reduce to lowest terms.

EXAMPLE 1 $3\frac{2}{3} \bullet 1\frac{1}{2} = \blacksquare$

Solution $3\frac{2}{3} \bullet 1\frac{1}{2} = \frac{11}{\cancel{3}_1} \bullet \frac{\cancel{3}^1}{2} = \frac{11}{2} = 5\frac{1}{2}$

Answer $3\frac{2}{3} \bullet 1\frac{1}{2} = 5\frac{1}{2}$

Exercise Multiply. Write your answers in lowest terms.

1. $2\frac{1}{2} \cdot \frac{1}{3}$ $\frac{5}{6}$
2. $\frac{1}{2} \cdot 1\frac{1}{5}$ $\frac{3}{5}$
3. $\frac{2}{7} \cdot 1\frac{1}{3}$ $\frac{8}{21}$
4. $\frac{1}{5} \cdot 1\frac{1}{7}$ $\frac{8}{35}$
5. $3\frac{1}{5} \cdot \frac{3}{4}$ $2\frac{2}{5}$
6. $5\frac{2}{3} \cdot \frac{1}{5}$ $1\frac{2}{15}$
7. $\frac{5}{7} \cdot 2\frac{3}{8}$ $1\frac{39}{56}$
8. $1\frac{1}{2} \cdot \frac{15}{18}$ $1\frac{1}{4}$
9. $4\frac{5}{7} \cdot \frac{7}{11}$ 3
10. $2\frac{3}{5} \cdot 1\frac{1}{5}$ $3\frac{3}{25}$
11. $2\frac{3}{7} \cdot 2\frac{1}{2}$ $6\frac{1}{14}$
12. $5\frac{1}{7} \cdot 2\frac{1}{5}$ $11\frac{11}{35}$
13. $5\frac{1}{6} \cdot 1\frac{1}{5}$ $6\frac{1}{5}$
14. $1\frac{5}{6} \cdot 1\frac{1}{3}$ $2\frac{4}{9}$
15. $1\frac{2}{7} \cdot 2\frac{1}{8}$ $2\frac{41}{56}$
16. $6\frac{1}{2} \cdot 2\frac{3}{4}$ $17\frac{7}{8}$
17. $2\frac{2}{5} \cdot 1\frac{3}{4}$ $4\frac{1}{5}$
18. $4\frac{1}{2} \cdot 1\frac{1}{4}$ $5\frac{5}{8}$
19. $3\frac{3}{7} \cdot 2\frac{1}{3}$ 8
20. $5\frac{2}{9} \cdot 1\frac{1}{8}$ $5\frac{7}{8}$

Review of Basic Skills 20

Dividing Fractions

Rule

To divide one fraction by another fraction, invert the divisor and multiply.

EXAMPLE 1 $\frac{4}{7} \div \frac{1}{2} = \blacksquare$

$\frac{4}{7} \div \frac{1}{2} = \blacksquare$ ← Invert the divisor. Then multiply.

$\frac{4}{7} \bullet \frac{2}{1} = \frac{8}{7}$

$\frac{8}{7} = 1\frac{1}{7}$

Answer $1\frac{1}{7}$

Exercise Divide. Write your answers in lowest terms.

Problem	Answer	Problem	Answer	Problem	Answer
1. $\frac{2}{5} \div \frac{2}{7}$	$1\frac{2}{5}$	**10.** $\frac{5}{11} \div \frac{2}{22}$	5	**19.** $\frac{1}{2} \div \frac{5}{7}$	$\frac{7}{10}$
2. $\frac{5}{6} \div \frac{1}{3}$	$2\frac{1}{2}$	**11.** $\frac{8}{11} \div \frac{5}{11}$	$1\frac{3}{5}$	**20.** $\frac{5}{7} \div \frac{5}{14}$	2
3. $\frac{2}{7} \div \frac{1}{8}$	$2\frac{2}{7}$	**12.** $\frac{5}{12} \div \frac{5}{6}$	$\frac{1}{2}$	**21.** $\frac{8}{9} \div \frac{3}{6}$	$1\frac{7}{9}$
4. $\frac{4}{5} \div \frac{1}{6}$	$4\frac{4}{5}$	**13.** $\frac{3}{8} \div \frac{5}{12}$	$\frac{9}{10}$	**22.** $\frac{3}{4} \div \frac{6}{7}$	$\frac{7}{8}$
5. $\frac{2}{7} \div \frac{5}{6}$	$\frac{12}{35}$	**14.** $\frac{2}{11} \div \frac{3}{22}$	$1\frac{1}{3}$	**23.** $\frac{13}{14} \div \frac{3}{7}$	$2\frac{1}{6}$
6. $\frac{3}{8} \div \frac{1}{2}$	$\frac{3}{4}$	**15.** $\frac{8}{13} \div \frac{24}{26}$	$\frac{2}{3}$	**24.** $\frac{8}{15} \div \frac{2}{5}$	$1\frac{1}{3}$
7. $\frac{4}{5} \div \frac{5}{6}$	$\frac{24}{25}$	**16.** $\frac{3}{9} \div \frac{1}{5}$	$1\frac{2}{3}$	**25.** $\frac{1}{2} \div \frac{1}{2}$	1
8. $\frac{8}{9} \div \frac{4}{5}$	$1\frac{1}{9}$	**17.** $\frac{11}{12} \div \frac{24}{30}$	$1\frac{7}{48}$		
9. $\frac{5}{6} \div \frac{2}{5}$	$2\frac{1}{12}$	**18.** $\frac{5}{7} \div \frac{48}{49}$	$\frac{35}{48}$		

MANIPULATIVES

Dividing Fractions

Materials: Cuisenaire Rods

Group Practice: Follow the example for dividing fractions. To perform the last step of changing improper fractions to mixed numbers, label a number line in $\frac{1}{7}$ units with improper fractions for mixed number values. Model $\frac{8}{7}$ by placing eight cubes on the number line. To model the mixed number equivalent, replace each group of seven cubes with a 7-rod. (The 7-rod is the whole unit.) Write the symbolic equivalent for the mixed number.

Student Practice: Have students use the rods to solve or check problems 1–3, 8, 11, 14, 16, 21, 23–24.

MANIPULATIVES

Dividing Mixed Numbers

Materials: Cuisenaire Rods

Group Practice: Using the example, label one number line in $\frac{1}{4}$ units and another in $\frac{1}{3}$ units. Model $2\frac{3}{4}$ by placing two 4-rods and three cubes on the first number line. Replace each 4-rod with four cubes and write the symbolic equivalent of the improper fraction. Repeat for $3\frac{1}{3}$. Divide as shown in the example. To change answers that are improper fractions to mixed numbers, review Basic Skill 16.

Student Practice: Have students use the rods to solve or check problems 1–14, 18, 21–23, 25–26.

Dividing Mixed Numbers

Rule

Rename the mixed numbers as improper fractions. Invert the divisor and multiply.

EXAMPLE 1 $2\frac{3}{4} \div 3\frac{1}{3} = \blacksquare$

Solution $2\frac{3}{4} \div 3\frac{1}{3} = \blacksquare$

$\frac{11}{4} \div \frac{10}{3} = \blacksquare$ ← Rename as improper fractions.

$\frac{11}{4} \bullet \frac{3}{10} = \blacksquare$ ← Invert the divisor and multiply.

$\frac{11 \bullet 3}{4 \bullet 10} = \frac{33}{40}$

Answer $\frac{33}{40}$

Exercise Divide. Write your answer in lowest terms.

	Problem	Answer		Problem	Answer		Problem	Answer
1.	$1\frac{1}{2} \div \frac{1}{2}$	3	**11.**	$1\frac{5}{7} \div \frac{6}{7}$	2	**21.**	$1\frac{1}{2} \div 2\frac{1}{4}$	$\frac{2}{3}$
2.	$3\frac{2}{3} \div \frac{1}{2}$	$7\frac{1}{3}$	**12.**	$2\frac{1}{3} \div \frac{2}{3}$	$3\frac{1}{2}$	**22.**	$3\frac{1}{4} \div 1\frac{1}{2}$	$2\frac{1}{6}$
3.	$1\frac{1}{5} \div \frac{1}{2}$	$2\frac{2}{5}$	**13.**	$3\frac{1}{5} \div \frac{2}{5}$	8	**23.**	$2\frac{1}{4} \div 1\frac{1}{4}$	$1\frac{4}{5}$
4.	$2\frac{1}{6} \div \frac{2}{3}$	$3\frac{1}{4}$	**14.**	$4\frac{1}{2} \div \frac{3}{4}$	6	**24.**	$6\frac{3}{8} \div 1\frac{1}{8}$	$5\frac{2}{3}$
5.	$\frac{3}{12} \div 2\frac{1}{2}$	$\frac{1}{10}$	**15.**	$2\frac{5}{8} \div \frac{3}{8}$	7	**25.**	$7\frac{1}{2} \div 2\frac{3}{4}$	$2\frac{8}{11}$
6.	$\frac{13}{15} \div 1\frac{1}{2}$	$\frac{26}{45}$	**16.**	$6\frac{1}{4} \div \frac{3}{4}$	$8\frac{1}{3}$	**26.**	$8\frac{1}{2} \div 1\frac{1}{2}$	$5\frac{2}{3}$
7.	$1\frac{2}{5} \div \frac{2}{3}$	$2\frac{1}{10}$	**17.**	$3\frac{5}{8} \div \frac{7}{8}$	$4\frac{1}{7}$	**27.**	$4\frac{3}{8} \div 2\frac{3}{8}$	$1\frac{16}{19}$
8.	$1\frac{3}{7} \div \frac{1}{7}$	10	**18.**	$5\frac{1}{3} \div \frac{3}{4}$	$7\frac{1}{9}$	**28.**	$7\frac{1}{4} \div 2\frac{5}{8}$	$2\frac{16}{21}$
9.	$3\frac{1}{2} \div \frac{1}{2}$	7	**19.**	$6\frac{3}{4} \div \frac{1}{2}$	$13\frac{1}{2}$	**29.**	$6\frac{3}{7} \div 5\frac{1}{7}$	$1\frac{1}{4}$
10.	$1\frac{1}{2} \div \frac{1}{3}$	$4\frac{1}{2}$	**20.**	$7\frac{9}{10} \div \frac{1}{2}$	$15\frac{4}{5}$	**30.**	$9\frac{1}{2} \div 3\frac{3}{8}$	$2\frac{22}{27}$

490 *Review of Basic Skills* *Algebra*

Review of Basic Skills 22

Adding Mixed Numbers with Like Denominators

EXAMPLE 1 $3\frac{1}{8} + 2\frac{3}{8}$

Solution

$$\begin{array}{r} 3\frac{1}{8} \\ +\ 2\frac{3}{8} \\ \hline 5\frac{4}{8} \end{array}$$

Step 1 Write in vertical form.
Step 2 Add numerators. 1 + 3 = 4
Step 3 Add whole numbers. 3 + 2 = 5
Step 4 Reduce fraction.

Answer $5\frac{1}{2}$

EXAMPLE 2 Add the sides to get the perimeter of the rectangle. Measurements are in feet.

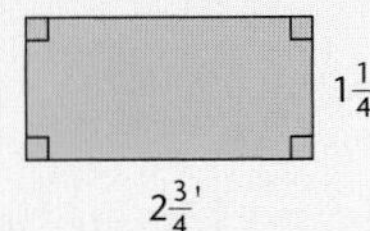

Solution $1\frac{1}{4} + 1\frac{1}{4} + 2\frac{3}{4} + 2\frac{3}{4}$ Add the four sides.

Step 1 Add numerators.
$1 + 1 + 3 + 3 = 8$ $\quad \frac{8}{4}$

Step 2 Add whole numbers.
$1 + 1 + 2 + 2 = 6$

Step 3 Simplify. $\frac{8}{4} = 2$ $\quad 6 + 2 = 8$ $\quad$ Answer 8'

Exercise Add the mixed numbers.

1. $1\frac{1}{2} + 1\frac{1}{2}$ 3
2. $3\frac{1}{4} + 2\frac{1}{4}$ $5\frac{1}{2}$
3. $6\frac{3}{4} + 1\frac{1}{4}$ 8
4. $5\frac{1}{2} + 7\frac{1}{2}$ 13
5. $3\frac{1}{3} + 4\frac{1}{3}$ $7\frac{2}{3}$
6. $7\frac{1}{8} + 1\frac{1}{8}$ $8\frac{1}{4}$
7. $3\frac{1}{4} + 6\frac{3}{4}$ 10
8. $7\frac{3}{8} + 1\frac{1}{8}$ $8\frac{1}{2}$
9. $5\frac{1}{16} + 3\frac{4}{16}$ $8\frac{5}{16}$
10. $1\frac{1}{8} + 2\frac{3}{8}$ $3\frac{1}{2}$
11. $5\frac{1}{16} + 6\frac{7}{16}$ $11\frac{1}{2}$
12. $3\frac{5}{16} + 1\frac{8}{16}$ $4\frac{13}{16}$
13. $4\frac{17}{32} + 1\frac{21}{32}$ $6\frac{3}{16}$
14. $8\frac{9}{15} + 1\frac{3}{15}$ $9\frac{4}{5}$
15. $6\frac{19}{32} + 1\frac{11}{32}$ $7\frac{15}{16}$

Find the perimeter of the rectangles.

16.
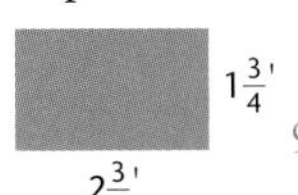

9'

17.
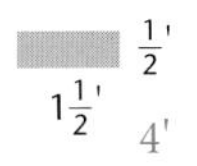

4'

18.
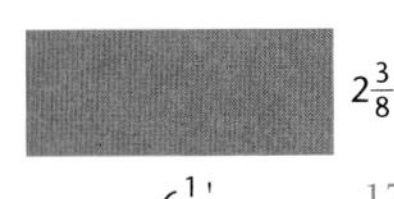

17'

19.
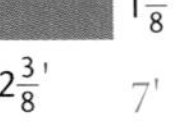

7'

20.
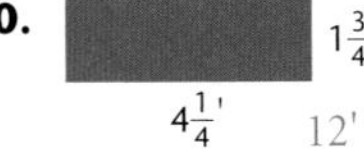

12'

Algebra *Review of Basic Skills* **491**

Manipulatives

Adding Fractions with Unlike Denominators

Materials: Cuisenaire Rods

Group Practice: Using the example, find the common denominator by building two rectangles—one with 3-rods, the other with 5-rods. Add rods to one or both rectangles until both have equal areas (15). This value represents the common denominator. To rewrite the fractions with common denominators, build $\frac{2}{3}$ by placing a 2-rod over a 3-rod. Add 3-rods to the denominator up to 15. Point out that 3 is added five times, or multiplied by 5. Next, "multiply" the 2-rod in the numerator by 5 also. Repeat for $\frac{1}{5}$. Write the symbolic equivalent for each step. Now that the denominators are the same, combine numerators to find the sum. Use the same procedure for adding the fraction portions of mixed numbers.

Student Practice: Have students use the rods to solve or check problems 1–5, 8–9, 11–12, 14–15, 17.

Review of Basic Skills 23

Adding Fractions with Unlike Denominators

To add fractions with *unlike* denominators, you must first rewrite the fractions so that they have *like* denominators. Then you can add.

Example 1 $\frac{2}{3} + \frac{1}{5} = \blacksquare$ $\qquad 3 \cdot 5 = 15$ is a common denominator

Solution

$$\frac{2}{3} = \frac{2 \cdot 5}{3 \cdot 5} = \frac{10}{15}$$
$$+\frac{1}{5} = \frac{1 \cdot 3}{5 \cdot 3} = \frac{3}{15}$$

Add $\frac{13}{15}$

Answer $\frac{13}{15}$

Adding Mixed Numbers with Unlike Denominators

Example 2 $1\frac{1}{2} + 2\frac{1}{3} = \blacksquare$

Solution

$1\frac{1}{2}$ $\quad \frac{1}{2} = \frac{1 \cdot 3}{2 \cdot 3} = \frac{3}{6}$ $\quad 1\frac{3}{6}$ Rewrite with common denominators.

$+\ 2\frac{1}{3}$ $\quad \frac{1}{3} = \frac{1 \cdot 2}{3 \cdot 2} = \frac{2}{6}$ $\quad +\ 2\frac{2}{6}$ Add.

$3\frac{5}{6}$ Simplify if needed.

Answer $3\frac{5}{6}$

Exercise Add the fractions. Watch for unlike denominators.

1. $\frac{1}{2} + \frac{1}{4}$ $\quad \frac{3}{4}$
2. $\frac{1}{3} + \frac{1}{5}$ $\quad \frac{8}{15}$
3. $\frac{3}{4} + \frac{1}{2}$ $\quad 1\frac{1}{4}$
4. $\frac{3}{5} + \frac{1}{10}$ $\quad \frac{7}{10}$
5. $\frac{7}{12} + \frac{1}{3}$ $\quad \frac{11}{12}$
6. $\frac{1}{10} + \frac{7}{15}$ $\quad \frac{17}{30}$
7. $\frac{3}{10} + \frac{1}{3}$ $\quad \frac{19}{30}$
8. $\frac{7}{12} + \frac{1}{6}$ $\quad \frac{3}{4}$
9. $\frac{3}{7} + \frac{1}{2}$ $\quad \frac{13}{14}$
10. $\frac{3}{8} + \frac{7}{24}$ $\quad \frac{2}{3}$
11. $1\frac{1}{2} + 2\frac{1}{3}$ $\quad 3\frac{5}{6}$
12. $6\frac{1}{2} + 1\frac{1}{3}$ $\quad 7\frac{5}{6}$
13. $3\frac{3}{4} + 1\frac{1}{2}$ $\quad 5\frac{1}{4}$
14. $3\frac{1}{4} + 2\frac{2}{3}$ $\quad 5\frac{11}{12}$
15. $5\frac{2}{5} + 1\frac{3}{10}$ $\quad 6\frac{7}{10}$
16. $3\frac{7}{12} + 1\frac{5}{6}$ $\quad 5\frac{5}{12}$
17. $1\frac{1}{12} + 3\frac{3}{4}$ $\quad 4\frac{5}{6}$
18. $4\frac{2}{5} + 6\frac{8}{15}$ $\quad 10\frac{14}{15}$
19. $5\frac{1}{2} + 6\frac{23}{24}$ $\quad 12\frac{11}{24}$
20. $5\frac{17}{32} + 6\frac{1}{2}$ $\quad 12\frac{1}{32}$

492 *Review of Basic Skills Algebra*

Review of Basic Skills 24

Subtracting Mixed Numbers with Like Denominators

Example 1

$14\frac{5}{11}$	**Step 1** Subtract numerators 2 from 5.	$5 - 2 = 3$
$-\ 6\frac{2}{11}$	**Step 2** Keep the denominator.	
$8\frac{3}{11}$	**Step 3** Subtract the whole numbers.	$14 - 6 = 8$

Answer $8\frac{3}{11}$

Exercise Subtract and write in lowest terms.

1. $\frac{3}{8} - \frac{1}{8}$ $\frac{1}{4}$

2. $\frac{5}{7} - \frac{2}{7}$ $\frac{3}{7}$

3. $4\frac{3}{8} - 1\frac{1}{8}$ $3\frac{1}{4}$

4. $5\frac{7}{8} - 1\frac{5}{8}$ $4\frac{1}{4}$

5. $3\frac{7}{10} - 2\frac{3}{10}$ $1\frac{2}{5}$

6. $5\frac{3}{4} - 3\frac{1}{4}$ $2\frac{1}{2}$

7. $6\frac{7}{12} - 5\frac{5}{12}$ $1\frac{1}{6}$

8. $7\frac{15}{32} - 5\frac{7}{32}$ $2\frac{1}{4}$

9. $9\frac{41}{100} - 6\frac{21}{100}$ $3\frac{1}{5}$

10. $5\frac{99}{100} - 2\frac{49}{100}$ $3\frac{1}{2}$

11. $6\frac{5}{16} - 4\frac{3}{16}$ $2\frac{1}{8}$

12. $\frac{3}{4} - \frac{2}{4}$ $\frac{1}{4}$

13. $2\frac{5}{8} - 1\frac{4}{8}$ $1\frac{1}{8}$

14. $5\frac{3}{4} - 3\frac{2}{4}$ $2\frac{1}{4}$

15. $6\frac{3}{5} - 3\frac{1}{5}$ $3\frac{2}{5}$

16. $2\frac{1}{2} - 1\frac{1}{2}$ 1

17. $3\frac{2}{17} - 1\frac{1}{17}$ $2\frac{1}{17}$

18. $10\frac{18}{39} - 5\frac{7}{39}$ $5\frac{11}{39}$

19. $3\frac{3}{10} - 1\frac{1}{10}$ $2\frac{1}{5}$

20. $4\frac{3}{4} - 2\frac{1}{4}$ $2\frac{1}{2}$

Algebra *Review of Basic Skills* **493**

MANIPULATIVES

Subtracting with Unlike Denominators

Materials: Cuisenaire Rods

Group Practice: Using the example, find the common denominator of the two fractions by building two rectangles—one with 3-rods, the other with 2-rods. Add rods to one or both rectangles until both have equal areas (6). This value represents the common denominator. To rewrite the fractions with common denominators, build $\frac{2}{3}$ by placing a 2-rod over a 3-rod. Add a 3-rod to the denominator to make 6. Point out that 3 is added two times, or multiplied by 2. Next, "multiply" the 2-rod in the numerator by 2 also. Repeat for $\frac{1}{2}$. Write the symbolic equivalent for each step. Now that the denominators are the same, place the rods from the numerator of the subtrahend on top of the rods from the numerator of the minuend. Find the rod that fits in the uncovered portion of the rods in the minuend (cube). Place the cube over the common denominator to model the difference of the fractions ($\frac{1}{6}$). Repeat the subtraction step with the whole numbers. Write the symbolic equivalent of the model.

Student Practice: Have students use the rods to solve or check problems 1–8, 11, 13–14.

Review of Basic Skills 25

Subtracting with Unlike Denominators

EXAMPLE 1 Rewrite fractions with a like denominator.

$$\begin{array}{r} 8\frac{2}{3} \\ -\,5\frac{1}{2} \\ \hline \end{array} \qquad \frac{2}{3} = \frac{2 \cdot 2}{3 \cdot 2} = \frac{4}{6} \qquad \frac{1}{2} = \frac{1 \cdot 3}{2 \cdot 3} = \frac{3}{6} \qquad \begin{array}{r} 8\frac{4}{6} \\ -\,5\frac{3}{6} \\ \hline 3\frac{1}{6} \end{array}$$

Subtract numerators and whole numbers.

Answer $3\frac{1}{6}$

Exercise Subtract and write in lowest terms.

Problem	Answer	Problem	Answer	Problem	Answer
1. $\frac{5}{8} - \frac{1}{2}$	$\frac{1}{8}$	**6.** $2\frac{1}{2} - 1\frac{1}{3}$	$1\frac{1}{6}$	**11.** $7\frac{3}{4} - \frac{1}{8}$	$7\frac{5}{8}$
2. $\frac{3}{4} - \frac{1}{2}$	$\frac{1}{4}$	**7.** $4\frac{3}{8} - 1\frac{1}{4}$	$3\frac{1}{8}$	**12.** $2\frac{6}{11} - \frac{1}{22}$	$2\frac{1}{2}$
3. $2\frac{5}{8} - 1\frac{1}{2}$	$1\frac{1}{8}$	**8.** $6\frac{7}{8} - 2\frac{3}{4}$	$4\frac{1}{8}$	**13.** $5\frac{7}{9} - 1\frac{1}{3}$	$4\frac{4}{9}$
4. $5\frac{3}{4} - 3\frac{1}{2}$	$2\frac{1}{4}$	**9.** $9\frac{3}{10} - 6\frac{3}{100}$	$3\frac{27}{100}$	**14.** $3\frac{1}{5} - 1\frac{1}{10}$	$2\frac{1}{10}$
5. $6\frac{3}{5} - 2\frac{1}{4}$	$4\frac{7}{20}$	**10.** $7\frac{51}{100} - 6\frac{1}{5}$	$1\frac{31}{100}$	**15.** $8\frac{1}{19} - 1\frac{2}{38}$	7

Review of Basic Skills 26

Subtracting with Renaming

Example 1 $\begin{array}{r} 12 \\ -\ 3\frac{1}{4} \\ \hline \end{array}$

You need to rename 12 to $11\frac{4}{4}$ first.
Then you can subtract the fractions and the whole numbers.

$$\begin{array}{r} 12 \\ -\ 3\frac{1}{4} \\ \hline \end{array} = 11 + 1 = \begin{array}{r} 11\frac{4}{4} \\ -\ 3\frac{1}{4} \\ \hline 8\frac{3}{4} \end{array}$$

Answer $8\frac{3}{4}$

Example 2 $\begin{array}{r} 5\frac{1}{4} \\ -\ 1\frac{3}{4} \\ \hline \end{array}$

You need to rename $5\frac{1}{4}$ to $4\frac{5}{4}$ first.
Then you can subtract the fractions and the whole numbers.

$$\begin{array}{r} 5\frac{1}{4} \\ -\ 1\frac{3}{4} \\ \hline \end{array} = 4 + 1 + \frac{1}{4} = 4 + \frac{4}{4} + \frac{1}{4} = \begin{array}{r} 4\frac{5}{4} \\ -\ 1\frac{3}{4} \\ \hline 3\frac{2}{4} \end{array}$$

Simplify.

Answer $3\frac{1}{2}$

Exercise Subtract and write in lowest terms.

1. $5 - 1\frac{1}{4}$	$3\frac{3}{4}$	**8.** $9 - 6\frac{3}{7}$	$2\frac{4}{7}$	**15.** $8\frac{5}{8} - 6\frac{3}{4}$	$1\frac{7}{8}$
2. $6 - 2\frac{3}{4}$	$3\frac{1}{4}$	**9.** $10 - 5\frac{3}{10}$	$4\frac{7}{10}$	**16.** $7\frac{1}{2} - 2\frac{3}{4}$	$4\frac{3}{4}$
3. $9 - 1\frac{1}{2}$	$7\frac{1}{2}$	**10.** $15 - 10\frac{2}{9}$	$4\frac{7}{9}$	**17.** $5\frac{1}{3} - 2\frac{1}{2}$	$2\frac{5}{6}$
4. $6 - 3\frac{1}{3}$	$2\frac{2}{3}$	**11.** $5\frac{1}{4} - 1\frac{3}{4}$	$3\frac{1}{2}$	**18.** $9\frac{1}{2} - 2\frac{2}{3}$	$6\frac{5}{6}$
5. $7 - 5\frac{2}{3}$	$1\frac{1}{3}$	**12.** $6\frac{1}{3} - 2\frac{2}{3}$	$3\frac{2}{3}$	**19.** $10\frac{1}{5} - 5\frac{7}{10}$	$4\frac{1}{2}$
6. $4 - 1\frac{3}{5}$	$2\frac{2}{5}$	**13.** $6\frac{3}{10} - 1\frac{7}{10}$	$4\frac{3}{5}$	**20.** $11\frac{1}{2} - 6\frac{9}{10}$	$4\frac{3}{5}$
7. $8 - 5\frac{1}{4}$	$2\frac{3}{4}$	**14.** $4\frac{5}{12} - 2\frac{7}{12}$	$1\frac{5}{6}$		

Manipulatives

Subtracting with Renaming

Materials: Cuisenaire Rods

Group Practice: Using the second example, label a number line in $\frac{1}{4}$ units. Place a model of $5\frac{1}{4}$ on the number line using five 4-rods and a cube. To regroup $5\frac{1}{4}$, remove the last 4-rod and replace it with four cubes. Write the symbolic equivalent ($4\frac{5}{4}$). To subtract the subtrahend, remove three cubes and one 4-rod ($1\frac{3}{4}$) and realign the remaining rods. Write the symbolic equivalent for the model of the difference. To rename fractions in simplest terms, review Basic Skill 15.

Student Practice: Have students use the rods to solve or check problems 1–6, 11–12.

Algebra Review of Basic Skills **495**

MANIPULATIVES

Identifying Place Value with Decimals

Materials: Base Ten Blocks

Group Practice: Tell students that the 100-Square Flat represents one whole and each square is $\frac{1}{100}$ of the whole. Explain that the unit cube (or 1-rod) represents 1 out of 100 and write the decimal form of the symbolic equivalent. Similarly, the 10-rod represents 10 out of 100 or $\frac{1}{10}$. Write the decimal form of the symbolic equivalent for one-tenth. Using the example, model 0.38 by placing three 10-rods (three $\frac{1}{10}$-rods) and eight cubes (eight $\frac{1}{100}$-rods) on one grid. Model 0.40 on the other grid placing four 10-rods (four $\frac{1}{10}$-rods). Compare rod values to see which model represents the larger decimal.

Student Practice: Have students use the rods to solve problems 11–17.

Review of Basic Skills 27

Identifying Place Value with Decimals

EXAMPLE 1 Write the place value of the underlined digits.

1. 23.0671 Hundredths
2. 105.1062 Ten-Thousandths

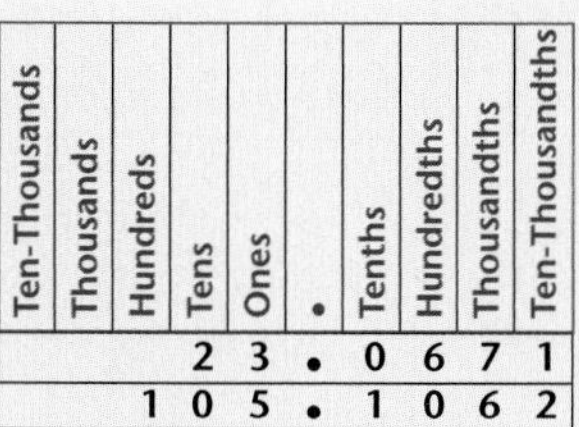

Ten-Thousands	Thousands	Hundreds	Tens	Ones	•	Tenths	Hundredths	Thousandths	Ten-Thousandths
			2	3	•	0	6	7	1
		1	0	5	•	1	0	6	2

EXAMPLE 2 Compare 2.38 and 2.4.
Use the symbol $<$ or $>$.
$<$ is "less than." $>$ is "more than."

Insert zeros to give each decimal the same number of places.

1. 2.38 and 2.4
2. 2.38 and 2.40 (after inserting zero)

Since 38 is less than 40, then $2.38 < 2.40$.

Exercise Write the place name for each underlined digit.

1. 35.06 tenths
2. 0.52603 thousandths
3. 5.6811 ten-thousandths
4. 1.0611 thousandths
5. 0.58111 hundred-thousandths
6. 0.401015 millionths
7. 0.002731 thousandths
8. 276.03 hundreds
9. 2.0835 hundredths
10. 0.28501 hundred-thousandths

Write $<$ or $>$.

11. 2.38 ■ 2.37 $>$
12. 6.19 ■ 6.91 $<$
13. 3.7 ■ 3.71 $<$
14. 6.8 ■ 6.81 $<$
15. 9.73 ■ 9.3 $>$
16. 4.03 ■ 4.3 $<$
17. 6.76 ■ 6.7 $>$
18. 4.801 ■ 4.81 $<$
19. 6.73 ■ 6.703 $>$
20. 8.701 ■ 8.71 $<$

Review of Basic Skills 28

Rounding Decimals

EXAMPLE 1 Round 2.7017 to the nearest thousandth.

Solution 2.7017 Number (7) to the right of the thousandths place is 5 or more, so add 1 to the thousandths place and drop all digits to the right.

Answer 2.7017 ≈ 2.702 (≈ means "approximately equal to.")

EXAMPLE 2 Round 8.1649 to the nearest hundredth.

Solution 8.1649 Number (4) to the right of the hundredth place is less than 5, so drop all digits to the right of 6.

Answer 8.1649 ≈ 8.16

Exercise Round each decimal to the places named.

	Tenths	Hundredths	Thousandths
1. 2.063	2.1	2.06	2.063
2. 0.0891	0.1	0.09	0.089
3. 1.0354	1.0	1.04	1.035
4. 0.15454	0.2	0.15	0.155
5. 32.70391	32.7	32.70	32.704
6. 7.63	7.6	7.63	7.630
7. 19.808964	19.8	19.81	19.809
8. 34.00354	34.0	34.00	34.004
9. 2.061155	2.1	2.06	2.061
10. 139.4181891	139.4	139.42	139.418

Algebra Review of Basic Skills **497**

Review of Basic Skills 29

Adding Decimals

Rule

Remember to line up all decimal points, then add.

Example 1 $13.11 + $2 + $1.91

Solution

```
  $13.11
   $2.00  ← Insert zeros
 + $1.91
  $17.02
```

Example 2 23 + .62 + 1.9

Solution

```
  23.00  ← Insert zeros
    .62
 + 1.90  ← Insert zero
  25.52
```

Exercise Write in vertical form, then add.

1. $13.10 + $3 + $1.93 $18.03

2. $5.10 + $1 + $7.63 $13.73

3. $6.03 + $7.17 + $5 $18.20

4. $3.41 + $4.01 + $6 $13.42

5. $3 + $14.63 + $1.01 $18.64

6. $4.63 + $5 + $6.15 $15.78

7. $9 + $18 + $6.09 $33.09

8. $16.09 + $7.17 + $3 $26.26

9. $10 + $0.05 + $16.20 $26.25

10. $14 + $6.37 + $9.56 $29.93

11. 4.3 + 6.02 + 5 15.32

12. 6.37 + 4 + 9.76 20.13

13. 5 + 3.01 + 4.1 12.11

14. 6.37 + 6 + 19.013 31.383

15. 41 + 16.1 + 7.303 64.403

16. 6.1 + 7.23 + 4.769 18.099

17. 4 + 3.01 + 4.607 11.617

18. 16.1 + 3.23 + 4.768 24.098

19. 19.02 + 4 + 63.0791 86.0991

20. 16.778 + 3 + 9.0734 28.8514

498 *Review of Basic Skills Algebra*

Review of Basic Skills 30

Subtracting Decimals

Rule

Remember to line up the decimal points first, then subtract.

Example 1 $29.48 − $5.15 — Write in vertical form.

Solution

```
  $29.48      Line up decimals.
− $ 5.15      Subtract.
  $24.33
```

Example 2 $12 − $3.74 — Write in vertical form.

Solution

```
  $12.00  ←   Insert zeros.
−  $3.74      Subtract.
   $8.26
```

Example 3 6.5 − 1.41 — Write in vertical form.

Solution

```
  6.50  ←   Insert zero.
− 1.41      Subtract.
  5.09
```

Exercise Write in vertical form, then subtract.

1. $21.48 − $5.15 $16.33
2. $13.41 − $10.30 $3.11
3. $16.71 − $5.36 $11.35
4. $14.70 − $4.70 $10.00
5. $18.41 − $16.30 $2.11
6. $41.86 − $14.68 $27.18
7. $12.00 − $3.74 $8.26
8. $15.00 − $6.72 $8.28
9. $19.00 − $5.63 $13.37
10. $15.00 − $9.81 $5.19
11. 6.5 − 1.41 5.09
12. 3.6 − 2.94 0.66
13. 6.7 − 5.61 1.09
14. 8.96 − 3.67 5.29
15. 10.46 − 4.67 5.79
16. 91.14 − 16.63 74.51
17. 41.62 − 19.81 21.81
18. 98.14 − 63.01 35.13
19. 43.1 − 6.37 36.73
20. 84.73 − 4.1 80.63

Algebra Review of Basic Skills 499

Review of Basic Skills 31

Multiplying Decimals

By adding the decimal places in the factors, you know exactly how many decimal places are in the product.

EXAMPLE 1 1.3 • 2 = ■

Solution	1.3	one place	
	× 2	no decimal	
Answer	2.6	one place	1 + 0 = 1

EXAMPLE 2 1.3 • 2.43 = ■

Solution	1.3	one place	
	× 2.43	two places	
	39		
	52		
	+ 2 6		
Answer	3.159	three places	1 + 2 = 3

Exercise Write in vertical form, then multiply.

1. 1.4 • 2 2.8

2. 2.4 • 5 12

3. 6.3 • 3 18.9

4. 4.9 • 3 14.7

5. 6.7 • 5 33.5

6. 1.3 • 2.4 3.12

7. 6.1 • 2.6 15.86

8. 3.9 • 4.1 15.99

9. 6.7 • 1.2 8.04

10. 8.6 • 6.8 58.48

11. 1.3 • 2.43 3.159

12. 6.8 • 2.61 17.748

13. 4.63 • 1.6 7.408

14. 9.84 • 2.7 26.568

15. 4.86 • 2.9 14.094

16. 6.7 • 1.79 11.993

17. 7.8 • 4.62 36.036

18. 4.91 • 1.8 8.838

19. 9.46 • 2.9 27.434

20. 6.3 • 8.76 55.188

500 *Review of Basic Skills Algebra*

Review of Basic Skills 32

Scientific Notation

Scientific notation expresses any number as a product of a number 1 or greater but less than 10 and a power of ten.

EXAMPLE 1 Express 2,800 in scientific notation.

Solution $2{,}800 = 2.8 \cdot 10^3$ Move the decimal point 3 places to the left.

Answer $2.8 \cdot 10^3$

EXAMPLE 2 Express 0.00039 in scientific notation.

Solution $0.00039 = 3.9 \cdot 10^{-4}$ Move the decimal point 4 places to the right.

Use the negative sign ($^{-4}$) when the decimal is moved to the right.

Answer $3.9 \cdot 10^{-4}$

Exercise Write these numbers in scientific notation.

1. 2,900 $2.9 \cdot 10^3$

2. 3,600 $3.6 \cdot 10^3$

3. 8,750 $8.75 \cdot 10^3$

4. 6,320 $6.32 \cdot 10^3$

5. 35,000 $3.5 \cdot 10^4$

6. 46,000 $4.6 \cdot 10^4$

7. 71,100 $7.11 \cdot 10^4$

8. 400,000 $4.0 \cdot 10^5$

9. 4,000,000 $4.0 \cdot 10^6$

10. 1,700,000,000 $1.7 \cdot 10^9$

11. 0.00038 $3.8 \cdot 10^{-4}$

12. 0.39 $3.9 \cdot 10^{-1}$

13. 0.41 $4.1 \cdot 10^{-1}$

14. 0.072 $7.2 \cdot 10^{-2}$

15. 0.0072 $7.2 \cdot 10^{-3}$

16. 0.0081 $8.1 \cdot 10^{-3}$

17. 0.00074 $7.4 \cdot 10^{-4}$

18. 0.000012 $1.2 \cdot 10^{-5}$

19. 0.00123 $1.23 \cdot 10^{-3}$

20. 0.000246 $2.46 \cdot 10^{-4}$

Algebra Review of Basic Skills **501**

Review of Basic Skills 33

Dividing Decimals by Whole Numbers

EXAMPLE 1 0.168 ÷ 14 = ■

Solution

```
     .012
14 ) .168    Place the decimal point in the quotient
   − 14      directly above the one in the dividend.
      28
    − 28
       0
```

EXAMPLE 2 68.6 ÷ 28 = ■

Solution

```
      2.45
28 ) 68.60   Add a zero to complete the division.
   − 56
     12 6
   − 11 2
      1 40
    − 1 40
         0
```

Exercise Divide each decimal by the whole number.

1. 4.7 ÷ 2 2.35

2. 0.78 ÷ 3 0.26

3. 1.25 ÷ 5 0.25

4. 6.34 ÷ 2 3.17

5. 19.5 ÷ 3 6.5

6. 21.7 ÷ 7 3.1

7. 35.5 ÷ 5 7.1

8. 1.68 ÷ 8 0.21

9. 42.6 ÷ 6 7.1

10. 18.9 ÷ 9 2.1

11. 12.4 ÷ 4 3.1

12. 23.1 ÷ 7 3.3

13. 184.5 ÷ 9 20.5

14. 36.36 ÷ 4 9.09

15. 42.7 ÷ 7 6.1

16. 8.414 ÷ 7 1.202

17. 36.6 ÷ 6 6.1

18. 25.5 ÷ 50 0.51

19. 25.5 ÷ 25 1.02

20. 12.5 ÷ 25 0.5

502 *Review of Basic Skills Algebra*

Review of Basic Skills 34

Dividing Decimals by Decimals

EXAMPLE 1 $8.04 \div 0.6 = ■$

Solution

$$\begin{array}{r} 13.4 \\ 6\overline{)80.4} \\ -6 \\ 20 \\ -18 \\ 2\,4 \\ -2\,4 \\ 0 \end{array}$$

Step 1 Make the divisor a whole number. Multiply both divisor and dividend by ten.
$8.04 \bullet 10 \div 0.6 \bullet 10 = 80.4 \div 6$

Step 2 Divide. Place the decimal point straight up into the quotient.

Answer 13.4

Exercise Divide each decimal. Watch where you put the decimal point.

1. 1.44 ÷ 0.2 7.2
2. 3.69 ÷ 0.3 12.3
3. 5.50 ÷ 0.5 11
4. 13.41 ÷ 0.9 14.9
5. 16.71 ÷ 0.3 55.7
6. 14.96 ÷ 0.4 37.4
7. 1.934 ÷ 0.02 96.7
8. 21.35 ÷ 0.05 427
9. 0.0014 ÷ 0.7 0.002
10. 6.315 ÷ 0.03 210.5
11. 42.10 ÷ 0.2 210.5
12. 32.30 ÷ 0.005 6,460
13. 56.7 ÷ 0.07 810
14. 5.67 ÷ 0.07 81
15. 5.67 ÷ 0.7 8.1
16. 636.3 ÷ 0.9 707
17. 13.2 ÷ 0.4 33
18. 132.4 ÷ 0.02 6,620
19. 159.6 ÷ 0.3 532
20. 7.938 ÷ 8.1 0.98

Algebra *Review of Basic Skills* **503**

MANIPULATIVES

Rewriting Decimals as Fractions

Materials: Cuisenaire Rods, two copies of Manipulatives Master 4 (Factor Frame) for each student

Group Practice: After writing the decimal as a fraction, write the fraction in lowest terms by building a rectangular model of the numerator inside the Factor Frame. Place rods representing the dimensions, or factors, of the rectangle on the left and top portions of the frame. Then use the second Factor Frame to build a rectangular model of 100 using one of the dimensions of the numerator. The largest dimension that can be used to build both rectangles represents the GCD. The remaining dimensions of each rectangle represent the simplest form of the numerator and denominator. If a rectangular model of 100 cannot be built using one of the dimensions of the numerator, then the fraction is already in lowest terms.

Student Practice: Have students use the rods to write fractions in lowest terms for problems 1–4, 6, 11–15, 17–18, 20.

Rewriting Decimals as Fractions

EXAMPLE 1 Rewrite 0.13 as a fraction.

Solution 0.1 3 means 13 hundredths.

↑ ↑ tenths hundredths

so $0.13 = \frac{13}{100}$ **Answer** $\frac{13}{100}$

Exercise Write these decimals as fractions. Then write the fractions in lowest terms.

1. 0.14 $\frac{14}{100}$ $\frac{7}{50}$
2. 0.15 $\frac{15}{100}$ $\frac{3}{20}$
3. 0.75 $\frac{75}{100}$ $\frac{3}{4}$
4. 0.36 $\frac{36}{100}$ $\frac{9}{25}$
5. 0.79 $\frac{79}{100}$
6. 0.150 $\frac{15}{100}$ $\frac{3}{20}$
7. 0.159 $\frac{159}{1,000}$
8. 0.375 $\frac{375}{1,000}$ $\frac{3}{8}$
9. 0.875 $\frac{875}{1,000}$ $\frac{7}{8}$
10. 0.999 $\frac{999}{1,000}$
11. 0.42 $\frac{42}{100}$ $\frac{21}{50}$
12. 0.65 $\frac{65}{100}$ $\frac{13}{20}$
13. 0.60 $\frac{60}{100}$ $\frac{3}{5}$
14. 0.45 $\frac{45}{100}$ $\frac{9}{20}$
15. 0.50 $\frac{50}{100}$ $\frac{1}{2}$
16. 0.168 $\frac{168}{1,000}$ $\frac{21}{125}$
17. 0.22 $\frac{22}{100}$ $\frac{11}{50}$
18. 0.98 $\frac{98}{100}$ $\frac{49}{50}$
19. 0.568 $\frac{568}{1,000}$ $\frac{71}{125}$
20. 0.72 $\frac{72}{100}$ $\frac{18}{25}$

504 *Review of Basic Skills* *Algebra*

Review of Basic Skills 36

Renaming Fractions as Decimals

Write decimals with denominators 10, 100, 1,000, and 10,000 or use a calculator to divide numerator by denominator.

EXAMPLE 1 Rewrite $\frac{2}{5}$ as a decimal.

Solution $\frac{2}{5} = \frac{2 \cdot 2}{5 \cdot 2} = \frac{4}{10}$ Rewrite with a denominator of 10.

$\frac{4}{10} = 0.4$ **Answer** 0.4

EXAMPLE 2 Rewrite $\frac{2}{7}$ as a decimal.

Solution Since 7 cannot be made into 10 or a multiple of 10, use your calculator.

2 ÷ 7 = 0.2857142 **Answer** 0.2857142

Exercise Write as decimals.

1. $\frac{1}{10}$ 0.1
2. $\frac{1}{5}$ 0.2
3. $\frac{1}{2}$ 0.5
4. $\frac{3}{25}$ 0.12
5. $\frac{9}{50}$ 0.18
6. $\frac{7}{20}$ 0.35
7. $\frac{9}{25}$ 0.36
8. $\frac{3}{500}$ 0.006
9. $\frac{6}{250}$ 0.024
10. $\frac{59}{500}$ 0.118

Use a calculator. Copy the display.

11. $\frac{3}{7}$ 0.4285714
12. $\frac{5}{7}$ 0.7142857
13. $\frac{2}{3}$ 0.6666666
14. $\frac{2}{9}$ 0.2222222
15. $\frac{5}{13}$ 0.3846153
16. $\frac{2}{17}$ 0.117647
17. $\frac{3}{19}$ 0.1578947
18. $\frac{5}{23}$ 0.2173913
19. $\frac{6}{29}$ 0.2068965
20. $\frac{5}{31}$ 0.1612903

MANIPULATIVES

Renaming Fractions as Decimals

Materials: Base Ten Blocks, Cuisenaire Rods

Group Practice: Using the example, remind students that $\frac{2}{5}$ means 2 parts out of 5. Build $\frac{2}{5}$ on the 100-Square Flat as many times as possible by placing one 2-rod on every five squares until each group of five squares has a 2-rod on it. Group the 2-rods together on the grid to model 0.40 or 0.4 and provide the decimal form of the symbolic equivalent.

Student Practice: Have students use the rods and flats to solve problems 1–7.

Measurement Conversion Factors

Metric Measures

Length

1,000 meters (m) = 1 kilometer (km)
100 centimeters (cm) = 1 m
10 decimeters (dm) = 1 m
1,000 millimeters (mm) = 1 m
10 cm = 1 decimeter (dm)
10 mm = 1 cm

Area

100 square millimeters (mm^2) = 1 square centimeter (cm^2)
10,000 cm^2 = 1 square meter (m^2)
10,000 m^2 = 1 hectare (ha)

Volume

1,000 cubic meters (m^3) = 1 cubic centimeter (cm^3)
100 cm^3 = 1 cubic decimeter (dm^3)
1,000,000 cm^3 = 1 cubic meter (m^3)

Capacity

1,000 milliliters (mL) = 1 liter (L)
1,000 L = 1 kiloliter (kL)

Mass

1,000 kilograms (kg) = 1 metric ton (t)
1,000 grams (g) = 1 kg
1,000 milligrams (mg) = 1 g

Temperature Degrees Celsius (°C)

0°C = freezing point of water
37°C = normal body temperature
100°C = boiling point of water

Time

60 seconds (sec) = 1 minute (min)
60 min = 1 hour (hr)
24 hr = 1 day

Customary Measures

Length

12 inches (in.) = 1 foot (ft)
3 ft = 1 yard (yd)
36 in. = 1 yd
5,280 ft = 1 mile (mi)
1,760 yd = 1 mi
6,076 feet = 1 nautical mile

Area

144 square inches (sq in.) = 1 square foot (sq ft)
9 sq ft = 1 square yard (sq yd)
43,560 sq ft = 1 acre (A)

Volume

1,728 cubic inches (cu in.) = 1 cubic foot (cu ft)
27 cu ft = 1 cubic yard (cu yard)

Capacity

8 fluid ounces (fl oz) = 1 cup (c)
2 c = 1 pint (pt)
2 pt = 1 quart (qt)
4 qt = 1 gallon (gal)

Weight

16 ounces (oz) = 1 pound (lb)
2,000 lb = 1 ton (T)

Temperature Degrees Fahrenheit (°F)

32°F = freezing point of water
98.6°F = normal body temperature
212°F = boiling point of water

506 *Measurement Conversion Factors*

Measurement Conversion Factors

To change	To	Multiply by	To change	To	Multiply by
centimeters	inches	0.3937	meters	feet	3.2808
centimeters	feet	0.03281	meters	miles	0.0006214
cubic feet	cubic meters	0.0283	meters	yards	1.0936
cubic meters	cubic feet	35.3145	metric tons	tons (long)	0.9842
cubic meters	cubic yards	1.3079	metric tons	tons (short)	1.1023
cubic yards	cubic meters	0.7646	miles	kilometers	1.6093
feet	meters	0.3048	miles	feet	5,280
feet	miles (nautical)	0.0001645	miles (statute)	miles (nautical)	0.8684
feet	miles (statute)	0.0001894	miles/hour	feet/minute	88
feet/second	miles/hour	0.6818	millimeters	inches	0.0394
gallons (U.S.)	liters	3.7853	ounces avdp	grams	28.3495
grams	ounces avdp	0.0353	ounces	pounds	0.0625
grams	pounds	0.002205	pecks	liters	8.8096
hours	days	0.04167	pints (dry)	liters	0.5506
inches	millimeters	25.4000	pints (liquid)	liters	0.4732
inches	centimeters	2.5400	pounds avdp	kilograms	0.4536
kilograms	pounds avdp	2.2046	pounds	ounces	16
kilometers	miles	0.6214	quarts (dry)	liters	1.1012
liters	gallons (U.S.)	0.2642	quarts (liquid)	liters	0.9463
liters	pecks	0.1135	square feet	square meters	0.0929
liters	pints (dry)	1.8162	square meters	square feet	10.7639
liters	pints (liquid)	2.1134	square meters	square yards	1.1960
liters	quarts (dry)	0.9081	square yards	square meters	0.8361
liters	quarts (liquid)	1.0567	yards	meters	0.9144

Measurement Conversion Factors **507**

Glossary

A

Absolute value (ab´ sə lüt val´ yü) the distance from zero of a number on a number line (p. 6)

$|-4|$ is read "the absolute value of negative 4."

$|-4| = 4$, 4 units from 0.

$|4| = 4$, 4 units from 0.

Acute angle (ə kyüt´ ang gəl) an angle which measures between 0° and 90° (p. 258)

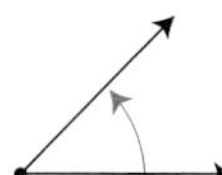

Acute triangle (ə kyüt´ trī´ ang gəl) a triangle with three acute angles (p. 368)

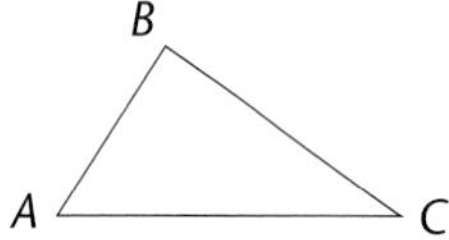

Addend (əd´ end) number to be added to another (p. 8)

$4 + 2 = 6$ The numbers 4 and 2 are addends.

Addition (ə dish´ ən) the arithmetic operation of combining two or more numbers to find a total (p. 8)

$3 + 5 = 8$

Addition property of zero (ə dish´ ən prop´ ər tē ov zir´ ō) a number does not change if 0 is added or subtracted (p. 46)

$2 + 0 = 2$ $2 - 0 = 2$

Additive inverses (ad´ ə tiv in´ vėrs es) numbers that equal 0 when added together; also called opposites (p. 46)

$6 + (-6) = 0$

$-6 + 6 = 0$

Adjacent angle (ə jā´ snt ang´ gəl)an angle that shares a vertex and a common side with another angle (p. 356)

∠*CAD* is adjacent to ∠*BAC*.

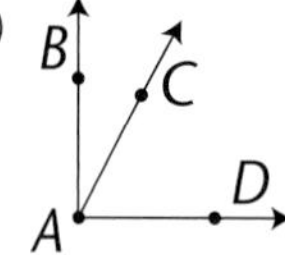

Algebra (al´ jə brə) the branch of mathematics that uses both letters and numbers to show relations between quantities (p. 2)

Algebraic expression (al´ jə brā´ ik ek spresh´ ən)—a mathematical sentence that includes at least one operation and a variable (p. 4)

$2x + 5$ $m \cdot 3$

Algebraic fraction (al´ jə brā´ ik frak´ shən) a single algebraic term divided by a single algebraic term (p. 222)

$\frac{x}{y}$ $\frac{a^2}{3b}$

Angle (ang´ gəl) a geometric figure made up of two rays with a common endpoint called a vertex (p. 356)

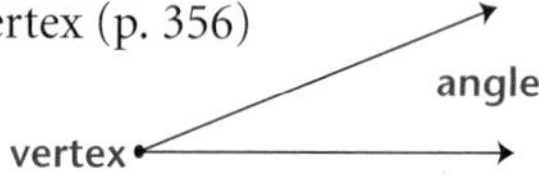

Arithmetic (ə rith´ mə tik) the study of the properties of numbers, using four basic operations—addition, subtraction, multiplication, and division (p. 2)

Associative property of addition (ə so´ shē ā tiv prop´ ər tē ov ə dish´ ən) the same terms added in different groupings result in the same answer (p. 34)

$(3 + 5) + 2 = 3 + (5 + 2)$

Associative property of multiplication (ə so´ shē ā tiv prop´ ər tē ov mul tə plə kā´ shən)the same terms multiplied in different groupings result in the same answer (p. 38)

$(3 \cdot 5)4 = 3(5 \cdot 4)$

Axis of symmetry of a parabola(ak´ sis ov sim´ ə trē) a perpendicular line that passes through the midpoint between the roots (p. 399)

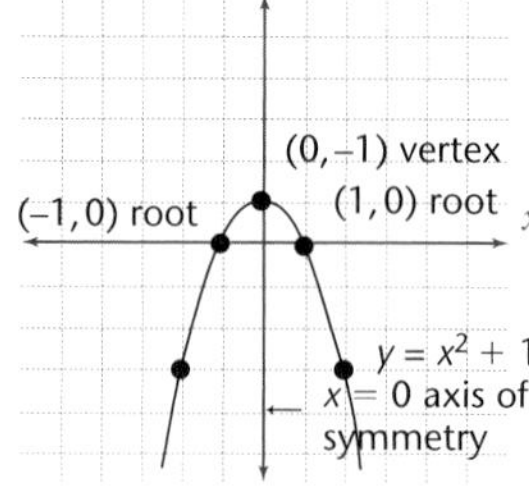

508 *Glossary Algebra*

B

Bar graph(bär graf) a way of showing how information can be compared using rectangular bars (p. 185)

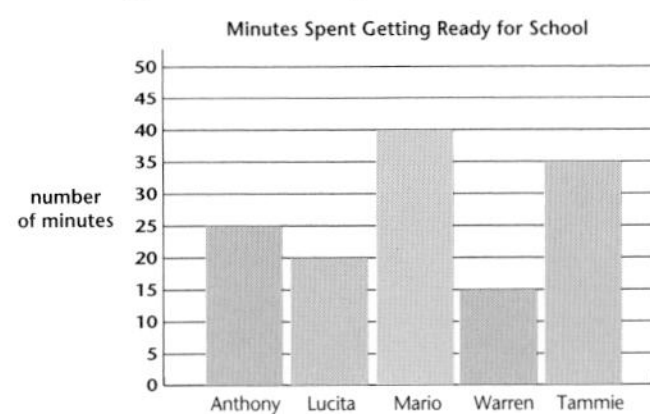

Base (b)(bās) the number being multiplied; a factor (p. 20) *a* is the base. a^2

Box-and-whiskers plot (boks and wis´ kərz plot) a way to describe the concentration and the spread of data in a set (p. 192)

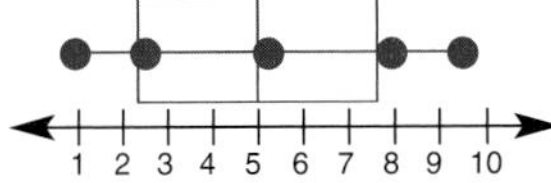

C

Circle graph (sėr´ kəl graf) a graphic way to present information using the parts of a circle (p. 101)

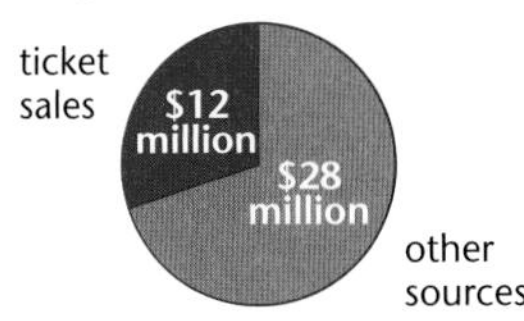

Coefficient (ko ə fish´ ənt) the number that multiplies the variable (p. 4)

$3x$ **3 is the coefficient.**

Common factor (kom´ ən fak´ tər) a multiplier shared by the terms in an expression (p. 44)

$4b + 3b$ ***b* is the common factor.**

Common solution (kom´ ən sə lü´shən)the ordered pair of real numbers that two intersecting lines share (p. 294)

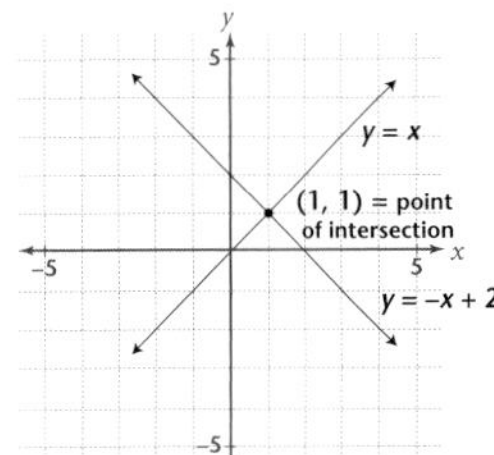

Commutative property of addition (kom´ yə tā tiv prop´ ər tē ov ə dish´ ən) the order in which two numbers are added does not change their sum (p. 32)

$3 + 4 = 4 + 3$

Commutative property of multiplication (kom´ yə tā tiv prop´ ər tē ov mul tə plə kā´ shən)the order in which two numbers are multiplied does not change their product (p. 34)

$3 \cdot 2 = 2 \cdot 3$

Complement of a probability event (kom plə ment´ ov ā prob ə bil´ə tē i vent´) the set of outcomes that are not in the event (p. 201)

Complementary angles (kom plə men´ tər ē ang´ gelz) two angles whose sum of their measures is 90 degrees (p. 357)

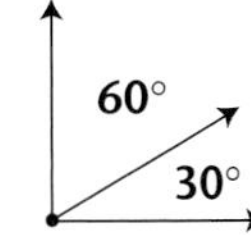

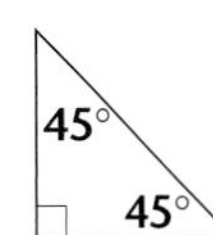

Completing the square (kəm plēt´ ing thə skwâr) a method of finding the roots of a perfect square trinomial (p. 392)

Complex fraction (kəm pleks´ frak´ shən) a fraction in which the numerator, the denominator, or both the numerator and the denominator are fractions (p. 226)

$\dfrac{\frac{3}{8}}{5}$ $\dfrac{10}{\frac{3}{5}}$ $\dfrac{\frac{2}{3}}{\frac{1}{2}}$

a	hat	e	let	ī	ice	ô	order	u̇	put	sh	she	ə { a	in about
ā	age	ē	equal	o	hot	oi	oil	ü	rule	th	thin	e	in taken
ä	far	ėr	term	ō	open	ou	out	ch	child	ᴛʜ	then	i	in pencil
â	care	i	it	ȯ	saw	u	cup	ng	long	zh	measure	o	in lemon
												u	in circus

Algebra Glossary **509**

Composite number (kəm poz′ it num′ bər) an integer that is not a prime number (p. 156)
$2 \cdot 2 \cdot 2 \cdot 2 = 16$ **16 is a composite number.**

Congruent (kən grü′ ənt) figures that have the same size and shape (p. 372)

Conjugate (kon′ jə git) a factor that when multiplied rationalizes (or simplifies) an expression (p. 340)
$(2 + \sqrt{3})$ and $(2 - \sqrt{3})$ **are conjugates**

Conjunction (kən jungk′ shən) two or more simple sentences connected by *and* (p. 306)

Consecutive (kən sek′ yə tiv) following one after the other in order (p. 96)

Constant (kon′ stənt) specific real number (p. 76)
$ax - by = c$ ***a*, *b*, and *c* are constants.**

Corresponding angles (kôr ə spon′ ding ang′ gəlz) interior and exterior angles on the same side of a transversal cutting through parallel lines (p. 361)

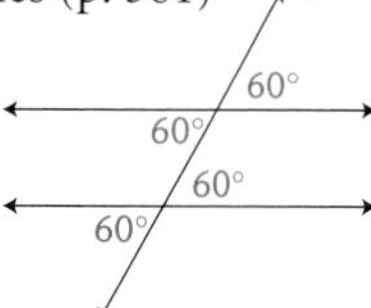

Cross products (krȯs prod′ əkts) the result of multiplying the denominator of one fraction with the numerator of another (p. 116)
$\frac{1}{2} \cdot \frac{2}{3}$ $2 \cdot 2 = 4$ $1 \cdot 3 = 3$

D

Data (dā′ tə) information given in numbers (p. 184)

Decimal expansion (des′ ə məl ek span′ shən) writing a number, such as a fraction, as a decimal (p. 329)
$\frac{3}{5} = 0.6\overline{0}$

Degree of a polynomial (di grē′ ov ā pol ē nō′ mē əl) greatest power of the variable (p. 134)
$2y^3 + 3y^2 + 2$ **degree 3**

Dependent event (di pen′ dənt i vent′) in a probability experiment, the outcome of one event is affected by the outcome of any other event (p. 207)

Dependent variable (di pen′ dənt vâr′ ē bəl) the value of the *y* variable that depends on the value of *x* (p. 265)

Difference (dif′ ər əns) the answer to a subtraction problem (p. 10)
$5 - 2 = 3$ **3 is the difference.**

Disjunction (dis jungk′ shən) a compound statement that uses the word *or* to connect two simple statements (p. 84)

Distributive property (dis trib′ yə tiv prop′ ər tē) numbers within parentheses can be multiplied by the same factor (p. 42)
$4(2 + 1) = 4 \cdot 2 + 4 \cdot 1$

Dividend (div′ ə dend) a number that is divided (p. 14)
$6 \div 3 = 2$ **6 is the dividend.**

Division (də vizh′ ən) the arithmetic operation that finds how many times a number is contained in another number (p. 14)
$12 \div 3 = 4$

Divisor (də vī′ zər) the number by which you are dividing (p. 14)
$10 \div 5 = 2$ **5 is the divisor.**

Domain (dō mān′) the independent variables, or set of *x*-values, of a function (p. 268)

E

Equality (i kwol′ ə tē) the state of being equal; shown by the equal sign (p. 84)
$2 \cdot 2 = 4 \cdot 1$

Equation (i kwā′ zhən) a mathematical sentence stating that two quantities are equal and written as two expressions separated by an equal sign (p. 64)
$4n + 4n = 8n$ $3x = 15$

Equiangular triangle (ē kwē ang′ gyə lər trī′ ang gəl) a triangle with three angles, each measuring 60 degrees (p. 368)

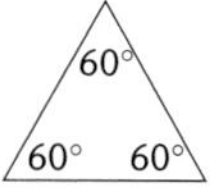

Equilateral triangle (ē kwə lat′ ər əl trī′ ang gəl) a triangle with three equal sides (p. 22)

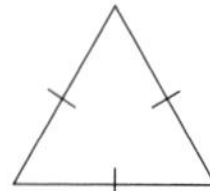

510 *Glossary Algebra*

Expanded notation (ek spand´ əd nō tā´ shən) an algebraic expression written to show its smallest terms (p. 32)

$2a + 3a = 5a$

$a \cdot a + a \cdot a \cdot a = a \cdot a \cdot a \cdot a \cdot a$

Exponent (ek spō´ nənt) number that tells the times another number is a factor (p. 20)

Exterior angles (ek stir´ ē ər ang´ gelz) angles that are formed outside two lines cut by a transversal (p. 361)

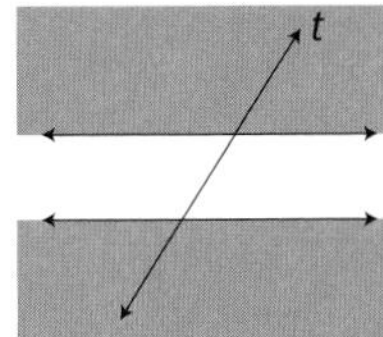

F

Factorial notation (fak tôr´ ē əl nō tā´ shən)the product of all positive integers from a given integer to 1 represented by the symbol [!] (p. 211)

$5! = 5 \cdot 4 \cdot 3 \cdot 2 \cdot 1 = 120$

Factoring (fak´ tər ing) using the distributive property to separate the common factor from the terms in the expression (p. 44)

$4x + 4y = 4(x + y)$

Factoring completely (fak´ tər ing kəm plēt´ lē) expressing an integer as a product of only prime numbers (p. 156)

$20 = 5 \cdot 2 \cdot 2$

Factor (fak´ tər) a number that is multiplied in a multiplication problem (p. 12)

$4 \cdot 3 = 12$ **4 and 3 are the factors.**

Frequency table (frē´ kwən sē tā´ bəl) a way of showing the count of items or number of times in different groups or categories (p. 184)

Frequency Table		
Interval	Tally	Frequency
0–9		0
10–19		0
20–29	𝍸 I	6

Function (fungk´ shən)a rule that associates every x-value with one and only one y-value (p. 265)

Fundamental principle of counting (fun də men´ tl prin´ sə pəl ov koun´ ting) a general rule that states that if one task can be completed p different ways, and a second task can be completed q different ways, the first task followed by the second task can be completed $p \cdot q$, or pq, different ways (p. 210)

G

Geometry (jē om´ ə trē) the study of points, lines, angles, surfaces, and solids (p. 34)

Graphing (graf´ ing) showing on a number line the relationship of a set of numbers or a plane (p. 84)

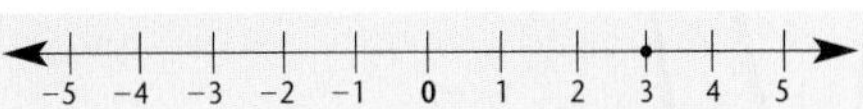

Greatest common factor (GCF) (grāt´ est kom´ fak´ tər) the largest factor of two or more numbers or terms (p. 157)

$10 = 5 \cdot 2$ **The GCF of 10 and 15**

$15 = 5 \cdot 3$ **is 5.**

H

Histogram (his´ te gram) a way of showing the frequency of data using rectangular bars and the area they contain (p. 186)

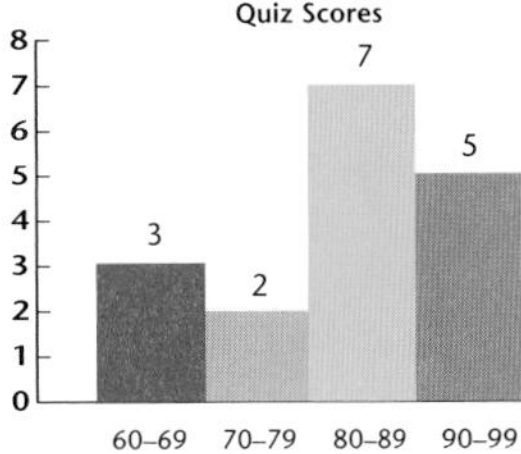

Hypotenuse (hī pot´ n üs) the longest side in a right triangle (p. 80)

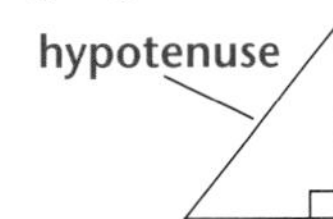

a	hat	e	let	ī	ice	ô	order	u̇	put	sh	she	ə { a	in about
ā	age	ē	equal	o	hot	oi	oil	ü	rule	th	thin	e	in taken
ä	far	ėr	term	ō	open	ou	out	ch	child	ᴛʜ	then	i	in pencil
â	care	i	it	ȯ	saw	u	cup	ng	long	zh	measure	o	in lemon
												u	in circus

Algebra Glossary **511**

I

Independent event (in di pen´ dənt i vent´) in a probability experiment, the outcome of any event does not affect the outcome of any other event (p. 208)

Independent variable (in di pen´ dənt vâr´ ē bəl) the value of x that determines the value of y (p. 265)

Inequality (in i kwol´ ə tē) the state of being unequal; shown by the less than, greater than, and unequal to signs (p. 84)

$5 > 2 \quad 5 < 7 \quad 5 \neq 4$

Integer (in´ tə jər) a whole number or its opposite, including 0 (... −2, −1, 0, 1, 2, ...) (p. 6)

Interest (in´ tər ist) the amount of money paid or received for the use of borrowed money (p. 111)

Interior angles (in tir´ ē ər ang´ gəlz) angles that are formed inside, or between, two lines cut by a transversal (p. 361)

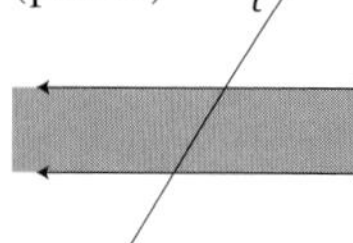

Intersecting lines (in tər sekt´ ing līnz) lines with one point in common (p. 294)

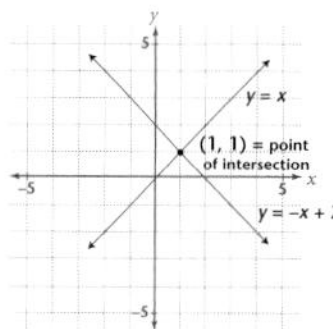

Irrational number (i rash´ ə nəl num´ bər) a real number, such as $\sqrt{2}$, that cannot be written in the form $\frac{a}{b}$ in which a and b are whole numbers and $b \neq 0$ (p. 328)

Isosceles triangle (ī sos´ ə lēz trī´ ang gəl) a triangle with two sides of equal length (p. 368)

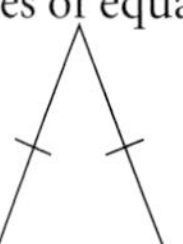

L

Least common multiple (LCM) (lēst kom´ ən mul´ tə pəl) the smallest number that two or more numbers can divide into without leaving a remainder (p. 226)

4: 4, 8, 12, . . . **The LCM of 4 and 6**
6: 6, 12, . . . **is 12.**

Like terms (līk tėrmz) terms that have the same variable (p. 16)

Linear equation(lin´ ē ər i kwā´ zhən) an equation whose graph is a straight line (p. 263)

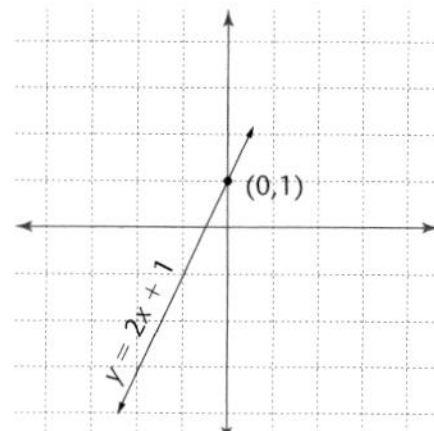

Literal equation (lit´ ər əl i kwā´ zhən) an equation that has only letters (p. 76)

$a + b + c = d$

Lower quartile (lō´ ər kwȯr´ tīl) the median of the scores below the median (p. 192)

{2, 3, 5, 6, 8, 9, 11} **3 is the lower quartile.**

M

Matrix (mā´ triks) any rectangular arrangement of numbers or symbols (p. 314)

Mean (mēn) the sum of the values in a set of data divided by the number of pieces of data in the set (p. 188)

{2, 3, 5, 6, 8, 9, 11} **6.3 is the mean.**

Measures of central tendency (mezh´ ərz ov sen´ trəl ten´ dən sē) the mean, median, and mode of a set of data (p. 190)

Median (mē´ dē ən) the middle value in an ordered set of data (p. 189)

{2, 3, 5, 6, 8, 9, 11} **6 is the median.**

Mode (mōd) the value or values that occur most often in a set of data (p. 190)

{2, 3, 5, 2} **2 is the mode.**

Monomial (mon ō´ mē əl) a single term that is a number, a variable, or the product of a number and one or more variables (p. 134)

$4 \quad x \quad 5b \quad 6y^2$

Multiplication (mul tə plə kā´ shən) the arithmetic operation of adding a number to itself many times (p. 12)

$3 \cdot 5 = 15 \qquad 5 + 5 + 5 = 15$

Multiplication property of 1 (mul tə plə kā´ shən prop´ ər tē ov wun) a number or term does not change when multiplied by 1 (p. 48)

$4 \cdot 1 = 4 \qquad 1x = x$

512 *Glossary Algebra*

Multiplication property of zero (mul tə plə kā′ shən prop′ ər tē ov zir′ ō) zero times any number is zero (p. 47)

$4 \cdot 0 = 0 \qquad x \cdot 0 = 0$

Multiplicative inverses (mul tə plik′ ə tiv in′ vėrs es) any two numbers or terms whose product equals 1 (p. 48)

$3 \cdot \frac{1}{3} = 1 \qquad x \cdot \frac{1}{x} = 1, x \neq 0$

Negative exponent (neg′ ə tiv ek spō nənt) for any nonzero integers a and n,

$a^{-n} = \frac{1}{a^n}$ (p. 126)

Negative integer (neg′ ə tiv in′ tə jər) a whole number less than zero (p. 6)... −3, −2, −1

Numerical expression (nü mer′ ə kəl ek spresh′ ən) a mathematical sentence that includes operations and numbers (p. 4)

$3 + 2 \qquad 6 - 4 \qquad 12 \div 3 \qquad 5 \cdot 2$

O

Obtuse (əb tüs′) an angle with a measure between 90 and 180 degrees (p. 258)

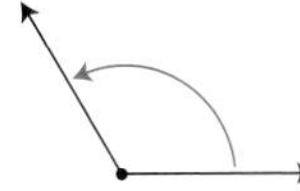

Obtuse triangle (əb tüs′ trī′ ang gəl) a triangle with one obtuse angle (p. 368)

Open statement (ō′ pən stāt′ mənt) a sentence that is neither true nor false (p. 2)

$6a = 30 \qquad 30 \div n = 5$

Operation (op ə rā′ shən) the mathematical processes of addition, subtraction, multiplication, and division (p. 4)

Opposites (op′ ə zits) numbers the same distance from zero but on different sides of zero on the number line (p. 6)

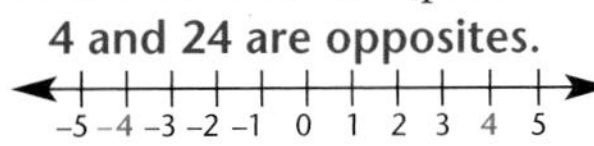

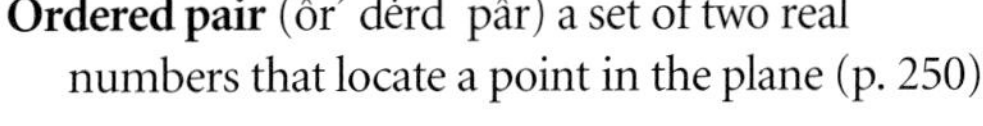

Ordered pair (ôr′ dėrd pâr) a set of two real numbers that locate a point in the plane (p. 250)

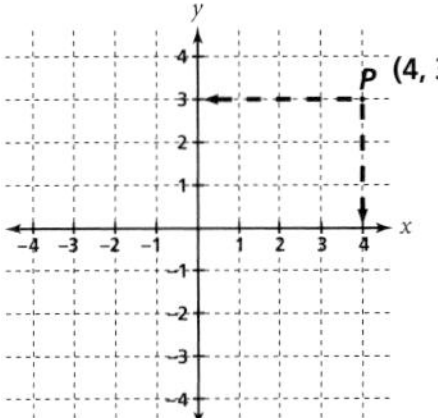

Origin (ôr′ ə jin) the point at which the axes in a coordinate system intersect (0,0)(p. 250)

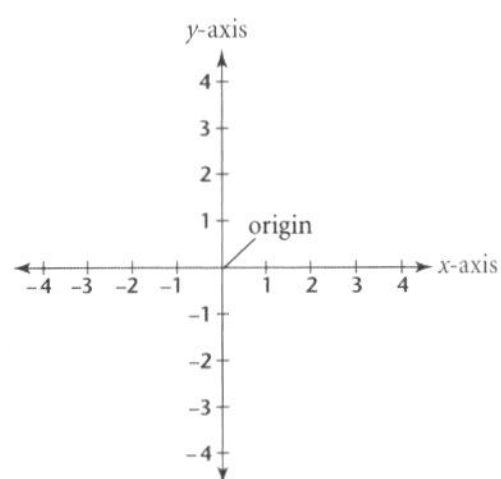

P

Parabola (pə rab′ ə lə) a plane curve generated by a point that moves so that its distance from a fixed point is always the same as its distance from a fixed line (p. 398)

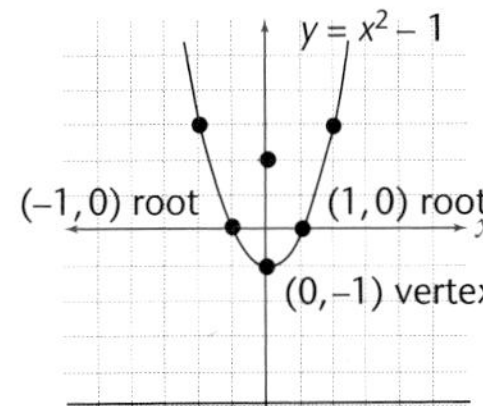

Parallel lines (par′ ə lel līnz) lines that have the same slope (p. 288)

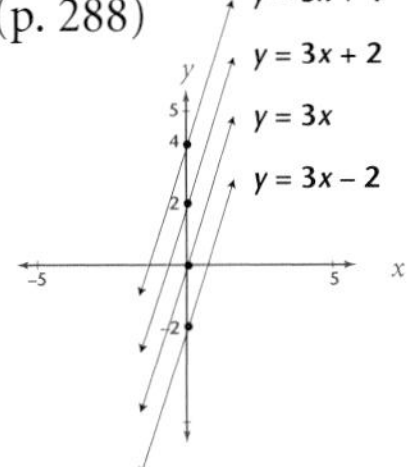

a	hat	e	let	ī	ice	ô	order	u̇	put	sh	she	ə	a in about
ā	age	ē	equal	o	hot	oi	oil	ü	rule	th	thin		e in taken
ä	far	ėr	term	ō	open	ou	out	ch	child	ŦH	then		i in pencil
â	care	i	it	ȯ	saw	u	cup	ng	long	zh	measure		o in lemon
													u in circus

Algebra Glossary **513**

Parallelogram (par ə lel′ ə gram) a four-sided polygon with two pairs of equal and parallel sides (p. 370)

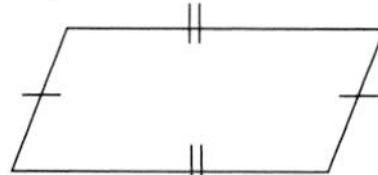

Percent (%) (pər sent′) part per one hundred (p. 98)

Perfect square (pėr′ fikt skwâr) the square of an integer (p. 166)

Perfect square trinomial (pėr′ fikt skwâr trī nō′ mē əl) the result of multiplying a binomial by itself or squaring a binomial (p. 168)

$(a + b)^2 = a^2 + 2ab + b^2$

Perimeter (pə rim′ ə tər) the distance around the outside of a shape (p. 22)

Permutation (pėr myü tā′ shən) an arrangement of some or all of a set of numbers in a specific order (p. 211)

Plane (plān) a two-dimensional flat surface (p. 360)

Polynomial (pol ē nō′ mē əl) an algebraic expression made up of one term or the sum or difference of two or more terms in the same variable (p. 134)

$2x^3 - 3x^2 + x - 3$

Positive integer (poz′ ə tiv in′ tə jər) a whole number greater than zero 1, 2, 3. . . (p. 6)

Power (pou′ ər) the product of multiplying any number by itself once or many times (p. 20)

$2^1 = 2 \quad 2^2 = 4 \quad 2^3 = 8 \quad 2^4 = 16$

Prime number (prīm num′ bər) an integer that can be divided only by itself and 1 (p. 156)

$7 = 7 \cdot 1$

Principal (prin′ sə pəl) the amount of money deposited, borrowed, or loaned (p. 111)

Probability (prob ə bil′ ə tē) the chance or likelihood of an event occurring (p. 196)

Product (prod′ əkt) the answer to a multiplication problem (p. 12)

$3 \cdot 4 = 12$ **12 is the product.**

Proportion (prə pôr′ shən) an equation made up of two equal ratios (p. 116)

$\frac{1}{2} = \frac{2}{4}$

Pythagorean theorem (pə thag′ ə rē ən thir′ əm) a formula that states that in a right triangle, the length of the hypotenuse squared is equal to the length of side b squared and the length of side a squared (p. 80)

$c^2 = a^2 + b^2$

Q

Quadrant (kwäd′ rənt) regions of a coordinate plane bounded by the x- and y-axes (p. 250)

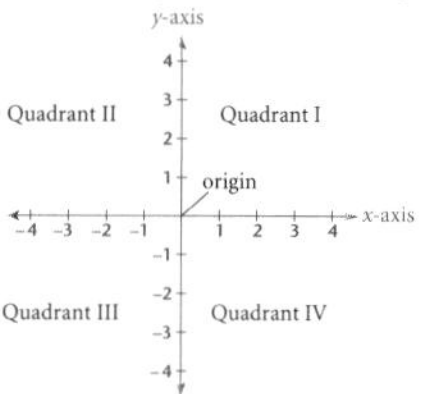

Quadratic equation (kwä drat′ ik i kwā′ zhən)an equation in the form of $ax^2 + bx + c = 0$ (p. 174)

$2x^2 + 3x + 4 = 0$

Quadratic formula (kwä drat′ ik fôr′ myə lə) the formula that can be used to find the roots of any quadratic equation $x = \frac{-b \pm \sqrt{b^2 - 4ac}}{2a}$ (p. 397)

Quotient (kwō′ shənt) the answer to a division problem (p. 14)

$20 \div 5 = 4$ **4 is the quotient.**

R

Radical (rad′ ə kəl) a number that is written with the radical sign (p. 334)

$\sqrt{9} \quad \sqrt[3]{8}$

Radical sign (rad′ ə kəl sīn) the mathematical symbol ($\sqrt{\ }$) placed before a number or algebraic expression to indicate that the root should be found (p. 334)

$\sqrt{16}$ $\sqrt{\ }$ is the radical sign.

Radicand (rad ə kand′) a number under the radical sign ($\sqrt{\ }$) (p. 346)

$\sqrt{3}$ **3 is the radicand.**

Range (rānj) the difference between the greatest and least values in a set of data (p. 188)

$\{2, 3, 5, 6\}$ $6 - 2 = 4$ **4 is the range.**

Range (of a function) (rānj) the dependent variables, or set of y-values, of a function (p. 268)

514 *Glossary Algebra*

Ratio (rā´ shē ō) a comparison of two like quantities using division (p. 116)

$a : b \quad \frac{a}{b} \quad a \text{ to } b$

Rational expression (rash´ ə nəl ek spresh´ ən) an algebraic expression divided by another algebraic expression (p. 222)

$\frac{(x^2 + 2)}{(x + 2)^3}$

Rationalizing the denominator (rash´ ə nə lī zing ᴛʜə di nom´ ə nā tər) changing a fraction with an irrational denominator to an equivalent fraction with a rational denominator (p. 340)

Rational number (rash´ ə nəl num´ bər) any number that is expressed as an integer or as a ratio between two integers when 0 does not serve as the denominator (p. 220)

$2 \quad \frac{1}{3} \quad -3 \quad \frac{-2}{5}$

Ray (rā) a set of points that is part of a line. It has one endpoint and extends infinitely in one direction. (p. 356)

ray

Real number (rē´ əl num´ bər) a number on the number line (p. 6)

−5 −4 −3 −2 −1 0 1 2 3 4 5

Reciprocals (ri sip´ rə kəlz) multiplicative inverses (p. 48)

$\frac{1}{2} \cdot 2 = 1$ $\quad \frac{1}{2}$ and 2 are reciprocals.

Rectangle (rek´ tang gəl) a four-sided polygon with four right angles and the opposite sides equal (p. 370)

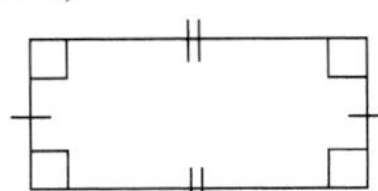

Repeating decimal expansion (ri pē´ ting des´ ə məl ek span´ shən) a decimal sequence in which the numbers repeat in exactly the same order (p. 329)

$\frac{1}{3} = 0.3333\ldots = 0.\overline{3}$

Rhombus (rom´ bəs) a four-sided polygon with four parallel sides the same length (p. 370)

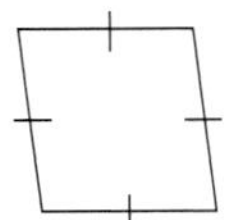

Right triangle (rīt trī´ ang gəl) a three-sided figure, or triangle, with one right, or 90°, angle (p. 80)

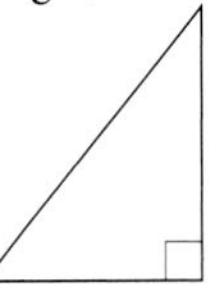

Root (rüt) an equal factor of a number (p. 50)

$\sqrt{25} = 5 \quad \sqrt[3]{64} = 4$

5 is the square root; 4 is the cube root.

S

Sample space (sam´ pəl spās) the set of all possible outcomes of an experiment (p. 204)

Scalene triangle (skā lēn´ trī´ ang gəl) a triangle with no equal sides (p. 368)

Scientific notation (sī ən tif´ ik nō tā´ shən) a number written as the product of a number between 1 and 10 and a power of ten; any number in scientific notation = $(1 \le x < 10)(10^n)$ (p. 129)

$5{,}000 = 5 \cdot 10^3$

Set of roots (set ov rüts)the set of numbers that make an equation true (p. 386)

Similar (sim´ ə lər) figures that have the same shape but not the same size (p. 374)

Simplest form (sim´ pəl est fôrm) a fraction in which the only common factor of the numerator and denominator is 1 (p. 220)

$\frac{1}{2} \quad \frac{1}{4} \quad \frac{2}{3}$

a	hat	e	let	ī	ice	ô	order	u̇	put	sh	she	ə { a	in about
ā	age	ē	equal	o	hot	oi	oil	ü	rule	th	thin	e	in taken
ä	far	ėr	term	ō	open	ou	out	ch	child	ᴛʜ	then	i	in pencil
â	care	i	it	ȯ	saw	u	cup	ng	long	zh	measure	o	in lemon
												u	in circus

Algebra Glossary **515**

Simplify (sim′ plə fī) combine like terms (p. 16)
$2a + 3a = 5a$

Slope (slōp) the measure of the steepness of a line (p. 258)

Solution (sə lü′ shən) the value of a variable that makes an open statement true (p. 174)

Square (skwâr) a polygon with four equal sides and four right angles (p. 370)

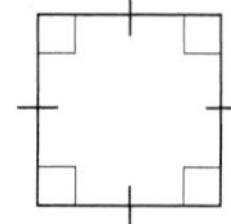

Standard form (stand′ dərd fôrm)arrangement of variables from left to right, from greatest to least degree of power (p. 135)
$x^3 + 2x^2 - x + 5$

Statement (stāt′ mənt) a sentence that is true or false (p. 2)
$5 \cdot 2 = 10 \quad 5 \cdot 2 = 8$

Statistics (stə tis′ tiks) numerical facts about people, places, or things (p. 196)

Stem-and-leaf plot (stem and lēf plot) a way of showing place value by separating the data by powers of ten (p. 184)

Stem	Time Spent Studying (in minutes)	leaves
1	0 0 5 5 5	
2	0 5 5	
3	0 0 0 5	
4	5	

Subtraction (səb trak′ shən) the arithmetic operation of taking one number away from another to find the difference (p. 10)
$10 - 3 = 7$

Sum (sum) the answer to an addition problem (p. 8)
$6 + 4 = 10$ **10 is the sum.**

Supplementary angles (sup lə men′ tər ē ang′ gəlz) two angles whose sum of their measures is 180 degrees (p. 358)

Symmetry (sim′ ə trī) the exact agreement of parts on opposite sides of a line (p. 399)

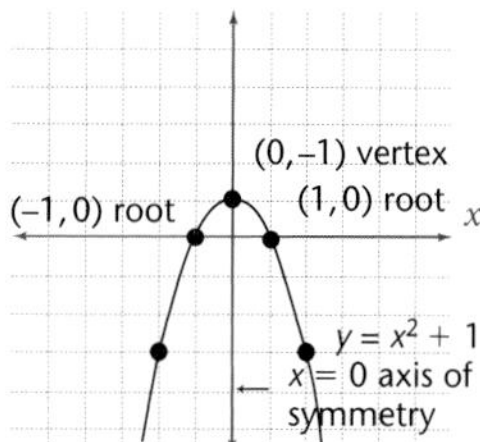

System of equations (sis′ təm ov i kwā′ zhənz) equations describing two or more lines (p. 294)

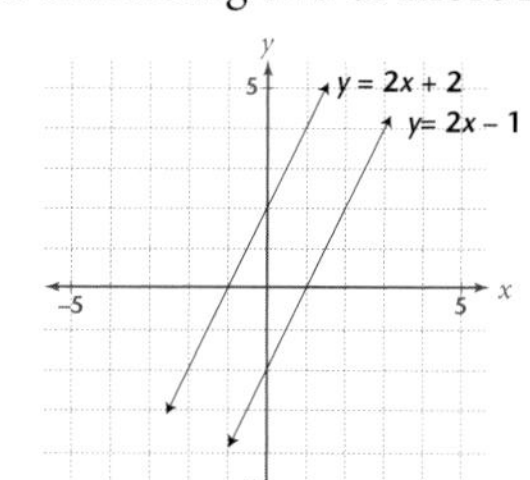

T

Terminating decimal expansion (tėr′ mə nā ting des′ ə məl ek span′ shən) a decimal sequence that ends in all 0s (p. 329)
$\frac{2}{5} = 0.4000... = 0.4\overline{0}$

Term (tėrm) part of an expression separated by an addition or subtraction sign (p. 16)
$3x + 2x + x$ **$3x$, $2x$, and x are terms.**

Theorem (thir′ əm) a statement that can be proven (p. 361)

Theoretical probability (thē ə ret′ ə kəl prob ə bil′ ə tē) the predicted likelihood of what should happen in an experiment (p. 197)

Transversal (trans vėr səl) a line that intersects two or more lines (p. 360)

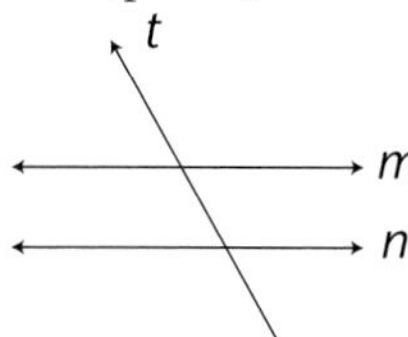

Trapezoid (trap′ ə zoid) a four-sided polygon with one pair of parallel sides and one pair of sides that are not parallel (p. 370)

516 *Glossary Algebra*

Trigonometric ratios (trig ə nə met´ rik rā´ shē ōs)angles measured by ratios of the sides of a right triangle (p. 376)

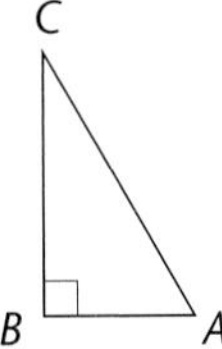

Truth table (trüth tā´ bəl) a table of true and false values (p. 85)

p	*q*	Disjunction *p* or *q*
T	T	T
T	F	T
F	T	T
F	F	F

Undefined (un di fīnd´) a term used without a specific mathematical definition (p. 242)

$\frac{1}{0}$ $\frac{a}{0}$

Unlike terms (un līk´ tėrmz) terms that have different variables (p. 18)

Upper quartile (up´ ər kwȯr´ tīl) the median of the scores above the median (p. 192)

{2, 3, 5, 6, 8, 9, 11} **9 is the upper quartile.**

Variable (vâr´ ē bəl) a letter or symbol that stands for an unknown number (p. 4)

$5x$ **x is the variable.**

Vertex (vėr´ teks) a point common to both sides of an angle (p. 356)

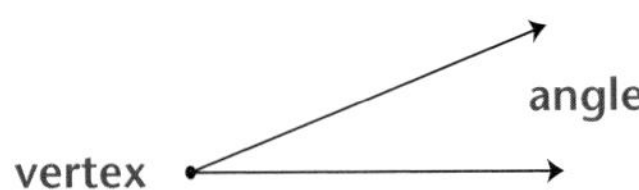

Vertical angles (vėr´ tə kəl ang´ gəlz) pairs of opposite angles formed by intersecting lines. Vertical angles have the same measure. (p. 357)

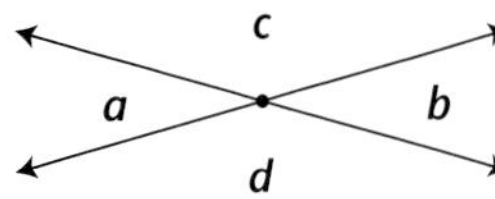

angles *a* and *b* are vertical angles; angles *c* and *d* are vertical angles

Vertical line test (vėr tə kəl līn test) a way of determining whether a graph is a function; if a vertical line intersects a graph in more than 1 point, the graph is not a function (p. 265)

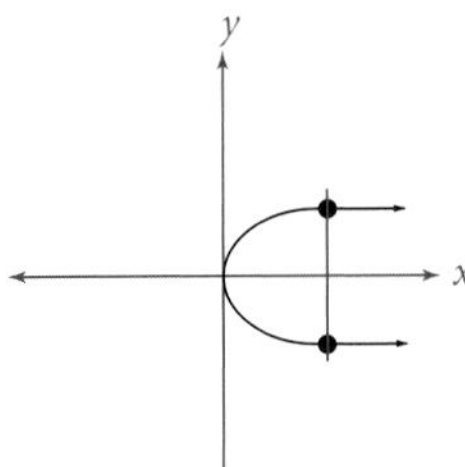

This graph is NOT a function.

***x*-axis** (eks´ ak sis) the horizontal axis in a coordinate system (p. 250)

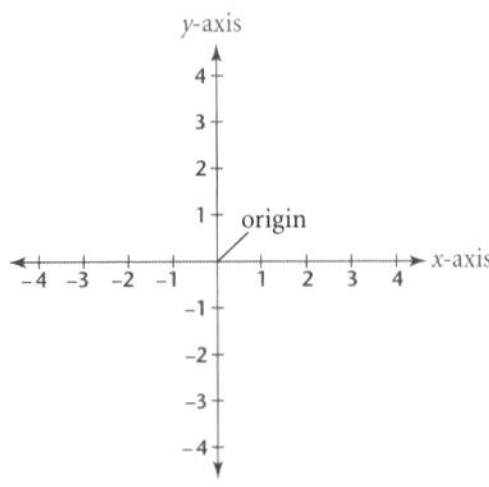

a	hat	e	let	ī	ice	ô	order	u̇	put	sh	she	ə { a	in about
ā	age	ē	equal	o	hot	oi	oil	ü	rule	th	thin	e	in taken
ä	far	ėr	term	ō	open	ou	out	ch	child	ᴛʜ	then	i	in pencil
â	care	i	it	ȯ	saw	u	cup	ng	long	zh	measure	o	in lemon
												u	in circus

Algebra Glossary **517**

***x*-intercept** (eks′ in tər sept′) the point at which a graph intersects the *x*-axis (p. 257)

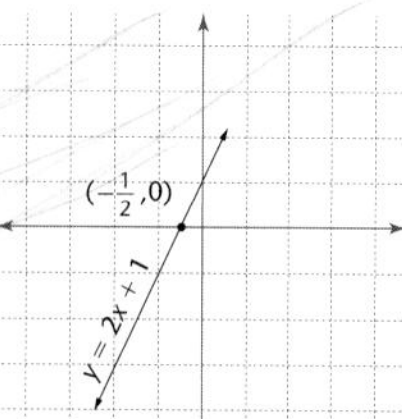

($-\frac{1}{2}$, 0) is the *x*-intercept.

Y

***y*-axis** (wī′ ak sis) the vertical axis in a coordinate system (p. 250)

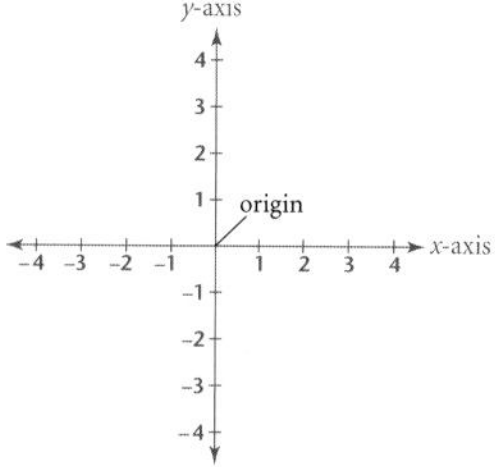

***y*-intercept** (wī′ in tər sept′) the point at which a graph intersects the *y*-axis (p. 256)

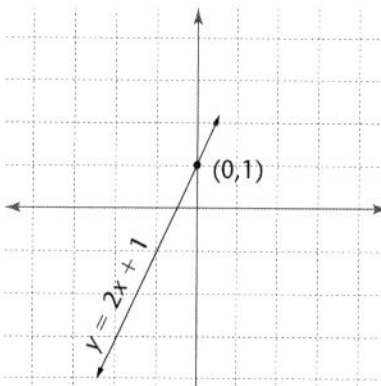

(0, 1) is the *y*-intercept.

518 *Glossary Algebra*

Index

A

B

C

Algebra Index **519**

520 *Index Algebra*

F

G

Algebra Index **521**

H

I

L

M

522 *Index Algebra*

Algebra Index **523**

Q

R

524 *Index Algebra*

S

T

Algebra Index **525**

Photo Credits

cover image: © Cosmo Condina/Getty Images; p. xviii, © MacDonald Photography/ Photri–Microstock; p. 5, © Bill Gallery/ Stock Boston; pp. 24, 244, © Photri–Microstock; p. 26, © Peter Vanderwarker/ Stock Boston; pp. 30, 354, © E.R. Degginger/ Color–Pic Inc.; p. 40, © Aaron Haupt/ Stock Boston; p. 47, © Inga Spence/ Visuals Unlimited; p. 49, © Ray Nelson/ Phototake; p. 57, © Jon Riley/ Stone; p. 58, © Mark Gibson/ Visuals Unlimited; p. 62, © Michael Dunning/ Taxi; p. 80, © Science Photo Library/ Photo Researchers, Inc.; pp. 83, 94, 326, © Tony Freeman/ PhotoEdit; p. 90, © Dwayne Newton/ PhotoEdit; p. 99, © J. Howard/ Stock Boston; p. 105, © Don Johnston/ Stone; pp. 107, 218, 241, 253, © David Young–Wolff/ PhotoEdit; p. 110, © Gary Randall/ Visuals Unlimited; p. 113, © Bob Daemmrich/ Stock Boston; p. 115, © Luis M. De La Maza, Ph.D. M.D./ Phototake; p.122, © Ken Fisher/ Stone; pp. 141, 237 (left), 379, © Gibson Stock Photography; p. 150, © Christopher Bissell/ Stone; p. 154, © S. Callahan/ Visuals Unlimited; p. 178, © Stephen Frisch/ Stock Boston; pp. 182, 350, © Minden Pictures; p. 185, © Doug Martin/ Stock Boston; p. 186, © Will Hart/ PhotoEdit; p. 196, © Neil Lavey/ Phototake; p. 209, © Roger Allyn Lee/ SuperStock; p. 212, © Joe Bator/ Corbis; p. 213, © Robert W. Ginn/ PhotoEdit; p. 214, © Courtesy NASA/ Color–Pic Inc.; p. 237 (right), © Glenn Oliver/ Visuals Unlimited; p. 248, © Jose Azel/ Aurora & Quanta Productions; p. 258, © Spencer Grant/Photo Edit; p. 262, © Royalty-Free/CORBIS; p. 282, © Alfred Pasieka/ Science Photo Library/ Photo Researchers, Inc.; p. 286, © Frederica Georgia/ Photo Researchers, Inc.; p. 297, © Thomas R. Fletcher/ Stock Boston; p. 300, © Michael P. Gadomski/ Dembinsky Photo Associates; p. 313, © Chuck Pefley/ Stock Boston; p. 344, © George Goodwin/ Color–Pic Inc.; p. 380, © Cary Wolinsky/ Stock Boston; p. 384, © Gerald & Buff Corsi/ Visuals Unlimited; p. 389, © Karl E. Deckart/ Phototake; p. 399, © A & E Morris/ Visuals Unlimited

526 *Index Algebra*

Midterm Mastery Test

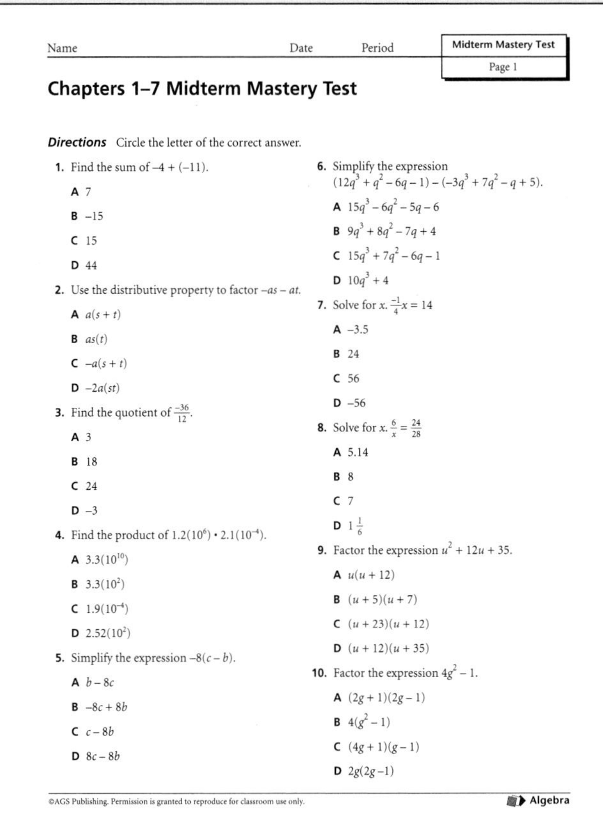

Name Date Period

Midterm Mastery Test
Page 1

Chapters 1–7 Midterm Mastery Test

Directions Circle the letter of the correct answer.

1. Find the sum of $-4 + (-11)$.

A 7
B -15
C 15
D 44

2. Use the distributive property to factor $-as - at$.

A $a(s + t)$
B $as(t)$
C $-a(s + t)$
D $-2a(st)$

3. Find the quotient of $\frac{-36}{12}$.

A 3
B 18
C 24
D -3

4. Find the product of $1.2(10^6) \cdot 2.1(10^{-4})$.

A $3.3(10^{10})$
B $3.3(10^2)$
C $1.9(10^{-4})$
D $2.52(10^2)$

5. Simplify the expression $-8(c - b)$.

A $b - 8c$
B $-8c + 8b$
C $c - 8b$
D $8c - 8b$

6. Simplify the expression $(12q^3 + q^2 - 6q - 1) - (-3q^3 + 7q^2 - q + 5)$.

A $15q^3 - 6q^2 - 5q - 6$
B $9q^3 + 8q^2 - 7q + 4$
C $15q^3 + 7q^2 - 6q - 1$
D $10q^3 + 4$

7. Solve for x. $\frac{-1}{4}x = 14$

A -3.5
B 24
C 56
D -56

8. Solve for x. $\frac{6}{x} = \frac{24}{28}$

A 5.14
B 8
C 7
D $1\frac{1}{6}$

9. Factor the expression $u^2 + 12u + 35$.

A $u(u + 12)$
B $(u + 5)(u + 7)$
C $(u + 23)(u + 12)$
D $(u + 12)(u + 35)$

10. Factor the expression $4g^2 - 1$.

A $(2g + 1)(2g - 1)$
B $4(g^2 - 1)$
C $(4g + 1)(g - 1)$
D $2g(2g - 1)$

Algebra

Midterm Mastery Test Page 1

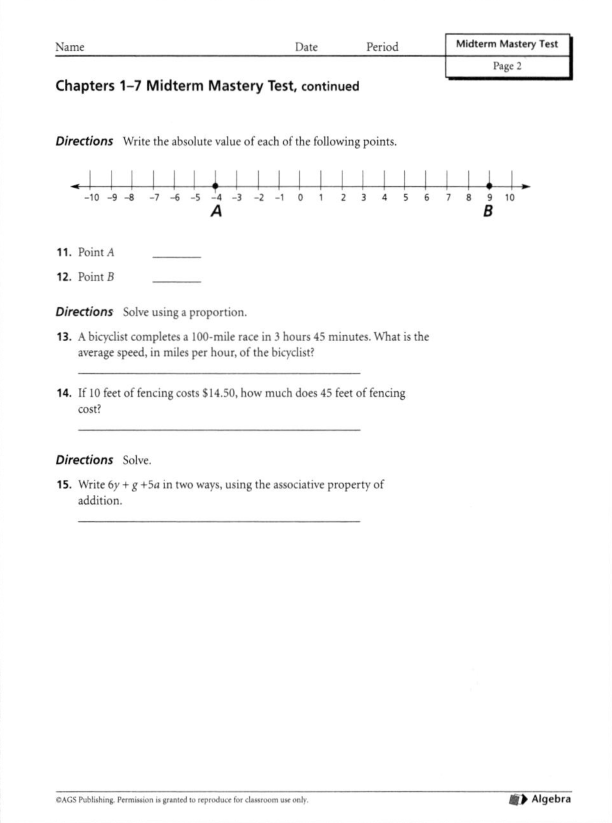

Name Date Period

Midterm Mastery Test
Page 2

Chapters 1–7 Midterm Mastery Test, continued

Directions Write the absolute value of each of the following points.

11. Point A ________

12. Point B ________

Directions Solve using a proportion.

13. A bicyclist completes a 100-mile race in 3 hours 45 minutes. What is the average speed, in miles per hour, of the bicyclist?

____

14. If 10 feet of fencing costs $14.50, how much does 45 feet of fencing cost?

____

Directions Solve.

15. Write $6y + g + 5a$ in two ways, using the associative property of addition.

____

Algebra

Midterm Mastery Test Page 2

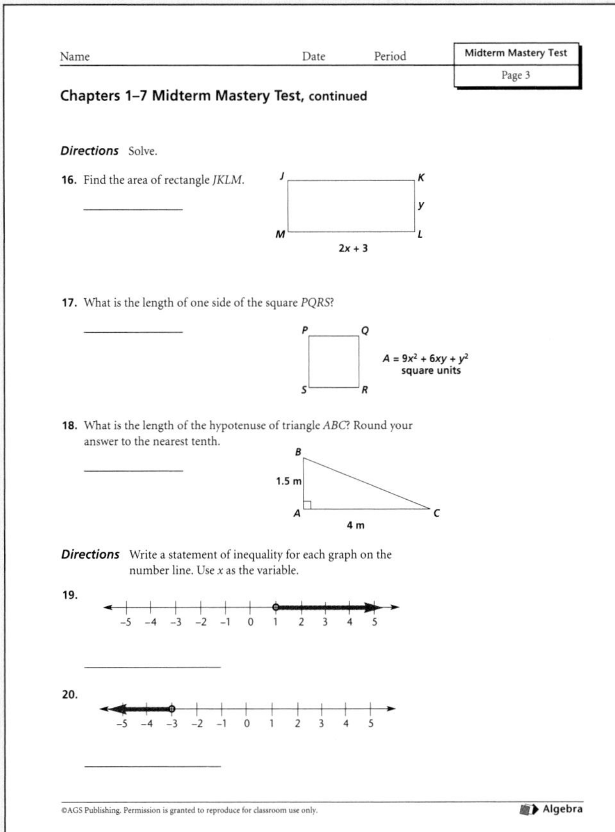

Name Date Period

Midterm Mastery Test
Page 3

Chapters 1–7 Midterm Mastery Test, continued

Directions Solve.

16. Find the area of rectangle $JKLM$.

____

17. What is the length of one side of the square $PQRS$?

____

18. What is the length of the hypotenuse of triangle ABC? Round your answer to the nearest tenth.

____

Directions Write a statement of inequality for each graph on the number line. Use x as the variable.

19.

____

20.

____

Algebra

Midterm Mastery Test Page 3

Name Date Period

Midterm Mastery Test
Page 4

Midterm Mastery Test

Directions Use the data in the table for problems 21–23.

15	8
13	11
15	4

21. Find the mean of the data. ________________

22. Find the median of the data. ________________

23. Find the mode of the data. ________________

Directions Refer to the spinner. Express the theoretical probability of each event below as a fraction in simplest form.

24. P (odd number) ________

25. P (not a variable) ________

x y 1 2 3 4 5 6

Algebra

Midterm Mastery Test Page 4

Final Mastery Test

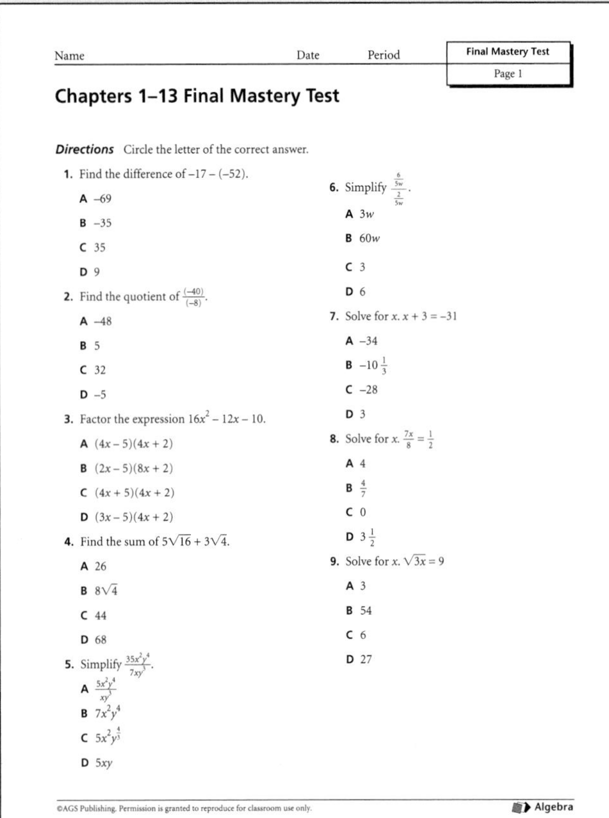

Name Date Period

Final Mastery Test
Page 1

Chapters 1–13 Final Mastery Test

Directions Circle the letter of the correct answer.

1. Find the difference of $-17 - (-52)$.

A -69

B -35

C 35

D 9

2. Find the quotient of $\frac{(-40)}{(-8)}$.

A -48

B 5

C 32

D -5

3. Factor the expression $16x^2 - 12x - 10$.

A $(4x - 5)(4x + 2)$

B $(2x - 5)(8x + 2)$

C $(4x + 5)(4x + 2)$

D $(3x - 5)(4x + 2)$

4. Find the sum of $5\sqrt{16} + 3\sqrt{4}$.

A 26

B $8\sqrt{4}$

C 44

D 68

5. Simplify $\frac{35x^2y^4}{7xy^3}$.

A $\frac{5x^2y^4}{xy^3}$

B $7x^2y^4$

C $5x^2y^{\frac{4}{3}}$

D $5xy$

6. Simplify $\frac{\frac{6}{5w}}{\frac{2}{5w}}$.

A $3w$

B $60w$

C 3

D 6

7. Solve for x. $x + 3 = -31$

A -34

B $-10\frac{1}{3}$

C -28

D 3

8. Solve for x. $\frac{7x}{8} = \frac{1}{2}$

A 4

B $\frac{4}{7}$

C 0

D $3\frac{1}{2}$

9. Solve for x. $\sqrt{3x} = 9$

A 3

B 54

C 6

D 27

©AGS Publishing. Permission is granted to reproduce for classroom use only. Algebra

Final Mastery Test Page 1

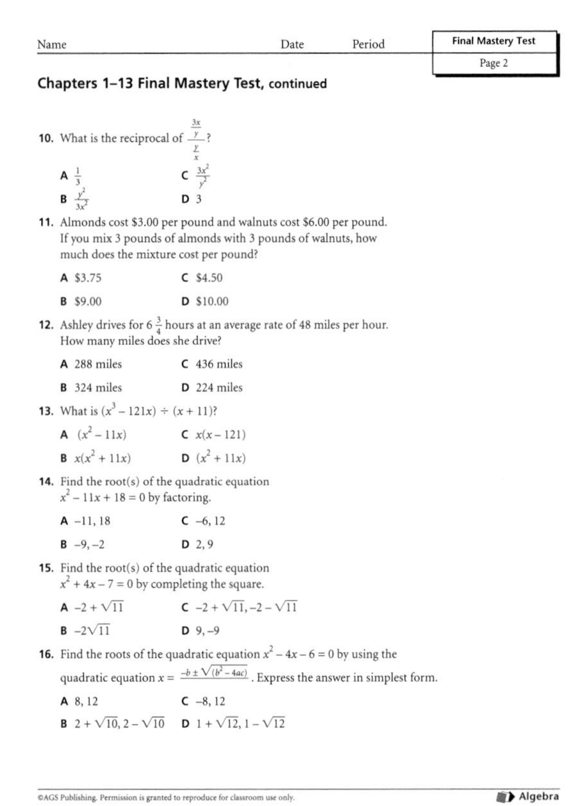

Name Date Period

Final Mastery Test
Page 2

Chapters 1–13 Final Mastery Test, continued

10. What is the reciprocal of $\frac{\frac{3x}{y}}{\frac{y}{x}}$?

A $\frac{1}{3}$ **C** $\frac{3x^2}{y^2}$

B $\frac{y^2}{3x^2}$ **D** 3

11. Almonds cost \$3.00 per pound and walnuts cost \$6.00 per pound. If you mix 3 pounds of almonds with 3 pounds of walnuts, how much does the mixture cost per pound?

A \$3.75 **C** \$4.50

B \$9.00 **D** \$10.00

12. Ashley drives for $6\frac{3}{4}$ hours at an average rate of 48 miles per hour. How many miles does she drive?

A 288 miles **C** 436 miles

B 324 miles **D** 224 miles

13. What is $(x^3 - 121x) \div (x + 11)$?

A $(x^2 - 11x)$ **C** $x(x - 121)$

B $x(x^2 + 11x)$ **D** $(x^2 + 11x)$

14. Find the root(s) of the quadratic equation $x^2 - 11x + 18 = 0$ by factoring.

A $-11, 18$ **C** $-6, 12$

B $-9, -2$ **D** $2, 9$

15. Find the root(s) of the quadratic equation $x^2 + 4x - 7 = 0$ by completing the square.

A $-2 + \sqrt{11}$ **C** $-2 + \sqrt{11}, -2 - \sqrt{11}$

B $-2\sqrt{11}$ **D** $9, -9$

16. Find the roots of the quadratic equation $x^2 - 4x - 6 = 0$ by using the quadratic equation $x = \frac{-b \pm \sqrt{(b^2 - 4ac)}}{2a}$. Express the answer in simplest form.

A 8, 12 **C** $-8, 12$

B $2 + \sqrt{10}, 2 - \sqrt{10}$ **D** $1 + \sqrt{12}, 1 - \sqrt{12}$

©AGS Publishing. Permission is granted to reproduce for classroom use only. Algebra

Final Mastery Test Page 2

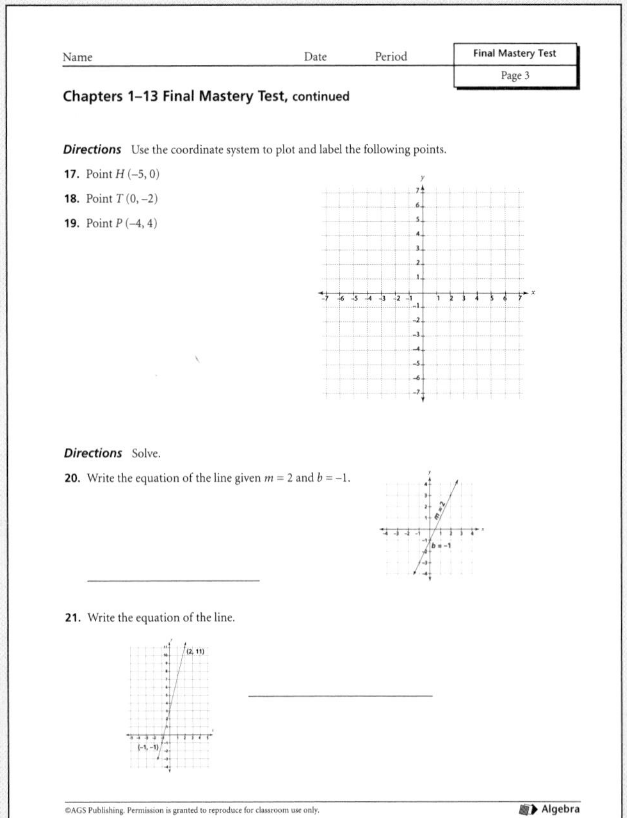

Name Date Period

Final Mastery Test
Page 3

Chapters 1–13 Final Mastery Test, continued

Directions Use the coordinate system to plot and label the following points.

17. Point $H(-5, 0)$

18. Point $T(0, -2)$

19. Point $P(-4, 4)$

Directions Solve.

20. Write the equation of the line given $m = 2$ and $b = -1$.

21. Write the equation of the line.

©AGS Publishing. Permission is granted to reproduce for classroom use only. Algebra

Final Mastery Test Page 3

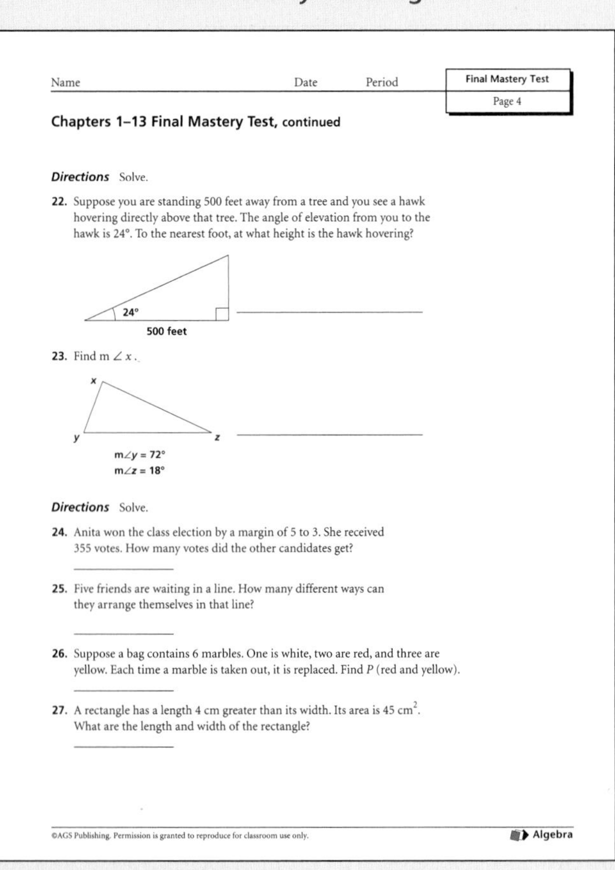

Name Date Period

Final Mastery Test
Page 4

Chapters 1–13 Final Mastery Test, continued

Directions Solve.

22. Suppose you are standing 500 feet away from a tree and you see a hawk hovering directly above that tree. The angle of elevation from you to the hawk is 24°. To the nearest foot, at what height is the hawk hovering?

23. Find m $\angle x$.

Directions Solve.

24. Anita won the class election by a margin of 5 to 3. She received 355 votes. How many votes did the other candidates get?

25. Five friends are waiting in a line. How many different ways can they arrange themselves in that line?

26. Suppose a bag contains 6 marbles. One is white, two are red, and three are yellow. Each time a marble is taken out, it is replaced. Find P(red and yellow).

27. A rectangle has a length 4 cm greater than its width. Its area is 45 cm^2. What are the length and width of the rectangle?

©AGS Publishing. Permission is granted to reproduce for classroom use only. Algebra

Final Mastery Test Page 4

Final Mastery Test

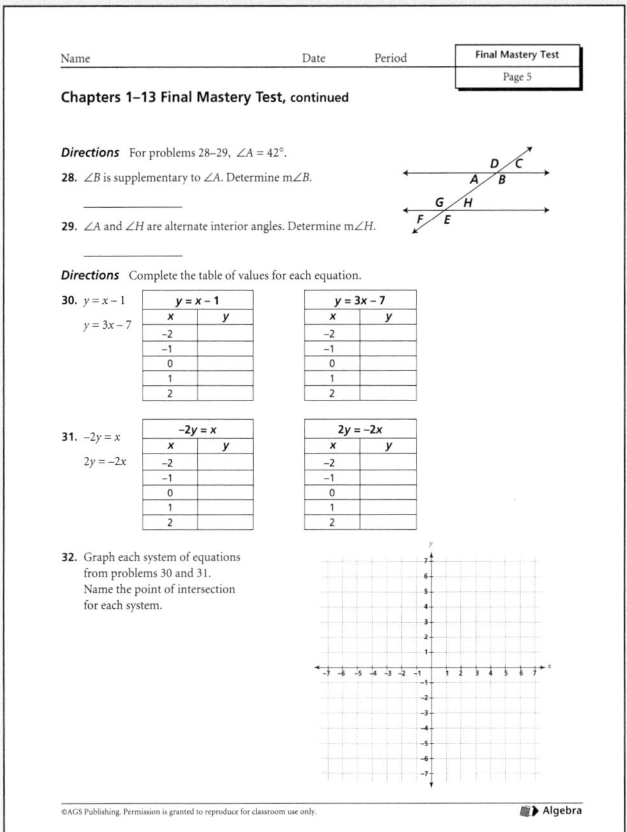

Name Date Period

Final Mastery Test
Page 5

Chapters 1–13 Final Mastery Test, continued

Directions For problems 28–29, $\angle A = 42°$.

28. $\angle B$ is supplementary to $\angle A$. Determine $m\angle B$.

____

29. $\angle A$ and $\angle H$ are alternate interior angles. Determine $m\angle H$.

____

Directions Complete the table of values for each equation.

30. $y = x - 1$
$y = 3x - 7$

$y = x - 1$	
x	y
−2	
−1	
0	
1	
2	

$y = 3x - 7$	
x	y
−2	
−1	
0	
1	
2	

31. $-2y = x$
$2y = -2x$

$-2y = x$	
x	y
−2	
−1	
0	
1	
2	

$2y = -2x$	
x	y
−2	
−1	
0	
1	
2	

32. Graph each system of equations from problems 30 and 31. Name the point of intersection for each system.

 Algebra

Final Mastery Test Page 5

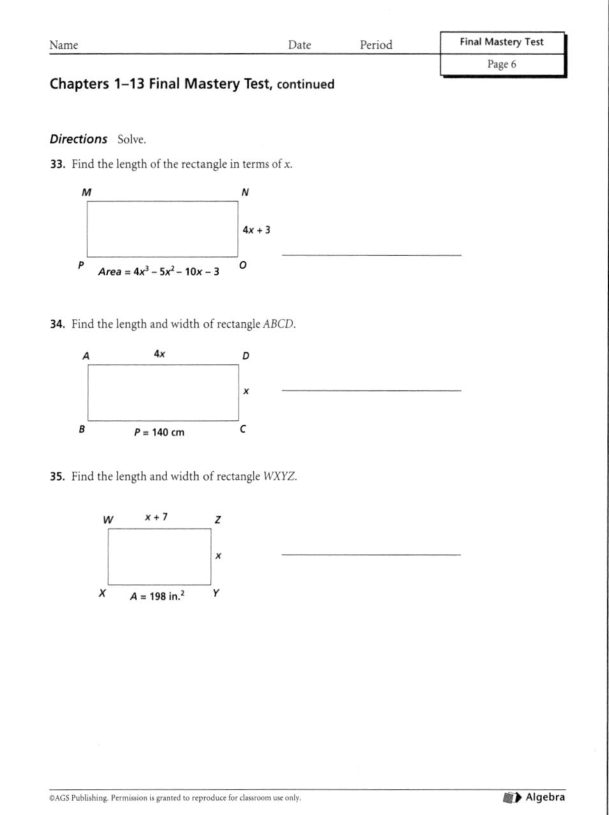

Name Date Period

Final Mastery Test
Page 6

Chapters 1–13 Final Mastery Test, continued

Directions Solve.

33. Find the length of the rectangle in terms of x.

34. Find the length and width of rectangle $ABCD$.

35. Find the length and width of rectangle $WXYZ$.

 Algebra

Final Mastery Test Page 6

The lists below show how items from the Midterm and Final correlate to the chapters in the student edition.

Midterm Mastery Test

Chapter 1: 1, 3, 11–12
Chapter 2: 2, 5, 15
Chapter 3: 7, 18–20
Chapter 4: 8, 13–14
Chapter 5: 4, 6, 16
Chapter 6: 9–10, 17
Chapter 7: 21–25

Final Mastery Test

Chapter 1: 1–2
Chapter 2: 10
Chapter 3: 7–8, 34
Chapter 4: 11–12
Chapter 5: 13, 33
Chapter 6: 3, 35
Chapter 7: 25–26
Chapter 8: 5–6, 24
Chapter 9: 17–21
Chapter 10: 30–32
Chapter 11: 4, 9
Chapter 12: 22–23, 28–29
Chapter 13: 14–16, 27

Teacher's Resource Library Answer Key

Activities

Activity 1—Arithmetic and Algebra

1. a and c **2.** b and c **3.** true **4.** open **5.** true **6.** false **7.** false **8.** true **9.** false **10.** true **11.** true **12.** false **13.** open **14.** false **15.** open **16.** true **17.** open **18.** false **19.** false **20.** true **21.** false **22.** false **23.** false **24.** true **25.** false **26.** false **27.** true **28.** false **29.** true **30.** false

Activity 2—Representing Numbers Using Letters

1. true **2.** false **3.** true **4.** false **5.** algebraic **6.** numerical **7.** numerical **8.** algebraic **9.** multiplication; subtraction **10.** division **11.** multiplication **12.** multiplication; addition **13.** $6 \cdot 10$ (or $10 \cdot 6$) **14.** $12 - 8$ **15.** $5m$ (or $5 \cdot m$)

Activity 3—Integers on the Number Line

1. algebraic **2.** x **3.** multiplication **4.** numerical **5.** division **6.** none **7.** multiplication; subtraction **8.** -3 **9.** -6 **10.** 2 **11.** -9 **12.** 15 **13.** 4 **14.** -7 **15.** 10 **16.** -10 **17.** -11 **18.** 5 **19.** -2 **20.** 1 **21.** 8 **22.** -21 **23.** A **24.** A **25.** 4

Activity 4—Adding Integers

1. 8 **2.** 8 **3.** 3 **4.** 5 **5.** 2 **6.** 1 **7.** 0 **8.** 1 **9.** 4 **10.** 4 **11.** 16 **12.** 12 **13.** -2 **14.** 9 **15.** -67 **16.** -24 **17.** -12 **18.** 28 **19.** -20 **20.** 71 **21.** 2 **22.** 0 **23.** -100 **24.** 80 **25.** -20

Activity 5—Choosing a Classroom Calculator

Responses will vary.

Activity 6—Subtracting Integers

1. 13 **2.** 3 **3.** -4 **4.** -10 **5.** 9 **6.** 0 **7.** -12 **8.** -14 **9.** -5 **10.** -10 **11.** 4 **12.** 2 **13.** 13 **14.** 0 **15.** 0 **16.** -10 **17.** -3 **18.** -4 **19.** 112° **20.** $28 - (-3) = 31$

Activity 7—Multiplying Integers

1. -11 **2.** 3 **3.** 14 **4.** -8 **5.** 1 **6.** -22 **7.** 4 **8.** 31 **9.** -12 **10.** 9 **11.** -8 **12.** 10 **13.** -7 **14.** -19 **15.** -14 **16.** 0 **17.** -42 **18.** -45 **19.** 39 **20.** 49 **21.** 15 **22.** 0 **23.** -16 **24.** 18 **25.** -33 **26.** 40 **27.** 28 **28.** -36 **29.** 50 minutes **30.** $(3)(-3)$

Activity 8—Dividing Positive and Negative Integers

1. -2 **2.** 1 **3.** -3 **4.** 17 **5.** -11 **6.** -7 **7.** 6 **8.** -13 **9.** -17 **10.** -4 **11.** 12 **12.** -9 **13.** 2 **14.** -10 **15.** -3 **16.** -10 **17.** -7 **18.** 3 **19.** -2 **20.** 6 **21.** 31 **22.** 7 **23.** -6 **24.** -5 **25.** b

Activity 9—Simplifying Expressions—One Variable

1. algebraic **2.** numerical **3.** numerical **4.** algebraic **5.** algebraic **6.** numerical **7.** numerical **8.** algebraic **9.** numerical **10.** algebraic **11.** $3 + (-4) = -1$ **12.** $6 + (-9) = -3$ **13.** $-8 + (-4) = -12$ **14.** $-8 + 4 = -4$ **15.** $12 + 1 = 13$ **16.** $9 + (-8) = 1$ **17.** $6y$ **18.** $3b + 15$ **19.** $10r + 11$ **20.** $8h - 15$ **21.** $7k + 4$ **22.** $3x - 1$ **23.** $-3m$ **24.** $13n + 14$ **25.** $-3w - 3$

Activity 10—Simplifying Expressions—Several Variables

1. 6 **2.** -7 **3.** -3 **4.** 5 **5.** -4 **6.** -3 **7.** 1 **8.** -7 **9.** 9 **10.** -11 **11.** $5x - 2y + 3$ **12.** $4k + y - 12$ **13.** $2h - 3w + 1$ **14.** $6n + 12p$ **15.** $8m + r$ **16.** $-d - 2j + 15$ **17.** $a + 5b + 5$ **18.** $-4y - 16$ **19.** $9r + 5w - 2$ **20.** 3 oranges + 3 apples + 1 peach (in any order)

Activity 11—Positive Exponents

1. d^2 **2.** k^5 **3.** w^3 **4.** c^6 **5.** b^7 **6.** x^{10} **7.** y (or y^1) **8.** a^{10} **9.** m^9 **10.** p^9 **11.** 6 **12.** 14 **13.** 8 **14.** 4 **15.** 11 **16.** 2 **17.** 4 **18.** 2, 2, 2, 2 **19.** 2^4 **20.** 16

Activity 12—Formulas with Variables

1. 21 m **2.** 120 cm **3.** 84 cm **4.** 3 km **5.** 10 m **6.** 55 mm **7.** 60 cm **8.** 500 mm **9.** $2l + 2w$ **10.** s^2

Activity 13—Commutative Property of Addition

1. 16 **2.** $3x$ **3.** $7p$ **4.** 7.7 **5.** g **6.** $31k$ **7.** $3y$ **8.** 31,774 **9.** $12h$ **10.** $700n$ **11.** $6q$ **12.** According to the commutative property of addition, their new total will be the same regardless of the order in which they add. **13.** 87 **14.** 87 **15.** commutative property of addition

Activity 14—Commutative Property of Multiplication

1. $(1.5)(36)$ **2.** $(3k)7k$ **3.** qp **4.** $32 \cdot 16$ **5.** dc **6.** $(4z)z$ **7.** $(12r)(11\text{m})$ **8.** $2(4b)$ **9.** Kim and Tomas should be circled. **10.** Designs a and b will give the same amount of memory. The commutative property of multiplication proves that both products will be equal.

Activity 15—Associative Property of Addition

In problems **1–6**, both sums must be correct for students to receive any credit. **1.** $1 + (14) = 15$; $(6) + 9 = 15$ **2.** $7 + (19) = 26$; $(18) + 8 = 26$ **3.** $(28) + 12 = 40$; $15 + (25) = 40$ **4.** $70 + (15) = 85$; $(75) + 10 = 85$ **5.** $14 + (12) = 26$; $(23) + 3 = 26$ **6.** $7 + (34) = 41$; $(29) + 12 = 41$ In problems **7–9**, both rewritten versions of the expression must be correct for students to receive any credit. The order of the rewritten expressions is irrelevant. **7.** $(d + h) + 2k$; $d + (h + 2k)$ **8.** $(x + y) + 4$; $x + (y + 4)$ **9.** $(6n + 5p) + 8r$; $6n + (5p + 8r)$ **10.** The same number. Because of the associative property of addition, the numbers of students can be added in various groupings without affecting the total.

Activity 16—Associative Property of Multiplication

1. (check) **2.** (check) **3.** (no check) **4.** (check) **5.** (no check) **6.** (no check) **7.** (check) **8.** (no check) **9.** (check) **10.** (check) **11.** (no check) **12.** (check) **13.** a **14.** b **15.** The statement is true. Box A and Box B do contain the same number of oranges.

Activity 17—The Distributive Property—Multiplication

1. *a* **2.** *a* **3.** *d* **4.** *d* **5.** *n* **6.** *d* **7.** *a* **8.** *a* **9.** *n* **10.** *n* **11.** *d* **12.** *a* **13.** *n* **14.** *d* **15.** Method 1

Activity 18—The Distributive Property—Factoring

1. $2j + 2k$ **2.** $36 + 9w$ **3.** $-7a + 7b$ **4.** $12q - 12r$ **5.** $24 + 6n$ **6.** $2.5d + dbw$ (or $2.5d + bwd$) **7.** $3(y - z)$ **8.** $7(p + r)$ **9.** $x(d + k)$ **10.** $-3(n + q)$ **11.** $a(x^2 + y^5)$ **12.** $16(m^4 - m^7)$ **13.** b **14.** b **15.** $3(x - y)$

Activity 19—Properties of Zero

1. true **2.** true **3.** true **4.** false **5.** neither true nor false **6.** true **7.** 0 **8.** 122 **9.** 11 **10.** 0 **11.** p **12.** 0 **13.** 18 **14.** 0 **15.** 9 **16.** 0 **17.** 68 **18.** 0 **19.** -3 **20.** c

Activity 20—Properties of 1

1. 1 **2.** 21 **3.** 0 **4.** 0 **5.** k **6.** 1 **7.** 33,244 **8.** 0 **9.** pq^3r^2 **10.** 0 **11.** g^2 **12.** 0 **13.** 0 **14.** 1 **15.** 0 **16.** b^6 **17.** 0 **18.** 0 **19.** a **20.** c

Activity 21—Powers and Roots

Check matching lines for **1–5.** **1.** d **2.** e **3.** a **4.** c **5.** b **6.** 9 **7.** 5 **8.** $\frac{1}{3}$ **9.** 106 ft **10.** 22,500 sq ft; 2,088.49 sq m

Activity 22—More on Powers and Roots

1. 25 **2.** −27 **3.** −4 **4.** 6, −6 **5.** 4 **6.** −25 **7.** 9 **8.** 125 **9.** −125 **10.** 4 **11.** 5, −5 **12.** −3 **13.** 8, −8 **14.** −8 **15.** 4 **16.** −4 **17.** 16 **18.** −32 **19.** 4, 5 **20.** No. An edge of one building block is $\sqrt[3]{27} = 3$ cm; 11 • 3 cm = 33 cm, which is longer than the shelf of 31 cm.

Activity 23—Order of Operations

1. 30 **2.** 1 **3.** −9 **4.** 41 **5.** 8 **6.** 16 **7.** 64 **8.** 1 **9.** −3 **10.** −33 **11.** 0 **12.** 63 **13.** a **14.** $14k$ **15.** $-7y$ **16.** $48y$ **17.** 0 **18.** $9n$ **19.** $8d^2$ **20.** $8d^2$ **21.** $-18x$ **22.** 0 **23.** b **24.** (1) exponent; (2) multiply **25.** 320

Activity 24—Writing Equations

1. $2y - 20 = 2$ **2.** $5y + 7 = 12$ **3.** $6 + y = 6$ **4.** $y - 13 = 2$ **5.** $3y + 17 = 56$ **6.** $6 + y = -2$ **7.** $4y - 12 = 0$ **8.** $2y - 2 = -6$ **9.** c **10.** b

Activity 25—Solving Equations: $x - b = c$

1. $k = 2$ **2.** $x = 2$ **3.** $w = 0$ **4.** $n = 4$ **5.** $d = 8$ **6.** 5 was added to one side of the equation only. It should have been added to both sides. **7.** 8 was added to one side of the equation and 7 to the other side. 8 should have been added to both sides. **8.** 15 **9.** 56°F **10.** 13

Activity 26—Solving Equations: $x + b = c$

1. $a = 2$ **2.** $x = 12$ **3.** $d = 3$ **4.** $n = 15$ **5.** $q = 14$ **6.** $b = 58$ **7.** $m = 18$ **8.** $y = 28$ **9.** $c = 17$ **10.** $j = 100$ **11.** $x = 1{,}000$ **12.** 590 miles **13.** $160.50 **14.** 4 **15.** 22

Activity 27—Solving Multiplication Equations

1. $5m = 45; m = 9$ **2.** $4d = 48; d = 12$ **3.** $9a = -45; a = -5$ **4.** $2j = -8; j = -4$ **5.** $-6k = 30; k = -5$ **6.** $10n = 500; n = 50$ **7.** 130 **8.** 1,300 m **9.** 93 **10.** 102.9°F

Activity 28—Solving Equations with Fractions

1. $\frac{1}{6}p = 6; p = 36$ **2.** $\frac{1}{9}x = 2; x = 18$ **3.** $\frac{9}{10}n = 18; n = 20$ **4.** $\frac{3}{4}q = -12; q = -16$ **5.** $-\frac{2}{3}w = 6; w = -9$ **6.** 150 **7.** 16 **8.** 300 cm **9.** 105 **10.** 280

Activity 29—Solving Equations—More Than One Step

1. correct **2.** incorrect; The 1 was added only to the left side. It should have been added to both sides. **3.** correct **4.** 3 **5.** 204

Activity 30—Equations Without Numbers

1. $x = \frac{c-b}{a}$ **2.** $x = \frac{a+c}{b}$ **3.** $x = \frac{-b}{a}$ **4.** $x = \frac{ab}{c}$ **5.** $x = \frac{bc}{a}$ **6.** $x = \frac{ab}{-c}$ **7.** $x = \frac{b}{a+c}$ **8.** $a = \frac{c}{b}$ **9.** 24 **10.** 18

Activity 31—Formulas

1. $c = P - a - b$ or $c = P - (a + b)$ **2.** $b = P - a - c$ or $b = P - (a + c)$ **3.** $s = \sqrt{A}$ **4.** $s = \sqrt[3]{V}$ **5.** $h = \frac{2A}{(b_1 + b_2)}$

Activity 32—The Pythagorean Theorem

1. 3.6 **2.** 5 **3.** 6.3 **4.** 26, 27 **5.** 26.9

Activity 33—Inequalities on the Number Line

1. $x < 6$ **2.** $x \geq -3$ **3.** $x = 7$ **4.** T **5.** F **6.** F **7.** T **8.** T **9.** F **10.** 50 m

Activity 34—Solving Inequalities with One Variable

1. $g \geq 0$ **2.** $r < 16$ **3.** $q < -4$ **4.** $m > 7$ **5.** $n \geq 11$ **6.** $y \geq 6$ **7.** $k \leq 200$ **8.** $n < \frac{2}{5}(100)$ (accept $n < 40$) **9.** $w \geq \frac{7}{10}(400)$ (accept $w \geq 280$) **10.** $k \geq \frac{1}{3}(18)$ (accept $k \geq 6$)

Activity 35—Writing Equations—Odd and Even Integers

1. Don 7; Jay 8; Brett 9 **2.** 8 **3.** Delia has 6 earrings (or 3 pairs). Reynal has 8 earrings (or 4 pairs). **4.** Mom's bag 9; Dad's bag 8 **5.** small 5; medium 7; large 9

Activity 36—Using the 1% Solution to Solve Problems

1. 4,320 **2.** 28 **3.** 1,360 **4.** 143 **5.** 40% **6.** 434 **7.** 400 **8.** 72% **9.** 396 **10.** 1,260

Activity 37—Using the Percent Equation

1. 28 **2.** 50 **3.** 26 **4.** 110 **5.** 48 **6.** 70% **7.** 300 **8.** 3,744 **9.** 8,900 **10.** 16%

Activity 38—Solving Distance, Rate, and Time Problems

1. r **2.** d **3.** t **4.** r **5.** 240 miles **6.** 44 km/h **7.** 27 miles **8.** 190 km/h **9.** 62.5 mph **10.** $2\frac{1}{2}$ hours

Activity 39—Using a Common Unit—Cents

1. 1,800 **2.** 3,513 **3.** 929 **4.** 32 **5.** 13 nickels, 13 quarters **6.** 8 coins of each type **7.** Lila—48 dimes; Marcie—24 dimes **8.** Gina—33 quarters; Antonio—11 quarters **9.** 5 quarters, 5 dimes, 10 nickels, 30 pennies **10.** 98 dimes, 49 nickels, 196 pennies

Activity 40—Calculating Simple Interest

1. $106.20 **2.** $31.35 **3.** $1,150.00 **4.** $900.00 **5.** Michael's account had the higher rate. Using the formula $r = \frac{I}{pt}$ and substituting I, p, and t for each person, we find that Kitra's rate was 6.5% (0.065) and Michael's was 7% (0.07).

Activity 41—Deriving a Formula for Mixture Problems

1. $1.00 per pound **2.** 4 ounces of raisins; 6 ounces of dried apples **3.** $0.80 (or 80¢) per pound **4.** 36 pounds of granola; 4 pounds of dried bananas **5.** 10 quarters, 20 nickels, and 60 dimes

Activity 42—Ratio and Proportion

1. 2:1 **2.** 1:2 **3.** 1:3 **4.** 3:1 **5.** $\frac{2}{1}$ **6.** $\frac{1}{10}$ **7.** $\frac{1}{3}$ **8.** $\frac{3}{400}$ **9.** Yes. To confirm, make an equation with the two ratios: $\frac{18}{9} = \frac{16}{8}$. Cross multiplication reveals that 18 • 8 = 16 • 9, because simplifying, 144 = 144. **10.** 21 pints

Activity 43—Exponents

1. 2^{10} **2.** x^8 **3.** y^6 **4.** m^0 or 1 **5.** r^8 **6.** k^1 or k **7.** $(n - m)^6$ **8.** n^5 **9.** Divide exponents by subtracting: $k^{2-2} = k^0$. The value of k^0 is 1. (accept "A fraction with identical numerator and denominator resolves to 1.") **10.** The answer is 3 cm. Calculation: $\frac{3^3}{3^2} = 3^{3-2} = 3^1 = 3$. (accept the calculation $\frac{3^3}{3^2} = \frac{27}{9} = 3$)

Activity 44—Negative Exponents

1. −1 **2.** 3 **3.** −1 **4.** −2 **5.** −3 (accept 3 − 6) **6.** −2 (accept 1 − 3) **7.** −6 (accept 2 − 8) **8.** −3 **9.** $y, y \neq 0$ **10.** −3 **11.** 2 **12.** −4 **13.** −2 **14.** −1 **15.** 0 **16.** −3 **17.** 10,000 **18.** 7 **19.** 9 **20.** $(2x + 3)$ **21.** 100 **22.** 0 **23.** k **24.** −3 **25.** −2

Activity 45—Exponents and Scientific Notation
1. 0.0227 **2.** 37,720 **3.** 0.56 **4.** 97,000,000 **5.** 133,586 **6.** 0.0000133586 **7.** 422 **8.** 8,960 **9.** $1.0(10^4)$ **10.** $9.3(10^7)$ **11.** $5.0(10^{-6})$ **12.** $4.0(10^9)$ **13.** $3.0(10^5)$ **14.** between $1.0(10^{-3})$ and $1.0(10^{-2})$ **15.** $6.0(10^9)$

Activity 46—Computing in Scientific Notation
1. $6.27(10^4)$ **2.** $3.84(10^5)$ **3.** $4.0(10^7)$ **4.** $3.0(10^3)$ **5.** $1.0(10^6)$

Activity 47—Defining and Naming Polynomials
1. 2 **2.** 2 **3.** 3 **4.** 3 **5.** 1 **6.** 4 **7.** 3 **8.** 5 **9.** 1 **10.** 6 **11.** 1 **12.** 3 **13.** 1 **14.** 2 **15.** 8 **16.** 5 **17.** has more than one variable **18.** has a negative exponent **19.** has a variable in the denominator **20.** has a negative exponent **21.** has more than one variable; Answers will vary in problems **22–25. 22.** Expression should include three terms in proper order, in which the first term contains k^2. Example: $k^2 - 2k + 5$. **23.** Expression should include two terms in proper order, in which the first term contains y. Example: $7y + 12$. **24.** Expression should include one term only. The single term should contain x^3. Example: $2x^3$. **25.** Expression should include five terms in proper order, in which the first term contains n^4. Example: $n^4 - 2n^3 + 3n^2 + 5n - 12$.

Activity 48—Adding and Subtracting Polynomials
1. $6a^4 - 2a^3 + 4a^2 - 3a + 9$ **2.** $16n^3 - 2n^2 - 11n - 22$ **3.** $3s^2$ **4.** $k^3 + 3k^2 + 3k + 4$ **5.** $6x^4 - 3x^3 + 3x^2$

Activity 49—Multiplying Polynomials
1. $7b^2 + 2b - 5$ **2.** $5n^4 + 40n^3$ **3.** $6y^7 + 10y^6 - 2y^4 - 14y^3 + 6y^2$ **4.** $x^3 + x^2 - 5x - 5$ **5.** $7x^3 - 13x^2 + 7x + 5$ **6.** $5n^4 + 8n^2 - 7n + 3$ **7.** $9k^3 + 11k^2 - 9k - 11$ **8.** $2d^3 + 5d^2 - 3d + 7$ **9.** $x^2 - 2x - 24$ **10.** $x^4 + 4x^3 + 3x^2 + 16x + 48$

Activity 50—Special Polynomial Products
1. $d - f$ (accept the exponent 2) **2.** k^3 **3.** – (the minus sign) **4.** m^2 **5.** $p + q$ **6.** $x + y$ (accept the exponent 2) **7.** $k^2 + 2kr + r^2$ square units **8.** $a^2 - 2ab + b^2$ square units **9.** $n^3 + 3n^2p + 3np^2 + p^3$ cubic units **10.** $(n + r)(n - r) = n^2 - r^2$

Activity 51—Dividing a Polynomial by a Monomial
1. $x^2 - 2x + 3$ **2.** $(x^2 - 2x + 3)(7x) = 7x^3 - 14x^2 + 21$ **3.** $4a^3 - 3a^2 - 7a + 6$ **4.** $(4a^3 - 3a^2 - 7a + 6)(-3) = -12a^3 + 9a^2 + 21a - 18$ **5.** incorrect, corrected answer $3x^2 - 7x + 27$ **6.** correct **7.** incorrect, corrected answer $2k^3 - 4k^2 - k + 7$ **8.** incorrect, corrected answer $n^3 + 8n^2 - 12n - 6$ **9.** correct **10.** correct

Activity 52—Dividing a Polynomial by a Binomial
1. 5 **2.** 7 **3.** 2 **4.** 3 **5.** 1 **6.** 4 **7.** 3 **8.** 1 **9.** 9 **10.** 2 **11.** $a + 3$ **12.** $(a + 3)(a + 3) = (a^2 + 6a + 9)$ **13.** $(x - 3)$ r–4 **14.** $(x + 2)(x - 3) + (-4) = (x^2 - x - 10)$ **15.** $x^2 + 4x + 4$ **16.** $(x^2 + 4x + 4)(x + 2) = (x^3 + 6x^2 + 12x + 8)$ **17.** $(n - 4)$ r3 **18.** $(n - 4)(n - 4) + 3 = (n^2 - 8n + 19)$ **19.** $(k + 7)$ **20.** $(k + 7)(k - 7) = (k^2 - 49)$

Activity 53—Polynomials in Two or More Variables
1. 9 **2.** 60 **3.** $111\frac{1}{4}$ **4.** 75 **5.** $49\frac{1}{16}$ **6.** 5 **7.** 3 **8.** 27 **9.** 412 **10.** 345 **11.** 120 **12.** –88 **13.** 0 **14.** 4,760 **15.** –150 **16.** 12 **17.** 192 **18.** –19 **19.** 15 **20.** –330

Activity 54—Greatest Common Factor
1. $2^2 \cdot 3$ **2.** 2^2 **3.** 5 **4.** $3p$ **5.** $11c^2$ **6.** $5a^2b^2$ **7.** $3m^3n^2$ **8.** 400 **9.** 3,528 **10.** 19,600 **11.** 576 **12.** 36,864 **13.** 864 **14.** 256 **15.** 144 **16.** 8,100 **17.** 6,125 **18.** 1,600 **19.** 1,296 **20.** You can rule out the even numbers in the range (146, 148, 150, 152, 154). You can also rule out numbers that can be divided by 5—numbers ending in 0 or 5. The remaining possibilities: 147, 149, 151, 153. (Accept any reasonable answer.)

Activity 55—Factoring Polynomials
1. x; $x(4x - 1)$ **2.** 8; $-8(r - 3s)$ or $8(-r + 3s)$ **3.** $3xy^2$; $3xy^2(x + 2y)$ **4.** 3; $3(f + 3g - 8h)$ **5.** $2ab$; $2ab(6a - 5b)$ **6.** $2n$; $2n(3m^2 + 11m - 4)$ **7.** $3n^2$; $3n^2(4n^2 - 2n + 1)$ **8.** $2j^2$; $2j^2(1 + 2k)$ **9.** $5k^2 + 7k + 11$; it cannot be factored because there is no GCF of these three terms other than 1 **10.** c; it is the factored form of $2a^2 + 4a + 4$

Activity 56—Factoring Trinomials: $x^2 + bx + c$
1. $(x + 9)(x + 1)$ **2.** $(n + 3)(n + 5)$ **3.** $(a + 2)(a + 6)$ **4.** $(x + 12)(x + 1)$ **5.** $(y + 2)(y + 11)$ **6.** $(r + 3)(r + 4)$ **7.** $2(x - 2)(x - 7)$ **8.** $2k(k + 8)(k - 2)$ **9.** $2y(x + 5)(x - 4)$ **10.** $a^2(a + 9)(a - 1)$ **11.** $3(x - 3)(x - 4)$ **12.** $m^2n^2(m + 7)(m - 8)$ **13.** $4x(x + 2)(x - 5)$ **14.** Two sides are $(x + 1)$ feet, and two sides are $(x - 4)$ feet. **15.** The GCF is 2, so factoring produces $2(x^2 - 3x - 4)$. This factored expression shows that the new piece is twice the size (area) of the original piece.

Activity 57—Factoring Trinomials: $ax^2 + bx + c$
1. $2(2x + 3)(3x - 5)$ **2.** $3c(2d - 3)(d + 5)$ **3.** $10(7a + 3)(a + 1)$ **4.** $x^3(5x + 1)(x - 1)$ **5.** $2(2n + 5)(4n + 3)$ **6.** $7(2b - 3)(b - 1)$ **7.** $4x^2(y + 3)(2y - 1)$ **8.** $-2x(x - 2)(4x - 3)$ **9.** $y^2(2y + 5)(6y - 1)$ **10.** two sides are $(2n - 3)$ cm, and two sides are $(n + 4)$ cm; the completely factored expression is $4(2n - 3)(n + 4)$

Activity 58—Factoring Expressions: $a^2 - b^2$
1. $(r^2 + 12)(r^2 - 12)$ **2.** $(5a + 3b)(5a - 3b)$ **3.** $(a^6 + 5)(a^6 - 5)$ **4.** $(r + 16)(r - 16)$ **5.** $(n^8 + 14)(n^8 - 14)$ **6.** $(2y^2 + 5z)(2y^2 - 5z)$ **7.** $(w + 15)(w - 15)$ **8.** $(x^2 + 4)(x^2 - 4)$ **9.** $(d^8 + 2x)(d^8 - 2x)$ **10.** $(7x + 8y)(7x - 8y)$ **11.** $(3m^2 + 11n^4)(3m^2 - 11n^4)$ **12.** $(x^{16} + 4)(x^{16} - 4)$ **13.** $(6k^2 + 5p)(6k^2 - 5p)$ **14.** $(t + 17)(t - 17)$ **15.** $(a^2 - 3^2)$ or $(a^2 - 9)$; factored expression $(a + 3)(a - 3)$

Activity 59—Factoring Expressions: $a^2 + 2ab + b^2$
1. 9 **2.** 27 **3.** 81 **4.** 27 **5.** 144 **6.** $(x - 5)^2$ **7.** $(2b - 4)^2$ **8.** $(3p + 10r)^2$ **9.** factored form $(a + b)(a + b)$ or $(a + b)^2$; unfactored form $a^2 + 2ab + b^2$ **10.** $(r^4 + 12)$ is a factor of $(r^8 + 24r^4 + 144)$ because $(r^8 + 24r^4 + 144)$ factors into $(r^4 + 12)(r^4 + 12)$; also accept $(r^4 + 12)$ is the square root of $(r^8 + 24r^4 + 144)$

Activity 60—Zero as a Factor
1. $v = 20$ **2.** $p = -17$ **3.** $n = -12$ or 16 **4.** $d = -5$ or 5 **5.** $m = 7$ or 8 **6.** $w = 22$ **7.** $x = -6$ or 6 **8.** $r = -13$ or -11 **9.** $n = 0$, Clarissa has no nickels. **10.** $4k = 0$, since $4 \neq 0$, k must $= 0$; If there are no crackers in the box, then surely there are none in the plastic tubes.

Activity 61—Solving Quadratic Equations—Factoring
1. 10, –1 **2.** $\frac{-5}{2}$, 4 **3.** $\frac{-13}{3}$, 4 **4.** factored trinomial $(2y - 3)(y - 5)$; solutions: $\frac{3}{2}$, 5 **5.** factored trinomial $(n + 8)(n - 5)$; The measurement of a side of a square (or other geometric figure) cannot be a negative value; of solutions –8 and 5, only 5 is reasonable.

Activity 62—Organizing Data

1. no **2.** students who read 6–10 books **3.** 6 **4.** 3 **5.** Though answers will vary, students should express the idea that the person who read 21–25 books was exceptional in the class. For instance, students may write something like "that person is very smart" or "that person can read fast." **6.** stem 1, leaf 4 **7.** stem 2, leaf 3 **8.** stem 3, leaf 6 **9.** stem 4, leaf 7 **10.** stem 5, leaf 5

Activity 63—Range, Mean, Median, and Mode

1. \$1.00, \$1.19, \$1.29, \$1.29, \$2.99, \$3.30, \$4.68, \$8.10 **2.** \$7.10 **3.** \$2.98 **4.** \$2.14 (Calculation: The two middle values in this even-numbered data set are \$1.29 and \$2.99. Taking their mean [\$1.29 + \$2.99] ÷ 2 = \$2.14.) **5.** \$1.29 **6.** 10, 16, 16, 19, 22, 24, 25, 32, 45, 61 **7.** 51 **8.** 27 **9.** 23 (Calculation: The two middle values in this even-numbered data set are 22 and 24. Taking their mean [22 + 24] ÷ 2 = 23.) **10.** 16

Activity 64—Box-and-Whiskers Plots

1. 1, 2, 3, 4, 6, 7, 7, 8, 9, 10, 10, 12, 18, 22, 24 **2.** 1 **3.** 24 **4.** 8 **5.** 4 **6.** 12 **7.** dot at 8 **8.** dots at 1 and 24 **9.** dots at 4 and 12 **10.** box enclosing the data between the lower quartile (dot at 4) and the upper quartile (dot at 12), whiskers extending from the box to 1 and 24, a vertical line at the median

Activity 65—The Probability Fraction

1. $\frac{1}{5}$ **2.** $\frac{2}{96} = \frac{1}{48}$ **3.** $\frac{1}{10}$ **4.** $\frac{1}{3}$ **5.** $\frac{40}{100} = \frac{2}{5}$

Activity 66—Probability and Complementary Events

1. $P = \frac{80}{90}$ or $\frac{8}{9}$ $C = \frac{10}{90}$ or $\frac{1}{9}$ **2.** $P = \frac{1}{2}$ $C = \frac{1}{2}$ **3.** $P = \frac{4}{12}$ or $\frac{1}{3}$ $C = \frac{8}{12}$ or $\frac{2}{3}$ **4.** $P = \frac{1}{7}$ $C = \frac{6}{7}$ **5.** $P = \frac{60}{480}$ or $\frac{1}{8}$ $C = \frac{420}{480}$ or $\frac{7}{8}$

Activity 67—Tree Diagrams and Sample Spaces

1. $\frac{1}{4}$ **2.** $\frac{1}{24}$ **3.** $\frac{1}{4}$ **4.** $\frac{1}{8}$ **5.** $\frac{1}{12}$ **6.** $\frac{1}{12}$ **7.** $\frac{2}{12}$ or $\frac{1}{6}$ **8.** $\frac{4}{12}$ or $\frac{1}{3}$ **9.** $\frac{3}{12}$ or $\frac{1}{4}$ **10.** $\frac{1}{12}$

Activity 68—Dependent and Independent Events

1. $\frac{1}{100}$ **2.** $\frac{1}{4}$ **3.** $\frac{1}{100}$ **4.** $\frac{1}{2{,}300}$ **5.** $\frac{11}{46}$

Activity 69—The Fundamental Principle of Counting

1. 7! = 5,040 **2.** 8 different outcomes **3.** 4! = 24 **4.** 2 • 4 = 8 **5.** will $\frac{4}{24} = \frac{1}{6}$; won't $\frac{20}{24} = \frac{5}{6}$

Activity 70—Fractions as Rational Numbers

1. $\frac{-16}{17}$ **2.** $\frac{7}{-9}$ **3.** $\frac{-1}{4}$ **4.** $-\frac{11}{12}$ **5.** $\frac{-3}{8}$ **6.** $-\frac{3}{10}$ **7.** $\frac{5}{9}$ **8.** $\frac{20}{26}$ **9.** $\frac{9}{12}$ **10.** $\frac{8}{42}$ **11.** $\frac{11}{16}$ **12.** $\frac{10}{32}$ **13.** They've both completed the same proportion of homework because $\frac{5}{8} = \frac{15}{24}$. **14.** The two companies are making the very same claim since $\frac{80}{100} = \frac{4}{5}$. **15.** $\frac{330}{2{,}970} = \frac{1}{9}$

Activity 71—Algebraic Fractions—Rational Expressions

1. no; $\frac{1}{3x^2}$ **2.** yes **3.** no; $\frac{1}{3p}$ **4.** no; $\frac{1}{6}$ **5.** yes **6.** yes **7.** no; $\frac{1}{b-9}$ **8.** yes **9.** no; $\frac{1}{1} = 1$ **10.** yes **11.** yes **12.** no; $\frac{1}{n-11}$ **13.** no; $\frac{1}{y+3}$ **14.** yes **15.** yes **16.** no; $\frac{1}{1} = 1$ **17.** no; $\frac{1}{1} = 1$ **18.** yes **19.** yes **20.** no; $\frac{1}{x-3}$ **21.** $\frac{x-8}{x+2}$ **22.** $\frac{(-1)(w-9)}{w-1}$ or $\frac{-(w-9)}{w-1}$ **23.** $\frac{1}{(2x+3)}$ **24.** factored $\frac{x+5}{(x+3)(x+5)}$; simplified $\frac{1}{x+3}$ **25.** $\frac{-1}{3}, -\frac{1}{3}$

Activity 72—Multiplying and Dividing Algebraic Fractions

1. $\frac{2}{21}$ **2.** $\frac{5}{12}$ **3.** $\frac{3}{8}$ **4.** $\frac{25}{6}$ or $4\frac{1}{6}$ **5.** $\frac{k^3}{m^3}$ **6.** $\frac{2}{(n-5)^2}$ or $\frac{2}{n^2 - 10n + 25}$ **7.** $\frac{d^2}{y^2 + d^2}$ **8.** $\frac{1}{2n^2}$ **9.** $\frac{3}{2}$ or $1\frac{1}{2}$ **10.** $\frac{4}{5}$ **11.** $\frac{39}{16}$ or $2\frac{7}{16}$ **12.** $\frac{9}{7}$ or $1\frac{2}{7}$ **13.** $\frac{3d}{5}$ **14.** $\frac{4}{m^4n^2}$ **15.** $7(z-6)$ or $7z - 42$ **16.** $\frac{1}{3b-4}$ **17.** $\frac{9}{w^2 - 81}$ **18.** $\frac{9}{2(w^2 - 81)}$ **19.** $\frac{3}{w^2 - 81}$ **20.** no; simplified $\frac{1}{x+y}$

Activity 73—Complex Fractions and the LCM

1. 12 **2.** 14 **3.** 6 **4.** 75 **5.** 36 **6.** 56 **7.** $96y$ **8.** $12n$ **9.** $54x$ **10.** $30a$ **11.** $\frac{4}{3}$ or $1\frac{1}{3}$ **12.** $\frac{1}{1}$ or 1 **13.** $\frac{7}{4}$ or $1\frac{3}{4}$ **14.** $\frac{36}{13}$ or $2\frac{10}{13}$ **15.** $\frac{7}{6}$ or $1\frac{1}{6}$ **16.** $\frac{63}{16}$ or $3\frac{15}{16}$ **17.** $\frac{50}{11}$ or $4\frac{6}{11}$ **18.** $\frac{36b}{5}$ **19.** $\frac{1}{10}$ **20.** $\frac{14}{15}$ **21.** $\frac{10x}{21}$ **22.** $\frac{7}{8y}$ **23.** $\frac{1}{4}$ dozen **24.** $\frac{1}{9}$ **25.** $\frac{17}{100}$

Activity 74—Least Common Multiples and Prime Factors

1. $\frac{4}{9}$ **2.** $\frac{18}{35}$ **3.** $\frac{14}{11}$ or $1\frac{3}{11}$ **4.** $\frac{3}{4}$ **5.** $\frac{33}{50}$ **6.** 9 **7.** a^2 **8.** $\frac{45}{44}$ or $1\frac{1}{44}$ **9.** $\frac{4b}{27}$ **10.** $\frac{7}{4(n-1)}$ **11.** $\frac{15}{14}$ or $1\frac{1}{14}$ **12.** $\frac{5a^2}{27}$ **13.** 72 seconds **14.** 168 cm **15.** every 18 months

Activity 75—Sums and Differences

1. 60 **2.** 18 **3.** 21 **4.** 22 **5.** 72 **6.** 54 **7.** 147 **8.** $18x$ **9.** $30w$ **10.** $63a^3$ **11.** $2d^5$ **12.** m^2n^4 **13.** $\frac{29}{24}$ or $1\frac{5}{24}$ **14.** $\frac{44}{45}$ **15.** $\frac{-2}{9}$ or $-\frac{2}{9}$ **16.** $\frac{29}{36}$ **17.** $\frac{29}{90}$ **18.** $\frac{2xy + 9}{3xy}$ **19.** $\frac{11r + 7w}{rw}$ **20.** $\frac{4d + 10}{15d}$ **21.** $\frac{3}{2r}$ **22.** $\frac{2}{21}$ **23.** $\frac{11}{3a}$ **24.** $\frac{53k}{42}$ **25.** $\frac{(-10y + 9m)}{90}$ **26.** $\frac{(5x - 1)}{10}$ **27.** $\frac{3p}{10}$ **28.** $\frac{a^2 + 4a + 1}{a^2b}$ **29.** $\frac{19}{45}$ **30.** $\frac{43}{60}$

Activity 76—Proportions and Fractions in Equations

1. $x = 45$ **2.** $w = 33$ **3.** $y = 6$ **4.** $n = -2$ **5.** $a = -3$ **6.** $c = 5$ **7.** 54 inches **8.** 12 inches **9.** 1,050 **10.** $\frac{35}{8}$ or $4\frac{3}{8}$ cups

Activity 77—More Solutions to Equations with Fractions

1. correct **2.** correct **3.** not correct **4.** correct **5.** not correct **6.** correct **7.** not correct **8.** correct **9.** $x = 30$ **10.** $y = 9$ **11.** $b = 33$ **12.** $w = 6$ **13.** $x = 60$ **14.** $\frac{46}{3}$ or $15\frac{1}{3}$ **15.** 25275

Activity 78—Denominators and Zero

1. $n = 14$ **2.** $m = \frac{1}{2}$ **3.** $d = \frac{-13}{14}$ **4.** $x = -15$ **5.** $a = 0$ **6.** $p = 0$ **7.** $n = 0$ **8.** $y = 0$ or $y = 1$ or $y = -1$ **9.** $a = 0$ or $a = \frac{1}{2}$ **10.** $a = 10$ or $a = -10$ **11.** $x = 2$ or $x = 5$ **12.** $r = 12$ or $r = -12$ **13.** $x = \frac{1}{2}$ or $x = -3$ **14.** $x = 0$ or $x = 3$ **15.** Lin is trying to divide by 0, but division by 0 is undefined.

Activity 79—The Coordinate System

1. III **2.** I **3.** IV **4.** I **5.** IV **6.** IV **7.** IV **8.** I **9.** II **10.** III **11.** *11* is located at (2, 1) **12.** *12* is located at (−2, 3) **13.** *13* is located at (3, 3) **14.** *14* is located at (−2, −3) **15.** *15* is located at (4, −2)

Activity 80—Graphing Equations

1. −7 **2.** −4 **3.** −1 **4.** 2 **5.** −10 **6.** −6 **7.** −2 **8.** 2 **9.** −4 **10.** −2 **11.** 0 **12.** 2 **13.** I **14.** a square **15.** the movement is straight up vertically, or "due north"

Activity 81—Intercepts of Lines

1. -1 **2.** 1 **3.** -2 **4.** 4 **5.** -5 **6.** -5 **7.** $-\frac{2}{3}$ **8.** 2 **9.** 1 **10.** -3 **11.** 0 **12.** 0 **13.** -4 **14.** 2

15.

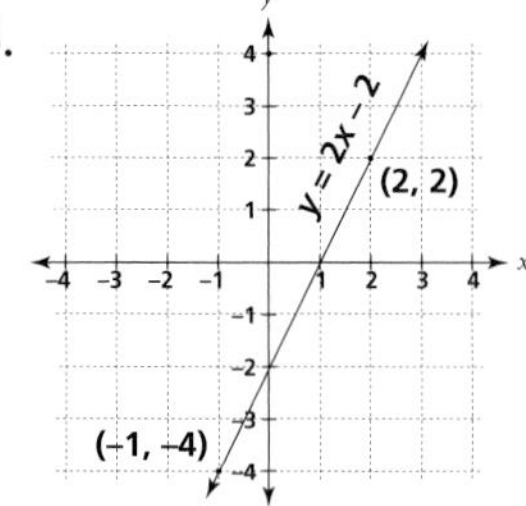

Activity 82—Slopes of Lines

1. negative **2.** positive **3.** neither **4.** negative **5.** 2 **6.** $\frac{5}{4}$ or $1\frac{1}{4}$ **7.** $\frac{1}{5}$ **8.** -2 **9.** accept any line with negative slope—that is, a line with end rays in quadrants II and IV **10.** accept any line with positive slope—that is, a line with end rays in quadrants I and III

Activity 83—Writing Linear Equations

1. $y = 3x - 1$ **2.** $y = -\frac{1}{2}x + 3$ **3.** $y = 3x - 5$ **4.** $y = 4x + 1$ **5.** $y = -\frac{2}{3}x + 7$ **6.** $y = -3x + 4$ **7.** $y = 2x + 7$ **8.** $y = -x + 5$ **9.** $y = \frac{3}{4}x + \frac{5}{4}$ **10.** $y = -\frac{2}{3}x$ **11.** $y = 3x - 4$ **12.** $y = -x + 5$ **13.** $y = 2x - 4$ **14.** $y = 3x - 2$ **15.** $y = -\frac{1}{2}x - \frac{3}{2}$, also accept $y = -\frac{1}{2}x - 1\frac{1}{2}$ **16.** $y = \frac{2}{3}x - 3$ **17.** $y = 2x$ **18.** $y = -\frac{1}{2}x + \frac{1}{2}$ **19.** $y = \frac{3}{2}x - 8$ **20.** $y = \frac{1}{2}x$

Activity 84—Lines as Functions

1. $-\frac{8}{3}$ or $-2\frac{2}{3}$; B **2.** $\frac{1}{5}$; A **3.** $\frac{7}{6}$ or $1\frac{1}{6}$; A **4.** $-\frac{5}{7}$; B **5.** $-\frac{1}{2}$; B **6.** 15 **7.** 0 **8.** -15 **9.** 0 **10.** 3 **11.** 8 **12.** -1 **13.** 9 **14.** $8\frac{1}{2}$ or $\frac{17}{2}$ **15.** -4

Activity 85—Domain and Range of a Function

1. 0, 1, 4, 8, 100 **2.** $-11, -10, 17, 206, 1{,}718$ **3.** $-6\frac{3}{8}, -6, -4\frac{1}{8}, -2\frac{1}{4}, 1\frac{1}{2}$ **4.** $104, 14, -4, -4, 24$ **5.** $-2, 13, 19, 25, 40$ **6.** $-19, -5, -3, 3, 15$ **7.** $-26, -20, -6, 16, 46$ **8.** $23, 9, -9, -7, 119$ **9.** $(-4, 5)$ $(-3, 6)$ domain: $-4, -3$ range: 5, 6 **10.** $(5, 3)$ $(6, -10)$ domain: 5, 6 range: $3, -10$ **11.** $(-123, 18)$ $(47, -190)$ domain: $-123, 47$ range: $18, -190$ **12.** $(2, 3)$ $(3, 7)$ $(4, 11)$ domain: 2, 3, 4 range: 3, 7, 11 **13.** $(-1, 9)$ $(9, 9)$ $(27, 9)$ $(43, 9)$ domain: $-1, 9, 27, 43$ range: 9 **14.** domain: $-6 \leq x \leq 6$ range: $-1 \leq y \leq 1$ **15.** domain: $-4 \leq x \leq 7$ range: $-2 \leq y \leq 4$

Activity 86—Graphing Inequalities: $y < mx + b$, $y > mx + b$

1. yes **2.** yes **3.** no **4.** no **5.** no **6.** no **7.** yes **8.** yes **9.** $y > 10$ **10.**

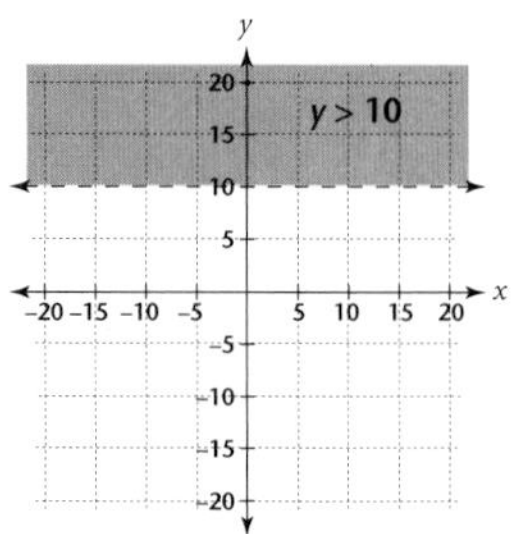

Activity 87—Graphing Inequalities: $y \leq mx + b$, $y \geq mx + b$

1. no **2.** yes **3.** yes **4.** yes **5.** no **6.** yes **7.** no **8.** no **9.** change the broken line of the equation to a solid line **10.** remove the shading below the broken line and add shading above the broken line

Activity 88—Graphs Without Numbers

1. D **2.** C **3.** A **4.** B **5.** accept any reasonable effort

Activity 89—Parallel Lines

1. $m = 3$ **2.** $m = -2$ **3.** $m = \frac{1}{2}$ **4.** $m = 1$ **5.** $m = 3$ **6.** $m = \frac{1}{3}$ **7.** $m = -1$ **8.** $m = -\frac{1}{2}$ **9.** rewrite as $y = 4x - 2$, $y = 4x + 3$ **10.** rewrite as $y = -x - 7$, $y = -x + 1$ **11.** rewrite as $y = 6x - 2$, $y = 6x - 4$ **12.** rewrite as $y = -\frac{3}{2}x - 3$, $y = -\frac{3}{2}x + \frac{1}{2}$ **13.** rewrite as $y = \frac{2}{5}x + 1$, $y = \frac{2}{5}x - \frac{3}{5}$ **14.** c **15.** b

Activity 90—Describing Parallel Lines

1. $m = \frac{3}{2}$ **2.** $m = 2$ **3.** $m = 5$ **4.** $m = 1$ **5.** $m = 3$ **6.** $m = \frac{5}{2}$ **7.** $m = -\frac{2}{3}$ **8.** $m = 1$ **9.** $m = 2$ **10.** $m = -\frac{2}{3}$ **11.** $m = -5$ **12.** $m = \frac{1}{2}$ **13.** $m = 2$ **14.** $m = -3$ **15.** a: Equation Set 2; b: Equation Set 1

Activity 91—Intersecting Lines—Common Solutions

1. yes, slopes are unequal, lines intersect **2.** no, slopes are equal, lines are parallel **3.** no, slopes are equal, lines are parallel **4.** yes, slopes are unequal, lines intersect **5.** yes, slopes are unequal, lines intersect **6.** yes, slopes are unequal, lines intersect **7.** no, slopes are equal, lines are parallel **8.** yes, slopes are unequal, lines intersect **9.** no, slopes are equal, lines are parallel **10.** yes, slopes are unequal, lines intersect **11.** match with *horizontal* **12.** match with *vertical* **13.** match with *slanting* **14.** yes, $y = -1$ describes a horizontal line, and $x = 2$ describes a vertical line **15.** no, both equations describe vertical lines, which are parallel and therefore cannot intersect.

Activity 92—Solving Linear Equations—Substitution

1. c **2.** $(1, 2)$ **3.** $(2, 3)$ **4.** $(4, -2)$ **5.** $(3, -1)$ **6.** $(4, 3)$ **7.** $(2, -\frac{3}{2})$ **8.** $(6, 6)$ **9.** $(3, 11)$ **10.** correct **11.** not correct **12.** correct **13.** not correct **14.** not correct **15.** correct

Activity 93—Solving Linear Equations—Elimination

1. yes, slopes are unequal, lines intersect **2.** no, slopes are equal, lines are parallel **3.** no, slopes are equal, lines are parallel **4.** yes, slopes are unequal, lines intersect **5.** no, slopes are equal, lines are parallel **6.** $(1, 1)$ **7.** $(-2, 3)$ **8.** $(1, 3)$ **9.** $(2, 5)$ **10.** $(4, 0)$ **11.** $(-2, -5)$ **12.** $(-3, 4)$ **13.** $(-\frac{9}{5}, \frac{18}{5})$ **14.** $(0, 8)$ **15.** $(3, 1)$

Activity 94—Graphing Systems of Linear Equations

1. Intersection: $(0, 1)$

2. Intersection: $(\frac{1}{2}, 2)$ **3.** Intersection: $(-2, 3)$ **4.** Intersection: $(0, 2)$ **5.** Intersection: $(4, 3)$

Activity 95—*And* Statements—Conjunctions

1. *T*—both are true **2.** *F*—both are false **3.** *T*—both are true **4.** *F*—second part is false **5.** *F*—first part is false **6.** *F*—first part is false **7.** *F*—both are false **8.** *T* **9.** *F* **10.** *T* **11.** *F* **12.** *T* **13.** *F* **14.** *T* **15.** *F*

Activity 96—Problem Solving Using Linear Equations

1. 215 cm and 105 cm **2.** 815 children's tickets, 2,445 adult tickets **3.** 94 white buttons, 30 black buttons **4.** 15, 5 **5.** small pizza—$6; salad—$2

Activity 97—Introduction to Matrices: Addition and Subtraction

1. 2×2 **2.** 3×3 **3.** 5×4 **4.** row 2, column 3 **5.** row 1, column 1 **6.** row 7, column 2 **7.** row 4, coulumn 7

8. $\begin{bmatrix} 20 & 30 \\ 0 & 3 \\ -40 & -70 \end{bmatrix}$ **9.** $\begin{bmatrix} 8 & 0 \\ -18 & -13 \end{bmatrix}$ **10.** $\begin{bmatrix} 891 & 735 \\ -739 & 409 \end{bmatrix}$

Activity 98—Multiplication of Matrices

1. $\begin{bmatrix} 6 & 16 \\ 10 & 18 \end{bmatrix}$ **2.** $\begin{bmatrix} 28 & 49 \\ 21 & 42 \\ 14 & 35 \end{bmatrix}$ **3.** $\begin{bmatrix} 10 & 50 \\ 20 & 60 \\ 30 & 70 \\ 40 & 80 \end{bmatrix}$

4. $\begin{bmatrix} 72 & 84 & 0 \\ 42 & 48 & 0 \\ 0 & 6 & 12 \end{bmatrix}$ **5.** $\begin{bmatrix} 2x & -x^2 \\ xy & 3x^2 \end{bmatrix}$ **6.** $\begin{bmatrix} 3a & 3b & 3c & 3d \\ 3y & 3x & 3z & 42 \end{bmatrix}$

7. $\begin{bmatrix} 137 & 135 \\ 179 & 177 \end{bmatrix}$

8. $\begin{bmatrix} xm + px + 12m & 2x + py + ma & 7x + pz + mb \\ ym + qx + 12a & 2y + qy + a^2 & 7y + qz + ab \\ zm + nx + 12b & 2z + ny + ab & 7z + nz + b^2 \end{bmatrix}$

9. $\begin{bmatrix} 1{,}168 & 291 & 315 & 1{,}050 \\ 972 & 634 & 253 & 2{,}832 \\ 1{,}608 & 574 & 479 & 2{,}764 \\ 5{,}575 & 1{,}346 & 1{,}166 & 5{,}078 \end{bmatrix}$

10. $\begin{bmatrix} 645 & 902 & 1{,}311 & 1{,}724 \\ 275 & 328 & 249 & 356 \\ 289 & 379 & 450 & 606 \\ 195 & 294 & 489 & 648 \end{bmatrix}$

Activity 99—Rational Numbers as Decimals

1. $0.\overline{36}$ **2.** $0.\overline{428571}$ **3.** $0.\overline{230769}$ **4.** $0.6\overline{0}$ **5.** $0.\overline{904761}$ **6.** $0.\overline{714285}$ **7.** $1.\overline{0}$ **8.** 40°C **9.** 84.2°F **10.** $123.\overline{3}$°C

Activity 100—Rational Number Equivalents

1. $\frac{2}{4}$ **2.** $\frac{18}{20}$ **3.** $\frac{1}{12}$ **4.** $\frac{4}{15}$ **5.** $\frac{7}{8}$ **6.** $\frac{6}{18}$ **7.** $\frac{9}{12}$ **8.** $\frac{11}{24}$ **9.** $\frac{8}{12}$ **10.** $\frac{1}{16}$ **11.** $\frac{7}{20}$ **12.** $\frac{11}{15}$ **13.** $\frac{17}{20}$ **14.** $\frac{11}{18}$ **15.** $\frac{31}{50}$ **16.** $\frac{17}{18}$ **17.** $\frac{9}{11}$ **18.** $\frac{189}{200}$ **19.** $0.1\overline{6}$ **20.** $0.8\overline{3}$

Activity 101—Irrational Numbers as Decimals

1. irrational **2.** rational **3.** rational **4.** irrational **5.** rational **6.** rational **7.** irrational **8.** irrational **9.** rational **10.** irrational **11.** irrational **12.** rational **13.** irrational **14.** rational **15.** irrational **16.** rational **17.** 20 inches **18.** 30.48 m **19.** 60 cm **20.** no, one side of the square tray is $\sqrt{112.4}$, or about 10.6 inches

Activity 102—Products and Quotients of Radicals

1. $\frac{6}{7}$ **2.** $a^2b^2\sqrt{a}$ **3.** $\frac{3}{5}$ **4.** $\frac{4}{11}$ **5.** $\frac{x}{8}$ **6.** $\frac{2}{9}$ **7.** $\frac{c}{6}$ **8.** $(a + b)^2$ **9.** $2\sqrt{13}$ **10.** $\frac{2a^3}{7b^4}$ **11.** $\frac{2x}{5y^2}$ **12.** $\frac{13}{w}$ **13.** $\frac{7}{12}$ **14.** $\frac{\sqrt{26}}{5}$ **15.** $\frac{\sqrt{15a}}{6a^2}$ **16.** $\frac{3y\sqrt{2}}{5}$ **17.** $2\sqrt{30}$ m

18. yes—the length of one side of a square is equal to the square root of the area of the square **19.** $7\sqrt{3}$ units **20.** $9\sqrt{5}$ feet

Activity 103—Sums and Differences of Radicals

1. $5\sqrt{7}$ **2.** $9\sqrt{3}$ **3.** $3\sqrt{5}$ **4.** $7\sqrt{5}$ **5.** $6\sqrt{10}$ **6.** $3x\sqrt{2x}$ **7.** $-7\sqrt{5}$ **8.** $2x\sqrt{7y} - 6y\sqrt{7y}$ **9.** $7\sqrt{10}$ feet **10.** $\sqrt{11}$ inches

Activity 104—Radicals and Fractions

1. $\frac{\sqrt{15}}{15}$ **2.** $3\sqrt{3}$ **3.** $\frac{\sqrt{10}}{10}$ **4.** $7\sqrt{2}$ **5.** $\frac{7\sqrt{3}}{6}$ **6.** $\frac{\sqrt{35}}{14}$ **7.** $\sqrt{2x}$

8. $\frac{3a\sqrt{5}}{5}$ **9.** $\sqrt{7} - 2$ **10.** $2\sqrt{2} - 2$ **11.** $\sqrt{3} + \sqrt{2}$ **12.** $\frac{k + k\sqrt{k}}{1 - k}$ or $\frac{k(1 + \sqrt{k})}{1 - k}$ **13.** $2 + \sqrt{6}$ **14.** $5\sqrt{3} - 5\sqrt{2}$ or $5(\sqrt{3} - \sqrt{2})$

15. $\frac{13\sqrt{35}}{350}$

Activity 105—Radicals in Equations

1. 36 **2.** 11 cm **3.** $5\sqrt{10}$ feet **4.** $2\sqrt{7}$ feet **5.** $2\sqrt{13}$ inches

Activity 106—Radicals and Exponents

1. $n^{\frac{1}{3}}$ **2.** $y^{\frac{1}{2}}$ **3.** $3^{\frac{1}{2}} \cdot d^{\frac{1}{2}}$ or $(3d)^{\frac{1}{2}}$ **4.** $x^{\frac{1}{5}}$ **5.** $k^{\frac{1}{4}}$ **6.** $9^{\frac{1}{3}} \cdot x^{\frac{1}{3}}$ or $(9x)^{\frac{1}{3}}$ **7.** $3^{\frac{1}{6}} \cdot a^{\frac{1}{6}}$ or $(3a)^{\frac{1}{6}}$ **8.** $7^{\frac{1}{5}} \cdot k^{\frac{1}{5}}$ or $(7k)^{\frac{1}{5}}$ **9.** $a^{\frac{7}{2}}$ **10.** $x^{\frac{7}{3}}$ **11.** $d^{\frac{7}{10}}$ **12.** $n^{\frac{13}{4}}$ **13.** $y^{\frac{4}{3}}$ **14.** 16 **15.** 9 **16.** 81 **17.** 9 **18.** 64

19. 125 **20.** 16 **21.** 1,000 **22.** 25 **23.** 10,000 **24.** 64

25. $4\sqrt{19}$ inches

Activity 107—Drawing and Using a Square Root Graph

1.

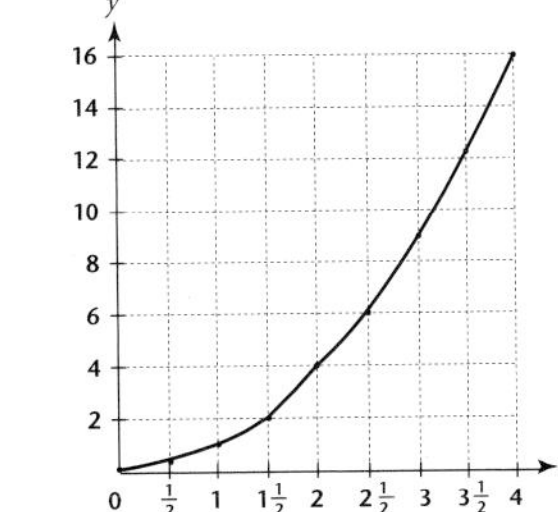

For problems **2–7** and **9–10**, accept any answer that is within 0.3 of the given answer and has the same whole number as the answer. Note that answer 8 must be exact. **2.** 1.7 **3.** 3.3 **4.** 2.8 **5.** 2.6 **6.** 3.5 **7.** 2.2 **8.** 3.0 (or 3) **9.** 3.6 **10.** 3.9

Activity 108—Angles and Angle Measure

1. 55° **2.** 125° **3.** 125° **4.** 60° **5.** 120° **6.** 120° **7.** 75° **8.** 105° **9.** 105° **10.** 18° **11.** 162° **12.** 162° **13.** 36°, 54° **14.** 70°, 20° **15.** 10°, 170°

Activity 109—Pairs of Lines in a Plane and in Space

1. alternate interior **2.** corresponding **3.** alternate interior **4.** supplementary **5.** 48° **6.** 132° **7.** 48° **8.** a **9.** c **10.** b

Activity 110—Angle Measures in a Triangle

1. 40° **2.** 30° **3.** list: *A, C, E, G*; list: *B, D, F, H* **4.** Cut out all the angles and fit them together, two at a time. Use a ruler to determine if any of the joined angles form a common straight line. Any such angle pairs are supplementary. **5.** The angles are equal because alternate interior angles of a transversal are equal.

Activity 111—Naming Triangles

1. yes **2.** yes **3.** no **4.** no **5.** no **6.** no **7.** yes **8.** Two of the sides are $8\frac{1}{2}$ inches and 11 inches, from the dimensions of the original sheet of typing paper. The third side is the hypotenuse of the triangle, so it will have a unique measurement. Accept any reasonable explanation for the hypotenuse—the cut side—such as "The slanted side goes sideways as well as up-and-down, so it must be longer than the long (11-inch) side of the original typing paper." **9.** The corner of the typing paper is squared off exactly—its angle measure must therefore be 90°. **10.** It is a right triangle, so one of the angles is 90°. That leaves only 90° for the other two angles, so no angle can be > 90°.

Activity 112—Quadrilaterals

1. b **2.** f **3.** a **4.** d **5.** c **6.** g **7.** h **8.** e **9.** each figure has 4 sides of equal length **10.** each figure has 4 sides; in each figure, at least 2 of the sides are parallel

Activity 113—Congruent and Similar Triangles

1. a, b **2.** a, c **3.** b, c **4.** a, b **5.** a, c

Activity 114—Trigonometric Ratios

1. 0.37 **2.** 0.93 **3.** 0.40 **4.** 0.98 **5.** 0.17 **6.** 5.67 **7.** 0.63 **8.** 0.78 **9.** 0.81 **10.** 0.85 **11.** 0.53 **12.** 1.60 **13–15.** Note: Students are not required to show the equations in their problem solutions. **13.** 11.3 feet, $\cos 20° = \frac{x}{12}$ **14.** 63 feet, $\sin 65° = \frac{x}{70}$ **15.** 17.5 feet, $\tan 70° = \frac{x}{6}$ Students must remember to add 1 foot to the solution of the equation.

Activity 115—Solutions by Factoring

1. $-6, 3$ **2.** $-4, -3$ **3.** $-10, 2$ **4.** 2, 4 **5.** $\frac{3}{2}$ (or $1\frac{1}{2}$), 8 **6.** $-3, -1$ **7.** 7 **8.** $-\frac{2}{3}, 1$ **9.** Tim is 7. Julio is 5. **10.** 4 cm [Equation: $x^2 + 32 = (x + 2)(2x)$]

Activity 116—Writing the Equations from Their Roots

1. $x^2 + 8x + 15 = 0$ **2.** $x^2 + 3x + 2 = 0$ **3.** $x^2 + 8x - 9 = 0$ **4.** $x^2 - 11x + 18 = 0$ **5.** $x^2 + 7x + 12 = 0$ **6.** $x^2 - 4x - 5 = 0$ **7.** $x^2 - 4x - 21 = 0$ **8.** $3x^2 - 4x - 4 = 0$ **9.** $x^2 - 9x + 14 = 0$ **10.** $3x^2 + 4x + 1 = 0$ **11.** $2x^2 + 5x - 3 = 0$ **12.** $6x^2 - x - 15 = 0$ **13.** $7x^2 + 10x + 3 = 0$ **14.** You can discard the negative root $(-3\frac{1}{3})$ because geometric figures cannot have negative dimensions. **15.** height = 9 inches; base = 4 inches[Equation: $2b^2 + b - 36 = 0$]

Activity 117—Solving by Completing the Square

1. $-6, 1$ **2.** 3, 5 **3.** $-4 - 2\sqrt{2}, -4 + 2\sqrt{2}$ **4.** 2, 4 **5.** $-3, -1$ **6.** $-1 - \sqrt{2}, -1 + \sqrt{2}$ **7.** $-\frac{3}{2}$ (or $-1\frac{1}{2}$), $\frac{1}{2}$ **8.** 5.3 inches, 2.3 inches [Equation: $x^2 + 3x - 12 = 0$] **9.** Terri, 4; Leah, 6 [Equation: $x^2 + 2x - 24 = 0$] **10.** long row, 17; short row, 9 [Equation: $x^2 + 8x - 153 = 0$]

Activity 118—Solving Using the Quadratic Formula

1. $-3, 6$ **2.** $-\frac{1}{2}, 2$ **3.** $-1, \frac{7}{2}$ (or $3\frac{1}{2}$) **4.** $-\frac{4}{3}$ (or $-1\frac{1}{3}$), 3 **5.** $-3, \frac{2}{3}$ **6.** $-\frac{2}{3}, 1$ **7.** $2 - \sqrt{11}, 2 + \sqrt{11}$ **8.** long row (length): 18 bushes; short row (width): 13 bushes. [Equation: $x^2 + 5x - 234 = 0$] **9.** large bag: 42 lb; small bag: 22 lb [Equation: $2x^2 - 2x - 924 = 0$] **10.** long row (length): 24 pieces; short row (width): 18 pieces [Equation: $x^2 + 6x - 432 = 0$]

Activity 119—Graphing Quadratic Equations

1. Chart: $(-1, 0)$, $(0, 3)$, $(1, 4)$, $(2, 3)$, $(3, 0)$.

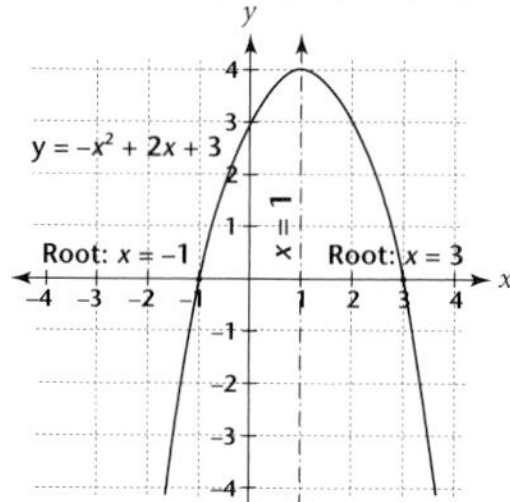

2. $x = 1$ **3.** see graph **4.** $-1, 3$ **5.** see graph

Alternative Activities

Alternative Activity 1—Arithmetic and Algebra

1. a and c **2.** b and c **3.** true **4.** open **5.** true **6.** false **7.** false **8.** true **9.** false **10.** true **11.** true **12.** false **13.** open **14.** false **15.** open **16.** true **17.** false **18.** true **19.** false **20.** false **21.** false **22.** true **23.** false **24.** false **25.** true

Alternative Activity 2—Representing Numbers Using Letters

1. false **2.** true **3.** false **4.** numerical **5.** algebraic **6.** algebraic **7.** multiplication; subtraction **8.** multiplication **9.** $6 \cdot 10$ (or $10 \cdot 6$) **10.** $5m$ (or $5 \cdot m$)

Alternative Activity 3—Integers on the Number Line

1. numerical **2.** none **3.** multiplication **4.** algebraic **5.** division; multiplication **6.** *n* **7.** -3 **8.** -6 **9.** 2 **10.** 7 **11.** 15 **12.** -7 **13.** 11 **14.** -13 **15.** 5 **16.** 1 **17.** 8 **18.** A **19.** A **20.** 4

Alternative Activity 4—Adding Integers

1. 32 **2.** 3 **3.** 5 **4.** 5 **5.** 1 **6.** 0 **7.** 1 **8.** 4 **9.** 4 **10.** -2 **11.** -1 **12.** -67 **13.** -12 **14.** 28 **15.** -20 **16.** 71 **17.** 2 **18.** -100 **19.** 80 **20.** -20

Alternative Activity 5—Choosing a Classroom Calculator

Responses will vary.

Alternative Activity 6—Subtracting Integers

1. 25 **2.** -2 **3.** 9 **4.** -10 **5.** 9 **6.** -12 **7.** -5 **8.** 4 **9.** 2 **10.** 9 **11.** 0 **12.** 8 **13.** -10 **14.** 112° **15.** $28 - (-3) = 31$

Alternative Activity 7—Multiplying Integers
1. −7 **2.** −7 **3.** −14 **4.** 1 **5.** −22 **6.** 4 **7.** 31 **8.** −12 **9.** 9 **10.** −8 **11.** 10 **12.** 15 **13.** 0 **14.** −42 **15.** −45 **16.** 39 **17.** 49 **18.** 15 **19.** 0 **20.** −16 **21.** 18 **22.** 40 **23.** −28 **24.** 50 minutes **25.** (3)(−3)

Alternative Activity 8—Dividing Positive and Negative Integers
1. 1 **2.** −5 **3.** −3 **4.** 17 **5.** −11 **6.** −7 **7.** −9 **8.** −4 **9.** 12 **10.** −9 **11.** 2 **12.** −5 **13.** −10 **14.** −7 **15.** 5 **16.** −2 **17.** 6 **18.** 31 **19.** −6 **20.** b

Alternative Activity 9—Simplifying Expressions—One Variable
1. numerical **2.** algebraic **3.** numerical **4.** algebraic **5.** numerical **6.** numerical **7.** algebraic **8.** numerical **9.** $3 + (-4) = -1$ **10.** $8 + (-12) = -4$ **11.** $-8 + (-4) = -12$ **12.** $-8 + 4 = -4$ **13.** $8 + (-9) = -1$ **14.** $8y$ **15.** $10r + 11$ **16.** $11h - 14$ **17.** $7k + 4$ **18.** $3x - 1$ **19.** $-3m$ **20.** $13n + 14$

Alternative Activity 10—Simplifying Expressions—Several Variables
1. −7 **2.** 8 **3.** −3 **4.** 5 **5.** −4 **6.** −3 **7.** 1 **8.** −7 **9.** $5k + y$ **10.** $2h - 3w + 1$ **11.** $6n + 12p$ **12.** $-d - 2j + 15$ **13.** $a + 5b + 5$ **14.** $-18 - y - 2x$ **15.** 3 oranges + 3 apples + 1 peach (in any order)

Alternative Activity 11—Positive Exponents
1. d^3 **2.** k^9 **3.** w^2 **4.** c^6 **5.** b^7 **6.** x^{10} **7.** a^{10} **8.** m^9 **9.** 10 **10.** 12 **11.** 4 **12.** 11 **13.** 2, 2, 2, 2 **14.** 2^4 **15.** 16

Alternative Alternative Activity 12—Formulas with Variables
1. 27 m **2.** 90 cm **3.** 84 cm **4.** 6 km **5.** 15 m **6.** 55 mm **7.** 60 cm **8.** 1,000 mm **9.** $2l + 2w$ **10.** s^2

Alternative Activity 13—Commutative Property of Addition
1. 17 **2.** $4x$ **3.** $7p$ **4.** 8.8 **5.** g **6.** 31,774 **7.** $700n$ **8.** 87 **9.** 87 **10.** commutative property of addition

Alternative Activity 14—Commutative Property of Multiplication
1. $(7k)(35)$ **2.** $(30)1.5$ **3.** ba **4.** $32 \cdot 16$ **5.** qp **6.** $(4z)z$ **7.** $(12r)(11m)$ **8.** $2(4b)$ **9.** Kim and Tomas should be circled. **10.** Designs a and b will give the same amount of memory. The commutative property of multiplication proves that both products will be equal.

Alternative Activity 15—Associative Property of Addition
In problems **1–6**, both sums must be correct for students to receive any credit. **1.** $(10) + 3 = 13; 8 + (5) = 13$ **2.** $(17) + 9 = 26; 10 + (16) = 26$ **3.** $(28) + 12 = 40; 15 + (25) = 40$ **4.** $70 + (15) = 85; (75) + 10 = 85$ **5.** $14 + (12) = 26; (23) + 3 = 26$ **6.** $7 + (34) = 41; (29) + 12 = 41$ In problems **7–9**, both rewritten versions of the expression must be correct for students to receive any credit. The order of the rewritten expressions is irrelevant. **7.** $(a + b) + 2c; a + (b + 2c)$ **8.** $(x + y) + 4; x + (y + 4)$ **9.** $(6n + 5p) + 8r; 6n + (5p + 8r)$ **10.** The same number. Because of the associative property of addition, the numbers of students can be added in various groupings without affecting the total.

Alternative Activity 16—Associative Property of Multiplication
1. (no check) **2.** (check) **3.** (check) **4.** (check) **5.** (no check) **6.** (check) **7.** (check) **8.** (no check) **9.** a **10.** b

Alternative Activity 17—The Distributive Property—Multiplication
1. n **2.** a **3.** d **4.** a **5.** a **6.** n **7.** d **8.** a **9.** d **10.** Method 1

Alternative Activity 18—The Distributive Property—Factoring
1. $36 + 9w$ **2.** $2j + 2k$ **3.** $-7a + 7b$ **4.** $24 + 6n$ **5.** $4(y - z)$ **6.** $9(p + 20)$ **7.** $7(x^2 + y^5)$ **8.** b **9.** b **10.** $3(x - y)$

Alternative Activity 19—Properties of Zero
1. false **2.** true **3.** true **4.** false **5.** 0 **6.** 122 **7.** 12 **8.** 0 **9.** p **10.** 0 **11.** 9 **12.** 0 **13.** 68 **14.** −3 **15.** c

Alternative Activity 20—Properties of 1
1. 1 **2.** 0 **3.** 17 **4.** 0 **5.** 1 **6.** 0 **7.** pq^3r^2 **8.** 0 **9.** g^2 **10.** 0 **11.** 0 **12.** 0 **13.** 0 **14.** 0 **15.** c

Alternative Activity 21—Powers and Roots
Check matching lines for **1–5**. **1.** d **2.** e **3.** a **4.** c **5.** b **6.** 8 **7.** 6 **8.** $\frac{1}{3}$ **9.** 106 ft **10.** 22,500 sq ft; 2,088.49 sq m

Alternative Activity 22—More on Powers and Roots
1. −27 **2.** 25 **3.** −4 **4.** 9 **5.** −25 **6.** 125 **7.** 8 **8.** 5, −5 **9.** −3 **10.** 4 **11.** 4 **12.** −4 **13.** 16 **14.** 4, 5 **15.** No. An edge of one building block is $\sqrt[3]{27} = 3$ cm; $11 \cdot 3$ cm $= 33$ cm, which is longer than the shelf of 31 cm.

Alternative Activity 23—Order of Operations
1. 50 **2.** 4 **3.** −9 **4.** 41 **5.** 16 **6.** 64 **7.** 1 **8.** −3 **9.** 10 **10.** 0 **11.** $14k$ **12.** $-7y$ **13.** $48y$ **14.** 0 **15.** $45n$ **16.** $8d^2$ **17.** $8d^2$ **18.** b **19.** (1) exponent; (2) multiply **20.** 162

Alternative Activity 24—Writing Equations
1. $4y - 20 = 2$ **2.** $6y + 7 = 12$ **3.** $7 + y = 8$ **4.** $y - 13 = 2$ **5.** $3y + 17 = 56$ **6.** $6 + y = -2$ **7.** $5y - 16 = 0$ **8.** $3y - 3 = -4$ **9.** c **10.** b

Alternative Activity 25—Solving Equations: $x - b = c$
1. $k = -1$ **2.** $x = 6$ **3.** $w = 0$ **4.** $n = 9$ **5.** $d = 8$ **6.** 5 was added to one side of the equation only. It should have been added to both sides. **7.** 8 was added to one side of the equation and 7 to the other side. 8 should have been added to both sides. **8.** 17 **9.** 56°F **10.** 13

Alternative Activity 26—Solving Equations: $x + b = c$
1. $a = 4$ **2.** $d = -9$ **3.** $d = 3$ **4.** $n = 22$ **5.** $q = 14$ **6.** $n = 24$ **7.** $c = 17$ **8.** $j = 88$ **9.** 590 miles **10.** 22

Alternative Activity 27—Solving Multiplication Equations
1. $9m = 45; m = 5$ **2.** $2d = 48; d = 24$ **3.** $9a = -45; a = -5$ **4.** $4j = -8; j = -2$ **5.** $-6k = 30; k = -5$ **6.** $10n = 500; n = 50$ **7.** 195 **8.** 1,300 m **9.** 93 **10.** 102.9°F

Alternative Activity 28—Solving Equations with Fractions
1. $\frac{1}{5}p = 5; p = 25$ **2.** $\frac{1}{8}x = 2; x = 16$ **3.** $\frac{9}{10}n = 36; n = 40$ **4.** $\frac{3}{4}q = -12; q = -16$ **5.** $-\frac{2}{3}w = 6; w = -9$ **6.** 150 **7.** 16 **8.** 300 cm **9.** 105 **10.** 280

Alternative Activity 29—Solving Equations—More Than One Step
1. incorrect; In step 1 you have to subtract 2 from each side; in step 2 the expression was simplified inaccurately. **2.** correct. **3.** correct **4.** 3 **5.** 204

Alternative Activity 30—Equations Without Numbers

1. $x = \frac{a+c}{b}$ **2.** $x = \frac{c-b}{a}$ **3.** $x = \frac{-a}{c}$ **4.** $x = \frac{ab}{c}$ **5.** $x = \frac{bc}{a}$ **6.** $x = \frac{ab}{-c}$ **7.** $x = \frac{b}{a+c}$ **8.** $a = \frac{c}{b}$ **9.** 24 **10.** 18

Alternative Activity 31—Formulas

1. $a = P - b - c$ or $a = P - (b + c)$ **2.** $c = P - a - b$ or $c = P - (a + b)$ **3.** $s = \sqrt{A}$ **4.** $s = \sqrt[3]{V}$ **5.** $h = \frac{2A}{(b_1 + b_2)}$

Alternative Activity 32—The Pythagorean Theorem

1. 4.5 **2.** 5.4 **3.** 7.3 **4.** 26, 27 **5.** 26.9

Alternative Activity 33—Inequalities on the Number Line

1. $x > 2$ **2.** $x \leq -1$ **3.** $x = 3$ **4.** T **5.** F **6.** F **7.** T **8.** T **9.** F **10.** 50 m

Alternative Activity 34—Solving Inequalities with One Variable

1. $g \geq 0$ **2.** $r < -4$ **3.** $q < -4$ **4.** $m > 7$ **5.** $n \geq 11$ **6.** $y \geq 6$ **7.** $k \leq 210$ **8.** $n < \frac{2}{5}(100)$ (accept $n < 40$) **9.** $w \geq \frac{7}{10}(400)$ (accept $w \geq 280$) **10.** $k \geq \frac{1}{3}(18)$ (accept $k \geq 6$)

Alternative Activity 35—Writing Equations—Odd and Even Integers

1. Don 8; Jay 9; Brett 10 **2.** 7 **3.** Delia has 6 earrings (or 3 pairs). Reynal has 8 earrings (or 4 pairs). **4.** Mom's bag 9; Dad's bag 8 **5.** small 5; medium 7; large 9

Alternative Activity 36—Using the 1% Solution to Solve Problems

1. 5,760 **2.** 144 **3.** 1,040 **4.** 143 **5.** 40% **6.** 434 **7.** 560 **8.** 72% **9.** 396 **10.** 1,260

Alternative Activity 37—Using the Percent Equation

1. 32 **2.** 100 **3.** 26 **4.** 30 **5.** 48 **6.** 80% **7.** 300 **8.** 3,744 **9.** 8,900 **10.** 16%

Alternative Activity 38—Solving Distance, Rate, and Time Problems

1. t **2.** r **3.** t **4.** r **5.** 168 miles **6.** 44 km/h **7.** 24 miles **8.** 190 km/h **9.** 62.5 mph **10.** $2\frac{1}{2}$ hours

Alternative Activity 39—Using a Common Unit—Cents

1. 1,900¢ **2.** 2,217¢ **3.** 848¢ **4.** 32¢ **5.** 13 nickels, 13 quarters **6.** 8 coins of each type **7.** Lila—48 dimes; Marcie—24 dimes **8.** Gina—33 quarters; Antonio—11 quarters **9.** 5 quarters, 5 dimes, 10 nickels, 30 pennies **10.** 98 dimes, 49 nickels, 196 pennies

Alternative Activity 40—Calculating Simple Interest

1. $88.50 **2.** $45.00 **3.** $1,150.00 **4.** $900.00 **5.** Michael's account had the higher rate. Using the formula $r = \frac{I}{pt}$ and substituting I, p, and t for each person, we find that Kitra's rate was 6.5% (0.065) and Michael's was 7% (0.07).

Alternative Activity 41—Deriving a Formula for Mixture Problems

1. $0.97 per pound **2.** 5 ounces of raisins; 5 ounces of dried apples **3.** $0.95 (or 95¢) per pound **4.** 36 pounds of granola; 4 pounds of dried bananas **5.** 10 quarters, 20 nickels, and 60 dimes

Alternative Activity 42—Ratio and Proportion

1. 3:2 **2.** 2:3 **3.** 1:3 **4.** 3:1 **5.** $\frac{3}{1}$ **6.** $\frac{1}{10}$ **7.** $\frac{5}{6}$ **8.** $\frac{3}{400}$ **9.** Yes. To confirm, make an equation with the two ratios: $\frac{18}{9} = \frac{16}{8}$. Cross multiplication reveals that $18 \cdot 8 = 16 \cdot 9$, because simplifying, $144 = 144$. **10.** 36 tulips

Alternative Activity 43—Exponents

1. 2^8 or 256 **2.** x^4 **3.** y^6 **4.** m^0 or 1 **5.** r^{15} **6.** k^1 or k **7.** $(n - m)^6$ **8.** n^9 **9.** Divide exponents by subtracting: $k^{2-2} = k^0$. The value of k^0 is 1. (accept "A fraction with identical numerator and denominator resolves to 1.") **10.** The answer is 3 cm. Calculation: $\frac{3^3}{3^2} = 3^{3-2} = 3^1 = 3$. (accept the calculation $\frac{3^3}{3^2} = \frac{27}{9} = 3$)

Alternative Activity 44—Negative Exponents

1. -1 **2.** 2^2 **3.** -2 **4.** -2 **5.** -6 (accept $2 - 8$) **6.** y, $y \neq 0$ **7.** -3 **8.** -3 **9.** 3 **10.** -4 **11.** -2 **12.** -2 **13.** 0 **14.** -3 **15.** 10,000 **16.** 7 **17.** 9 **18.** 1,000,000 **19.** k **20.** -3

Alternative Activity 45—Exponents and Scientific Notation

1. 0.00227 **2.** 377,200 **3.** 97 **4.** 1,335,860 **5.** 0.0000133586 **6.** 0.422 **7.** $1.0(10^4)$ **8.** $9.3(10^7)$ **9.** $4.0(10^9)$ **10.** $3.0(10^5)$

Alternative Activity 46—Computing in Scientific Notation

1. $7.43(10^4)$ **2.** $4.18(10^5)$ **3.** $4.0(10^7)$ **4.** $3.0(10^3)$ **5.** $1.0(10^6)$

Alternative Activity 47—Defining and Naming Polynomials

1. 3 **2.** 4 **3.** 7 **4.** 3 **5.** 1 **6.** 4 **7.** 3 **8.** 6 **9.** 1 **10.** 3 **11.** 3 **12.** 4 **13.** 8 **14.** 5 **15.** has more than one variable **16.** has a negative exponent **17.** has a variable in the denominator **18.** has a negative exponent Answers will vary in problems **19–20.** **19.** Expression should include three terms in proper order, in which the first term contains k^2. Example: $k^2 - 2k + 5$. **20.** Expression should include two terms in proper order, in which the first term contains y. Example: $7y + 12$.

Alternative Activity 48—Adding and Subtracting Polynomials

1. $7a^3 - a - 2$ **2.** $18n^3 - 2n^2 - 11n - 17$ **3.** $3s^2$ **4.** $k^3 + 3k^2 + 3k + 4$ **5.** $6x^4 - 3x^3 + 3x^2$

Alternative Activity 49—Multiplying Polynomials

1. $6b^2 + 5b - 14$ **2.** $6n^4 + 12n^3$ **3.** $3y^7 + 5y^6 - y^4 - 7y^3 + 3y^2$ **4.** $x^3 + x^2 - 5x - 5$ **5.** $7x^3 - 7x^2 + 5$ **6.** $5n^4 + 8n^2 - 7n + 3$ **7.** $9k^3 + 11k^2 - 9k - 11$ **8.** $2d^3 + 5d^2 - 3d + 7$ **9.** $x^2 - 2x - 24$ **10.** $x^4 + 4x^3 + 3x^2 + 16x + 48$

Alternative Activity 50—Special Polynomial Products

1. $-$ (the minus sign) **2.** $d - f$ (accept the exponent 2) **3.** $-$ (the minus sign) **4.** m^2 **5.** $p + q$ **6.** $x + y$ (accept the exponent 2) **7.** $k^2 + 2kr + r^2$ square units **8.** $a^2 - 2ab + b^2$ square units **9.** $n^3 + 6n^2 + 12n + 8$ cubic units **10.** $(n + r)(n - r) = n^2 - r^2$

Alternative Activity 51—Dividing a Polynomial by a Monomial

1. $4a^3 - 3a^2 - 7a + 6$ **2.** $(4a^3 - 3a^2 - 7a + 6)(-3) = -12a^3 + 9a^2 + 21a - 18$ **3.** $x^2 - 2x + 3$ **4.** $(x^2 - 2x + 3)(7x) = 7x^3 - 14x^2 + 21x$ **5.** incorrect; corrected answer $3x^2 - 7x + 27$ **6.** correct **7.** incorrect; corrected answer $2k^3 - 4k^2 - k + 7$ **8.** incorrect; corrected answer $n^3 + 8n^2 - 12n - 6$ **9.** correct **10.** correct

Alternative Activity 52—Dividing a Polynomial by a Binomial
1. 6 **2.** 8 **3.** 1 **4.** 3 **5.** 4 **6.** 4 **7.** 3 **8.** 2 **9.** 9 **10.** $a + 5$ **11.** $(a + 5)(a + 5) = (a^2 + 10a + 25)$ **12.** $(x - 3)$ r-4 **13.** $(x + 2)(x - 3) + (-4) = (x^2 - x - 10)$ **14.** $(n - 4)$ r3 **15.** $(n - 4)(n - 4) + 3 = (n^2 - 8n + 19)$

Alternative Activity 53—Polynomials in Two or More Variables
1. 7 **2.** 19 **3.** $8\frac{1}{9}$ **4.** 31 **5.** $68\frac{1}{4}$ **6.** 49 **7.** 37 **8.** 64 **9.** 138 **10.** 66 **11.** 0 **12.** 2,240 **13.** 95 **14.** 16 **15.** 0

Alternative Activity 54—Greatest Common Factor
1. 46 **2.** 5 **3.** $12p$ **4.** $11c^2$ **5.** $5a^2b^2$ **6.** 144 **7.** 3,528 **8.** 6,400 **9.** 576 **10.** 36,864 **11.** 864 **12.** 144 **13.** 8,100 **14.** 12,544 **15.** You can rule out the even numbers in the range (146, 148, 150, 152, 154). You can also rule out numbers that can be divided by 5—numbers ending in 0 or 5. The remaining possibilities: 147, 149, 151, 153. (Accept any reasonable answer.)

Alternative Activity 55—Factoring Polynomials
1. y; $y(5y - 1)$ **2.** 6; $6(-r + 3t)$ or $-6(r - 3t)$ **3.** $3xy^2$; $3xy^2(x + 2y)$ **4.** 4; $4(a + 2b - 3c)$ **5.** $2ab$; $2ab(6a - 5b)$ **6.** $2n$; $2n(3m^2 + 11m - 4)$ **7.** $3n^2$; $3n^2(4n^2 - 2n + 1)$ **8.** $2j^2$; $2j^2(1 + 2k)$ **9.** $5k^2 + 7k + 11$, it cannot be factored because there is no GCF of these three terms other than 1 **10.** c; it is the factored form of $2a^2 + 4a + 4$.

Alternative Activity 56—Factoring Trinomials: $x^2 + bx + c$
1. $(x + 2)(x + 8)$ **2.** $(x + 5)(x + 2)$ **3.** $(x + 16)(x + 1)$ **4.** $(r + 3)(r + 4)$ **5.** $2(x - 2)(x - 11)$ **6.** $2k(k + 8)(k - 2)$ **7.** $2y(x + 5)(x - 4)$ **8.** $b^2(b - 3)(b + 6)$ **9.** $3(x - 3)(x - 4)$ **10.** The GCF is 2, so factoring produces $2(x^2 - 3x - 4)$. This factored expression shows that the piece is twice the size (area) of the other piece.

Alternative Activity 57—Factoring Trinomials: $ax^2 + bx + c$
1. $x^3(5x + 1)(x - 1)$ **2.** $7(2b + 3)(b + 1)$ **3.** $10(7a + 3)(a + 1)$ **4.** $2(2x + 3)(3x - 5)$ **5.** $2(2n + 5)(4n + 3)$ **6.** $3c(2d - 3)(d + 5)$ **7.** $4x^2(y + 3)(2y - 1)$ **8.** $-2x(x - 2)(4x - 3)$ **9.** $y^2(2y + 5)(6y - 1)$ **10.** two sides are $(2n - 3)$ cm, and two sides are $(n + 4)$ cm; the completely factored expression is $4(2n - 3)(n + 4)$

Alternative Activity 58—Factoring Expressions: $a^2 - b^2$
1. $(r^2 - 8)(r^2 + 8)$ **2.** $(5a + 4b)(5a - 4b)$ **3.** $(a^6 + 5)(a^6 - 5)$ **4.** $(r + 12)(r - 12)$ **5.** $(n^8 + 14)(n^8 - 14)$ **6.** $(2y + 6z)(2y - 6z)$ **7.** $(x^8 + 4)(x^8 - 4)$ **8.** $(d^8 + 2x)(d^8 - 2x)$ **9.** $(x^{16} + 4)(x^{16} - 4)$ **10.** $(a^2 - 3^2)$ or $(a^2 - 9)$; factored expression $(a + 3)(a - 3)$

Alternative Activity 59—Factoring Expressions: $a^2 + 2ab + b^2$
1. 16 **2.** 48 **3.** 144 **4.** 48 **5.** 256 **6.** $(x - 5)^2$ **7.** $(2b - 4)^2$ **8.** $(3p + 10r)^2$ **9.** factored form $(a + b)(a + b)$ or $(a + b)^2$; unfactored form $a^2 + 2ab + b^2$ **10.** $(r^4 + 12)$ is a factor of $(r^8 + 24r^4 + 144)$ because $(r^8 + 24r^4 + 144)$ factors into $(r^4 + 12)(r^4 + 12)$; also accept $(r^4 + 12)$ is the square root of $(r^8 + 24r^4 + 144)$

Alternative Activity 60—Zero as a Factor
1. $v = 16$ **2.** $p = -8$ **3.** $n = -12$ or 16 **4.** $d = -7$ or 5 **5.** $m = 7$ or 8 **6.** $w = 22$ **7.** $x = -6$ or 6 **8.** $r = -13$ or -11 **9.** $n = 0$, Clarissa has no nickels. **10.** $4k = 0$, since $4 \neq 0$, k must $= 0$; if there are no crackers in the box, then surely there are none in the plastic tubes.

Alternative Activity 61—Solving Quadratic Equations—Factoring
1. $-10, 1$ **2.** -4 **3.** $\frac{-13}{3}, 4$ **4.** factored trinomial $(2y - 3)(y - 5)$; solutions: $\frac{3}{2}, 5$ **5.** factored trinomial $(n + 8)(n - 5)$; The measurement of a side of a square (or other geometric figure) cannot be a negative value; of solutions -8 and 5, only 5 is reasonable.

Alternative Activity 62—Organizing Data
1. yes **2.** students who read 21–25 books **3.** 3 **4.** 10 **5.** Though answers will vary, students should express the idea that the person who read 21–25 books was exceptional in the class. For instance, students may write something like "that person is very smart" or "that person can read fast." **6.** stem 1, leaf 7 **7.** stem 4, leaf 4 **8.** stem 3, leaf 6 **9.** stem 4, leaf 7 **10.** stem 3, leaf 2

Alternative Activity 63—Range, Mean, Median, and Mode
1. \$1.29, \$2.00, \$2.10, \$2.19, \$3.30, \$3.99, \$5.71, \$5.71 **2.** \$4.42 **3.** \$3.29 **4.** \$2.75 (Calculation: The two middle values in this even-numbered data set are \$2.19 and \$3.30. Taking their mean [\$2.19 + \$3.30] ÷ 2 = \$2.75.) **5.** \$5.71 **6.** 10, 16, 16, 19, 22, 24, 25, 32, 45, 61 **7.** 51 **8.** 27 **9.** 23 (Calculation: The two middle values in this even-numbered data set are 22 and 24. Taking their mean [22 + 24] ÷ 2 = 23.) **10.** 16

Alternative Activity 64—Box-and-Whiskers Plots
1. 0, 2, 3, 7, 8, 8, 9, 13, 15, 15, 16, 21, 22, 23, 24 **2.** 0 **3.** 24 **4.** 13 **5.** 7 **6.** 21 **7.** dot at 13 **8.** dots at 0 and 24 **9.** dots at 7 and 21 **10.** box enclosing the data between the lower quartile (dot at 7) and the upper quartile (dot at 21), whiskers extending from the box to 0 and 24, a vertical line at the median (13)

Alternative Activity 65—The Probability Fraction
1. $\frac{4}{5}$ **2.** $\frac{2}{75}$ **3.** $\frac{1}{10}$ **4.** $\frac{1}{3}$ **5.** $\frac{40}{100} = \frac{4}{10}$

Alternative Activity 66—Probability and Complementary Events
1. $P = \frac{90}{100}$ or $\frac{9}{10}$ $C = \frac{10}{100}$ or $\frac{1}{10}$ **2.** $P = \frac{1}{3}$ $C = \frac{2}{3}$ **3.** $P = \frac{4}{12}$ or $\frac{1}{3}$ $C = \frac{8}{12}$ or $\frac{2}{3}$ **4.** $P = \frac{1}{7}$ $C = \frac{6}{7}$ **5.** $P = \frac{60}{480}$ or $\frac{1}{8}$ $C = \frac{420}{480}$ or $\frac{7}{8}$

Alternative Activity 67—Tree Diagrams and Sample Spaces
1. $\frac{1}{4}$ **2.** $\frac{1}{4}$ **3.** $\frac{1}{2}$ **4.** $\frac{1}{48}$ **5.** $\frac{1}{12}$ **6.** $\frac{1}{12}$ **7.** $\frac{2}{12}$ or $\frac{1}{6}$ **8.** $\frac{4}{12}$ or $\frac{1}{3}$ **9.** $\frac{3}{12}$ or $\frac{1}{4}$ **10.** $\frac{1}{12}$

Alternative Activity 68—Dependent and Independent Events
1. $\frac{1}{25}$ **2.** $\frac{1}{4}$ **3.** $\frac{1}{100}$ **4.** $\frac{1}{2{,}300}$ **5.** $\frac{11}{46}$

Alternative Activity 69—The Fundamental Principle of Counting
1. $5! = 120$ **2.** $7! = 5{,}040$ **3.** $4! = 24$ **4.** $2 \cdot 4 = 8$ **5.** will $\frac{4}{24} = \frac{1}{6}$; won't $\frac{20}{24} = \frac{5}{6}$

Alternative Activity 70—Fractions as Rational Numbers
1. $-\frac{16}{17}$ **2.** $\frac{-7}{9}$ **3.** $-\frac{11}{12}$ **4.** $\frac{3}{-8}$ **5.** $-\frac{5}{9}$ **6.** $\frac{9}{12}$ **7.** $\frac{1}{6}$ **8.** $\frac{11}{16}$ **9.** Terry's claim is true, because $\frac{5}{8} = \frac{15}{24}$ and $\frac{5}{8} < \frac{7}{8}$ **10.** $\frac{330}{2{,}970} = \frac{1}{9}$

Alternative Activity 71—Algebraic Fractions—Rational Expressions

1. no; $\frac{1}{4x^2}$ **2.** no; $\frac{1}{2x}$ **3.** yes **4.** no; $\frac{1}{6}$ **5.** no; $\frac{r}{5}$ **6.** yes **7.** no; $\frac{1}{b-9}$ **8.** yes **9.** yes **10.** no; $\frac{a^2}{6b^2}$ **11.** no; $\frac{1}{n-11}$ **12.** yes **13.** yes **14.** no; $\frac{1}{1} = 1$ **15.** yes **16.** yes **17.** $\frac{x-8}{x+2}$ **18.** $\frac{(-1)(w-9)}{w-1}$ or $\frac{-(w-9)}{w-1}$ **19.** factored $\frac{x+5}{(x+3)(x+5)}$; simplified $\frac{1}{x+3}$ **20.** $\frac{-1}{3}, -\frac{1}{3}$

Alternative Activity 72—Multiplying and Dividing Algebraic Fractions

1. $\frac{3}{35}$ **2.** $\frac{1}{8}$ **3.** $\frac{3}{8}$ **4.** $\frac{25}{6}$ or $4\frac{1}{6}$ **5.** $\frac{2}{(n-5)^2}$ or $\frac{2}{n^2-10n+25}$ **6.** $\frac{y^2}{y^2+d^2}$ **7.** $\frac{8}{3}$ or $2\frac{2}{3}$ **8.** $\frac{6}{5}$ or $1\frac{1}{5}$ **9.** $\frac{39}{16}$ or $2\frac{7}{16}$ **10.** $\frac{3d}{5}$ **11.** $\frac{4}{m^4n^2}$ **12.** $7(z-6)$ or $7z-42$ **13.** $\frac{9}{w^2-81}$ **14.** $\frac{9}{2(w^2-81)}$ **15.** no; simplified $\frac{1}{x+y}$

Alternative Activity 73—Complex Fractions and the LCM

1. 6 **2.** 24 **3.** 6 **4.** 75 **5.** 36 **6.** 56 **7.** $96y$ **8.** $60n$ **9.** $36x$ **10.** 2 **11.** $\frac{1}{1}$ or 1 **12.** $\frac{7}{4}$ or $1\frac{3}{4}$ **13.** $\frac{7}{6}$ or $1\frac{1}{6}$ **14.** $\frac{63}{16}$ or $3\frac{15}{16}$ **15.** $\frac{80}{11}$ or $7\frac{3}{11}$ **16.** $\frac{1}{10}$ **17.** $\frac{14}{15}$ **18.** $\frac{10x}{21}$ **19.** $\frac{1}{4}$ dozen **20.** $\frac{17}{100}$

Alternative Activity 74—Least Common Multiples and Prime Factors

1. $\frac{5}{6}$ **2.** $\frac{3}{4}$ **3.** $\frac{14}{11}$ or $1\frac{3}{11}$ **4.** $\frac{9}{8}$ or $1\frac{1}{8}$ **5.** 4 **6.** $\frac{1}{a^2}$ **7.** $\frac{4b}{27}$ **8.** $\frac{7}{4(n-1)}$ **9.** 72 seconds **10.** every 18 months

Alternative Activity 75—Sums and Differences

1. 96 **2.** 18 **3.** 6 **4.** 22 **5.** 72 **6.** 54 **7.** 147 **8.** $18x$ **9.** $50w$ **10.** $63a^3$ **11.** $2d^5$ **12.** $\frac{7}{12}$ **13.** $\frac{44}{45}$ **14.** $\frac{-2}{9}$ or $-\frac{2}{9}$ **15.** $\frac{29}{36}$ **16.** $\frac{29}{90}$ **17.** $\frac{2xy+9}{3xy}$ **18.** $\frac{3}{2r}$ **19.** $\frac{7}{30}$ **20.** $\frac{11}{3a}$ **21.** $\frac{53k}{42}$ **22.** $\frac{(-10y+9m)}{90}$ **23.** $\frac{(5x-1)}{10}$ **24** $\frac{19}{45}$ **25.** $\frac{43}{60}$

Alternative Activity 76—Proportions and Fractions in Equations

1. $x = 40$ **2.** $w = 39$ **3.** $y = 2$ **4.** $n = -2$ **5.** $a = -3$ **6.** $c = 5$ **7.** 60 inches **8.** 12 inches **9.** 1,050 **10.** $\frac{35}{8}$ or $4\frac{3}{8}$ cups

Alternative Activity 77—More Solutions to Equations with Fractions

1. not correct; $n = 10$ **2.** not correct; $n = 252$ **3.** not correct; $y = 49$ **4.** correct **5.** correct **6.** correct **7.** $x = 20$ **8.** $y = 9$ **9.** $w = 6$ **10.** 25275

Alternative Activity 78—Denominators and Zero

1. $n = 8$ **2.** $m = \frac{3}{4}$ **3.** $d = \frac{-13}{14}$ **4.** $a = -11$ **5.** $p = 14$ **6.** $n = 0$ **7.** $y = 0$ or $y = 1$ or $y = -1$ **8.** $a = 0$ or $a = \frac{1}{2}$ **9.** $a = 10$ or $a = -10$ **10.** Lin is trying to divide by 0, but division by 0 is undefined.

Alternative Activity 79—The Coordinate System

1. I **2.** II **3.** III **4.** II **5.** IV **6.** IV **7.** I **8.** *8* is located at $(4, -1)$ **9.** *9* is located at $(-2, 3)$ **10.** *10* is located at $(3, 3)$

Alternative Activity 80—Graphing Equations

1. -3 **2.** -1 **3.** 1 **4.** 3 **5.** -10 **6.** -6 **7.** -2 **8.** 2 **9.** -4 **10.** -2 **11.** 0 **12.** 2 **13.** I **14.** a square **15.** the movement is straight up vertically, or "due north"

Alternative Activity 81—Intercepts of Lines

1. -2 **2.** 2 **3.** -2 **4.** 6 **5.** 7 **6.** 7 **7.** 1 **8.** -3 **9.** -4 **10.** 2

Alternative Activity 82—Slopes of Lines

1. neither **2.** negative **3.** negative **4.** positive **5.** 2 **6.** $\frac{5}{4}$ or $1\frac{1}{4}$ **7.** $\frac{1}{5}$ **8.** -2 **9.** accept any line with negative slope—that is, a line with end rays in quadrants II and IV **10.** accept any line with positive slope—that is, a line with end rays in quadrants I and III

Alternative Activity 83—Writing Linear Equations

1. $y = 3x - 2$ **2.** $y = -\frac{1}{2}x - 1$ **3.** $y = 3x + 5$ **4.** $y = 4x + 1$ **5.** $y = -\frac{2}{3}x + 7$ **6.** $y = 7x - 7$ **7.** $y = -x - 2$ **8.** $y = \frac{3}{4}x + \frac{5}{4}$ **9.** $y = 3x - 4$ **10.** $y = -x + 5$ **11.** $y = 2x - 4$ **12.** $y = 3x - 2$ **13.** $y = -\frac{1}{2}x - \frac{3}{2}$, also accept $y = -\frac{1}{2}x - 1\frac{1}{2}$ **14.** $y = 2x$ **15.** $y = -\frac{1}{2}x + \frac{1}{2}$

Alternative Activity 84—Lines as Functions

1. $-\frac{5}{7}$; B **2.** $\frac{7}{6}$ or $1\frac{1}{6}$; A **3.** $\frac{1}{5}$; A **4.** $-\frac{8}{3}$ or $-2\frac{2}{3}$; B **5.** 15 **6.** 0 **7.** -15 **8.** 0 **9.** 3 **10.** 8

Alternative Activity 85—Domain and Range of a Function

1. 1, 2, 5, 9, 82 **2.** $-7, -8, 1, 28, 136$ **3.** $-6\frac{3}{8}, -6, -4\frac{1}{8}, -2\frac{1}{4}, 1\frac{1}{2}$ **4.** $104, 14, -4, -4, 24$ **5.** $-21, -1, 7, 15, 35$ **6.** $-19, -5, -3, 3, 16$ **7.** $15, -85, -84, -49, 15$ **8.** $11\frac{7}{8}, 12, 12\frac{1}{8}, 12\frac{1}{2}, 14\frac{1}{2}$ **9.** $(-7, 6)$ $(-2, 5)$ domain: $-7, -2$ range: 5, 6 **10.** $(5, 3)$ $(6, -10)$ domain: 5, 6 range: $3, -10$ **11.** $(-123, 18)$ $(47, -190)$ domain: $-123, 47$ range: $18, -190$ **12.** $(2, 3)$ $(3, 7)$ $(4, 11)$ domain: 2, 3, 4 range: 3, 7, 11 **13.** $(-1, 9)$ $(9, 9)$ $(27, 9)$ domain: $-1, 9, 27$ range: 9 **14.** domain: $-6 \leq x \leq 6$ range: $-1 \leq y \leq 1$ **15.** domain: $-4 \leq x \leq 7$ range: $-2 \leq y \leq 4$

Alternative Activity 86—Graphing Inequalities: $y < mx + b$, $y > mx + b$

1. yes **2.** yes **3.** no **4.** no **5.** no **6.** no **7.** yes **8.** yes **9.** $y > 10$ **10.**

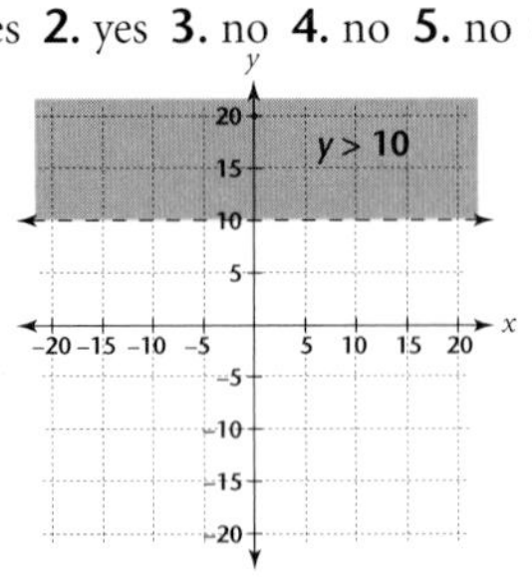

Alternative Activity 87—Graphing Inequalities: $y \leq mx + b$, $y \geq mx + b$

1. yes **2.** no **3.** yes **4.** yes **5.** no **6.** yes **7.** no **8.** no **9.** change the broken line of the equation to a solid line **10.** remove the shading below the broken line and add shading above the broken line

Alternative Activity 88—Graphs Without Numbers

1. C **2.** D **3.** A **4.** B **5.** accept any reasonable effort

Alternative Activity 89—Parallel Lines

1. $m = 4$ **2.** $m = -7$ **3.** $m = -1$ **4.** $m = 3$ **5.** $m = 1$ **6.** rewrite as $y = 4x - 2,\ y = 4x + 3$ **7.** rewrite as $y = -x - 7,\ y = -x + 1$ **8.** rewrite as $y = 6x - 2,\ y = 6x - 4$ **9.** c **10.** b

Alternative Activity 90—Describing Parallel Lines

1. $m = \frac{7}{2}$ **2.** $m = 4$ **3.** $m = -2$ **4.** $m = -1$ **5.** $m = 32$ **6.** $m = \frac{5}{2}$ **7.** $m = -\frac{2}{3}$ **8.** $m = 1$ **9.** $m = 2$ **10.** a: Equation Set 2; b: Equation Set 1

Alternative Activity 91—Intersecting Lines—Common Solutions

1. no, slopes are equal, lines are parallel **2.** yes, slopes are unequal, lines intersect **3.** yes, slopes are unequal, lines intersect **4.** yes, slopes are unequal, lines intersect **5.** yes, slopes are unequal, lines intersect **6.** yes, slopes are unequal, lines intersect **7.** match with *horizontal* **8.** match with *vertical* **9.** match with *slanting* **10.** yes, $y = -1$ describes a horizontal line, and $x = 2$ describes a vertical line

Alternative Activity 92—Solving Linear Equations—Substitution

1. b **2.** $(1, 2)$ **3.** $(4, -2)$ **4.** $(-17, 24)$ **5.** $(2, -\frac{3}{2})$ **6.** $(6, 6)$ **7.** correct **8.** not correct **9.** not correct **10.** not correct

Alternative Activity 93—Solving Linear Equations—Elimination

1. no, slopes are equal, lines are parallel **2.** yes, slopes are unequal, lines intersect **3.** no, slopes are equal, lines are parallel **4.** $(\frac{1}{2}, 0)$ **5.** $(-1, 4)$ **6.** $(1, 3)$ **7.** $(4, 0)$ **8.** $(-2, -5)$ **9.** $(-3, 4)$ **10.** $(0, 8)$

Alternative Activity 94—Graphing Systems of Linear Equations

1. Intersection: $(0, 1)$.

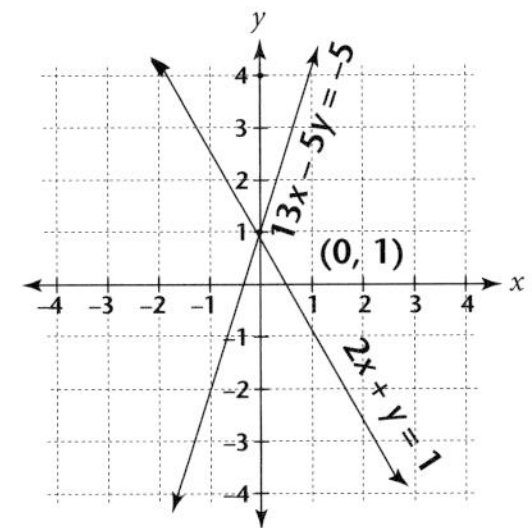

2. Intersection: $(\frac{1}{2}, 1\frac{1}{2})$ **3.** Intersection: $(-2, 3)$ **4.** Intersection: $(0, 2)$ **5.** Intersection: $(4, 3)$

Alternative Activity 95—*And* Statements—Conjunctions

1. *F*—second part is false **2.** *T*—both are true **3.** *F*—second part is false **4.** *F*—second part is false **5.** *F*—first part is false **6.** *T* **7.** *F* **8.** *T* **9.** *F* **10.** *T*

Alternative Activity 96—Problem Solving Using Linear Equations

1. $146\frac{2}{3}$ cm and $303\frac{1}{3}$ cm **2.** 1,090 children's tickets, 2,180 adult tickets **3.** 94 white buttons, 30 black buttons **4.** 15, 5 **5.** small pizza—\$6; salad—\$2

Alternative Activity 97—Introduction to Matrices: Addition and Subtraction

1. 3×3 **2.** 2×2 **3.** 4×4 **4.** 2×7 **5.** row 4, column 2 **6.** row 2, column 8 **7.** row 7, column 2

8. $\begin{bmatrix} 91 & 85 \\ -80 & 99 \end{bmatrix}$ **9.** $\begin{bmatrix} 20 & 30 \\ 0 & 3 \\ -40 & 52 \end{bmatrix}$ **10.** $\begin{bmatrix} 8 & 0 \\ -18 & -13 \end{bmatrix}$

Alternative Activity 98—Multiplication of Matrices

1. $\begin{bmatrix} 56 & 48 \\ 32 & 24 \end{bmatrix}$ **2.** $\begin{bmatrix} 52 & 26a \\ 13x & 130 \end{bmatrix}$ **3.** $\begin{bmatrix} ya & yb & yc \\ yd & ye & yf \end{bmatrix}$

4. $\begin{bmatrix} 72 & 84 & 0 \\ 42 & 48 & 0 \\ 0 & 6 & 12 \end{bmatrix}$ **5.** $\begin{bmatrix} 14c & 12c & 10c \\ 8c & 6c & 4c \\ 2c & 18c & 16c \end{bmatrix}$ **6.** $\begin{bmatrix} 3a & 3b & 3c & 3d \\ 3y & 3x & 3z & 42 \end{bmatrix}$

7. $\begin{bmatrix} 137 & 135 \\ 179 & 177 \end{bmatrix}$ **8.** $\begin{bmatrix} 334 & 359 \\ 467 & 498 \end{bmatrix}$

9. $\begin{bmatrix} mx + px + 12m & 2x + py + ma & 7x + pz + mb \\ ym + qx + 12a & 2y + qy + a^2 & 7y + qz + ab \\ zm + nx + 12b & 2z + ny + ab & 7z + nz + b^2 \end{bmatrix}$

10. $\begin{bmatrix} 6r + 130 & 14r + 12y & 2rx + 4x + 99 \\ 30x + 5y + 10\pi & 70x + 3y^2 & 10x^2 + yx + 9\pi \\ 233 & 7 & x + 207 \end{bmatrix}$

Alternative Activity 99—Rational Numbers as Decimals

1. $1.\overline{0}$ **2.** 0.375 **3.** $0.\overline{230769}$ **4.** $0.6\overline{0}$ **5.** $0.\overline{904761}$ **6.** $0.\overline{714285}$ **7.** $0.\overline{36}$ **8.** $42.\overline{2}$°C **9.** 84.2°F **10.** $123.\overline{3}$°C

Alternative Activity 100—Rational Number Equivalents

1. $\frac{2}{3}$ **2.** $\frac{4}{5}$ **3.** $\frac{1}{12}$ **4.** $\frac{4}{15}$ **5.** $\frac{7}{8}$ **6.** $\frac{7}{18}$ **7.** $\frac{9}{13}$ **8.** $\frac{8}{12}$ **9.** $\frac{9}{20}$ **10.** $\frac{11}{15}$ **11.** $\frac{17}{20}$ **12.** $\frac{11}{18}$ **13.** $\frac{31}{50}$ **14.** $\frac{17}{18}$ **15.** $0.1\overline{6}$

Alternative Activity 101—Irrational Numbers as Decimals

1. rational **2.** irrational **3.** rational **4.** rational **5.** irrational **6.** irrational **7.** irrational **8.** rational **9.** irrational **10.** irrational **11.** rational **12.** irrational **13.** 20 inches **14.** 60 cm **15.** no, one side of the square tray is $\sqrt{112.4}$, or about 10.6 inches

Alternative Activity 102—Products and Quotients of Radicals

1. $\frac{7}{8}$ **2.** $ab^2\sqrt{a}$ **3.** $\frac{6}{7}$ **4.** $\frac{5}{11}$ **5.** $\frac{2}{9}$ **6.** $\frac{b}{2}$ **7.** $(a + b)^2$ **8.** $2\sqrt{13}$ **9.** $\frac{2a^3}{7b^4}$ **10.** $\frac{3x}{5y^2}$ **11.** $\frac{13}{w}$ **12.** $\frac{\sqrt{26}}{5}$ **13.** $\frac{\sqrt{15a}}{6a^2}$ **14.** yes—the length of one side of a square is equal to the square root of the area of the square **15.** $7\sqrt{3}$ units

Alternative Activity 103—Sums and Differences of Radicals

1. $9\sqrt{3}$ **2.** $5\sqrt{7}$ **3.** $3\sqrt{5}$ **4.** $7\sqrt{5}$ **5.** $6\sqrt{10}$ **6.** $2x\sqrt{7y} + 6y\sqrt{7y}$ **7.** $-7\sqrt{5}$ **8.** $-x\sqrt{2x}$ **9.** $7\sqrt{10}$ feet **10.** $\sqrt{11}$

Alternative Activity 104—Radicals and Fractions

1. $\frac{\sqrt{7}}{7}$ **2.** $\frac{7\sqrt{3}}{6}$ **3.** $3\sqrt{3}$ **4.** $\frac{\sqrt{35}}{14}$ **5.** $\sqrt{2x}$ **6.** $\frac{k + k\sqrt{k}}{1 - k}$ or $\frac{k(1 + \sqrt{k})}{1 - k}$ **7.** $2\sqrt{2} - 2$ or $2(\sqrt{2} - 1)$ **8.** $\sqrt{3} + \sqrt{2}$ **9.** $5\sqrt{3} - 5\sqrt{2}$ or $5(\sqrt{3} - \sqrt{2})$ **10.** $\frac{13\sqrt{35}}{350}$

Alternative Activity 105—Radicals in Equations

1. 25 **2.** 12 cm **3.** $5\sqrt{10}$ feet **4.** $2\sqrt{7}$ feet **5.** $2\sqrt{13}$ inches

Alternative Activity 106—Radicals and Exponents

1. $n^{\frac{1}{5}}$ **2.** $a^{\frac{1}{2}}$ **3.** $3^{\frac{1}{2}} \cdot d^{\frac{1}{2}}$ or $(3d)^{\frac{1}{2}}$ **4.** $x^{\frac{1}{6}}$ **5.** $k^{\frac{1}{4}}$ **6.** $9^{\frac{1}{3}} \cdot x^{\frac{1}{3}}$ or $(9x)^{\frac{1}{3}}$ **7.** $7^{\frac{1}{5}} \cdot k^{\frac{1}{5}}$ or $(7k)^{\frac{1}{5}}$ **8.** $a^{\frac{7}{2}}$ **9.** $x^{\frac{7}{3}}$ **10.** $d^{\frac{7}{10}}$ **11.** $n^{\frac{13}{4}}$ **12.** 36 **13.** 9 **14.** 81 **15.** 9 **16.** 64 **17.** 125 **18.** 16 **19.** 25 **20.** $4\sqrt{19}$ inches

Alternative Activity 107—Drawing and Using a Square Root Graph

1.

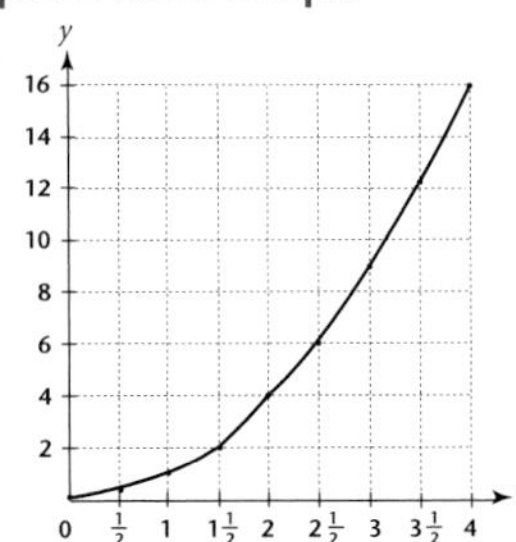

For problems **4–7** and **9–10,** accept any answer that is within 0.3 of the given answer and has the same whole number as the answer. Note that answers 2, 3, and 8 must be exact. **2.** 2.0 (or 2) **3.** 4.0 (or 4) **4.** 2.8 **5.** 2.6 **6.** 3.5 **7.** 2.2 **8.** 3.0 (or 3) **9.** 3.6 **10.** 3.9

Alternative Activity 108—Angles and Angle Measure

1. 65° **2.** 115° **3.** 115° **4.** 57° **5.** 123° **6.** 123° **7.** 80° **8.** 100° **9.** 100° **10.** 10°, 170°

Alternative Activity 109—Pairs of Lines in a Plane and in Space

1. corresponding **2.** corresponding **3.** alternate interior **4.** supplementary **5.** 42° **6.** 138° **7.** 42° **8.** a **9.** c **10.** b

Alternative Activity 110—Angle Measures in a Triangle

1. 42° **2.** 41° **3.** list: *A, C, E, G*; list: *B, D, F, H* **4.** Cut out all the angles and fit them together, two at a time. Use a ruler to determine if any of the joined angles form a common straight line. Any such angle pairs are supplementary. **5.** The angles are equal because alternate interior angles of a transversal are equal.

Alternative Activity 111—Naming Triangles

1. no **2.** no **3.** yes **4.** yes **5.** yes **6.** no **7.** yes **8.** Two of the sides are $8\frac{1}{2}$ inches and 11 inches, from the dimensions of the original sheet of typing paper. The third side is the hypotenuse of the triangle, so it will have a unique measurement. Accept any reasonable explanation for the hypotenuse—the cut side—such as "The slanted side goes sideways as well as up-and-down, so it must be longer than the long (11-inch) side of the original typing paper." **9.** The corner of the typing paper is squared off exactly—its angle measure must therefore be 90°. **10.** It is a right triangle, so one of the angles is 90°. That leaves only 90° for the other two angles, so no angle can be > 90°.

Alternative Activity 112—Quadrilaterals

1. b **2.** f **3.** a **4.** d **5.** c **6.** g **7.** h **8.** e **9.** each figure has 4 sides of equal length **10.** each figure has 4 sides; in each figure, at least 2 of the sides are parallel

Alternative Activity 113—Congruent and Similar Triangles

1. a, c **2.** a, b **3.** b, c **4.** a, b **5.** a, c

Alternative Activity 114—Trigonometric Ratios

1. 0.54 **2.** 0.84 **3.** 0.65 **4.** 0.98 **5.** 0.17 **6.** 5.67 **7.** 0.77 **8.** 0.64 **9.** 1.19 **10.** Note: Students are not required to show the equations in their problem solutions. **10.** 63 feet, $\sin 65° = \frac{x}{70}$

Alternative Activity 115—Solutions by Factoring

1. 2, −10 **2.** −4 **3.** −5, 4 **4.** 2, 4 **5.** $\frac{3}{2}$ (or $1\frac{1}{2}$), 8 **6.** −3, −1 **7.** 7 **8.** $-\frac{2}{3}$, 1 **9.** Tim is 7. Julio is 5. **10.** 4 cm [Equation: $x^2 + 32 = (x + 2)(2x)$]

Alternative Activity 116—Writing the Equations from Their Roots

1. $x^2 + 11x + 28 = 0$ **2.** $x^2 + 4x + 3 = 0$ **3.** $x^2 - 81 = 0$ **4.** $x^2 - 11x + 24 = 0$ **5.** $x^2 - 4x - 12 = 0$ **6.** $x^2 - 4x - 21 = 0$ **7.** $3x^2 - 4x - 4 = 0$ **8.** $3x^2 + 4x + 1 = 0$ **9.** $6x^2 - x - 15 = 0$ **10.** height = 9 inches; base = 4 inches[Equation: $2b^2 + b - 36 = 0$]

Alternative Activity 117—Solving by Completing the Square

1. −6, 2 **2.** 10, −1 **3.** −6, 1 **4.** 2, 4 **5.** −3, −1 **6.** $-1 - \sqrt{2}$, $-1 + \sqrt{2}$ **7.** $-\frac{3}{2}$ (or $-1\frac{1}{2}$), $\frac{1}{2}$ **8.** 5.3 inches, 2.3 inches [Equation: $x^2 + 3x - 12 = 0$] **9.** Terri, 4; Leah, 6 [Equation: $x^2 + 2x - 24 = 0$] **10.** long row, 17; short row, 9 [Equation: $x^2 + 8x - 153 = 0$]

Alternative Activity 118—Solving Using the Quadratic Formula

1. −4, 6 **2.** −3, 2 **3.** 1, 7 **4.** $-\frac{4}{3}$ (or $-1\frac{1}{3}$), 3 **5.** −3, $\frac{2}{3}$ **6.** $-\frac{2}{3}$, 1 **7.** $2 - \sqrt{11}$, $2 + \sqrt{11}$ **8.** long row (length): 18 bushes; short row (width): 13 bushes [Equation: $x^2 + 5x - 234 = 0$] **9.** large bag: 42 lb; small bag: 22 lb[Equation: $2x^2 - 2x - 924 = 0$] **10.** long row (length): 24 pieces; short row (width): 18 pieces [Equation: $x^2 + 6x - 432 = 0$]

Alternative Activity 119—Graphing Quadratic Equations

1. Chart: (−1, 0), (0, 2), (1, 2), (2, 0), (3, −4)

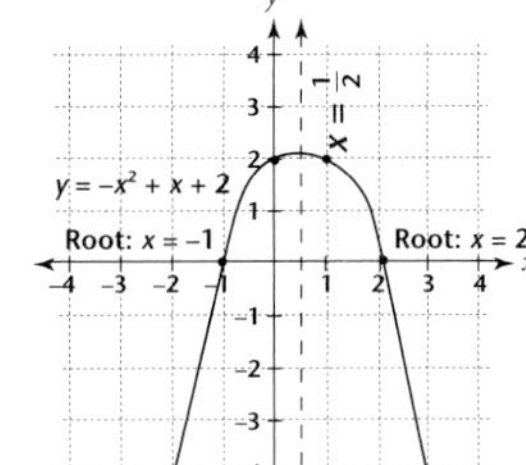

2. $x = \frac{1}{2}$ **3.** see graph **4.** −1, 2 **5.** see graph

Workbook Activities

Workbook Activity 1—Arithmetic and Algebra

1. true **2.** false **3.** true **4.** true **5.** open **6.** true **7.** false **8.** false **9.** false **10.** open **11.** true **12.** open **13.** open **14.** false **15.** false **16.** true **17.** true **18.** true **19.** open **20.** true **21.** true **22.** false **23.** open **24.** false **25.** true **26.** open **27.** false **28.** open **29.** true **30.** false

Workbook Activity 2—Representing Numbers Using Letters

1. *y* **2.** *k* **3.** *x* **4.** *n* **5.** *m* **6.** *d* **7.** *r* **8.** *k* **9.** *x* **10.** *p* **11.** *y* **12.** *m* **13.** numerical **14.** division **15.** algebraic **16.** multiplication **17.** numerical **18.** addition **19.** numerical **20.** division **21.** algebraic **22.** multiplication; subtraction **23.** algebraic **24.** multiplication; addition **25.** $k - 17$

Workbook Activity 3—Integers on the Number Line

1. positive **2.** positive **3.** negative **4.** positive **5.** positive **6.** negative **7.** zero **8.** negative **9.** positive **10.** positive **11.** positive **12.** negative **13.** 5 **14.** 6 **15.** 2 **16.** 2 **17.** 18 **18.** 5 **19.** 11 **20.** 12 **21.** 12 **22.** 4 **23.** 9 **24.** 9 **25.** +5; −5

Workbook Activity 4—Adding Integers
1. left **2.** right **3.** 0 **4.** -6 **5.** 6 **6.** 6 **7.** -6 **8.** -6 **9.** -2 **10.** -3 **11.** -1 **12.** -6 **13.** 0 **14.** 0 **15.** 4 **16.** 6 **17.** 4 **18.** 6 **19.** 14 **20.** -6

Workbook Activity 5—Subtracting Integers
1. $-4 + 11 = 7$ **2.** $9 + (-3) = 6$ **3.** $-1 + (-13) = -14$ **4.** $-6 + (-10) = -16$ **5.** $7 + 10 = 17$ **6.** $4 + (-4) = 0$ **7.** $2 + (-8) = -6$ **8.** $-11 + 1 = -10$ **9.** $6 + (-2) = 4$ **10.** $-5 + 5 = 0$ **11.** $2 + (-9) = -7$ **12.** $1 + (-4) = -3$ **13.** $6 + (-8) = -2$ **14.** $-8 + 3 = -5$ **15.** $-3 + (-7) = -10$ **16.** $8 + 7 = 15$ **17.** $10 + (-5) = 5$ **18.** $5 + (-6) = -1$ **19.** $67 - 40 = 27$ feet **20.** $60 - (-30) = 90$ m

Workbook Activity 6—Multiplying Integers
1. negative **2.** negative **3.** zero **4.** positive **5.** negative **6.** negative **7.** positive **8.** zero **9.** negative **10.** positive **11.** positive **12.** positive **13.** negative **14.** positive **15.** negative **16.** 18 **17.** -45 **18.** -27 **19.** -20 **20.** 63 **21.** -50 **22.** 24 **23.** 0 **24.** -24 **25.** 22 **26.** -32 **27.** 80 **28.** -25 **29.** 1 **30.** 70

Workbook Activity 7—Integers
1. 10,822 feet **2.** 22,480 feet **3.** 18,488 feet **4.** 15,790 feet **5.** 23,466 feet **6.** 24,798 feet **7.** 20,974 feet **8.** 24,966 feet **9.** 28,434 feet **10.** 12,399 feet

Workbook Activity 8—Dividing Positive and Negative Integers
1. negative **2.** positive **3.** negative **4.** positive **5.** negative **6.** positive **7.** negative **8.** negative **9.** negative **10.** zero **11.** positive **12.** negative **13.** positive **14.** positive **15.** negative **16.** 3 **17.** -3 **18.** -6 **19.** -5 **20.** -12 **21.** 2 **22.** -5 **23.** 1 **24.** -5 **25.** -3 **26.** -7 **27.** 0 **28.** 8 **29.** 1 **30.** 3

Workbook Activity 9—Simplifying Expressions—One Variable
In problems **1–10,** look for correct underlining. **1.** $3k, 2k$ **2.** p, p **3.** $4w, 4w$ **4.** $5m, 2m$ **5.** $7x, 5x$ **6.** $11c, c$ **7.** $2m, 3m$ **8.** $2y, -3y$ **9.** $4x, 5x$ **10.** $8r, -3r$ **11.** $4b$ **12.** $14y$ **13.** $8j$ **14.** $3k - 17$ **15.** $12x - 14$ **16.** $10d + 22$ **17.** $7g + 4$ **18.** $12h - 3$ **19.** $-6m$ **20.** $k + 3$ **21.** 5 **22.** $2n - 5$ **23.** $13x - 13$ **24.** $6h$ **25.** $4k - 11$ **26.** $6d + 40$ **27.** $4m + 8$ **28.** $-2w$ **29.** $3x + 2$ **30.** $3g - 6$

Workbook Activity 10—Simplifying Expressions—Several Variables
In problems **1–5,** look for check marks in the indicated columns. **1.** all three columns **2.** y terms, Integers **3.** all three columns **4.** Integers **5.** x terms, Integers **6.** $k + 5r + 12$ **7.** $11b + 3c$ **8.** $2j + 4k + 1$ **9.** $2m + 2p + 1$ **10.** $2d - 3n - 1$ **11.** $-7x + 8y + 19$ **12.** $4w + 18y - 22$ **13.** $-3h + 5k - 12$ **14.** $-6m - 11p + 3$ **15.** $3y - 7$

Workbook Activity 11—Positive Exponents
1. true **2.** true **3.** false **4.** true **5.** true **6.** false **7.** false **8.** true **9.** k^6 **10.** w^3 **11.** j^4 **12.** n^7 **13.** d^{14} **14.** y^6 **15.** x^{13} **16.** a^{12} **17.** 289 **18.** 32 **19.** 243 **20.** 0.512

Workbook Activity 12—Formulas with Variables
1. 24 cm **2.** 12 m **3.** 20 km **4.** 72 cm **5.** 36 m

Workbook Activity 13—Commutative Property of Addition
1. $k + k + k + k = 4k$ **2.** $r + r + r = 3r$ **3.** $y + y + y + y + y = 5y$ **4.** $n + n + n + n + n + n = 6n$ **5.** $17 + b$ **6.** $5 + 3k$ **7.** $5x + x$ **8.** $1.2 + 2.7$ **9.** $3p + 5m$ **10.** $6 + 7q$ **11.** $133 + 164$ **12.** $4y + 8y$ **13.** 214 pounds **14.** 214 pounds **15.** commutative property of addition

Workbook Activity 14—Commutative Property of Multiplication
In problems **1–2,** students must write both products correctly to receive credit. **1.** $1 \cdot 7 = 7; 7 \cdot 1 = 7$ **2.** $3 \cdot 6 = 18; 6 \cdot 3 = 18$ **3.** 48 **4.** 48 **5.** commutative property of multiplication

Workbook Activity 15—Associative Property of Addition
1. $(3k + 2k) + 5$ **2.** $1.3 + (8.1 + 6.6)$ **3.** $11x + (10y + 4)$ **4.** $(7 + 5) + q$ **5.** $3 + (12n + 2)$ **6.** $(g + 21) + h$ **7.** $(3 + 5) + 4 = 12$ **8.** $3 + (5 + 4) = 12$ **9.** yes **10.** associative property of addition

Workbook Activity 16—Associative Property of Multiplication
In problems **1–7,** both rewritten versions of the expression must be correct for students to receive any credit. The order of the rewritten expressions is irrelevant. **1.** $(mn)q; m(nq)$ **2.** $(ab)c; a(bc)$ **3.** $(4s)t; 4(st)$ **4.** $(kv)z; k(vz)$ **5.** $(1.5b)c; 1.5(bc)$ **6.** $(9m)n; 9(mn)$ **7.** $(ak)s; a(ks)$ **8.** Plan A **9.** Plan B **10.** yes

Workbook Activity 17—The Distributive Property—Multiplication
1. 2 **2.** m **3.** 7 **4.** $5c$ **5.** $-p$ **6.** 8 **7.** $2j$ **8.** 300 **9.** $-2q$ **10.** 12 **11.** $3b$ **12.** $14k$ **13.** -20 **14.** $-11n$ **15.** km (or mk) **16.** by **17.** $32 + 16 = 48$ **18.** $6r + 6z$ **19.** $-d - k$ **20.** $33 + 3w$ **21.** $8 - 2m$ **22.** $-8a - 24$ **23.** $-9x - 9y$ **24.** $7g + 70$ **25.** $8v - 64$

Workbook Activity 18—The Distributive Property—Factoring
1. 11 **2.** n **3.** -2 **4.** b **5.** p **6.** d **7.** 1.9 **8.** r **9.** 7 Check matching lines for **10–14. 10.** d **11.** a **12.** e **13.** b **14.** c **15.** $2(d + n)$

Workbook Activity 19—Properties of Zero
1. true **2.** true **3.** false **4.** true **5.** false **6.** true **7.** 9 **8.** 27 **9.** -14 **10.** k **11.** -16 **12.** m^2 **13.** -37 **14.** k^5 **15.** $-y^2$ **16–24.** All answers are 0. **25.** c

Workbook Activity 20—Properties of 1
To receive credit in **1–8,** students must include the checking. **1.** $4; \frac{1}{4} \cdot 4 = 1$ **2.** $9; \frac{1}{9} \cdot 9 = 1$ **3.** $\frac{1}{7}; 7 \cdot \frac{1}{7} = 1$ **4.** $12; \frac{1}{12} \cdot 12 = 1$ **5.** $\frac{1}{k}; k \cdot \frac{1}{k} = 1$ **6.** $m; \frac{1}{m} \cdot m = 1$ **7.** $\frac{1}{c^2}; c^2 \cdot \frac{1}{c^2} = 1$ **8.** $\frac{1}{3}; 3 \cdot \frac{1}{3} = 1$ **9.** 5 **10.** $\frac{1}{6}$

Workbook Activity 21—Powers and Roots
1. 19 **2.** 17 **3.** ^{3} **4.** root **5.** ^{5} **6.** 11 **7.** 7 **8.** 9 **9.** 4 **10.** 15 **11.** 27 **12.** 2 **13.** 77 **14.** 1.9 **15.** 3.2 **16.** 10 **17.** 13.5 **18.** 6 **19.** 6 **20.** a

Workbook Activity 22—More on Powers and Roots
1. $64d^2$ **2.** $100n^2$ **3.** $-8y^3$ **4.** $81m^4$ **5.** $4, -4$ **6.** $3, -3$ **7.** 2 **8.** -2 **9.** $k, -k$ **10.** $10, -10$ **11.** -3 **12.** -6 **13.** 6 **14.** 100 square units (accept 100) **15.** $-1{,}000$ cubic units (accept $-1{,}000$)

Workbook Activity 23—Order of Operations
1. 5 **2.** 58 **3.** 70 **4.** 0 **5.** 10 **6.** 6 **7.** 109 **8.** 102 **9.** 29 **10.** 3 **11.** 3 **12.** 15 **13.** c **14.** (1) calculate the exponent; (2) multiply; (3) add **15.** 231

Workbook Activity 24—Order of Operations
1. first multiply, then add; 22 **2.** first divide, then add; 9 **3.** first multiply, then subtract; 98 **4.** first divide, then add; 26 **5.** first divide, then multiply; 4 **6.** first multiply, then add; 41 **7.** first divide, then add or subtract; 125 **8.** first divide, then multiply; 49 **9.** first divide, then add the fours; 10 **10.** first multiply, then divide and add; 21

Workbook Activity 25—Writing Equations
1. $6x = 30$ **2.** $2x + 5 = 9$ **3.** $3x - 8 = 1$ **4.** $x - 17 = 14$ **5.** $10x + 7 = 87$ **6.** $x - 11 = 2$ **7.** (5)(1) = 15, F; (5)(2) = 15, F; (5)(3) = 15, T **8.** (7)(5) = 49, F; (7)(6) = 49, F; (7)(7) = 49, T **9.** (10)(7) = 80, F; (10)(8) = 80, T; (10)(9) = 80, F **10.** (2)(11) = 22, T; (2)(12) = 22, F; (2)(13) = 22, F

Workbook Activity 26—Solving Equations: $x - b = c$
1. $x = 24$ **2.** $b = 8$ **3.** $n = 9$ **4.** $k = 16$ **5.** $d = 200$ **6.** $c = 11$ **7.** $y = 18$ **8.** $r = 100$ **9.** $w = 8$ **10.** b

Workbook Activity 27—Solving Equations: $x + b = c$
1. $w = 1$ **2.** $r = 4$ **3.** $y = 5$ **4.** $c = 3.0$ **5.** $k = 38$ **6.** $d = 9$ **7.** $n = 35$ **8.** $b = 7$ **9.** $x = 6$ **10.** b

Workbook Activity 28—Solving Multiplication Equations
1. $q = 7$ **2.** $k = 3$ **3.** $x = 4$ **4.** $d = 6$ **5.** $w = 11$ **6.** $j = -4$ **7.** $y = 6$ **8.** $n = 4$ **9.** $p = 4$ **10.** c

Workbook Activity 29—Solving Equations with Fractions
1. $x = 4$ **2.** $w = 24$ **3.** $q = 14$ **4.** $r = 15$ **5.** $m = 25$ **6.** $k = 48$ **7.** $d = -15$ **8.** $y = 48$ **9.** $a = 20$ **10.** b

Workbook Activity 30—Solving Equations—More Than One Step
1. $b = 4$ **2.** $c = 3$ **3.** $x = 1$ **4.** $p = 10$ **5.** $v = 5$ **6.** $w = 8$ **7.** $g = 6$ **8.** Divide both sides of the equation by 7. **9.** Subtract 1 from both sides of the equation. **10.** Divide both sides of the equation by 3.

Workbook Activity 31—Equations Without Numbers
1. $x = \frac{b+c}{a}$ **2.** $x = \frac{bc}{a}$ **3.** $x = c + b - a$ **4.** $x = -\frac{c}{ab}$ **5.** $z = x - y - 2$

Workbook Activity 32—Formulas
1. $s = \frac{P}{6}$ **2.** $m = \frac{2A}{h} - n$ **3.** $b = \frac{P}{2} - h$ **4.** $l = \frac{A}{w}$ **5.** $b = P - a - c$ or $b = P - (a + c)$ **6.** $n = \frac{2A}{h} - m$ **7.** $m = \frac{V}{h}$ **8.** $h = \frac{P - 2b}{2}$ **9.** $s = \frac{P}{4}$ **10.** square; $P = 4s$ is the formula for the perimeter of a square. Also, the formula itself indicates that all sides are equal—therefore, the deck is a square.

Workbook Activity 33—The Pythagorean Theorem
1. 7.3 **2.** 8 **3.** 11.5 **4.** 34.9 **5.** $c = 4.5$ m

Workbook Activity 34—Using the Pythagorean Theorem
1. no **2.** yes **3.** no **4.** yes **5.** yes

Workbook Activity 35—Inequalities on the Number Line
1. $x > -1$ **2.** $x \geq 4$ **3.** $-4 < x < -1$ **4.** $x \leq 0$ **5.** T **6.** T **7.** F **8.** F **9.** T **10.** T

Workbook Activity 36—Solving Inequalities with One Variable
1. $x > 3$ **2.** $d > 2$ **3.** $k < 1$ **4.** $q > 12$ **5.** $c \leq 37$ **6.** $g < 7$ **7.** $p < 3$ **8.** $w \geq -7$ **9.** $t \leq 25$ **10.** $f \geq 200(5)$ (accept $f \geq 1{,}000$)

Workbook Activity 37—Writing Equations—Odd and Even Integers
1. $2 + 3n = 5$ **2.** $4n - 5 = 15$ **3.** $8n + 5 = 53$ **4.** $7n - 2 = 40$ **5.** $10 + 11n = 32$ **6.** $8n - 25 = -1$ **7.** $4 + 9n = 76$ **8.** $10n - 1 = 99$ **9.** $9n - 14 = 22$ **10.** 18

Workbook Activity 38—Using the 1% Solution to Solve Problems
1. 800 **2.** 300 **3.** 700 **4.** 300 **5.** 900 **6.** 200 **7.** 100 **8.** 300 **9.** 700 **10.** 3,000,000

Workbook Activity 39—Using the Percent Equation
1. 4 **2.** 12 **3.** 17 **4.** 50 **5.** 12 **6.** 21 **7.** 9 **8.** 70 **9.** 130 **10.** 18

Workbook Activity 40—Using Percents
1. Bombay (Mumbai), India; 12,904,000 **2.** New York City, U.S.; 1,329,000 **3.** Bombay (Mumbai), India; 89% **4.** Tokyo, Japan, and New York City, U.S.; 8% **5.** 32%

Workbook Activity 41—Solving Distance, Rate, and Time Problems
1. $2\frac{1}{2}$ miles **2.** 114 km **3.** $1\frac{1}{2}$ hours **4.** 82 km/h **5.** 3 hours **6.** 9 km **7.** 83 km/h **8.** $\frac{1}{5}$ hour **9.** 411 mph **10.** 72 km

Workbook Activity 42—Using a Common Unit—Cents
1. 192¢ **2.** 746¢ **3.** 1,100¢ **4.** 225¢ **5.** 2,295¢ **6.** 89¢ **7.** a **8.** b **9.** b **10.** $n(10) + \frac{1}{5}n(25)$ (accept $10n + 5n$)

Workbook Activity 43—Calculating Simple Interest
1. \$6 **2.** \$28.80 **3.** \$196 **4.** \$500 **5.** \$900 **6.** \$3,200 **7.** 9% (or 0.09) **8.** 4% (or 0.04) **9.** 5% (or 0.05) **10.** \$52.40

Workbook Activity 44—Deriving a Formula for Mixture Problems
1. price per pound $= \frac{7(\$2) + 1(\$6)}{7 + 1}$ **2.** \$2.50 per pound **3.** price per pound $= \frac{2(\$9) + 1(\$3)}{2 + 1}$ **4.** \$7 per pound **5.** \$1.92 per pound

Workbook Activity 45—Ratio and Proportion
1. yes, $1 \cdot 8 = 2 \cdot 4$ **2.** yes, $1 \cdot 14 = 2 \cdot 7$ **3.** no, $2 \cdot 14 \neq 3 \cdot 7$ **4.** no, $4 \cdot 20 \neq 15 \cdot 5$ **5.** yes, $3 \cdot 16 = 12 \cdot 4$ **6.** no, $3 \cdot 30 \neq 6 \cdot 10$ **7.** yes, $1 \cdot 6 = 2 \cdot 3$ **8.** yes, $1 \cdot 18 = 3 \cdot 6$ **9.** 5 **10.** 12 **11.** 6 **12.** 5 **13.** 6 **14.** 4 **15.** 1

Workbook Activity 46—Exponents
1. 4^1 or 4 **2.** y^2 **3.** m^4 **4.** r^8 **5.** 6^4 **6.** $(j + k)^2$ **7.** 10^0 or 1 **8.** w^0 or 1 **9.** 3^2 or 9 **10.** 81

Workbook Activity 47—Negative Exponents
1. 8^{-2} **2.** 2^{-1} **3.** 3^{-1} **4.** 10^{-5} **5.** 10^{-3} **6.** c^{-2} **7.** 8^{-3} **8.** y^{-7} **9.** 18^{-3} **10.** $(3j - 2k)^{-4}$ **11.** $\frac{1}{5^3}$ **12.** $\frac{1}{10^3}$ **13.** $\frac{1}{x^5}, x \neq 0$ **14.** $\frac{1}{8^5}$ **15.** $\frac{1}{y^7}, y \neq 0$ **16.** $\frac{1}{10^7}$ **17.** $\frac{1}{(2d + 3k)^3}, (2d + 3k) \neq 0$ **18.** $\frac{1}{n^4}, n \neq 0$ **19.** $\frac{1}{7^2}$ **20.** $\frac{1}{(m - 3n)^2}, (m - 3n) \neq 0$ **21.** 4 **22.** 2 **23.** 1 **24.** $\frac{1}{2}$ **25.** $\frac{1}{4}$

Workbook Activity 48—Exponents and Scientific Notation
1. $2.99(10^4)$ **2.** $1.6(10^{-3})$ **3.** $1.99(10^{-2})$ **4.** $8.83(10^2)$ **5.** $1.1(10^4)$ **6.** $2.23(10^6)$ **7.** $1(10^{-3})$ **8.** $3.14(10^{-5})$ **9.** $9.999(10^{-4})$ **10.** $3.04922(10^5)$ **11.** $1.725(10^4)$ **12.** $2.983925(10^7)$ **13.** $3.3(10^{-9})$ **14.** $3(10^9)$ **15.** $2.226(10^2)$ **16.** $2(10^{-7})$ **17.** $2.6(10^8)$ **18.** $7(10^{-5})$ **19.** $8(10^{-4})$ **20.** $6.5(10^7)$

Workbook Activity 49—Computing in Scientific Notation
1. $1.33(10^{-1})$ **2.** $1.44(10^4)$ **3.** $9.72(10^{-5})$ **4.** $4.1625(10^7)$ **5.** $1.8(10^{-4})$ **6.** $3(10^4)$ **7.** $3.08(10^6)$ **8.** $1.12(10^{-3})$ **9.** $3.44(10^{-2})$ **10.** $6.6(10^4)$

Workbook Activity 50—Defining and Naming Polynomials
1. binomial **2.** 3 **3.** 1 **4.** monomial **5.** 2 **6.** polynomial **7.** 3 **8.** monomial **9.** trinomial **10.** 2 **11.** binomial **12.** 2 **13.** "degree 1" **14.** "binomial" **15.** "polynomial in r"

Workbook Activity 51—Adding and Subtracting Polynomials
1. $6k^3 + k^2 + 13k + 11$ **2.** $3y^4 + 5y^3 - 5y + 9$ **3.** $n^2 - 13n + 7$ **4.** $6x^4 - 6x^3 + 12x - 18$ **5.** $4x^2 + 3x + 2$

Workbook Activity 52—Multiplying Polynomials
1. $3k^2 + 6k - 24$ **2.** $2x^2 + 15x - 50$ **3.** $c^4 + 2c^3 + c^2$ **4.** $d^3 + 5d^2$ **5.** $y^3 + 7y^2 - 12y + 54$ **6.** $n^4 - 3n^3 + 6n^2 - 21n + 9$ **7.** $w^5 - 4w^3 + w^2 - 4$ **8.** $-6x^6 - 17x^5 + 3x^4 + 8x^3 - 30x^2$ **9.** $c^5 - 3c^4 + 9c^3$ **10.** $4k^2 + 4k - 35$ **11.** $m^5 - 6m^4 + 9m^3 - 7m^2 + 20m + 3$ **12.** $16b^2 - 66b - 27$ **13.** $k^9 + 2k^8 - 3k^7 - 8k^6 + 4k^5 - 9k^4 - 9k^3$ **14.** $21n^4 - 68n^3 - 3n^2 + 76n - 32$ **15.** $6x^2 + 15x - 36$

Workbook Activity 53—Special Polynomial Products
1. $(m + n)^2$ or $(m + n)(m + n)$ **2.** $(j + k)(j - k)$ **3.** $(x + y)^2$ or $(x + y)(x + y)$ **4.** $(c + d)^3$ or $(c + d)(c + d)(c + d)$ **5.** $(w + x)(w - x)$ **6.** $(g - h)^2$ or $(g - h)(g - h)$ **7.** $p^2 - r^2$ **8.** $f^2 + 2fg + g^2$ **9.** $y^3 + 3y^2z + 3yz^2 + z^3$ **10.** $a^2 - d^2$ **11.** $p^2 - 2pq + q^2$ **12.** $t^3 + 3t^2u + 3tu^2 + u^3$ **13.** $n^2 + 2np + p^2$ **14.** $c^2 - 2cd + d^2$ **15.** $k^2 - m^2$

Workbook Activity 54—Exponents and Complex Fractions
1. $\frac{1}{a}$ **2.** $\frac{c^2d}{4}$ **3.** $\frac{b}{a^3}$ **4.** $\frac{1}{g^2}$ **5.** $2y$ **6.** $\frac{5m^3n^3}{p^3}$ **7.** $3cde$ **8.** $3rst^2$ **9.** $\frac{12g^3i^3}{h^2}$ **10.** $\frac{4c}{9b^2d^2}$

Workbook Activity 55—Dividing a Polynomial by a Monomial
1. $3n^2 - n + 9$ **2.** $4y^2 - 1$ **3.** $k^5 - 2k^4 + 8k^3 - 11k - 3$ **4.** $x^4 + 2x^3 + 8x - 64$ **5.** $2k^4 + k^3 + 3k^2 - 4k$

Workbook Activity 56—Dividing a Polynomial by a Binomial
1. $(x - 3)$ **2.** $(2a - 4)$ **3.** $(5y - 6)$ **4.** $(3d - 9)$ r13 **5.** The student failed to mark the places for the 4th, 3rd, and 2nd powers of x with a 0. The dividend should be changed to the following before division is performed: $x^5 + (0 \cdot x^4) + (0 \cdot x^3) + (0 \cdot x^2) + 3x - 9$ or $x^5 + 0 + 0 + 0 + 3x - 9$

Workbook Activity 57—Polynomials in Two or More Variables
1. 3 **2.** 31 **3.** $8\frac{1}{9}$ **4.** 31 **5.** $68\frac{1}{4}$ **6.** 14 **7.** −102 **8.** 0 **9.** 2,240 **10.** 95 **11.** 16 **12.** 0 **13.** −41 **14.** −5 **15.** −128

Workbook Activity 58—Greatest Common Factor
1. $2 \cdot 3$ **2.** 7 **3.** $3^2 \cdot 5$ **4.** 2 **5.** $2 \cdot 3$ **6.** $7xy^3$ **7.** $3j^2k^4$ **8.** $2a^2b$ **9.** $5m^5n$ **10.** Dad's new age is an even number. You know this because his previous age was an odd number (it left a remainder when divided by 2), and odd and even numbers alternate in a series. Since Dad's new age is even, it cannot be prime because it is divisible by 2.

Workbook Activity 59—Factoring Polynomials
1. $3a$; $3a(2a + 3)$ **2.** $2b^2$; $2b^2(b^2 - 2)$ **3.** $2d$; $2d(2d + 4 - c)$ **4.** $3x^2$; $3x^2(2x - 3y)$ **5.** $3a$; $3a(4a - b + 3ab^2)$ **6.** jk; $jk(jk - 1)$ **7.** $6xyz^2$; $6xyz^2(2z - 3y)$ **8.** $3mp$; $3mp(4m^2n^2 + 2mn - 1)$ **9.** $x(2x + 7)$ **10.** $2x^2 + 6x$; $2x(x + 3)$

Workbook Activity 60—Factoring Trinomials: $x^2 + bx + c$
1. $(y + 3)(y + 4)$ **2.** $(w - 7)(w + 3)$ **3.** $(b - 7)(b - 2)$ **4.** $(x - 9)(x - 2)$ **5.** $(n - 4)(n - 3)$ **6.** $(z - 6)(z + 5)$ **7.** $(d + 3)(d + 2)$ **8.** $(a - 10)(a + 5)$ **9.** $(m - 5)(m + 3)$ **10.** $(x + 3)(x - 9)$

Workbook Activity 61—Factoring Trinomials: $ax^2 + bx + c$
1. $(3a + 1)(a + 1)$ **2.** $(3x + 2)(x - 2)$ **3.** $(3d - 5)(2d + 3)$ **4.** $(4x - 3)(2x - 3)$ **5.** $(n + 3)(4n + 1)$ **6.** $(2y - 1)(y - 3)$ **7.** $(4x - 1)(x + 3)$ **8.** $(2n - 3)(n - 1)$ **9.** $(3b - 4)(2b + 5)$ **10.** $(4k + 9)(k + 2)$

Workbook Activity 62—Factoring Expressions: $a^2 - b^2$
1. $(y + 12)(y - 12)$ **2.** $(x + 4)(x - 4)$ **3.** $(w + 20)(w - 20)$ **4.** $(4b + 9)(4b - 9)$ **5.** $(3x + 2y)(3x - 2y)$ **6.** $(2m + 3n)(2m - 3n)$ **7.** $(j^2 + k)(j^2 - k)$ **8.** $(ab + 10)(ab - 10)$ **9.** $(5c + 13)(5c - 13)$ **10.** $(6n^2 + 5p)(6n^2 - 5p)$ **11.** $(22x + 30y)(22x - 30y)$ **12.** $(6a^4 + 7b^4)(6a^4 - 7b^4)$ **13.** $(7k^8 + 5k)(7k^8 - 5k)$ **14.** $(11n + 7p)(11n - 7p)$ **15.** $(p + 11)(p - 11)$

Workbook Activity 63—Factoring Expressions: $a^2 + 2ab + b^2$
1. $(r + 5)^2$ **2)** $(b + 10)^2$ **3.** $(k + 1)^2$ **4.** $(y + 7)^2$ **5.** $(x + 2y)^2$ **6.** $(3v + 7w)^2$ **7.** $(c + d)^2$ **8.** $(2m + 7n)^2$ **9.** $(w^2 - x)$ feet **10.** $(k + 4)$ cm

Workbook Activity 64—Zero as a Factor
1. $y = 0$ **2.** $k = 0$ **3.** $p = 0$ **4.** $x = 0$ **5.** $v = 0$ **6.** $b = 0$ **7.** $x = 0$ **8.** $r = 0$ **9.** $n = 0$ **10.** $n = 0$ **11.** $b = -5$ **12.** $n = 30$ **13.** $a = -4$ or 5 **14.** $x = -4$ or -7 **15.** $x = 30$ or 120 **16.** $d = 3$ or -1 **17.** $x = \frac{1}{2}$ or -2 **18.** $x = -6$ or 1 **19.** $y = -\frac{2}{3}$ or 1 **20.** $k = \frac{5}{2}$ or -2

Workbook Activity 65—Solving Quadratic Equations—Factoring
1. 3, −1 **2.** −4, 3 **3.** 8, −2 **4.** $\frac{5}{2}$, −2 **5.** 7, −3 **6.** −2, $\frac{3}{4}$ **7.** $-\frac{1}{3}$, $\frac{3}{2}$ **8.** $\frac{1}{2}$, −3 **9.** −7, 2 **10.** $d^2 + 5d + 6 = 0$; $d = -2$ or -3

Workbook Activity 66—Organizing Data
1. dog **2.** snake **3.** yes; by comparing the relative heights of the bars **4.** 4 **5.** 3 **6.** no, to determine a specific number value for a bar's data, you must read the number scale opposite the top of the bar **7.** Tally and Frequency of 6 **8.** Tally and Frequency of 3 **9.** Tally and Frequency of 2 **10.** Tally and Frequency of 1

Workbook Activity 67—Range, Mean, Median, and Mode
1. 16 **2.** 102.5 **3.** 8.3 **4.** 478.6 **5.** 350 **6.** 20.5 **7.** 15 **8.** 9 **9.** 7 **10.** 6

Workbook Activity 68—Box-and-Whiskers Plots
{\$4.88, \$6.95, \$8.15, \$9.29, \$10.99, \$12.79, \$13.12, \$14.69, \$23.95, \$24.20, \$27.67} **1.** \$12.79 **2.** \$4.88 **3.** \$27.67 **4.** \$8.15 **5.** \$23.95 {15, 19, 21, 27, 30, 35, 39, 40, 44, 45, 48, 55, 58, 66, 72} **6.** 40 **7.** 15 **8.** 72 **9.** 27 **10.** 55

Workbook Activity 69—The Probability Fraction
1. $\frac{1}{2}$ **2.** $\frac{1}{24}$ **3.** $\frac{1}{24}$ **4.** $\frac{2}{24} = \frac{1}{12}$ **5.** $\frac{1}{2}$

Workbook Activity 70—Probability and Complementary Events
1. not likely **2.** certain **3.** not likely **4.** not likely **5.** impossible **6.** not likely **7.** not likely **8.** certain **9.** not likely **10.** likely

Workbook Activity 71—Tree Diagrams and Sample Spaces
1. $\frac{1}{6}$ **2.** $\frac{1}{6}$ **3.** $\frac{2}{6}$ or $\frac{1}{3}$ **4.** $\frac{1}{6}$ **5.** $\frac{2}{6}$ or $\frac{1}{3}$ **6.** $\frac{2}{6}$ or $\frac{1}{3}$ **7.** $\frac{3}{6}$ or $\frac{1}{2}$ **8.** $\frac{6}{6}$ or 1 **9.** $\frac{1}{4}$ **10.** $\frac{2}{4}$ or $\frac{1}{2}$

Workbook Activity 72—Dependent and Independent Events
1. dependent **2.** independent **3.** dependent **4.** dependent **5.** independent **6.** dependent **7.** dependent **8.** independent **9.** dependent **10.** independent

Workbook Activity 73—The Fundamental Principle of Counting
1. 40,320 **2.** 39,916,800 **3.** 362,880 **4.** 120 **5.** 5,040 **6.** 6 **7.** 720 **8.** 3,628,800 **9.** 6! = 720 **10.** 4! = 24

Workbook Activity 74— Choosing the Best Measure of Central Tendency
1. 28 **2.** 20 **3.** 0 and 10 **4.** 80 **5.** sample answer: the median and/or the mode; explanations will vary.

Workbook Activity 75—Fractions as Rational Numbers
1. $\frac{1}{8}$ **2.** $\frac{1}{4}$ **3.** $\frac{4}{13}$ **4.** $\frac{5}{8}$ **5.** $\frac{2}{3}$ **6.** $\frac{1}{21}$ **7.** $\frac{3}{4}$ **8.** $-\frac{1}{3}$ **9.** $\frac{7}{12}$ **10.** $\frac{1}{3}$ **11.** $-\frac{1}{8}$ **12.** $\frac{59}{100}$ **13.** $\frac{3}{27} = \frac{1}{9}$ **14.** $\frac{18}{48} = \frac{3}{8}$ **15.** $\frac{15}{36} = \frac{5}{12}$

Workbook Activity 76—Algebraic Fractions—Rational Expressions
1. $\frac{1}{c^2}$ **2.** $\frac{5}{9x^2}$ **3.** $\frac{1}{m^5}$ **4.** $\frac{1}{3c^2d}$ **5.** $\frac{3}{4a^2}$ **6.** $\frac{7}{11wy^3z^5}$ **7.** $\frac{x+3}{y(x+8)}$ **8.** $\frac{1}{x+2}$ **9.** $\frac{1}{y-2}$ **10.** $\frac{5}{x+3}$ **11.** $\frac{1}{r-10}$ **12.** $\frac{1}{a+4}$ **13.** $\frac{k-33}{k+14}$ **14.** $\frac{1}{x+5}$ **15.** $\frac{z+1}{y(z-1)}$ **16.** $\frac{1}{w-3}$ **17.** 1 **18.** $\frac{(-1)(k+7)}{(5k^5+7)}$ or $\frac{-k-7}{5k^5+7}$ **19.** no, $\frac{1}{x-y}$ **20.** $\frac{4x^2}{6x^3} = \frac{2}{3x}$

Workbook Activity 77—Multiplying and Dividing Algebraic Fractions
1. $\frac{2}{7}$ **2.** $\frac{3}{4}$ **3.** $7\frac{1}{2}$ **4.** $3\frac{7}{9}$ **5.** $1\frac{1}{9}$ **6.** $\frac{5}{4k}$ **7.** $\frac{c^3}{d^5}$ **8.** $\frac{9}{8w^2}$ **9.** $\frac{11}{x^2y^3}$ **10.** $\frac{5n^2}{3}$ **11.** $\frac{1}{mn}$ **12.** $\frac{7ab}{3cd}$ **13.** $\frac{5b^3}{2c^3}$ **14.** $\frac{3}{x}$ **15.** $\frac{1}{x-1}$ **16.** $\frac{1}{(w+3)^2}$ or $\frac{1}{w^2+6w+9}$ **17.** $\frac{1}{8}$ **18.** 10 **19.** $\frac{1}{22}$ **20.** 7

Workbook Activity 78—Complex Fractions and the LCM
1. 6 **2.** 42 **3.** 30 **4.** 44 **5.** 90 **6.** 51 **7.** 24 **8.** 32 **9.** 154 **10.** 45 **11.** $60x$ **12.** $21a$ **13.** $40b$ **14.** $12k$ **15.** $26n$ **16.** $28k$ **17.** 1 **18.** $\frac{3}{4}$ **19.** $\frac{7}{6}$ or $1\frac{1}{6}$ **20.** $\frac{6}{7}$ **21.** $\frac{6}{5}$ or $1\frac{1}{5}$ **22.** $\frac{7}{6}$ or $1\frac{1}{6}$ **23.** $\frac{3n}{4}$ **24.** $\frac{8}{15}$ **25.** $\frac{9}{16a}$

Workbook Activity 79—Least Common Multiples and Prime Factors
1. 24 **2.** 75 **3.** 266 **4.** 42 **5.** 80 **6.** 35 **7.** x^4y^2 **8.** c^2d^4 **9.** 60 seconds **10.** 12 inches

Workbook Activity 80—Sums and Differences
1. $1\frac{6}{35}$ **2.** $\frac{19}{42}$ **3.** $\frac{7n}{60}$ **4.** $\frac{53y}{42}$ **5.** $\frac{3w}{10}$ **6.** $\frac{2-3c^2}{c}$ **7.** $\frac{m+n^2}{mn}$ **8.** $\frac{k^2-3k-3}{k(k+1)}$ or $\frac{k^2-3k-3}{k^2+k}$ **9.** $\frac{19}{35}$ **10.** $\frac{19}{40}$

Workbook Activity 81—Proportions and Fractions in Equations
1. $a = 12$ **2.** $x = 15$ **3.** $k = 9$ **4.** $y = -10$ **5.** $x = 6\frac{2}{3}$ **6.** $n = -6$ **7.** $r = 0$ **8.** $w = 65$ **9.** 14 cups **10.** $9\frac{1}{3}$ bushels

Workbook Activity 82—More Solutions to Equations with Fractions
1. $b = 9$ **2.** $k = 21$ **3.** $a = 22$ **4.** $m = -2\frac{2}{5}$ **5.** $x = 10$ **6.** $p = 6\frac{3}{4}$ **7.** $a = 39$ **8.** $y = 25$ **9.** $3\frac{3}{8}$ **10.** 2,475

Workbook Activity 83—The Greatest Common Factor of Large Numbers
1. 17 **2.** 27 **3.** 36 **4.** 9 **5.** 24 **6.** 90 **7.** 72 **8.** 106 **9.** 288 **10.** 1,365

Workbook Activity 84—Denominators and Zero
1. $d = 3$ **2.** $a = -5$ **3.** $w = 9$ **4.** $x = 0$ **5.** $y = 0$ **6.** $b = 4$ or -4 **7.** $x = 5$ or -5 **8.** $k = 0$ **9.** $x = 2$ or 7 **10.** $a = 0$ **11.** $x = 0$ **12.** $y = -5$ **13.** $y = 0$ **14.** $x = 0$ **15.** $k = 0$ **16.** $c = 6$ or -6 **17.** $b = 0$ **18.** $x = -2$ or 5 **19.** $x = 0$ **20.** $x = 15$

Workbook Activity 85—The Coordinate System
1. $(-3, -3)$ **2.** $(-3, -1)$ **3.** $(-2, 1)$ **4.** $(-4, 2)$ **5.** $(1, -2)$ **6.** $(3, -2)$ **7.** $(-2, 4)$ **8.** $(1, 1)$ **9.** $(3, 2)$ **10.** $(4, -4)$

Workbook Activity 86—Graphing Equations
1. -2 **2.** 0 **3.** 0 **4.** -6 **5.** $y = -1, y = 3$ $y = 2x + 1$; line passes through $(-1, -1)$ and $(1, 3)$

Workbook Activity 87—Intercepts of Lines
1. $-\frac{3}{2}$ **2.** 3 **3.** $\frac{4}{3}$ **4.** -4 **5.** 1 **6.** 2 **7.** $-\frac{7}{2}$ **8.** 7 **9.** 3 **10.** 3

Workbook Activity 88—Slopes of Lines
1. 1 **2.** 2 **3.** $\frac{3}{4}$ **4.** -1 **5.** $-\frac{2}{3}$ **6.** $\frac{3}{4}$ **7.** $-\frac{3}{2}$ or $-1\frac{1}{2}$ **8.** $\frac{-3}{5}$ **9.** negative **10.** positive

Workbook Activity 89—Writing Linear Equations
1. $y = -\frac{1x}{3} + 2$ **2.** $y = -3x - 6$ **3.** $y = \frac{3}{2}x + \frac{1}{2}$ **4.** $y = \frac{4}{3}x - 2$ **5.** $y = 2x + 4$ **6.** $y = \frac{2}{3}x + \frac{13}{3}$ **7.** $y = -\frac{3}{2}x + 4$ **8.** $y = -\frac{3}{2}x + 15$ **9.** check that the line is labeled with the equation: $y = \frac{3}{4}x - \frac{1}{2}$; line passes through $(-2, -2)$ and $(2, 1)$ **10.** check that the line is labeled with the equation: $y = -\frac{2}{3}x + \frac{4}{3}$; line passes through $(-4, 4)$ and $(2, 0)$

Workbook Activity 90—Lines as Functions
1. yes, any single vertical line crosses it only once **2.** no, a vertical line may cross it more than one time **3.** yes, any single vertical line crosses it only once **4.** yes, any single vertical line crosses it only once **5.** no, a vertical line may cross it more than one time.

Workbook Activity 91—Domain and Range of a Fraction
1. 3, 5, 11, 19, 25 **2.** $-1, 0, 8, 125, 512$ **3.** $-2\frac{1}{4}, -2, -\frac{1}{2}, \frac{1}{2}, 2\frac{1}{2}$ **4.** $-4, -4, 6, 24, 50$ **5.** $-21, -18, -9, -6, 15$ **6.** 12, 2, 0, 2, 6 **7.** Domain: $-3 \le x \le 5$ Range: $-3 \le y \le 4$ **8.** Domain: $-5 \le x \le 4$ Range: $-2 \le y \le 7$ **9.** Domain: $-4 \le x \le 6$ Range: $y = -3$ **10.** Domain: $x = -2$ Range: $= -2 \le y \le 4$

Workbook Activity 92—Graphing Inequalities: $y < mx + b$, $y > mx + b$
1.

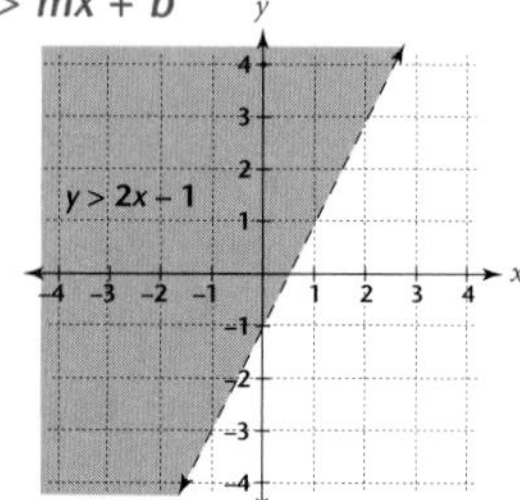

2. broken line passes through $(0, 2)$ and $(-2, 0)$; region below broken line is shaded **3.** broken line passes through $(0, 3)$ and $(3, 0)$; region above broken line is shaded **4.** $y < 1$ **5.** $x > -2$

Workbook Activity 93—Graphing Inequalities: $y \le mx + b$, $y \ge mx + b$

1. $y \le 3x - 2$ **2.** $y < -\frac{1}{3}x + 3$ **3.** $y \ge -\frac{1}{2}x + \frac{1}{2}$ **4.** $y > 2x + 4$ **5.** the line of the equation would be solid in $y \le 2x$, but the line would be dashed in $y < 2x$.

Workbook Activity 94—Graphs Without Numbers

1. C **2.** A **3.** B **4.** (0, 0) **5.** For many applications, negative values have no meaning or have a nonsensical meaning. For example, weights and measurements cannot be negative, nor can time (unless we imagine backward time, which does not exist as far as we know).

Workbook Activity 95—Parallel Lines

1. $y = x + 4$ **2.** $y = 2x + 2$ **3.** $y = 4x - 4$ **4.** $y = 2x + 5$ **5.** $y = 3x - 3$ **6.** $y = 4x - 1$ **7.** $y = x + 1$ **8.** $y = 5x + 1$ **9.** h; It describes a diagonal line (line on a slope). The other equations all describe either horizontal or vertical lines. **10.** yes, in both equations, 6 is the coefficient of x, so the equations have the same slope, and the graphed lines will therefore be parallel

Workbook Activity 96—Describing Parallel Lines

1. $y = x + 3$ **2.** $y = 3x + 1$ **3.** $y = 2x + 4$ **4.** $y = x + 2$ **5.** $y = 3x + 1$ **6.** rewrite as $y = \frac{1}{2}x - 2$, $y = \frac{1}{2}x - 5$ **7.** rewrite as $y = 6x$, $y = 6x + 3$ **8.** rewrite as $y = \frac{4}{5}x + 1$, $y = \frac{4}{5}x$ or $y = \frac{4}{5}x + 0$ **9.** rewrite as $y = -2x - 2$, $y = -2x - 1$ **10.** rewrite as $y = x + 4$, $y = x - 6$

Workbook Activity 97—Intersecting Lines—Common Solutions

1. no, slopes are equal, lines are parallel **2.** yes, slopes are unequal, lines intersect **3.** yes, slopes are unequal, lines intersect **4.** no, slopes are equal, $m = 3$ **5.** yes, slopes are unequal, $m = 3$ and $m = 1$

Workbook Activity 98—Solving Linear Equations—Substitution

1. $(3, -2)$ **2.** $(\frac{1}{3}, -\frac{2}{3})$ **3.** $(-1, -2)$ **4.** $(-1, 1)$ **5.** $(3, 1)$ **6.** $(17, 23)$ **7.** $(1, -\frac{1}{2})$ **8.** $(2, 6)$ **9.** $(1, 2)$ **10.** $(\frac{1}{2}, 2)$

Workbook Activity 99—Solving Linear Equations—Elimination

1. $(15, 5)$ **2.** $(3, 5)$ **3.** $(1, 4)$ **4.** $(3, -1)$ **5.** $(-2, 1)$ **6.** $(3, 11)$ **7.** $(2, 0)$ **8.** $(-2, 4)$ **9.** $(\frac{1}{2}, \frac{1}{3})$ **10.** $(-5, -4)$

Workbook Activity 100—Graphing Systems of Linear Equations

1. x-intercept $= 4$; y-intercept $= 8$ **2.** x-intercept $= -4$; y-intercept $= -2$ **3.** x-intercept $= \frac{11}{5}$; y-intercept $= -\frac{11}{3}$ **4.** point of intersection $(-2, 1)$ **5.** point of intersection $(3, -1)$

Workbook Activity 101—*And* Statements—Conjunctions

For answers **1–4**, true statements are from the left side of the Statement Box on the work page; false statements are from the right side. **1.** any true statement **2.** any false statement **3.** any false statement **4.** any true statement **5.** accept any conjunction having 2 true parts and the following structure: statement and statement.

Workbook Activity 102—Problem Solving Using Linear Equations

1. $(4, 5)$ **2.** $(12, 2)$ **3.** $(\frac{1}{2}, \frac{1}{3})$ **4.** 100 acres of wheat, 80 acres of oats **5.** 36, 12

Workbook Activity 103—Introduction to Matrices: Addition and Subtraction

1. $\begin{bmatrix} 12 & 23 \\ 4 & 100 \end{bmatrix}$ **2.** $\begin{bmatrix} 14 & 51 \\ 10 & 39 \\ 84 & 26 \end{bmatrix}$ **3.** $\begin{bmatrix} 41 & 47 & 48 & 66 \\ 70 & 3 & -11 & 0 \\ 75 & 75 & 75 & 75 \\ -17 & -14 & -86 & -100 \end{bmatrix}$

4. $\begin{bmatrix} 25 & 9 \\ -23 & -1 \end{bmatrix}$ **5.** $\begin{bmatrix} 48 & -24 & 0 \\ 12 & 31 & -29 \end{bmatrix}$

Workbook Activity 104—Multiplication of Matrices

1. $\begin{bmatrix} 9 & 24 \\ 27 & 15 \end{bmatrix}$ **2.** $\begin{bmatrix} 70 & 105 & 140 \\ 42 & 56 & 70 \\ 28 & 14 & 0 \end{bmatrix}$ **3.** $\begin{bmatrix} xy & 4y & 17y \\ 2xy & 9y & 0 \\ 3xy & y & y^2 \end{bmatrix}$

4. $\begin{bmatrix} 4x + 6y & 5x + 7y \\ 4n + 6r & 5n + 7r \end{bmatrix}$ **5.** $\begin{bmatrix} 216 & 41 \\ 321 & 63\frac{1}{2} \end{bmatrix}$

Workbook Activity 105—Rational Numbers as Decimals

1. $0.25\overline{0}$, terminating **2.** $0.8\overline{0}$, terminating **3.** $0.95\overline{0}$, terminating **4.** $0.8\overline{3}$, repeating **5.** $0.1\overline{3}$, repeating **6.** $0.\overline{1}$, repeating **7.** $0.875\overline{0}$, terminating **8.** $0.44\overline{0}$, terminating **9.** $0.2\overline{0}$, terminating **10.** $0.\overline{285714}$, repeating **11.** $0.\overline{09}$, repeating **12.** $0.\overline{8}$, repeating **13.** $0.375\overline{0}$, terminating **14.** $0.0625\overline{0}$, terminating **15.** $0.75\overline{0}$, terminating **16.** $0.\overline{076923}$, repeating **17.** $0.7\overline{0}$, terminating **18.** $0.8\overline{6}$, repeating **19.** $0.\overline{857142}$, repeating **20.** $0.8625\overline{0}$, terminating

Workbook Activity 106—Rational Number Equivalents

1. $\frac{2}{15}$ **2.** $\frac{5}{6}$ **3.** $\frac{1}{9}$ **4.** $\frac{2}{3}$ **5.** $\frac{13}{15}$ **6.** $\frac{8}{9}$ **7.** $\frac{1}{6}$ **8.** $\frac{4}{11}$ **9.** $\frac{2}{11}$ **10.** $\frac{4}{9}$

Workbook Activity 107—Irrational Numbers as Decimals

Note: Irrational roots are approximate.

1. 7 **2.** rational **3.** 3.87298. . . **4.** irrational **5.** 3.31662. . . **6.** irrational **7.** 2.44948. . . **8.** irrational **9.** 12 **10.** rational **11.** 11 **12.** rational **13.** 7.07106. . . **14.** irrational **15.** 3.68403. . . **16.** irrational **17.** 6 **18.** rational **19.** 2.62074. . . **20.** irrational **21.** 13 **22.** rational **23.** 5 **24.** rational **25.** 9

Workbook Activity 108—Products and Quotients of Radicals

1. $2\sqrt{3}$ **2.** $2\sqrt{5}$ **3.** $4\sqrt{3}$ **4.** $3\sqrt{2}$ **5.** $4\sqrt{2}$ **6.** $5\sqrt{2}$ **7.** $2\sqrt{21}$ **8.** $6ab\sqrt{5b}$ **9.** $7\sqrt{2}$ **10.** $3\sqrt{5}$ **11.** $4y\sqrt{x}$ **12.** $4\sqrt{6}$ **13.** $a\sqrt{3}$ **14.** $3xy\sqrt{5y}$ **15.** $2xy\sqrt{2xy}$ **16.** $5xy\sqrt{y}$ **17.** $10\sqrt{10}$ **18.** $6x\sqrt{11}$ **19.** $3x\sqrt{y}$ **20.** $4k\sqrt{2k}$ **21.** $2a^3b^3\sqrt{3ab}$ **22.** $3xy^2\sqrt{2xy}$ **23.** $5ab^2\sqrt{2ab}$ **24.** $8\sqrt{3}$ **25.** $6\sqrt{11}$ inches

Workbook Activity 109—Sums and Differences of Radicals

1. $8\sqrt{2}$ **2.** $5\sqrt{5}$ **3.** not possible **4.** $\sqrt{2}$ **5.** $4\sqrt{21}$ **6.** $6\sqrt{2}$ **7.** $5\sqrt{3}$ **8.** not possible **9.** $2\sqrt{2}$ **10.** $8\sqrt{5}$ **11.** $13\sqrt{2}$ **12.** $-2\sqrt{3}$ **13.** $3x\sqrt{2}$ **14.** $8\sqrt{6}$ **15.** $5x\sqrt{2y}$ **16.** not possible **17.** $22\sqrt{6}$ **18.** $7\sqrt{5}$ **19.** $4\sqrt{10}$ **20.** $-2x\sqrt{6}$

Workbook Activity 110—Radicals and Fractions

1. $\sqrt{3}$ **2.** $\frac{\sqrt{2}}{2}$ **3.** $\sqrt{5}$ **4.** $\frac{\sqrt{5}}{2}$ **5.** $\frac{\sqrt{7}}{7}$ **6.** $\frac{2\sqrt{3}}{3}$ **7.** $\frac{\sqrt{5}}{5}$ **8.** $\frac{10\sqrt{x}}{x}$ **9.** $\sqrt{3}$ **10.** $\frac{3\sqrt{2x}}{2x}$ **11.** $\sqrt{3} + 1$ **12.** $\frac{6+2\sqrt{2}}{7}$ **13.** $\frac{3(\sqrt{3} + 1)}{2}$ **14.** $2 + \sqrt{2}$ **15.** $6 + 2\sqrt{3}$

Workbook Activity 111—Radicals in Equations

1. $x = 25$ **2.** $n = 64$ **3.** $k = 1$ **4.** $a = 169$ **5.** $r = 136$ **6.** $y = 30$ **7.** $m = 256$ **8.** $n = 3$ **9.** $\sqrt{n} + \sqrt{100} = 19, 81$ **10.** $n^2 = 800$, $20\sqrt{2}$ inches

Workbook Activity 112—Simplifying Equations with Radicals

1. 40.5 feet or 40 feet 6 inches **2.** 162 feet **3.** 16 inches **4.** 7.2 inches **5.** 13.9 feet

Workbook Activity 113—Radicals and Exponents

1. $5^{\frac{1}{3}} \cdot x^{\frac{1}{3}}$ **2.** $7^{\frac{1}{2}} \cdot b^{\frac{1}{2}}$ **3.** $13^{\frac{1}{4}} \cdot d^{\frac{1}{4}}$ **4.** $5^{\frac{1}{3}} \cdot y^{\frac{1}{3}}$ **5.** $17^{\frac{1}{2}} \cdot x^{\frac{1}{2}} \cdot y^{\frac{1}{2}}$ **6.** $11^{\frac{1}{7}} \cdot a^{\frac{1}{7}} \cdot b^{\frac{1}{7}}$ **7.** $c^{\frac{3}{2}}$ **8.** $n^{\frac{4}{3}}$ **9.** $d^{\frac{7}{3}}$ **10.** $x^{\frac{7}{2}}$ **11.** $y^{\frac{13}{6}}$ **12.** $b^{\frac{22}{7}}$ **13.** $a^{\frac{2}{3}}$ **14.** $k^{\frac{5}{3}}$ **15.** $n^{\frac{2}{5}}$ **16.** $m^{\frac{3}{7}}$ **17.** $c^{\frac{3}{5}}$ **18.** $b^{\frac{5}{4}}$ **19.** $x^{\frac{5}{2}}$ **20.** $n^{\frac{4}{3}}$

Workbook Activity 114—Drawing and Using a Square Root Graph

Accept any answer that is within 0.3 of the given answer and has the same whole number as the answer. **1.** 1.4 **2.** 5.5 **3.** 3.2 **4.** 5.2 **5.** 3.5 **6.** 4.8 **7.** 3.7 **8.** 2.8 **9.** 4.1 **10.** 5.3

Workbook Activity 115—Angles and Angle Measure

1. supplementary **2.** vertical **3.** complementary **4.** supplementary **5.** yes **6.** no **7.** yes **8.** yes **9.** no **10.** yes

Workbook Activity 116—Pairs of Lines in a Plane and in Space

1. parallel **2.** skew **3.** intersecting **4.** parallel **5.** intersecting **6.** skew **7.** no **8.** no **9.** yes **10.** yes

Workbook Activity 117—Angle Measures in a Triangle

1. 20° **2.** 15° **3.** 30° **4.** 45° **5.** 105°

Workbook Activity 118—Naming Triangles

1. scalene **2.** scalene **3.** isosceles **4.** equilateral **5.** isosceles **6.** equiangular **7.** obtuse **8.** obtuse **9.** right **10.** acute

Workbook Activity 119—Quadrilaterals

Explanatory note for answers **1–3**: the angle measurements in **1–3** are derived as follows. You know that $\angle B$ and $\angle C$ are supplementary, because of the properties of transversals. This means that you can find $m\angle C$. And since $\overline{DA} = \overline{CB}$ (definition of isosceles trapezoid), you know that $\angle B$ must equal $\angle A$ and $\angle D$ must equal $\angle C$. Otherwise, either $\overline{DA}$ and $\overline{CB}$ could not be equal or $\overline{DC}$ and $\overline{AB}$ could not be parallel. Students are not required to give an explanation for their answers. **1.** 45° **2.** 135° **3.** 135° **4.** Enough. By definition, a rectangle has all right angles (90°). **5.** Not enough. You can calculate $m\angle D$—it is supplementary to the given $\angle A$ (definition of trapezoid and property of transversals). But you cannot calculate $m\angle B$ or $m\angle C$ from the given data.

Workbook Activity 120—Congruent and Similar Triangles

1. yes—SAS **2.** yes—SSS **3.** yes—ASA **4.** no **5.** No. The only requirement for a right triangle is to have one right angle. Each of the other two angles can be any measure that is $< 90°$.

Workbook Activity 121—Trigonometric Ratios

Note: Students are not required to show their equations.
1. $x = 12.4$, $\tan 68° = \frac{x}{5}$ **2.** $x = 21.9$, $\cos 43° = \frac{x}{30}$ **3.** $x = 59.8$, $\sin 50° = \frac{x}{78}$ **4.** $x = 49.4$, $\tan 66° = \frac{x}{22}$ **5.** 29.9 m, $\tan 75° = \frac{x}{8}$

Workbook Activity 122—Solutions by Factoring

1. $x^2 + 5x + 6 = 0$ **2.** $x^2 - 2x - 15 = 0$ **3.** $y^2 - 7y + 10 = 0$ **4.** $2x^2 + 3x - 2 = 0$ **5.** $-2, -3$

Workbook Activity 123—Writing the Equations from Their Roots

1. $x^2 + x - 6 = 0$ **2.** $x^2 - 3x - 4 = 0$ **3.** $x^2 + 3x - 18 = 0$ **4.** $x^2 - 7x + 10 = 0$ **5.** $x^2 + 5x - 6 = 0$ **6.** $x^2 + 8x - 20 = 0$ **7.** $x^2 - 5x + 6 = 0$ **8.** $x^2 + 7x + 10 = 0$ **9.** $x^2 - 2x - 15 = 0$ **10.** $x^2 - 13x + 12 = 0$ **11.** $x^2 + 6x - 16 = 0$ **12.** $x^2 - 5x - 50 = 0$ **13.** $x^2 + 2x - 35 = 0$ **14.** $x^2 - x - 30 = 0$ **15.** $x^2 + 4x - 32 = 0$

Workbook Activity 124—Solving by Completing the Square

1. $-3, -1$ **2.** $0, 2$ **3.** $-1, 7$ **4.** $-12, 0$ **5.** $-9, 1$ **6.** $0, 10$ **7.** $3 - \sqrt{7}, 3 + \sqrt{7}$ **8.** $-2, 6$ **9.** $-3, 5$ **10.** $-4, 6$

Workbook Activity 125—Solving Using the Quadratic Formula

1. 2, 3 **2.** $-3, -4$ **3.** $-\frac{1}{2}, 1$ **4.** $-1, 4$ **5.** Both roots are valid.

Workbook Activity 126—Graphing Quadratic Equations

1. a **2.** yes **3.** no **4.** $x = \frac{3}{2}$ (or $x = 1\frac{1}{2}$)
5.

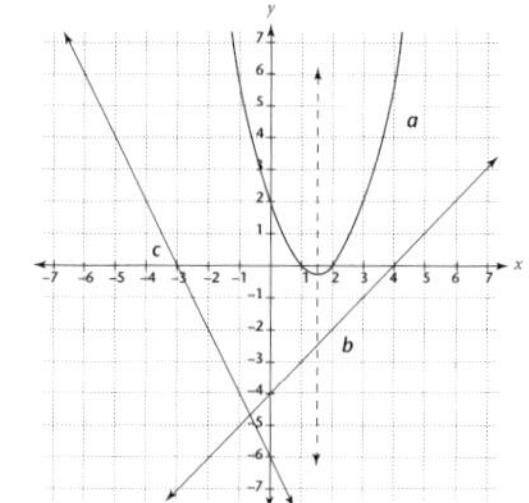

Application Activities

Application Activity 1—Using a Formula

1. 193 mph **2.** 12 mph **3.** 179 mph **4.** 113 mph **5.** 256 mph **6.** 331 mph **7.** 32 mph **8.** 57 mph **9.** 150 mph **10.** 225 mph **11.** 17 mph **12.** 26 mph **13.** 111 mph **14.** 584 mph **15.** 273 mph

Application Activity 2—Using Square Root

1. 11 miles **2.** 18 miles **3.** 27 miles **4.** 63 miles **5.** 44 miles

Application Activity 3—Using Equations

1. The Bank of China Tower is 1,209 feet tall. **2.** The Sears Tower has 110 stories. **3.** Moscow State University has 26 stories. **4.** Petronas Twin Towers are 1,483 feet tall. **5.** One Ninety-One Peachtree Tower is 770 feet tall.

Application Activity 4—Using Proportions

1. 32 laps **2.** 65 miles **3.** $14.96 **4.** $15\frac{3}{4}$ cups of flour **5.** 35 laps **6.** 40 laps **7.** 150 miles **8.** $9\frac{3}{5}$ inches **9.** $18\frac{7}{16}$ miles **10.** 16 cm

Application Activity 5—Polynomial Interest

1. $520.30 **2.** $520.20 **3.** $541.22 **4.** $595.51 **5.** $633.39

Application Activity 6—Frame Factor

1. The matte is $\frac{1}{2}$ foot wide. **2.** The path is 1 meter wide. **3.** The length of the side of the original square is 8 feet. **4.** The length is 16 cm and the width is 4 cm. **5.** The length of one side of the square is 3 or 1. Both solutions are acceptable.

Application Activity 7—Multistage Experiments

1. First stage, because it fails once for every 5 times it is used. $\frac{1}{5} > \frac{1}{10} > \frac{1}{50}$ **2.** Third stage, because the probability for success is $\frac{49}{50}$ which is $> \frac{45}{50}$ for the second stage and $> \frac{40}{50}$ for the first stage. **3.** $\frac{1764}{2500}$ **4.** The third stage is 10 times less likely to fail than the first stage and 5 times less likely to fail than the second stage. This is because the denominator of the probability for failure in the third stage is 10 times larger than the denominator in the first stage and 5 times larger than the denominator in the second stage. **5.** 400 failed launches for every 1,000,000 attempted.

Application Activity 8—Working Fractions

1. $1\frac{1}{5}$ hours **2.** $2\frac{2}{5}$ days **3.** $1\frac{4}{5}$ hours **4.** $3\frac{15}{16}$ hours **5.** $2\frac{4}{7}$ hours

Application Activity 9—Graphing

1. triangle **2.** pentagon **3.** Answers will vary. Check students' work for accuracy. **4.** Answers will vary. Check students' work for accuracy. **5.** Answers will vary. Check students' work for accuracy.

Application Activity 10—Using Venn Diagrams

1. $U = \{1-8\}$
$A \cup B = \{1, 2, 3, 5, 6, 7, 8\}$
$A \cap B = \{1, 8\}$

2.

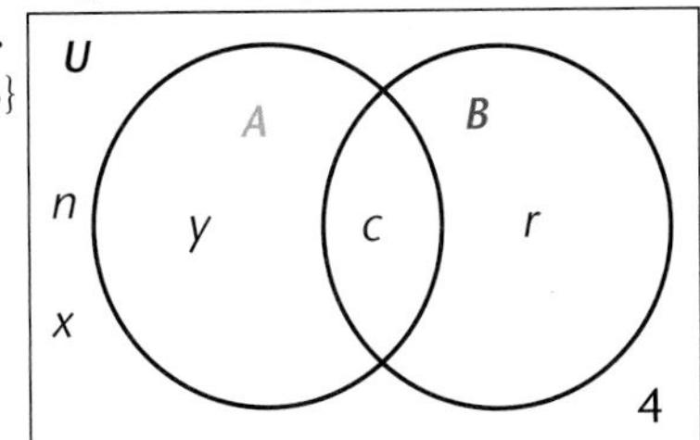

3. Two different Venn diagrams can be created. **4.** Five students were taking no math or science. **5.** Answers will vary.

Application Activity 11—Falling Objects and Soaring Rockets

1. 80 feet per second **2.** 31.30 meters per second **3.** 132.82 meters per second **4.** 113.14 feet per second **5.** 11.18 kilometers per second

Application Activity 12—Using Geometric Shapes

1. The octagon should have 20 diagonals drawn. **2.** The pentagon should have 5 diagonals drawn. **3.** 54 **4.** 14 **5.** 35

Application Activity 13—Using Quadratic Equations

1. The rocket is 60 feet above the ground at 1.02 seconds and 3.66 seconds. **2.** The rocket is 75 feet above the ground at 1.45 seconds and 3.24 seconds. **3.** There are two times when the rocket is at a certain height because it must go up and down. **4.** You could estimate the total flight time by adding together the two times, no matter what height you are using. **5.** About 4.68 seconds

Everyday Algebra

Everyday Algebra 1—Using Basic Operations

Check Number	Payment or Withdrawal	Deposit or Interest	Balance
1529			$776.96
1530	$47.61		
1531			$79.35
1532	$22.00		
1533			−$24.95
		$541.88	
1534			$246.93
			$216.93
1535	$17.91		
1536			$64.27
		$1.26	

1. subtraction **2.** addition **3.** The check to the hardware store should not have been written. At the time, the amount of money in the account was less than the amount of the check. The bank charged $30 for this error.

Everyday Algebra 2—Finding Volume

1. 15 units^3 **2.** 112 units^3 **3.** 210 units^3 **4.** 1080 unit cubes **5.** 7 units

Everyday Algebra 3—Calculating Distances

1. 8.1 units **2.** 16.2 units **3.** 8.2 units **4.** 14.3 units **5.** 15.7 units **6.** 10.2 units **7.** 6.1 units **8.** 14.9 units **9.** 18 blocks **10.** 770 miles

Everyday Algebra 4—Using Proportions

sample answer: $y = \frac{1}{4}x$ where x = weight in pounds and y = force in pounds **1.** 12.5 pounds **2.** 250 pounds **3.** 4 pounds **4.** 2,000 pounds **5.** sample answer: $y = \frac{3}{8}x$ where x = weight in pounds and y = force in pounds

Everyday Algebra 5—Using Scientific Notation

Sample estimates shown. **1.** 2.26 (10^8) mi **2.** 4.22 (10^8) mi **3.** 5.84 (10^8) mi **4.** 8.9 (10^8) mi **5.** 2.31 (10^{10}) mi

Everyday Algebra 6—Using Formulas

1. length $= x$ or y units; width $= x$ or y units; Area $= xy$ units
2. length $= 2x$; width $= 1$; Area $= 2x$ or length $= x + 1$; width $= x$; Area $= x^2 + x$ **3.** length $= x + y$ units; width $= x - y$ units
4. length $= x$ units; width $= x - 2$ units; Perimeter $= 4x - 4$ units
5. length $= a - 3$ or $b + 5$ units; width $= a - 3$ or $b + 5$ units

Everyday Algebra 7—Studying Graph Impressions

1.

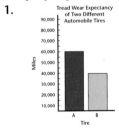

Tread Wear Expectancy of Two Different Automobile Tires
Miles: 90,000 80,000 70,000 60,000 50,000 40,000 30,000 20,000 10,000
Tire: A B

2. Check students' graphs. **3.** Check students' graphs. **4.** Check students' graphs. **5.** Answers will vary. Check students' responses.

Everyday Algebra 8—Solving Distance Problems

1. $54\frac{9}{20}$ km **2.** 161 mm **3.** $16\frac{5}{16}$ mi **4.** $2\frac{1}{2}$ in. **5.** $36\frac{27}{80}$ km

Everyday Algebra 9—Comparing Slopes

1. $\frac{3}{4}$ **2.** the eight-foot staircase **3.** the 3.5 km trail **4.** line *N*; since the slope of the *x*-axis is zero, and $\frac{1}{30} < \frac{7}{200}$, line *N* with a slope of $\frac{1}{30}$ is most nearly parallel to the *x*-axis. **5.** no; to determine the height of each kite, the length of each string must be known in addition to the given data.

Everyday Algebra 10—Graphing Linear Equations

1. possible answer: $C = \$7.50v$ where C = cost in dollars and v = number of visits; $C = \$50 + \$2.50v$ where C = cost in dollars and v = number of visits **2.** Answers will vary. **3.** Check students' graphs. The common solution of each graph should be (10 visits, $75.00). **4.** Plan A is most cost-effective when fewer than ten visits are made each month. **5.** Plan B is most cost-effective when more than ten visits are made each month.

Everyday Algebra 11—Converting Measurements

1. 3.105 miles **2.** 9.18 cubic meters or 9.18 m^3 **3.** 2.114 quarts **4.** 9.361 yards **5.** 5 feet 11 inches or 71 inches

Everyday Algebra 12—Finding the Sum of Angle Measurements in a Figure

1. 540° **2.** 720° **3.** $x = 45°$; $y = 5°$ **4.** $x = 45°$; $y = 30°$ **5.** $x = 20°$; $y = 10°$

Everyday Algebra 13—Graphing Quadratic Equations

1. *b*; $y = x^2$ is a parabola that opens upward **2.** 8 feet **3.** 8 feet **4.** 7.5 inches **5.** 176.625 square inches

Community Connections

Community Connection 1—Landscaping

1–5. Answers will vary. Check students' responses.

Community Connection 2—Transportation and Shipping

1–2. Answers will vary. Check students' responses. **3.** 3,465 $feet^3$ **4–5.** Answers will vary. Check students' responses.

Community Connection 3—Understanding Pricing

1–9. Answers will vary. Check students' responses. **10.** Sample answer: The package with the smaller unit cost is the better buy regardless of size.

Community Connection 4—Automobile Leasing

1–5. Answers will vary. Check students' responses.

Community Connection 5—Careers and Scientific Notation

Answers will vary.

Community Connection 6—Exact or Estimated Measurements

Answers will vary.

Community Connection 7—License Possibilities

Answers will vary.

Community Connection 8—Weather Forecasts

Answers will vary.

Community Connection 9—Slope in Construction

1–5. Answers will vary. Check students' responses.

Community Connection 10—Line Graphs

1–5. Answers will vary. Check students' responses.

Community Connection 11— Measurement Conversion

1–5. Answers will vary. Check students' responses.

Community Connection 12—Geometric Shapes

1–30. Answers will vary. Check students' responses.

Community Connection 13—CAD—Computer-Aided Design

1–5. Answers will vary. Check students' responses.

Estimation Exercises

Estimation Exercise 1—Estimating Answers to Operations on Positive and Negative Integers

Student estimates may vary. Sample answers are given.

1. $600 \div 10 = 60$; 49.42 **2.** $800 \div 50 = 16$; 17.30 **3.** $40 \times -80 = -3{,}200$; $-3{,}608$ **4.** 25, 125, 130 **5.** 39, 390, 404

Estimation Exercise 2—Estimating Square Roots

2. 25, 36, less, 6 **3.** 16, 25, more, 4 **4.** 64, 81, less, 9 **5.** 100, 121, more, 10 **6.** 256, 289, less, 17 **7.** 361, 400, less, 20 **8.** 27, 64, more, 3 **9.** 125, 216, more, 5 **10.** 512, 729, less, 9

Estimation Exercise 3—Estimating the Value of a Variable in an Equation

Student estimates may vary. Sample estimates are given.

1. $p = 4, p = 4$ **2.** $x = 6, x = 8$ **3.** $a = 10, a = 9$ **4.** $s = 11, s = 12$ **5.** $g = -2, g = -3$ **6.** $x = 5, x = 7$ **7.** $r = 12, r = 10$ **8.** $b = -7, b = -7$ **9.** $k = 2, k = 2$ **10.** $t = -1, t = -1$ **11.** $n = 9, n = 9$ **12.** $c = -2, c = -2$ **13.** $r = -4, r = -4$ **14.** $x = 3, x = 2$ **15.** $m = 4, m = 6$ **16.** $h = -2, h = -2$ **17.** $w = 0, w = 1$ **18.** $f = 3, f = 3$ **19.** $q = 0, q = 0$ **20.** $d = 4, d = 4$

Estimation Exercise 4—Estimating Distance, Rate, and Time

Answers will vary. Sample answers are given.

1. 64 is the closest number to 65 that evenly divides by 4. So divide 64 by 4 to get 16. She must average a little more than 16 mph. **2.** 2 hours 54 minutes is about 3 hours. Divide 3 into 33 to get 11. That means Yen ran a little more than 11 kilometers per hour. **3.** 4 minutes 16 seconds is about 4 minutes, which is $\frac{1}{15}$ of an hour. 28 mph is about 30 mph. So, to find the distance, multiply 30 mph times $\frac{1}{15}$, which is 2. So the run is about 2 miles long. **4.** $60 \times 6 = 360$ and $60 \times 7 = 420$. So the trip will take less than 7 hours but more than 6. 385 is closer to 360 than it is to 420. So Kunal's trip will be about 6.5 hours, meaning he should plan to leave town around 12:30 p.m. in order to meet his cousin at 7 p.m. **5.** 2 hours 18 minutes is about $2\frac{1}{3}$, or $\frac{7}{3}$, hours. 58 mph is about 60 mph. Multiply $\frac{7}{3}$ times 60 to get 140 miles. So the trucker drove about 140 miles.

Estimation Exercise 5—Estimating Quotients of Polynomials Divided by Monomials

1. $\frac{24x^2 - 8x + 16}{8} = 3x^2 - x + 2$ **2.** $\frac{20p^2 + 15p - 40}{5} = 4p^2 + 3p - 8$ **3.** $\frac{33n^3 - 12n^2 - 18n}{3n} = 11n^2 - 4n - 6$ **4.** $\frac{28r^4 - 21r^3 + 14r^2}{7r^2} = -4r^2 + 3r - 2$ **5.** $\frac{16x^2y^2 + 8xy - 4}{4} = 4x^2y^2 + 2xy - 1$

Estimation Exercise 6—Estimating Factors

1. $(m + 9)(m + 10)$ **2.** $(p + 2)(p + 45)$ **3.** $(r - 2)(r - 12)$ **4.** $(b - 3)(b - 48)$ **5.** $(x + 5)(x - 20)$ **6.** $(c + 5)(c + 12)$ **7.** $(n - 2)(n + 50)$ **8.** $(s + 9)(s - 16)$ **9.** $(v + 5)(v - 16)$ **10.** $(d - 8)(d + 10)$

Estimation Exercise 7—Estimating Probability with a Spinner

1. $\frac{1}{15}$ **2.** $\frac{9}{15}$ or $\frac{3}{5}$ **3.** $\frac{3}{15}$ or $\frac{1}{5}$ **4.** $\frac{6}{15}$ or $\frac{2}{5}$ **5.** Answers will vary. Sample answer: No. Even if Andrew wins, he still "loses" $50 because he's paid $100 for something that's worth only half that amount.

Estimation Exercise 8—Estimating Products and Quotients of Fractions

1. less, 17 **2.** less, 2 **3.** greater, 99 **4.** greater, 75 **5.** less, $\frac{1}{2}$ **6.** greater, $\frac{8}{9}$ **7.** less, $\frac{3}{10}$ **8.** greater, $\frac{28}{27}$ or $1\frac{1}{27}$ **9.** greater, $\frac{2}{3}$ **10.** less, $\frac{1}{30}$ **11.** greater, $\frac{2}{5}$ **12.** less, $\frac{1}{2}$ **13.** greater, $\frac{1}{3}$ **14.** less, $\frac{9}{32}$ **15.** greater, $\frac{19}{18}$ or $1\frac{1}{18}$

Estimation Exercise 9—Estimating Slope

1. $(-3, 0),(0, 3)$, m is approximately 1 **2.** $(1, 0),(0, 6)$, m is approximately -6 **3.** $(-5, 0),(0, 2)$, m is approximately $\frac{2}{5}$ **4.** $(3, 0),(0, 5)$, m is approximately $-1\frac{2}{3}$ **5.** $(8, 0),(0, 3)$, m is approximately $-\frac{3}{8}$

Estimation Exercise 10—Estimating Intersection

1. intersect, slopes are different positive integers **2.** parallel, slopes are the same **3.** intersect, slopes are positive and negative **4** intersect, slopes are different negative integers **5.** parallel, slopes are the same **6.** For question 2, answers will vary. Sample answer: $y = 6x + 6$ **7.** For question 5, answers will vary. Sample answer: $y = x + \frac{1}{5}$ **8.** For question 1: $y = 5x + 3$ and $y = 5x + 2$ Note: The intercept should change here so that the lines aren't the same. **9.** For question 3: $2y - 4x = 5$ and $y = 2x + 9$ **10.** For question 4: $\frac{1}{3}y = -4x - 2$ and $\frac{1}{3}y = -4x - 3$ Note: The intercept should change here so that the lines aren't the same.

Estimation Exercise 11—Estimating the Dimensions of a Square Given Its Area

1. 7' × 7' because 8' × 8' would be too big and 6' × 6' would be too small **2.** a little less than 7 feet long **3.** 40 feet because 56 is close to the perfect square 64, so each side of her garden is about 8 feet long; 8 × 4 = 32, the perimeter of her garden **4.** 60' × 60' because the square root of 930 is a little more than 30. The length of two squares will make up the length of one side of the building. **5.** 40 cm because 97 is close to the perfect square 100, so each side of his card is approximately 10 cm; 10 × 4 = 40, the perimeter of the card

Estimation Exercise 12—Estimating the Measure of Angles

Estimates will vary. Actual measures are given.

1. 45° **2.** $22\frac{1}{2}$° **3.** 15° **4.** $67\frac{1}{2}$° **5.** 80° **6.** 120° **7.** 135° **8.** 165° **9.** 90° **10.** 175°

Estimation Exercise 13—Estimating Whether a Quadratic Equation Has a Solution

1. $\sqrt{-354}$, no solution **2.** $\sqrt{161}$ **3.** $\sqrt{-4}$, no solution **4.** $\sqrt{-347}$, no solution **5.** $\sqrt{32}$ **6.** $\sqrt{33}$ **7.** 20 **8.** $\sqrt{-20}$, no solution **9.** $\sqrt{576}$ **10.** $\sqrt{-99}$, no solution

Chapter Mastery Tests

Chapter 1 Mastery Test A

1. C **2.** D **3.** C **4.** A **5.** B **6.** open **7.** false **8.** true **9.** algebraic **10.** numerical **11.** algebraic **12.** -24 **13.** $+\frac{4}{5}$ or $\frac{4}{5}$ **14.** 0; zero has no opposite **15.** +2.1 or 2.1 **16.** 8 **17.** 4.09 **18.** $\frac{11}{15}$ **19.** 1.7 **20.** -50 **21.** -23 **22.** +11 or 11 **23.** -28 **24.** +60 or 60 **25.** -4 **26.** $+9y$ or $9y$ **27.** m^9 **28.** r^{12} **29.** $25a + 2$ **30.** $6n^3$

Chapter 1 Mastery Test B

1. B **2.** C **3.** B **4.** C **5.** A **6.** open **7.** false **8.** true **9.** algebraic **10.** numerical **11.** algebraic **12.** –18 **13.** $\frac{3}{7}$ **14.** 0; zero has no opposite **15.** 1.6 **16.** 5 **17.** 3.78 **18.** $\frac{14}{23}$ **19.** 5.9 **20.** 60 **21.** -14 **22.** 12 **23.** -27 **24.** 72 **25.** -3 **26.** $8x$ **27.** c^7 **28.** b^{12} **29.** $22p + 4$ **30.** $7r^3$

Chapter 2 Mastery Test A

1. D **2.** A **3.** A **4.** C **5.** B **6.** e **7.** a **8.** b **9.** a **10.** b **11.** 64 **12.** $-12p - 12r$ or $-(12p + 12r)$ **13.** $6(c + d)$ **14.** $h(g^2 + j^3)$ **15.** 5 **16.** 1 **17.** g **18.** $-\frac{1}{2}$ **19.** $\frac{1}{b^4}$ **20.** $\frac{m}{n}$ **21.** $-8m^3$ **22.** $10{,}000z^2$ **23.** $-6e$ **24.** $-9a$ **25.** $520z$

Chapter 2 Mastery Test B

1. C **2.** D **3.** A **4.** B **5.** A **6.** e **7.** a **8.** b **9.** a **10.** b **11.** 72 **12.** $-8n - 8p$ or $-(8n + 8p)$ **13.** $3(g + h)$ **14.** $m(c^2 + d^3)$ **15.** 6 **16.** 1 **17.** x **18.** $-\frac{1}{7}$ **19.** $\frac{1}{a^3}$ **20.** $\frac{2}{y}$ **21.** $-64q^3$ **22.** $6400b^2$ **23.** $-2a$ **24.** $-17r$ **25.** $850y$

Chapter 3 Mastery Test A

1. B **2.** D **3.** D **4.** A **5.** D **6.** $4x = 32$ **7.** $7x = 161$ **8.** $2x = \frac{1}{2}$ **9.** $10x = -40$ **10.** 7 **11.** 29 **12.** -24 **13.** -6 **14.** 42 **15.** -2 **16.** $b = \frac{2A}{h}$ **17.** 12 cm **18.** $x = -2$ **19.** $x > -1$ **20.** $x \geq -6$

Chapter 3 Mastery Test B

1. A **2.** B **3.** D **4.** B **5.** D **6.** $3x = 27$ **7.** $9x = 210$ **8.** $5x = \frac{1}{5}$ **9.** $12x = -36$ **10.** $a = 8$ **11.** $w = 8$ **12.** $z = 33$ **13.** $r = -6$ **14.** $m = 51$ **15.** $q = -2$ **16.** $b = \frac{2A}{h}$ **17.** 12 cm **18.** $x = -2$ **19.** $x > -1$ **20.** $x \geq -6$

Chapter 4 Mastery Test A

1. A **2.** D **3.** B **4.** A **5.** B **6.** $4n - 3 = 13$; $n = 4$ **7.** $-10 + n = 6$; $n = 16$ **8.** $\frac{n}{10} = -5$; $n = -50$ **9.** $n - (-3) = 21$; $n = 18$ **10.** 25% **11.** 45 miles **12.** 12.5% or $12\frac{1}{2}$% **13.** $530 **14.** 4 to 1, 4:1, or $\frac{4}{1}$ **15.** 12% **16.** 40 pennies, 16 nickels, 8 dimes **17.** $7.25 **18.** 52 miles per hour **19.** The length of the rectangle is 21 inches and the width is 6 inches. **20.** $9.00

Chapter 4 Mastery Test B

1. D **2.** A **3.** A **4.** B **5.** B **6.** $3n - 5 = 19$; $n = 8$ **7.** $n + (-15) = 11$; $n = 26$ **8.** $\frac{n}{7} = -6$; $n = -42$ **9.** $n - (-2) = 13$; $n = 11$ **10.** 20% **11.** 48 miles **12.** 8% **13.** $432 **14.** 3:1 **15.** 16% **16.** 50 pennies, 30 nickels, 10 dimes **17.** $6.50 **18.** 44 mph **19.** 24 inches by 9 inches **20.** $7.50

Chapter 5 Mastery Test A

1. D **2.** C **3.** D **4.** B **5.** A **6.** p^{-2} **7.** $(r + 2s)^{-4}$ **8.** $5.3(10^{-2})$ **9.** $4.1(10^{-3})$ **10.** $4.0(10^5)$ **11.** $10y^5 + 5y - 6$ **12.** $w^7 - w^6 - w^3 - w^2 + 2w$ **13.** $22p^4 - 4p^3 - 4p^2 + 2p - 11$ **14.** $3y^3 - 12y^2$ **15.** $-14h^2 + 8h + 6$ **16.** $-8c^3 + 9c^2 - 6c + 5$ **17.** $6d^3 - 10$ **18.** $-11z^2 + 7$ **19.** $2w + 3$ **20.** $3a^2 - 2a - 4$

Chapter 5 Mastery Test B

1. B **2.** D **3.** B **4.** A **5.** D **6.** x^{-3} **7.** $(n + m)^{-2}$ **8.** $4.2(10^{-4})$ **9.** $6.44(10^{-2})$ **10.** $4.2(10^8)$ **11.** $10y^6 - 4y^5 + 4y^3 + 3y^2 + 7y - 2$ **12.** $-n^{88} + n^5 - n^4 - n^{33}$ **13.** $7z^7 + 10z^6 - 2z^{44} - 3z^2 - 11$ **14.** $2r^4 - 4r^3$ **15.** $-18d^2 - 39d + 7$ **16.** $-6m^3 + 14m^2 - 13m + 18$ **17.** $q^2 - 3$ **18.** $-4a + 6$ **19.** $3z + 8$ **20.** $2c^2 - c - 3$

Chapter 6 Mastery Test A

1. C **2.** B **3.** D **4.** A **5.** C **6.** 5 **7.** $3a^2$ **8.** $2y$ **9.** 8 **10.** $(3q - 1)(2q + 2)$ or $2(3q - 1)(q + 1)$ **11.** $(-4u + 1)(u - 1)$ **12.** $(y + 12)(y - 12)$ **13.** $(d - 8)(d - 8)$ or $(d - 8)^2$ **14.** $r = 0$ **15.** $a = 1$ or -1 **16.** $m = 1$ or 2 **17.** $k = 3$ or -2 **18.** $y = \frac{3}{4}$ or $-\frac{3}{2}$ **19.** $xy + 6y$ square units **20.** $2x - y$

Chapter 6 Mastery Test B

1. D **2.** C **3.** B **4.** C **5.** A **6.** 3 **7.** $5x^2$ **8.** $4m$ **9.** 9 **10.** $(4y + 2)(3y - 1)$ or $2(2y + 1)(3y - 1)$ **11.** $(-3c - 2)(c - 2)$ **12.** $(z - 11)(z + 11)$ **13.** $(a - 20)(a - 5)$ **14.** $k = 0$ **15.** $d = \frac{1}{3}$, $d = -2$ **16.** $n = 1\frac{3}{4}, n = 2\frac{1}{2}$ **17.** $t = -3, t = 4$ **18.** $m = -2$, $m = \frac{3}{5}$ **19.** $xy + 3y$ **20.** $3x - y$

Chapter 7 Mastery Test A

1. D **2.** B **3.** A **4.** B **5.** D **6.** $\frac{1}{6}$ **7.** $\frac{2}{3}$ **8.** $\frac{0}{6}$ or 0 **9.** $\frac{1}{3}$ **10.** $\frac{3}{4}$ **11.** $\frac{4}{4}$ or 1 **12.** $\frac{1}{30}$ **13.** $\frac{2}{5}$ **14.** $\frac{1}{16}$ **15.** 40,320 ways

Chapter 7 Mastery Test B

1. A **2.** D **3.** B **4.** B **5.** B **6.** $\frac{2}{3}$ **7.** $\frac{1}{6}$ **8.** $\frac{1}{3}$ **9.** 0 **10.** 1 **11.** $\frac{3}{4}$ **12.** $\frac{2}{5}$ **13.** $\frac{1}{30}$ **14.** $\frac{1}{8}$ **15.** 362,880

Chapter 8 Mastery Test A

1. C **2.** B **3.** C **4.** A **5.** B **6.** $-\frac{4}{9}$ **7.** c^2 **8.** $3ab$ **9.** $\frac{1}{n + 5}$ **10.** $(p - 8)$ **11.** $\frac{-1}{w - 2}$ **12.** b **13.** $\frac{1}{(c + 2)^2}$ or $\frac{1}{c^2 + 4c + 4}$ **14.** $(p + 3)(q - 4)$ or $pq - 4p + 3q - 12$ **15.** $\frac{7}{2}$ or $3\frac{1}{2}$ **16.** $\frac{g^2}{h^5}$ **17.** $(y - 2)$ **18.** 12 **19.** $\frac{1}{50}$ **20.** $\frac{1}{2}$ **21.** b^2 **22.** $c = -2$ **23.** $k = 0$ **24.** $n = +7$ and -7 **25.** 280 balls

Chapter 8 Mastery Test B

1. B **2.** B **3.** C **4.** C **5.** A **6.** $-\frac{1}{3}$ **7.** d^3 **8.** $4m^2n^2$ **9.** $\frac{1}{(t + 3)}$ **10.** $s - 3$ **11.** $\frac{-1}{(c - 3)}$ **12.** y **13.** $\frac{1}{(m + 3)^2}$ **14.** $(d + 3)(c + 2)$ **15.** $2\frac{2}{3}$ **16.** $\frac{p^2}{q^9}$ **17.** $a - 2$ **18.** 12 **19.** $\frac{1}{27}$ **20.** $\frac{7}{10}$ **21.** n^2 **22.** $n = -3$ **23.** $c = 0$ **24.** $z = 8, z = -8$ **25.** 288 balls

Chapter 9 Mastery Test A

1. A **2.** D **3.** B **4.** A **5.** B **6.** (2, 5) **7.** (−5, 1) **8.** (−1, 0) **9.** (0, −2) **10.** Quadrant II **11.** Quadrant IV **12.** Quadrant III **13.** Quadrant I

14.

$y = -x$	
x	y
−2	2
−1	1
0	0
1	−1
2	−2

15.

$y = 4x$	
x	y
−5	−20
−3	−12
−1	−4
1	4
3	12

16.

$y = -2x + 5$	
x	y
−7	19
−4	13
−1	7
2	1
5	−5

17. broken line passing through points (0, 1) and (−2, −5); region to the left of the broken line is shaded **18.** solid line passing through points (4, 4) and (−4, 4); region below the solid line is shaded **19.** solid line passing through points (0, 0) and (1, −2); region to the right of the solid line is shaded **20.** $y > 3x - 3$

Chapter 9 Mastery Test B

1. A **2.** B **3.** A **4.** B **5.** D **6.** (4, 4) **7.** (−3, 4) **8.** (0, −2) **9.** (−1, 0) **10.** Quadrant II **11.** Quadrant III **12.** Quadrant IV **13.** Quadrant I **14.** 3, 2, 1, 0, −1 **15.** −15, −9, −3, 3, 9 **16.** 30, 18, 6, −6, −18

17.

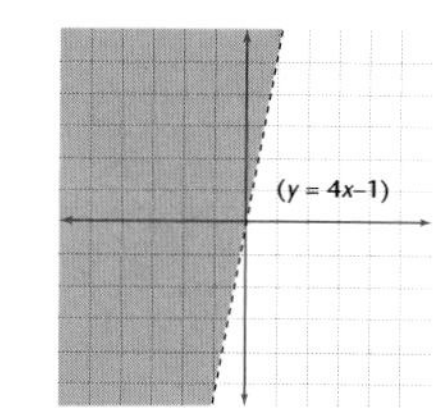

18.

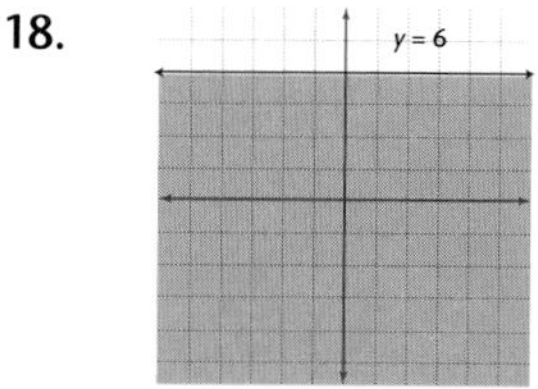

19.

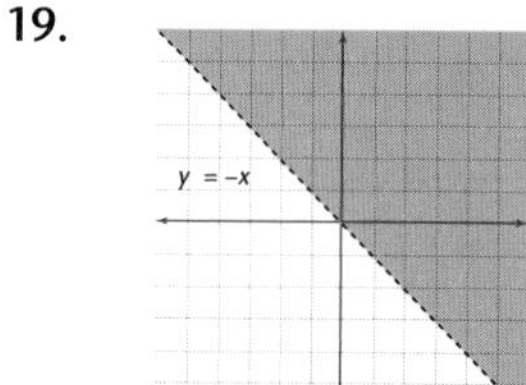

20. $y > 3x - 3$

Chapter 10 Mastery Test A

1. C **2.** A **3.** A **4.** B **5.** C **6.** (4, 3) **7.** (10, −2) **8.** Check students' graphs; (2, 3) **9.** Check students' graphs; (0, −2) **10.** true; both statements are true **11.** false; the second statement is false **12.** false; the first statement is false **13.** 20 feet and 40 feet **14.** 12 m and 48 m **15.** −6 and 2

Chapter 10 Mastery Test B

1. B **2.** C **3.** A **4.** C **5.** B **6.** $(1\frac{1}{2}, 2\frac{1}{2})$ **7.** $(9, -3)$
8. $(-1, -2)$

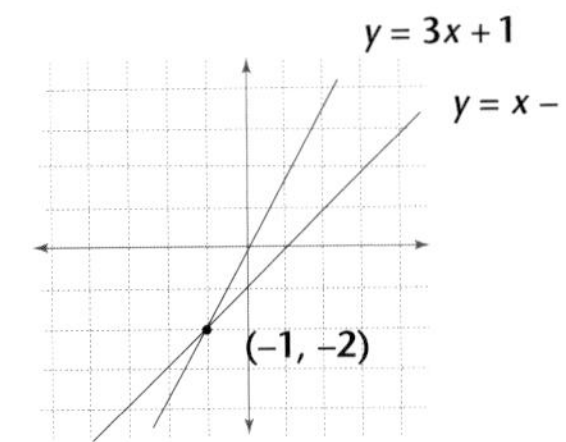

9.

$y = \frac{1}{3}x - 2$

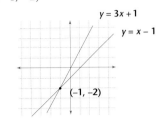

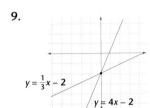

$y = 4x - 2$

10. true; both statements are true **11.** false; the second statement is false **12.** false; the first statement is false **13.** length = 60 feet, width = 30 feet **14.** length = 32 feet, width = 8 feet **15.** -4 and 2

Chapter 11 Mastery Test A

1. *B* **2.** B **3.** A **4.** D **5.** C **6.** 0.8 **7.** $0.\overline{21}$ **8.** $\frac{5}{33}$ **9.** $1\frac{16}{55}$ **10.** $4a$
11. $\frac{3}{x}$ **12.** $\frac{3w^8}{5z^2}$ **13.** $10\sqrt{2}$ **14.** $5\sqrt{2}$ **15.** $42a^4\sqrt{a} - 30b$

Chapter 11 Mastery Test B

1. D **2.** A **3.** C **4.** B **5.** B **6.** 0.4 **7.** 0.348 **8.** $\frac{1}{9}$ **9.** $1\frac{2}{11}$
10. $3m$ **11.** $\frac{\sqrt{7}}{c}$ **12.** $\frac{2b^6\sqrt{3}}{5a\sqrt{a}}$ **13.** $7\sqrt{3}$ **14.** $2\sqrt{3}$
15. $24p^8 - 12q$ or $4(6p^8 - 3q)$

Chapter 12 Mastery Test A

1. C **2.** B **3.** D **4.** A **5.** B **6.** obtuse **7.** acute **8.** right **9.** adjacent **10.** adjacent **11.** vertical **12.** interior **13.** exterior **14.** interior **15.** corresponding **16.** alternate interior **17.** supplementary **18.** alternate interior **19.** 118° **20.** 118° **21.** 118° **22.** 62° **23.** 118° **24.** obtuse scalene **25.** equilateral and equiangular **26.** right isosceles **27.** SAS **28.** ASA **29.** 145 feet **30.** 13.9 feet

Chapter 12 Mastery Test B

1. B **2.** D **3.** A **4.** C **5.** B **6.** acute **7.** right **8.** obtuse **9.** adjacent **10.** vertical **11.** adjacent **12.** exterior **13.** interior **14.** interior **15.** alternate interior **16.** supplementary **17.** corresponding **18.** alternate interior **19.** 118° **20.** 118° **21.** 62° **22.** 118° **23.** 118° **24.** obtuse scalene **25.** equilateral and equiangular **26.** right isosceles **27.** SAS **28.** ASA **29.** 145 feet **30.** 13.9 feet

Chapter 13 Mastery Test A

1. A **2.** D **3.** B **4.** C **5.** C **6.** 3, 5 **7.** $4, -\frac{3}{2}$ **8.** $x^2 - 3x + 2$ **9.** $x^2 - \frac{15}{2}x - 4$ or $2x^2 - 15x - 8$ **10.** $x^2 + \frac{38}{3}x + 8$ or $3x^2 + 38 + 24$ **11.** $-7, 3$ **12.** 4, 0 **13.** $5 \pm \sqrt{19}$ **14.** $-4 \pm \sqrt{18}$ or $-4 \pm 3\sqrt{2}$ **15.** $4, -2$ **16.** $\frac{1}{2}, 1$ **17.** $-\frac{3}{2}, -1$ **18.** $-\frac{3}{4}, -\frac{1}{2}$ or $-0.75, -0.5$ **19.** $x = 0$; $(0, 0)$ The graph is a parabola opening upward. The *y*-axis is the axis of symmetry—it divides the graph exactly in half. The vertex of the parabola is at $(0, 0)$ and the parabola passes through $(1, 2)$, $(2, 8)$ $(3, 18)$ $(-1, 2)$, $(-2, 8)$, $(-3, 18)$. **20.** $x = 1$; $(1, 0)$ The graph is a parabola opening upward; $x = 1$ is the axis of symmetry—it divides the graph exactly in half. The vertex of the parabola is at $(1, 0)$ and the parabola passes through $(0, 1)$, $(1, 0)$ $(2, 1)$ $(3, 4)$, $(-1, 4)$, $(-2, 9)$, $(-3, 16)$.

Chapter 13 Mastery Test B

1. D **2.** B **3.** D **4.** B **5.** C **6.** $x = 2, x = 4$ **7.** $x = -4, x = 6\frac{1}{4}$
8. $x^2 - 5x + 6$ **9.** $x^2 - 5\frac{1}{3}x - 4$ or $3x^2 - 16x - 12$
10. $x^2 + 8\frac{3}{4}x + 6$ or $4x^2 + 35x + 24$ **11.** $x = -4 + \sqrt{29}$, $-4 - \sqrt{29}$ **12.** $r = 6, 0$ **13.** $t = 10, 2$ **14.** $c = -2 + \sqrt{11}$, $c = -2 - \sqrt{11}$ **15.** $x = 2 - \sqrt{10}, x = 2 + \sqrt{10}$
16. $x = \frac{1}{3}, x = 1$ **17.** $x = 1, x = \frac{1}{2}$
18. $x = -1 + \frac{\sqrt{6}}{6}, x = -1 - \frac{\sqrt{6}}{6}$
19. root $x = 0$, axis of symmetry $= 0$

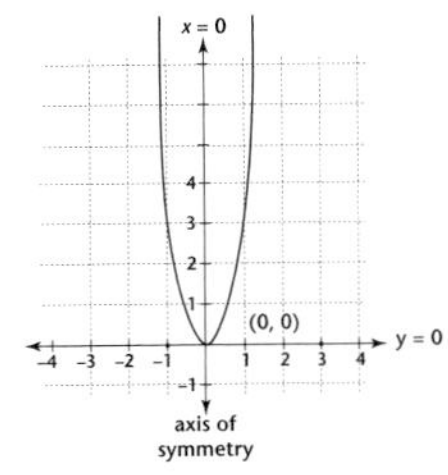

20. roots $x = -1$ and $x = 2$, axis of symmetry $= \frac{1}{2}$

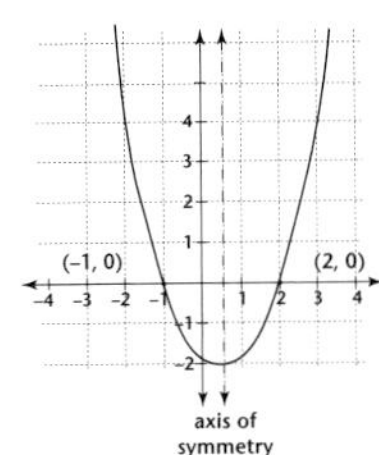

Midterm Mastery Test

1. B **2.** C **3.** D **4.** D **5.** B **6.** A **7.** D **8.** C **9.** B **10.** A **11.** 4 **12.** 9 **13.** $26\frac{2}{3}$ mph **14.** $65.25 **15.** $6y + (g + 5a)$, $(6y + g) + 5a$ **16.** $2xy + 3y$ square units or $3y + 2xy$ square units **17.** $(3x + y)$ **18.** 4.3 m **19.** $x > 1$ **20.** $x \leq -3$ **21.** 11 **22.** 12 **23.** 15 **24.** $\frac{3}{8}$ **25.** $\frac{3}{4}$

Final Mastery Test

1. C **2.** B **3.** A **4.** A **5.** D **6.** C **7.** A **8.** B **9.** D **10.** B **11.** C **12.** B **13.** A **14.** D **15.** C **16.** B **17–19.** Check students' graphs. Each graph should display Point H at $(-5, 0)$, Point T at $(0, -2)$, and Point P at $(-4, 4)$. **20.** $y = 2x - 1$ **21.** $y = 4x + 3$ **22.** 223 feet **23.** 90° **24.** 213 votes **25.** 120 ways **26.** $\frac{1}{6}$ **27.** length = 9 cm width = 5 cm **28.** 138° **29.** 42° **30.** $y = x - 1, y = -3, -2, -1, 0, 1$; $y = 3x - 7, y = -13, -10, -7, -4, -1$ **31.** $-2y = x, y = 1, \frac{1}{2}, 0, -\frac{1}{2}, -1$; $2y = -2x, y = 2, 1, 0, -1, -2$ **32.** Check students' graphs; $(3, 2)$ is the intersection of the system $y = x - 1$ and $y = 3x - 7$; $(0, 0)$ is the intersection of the system $-2y = x$ and $2y = -2x$ **33.** $x^2 - 2x - 1$ **34.** 14 cm, 56 cm **35.** 11 in., 18 in.

Teacher Questionnaire

Attention Teachers! As publishers of *Algebra,* we would like your help in making this textbook more valuable to you. Please take a few minutes to fill out this survey. Your feedback will help us to better serve you and your students.

1. What is your position and major area of responsibility? ____________________

____

____

2. Briefly describe your setting:

____ regular education ____ special education ____ adult basic education

____ community college ____ university ____ other ____________________

3. The enrollment in your classroom includes students with the following (check all that apply):

____ at-risk for failure ____ low reading ability ____ behavior problems

____ learning disabilities ____ ESL ____ other ____________________

4. Grade level of your students: ____________________

5. Racial/ethnic groups represented in your classes (check all that apply):

____ African-American ____ Asian ____ Caucasian ____ Hispanic

____ Native American ____ Other

6. School Location:

____ urban ____ suburban ____ rural ____ other ____________________

7. What reaction did your students have to the materials? (Include comments about the cover design, lesson format, illustrations, etc.)

____

____

____

8. What features in the student text helped your students the most?

____

____

____

9. What features in the student text helped your students the least? Please include suggestions for changing these to make the text more relevant.

____

____

10. How did you use the Teacher's Edition and support materials, and what features did you find to be the most helpful?

____

____

11. What activity from the program did your students benefit from the most? Please briefly explain.

____

____

____

12. Optional: Share an activity that you used to teach the materials in your classroom that enhanced the learning and motivation of your students.

____

____

____

Several activities will be selected to be included in future editions. Please include your name, address, and phone number so we may contact you for permission and possible payment to use the material.

Thank you!

▼ fold in thirds and tape shut at the top ▼

Name: ______________________

School: ______________________

Address: ______________________

City/State/ZIP: ______________________

Phone: ______________________

NO POSTAGE
NECESSARY
IF MAILED
IN THE
UNITED STATES

BUSINESS REPLY MAIL

FIRST-CLASS MAIL PERMIT NO.12 CIRCLE PINES MN

POSTAGE WILL BE PAID BY ADDRESSEE

AGS PUBLISHING

AGS Publishing ATTN: Marketing Support
4201 WOODLAND ROAD
PO BOX 99
CIRCLE PINES MN 55014-9911